The Big Show in Bololand

THE BIG SHOW IN BOLOLAND

The American Relief Expedition to Soviet Russia in the Famine of 1921

BERTRAND M. PATENAUDE

Stanford University Press
Stanford, California 2002

Stanford University Press
Stanford, California

© 2002 by the Board of Trustees of the
Leland Stanford Junior University.
All rights reserved.

Published with the assistance of the Hoover Institution
at Stanford University.

Except where noted, all illustrations are courtesy of the
Hoover Institution Archives.

Printed in the United States of America on acid-free,
archival-quality paper.

Library of Congress Cataloging-in-Publication Data

Patenaude, Bertrand M.
    The big show in Bololand : the American relief expedition
to Soviet Russia in the famine of 1921 / Bertrand M. Patenaude.
        p.   cm.
    Includes bibliographical references and index.
    ISBN 0-8047-4467-X (cloth : alk. paper)—
ISBN 0-8047-4493-9 (pbk. : alk. paper)
        1. Famines—Soviet Union—History.   2. American Relief
Administration.   3. Reconstruction (1914–1939)—Soviet Union.
I. Title.
    HC340.F3 P38 2002
    947.084'1—dc21   2002005860

Original Printing 2002
Last figure below indicates year of this printing:
11   10   09   08   07   06   05   04   03   02

Designed by Eleanor Mennick
Typeset by James P. Brommer in 10/13 Caslon and
Copperplate display

On ruined towns and desolated villages across the bleak, dreary steppes had fallen the heavy pall of black misery, of inert despair. Into this atmosphere of fatalistic hopelessness came the representatives of that distant incredible land—America.

—Harold Fisher, *The Famine in Soviet Russia*, 1927

CONTENTS

ILLUSTRATIONS

Frontispiece

American relief workers at Samara, spring 1922. *Seated, left to right*: Henry Wolfe, Ronald Allen, Will Shafroth, Frederick Foucar, and Louis Landy. *Standing, left to right*: George McClintock, Dudley Hale, Charles Willoughby, William Smith, and Oscar Anderson. Courtesy of Stephen Shafroth.

Maps

Photographs

Photo sections follow pages 199, 323, 490, and 710.

When a devastating famine descended on Soviet Russia in 1921, the United States responded with a massive two-year relief campaign that battled starvation and disease, and saved millions of lives. By summer 1922, American kitchens were feeding nearly eleven million Soviet citizens a day. At the time, the American rescue operation was hailed as "the *beau geste* of the twentieth century." Today, it is all but forgotten.

The American expedition took place as the embers of the 1917 Russian Revolution still smoldered. The nearly 300 American relief workers, most of them veterans of the Great War, were the first group of outsiders to break through Russia's isolation and to witness and record the impact of the revolution. They did so in a most remarkable way. Penetrating the heartland in and beyond the Volga valley, their mobility and access unrestricted, these young men came into daily contact with all classes of society, from impoverished former aristocrats to the poorest peasants. They were the first as well to have sustained exposure to the strange new phenomenon of Russian Bolshevism, known to the American public from terrifying and sensationalistic newspaper stories.

The present volume narrates this epic tale set in exotic Bololand, as the relief workers liked to call Bolshevik Russia. The book consists of four parts. Part I's chronologically arranged chapters recount the essential story of famine and relief. This is followed by three thematically organized sections which examine—chiefly though by no means exclusively—in Part II the *personal* triumphs and tragedies of the relief workers and their beneficiaries, in Part III the *political* confrontations between these emissaries of American capitalism and the Bolshevik commissars who struggled to gain control over their operations, and in Part IV the American-Russian *cultural* encounter occasioned by the relief mission.

In resurrecting this extraordinary episode, this book relates the larger story of the Russian Revolution and lays bare the roots of the U.S.-Soviet rivalry that would dominate the second half of the twentieth century.

The Big Show in Bololand

FUTURE CORPSES

Early in December 1921, a twenty-nine-year-old American by the name of Will Shafroth entered a village not far from the Russian city of Samara on the Volga River. There he came upon a group of peasants digging a large pit. He noted that the men were weary and "rested often in their work," which did not seem out of the ordinary to him since he knew they were starving. Samara was in the midst of the deadliest famine in modern European history, and many inhabitants of the Volga valley were engaged in a desperate struggle for survival. Being Russians, most were veterans of that struggle, but in 1921 its scope and intensity were as nothing in living memory. The men laboring in their pit, like very many people in the famine region, were getting by on food substitutes—grass, weeds, acorns, twigs, bark, roots, and worse.

Rumors of corpse eating were in the air. The number of authenticated cases would grow during the winter, when the Samara city government would shut down ten butcher shops for selling human flesh. One account of outright cannibalism that would prove to be unfounded was an especially sensationalistic story given publicity by the European and American press. It claimed that the supervisor of the American famine relief mission in Samara had been killed and eaten by cannibals. The victim was unnamed, but from the job title he could only have been Will Shafroth.

It was Shafroth, along with a team of several dozen fellow Americans, who had entered Russia as a relief worker in late summer 1921 after an appeal came out of Moscow for help in combatting a raging famine on the Volga. He undertook this assignment as a member of the American Relief Administration, the much-heralded ARA, under the chairmanship of Herbert Hoover. Since the end of hostilities in the Great War, Hoover's ARA had successfully executed a massive food relief campaign across Central and Eastern Europe. Shafroth had served in ARA missions in Germany, Czechoslovakia, and Poland. But the hardship he had worked to alleviate there did not compare to the horrors he now witnessed in Soviet Russia. He had considered himself to be pretty "hard-boiled" until he encountered the suffering of Samara's starving children, with their toothpick legs and swollen "hunger bellies." Most horrifying were the gaunt, aged faces. Walking into the so-called children's homes—collection points for children abandoned by their parents—he was shocked to find there wizened old men and women, most of them under ten years of age.[1]

It was these unfortunate ones that the Americans had come to save, their mission being to sustain one million children through the winter of 1921–22. But soon after reaching the Volga provinces in early September, the ARA men sent word back to Moscow headquarters that the Russian famine was a catastrophe of proportions that would overwhelm even the ARA's mammoth undertaking. Shafroth and his four fellow Americans in Samara were, within a short time, directing a staff of nearly eight thousand local citizens and operating throughout a province about four-fifths the size of New York State, with a population estimated to be nearly 2.8 million. By mid-December the Samara Americans reached their maximum allocation of two hundred thousand children's meals a day served in some nine hundred ARA kitchens.

To Shafroth, on an inspection trip in early December through the villages south of Samara city, it was disturbingly obvious that this effort was not going to be nearly enough to stem the tide of famine. Recent snows hindered the search for food substitutes, and peasants were consuming their last draught animals in order to stay alive. In many villages in this region almost all the horses would soon be slaughtered for food, as would the cows, many of which had by then become too weak to serve any other purpose.

Across southern Samara province, where Shafroth was now making his way, camels did duty as beasts of burden. He had been surprised to find camels in the heartland of Russia, having always associated them with "hot countries"—yet here they were, "these awkward beasts, with their slow, almost meticulous step, pulling heavily laden sleds over the snowy crust." No matter how deserved their reputation for endurance, even camels require fodder to keep going; and so they, too, lost strength and their numbers dwindled.

Along his route, Shafroth came to a village of about three thousand residents, which was down to nine camels and eight horses. Cows numbered 150 but were being slaughtered at a rate of ten per day. Human residents also were rapidly disappearing. Of the 400 homes in the village, 175 had been deserted, the inhabitants having died or gone off in search of food. Shafroth observed that those who remained behind acted as if condemned to death: "The weariness and the hopeless resignation of the peasants were very depressing. Seeing the weaker members of the community dying, they said in their fatalistic way, 'There is no more food. We must die too. Only our children who eat at the American kitchens will be saved.'"

By now in most of these villages the dead were so numerous they were buried in common graves. "I have seen piles of the corpses stark naked and frozen into the most grotesque positions, with the signs of having been preyed upon by wandering dogs. I have seen these bodies—and it is a sight that I can never forget—taken by two men and tossed like sticks of cordwood into a yawning hole." Elsewhere corpses were "simply piled in warehouses to rot and corrupt." And there were "horrible stories," "told and often verified," of people entering these places at night and cutting off limbs to eat.

Perhaps such nightmarish images served to sustain the weary peasants Shafroth found digging their large pit. Missing from the scene were the deceased whose burial had presumably brought these men together in their common enterprise. He asked them about this, and they told him that they were preparing a mass grave for the dead to come: "We are afraid we won't have the strength to do it later, so we are trying now to make a place to put the future corpses."

Here was grim testimony to a fact that haunted Shafroth throughout his tour of inspection: without urgent and extreme intervention in the Volga valley, hundreds of thousands of Russian children and many more adults would surely die by winter's end. It seemed likely that the victims would include some of the peasants struggling inside the pit before him. In fact, it seemed inescapable. "As I looked at them I wondered if any of those men thought he might be digging his own grave."

PART ONE

THE BATTLEFIELD OF FAMINE

Russia's Crisis and America's Response

The A.R.A. Russian operation was in the strictest military sense of the word
a campaign, and like the English at Gallipoli the Administration had to begin
firing the moment it landed.

—John Ellingston, Moscow, 1923

Trying to kill people may sound more exciting than trying to keep them alive,
but don't you ever believe it's so.

—George McClintock, Samara, 1922

CHAPTER I

GOING IN

America's postwar famine fighters tended to be well-educated former doughboys in their twenties, and Will Shafroth fits this rough profile. Son of the former governor of Colorado, he graduated from the University of Michigan in 1914
and received a law degree from the University of California in 1916. A good number of the relief workers had their undergraduate studies interrupted by the call
to war. Shafroth joined the U.S. Army with a commission as a Second lieutenant
in August 1917, four months after President Wilson had brought the country into
the Great War. In June 1918 Captain Shafroth was off to France with the American Expeditionary Force (AEF), assigned to the Seventy-eighth Field Artillery,
Sixth Division.

It was a short war for the AEF. In November came the armistice, and Pershing's soldiers took up various occupation duties. Shafroth's assignment took him
to Hungary, where he served for three months with the interallied military mission. Demobilized after the signing of the Treaty of Versailles in June 1919, he
joined the American Relief Administration (ARA). This meant putting off his
return to the States and his law career, but like many other doughboys Shafroth
had become hooked on Europe and preferred to continue the Great Adventure.
And service with Hoover's boys was about the most splendid way to do so. As an
ARA man he was stationed for a month in Hamburg and then ten months in
Prague before his transfer to the Poland mission, headquartered in Cracow. This
is where he was in August 1921, when a telegram arrived instructing him to prepare for reassignment to Russia.[1]

Shafroth proceeded to Riga, capital of Latvia, which had only recently become
an independent country, having been detached from the Russian empire during
the war. The ARA had been feeding people throughout the Baltics since the armistice, and so it could now count on the cooperation of the Latvian authorities
in setting up its formidable Russian undertaking. The advance party of seven
Americans, ARA veterans all, assembled at Riga in the final week of August and
made hurried preparations for their expedition.

The men were led by Philip Carroll of Hood River, Oregon; that is, Hood
River was what he filled in under "home address" in his ARA personnel questionnaire. For most of these wanderers, by 1921 home was somewhere long ago and far
away. At thirty-six, Carroll was about ten years older than the average relief
worker. A graduate of West Point in 1908, he joined the colors in 1917 with a com-

mission as a major. His ARA biographical sketch gives no details about his AEF activity but has much to say about his food relief experience, which was considerable. He served in 1919 with Allied missions based in the Black Sea ports of Novorossisk, Batum, and Constantinople, and subsequently was chief of ARA operations in Serbia in 1919–20, before taking charge of the ARA's Hamburg unit. Carroll was considered within the organization to be the leading candidate to take the helm of any future ARA mission to Russia—Bolshevik or post-Bolshevik— for which he was charged with drawing up contingency plans in 1920. Yet, though he was to head the advance guard into Moscow and lay the foundation for the Russian unit, he was not to be its chief.[2]

Before setting off, Carroll, Shafroth, and the others were given the benefit of the latest reports on conditions in Russia from the American relief workers posted in Riga and from that city's resident diplomats and journalists. Since 1918 an information blockade had made it impossible to get regular, credible, first-hand testimony on developments inside Bolshevik Russia. During that time, Riga had been serving as the West's primary "listening post" into that forbidden land. Geographic proximity, it turned out, gave no advantage to those doing the listening. The city became a primary source of sensationalistic stories about the horrors of Bolshevism in Red Russia, indeed inside the very walls of the Kremlin. It was frequently reported that the Bolsheviks had at last fallen from power, or were about to, and such rumors were regularly published as fact in the most respectable European and American newspapers. Now, in 1921, the press blockade was about to fall, as foreign correspondents not vetted by the Kremlin for their sympathy to Bolshevism were to be allowed to enter Russia and report to the world on the famine and other topics.

Whatever insights they gained from their Riga briefings, once Shafroth and his ARA colleagues crossed over and had a few weeks to see things for themselves, they understood the extreme difficulty of trying to comprehend, let alone convey, the truth about Russia. For the rest of their days, they would never again take newspaper stories on the Soviet Union, not least those of Moscow-based reporters, at face value.

They did take away from Riga a few durable expressions, however. One was the nickname for the Bolsheviks fashionable in relief and diplomatic circles in East-Central Europe: the Bolos. Shafroth would have been familiar with it from his Cracow days, and now the entire advance party got into the habit. Not long into their stay in the land of the Bolos, the Americans would develop the word into an irreverently exotic appellation for Bolshevik Russia: Bololand.

What also stuck with them were the terms the Latvians in Riga used for making the trip into Russia, "going in," and for leaving it, "coming out"—phrases that suggested something vaguely ominous about the act. The relief workers would adopt this terminology to refer to their own passages in and out of Bololand, though two of their number would never experience coming out.

Carroll's team departed Riga for Moscow at 10:00 P.M. on Thursday, August 25. In the words of a colleague later imagining the moment, it was "Off to Russia— and with quiet hopes and convictions that as representatives of the ARA they would 'make the show a go.'"[3] On the following day at about 1:30 P.M. they arrived at the town of Sebezh, on the Russian frontier. Here they were held up for four hours, a delay they could not explain since their papers from the Latvian authorities and from the Soviet mission in Riga exempted them from customs inspection. Nervous impatience to discover what was on the other side sent them pacing the platform, but in fact, without realizing it, they were already beginning the process of discovery. Within a few days they would understand that delays, impatience, and frustration were unavoidable features of Russian reality. By then their four-hour wait at the border was a very old story. By the next summer Shafroth would characterize it as "four hours doing nothing in the customary busy Slav fashion."

Their eagerness to get on with the mission was heightened by the fact that ARA veterans like Shafroth had been anticipating this moment for over two years. Not that the allure of Russia was confined to American relief workers, as many Europeans also were intensely curious to have a look in. Even before the earthshaking events of 1914 and the blood-curdling tales of Bolshevism told in the West over the previous four years, going into Russia was considered something of an adventure by inhabitants of the "civilized" world. The fanfare accompanying the send-off of the ARA party served to reinforce this impression, as Shafroth indicated in his first letter out to his mother: "With us was a 'movie' man from the Universal News and he filmed us one by one on the Latvian border and sent back the pictures, so we may appear on the screen. The great number of people in Riga who wanted to go in with us, the excitement of preparation and departure, the special cars and the movie man, all put a great atmosphere of adventure into the thing."[4]

The delay gave the new celebrities an opportunity to put the moment in perspective. They were the first quasi-official delegation of Americans to enter Bolshevik Russia in two and a half years—that is, if one overlooks the several thousand uninvited soldiers of the American Expeditionary Force who landed in the Russian north and far east in 1918, lingering in Siberia for a year and a half. This intervention, unprecedented in the history of relations between the two countries, would for decades afterward serve as a symbol of U.S.-Soviet animosity.

SUCH AN UNHAPPY TURN in American-Russian affairs could not have been anticipated in March 1917, when the Romanov dynasty collapsed unexpectedly and with little bloodshed—an event known as the February Revolution because the Russian calendar at the time, thirteen days behind that of the West, made it fall in that month. The February Revolution began with workers' protests against food shortages, which then turned into industrial strikes and escalated into mass political demonstrations against the war and the autocracy. The refusal of the Petrograd garrison to fire on crowds of protesters signalled the end of imperial authority. Tsar Nicholas II, returning to the capital from his personal command of Russia's crumbling war effort at the front, was pressed to abdicate in favor of his brother, who refused the throne. Quite suddenly, Russia was no longer an absolute monarchy.

In Washington this was very good news to Woodrow Wilson, who was seeking to overcome isolationist sentiment among the American public and justify bringing the United States into Europe's war. The Russian autocracy had since the last decades of the previous century become increasingly unpopular with Americans for its despotic ways and would hardly have inspired enthusiasm as a potential wartime ally. Now with the Tsar out of the way—not to mention the German-blooded Empress Alexandra and, several months earlier, the preposterous figure of Rasputin—Wilson could pronounce Russia to be a "fit partner for a league of honour" in the struggle against the Kaiser. The way was cleared for Wilson's idealistic portrayal of the war as a fight to "make the world safe for democracy."[5]

On a more practical level, U.S. and Allied officials believed that this newly liberated Russia, swept clean of its repressive and inefficient autocracy and of German influence and intrigue at the court of the Romanovs, would put up a more effective fight on the battlefield, one that would be wholeheartedly supported by the Russian people, who now controlled their own destiny. Wilson did much to encourage such thinking among Americans by making intemperate public remarks about the allegedly democratic nature of the Russian people, as if the imperial regime had had no legitimate roots in Russia. Such optimism was misplaced, however, and after the February Revolution the country rapidly unravelled.[6]

The Provisional Government that succeeded the autocracy, composed at first of conservative and liberal figures of the old regime, proved unable to establish its authority over the country. Isolated in Petrograd, it failed to organize local branches of power as Russia's political and social structures simply broke down. Greatly complicating matters, in Petrograd the Provisional Government's authority was challenged from the start by the Soviet of Workers' and Soldiers' Deputies. The Petrograd soviet was made up of members of the social democratic and radical parties and groupings, representing the workers and the soldiers' garrisons of the capital. They refused to take power for themselves, preferring instead to act as a watchdog over the activities of the Provisional Government. This standoff, which goes by the name of "dual power," resulted in an eight-month duel of nerves. Soon other soviets sprang up across the country—soviets of workers, of soldiers, and later of peasants.

In Petrograd, 1917 saw the progressive deterioration of the tentative authority of the Provisional Government in a series of increasingly leftward-leaning cabinets, each in turn undermined by its failure to reverse the Russian army's defeats at the front and to manage the economic distress related to the prosecution of the war, especially a deepening food crisis. Workers and soldiers became increasingly radicalized as Russian politics as a whole slid to the left. Slid, and then lurched in August, when General Lavr Kornilov turned and marched his troops on Petrograd, causing Prime Minister Alexander Kerensky to enlist the support of, indeed provide arms to, the radicals in order to defend the capital. Kornilov never made it to Petrograd, but the days of Kerensky and the Provisional Government were now numbered.

The greatest beneficiaries of the Kornilov affair were Lenin's Bolsheviks. Of marginal influence early in the Revolution, their prospects appeared bleak in July after their half-hearted effort to take power led to the arrest of Trotsky and other Bolsheviks and sent Lenin into hiding in Finland. Kornilov's advance on Petrograd reversed their fortunes by removing their outlaw status and allowing the Red Guards to arm themselves. Bolshevik promises of "Land, Bread and Peace" and Lenin's slogan "All Power to the Soviets" helped win them increasing support among workers and soldiers. In September the Party captured a majority in the Petrograd soviet, and it continued to gain political strength in other city soviets.

This was now more than enough for Lenin. From his Finnish hideout he urged his Party lieutenants to overthrow the Provisional Government. Some of them resisted this call to revolution, but on the night of November 6–7, with Trotsky executing brilliantly, the Bolsheviks seized power in the name of the Congress of Soviets, which had convened in the capital. This October Revolution—another designation determined by the old calendar—met with little resistance in Petrograd, where the Party, in Lenin's phrase, "found power lying in the streets and simply picked it up."[7] The "storming" of the Winter Palace was in fact a decidedly unromantic event, and before it began Kerensky took flight and made his way out of the country. The Bolshevik Revolution succeeded in other cities with greater difficulty and in Moscow with considerable violence and the loss of several hundred lives. Lenin proclaimed the formation of the first workers' state—the "dictatorship of the proletariat"—and called upon the workers of the rest of the world to unite and overthrow their capitalist oppressors.

At first the Bolsheviks ruled in an uneasy coalition with the left wing of the populist Socialist Revolutionary Party, known as the Left-SRs. This was destined to be a short-lived arrangement. The break came in spring 1918 and led to violence in summer when the Bolsheviks moved to suppress a Left-SR revolt. The immediate cause of the split with the Left-SRs was a disagreement over matters of foreign and agrarian policy, but a rupture was inevitable because Lenin's party was in any case predisposed, ideologically and programmatically, to a single-party dictatorship. In January the Bolsheviks abolished the Constituent Assembly, up to then Russia's most democratically elected national body, in which they held only a minority of seats. The assembly was dispersed on the second day of its existence. By summer 1918 the Bolsheviks had eliminated their rivals for power through repressive measures, which escalated into the Red Terror after August 30, the date an assassin's bullet left Lenin gravely wounded. The Party was the supreme ruling authority, though it chose to exercise power through the mechanism of the soviets, locally and at the center, where government ministries were formed. Trotsky gave them the subversive label "People's Commissariats."

In the West all of this was greeted with expressions of horror and scoffing disbelief. Few expected the experiment to last longer than a few days or weeks, at which point reasonable men would emerge to rule Russia. But the nightmare continued.

The Bolsheviks came to power denouncing the "imperialist" war and calling for peace. On the first full day of their revolution they issued a Decree on Peace, which called for an end to hostilities with no annexations and no indemnities and which effectively ended Russian involvement in the war. To demonstrate that they had no intention of playing by the established rules they set about publishing the secret treaties between Russia and the Allies.

The Allies' worst fear was not actually realized until March 1918, when the Soviet government signed a separate peace with the Germans, the Treaty of Brest-Litovsk. Lenin's idea—which won the day despite fierce opposition within the Party leadership—was that such a peace was necessary in order to stave off a German advance and save the Revolution, giving it a "breathing spell." In the end the Bolshevik gamble of trading space for time would pay off, though in the short run Soviet Russia paid a very high price, sacrificing about a third of European Russia's territory—including Ukraine, the Baltic provinces, and Russian Poland—and about half of imperial Russia's industrial capacity and food production. And from now on Bolshevik deliberations would take place inside the Kremlin: the German advance on Petrograd had helped to prompt the removal of the seat of government to Moscow on March 10.

Within weeks of Brest-Litovsk, White armies were organizing on the periphery and civil war was brewing in Russia. In late summer, the United States and Great Britain would land expeditions in the Russian north, at Archangel and Murmansk, and in Siberia. The connection between the Russian Civil War and this Allied intervention has been a source of contention among historians.[8]

The Allied landings in the north were prompted by fear that war munitions that had been shipped to pre-Bolshevik Russian governments and stored there might fall into the hands of the Germans. Thus, the operation was not anti-Bolshevik in origin—indeed, there was initially open military collaboration between the Allied forces and the Soviet authorities in Murmansk—though it soon became so. The most serious fighting was seen at Archangel, where on September 4, 1918, forty-five hundred Americans went ashore under British command and clashed with Soviet forces. The Great War ended on November 11, but weather conditions made an immediate withdrawal impossible and the joint American-British force stayed on through the frozen winter. The Americans departed by July 1919; the British by September. In total, at Archangel, nearly five hundred British and Americans died of various causes, related and unrelated to battle.

There were far fewer casualties in the Siberian intervention, but the political fallout it produced was far greater. George F. Kennan devoted himself to a thorough study of the complex series of events leading up to the decision to intervene in Siberia; as he would say, it is a story that defies brief description. Here, as in the north, the primary motivation of the Allies initially—or at least of the principal statesmen in Washington—was anti-German, based on a fear that German and Austrian war prisoners inside Russia might somehow stir up trouble on the former eastern front. This tends to sound suspect, even ridiculous, to later generations but only because we know how the war turned out and how little fight the Germans had left in them.

The actual trigger for the Allied intervention in Siberia was a crisis involving a Czechoslovak legion of about thirty-five thousand that had been cut off from the anti-German struggle after the eastern front was shut down and which was now attempting to exit Russia by way of Siberia. The Czechoslovak soldiers were strung out along the Trans-Siberian railway from the Volga to Siberia when, in May, they got into a scrape with Red Army forces trying to disarm them. Hostilities broke out along a large stretch of the Trans-Siberian, which the Czechoslovak corps essentially seized, presenting the Bolsheviks with a military crisis just as the Civil War was getting underway.

Unlikely though it might seem, the immediate cause of the American decision to intervene in Siberia was a desire to come to the aid of these embattled Czechoslovaks, not least because it appealed to Wilson's notion of America coming to the defense of the "little peoples" of Europe—selected ones, anyway. Of course this was not the president's sole consideration. Officials in Washington were also somewhat anxious that the Japanese might try to take advantage of the unstable moment and extend their influence into the Russian far east. Other statesmen, American and especially European, doubtless from the beginning had it in mind to use the crisis of the Czechoslovak legion as a pretense to intervene and restore the eastern front. And if this required giving the Bolshevik regime a shove out of power, then so much the better.

It is impossible to gauge the relative weights Wilson assigned to each of these considerations at any one time in his overburdened and inscrutable mind. The difficulty in making a case that the American intervention was anti-German in motivation has to do with the calendar. The decision to intervene in Siberia was made in the first week of July, and American troops landed at Vladivostok in August. By November Germany had been defeated, yet the nearly seven thousand soldiers of the American Expeditionary Force remained in Siberia for a year and a half, departing only in April 1920. Clearly the intervention *became* an anti-Bolshevik enterprise, though at precisely what point and to what degree it did so are matters of scholarly dispute.

Wilson himself was a reluctant interventionist to begin with. Physically unwell and mentally preoccupied with the peace of Versailles and his plans for the League of Nations, he was persuaded by the British to redefine the Siberian expedition and lend American support to the White army of Admiral Alexander Kolchak when it scored military successes against the Reds in spring 1919. The AEF ostensibly stayed on as well to fulfill a commitment to assist an interallied committee in operating the Trans-Siberian and Chinese Eastern railways, but few today would attempt to make very much out of this.

Whatever the motivations of the officials who sent them, the American soldiers on the ground saw little action, engaging in only a few skirmishes with Bolshevik forces. A bigger concern was keeping the peace with bands of local Cossacks and conducting delicate diplomacy with British and Japanese officers. In the end the military effect of the intervention was negligible, but politically its influence was poisonous. It enabled the Soviet government to rally Russian patriotic support to the Red cause by sounding the alarm against the foreign invader, and for decades afterward it served the Kremlin as a propaganda club against the imperialists for having tried to smother the infant Revolution in its crib.

The real action, the Civil War of Reds versus Whites, was a savage struggle that lasted nearly two years. The most intense fighting took place from mid-1918 to the end of 1919. The Bolsheviks met the White challenge by creating an initially ragtag Red Army under the forceful leadership of the charismatic Trotsky, who enlisted in the cause former tsarist army officers, kept under the watchful eye of political commissars. At the onset few would have given this hastily improvised army a fighting chance, but the White forces were never as formidable as they appeared, with three separate armies in the field—Kolchak's advancing from Siberia, Denikin's from Ukraine, and Yudenitch's from the northwest—each vying for political supremacy and each more or less hampered in the rear by the intermittent resistance of peasants who had no desire to see the return of the landlord and to the old ways. Trotsky, as people's commissar of war, made the best of this White disunity and of Soviet mastery over a consolidated geographic entity with Moscow at its center. The White tide was turned back in autumn 1919, and final victory was won by the end of the year, though sporadic fighting continued well into 1920.

The last significant military episode of the revolutionary period was the Russo-Polish War of 1920. Poland had been made an independent state at Versailles, having previously been divided between Russia, Austria, and Germany. The Poles initiated hostilities in April 1920, when Marshal Pilsudski launched an offensive, taking Kiev on May 7. But the Polish army overextended itself, and Pilsudski's advance was reversed by June, when the Red Army began to march westward, reaching the outskirts of Warsaw in July. This set heads spinning in the Kremlin, most importantly Lenin's, as the realist of Brest-Litovsk now became intoxicated with the possibility of inciting revolution across Europe by bringing Soviet rule to Poland. This time it was the Red Army's turn to overreach itself, which opened the way for a successful Polish counteroffensive. By October the war was over, and Poland's frontier with Russia had shifted considerably to the east of what the Allied diplomats at Versailles had proposed.[9]

By the end of 1920 Soviet Russia was no longer at war. It had managed to regain the eastern territories all the way to the Pacific and, in the early 1920s, through hard political work and some military muscle flexing would reincorporate the southern territories of the old empire. On the western frontier the Bolsheviks had managed to undo much of the humiliation of the Brest-Litovsk settlement by reacquiring Ukraine, which had been a continuous battleground for three years and was now rife with anti-Soviet partisans. Otherwise, Russia had lost its Polish domain and the Baltic States to independence and Bessarabia to Romania. Regaining these lands would have to wait until the end of the next world war.

This is why, in August 1921, Shafroth and the other American relief workers performed their restless ruminations on a railroad platform in a town called Sebezh on the Latvian-Russian border.

THE MEN IN THE ARA PARTY had worked on the periphery of the Russian Revolution. From all that they had heard about it they could not help now but feel somewhat apprehensive. The fighting had stopped but apparently not the operations of the infamous Cheka, the political police that had conducted the Red Terror. The days of the Terror were supposed to be over, but who could say for sure?

For the moment the most unsettling object in their sights was the camel-peaked woolen headgear that served as the helmet of the Red Army soldier. At Sebezh and at every other station along their route they found Trotsky's troops much in evidence. In the flesh the Red warriors turned out to be hardly at all the imposing figures of Western myth: their uniforms were shabby, ill-fitting, and often incomplete; their rifles seemed to burden their bony shoulders; most seemed to be mere boys. But to take in these details one's attention had to get beyond the distracting headgear. Shafroth described it as "the peaked aviator's helmet type of hat, with tucked up ear-flaps and bearing a large red star over the visor, the design of which rumor has attributed to Trotzky." On some, the sight of this Bolo innovation had a comic effect. Harold Fisher, the ARA's official historian, who entered Russia some months later, said it looked "for all the world like a nightcap ineffectually disguised."[10]

Underway again after their detention at the border, the travelers gazed through their railway car windows, on the qui vive for signs of the famine that had brought them there. Shafroth noted that the peasants were a bit more ragged than he was used to seeing in Poland, that cattle were few, and that mostly women worked the fields. But as yet there was no indication of starvation conditions in the country-side; on the contrary, at every railway station they found fruit, bread, and vegetables for sale.

Yet it was at these same stations that the advance party came in contact with the first signs of hardship, including hunger, in the form of trainloads of pitiful refugees journeying out of Russia. Each train consisted of twenty to thirty freight cars jammed with tattered, starving people. They were not refugees in flight from the famine, however. These unfortunates were Poles, Lithuanians, Letts, Estonians, and others, who had fled to the Russian interior before the advancing German army and who were now returning home after five years in southeastern Russia as exiles—first internal, then foreign. To say they were being repatriated is not entirely accurate since their countries had not existed as independent states at the time of their departure. Miserable as they were in their present state, some must have been achingly curious as to what had become of their homelands, not to mention their homes, in their absence.

The Americans listened to translations of individual tales of woe. One train had been en route from Turkestan since July 2, a fact that got the Americans thinking about the state of Russian transport on the far side of Moscow. Carroll noted that the trains and equipment employed on the Riga-Moscow line, presumably among the best available, appeared to be badly run down, which did not bode well for conditions in the interior.[11] The trip from Riga to Moscow was about the same distance as that from New York to Cleveland, a fifteen-hour journey in the United States in those days. In Russia before the war the trip took about twenty-two hours, whereas the ARA advance party—making good time, it turned out, even with their border delay—rolled into Moscow almost two days after setting out, on Saturday evening, August 27, around 6:00 P.M..

Upon arrival at Moscow's Windau station, Carroll and his men were met by two unnoteworthy Soviet officials, one representing the People's Commissariat of Foreign Affairs, the other the Soviet government's famine relief committee. The hosts observed that there were seven Americans in the party and remarked that they had made preparations to receive only three: housing was not immediately available for all. This was, at minimum, a forceful introduction to the frightful scarcity of housing in Moscow. Far more disturbing, however, was what it seemed to portend for the future of cooperation between the ARA and the Soviet authorities. For on this, the extraordinary occasion of the arrival in Bolshevik Russia of American famine relief workers charged with the task of rescuing one million children from starvation, sleeping quarters were unavailable for more than three of the saviors.

Carroll told these officials that it was a case of all or none and that the entire ARA party would stay in its railroad car another night and settle the matter of housing the next day. At that point the officials reminded Carroll that the following day was Sunday. It being a day of rest, even in the capital of godless communism, nothing could be done to secure accommodations for the American guests until Monday.

A famine was reportedly raging a few hundred miles to the east of Moscow, affecting nearly thirty-five million people. These American famine fighters were in a big hurry to get on with the fight. Soviet officials had a different conception of what it meant to be in a hurry.

Their reception took some of the spirit out of the Americans. Carroll, Shafroth, John Gregg, Van Arsdale Turner, John Lehrs, Columba Murray, and Harry Fink could only shake their heads and wonder if that was not the damnedest thing they had ever heard of. Maybe it was, but they were destined to experience stranger things in the months ahead.

The enforced day of leisure gave the Americans an opportunity to have a look around Moscow. Shafroth had never been to Russia, so his day was filled with a tourist's first impressions of, for example, the Byzantine onion domes of the Russian Orthodox churches. The gaudy St. Basil's on Red Square he thought looked like Coney Island or Luna Park. The Kremlin appeared much like the Baedeker's description of it: although one tower was in scaffolding, its red brick walls showed no signs of damage from the Revolution. Moscow suffered not nearly as much from street fighting as from neglect and economic hardship. While the main administrative buildings had come through in decent shape, many office and residential structures were bad off. Some had been burned out already several years earlier; others had been torn down or gutted for fuel; many were windowless.

The city streets were in a discouraging state of disrepair. Trolley cars were running, but there were few street lights, giving the city a deserted feel after dark. Moscow in these days was not a place of suffering and misery but rather of dullness and hopelessness, dirtiness and decay. The arriving foreign correspondents, who discussed it among themselves, agreed that the most apt comparison was Lille after four years of German occupation. Everywhere was ruin.

After having a look around, Shafroth wrote to his mother that Moscow was "the most depressing city in the world today." It appeared to him that the regular residents had abandoned the metropolis and had their places taken by peasants from the surrounding countryside, "with no notion of cleanliness or sanitation." The city, he wrote, "seems to have started back on the road to the civilization of the middle ages." For an American, even a European, who had never been to Russia, the rustic appearance of Muscovites in 1921 could easily mislead, for Moscow had always been something of a big village. People on the streets wearing "the most nondescript outfits it is possible to imagine" and the preponderance of peasant types, especially women with scarves, wearing sandals or going barefoot—this sounds like Moscow's pedestrians in travelers' accounts from before 1914.

Nonetheless, appearances had changed, one major difference being the pronounced military note in the attire of the men. Most were not actively serving in the Red Army but were demobilized soldiers of the Imperial and Red Armies or other civilians wearing these armies' uniforms, or bits and pieces of them: a soldier's cap here, breeches and puttees there, a military coat there, or some combination of these. Even Trotsky's pride, according to Shafroth, was outfitted rather pell-mell: "And the troops of the Red Army were everywhere. Their uniforms are as assorted as those of the enemies they have fought against for the last three years."[12]

At least one of these ragtag specimens negotiating Moscow's cobblestones was partly decorated in an American Army uniform. He was in fact an American soldier by the name of Vikoren, who had gone into Siberia two years earlier with the American Expeditionary Force, Thirty-first Infantry. As he related his story to Carroll, "after a party" he was unable to rejoin his regiment. It seems to have been a farewell party, but not the kind Vikoren had imagined, because the Thirty-first sailed from Vladivostok without him. Left to his own resources, he decided to cross Siberia, arriving in Moscow sixteen months later. He expressed an interest in going home.[13]

In the evening of their Sunday holiday, Shafroth and a colleague took a horse carriage to the Bolshoi theater and back. They found it odd to have gone half a mile before seeing anyone in a white collar. "There is no middle class left, there are no bourgeois left. There are only the commissars and the people."

In one sense he was right about this. The Revolution had caused Russia's intricately layered social structure to collapse in a heap, hurling the privileged classes into the lower depths. The aristocracy, the clergy, and the bourgeoisie ceased to exist as organized entities, leaving only workers, peasants, and government bureaucrats. But of course the individual remnants of the once-privileged classes still walked the streets in 1921. The former well-to-do had pawned off their old clothing or otherwise made an effort, as a matter of self-preservation, to dress themselves so as to blend in, more or less, with the laboring masses. Shafroth's untrained eye could not as yet detect the difference, but in time he would learn to distinguish people from "former people," as the dispossessed came to be called.

Like Shafroth, Carroll found the Moscow landscape "most depressing." He, too, remarked on the shabby clothing, though Moscow's residents appeared to be much better fed than he had expected. He might have thought this because he had such low expectations going in. The men of the ARA, in their encounters with hardship across Central Europe, had found conditions worst in the urban centers, not least in the capital cities, where bread was scarcest, whereas the countryside was, generally speaking, not nearly as bad off. Thus, the Russian situation required of these relief workers some mental adjustments, beginning with the fact that the crisis at hand was a full-blown famine, striking directly at the actual producers of food. Moscow itself was as yet hardly affected since the actual scene of the catastrophe was five hundred miles east of the capital. Once they arrived on that scene they would discover that it was those who worked the land, the peasants themselves, and not the town dwellers, who were starving in large numbers. This realization would occur soon enough, but for now, observing the relative contentment of the residents of Moscow—the city's depressing air notwithstanding—the men of the advance party registered mild expressions of relief.

Carroll's reaction would have been entirely different had he arrived in Moscow and Petrograd in 1919, when actual starvation prevailed, cholera was epidemic, and people were dropping dead in the streets. This occurred during the most intense period of the Civil War, when Red Russia was cut off from the principal grain-growing regions, causing food supplies in the cities to dry up. The Bolshevik regime's priority was to feed its essential constituencies: Red Army soldiers, factory workers, and the fast-growing legions of government bureaucrats. Most everyone was hungry during the troubles, but especially vulnerable were the former aristocrats and members of the middle classes—merchants, teachers, professors, writers, lawyers, architects, engineers, and others. Though many found work in the ballooning state bureaucracy and could therefore claim a government food ration, and while some well-connected intellectuals found benefactors among the more enlightened Bolsheviks, such people died in disproportionately large numbers during the Civil War. The victims usually expired slowly, of hunger, cold, and disease, during what the survivors now remembered as the black years of 1918 to 1920.

Muscovites were eager to unload stories of their sufferings during those dark days on the arriving Americans, but as they spoke, in August 1921, they were merely severely undernourished, sick, and weary. Carroll observed, "The people are listless to a degree even greater than the easiest going of Serbians." Listless, but not lifeless.

Food could be gotten, if one had the means, but not in the usual retail stores since most were boarded up—that is, where the boards were still in place. On Kuznetskii Most, once the principal shopping avenue, Shafroth counted only one open store out of every ten or fifteen, most of those in operation being flower and barber shops. The fact that so many barbers were so quickly back in business struck him as strange. In fact, not a few of these salons were fronts for bootleggers, but Shafroth departed for the Volga before he had time to solve this little mystery.[14]

As for the food and other shops that had opened, in most cases the extent of their wares was on display in their windows. Much more buying and selling was going on outside the established stores. On Kuznetskii Most and on many other streets old women and children hawked small basketfuls of apples, pears, and plums. They squatted along the sidewalk, five or six on every block.

By far most trading was done in the open-air markets, which were sometimes as large as two or three city blocks, and contained hundreds of stalls. Here, within view if not always within price range, one found on sale bread, vegetables, meats, fruit, eggs, and other delicacies of hard times. Food was not all that was on offer at these bazaars, which resembled enormous flea markets. People brought their trinkets, knickknacks, old clothing—"practically anything that can be bought or sold"—which meant whatever they had managed to salvage from the old days. Shafroth called the big market, by which he must have meant the well-known Sukharevka, "a very remarkable sight."

Most exchange was conducted in the form of barter, the ruble having become devalued nearly out of existence by inflation. The rate of exchange on that particular day—and one could never be too time-specific—was thirty-four thousand rubles to a dollar. A person could get a meal in one of the few open restaurants for fifty to sixty thousand rubles. Using the currency meant carrying around a thick wad of thousand-ruble notes, which one customarily counted out as "five," "ten," or "twenty," the "thousand" being understood. How so many resourceful Muscovites accumulated such large quantities of paper money was puzzling to the Americans, as it was to many Russians, yet somehow they did it. The government paid most wages in food rations—at that time usually black bread and some sugar—supplemented once a month by a wispy thousand-ruble bill, which could not take you very far: at the market, on August 28, eggs cost twenty-five hundred rubles each, black bread seven hundred rubles a pound.

The Americans wondered where this food came from in a famine and how it found its way into Moscow. They were able to discover this for themselves after they returned from their Sunday sight-seeing to spend the night in their railroad car. It was late evening by the clock, but since they had advanced their watches by three hours at the border in order to put themselves on Russian time, it was still daylight. This enabled them to observe an unforgettable scene as a train pulled into the station and "a perfect mob" of men, women, and children clambered into and onto its empty box cars, presenting "a very fantastic sight in the half twilight."

What the relief workers were witnessing in this desperate scramble was graphic evidence of the near-total collapse of Russia's food distribution system. In fact the years of turmoil had almost completely severed the economic nexus between the cities and the countryside.

THE FOOD SUPPLY CRISIS in Russia had already begun during the war, partly as a consequence of the displacement caused by the wartime mobilization but as well due to the administrative incompetence and corruption of the tsarist government. The wartime blockade of its Baltic and Black Sea ports by the Central Powers put a halt to Russia's export of grain and raw materials as well as its import of industrial and consumer goods, resulting in a glut of foodstuffs, which the peasants had no incentive to sell because agricultural prices were low and because there was nothing for which to exchange their produce. This led to severe food shortages in the cities, as hunger came to Moscow and Petrograd already in 1916. In response, the government was forced to fix food prices and take measures to compel peasants to deliver grain to the state.[15]

Food was a central factor in the outbreak and course of the Revolution of 1917. The February Revolution that toppled the Romanovs began as a bread riot, and the scarcity of food did much to fuel political radicalization during 1917. In its own increasingly desperate attempts to find a solution to the problem, the Provisional Government established a state monopoly on grain. Yet it refused to act on the crucial, related question of the redistribution of the land, preferring to wait until the convening of the Constituent Assembly, an extraordinary body whose purpose would be to resolve such fundamental issues. But revolution in the countryside would not await the deliberations of democratically elected bodies. Peasants took matters into their own hands, dividing up among themselves gentry estates and church lands, a process catalyzed by the return to the villages of peasant soldiers deserting the front to take part in what rumor claimed was the mythical "black partition" of the land—to the land-starved Russian peasantry the equivalent of the proverbial Holy Grail.

An agrarian revolution was already in full swing, then, by the time the Bolsheviks came to power in November, a revolution their policies only served to accelerate. The Soviet decree "On Land" declared that the soil belonged to those who worked it, something the peasants deep in their Russian souls had always held to be true and thus needed little encouragement to act on. At this stage the Bolsheviks merely rode the wave of revolution, letting the peasants have their way in the breaking up of the large landed estates and the plundering of the manor houses. The populist "On Land" decree, which *socialized* the land and which the Bolsheviks essentially lifted from the program of their temporary Left-Socialist Revolutionary allies, "gave" the land to the peasants in an act of political expediency. Only in February 1918 did Lenin's government begin to assert its Marxist principles by *nationalizing* all the land—that is, claiming legal title to it for the state. Of course, that state was as yet incapable of acting upon any such paper nationalization, but the February decree signalled the direction the Bolsheviks intended to go.

The escalating agrarian revolution had the effect of greatly exacerbating the food supply crisis, which in turn encouraged the Soviet regime to take progressively more intrusive action. This drift toward state control did not start with the Bolsheviks, for the tsarist and provisional governments, too, had been forced to substitute control and coercion for market forces—as had, to a greater or lesser extent, all the wartime European governments. The White armies as well would employ coercive methods in the territories under their control in order to feed their troops. But the Bolsheviks, being Marxists, were different in that they aspired to create a communist society, that is, eventually to extinguish all elements of capitalism from the Russian economy. And so, although it was often the pressures of immediate circumstances that induced them to adopt increasingly radical economic measures, the fact that their draconian policies appeared to be speeding Russia's advance along the road to communism inspired them to see inevitability and opportunity where others saw mere expediency and exigency.

The Soviet government reaffirmed the state grain monopoly and the fixed food prices established by the Provisional Government. When hunger came to the northern, grain-consuming regions early in 1918, the Bolsheviks went over to more aggressive methods of grain collection, which helped bring about the split with their Left-SR coalition partners and hastened the onset of civil war. The decisive turn came in May with the establishment of a "food dictatorship," which gave the central government sweeping powers to extract grain from the countryside. Workers and peasants were called upon to unite in a relentless battle against the "rich" peasants, called *kulaks*—a traditional term used for better-off peasants but one sufficiently ambiguous to target anyone possessing a surplus. In order to enforce this "dictatorship," the government sponsored the formation of food requisition detachments, made up of Party members and workers recruited from the consuming regions. Lenin called for a "grain war," a "crusade" for bread, which he defined as a "merciless and terroristic struggle and war against peasants and other bourgeois concealing grain surpluses."[16]

The following month the government announced the creation of "committees of poor peasants," whose members were to take the lead in the collection of grain in return for a share of the spoils. The intention was to bring "class war" to the countryside, pitting the "poor" peasants against the "rich." In fact, what transpired was the plunder of the "haves" by the "have-nots," whose ranks were swelled by returning soldiers and hungry peasant-workers abandoning the factories. The result was the further spread of destruction and chaos in the countryside so that within a few months the committees had to be disbanded and the entire campaign abandoned. By summer the Civil War was beginning, and for the Bolsheviks to continue alienating the bulk of the peasantry would be to court disaster.

This ended, for now, the experiment of class war in the countryside, but the regime nonetheless found it necessary to proceed to squeeze the peasantry as a whole. As the Civil War intensified, in order to feed the Red Army and the cities the Bolsheviks had to rely increasingly on the forcible requisition of grain. Most of this work was done by armed food detachments, entering villages and uncovering grain "surpluses" at the point of a gun or bayonet, though by 1920, when the reputation of these units for ruthlessness had spread far and wide, it was said that their mere arrival on the scene was enough to make grain "appear." None of this caused the Bolsheviks to suffer pangs of ideological conscience. They had, after all, established a "dictatorship of the proletariat," and despite the spirit of collaboration implied in the emblematic hammer and sickle, the peasantry was never intended to be more than the junior partner in the revolutionary enterprise.

In the course of 1918 to 1920, the Soviet government assumed responsibility—on paper, anyway—for the provisioning of Red Russia's entire urban population and all the inhabitants of the grain-consuming provinces in the north. But with food increasingly scarce, the regime found it more and more difficult to supply adequate food rations even to its class allies in the cities, despite the gradual extension of its grain monopoly to cover all the more important food products, making them as well subject to requisition.

The official line was that the requisitioned food was a "loan" from the peasants to the cities until such time as there would be sufficient industrial goods to pay them back. The scarcity of such goods was due to a breakdown of industrial production, partly from the effects of the German war and the Civil War but also as a result of the chaos caused by the introduction of "workers' control" in the factories during the initial phase of the Revolution. In industry, too, the twin forces of circumstance and ideology encouraged a trend toward state control. In June 1918 the government nationalized all heavy industry, then proceeded incrementally to nationalize every other category—light industry, wholesale trade, retail trade, and cooperatives—until, near the end of 1920, state control had been extended to every enterprise hiring at least five employees. This is the order of affairs the paper decrees describe, but in reality the government lacked the apparatus to nationalize small industry and retail trade, and in any case by 1920 there was little active industry and no large-scale trade left to bring under control. Again, though, the laws indicate the direction of Bolshevik economic policy after the Civil War.

Here, then, was the basic mix of policies in agriculture and industry that would become known as War Communism, though only after they had been abandoned in 1921.[17] The term conveys the impression of a blueprinted program, when in fact the economic system in place at the end of 1920 had resulted from a spiralling series of ad hoc responses to the exigencies of civil war adopted with the general sanction of Marxist ideology. The fact that Lenin's government had built this War Communist structure under the pressures of war did not dampen Bolshevik enthusiasm for the end result. For what was the Civil War if not a class war on the battlefield? Thus, the emergency measures introduced during the struggle were not so much caused by war as forged in the fires of war, a war against the class enemy on an international scale. Taken together, they amounted to an accelerated approach toward "communism," albeit of a heroic-martyr variation unanticipated before the Revolution. As one Bolshevik put it in November 1920, if anyone was to blame for this, it was "the socialist logic of history."[18]

The fate of the ruble illustrates the dialectical interplay of ideology and circumstance. Serious inflation was not a product of the Soviet period, having already come to Russia during the war, when the imperial government set the printing presses turning in order to meet its expenses. Lenin's government, which nation-alized the State Bank and all private banks in 1917, also was forced to rely on this practice, until by the end of 1920 the ruble had become nearly worthless. To the Bolsheviks, the undermining of the currency, while it may not have been part of their short-term design, fit into their long-term plans. Any good Marxist could tell you that the future communist society would hold no place for this symbol of the exploitation of man by man. And because, by 1920, the communist utopia seemed suddenly very near indeed—nearer still because of the near-extinction of the ruble—it was felt that monetary relations, including all forms of taxation, should be allowed to wither away. Far be it for the world's first socialist govern-ment to rescue this remnant of the old order.

War Communism did not bring about the eradication of trade, however. Though the Bolsheviks were intent on the complete elimination of an activity they demonized as "speculation," they had of necessity to tolerate small-scale pri-vate trade in order to avoid a complete breakdown of food distribution. One manifestation of this relative tolerance was the open-air market, though its buy-ers and sellers were vulnerable to occasional sweeps conducted by the Cheka or Red Army soldiers. Another was an arrangement whereby residents of cities and towns were permitted to venture into the grain-growing regions to procure small amounts of food. The size of the allowance varied: now one-and-a-half poods, now two poods, or about eighty pounds. People desperate enough to have to take advantage of this opportunity were called *meshochniki*, or sackers, because of the sacks they used to transport the grain, potatoes, lard, or whatever it was they had managed to procure.

The Bolsheviks called them "speculators," but in fact most sackers were sim-ply trying to survive. Many were peasants from the north who journeyed south, mostly to Ukraine, to exchange the last of their possessions for food. This in-volved travel by rail for long periods of time under wretched conditions, includ-ing the punishing Russian winter. One veteran left behind a description of these sackers, who, he believed, faced hardships and dangers surpassing those of "the most risky expeditions to the African jungles or the North pole."

Hanging between the buffers of the cars with their sacks upon their shoulders, de-voured by lice, these spreaders of typhus, the people perished among the snow drifts. Scores and hundreds of corpses were taken from the tops of the ice-covered trains which crept from one station to another without any time-table: the corpses of unhappy "speculators" whose speculation consisted only in that they exchanged in some village their last shirt, blanket, or pan for two, three pounds of millet or a measure of peas.

All kinds of people, belonging to different classes of society, took part in these ex-peditions, all professions and all ages, men, women, and children: cabman and com-poser of music, journeyman and university professor, old [seamstresses] and school-boys—all formerly decent people now mix in one crowd of hungry, ragged beggars.[19]

Such activity served to hasten the deterioration of Russia's railway system. There are many descriptions from the period 1919 to 1921 of moving trains over-burdened with sackers, some so loaded down that from a distance they resembled swarms of bees. The "perfect mob" that Shafroth and his ARA colleagues ob-served at the Moscow train station was one such gathering swarm.

In the frigid winter of 1920–21, normal channels of distribution having broken down, sackers were an essential lifeline between town and village. Yet the Bolsheviks, riding the enthusiastic wave of War Communism and increasingly desperate to capture shrinking food supplies, chose to crack down on such activity. Special guard detachments stationed along the railway lines and major roads stepped up their confiscation of food carried by sackers returning home from the countryside. This highly unpopular practice played no small role in sparking political turmoil in January–February 1921, which briefly appeared to threaten the very existence of the regime. By this point, the Bolsheviks, in soldiering on with their War Communism even after the Civil War had ended, had become seriously out of touch with the mood of the country.

Ever since March 1918, when the Bolsheviks changed their official name from the Russian Social Democratic Workers' Party to the Communist Party, it was common to hear a peasant state that he was "for the Bolsheviks"—remembered as having decreed in 1917 that the land belonged to the peasants—but "against the Communists"—who since 1918 had been requisitioning grain. On the whole, though, the peasantry could tolerate a great deal at the hands of its new masters as long as the White armies were in the field threatening a restoration of the landlord. Once the fighting stopped, however, the villages met the requisition squads with stiffening resistance, and violence broke out, especially in the central provinces and in western Siberia, where it took the form of large-scale, organized revolts.

Meanwhile, for residents in the cities, exhausted after years of deprivation, the food situation was growing more desperate. Moscow required a minimum of 44 cars of grain per day to feed itself, but between January 20 and February 1 the daily average was only 33.4 incoming cars. At the same time, in the midst of an especially severe winter the city was running seriously short on fuel. Moscow's minimum need was 469 cars of fuel per day, whereas by mid-February it had to get by on only 380 cars.[20] The math was similarly dismal in other cities, where the governments responded by reducing food rations and clamping down on the individual self-provisioning of the sackers. It was in response to these measures that the workers in Moscow and Petrograd turned against their self-proclaimed Communist vanguard.

The Bolsheviks had justified making their proletarian revolution in backward Russia, where 80 percent of the population was rural, with the argument that this act would trigger a revolution across Europe, starting with Germany. But by 1920 political stability had returned to Central Europe, and it dawned on the men in the Kremlin that the workers of the world were not going to unite anytime soon. For now, Soviet Russia would have to go it alone. The uncertain future of the first socialist state was clouded further by the fact that its relatively tiny working class, which in 1917 had numbered 3 to 3.5 million out of a total population of 170 million, had shrunk by 1920 to as few as 1.2 million. Many workers had been called up into the army, others drafted into the Party and state bureaucracies, while still others had melted away into the countryside as industry came to a near-standstill. The disappearance of the proletariat reflected a general and equally precipitous decline in the population of urban Russia, with the number of Moscow's residents falling by nearly one-half and Petrograd's by more than two-thirds since the onset of the troubles.[21]

Just as the number of workers declined, so too did the quality of those who remained at the bench. Russia's workers had been a peasantized lot even before the Revolution, retaining strong ties to the land that were most apparent at harvest time, when many returned to the village to help bring in the crop. The large exodus of skilled workers from the ranks of the proletariat during the Civil War reinforced this rustic quality: the epithet "peasants in the factories" was even more apt in 1920 than in 1917.

The Bolsheviks were not unaware of these developments, but were nonetheless taken aback in the first week of February 1921, when Moscow's workers began to pass resolutions demanding the right to engage in free trade and heckled and shouted down Party speakers, even Lenin himself on one occasion. The Party faithful, who never stopped thinking in ideological categories, recoiled in horror and agonized aloud that the Russian proletariat, in whose name they had made a revolution, had become "déclassé." That is to say, workers were exhibiting a petty-bourgeois, or peasant, mentality. In fact all that these cold and hungry people wanted was the freedom to try to feed themselves in order to stay alive.

The jolt provided by these rowdy protests, occurring as they did against a backdrop of growing violence in the countryside, convinced Lenin and key Party leaders of the absolute necessity to embark on a retreat in economic policy. Before they could act, however, in the last days of February there came the greatest shock of all in the form of a rebellion of the sailors at Kronstadt, the tiny island in the Gulf of Finland, near Petrograd. The Kronstadt sailors had provided crucial support to the Bolsheviks in 1917 and remained a symbol of Red October, and thus their defection was especially dramatic and portentous. They, too, were now hungry and, maintaining their own close ties to the village, had seen for themselves or heard about the work of the food requisition squads and guard detachments. Thus, their principal demand was for the right to trade, but they did not stop there. Eerily echoing 1917, they revived Lenin's revolutionary slogan "All Power to the Soviets," turning this political weapon back on the Bolshevik regime. Trotsky, who had been loud in praise of the Kronstadt sailors as the pride and glory of the Revolution, ordered his Red Army soldiers across the ice to put down the rebellion, which was accomplished only with considerable loss of life.[22]

Even as Kronstadt was being pacified, in the second week of March Lenin was taking steps to meet the chief economic demand of the rebels. At the Tenth Party Congress in Moscow, surmounting the doubts and fears of the assembled delegates, he initiated a retreat from War Communism by muscling through a resolution ending grain requisitions and allowing limited free trade. The measure was intended merely to give peasants the right to trade their individual surpluses at the market, thus restricting trade to forms of local exchange. But once the door was opened a crack, private trade burst through—"broke loose," as Lenin put it. Through the spring and summer the market spread like wildfire—behaving "according to Marx," in the phrase of Politburo member Lev Kamenev.[23]

The concession on trade was merely the first step of a yearlong transition to a first-of-its-kind partial market economy called the New Economic Policy, popularly known by the acronym NEP. Retail trade and small-scale industry were left unfettered, while the state retained control over the economy's "commanding heights": heavy industry, the railroads, the utilities, and foreign trade.

A major threshold was crossed on August 9 when state industry was allowed to sell part of its production on the market. By the end of the month, when the American relief workers came on the scene, Moscow had become a "pit of speculation," in Shafroth's words. All the same, the New Economic Policy was still new, and many were as yet hesitant to display their wares for fear of confiscation. The boundaries of the permissible were still undefined. And—who could tell?—NEP itself might be, as some whispered, a clever Bolshevik trick to lure people into bringing their valuables out of hiding.

Such doubts were largely dispelled in the autumn, when Lenin delivered a pair of shocking public speeches to fellow-Bolsheviks, in which he judged War Communism to have been "a mistake," and called on all Party members to learn to "master trade" and to prepare for a "transition to commercial principles"—in other words, for a further retreat into capitalism.[24]

What confounded many observers at the time was that the same leaders who had guided the Revolution through its most radical phase were now overseeing the reaction, as if Robespierre had kept his head in 1794 and himself introduced Thermidor. Lenin the extreme radical of 1917 had transformed himself into Lenin the extreme moderate of 1921. Quite predictably, the Bolshevik leader's blunt talk about the return to capitalism sowed confusion and disillusionment within the Party, as the faithful struggled to understand why they should now tolerate the private trader—the speculator—after three years of hard work to liquidate his kind. Communism itself had seemed within grasp, yet Lenin could now be heard classifying the Soviet economy as "state capitalism," a term that met with prickly resistance within the ranks, as did the NEP reforms themselves in some quarters.[25]

It was at this point, with Bolshevism in panicky retreat, that the ARA entered the country and began to mount its operations across a large swath of the Russian heartland. Of course the very presence of famine relief workers from the world's foremost capitalist country only aggravated the Party's general state of anxiety. Politically speaking, it was worse than the famine itself.

THE GREAT FAMINE OF 1921 was not a factor in the Bolshevik decision to abandon War Communism, though perhaps it would have been had the government paid earlier and more serious attention to omens of the looming catastrophe. At the beginning of January 1921 the writer Vladimir Korolenko addressed an anxious letter to culture commissar Anatolii Lunacharsky and writer Maxim Gorky, in which he warned, inconsonantly, that "an unprecedented calamity is impending such perhaps as we have not seen since the days of Czar Alexis."[26]

This was a remarkable statement, considering that Alexis had been tsar in the mid-seventeenth century and that Russia had had since that time a rich history of famine. Several factors explain this historic vulnerability. Although it covered a vast territory, Russia had a limited agricultural area and a relatively dense population and thus considerable "land hunger" in the grain-growing provinces, which the end of serfdom in 1861 did little to alleviate. Nor did the emancipation of the peasantry bring reform to the traditional peasant commune, whose structure and conventions enforced a debilitating inefficiency on the countryside and discouraged the development of modern farming methods. Right up to the Revolution most peasants still farmed their land according to the ancient three-crop rotation. Late in the day, the tsarist government finally undertook a serious effort to break up the communes and form a class of independent, large-landholding peasants, but it was too little, too late.

The result of all this was that Russian agriculture easily produced the lowest yield per unit of any European country. Russia enjoyed a reputation as a great exporter of grain, but most peasants lived in poverty. The grain sent abroad came chiefly from the great estates of landed proprietors and a few rich peasants—in other words, those who would take the biggest fall in the Revolution.

This state of affairs, combined with the harsh climate, left Russia prone to periodic famine. In living memory were three series of major crop failures—1890–93, 1906–08, and 1910–11—as well as local famines in 1898 and 1900–01. The peasant was usually able to carry over a reserve for one year, but if two bad years came in succession, he might starve.

The devastating famine of 1921 was indeed the largest in modern Russian history—that is, up to that time. Its significance has been obscured by the similarly deadly but politically more notorious famine of 1932–33, centered in Ukraine. Robert Conquest has called that calamity the "terror-famine" because of its man-made character, though the extent of Stalin's culpability and whether the crime deserves to be called "genocide" are subjects of learned and emotional debate. The 1921 famine does not carry this political baggage, though it, too, was no simple act of nature.[27]

The roots of the disaster can be traced to the disruption caused by the Great War, which mobilized eleven million men and two million horses, drawing them away from agricultural production. A combination of unavoidable economic dislocation and the unwise food policies of the tsarist government reduced the incentives of the peasants to plant crops, so that between the outbreak of the war and the February Revolution the area under cultivation in European Russia reportedly declined by 25 percent, in Ukraine by 10 percent, and in Asiatic Russia by 25 percent. This downward trend continued during the revolutionary years as a result of the agrarian upheaval of 1917–18, the Civil War—which was fought on the greater part of the country's most fertile agricultural areas—and, as well, War Communism in the countryside.

Peasants responded to Bolshevik food requisitions with a great "strike," reducing the land under cultivation to a bare minimum, enough to feed themselves and, if they wanted to risk it, a bit more for a safe hiding place. It has been estimated that the area of sown acreage in the consumer provinces of the north fell by 18 percent from 1917 to 1921, while in the producing regions the decline was 33 percent.

When disaster struck, many peasants, not surprisingly, were quick to blame the government, complaining bitterly that "The Bolsheviks know how to take, but not how to give." Typically, though, when it came to pointing fingers, these same peasants were apt to aim skyward. As they understood it, God had inflicted the drought of 1920–21 upon them. As Fisher recounts, "The spring [of 1920] was hot and almost rainless, and the land at the time of spring planting was caked and dry. The summer followed with scant rain, cereals ripened before their time, and the crops were far from satisfactory. In the autumn, again, there was insufficient rain, and the winter crops were sown in soil too dry to promise fruition." Winter brought only light snow, and in spring 1921 rainfall was slight and hot weather came early. By then Russia was in the midst of a major drought, most seriously affecting the Volga Basin, the Asiatic frontier, and southern Ukraine. The drought produced a second successive crop failure, and that meant famine.[28]

Of course the Bolsheviks cannot be held accountable for acts of God. Still, on the matter of the drought they are culpable for having failed to take timely action in the face of unmistakable signs of danger, which should have been evident as early as autumn 1920 even to readers of the Soviet press. Worse still, grain requisitioning, which was supposed to have been ended in March 1921, continued in some especially vulnerable regions of the Volga valley into the summer. Only by early summer did the government at last seem to recognize the enormity of the problem and begin to act, though it took longer still to arrive at the decision to request outside assistance. Having to seek food relief from abroad would have been embarrassing enough for any great power in eclipse, but for the pariah government in the Kremlin the prospect was supremely humiliating.

The first official acknowledgment of the crisis appeared in *Pravda* on June 26, which described a famine worse than that of 1891, affecting about twenty-five million people, a total later raised to thirty-five million. Subsequently, on June 30, *Pravda* reported that a mass flight from the famine regions was underway. Such articles multiplied in July when they were picked up by the European press; American awareness of the catastrophe came more slowly.

Initially, Bolshevik publicists openly scorned the idea of applying to Western governments for aid and claimed at most to be counting on the contributions of the international proletariat. But the leadership understood that the workers of the world were in no position to save Soviet Russia from starvation and that any significant relief from abroad would have to be sponsored by imperialist governments. In the first week of July two appeals went out from Moscow, one from Patriarch Tikhon of the Russian Orthodox Church and the other, of far greater consequence, from Maxim Gorky.

Gorky, who had had by this time a long and complicated relationship with Lenin and the Bolsheviks, had since 1917 been serving as a kind of intercessor for the intelligentsia with the regime, a role facilitated by his personal access to the Soviet leader. This involved him in situations of political and moral ambiguity sufficient to earn him detractors and enemies among anti-Bolsheviks. He had only recently been instrumental in obtaining official permission for the establishment of a home-grown famine relief committee led by "bourgeois" former political figures, an experiment that was destined to be short-lived. His ambiguous political status suited him to the job of petitioning the outside world on behalf of Soviet Russia.

Gorky's appeal, "To All Honest People," was published in the West in late July.[29] In typically dry prose its author announced that a crop failure caused by drought was threatening the lives of millions of Russians. He invoked the common cultural heritage of Europeans and Americans. "Gloomy days have come to the country of Tolstoy, Dostoevsky, Mendeleev, Pavlov, Mussorgsky, Glinka, etc." In other words, forget for the moment the names of Lenin and Trotsky: "I ask all honest European and American people for prompt aid to the Russian people. Give bread and medicine."

CHAPTER 2

FOOD AND WEAPONS

Gorky's appeal was read by millions in the West, but only one man was in a position to meet the emergency that inspired it. Time passes, and the more puzzling it is to discover that Herbert Hoover, whose name is forever joined in the American mind with images of the Great Depression, was in an earlier day regarded at home and abroad as the Great Humanitarian of the age. Millions of hungry children and adults in war-ravaged Europe were sustained by food relief he organized and administered. Gorky was quite aware of this, and he must have wondered now what effect his alarm about a Russian famine would have on this towering figure, who also happened to be famously anti-Bolshevik.

Hoover rose to prominence by overcoming his humble beginnings as a poor Iowa orphan and achieving enormous wealth and international renown as a mining engineer.[1] He had a reputation in the business world as a technical innovator, a skillful manager of money, and a brilliant administrator. His rags-to-riches story sounds quintessentially American, yet by 1914 his mining operations had kept him occupied outside the United States for most of his adult life, and it was his actions abroad that would establish his credentials as a humanitarian.

The outbreak of the Great War, which found Hoover at his mining company's London headquarters, served to catapult him onto the world stage. The guns of August 1914 stranded nearly two-hundred thousand American tourists, who gathered in England with dwindling resources and no means to get home. Hoover was asked by the U.S. ambassador to Great Britain to apply his energies to their predicament, which he did by arranging to furnish them with emergency funds and transportation to the States.

Having thus aided his fellow countrymen, Hoover was making his own preparations to sail for home when, in December, his services were requested to help manage a much more formidable crisis: the fate of the hungry Belgians living under German occupation. Was Hoover willing to bring his international contacts and his business talents to bear on alleviating their plight? His decision to accept this challenge profoundly changed the course of his life. It led him to establish the neutral Commission for Relief in Belgium, the CRB, which undertook with surprising success the feeding of the citizens of occupied Belgium across the British blockade and numerous political and diplomatic minefields. Before long the CRB acquired the attributes of an independent state: it flew its own flag, issued its own passports, and operated its own fleet of cargo ships under an immunity agreed to by all the belligerent powers. Hoover's own American agents distributed CRB food within Belgium until the United States entered the war, at which point operations on the ground were handed over to a neutral Spanish-Dutch committee.

The CRB marked the inauguration of a unique brand of humanitarian enterprise, which was soon to become familiar to, though not always fully understood and appreciated by, Europeans and Americans. Hoover conducted his relief programs along the same lines as his mining operations, employing the same creatively aggressive financing strategies, strict accounting methods, efficient administration, and even commercial principles. The CRB operated on funding from the governments of Great Britain, France, and the United States, from private sources, and from the modest profits of its own commercial activities, chiefly the sale of food. Over its four-and-a-half-year existence it provided relief worth more than $880 million.

This was the beginning of a marriage of convenience between philanthropy and business, one engineered and sustained by the unmatched resourcefulness of "the Chief," as Hoover was called by the men serving under him. Hoover was no committee man. In the name of executive efficiency he maintained supreme authority over the CRB, though operations were decentralized, with the men in the field given a good deal of leeway within the general principles laid down by Hoover. The commission's central staff consisted mostly of past and present business associates, while the several dozen relief workers were recruited heavily from among the nearly one hundred Rhodes Scholars enrolled at Oxford, who were eager to see something of the war. These CRB volunteers developed a keen sense of loyalty to the Chief—another hallmark of every Hoover enterprise—and several of them would go into Soviet Russia in 1921 as ARA men.

In May 1917, a month after the United States entered the war, Hoover arrived in Washington, welcomed as "the savior of Belgium." Wilson appointed him head of the new Food Administration, placing him in charge of the country's wartime food supply, which meant both the military and the civilian populations as well as the provisioning of the Allied countries. As food administrator, Hoover employed a mixture of compulsion and appeals for voluntary rationing in order to encourage food conservation. Americans underwent "meatless" and "wheatless" days and were subject to hortatory and moralistic advertising campaigns built around the theme "Food Will Win the War."

So closely identified was the name of the food administrator with his program that the verb "to Hooverize" for a time almost replaced "economize" in the American vocabulary. Hoover brushed off the "food dictator" label applied to him by both supporters and critics, but his manner of directing the Food Administration earned him this badge. He made enemies in and out of the Wilson administration, usually as a result of jealousy engendered less by his high profile than by his fierce instinctive drive for bureaucratic control.

When the war ended, Hoover accompanied Wilson to Paris to act as adviser to the American delegation to the peace conference, his principal duties involving the administration of American relief to Europe. Thus, entering through the food-supply door, Hoover joined the ranks of the statesmen responsible for settling the peace and shaping the postwar order.[2]

In Paris Hoover continued to serve as food administrator, though he accumulated other titles. In November 1918 he was made director general of relief for the Allied governments, essentially confirming his status as food administrator for the Allies, and in January 1919 he was named principal executive of the Allied Supreme Economic Council. However he was addressed, he felt duty-bound to retain American control over food distribution, resisting the encroachments of those "pinheads of bureaucratic Europe," as he called them. The United States having the food, Hoover was able to have his way. He conducted himself not as the Allies' chosen representative to administer relief to Europe but as the U.S. food administrator working out of the Paris branch office. And he did it in true Hoover style, undertaking the economic reconstruction of Europe with what biographer David Burner calls his "typical cold aggressiveness."[3] European statesmen recoiled in horror at the effect produced by Hoover's sturdy American fingers on the piano keys of old-world diplomacy.

In January 1919, at Hoover's suggestion, Wilson asked Congress for an appropriation of $100 million for European relief, which was granted on February 25. To manage these funds, Hoover arranged for the president to establish a separate government agency, the American Relief Administration, with Hoover as its director general. He built a staff from among his CRB and Food Administration veterans and enlisted as his field workers some fifteen hundred U.S. Army and Navy officers, demobilized during their time of service with the ARA.

During the nine months following the armistice, Hoover organized the distribution of over $1 billion in relief, which translates into over four million tons of food and other supplies delivered to children and adults across Europe all the way to the inconstant borders of Bolshevik Russia. Except for the portion purchased with funds from the congressional appropriation, these massive quantities of relief administered by the ARA were supplied through the U.S. Food Administration.[4]

This sketches the food relief story only through the armistice period. Upon the signing of the Treaty of Versailles, on June 28, the Food Administration expired by law. Three days later, the ARA's distribution of the congressional $100 million having been completed, Hoover created a private successor to that public agency: the American Relief Administration European Children's Fund, the A.R.A.E.C.F., though its full name and initials were used only on paper and within the organization. Everyone knew it as the ARA.

During the next two years, the quasi-private ARA delivered food worth over $150 million to children in twenty-one countries in central, eastern, and southeastern Europe and the Near East, functioning either independently or in conjunction with other private relief organizations. Its operations required a close involvement in matters of transportation and communications. This was of course unavoidable on a continent torn apart by war, but Hoover had a knack for making the most of it, as Burner describes:

Hoover coordinated the distribution of food and the means of financing its purchase, restored to useful service river craft and rolling stock, took charge—or attempted to—of ports and canals and traffic on the Rhine, the Elbe, the Vistula, the Danube, rebuilt telegraphic and postal communication, renewed coal production for homes and industry, eradicated much contagious disease including typhus, and arranged barter where food could be moved in no other way. He coordinated Congress, the Treasury, the Shipping Board (where he could), the armed forces, and his own food agencies. Anyone who wished to communicate among European countries had to do so through Hoover.[5]

The ARA employed in all these countries only skeletal staffs of Americans to supervise much larger numbers of local citizens. The philosophy behind its modus operandi was to encourage the initiative of the population, emphasize the idea of self-help over charity, and at the same time keep overhead costs as low as possible. The American relief workers, as dispensers of food in a time of great hunger, commanded extraordinary authority. They enjoyed access to the highest government officials and remarkable influence in political matters, while their "Hoover passports" served them as laissez-passer to points on the map off-limits to ordinary mortals. Acting in tandem with the relief workers in Poland, Austria, Czechoslovakia, and Yugoslavia were teams of unofficial American "technical advisers," who counseled government officials on economic reconstruction, with an emphasis on the revival of transport. Their secondary agenda was to promote U.S. commercial interests in these countries, a consideration that always had a place in Hoover's crowded mind.

General Pershing called Hoover the "food regulator of the world." Wilson remained wary of him, while regarding his services as indispensable. The president had been warned by Colonel House, a Hoover booster, who had written Wilson in April 1917 that the savior of Belgium was "the kind of man that has to have complete control in order to do the thing well."[6] Hoover's correspondence with heads of state and government and with other political, military, religious, and business leaders conveys a sense of the driving energy he applied to matters of food relief and to securing America's—and thus his own—control over its administration. Hoover's achievement earned him the eternal gratitude of millions; his methods ruffled as many feathers.

The authoritative voice of this aggressive correspondent seems strikingly out of character with that shy, awkward, figure of the silent newsreels, the only Hoover known to most Americans of later generations. To them the President Hoover of 35 mm appears distinctly unpresidential as he stands there, self-conscious, blinking uncomfortably at the camera. Of course, the image suffers from the unavoidable associations with hard times and from the inevitable unfortunate contrast with the face of his nemesis, the candidate FDR, with its ferocious smile and jutting chin projecting confidence in every frame. Hoover once wrote: "I have never liked the clamor of crowds. I intensely dislike superficial social contacts. . . . I was terrorized at the opening of every speech."[7] Motion pictures were unkind to him; television would have been unkinder still. But on paper, in earlier and better times, he could move the world. Perhaps not quite the world: there was the small matter of Russia.

NO AMERICAN FOOD was delivered to Bolshevik Russia in the armistice and post-Versailles periods, but Bolshevik Russia was at the heart of the story of postwar American relief to Europe.

America's benevolence, as orchestrated by Hoover, was inspired by a combination of interrelated motives. The most apparent was pure humanitarianism, which was by then becoming a peculiarly American vocation. Central as well was a concern to speed the economic and political reconstruction of Europe, not least in order to revive the market for U.S. goods. Less elevated, but not inconsiderable, was the desire to unload America's sizable agricultural surpluses, whose accumulation was largely attributable to the policies of food administrator Hoover. And inseparable from these considerations, and suffusing the distribution of food aid with a crusading spirit, was a determination, as Hoover phrased it, "to stem the tide of Bolshevism."

Of immediate concern were the destitute peoples of Central Europe—the term used in that era to designate the stretch of territory from the Rhine to the western border of Red Russia. The economic and political instability of these mostly fledgling states, risen from the ashes of old empires, made them vulnerable to the spread from the East of "the disease of Bolshevism," in a popular conception of the day. It was generally assumed that this malady was caused by hunger. The Russian Revolution itself was thus diagnosed—certainly by Hoover, who reduced it to a "food riot." The failure to relieve food shortages during the course of 1917 had cleared the way for the monstrous Lenin and Trotsky to take power. Bolshevism, then, was what happened when good people went hungry, even the instinctively democratic Russians of Wilson's imagination.

"Bolshevism," Harold Fisher wrote in 1927 of the immediate postwar years, "in most minds did not represent a political or economic theory, but the destruction of public order, the end of all security of person and property, the reign of bloody violence." This simplified understanding of the phenomenon led reasonable people to believe that if Central Europe succumbed to Bolshevism, it would be hard to save the rest of Europe from the same fate. Thus on April 25, 1919, in the midst of the crisis, Hoover wrote: "Of course, the prime objective of the United States in undertaking the fight against famine in Europe is to save the lives of starving people. The secondary object, however, and of hardly less importance, was to defeat Anarchy, which is the handmaiden of Hunger."[8] It is telling that the word "anarchy" was used interchangeably with "Bolshevism" in these early days. Hoover was casually aware of the elaborate theoretical foundations of the Soviet experiment, but like most people he understood that whatever mass appeal it enjoyed could only be the result of misery and a breakdown of order.

Everyone assumed that the Bolsheviks in Russia were making every effort to spread this anarchy. Ever since their October coup, they had been forecasting an imminent worldwide revolution, declaring, like true Marxists, that it was inevitable but also, like true Leninists, that it was essential in the short term to the survival of Bolshevik rule in Russia. Thus, any government not made in the Soviet image was considered illegitimate, not to mention inherently dangerous, and had to be overthrown. The organizational mechanism set up to coordinate this effort was the Communist International, the Comintern, whose membership included all Communist parties but which was based in Moscow and dominated and controlled by the Bolsheviks. The Comintern's heaviest weapon by far was propaganda, which it targeted mostly at Germany, assumed to be the best and strategically the most important prospect for a socialist revolution.

"Bolshevism is steadily advancing westward, has overwhelmed Poland, and is poisoning Germany," Wilson cabled congressional leaders from Paris in January 1919. "It cannot be stopped by force but it can be stopped by food."[9] This conviction did not apply to the Russian mecca itself, where Wilson apparently came to believe that the disease could be conquered by force of arms. Otherwise the American Expeditionary Force would not have become entangled in the Russian Civil War. In the debate over Allied intervention, Hoover stood by the antidote of food—predictably, perhaps, for someone who commanded not soldiers but relief workers. In a memorandum to Wilson dated March 28, 1919, he argued that it was a mistake to send troops into Russia, thereby giving the Bolsheviks an excuse for their failures. Left undisturbed, they would make a big enough mess on their own: "No greater fortune can come to the world than that these foolish ideas should have an opportunity somewhere of bankrupting themselves."

For this reason as well he opposed the Allied economic blockade of Russia, imposed as a war measure in the summer of 1918 to prevent cooperation between Germany and Russia, and then maintained as a *cordon sanitaire* for a year after the peace treaty. Better to "lift the curtain on this experiment in economics," Hoover believed.

In his March 28 memo to Wilson, which was an extended essay on America and Bolshevism, he wrote that if it happened that the Kremlin undertook a military crusade in order to advance communism westward, then the United States had to be prepared to fight, and for the same reasons that it had entered the war against Germany. Absent such an offensive, however,

[W]e should not involve ourselves in what may be a ten-year military entanglement in Europe. The American people cannot say that we are going to insist that any given population must work out its internal social problems according to our particular conception of democracy. In any event, I have the most serious doubt that outside forces entering upon such an enterprise can do other than infinite harm, for any great wave of emotion must ferment and spread under repression. In the swing of the social pendulum from the extreme left back toward the right, it will find the point of stabilization based on racial instincts that could never be established by outside intervention.

The pendulum analogy was Hoover's favorite for explaining political developments in Central Europe. He found it unsurprising that radicalism, which was "based on a foundation of real social grievance," was ascendant in those lands where reactionary tyranny once ruled. "If former revolutions in ignorant masses [*sic*] are any guide, the pendulum will yet swing back to some moderate position when bitter experience has taught the economic and social follies of present obsessions." The interference of the Allied armies in Russia might serve to halt or even reverse the swing of the pendulum.

On the other hand, there could be no thought of the United States granting political recognition to "this murderous tyranny" in Moscow, a step that would only serve to stimulate "actionist radicalism" in Europe.[10] Hoover had in mind the very thing going on at that moment in northern Germany, the scene of radical-socialist disturbances, including a failed uprising by the Sparticist League in Berlin. Yet his idea to crush this "incipient Bolshevism" by importing food ran against the grain of public sentiment in Europe and America, which opposed giving succor to a defeated enemy, especially the bestial Hun. Such assistance was explicitly circumscribed in the $100 million congressional appropriation of January 1919, forcing Hoover to improvise its funding until June, when the signing of the Treaty of Versailles made it easier to raise money directly for the relief of Germany and Austria.[11]

Northern Germany was not the only scene of revolutionary activity in the first half of 1919. In Hungary a Soviet regime was established in March under Bela Kun and endured a troubled four months before being overturned by invading Romanian troops with Allied encouragement. Bavaria saw a leftist uprising in April, followed by the declaration of the Bavarian Soviet Republic, which survived only a few weeks. In Vienna in mid-June there was an attempted Communist rising, which was shortly crushed.[12]

In the end, American food was widely seen as having prevented this period of crisis from becoming Europe's "October." Hoover was never shy about taking the credit for the United States. Several years later, in a private letter, he wrote that "at no time were we of any other mind than that the European relief in 1919 was the greatest battle ever made against Bolshevism."[13] While the battle was underway, however, this kind of talk was muted in favor of the more uplifting message of rescuing Europe's children from starvation. Hoover's anti-Bolshevism caused people at the time, as it has ever since, to question the authenticity of his humanitarianism. If the purpose of American relief was to stem the Bolshevik tide, then all the affecting words about Europe's starving children could not have been entirely to the point. In other words, the Great Humanitarian had a political agenda. But in understanding Hoover's motives it is not helpful to insist on a dichotomy of humanitarianism versus anti-Bolshevism. To Hoover, just as to Wilson and to most Western statesmen at the time, Bolshevism was a symptom of people in distress; thus, fighting Bolshevism *was* humanitarian.

WHERE HOOVER STANDS OUT from the rest is in the typically muscular way he acted on his ideas. It was not enough to use food simply to contain Bolshevism; his mind worked overtime on ways to deploy the weapon inside the enemy's territory. Among the several proposals for dealing with the Russia problem discussed by the diplomats in Paris was one put forward by Hoover in March 1919 to establish a neutral commission to administer food relief inside Bolshevik Russia, along the lines of the wartime mission to Belgium. The plan called for a halt to the fighting in the Russian Civil War and for the Bolsheviks to cease their "propaganda" in the West. With hostilities suspended, the commission would take control over all distribution and transportation within Russia, Red and White. To lead this effort Hoover proposed Fridtjof Nansen, the Norwegian explorer, scientist, and humanitarian—a man considered likely to be an acceptably neutral figure to the Bolsheviks—though there was no doubt who was to be the moving force behind the scenes. Wilson approved the plan and brought it to the other Allied chiefs for action.[14]

How Hoover and Wilson could believe that the Soviet government might find such an arrangement acceptable is hard to fathom. Kennan characterizes the plan as an attempt to extort an end to the Civil War on terms favorable to the Allies by using "food as a weapon." One states one's conditions and leaves it to the putative beneficiary to take it or leave it. In revolutionary Russia, where food was rationed in favor of class allies, the notion of its "fair and impartial" distribution meant necessarily feeding class enemies. There was in fact nothing neutral about the proposed commission. It was a design for intervention of the most extreme kind and was tantamount to ordering the Bolsheviks to call off the Revolution.

Nevertheless, the Big Four endorsed the plan on April 17, on which date they signed a letter addressed to Nansen, spelling out some of the details. The distribution of food in Russia was to be under the control of local food committees consisting of citizens selected within each community, the system employed by the ARA in all its European operations. Yet Russia was not like anywhere else, as even a cursory knowledge of events since 1917 should have made apparent. The entire scheme strikes Kennan as preposterous: "Was there ever, one wonders, any greater nonsense than this curious document, bearing the signatures of Orlando, Lloyd George, Wilson, and Clemenceau? . . . The very suggestion of local community action of this sort reflected a terrifying naïveté as to what the Russia of that hour was really like." The commission idea, it hardly needs to be said, came to nothing.[15]

It is revealing that in advancing his proposal, Hoover repeatedly cited as the precedent the Commission for Relief in Belgium, where neutral relief workers fed a country's citizens with the permission of its foreign occupiers. And the CRB conducted its operations without recognizing the German authorities in Belgium as the legitimate government. That Hoover—and indeed the Big Four—assumed such a parallel underscores the fact that they were under a serious misapprehension about the significance of the Russian Revolution.

Not long after this, Hoover became involved in a Russian relief project of a very different sort, by providing food to the White armies in the Civil War. During the armistice period, the ARA supplied Denikin's army on credit at the request of the Supreme War Council. Of greater potential consequence, at the direction of the U.S. State Department, in the summer and autumn of 1919 the by now private ARA provisioned Yudenitch's Northwestern Army as it advanced through the Baltic region toward Petrograd. This American food was paid for by Kolchak's provisional government, and its distribution was coordinated by the ARA's Baltic chief, John Miller, with the ultimate goal of delivering food to the residents of Petrograd as soon as Yudenitch's forces entered that city. They never got there, coming only as far as the outskirts. In the critical hour, in October, with Lenin prepared to abandon the cradle of the Revolution, Trotsky arrived on the scene to rally the Red forces and push Yudenitch back—much in the style, one cannot help but imagine, of one of Moor's heroic-revolutionary posters.

As defiantly proud as he was of his role in the struggle against Bolshevism, Hoover never owned up to his involvement in the failed Yudenitch offensive. He claimed on many occasions afterward that the ARA had fed only civilians behind the lines of the Northwestern Army. Yet he would have known full well that even had this been the letter of the plan, it would have been impossible to execute, as Yudenitch's men could not have been encouraged to charge at Petrograd on empty stomachs while abundant food supplies pulled up the rear. Fisher's 1927 official ARA history has not a word to say about this episode, nor about the fact that in August 1919 Hoover urged the State Department to provide arms and supplies to Yudenitch—which it did, though without influencing the outcome on the Baltic front. This dilutes somewhat the force of Hoover's admonitions against using military force to defeat Bolshevism, even though in this case it was Russians themselves doing the actual fighting. All the same, it is a safe bet that had Yudenitch's offensive broken through, altering the course of the Civil War and even bringing down the Bolshevik regime, the story of that triumph would have been inseparable from the role played by American food. The Chief would have made sure of that.[16]

The outbreak of the Russo-Polish war in the summer of 1920 provided Hoover with a different kind of opening to Russia. In August, toward the end of the conflict, as the Red Army's counteroffensive brought it westward into Polish territory, he directed two of his relief workers stationed in the area to remain on the scene as the Red forces moved in and then to accompany the Polish armistice delegation to Minsk. From there the Soviets allowed the two Americans to proceed to Moscow, where they held discussions with officials in the People's Commissariat of Foreign Affairs.[17] Their purpose was to gain official permission to continue child-feeding operations in the territories in eastern Poland only just occupied by the Bolsheviks, but also to explore the possibility of the ARA administering relief in the central cities of European Russia. These talks came to nothing when the Bolsheviks stipulated that the food had to be distributed through their own relief machinery and that the Soviet government had to be contacted officially by the U.S. State Department. The point of demanding such contact, of course, was to use it to secure political recognition. One year later the Kremlin leaders would not be in a position to hold out for either condition.

In Washington in mid-1920 the idea of extending diplomatic recognition to the Soviet regime was still completely out of the question, even though by then all American troops had officially left Russian soil and the White cause was lost. As it happened, just at the time that Hoover's emissaries were on their way to Moscow, the U.S. government issued the first clear statement of its Russia policy since the Revolution. This took the form of a diplomatic note by Secretary of State Bainbridge Colby, which presented a clear and vigorous statement of the reasons the United States would not establish official relations with the current rulers of Russia. It had nothing to do, Colby declared, with Soviet Russia's internal political or social system. Rather, the problem was that "the existing regime in Russia is based upon the negation of every principle of honor and good faith, and every usage and convention, underlying the whole structure of international law." Soviet spokesmen had many times declared that "it is their understanding that the very existence of Bolshevism in Russia, the maintenance of their own rule, depends, and must continue to depend, upon the occurrence of revolutions in all other great civilized nations, including the United States." It was not possible to maintain official relations with men "determined and bound to conspire against our institutions."[18]

This unambiguous declaration of principle left Soviet diplomacy no room for maneuver. The men in the Kremlin wondered if the U.S. position might soften under the new Harding administration, although the designation of Hoover as secretary of commerce was not a good omen. Soon after Harding's inauguration in March 1921, the Soviets made an overture, in the form of a letter from the titular Soviet president, Mikhail Kalinin, to the Congress and the president, appealing for a reconsideration of America's Russia policy. Lenin's government had recently been buoyed by the signing, on March 16, of a trade agreement with Great Britain, which involved the exchange of trade representatives and amounted to de facto British recognition of the Soviet government. Other governments would follow London's lead, and before the end of 1921 Moscow would reach similar agreements with Germany, Norway, Austria, and Italy.

But the new administration was determined to hold the line. Secretary of State Charles Evans Hughes delivered a stiff rebuff to the Soviet feeler, stating that the United States could not enter into relations with Soviet Russia until the Bolsheviks did certain things: namely, agree to pay Russia's pre–October 1917 foreign debts, which they had renounced; settle claims by U.S. nationals for property confiscated since the Revolution; and cease their revolutionary propaganda. In other words, Russia's leaders must start behaving in a civilized fashion.[19]

This was to be Washington's basic position, with variations in emphasis, for the next three years. But the administration's rhetoric marked a shift from the Colby note's concern with general principles of international law to a special focus on the unorthodoxies of the Soviet economic system. Hughes famously called Soviet Russia a "gigantic economic vacuum," whose recovery could not begin until it adopted normal economic principles, not least the introduction of proper legal guarantees of private property and the sanctity of contracts. The new tone was partly a reflection of the pressures created by the Anglo-Soviet trade agreement and also by the influence of the secretary of commerce. Hoover made statements equally dismissive of the "foolish" Soviet economic practices. Although they addressed their requirements to the current occupants of the Kremlin, both Hughes and Hoover still believed in 1921 that the return to economic sanity they were demanding, inevitable though it was, was impossible under Bolshevik rule.

A major reason for the administration's immediate stress on economic principles was that simultaneous with Harding's inauguration, the Bolsheviks began their New Economic Policy. Even the very restricted return to capitalism envisioned in the initial decrees opened up prospects for foreign trade and business in Russia. And in the course of 1921, one of Lenin's goals as he broadened and deepened the reforms, trying to keep pace with the explosive spread of the market, was to attract Western capital to participate in the reconstruction of Soviet industry. Not that the author of the Great October Socialist Revolution was abandoning the path to the communist utopia: this was merely a new tack, made in the spirit of a possibly apocryphal statement attributed to him about selling the capitalists the rope with which to hang themselves. Still, many outsiders saw in the new policies a permanent conversion to common sense.

The view from Washington, however, was that the introduction of NEP was not a sign that the Bolsheviks had come to their senses but merely that they were desperate. NEP was a panicky response to popular opposition to the regime, which had reached a flash point in the Kronstadt rebellion, an event that grabbed the attention of U.S. officials, who wondered if it might finally signal the beginning of the end. Thus, it made no sense to talk of a trade agreement with Moscow. For Hoover it was a matter of the pendulum at last beginning to swing back in Russia: why halt its progress by easing the burden on the Bolsheviks?

First rumors, then credible word of a famine raised expectations further. The ARA's internal correspondence in and out of New York headquarters at the time shows the chiefs were preparing for the possibility of a major Russian expedition, a prospect that Hoover discussed with Hughes in mid-June.[20] American relief in Europe was now being phased out, though operations were still underway in ten countries involving the support of three and a half million children. As things stood in July, the ARA had somewhere between five and seven million dollars available for a mission to Russia.

THESE WERE THE CIRCUMSTANCES in place when Gorky's call for help was publicized in the West. Gorky's appeal and one he solicited from Patriarch Tikhon were written on or near July 6 and sent together in the same telegram to Nansen in Norway, who received them on July 13. Tikhon's appeal was directed both to the British people, through the archbishop of Canterbury, and to the American people, through the archbishop of New York. Nansen seems to have relayed Tikhon's message to the intended recipients, and it found its way into the American press prior to July 21, according to the *New York Times*, which published it on July 31.[21]

On July 14 Nansen replied by wire to Gorky that only the Americans could provide substantial assistance and that he had better concentrate his efforts on that audience. At the same time, Nansen passed Gorky's appeal on to the American minister in Norway, who forwarded it to the State Department, where it would arrive on July 29—only after it had been published in the Unites States. Hoover had seen Gorky's appeal, or a description of it, in the newspapers on or before July 22, on which date he wrote a note to Hughes asking for permission to respond to it, which was granted.

These details make nonsense of the standard version of the story, which talks of "Gorky's telegram to Hoover." That simplified and more satisfyingly dramatic reconstruction of events would originate with Hoover and was intended to serve political ends not yet evident in late July.

In any event, on July 23 Hoover sent Gorky a lengthy and momentous telegram. Gorky's well-known connections to the Bolshevik leadership led some to believe that in writing his appeal he was acting as a stalking-horse for the Soviet government, something that Hoover, in responding to it, took for granted. His message asserted that the ARA, "an entirely unofficial organization," was prepared to offer assistance but that a prerequisite for any discussion of famine relief was the immediate release of all American citizens being held prisoner in Russia.[22]

These Americans had been a subject of warm feeling in Washington for nearly a year, with the temperature occasionally turned up by newspaper stories about their alleged mistreatment in Soviet "dungeons." Hoover himself had been making inquiries about their circumstances and about the possibilities of supplying them with food—inquiries he made through the American Quakers, who maintained a small presence in Moscow. The confirmed number of American prisoners was eight, though there was speculation that there might be more either in confinement or in hiding. These unlucky eight had been arrested for various forms of espionage. This term was used rather loosely in 1921 Russia, though in fact the Cheka had hooked several genuine spies, among them the *Baltimore Sun's* Marguerite Harrison, an agent for U.S. Military Intelligence.

Were the prisoners issue to be settled, Hoover informed Gorky, the ARA was prepared to distribute food, clothing, and medical supplies to one million Russian children. Before that could happen, however, "the Moscow Soviet authorities" would have to make a direct application to the ARA. Beyond that, the ARA would insist that certain conditions be agreed to before it embarked on a Russian mission, the same ones enforced in all twenty-one countries in which it had served. The essential arrangement Hoover proposed was that the Soviet government would allow the ARA the freedom to organize its relief operations as it saw fit, while the ARA would promise to feed impartially and stay clear of politics. This was in fact the basis of the agreement the two parties would shortly sign, though time would demonstrate that neither side would be able to uphold its end of such a bargain because Soviet Russia was not remotely like any of those twenty-one beneficiary countries.

Hoover's telegram was received in Russia on July 26, and two days later Gorky cabled a reply to Hoover, which included the text of the formal acceptance of the ARA's offer by Politburo member Lev Kamenev, acting here in his capacity as deputy chairman of the official Soviet relief committee. Kamenev proposed that an ARA representative come to Moscow, Riga, or Reval—later-day Tallinn—to conduct negotiations.[23]

Hoover decided on Riga, the ARA's Baltic base of operations, and dispatched there his chief of European operations, Walter Lyman Brown, who was to play a central role in the Russian relief story, mostly from headquarters in London. It was there that he had, during the previous year, become acquainted with Kamenev, who must have found the American agreeable since the Soviet leader suggested him specifically for the role.

Brown was assisted by Cyril Quinn, chief of the ARA Poland mission, Miller of the Baltic mission, and Carroll of the German mission. Representing the Soviet government in Riga was Maxim Litvinov, assistant people's commissar of foreign affairs, a formidable negotiating talent with ample experience at playing a weak hand.

Negotiations began at Riga on August 10, the same day that seven of the American captives were released from Russia. Despite the repeated reminders by the secretary of commerce of the private status of his ARA, from the outset the talks unavoidably had the feel of an intergovernmental exercise, a perception the Soviet side was eager to encourage. It would be like this for the next ten days, and then the next two years: the ARA at pains to emphasize its technically unofficial standing and the Bolsheviks using every opportunity to identify Hoover's organization with the U.S. government.

Brown started things off by presenting Litvinov with a draft agreement prepared by Hoover based on the points set out in his telegram to Gorky. Litvinov raised several objections, and the game was on. Each side was in close communication with its home base, with Chicherin and Lenin advising and encouraging Litvinov from Moscow and Hoover, that relentless micromanager, instructing Brown from Washington.[24]

The thorniest disagreements had to do with the ARA's freedom of action: its right to choose its American and Russian personnel and where it could operate inside Russia. The discussion of both issues indicates an understandable Soviet trepidation about the imminent prospect of Hoover's agents being let loose in Russia. Litvinov demanded a Soviet veto over the selection of Americans, which Brown rejected, as he did the Soviet proposal to limit their number to one hundred.

Absolute liberty to inspect and otherwise operate in all regions of the target country had been a condition of every previous ARA mission, and Hoover insisted on it for Russia, territorially by far the largest of the lot. The Soviet government, on the other hand, was apprehensive about having a large contingent of foreigners, especially of the bourgeois American variety, establishing itself in Moscow and Petrograd and just anywhere else it might choose. Thus Litvinov suggested that the agreement specify the ARA's primary area of activity as the Volga region. Brown and company resisted, suspecting that the Soviets would later use this clause to limit the American presence in Moscow and Petrograd. These suspicions, fed by the mistaken assumption that Russia's capitals would be the scene of greatest hardship, were somewhat misplaced. In fact, in seeking to write this restriction into the accord, the Soviets had in mind primarily other territories, though this would become apparent to the Americans only after the mission was underway.

Sticking points accumulated. Hoover wanted any ARA-Soviet agreement to shield his relief workers from arrest. The American side would pledge to remove those personnel who the authorities could demonstrate had mixed in Soviet politics. Litvinov maintained that his government should be able to oust any foreign citizens it wished, American relief workers included, just as it had the right to expel all foreign diplomats—in other words, that this was a matter of sovereignty. Similarly, Litvinov claimed for his government the right to search the Americans' quarters, citing the possibility that the ARA's Russian personnel would store contraband there. Later on, once their deepest suspicions had been allayed, Soviet officials admitted that some among them had feared that the Americans might import weapons with the food supplies, and this may well have been what was in the back of Litvinov's mind.

Even more problematical was the ARA's ethos of promoting self-help and local initiative by establishing committees of local citizens to administer relief. This had been the most unrealistic feature of Hoover's proposed 1919 relief commission to Russia and the one that Kennan found so terrifyingly naive. Hoover had not changed his view since those days in Paris, but now, two years on, Lenin's government was unable to dismiss outright the fanciful notions of every capitalist statesman, this one in particular. So here was an extraordinary moment. In no country in Europe had there been a social revolution as thoroughgoing as Russia's. Since 1917 the Bolsheviks had succeeded in shackling all previously independent social organizations. The church, arguably the one limited exception, was about to have its turn. Yet Hoover and the ARA, taking for granted the continued existence, indeed vitality, of civil society in Russia, now come along and demand the right to establish independent committees of Russians under American control.

One wonders what thoughts crossed Litvinov's mind as Brown attempted to reassure him that the ARA would fill its committees with "neutral" individuals and feed in a "nonpartisan" manner. Tightening the rein on his exasperation, the seasoned diplomat patiently attempted to explain to his earnest interlocutor that there could be no such thing as nonpartisan food relief in Russia's utterly politicized society.

It was in this context that Litvinov—who, according to one ARA official, spoke fluent English in a "Semitic, cockney accent"—first pronounced the conference's signature line, between drags on the inevitable cigarette, instructing his

American counterparts in a didactic tone and in his distinct lisp, "Gentlemen, food is a weapon."[25] Or, as the Americans rendered it phonetically, "Food iz a veppon." Of course, Litvinov, as a Bolshevik, was speaking from several years of his own government's experience at wielding this weapon among its own people.

Of the several unresolved issues in the negotiations this became the outstanding one: the ARA's desire to establish independent food committees, whose very existence the Soviet side regarded as a counterrevolutionary threat. Litvinov remonstrated that the Soviet government had its own distribution machinery, which the ARA's committees would merely duplicate, thereby creating "parallelism"—a rich term in the Soviet context, a Bolshevik cousin of the Nazis' *Gleichschaltung*. If such committees had to be formed, Litvinov added, then his government would require control over the selection of their participants. Brown countered by making a case for the ARA's trustworthiness, as if this was a matter of trust.

Brown's credibility was undermined, and Soviet paranoia magnified, by the appearance of a series of articles in the April, May, and June 1921 issues of the journal *The World's Work* by one of Hoover's ARA lieutenants, Tom Gregory, under the epic title, "Stemming the Tide of Bolshevism." At great length, Captain Gregory told of how he and Hoover had used the weapon of food in Hungary to cause the downfall of Bela Kun's Soviet regime in the summer of 1919. At the time of their publication, these articles aroused the indignation of liberals and radicals in America. Ever since, Gregory's handiwork has been regularly cited as incontrovertible proof that Hoover was not the innocent humanitarian he always claimed to be.

Among his fellow relief workers Gregory was regarded as something of a cowboy—a damned good ARA man, all in all, but temperamentally far from the ideal candidate to deliver a reliable, not to mention circumspect, account of the Chief's accomplishments, let alone his own, in Hungary or anywhere else. So at ARA headquarters in New York this cowboy's unauthorized foray into journalism drew sighs of exasperation.[26]

Hoover had indeed influenced the outcome of the revolutionary events in Hungary, mostly by withholding food from the country while Kun was in power. Yet, as historian Burner points out, his most striking intervention in Hungary was his almost single-handed ouster of the reactionary Habsburg Archduke Joseph, who took power in a coup after Kun had fled to Moscow. In the critical moment and with the permission of the Big Four, Hoover wired a message to Budapest for Gregory to relay to the archduke, notifying him that the Allies would not recognize his authority. Gregory did as instructed and then informed Hoover of the outcome in a coded telegram: "Archie on the carpet at 7 P.M. Went through the hoop at 7:05 P.M." At home the left-wing editors of the *Nation* cheered, "Bravo, Mr. Hoover!"—one of the few occasions they would have to applaud the chairman of the ARA.[27]

Whatever the truth behind it, Gregory's version of events stiffened the resolve of the Bolshevik leaders to restrict the movements and activities of the potential Gregorys about to enter Soviet Russia. At the same time, the controversy now swirling around Hoover's role in the Hungarian events strengthened the Bolsheviks' bargaining position vis-à-vis the ARA during the Riga talks, and well afterward. Litvinov had been handed an ideal pretext for dismissing Brown's invocations of the ARA's previous arrangements in Central Europe as he pressed for tighter ground rules to govern its Russian mission.

Even absent the Gregory episode there was considerable uneasiness among the leading Bolsheviks about embarking on the path before them. The record shows that the Politburo was initially inclined to accept every one of Hoover's conditions lest the failure to reach an accord sink the entire government campaign for foreign food relief. Yet, having detected a certain softness in the ARA position, the Soviet leaders adopted a harder line.[28] Lenin, for one, was quite skittish. He believed he saw a connection between the Riga negotiations and the concurrent deliberations on the Russian famine by the Allied Supreme Council in Paris. On August 11, the second day of the negotiations, he had a message sent to Litvinov cautioning him to be doubly vigilant because the Americans were collaborating with the Supreme Council. On the same day he wrote an agitated note to the Politburo, warning that there was a "highly complex game going on" involving the trickery of America, Hoover, and the League of Nations, by which he meant the Allied Supreme Council. It was absolutely essential, he wrote, to name a special Politburo commission to deal with the day-to-day questions of foreign relief. "Hoover must be punished, must be *publicly* slapped so that *the whole world* can see, and the Council of the League as well."

Lenin's illness, of which he complained in numerous letters during this period, must have sharpened his edginess by exacerbating both his sense of personal vulnerability and the confusion in his mind about just what the ARA was up to in Riga. "Delicate maneuvers are needed," he told the Politburo. "A series of measures, especially strict. Hoover and Brown are insolent liars." As for the relief workers, "We must establish superstrict conditions: for the slightest interference in internal matters—expulsion and arrest."[29]

As Lenin's aching head feverishly sorted through the options, it occurred to him that there might be a way to keep the number of Hoover's agents in Russia to a minimum and yet still have the benefit of American food. On August 13 Lenin and Kamenev instructed Litvinov to propose to Brown that the Soviet government give the ARA a security deposit—made in New York, in gold—of 120 percent of the value of one month's supply of foodstuffs, in return for which the ARA would leave the distribution of its food entirely in Soviet hands. The American relief workers would have the right of inspection and control, jointly carried out with Soviet government officials. Litvinov placed such a proposal before Brown, but he must have known that it would be instantly rejected.

The effect of this and other indications of insecurity in the Kremlin was to make Brown redouble his efforts to demonstrate that the ARA had no intention of meddling in Soviet politics. He showed Litvinov a cable from Hoover, dated August 9, stating that any American that involved himself in politics in Russia would immediately be withdrawn from the mission.

The fact is that Hoover was playing this entirely straight. The idea that his relief workers *themselves* should attempt to influence Russian politics was unacceptable to him. Hoover did indeed intend to use food as a weapon in Russia but not in the crude way his enemies in Moscow and his critics at home imagined. His plan was to accomplish political ends in Russia not *under the guise of* famine relief, as they suspected, but rather *by means of* it. Hoover believed that if he could only relieve the Russians' hunger they would return to their senses and recover the physical strength to throw off their Bolshevik oppressors. The ARA example of energy and efficiency would itself serve to bring further discredit upon the "foolish" Soviet system in the eyes of the people and serve to catalyze the inevitable political healing process. All Hoover needed was to set up his operation inside the country, a goal that now lay so tantalizingly near.

Yet by August 17 the Riga negotiations were threatening to break down, as Litvinov and especially Brown conferred by wire with their respective chiefs in search of maneuvering room. The parties faced no firm deadline, but while they talked, millions of Russians were facing starvation. Adding to the mounting pressure for a quick settlement was the bustle of activity outside the negotiating room. Representatives of foreign governments and relief organizations were on hand to monitor developments, while reporters from America and from across Europe had descended on the city to cover this unusual diplomatic event, some angling to be among the first correspondents to go into Russia and tell the fact story of the famine.

The ARA team found the spotlight decidedly more uncomfortable. As the rumor of a stalemate circulated, Litvinov was able to draw upon his formidable talent for what in a later day would be called spin control. He used the press to score points against Brown and prepare the ground in the event that the talks collapsed. Just as he had already stated to the American negotiators on several occasions, Litvinov told reporters that the parties suffered from a "lack of confidence on one side and suspicion on the other." To Brown he explained that this meant the ARA's lack of confidence in the Soviet government and Bolshevik suspicion of the ARA, but now he told the press, "If you apply my remark to either side you will not be incorrect."

With the outcome in suspense, Litvinov seemed to thrive, though his posturing did not win him support all around. The correspondent of the *Manchester Guardian* characterized his attitude as "looking a gift-horse in the mouth, complaining of the sharpness of its teeth and suggesting that it has an uncertain temper."[30]

While the major disagreements simmered, the negotiators took up two less-sensitive, related matters. One was the size of the proposed ARA ration. Hoover's plan called for the ARA to deliver a supplementary ration, as was the standard practice in its other child-feeding operations: most children were fed one daily meal, usually served at noon. The question for Russia was, supplementary to what? Somehow Hoover and Brown had been led to believe that all Soviet citizens, even peasants, were receiving a daily ration from the government approximately the size of the Red Army ration—an assumption that reveals just how shockingly ignorant supposedly informed outsiders could be of the actual state of affairs in Soviet Russia. The fact is that even at the height of War Communism most of the rural population had never been included on the ration rolls. The rations distributed to urban dwellers, seldom as numerous and generous as official decrees indicated and Bolshevik propaganda seemed to advertise, were now rapidly dwindling under the force of NEP economizing.

The ARA's stand was greeted with irritation in Moscow, where Lenin offered to dispatch to Riga a Soviet food-supply official to enlighten the misinformed Americans. Instead, Foreign Affairs Commissar Georgii Chicherin suggested that

Litvinov ask them to consider the fact that if most Russians were receiving the equivalent of the Red Army ration there would be no famine to talk about. Brown saw the light and brought Hoover around, and the final agreement contained protective wording to the effect that no beneficiary of an ARA ration was to be deprived of such local food supplies as were available to the rest of the population.

A related dispute involved whether the ARA would obligate itself to come to the aid of a certain number of Russians. Litvinov wanted a commitment to feed one million children, the figure Hoover had used in his telegram to Gorky. But Hoover had written in a general way about providing one million children with food, clothing, and medical supplies, a statement based on his assumption that all food relief would be supplementary. This was not the same as a pledge to "feed"—in the sense of sustain—one million children. This sounds like a reasonable rejoinder, but Litvinov would not let go. He told Brown, presumably in confidence, that the primary reason for his insistence on securing the one-million figure in writing was that it would enable Lenin to justify to the radical element within the Bolshevik Party the signing of an accord granting such wide latitude inside Russia to an organization run by the inimical Hoover.

This was to become a familiar story to the relief workers in the coming months: the Bolshevik "moderates" would apply to the ARA for one or another concession in the name of keeping the "radicals" from causing it far greater trouble and perhaps even jeopardizing the entire relief mission. In most cases, such as this one, the concerns of the moderates were partly genuine, but it would not be long before the ARA chiefs would grow impatient with the many entreaties of the good cop. Here Litvinov was met halfway: the final agreement recorded that Hoover had "suggested" in his reply to Gorky that the ARA would provide "supplementary relief" to "up to a million children in Russia."

So the parties managed to reach agreement on several outstanding issues, even as they remained far apart on the more delicate ones. On August 18, after he had compromised on the Soviet rights to search ARA premises and remove objectionable Americans, Litvinov declared that the Kremlin would let him retreat no further, something the Soviet documentation bears out. In Moscow Chicherin drew up a protective memorandum to make public in case the negotiations failed. Rehearsing all the points of the Riga discussions, it charged that Hoover's demands were aimed at violating Russia's sovereignty and independence. The Soviet government could not recognize the "extraterritoriality" of the ARA and allow it to "create within the Soviet state its own independent state."[31]

This is a fair description of what Hoover had gotten away with everywhere else in Europe. But again, as Hoover was now discovering, Soviet Russia was not like anywhere else. Although the Bolshevik government was greatly in need of famine relief, it had a distinctly lower tolerance level for the intrusiveness of outsiders. And Russia was different for Hoover in still another way. His anti-Bolshevik credentials, recently fortified by the appearance of Gregory's articles, placed a special burden on him now to demonstrate fair play vis-à-vis the Soviet government. The collapse of the Riga negotiations over a dispute about ARA control, leaving millions of children to starve, would certainly have provoked a storm of controversy in America.

So in any negotiating game of chicken, Litvinov had the advantage. Sitting directly across from him, Brown could see this more clearly than Hoover, whom he persuaded to give way on a few substantial points. The key compromise allowed the Soviet government to be represented on the ARA's local food committees. The Americans were surprised at how suddenly Litvinov's opposition to their committee plan crumbled once he was assured of Bolshevik representation. After but a few weeks' time on the ground in Russia, however, they would see why his instant conversion had made perfect sense.

The deadlock over the privileged status Brown sought for the American relief workers had been broken by means of some artfully ambiguous prose. The ARA men would enjoy immunity from personal search and arrest, though anyone caught engaging in political or commercial activity would be withdrawn from the mission at the request of the "Central Soviet Authorities" after they had submitted the reasons and the evidence to the appropriate ARA chief, who presumably would have an opportunity to pass judgment on the veracity of the charges. As well, the Soviet authorities would have the right to search ARA premises if they had definite proof of foul play and if they conducted their search in the presence of an official of the ARA. If such an investigation failed to turn up anything incriminating and was thus proved to have been unwarranted, the Soviet official who had instigated the search was to be punished.

Regarding the question of Soviet approval of American personnel, the agreement was that any non-Americans or Americans who had been detained in Russia since 1917 would have to be cleared for the mission by the Soviet government. As for the freedom of the Americans to move about the country in order to conduct their investigations, here too an acceptably ambiguous formulation was found. Paragraph 26 of the agreement states that the ARA "will carry on its operations where it finds its relief can be administered most efficiently and to secure best results. Its principal object is to bring relief to the famine stricken areas of the Volga." Events would demonstrate the importance to hundreds of thousands of Ukrainians, among others, of the ARA's determination to keep its options open.

Otherwise the Riga Agreement, as it was called, represented the standard ARA arrangement. Making no exception for Russia's frightful economic condition, exclusive of the famine, it obligated the Soviet government to bear all the expenses for the operation—transportation, facilities, supplies, and so on—except for the cost of the relief supplies at port and the direct expenses of the American personnel. Brown and Litvinov agreed on the final wording of their twenty-seven-paragraph document, announced their accord on August 19, and signed it in a public ceremony on August 20.

It was an awkward contract between a relief organization trying very hard not to be perceived as a U.S. government agency and a regime trying even harder to be recognized as the legitimate government of Soviet Russia. In drafting the agreement, Brown was careful to make no reference to a "Soviet government," employing instead the legally neutral "Soviet Authorities." This was more than enough to enable Litvinov to get a foot in the door. While it was undoubtedly a deep humiliation for the Bolsheviks to have to accept foreign food relief, an agreement with a quasi-official American organization gave the Soviet leaders an opportunity to press the case for their government's legitimacy. At the signing ceremony, addressing a crowd of reporters, Litvinov sought to endow the occasion with political significance by remarking that the United States was free to regard the Riga accord as a U.S.-Soviet trade agreement. Brown followed by pouring diplomatic cold water on this gambit.

When it was over, Quinn of the American team sized up Litvinov as "an extremely clever man and a very able negotiator—if the Soviet regime is directed by men of his type it is easier to understand their apparently soulless cleverness." Brown wrote to Hoover a week later, "I think that before we got through we convinced Litvinoff personally that we were straight, but it took a bit of doing, which is understandable when one considers how, even in the countries where we have been operating for the last two years, this phase is not always understood." What Brown as yet did not grasp was that, even straight as an arrow, the ARA posed a considerable danger for the Kremlin. In the midst of the negotiations, Litvinov cabled Moscow: "Received impression that ARA comes to us without ulterior motives, but will cause us much trouble."[32]

IN LOBBYING THE ARA to insert the figure of one million children into the agreement, Litvinov cited as an additional consideration the fact that it would help the Soviet government avoid having to award the same privileges to other, much smaller, relief organizations that would also be applying to work in Russia. Yet Litvinov's concern about a long queue of applicants proved to be unfounded.

Two initiatives came out of Europe.[33] While the Riga negotiations were underway, a joint committee representing the International Red Cross and the League of Red Cross Societies called a meeting of the various national relief associations for August 15 at Geneva, where over one hundred delegates representing twenty-two countries and thirty organizations met to discuss Russian relief. The conference established the International Committee for Russian Relief, of which Nansen was appointed high commissioner on August 18. There were supposed to be two high commissioners, but Hoover, true to his principle of avoiding all unnecessary European entanglements, turned down the nomination.

Nansen immediately set off for Moscow, where he worked out an agreement governing the operations of what came to be called the Nansen mission. This accord left the control of food supplies in the hands of the Soviet government, an arrangement that raised a fuss in European relief and political circles. Compared to the ARA's contract, it seemed like a bad deal, yet Nansen had not arrived in Moscow carrying a proposal to relieve one million children. His mission would make only a modest contribution to the famine relief effort, while it unwittingly served as a propaganda boon to the Soviet government.

Meanwhile, the Allied Supreme Council—whose deliberations so rattled Lenin —created an International Commission for Russian Relief on which the principal allies were represented. It held its first meeting in Paris on August 30, with Brown representing the U.S. government, though only as an unofficial observer, in keeping with American aloofness. The delegates called for an investigation of famine conditions to be led by Joseph Noulens, the French diplomat whose actions in the Russian Revolution had earned him the eternal hatred of the Bolsheviks. Predictably, Moscow condemned the very idea of a Noulens commission of inquiry, but in any case nothing very substantial could have resulted from it because Europe lacked the economic resources to undertake a large-scale relief effort.

So Hoover held all the cards—or was about to. Once it was certain that there would be an ARA-Soviet accord, he moved quickly to centralize all American relief under his control.[34] He helped himself by the inclusion of the second "whereas" of the Riga Agreement, which created the myth that Gorky had "appealed through Mr. Hoover to the American people." Two days before Brown and Litvinov signed their accord, Hoover engineered it that Harding designate the ARA as the sole vehicle for American relief to Russia, the rationale being that such an arrangement would provide the best use of funds under the umbrella of the Riga Agreement and, not incidentally, prevent the Soviets from playing off American agencies one against another. The secretary of state was instructed to issue passports to Russia only to individuals in the service of the ARA. Hoover then called a meeting in Washington on August 24 of the American relief organizations comprising the European Relief Council, a body he had formed in autumn 1920 to coordinate the financing of American relief and reconstruction work in Europe and of which he served as chairman.

The European Relief Council had raised close to $30 million during the previous winter. The ARA aside, the most important organizations represented in the council were the American Red Cross, the Jewish Joint Distribution Committee, or JDC, and the American Friends Service Committee, known simply as the Friends or the Quakers. The JDC and the Friends were significant contributors to European postwar relief, working both on their own and in conjunction with the ARA, and had distributed small amounts of food in urban Russia since the war, the Quakers almost uninterruptedly into spring 1921.

At the August 24 conference it was agreed that each of the member organizations was to have a representative on the staff of the ARA director in Russia, and that the ARA would have ultimate control over the distribution of the personnel of these organizations. Subsequently, other American relief societies entered into this arrangement, bringing the number of "affiliates" to ten. In practice, except for the JDC and the Quakers, their programs in Russia were effectively absorbed by the ARA.

Hoover had managed to clear the field for himself and his ARA, which at long last was going into Bolshevik Russia. Brown wrote to Hoover, "It is going to be by far the biggest and most difficult job we have yet tackled and the potentialities of it are enormous, but I think we can pull it through."[35]

Few as yet understood its true potentialities because the famine itself was a good deal worse than most people in the West realized at that moment, despite the dire forecasts of the appeals for assistance. The American public's first unfiltered view of starvation among the Russians was provided by the famous American war correspondent Floyd Gibbons. This intrepid headline hunter came to Riga during the talks and coerced a visa out of Litvinov, apparently by threatening to enter Russia illegally by airplane. He wore a black patch over his missing left eye, a decoration he had earned covering the war and which must have helped persuade Litvinov that the man seated before him was no bluffer. Gibbons was first to the Volga and first to send stories out on the wire in what was considered the greatest newspaper scoop since the war.[36]

The ARA had not made Western press access to Russia part of the negotiated agreement, but Hoover had Brown suggest to Litvinov that it was in his government's interest to let the reporters in. Should the ARA conduct a public appeal for funds, it would have a better chance of success if Americans were informed of famine conditions by journalists who could not be dismissed as "Bolshevik sympathizers." Litvinov went along with this, perhaps with some inducement from Gibbons, whose path to the Volga was soon followed by a dozen more glory seekers.

The end of the press blockade and the fact that dozens of foreign relief workers were set to enter Soviet Russia marked the opening up of the country for the first time since 1918. The fire curtain that had descended between Russia and the West during the most incendiary days of the Revolution was now to be lifted.

CHAPTER 3

THE KINGDOM OF HUNGER

Once Hoover's telegram to Gorky was made public, the ARA's offices in New York, London, and Paris were inundated with applications for the prospective Russian mission. Already on August 3, one week before the Riga negotiations, Frank Page of New York headquarters remarked to ARA publicity chief George Barr Baker, "All of your friends, my friends, the office boy's friends and everybody's friends want to get a job in Russia." That was how it seemed; in fact, by August 18 the number of applications received at 42 Broadway was 450.

Naturally, those at the head of the line were the veteran ARA relief workers, some of whom were still on the job in Europe. They were the most qualified candidates and certainly the most eager. Russia had been, in the words of one who had served in the Poland mission, "the romantic goal of all the old timers." They considered it "the ultimate show."[1]

This word "show" was indispensable to the ARA man's everyday vocabulary, evidence of his service with the American Expeditionary Force in France. Soldiers referred to trench raids as "shows" and "stunts," and when the fighting stopped, former soldiers often used these words to designate even the most harmless activities.

The Great War itself they still called "the show," or "the Big Show." Dos Passos's answer to why he went over there was; "[H]ell, I wanted to see the show." Others were less definite about it. In Dos Passos's 1921 *Three Soldiers*, one of them remarks when asked why he enlisted: "I was restless-like. I guess I wanted to see the world. I didn't care about the goddam war, but I wanted to see what things was like over here." Historians attest that this pretty well sums up the attraction to wartime Europe of the majority of America's fighting men. There was no shortage of committed idealists among them, but most went over less for the cause than for the adventure, to see the war and the world.[2]

Once the show was over, hundreds of thousands of American soldiers lingered in Europe, assigned to post-armistice occupation, graves registration, and food relief duties. A good number of these men believed they had had enough of Europe and adventure and, after the Versailles peace was signed, became impatient when an insufficiency of transport ships delayed their departure for the States. Others, however, were filled with wanderlust and an insatiable hunger for still more experiences. Such men were seriously hooked on Europe, or perhaps on their privileged position as American soldiers in Europe—it was hard to tell.

Very many doughboys were from small towns back home, and having seen "Paree" they resisted the prospect of being kept down on the farm.

After Versailles, then, thousands of Americans, some still attired at least partly in military uniforms, roamed across Europe engaging in worthy and less worthy enterprises. One occupation that offered to satisfy the desire for discovery and adventure was food relief work. In a post-armistice bull session in Paris, Dos Passos's three soldiers speculate as to whether Wilson will walk out of the Peace Conference. One of them imagines that if he does, he'll recognize the Soviet government. "Me for the Red Cross Mission that goes to save starving Russia."[3]

The recruits of the ARA were mostly enlisted men and, like Shafroth, commissioned officers who went to work for Hoover right out of the AEF, without returning home. By 1921 those still on the job referred to themselves as "veteran babyfeeders," although they were relatively young. Shafroth, at twenty-nine, was a few years older than the average relief worker in the Russian mission, once it got up to speed. Several of the "old-timers" had begun their food relief service in wartime Belgium. These veterans joined the ARA in 1919 in the same spirit of adventure they had enlisted in the U.S. Army in 1917. As relief workers it was not long before they were inspired by a sense of dedication to the ARA cause. Most of them would never meet Hoover, but their references to him in private correspondence during and long after these years testify to a genuinely felt loyalty to "the Chief."

Hoover's name had come to be associated in the United States with the idea of "service," and the writings left behind by the higher-minded ARA men make plain that they went about their duties conscious of rendering a service to mankind.[4] Of course, such affirmations may merely have sounded satisfying, especially in letters to the folks back home—though even there, uplifting sentiments had to make room for the romantic imagery of riding the coattails of fate. Loyalty to Hoover, service to mankind, the pursuit of fresh adventure—all of these were part of what made the ARA man tick, and it is doubtful that any relief worker truly understood the particular mix of his own motivations at any given moment.

The Russian mission had a sizable pool of experienced candidates to draw upon, though it would not be enough to satisfy the demand since even the one-hundred-strong force originally anticipated would have made this by far the largest ARA expedition yet. And because European operations, though winding down, were still ongoing, the Russian unit would have to tap other sources for its personnel: mostly veterans of non-ARA relief missions but also the untried former enlisted men of the Graves Registration Service; and there would be other raw recruits sent from the States.

The ARA followed two rules for staffing the Russian unit—that is, aside from the publicly known restrictions agreed upon at Riga. The first, the exclusion of women, had applied to all previous missions. Here a partial exception would have to be made because the ARA could not reasonably demand that the Quakers bar their experienced staff of female relief workers; otherwise, Russia was considered no place for women folk. The second restriction, which had special application to Russia, was that the ARA should employ no members of the Jewish "race," in the parlance of the day. This was based on the well-founded assumption that should order completely break down, there would ensue large-scale pogroms, which in Russia in troubled times was an especially savage version of rounding up the usual suspects. Pogroms had become part of the American image of Russia during the last quarter of the previous century, pounded in by waves of Jewish immigrants. The Bolsheviks were widely assumed, at home and abroad, to be predominantly Jews; true or not, who could tell what a horrible bloodbath of innocents their downfall might inspire?[5]

Of course, discriminating by "race" was not as straightforward a matter as by gender. Regardless, here as well the ARA would have to compromise when, in 1922, the Jewish Joint Distribution Committee set up a semi-autonomous unit in Ukraine and American Jews partially staffed the operation. Their involvement aside, the very fact of a distinct JDC presence would arouse predictable anti-Semitic sentiments among local citizens and officials, which would complicate matters in Ukraine, Moscow, and New York.

CARROLL AND THE ADVANCE PARTY knew they were to prepare the ground for scores of relief workers to follow. And so they must have wondered, as they retired to their railroad car after their first day in Moscow, how they would manage to secure sufficient headquarters and housing for so many when the Soviet government was hard-pressed to accommodate a team of seven. Their initial suspicions that this might be purely a reflection of official inhospitality quickly evaporated as their own search for working and living quarters revealed the appalling housing conditions in the capital.

For the previous two and a half years Moscow had had no running water and thus no possibility of steam heat. Nor was there sufficient wood to fuel the big tile stoves found in the larger buildings. The partition of houses into numerous individual, often single-room apartments put an even greater strain on the scarce supply of fuel. Occupants improvised crude stoves in each room—several to a room if space required it—burning whatever fuel they managed to forage in or out of town. Ventilation was arranged by passing the stove pipe through a hole in a window or by knocking one through a wall. For most it was enough to keep from freezing to death. Muscovites told Walter Duranty of the *New York Times* in 1921 that during the darkest days of the Civil War, it was the collapse of the water supply and sanitation more than hunger and cold that made life so nearly intolerable.[6]

Despite the precipitous decline in Moscow's population, the city's housing crisis after the Civil War was acute. One reason was that once the city became the capital, in spring 1918, it had to make room for the big and bloating central government bureaucracy, which requisitioned choice office and residential buildings. At the same time, houses abandoned by their occupants were often as not cannibalized for firewood. The Americans got to see this practice for themselves as it was still going on through the winter of 1921–22.

So the relief workers would have to spend more time and energy settling themselves in than they had anticipated. For a headquarters building Carroll decided on a former residence of a wealthy Muscovite. This was a square-block greystone mansion at the address Spiridonovka 30, near the Arbat in the city center. In its day, when the tsar still ruled, it was quite a place; but in recent years its thirty rooms had had to endure a variety of tenants and lately had served as a workers' club, which explained the presence of all manner of props and makeshift studios and stages. Carroll found it to be in "an absolute state of filthiness," its plumbing "only a memory," its electricity "on a strike." He hired a team of workers to undertake repairs, while his men contrived a part-office, part-residence arrangement, which lent these inaugural weeks the feel of a "camping party."

Shafroth was rather taken by it, despite its state of deterioration. He wrote to his mother that after two nights in their sleeping car, he and his colleagues had moved into a "palace . . . with its marble staircases, salons with painted ceilings and all that sort of stuff." Of this imposing edifice Carroll is supposed to have said to one of the Americans arriving with the second ARA contingent, "It should be able to withstand a long siege," a remark that may reflect the grave atmosphere of those early days or was simply a bit of dark humor.[7]

Spiridonovka 30 would eventually have to serve exclusively as ARA headquarters, so there remained the challenge of locating adequate living space. The search was protracted, and after several weeks Carroll voiced the threat, hardly credible, to get his men on the train and go back to Riga. This prompted Litvinov to suggest, perhaps more in earnest, that they move to Petrograd, where the accommodations were ample.[8]

Petrograd's advantage was its having shed the central government, the agent of so much congestion in Moscow, but that was the only benefit it gained from this turn of events, which hastened its decline and sealed its fate. Petrograd, which had become the new Russian capital shortly after its founding in 1703, had been established, as St. Petersburg, not in the usual way metropolises arise and prosper, which is to say, on commerce. Peter the Great built his city on the swamps along the Neva River for the purpose of giving Russia a "window on the West," in that well-worn phrase. It was thus a most unnatural creation. Once it was abandoned by Lenin's government and ceased to be the capital, it was in a sense doomed. As its trade and industry progressively became paralyzed in the course of the Revolution, its residents vacated the city in even greater numbers than did Muscovites from the new capital, the evacuation of government and Party bureaucrats amplifying the exodus.

Shafroth passed through Petrograd in spring 1922 and sensed this irretrievable loss: the city did not have "the same busy air as Moscow, and around its wide streets there was an air of grandeur which had departed not to return again."[9] Of course, Petrograd would once again become, as Leningrad, an industrial center and would survive in the Second World War, a trial worse than that of 1918 to 1920. But without a central Russian government to give purpose to its grand imperial architecture and compensate for its frontier location, the second capital would never regain its former spiritual vitality. Eighty years later, once again as St. Petersburg, though it retains much of its original eerie beauty, it is marked by the same air of lost grandeur Shafroth discerned in 1922.

Anyway, Litvinov knew what he was talking about. Although Petrograd had seen an estimated five thousand buildings demolished and consumed as fuel, its steep population decline more than offset its vanishing architecture. So the matter of housing did not preoccupy the Americans who arrived in Petrograd in the final days of August, just before the landing, on September 1, of the first food supply ship, the S.S. *Phoenix*. The chief of the ARA Petrograd district, Carlton

Bowden, was a former Rhodes Scholar who served with the Commission for Relief in Belgium and the ARA in Hungary. Arriving by rail directly from Reval, he took quick action, combing the city for suitable space for kitchens, selecting local personnel to run them, hiring clerks, secretaries, chauffeurs, and others for his headquarters staff, and attending to a whole host of other tasks associated with getting a food relief operation up and running.

Bowden was one of the ARA's take-charge sort, incurably impatient and not completely satisfied unless he was running his own show. His first message to London after he had had a look around town announced, "We have certainly come to the right place." On September 6 he opened the first ARA kitchen in Soviet Russia—in School No. 27, at 108 Moika Street—boasting that "any doubts which the Soviet authorities may have had as to whether Hoover's men meant business have been dispelled by the rapidity with which the machinery has been set in motion."[10]

These American kitchens, which soon began to sprout up by the thousands in hundreds of Soviet Russian cities, towns, and villages, served balanced meals consisting of some combination of white bread, corn grits, rice, lard, milk, cocoa, and sugar. Four days after Petrograd, Moscow opened its first and largest kitchen— big enough to be called a child-feeding station—in the former Hermitage restaurant, a famous gathering place before the Revolution where the well-to-do ate extravagantly and danced to gypsy music, *à la Russe*.

Bowden was off to a racehorse start. Within a couple of weeks his team of local doctors had examined about one hundred thousand children, accepting forty-two thousand to be fed in 120 ARA kitchens with the intention of increasing the total to fifty thousand as soon as enough food arrived. Meanwhile, in Moscow they were figuring on feeding one hundred thousand children in the month of September. There was without doubt severe undernourishment in the capitals, even cases of children dying of starvation. These cities, Moscow in particular, had to cope with an increasing number of refugees arriving by the trainload in flight from famine.

Bowden's understanding was that the principal feeding was to be done in the major cities, where it was most needed, that the peasants had done quite well for themselves up to the famine and would manage just fine on their own. Of course he could not have known this from first-hand knowledge, so he must have gotten an earful from the Petrograd intelligentsia and former well-to-do. How rude a shock it must have been then toward the end of September when Moscow headquarters instructed him to reduce the Petrograd kitchen rolls to fifteen thousand children.[11] There had been a change of plan. The first American reports had arrived from the Volga, where an ARA scouting party had encountered starvation on a mass scale.

FIVE DAYS AFTER Carroll reached Moscow, he dispatched the first team of relief workers to the Volga, a threesome of Shafroth, John Gregg, and Frank Golder. Gregg hailed from Portland, Oregon, and was a graduate of Stanford, Class of 1913. He was commissioned a lieutenant in the war, after which he served with the ARA in the Baltics and in Poland.[12]

Golder was not a relief worker, but a Stanford University historian who had come into Russia to collect books and documentary material for the Hoover War Collection, established by Hoover at Stanford in 1919. He had been engaged in these collecting duties for about a year, using the good offices of the ARA in the various capitals of Central Europe to acquire and ship to Stanford materials that were part of the extraordinary founding collections of what later became known as the Hoover Archives. He was already a familiar figure then to many of the old ARA hands. His greatest glory as a collector would come during the next two years in Russia, but for the time being his peculiar background made him valuable to the cause of famine relief. Golder was born near Odessa in 1877, the son of German-Jewish parents, and left Russia when he was eight years old in the wake of the pogroms brought on by the assassination in St. Petersburg of Tsar Alexander II. He went on to get a Ph.D. in Russian history from Harvard and visited Russia in 1914 and in 1917 during the Revolution. His familiarity with Russia and facility with the language led Carroll to co-opt his services to assist Shafroth and Gregg on the Volga.[13]

The three Americans were accompanied by the inevitable Soviet government minder and a Russian chauffeur to drive the Ford camionette, which they brought along from Moscow on a flat car. Their assignment was to investigate conditions on the Volga and as soon as possible to telegraph their findings to the Moscow chiefs, who could then release the first food trains to the famine zone and advise London and New York of any needed adjustments to the program.

The city of Kazan on the northern Volga was their first destination, a distance of about 650 miles directly due east of Moscow, which they managed to cover in the very respectable time of about thirty-six hours. Kazan had since the Revolution become the capital of the Autonomous Tatar Soviet Republic, one of the federated republics of the RSFSR, the Russian Soviet Federated Socialist Republic. This new, postrevolutionary entity was in territorial configuration very similar to the old Kazan province. Indeed, this is what the Americans found to be the case in most places in Russia: the Soviet government had essentially adopted the old administrative units of tsarist Russia—though with numerous minor boundary adjustments and several name changes—and casted them as constituent parts of a federal structure, one more decentralized in theory than in fact. The Tatar Republic was so designated as part of a policy of accommodating the aspirations for self-determination among the ethnic groups of the old empire, in this case the Tatars, who composed about 60 percent of the population of the republic, the remainder being mostly Russians. In the larger Bolshevik scheme of things, such national self-determination was for the time being to be allowed, even encouraged to flourish, with the understanding that it would eventually die out and be replaced by class solidarity, federalism inevitably giving way to socialist unitarianism.

The American investigators got their first look at actual famine conditions at the Kazan railway station, which was overflowing with refugees, most lying on the floor and waiting—many now for weeks—for a train that would take them to "some mythical land of bread and honey," in Shafroth's pungent phrase.[14] Some had first deserted their homes in 1915, fleeing the territories on the Russo-German front and settling in villages in Kazan and Ufa provinces; now it was famine that had them on the move. Shafroth reports that in the railway yards they came upon a "terribly pitiful refugee camp," whose occupants had no shelter except the graveyard of decomposing box cars that they crawled under at night or to escape the rain. These people were part of the summer 1921 panic migration to escape the famine. They had sold off whatever farm animals and field implements they still possessed and moved toward railway and river stations. Some intended to head west to Moscow, many more east to Siberia or southeast to Turkestan, and others down the Volga and then over to Ukraine.

Golder observed that these wretched creatures were "huddled together in compact masses like a seal colony, mothers and young close together." Most were little children whose parents had deserted them or had died on the way to, or after reaching Kazan. Local officials told the Americans that this particular refugee station was under control, that they had evacuated seventy-two thousand out of the Kazan region, though they guessed that probably an equal number had left without being registered.

The scene at the station having delivered the first shock, the trio braced themselves to enter the city, whose recent degeneration only Golder's seasoned eye could fully appreciate. "What a change, what a ghost of its former self! Rusty tracks and dangling wires indicate that the city had at one time a street-car system, and shabby signs over ruined buildings tell the story of banks, theaters, and shops that are no more." On the streets one encountered "pitiful-looking figures dressed in rags and begging for a piece of bread in the name of Christ."[15]

In the company of local officials, the Americans began the business of inspecting the city's hospitals and children's homes. Of these the most revolting were the emergency institutions known as "collectors" or "receiving homes," where refugee children orphaned or abandoned by their parents were taken in. Here Shafroth and Gregg witnessed scenes of horror unlike any they had encountered in Central Europe. Shafroth tells of "emaciated little skeletons, whose gaunt faces and toothpick legs, around which their rags were fluttering, testified to the truth of the report that they were dying off daily by the dozen." The stench in these rooms was nauseating. About one-third of Kazan's children were being fed, in government homes and kitchens, a meager ration of mostly black and rye bread, but officials told the visitors that they would soon be forced to reduce the size of the ration and the number of recipients. Shafroth wrote in his trip report, "Poland has no children reduced to this degree of starvation."

The hospitals were in a dreadful state of filth and lacked the most basic medicines, such as quinine, aspirin, castor oil, and cod liver oil. There were numerous cases of tuberculosis and scurvy and a great many of malaria and dysentery. Typhus, the cause of such terror in the coming winter, had not as yet been diagnosed, though several patients were under isolation as suspected cases.

So much for Kazan city. A trip by Ford into the countryside revealed the situation in the villages to be considerably worse than the Americans had expected. Actually, as they drove across the rolling plains, the landscape belied the reports of mass starvation. Shafroth beheld "as fertile and rich a black soil as I have ever seen." But he noted as well the primitive agricultural methods that had helped to bring on the present catastrophe: "If they used dry farming, or irrigation, crop failures would be impossible, but they don't even know how to plow, and usually only scratch the surface with some makeshift implement. Crop rotation or summer fallow is unheard of."[16] Upon entering the villages, the Americans quickly recognized the desperate condition of the inhabitants. Food stocks were practically exhausted, and it seemed impossible that the peasants could last the winter.

The local government was supposed to be distributing two poods, about eighty pounds, of seed grain for every *dessiatina*, about 2.7 acres, of land plowed. Gregg learned that despite their predicament the peasants were planting, not eating this seed, even though it was doubtful that they themselves would last until the harvest if nothing was done to save them.[17] Some of these peasants were already dying, others preparing to join the migration. Many were suffering from edema, the distended stomach caused by eating grass and weeds and various other food substitutes.

These substitutes were testimony to the intestinal fortitude of the Russian peasant. What passed as food typically resembled black or green bread and usually contained only the slightest bit of flour, if any, the rest being grass or some similar ingredient. During the winter, the menu came to include such indelicacies as straw from the roofs of peasant huts ground into powder and baked, wood ground into sawdust, cattle dung, and bones from decaying carcasses. Starving horses would turn down such offerings, as would other domestic animals, even the few remaining dogs and cats. A very popular source of sustenance was a weed called *lebeda*, which grows among rye and resembles oats. Unlike either cereal, however, it might produce the swollen "hunger belly," the swelling sometimes affecting the legs. Children were especially vulnerable. Substances that could sustain adults could kill their young offspring. The northern Volga region, unlike the south, was wooded, and once the snows fell and obscured the forage, peasants entered the forests to help themselves to the bark of the trees.

After their depressing excursion into the countryside, the Americans journeyed by boat some forty miles down the Volga to a place called Bogorodsk, where they came upon what Shafroth calls "another unforgettable sight": over four thousand refugees, most of them Tatars, encamped on the river bank "in an appalling state of wretchedness." Each family had constructed its own makeshift shelter with roofs of blankets, rugs, mattings, whatever was to hand. "A light rain which was falling made the sight of their pitiable condition even more depressing." The officials said they were feeding the children and would start evacuating them at a rate of five hundred per day to Turkestan within a week. About a quarter of their total were children.

Golder called this place a "nightmare." He found that most of the uprooted were "in a state of stupor, indifferent to what happens to them," yet he also recorded that "Women surrounded us and wept over their miserable lot, and the death of their children." Some of the Bogorodsk refugees had been there for four weeks. And there were said to be many other river stations just like this, beaches covered with human driftwood. There were few signs of panic among them; most sat and waited, either for a vessel to come and take them away or for death. "We went into the hospital and saw tiny tots lying four in a cot, and the poor things were mere skeletons with just a breath of life in them."

Three days of taking in such horrors had left their mark on the investigators. Gregg was in no doubt: "The need for relief in this country is beyond anything I have ever seen." His first telegram to Moscow headquarters, sent from Kazan on September 5, emphasized the urgency of the situation: "Speed is of utmost repeat utmost importance as without exaggeration children dying actual starvation every day." On the following day, with the help of his colleagues he composed a full report, sent to Moscow by courier, which sought to impress upon the chiefs the severity of the crisis: "If Petrograd and Moscow show no greater need than was seen in Moscow, it will not be in accordance with our principles to feed in either place." Gregg advised that Moscow recruit experienced relief workers from other ARA missions for immediate service on the famine front. "We repeat, speed is vital."[18]

Shafroth wrote in his trip notes that the projected allocation of one million rations for the Volga would not be enough to provide for even half the children needing attention. He thought five hundred thousand should be the minimum number for Kazan province alone, that its planned allocation of two hundred thousand was "wholly inadequate to cover the need." Along with Gregg, he put great stress on the necessity for quick action: "Speed is the essence of our problem. . . . Food must be gotten out into the country with the least delay possible; but meanwhile the need for a greater number of rations should at no time be forgotten and every opportunity should be taken to impress it on New York as further investigation substantiates the truth of this conclusion—and we already feel certain that it will."

And indeed it would. The troika continued south by rail to Simbirsk, taking three-and-a-half days to cover the distance of 150 miles. Why they chose not to float down the Volga is not clear, but it probably had to do with the hazards of navigating a river that had not been dredged for years. Still, en route they must have had second thoughts. There being no direct line, their car was changed several times from one slow train to another. At one point they arrived just too late to be attached to a train that got into a wreck down the line, killing ten passengers and delaying all rail traffic for a full day.

The station stops gave the travelers a chance to continue their investigations. In the town of Kanash, Golder and Shafroth went to the marketplace and found food plentiful, though costly. Meat was less expensive than bread, which indicated the presence of famine. They attracted a small crowd of locals, including two militiamen and a Red Army soldier, eager to give vent to their many grievances, which the faithful diarist Golder dutifully recorded: "They showed us and gave us a piece of the bread they made for themselves out of grass and acorns, which looked like a piece of horse manure." Further along the route, at the village of Krasnyi Uzel, two long-bearded peasants told Gregg and Golder that the people had enough potatoes and cabbage to last another two to three months; then they would have to kill their livestock for food.

Arriving in Simbirsk, where once again the railway station doubled as a refugee camp, the Americans made the rounds of children's homes and hospitals and found conditions even worse than in Kazan. Their first stop was at one of the dreaded receiving homes for abandoned children. How many of its six hundred inmates had lost their parents to starvation was impossible to guess; even if they knew, many were too young to say. Golder was told that it was "quite common" for mothers to leave their young ones in the market square or on the doorstep of a children's home. "We saw one pitiful case of two Tartar children, about five and three years of age, who did not understand a word of Russian, and when the nurse, who could not talk Tartar, tried to separate them to feed them, they clung to each other and wept most piteously, as if she were doing them harm."[19] Here, as in the regular children's homes, the single meal of the day consisted of a small chunk of black bread and a bowl of watery soup.

In the city of Simbirsk, just as in Kazan and everywhere else in Russia, there was tremendous filth all around, the practice of street cleaning having by now become a distant memory. Something else about this troubled land struck the Americans just as forcefully: the maintenance of what appeared to be absolute law and order. This was not at all what they had expected to find, and it came as a distinct relief, as Shafroth later recalled: "After the stories which we had heard of unorganized mobs of peasants burning villages and moving on toward the big cities and of the anarchy and lawlessness which existed in the provinces, it was impossible not to be impressed by the absolute authority of the local Governments and their entire control over the people."[20] Only the famine was out of control.

By car the Americans drove into the Simbirsk countryside to the town of Sengilei in one of the most distressed regions in the province, where they were shown sixteen varieties of "bread" made mostly of grass but also of acorns, leaves, and other substitutes. In a matter of weeks the first snows would fall and end the consumption of grass bread; horses as well would be cut off from their food supply and would have to be slaughtered and consumed.

After two-and-a-half days in Simbirsk province, the party boarded a dirty twenty-five-foot steamer and headed south toward Samara. This was their first extended voyage on the Volga, the longest river in Europe, which the peasants called Mother Volga, or little mother of Russia, and were said to regard as sacred, or as possessing supernatural powers. The visitors could not argue with superstition but neither could they register much enthusiasm about the river's natural beauty, which disappointed even an old hand like Golder: "There is not much scenery to thrill over." This was partly due to the river's languid flow and extraordinary breadth, which gave it the appearance of a narrow lake. Shafroth and Gregg began to ponder how this fact of nature might complicate their mission. On the stretch from Simbirsk to Samara the Volga was in places a mile across; below Samara it was generally two miles wide, until at Saratov it gradually widened so that by the time it reached Tsaritsyn it spanned three miles. How much time, they wondered to themselves, before the little mother of Russia froze and brought river traffic to a stop?

After navigating the lazy waters for thirty-six hours, two of which they spent aground on a shoal, the men came to Samara, before the war the richest grain-growing province in the river valley, now the seat of the Volga famine. The beach near the boat landing was dense with peasant families hoping to reach Ukraine or Turkestan. Golder says they "had only a very faint idea as to the distance." They had been in the same location for weeks, existing on watermelon and pumpkin rinds and distracted by the endless exercise of delousing themselves and their neighbors.[21]

Samara being a railroad junction on the Trans-Siberian, the train stations were teeming with refugees. Some were headed toward Moscow, many more toward Siberia—again, with little sense of the actual distance involved—and of course there was the usual quota destined for Ukraine, the proverbial breadbasket of Russia. It was a scene, like so many others, of misery, suffering, and filth but on a scale and of a severity surpassing anything they had witnessed thus far. F. A. Mackenzie of the *Chicago Daily News*, who came to this planet-stricken spot shortly afterward, described what he saw:

Here were lads, gaunt and tall, thin beyond any conception a Westerner can have of thinness, covered with rags and dirt. Here were old women, some of them sitting half-conscious on the ground, dazed by their hunger, their misery and their misfortune. The little children played feebly around. Some had lost their parents. Other women tried to mother them a bit as best they could. Here were pallid mothers seeking to feed dying babies from their milkless breasts. Were a new Dante to come among us, he could write a new Inferno after visiting one of these railway stations.

People were dying off daily by the score, perhaps by the hundred; "The children died like flies."

There were sad scenes when the trains came into the stations. People rushed to the doors of the third-class carriages. Every place was soon taken, every space filled, corridors packed, the platform full. Children were separated from their parents, never to see them again; old folk were left behind to die. Some tried to climb up on the buffers or on the roofs. The guards beat them off. Only the strongest and the luckiest remained on. When the train began to move off, people ran after it, clinging to the steps, trying to drag themselves along with it. Then there came a cry, a mournful cry, from the women left behind.[22]

Samara was conspicuously scarred by the invading armies in the Civil War. As Golder saw it, "the city is a wreck, a shadow of its former self," an appraisal that owed something to his memories of previous visits, though the evidence was plain to any first-time visitor. "Dirt and ruins are everywhere; windows are smashed; streets are torn up and littered with rubbish and dead animals. Hotels which at one time compared well with the best of Europe, are today empty shells; church steeples are turned into wireless stations and palatial homes into barracks." Here, as everywhere else in Russia, the foreign visitor was pressed by individuals of all classes, momentarily pausing in the never-ending search for bread, to satisfy a special curiosity: "What does the world think of us? Does it think we are crazy or a lot of wild savages?"

Just as the plight of the refugees was more extreme in Samara, so were conditions in the children's receiving stations. Shafroth and his colleagues visited six of these "hell-holes," one of which he described as "a nightmare of filth, lack of equipment, unbelievable overcrowding and criminal lack of the most elementary sanitary measures." Another, formerly a children's home with a capacity of sixty, presently housed 630 shriveled bodies. The disgusted Americans walked through the close, "vile-smelling" rooms, studying these pathetic creatures, "their skinny legs hanging over the edge of the wooden cot where three or four of them would be huddled together, an aged-look of suffering on their pale and emaciated faces."

Eight months later Shafroth departed Russia but could not leave these images behind: "I shall never forget the sights I saw in September, in Samara."[23]

The time for investigations was over. There was indeed a great famine, "the greatest in Russia since the time of Boris Godunoff, in the sixteenth century," in Shafroth's dark assessment.

As soon as the investigators' report from Kazan reached Moscow, the first food trains were sent out to Kazan, Simbirsk, and Samara, escorted by the relief workers who were to staff these districts. The three Americans did not know this and, having received no instructions by wire and unsure that their own communications had gotten through, decided that Gregg should proceed at once to Moscow. Shortly after his departure, a telegram came through from headquarters instructing Shafroth to remain in Samara as supervisor of the district. At long last he was to run his own show in the heart of Russia—though in his Cracow days he could never have imagined that the job itself would be such a formidable adventure.

Gregg arrived in Moscow full of stories about the catastrophe on the Volga, only to receive a new shock: ARA headquarters at Spiridonovka 30 had been taken over by a party of hostile forces—and it was not the Bolos.

JUST AFTER SHAFROTH, Golder, and Gregg had left Moscow for the Volga, Carroll received a telegram informing him that a large company of Americans was en route to Russia from the United States. They were led by Colonel William N. Haskell, who was to direct the ARA mission. This news was not unanticipated, for Haskell's selection had already been determined before the Riga negotiations and been made public right afterward.

Haskell qualified for the Russian assignment by following a path markedly different from the veteran ARA men. A graduate of West Point, Class of 1901, he was a career soldier with a distinguished record of service. In 1912 he was sent to the Philippines, his third spell there, where he was stationed for three years, with the Fourteenth, Eighth, and Seventh cavalry regiments, serving as adjutant of the Seventh, Custer's old regiment. He first came to national attention when, loaned to the New York national guard in 1916, he was named colonel of the famous Irish regiment, the 69th New York, in the war with Mexico in 1916–17. In the Great War he was a line officer in the St. Mihiel offensive, before becoming deputy chief of staff and chief of operations of the Second U.S. Army corps on the British front.[24]

This is but a partial record of Haskell's impressive credentials as a soldier. As a relief worker too he had, as they used to say, large experience. After the signing of the armistice, Hoover made him chief of the American relief mission to Romania, an operation of the U.S. Food Administration, and subsequently, in July 1919, he was selected by the Chief—though formally by the Allied Supreme Council— to be Allied high commissioner to Armenia, where he served also as director general of all American and European relief agencies in Transcaucasia. These included, among the American ones, the Near East Relief and the American Red Cross, as well as the ARA, which his own project essentially absorbed.

The Armenia campaign lasted about a year, and it sounds as if it was a busy, complicated, and generally unpleasant time. Haskell had to coordinate his relations with, among others, the representatives of the American Commission to Negotiate Peace, the American vice-consul at Tiflis, and the U.S. high commissioner at Constantinople, and with envoys of Russia's White armies and of the governments of France, Britain, Italy, Greece, Turkey, Georgia, Azerbaidzhan, and Armenia—these last three being new entities spawned by the break-up of the Russian empire. Actually, Armenia itself was a special case, as Haskell made clear in a letter from Tiflis, the Georgian capital, in February 1920: "As far as Armenia is concerned, I have taken things pretty much in my own hands, due to the fact that the whole country simply exists as a result of our efforts."[25] This is only somewhat exaggerated as in fact the fledgling state contained neutral zones where no established authority was recognized and where the high commissioner practically exercised sovereign powers. Operating within this diplomatic whirlwind, Haskell could not but become a controversial figure in many quarters.

This was indeed large relief experience, and it was service under Hoover, but it was not the same thing as conducting an ARA child-feeding operation. One difference was that the Romania and Armenia missions entailed relief to adults as well as children. Another, of far greater significance, was that both Haskell-led missions were heavily staffed with career U.S. Army officers.

In selecting Haskell to lead the Russian mission, Hoover's main concern was that the Soviets would object to the appointment of a well-known military man, so he telegraphed Brown to give Litvinov a proper introduction to the news, one stressing that Haskell had an exemplary record of cooperating with local authorities and staying clear of politics. Brown was worried that, Haskell's nomination aside, the Bolsheviks would be unnerved by the fact that most ARA men—and most other potential candidates for service in Russia—had been soldiers in the war. Yet they had long since been demobilized; Haskell, on the other hand, would merely be on loan from the army.[26] Nonetheless, for whatever reason, Litvinov offered no resistance to the selection of the colonel.

The audience Hoover should have been most concerned about was not the Bolsheviks, however, but his own relief workers. The question they would ask themselves in the coming months was why the Chief had not given the nod to an experienced ARA man to lead the largest ARA mission of them all. Hoover justified his choice privately within the organization by pointing to the fact that the Russian show would be very much in the public spotlight. Because positive publicity would play a vital role in winning the support—financial and otherwise—of the American public, it was important that the head of the mission be a man of prestige. This meant necessarily the selection of a man older than the relatively young ARA set, someone, that is, of more mature judgment. Haskell turned forty-three on August 13; Carroll was thirty-six.

In other words, Hoover wanted a big man for the ARA's biggest and politically most perilous mission. Haskell's reputation of avoiding political entanglements wherever possible was well deserved, he having managed during his time in the Caucasus to alienate virtually every party on the scene. His ego was very much intact, yet this deliberate, stiff, and taciturn soldier was by temperament nothing like the irrepressible Tom Gregory. Their paths had crossed in Trieste in spring 1919, and the colonel found the captain to be insufferable: "He impressed me as being overcome by the great power being wielded by himself for the moment and gave the impression to all who met him of having succeeded the Hapsburg dynasty."[27]

These factors in the selection of Haskell, whatever the order of their importance, are ones that can be gleaned from the ARA's internal correspondence. Perhaps Hoover was influenced as well by the fact that from the start he quietly anticipated expanding the Russian operation to include the feeding of adults, not customarily an ARA undertaking.

Although there is not a hint of it in the documentation, the choice of Haskell might say something about how Hoover thought Russia's political situation could develop. Reports that summer of a famine on the Volga seemed to indicate that the Bolshevik regime might finally be using up the last of its many lives. If authority broke down, it would be advantageous to have a veteran American soldier on the scene, one with some experience at directing political traffic in a failed state.

Considered though Hoover's decision may have been, inside the ARA the Haskell nomination was received like a slap in the face. Brown in London wrote to the New York office on July 30 to express his reservations, which indicates a troubled state of mind in view of the fact that he came near to doing the unthinkable: openly opposing a major decision of the Chief. He speculated that the Soviets would balk at the selection of Haskell because he was U.S. Army, which automatically associated him with the Allied intervention in the Russian Civil War. He wondered also if the colonel's having served as high commissioner in Armenia might lend an inexpedient official aura to the Russian unit. Much more to the point, Brown expressed apprehension at the fact that Haskell, not being an ARA man, was not "sufficiently one of us" to ensure a smooth and efficient operation in Russia.[28]

This still did not quite get at the fundamental reason behind Brown's dissent, whose delicacy prevented him from registering it outright, but which he most certainly had in mind in asserting that the director in Russia should be "one of us." Haskell was a Regular Army officer designated to take command of a group of former nonregulars. Such an arrangement was, as Brown knew, problematic, to say the least. Pivotal to the American soldier's experience in World War I was the bad blood between, on the one hand, enlisted men and commissioned officers and, on the other, Regular Army officers. Generally speaking, all nonregulars bridled at the caste and privilege in the AEF. To be sure, the enlisted men were estranged from the commissioned officers, too, partly due to the fact that these superiors were also their educational and social betters. But relations were far more strained with the non-coms because such officers were their social peers, even while outranking them in uniform. On their part, the commissioned officers chafed at having to take orders from their less-educated and socially inferior Regular Army superiors.

Even Henry Stimson, the once and future secretary of war, grew irritable while serving as a staff officer in France, complaining to his diary, "I am getting a little tired of kow-towing to regulars just because they are regulars."[29]

The American soldier's antipathy for the discipline and hierarchy of army life would become a theme of the disillusionment fictional literature of the 1920s. Baker of the New York office, having just put down Dos Passos's *Three Soldiers*, was inspired to send off copies to a few friends. Among them was Charles Field of *Sunset* magazine in San Francisco, to whom Baker wrote in an accompanying note on September 26, five days after Haskell arrived in Moscow, that the new book was "at once an exquisite literary production of great charm and incidentally a fine analysis of the state of mind and body of one who has served under the illiterate and irresponsible non-com."[30] One of the eponymous three soldiers uses a grenade to get rid of his sergeant.

This was not how the Great War was remembered, two years after Versailles by someone like Hoover, who may have been only vaguely aware of incendiary psychodynamics at work inside the AEF. Brown, however, immediately understood that appointing Haskell was like lighting a fuse.

Only with this background is it possible to understand why the air was electric with enmity when Haskell and his party, twenty-one-strong, arrived in Moscow on September 21. The reception at headquarters by Carroll and company was ice cold. The men already in place had been given advance warning that the colonel was to be their chief, but what was unexpected was the strong military flavor of his party, which included, counting Haskell, seven regulars: Colonels Lonergan, Telford, Winters, Bell, and Beeuwkes, and Major Dodge. Of these, Lonergan, Telford, and Dodge had served under Haskell in the Caucasus.

At the outset it was unclear which of these men were active officers, whose services Haskell had requested from the secretary of war, and how many were retired from the army. The active-duty men were out of uniform, while the others retained their military titles, making it hard to distinguish between the two. Gregg counted "three army officers in the party out and out, and some four more that are called major and captain by their friends and compatriots," but he was upset at the time and may have been wrong about this. Among those who had come in with the Haskell party was John Clapp, a veteran of ARA missions in Paris, Trieste, Belgrade, Bucharest, Prague, and Vienna. Clapp, who had been commissioned a captain in the Signal Corps, told his diary during these disorienting first days: "Office at Moscow very military. . . . Esprit de corps is not very good. Questions of relative rank always popping up."[31]

The matter of living space for those already in Moscow had not yet been settled, and this did not make the arrival of twenty-one more men—army or otherwise—any easier to take. At first the newcomers were forced to utilize their railroad cars as living quarters, just as the advance party had done the month before. This might have seemed to Carroll's crowd like fair treatment, but from Haskell's point of view the fact that their American hosts had not found space for them was an especially petty manifestation of their undisguised hostility for the new arrivals. John Sellards, one of the intruders, remarked that some of Carroll's men were occupying rooms of their own, yet no place was offered to the man who was to direct the mission.

Passing four nights in the railway yards seems to have stuck in the colonel's gullet, though he made no mention of it at the time in official correspondence. On September 30 he wrote to Brown that he had arrived to find that Carroll and his team had "accomplished a great deal"; yet, as he recalled it ten years later, they "had been able to accomplish very little in the way of preliminary organization, nor had they succeeded in obtaining sufficient living quarters for us." So the lack of accommodations was taken as a message, and with a good deal more justification than Carroll's earlier imputation of inhospitality to the Soviet government.

From the first moment, Sellards observed, there were "two distinct factions." Carroll and the ARA veterans saw Haskell and his Caucasus men as tyros in the job of child-feeding; Haskell, on the other hand, believed that the Armenian experience was more relevant to Russia's circumstances than a background in the ARA. Haskell made this point openly a decade later in his unpublished memoir, in which he remarked that only in Armenia had there been actual famine conditions, whereas in Europe the ARA had provided merely supplementary rations; only in Armenia had the Americans found the machinery of distribution completely broken down and local authorities, where they existed, withholding cooperation. This more or less tacit running dispute over who was more qualified to lead the Russian show, energized as it was by the visceral animosity between army and ARA, kept tensions simmering at Moscow headquarters.[32]

By previous agreement, once Haskell took command, Carroll assumed the post of chief of the supply division. This was a vitally important job, but it still left Carroll subordinate to Haskell, and both men seem to have understood from the first moment that their relationship was destined to end badly. Haskell sensed right away that Carroll was an unwilling subordinate. In his initial letters to London and New York he could not avoid mentioning how difficult it was for the "old A.R.A. men" to adjust to his leadership and system, that it would take time for them to fall into rank. As for Carroll, "I wish he would cheer a bit. It is quite difficult for him to concentrate on a part of a thing of which he had the general management." On October 5 Haskell reports that all is going well, that everyone is "playing the game," and that he is perfectly satisfied with Carroll—although if Carroll wants "a separate independent show," he hopes Brown will try to find him one. Perhaps the Colonel hoped that the ARA was planning a move into China or points further east. For now, Haskell in his correspondence adopted an attitude of pressing on gamely, promising Edgar Rickard, the ARA's director general in New York, on September 28, that "the job is going to be put over in excellent shape."[33]

This is where matters stood when Gregg returned from the Volga in the last days of September to find "Carroll's carefully built up plans knocked higher than a kite." That is how he described it in a rather overwrought letter to Shafroth, in which he announced that "the blow has fallen with full force." The blow, of course, was the arrival of Haskell and his retinue: "She is some party, and I am ready for Poland, if it were not for the Chief and London." Gregg indicates that the two men had anticipated such an incursion: "We were absolutely right in assuming that there would be a large crowd of new people, with new ideas, which they think are exactly like ours, and with army manners and discipline that make every order they give rather a burden"; nonetheless, "It is worse than we imagined and that is going some."

They were arrogant, these outsiders, with their talk of "bringing order out of chaos," as if those who preceded them had simply been marking time. "Carroll and I are both disgusted and it looks to me as if the party were about to end for us in a grand finale of resignations." The ARA men were used to a loose, decentralized organization; Haskell meant to impose on them a centralized, military-style system. They were avoiding a break, Gregg says, hoping things would improve, but the outlook was not good: "Carroll and I may be on our way at any moment so prepare for the news and be ready to move if you so desire. They are a hard boiled crowd and there are lots of them."

This was more than simply starting out on the wrong foot, for on October 7 Gregg, though still in Moscow, sounds even more agitated. Haskell's plan of operation, he confirms for Shafroth, is "foreign to all our ideas." By now there were forty-nine Americans in the mission, most gathered in Moscow. "There are a mass of people here that have little or nothing to do with Child Relief, and with the strong army atmosphere we could believe that we are back in France." Among other things, Gregg had in mind Haskell's appointment of a chief of staff, through whom all business between the director and his subordinates was to be conducted —an army arrangement entirely alien to the ARA. What is more, Haskell and his adjutant delivered their instructions, both verbal and written, in a clipped, unmistakably military fashion, that is to say, as if they were giving orders. Beyond the fact that all of this broke with the ARA's customary way of doing things, what truly enraged was that this, the stress on hierarchy and the disciplinary tone, was precisely what the relief workers of the ARA thought they had put behind them forever once demobilized. It revived memories of their inglorious days in boot camp.

Without this context, Gregg's outbursts would seem merely histrionic. "We are certainly convinced that the Chief has sold us out." This is a shocking statement coming from one of the outstanding performers in an organization whose ethos assumed an unquestioning loyalty to the Chief. Shafroth himself may have been surprised to read it, though perhaps the urgent business of saving tens of thousands of starving people and the countless practical details it involved—locating warehouses, establishing kitchens, organizing food committees, hiring a staff, and so on—perhaps these distractions did not allow him to consider the significance of Gregg's stream of overexcited sentences. One passage, however, must have given him pause: "To get to the point: if it comes to a show down as to whether this is to be an Army show or an A.R.A. show, we will let you know by a short wire along lines such as 'may be able to take leave' or something similar indicating that the jig is up so far as we are concerned and we are on our way."[34]

Of course, threatening to desert the mission was a long way yet from the actual thing. But the record indicates that it might have come to an open break if not for the arrival in Moscow of Vernon Kellogg on the morning of October 2, just as the lid was about to blow off. Kellogg had accompanied the first food train to the Volga and made his own famine investigation before returning to Moscow and proceeding from there to London and the United States, where he would brief the ARA chiefs and Hoover himself on the Russian situation.

Kellogg, professor of entomology at Stanford and a longtime friend and associate of Hoover, had directed Belgian relief from Brussels as his chief deputy in 1915–16, then became his assistant at the Food Administration from 1917 to 1919, before serving with the ARA in Europe, for a time heading up the Poland mission. Even prior to going in, he anticipated the rough weather that lay ahead. From London on September 8 he wrote to Hoover of the uneasiness among Brown's staff about Haskell, who was at that moment on a ship bound for England. "I shall be in Russia when Haskell and his party come in—and shall see him and try to have him understand our way of working. . . . I know Haskell and can talk frankly with him." As it happened, it was Kellogg's frank talk that saved the situation in the first days of October, as he was able to patch together an understanding between the factions.[35]

The bad feeling in Moscow, which subsided only temporarily, was compounded in those initial weeks by the tremendous strain involved in organizing a relief operation in a country where everything seemed broken down, the people were listless, and it was impossible to get action the way the Americans were used to getting it. It did not help matters that the relief workers had to keep such close quarters. After their four nights in the railroad cars, Haskell moved his party into cramped lodgings, where most of the men were billeted dormitory-style and fed in a single crowded mess. Haskell informed New York one week after arrival that "such things as baths are unknown and no one has had a real one since leaving London." Gregg called headquarters a "madhouse."

Securing more spacious accommodations was considered such a priority that Haskell himself took on the responsibility. Soviet officials brought him around to inspect several potential candidates for occupancy, including a very large house. The woman who once owned it, a former aristocrat close to the Romanov court circles, now lived in the basement, the remaining rooms having been converted into individual apartments, each inhabited by a family of laborers. This fact of life under the Revolution would later become familiar to millions of moviegoers from a scene in which Doctor Zhivago returns home from a long absence to discover he has acquired a strange assortment of new neighbors—living inside his own house. Haskell entered and found the structure spacious enough to suit the ARA's purposes but in an unacceptable state of disrepair. Each of the rooms had its own makeshift stove with ventilation pipe penetrating an exterior wall. The building was terribly filthy and would take weeks to get in shape. Besides, requisitioning it would entail the unpleasant business of having to dislodge its destitute working-class tenants, an unappealing prospect even for this representative of capitalist America.

So the structure was unfit for the ARA, but something made Haskell hesitate. At the entrance to her basement apartment stood the former owner of the house, her children at her back, the family's careful grooming in stark contrast to the squalid surroundings. The mother, standing erect and fearless before the Soviet officials, followed Haskell pleadingly with her eyes. No words were spoken, but he understood that she wanted him to appropriate the building, which would mean security and sustenance for herself and her children and the restoration of her house. The colonel lingered, contemplating the ceiling, the walls, the floor, the scuff marks on his boots, struggling to imagine a satisfactory solution to this unexpected dilemma. But there was none.

It was the kind of choice these Americans would be faced with time and again in the course of the next two years, many far more heartrending than the one that now tested Haskell. The company left the building, the woman still posted in her doorway. Four months later Haskell had still not managed to put the episode behind him. An American visitor to Moscow found him obsessed with it, returning to the subject "at least once every day" at mealtime, and "he touched upon it again almost every evening."[36]

Haskell's reconnaissance mission disclosed that the only buildings fit for immediate occupancy were those private homes that had been nationalized and converted into state museums and whose interiors had been maintained intact, including furniture, paintings, and objets d'art. These museums were open to the public so that the newly empowered people could come and gaze upon not only works of art but the relics of a way of life relegated to the dustbin of history. Haskell asked that the ARA be allowed to take over two of these buildings. His request was opposed by Madame Trotsky, whose job it was to administer such cultural establishments, but she was overruled on one of the two, which was placed in the charge of the ARA in exchange for a pledge to guarantee the safety of the art collection.[37] This capacious residence was located in the Arbat neighborhood, a ten-minute walk from headquarters. Within three weeks came three more houses, and the ARA's congestion was alleviated.

Trying his hand at Moscow real estate had accelerated Haskell's introduction to the difficulties of getting things done in Russia. Completing even minor tasks seemed to take forever, giving the Americans the sensation of walking in place. There was much to do, but the government appeared incapable of action or even to be dragging its feet; even when it cooperated, orders given by responsible officials seemed, in Carroll's words, to "vanish in thin air once outside the office." Haskell had this uninspired performance in mind when he wrote to the New York office on September 28: "The whole situation in Russia at present seems to be that everything is old, broken, worn out, gutted, nothing works and everybody seems to be milling about in a semi-dazed condition with only one thought in mind, that is, where are they going to get food to eat, shelter and clothing."[38]

That was the view from Moscow, anyway, yet from what Gregg and Kellogg had told him, he knew that the situation of the Muscovites was incomparably better than that of the inhabitants of the Volga valley, which he pictured as "another Armenia of 1918–19 multiplied in size and population to an extent not yet determined." And so, having brought order out of chaos in Moscow, Haskell went to have a look for himself at the kingdom of hunger.

BY NOW THE SCALE of the problem in the capitals and on the Volga, at least the stretch north from Samara, had been roughly ascertained. The rations established for the month of October were: Kazan, 150,000; Samara, 150,000; Simbirsk, 75,000; Saratov, 75,000; Moscow, 20,000; and Petrograd, 15,000. These totals were to be built up, as incoming food supplies allowed, to the one million maximum target. But as Haskell indicated, the geographic boundaries of the famine had yet to be confirmed. The Soviet government defined the "famine zone"—meaning the territory affected by drought—to be an area covering roughly 800 miles long, from Viatka in the north to Astrakhan on the Caspian Sea, and 350 miles across at the widest point, between Penza and Ufa. This meant that drought had afflicted the greater part of the so-called black earth region, encompassing the most fertile soil in Russia, where food production in 1921 was already less than half of what it had been in 1913, and which was also the most populated section of the country.[39]

At this point the government was saying nothing about the situation in southern Ukraine, where ten million people were dealing with a famine as bad as anything on the Volga. Haskell's relief workers were not aware of this, nor did they have a fix on the severity of the situation east of the Volga, the source of thousands of refugees fleeing westward. Word of American famine relief might turn this exodus into a stampede, which meant that it was important for the ARA to determine the extent of the problem in the east and to decide whether to establish relief operations there.

Haskell needed to be able to visualize the job ahead and to give Hoover a first-hand report. He left Moscow on October 5 and made a brief swing through Samara and across to Ufa province in the Ural Mountains, then back—a round trip that was to last nine days. In his company as he departed the capital was Lincoln

Hutchinson, professor of economics at the University of California, who had been drafted as a special investigator for the Russian unit. Hutchinson had been, before and since the war, a U.S. commercial attaché and had been stationed in Prague with the ARA. He was brought on board the Russian mission to act as chief economist and statistician in a land of notoriously unreliable statistics, something he had learned for himself during an extended visit in 1913.[40]

At Samara Hutchinson split from Haskell and teamed up with Golder, who now also assumed the title special investigator. This pair would in the coming year become the two most-traveled Americans in Soviet Russia as they criss-crossed the famine zone by rail, collecting statistics from local authorities and recording their observations and interviews with officials and citizens, most of which is chronicled in their 1927 book, *On the Trail of the Russian Famine*.

Near the end of their wanderings together, Golder indicated in private correspondence that despite all their shared experiences, he had barely gotten to know his traveling companion. Long periods of silence passed between the two during their interminable train rides. Golder referred to him as "the careful economist and cautious statistician," and a reading of Hutchinson's reports from autumn 1921 demonstrates that Golder, in fact, knew whereof he spoke.[41] The uninitiated might easily be led to believe that Hutchinson and Shafroth walked through different lands. There is "no real famine yet," Hutchinson wrote to Brown from Samara on October 13. "There is a shortage of food and a lot of suffering and disease, but about nine-tenths of it is due to official inefficiency and indifference." Food was available in Russia; the trouble was that the distribution system had broken down. As a consequence, people were starving at points not fifty miles away from areas of abundance. The root of the problem was that for those holding the grain there was nothing to sell it for. There was certainly much more food than was indicated in the reports of local officials, because the peasants, true to their "Oriental" character, were concealing it.

Hutchinson advised that the ARA focus its energies on reviving distribution, that it apply to the Soviet government for permission to import a few cargoes of consumer goods and agricultural supplies in order to barter these for food, which could then be used to feed the hungry. On November 9, after returning to Moscow from his initial investigations, he assured Brown that there was as yet still no famine, "if we mean by 'famine' that food supplies are exhausted"; instead there was "merely a panic fear that famine will come before the winter is over, plus real privation and to a certain extent real starvation on the part of those who either have not the wherewithal to purchase food or who live too far from regions of surplus to be able . . . to get what they need."

Of course, if one wanted to assemble "sob photographs," one could make quite a collection, but "the 'intrinsic' situation is a hopeful one." The crisis, he reiterated, was one of food distribution, not production: "The fact is that the whole communistic system of exchange has broken down. This is what I have seen everywhere I have been; trade in our ordinary sense of the word can hardly be said to exist at all." Again he recommended that the ARA win Soviet approval for a concession to trade in breadstuffs, which would enable it "to feed the entire needy population of the famine area."[42]

Hutchinson was to become known among his colleagues within the Russian unit as "the Professor," which correctly states his title, but which was intended to imply—as it often does—a certain aloofness, a remoteness from reality, and of course absent-mindedness. In Hutchinson's case the particular object of this sniggering was his obsession with statistical information and economic analysis of a kind that at times seemed far removed from the real-world problems they were intended to help solve. His diagnosis of Russia's economic disorder was arguably sound, but his promotion of a commercial solution over straightforward philanthropy, while very much in the Hoover spirit, was hardly a realistic prescription for meeting the emergency at hand.

Nonetheless, even the professor's analysis allowed that famine would shortly be upon the Russians, fifteen million of them by his estimate. "Something will have to be done to get into the famine area within the next few months, from somewhere either in other parts of Russia or from outside countries, from three quarters of a million to one million tons of food."

Golder and Hutchinson had been joined in Samara by James P. Goodrich, a third special investigator—special for reasons completely different from the others. Goodrich, the former Republican governor of Indiana, was a banker and a well-connected Republican, partly on the strength of his personal friendship with President Harding. Hoover had enlisted his services in the ARA to conduct an independent survey of the famine. Summoned to Washington for an interview, Goodrich pleaded ignorance about Russia, to which Hoover responded that this was precisely why he wanted him for the job. What could be better than to have a plain-spoken, red-blooded American, untainted by any previous exposure to Russia or to Bolshevism, go and see for himself the utter foolishness of the Soviet economic system and report back to the American people? But Hoover had a far more important and more practical motive for sending a relative innocent like the governor to Bolshevik Russia: he was anticipating the value of the public testimony on the Volga famine from an eyewitness credible with the American people and, even more significantly, influential in official Washington.[43]

Goodrich reached Moscow in the first week of October and, after taking a few days to look around, headed for the Volga. From Samara, he journeyed south with Hutchinson and Golder to Saratov, where he split off from the pair and, accompanied by a Soviet guide and a translator, followed a trail of the famine. Goodrich appears to have been influenced by the opinions aired by the professor during their few days together on the road. In any event, like Hutchinson he proved to be an immovably cold-blooded observer. This quality is more unexpected in the governor, who was new to both Russia and hunger on a mass scale. He had been in the States when Gibbons's first reports from the Volga appeared in the newspapers; now at the scene, he agreed with Hutchinson that these articles sensationalized the famine.

In his first memorandum to Hoover, dated November 1, Goodrich declared that the peasants actually had a surplus of grain; in fact they had a four or five months' reserve of food, maybe more, for the entire population. No statistics provided by local officials would have led him to such an estimate; rather he drew heavily upon his personal powers of observation, in which he put great stock. He described for Hoover the varieties, amounts, and prices of food in the bazaars of Samara, Saratov, and nearby Markstadt. The plenitude of the marketplace, he believed, was a fair index of Russia's food supply; one got a distorted view of the situation from the children's homes and public institutions.

This judgment directly contradicted that of the experienced relief workers, who understood that in a time of famine an abundance of food in the marketplace was a false sign of prosperity—especially an abundance of meat, which typically meant that draught animals were being slaughtered, either because their flesh was now the difference between life and death or because of a lack of fodder. A Shafroth or a Gregg would have agreed that the children's homes were indeed the site of some of the worst suffering, but they knew as well that making inventories of the food on sale in the markets was not going to save those children.

So Goodrich tended to see the cup as half full. He wrote in his report for Hoover that he arrived at his general assessment of the Russian condition not by relying solely on government statistics, or his inspections of bazaars, or his visits to children's homes, but only after he had personally entered the villages and talked with the peasants, consulted their records, inspected their kitchens and hospitals, "slept in their homes and ate their bread." He claimed to have carried out this procedure in five villages in Samara province and twelve in Saratov. It begins to sound as if he had camped among the natives for months on end, yet what he himself allowed was a "hurried investigation" lasted only two weeks. Still, where his empirical research fell short, he relied on deductive logic in order to draw sweeping conclusions. This enabled him to become a remarkably quick study of the mentality of the Russian peasants: "They tell you there is no concealed supply. I question the correctness of this for it is contrary to human nature and the semi-Oriental character of the famine provinces." Echoes of the professor.

Like Hutchinson, Goodrich was not blind to the suffering around him, especially that of the many thousands of refugees he saw along his route. He sketched a few choice hardship scenes for Hoover and observed that in the village of Baro, in Saratov province, every single dog had been made into sausages. "I could tell you these things until you would be sick of heart as I have been as I saw them, but that would not help the situation, nor aid in the solution of the problem." His recommendations did not stray beyond the bounds of philanthropy. He urged that the number of rations be increased to 1.5 million and the program include adult feeding.[44]

Even as he wrote these lines on November 1, and well before they arrived on Hoover's desk, a far more ambitious plan to expand American relief to Russia was in the works in Washington and New York.

Having arrived back in Moscow, on October 20 Haskell sent Hoover his first telegraphic report on conditions in Russia. He agreed with his investigators about one thing: "Newspaper stories exaggerate present general condition and photographs are selected from worst cases." The actual number of people affected was not twenty-five million, but nearer to sixteen million. "Starvation present but not yet general; peak will arrive December January and continue August. . . . Greatest need program adult feeding limited to cereals. . . . Estimate two thousand tons flour daily judiciously distributed, commencing January first would meet requirements Volga." That and a seed program, he added in a telegram of November 5, and "Russia will have surplus August."[45]

Shortly after receiving Haskell's first telegram—though not as a direct consequence of it—Hoover made his carefully considered move to expand the mission. Precisely when this decision was taken is impossible to determine. Haskell's call for adult feeding was a necessary step, but Hoover had been contemplating this possibility even before the Riga talks began; he had also discussed it with Haskell before the mission, so the colonel's recommendation had in fact been prompted. Support for the idea had been provided by the reports of Gregg and Shafroth, which had been passed on to New York and Washington. Even earlier still, the return of Kellogg from Russia in the second week of October had probably clinched the matter. Hoover had absolute faith in his colleague's judgment based on their years together in the business of relief, from Belgium to Poland. The essence of the message Kellogg brought back to Washington is captured in an undated diary entry from his September sojourn along the Volga, in which he wonders: "Can we stop with feeding children alone while their natural protectors (mother and father) are allowed to die?"[46]

This was all the inducement Hoover needed to move forward with a plan for adult feeding sufficient to carry the Volga population through to the 1922 harvest and a seed program to give that harvest a chance. On October 27 he telegraphed Brown in London that the ARA program as conceived was inadequate and that the European countries were unlikely to make up the difference. "Therefore only practicable hope lies in large response U.S. people." By this he meant through their elected representatives; in other words, it was time to go to Congress for an appropriation for Russian relief. Brown was instructed to relay word to Haskell that as soon as Goodrich had been able to satisfy himself as to the great scope of the famine he should return to assist with the preparations on the U.S. end.[47] Thus, the decision to expand was taken before Goodrich had even sat down to compose his first memorandum from Russia. But then, the governor's role was less about suffering on the Volga than it was about politics along the Potomac.

BEFORE THE SOVIET TELEGRAPH became reliable, Haskell's telegrams in this early phase of operations—and the most sensitive of them for the duration of the mission—were sent by courier to Riga and from there in cipher to the State Department, where the secretary of state passed them on to Hoover in the form of a close paraphrase. Hoover, and in fact Hughes and other officials at State and Commerce, had been waiting for Haskell's analysis of the political situation in Russia, their curiosity peaked by recent newspaper stories out of Moscow about a further phase of radical economic reform initiated by Lenin. Haskell's cable of October 20 confirmed the general trend: "Rapid drifting from communistic ideals indicated by recent free trade, rent authorization, car fares, etcetera."

The reforms seemed to spill over into the international political arena toward the end of October when a diplomatic note issued by Chicherin indicated a willingness on the part of the Soviet government to acknowledge its responsibility to pay Russia's prewar foreign debt and proposed an international conference to negotiate an agreement.[48] Even more strikingly, it was in the last two weeks of October that Lenin scandalized his fellow Bolsheviks with his blunt statements, published in the Soviet press, declaring that heroic War Communism had been a mistake and that Soviet Russia needed to make more room for capitalism.

Chicherin's note and Lenin's "remarkably bold" speeches influenced the tone of

Haskell's November 5 telegram to Washington: "Government now anxious repair mischief save peasants and hold their own jobs at any price. Scarcely day passes without some new concession to private ownership and right to trade." Haskell's wording may have encouraged the wishful thinking in Washington that the Bolshevik hold on power was fast slipping. In his earlier report he had even used the formulation "Complete economic breakdown." Yet there he also stated flatly that the central Bolsheviks were solidly in control. "Bureaucracy functioning under dictation group Jewish opportunists as severe as Imperial regime. . . . Dazed population accepts situation calmly."

For Hoover and Hughes, this, more than his confirmation of the accelerating economic retreat from communism, was the critical message of Haskell's communications out of Moscow: the Bolsheviks were not going to fall from power. In fact, the colonel wrote, the Soviet government had a "strangle hold on Russia" even though it "lacks support and confidence of people. No opposition dares raise its head." In his October 20 cable he identified two competing Bolshevik factions, Lenin's moderates and Trotsky's radicals. This was common speculation at the time and completely baseless. By November 5 his analysis had progressed beyond this: "Soviet control complete and none to oppose it. No sign serious division in ranks communists though obvious there must be some discontent at turn of affairs." So there was no hope after all that Comrade Trotsky might shoot Comrade Lenin and at last end the whole Bolshevik project in a paroxysm of self-destructive violence.

All the investigators' reports agreed with Haskell that Russia's experiment in communism was over. Goodrich informed Hoover that although Lenin was assuring his colleagues that NEP was merely a strategic retreat, it marked "such a complete abandonment of the underlying principles of communism that I care not by what name they call it, tactics or not, it marks the complete failure of communism." His ARA colleagues were unanimous on this point. Lenin "blew the gaff," in the slang favored by the relief workers, who read translations of newspaper summaries of his October speeches. At the same time, all could see that the Bolsheviks remained, in the ARA man's phrase of choice, "firmly in the saddle."

Here was a strange and unsatisfyingly mixed message. Communism was dead, but Communist power was unchallenged. There were no more Kronstadt rebellions in Russia's future. The revolutionary radicals were not to suffer the same fate as their victims in the way Robespierre himself had eventually been escorted to the guillotine. This was not the way things were supposed to turn out.

Haskell's advice was that the United States ought to take advantage of the opening through "constructive action." Hutchinson, writing privately to Brown, could afford to be more direct: the United States ought to recognize the Soviet government as the de facto government of Russia. "Things seem now, in view of Lenin's and Tchicherin's statements, to indicate that the present may be the psychological moment for this step too."[49] Goodrich, returning to Washington, began to make the same case.

But Hoover and Hughes resisted, unable to imagine that Bolshevik power would endure. In Hoover's analogy it was still a matter of the pendulum's inevitable progress. A mixed economic system like NEP was an unnatural creation, destined to evolve into a genuine market. Washington could encourage this evolution by maintaining a policy of watchful waiting, forcing the Bolsheviks to retreat still further by continually reiterating the demands that the Soviet authorities must recognize their foreign debts, restore nationalized property, cease their campaign of propaganda, and return to a sane economic system, one based on the legal protection of property. The assumption was that it would be impossible for Lenin's government to meet these requirements and retain its hold on political power. So watchful waiting meant in essence waiting for the Bolsheviks to fall. With the ARA organization now in place inside Russia, the U.S. government had a special instrument that enabled it to monitor these developments—and perhaps to act when the time came.

CHAPTER 4

MAKING THE SHOW A GO

The relief workers on the famine front had no idea about the impending expansion of their mission, and most remained in the dark until it became a reality, in January 1922. As it was, the men in the field had their hands full with the enormous task of feeding one million children through the winter.

Food trains were arriving in Kazan, Samara, Simbirsk, and, by mid-October, Saratov, followed at the end of the month by Tsaritsyn, situated on the lower Volga where the river turns left toward the Caspian. These were the Volga "districts," as the ARA called its administrative-territorial units. They were roughly coterminous with the corresponding Russian provinces, *gubernii*, which were named after their capital cities. The ARA adjusted boundaries here and there, where practical considerations such as the location of a warehouse or a railroad line argued in favor of the disposition of one or another provincial region to a contiguous district.

Alone the five Volga districts would have constituted a sizable mission, yet as American investigations had confirmed, the popular expression "famine on the Volga" understated the scale of Russia's crisis. By late October the ARA had established two sprawling districts to the east. One was centered at Ufa, on the western slopes of the Ural Mountains, and included most of the Bashkir Autonomous Republic. Feeding children at Ufa began on November 16, with food supplies for fifty thousand. Subsequent investigations revealed that starvation in the region was epidemic, so the following month this allotment was increased to seventy thousand. This was just the beginning: within a few months Ufa would become the largest ARA district, both territorially and as measured by volume of relief, providing daily meals to more than 1.6 million children and adults.[1]

The other trans-Volga district was Orenburg, capital of the Kirghiz Autonomous Republic, situated at the southeastern edge of European Russia, where the southern ranges of the Ural Mountains descend into the scrub and brush of the steppe, back then Russia's Badlands. Unlike Ufa, Orenburg province was not included in the official Soviet famine zone.

Both district capitals were nearly a thousand miles removed from Moscow, a circumstance that would create special problems, opportunities, and adventures for the men stationed there. For everyone involved, the problem of distance was compounded by the sparseness and wretched state of Russia's transportation and communication systems. (See map, page 200.)

The network of railroads to and along the Volga was sufficient, but further east it thinned out considerably. The city of Ufa is on the Trans-Siberian line, which crosses the Volga at Samara; but in the Bashkir republic, which composed a large part of the ARA's Ufa district, there was in those days no railroad and only one navigable river—and that for only a few weeks in spring. The city of Orenburg was located on a single-track line that broke off from the Trans-Siberian just east of Samara. At Orenburg the line forked, one branch heading southeast to distant Tashkent, the other projecting eastward 150 miles into the Kirghiz republic, where it dead-ended. Otherwise one traveled by river or road or, more commonly, over the flatlands.

The ruinous condition of Russia's railroads, first reported by Carroll upon his arrival in Moscow, was graphically conveyed in Haskell's October 20 telegram to Washington: "Railroads hanging together, roadbeds unrepaired, derailed cars ditched. Thousands cars deteriorating on sidings where rails and ties have been removed from under them." As the colonel feared, this state of affairs greatly complicated the shipment of relief supplies, especially once the snows began to fall. It also hampered the movement of ARA personnel, Americans and Soviets, within their districts as well as between districts and to and from Moscow. Travel in winter was hazardous, even perilous. Most vulnerable were the ARA's locally recruited couriers, underfed, underclothed, and forced to cover ground in unheated boxcars, where they were prey to the typhus louse and in danger of freezing to death if their train's engine ran out of fuel or they became stuck in a blizzard in the middle of nowhere.

These couriers were a chief means of communication between Moscow and the districts, especially in the early going when the telegraph was slow and unreliable. In autumn 1921 it generally took five days for a telegram from Moscow to reach Kazan, Simbirsk, or Samara; to Tsaritsyn it took fifteen days; to Orenburg fourteen. International communication was initially slow as well: a wire from Moscow to London took six or seven days. Only by summer 1922 did this become a twenty-four-hour service.[2]

Distance from Moscow complicated the uphill assignment of establishing a district headquarters. Although the provincial capitals had endured their share of physical destruction, the relief workers encountered little difficulty getting situated, even if they often had to expend considerable effort in the repair of their new offices and residences. Empty warehouses also were easy to come by, since there was neither grain nor goods to occupy them, the chief concern being their frightful state of disrepair. It was the basic items—furniture, tools and equipment, office supplies, and the like—which proved more difficult to procure in the provinces than in the capitals. Their provision was the responsibility of local officials, not every one of whom could quite fathom why, all of a sudden, it should be such an urgent matter to locate, say, a typewriter just because some agitated American had appeared on the scene and demanded one.

And the struggle for a typewriter was only the beginning. As Fisher wrote, "It took persistent nagging, expostulations, and search to get proper locks for storerooms, scales or measures for the kitchens, paper and pens for keeping kitchen accounts, kettles, and fuel." What, wondered the locals, was the big hurry? "The Russians, for whom famine was a familiar catastrophe, naturally could not understand the nervous impetuosity of the young Americans who seemed to think

that if things were not done at breakneck speed all would be lost, whereas the
natives knew that there would be hungry to feed next week, the week after, and
next year."[3]

The Americans attempted to overcome inertia by explaining to local authorities why the ARA had come into Russia, how many children it hoped to rescue
from starvation, and so on. If this did not produce the desired effect, they reminded these same officials of their obligation under the Riga Agreement to assist the relief workers in securing all facilities and equipment, and—perhaps adding for good measure—to respect the ARA's freedom to hire its employees and
assemble its food committees. Far from getting action, this argument was apt to
confound the local chiefs, many of whom, it turned out, had only a vague idea
about the coming of the ARA, and few of whom seemed to have even heard of
the Riga Agreement. For the moment, there must have been at least one especially puzzled Bolo trying to fathom what possible connection the obtuse American before him saw between his demand for a typewriter and the recently won
independence of Latvia.

One must consider the state of mind of these local officials, Party and soviet, at
this juncture in the Revolution. For several months now the Kremlin had been issuing heretical decrees, first ending grain requisitions, then authorizing free trade
and resurrecting other forms of the infernal capitalism. More recently, Comrade
Lenin had come out and called the economic policies of War Communism a mistake. For many smaller-fry Communists—most of whom, having joined the cause
only since 1917, knew only a revolutionary-heroic brand of Bolshevism—it was almost too much. Fisher likened the effect to a game of snap-the-whip: the further
down the line—in this case removed from the political center—the more violent
the jolt.[4] Some provincial officials found the retreat to the market so unbelievable
or simply unacceptable that they routinely chose to ignore the early reform decrees, which delayed the implementation of NEP in the hinterland.

Then, at this moment of terrific confusion, even panic, there arrived from
America, the stronghold of capitalism, an army of so-called relief workers with
pretensions of operating independently of the dictatorship of the proletariat. After four years of supreme struggle to defeat the imperialist armies and class enemies and to extinguish all privately organized activity, suddenly some insolent
Americans were to be allowed to roam freely about and make brazen demands of
Soviet power.

The initial reaction of local authorities toward the ARA was seldom one of
outright hostility but merely reflexive suspicion and a defiant disbelief that the
mandate of these bourgeois relief workers was really as extensive as they claimed.
None of the Americans had left Moscow with a duplicate of the Riga Agreement, and so a standard request in the initial telegrams from the Volga districts
to Haskell's office was for authenticated copies of the document—the wire from
Saratov adding a plea for a Latin-script typewriter.

The districts that opened later were able to learn from this experience, though
the results were not always satisfactory. Moscow dispatched Freddie Lyon to
Orenburg armed with English and Russian versions of the Riga accord. Yet a
simple reading of the sacred text to the natives, he discovered, did not work the
intended miracles. Lyon's own performance of it to a gathering of Orenburg of-

ficials and residents was greeted with total silence. "The 'whereas'es, 'inasmuch as'es and 'therefore's quite bewildered them and I am sure that not one man present fully comprehended this document—were they to understand it one would have to put it to music and sing it to them." Recovering their tongues, members of the local famine committee read aloud a lengthy counterproposal describing their own plan for organizing foreign relief. Lyon claims he cut short this exercise with the suggestion that they either frame their proposal or burn it.[5]

Drafted from the Graves Registration Service, Lyon had absolutely no background in food relief, and his charge was merely to get operations in Orenburg up and running until an experienced man could take over. In Simbirsk the Americans had among their number no seasoned baby feeders, whereas Kazan, Samara, and Tsaritsyn were all led by old ARA hands and a veteran of the Armenian expedition ran the show in Saratov. The chief American in each district was called the district supervisor and within his realm he was supreme. The other relief workers performed various duties at district or subdistrict headquarters or on the road as inspectors. In each district the Americans initially numbered only a few, by year's end no more than a half-dozen, and even at the peak of activity, in summer 1922, never more than a dozen.

Despite the efforts of the Moscow chiefs to enforce organizational uniformity across the districts, the mission developed so rapidly, the personnel was such a heterogenous mix, and the distances to be covered were so great that beyond adhering to the ARA's fundamentals, each district ended up improvising the particulars. Lines of command and divisions of responsibility beneath the district supervisor varied, depending in part on the personalities involved and on the quality of local cooperation.

A FEATURE COMMON to all districts, to a greater or lesser degree, was the central involvement of the local population, a hallmark of the ARA. Decision-making authority on vital matters—where to feed, in what numbers, and so on—was retained by the Americans, who supervised the execution of relief by native hires. As the organization's name implied, the men of the ARA were supposed to be genuine "administrators" of others' work. Thus, their numbers were kept low and a great burden placed on a far larger force of local inhabitants. The model for this arrangement was Poland, where at peak in June 1920 a mere twenty-four Americans supervised the work of 27,890 Polish nationals in the feeding of 1.3 million children.[6]

The Soviet citizens who became involved in the enterprise were of two kinds: regular ARA employees, who performed clerical work, ran kitchens and warehouses, and served as couriers, inspectors, and so on; and the unpaid volunteers who composed the food committees that selected the children to be fed.

The Americans were naturally disposed to take on employees from among Soviet Russia's "former people"—the castaways from the old aristocracy, bourgeoisie, and the so-called intelligentsia, an elastic term which the relief workers usually stretched to cover Soviet society's educated classes in general, as opposed to its narrower sense of "intellectuals," as in professors, writers, artists, and the like. These were often the most qualified candidates for employment, on the strength of their familiarity with, if not experience in, office systems and their abilities, actual or merely professed, in English, French, and German. Above and beyond considerations of efficiency, the Americans naturally felt a certain sympathy toward these unwilling occupants of history's dustbin, who appeared on the scene rehearsing their tales of tragedy and woe. For them the arrival of the ARA was a godsend.

Unsurprisingly, it proved relatively easier to staff headquarters in Moscow and Petrograd, where there was a large pool of candidates from the former professional classes, many having worked before the Revolution in commercial offices and since then, perhaps, in the state bureaucracy. There was no shortage of clerks, whose expertise was highly prized by the ARA, an organization proudly run on business principles and thus, inevitably, obsessed with paperwork. Bowden of Petrograd had no complaints: "Our office staff compares favorably to anything which I have seen in Europe."[7]

The pickings were slimmer in the provincial cities, where the ARA drew heavily on the services of refugees from the capital cities. During the black years of 1919–20, teachers, artists, professors, engineers, former merchants, and others fled to the provinces in large numbers. Some ended up occupying key administrative positions in the local governments. Now in 1921, with famine descending on the Volga provinces even as conditions had improved in Moscow and Petrograd, many of these displaced citizens were making plans to return home. But not all: some were too destitute to make the move, others were dissuaded by the depressing prospects at the other end, and still others were forbidden to leave, their talents having come to be considered indispensable to the local authorities.

The Bolos understandably objected to the ARA's heavy reliance on enemies of the people, many of whom had demonstrably anti-Bolshevik pasts, meaning affiliation with one of the outlawed political parties or service with one of the White armies. On September 22, reacting to Soviet protests, Haskell issued a circular letter to the district supervisors advising them to staff their offices with Russians of diverse backgrounds, lest the local governments come to see ARA headquarters as hotbeds of anti-Bolshevism.[8]

Native personnel filling the most important positions in each district would have to be at least minimally acceptable to the authorities if the operation were going to be a success. This was particularly true of the "Russian executive," after the American supervisor the principal executive of the district, at least in theory, as the power of its holder in fact varied widely by district. The post was another questionable carryover from European operations. In any land this was a sensitive assignment; in Bolshevik Russia, extremely so.

Shafroth intended to invest the Russian executive in Samara with genuine authority, and his account of the troubles he encountered in making the appointment is instructive.[9] He discussed the position with the provincial Soviet chief, whom he called "the governor," at their first meeting, at which time the two men agreed that a candidate would be nominated by Shafroth and approved by the soviet. At a subsequent session, however, held in the presence of the soviet's executive committee, Shafroth was informed that after careful deliberation, that august body had proceeded to nominate two candidates for the job: one of them the head of the transportation department, the other the director of the local state-run cooperative society. This was, of course, not at all what Shafroth had in mind.

Perhaps anticipating resistance, the governor urged that the selection be made immediately, since the food had now arrived and there were lives to be saved. Shafroth expressed agreement on the importance of quick action, later remarking "that up to that time my repeated requests for furniture and equipment for the house and office which had been furnished to us had met only with delays and excuses." He thanked the executive committee for the names of its nominees and promised they would receive due consideration.

At this the governor's mood soured, and he pressed Shafroth to choose one of the two proposed candidates for Russian executive before leaving the meeting. This got the American's back up and "for a minute the situation was very tense." He recalled afterward that the members of the executive committee, sitting around the big table, were watching to see the effect the governor's statement would have on him, "but in spite of it, I had difficulty in keeping my temper." Keep it he did, however, calmly assuring the assembly that he would make his decision after careful deliberation, at which time he would notify the governor, who would then be invited to express his opinion. "This caused rather a stir of surprise as the government was not used to having its wishes opposed, and the meeting broke up spontaneously."

Shafroth now fully recognized that he had to come up with a formidable figure, one that would trump the Soviet candidates being urged upon him. He consulted the rector of Samara University, the foremost doctors in the city, and several other individuals "of good standing"—in former times, anyway—before deciding on the ideal candidate: Dr. Andrei Glasson, director of the general hospital in Samara, a surgeon with long executive experience, and a man of forceful personality highly regarded throughout the province.

Shafroth had done his homework, so he may not have been surprised when the Soviet chiefs raised no objection to Glasson. It was certainly not incidental that he decided on a doctor. The Americans in all the districts quickly concluded that of all the professionals they encountered in Russia, doctors were generally men of unusually strong character. This may have been partly a function of uniquely favorable circumstances, in that, their expertise being impenetrable to the influence of Marxist-Leninist ideology, their professional practice was immune to the intrusions of Bolshevik politics, at least for the moment. Whatever the actual role played by the hand of Hippocrates, most relief workers would have agreed with Simbirsk's James Somerville that physicians were "as independently minded as any citizens of Soviet Russia can be expected to be."[10]

Aside from Glasson, Shafroth staffed his headquarters with a former inspector in the cooperative organization, a lawyer, a colonel in the Red Army who had once held the same rank under the tsar, the former head bookkeeper of Samara's largest bank, a female interpreter from one of the province's oldest and richest families, a Russian-American who had wandered in from Siberia, and, initially, a half-dozen others. Of course, he drew heavily on "former people," and he hired no Bolsheviks, although he maintained that prospective personnel were never asked their political affiliations or opinions. "It was rather that the intelligentsia saw in our work a chance to live again and possibly to find some connection with the outside world, and they flocked to us for employment." This was not good enough for Samara officials, who demanded that the ARA apply to the state employment bureau for its personnel, and the matter was settled only after Shafroth wired Moscow headquarters and was able to get the central government to endorse his interpretation of the appropriate clause of the Riga Agreement.

Shafroth's experience is fairly representative of that of his fellow district supervisors. Local officials tended to object most strenuously to the recruitment of priests for service on either the ARA's staff or its food committees, and the relief workers treaded cautiously here. Not in Tsaritsyn, though, where the ARA hired two Orthodox priests and, along with the usual numbers of lawyers, doctors, and others, several Bolsheviks as well, thus giving "queer jerks" to the Bolos and the public alike.[11]

In addition to these willing and relatively able applicants from the intelligentsia, there was a second, radically different group of candidates for employment. These were former émigrés to America who had returned to Russia after the Revolution. Though less numerous, they turned out to be much more important to staffing the mission than the ARA anticipated going in. Some had been engaged in radical politics while in the States; lured back by the mirage of the communist utopia, they arrived in Bolshevik Russia expecting "to find heaven, but found only hell," in the words of one relief worker. Some landed safely within the Soviet establishment but others discovered that being ideologically more akin to the outlawed anarchists, they were regarded with suspicion. Most were Jewish—the reason they had abandoned Russia in the first place—and a large number were accurately described by the coarsely euphemistic epithet the ARA men applied to all returned Russian Jews: "ex-New Yorkers of the east side variety."[12]

Carroll was the first to consider them for employment, instantly recognizing their potential value to the Russian unit. For one they were proficient in English—and not the kind absorbed from Victorian novels but practical American English. Many had taken courses in commercial schools in the United States and were thus better qualified to perform the kind of office work the ARA required. Moreover, because they had lived and worked in America, they understood the premium Americans—especially of that day—placed on energy and efficiency and what was meant by American work methods. This gave them a crucial psychological edge over rival candidates for hire. They were, as well, generally younger than the intelligentsia applicants, and quite a few had only recently returned to Russia so their stamina and spirit had not been worn down by the extreme hardships of the Civil War years. The Bolsheviks were not especially pleased to see the Americans enlist such awkward characters but could hardly stand in the way since nothing in the Riga Agreement forbade the ARA from hiring them.

EVEN AS THE AMERICANS hurried to assemble their staffs, their top priority was to get kitchens up and running.[13] The first step was to secure from provincial officials the most recent statistics on famine conditions in each *uezd*—the Soviet administrative-territorial unit, which the ARA called a subdistrict. With these in hand, the district supervisor allocated food by subdistrict and made preparations for its delivery. Americans were dispatched to the principal subdistrict towns, which served as regional bases for the neighboring villages. A relief worker would set out from district headquarters with a trainload or boatload of food sufficient to supply a subdistrict for one month. Though word of his coming had been wired ahead, his arrival in town might set off a Gogolian mad scramble to locate warehouses and kitchen facilities and to organize food committees—all within a week because the impatient American had many other promises to keep.

The further from the provincial capital, as a general rule, the more onerous the undertaking. Warehouses were fewer and, after years of neglect, further gone. Qualified personnel were that much harder to come by. Most everything else was in shorter supply, down to the kitchen utensils, which, when available, were of a more primitive sort. Decimal scales, which the ARA considered essential because all the food had to be precisely measured out, were extremely scarce in the smaller towns and villages.

The most delicate and time-consuming task of the itinerant American was the organization of the subdistrict food committee, whose job it would be to assemble lists of needy children eligible for American food and to supervise its transportation and distribution. Much care had to be given to selecting the committee and installing it in a building separate from the headquarters of the executive committee of the soviet, which on this occasion was naturally most eager to demonstrate its hospitality.

It was also critically important to hire reliable inspectors to monitor ARA operations in the region. As there was to be no permanent American presence in most of the subdistricts, these inspectors were responsible for enforcing the rules and serving as whistle-blowers in the event of foul play. They were charged as well with organizing food committees in those smaller towns and villages the relief workers had no time to visit.

The open opposition of provincial soviet chiefs to the very idea of ARA food committees did not bode well for their sustained independence in the back country. Again, Shafroth's experience was rather typical. At a meeting of the presidium of the executive committee of the soviet, he and two American colleagues presented their plan to set up committees in Samara city and at the subdistrict and village levels. "An objection was made that we were paralleling an already existing organization, that the government at that time had in every village a hunger committee which could perfectly well perform the functions delegated to our committees, and that the transport organs of the government were exactly fitted for distributing the food to these committees."[14]

Echoes of Riga. Shafroth had been briefed by Carroll on those negotiations so he must have anticipated some such trouble. In response he explained that the ARA's previous operations had demonstrated the wisdom of appointing enlightened individuals in the towns and villages to independent food committees that would report directly to the ARA. This statement "was received in silence," prompting Shafroth to direct the attention of his dumbstruck audience to the relevant clauses in the Riga Agreement, using the occasion to refresh their memories on those sections entitling the ARA to the free use of government storage facilities and transportation, and to direct control over all warehouses assigned to it and all carriers transporting American food.

These Americans certainly made a lot of demands. The Samara chiefs decided to talk it over among themselves, then arranged a second meeting, at which, rising to meet the challenge, they raised "a rather decided opposition" to the ARA plan. "The governor expressed the opinion that we had no right to organize our own committees and it was only after some rather sharp telegraphic communication with Moscow, for which we were given every facility, that he acknowledged this right was given us by the Riga agreement." This was how the matter played out in other districts and subdistricts: initial government resistance might stiffen into open opposition, which would spark telegraphic appeals to higher authorities, leading inevitably to official acquiescence.

This proved to be just the opening battle, however. Controversy dogged the selection of individual committee members, an exercise even more ticklish than the hiring of employees because candidates had to possess the confidence of their communities yet not be completely objectionable to the authorities. As in so many other particulars, the ARA veterans in the Russian unit had unreasonable expectations of success based on their practice in Central Europe of relying on the assistance of nonpolitical "prominent citizens." In Soviet Russia such a species had become all but extinct.

Some had fled or been exiled abroad; of those who stayed behind, many did not survive and most who did were in no condition to take up philanthropic work. During the Revolution, refined people who had never had to perform physical labor were forced to sweep snow from the railway lines, clear forests, remove rubbish heaps—whatever it took to get a food ration and stay alive. The search for bread was everything. Now, in 1921, these were among the first people to turn to the ARA for help. Somerville described this situation from Simbirsk:

For Americans, accustomed to a large class of people with comfortable incomes and plenty of leisure time, to whom voluntary welfare work is a pastime, it is hard to conceive that in Russia the levelling down process of war and revolution had completely done away with any such class—most of those who had done such work before having now become themselves the neediest objects of charity.[15]

Those who might be able to contribute had to weigh the risks of associating themselves with a foreign "bourgeois" organization.

Setting up committees in the villages was generally less complicated because village politics and society tended to be less tangled. Typical village committees consisted of a school teacher, a doctor or doctor's apprentice, a representative of the village famine committee, a priest perhaps, and, as agreed at Riga, a representative of the village soviet. In the event that any of these types were found wanting, their places were to be filled either through election by those members of the committee already chosen or by appointment by an ARA inspector.

ONCE COMMITTEES WERE in place at the village, town, regional, and provincial levels, the ARA intended to cap this structure with a national committee in Moscow, which would bring together prominent Russians who would direct all aspects of the relief program. The national committee, like the local versions, was to operate independently of the government, with the American relief workers there principally to supervise the work and perform tasks of inspection and control. This was the plan in theory, in which realm it was destined to remain.

The model for Russian operations was supposed to be the ARA Poland mission, with its PAKPD, the Polish acronym for Polish-American Children's Relief Committee, established by a Polish government statute in the summer of 1920. The PAKPD was actually an entire network of food committees organized across the country by the relief workers with the help of local mayors and Catholic priests and other respected citizens in each community. The committees were responsible for selecting the children to be fed and overseeing matters of transportation, kitchens, staffs, and so on. Other such bodies coordinated the work at the provincial level, while in Warsaw the central PAKPD, made up of public figures well known throughout the land, directed operations nationally.

On paper the job of the Americans in Poland was to ensure that ARA food was distributed without regard to politics, "race," or religion, while retaining ultimate control over all relief supplies. Similar national organizations were established in Austria and Czechoslovakia. The committee system was successful in part because it mobilized citizens in good standing in their communities, notably doctors and teachers and even a sizable number of civil servants. In practice, though, even the flagship Poland mission did not operate as it was designed: far from serving merely as watchdogs, or even as administrators, the Americans ended up having to play an active role in the distribution of the food.

However mixed were the results farther west, the principles of the PAKPD were completely impractical for Russia in 1921, no less so than they had been two years earlier when Hoover put forth his proposal at Versailles. It would take the relief workers some time to adjust to the reality that Russia was not Poland, that it made no sense to talk of placing large responsibilities in the hands of Russians free of "political entanglements," because in the land of the Bolos such people did not exist. Litvinov had spoken the truth at Riga in warning Brown that there were "no neutrals" in his country. In an environment thoroughly saturated with politics, the notion that it was possible to organize "independent" food committees immune from Soviet manipulation was a dangerous delusion.

As Fisher recounts, "After a few months experience in Russia, the ARA Russian Unit would have regarded the suggestion that the precedent of western Europe be followed in Russia as fantastic, but in these early days they were innocently unaware of the devious workings of government under the proletarian dictatorship."[16]

In those early days the central Bolshevik leadership cooperated with the ARA in setting up local food committees, helpfully bringing wayward provincial officials into line when so requested by the Americans; the ARA lived up to its end of the bargain by allowing a government representative to sit on each committee. The Bolsheviks balked, however, at the ARA's proposal for a national committee, or central RAKPD, the Russian acronym for Russian-American Children's Relief Committee, which was intended to be an adaptation of the Polish precedent but which had not been written into the Riga Agreement. Kamenev, the Politburo's point man on American relief matters, insisted that only government officials should sit with the ARA chiefs on the central committee, that the participation of non-Communist Russians was out of the question. Elmer "Tommy" Burland, who took part in the RAKPD discussions, remarked to London on September 11 that "The Soviet government is suspicious to the nth degree" of all organizations not under its direct control.[17]

This was explanation enough, though Burland may not have been aware of the bearing of very recent events on the fate of the RAKPD proposal. In July, as part of an effort to attract foreign relief, the Bolsheviks had taken the unorthodox step of allowing the establishment in Moscow of a quasi-independent national relief organization, the All-Russian Famine Relief Committee. The idea was conceived by a group of non-Bolshevik socialists and liberals, on whose behalf Gorky interceded with Lenin, who gave his approval. Although Kamenev held the chairmanship of this committee, which included other prominent Bolsheviks and Gorky himself, most of its sixty-three members were non-Party public figures, which often meant that at one or another time since the October Revolution they had been openly opposed to Bolshevik power.

The Politburo, evidently horrified at the prospect of allowing such ghoulish characters to reemerge onto the historical stage, approved the project with great reluctance and only at Lenin's urging. Attempting to placate an especially bitter colleague, Lenin offered cynical reassurance that the committee would be used to attract "a couple of carloads" of food from the West and then quashed. When the Soviet government finally issued its own official appeal for famine relief, from Berlin in late July, it cited the existence of this committee as evidence of its good faith.

In its very brief lifetime, the All-Russian Famine Relief Committee enjoyed considerable freedom of activity by the standards of Soviet Russia in 1921—at least according to its written mandate. It was empowered to raise funds, publish its own newspaper, set up local chapters, and make applications abroad for food. Perhaps inevitably, émigré and other Western opinion of every stamp freely speculated about the potential of this famine committee to become the core of a post-Bolshevik government in Russia. In retrospect such hopes seem like senseless dreams, but given the drift of events in that bleak summer, who could tell? According to Victor Serge, even Gorky believed that this new creation might be "the germ of tomorrow's democratic government."

Such talk could only hasten the inevitable end. Once the Riga Agreement was signed, the public relief committee's days were numbered, for it had served its propaganda purpose and thus had outlived its usefulness. In fact its further existence might prove to be dangerous. Nansen was in Moscow proposing to link his relief mission with the committee, the Americans were about to arrive in the capital, and the committee was preparing to send a delegation abroad. On August 26 an anxious Lenin sent a note to Stalin for distribution to all Politburo members conceding that the little experiment had been a mistake, or was about to become one. The "bad tooth" had to be removed without delay.[18]

Lenin ordered that the committee be dissolved and its non-Bolshevik members arrested on various pretexts and, in certain cases, exiled from Moscow—this to the accompaniment of an appropriately orchestrated propaganda campaign. Indeed, on the following day, August 27, only hours before Carroll and the advance guard rolled into Moscow, the government decreed the dissolution of the committee. As some of its non-Bolshevik members gathered for a final meeting, a Cheka detachment moved in, making arrests and pronouncing death sentences. The same fate befell the members of the committee's local chapters.

Kamenev's chairmanship of this ill-starred "public" committee has been the cause of some confusion because he was also associated with the official Soviet relief organ, the Central Commission for Relief of the Starving, known by the Russian acronym Pomgol. When, through Gorky, he telegraphed an official Soviet response to Hoover in July, he signed as deputy chairman of that body. It was the Pomgol and its local organs that the Bolsheviks had in mind when they argued against the establishment of "parallel" ARA committees. As it happened, however, the Pomgol ended up functioning chiefly as a fund-raising agency, its actual contribution to famine relief never remotely commensurate with the prominence it was given in the Soviet press.[19]

The abortive All-Russian Famine Committee had had no bearing on the ARA's intention to establish an RAKPD. Yet the episode of this ill-starred committee turned out to be quite relevant to the fate of the proposed RAKPD. For one, its example had brought home to the Bolsheviks the dangers of experimenting with "bourgeois" national bodies. As well, it all but eliminated any possibility that well-respected non-Communist Russians would agree to sit on the RAKPD's central board. Carroll and his colleagues interviewed prominent Muscovites, including leading professors at Moscow University, each of whom "politely but firmly" declined to take part.

Tommy Burland reported to London on September 11 that there were two factors behind the refusal of Moscow's professional men to be part of the RAKPD: an apprehension that American relief might prop up the Soviet regime—which meant that their resistance constituted "a mild form of sabotage"—and a thoroughgoing intimidation of the intelligentsia. The second point was explanation enough for Fisher, who wrote that "The terror, that relentless steam-roller" had crushed any impulse to public service.[20] It might land you in internal exile, like the unfortunate members of the public relief committee, or even get you killed, like a group of sixty-one public figures in Petrograd only a few weeks earlier, charged with membership in a "counterrevolutionary" organization and shot.

The Americans approached Gorky, believing that his assumption of the chairmanship of the RAKPD central committee would provide sufficient political cover to embolden others to sign on. Gorky turned down the offer. He could credibly plead poor health, but in any case he knew that nothing meaningful could come of the project. Soon he would depart Russia for Berlin and a convalescence that would turn into eight years of emigration.

By the time Haskell arrived on the scene, the ARA had already retreated from its original plan by agreeing that, while the formation of local committees would proceed as planned, the central committee of the RAKPD would be composed exclusively of Soviet government and ARA representatives. Before long, however, it became clear that even in this modified form the RAKPD system was unsuitable for Russia. The ARA's local committees proved incapable of acting independently. Worse, the authorities had little difficulty rigging their memberships, with the result that many were "as obviously packed as any Tammany convention," in the words of a relief worker in Kazan.[21] As such, they threatened to become, more than a mere nuisance, a vehicle for government control over ARA operations.

So it was welcome news to the Russian unit when at the beginning of November Hoover directed that the RAKPD name be dropped and that the mission proceed as a strictly ARA operation. Food committees were to be handled as mere affiliated bodies of the ARA, and any impression of a joint Russian-American endeavor avoided. Hoover's reasoning was that circumstances in Russia were vastly different from those in Poland, where substantial funding for American relief had been generated locally and Polish citizens had been vital participants—and, thus, where the ARA had been willing to "obscure our light."

But Hoover's instruction amounted only to a change in nomenclature. In relaying the Chief's message on to Moscow, Brown instructed Haskell to set about "eliminating R.A.K.P.D. from our vocabulary," nothing more: "Of course, it is the name only that is involved, the type of organization remaining the same."[22] Haskell, however, had already become convinced of the need for surgery more radical than simply the removal of some inconvenient initials.

The colonel explained his thinking to Hoover in a November 14 memorandum, in which he used the failure of the RAKPD scheme as a club with which to beat Carroll and the ARA veterans, though not by name. When he first arrived in Moscow, Haskell wrote, he found that the men in charge had certain ideas about how to run "the Russian proposition." They were attempting to apply methods they had used in Poland, which, as anyone with any common sense could apprehend, were totally inappropriate to Russia. Had he permitted this to continue, it would have put the ARA in a position of handing over American food to the Soviet government at the ports and surrendering all control over its distribution. He admitted that at first he had allowed himself to be persuaded to go along with the plan to create district-level committees, but he soon came to see the error in this.

Recognizing the danger, Haskell sent a confidential circular letter to the district supervisors ordering them to "take the necessary means to kill the entire R.A.K.P.D., to take all the Russian personnel directly under their own charge and to run the entire show themselves." All placards and printed materials were revised accordingly, and "RAKPD"—which the Americans dubbed "Rockpud"—was replaced with "ARA"—which the Russians pronounced as one word, "Ahra." Unfortunately, the colonel related, certain expectations had been created among the Russians, but "eventually they will be told that such an organization is impracticable for Russia and it is in fact impracticable for the simple reason that the necessary people do not exist in Russia with the ability and integrity to carry out this work as they do in other countries even if the scheme itself were otherwise acceptable which in my opinion it is not."[23]

Haskell seems to have been under the impression that the enlistment of local citizens in food committees was an invention of Carroll and the Polish mission, when in fact it was a feature common to all ARA operations and, as he must have known, had been raised at the negotiating table by Brown, then written into the Riga Agreement. Moreover, from the colonel's exasperated tone one could not have guessed that the retreat from the RAKPD was a collective and spontaneous one on the part of most of the relief workers, once they realized its impracticability. Even Bowden, a torch-bearer of the old ARA guard, having been transferred from Petrograd to Tsaritsyn, wrote in one of his first communications to Haskell in early November that the Rockpud had been "an unfortunate mistake"; he urged Haskell to kill it "before we have weakened our position too much."[24]

Some of the committees were abolished outright. Others were allowed to carry on as honorary bodies, minus the RAKPD label, and assist in assembling the first lists of children eligible to receive American relief.

WHILE THE ARA was to feed primarily in its own kitchens, in the interest of saving time it intended as well, especially in the early going, to distribute food through the government-run children's homes. Its only stipulation was that the administrators of these establishments maintain reasonable standards of cleanliness and that local governments use their best efforts to make all necessary repairs on the facilities. When, as sometimes happened, the ARA decided that these requirements were not being met, it could suspend food deliveries. Shafroth once felt compelled to cut off supplies to all the children's homes in Samara city, which spurred the authorities to give immediate attention to matters of sanitation. This use of American food as leverage, above and beyond its life-saving sustenance, was later credited with having inspired a marked improvement in the overall performance of these institutions, thereby lifting the morale of their staffs and further promoting the health of the children.

Food and medicine channeled directly to children's homes and hospitals—collectively identified as "closed" institutions—would account for a much greater percentage of overall relief during the mission's second year, when operations were radically scaled down. While the famine raged, however, the ARA relied chiefly on its own kitchens, referred to as "open" institutions. These appeared in many varieties, from the largest, a dining hall seating several hundred located in Moscow's former Hermitage restaurant, to the lowliest peasant hut in the deep recesses of the Russian interior.[25]

In cities and towns the operation involved a central ARA bakery supplying anywhere from a few to over a dozen kitchens. Dishes and utensils used to prepare, serve, and consume the food were usually available. American trucks made deliveries from warehouses to bakeries and kitchens. Children who qualified for assistance were given food cards entitling them to a daily meal.

Only in the urban centers, and there only in the beginning, did the ARA introduce the method it had employed in Central Europe to identify the neediest children: the so-called Pelidisi system. This was the creation of a Viennese medical doctor, Professor Clemens Pirquet, who served as chairman of the Austrian equivalent of the RAKPD. Pirquet devised a formula for determining the degree of undernourishment in children up to the age of fifteen. The measurement was the cubic root of the tenfold weight of the body divided by that body's sitting height. For adults the average would be 100, for children 94.5—anything below that signified undernourishment. In Austria the cutoff figure used was 94; in Russia, where there were tens of millions of hungry people, the standard had to be lowered to 92, and in some places less.[26]

Here was another application of previous ARA practice that did not translate well to the Russian setting. This may have been partly due to the difference between hunger and starvation, because whereas Pirquet's system seems to have worked reasonably well in Central Europe, the relief workers in the Volga cities complained that it proved accurate only half the time. Others objected that it was too impersonal a method for dealing with starving children, even for the businesslike ARA. In any event, the severe shortages of time, staff, and scales prohibited the widespread introduction of the Pelidisi system into Russia.

In the villages relief operations were of necessity less standardized and regulated than the ARA was used to. For one, the scarcity of decimal scales meant that the measurement of individual food portions was less than exact. On the other hand, in such small communities, where everyone was known to everyone else, there was no need to calculate the cubic root of anything in order to determine who was deserving of American food. Nor were food cards available for use in the villages, though here again they would have served no useful purpose, as kitchen managers personally knew all the children.

The larger village kitchens were often established in the schoolhouses, in which case the teachers themselves often stepped into the role of manager. Since many schools had by then ceased functioning, this arrangement not only kept the teachers and students from starving, but the children could stay for their lessons after the noon meal. In the smaller villages kitchens were set up in huts left vacant by the death or departure of their inhabitants. Motor vehicles being unknown in most villages, food supplies were transported in peasant carts. Bread for each kitchen was prepared on the premises. Utensils were everywhere in short supply, and children might be asked to bring their own dishes at mealtime.

ARA meals consisted of white bread, rice, lard, corn grits—*kasha* in Russian—milk, sugar, and cocoa. The menu was adjusted during the course of the week based on the availability of these products and for the sake of variety. The "serious business" of eating was performed in silence. Fisher, himself a witness to such scenes, testified: "The sight of these ragged rows of thin bodies, desperately concentrated, was undoubtedly the greatest inspiration that the relief workers had." And not only the relief workers: a Russian professor of history employed by the ARA in Simbirsk observed, "One could scarcely keep from tears when these little folks trembling all over from the bitter winter wind, wrapped up in their rags, almost barefoot, received into their miserable earthen pots the smoking cocoa and gruel and brought it to their dining place holding in the other hand a slice of bread."

Not all of the initial testimony is so heartwarming. From across the Samara district came reports that some children were not able to ingest their food; others suffered from diarrhea and dysentery.[27]

The distribution of food in a famine country being an especially sensitive business, ARA kitchens were regulated by a strict set of rules aimed at ensuring that the children were properly fed. Hundreds of Russians were hired as inspectors to help enforce this regime. Shafroth indicates that his Samara district by spring 1922 had a team of forty traveling inspectors continuously making the rounds of the villages and reporting their findings back to the Americans at subdistrict or district headquarters.[28] The relief workers themselves often took a hand in this work, making flying visits into the countryside in order to carry out unannounced inspections of ARA kitchens.

The inspectors' chief tasks were to check feeding rolls for the presence of dead souls and to test the quality of the food, such as the consistency of the cocoa and the grits—in other words, to look for evidence of graft on the part of kitchen managers and staffs. They were also charged with reviewing and where necessary adjusting the composition of food committees. The power of these native inspectors varied by district. In expansive Ufa, where the relief workers were spread very thin, the hired local hands had the authority to shut down delinquent kitchens without first securing American approval. Elsewhere, they could only pass their findings on to headquarters.

Reading through their reports, most of which are tediously routine, one gets a sense of the striking mix of empowerment and ostracism that characterized the daily existence of these inspectors. Resented by Soviet officials and kitchen managers alike, all the more so because of their generally superior education, they were among the quiet heroes of the Russian mission. An American of the Tsaritsyn district recalled how "They tramped around from village to village in all sorts of weather—and in all sorts of clothing and shoes—with or without—attending to the business in hand." Turnover among them was high, with sickness and death claiming many of their number.

Graft was not the only object of an inspector's inquiries. Trouble often appeared in the form described by an investigator in Saratov, who discovered in one village that the cocoa was "more like some red dishwater," that the bread was not baked through, and that "for the most part the food is taken home and I don't know what I have to do and how I must struggle against this evil."

The inspector was agitated because he could not enforce one of the ARA's strictest rules: that all food was to be cooked and eaten at the kitchen; no one was allowed to bring home any part of a meal, nor could food be delivered to those children too sick to leave home. This turned out to be the most unpopular of all ARA regulations, especially so when cold weather set in, as children lacked the proper clothes, especially shoes, for the walk to the kitchens. In fact many inspectors' reports underscored this crying need for clothing and footwear. From the ARA's point of view, it was unwise to allow children to bring food home, where it would likely be shared among hungry parents and siblings, thus spreading the nutrition too thin. In the more clinical language of one relief worker: "The ARA ration is scientifically prescribed and contains exactly the proper number of calories to maintain one child, so it will be seen that it is necessary to know that he consumed all of it."[29]

But everyday life in the valley of the shadow was hardly subject to scientific prescription, and as the lament of the Saratov inspector indicates, the ban on feeding outside the kitchens was frequently disregarded, especially in the villages. Efforts at enforcement might provoke loud protests from beneficiaries and officials alike, and in the deep freeze of the Russian winter district supervisors were besieged with appeals to modify or withdraw this heartless restriction. In most districts the Americans yielded, allowing meals to be taken home, uncooked, to underclothed or ill children. Strictly speaking, all exceptional cases were supposed to be certified by a doctor's note, but that assumed the presence of a doctor. Not a few cases came to light, even one in Petrograd, of family members concealing a dead body at home for several days so that they could consume the recently departed's home-delivered food ration.[30]

Such were the obstacles and challenges the relief workers had to overcome in getting their Russian operation up and running. By November kitchens in all the Volga districts were serving American food. By December 1 the ARA was over halfway toward reaching its one-million mark: each day 568,020 children were being served a balanced ration in 2,997 feeding points set up in 191 towns and villages in the regions of greatest need, from Petrograd on the Baltic to, by midmonth, Astrakhan on the Caspian. Still ahead lay a great expansion of the mission, but for now, in the ARA man's parlance, the show was a go.

FOOD MIGHT SAVE hundreds of thousands of children from starvation, but an equal number might be carried off by hunger-related disease. In order to meet this danger, the ARA mounted a large-scale medical relief effort, one of two large supplementary programs it carried out in Russia.[31]

The ARA had not conducted a medical program in any of its previous missions, but Russian conditions demanded it. Not only were millions vulnerable to life-threatening disease, but Russian medicine was severely underequipped to deal with the emergency, to such an extent that the ARA spoke in terms of a "medical famine." In tsarist times, Russia acquired most of its medicines and medical equipment from abroad. The Great War cut off this supply at the same time that the ravages of war sharply increased the demand. With the Revolution came a breakdown in basic sanitation in the cities and the attendant appearance of epidemic diseases. The carnage of the Civil War severely overstretched the country's medical personnel and unreplenished supplies.

Meanwhile, the ranks of Russia's doctors steadily thinned. Some fled the country. Others perished, weakened by hunger, disease, and demoralization. The relief workers recorded several cases in which physicians with long and distinguished careers as directors of hospitals and local health departments had been, after the Revolution, replaced by veterinarians holding the proper Communist credentials. Fisher, employing a military analogy, took the measure of the heroism of those doctors who remained at their posts: "Hundreds met death fighting disease, without weapons, with the same dogged courage that Russian soldiers, without ammunition, met death trying to stay the German advance."

In October 1921 the relief workers in some famine regions were told that the mortality rate of doctors in recent years had been nearly 50 percent. This and other symptoms of the medical famine were shockingly evident to the newly arrived Americans. Hospitals lacked even basic supplies. There was no chloroform or ether, so surgery was being performed without anesthesia. Because there were no bandages, wounds and incisions had to be closed with newspaper. Governor Goodrich paid a visit to a hospital north of Kazan, the largest in the region. This facility of eight hundred beds had but two thermometers and was without the most essential drugs. The hospital's best physician, "underpaid, underfed, and overworked, unable to stand the work," committed suicide the day before Goodrich arrived. Like every other American in Russia, Goodrich was struck by the fortitude and courage of the doctors and feldshers, their assistants, who carried on under what appeared to be impossible conditions. Bowden found them to be "excellent people," which was consistent with his experience in other countries: "If it were not for doctors and school teachers in Europe, one would almost lose faith entirely."[32]

The foundation of the ARA's medical program was an agreement it made with the American Red Cross on September 2, 1921, by which the latter undertook to furnish the Russian unit with supplies and funds totalling $3 million, a sum later increased to $3.6 million. The medical division began work in November 1921 in Moscow, Petrograd, Kazan, and Samara and in December extended its activities to Simbirsk, Saratov, Tsaritsyn, and Orenburg, then in January to Ufa. The program was directed from Moscow by a retired army doctor, Colonel Henry Beeuwkes.

Assigned to each district was an American physician, whose chief responsibility was to supervise the distribution of the 1,222 varieties of medical supplies imported by the ARA. That is, the district physicians were intended to be bureaucrats and not to practice medicine unless an ailing relief worker required their professional attention. Most became quickly bored with all the monotonous paperwork. What usually kept the job interesting and sometimes rewarding was the opportunity to observe and favorably influence the work of their Russian colleagues. Kazan's district physician, William Dear, who was endlessly fascinated by the daily triumphs and tragedies of Russian medicine, notes that the medical laboratories in the region would have been totally useless but for the equipment provided by the ARA: "What became of equipment that formerly existed in these hospitals and laboratories I am unable to say. In answer to questions the reply was always that they had been 'taken'. By whom or for what purpose no one seemed to know. I do know that what apparatus from the former equipment remained on hand was almost invariably obsolete and worn out."[33]

Dear and the other Americans in the famine zone took the lead in addressing another aspect of the medical famine. For years unable to inform themselves of, let alone apply, advances in scientific research in their fields of specialty, Russian doctors now appealed individually to their benefactors for the most important recent medical literature. The districts passed these requests on to Moscow headquarters, and by spring 1922 the ARA began to relieve this kind of hunger as well. In Kiev the most interesting and important of such journal articles were translated and republished locally, and conferences were organized to discuss their findings.

The first priority was to check hunger-related disease. Russia's cities had seen epidemic outbreaks of typhus, relapsing fever, cholera, smallpox, and typhoid during the Civil War years. These had largely subsided by 1920. Typhoid fever and dysentery, the latter frequently resulting from the consumption of food substitutes, were still widespread, as was relapsing fever, while cholera had almost completely disappeared by the time the ARA came on the scene. Tuberculosis, meanwhile, continued to wage the war of attrition it had begun in 1914. Malaria was widespread, and numerous cases were chronic because there was no quinine to treat it. There was as well a marked increase in the deficiency diseases, especially among children, including rickets, scurvy, hunger edema, plus any variety of mental illnesses.

The famine portended a second, much deadlier wave of pestilence. Cholera posed the most immediate threat, but there was far greater concern about an inevitable and looming epidemic of typhus, which was in fact to become the chief object of the ARA's medical program.

THE ARA'S OTHER LARGE supplementary activity—the delivery of food packages—proved to be much more difficult to launch.[34] Here the precedent was the food draft program the ARA had organized for Central Europe in 1920–21, whereby a donor living outside the distressed country could purchase a food draft—that is, a coupon—on sale in many American banks and at the ARA's European offices. The benefactor, most often someone residing in the United States, then sent the coupon through the post to the intended beneficiary, who brought it to the nearest ARA warehouse and redeemed it for one or more food packages, the precise number depending on the amount of the draft. In order for the system to work, it was necessary to maintain a dense network of these warehouses, each stocked with the right amounts of the necessary products, operating throughout the beneficiary country; thus the ARA's internal designation for the food draft program, the "warehouse system."

Because the ARA purchased the food in bulk, it was able to sell to donors at wholesale prices. The market value of the products in the food packages was often worth up to three times what the donor had paid for it. Prices being so favorable, the ARA was able to arrange to make a small profit on each $10 food package it sold, which proceeds it used to expand its child-feeding operation. All those purchasing food drafts were advised of this "commercial" dimension of their act of charity.

All told, in Central Europe in 1920–21 the ARA delivered $8.3 million worth of food packages. The benefits of the program were greater than the sum of those derived directly by the individual recipients. The operation produced a profit margin of $2.5 million, all of which went toward the purchase of additional food for the children.[35] Moreover, the large volume of food products made available through these packages helped to stabilize prices and hasten the general economic recovery. The food draft program was an integral and very popular component of the ARA's undertaking in Central Europe, where appreciative governments worked to facilitate it. This was not to be the case with the Bolshevik government, however.

From the outset Soviet officials were resistant to the idea of food package deliveries. Brown had tried to write it into the Riga accord, but Litvinov put him off, saying it could be taken up in Moscow once the mission was underway. Litvinov and his fellow commissars knew that a food draft program, unlike child-feeding, would leave them almost no influence over the selection of beneficiaries, and they could assume that the majority of recipients would not likely be from among the laboring masses—thus their instinctive hostility.

It was the job of Tommy Burland to devise a warehouse system for Russia and then to implement it. Burland, who had drawn up the general arrangement for the RAKPD, had earlier created and managed the food draft program for the Austrian mission. His plan for Russia had to take into account that country's special circumstances. A food draft operation, he recognized, might break down completely in Russia, where the mail delivery and the communications and transportation systems were in a state of disruption, especially given the long distances involved. What is more, many people in Russia had been displaced since 1915, which meant that there would likely be a large percentage of refunds for undeliverable packages.

In order for a food package program to stand any chance of success the ARA itself would have to maintain a degree of control over the notification process and not be completely reliant on the Russian mail service. The solution, then, was a food *remittance* program, which would work as follows: relatives, friends, and other benefactors could put money down for a package at the ARA's New York headquarters or at one of its European offices. A statement of payment would then be sent by ARA courier to Moscow headquarters, which would in turn contact the appropriate district office, where the responsible American would send, by post or courier, a notification card to the intended beneficiary. This fortunate individual or family could collect one or more standardized food packages at one of the many ARA delivery stations spread out across the districts.

During the second week of October, Burland presented this proposal to officials of the Soviet government, who received it, as an American in Moscow remarked, like a French court does an alleged criminal: guilty until proven innocent.[36] Uppermost in the mind of the Bolsheviks was the disagreeable fact that many purchasers were bound to be individuals who had fled Russia during the Revolution. The beneficiaries of their charity would thus by definition be hostile to Soviet power. Burland the engineer had designed a system with an eye toward maximizing the volume of imported food and the efficiency of its delivery, while the Bolos, engineers of a different sort, saw his scheme as a potential vehicle for counterrevolution.

Further prejudicing the Soviets against the food remittance proposition was the fact that, like its food draft forerunner, it contained a built-in profit mechanism—in other words it was, as Fisher wrote, aping the communist idiom, "shamelessly capitalistic in its methods."[37]

Despite the troubled reception, after one exhausting week of negotiations an agreement between the ARA and the Soviet government to establish a food package program was completed and made ready for signing. On October 18 this document, which was proposed as an addendum to the Riga Agreement, was circulated among the members of the Politburo for initialing. Among those polled, Stalin commented that, since this was after all a question of commerce, not philanthropy, the Soviet government should demand payment for the transport of the products from ports to warehouses. Lenin's own inscription rejected this suggestion, pointing out that, even if this was indeed a matter of trade, the Soviet government was to reap the profits in the form of additional food for the starving. In any case, the arrangement gave the government ultimate control over the program and the right to terminate it after three months. Beyond offering his colleagues these reassurances, Lenin urged them to take advantage of this opportunity to acquire "experience" from the Americans—this in the spirit of his admonition to fellow Bolsheviks to "learn to trade."

One of the fears expressed by the Bolshevik negotiators was that large numbers of packages would fall into the hands of speculators, so the agreement stipulated that should the ARA receive orders for more than five food packages for a single beneficiary, the Soviet government would have the right to stop delivery if it believed the products would be sold on the market. Lenin instructed the Politburo to appoint an individual to monitor the food package program at ARA headquarters.[38]

The Politburo approved the agreement on October 19. Remittances began to sell immediately, notably in Riga, where most of the charity was directed at residents of Petrograd. Once a buyer put his money down, the ARA was obligated to locate the designated beneficiary in Russia and deliver the notice of a package. If that individual could not be found and the package handed over within ninety days, the ARA had to give a full refund to the buyer. The first food package deliveries were made on November 21 in Moscow.

The precise contents of the packages were occasionally adjusted according to the availability of certain food products and the market demand for them, but the standard ARA package during the first year of the mission consisted of the following: flour, 49 lbs.; rice, 25 lbs.; tea, 3 lbs.; fats, 10 lbs.; sugar, 10 lbs.; preserved milk, 20 one-pound cans—for a total weight of 117 pounds. Upon receiving this package at one of the ARA delivery stations, the beneficiary would sign duplicate receipts, one of which was sent to the purchaser.

While the monetary value of the package fluctuated over time, in the early months the contents of a single package cost the ARA $6.75; the prices of transportation into Russia, insurance, and overhead added another $1.00, bringing the total cost to $7.75, which left $2.25 as a contribution to child-feeding. The food remittance program could be used as well for group relief, whereby individuals, organizations, and communities in the United States could purchase a large number of packages for specific professional or other groups in Russia. Similarly, the relief societies affiliated with the ARA could purchase packages in bulk for distribution by their representatives inside Russia.

In still other ways was the ARA's food package operation in Russia tailored to local conditions. In Europe the various missions received the food packages as assembled parcels; in Russia, due to the size of the operation and the state of Russian transport, the individual components of the food packages were imported separately in bulk. While child-feeding supplies could be transshipped at Moscow without being unloaded from freight cars, all food package stocks had to be repacked before being sent on to the districts. This meant that Moscow headquarters had to procure containers for the food—namely, sacks and tins—plus items like paper, string, and nails, none of which was in ready supply in Russia in 1921. Eventually, the quantity of food entering the country became overwhelming and Moscow, unable to keep pace, chose to pass the buck and place the burden of creating individual packages from bulk supplies on the districts. And the buck did not always stop there: some food remittance stations were forced to require recipients to provide their own containers. It sometimes happened that the shortage of receptacles held up the consignment of packages.

Another feature improvised by the Russian unit was the printing and distribution within Russia of some 1.5 million appeal cards, post cards inscribed with a printed appeal for food packages, which Soviet citizens could send to potential benefactors in the West. This innovation was necessitated by the great dislocation of Russians since 1914, which increased the likelihood that families and friends on the outside would provide the ARA with incorrect addresses. The estimate is that six to seven hundred thousand such cards were forwarded out of Russia by the ARA via its courier service to addresses in Europe and America, while an undetermined number were sent out of Russia through the regular post.

Food remittance operations were encumbered at the start, almost terminally, by the wretched state of Russia's transportation system. Of course this hampered all phases of the mission, but because the government gave low priority to the delivery of food packages, it made little effort to provide the empty cars necessary to ship the readied packages from Moscow to the districts. Before long, word began to get through to Russians living in the major cities that relief packages had been bought for them by their loved ones. This information might have been conveyed by post, but not a few anxious citizens must simply have come forward on the presumption that they had not been forgotten. One must also allow for the inevitable quota of bluffers.

Whatever the substance behind their petitions, a growing number of beneficiaries-in-waiting figured they had been swindled, and they came to the ARA remittance stations clamoring to be given what belonged to them. The experience of the previous few years would have made them naturally suspicious that some functionary—in Moscow, at the ARA's warehouses, or somewhere in between—was growing fat off the flour, rice, tea, lard, sugar, and milk intended for them. Somehow their complaints became known to those who had purchased the packages, and these individuals began, in December, to present themselves at ARA offices angrily demanding their money back. For several weeks the situation was touch-and-go. By January the ARA was preparing to make refunds and threatened the Soviet government with liquidating the remittance program unless it furnished the necessary trains. This ultimatum had the desired effect, stirring the authorities to action, and the crisis passed.

The ARA made a special arrangement with the Soviet postal authorities to deliver food packages, but in the hungry winter of 1921–22 few people chose to entrust the safe passage of their life-saving parcels to a half-starved mail carrier, preferring instead to pick up the package in person. This might mean covering a considerable distance each way or sending an agent in their place. Upon arrival at the delivery station, they found that they were hardly alone in their quest and that, in fact, the nearer they came to attaining their final goal, the more intense became their struggle. John Ellingston, who served with the Russian unit in Saratov and in Moscow, where toward mission's end he wrote a survey of the food remittance operation, described the mix of social types who gathered into Russian-style queues at the remittance counters:

They came from every class, profession, age, reduced to one by the common leveller—hunger and the fear of it. Most of them knew that packages had been sent them from abroad, many only hoped, and others knew merely that "A.R.A." meant food. The peasant from the village came sewed up in his bulky, mud-colored, sheepskin great coat, long bearded, gaunt, with the heavy movements of toilers of the soil, bewildered in the commotion. The former bourgeoisie came, men who had been generals, governors, professors, lawyers, doctors; and the wives of these people, drawn-faced women marked by a threadbare cleanliness. Jewish rabbis elbowed the priests of Russia's church; the secret speculator fought for a place in line with the completely destitute, tied up in dirty rags.

Everything seemed to ride on reaching that counter. A single package meant enough food to sustain three people for one month. A false rumor could set off a wave of panic through the crowds, and "a spirit of frenzy would drive them into a small riot." When, as often happened, it was announced that food stocks were temporarily exhausted, many applicants chose to remain in place, sleeping out overnight if necessary to be positioned near the entrance in the morning.

Reaching that counter did not always bring relief, however. The Americans in Elizavetgrad, in Ukraine, record an entirely unexpected complication: "astonishing" similarities in the names of beneficiaries. "There were cases where not only the first and second names of persons were the same, but also two persons having exactly the same names living in the same house and the same street and were in no way related to each other. For several days two 'Gersh Finkels' stood before the identification window, each trying to assure the clerk that he was the proper consignee."[39]

Though most of them were probably never made aware of it, all beneficiaries, by signing the receipts for their packages, agreed not to sell their contents on the market. Of course there was no practical way for the ARA to enforce this contract, and it appears that significant quantities of American products were bartered away, some finding their way into the bazaars and store windows. This never became a source of concern, however, the ARA's attitude being that anything that brought more goods onto the market and thereby drove down the price of food served to lighten everyone's load. In any case, much of the trading in American food was of the kind that only a Bolo would dare to classify as speculation: many recipients were without the means or the might to transport a 117-lb. food package—let alone two or three—and simply had to sell a portion of their prize along the way in order to arrive home with the remainder of it.

MOST OF THOSE RECEIVING food packages were poor Jews, something the Americans had been able to anticipate. Two weeks before the remittance agreement was signed, the New York office wired Moscow to say that 40 percent of all inquiries directed to the ARA regarding food packages identified Ukraine as the point of destination. The initial reports of remittance sales in the United States and Europe confirmed that by far the largest number of beneficiaries would be in Ukraine, as well as in White Russia and its neighboring provinces—regions that, taken together, had in tsarist times made up the greater part of the Jewish Pale of Settlement, the chief source of emigration out of Russia during the troubles and now still home to the greatest number of Russian Jews.[40]

What this meant for the ARA was that food remittance delivery stations would have to be set up in the principal cities of these regions even though they lay outside what was generally recognized as the famine zone. Technically this should not have raised any problems, as the Riga Agreement allowed the ARA to establish its operations in Russia wherever it saw fit. Or did it? This was the question at the heart of one of the most curious subplots of the entire relief story.[41]

There had been no discussion at Riga of including Ukraine in the famine zone. During the initial weeks of the mission, the relief workers came across no evidence to suggest the need to revise Ukraine's status. Indeed, the Soviet government informed the Americans that grain was being shipped from Ukraine to the famine victims on the Volga. And many of the thousands of hungry refugees they encountered in the starving regions, desperate to reach Ukraine, spoke of it as the promised land. There was, in other words, little hint of the dire reality.

Even by contemporary Russian standards, Ukraine had just passed through especially troubled times, overrun during the period from 1917 to 1920 by successive armies of Germans, Russian Whites and Reds, and Ukrainian nationalists, as well as an assortment of bandits and outlaws. Power changed hands eleven to thirteen times, depending on which city you counted from. Fisher likened the devastation inflicted in three years to that of the Thirty Years' War.[42] Then came the drought of 1920–21, which led to a crop failure in southeastern Ukraine and, by summer 1921, famine.

The start-up of the food remittance program at the end of October, with its promise of a large number of deliveries to Ukraine, necessitated an ARA survey of the region's food supply. An American presence in Ukraine was probably inevitable, for at about this same time the Joint Distribution Committee, whose New York office had been receiving reports of widespread starvation there, asked the

ARA to have its Russian unit look into the matter. In any case, in mid-November Haskell requested that the Soviet government allow Golder and Hutchinson to conduct investigations in Ukraine.

Permission denied. Moscow officials wondered what the point was, in view of the fact that the northwestern Ukrainian provinces of Kiev, Volhynia, Chernigov, Podolia, and Poltava, far from experiencing food shortages, had produced a combined surplus of grain so large that they could afford to contribute a portion of it to the relief of the Volga. No, Ukraine did not require American charity.[43]

Haskell persisted, invoking the ARA's rights under the Riga Agreement, and after some correspondence back and forth permission was granted to send Golder and Hutchinson into Ukraine.[44] The pair arrived on November 26 in Kiev, where local officials directed them east to Kharkov, capital of the Ukrainian Soviet Socialist Republic. Moscow had settled on this city as the republic's seat of power because the "Mother of Cities," Kiev, had achieved notoriety through its fierce resistance to Bolshevik rule and because Kharkov was the center of Ukrainian industry and thus had a larger proletariat.

Upon arrival in Kharkov on November 30, the two Americans sat down with the acting Bolshevik chief, Commissar Mykola Skripnik, to spell out to him their intentions. Here they were met with a rude jolt. Skripnik informed them, "much to our astonishment," that there was no official basis for their investigations, as the Ukrainian republic was not a party to the Riga Agreement. The investigators explained that the document signed at Riga applied to all the federated republics of Soviet Russia, an interpretation supported by the central government in Moscow, they pointed out, which had after all sanctioned their trip. Skripnik, an ethnic Ukrainian, countered that Ukraine was no ordinary federated republic, that Russia and Ukraine were in fact political equals, and that the Ukrainian republic conducted its own foreign relations—and, he reiterated, it was not a signatory to the Riga Agreement.

Golder and Hutchinson at first assumed that these were merely the ravings of a backwoods commissar, but Skripnik's argument was wholly defensible, at least in the abstract. The legal relationship of the Ukrainian republic, established in March 1919, to the RSFSR, to which it was formally linked by treaty, was ambiguous.[45] The constitution of the Russian federation—which, despite the name, was not a genuinely federal structure—had been adopted in spring 1918 when the German armies were occupying Ukraine, as well as the Baltics, most of White Russia, and the North Caucasus. When Ukraine joined the union one year later, it, along with Azerbaidzhan, earned a place near the top of the administrative hierarchy in that it enjoyed some of the privileges of independent statehood. For a short time its diplomats represented it in Berlin, Prague, and Warsaw, and Ukrainian leaders were able to resist the Kremlin's efforts to subsume their foreign policy within its own. The uncertainty of this arrangement would be resolved only with the formation, in December 1922, of the Union of Soviet Socialist Republics, a true federation of Russia, Ukraine, White Russia, and Transcaucasia. But for the moment Ukraine was still, technically anyway, a sovereign state.

The Bolsheviks were federalists only up to a point, however. They embraced federalism as the political-administrative corollary to their calculated support for the self-determination of the major ethno-national groups of the former Russian empire. Their assumption was that if nationalism were allowed, even encouraged to blossom, it would all the sooner expend itself and be supplanted by class allegiance, eventually leading, in the words of People's Commissar of Nationalities Stalin, to "the voluntary and fraternal union of the working masses of all nations and peoples of Russia."[46] This would turn out to be an enormous miscalculation. As it happened, the Soviet federal system had the effect of nurturing ethnonational identity, in some instances rescuing it from extinction. Seven decades later the illusoriness of Bolshevik "nationality" policy would be dramatically and conclusively confirmed.

In Ukraine nationalist sentiment among the intelligentsia had been gathering strength in the decades before the war, which event served to catalyze the phenomenon and broadened its social base. The establishment by the occupying German forces of an independent Ukrainian state further aroused this spirit of nationalism, as did the subsequent formation by the Moscow Bolsheviks of a distinct, semisovereign Ukrainian "republic."

No amount of nationalist pride could fill Ukraine's need for famine relief, however, which was substantial. Skripnik told Golder and Hutchinson that the situation was critical in the southern regions of his republic, where over seven million people were threatened by hunger. He requested the ARA's assistance, but only on condition that a separate ARA-Ukraine agreement first be negotiated and signed. The two Americans, partly amused, partly irritated, refused to play along, dismissing the very notion of Ukraine's independence as "a make-believe." They had not, they said, come to Kharkov to discuss politics, only to fight starvation. But, Skripnik replied, "you are mixing in politics when you differentiate between the two Republics; when you treat with one, and refuse to do so with the other; when you regard one as a sovereign state, and the other as a subject state." The discussion went back and forth like this until the Americans asserted that they had no authority to sign any agreements and ended the meeting.

Before departing, the investigators were able to get hold of local agricultural statistics. These confirmed that northern Ukraine, more wooded and blessed with normal rainfall during the previous year, did indeed have a good crop, while the unforested southern provinces, where the steppe descends into the Black Sea, had been badly affected by drought. On top of this, the south was having to absorb a large number of refugees from the Volga. Ukraine had always been a mecca for refugees in hard times, and recent years had witnessed a succession of migrant waves, beginning with the arrival of the Polish war evacuees in 1915 and now culminating in the largest influx of all, the droves of ragged creatures in flight from the famine.[47]

The Moscow government's reticence about this state of affairs, together with its initial outright denial of access to Odessa for the import of American food supplies, indicated a determination to keep the ARA out of Ukraine. When asked to explain, a Kremlin official responded that the government preferred to see the ARA defeat the Volga famine decisively and not "split its forces"—adding incidentally that Kiev was under martial law.[48] In fact politics was at the heart of the matter. Across Ukraine the dying embers of the Civil War still smoldered and occasionally flared up. Pockets of armed anti-Bolshevik resistance persisted, with partisan bands still roaming the countryside, while Ukrainian peasants, by nature a defiantly individualistic lot who put up a fierce struggle against grain requisitions, remained bitterly hostile. Only this could explain why the infamous anti-Bolshevik rebel leader Nestor Makhno was able to hold out for so long, fleeing Ukraine for Romania as late as August 28, 1921.

Golder was inclined to attribute such restiveness, which the Soviet government disparaged as "banditism," to national character: "The Ukrainian is the descendant of the unruly Cossack and still chafes under discipline."[49] Whatever the basis for it, Moscow had good reason to be wary of Ukraine's peasants and therefore of having American relief workers at liberty among them. At minimum these outsiders would learn of the limited reach of Soviet power. Worse, suppose the inquisitive Americans came into contact with bandits of one or another stripe? Why, there was no telling what kind of trouble the mere presence of these foreign bourgeois might instigate.

This much was understandable. What Golder and Hutchinson, and the American relief workers who followed in their wake, found incomprehensible was the fact that while tens of thousands of Ukrainians were literally starving, the local Bolsheviks were nonetheless exhorting the people to come to the aid of their famishing brethren on the Volga. To what extent this call was voluntarily or involuntarily heeded is a matter of conjecture. According to the figures of the Pomgol, the Soviet famine committee, the republic's northern provinces shipped a total of 1,127 cars of food products out to the famine zone between autumn 1921 and August 1922. These were sent hundreds of miles across country to the Volga when their shipment a few dozen miles south to famishing Odessa and Nikolaiev would have saved at least as many lives and done so more efficiently.

Official Soviet statistics of this kind invite skepticism, but the accuracy of the figures aside, the very fact of their public advertisement is itself remarkable. The province of Odessa, whose autumn 1921 crop was only 17 percent of normal, was credited with having exported sixty-five cars of food as famine relief; meanwhile, Nikolaiev, where the crop was estimated to be a mere 4 percent of normal, reportedly sent eight cars to the starving on the Volga. The Pomgol report states uncannily, "It is important to observe that even the famine provinces sent bread to the Volga regions."

As late as March 1922, the ARA men in the region encountered exhortatory posters such as, "Workers of Nikolaiev, help the starving of the Volga." At that time there were three million Ukrainians facing the threat of starvation, and in cities like Odessa the corpses of the victims, too numerous for immediate burial in the frozen earth, were being stored like cordwood. Yet the propaganda presumed that the living might somehow be prevailed upon to help ease the plight of the suffering on the Volga.

The logic behind this was unfathomable to the ordinary American relief worker, who wondered why the Ukraine government—which after all was so eager to demonstrate its independence from Russia—would deny food to its own starving in order to come to the aid of needy Russians. One interpretation was that this was a way for Ukraine to prove its worthiness as a "sovereign" state. But most of the Americans on the scene perceived the hand of Moscow behind these bizarre doings. Fisher's judicious assessment of the Bolshevik attitude toward the famine in Ukraine is that Moscow was, first, "not unconscious of the salutary effect of the frightful visitation, and, second, willing to let the Ukraine suffer, rather than take the chance of new uprisings which might follow foreign contact."[50]

The question remains an especially sensitive one in light of the fact that, a decade later, in the aftermath of the all-out collectivization drive, Ukraine was the principal locus of Soviet Russia's next massive famine, the primary responsibility for which has been laid at the gates of the Kremlin. Ukrainians perished by the millions, perhaps as many as ten million, and Stalin's regime has been charged with "genocide." Whether or not this latter judgment is supported by the known facts is a debate that is destined to continue. With regard to the 1921–22 tragedy, however, the worst that can be said about the Soviet government's behavior vis-à-vis Ukraine, beyond the ill effects resulting from its Civil War agrarian policies, is that it was particularly slow to come to the aid of the famine victims there, at least to the extent that it inhibited the ARA from doing so, and that with the famine in progress, it diverted potentially life-saving food to other regions.

Their investigations cut short, Golder and Hutchinson returned to Moscow, where their chiefs at headquarters had by now become aware of a dispute between Moscow and Kharkov over the Soviet government's unilateral decision to permit the ARA to enter Ukraine. Haskell, ever impatient with matters of politics, failed to see the point. "Governmental relations and diplomatic relations are too deep for us to fathom," he wrote to Brown. None of the Americans in Russia could work up any sympathy for the cause of Ukrainian independence, which struck them as fairly ridiculous and which, worthy or not, was now threatening to hinder the efficiency of their operation. Haskell reduced it to "a matter entirely of diplomatic pride or privileges" between the two governments. Moscow officials, somewhat embarrassed, told him that it was "simply a family row," that Ukraine, though in fact only a federated republic of the RSFSR, held a more elevated status than the other republics, but just how elevated was not always clear.[51]

Clarity, the Americans had little doubt, would very soon be imposed by the heavy hand of the Kremlin. It came as a distinct shock therefore when the authorities in Moscow backed down. They admitted to having erred, in allowing Golder and Hutchinson to undertake their journey, by not consulting with Ukrainian officials beforehand. Moreover, they acknowledged the correctness of Kharkov's understanding that Ukraine was not included in the Riga Agreement. As Golder understood it, "The matter should have been arranged en famille. The Commissars acknowledge that the Ukraine is within its rights and regret that the Ukraine has that much right."[52]

After some hesitation, the ARA decided it had no choice but to accede to the Kremlin's wishes. There ensued a series of conferences in Moscow with the chairman of the Ukrainian Council of People's Commissars, Christian Rakovsky—an ethnic Romanian—who patiently explained to the Americans that Ukraine was not merely some autonomous republic but a sovereign state with its own diplomatic corps and the right to make treaties with foreign powers. The Americans inserted into the Riga text an additional "whereas" recognizing Ukrainian "independence" and added a paragraph to cover the October 19 food remittance agreement. This new Riga-via-Moscow agreement, signed by Rakovsky and Haskell, went into effect on January 10, 1922.[53] Of most immediate importance to the ARA, it cleared the way for the establishment of food remittance stations in Ukraine.

Hutchinson had meanwhile been cleared to conduct another investigation of the region, and in mid-January he returned to Moscow and informed headquarters of the dire situation in the south. In numerical terms, the famine zone now had to be extended by eighty-five thousand square miles and include an additional ten million people. Hutchinson recommended that the ARA introduce a child-feeding program in Ukraine, citing the extreme need but something else as well. He believed that even a relatively thin network of American kitchens would act as an "effective lubricator" for the food package program, which Ukrainian officials had received as coolly as had their comrades in Moscow.

Events were to bear out Hutchinson's supposition. Relations between the relief workers and Ukrainian officials were in any case somewhat tense in the early period owing to local sensitivity about the status of the republic. Upon his arrival at his post in Kiev, district supervisor Kenneth Macpherson was informed that his papers were not in order: "You know this is not Russia, but the Ukraine. Where is your visa to enter this country?" The reception was that much frostier due to the fact that the ARA had at first announced that it intended to restrict its activities in the region exclusively to food remittance work. The first American in Ekaterinoslav, Tom Barringer, was told by an official that the ARA was a great disappointment because its food packages helped "only the speculators."[54] The fact is that most packages went to destitute Jews, but there was no use arguing the point. Once American kitchens began to open and the medical relief program got under way, relations with the Ukrainian authorities markedly improved.

The ARA's use of child-feeding to grease the wheels of food remittance was even more conspicuous in White Russia and neighboring Gomel and Vitebsk provinces, which though certainly hungry, were largely untouched by famine. The White Russian government at first made some noises about the necessity of negotiating its own separate agreement with the ARA, but it did so without apparent conviction. Unlike Ukraine, White Russia had no legal claim to even the most limited sovereignty, and what partly explains that fact, local nationalism was a feeble force.

In the months ahead, the ARA would expand its operations south to Crimea, and southeast into the Don, Kuban, and Stavropol territories. During the spring of 1922, when the situation was most dire, the ARA would contribute modest supplies of food and medicine to the Caucasus republics—Georgia, Azerbaidzhan, and Armenia—delivered through the agency of the Near East Relief.

THIS BURGEONING OPERATION was directed from Moscow headquarters at Spiridonovka 30—and later Spiridonovka 32 and 17 as well—where the staff was apportioned among various administrative "divisions," each charged with the execution and oversight of a particular set of duties intrinsic to the standard child-feeding mission in addition to the two supplementary divisions, food remittance and medical.[55] Of the departments concerned with the feeding program, the most important were supply and traffic.

Supply, headed by Carroll, monitored the movement of ARA food from the time it left American ports until it was delivered to the kitchens in the famine zone. When the food trains arrived in Moscow, they were brought into the Boinaia station, the former stockyards and meat business district where the ARA commanded a huge warehouse situated in a railroad yard and capable of accommodating several hundred cars per day. It was the responsibility of the supply division to procure food trains and determine their cargoes and destinations. As well, it had to ensure that each district was provided with sufficient stocks of all products so that balanced rations could be served, and that district supervisors were able to increase their feeding programs promptly upon authorization by Haskell's office. District supply chiefs coordinated these matters with Moscow and regulated the distribution of food below the district level.

The job of the traffic division was to see that the trains arrived—eventually, if not on schedule—at destination, which was the district warehouses, where the local traffic chiefs took over and arranged for through- and transshipments to subdistrict warehouses.

The accounting division recorded the many financial and other business transactions of the unit. Its principal concern was to document the disposition of all food and medical supplies. Toward that end, the relief workers in the field were required to obtain receipts from all food committees and public organizations and institutions serving as the final distribution points for individual beneficiaries. This being the "business of relief," the Americans took matters of accounting very seriously, which was a source of unceasing wonder and suspicion to Soviet officials and citizens alike.

The motor transport division was responsible for keeping track of the large fleet of cars and trucks the ARA brought into Russia—transport that proved to be invaluable to the relief operations—and for servicing the dozen or so vehicles the Americans maintained in Moscow.

The liaison division was established to facilitate relations between the ARA and the Soviet government. An inspection division enjoyed a brief existence at the very outset, when a central role was envisioned for the RAKPD committee structure. This department was to be revived, as inspection and control, during the second year of the mission when large amounts of food were distributed through Soviet institutions, which necessitated an increased emphasis on American supervision. In January 1922, a communications division was created to handle ARA publicity vis-à-vis the Soviet press and the Western correspondents in Moscow. Finally, in July 1922, when the mission appeared to be nearing an end, a historical division was formed for the purpose of gathering and preserving the records of the unit, which functions it continued to perform after the decision was made to continue operations for a second year.

The organizational structure of the Russian unit was crowned by the office of the director, Haskell, whose personnel at Moscow headquarters by spring 1922 numbered some fifty Americans, with another 150 stationed in the various districts or serving as couriers. They were supported by a staff of local citizens whose total number would peak at some 120,000. By such measures alone, Russia was by far the largest of the Hoover relief missions.

Any sketch of the administrative machinery of the Russian unit would be incomplete, however, if it failed to consider the contribution of the Soviet government. This took the form of a shadow organization whose purposes were several: ostensibly to assist, essentially to monitor, maximally take the credit for, and ideally to win control over American operations.

CHAPTER 5

THE NECK OF THE BOTTLE

In his telegraphed report to Hoover of October 20, Haskell had this to say about official Soviet cooperation with the ARA: "Government attitude in the main friendly and helpful but constant effort inject government machinery into our relief operations under pretext more efficient and quicker; purpose create impression among simple peasants government operation. Every move we make scrutinized by Chekka. Our telegrams vised. Our agents constantly watched. Trusted Bolsheviks highly recommended to us for employment, others discredited."[1]

No one in Washington would have found anything remarkable in this. It was not expected that the Bolsheviks would give free rein inside Russia to a foreign relief agency, especially one directed by Hoover. Even had the leading Bolsheviks believed that the ARA was the "nonpartisan" organization it claimed to be, they would still have mounted an effort to control it—or at least to appear to do so—partly, as Haskell suggested, to save appearances before the Soviet people. Toward that end, it served the government's interest to exaggerate its suspicions of the ARA's motives, to play up the bogeyman Tom Gregory, in order to lend legitimacy to its campaign for control. Such deviousness aside, however, in the initial weeks of the mission there was a good deal of genuine official anxiety that Hoover's men had evil designs in Russia, even more sinister than delivering bread to the bourgeoisie.

The Soviet press started banging the drum during the Riga negotiations. On August 11 *Krasnaia gazeta—The Red Gazette*—published an article titled "The Greek Hoover and His Gifts," which expressed outrage at the conditions Hoover had laid down in his telegram to Gorky. The author urged that if the Soviet government were going to accept America's gifts, it should beware that the belly of the ARA wooden horse was not stuffed with "contraband," either tomorrow or the day after. The only guarantee that the relief workers would not interfere in political matters was not some promise made by Hoover but Bolshevik "control." Other press articles criticized the plan for a distinct ARA apparatus, repeating Litvinov's objection at Riga to the introduction of "parallelism."

The day before Carroll's arrival in Moscow, *Krasnaia gazeta* informed its readers about Gregory's Hungarian adventures, under the defiant title "That Was Hungary, But This Is Russia." At the same time and on the same note, Trotsky called on all Soviet organs to "demonstrate real vigilance in order to prevent adventurists and rogues from using the famine to mount an attempt at counterrevolutionary overthrow in Russia." A few days later he gave a speech in Moscow in which he said that America, the citadel of capitalism, had always opposed the Bolshevik Revolution and that now it sought "to whiten its soiled hands with flour and milk." One week after that, in a speech in Odessa, he assured his audience that the ARA's "Captain Gregorys" would be met with the full force of the Cheka.[2] In this as in most other official Soviet utterances, the ARA was presented as an official U.S. government organization.

Meanwhile, the case of nerves that afflicted Lenin during the Riga talks had not abated. Three days after the accord with Hoover was signed, he wrote to the Politburo urging that in anticipation of the coming into Soviet Russia of "a lot of Americans," a commission be formed to organize the surveillance of these foreigners through the Cheka. "The main thing is to identify and mobilize the maximum number of Communists who know English, to introduce them into the Hoover commission and for other forms of surveillance and intelligence." Two weeks later, reacting to a report of suspect behavior on the part of individual relief workers, Lenin wrote to Chicherin that "as for the hooverites, we must shadow them with all our might." The most unsavory among them had to be compromised by creating scandals around them. "This calls for a brutal, *sustained* war."[3]

In fact it did not call for any such thing, as Lenin and his colleagues soon enough came to realize. The relief workers busied themselves with feeding hungry children and showed bafflingly little interest in Soviet politics. A September 21 *Pravda* article remarked upon this in a tone of undisguised relief. There was the obligatory reference to Hungary 1919 and the assertion that Americans of the Gregory type had indeed come into Russia; "but still, the 'administration' is behaving for now strictly loyally, apolitically. To all overtures of the 'white' party, which remained here under different flags, they don't answer, but are doing their necessary and great work, without looking to the right or to the left."

Still, this was no cause for celebration. "Without joy and contentment do we accept the gifts of the American benefactors. The bread of alms is not sweet.

"We know it well: you pay the most for charity."

Nor was it a cause for complacency. The relief workers themselves may have been playing it clean, "for now," but the various "Whites" in their employ could be expected to use the ARA as a cloak for their anti-Soviet activities. Beyond that, there was the prospect that the high-profile operations of this singular non-government organization might give people dangerous ideas at a time when ideological precepts seemed to be falling like kingpins. What is more, as the *Pravda* writer indicated, having to accept American charity was a humiliation, most of all for the Bolshevik government, which found itself in the acutely embarrassing position of being bailed out by the alms of the international class enemy.

For all these reasons, no matter how "apolitically" the relief workers themselves might behave, in the Bolshevik mind the very presence of the ARA in Russia was fraught with danger and it could not be left unattended. Lenin's feverish call for a brutal war notwithstanding, what was in fact needed was a quietly aggressive political operation that would enable the Soviet government to exert its influence over and effectively dominate the ARA.

COMPLICATING MATTERS was the fact that the Bolsheviks were divided among themselves—indeed, *within* themselves—as to what the Soviet government's posture should be vis-à-vis the ARA. The Bolsheviks were hardly the tightly held party of Lenin's dream and of so many misinformed history books, although already in 1922 the institutions were in place for the rise of Stalin's one-man dictatorship. Soviet Russia was supposed to be a dictatorship of the proletariat, for now run by its vanguard, the Bolshevik Party. But the vanguard needed a vanguard, and Party policy, while ostensibly decided at the periodic Party congresses and conferences attended by delegates from across the country, was in reality set at the top by the Central Committee and increasingly its five-member executive arm, the Politburo.

This hierarchy of Party organs paralleled that of the Soviet government, the machinery through which the Party ruled. At its base was the All-Russian Congress of Soviets, consisting of representatives of local soviets, which convened annually to discuss and ratify policies already worked out at Party gatherings. At the top of the Soviet government structure was the Council of People's Commissars, Lenin's "cabinet," comprised of leading Bolsheviks.

The Party was politically in control, but it was deficient both in numbers and know-how. Membership had grown from under 25,000 in 1917 to, by some counts, 775,000 in 1921, at which point a first-ever purge—of the bloodless sort—thinned the ranks by as much as one-third.[4] The resulting total represented less than 1 percent of the general population and was not nearly large enough to enable the Party to staff the central state bureaucracy, which had grown enormously since the Revolution. Numbers aside, the Party did not command the expertise to run government and industry on its own and was thus forced to rely on non-Party experts to keep the administrative wheels turning. The essential consideration was to have reliable Bolsheviks either manning the key posts or keeping an eye on those non-Bolsheviks who did. The best-known example of this pairing of Reds and experts was the Red Army, where Trotsky, forced to call upon the services of former imperial army officers to command his forces, attached to them political commissars: Party loyalists charged with conducting the most essential kind of political quality control.

Thus, although the Soviet constitution was completely silent on the leading role of the Party, Soviet Russia was in fact a Party-state. As Fisher conceived it, the Politburo was to the ostensible government of Russia what the cow with the crumpled horn was to the house that Jack built[5]:

> This is the cow with the crumpled horn
> > That tossed the dog
> > That worried the cat
> > That killed the rat
> > That ate the malt
> That lay in the house that Jack built.

That was how it appeared to him in the early 1920s. As the decade progressed, another arm of the Central Committee, the Secretariat, established just after the October Revolution, would become the dominant political force. Soon to be headed by a general secretary, the Secretariat was responsible for managing the Party's own expanding bureaucracy, and it would exploit its authority over the appointment of cadres to achieve control over the entire Party—and thus state—establishment. This was chiefly the handiwork of that supreme intriguer, Stalin, whom Lenin appointed the first general secretary in 1922. By the end of the decade he would succeed in displacing the Politburo as stand-in dictator for the proletariat. Eventually he and his minions would thoroughly terrorize the ranks of the Party-state that Lenin built.

Where the power lay in Soviet Russia in 1921 was readily apparent to the incoming Americans, both at the center and in the provinces. Childs of the Kazan ARA, who was still morose about the previous year's election as U.S. president of the uninspiring Warren G. Harding, observed dryly: "There is not much doubt that it is the Communist party which controls all elections in Russia and in as effectual a manner as elections are controlled in New York by Tammany Hall or as American presidential candidates are engineered to election by a Penrose or a Smoot in a national convention."[6]

With the introduction of NEP a few months earlier, the Party had moved to tighten discipline within its own ranks by placing a ban on internal factions. The Bolsheviks had a weakness for endless polemical debate, which is a pernicious habit for any ruling political party but which threatened to have fatal consequences for this single-party dictatorship when it diverted the leadership's attention and energies from the rapidly escalating political and economic crisis of the winter of 1920–21 and began to fractionalize the Party. Now, with a dangerous retreat underway, a premium was to be placed on Party unity.

But the March 1921 ban on factions could not prevent the emergence of divisions within the Party over the wisdom, limits, and theoretical interpretation of the New Economic Policy. Party journals reflected the profound sense of disillusionment among many of the faithful at the death of revolutionary romance. After four years of beating the bourgeoisie—of sweeping away the capitalists with the broom of revolution, in the imagery of the propaganda poster art of the period—now some of these very bourgeois were to be invited back to the table. And it quickly became evident that this entailed more than the rehabilitation of deposed factory managers. By autumn Moscow and Petrograd were witnessing the return of *cafés chantants*, night clubs, and casinos, where genuine speculation on a grand scale was carried on by so-called NEPmen, nouveaux riches who came into their fortunes by unfathomable means. In the face of this, Bolshevik true-believers wondered aloud whether the October Revolution had been made in vain. The whole communist experiment seemed at a dead end and, worse, about to be inundated by a resurgent capitalist tide.[7]

Golder was tuned in to the Party's dilemma: "The poor Bolos are up against it. They have used up their resources, their gold, their propaganda, their tricks; they can no longer play off one foreign power against the other. They can not even appeal to the proletariat to rise and shake off the yoke of the capitalists, for they themselves are now putting on that coat." Lenin's awkward attempts to speak the plain truth about the need to cede hard-won positions while at the same time offering hope for the future seemed only to deepen the confusion, even to sow panic in the ranks. His label for NEP, "state capitalism," was rejected by the Party's leading ideologues, and his attempt to portray it as a mere "breathing spell" and a "strategic retreat" failed to reassure, as Golder detected. "No matter how hard they try it is difficult to convince the average Communist that the New Economic Policy leads to Utopia and not to Capitalism."[8]

Haskell was correct to report to Hoover that there was an essential unity within the Bolshevik government. Yet as he presently came to realize, the shock waves produced by NEP created a discernible, if indistinct, division of the Party's orthodox members into two strains: to use the Americans' terms, the "moderates," including Lenin and Trotsky, took a more tolerant view of the reforms, while the "die-hards," or "radicals," on the Left displayed at best a grudging acceptance of the letter of NEP, but remained constitutionally incapable of observing its spirit. In his effort to maintain Party unity and morale Lenin sometimes gave his rhetoric a sharper edge in order to satisfy the radicals, who could also be appeased by being tossed political red meat such as the 1922 show trial of the remnants of the Socialist Revolutionary Party.

This rough differentiation of hard and soft lines on NEP was reflected in Bolshevik attitudes toward the ARA, whose presence in Russia after all would have been unthinkable had the dramatic compromise with capitalism not already taken place. The die-hards, more numerous among the middle- and lower-level cadres, tended to be more openly hostile to the ARA and more apt to make life difficult for the relief workers, seeing in them carriers of political contamination if not worse. Lenin, on the other hand, after overcoming his initial paranoia about Hoover's designs in Russia, tended to think of the American mission as an opportunity—that is, beyond the actual food and medical supplies it was delivering to Russia.

One of principal rationales for the NEP reforms was the realization that, the prospects of revolution in the West having dimmed, Soviet Russia would not be able to revive its industrial base—and thus build socialism—without attracting foreign trade, credits, and investment. The Bolsheviks in the Kremlin understood that the United States was the only country to have emerged from the Great War in any condition to bring significant capital investment into Russia. The ARA-Soviet contract was not, of course, a trade agreement—Litvinov's nudging commentary notwithstanding—but Lenin came to see it as a foot in the door to official trade relations with the United States and perhaps even to political recognition: after all, Hoover was the U.S. secretary of commerce.

In a note to Chicherin on October 16 Lenin pressed this very point—"*Hoover* is a real plus"—as he did again several days later: "Agreements and concessions with the Americans are super-important to us: with Hoover we have something worthwhile."[9] It was at this same time that he countered Stalin's small-minded advice regarding the ARA's food remittance proposition with the argument that the Bolsheviks, in seeking to master trade, could benefit by watching the Americans in action. What is more, cooperation with the ARA in such a program was a way to demonstrate to the Americans, and to the West generally, that the Bolsheviks were capable of collaboration in "commercial" enterprises. This is precisely what Haskell and company were counting on: that in order to build up its bona fides with Western governments and business the Soviet government would make every effort to come across with efficient and friendly cooperation.

Yet this would prove to be impossible. While the more "enlightened" Bolsheviks usually worked to maintain stable relations with the ARA, they often could not control the destructive inclinations of radical subordinates. Beyond that, the moderates themselves proved incapable of holding to a consistently cooperative line toward the ARA. Apprehensive about the capitalist wave they had unleashed and impatient with the slow progress of their effort to attract foreign trade and recognition, the Bolo "friends" of the ARA were not above roughing up the Hoover crowd as a way of rallying the faithful and in the hope of drawing in and entangling the U.S. State Department. In the end, no matter how compelling the argument for demonstrating tolerance and goodwill, the Bolshevik proclivity for suspicion and control often got the upper hand. The Soviet government was inherently incapable of cooperation in the spirit of the Riga Agreement.

THE SOURCE OF THE GREATEST strain in ARA-Soviet relations was the constellation of commissars the Bolsheviks put in place to play the Reds to the ARA's experts. Despite Lenin's call for a war against American relief workers, this machinery of control was a bit slow in coming together, perhaps because the Americans made an unexpectedly fast start. Curiously, the ARA itself unwittingly aided and abetted the government in its intrusive designs.

Carroll and the advance guard wrongly assumed that their principal contact in the government would be Kamenev, officially in his capacity as deputy chairman of the Soviet famine relief committee, though actually because of his standing as a member of the Politburo. The ARA was quite accustomed to dealing with the top echelons of leadership in the various states of Europe, so it seemed quite reasonable to assume that the administration would have daily access to one of the five most powerful men in the Kremlin. This expectation was attractive as well because Kamenev was, in the flesh, not at all like the Western newspaper image of the bloodthirsty Bolshevik. There was nothing "proletarian" about him, except of course for passages in his articles and speeches printed in *Pravda*. Like most of the Bolshevik old guard he was a man of petty-bourgeois appearance and taste who would have looked very much at home in the capitals of Western Europe—as indeed he did during his many years as a political exile. His pre-1917 enlistment in the Party made him one of the so-called Old Bolsheviks, those who had experienced the vicissitudes of the revolutionary underground. As such they were mentally better equipped to deal with the head-spinning "revolution" of NEP than was the great majority of their fellow Communists, who had joined their ranks after Red October.

Whatever were Carroll's precise expectations, the fact is that Kamenev was far too busy tending to affairs at the center of Soviet politics, not to mention his responsibilities as administrator of Moscow city and province, to concern himself with the day-to-day requirements of a foreign relief organization. At minimum, Carroll assumed that someone from Kamenev's office would serve as the government's liaison with the ARA, expediting and simplifying its operations.

On the very evening of his arrival in Moscow, Carroll had a letter delivered to Kamenev requesting that the ARA be provided with a government representative to help it coordinate and manage its dealings with all the many Soviet bureaus. This was to be only the first of several increasingly impatient such applications, reflecting a mounting frustration with the inefficiency of the state bureaucracy. On September 2 Carroll again asked that Kamenev appoint a "liaison officer" to assist the ARA, "someone with sufficient power to get results." Two weeks of further entanglement in Soviet red tape and Carroll's petition is now soaked in sarcasm:

what was required was a man "with sufficient authority to make the average pro-crastinating, petty public servant realize that we are not here to play but to carry on a large undertaking in child feeding in which speed is of vital importance."[10]

Finally, on September 24, the Soviet government appointed Johann Palmer as plenipotentiary representative to the ARA. The effect of this step was minor as Palmer had but a slight political stature and none of the personal force of charac-ter the assignment demanded. His written "mandate," however, was far-reaching, though it is unclear if the Americans paid much attention to it. It gave him, among other things, the authority to appoint his own representatives in each of the districts and, with their assistance, to act as intermediary between the ARA and all government agencies and to ensure that the ARA enlist only acceptable lo-cal personnel.[11] So the power of the plenipotentiary was on paper substantial; all that was required was a forceful individual to fill the position.

That man made his appearance in the second week of October, when Palmer was replaced by Aleksandr Eiduk, who bore the title "representative plenipoten-tiary of the Russian Socialist Federated Soviet Republic with all foreign relief or-ganizations," which meant essentially the ARA. He brought to the job the nec-essary political and personal qualities his predecessor lacked. Eiduk—a Latvian name, pronounced Eye-DOOK—was a member of the collegium of the Cheka and, to match, had a reputation for bloodthirstiness in the Revolution.[12] Despite the recent economic reforms, in 1921 the Cheka—the Russian acronym for "Ex-traordinary Commission"—was still very much a dreaded institution. In his Oc-tober 20 telegram to Hoover, Haskell self-contradictorily characterized it as "all powerful, inclined to get out of hand but still controlled"—wording that indi-cates its awkward place in NEP Russia.

The Extraordinary Commission had fallen on hard times, relatively speaking. Gone were the days of uninhibited Red Terror. The priority in autumn 1921 was the creation of a climate conducive to promoting domestic trade and private en-terprise and, as importantly, attracting foreign investment and political recogni-tion. That meant curbing the excesses of the Cheka, most immediately calling a halt to the practice of arresting, executing, or otherwise terrorizing those guilty of committing the crime of "speculation." This was now technically legal and went by the name of "trade," a word only slightly less repellent to the Bolshevik ear. As economic policy was recast to accommodate the presence of a growing market, it became apparent that in order to shed its image of lawlessness, Soviet Russia needed to establish proper legal codes protecting the sanctity of private property. The Cheka, with its own courts and prisons, its arbitrary ways and shoot-first mentality, understood only "revolutionary legality." In any case, regardless of how earnestly it might try to adjust to the new spirit of the times, its blood-stained reputation was indelible.

The unavoidable step, the Cheka's abolition, came almost a year after NEP began, in February 1922, at which time most of its responsibilities were trans-ferred to the People's Commissariat of Internal Affairs, where a new "state polit-ical administration"—GPU, in the Russian initials—was formed to take over se-cret police functions, while the Cheka's quasi-judicial powers were absorbed by the regular courts.[13]

Few Soviet citizens took comfort in what seemed to be little more than a change of nomenclature. After all, the chief of the new GPU was the founding head of the Cheka and the very personification of the Red Terror, Feliks Dzerzhinskii, who in his new job surrounded himself with seasoned Chekkists. For as long as the ARA was in the country, most Russians continued to call the political police the Cheka, even though the bad old days of drumhead executions were over.

As a veteran Chekkist, Eiduk was by definition a die-hard. Both he and Kamenev were orthodox Bolsheviks, but beyond that they had little in common. Kamenev belonged among the Party's three-piece-suited intellectuals; Eiduk was one of its leather-jacketed toughs. As such, his own personal "transition to NEP" must have been more unpleasant. He was known as an "executioner," a talent unlikely to be in great demand in the new era of "state capitalism." That term may have sounded to his ear like an occupational death sentence. His reprieve came in the form of a call to shepherd the bourgeois relief workers of the ARA.

Initially, the ARA chiefs were encouraged by his appointment. What they saw in Eiduk—now moving his ample staff into headquarters at Spiridonovka 30— with his gruff manner and fearsome reputation, was a man who would positively terrorize obstructionist officials out of their lethargy and inefficiency. Even more promising, he began at once to assign to the ARA's various district headquarters his own agents, charged exclusively with expediting relief matters. Yes, Eiduk was going to get things moving. The Americans would be able to go to him for all their needs, from warehouses and living space to rail and water transportation, to fuel, supplies, and repairs—and the Russian relief job would be put over in fine shape. In Fisher's words, "It seemed—as it proved—too good to be true."[14]

Unexpectedly, by October the critical need of the Russian unit was money. This was something entirely unanticipated going in, but the inflationary policies of War Communism had been replaced by a spirit of stringency and fiscal responsibility. The central government was in the process of financially cutting loose the local soviets, forcing them to fend for themselves in the new pay-as-you-go environment. This placed the cash-strapped local governments in the position of having to cover the operating costs of the ARA, as the Riga Agreement required of the "Soviet Authorities."

The precariousness of this arrangement was obvious to the relief workers soon after their arrival in the districts. Provincial officials threw up their hands when pressed by the Americans to come up with the funds to pay for the personnel, transport, services, and equipment necessary to move the food from the railway yards of the provincial capitals to the ultimate distribution points. Unpaid workmen began refusing to unload supplies, and some of the ARA's own employees threatened to quit unless they received their wages. Telegrams to Moscow headquarters from the district supervisors told of their distress and requested urgent assistance, but the ARA chiefs at the center could themselves get no satisfaction.

So the appearance on the scene of Eiduk, the man of action—or rather, at the moment, promises of action—inspired the Moscow Americans to visions of railroad cars loaded with cash and piloted by his intrepid subordinates on their way to the districts. In fact Eiduk's men showed up without funds and without much real ability to squeeze any out of the local governments. By design, these men were usually not from the regions to which they were assigned. Most were of a Cheka or Red Army background, as were the agents they in turn appointed to the subdistricts. In almost every instance their arrival at district headquarters was distinctly unwelcome to the relief workers, most of whom recognized immediately about Eiduk's satellites what the chiefs in Moscow were slow to grasp about Eiduk himself: that the plenipotentiary's role was as much about control as assistance.

A few of the district Americans, evidently prompted by their Russian employees, believed that the inspiration for assigning Eiduk and his "plenipotentiaries" to the ARA had come from Trotsky's appointment of political commissars to the Red Army. In this case the purpose was to shield comparatively untried local officials, Party and soviet, "from the subtle poison of contact with these unregenerate bourgeois democrats," as Fisher put it, affecting the Bolshevik style. He believed that the establishment of the plenipotentiary system was a concession to influential Bolshevik opponents of the Riga accord. Maybe so, but it was also perfectly good Leninism.

IT IS DIFFICULT TO GET a precise fix on when the Moscow Americans finally took the proper measure of Eiduk. Fisher says that the first intimation of trouble came within days of his appearance, when Haskell presented him with an outline of the ARA's medical relief program. The Great Expediter dragged his feet, first contending that the People's Commissariat of Health was quite capable of distributing American supplies on its own, and then, when this line of defense failed to hold, arguing that a medical program would require an addendum to the Riga Agreement.[15] More troubling was his openly hostile reception to the proposed food package program, though eventually both projects won government approval.

On October 20 Eiduk informed Haskell's chief of staff that he wanted to have a say in the selection of employees at Moscow headquarters in order to "save the ARA any kind of unexpected trouble."[16] The right of the plenipotentiary to be involved in the hiring of staff had been part of Palmer's original mandate; now Eiduk intended to act upon it and, as well, to have his agents provide similar guidance to the Americans in the districts. This was not an offer the ARA could simply refuse, and it turned out to be the opening move in a struggle for control over the native personnel of the relief administration, one that would last, in harder and softer phases, for the duration of the mission.

Evidently feeling that his generosity was not sufficiently appreciated, Eiduk fired off a warning shot in the form of a declaration called Order No. 17. This document laid out in a series of eight points the program of the ARA and the obligation of the local authorities to offer it every assistance—strictly under the guidance of Comrade Eiduk, of course. Its most noteworthy feature was a message directed at the native employees of the ARA, whom it warned not to abuse their positions, either for personal aggrandizement or in order to conduct anti-Bolshevik propaganda. If they did, they would be "prosecuted by me in the most merciless manner." Eiduk reminded these prospective outlaws that they were ultimately responsible not to the ARA but to the Soviet government. Meanwhile, the general population was urged to be vigilant and report any improper activities to Eiduk's district representatives or to telegraph him directly in Moscow at Spiridonovka 30.[17]

Order No. 17 made it plain that Eiduk was on the job principally as a policeman. This would have been troubling enough even had he met American expecta-

tions by delivering efficiency-through-terror, but this was not to be. It was a desire
to avoid red tape that had moved Carroll to request the services of a liaison officer
in the first place, but in fact Eiduk's plenipotentiary system itself turned out to be
a bureaucratic bottleneck. His satellites forbade direct dealings between the ARA
and local government departments, demanding that all business be conducted
through them, thus extending to the districts the arrangement Eiduk and his staff
enforced in Moscow. Yet in the districts just as in the center the plenipotentiaries
seemed incapable of getting action, and the relief workers, growing increasingly
frustrated, repeatedly requested permission to work directly with local officials.

Haskell reached the limit of his patience on or before November 11, the date
he signed a memorandum to Eiduk rehearsing a long list of grievances, which in
the colonel's view argued convincingly that the Soviet authorities were reneging
on their obligations under the Riga Agreement. "It would be impossible to enu-
merate all the broken promises and the obstacles placed in the way of progress in
our work by officials of the Soviet Government." Though Haskell aimed most of
his criticism at "subordinates in the various bureaus," he rebuked Eiduk's Moscow staff for failing to provide the ARA with adequate living quarters in the capital, for the deplorable quality of the rail transportation made available to the relief workers, for the failure to give the mission appropriate publicity in the Soviet
press—"I could go on indefinitely. . . . "

This intolerable state of affairs, Haskell's memo alliterated, was "discouraging,
disappointing and disheartening to the Americans." He indicated that although
plans were underway in the United States to expand the Russian relief program,
given the poor record of Soviet cooperation thus far, he was not inclined to encourage this. "If it requires so much pleading, letter writing and delay to accomplish our present program, I view with great doubt the ability of the Russian
Government to carry through any relief program which might double, triple or
quadruple the cooperation necessitated at the present time."[18]

Meanwhile, similar dramas were being acted out in the districts, with subplot
lines written into the script for local Party and Soviet officials, whose resentment
of the outsiders Eiduk sent from Moscow inspired some to take the side of the
Americans and others to defy both parties to the contest.

Shafroth relates that when Eiduk's man in Samara, Karklin, took up his post, he
ordered that all arrangements made prior to his arrival be redone, including the establishment of kitchens in Samara city. Had the Soviet system been better organized, Shafroth believed, the plenipotentiary might have been able to play a useful
troubleshooting role; as things stood, Karklin's presence only generated more red
tape. His obstructions cost the Samara Americans precious time in the drafting of
official memorandums and protocols, the lifeblood of Soviet officialdom. "Moreover, this particular representative thought it his duty not merely to see my requests
were fulfilled, but to control the manner in which the show was run. Tho disabused
of this idea twice weekly, he always came back with it at the next meeting."[19]

A crisis point was reached on November 4 when Karklin had one of Shafroth's
key Russian staff members arrested, the second such incident in two days, followed the next day by the arrest of an ARA inspector. A few days after that came
the arrests of two ARA employees in Kazan: the Russian office manager and the
chief kitchen inspector of Kazan city. In Saratov it was the manager of the prin-

cipal warehouse. In Simbirsk Eiduk's man tried to have district supervisor Eddie Fox recalled to Moscow. A few weeks later the Russian executive in the Tsaritsyn office was put in prison.[20] The effect of all this on the morale of the native personnel of each district headquarters was, as intended, chilling.

News of the arrests, which turned out to be merely the first such wave, reached Moscow just as the chiefs had lost all patience with Eiduk, and it provoked Haskell to a vigorous written protest. Eiduk replied matter-of-factly, in a letter dated November 20, that service with the ARA did not entitle its native employees to immunity from arrest and that the administration had made the mistake of enlisting too many representatives of the former bourgeoisie, an element inherently hostile to the very children they were hired to feed.[21] By now it was clear what Eiduk had meant by his earlier offer to help the ARA avoid "unexpected trouble."

Three days later, a letter drafted over Haskell's name and addressed to Kamenev put forward the most severe indictment yet of the Soviet government for its unwillingness to cooperate with the ARA. The document catalogued all of the Russian unit's many complaints, linking each grievance to the specific paragraph in the Riga Agreement the Soviet government was charged with having violated. Topping Haskell's list was the now burning issue of the arrests of local employees, but it was the second article of impeachment that stood out boldly: Eiduk himself, or rather, the office of plenipotentiary. The ARA, the letter maintained, was not to be restricted to conducting its relief operations "through and upon the approval of" any one government representative. "In fact I may add frankly that the activities of the A.R.A. can not be subjected to the supervision of any individual or any government organization including the Extraordinary Commission itself. This condition now exists and is a distinct violation of *Paragraph XII of the Riga Agreement*."[22]

What kind of ARA-Soviet crisis this bill of particulars might have produced must remain in the realm of speculation, because it was never delivered, at least not officially. It appears, however, that Eiduk may have been allowed to read a copy or in some other way must have been made to feel the heat; otherwise it is difficult to explain the publication in *Izvestiia* on November 30 of a strikingly pro-ARA article credited to him. It praised the American mission for fully living up to Soviet expectations in the delivery of famine relief, and thereby vindicating Moscow's signing of the Riga Agreement. But it was sharply critical of the lackluster performance in relief matters on the part of Soviet officials, including even some of Eiduk's own agents in the districts. Especially odious were those dull-witted bureaucrats, "tangled in red tape," who either did not take the work of the ARA with due seriousness, did not understand it, or had not even heard of it. Many were as yet unable to shed their pre-NEP work habits, remaining mired "in paper routine, eternal commissions, interminable meetings." As a result, there were cases where American food stood idle in one place while people nearby died of starvation. The ARA deserved active cooperation, "not a thoughtful-dreamy attitude."

This was an unexpected and welcome blast, indeed. One of the ARA's routine complaints was the Soviet government's failure to give its relief operations appropriate publicity as required under the Riga accord, but this was certainly a big step in the right direction—as was a similar contribution to *Izvestiia* by Eiduk on December 8, which again portrayed the ARA in a positive light: "There is actual food, there is real aid."

Regardless of whether these articles succeeded in lighting a fire under indifferent local officials, Eiduk's plenipotentiaries continued in their meddling ways. Much of their energy seemed to be devoted to giving the impression that the ARA was a joint Soviet-American operation. While this was to remain a source of strain throughout the course of the mission, in the early going the principal battleground for the struggle to take the credit was the RAKPD. Although Haskell would give the order to the districts in late November to eliminate that ill-considered institution, at least to the extent of erasing its name, Eiduk's men and certain local officials found it advantageous to keep it alive.

Local ignorance worked in their favor. The "Russian-American" in "RAKPD" was supposed to recognize the contribution to the relief effort of tens of thousands of local citizens. But from the beginning "Russian-American" was widely understood to mean an equal share of control for the ARA and the Soviet government, which would inevitably have given the latter the upper hand. In Simbirsk, where the RAKPD's demise was an especially protracted affair, the Americans were confounded by the fact that ordinary people simply could not conceive of the existence of a public body in which the Soviet government was not the controlling factor. To them, Somerville reports, the "Russian" in "Russian-American" could only have meant the government, "for who could be expected to think that Russian referred to anything so obsolete as the Russian people!"

Party and Soviet officials may or may not have known better, but either way they were not about to let go of such a good thing without putting up resistance. In Simbirsk as elsewhere neutralizing the RAKPD was supposed to be as simple as changing its name to ARA. Yet according to Somerville, removing "the five troublesome letters" was easy only in theory, for "in practice they proved as difficult to get rid of as the proverbial nine-lived cat. They would pop up in the most unexpected and exasperating ways."[23]

Bowden of Tsaritsyn complained to Haskell that his effort to eliminate the RAKPD was impeded by the machinations of two men, each claiming to be Eiduk's plenipotentiary: "I am now faced with the necessity of getting rid of, or sidetracking, a committee which had been led to believe that its powers and dignities were to be very great. This is made more difficult by the presence of two representatives from the Central Government in Moscow, who seem to think that the functions of the A.R.A. are to be limited to inspection and control."[24]

BY THIS POINT IN TIME—midautumn—the institutional interface between the ARA and the Soviet government at Moscow was wholly different from what the chiefs in the United States and London had planned for in organizing and staffing the Russian unit. The man recruited to conduct those relations for the ARA was the chief of the liaison division, Archibald Cary Coolidge, who cut a peculiar figure at Moscow headquarters. Coolidge was a distinguished professor of history at Harvard—where Golder had been one of his Ph.D. students—and director of the university library. He had traveled extensively in tsarist Russia, where he served for six months in 1890–91 as acting secretary with the American legation at St. Petersburg. Hoover himself had cabled Coolidge in Cambridge to enlist his services with the Russian unit as its "political adviser and diplomatic go between" with the Soviet authorities. Coolidge understood this to mean that he would be the chief political figure of the mission, which may well have been Hoover's desire initially.[25] Soon after arriving in Moscow, however, Coolidge understood that his was to be a secondary role. Two people were responsible for this: Haskell and Eiduk.

Immediately upon meeting Haskell, Coolidge sensed that this was the kind of man who needed to be in total command. Personal relations between them were apparently always cordial and in fact started out especially well, Coolidge being relieved to discover at their first encounter in New York that Haskell did not live up to the reputation of the general run of career army men. "He pleased me as he seemed clear cut, intelligent, energetic. I fancy he is extremely capable. He was most friendly and I did not discover any of the arrogance one so often finds in our regular army officer of a certain type." But it was not long before Coolidge was remarking privately that the colonel was not apt to listen to advice—"this is his show"—and that contrary to what Coolidge had been led to believe, the chief of the liaison division was made subordinate to the director of the mission, same as the other division heads.[26]

Haskell's personality and administrative style aside, the very existence of the Soviet liaison system would in itself have had the effect of sidetracking Coolidge, since Eiduk intended to deal directly with the chiefs of the various ARA divisions and with Haskell. This left Coolidge and his staff with a greatly reduced role, principally the job of repatriating American citizens living in Russia. This was an unprecedented activity for the ARA, one which fell to it due to the absence of official U.S.-Soviet relations and to the fact that paragraph 27 of the Riga Agreement obligated the Soviet government to facilitate the departure from Russia of all Americans. Their number was not insubstantial, owing to the presence of so many former Russian émigrés to the United States. So ARA headquarters assumed the functions of a consular office, coordinating its repatriation activities with the American mission at Riga. The liaison division was further marginalized by the creation, in January 1922, of the communications division to handle publicity matters.

By then Coolidge was already packing his bags for his return to Harvard, where within a year, and in large part inspired by his experience in Soviet Russia, he would launch the journal *Foreign Affairs*. So in one sense the Russian unit's loss was our gain. Still, in a way it is a pity that his part was written out of the script because we can only imagine how the ARA drama would have played out had this practitioner of old-world diplomacy been pitted against that symbol of the brave new world of antidiplomacy, Eiduk. The one was a refined gentleman, the other "a tough egg and a killer," as an American relief worker sized him up. Coolidge himself wrote of the Lett, "With some geniality and a pleasant smile, he has a cruel mouth and a certain, underlying brutality cropped out rather easily."[27]

Yet this Boston Brahmin was as much out of his element among the young bloods and soldiers at ARA headquarters. One improbable manifestation of this was his remarkably mild judgments of Eiduk and of Bolshevik power generally. Coolidge turned out to be far more tolerant politically than his colleagues. He was not the author of Haskell's November 23 missive citing the liaison system itself as a violation of the Riga Agreement—quite the contrary, he composed a stiff rebuttal to it.[28]

In Coolidge's view, Eiduk was "vigorously aiding us," and in carrying out his job was facing many more difficulties than the Americans recognized. Yes, the chief plenipotentiary was also intent on establishing control over the ARA; nonetheless, the liaison system was essential to the American operation and ought not to be scrapped. Echoing Carroll's rationale for requesting such an arrangement in the first place, Coolidge pointed out that it spared the ARA the burden of having to carry on relations with an assortment of government departments spread out across Moscow, allowing it instead to concentrate all its energy on Eiduk, the "neck of the bottle."

Nor would it do any good to replace Eiduk with some mere secretary, as only a figure of authority could get results out of the government bureaucracy, as the sojourn of Palmer had made abundantly clear. Coolidge disagreed as well with the notion, widely shared at ARA headquarters, that Kamenev was the answer to their problems: "Kamenev might be willing to sacrifice Eiduk personally, but he probably has no desire to have us continually getting at him, and it is not unlikely that he himself invented the idea of creating a plenipotentiary."

Nothing Coolidge observed over the next six weeks caused him to change his position. Near the time of his departure from Russia he wrote that all in all the chief plenipotentiary delivered almost everything the ARA asked of him, which was a great deal. "He showed plenty of intelligence; his criticisms were sagacious, his own demands reasonable, he was quick in decision, and he knew how to distinguish essentials from non-essentials. . . . When all is said and done, if we might have had a better man to deal with, we might easily have had a worse one." This assessment was breathtakingly at odds with those of his American colleagues, both at Moscow headquarters and in the districts, which Coolidge did not visit during his time in Russia.

This seems counterintuitive if one assumes that Coolidge's social class and seniority would predispose him to feelings of hostility toward the revolutionaries occupying the Kremlin. The explanation lies in his exposure to Russia under the old regime. Where his colleagues detected intentional obstructionism on the part of Eiduk and other Soviet officials, Coolidge was apt to see mere inefficiency. And inefficiency, he understood from long experience, was a quality ingrained in the Russian national character, however much it was now accentuated by a Soviet system that gave loyal Bolsheviks authority over politically unreliable experts. Much of the bureaucratic red tape the ARA had to contend with had been present before the Revolution: "I sometimes wonder if the obstacles we encounter would not have been as great then as now, in spite of all the disorder and demoralization consequent to the present revolution."

As for Haskell's charge that the Soviet government's deployment of plenipotentiaries constituted a violation of the pledges it made at Riga, this was dubious. "The Riga Agreement, while binding them to aid us, does not prescribe that they shall subordinate their judgment to ours in such matters."

It is impossible to say for certain whether Coolidge would have continued to preach such tolerance had he remained in Russia through the ARA's corn campaign the following spring, when the crisis of the railways brought matters to a head between Haskell and Eiduk. Regardless of his opinions, his counsel would likely have had little effect on the ARA chiefs. By November he was without any political influence on the colonel, who excluded him from the important conferences with Eiduk. On his own initiative Coolidge conferred with some of the big Bolos, notably Chicherin and especially Karl Radek, recounting these discussions in private letters to the secretary of state and to Senator Henry Cabot Lodge. Haskell was unaware of such correspondence until word arrived from Hoover's office in Washington advising that such freelancing was causing embarrassment to the Chief.

Haskell had only recently, in mid-November, requested that Hoover clarify Coolidge's status, claiming it was difficult to find anything for him to do that "the Professor considers of sufficient importance": he prefers to leave the details of repatriation to subordinates "while he holds conferences with the heads of the Russian Government."[29]

The final straw for Coolidge, it appears, was the fact that the ARA-Ukraine agreement of January 10 had been negotiated without his knowledge. By then, according to an American who worked alongside him, within the ARA he was treated by "the powers" with "amused tolerance." He served in the Russian unit, but he departed Moscow in February 1922 without ever having become part of the show.

Farmer Murphy, one of Coolidge's subordinates in the liaison division, more accurately reflected the collective state of mind at headquarters. In his view, "everything is stopped and clogged at the neck of the bottle, which is Eiduk." Because of this, he believed, the ARA was little by little losing its independence:

Although we are getting a great deal done in spite of this red-tape obstruction I cannot help but feel that they are gradually winding their tentacles around us and unless some vigorous, masterful action is shown soon they will have us entirely in their power and make a sideshow of us. I feel also that we are in a position to make vigorous representations, because the big men in the government desire above all things recognition from us and they desire also financial and commercial assistance, so that they cannot afford not to please us.

Murphy's complaint, one shared by a growing number of relief workers, was that the ARA chiefs, rather than using this political leverage to secure the required cooperation from the Soviet government, were allowing the administration to be pushed around. Witness the reaction to the recent arrest of a Russian secretary in his office: Murphy wanted a "vigorous" response; instead, "Coolidge has written another note about it to Eiduk, but so far without result. It was an excellent note if you were dealing with civilized people instead of a lot of ruffians like the Eiduk bunch." It was high time for the Chief himself to weigh in. "In my belief a good strong intimation from Hoover that further benefits will depend on the conduct of the Russian representatives in their dealings with the ARA in Russia, is just about due. The Eiduk crowd is getting cockier every day."[30]

Murphy's sarcasm may have been directed at Coolidge, but his charge that the ARA was failing to stand up to the Bolos was leveled implicitly at the hard-boiled soldier running the show. Mounting frustration with Haskell's conduct of what the relief workers called "government relations" was about to kindle the smoldering feud between the ARA veterans and their Regular Army superiors.

CHAPTER 6

HASKELL AT THE BAT

Among the howls of protest emanating from the districts over the encroachments of Eiduk's liaisonites, one that may have annoyed Haskell was a letter sent to him from Bowden of Tsaritsyn in January 1922. Bowden was writing in regard to Eiduk's Order No. 84, just published in the local newspaper, which stated that all mandates signed by American representatives of the ARA were null and void and that persons using them were liable to prosecution. Eiduk's purpose was to require the ARA's Russian inspectors to secure official Soviet mandates. Bowden informed Haskell that there were regions of the Tsaritsyn district where anyone caught with a Soviet mandate would be "immediately and violently put to death." This statement, which was technically true, was bound to attract the attention of its reader, but it was Bowden's parting shot that could have provoked the colonel: "Is it not possible for you to hold Eyduck in check a bit more?"[1]

Bowden was one of the unit's Old ARA men, and as such he was used to having his way with government officials of every rank. By January there were more than a dozen ARA veterans like him stationed in the districts, and they tended, more than the other relief workers, to attribute Eiduk's ascendancy to the failure of the veteran officer at the head of their mission to defend the interests of the baby feeders on the famine front. Their distress at having a Regular Army man impose a military brand of authority on an ARA operation was bad enough. It is doubtful, however, that this unhappy marriage would have proved to be so incendiary had the ARA's old guard believed that Haskell was standing up to the Bolos. Unlike the rude intrusion of military culture, the colonel's deference to the Soviet authorities was entirely unanticipated because it seemed out of character with that culture and especially with the colonel's reputation for toughness.

The staffs in New York and London remained anxious about the state of morale inside the Russian unit, which they attempted to monitor from Haskell's official correspondence and from private letters the men were sending out of Russia to ARA colleagues in Europe and America. It is remarkable indeed, given the enormity and complexity of the relief operation itself, how much time and mental energy the chiefs expended in autumn 1921 trying to understand where they had gone wrong in assembling the Russia team and what steps they should take to ensure that this, the largest and last ARA mission, would not fall on its face and tarnish the entire proud record of Hoover's humanitarian achievements since Belgium.

Edgar Rickard, the ARA's director-general in New York, must have had a disturbing sense of déjà vu as he read the incoming reports about the chilly reception afforded Haskell, first in Riga by Miller, then in Moscow by Carroll. For this is what had happened in July 1919 when the colonel took up his assignment as Allied high commissioner to Armenia. His arrival in the Caucasus did not sit well with, among others, the head of the ARA mission there, Major Joseph C. Green, a commissioned officer who at that moment effectively became Haskell's subordinate. The two men evidently never got along. Six months later matters had deteriorated to the point where Haskell felt compelled to address a lengthy memorandum to Rickard defending his conduct as high commissioner.[2] Among the several unnamed objects of his displeasure was the discernible figure of Major Green. The colonel wrote that he could easily see why certain men under his authority might believe "that an officer of the Regular Army, arriving with considerable powers, might, in their opinion, be absolutely incapable of carrying on without their able assistance and advice."

Whatever the merits of the complaints about him, word of Haskell's allegedly high-handed treatment of the ARA spread throughout the organization's European offices, where relief workers were prepared to believe the worst about the soldier from West Point. Thus, even before his nomination to head the Russian mission, Haskell enjoyed a poisonous notoriety within the organization. One of members of the Russian unit recalled in the 1930s, "we had heard stories of him from Georgian Russia, stories which we did not like."

Compounding the problem was the gossip surrounding Haskell's direction the year before of the relief mission to Romania. The former chief of the ARA Poland unit enlightened the chiefs in New York as to the perniciousness of this Romanian strain of the virus and the means of its transmission: "Now, a few scattering members of this ex-Rumanian personnel have been drifting across Europe from time to time ever since 1919 and, over the coffee cups or the sliwowic glasses, have gossiped a good deal about the Colonel, his ability, his methods and certain personal characteristics evident at least while in Rumania."[3] The precise allegations remain obscure, but the presumption of guilt no doubt derived from the military pedigree of the accused.

Thus, in assuming command of the Russian mission, Haskell was handicapped not only by the inevitable animosity of the enlisted man for the army regular but by the shadow cast over his past performance as an administrator of food relief.

That all of this was a source of deep apprehension among ARA officials in Europe is documented in a remarkable letter written to Haskell by one of his own, Col. James A. Logan. During the war, Logan had been head of the United States mission in Paris, where he served in 1919 as U.S. unofficial representative on the Reparations Commission, while at the same time running the ARA's headquarters there. He knew Haskell well and had taken a hand from Paris in sorting out the Caucasus imbroglio. Haskell's selection to head the Russian mission inspired his superior officer, still in Paris, to offer words of advice in a letter dated September 9—as Haskell was steaming toward Europe—whose admonitions suggested past difficulties and present dangers.

As both career soldier and ARA insider, Logan was in a unique position to deliver some straight talk to the newly designated director of the Russian unit. A "splendid morale" had been built up within Hoover's organization, he instructed

Haskell; what a "great pity" it would be were it now to suffer a decline. Yet the present circumstances held the potential for just such an eventuality. He reminded Haskell that a large number of ARA men, having once been volunteer officers, had had many unfortunate experiences during their time in the AEF while serving under Regular Army officers: "You know the class of Regular Officers of which I speak and also know that there are far too many of this type in existence. These civilians, while under their orders, were in many cases their intellectual superiors." As a result, they developed "a rather instinctive distrust of Regular Army Officers and Regular Army methods. Confidentially and generally I share their views." Men such as Carroll, Miller, and Quinn had at first felt this way about Logan, but "I believe by this time I have proved that I am human."

The ARA veterans recruited for the Russian mission, Logan cautioned Haskell, would start out distrustful of him, and he would have to earn their confidence.

> I therefore venture to suggest the following list of DON'TS viz:
>
> Don't wear a uniform yourself and don't allow anybody else to
> Don't use your military title—call yourself "Mister"
> Don't use your military form of letter writing or military language in your letters or instructions
> Don't take a military attitude in handling your men (I know you won't do this anyhow, but it is a very important "Don't" to remember)

On a completely different note Logan warned that "it will be a great mistake to take any women folks, family included, into Russia, and on this particularly you should set an example." To place such weight on such an apparently trivial point seems incongruous, but in fact its inclusion also was prompted by bad memories and foreshadowed future troubles.

Logan closed with an emphatic postscript: "To sum up, you are a DAMN GOOD SOLDIER but forget it while you are in Russia and be a DAMN GOOD MISTER. I would not write you this way but that I am your good and true friend and interested in your doing the biggest possible things in Russia."

It is impossible to say for sure, but perhaps had this warning actually been delivered, it would have thrown a switch inside Haskell's head and the ARA might have been at least partly spared from the unpleasantness that lay ahead. In fact, though, Logan's letter was placed in the care of Brown, who, though he may well have commissioned it, decided that its condescending tone might alienate the colonel, so he suppressed it. He disclosed this fact to Rickard in forwarding him a copy of the document several weeks later when the very trouble it was intended to head off was threatening to cripple the Russian unit.[4]

TO BE PRECISE, at that point in time the ARA veterans in Moscow were less hostile to Haskell than to Col. Tom Lonergan, his chief of staff. Lonergan belonged to that unattractive "class of Regular Officers" that so exercised Logan: he was long on arrogance and short on tact. His circulars and instructions, many issued over Haskell's signature, were composed in the style of military orders. Col. Logan's DON'TS were Col. Lonergan's DOS. And since the men in the districts, and even those in the capital, could not always see the hand of the executive assistant in the signed communications of the director, Haskell's standing among the old ARA guard was the worse for it. Nor did the army officers take to Lonergan: it was said that he had "not a friend in the show."

Stories about the discontent inside the Russian unit spread to the ARA missions in Europe and to former ARA men in the United States. Gregg of Saratov regularly corresponded with Phil Baldwin in Warsaw, who wrote to W. Parmer Fuller, the former chief of the Polish mission, in San Mateo, California, that the same mistake was being made in Russia as had been made by the Red Cross after the armistice: namely, that "the show is being run too much 'à la militaire.' One would almost think that the Russian show was a second army of occupation."

Long after all the bad feeling had had time to wear off, in 1929, the ARA's alumni newsletter printed, under the heading "Non-Statistical Notes of the A.R.A." an elliptical string of phrases that humorously and, to the uninitiated, cryptically evoked the settings and circumstances of the various missions. Among the several dozen items devoted to the Russian unit was the outburst: "What is this, the U.S. Army?"[5]

The offensive manner of its occupant aside, the office of executive assistant was itself objectionable to the ARA veterans, who resented the presence of a filter between the director and the division and district chiefs and who otherwise chafed under Haskell's centralized administration of the Russian unit. The modus operandi of Hoover relief, beginning with the Belgium mission, was a less ordered arrangement whereby the men in the field were required to follow the general policy set at the top by the Chief, yet, in Brown's words, were given "a relatively free hand as long as they make good."[6] This was the kind of operation Carroll was in the process of establishing in the early period, and it was what Bowden had in mind as he set about organizing the Petrograd district.

Ever since his Belgian days, Bowden had enjoyed considerable latitude in matters of relief. In Russia, though, once Haskell and company arrived in Moscow, he seems to have been intent on further enlarging this independence, initiating a "Petrograd-London" correspondence series, a move that surprised the London office. Perhaps this reflected a simple misunderstanding of the actual chain of command within the Russian unit, but more likely it was a conscious attempt by Bowden to bypass Moscow. Whichever it was, when Haskell complained about it, Brown chose to attribute Bowden's behavior to overenthusiasm—"He has always fought hard for his pet show, whatever it was"—and backed the colonel unequivocally: "We have each time told him that Petrograd is simply a part of the Russian show, and referred him always to you."[7]

On this as on other such occasions Brown made a special effort to make Haskell feel that he enjoyed the solid backing of the chiefs, repeatedly congratulating the colonel on his "tact," "fairness," and "good judgment." But these expressions of support, as well as the encouraging statements he addressed to New York about how well Haskell was "playing the game," masked Brown's growing anxiety about the state of affairs at Spiridonovka 30. On November 9 he shared his concerns with Billy Poland in a letter to 42 Broadway. "The job is certainly 'going', and I believe equally certainly will continue to 'go', but as one newspaper correspondent who knows us well expressed it: 'it looks now more like a Red Cross than an A.R.A. show'"; namely, "with everything carried out on military orders." What was most depressing was that the ARA's old hands like Carroll and Burland had lost their fire.

A wonderfully fine spirit of devotion and service under the inspiration of the Chief has been built up in our crowd over here. Nothing was too much to ask of them, no hours too long, and they gave the job the best they had in them for the love of it and the ideals which it expressed. Something of that has gone, and it's the sort of thing that tends to spread, and undoubtedly is spreading, to other Missions than Russia. Getting it back will be a stiff fight.[8]

Meanwhile, in Moscow, Haskell had become sufficiently disconcerted by the disunity within the ranks to decide to bring the matter to Hoover's attention. He entrusted Goodrich with a lengthy memorandum, dated November 14, reviewing the issues the governor should take up with the Chief upon his return to Washington.[9] Several items had to do with unacceptable behavior and attitudes on the part of the personnel, including the fact that unnamed "subordinates" were expressing their individual views on matters of policy to correspondents outside Russia and disturbing evidence that some of the men were speculating in diamonds and furs.

The centerpiece of this aide-mémoire was a combative defense of the administrative organization of the Russian unit which doubled as an offensive thrust against the ARA's old guard. Some members of the Moscow staff, Haskell informed Hoover, were still under the misapprehension that Russia was no different from Austria, Hungary, Poland, Belgium, "and other highly organized countries of smaller size," where relief missions could be administered by relatively few Americans. "It must be clearly understood that the Russian proposition is entirely different from other operations." Each district within Russia was in itself the size of a large country, and "we are really up against it at the present moment for the proper American supervision of our supplies. The idea of having an organization like Poland or Austria with only a handful of Americans in the country is utter nonsense and such an idea should be busted at once all along the line."

Haskell's memorandum, augmented by whatever personal observations and commentary Goodrich may have contributed verbally, provoked the Chief to issue a thundering edict "To Whom It May Concern." The Russian mission, Hoover declared, required "a definite leadership" and "completely centralized direction," which included authority to regulate the personal correspondence sent out through the ARA courier—a prerogative that seems completely impractical. The original copy of this carte-blanche, together with a cover letter to Haskell empowering him to use it as he saw fit, are in a file folder in the ARA collection at the Hoover Archives. Each page is torn into four equally sized pieces, the word "Destroy" handwritten across the top of the mandate. Somebody in the Washington or New York office must have considered its present state sufficiently destroyed.[10]

In any case, like several other potentially significant communications in the Russian relief story, it went undelivered. Yet it survives as testimony to the fact that Hoover and other top ARA officials like Goodrich had reached the limits of their patience with what appeared to be acts of near-insubordination by members of the Russian mission. Rickard felt that some of the Old ARA men were demonstrating "disloyalty to the Chief and we cannot stand for that." He cited as evidence remarks such as, "The Chief is not the same old Chief."[11]

Rickard had evidently read the contents of letters sent by the men in Russia to colleagues at 42 Broadway. Taken together they would have painted a frightful picture of demoralization and disunity inside the Russian unit. Farmer Murphy wrote to publicity chief Baker in New York on December 12 that "the machine is still creaking badly," which everyone knew, but he then added this Machiavellian twist: "At present there is almost an open break between Lonergan and Haskell and each seems trying to strengthen himself with the other elements in the organization. There will always be this kind of intriguing and 'kitchen cabinets' where a little court is set up and some one tries to play king."[12] No one else in Moscow seems even to have hinted at a power struggle between the two colonels, but whether Murphy's gossip was idle or not, it was another compelling reason for Baker to undertake the visit to Moscow he was planning for the following month.

Brown would get there first, from London. At a moment when the entire show seemed about to fall apart and with the congressional appropriation for Russian relief imminent, he traveled to Riga in the second week of December to meet with Haskell in order to sort out issues of personnel and policy, and to propose a general solution to the ARA's crisis, one he had been considering for some time. By now the situation had become further aggravated as a result of a matter of some delicacy, having to do with loyalties more sacred than army or ARA; namely, the recent visit to Moscow of Mrs. Haskell.

The ARA had laid down the law that no wives of relief workers were allowed to enter Russia, but this did not stop the intrepid Winnifred Haskell from descending on Moscow for a visit with her husband. The concern of the ARA leadership was, first, that this act would arouse resentment among the men and, second, that it would inspire imitators. Arriving now in Riga, Brown's immediate task was to make sure that Mrs. Haskell had made her last such Russian sojourn. He and Haskell wrestled with the problem for an hour, apparently failing to come to a resolution. The beleaguered colonel, who had been pressured into curtailing her visit, announced that he would prefer to fight the ARA for twenty days than his wife for twenty years.

This new round of Riga negotiations brought together Brown, Haskell, Carroll, and, from the Riga mission, Miller, to whom the colonel had never taken a liking, and vice-versa. Afterward Brown felt it had gone well. "It looked like old times to see them arguing out matters of policy in the handling of the work."[13] He then accompanied the men to Moscow, where he contrived to have Haskell recommend that Cyril Quinn be brought on board as a second executive assistant, complementing Lonergan. Quinn's name had been mentioned in such a context from the first moment London learned of the disaffection within the Russian unit. He had wide experience throughout the organization, including as Brown's assistant in the London office and, since July 1921, as chief of the Poland mission. Thus he was well known to most of the men with experience in the European theater of relief, who generally liked and respected him. Quinn was endowed with certain personal qualities that Lonergan lacked, most importantly the ability to manage unlike-minded people. Of crucial significance, Captain Quinn had served under Haskell in the Great War, and the colonel had a high regard for his abilities.

So Quinn was uniquely qualified to bridge the army-ARA divide and rally the Russian unit. As early as October 15 Brown had suggested to Rickard the idea of inserting Quinn into the executive assistant position. "If he could take the place of Lonergan I would be perfectly satisfied that the show would run as we want it to."[14] At the time, it was considered unrealistic to think that Haskell would agree to replace his chief of staff. By December, however, perhaps worn down by the endless intrigue, the colonel was ready for a change of personnel, and Brown's achievement was to present it to him in a way that made it seem like his own idea.

Brown was extremely pleased by Quinn's appointment. Back in London on December 16, he wrote to Rickard that it marked "a big step away from the military organization." Getting rid of Haskell himself was out of the question, but Quinn might be able to raise the quality of the operation to the administration's standards. "Our function is to make the show go as a 100% A.R.A. job, if possible."

As it turned out, Quinn's steady hand was critical to the eventual success of the Russian mission, but that phase of the story could unfold only after Carroll and Lonergan had left the scene, virtually simultaneously, having each been brought down by great acts of self-destruction.

THE LONG FUSE leading from this bomb was lit by one Thomas Dickinson, by means of a letter he addressed to Hoover from Riga on January 7, just after his retirement from the Russian unit. On a single typewritten page Dickinson made some shocking statements about the situation he had left behind in Russia, among them that the ARA mission was in the grip of Eiduk and his plenipotentiaries; that a consequence of American relief was the strengthening of Soviet power; and that the famine in Russia was an "economic," not a "natural" one—meaning that it had been caused by Soviet government policies and implying that these were still in force.

Hoover found the contents of this report disturbing enough to warrant taking an extraordinary step. He instructed Brown to arrange the solicitation of signed statements from members of the Moscow staff—"not alone Haskell's views"—on how matters stood with respect to Russian relief. "If Dr. Dickinson's statements are true, then every assurance we have given the American public is unfounded."[15]

Dickinson had a Ph.D. in English from the University of Wisconsin, was the author of two plays and three books on the theater in America and Britain, and had edited several volumes of plays before, at age forty, placing his writing talents in the service of the U.S. Food Administration in Washington in 1917. From there he went on to work, from 1919 to 1921, in the ARA's Paris and then New York headquarters, where in 1920–21 he authored a five-volume history of the ARA's European operations. This exhaustively detailed study, prepared for publication by Macmillan, reached the galley-proof stage before being withdrawn by the ARA, presumably for political reasons, possibly because of the dust kicked up by Tom Gregory's own publishing feat. Dickinson's new assignment was to write the history of the Russian operation, which explains his appointment to the liaison division in Moscow.

A man capable of turning out such a colossal manuscript was not about to limit himself to a one-page letter on such an explosive topic. Dickinson gave it more elaborate coverage in "A Short Survey of the Russian Unit, A.R.A. Operations in

Russia," a ten-page memorandum that he sent ahead to the New York office from Europe.[16] Its cardinal point was that the Russian mission was being done immeasurable harm by the schism between the Regular Army officers and the Old ARA men, the latter judged to be of higher caliber. Neither side was deliberately trying to sabotage the other, "but the gulf is so deep that it cannot be bridged."

For the first time in a formal ARA document, Haskell was accused of lacking firmness in his dealings with the Soviet government. "The Director of the Russian Unit assumed from the start the burden of proving that the Administration was politically respectable. This has led to the appearance of an excessive caution and has come to give the effect of timidity. I believe it has been a limiting factor upon imagination and the adjustment of the administration to Russian needs." Haskell failed to understand the distinction between "political aggressiveness which was taboo, and aggressiveness in relief." He should have been pursuing a policy of "friendly audacity in helpfulness" but instead was allowing the government to intimidate the ARA.

The Russian government got the drop on the Americans at the beginning. They have kept the Americans with their hands in the air ever since. The policy has been to view everything with suspicion, to grant little, and to be grateful for nothing. By doing so they have kept the Administration always in a position of being the suppliant.... The concealed weapon in the hip pocket of the Russian Unit was withdrawal, the concealed weapon carried by the Soviet government was "summary action" which vaguely suggested "expulsion". Of the two there is no doubt that the former was the better weapon. By getting the jump on the Director at the start, the government showed him to be afraid to use his weapon. Thereafter the Soviet weapon was always half in view and the Soviet attitude became more provocative.

Haskell's watchword, "We cannot quit for Hoover's sake," was appropriate to a defensive posture, while the circumstances called for offensive-mindedness. The Bolos discovered early on that they could afford to be "churlish, niggardly of cooperation and praise, officious, suspicious, high and mighty in attitude.... For they conceive that the Americans are afraid to quit."

Dickinson believed that the Kremlin was so "keenly sensitive to opinion in Europe and America," was so eager "to prove itself respectable," that the ARA had the upper hand. "The withdrawal of the A.R.A. upon an issue related to the welfare of the Russian people if that issue had been clearly made and documented, would have been fatal to the Soviet power. But they would not have permitted this issue to arise. They would not have permitted withdrawal." This analysis exaggerated the Bolsheviks' sense of vulnerability, misread their political priorities, and in any case overlooked their propensity for behaving in ways detrimental to their own interests. Moreover, it failed to take into account the political pressures acting upon the ARA on the American home front. Dickinson, though, was just warming up.

Eiduk and his commissars, he testified, had become "a machine for co-administration." The first mistake had been to allow the chief plenipotentiary to have an office in the same building as the ARA director. Ever since, this Communist creature had been winding his tentacles around the nerve center of the organization. "Everything required by the Administration must come through the Plenipotentiary's office, be it a bookcase, a chair, a box of nails, street car tickets for Moscow personnel, travel orders, orders for inspection tours, and permission to make investigations and take photographs."

Worse still was the situation in the districts, where each supervisor, overextended and overworked, was at the mercy of Eiduk's agents: "a lonely American surrounded by men who know their field perfectly."

The responsibility for this deplorable state of affairs lay with Haskell, whose policies lacked "that largeness of initiative, that liberality of suggestion and counsel, that adaptiveness of resource" necessary to the success of such an enormous undertaking. For some reason Dickinson chose not to mention the accused by name. "The Director is colorless. He does not register in relation to the government and the Russian people. His influence is not felt in his own organization."

At the same time, Lonergan, identified only as "the Chief of the Executive," was said to be "left too much in charge. A hard worker, he is at times violent in temper and intemperate in personal habits." Dickinson's precise meaning here is suggested by a blunt assertion found on the same page: "In the group as a whole (manifest exceptions being understood) there is too much drinking. The Moscow Unit gives the impression of a junket." This is qualified by the observation that "the old A.R.A. group measure up far better in every way than does the military group."

It is unclear if this scandalous exposé was shown to Hoover, but regardless, Dickinson's private letter had gotten his attention, and he wanted some questions answered. Brown relayed to Haskell Hoover's instructions to survey opinion among the Moscow personnel on a number of sensitive topics, and though no explanation was given for this unusual request, the men at Spiridonovka 30 guessed immediately what was behind it. Haskell cabled Brown in reply: "I hope you have not based your worry on any statements made by Doctor Dickinson whose many peculiarities and general attitude while in Russia convinces me he incompetent render unbiased and accurate report situation. He left Russia in threatening attitude."[17]

Haskell was said to feel humiliated and aggrieved that Dickinson was being taken seriously, because he knew it implicitly called his judgment into question. In his defense he marshaled the testimony of a Moscow loyalist who had decided that "no thoroughly healthy man" could have aroused such concerns in the Chief. So they were casting shadows over Dickinson's mental health, which is a time-worn method for discrediting one's enemy, though in this instance the allegation may not have been entirely unfounded. Mowatt Mitchell of the London office was in Moscow several weeks later and heard enough all around to convince him that Dickinson had indeed gone over the edge. From what he told Brown, it would appear that the erstwhile playwright had not entirely abandoned theatrics after all:

Many stories afloat here, by the way, which go to prove that Dickinson was a bit of a paranoiac—had crying fits, sat down on the floor and had hysterics in Haskell's office because he didn't get the treatment he thought himself entitled to, used language to one of the men at Samara which resulted in his being knocked flat on his back, and so on. Don't wonder the people in here are sore at his criticisms—and they spotted the source of the Chief's cable at once.[18]

WHETHER OR NOT Dickinson was daft, Hoover needed reassurance that his assertions were without foundation. Brown decided to respond to the Chief's concerns, cabling him directly on February 5.[19] Yes, he believed, by saving lives American famine relief had the unavoidable effect of stabilizing the Soviet government. As to whether that government had the ARA in its grip, "Tendency to place Administration in hands Russians is apparently true and was perhaps at one time largely true and has almost certainly been aimed at." Still, the Russian unit was now managing to hold its own, and there was no question that "our main jobs childfeeding and food remittances are marching and that we are now putting this job across and will continue to do so."

Brown presumed that the famine was due to "economic causes in the past years coupled with present natural causes." Hoover's query about the origins of the famine was far from purely academic. He evidently understood Dickinson's use of "economic" to mean that the present catastrophe, more than simply having been brought on by past Bolshevik practices, was being perpetuated by continuing policies, such as grain confiscation, even as the ARA was importing food into the country. Brown countered that, on paper at least, the Moscow government's tax on the peasants amounted to only a standardized 10 percent of their output— nowhere near the scale of the War Communist requisitions.

Haskell, in his first telegram to Hoover in October, had stated unequivocally that the famine was primarily the result of the government's exploitation of the peasantry, rejecting as "ridiculous" the suggestion that the drought or military operations were largely to blame. But in a cable of February 15 prompted by Hoover's inquisition, he averred that the famine was due principally to "natural" factors, aggravated by economic ones. On other matters the colonel's tone was defiant. He dismissed the notion that the ARA was under the Bolsheviks' thumb and declared that the Soviet government was "absolutely" adhering to the Riga Agreement.[20] Neither Haskell nor his staff was asked to address the question of whether American relief was serving to bolster Soviet power, because London considered the point too sensitive to transmit to Moscow by telegram.

In order to canvas the American personnel as the Chief required, Haskell distributed a questionnaire to all division chiefs and district supervisors. The London office later expressed doubt as to the value of this poll, feeling that the questions were phrased in a leading way. With respect to the critical issues, most of the respondents agreed with Haskell that the famine was due mostly to natural causes, and most attributed the lack of Soviet government assistance to shortages and chaos, not ill will. Carroll alone refused to go along with the exercise, maintaining that the questions were unfair because "they invite signed comments by subordinates on the work of the director." He used the occasion to put in a good word for the RAKPD, which sounds strangely perverse in view of the fact that every other American in Russia had long before recognized that the committee structure was dangerously inappropriate for Russia.[21]

When Professor Coolidge reached Washington, he had a conversation with Hoover about the Dickinson business. Afterward, on March 9, he wired Haskell to reassure him that the Chief had the highest confidence in him and his work: "inquiry regarding Dickinson statement not made in reflection upon you but in preparation for defense here against a neurotic." This interpretation has some merit. Dickinson was known within the organization as a temperamental sort; he had been resigning from the organization periodically over the previous couple of years. ARA officials appear to have been nervous that he would circulate his observations on the Russian unit and create a public relations disaster.[22]

As it happened, he published a series of prickly but altogether harmless articles in the *New York Herald Tribune*, which had been cleared by the publicity men at 42 Broadway. He left the ARA on March 1, replaced as official historian of the Russian mission by Harold Fisher, whose sturdy volume has nothing to say about the perilous discord within the unit, Dickinson's histrionics, or the scandalous conduct of numerous famine fighters.

Whatever else it served to do, the Dickinson affair for the first time brought front and center the question of whether Haskell was standing up to the Bolsheviks. The fact is, however, that anyone in command of relief operations in Russia would have been constrained by Hoover's—and thus the ARA's—reputation for anti-Bolshevism. From the start the Russian unit was automatically placed on the defensive, burdened with the onus of continually having to demonstrate to the Soviet government, as well as to watchful Americans, that it was playing fair.

The colonel and his supporters defended his restraint as prudent realism. Although some on his staff had repeatedly urged him to go over Eiduk's head to Lenin, Trotsky, Chicherin, or at least Kamenev, he had decided that because the unsavory Lett was capable of causing the ARA great trouble, it made more sense to work through him and to appeal to the higher-ups only on vital matters. Otherwise, in a truly tight spot the director would find himself crying wolf.

One who arrived at some definite opinions about these matters was Mitchell, who was dispatched from London to Moscow in the third week of February in order to assess the situation inside the Russian unit in the wake of the Dickinson blast. By then the first American corn was about to reach the Volga, and it was becoming critically important to close the ranks before the corn campaign got seriously under way. Mitchell, who personally knew all the principals in the mission, sent lengthy reports to Brown during his extended stay in Russia—breezily written, informative accounts of the play of personalities inside Moscow headquarters. These eventually reached an avid, though restricted readership at New York headquarters, whence a few copies were quietly passed on to former ARA men west of the Hudson.

Granted, Mitchell had great material to work with, starting with the peripatetic Mrs. Haskell, who had once again become the object of controversy: she was about to re-enter Russia, and it fell to Mitchell to persuade her husband to forbid her a second visit. The colonel, it appears, would sooner have squared off with the entire Cheka. "I really don't give a damn whether she comes or not—I threw her out once and I wouldn't go to the bat with her again on the subject for the sake of all the principles in the world."

It was Mitchell's first trip to Russia and thus his first look at a Haskell-run ARA show. Very quickly he understood Dickinson's point about the director's ineffectiveness at holding the Bolsheviks at bay, as he explained to Brown on February 23. "Ever since I have been here I have been accumulating the atmosphere of the hindering and hampering effect of this liaison system." Haskell, he felt, was much too willing to take the Soviet word for things and "not enough inclined to exert the constant pressure which is the only way to get accomplishments." He did not seem to understand that "he can get anything of that sort he wants if he will only insist upon it." The ARA way was to push and persist—Dickinson's "aggressiveness in relief"—but this was clearly not the Haskell way.

The longer I am here the better I realise what men like Burland and Gregg and Carroll—men who have always stepped out and demanded and got what they wanted—have had to put up with in the matter of what seemed to them to be inefficiency and lack of punch. Their constant cry is that they can get anything they want and need if they are only allowed to go after it.

Mitchell acknowledged several days later that the Russian unit would not be able to do without some sort of liaison officer of the Eiduk kind; the problem was that Haskell did not keep the chief plenipotentiary in check, a point underscored, Mitchell believed, by the outcome of the most recent dispute between the two men. Perhaps influenced by Mitchell's presence, Haskell decided to go around Eiduk and take his case directly to Kamenev, whom he showed a draft cable addressed to Hoover requesting the Chief's authority to curtail all further relief activity in view of the government's lack of cooperation. According to Mitchell, Kamenev threw a fit, begging Haskell not to transmit his message and promising to grant all of the ARA's outstanding requests, including for better communications links with the Black Sea ports and for another residence for the American personnel in Moscow. The success of this act of coercive diplomacy, which anticipated the decisive showdown of six weeks hence, did not surprise Mitchell at all.

This has been the case every time he has gone to the bat, and my principal criticism of the Colonel is that he has the same fault that so many army people have—instead of insisting on complete and immediate performance always and all the time, even in minute details, and thus insuring that the larger things would be taken care of as a matter of course, he is inclined to let the little things slide and the big ones accumulate until there is a big jam, and then he goes "lust" and starts in swinging in all directions and gets them straightened up again, but with a lot of fuss and a great expenditure of cuss words and energy while a little consistent pressure would keep things moving smoothly. He does not keep as closely in touch with the details of the show as he might, and as a result things can get pretty bad in some department before he knows anything about it, and then he raises a row.

In Mitchell's view the ARA's biggest liability in Russia was not its reputation for anti-Bolshevism but the limited abilities of its director.

MITCHELL HAPPENED TO BE in Moscow when Carroll and Lonergan met their ends, each man's downfall smoothed by demon alcohol. It seems that Lonergan had thrown a big Christmas bash after Haskell had left Russia for the holidays. As Mitchell learned at the scene of the crime that had become known as "the Christmas incident," the hard-drinking executive assistant had been "in a state of coma on several occasions during that historic week."[23]

Dickinson dutifully passed this information on to Hoover, prompting the Chief to address a memo to Haskell, dated February 16, in which he expressed his deep concern over reports of unacceptable behavior exhibited by the personnel, including "an account of heavy drinking bouts on the part of some of our Moscow staff." The thought of the newspapers getting hold of such material "gives me utmost anxiety, as the publication of a story of this kind would smear the whole reputation of American effort in Russia to a degree I cannot possibly describe." It was therefore "practically mandatory" that Lonergan be relieved of his duties and that Quinn should become the sole adjutant.

And one other thing was troubling the Chief: Haskell's staff was dominated by Catholics. "I haven't any prejudice in any religious matters as you know, but if we are going to have peace in the United States we need to have a sprinkling of Protestants on the job somehow."[24] Thus spake the Master of Emergencies.

Hoover entrusted this letter to Goodrich, who was about to head back to Russia. Until the governor arrived in Moscow, Haskell had no idea that Lonergan was a doomed man. In the meantime, the colonel had himself become very much preoccupied by the matter of booze and the Russian unit, though the particular object of his scrutiny was his ARA nemesis, Carroll. One month earlier, on January 16, Haskell had sent a confidential memo to Brown concerning Carroll's placements of orders for large amounts of liquor, which he was importing with the ARA commissary supplies. The shipments were sent to Moscow in Carroll's name; on the receiving end he would fill the orders of and collect payments from ARA colleagues, apparently for only a negligible profit, if any.[25] Haskell's exclusive focus on the Moscow personnel indicates that he was in the dark about the abundant supplies of whiskey and gin regularly being shipped into the districts, also apparently through the good offices of the supply chief.

Haskell could invoke paragraph 27 of the Riga Agreement, which states that the ARA "will import no alcohol in its relief supplies," yet at Riga Litvinov had given informal consent to the import of liquor for the personal consumption of the relief workers. Carroll, who was present, must have developed an instant appreciation for the virtuoso diplomatic skills of the Soviet commissar—later he would argue in his own defense: "Am all ARA but half Irish."[26]

During the autumn, Haskell had ordered a halt to the use of the Moscow commissary for the import of liquor, which he wanted kept off the ARA's books, but in mid-January something or someone tipped the colonel off to the fact that the practice was continuing. He believed this to be, as he told Brown,

a matter so heavily loaded that it would create a tremendous amount of trouble and embarrassment should any critics desire to make adverse capital out of it. You can imagine how we would all feel to read in the New York papers some morning that the limited transportation of Russia was being utilized to carry "booze" to the American Relief officials in Moscow, while the children starve in the Volga valley and while medicines were kept from the dying due to lack of means of transportation.[27]

At that moment, Haskell had just had Carroll in his office and had told him to run his rum any way but through the ARA. It was fine, however, if someone coming from London wished to carry in a bottle for a colleague on the inside, a remark that betrays a shocking ignorance on the part of the director as to the grand consumption of spirits going on throughout the Russian unit. Anyway, the colonel requested that all further orders of liquor from London be canceled, and Brown backed him up completely.

Stories about Carroll's bibulous feats, including a noteworthy performance during "that historic week" at Christmas, leave no doubt that his involvement in the liquor import business was more than a courtesy operation for fellow relief workers. Whether or not it was boozing that had impaired his efficiency on the job, everyone could see he was slipping. Mitchell reported to Brown quite out of the blue that he was sorry to say that Carroll had stumbled badly, so badly in fact that when he went out on leave the following month he would not have a job to return to.[28] The matter-of-fact tone of this statement indicates that Mitchell believed such punishment was deserved, which means that Carroll must really have hit bottom because the two men were best friends.

So Carroll's days with the Russian mission were numbered. It was at about this time, on March 9, that Goodrich arrived in Moscow bearing the letter that sealed Lonergan's fate. Goodrich—not incidentally a notorious bluenose in the estimation of the American personnel—had picked up new information during his stopover in Riga, which he felt an urgent need to convey to Hoover before resuming his journey. It turned out, the indignant governor reported, that Carroll too was implicated in these Christmastime drinking bouts; in fact he drank even more than the unquenchable Lonergan, yet managed to stay on his feet, or at least conscious, as "he seemed to be able to carry a heavier load than some of the others." Haskell still had no idea of what had transpired in his absence over Christmas, Goodrich informed the Chief, and Quinn did not feel that he could bring it to the colonel's attention after his return to Moscow because of the "peculiar hierarchy" at headquarters.

All this and more Goodrich ascertained in Riga, both from the ARA staff there and from relief workers who had recently been in Russia. As for Lonergan, the governor learned that he was guilty also of carrying on an illicit relationship with a Russian woman, maintaining her in an apartment close to his ARA residence. Then there was the case of Saunders of Petrograd, who was frequently drunk and consorted with prostitutes at ARA headquarters. Also, the Chief should know that one of Haskell's army men got drunk at a party given by Eiduk and attempted to do physical harm to Professor Coolidge. As well, he should be aware of the many rumors going about that several relief workers were involved in speculation.

This collection of revelations formed the contents of an official memorandum from Special Investigator Goodrich to Chairman Hoover—this before the governor had even arrived in Gomorrah.[29]

No doubt Goodrich had heard enough to want to press for the excommunication of Carroll as well as Lonergan, but he was spared the trouble, arriving in Moscow six days after the supply chief had reached the end of the road. Haskell, Quinn, and Mitchell had been deliberating how best to demote or remove their wayward colleague when he resolved matters himself by openly criticizing the director's handling of Eiduk in the presence of an army loyalist. This man took it right to Haskell, who "blew up entirely" and fired this insubordinate straightaway. To make it official, the colonel issued Special Memorandum No. 66:

On account of his inability to comprehend the duties and responsibilities of his position on the staff of the Director in Russia and further, for continued incompetency in the conduct of the Supply Division, notwithstanding repeated reductions in the scope of its work, Mr. Philip H. Carroll is relieved from further duty with the American Relief Administration in Russia and will proceed by the first available transportation to London.[30]

While everyone had come to recognize by that point that Carroll had to go, the notably censorious manner of his termination left the ARA chiefs stunned. Mitchell wrote Brown that the wording of Haskell's order was unacceptable and should not be allowed to ruin Carroll's otherwise estimable record of service with the ARA. In a letter to Baker in New York, Brown affirmed that Carroll's release was justified,

But, Oh, Lord! it could have been done so differently considering the past service and loyalty of the man and the extraordinary conditions of the start-out of the job on which we have talked "ad nauseam." It looks like a case of two incompatible spirits which could not get together considering this background; but it could have been handled in so much more a generous and broadminded way.

Rickard called Haskell's special memorandum a "cruel order," one that would make it difficult for the ARA to employ Carroll elsewhere in the organization: "it is beyond my comprehension as to his state of mind when putting out a more or less public document of this kind."[31]

Next it was Lonergan's turn. Once Goodrich had produced the Chief's censorious letter, Haskell had no choice but to dismiss his intemperate executive. When the news was broken to him, on March 12, Lonergan took it hard, especially in view of the fact that it was caused by something that had happened two-and-a-half months earlier and whose details he could probably only vaguely recall. Mitchell's assessment was that Lonergan "has been accustomed to getting drunk, periodically, all his life, and the fault is Haskell's in having brought him in and left him in charge, more than it is his, in merely acting naturally."[32]

Haskell's housecleaning, which placed the versatile Quinn in a position of considerable authority, would go a long way toward bridging the army-ARA gap within the Russian unit. And even though it did not succeed in driving the spirit of Bacchus from the mission, it at least allowed Hoover the comfort of this illusion. The Chief's anxiety that the personal behavior of his relief workers in Russia might cause him great trouble in the United States was well founded. The American scene was in fact fertile soil for a scandal about the ARA.

CHAPTER 7

HOME FRONT

As concern mounted among ARA officials on both sides of the Atlantic over the worrisome dissension within the Russian unit, Brown wrote to Billy Poland in the New York office: "The Chief has put in Haskell, who is well-known in America, a great deal of publicity has been built up around him, and on no account can we allow any friction to develop or any action which could possibly cause comment or scandal on the A.R.A. in America."[1]

Poland did not need to be told any of this. From his vantage point at 42 Broadway, he understood full well that adverse publicity about the conduct of American relief workers in Moscow might easily escalate into a public relations nightmare for the ARA at home. Hoover and his relief missions had weathered a fair amount of public criticism in the past, but this operation was unlike any other because it engaged the twin lightning rods of Russia and Bolshevism.

In the course of the final two decades of the nineteenth century, after more than a century of cordial, if distant, Russian-American relations, Americans began to develop a particular aversion to the tsarist government as they became acquainted with manifestations of its authoritarian character. The evidence arrived on American shores in the form of tens of thousands of Russian Jews, who had fled their homeland to escape pogroms in the wake of the assassination of Tsar Alexander II in 1881. Official relations deteriorated accordingly, to the point where in 1911 the U.S. Congress unilaterally abrogated its commercial treaty with Russia dating back to 1832.[2]

Those Americans who gave any thought to such matters placed the blame on Russia's despotic political system, not on the suffering masses who endured it. This perception of the Russian condition was perhaps most famously articulated shortly after the fall of the Romanovs in March 1917, when President Wilson made his ill-advised remarks about how the democratic "natural instinct" of the Russian people was about to reveal itself now that the alien autocracy had been "shaken off"; how the new Russia would be a "fit partner for a league of honour" in the war to "make the world safe for democracy." Such expectations, however widely they may have been shared by the American public, were cruelly and utterly disappointed, as political authority in Russia disintegrated, the Eastern Front collapsed, and the Bolsheviks took power, signing a separate peace with Germany.

It was not long before Bolshevism became the Unspeakable Thing to Americans, who were shocked by sensationalistic newspaper stories about the nationalization of women and the mass production of children out of wedlock, as well as by blood-curdling tales of the Red Terror and of the barbarities of the Civil War. That was all happening over there, but it soon developed that Americans believed they were faced with the specter of Russian Bolshevism in their own cities and towns. The fear this incited and the overwrought government actions it provoked have come down to us as the Red Scare of 1919–20.[3]

Its prologue was the growing industrial unrest of the winter of 1918–19, whose high-water mark was the Seattle general strike in the first week of February. Then came a month-long set of public hearings conducted in February–March by a U.S. Senate judiciary subcommittee investigating "Bolshevik propaganda," which in 1,200 pages of published testimony and other evidence documents the state of mind of official Washington as it struggled to make sense of the Red Menace. "Bolshevist," "anarchist," "radical," "socialist," "communist," "red"—the labels were applied promiscuously by the five uncomprehending senators and by most of their two dozen witnesses, some of them not long out of Red Russia, who testified about the nature of the Bolshevik beast and the threat it posed to "civilization" in America. Senators wondered, Could it happen here?[4]

The scare as such began with the discovery of the so-called May Day bombs, thirty-six in all, sent by mail from a single source to a variety of serving and former government officials. Only two got through: one was delivered to the office of the mayor of Seattle, the other, the only device to go off, arrived at the home of a former senator in Atlanta, where it was opened by the maid, who lost both hands in the explosion. Thirty-four more package bombs were subsequently recovered from local post offices.

May Day itself was unusually active, as mass meetings, rallies, and parades led to rioting when marchers raising the red flag provoked antiradical violence. June 2 was especially eventful. In the late evening hours, anarchists set off explosions at public buildings and the private homes of federal judges, businessmen, and politicians—most spectacularly, the Washington, D.C., residence of Attorney General A. Mitchell Palmer, leader of the anti-Red crusade. Thus provoked, the attorney general launched the so-called "Palmer raids" against suspected radicals. In New York the state legislature established the Lusk committee, which conducted its own antiradical investigations and staged a sensational series of raids, most notably of the Soviet Bureau in New York City.

In December, 249 of the most notorious radicals nabbed in these operations, including the "Red Queen," Emma Goldman, were escorted down to New York harbor and loaded on an army transport ship, dubbed the "Soviet Ark," which sailed to Hango, Finland, from where the exiles could make their way to the homeland of Bolshevism. Thus were the most American of civil liberties given a roughing up in the name of "100 Per Cent Americanism."

Robert K. Murray's 1955 history of the Red Scare takes as its subtitle "A Study in National Hysteria, 1919–1920," which seems to have been inspired by the anti-Communist delirium gripping the country as he wrote his book. For, as Murray understood, by comparison with the events associated with a certain senator from Wisconsin, the earlier episode was of minor significance. There simply was not much scare in the Red Scare; nor, as Murray demonstrates, was there much substance to the red specter in 1919.

One strand of continuity stands out. In 1919 Palmer appointed J. Edgar Hoover to head the new General Intelligence Division of the Justice Department's Bureau of Investigation. Murray tells us that the Red Scare "made" the bureau, starting it on its evolution toward the modern-era FBI. The investigatorial Hoover, whose task was to gather information on the activities of radicals in America, would still be in place in the 1950s to feed the fantasies of Senator McCarthy, as he had those of Attorney General Palmer.

As for the other Hoover, who led the crusade against the spread of Bolshevism in foreign lands, he did not even make the index in Murray's book. The chairman of the ARA looked upon the entire affair as disconcertingly un-American. His judgment can be seen to have been summed up by Fisher, who wrote that the excitement stirred up by the Red Scare was "as grotesque as the terror of an elephant at the sight of a mouse. . . . "

BY 1921 POPULAR American attitudes toward the Russians had evolved to the point where Wilson's promotion of them as instinctively democratic would have been a hard sell. Fisher observes that "Russian and Bolshevik were terms that were rapidly acquiring the same connotation" in the American mind. The Bolshevik regime having held on to power for four years, long enough to invite comparison with its undemocratic tsarist predecessor, some Americans appear to have arrived at the conclusion that the Russian people had, after all, been getting the kind of government they wanted and therefore deserved. Fisher tells us that "Russian atrocities were now as dear to the sensationalists of press and platform as German atrocities had been a few years before."[5]

This blurring of the line between Russia's rulers and ruled helps explain the opposition toward famine relief evinced by a vocal minority of Americans, who wondered why their country should provide, in a phrase of the day, "soup to nuts."[6] Others, perhaps persuaded of a vital distinction between the regime and the people, worried that American relief to Russia, though it would give sustenance to innocent children, would at the same time serve to legitimize, bolster, or even bail out, the morally, politically, and economically bankrupt Soviet government.

Some of these concerned Americans addressed themselves on the subject directly to Hoover, among them a Boston businessman named James Mcnaughton, who believed that the United States ought to let the Bolsheviks know that "we will intervene with military authority, unless they conduct themselves like the balance of the civilized world." Hoover's rejoinder was one he would feel compelled to state repeatedly during the first year of the mission: "We must make some distinction between the Russian people and the group who have seized the Government."

W. Hume Logan, president of The Dow Co., complained to Hoover in May 1922 from his Louisville headquarters that there was no reason for America to be sending millions of dollars worth of food to Russia when that country was "inviting unmarried women to become mothers" and kept a large standing army. "It seems to me that in helping Russia, that we are strengthening a dangerous enemy." Hoover instructed gently: "I think you will need to separate in your mind the 200,000 Communists in Russia from the 150,000,000 of Russian people." Such alarums would be warranted, he argued, were the ARA's goal to restore the

Russian economy or to stabilize the political situation to the benefit of the Bolsheviks, whereas in fact its sole objective was famine relief.[7]

In fact, by that point in time—three months after Dickinson's warning that American relief was strengthening the Soviet government—Hoover must have begun to entertain his own doubts, though he seems still to have believed, as perhaps most Americans did with him, that feeding the Russians would eventually serve to weaken their attraction to and, better yet, their tolerance of Bolshevism. Time would tell. In any case, unlike Mr. Logan, few Americans were worried that the nation's most accomplished anti-Bolshevik was playing into the hands of the Reds in the Kremlin. Hoover was immune to such suspicion in the same way that half a century later Richard Nixon's unimpeachable anti-Communist credentials uniquely qualified him to make a historic presidential visit to Red China.

A few detractors questioned the sincerity of Hoover's humanitarianism. The most vociferous of these was the crotchety Senator Thomas E. Watson, Democrat of Georgia, *bête noire* of Hoover and the ARA, which he routinely denounced as an organization of "professional charity brokers" that was once again bamboozling the U.S. Congress and the American people.[8]

The man responsible for parrying the blows of the likes of Senator Watson was Baker, as head of the ARA's publicity department in New York. After several years of experience in the contentious business of famine relief, the ARA had become well practiced in the performance of public relations. A continuous stream of press releases generated in Moscow and New York drummed the message into the American people that their relief workers were right on the job, distributing life-saving food to many thousands of starving Russian children with quintessential American efficiency. Local newspapers, meanwhile, were accommodated with uplifting feature material on the contributions of their particular boys at the famine front.

Managing publicity naturally entailed keeping certain kinds of stories out of the papers. Nothing should be allowed to stir up the American pot. Once the corn drive got under way, a guiding principle was to play down famine horror stories and promote the coverage of the rescue operation. Toward that and other ends, Baker's Moscow staff was careful to cultivate the foreign correspondents. One of the fruits of this was an arrangement whereby the reporters agreed not to publicize the ARA's troubled relations with the Soviet authorities, stories about which might turn opinion at home against the mission and thus, the rationale went, jeopardize the lives of millions of children.

Earning the cooperation of the Moscow correspondents was greatly facilitated by ARA largesse. Haskell allowed at least the Americans among them to make use of the ARA's usually secure courier pouch to file stories to their European or home bureaus, enabling them to circumvent the Soviet censor. Additional leverage was won by offering access to the American commissary, where highly prized items like food, cigarettes, and—off the books—liquor could be purchased, and by extending invitations to ARA-sponsored social events spanning the cultural gamut from private performances of Bolshoi ballerinas to Lonergan's Christmas blowout. Thus, spreading the word about the extracurricular activities of relief workers in Russia would run counter to an American correspondent's self-interest—indeed, might well be self-incriminating.

Back in the United States, free and welcome publicity was generated by the Russian émigré artistic community, mostly in New York, where the partially reconstituted Chauve Souris performed, Chaliapin sang, and Pavlova danced at benefits for the ARA. Such events contributed more in the way of favorable press notices than in the modest number of dollars they raised.

The regularity of Senator Watson's broadsides notwithstanding, the ARA's New York office spent far more time contending with the politically colored allegations and insinuations of the liberal and especially the radical press. Many of Hoover's liberal critics, like those at the *New Republic*, believed that food relief to Russia was the way to nurture the forces of political moderation in that country. Hoover, of course, saw it the same way, though with the fundamental difference that he envisioned these forces emerging from outside the Bolshevik regime, which made liberals suspicious that the ARA had a concrete political agenda in Russia.

Hoover's radical critics, on the other hand, had no doubt that his principal motives in Russia were political, for which his humanitarianism served principally as a cover. This was considered cause for alarm in radical circles at the time of the Riga negotiations when Bolshevik power was thought to be precarious. If the Bolsheviks were indeed slipping, Hoover could be expected to position himself to give them a shove, and this he seemed to be doing, first by laying down conditions for the start of the Riga talks and then by negotiating an elaborate and legalistic agreement that won his organization extraterritorial rights inside Russia—behavior that came in for loud criticism from the left. Once the mission got under way, though, and the essential stability of the Soviet regime was no longer in doubt, it is difficult to understand what radical opinion thought Hoover might actually do to undermine the Bolsheviks, beyond spreading hostile propaganda among the ARA's beneficiaries. Since the appearance of the Gregory articles, anything must have seemed possible, and it did no harm to keep ringing the tocsin.

Some of the harshest criticism appeared in the *Nation*, whose editorials portrayed the ARA, not without cause, as an association of Bolshevik-killers. In a letter to editor Oswald Garrison Villard of August 17, 1921, Hoover embraced the charge of anti-Bolshevism:

I am glad to say that my understanding is that the whole of American policies during the liquidation of the armistice was to contribute everything it could to prevent Europe from going Bolshevik or being overrun by their armies. I believe this contribution was one of the greatest services that Americans accomplished to the world as witnessed by the comparative situation in Europe with that of Russia to-day.

As for the impending expedition to Russia, the purpose was "to save the lives of a few children from Bolshevism," not to interfere with the political system.

In the same vein, on September 5 Hoover wrote to Herbert Croly, editor of the *New Republic*, defending his Riga preconditions as being entirely consistent with past administration practice and certainly essential in view of the fact that the country in question was one in which "an unlimited terrorist communism is in control." As for the Gregory affair, Hoover denied responsibility for the downfall of Bela Kun and his Soviet regime but openly expressed his satisfaction with that outcome.

So far as Russia's politics are concerned you know that I am one who has maintained from the beginning that Bolshevism is a Russian fever that must burn itself out in Russia and that I have constantly opposed any pressure upon it. I have insisted on this, not only because such pressure lost many human lives but also because I have no doubt that sooner or later this spectacle will bankrupt the socialist idea despite all its apologists.[9]

This is almost right. The record shows that even Hoover succumbed for a while to the temptation to try to influence the course of events inside Russia, both by supplying food to and by lobbying Washington to provide munitions to the White armies. Nor should Hoover be credited with exceptional powers of prognostication for his firm prediction that Soviet socialism would discredit itself "sooner or later": seventy years was a full two generations later than Hoover actually had in mind.

The amount of time Hoover spent addressing his critics is extraordinary when one considers that as secretary of commerce and chairman of the ARA he was a very busy man, indeed. It is all the more remarkable when one discovers that so much of his energy was expended joining battle with insubstantial figures, men at the head of radical relief organizations that gained attention, if not financial contributions, principally by maligning the ARA.

Among these peculiar individuals was Paxton Hibben, secretary of the Russian Red Cross, whom Hoover and company regularly accused of furnishing anti-ARA ammunition to American radicals. Further to the left was D. H. Dubrowsky, who had replaced the unofficial Soviet representative to Washington, Ludwig Martens, after his deportation in January 1921. Dubrowsky organized the Friends of Soviet Russia, which established a network of collecting agencies for Russian relief targeted at American labor. Part of its take was used to support a propagandistic periodical called *Soviet Russia*. Its letterhead made plain where its loyalties lay: "Our principle: We make the working-class appeal. Give not only to feed the starving but to save the Russian workers' revolution. Give without imposing imperialist and reactionary conditions as do Hoover and others."[10]

Also out on the pro-Bolshevik fringe was Walter Liggett, who together with Dubrowsky organized the American Committee for Russian Famine Relief, a thinly veiled Soviet organization. This committee assembled a very respectable advisory board, which included ten senators, eight congressmen, thirteen governors, two ex-governors, one cardinal, and twenty-three bishops. Unaware when they signed on to the project that it was intended as much to rally the prorecognition and anti-Hoover cause as to save famine victims, many of these well-meaning personages were said to be surprised and embarrassed upon learning the truth—which revelation effectively put an end to Liggett's committee.

The ponderous correspondence between Hoover and Liggett is quoted extensively in Fisher's history, whose detailed attention to such marginal characters and the aggravations they caused the Chief is nothing if not obsessive.[11] From this distance it all seems beneath the dignity of the man who had organized the great enterprise then underway in Russia. One is reminded of Fisher's own admonition about an elephant and a mouse. Much is explained by the salience of personal attacks on Hoover, who was endowed with a rather thin skin. Privately, as in February 1922, he complained bitterly about the cost to him of his

Russian project: "From a personal point of view I have every reason to regret that I ever touched a situation that is so pregnant with mud and personal vilification from all sides as this appears to be."[12] That may have been how things looked from the inside on a bad day, but the big picture told quite a different story altogether. To judge from the reporting and the editorial coverage in the mainstream press, by far most Americans enthusiastically supported the ARA's work in Russia, which they regarded as emphatic confirmation of their self-image as the philanthropic nation.

In the end, the definitive judgment regarding Hoover's fixation on his radical critics came from Bessie Beatty, a.k.a. Lizzy Bach, the onetime radical journalist from Seattle and witness to the Russian Revolution, who was living in Petrograd when Bowden arrived and drafted her to run the first ARA kitchen opened in Russia. In May 1922 she returned to the United States, stopping at 42 Broadway where she gave Baker an earful on this subject, which went, he recounts, "something like this":

I wish I knew the A.R.A. personnel in New York City and Washington intimately enough to act like a mother to them. What I would do first would be to spank Mr. Hoover. He is at the head of the greatest thing in the world, and his organization is doing the finest thing in the world, and, therefore, ought never to be worried about any of the pinpricks, such as Hibben, Dubrowsky, Liggett, etc., etc. Therefore, when I find you all taking these things to heart, I feel that you are just a little tired, quite a little sensitive, and in need of just what I suggested.[13]

MUCH MORE INTERESTING and illuminating than these epistolary engagements was Hoover's ongoing quarrel behind the scenes with the American Quakers, a subject to which Fisher's book could only allude, such was its delicacy in that day.

The American Friends Service Committee (AFSC), in conjunction with Quaker organizations of other countries, notably Britain, had been performing relief work in Russia on a minor scale since 1916, with a break of fifteen months in 1919–20. Over that period Quaker relief was distributed almost exclusively through the existing institutions of the Soviet government.

The ARA had been working in association with the AFSC in Europe since 1919, and Hoover was responsible for channeling millions of dollars into Quaker operations under the general flag of American relief. In January 1921 he offered to contribute $100,000 toward Russian food relief to be administered through the Friends, if the Soviet government would agree to release all of its dozen or so American prisoners. Nothing came of this proposal, but Hoover complained at the time to the AFSC that it was not being forceful enough with the Moscow authorities by insisting on the right to feed the imprisoned Americans. The Friends' defense was that while they were not in principle against assuming such a responsibility, in view of the fact that apparently not all of the prisoners were innocent of the charges brought against them, a strong demonstration of interest in their fate on the part of the AFSC might leave the organization open to the charge of meddling in Soviet politics.[14]

The Friends were wary of Hoover in the way that a mouse might be of an elephant. They recognized that conducting operations in the vicinity of the ARA—

let alone entering into a joint endeavor with it—would mean virtually complete obscurity in its shadow. So great was this concern that when it became apparent in August 1921 that the ARA was going into Russia, the AFSC considered not mounting any operation at all. This option must have seemed even more attractive when Hoover insisted that the Friends completely sever their connection to the British Quakers inside Russia—this in order to comply with Hoover's "united front" principle, sanctioned by President Harding, which required that for the sake of security and efficiency and in the name of patriotism, all American relief be administered through the ARA under the auspices of its Riga Agreement.

The Friends complied reluctantly. Like all the ARA's "affiliated organizations," the AFSC was not permitted to enter into direct contact with the Soviet authorities; however, like only the Jewish Joint Distribution Committee, it was allowed to maintain its identity in Russia as a distinct unit, operating in a specially designated region of the Volga valley where it could employ its own relief methods so long as these conformed to the principles agreed to at Riga.

Another source of the Friends' reluctance to be tied to Hoover was the expectation that it would cost them the financial support of liberal and radical groups that might otherwise wish to contribute funds to the AFSC by virtue of its independence from the ARA. The attraction of a distinct AFSC mission, it was believed, would have been unusually strong among liberals, some of whom had soured on the ARA after the "revelations" of the Gregory articles. A September 1921 circular letter distributed within the organization lamented that because of its involuntary ARA connection, the AFSC's fund-raising prospects would be much diminished since "Practically all of the Soviet sympathizers are opposed to Mr. Hoover."

A special strength of the Friends was their success at conducting public appeals for funds, yet once the ARA entered the Russian relief picture no such appeals were possible as long as Americans anticipated that Hoover would organize a national drive of his own—something widely expected in August 1921. When, however, several weeks into the mission Hoover declared that in light of economic difficulties at home and the past generosity of Americans, the ARA would undertake no such appeal but that other relief organizations were welcome to do so, the announcement effectively precluded such a possibility. Then, in December, came the $20 million congressional appropriation for Russian relief, whose magnitude seemed to rule out prospective donations from individuals and most organizations. This did not put to rest the matter of an appeal, however, and it would stir up controversy between Hoover and the AFSC staff in Philadelphia several times into the spring of 1923.

These differences alone were enough to place a strain on ARA-AFSC relations, but matters were further complicated by Hoover's objection to the "pink" political company kept by the AFSC. His own Quaker upbringing made Hoover particularly sensitive on this point. "If there is anything in which I have implicit confidence, it is the right-mindedness of the people with whom I have been born and raised," he wrote on September 21, 1921, to Friends chairman Rufus Jones, protesting the AFSC's basic wrongheadedness on Russia.

Hoover was incensed when editorials in liberal-to-left-wing publications cast aspersions on the integrity of the ARA in a manner that compared it unfavorably to the AFSC. He complained to Jones that the Friends not only ran with a radical crowd but failed to issue denials when the "red-minded" papers slandered him by charging that he was behaving imperially toward the AFSC. "[T]he propaganda in the New Republic and in the Red Press is enough to cause some anxiety lest through such intrigues conflict would be created between American organizations and do infinite harm to the whole cause of saving life in Russia." Jones stood his ground: "I have no affiliation with or leaning toward reds or pinks." But as this was demonstrably not the case, the unpleasantness was bound to continue. In February 1922, when Hoover was once again under fire from the AFSC and its supporters on the Left for his refusal to back a public appeal for Russian relief, he wrote to Jones: "I cannot conceive a greater negation of all that the Quakers stand for than a regime that carries on its banners, 'Religion is the opiate of the people.'"[15]

Nor was this the extent of the discord. Hoover's disdain for the AFSC's relief methods was always threatening to become an issue. The Friends' unit was stationed at Sorochenskoe, one of the hardest-hit regions in the famine zone, where fewer than a dozen Quakers were responsible for a district about the size of the state of Indiana. Though women were not allowed to serve in the Russian unit, Hoover could not very well have insisted that the Friends leave behind their integral corps of experienced female relief workers. Their presence on the Volga had the effect of accentuating the AFSC's image as a practitioner of a more traditional, "softer" brand of relief, as opposed to the impersonal, business-like version of the ARA.

The Friends in Russia were not subject to the directives of ARA headquarters in Moscow, but that did not prevent Hoover from offering advice to their superiors in Philadelphia. On November 1 he informed Jones that, judging from early reports out of Russia, the Friends' operation amounted to "house to house relief"; he suggested that they avoid spreading out their contribution and focus on saving a specific number of people. "Otherwise it is a question of giving a man his breakfast and letting him die before dinner." Far better to feed ten thousand people until they were back on their feet than to feed one million people for a week and watch them die.[16]

Hoover must have tired of the struggle. In February 1922 he directed Haskell to prompt the AFSC's chief in Moscow to suggest to Philadelphia a separation from the ARA and an amalgamation with the British Quakers operating in nearby Buzuluk. This was the start of divorce proceedings. The realignment took effect only on September 1, as the second year of the mission began.[17]

So much for the discord between Washington and Philadelphia. One will search in vain for evidence of parallel strife at the scene of the famine. In fact, while contact between the Friends and the ARA men in Samara province was infrequent, relations were genial. Perhaps the most noteworthy fact to be reported is that relief workers from other districts passing through Samara expressed a desire to get a glimpse of those Quaker girls—who it was said wore pants. After their separation from the ARA, the Friends on the Volga chafed under their new arrangement, complaining to Philadelphia of an incompatibility between American and British relief methods, citing the "inefficiency" of the British Quakers and a "difference in the temperament of the two units," and calling the ARA-AFSC split a mistake.[18] The Quaker from West Branch would have savored the irony in this.

THE REASONS for Hoover's resistance to the idea of a public appeal for Russian relief changed over time, but in 1921 the paramount consideration in his mind was the health of the American economy, which was one year along into a business depression. Fisher summarizes the problem succinctly: "America had expanded production to meet the needs of Europe during the war. The end of hostilities and subsequent collapse of the European market demonstrated with painful emphasis that a quart would not go in a pint measure."[19] Bankruptcies multiplied and unemployment rose to five million in September 1921. Agricultural prices dropped steeply or collapsed, a development for which Hoover as food administrator was partly responsible as he had encouraged the increased production that had created the large surpluses for which there was now no market outlet.

So it is unsurprising that Hoover the secretary of commerce was disinclined to take the lead in organizing a public appeal for Russian relief. It was a moment, moreover, after three years of American beneficence abroad, when one began to hear it said that "charity begins at home"—a sentiment expressed in letters to the chairman of the ARA at the time of the Riga negotiations.[20] The collection taken for the European Relief Council, under Hoover's chairmanship, had brought in by February 1921 nearly $30 million. There was reason to believe that another such appeal would fail, that Americans had come to feel that they had done their duty. And, after all, this was about Russia, a subject that did not arouse the most charitable impulses in all Americans. Besides, even had the success of a national drive been guaranteed, there would still have been a problem of time: the collection for European relief took over three months to complete; the Russian emergency, once confirmed by ARA investigations in October 1921, required more urgent action.[21]

The only alternative to undertaking a national appeal was to seek an appropriation of funds from Congress, a course of action Hoover seems to have had in mind even before the mission got under way. His enlistment of Governor Goodrich as special investigator is strong indirect evidence of this. The selection of Haskell may also have been partly influenced by this prospect, and not only because of his reputation as an outstanding soldier of war and peace. During the hearings on relief to Russia, Baker indicated that Haskell's name was a big help in winning support in Congress because of his "immense following" in the National Guard and his "great influence with the high class and powerful Roman Catholics," who previously had been "indifferent to our work, or positively antagonistic."[22]

Hoover's intention was to get Congress to release the funds remaining in the coffers of the U.S. Grain Corporation, totaling some $20 million, which would be used to purchase food from American farmers for Russian relief as part of an expanded ARA program that would encompass adult feeding. Thus, not only would starving Russians be fed, but American farmers would be partly relieved of their unmarketable crops. This, it was thought, would stimulate purchases by other, especially foreign, buyers, thereby raising farm values. That, in turn, would encourage farmers to increase purchases of manufactured goods, giving a boost to industry and helping to ease unemployment.

Hoover's case, which he now presented to the U.S. Congress and public, thus laid a sturdy foundation of self-interest beneath a lofty appeal to American altruism. Fisher employed a dichotomous set of images commonly invoked at the time to demonstrate the reciprocal nature of the enterprise: "The Government appropriation would thus indirectly put an end to the tragic anomaly of the farmers of one part of the world using food grains for fuel, while the farmers of another part of the world were starving. And 'charity,' both abroad and at home, would be served."[23] And the chairman of the ARA and the secretary of commerce would each be able to have his way.

The political wheels began turning at the end of October, but the first formal and public step was made on December 6 when the president, in a move orchestrated by Hoover, requested that Congress appropriate an amount of money sufficient to supply the ARA with ten million bushels of corn and one million bushels of seed for Russian relief. Hoover expected resistance from Congress, though given the economic soundness of the proposition, and in light of the relatively uneventful passage of the bill, his pessimism appears to have been unwarranted. He was especially concerned about the debate in the House of Representatives, where he had been hoping to get a hearing before the Ways and Means Committee but learned instead that he would have to face the reputedly less sympathetic members of the Foreign Affairs Committee. Goodrich, on the other hand, arriving back from Russia to provide the legislators on Capitol Hill with credible eyewitness testimony about the famine, was a study in optimism. Congressional opposition, he felt confident, would be negligible.[24]

Perhaps someone had spooked Hoover by informing him of the outcome of an earlier such congressional episode back in the time of the Russian famine of 1891–92. President Benjamin Harrison had urged passage of a joint resolution, introduced in Congress on January 5, 1892, to authorize the U.S. Navy to transport to Russia relief supplies already collected privately—and eventually amounting to over $700,000—which the railroads had agreed to deliver without charge to the eastern seaboard. The Senate passed the resolution, attaching an amendment limiting the appropriation to $100,000, at which point the House talked the proposal to death, using the occasion to condemn the authoritarian ways of the tsarist government, notably its persecution of Jews.[25]

There were some obvious parallels with the situation in 1921. The Soviet government, like its tsarist predecessor, could be blamed for policies that had caused the famine, for failing to take measures to combat it early enough, and for stifling nongovernment relief initiatives at home. But the contrasts were more conspicuous, and they worked in favor of Hoover's undertaking. Unlike in 1892, there was in 1921 the compelling argument of U.S. economic self-interest; there was also a proud three-year record of American philanthropy in Europe on which to build; and, not least, there was Hoover himself, the face of that philanthropy and, behind the scenes, its consummate political impresario.

Two days after Harding's letter to Congress, and by earlier arrangement, Haskell sent Hoover a telegram, promptly released to the public, depicting the Russian emergency in dire terms: somewhere between five and seven million people, over half of them children, must die unless they receive outside assistance. "As a Christian nation we must make greater effort to prevent this tragedy. Can you not ask those who have already assisted this organization to carry over eight million children through famine in other parts of Europe to again respond to the utmost of their ability?"[26]

On December 10 a bill "for the relief of the suffering people of Russia through the American Relief Administration" was introduced in the House and referred to the Foreign Affairs Committee, where hearings were held on December 13 and 14.[27] Hoover appeared before the committee, as did Goodrich and Kellogg, both of whose special investigations in Russia now paid off handsomely. The original bill called for an appropriation of $10 million, but Goodrich told the panel that this would not be enough and urged that the intended purchase of ten million bushels of corn and one million of seed be doubled, boosting the appropriation to $20 million. In his own testimony, Hoover estimated that twenty to twenty-two million bushels would be the maximum feasible program because Russia's transport would be unable to carry more. He suggested that the funds be used to purchase, in addition to corn and seed, canned milk for Russian children. Harding gave his approval to these amendments and the Foreign Affairs Committee reported the bill favorably to the House on December 14.

The debate on the floor of the House took place three days later. Among the bill's critics, most thought it was a bad idea to be spending money on foreign relief at a time when Americans themselves were in need; some contended that using taxpayers' money for the benefit of non-Americans was unconstitutional, an argument heard in 1892; still others expressed the fear that the relief would serve to sustain, or at least sanction, the Bolshevik regime. By the end of the day, three minor amendments had been attached to the bill, and it passed the House by a margin of 181–71, with 175 abstaining—the vote heavily divided along partisan lines, with Republicans in favor.

The Senate debated the measure on December 20.[28] Here too its constitutionality was questioned; senators added amendments to provide funds for World War I veterans and the unemployed; and Senator Watson made familiar noises about ARA "charity" serving as a mask for business. Yet the bill passed without a roll call. In the House-Senate conference the Senate's amendments were dropped, and the bill was reported back to the Senate where it was approved in this form on December 22. Harding signed it on the same day and two days later issued an executive order stipulating how the $20 million appropriation was to be disbursed.

An executive order prepared by Hoover and signed by Harding on December 24 created a Purchasing Commission for Russian Relief—whose five members included Hoover, Rickard, Goodrich, and ARA comptroller Edward Flesh—charged with overseeing the purchase, transport, and delivery to Russia of all commodities procured through the appropriation, with the U.S. Grain Corporation acting as the fiscal agency of the commission. The ARA was designated as the sole agency authorized to distribute within Russia those commodities purchased for it by the commission. Shortly after these arrangements were put in place, Brown and the Soviet diplomat and trade representative Leonid Krassin signed a document in London extending the Riga Agreement to cover this expanded relief program.

There remained one final transaction involving the Congress. Earlier in the autumn, Hoover had begun to take steps to win the release from the War Department of a large surplus of medical and hospital supplies for use by the ARA. The Senate passed a bill to this effect on December 6, but the initiative was put on hold when on that same day Harding sent his message to Congress requesting the much larger appropriation. The decks having been cleared, on January 17 Congress approved legislation allowing the War Department and any other appropriate government agencies to donate up to $4 million in medical surpluses to the ARA.[29]

THUS WERE THE RESOURCES assembled for the massive corn campaign that was to be the centerpiece of the ARA's Russian mission. The choice of corn was not uncontroversial. From the start corn had been included in the ARA's child-feeding program, in the form of grits. A helpful executive of the Aunt Jemima Mills Company wrote to Hoover in August 1921 to suggest that the corn be packaged and recipes provided. This, like some other alimentary advice from concerned citizens, was perhaps not entirely disinterested. Someone from the Quitman Packing Company suggested that the ARA use canned sweet potatoes for Russian relief. A prominent Montana rancher informed Hoover that there was a million head of horses running the range in his own and nearby states, "fat as butter"; he proposed that these wild beasts be canned and shipped to the Volga.

The Aunt Jemima representative said he had come forward out of concern that the Russians, being unfamiliar with corn, would not know how to prepare it, with the result that much would go wasted. Recommendations as to how the starving Russians on the Volga could make the most of America's gift came in from unlikely sources. The president of the Phelps Publishing Co. of Springfield, Missouri, whose authority on culinary matters cannot be verified, wrote to Hoover to suggest that Russians be encouraged to make tortillas, which did not require grinding the corn, just soaking it and frying or baking the dough.[30]

From Moscow came word through ARA channels that Soviet officials deemed corn to be "unusable" in Russia because the peasants would refuse to eat it. They suggested yellow peas, buckwheat grain, rye as rye meal or flour, wheat flour, wheat grain, or millet grain—any of these would be better than corn. Hoover was said to be amazed that the Soviet government would exhibit such fastidiousness in the midst of a famine. Should this fact become widely known among Americans, he warned, it would raise doubts as to the severity of the crisis in Russia.

Actually, Hoover could not have been completely surprised: he had encountered similar resistance several years earlier when Belgians initially refused to eat the great American cereal, pronouncing it fit only for cattle.[31]

Haskell, in a report of October 14, listed the most desirable cereals for Russia in order of importance as: rye flour, wheat flour, corn, barley, and millet.[32] But Hoover had American interests to take into account, and he had decided that the optimal use of the congressional appropriation was toward the purchase of corn, due to its exceptionally low price. The announcement aroused protests from other agricultural interests, notably wheat growers.

William C. Edgar, editor of the *Northwestern Miller*, wrote to the president on December 12 to warn that the selection of corn was a serious mistake in view of the fact that there were no mills in Russia equipped to grind it, that it was apt to spoil in transit and in storage, that it was not suitable as a daily food ration, that it tended to produce stomach disorders, and that the difficulties involved in teaching the Russian people how to prepare corn were "insuperable." The Russians wanted and needed wheat flour, of which there was a large surplus. "I took a trainload of corn meal to Russia during the famine of 1892. The experiment was a failure."

Two years later, Edgar published an article in his journal under the title "Old King Corn Vindicated," in which he good-naturedly admitted to having been wrong about the impracticability of importing corn into Russia—but in December 1921 he spoke for a large and influential farm group.[33]

Hoover defended his choice of corn in a response to Maryland Senator Joseph France, one of his most persistent critics on Russian affairs: "The primary reason for the use of corn instead of wheat was that nearly double the food values can be delivered in corn as could be delivered in wheat for the same money." Besides, "Corn is not unknown in many parts of Russia. In any event, they are all familiar with non-glutinous cereals, such as buckwheat and millet, the preparation of which in the household is identical with many corn dishes."[34] Here Hoover was stretching his argument a bit. The fact is that *kukuruza*, as the Russians call it, was in those days virtually unknown to the inhabitants of the Volga valley.

The selection of seed was necessarily less subjective, as considerations of climate and soil had to be taken into account. The Soviets expressed a strong preference for wheat seed, a request supported by Haskell, who advised New York that American corn could not grow in the soil of the northern reaches of the famine zone, including Kazan province. In the event, the Purchasing Commission bought both wheat seed and corn seed, selected from northwestern states where climatic conditions approximated those of central Russia.[35]

On the matter of seed, the Soviet government's opinion held greater weight because it was footing most of the bill. This arrangement was concluded near the time of the congressional appropriation, but only after drawn-out negotiations that had begun the previous August. Within a week of the signing of the Riga Agreement, Hoover had directed Brown in London to inquire of Krassin as to the veracity of reports that the Kremlin was in possession of several million dollars worth of gold and platinum. These assets, Hoover suggested, could be used to purchase surplus grain in the Balkans, an act that would help convince the American people that the Soviet government was making an effort to aid its own people. "We wish to force their hand to do their share in adult feeding" is how he framed the matter for Brown. The Bolsheviks, he wrote to Haskell, "can scarcely expect the rest of the world to make sacrifices until they have exhausted their own resources."[36]

To his query Brown received the reply that while the rumors about a reserve of platinum were unfounded, the Soviet government was interested in discussing the expenditure of several million dollars in gold toward the purchase of food from the United States. Negotiations with Krassin dragged on through late October, at which time Hoover cabled Brown of his intention to seek congressional funding. In light of this and with a view toward greasing the political wheels, he now insisted that the Soviet government "make strong demonstration of self-help" in the form of a $10 million food purchase, asserting that U.S. government assistance would be contingent on it. Indeed, this is what Krassin was led to believe and so informed his government right up to the announcement of the appropriation.[37] Still, the talks progressed slowly and a deal was reached only on

December 30, too late to influence the congressional hearings. The Soviet government agreed to buy $10 million in food, which it opted to acquire in the form of seed. The Ukrainian Republic signed a similar contract, on February 1, in the amount of $2 million. From there it remained for Hoover to see to it that both purchases were cleared with the State and Treasury Departments as an exception to the U.S. embargo on Soviet gold.

This Soviet expenditure, which capped the funding for the expanded Russian relief mission, exemplifies Hoover's special talent for enlisting support from every corner in order to build a maximum program. Many followed enthusiastically, some needed jollying along, and there were always those requiring forceful persuasion. In each case Hoover had no doubt where the credit belonged. In a memorandum he wrote in 1925 concerning the official history of the Russian unit, a work then in progress, he objected to how Fisher had drafted the section dealing with the Soviet seed program. Yes, the Bolsheviks put up the money, he allowed, but one had to remember that the ARA had given them an "ultimatum" and thus deserved the recognition. "In other words, whether a man gives you assistance by charity or whether you force him to do it at the point of a gun makes no difference in the account of the assistance given."

It is no wonder that his Quaker brethren were spiritually so estranged from Hoover. As the chronicler of the Friends' Russian relief efforts wrote of him many years later, "Clearly, Herbert Hoover is not to be summed up over a dish of pears."[38]

Thus did Hoover set the stage for a mighty drama whose essential plot line was a race to transport tens of thousands of metric tons of corn and seed from the American Midwest to the Russian heartland in time to save millions from starvation. Before moving on to recount that epic tale as it unfolded inside Russia, Fisher paused to pay tribute to those responsible for the success of the American end of the corn campaign, "men experienced in large affairs and skilled in the details of their management. They applied to this enterprise of philanthropy the minds and energies developed in the building of great industrial and commercial operations and translated into facts the vision they shared with their chief." And they performed this service out of the spotlight:

No glamour, no bright element of human interest attaches to the sober business of buying grain, chartering ships, and keeping accounts. These activities are dull beside the stories of political manoeuvres, of ardent controversies, and adventures in Russian outposts; yet they contributed a vital part to the A.R.A.'s success and the manner of their execution was a characteristic feature of the international humanitarianism exemplified by the A.R.A.[39]

It was now up to the men stationed in the Russian theater of action to make good on their countrymen's vital efforts on the home front.

CHAPTER 8

PUTTING THE JOB OVER

Most of the relief workers in the famine zone had no inkling that an expansion had been in the works for over two months. As Christmas approached, Piet Hofstra arrived back in Ufa city, having completed an excursion into the interior. On December 27, five days after President Harding signed the appropriation, an unaware Hofstra wrote in his trip report to Moscow: "The question is raised all along the route, 'What is America going to do to give us seed and to feed the adults?' I myself am also raising this question. Is anything going to be done during the coming year?"

Relief workers in every district were asking the same question, including Shafroth, who had recently returned to headquarters from his inspection tour of the lower reaches of Samara, where he had observed a group of peasants hollowing out a large burial pit in anticipation of future corpses. Black clouds were gathering, he later recalled, "And then into the pervading gloom of this situation, like a shaft of light came the Christmas message from Mr. Hoover." The news spread quickly into Samara's villages that the Americans were promising to supply corn to adults. "Altho it was known that this food could not reach the Volga before March, the announcement put heart into the peasants who had already learned to trust our word."[1]

The peasants may have had faith, but a good number of relief workers—some after an initial burst of unrestrained enthusiasm—were unsure that this time they would in fact be able to deliver on their promise. For the task before them seemed Herculean: move twenty million bushels of corn, not to mention unspecified thousands of tons of seed, by rail from the ports into the famine zone, then from the railheads to the villages, and do so in time for the spring planting. All at once, the decrepit state of Russia's railways loomed over the mission.[2] Upon arrival in Russia the previous August, the ARA found the railway crisis to be severe, as had been expected, but concern had been tempered by the relatively modest size of the initial relief program. Now in the face of a drastic increase in that program—of a kind, moreover, that hinged on a successful race against the seasonal clock—there was cause for grave apprehension.

The German War, the Revolution, the Civil War, and the Polish War had exacted a terrific toll on Russia's railroads, while since 1914 few repairs had been made to the rolling stock, rails, or roadbeds. The engineer-minded American relief workers recorded with a horrified fascination the evidence of this destruction.

A country's railway network, they would not hesitate to tell you, was a fair index to its standard of "civilization," and Russia's had suffered a crippling blow.

Of course, by this measure civilization had never penetrated very deep in Russia, even before the time of troubles. A country several times the size of the United States in 1914, it had less than one-sixth the railway mileage; by European standards its railroads ranked last in total miles and technical standards. Except for the most important lines—Moscow-Riga, Moscow-Danzig, Moscow-Rostov, and Moscow-Nizhnii Novgorod—the entire network consisted of single-track lines. This made running times relatively slow before the war but much slower still by 1921 when trains had to pass cautiously over the many rough patches of track. In European Russia no more than one-third of the pre-1914 track was still in use, many of the secondary lines having long before been shut down, and service on the main and larger branch lines in operation was extremely reduced.

By 1921 only about 20 percent of prewar rolling stock was in service, a drop partly explained by Russia's loss of Estonia, Latvia, Lithuania, Finland, and Poland, each of which inherited portions of imperial Russia's cars and locomotives. Much of what Soviet Russia had managed to retain for itself was now in an advanced stage of deterioration due to the demands and destruction of war and the progressive ruin of Russian industry, which left many engines and cars to die of idleness, exposure to the elements, and the enterprise of scavengers.

In the course of their train travels, the relief workers listened to the conductors' Civil War tales of how soldiers, Red and White, had made it their mission to break every pane of glass and to strip the cloth from every seat on every car of every train. An ARA man who briefly entered Kiev in June 1920, during the Russo-Polish War, elaborated on this spirit of destruction: "The favorite amusement of the 'Bolos' seemed to have been the old moving picture stunt of getting two trains facing each other and turning them loose to see the crash. Some engines had the front ends and frames badly bent and the beautiful big Russian passenger cars were telescoped and bent in all directions." In those days the Soviet government had abolished passengers fares, which exacerbated the overcrowding of the trains and thus accelerated the deterioration of the cars.

A year later, journalist Hullinger observed "miles of these sick box cars, on sidings, their walls and floors partially or wholly gone, their wheels red with rust, standing there like rows of skeletons against the snowy steppes." In the railroad yards of European Russia, especially around Moscow, one came upon "locomotive graveyards," rows of rusted and dilapidated locomotives that had gone unused for years, their tenders missing, piston rods removed, and boilers open, "resting there soundlessly, like sleeping monsters."[3]

An inevitable accompaniment to this physical destruction was a crisis of morale among the railway personnel, although the relief workers and foreign journalists were generous in their praise of the railroad specialists, many of whom were holdovers from the old regime left in place by the Soviet government because their expertise was irreplaceable. The Americans credited the dedication of these men with preventing the complete collapse of the system. Still, no amount of loyalty and personal integrity would enable the railroads to support the impending corn campaign. Putting the job over required the mobilization of the entire railway system and administration, including the repair of roadbeds and rolling stock, the provisioning of labor and fuel, improved traffic management, and close coordination with the ARA. Such a prospect seemed utopian at the moment when the relief workers learned that ships bearing American grain were steaming toward Russia.

Haskell went to London to talk it over with Brown, leaving the Moscow staff to brood about the troubling prospects. Golder voiced the general concern in a letter to a Stanford colleague on December 29: "For the life of me I do not now see how the transportation is going to take care of all the grain that may come in." A day later his mind is burdened by an accumulation of disquieting details:

Our friends in New York are rushing things a bit. Yesterday or the day before a telegram came that ships with grain are on the way or about to start. No arrangements have been made for unloading or for transportation, no arrangements have been made for milling, for sacking, for a dozen and one things and it is a serious question whether the grain can be milled and so on. It sounds good in the papers that the next day after Congress appropriated the money the grain was shipped.[4]

In fact, although no American who had not seen it for himself could possibly imagine the state of affairs on the Russian end, the staff at 42 Broadway thought ahead. For the sake of speed it was decided to purchase and ship the corn in bulk rather than to wait to have it milled and sacked in America. Aware that the Russian ports were ill-equipped to handle bulk corn and that many Russian freight cars were in no condition to transport it, the New York office arranged for the first corn ships to carry over a large supply of grain sacks, along with lumber, nails, slings, and tarpaulins—items in scarce supply in Russia. The idea was that all corn would be sacked at ports prior to rail shipment, but the districts were notified that at the peak of the campaign it might become necessary to make bulk shipments and have sacking done at the district end—which would indeed turn out to be the case. The corn was to be issued whole, unless facilities for milling were available at the distribution points.[5]

The average haul by rail from port to final destination was one thousand miles; among the farthest of the regular routes was the fourteen-hundred-mile stretch from Novorossisk, on the Black Sea, to Ufa. Bill Kelley arrived there on New Year's Day after a rail journey that was most memorable for its grueling ten-day Riga-Moscow leg. After a week at his post he informed his correspondent in the States of the ARA's impending expansion, which he understood would involve the large-scale distribution of wheat. The Ufa district was to get 350 tons a day for six months, meaning twenty cars per day as compared to the current average of two.

Knowing the condition of the Russian railroads as we do (and I am an authority on the Riga-Moscow roadbed) it is inconceivable that the roads can move such an enormous quantity of wheat. There is not the slightest doubt that our district needs 350 tons a day and more too, but whether they can ever deliver it to us or not is the mighty question. Even if these daily trains pull into Ufa, somehow—God knows how—can we move this wheat into the interior villages by sleds, drawn by horses that are almost dead on their feet now? Some of our villages are 60 and even a hundred miles from a railroad. Isn't it an appalling task?

One week later his pessimism is undiminished: "the entire railway system may collapse under the strain."[6]

KELLEY WOULD HAVE BEEN more disturbed still had he arrived in Russia by ship and cast his skeptical eye on one of Russia's ports, which like the railways were suffering the effects of war, neglect, and wanton destruction. There was good reason to doubt that the Baltic and Black Sea ports would have the combined capacity to receive the grain ships, the equipment for the handling and storage of cargoes, or adequate rail facilities to evacuate supplies to the interior.[7] (See map, page 210.)

Of the northern ports, Petrograd was in the best condition, but it was equipped for the export, not import, of grain. The ARA converted its export grain elevator to perform import duty during the time it used the port, which was brief because ice closed the port down for the winter in early December. Of the other, non-Russian, Baltic ports Reval—today's Tallinn—was the best equipped for the ARA's purposes but presented the problems of insufficient warehouse space and of having to secure rolling stock from the Estonians, who were resistant to the idea of releasing their precious cars into the black hole of Bolshevik Russia. These were the same principal drawbacks to the port of Riga, which was of greater potential value to the ARA because shipments from Riga could be sent directly to Moscow and from there be transshipped, without unloading, to the Volga districts. Two other Latvian ports, Windau and Libau, offered certain advantages—especially the former, being ice-free—but shared a major handicap: the occupying German armies had changed the railroad gauge in Poland and much of Latvia to have it correspond to the narrower continental width, and this necessitated unloading and reloading supplies into Russian cars at Riga—just as shipments from Danzig had to be transferred at Stolpce on the Polish border.

Thus far the situation on the Baltic. The outlook for the Black Sea ports was brighter, with Novorossisk offering the best facilities and the closest proximity to the famine districts of the lower Volga. Theodosia, the only Crimean port with adequate rail connections, could also be utilized, though only minimally because of the poor condition of the lines running into the peninsula. Odessa, in the worst shape and situated farthest from the famine zone, was to be used chiefly to take on overflow shipments from the other two Black Sea ports, which would turn out to be substantial.

The Baltic ports were to supply Kazan, Simbirsk, and part of Samara, while the Black Sea ports were responsible for the rest of Samara plus Saratov, Tsaritsyn, Orenburg, and Ufa. As for the seed purchased by the Soviets through the ARA, upon its arrival at port it was to be unloaded, shipped, and distributed under the exclusive control and supervision of the government.

Of crucial importance to the port operations on the Black Sea would be the contribution of the U.S. Navy in facilitating the movement of American supply ships. The question of the navy having a role in the relief program was at first considered a matter of some delicacy. In September 1921 Secretary Hughes advised the secretary of the navy that the presence of American destroyers in Soviet ports "might lead to undesirable complications or be subject to serious misinterpretations, in view of the absence of official relations between this Government and the Soviet authorities and the disposition of the Bolsheviki to ascribe ulterior motives to the American Relief activities." The State Department's chief concern was that official American contact with Soviet authorities might somehow compromise the U.S. government's heretofore unbending nonrecognition stance toward Soviet Russia. Hughes authorized the navy to be called in only for "extraordinary emergency" situations.

This regime had to be relaxed, however, once the mission was expanded and there was found to be no acceptable alternative to having American naval vessels perform the vital function of coordinating the import of large shipments of food into the Black Sea ports. So American destroyers under the command of Rear Admiral Mark Bristol, U.S. high commissioner at Constantinople, delivered sailing orders to American ships destined for port. At the same time, a destroyer was made to serve as a station ship at Novorossisk for the purpose of conducting radio communication with Constantinople, London, and, somewhat later, Moscow.

In performing these services, the navy proved to be indispensable to the port end of the relief operations, though this was not the extent of its activity. Naval intelligence officers, taking advantage of the opportunity, monitored wireless broadcasts, including Soviet government diplomatic communications, whose contents were passed on to Washington. The Soviet government, in the person of Eiduk, periodically registered its discomfort with one or another of the navy's doings, most often the imperious behavior of its hard-drinking sailors in port, but the political entanglements initially feared by Hughes never materialized.[8]

That was on the Black Sea, where the first corn ship, the *Winnebago*, arrived in Novorossisk on February 6. The southern ports were able to handle their cargoes as well as was expected, but in the north there were problems beyond the many already anticipated. The winter of 1921–22 in the Baltic region was the coldest in fifteen years. Relief ships became ice-bound in the Kiel Canal and the Skagerrack. The approaches to Reval harbor froze and ice blocked the ports of Riga and Petrograd, which were closed until the end of April. Quinn mused on February 26: "The Lord seems to have a particular animus toward the Russian people; He cuts off the rain in the summer and freezes up the Baltic in winter." As if to prove him wrong, just at that time there came a thaw, and the relief ships were able to advance toward the ports, though this meant that they arrived in clusters rather than in staggered fashion, thereby complicating the tasks of evacuating and storing grain.[9]

AS IT HAPPENED, storing the corn at port was the more pressing concern due to a severe shortage of empty cars to transport it to the interior. In early January the Soviet government had promised the ARA to supply the ports with 400 empty cars per day, which would allow the movement of 150,000 tons of corn per month—but it could not meet its commitment and almost immediately began to retreat from this figure. In February it pledged to supply the Baltic ports with 80 cars per day but delivered on average fewer than 15. For the Black Sea ports it was 236 cars promised but an average of only 58 delivered.

The failing car program was threatening to scuttle the entire corn campaign. Haskell pressed the government to take emergency measures, with the result that in early March it formed an extraordinary commission to manage the transportation crisis. The man chosen to head the effort was Krassin, lately relocated from London, and his appointment gave encouragement to the ARA chiefs, who appreciated his diplomatic skills and were aware of his reputation as an efficient administrator and of his engineering expertise, acquired under the old regime. Brown knew him better than any other ARA official from several months of negotiations in London; nonetheless, he remained doubtful, writing to New York that the Bolsheviks were said to be optimistic regarding the supply of empty cars, "and they may fool us yet. But it doesn't look like it to me."

Krassin himself did not much like the looks of things, admitting to Haskell straightaway that the government could not fulfill the original program of 400 cars per day. The two men agreed on a reduced program of 250 cars, though even this number would not hold up for long.[10]

One reason for the shortage of empties was the amount of time it took the trains carrying corn and other ARA food and supplies into the famine zone to reach their destinations—if they managed to get there at all. Some food trains from Petrograd took up to a month to reach Moscow, a distance covered by passenger trains in fourteen hours. The first corn train out of Odessa, consisting of 43 cars, took one month to reach Simbirsk, less than fifteen hundred miles distant. Deteriorated track was mostly to blame but so was the decaying rolling stock, which now buckled under the burden. Fuel was in short supply, and what was available was of poor quality. Coal ordered from England especially for the corn campaign was late in arriving, a result of the backup at the ice-clogged Baltic ports, and often the best fuel on hand was frozen logs.

Human error was also a factor. When the first corn train arrived in Ufa from the port of Novorossisk in the first week of March, Kelley learned from the Red soldiers assigned to escort the train that their journey of several weeks had, he concluded, taken them over most of European Russia. They were broke and hungry, having gone the previous three days without bread. Kelley gave the head of the Soviet squad two million rubles, enough to purchase one pood, about 40 lbs., of black flour. "These South Russia convoys resemble Italians. I enjoy their dramatic accounts of their trip. After tracing the route of the first train, I wired Novorossisk to equip future convoys with a map of the world and a compass." Kelley's dig had probably lost most of its force by the time his telegram arrived in Novorossisk, two months later.

Fisher likens the dispatch of food trains into the interior to "shots in the dark." He recounts that when 18 of 32 cars of an ARA food train failed to arrive at Kazan, a relief worker set out from Moscow to locate them. A few miles outside the capital he came upon the first of them and found the others not far down the line, some having been sidetracked on account of hot boxes. The ARA's records show that of the cars shipped east of Moscow in October 1921, 11 percent had failed to reach their destinations; by December the number of errant cars had increased to 23 percent; and by the end of January it was up to 35 percent.

At destination there were further complications. In Saratov the main supply base for the district was across the Volga at Pokrovsk, where in the month of January only one locomotive was available to service the railroad yards, so camel power had to be harnessed to shift ARA cars. From Pokrovsk it took as long as seventeen days for trains to make the trip to Pugachev, in the very heart of the valley of the shadow, a distance of less than 150 miles.

Even before the corn started to arrive on the Volga in the third week of February, the transportation crisis had twice nearly forced the ARA to terminate its food remittance service and was threatening to starve the child-feeding program. Frantic telegrams in January and February from the subdistricts to district headquarters, and from the districts to Moscow headquarters, warned that operations would have to be suspended if food supplies were not forthcoming. At Uralsk, on the eastern edge of the Saratov district, John Clapp was within days of having to close all American kitchens in the region, when at the urging of local officials he convinced the Red Army commander of an armored train to transport him to Pokrovsk in search of missing cars of ARA food—which they soon found, standing idle in a way station.[11]

On the Volga, trains seemed to arrive in large numbers or not at all, making for alternating periods of, quite literally, feast or famine. Farther east at Orenburg it was mostly famine because over a period of nearly five weeks in February–March only a single car—sixteen tons—of food supplies got through. In Ufa, district supervisor Bell for a time put the children's kitchens on half-rations, and when the first corn arrived he diverted some of it to the child-feeding program, ordering that it be ground and served as grits. After its long dry spell, Orenburg did the same, serving a menu of corn grits with lard and milk and reducing children to two-thirds rations until adequate supplies came in.

By the middle of March there were, according to ARA figures, 6,828 cars en route containing over one hundred thousand tons of corn and other relief supplies. Where many of these cars were, precisely, was a deepening mystery. And there were mysterious subplots as well. Haskell received reports from Samara and Simbirsk that some empty cars were being sent not back to the ports but farther on to Siberia, which if true was disturbing news: given the even more wretched condition of the railway lines to the east, this amounted to sending these cars over a cliff. American food, meanwhile, continued to accumulate in the ports. By the end of March there were some sixty thousand tons of relief supplies awaiting empty cars.[12]

Another troubling sign was that the Soviet government seemed to be taking a greater interest in the delivery of the seed it had purchased, despite its understanding with the ARA that the seed was to follow the corn so as not to be consumed by the starving planters. Ideally the seed would finish a close second in the race to the countryside, but word was coming through to the center from various ports and railway junctions that Soviet officials were giving priority to seed trains.

FROM MOSCOW HEADQUARTERS it began to appear as if the entire Russian project was swiftly unraveling. These dire circumstances crystallized into a full-blown crisis as a result of a revelation produced in an unlikely place, the Ukrainian capital, Kharkov. It was there, one afternoon in the third week of March, that a Red Army soldier, hungry and exhausted, entered ARA headquarters and told the disbelieving Americans a fantastic tale. He was one of a party of soldiers that had during the previous month passed through Kharkov escorting a corn train from Odessa bound for the Volga. Advancing northeast of Kharkov at the usual crawl, their train came to the junction at Balashov, about 160 miles west of Saratov, where it came to rest among numerous other ARA trains. Three weeks later it was still standing in the Balashov yards, unable to move forward or back.

During that time, trains had pulled in behind and alongside it until the yards and sidings were jam-packed with trains for several miles. Each had its Red Army convoy, all running low on food rations. The soldier who dragged himself into the ARA office in Kharkov had been enlisted by his comrades to double back and alert the Americans.

In fact, at about this time two American relief workers happened upon the Balashov jam. Joe Driscoll and John Foy had departed Tsaritsyn on March 16, escorting a corn train of twenty-five cars to Nikolaevsk on the Volga, a trip of three hundred miles by rail. Three days later they rolled into Balashov and became part of the problem. Driscoll dispatched a letter to supervisor Bowden in Tsaritsyn reporting that the backup—which the station manager estimated to be thirty ARA trains—was caused by the expeditious evacuation of corn from Odessa and by the partiality shown to trains carrying seed.

In breaking this news, Driscoll gives no indication of appreciating the enormous implications of what he has discovered. He does, however, display a keen interest in the soldiers stranded along with their cargoes—onetime convoys reduced to simple guard duty. They were, he wrote, "in hard straights"; moreover, their mood was turning ugly, and "several hungry looking crowds of convoys made long speeches to me, waving paper in their hands. John said they were hungry, and after looking over the papers with John's help, I rather believe them." One party of seven had left Odessa on March 1 with five million rubles for fourteen days' rations, having been assured they would be back in Odessa with their empty trains within that period of time. It was March 22 and they were stuck many miles west of the Volga. Driscoll, like Kelley and other relief workers, praised the grit and incorruptibility of these men and urged that they be better dressed and supplied for their long journeys.

Driscoll made his way through the yards, inspecting the seals on the corn cars and finding all of them in order. An interview with the station chief revealed that there were but two engines in running order and that his instructions were to give preference to seed trains. Driscoll convinced him to hook his own cars onto the weekly passenger train toward Nikolaevsk, and on March 24, after wiring Moscow of the situation, he and Foy were able to extricate themselves from the quagmire.[13]

An urgent telegram from the Kharkov Americans reached Moscow first, and this was followed by reports of similar jams, one at Kozlov, a junction nearly 200 miles northwest of Balashov, and another about 150 miles to the north, at Penza. None of the three locations was within the ARA's administrative range, and Haskell's immediate response was to dispatch American traffic controllers to these "congested division points," overriding Eiduk's objections that his own men had everything under control. At the same time he instructed the district supervisors to set up their own traffic controls at "strategic points" along the railways.

The congestion was most severe at Balashov and Kozlov. The problem began with the detention—for reasons that are not clear—of several corn trains, likened by Fisher to floating logs "held up by an obstruction," damming up a river. At Kozlov on March 5 there were nine trains; on March 16 there were thirteen; on March 21 twenty; and on April 3 twenty-six, in addition to fourteen more "held up in the immediate vicinity." The Balashov jam was worse: from eight trains on

March 5 to twenty-two on March 16, to forty-six on March 26.[14] Here was a corn surplus of a new type. (See map, page 212.)

As anxiety mounted, Haskell several times petitioned, with increasing importunity, for a meeting with Kamenev, but without success. The fact that the ARA's contact in the Politburo would become scarce just as it seemed that the entire corn campaign was about to go under was now a matter of some speculation at Spiridonovka 30.

Word of the Balashov and Kozlov jams was conveyed to London, where Brown sensed that his worst fears were becoming a reality. On top of this came a report from Miller in Riga on March 27 that the Red Army was preparing for war. It appeared as though a simmering dispute between Finland and Russia over the contested border region of Karelia was about to boil over into armed conflict. Soviet troops were said to be gathering in the area, and there were even rumors of a Red Army mobilization along the entire western frontier. Haskell, who loathed Miller, contemptuously dismissed his information, but the London chiefs took it seriously: a mobilization of the Red Army would divert precious rolling stock from the ARA's corn drive.

One piece of evidence that hostilities might indeed be imminent was the text of Trotsky's speech before the Moscow soviet on March 12, in which he warned the Finns against inciting a Karelian rebellion and offered a pessimistic assessment of Soviet relations with the Baltic States and Romania, portraying all as hostile and even prone to war. In his address Trotsky had some appreciative words for the work of the ARA, though he also charged it with subsidizing the forces of White General Wrangel. In view of the fact that Wrangel was in exile and his army extinct, Trotsky could only have been referring to scattered remnants of the former White Guard now in the employ of the ARA. The Moscow soviet passed a resolution supporting the ARA but at the same time calling for vigilance against the counterrevolutionary elements it harbored.[15]

In fact, vigilance had been stepped up at the time of the congressional appropriation, an act that was regarded as a mixed blessing in Bolshevik quarters. Just as the bill was clearing the Congress, Eiduk stepped forward to warn the Soviet leadership, in a letter of December 21, that Hoover's plan to introduce adult feeding might well endanger the government since it would mean a significant increase in the ARA's local staffs—"a bunch of White-Guardists"—and thus produce an intolerable increase in anti-Bolshevik activity. Besides, "according to my sources," the ARA is in fact a "secret joint stock company" responsible to its entrepreneur-shareholders, which could only mean that the Soviet government, in advancing it $10 million in gold for the purchase of seed, was bound to get a raw deal. Eiduk recommended that the congressional appropriation be rejected. In the event that the Soviet government found it necessary to accept the ARA offer, however, then the Riga Agreement would have to be subject to a fundamental revision.

Lenin of course rejected the policeman's advice but shared enough of his paranoia to recommend the circulation of his letter among the Politburo as background material for that body's discussion, on December 31, of "political measures in connection with the ARA." A result of these deliberations was the secret formation of an extraordinary troika—made up of the deputy head of the Cheka, a

Central Committee secretary, and Eiduk—under the supervision of Kamenev "to work out special precautionary measures in the event of an expansion of the apparatus of the ARA and the enlistment by it of unreliable elements."[16]

None of these facts was known to the ARA, and in any case nothing transpired over the course of the subsequent two months to indicate a change in the Soviet policy of grudging cooperation. Then, in the midst of the railroad crisis, came a wave of arrests of key native staff members in the districts, all stemming from political charges and several with the direct involvement of Eiduk's plenipotentiaries. When the distress signals from the supervisors reached Moscow, Haskell brought the matter to Eiduk, who explained that the Soviet government was rounding up all members of the defunct Socialist Revolutionary Party in preparation for what would become, that summer, the first Soviet show trial. The relief workers in the field, who generally disdained politics and who therefore did not appreciate the value to the Bolsheviks of such political theater, could only assume that the arrests were intended to undermine the efficiency of their operations.

It was at this same time that Eiduk, who had initially brushed aside reports of the gravity of the corn jam, suddenly changed tack and told Haskell that he supported a proposal by railway officials at Balashov and Kozlov to unload ARA corn into warehouses there in order to free up empty cars for the ports and relieve the congestion. Haskell, able to imagine no end of trouble once the corn was discharged from the ARA's sealed cars, rejected the idea. Eiduk then suggested that trains at these two junctions be moved in various directions away from the congested points, and again Haskell balked, fearing that chaos would ensue. Since no better solution presented itself, however, with great reluctance the colonel agreed to allow the temporary storage of the contents of eleven hundred cars into Soviet warehouses at Balashov and Kozlov. But before this plan could be finalized, the telegraphic wires produced another series of jolts: railroad workers at various locations had begun seizing corn cars.

From the outset of the mission the ARA had had recurrent difficulties moving its supplies at ports, railway stations, and warehouses because Soviet hands refused to work until they were paid. No longer able to revert to the printing press to cover its debts, the government had fallen months behind in paying the wages of its employees, and among the most hard up were the railroaders: in February 1922 many were still waiting on their salaries from the previous November. Yet here they were, charged with transporting trainloads of food imported for the benefit of other people, mostly peasants. In December Eiduk had requested that Haskell allot a portion of relief supplies to stevedores and railway men, but the colonel was unwilling. When Eiduk raised the matter again in February, however, the railway crisis had become serious enough for Haskell to agree to a small loan of corn for workers at Kozlov, at the Baltic ports, and at Novorossisk. The arrangement, written up as a contract, required the Soviet government to deposit with the ARA in London the replacement price of the corn, whose total volume was forty-five hundred tons, later supplemented by an additional four thousand tons.

So a small proportion of American corn had in fact been set aside for Soviet transportation workers, but what occurred in the first days of April fell outside the bounds of this agreement. Walker in Petrograd wired Moscow that Eiduk's office had evidently directed local railroad officials to confiscate the first forty corn cars arriving from Reval; he wished to know if this act had been sanctioned by the ARA. Then came a telegram from Shafroth with the news that Samara officials had commandeered thirty-four ARA corn cars at Russaevka, fifty at Balashov and another eleven at Penza—all for the benefit of railroad employees. Shafroth had in hand copies of the telegrams sent out from the Moscow railway administration authorizing these seizures, which he passed on to Haskell.

The colonel responded by instructing ARA officials at the ports to stop the delivery of corn to the railroads. At the same time, the ARA made yet another application for a conference with Kamenev, and once again word came back that he was busy tending to affairs of state. This was no doubt true, but the matter of ARA corn was itself about to land at the center of the political stage.

Eiduk sent his chief railroad deputy to Petrograd to investigate the corn seizures, and this man, having had a look around, took the bizarre step of ordering the railway officials to confiscate eleven additional cars of corn. Haskell issued a written protest to Eiduk against this "flagrant breach of the Riga Agreement," and warned that in light of such developments it would be difficult for him to recommend to the ARA in America that it direct any further food shipments to Russia. Fisher assumed that Eiduk was "impervious" to the colonel's protests, but in fact two days later he informed the Politburo that the railway crisis, which he blamed on the People's Commissariat of Transportation, had placed the entire famine relief program and thus many thousands of lives in "serious danger." He called for "extraordinary measures," using Haskell's letter to support his case.[17]

The central railway authorities, meanwhile, in an attempt to relieve the jam of corn trains, ordered that forty-four cars per day be unloaded and placed in storage at Petrograd and that fifty-two cars en route from Petrograd to Kazan be redirected to Rybinsk—directly north of Moscow at the source of the Volga—and unloaded there, as should all further shipments from the port of Reval. Haskell had agreed in principle to the unloading and storing of corn in Soviet warehouses but only at Balashov and Kozlov, and in any case the colonel had withheld his final approval of this plan upon learning of the corn seizures. Nonetheless, railroad officials in Kozlov, where the preliminary agreement called for the storage of four hundred cars of corn, proceeded to unload the cars anyway, and when the American who had been dispatched there, Alonzo Darragh, tried to prevent the breaking of the ARA seals, the Cheka placed him briefly under arrest.

In his letter to London of April 10 detailing these developments, Quinn wrote, "For some inexplicable reason we have been unable to secure an interview with Mr. Kameneff in spite of the fact that a request was made at least ten days ago." Later that same day Haskell decided that it had become necessary to get Kamenev's attention by more radical means—indeed, that it was high time to force a showdown with the Bolos.

THE COLONEL DELIVERED a tacit ultimatum to the Soviet authorities in the form of a telegram to Hoover, transmitted *en clair* over the Soviet wire service on April 10. The usual practice was for the ARA to send all sensitive telegrams first by courier to Riga and from there in code to London or New York, but as the primary audience on this occasion was only a mile or so away in the Kremlin, measures of secrecy were intentionally disregarded. In his communication, Haskell apprised Hoover of the facts of the transportation crisis, a situation which "leads me to seriously doubt the ability of Russian railways to deliver our program." What is more, the Soviet government's attitude toward the ARA had "grown steadily more indifferent and disagreeable" in the previous two weeks to the point where officials were sanctioning the confiscation of American corn. While this was transpiring, Kamenev was apparently too busy with political matters to grant ARA officials an audience. "I can positively recommend that not another pound of relief supplies should be added to our existing program and I recommend that all pending shipments from America be stopped beyond actual present commitments until such time as I see and can advise how present difficulties are met here and whether a sincere effort to cooperate with us manifests itself."[18]

Coincidentally, at the moment Haskell's telegram arrived, Hoover was embroiled in a controversy at home about whether he was doing enough for Russian relief. At the congressional hearings the previous December Hoover had estimated that $20 million worth of American grain was the maximum amount that Russia's transportation system could handle. His critics claimed that he was intentionally underestimating the capacity of Russia's ports and railways, and in March and April he was accused of exaggerating the scale of the railway crisis in order to stifle the funding drives of other relief organizations, notably the Friends. Radicals charged that Hoover had "sabotaged" Russian relief.[19]

The Chief now called upon the ARA's staff to generate publicity about the clogging of ports, the congestion at railroad junctions, and the poor conditions of Russia's roads; yet the one document that would have clinched his case, Haskell's telegram, was never made public. Nor, several weeks later, was an incriminating "strictly confidential" memorandum issued in April by the People's Commissariat of Transportation, which someone in Moscow had divulged to the Russian unit. This document criticized railroad officials in various regions for inefficiency and for the unauthorized requisitioning of ARA corn and warned that they would be held accountable for their actions. Some members of the ARA's New York staff wanted to send copies to the *Nation* and the *New Republic*, even though the fact of its possession by the ARA might have suggested Gregory-style behavior among the relief workers in Russia. Whatever the political calculations at 42 Broadway, the official position as stated by Fisher five years later was that publishing Haskell's telegram would have been beneath the dignity of the ARA, which "was engaged in the business of saving human life."[20]

Still, the publication of Haskell's telegram, whatever the repercussions in Moscow, would have clarified matters and put Hoover instantly in the clear. Walter Lippmann, after accepting an invitation from New York headquarters to examine the ARA's internal correspondence concerning the whole business, announced to readers of the New York *World* on May 14 that the charge that Hoover had sabotaged Russian relief was "a cruel absurdity." The chairman of the ARA deserved the highest praise for his enormous achievement in Russia. There was, however, one aspect of his performance that was not above criticism.

Mr. Hoover has every great gift of the statesman except the politician's art. He has been right, I think, in all the controversies about relief, but his judgment of the psychology of his critics has been lamentable. He has quite underestimated the strength of the passions evoked by the word Russia. He has never taken the trouble to make it sufficiently plain why he was doing one thing rather than another which seems more obvious.

Hoover, Lippmann believed, should have presented the public with a clear explanation for his opposition to a national appeal at a time when one of the worst famines in history was raging. Because he did not, reasonable-minded citizens gave credence to the most outrageous charges made against him. "He must not be surprised if people who are deeply concerned misunderstand."

So much for the ARA's public relations prowess.

In Moscow, meanwhile, Haskell's telegram produced the desired effect. For Lenin's government this would have been an especially inopportune moment to be accused by the head of the ARA in Russia of bad faith and incompetence. The Genoa Conference was in session, and the Bolsheviks were eager to make a good impression. Genoa was the first diplomatic conference to which the Soviet government had been invited. It was called to discuss the European economic situation in general, though its particular business, aside from a further round of agonizing over German war reparations, was to seek a resolution to several inter-related issues: Soviet Russia's pre-Bolshevik monetary debt to the West, property claims against the Soviet state by Western governments and business, and the Bolsheviks' application for Western credits as well as their own claims against the Allies for the Civil War intervention. In the end, the conference would resolve none of these matters, though it would be the occasion for a burst of scandalous excitement in the form of the Rapallo Treaty, an agreement providing for economic cooperation between the two outcasts of the Versailles peace, Soviet Russia and Germany.[21]

Genoa ended Russia's diplomatic isolation, but behind the gush of triumphant propaganda over the Rapallo breakthrough there was little celebration in the Kremlin. For the results of Genoa were nothing as compared to the sense of expectation that had been aroused in January when the invitation was issued. Here was the proof, the Bolshevik leadership was convinced, of the West's recognition that it could not recover from its postwar economic slump without Russia. Enthusiasm took a plunge on March 8, however, when Secretary Hughes formally declined the U.S. invitation to attend the conference. This was a blow to Lenin and his colleagues because the United States was seen as key to Russia's industrial revival, and the Soviets coveted economic rehabilitation above all, seeing diplomatic recognition as merely a means to that end. At once the idea of Genoa lost a good deal of its lustre.

When the conference got under way, monitoring its day-to-day proceedings and guiding the diplomacy of the Soviet delegation was a major preoccupation of the Bolshevik leaders, especially the ailing Lenin, and because of this Kamenev was indeed, as reported, busier than usual with administrative duties. Haskell observed that he "seems to be running the whole government at present." Still, his unavailability to the ARA may have been calculated. At his previous meeting with the colonel he had responded to several complaints concerning the Soviet treatment of the ARA with the remark that since the United States did not recognize Soviet Russia, the ARA was not entitled to the freedom of action it demanded. The Bolsheviks had a habit of taking out their frustrations with the Harding administration on the ARA, the idea being to send a message to Washington about the cost in the short term of sitting out Genoa and, more generally, of nonrecognition. So Kamenev's scarceness at that juncture could have been deliberate.

In fact, though, it was Haskell who held the Genoa card. As he put it at the time, "I did not forget of course that the Genoa conference was in session and that the psychological moment for this matter was at hand." Seizing that moment, he contrived his telegram to Hoover as "the final punch to settle for all time American control and inviolability of our supplies."[22]

Within hours of its transmission, Eiduk telephoned Haskell to say that Kamenev was eager to see him the next day. Their conference, which lasted two and a half hours, turned out to be a most satisfying episode for the Americans present. Kamenev was apparently surprised at much of what the colonel had to tell him, and he blamed Eiduk for keeping him in the dark about the seriousness of the railroad crisis. When Haskell informed him of the seizures of corn cars, Kamenev declared, "There is a criminal thing here, and I am surprised that Mr. Eiduk has let it go for ten days without taking severe steps." Every time Eiduk tried to interject an explanation Kamenev silenced him.

Kamenev promised to provide by the next day written statements from the railroad authorities outlining a program for delivery of the corn, but this was no longer good enough for Haskell, who declared: "It is not a question of promises. The only proof I have is the arrival of food in the Volga valley." Kamenev proposed a renewed Soviet commitment to supply the ARA with 250 empty cars per day, to which Haskell responded that since the earlier-promised 250 cars had not materialized, the new minimum requirement was 450 cars. Kamenev then suggested a conference between the ARA and the railroad authorities, and Haskell readily accepted. Thus, at least when it came to the railroads, Eiduk was no longer to be the neck of the bottle.

Pressing his advantage, Haskell proceeded to indict the apparatus of government plenipotentiaries. Kamenev, on an ultra-appeasement roll, threatened to fire Eiduk's entire staff—which may or may not have implied a threat to the chief plenipotentiary himself—and he promised to furnish a written statement delimiting the powers of Eiduk's district satellites and to issue them new instructions, which Haskell would be allowed to read and endorse. The subject of the arrests of ARA employees was raised, and Eiduk, permitted to speak, announced that he had just ordered his local agents to make no further arrests without his prior approval.

Eiduk had been routed, if only for the time being. Kamenev closed the meeting with an expression of gratitude for the generous humanitarian work of the ARA in Russia, but the colonel was not in the mood: "I am following results, and the minute I get them, I will advise my people at home."

Immediately after the conference Haskell wired Hoover, again *en clair*, characterizing his meeting with Kamenev as satisfactory but insisting that until he got results he could not reverse his recommendation that the ARA suspend all further relief shipments. Nonetheless, the moment marked the turning point in the corn campaign, for results were indeed forthcoming.[23]

One of the issues Haskell raised in the conference was the Soviet failure to give the ARA sufficient publicity through the press, a stipulation of the Riga accord. Kamenev vowed to rectify this, and on the following day an informational article about American relief, which had weeks earlier been submitted to *Izvestiia* by Farmer Murphy, appeared in print. Murphy, pondering the fruits of the ARA's conference diplomacy that week, was at some pains to make sense of the behavior of the Soviet government from the point of view of its self-interest. Had the Bolos treated foreigners, especially famine relief workers, with civility, he believed, they would by now have been recognized by the major powers as the legitimate rulers of Russia. Surely they understood this. Trotsky and Chicherin had publicly stated the previous month that the men of the ARA would return home and make known to the American public that the Bolsheviks were not devil figures after all and that this would have a mellowing effect on U.S. policy toward Soviet Russia. Why then did the Soviet government seem intent on spoiling the impression it made on these potential goodwill ambassadors?

I've puzzled and puzzled over this, why such an easy, obvious and effective means of gaining the world's good will should be neglected. I could never find a satisfactory answer until I came to the conclusion that the mass of those in power now are a lot of blackguards and cut-throats who would not last ten minutes after contact with the civilized world was established and that the only way they can keep their jobs, which are the only thing that means anything to them, is to employ the same methods of insolence and terrorism which put them into power. That is the only way one can explain their insolence here at the very moment when their statesmen (?) are at Genoa trying to secure a place for themselves among other nations.[24]

This is roughly how most of the ARA's Moscow Americans, early amateur Sovietologists, saw the matter. They sensed that a few enlightened Bolos like Kamenev could see the big picture well enough and understand what needed to be done but that the bulk of the lesser lights, most of them die-hards like Eiduk—who, after all, had opposed even accepting the gift of American corn—stood in the way of good relations and reasonable efficiency. Professor Coolidge was no longer in Moscow to remind his colleagues of the weight of Russian tradition in these matters.

The Kamenev meeting led to a conference on April 12 between the ARA and the railroad authorities, and this meant most importantly with Feliks Dzerzhinskii, people's commissar of transportation, though far better known as the founding head of the Cheka. Kamenev and Eiduk were present as well at this gathering, which the ARA's record describes as "three hours of struggle." Dzerzhinskii began by attributing the corn seizures to a miscommunication between him and Eiduk. Haskell accepted this explanation, and this allowed the parties to get on with discussing the urgent problem of the obstructed corn trains.

By this point in time, there were 56 trains backed up at Balashov, which were being evacuated at a rate of two per day, the same number as was daily arriving. More trains loaded with corn and child-feeding supplies were on their way from the ports, and the Soviet government had some 330 trains of seed en route. Dzerzhinskii maintained that the only solution was to place some of the corn in storage and evacuate the empty cars, and Haskell consented to this, authorizing the discharge of 1,100 cars of corn—500 at Kozlov, where 400 had already been unloaded over Darragh's futile protest, and 600 at Balashov—into warehouses placed under American supervision, with the understanding that the empty cars required to move this corn would be furnished on or before May 15.

Dzerzhinskii made an ironclad agreement to provide 160 empty cars per day at the ports—far more modest than Krassin's already scaled-back promise of 250—and the ARA was counting on the author of the Red Terror to make good on his word.[25] Indeed, within two weeks trains were moving, empties were appearing at the ports, and Haskell was able to notify Hoover that the transportation crisis had passed and to recommend that food shipments from the United States be resumed. Not until the harvest would the railroads actually catch up and be able to meet the needs of the ARA at the ports, but the tide had turned.

THE RAILROAD CRISIS WAS the greatest obstacle to be overcome in order to deliver the food and seed to the beneficiaries, but there were other hurdles along the way. Once the corn trains arrived by rail at their final destinations, their contents had to be conveyed from the railheads to the villages. Most of the corn was in bulk and had to be sacked—and in most cases was milled—before distribution, the supply of sacks being the responsibility of the ARA. It was up to representatives of villages and food committees to arrange the necessary means of transportation, which meant principally carts or sledges and draught animals.

Then it was a matter of negotiating roads, which were sparse and primitive. Fisher, who had some experience in the Russian outback in those days, observes that due to a combination of the character of the soil, the severity of the climate, and the material used in their construction, the roads of central Russia were barely worthy of the name.

The majority are dusty zigzag routes, wavering across the steppes, with none of the attributes of a road, except a beginning and an end. There are, in some parts of the country, military roads, the "*chaussées*," which are surfaced with cobblestones and consequently so rough that even a Russian peasant, who can sleep on his cart under almost any circumstances, slumbers fitfully as he drives along. The *chaussées*, therefore, serve principally as brilliant examples of what a road should not be, and as guides to the wagon tracks which the peasants have made on either side.

It was during this leg of the journey that the elements posed their gravest threat. The chief worry was not the fabled Russian winter but the coming of spring, for when the thaw set in, the roads would become impassable. The change could be abrupt, as Fisher understood: "The cold weather stops; then come a few hot days; the snow melts; and the whole country becomes a sea of black, tenacious mud, which for a period of two weeks or a month holds up communication as effectively as an inundation."[26]

No wonder the weather—seldom a mere conversational crutch in Old Russia, even in normal times—was a particular obsession of the residents and relief workers of the famine zone from the moment they learned of the congressional appropriation. By late February, when the corn began to arrive, the mood was tense. From Tsaritsyn, Bowden wired Moscow on February 28: "For once people this district praying for late spring enable ARA effect delivery."[27] In Russia "praying" was meant literally.

Bowden's message was received in Moscow just as the weather took a milder turn in northern Europe, freeing up corn ships to enter the Baltic ports. This was good news on the port end, but in Bowden's part of the world this omen of an early spring threatened not only to turn the entire valley into a sea of mud but to melt the ice on the Volga and thereby obstruct the movement of supplies across the river. The one exception was the Kazan district, where an early thaw would serve to expedite the delivery of relief along the region's many small rivers. Otherwise, up and down the Volga the fervent hope was that this was merely a false spring, as it indeed turned out to be. Goodrich, now returned to Russia and the famine zone to resume his investigations, was able to report to Brown in a letter of March 16: "Winter has tightened up again here in Russia. It is very cold now. More snow has fallen in the last two days and covers the country everywhere from the railheads to the communes." Five days later Kelley relayed the good news from Ufa: "Signs of spring have vanished. The snow continues to fall and the blasts are decidedly chilly." Pace Quinn, for once the Lord had decided to cut the Russians a break.

The cold weather continued into April. Only to the south at Tsaritsyn, on the lower Volga, did the ice begin to break before the distribution of the corn was completed. When the river became unsafe for horses, men volunteered to move supplies across using long poles to advance the hand sleds placed well ahead of them.

At Orenburg, at a critical moment of the corn drive and without informing the ARA, the local authorities removed the bridge over the Sakmarskaya River, the only means of transportation across into the Bashkir Republic. This was the usual practice every year on the eve of the spring river rush, but the ice had not as yet melted through—and in any case even the notoriously thick-headed bureaucrats running Orenburg might have considered that circumstances this year were different. As a consequence, the ARA dispatched runners out to the villages, where all available animals, sledges, and carts were mobilized for a big haul of corn across the liquefying surface of the river.[28]

Weather and road conditions aside, there was a severe shortage of draught animals to power the final stage of the corn delivery. The number of horses, by reasonable estimates, had been reduced by as much as one-half since prewar days, with the largest decreases occurring in the now-famishing regions. The loss of all draught animals seems to have been near 40 percent. Many of those still among the living were, like the human population, so weakened as to be unfit for sustained strenuous labor. What is more, the majority of the sturdiest horses belonged to the better-off peasants, who had no interest in offering their teams to perform a service of no direct benefit to them. A year earlier, before NEP, the government would have been able simply to conscript these horses—indeed to requisition the labor of the peasants who owned them—but now it was out of the question.

Even if the self-interest of these better-off peasants could somehow have been engaged, the drought and the famine had caused such a shortage of fodder that they would anyway have been extremely reluctant to employ their weakened animals in the essentially life-threatening job of hauling heavy loads over long distances. The ARA, together with the Nansen mission, arranged for the Soviet government to purchase several thousand tons of oats from Estonia. These oats were then used as a magnet, stored at district warehouses alongside the corn supplies and made available only to those peasant representatives from the villages who came to pick up their corn or child-feeding supplies with animal transport.[29]

Pressed into service along with the horses and the far less numerous cattle were camels, which numbered in the thousands in the districts of Tsaritsyn, Samara, and Orenburg, where they drew sleds or carts according to the season. In the city of Ufa starvation and slaughter had all but wiped them out, although they still survived in some regions of the district, as Kelley soon learned. He first caught sight of them on the edge of the city of Kustanai, where he found a camel team struggling up an incline. There was little romance about the scene. "Camels are led by an iron ring driven through their noses, but not easily, and much blood was spilled about this slope."

The Americans were not expecting to find these exotic beasts of burden in the Russian heartland, and this discovery seemed to reinforce in their minds the notion that they had indeed landed outside "civilization." Dudley Hale wrote from the interior of Samara province on March 5, "The most striking thing about Samara is the sight of great furry camels in the snow dragging little sleds loaded with goods and bossed by great furry peasants in the most alarming headgear of the picture-book Cossack type." Much was made of their legendary stamina, which in a time of famine assumed vital importance. Mackenzie of the *Chicago Daily News* confirmed that "The camel can live where the horse dies. It grubs up herbage from under the snow. It will exist on anything. The horses had died wholesale all over Samara during the autumn from lack of food. The camels still lived." It turned out that the camel's reputation for stubbornness also was well deserved, as Kelley had seen for himself and as Tsaritsyn's George Cornick reported to his father after observing camel caravans crossing the thawing Volga: "It really beats any circus parade you ever saw, as the camels don't like to go through water at all and cut all sorts of capers."[30]

All the testimony about their unruly individualism would appear to render oxymoronic the notion of a camel caravan, but in fact this was, and remains, the singular romantic image of the corn campaign, perhaps of the entire ARA mission. It appears in numerous letters and reports written by relief workers and has been preserved in several dozen photographs. Most impressive are camel-and-sleigh transport columns extending out of sight into the snowy expanse of the steppe. Some of the shots are posed, the caravan having been momentarily halted. The woolly creatures in the foreground, near the head of the column, appear to stand patiently, cooperatively, as if they are aware of the purpose of the exercise. All the same, in every pose they seem out of their element, their bushy coats merely a seasonal adaptation, like the outsized headgear of their reinsmen.

Their mobilization on such a scale was as extraordinary as the purpose for which they had been drafted. This is confirmed by a Russian inspector of the ARA who was present in a Tsaritsyn village when the locals received word that the Americans were waiting for them to come to a distribution point and collect their first monthly ration of corn, the standard thirty *funts*—about twenty-seven pounds—per person. Within an hour a wagon train was en route.

This is always an impressive spectacle—a transport train loaded with American supplies. At one time 2500 wagons were loaded in Tzaritzin and despatched to Leninsk. Every available animal, mostly camels, was utilized for this transport. In spite of the immensity of the steppes it was impossible to see the beginning or the end of this train. Even the oldest and most experienced teamsters admitted that they had never seen such a sight.[31]

Where draught animals were lacking, man power filled the need, as Hale recorded on April 24 from Samara: "The other day three hundred men arrived at our Corn Warehouses here on foot, each man with a sack. They had walked twenty-five miles, on account of the lack of horse transport, and walked back the same twenty-five miles, each with a forty pound sack of corn on his back."

THE RECEPTION GIVEN this lifesaving corn by the starving Russians was by no means universally uplifting, although, perhaps inevitably, it is the inspirational accounts that endure. The "New York News Letter," the internal organ of 42 Broadway, displayed a weakness for the melodramatic: "Nothing is more beautiful in history than is the picture of the moujik waiting, waiting, waiting, and then rising to exclaim: 'They come! The Americans come!'"[32] The ARA's press releases favored scenes of emotional gratitude as witnessed by the American saviors. Yet the arrival of the corn did not everywhere evoke the affecting response so dear to the ARA's publicity hawks.

Henry Wolfe might well be the most satisfying ARA chronicler of the immediate effect on the beneficiaries of the advent of the corn. At the time, he was on a tour of inspection through the Melekes region of the Samara district. Melekes was in desperate straits, and along his route Wolfe recorded stories—and soon the evidence—of corpse eating and cannibalism. The first corn train arrived in the town of Melekes on April 18. "To say that there was great rejoicing is to put it mildly. The news quickly spread through the town and out into the Uyezd. At first people refused to believe it and then when it became known that corn had really arrived their joy and gratitude cannot be described adequately."

The corn having at last become a reality, the mill began operating and continued to turn all night so that by the time morning came a large amount of very fine flour had been produced and was ready for distribution. Local committees from the villages, given the option of receiving corn or flour, asked for flour in every case. Roads near the mill were packed with people, wagons, and horses, which were emaciated and appeared to walk with great difficulty. The majority of the recipients were Russians, but there were also Tatars, Kalmyks, and Mordvas. In view of the general excitement and the lack of preparedness, Wolfe was surprised by the speed and precision of the operation.

He was one of many relief workers to remark upon the unexpected sense of calm and order that attended the corn distribution. It was nothing like the scenes of fervid chaos they had imagined for themselves during the previous months. Fisher's observation on this was also a subtle commentary on the political culture of old- and new-regime Russia: "When help really came, there was in the great decisive struggle against hunger a greater degree of cooperation, of unity in a common cause, than the Russian towns had known for many years; greater perhaps, than they had ever known. Under the leadership of politically disinterested foreigners, men of all classes could and did join in the accomplishment of a supremely arduous task."

Wolfe noted that each sack of flour was handled with utmost caution "and much as a mother handles a baby." Or, in less benign imagery, "No miser ever guarded his gold with more care than these famished peasants watched over their flour." Where horses were wanting, the corn was conveyed on the bony shoulders of men, women, and children. This was the case in the village of Yakushskii, where all the horses had been eaten. At the news of the coming of the corn, every villager able to walk the ten miles into town—from little children to the elderly—was on the move. Having reached their destination and been loaded down with flour, they turned to walk home. "In looking at this feat it should be kept in mind that these people had been starving for months. They are subnormal physically and for people in their condition this accomplishment can only be described as wonderful."

Wolfe, like most of the relief workers serving at the famine front, would have readily concurred with Fisher's estimation that "The bringing of the corn to the villages is chiefly a tale of peasant fortitude. Those peasant qualities which in the past have made Russian armies strong in battle, revived and, under American and native leadership, brought victory under conditions as formidable as war."[33] ARA veterans would have occasion to reflect upon the stamina of the Volga peasants two decades hence in the time of the Battle of Stalingrad.

The chairman of the local food committee of Novo-Maina paid a call on Wolfe in Melekes and told him that American corn had saved the lives of the fifteen thousand residents of his volost. "When the wagons came in sight of the village all of the people able to walk dragged themselves after the others. The people knelt on the ground crossing themselves and thanking God and America for this delivery from the grave. Many of the people were crying, he said." Before departing he asked Wolfe for a piece of paper on which he inscribed a brief tribute, which was later translated into English:

TO THE AMERICAN PEOPLE

Great Land, Great People,
Greetings to you from the edge of the grave;
Only in you we found our Saviour,
And at the edge of the grave you saved us.

E.V.D.

The symbolism of deliverance was reinforced by the fact that in many towns and villages the distribution of the corn was accompanied by the peal of church bells in celebration of Easter. Clapp, for example, wrote from Uralsk, "The folk will always connect the ringing of the Easter bells with the yellow American corn which came at that season in 1922 to save their lives."

Russians being culturally so constituted, even without the coincidence of Easter they were likely to perceive their salvation as an act of God. The report of an ARA Russian inspector in Penza describes the mounting tension among the starving peasants awaiting their rescue, building to this climax: "But then came the long awaited day, April 27, and there arrived five cars of corn; but here there were no feverish raptures, but only a single prayerful ecstasy: those who, like skeletons standing on the edge of the grave, offered prayers, crossed themselves and said Praise the Lord, there has come a deliverance from starvation for us and our children."

Many, many others, however, kept such thoughts to themselves, if such were indeed their thoughts. When the communications division in Moscow pressed the men in the field for compelling publicity material on the corn distribution, not everyone could readily oblige. From Orenburg Coleman wrote, with apparent reference to the Kirghiz: "these are the most phlegmatic, stoic and undemonstrative clan I've ever met." In Ufa, according to Kelley, the corn was spread so thin over a vast area that local expressions of gratitude were bound to be relatively subdued.

The Kazan ARA's district history states that "No one who was permitted to watch the first distribution of corn in a village of the famine area is likely to forget the sight no matter how long the life he may be blessed with." Yet the author notes that on the whole the beneficiaries showed conspicuously little outward feeling. "Apparently hunger after a certain period mercifully deadens the nerves of man."[34]

The Kazan district at that point comprised an area as large as the state of Ohio, with a population of up to 3.5 million, of which over 350,000 were receiving corn. Given that this sizable territory was under the administration of only six Americans, who could have witnessed the delivery of only a small percentage of the corn, there must have been many emotional episodes unseen by American eyes. Although perhaps not so many. District physician William Dear was in a small village in Norkeyevskaya volost when the first corn arrived. To his surprise, the occasion created very little stir.

These people have borne so much that their emotions have long since exhausted. Contrary to the popular imagination the corn was not heralded with the ringing of church bells but crept slowly through the village drawn by tired horses piloted by earnest men. When I informed the group of drivers and warehousemen clustered around the Volost warehouse that other shipments were to come and that continual protection would be assured them they received the news with apathy and seemed to take it for granted.

In a village in the next volost he spots a woman in a crowd weeping, "a living skeleton, yellow and emaciated." He learns that she is the only surviving member of a family of five, all of whom have perished from hunger. She cries as she clutches her twenty-day ration of corn. "This remarkable display of emotion in one so far gone towards the valley of the shadow was indeed unusual."

His peregrinations at an end, in a single epic sentence Dear reflects on the enormity of the Russian undertaking:

After passing through the Volosts of one of these cantons, living in the village and talking with the people whose hopes of life have been built on the possibility of securing American corn one cannot refrain from thinking of the vast chain, administrative and physical, which has been forged link by link for thousands of miles from American elevators in the Middle West where corn was being used as fuel, to the seaboard across the Atlantic, to ports in the Black Sea and in the Baltic, and thence, drawn by crippled engines in broken down cars over many snowy miles of a decadent rail system, manned and guarded by half starved crews to serve villages such as those I had been through where life and hope was almost extinct.[35]

IN SOME PLACES the corn arrived too late to have maximum impact, and in a number of regions this meant that in the race between the corn and the seed, the corn lost. Orenburg was especially unfortunate in this way. By the time the corn reached the famine zone, the Tashkent line, the sole artery connecting the district to the Volga, was snowbound, and thus much of the corn intended for Orenburg had to be diverted to Samara and Ufa. Only thirty corn cars managed to roll in just before the spring thaw broke up the roads, and most of it had to be used for child-feeding. When the seed arrived at Kunel, the junction point where the Tashkent line broke off from the Trans-Siberian, Coleman requested that it be held up and that the corn be shipped in first in order that the starving peasants not be tempted to consume the seed. The Soviet authorities agreed to do this but in fact did not, with the result that a large amount of the seed that reached the peasants never made it into the ground.

There was better ARA-Soviet cooperation in Simbirsk, where the situation in April was very tense because much of the seed was stored in warehouses and ready for distribution two to three weeks before the corn—which then made its appearance at the last moment, leaving a "very small margin of escape." At last, Somerville exulted, "the kukuruza was no longer a myth." Even when it happened that the corn was actually delivered shortly after the seed, the Simbirsk peasants trusted the word of the ARA, it was said, and had begun planting.[36]

It was never a question of the proper sequence for the residents of the Samara district's ill-fated Pugachev region, "the plague spot of the Volga," where both corn and seed arrived too late to prevent the loss of many thousands of lives, a calamity which one relief worker on the scene termed a "holocaust." The outcome for the Samara district as a whole was far better, with Shafroth able to report on May 5 that "In many places American corn arrived just in time to save the seed, which was distributed shortly after, from being eaten." In Tsaritsyn the ARA determined that although the corn made it in time, part of the seed was still used for food: "Many of the starving could not resist the temptation." Colonel Bell estimated that 25 percent of the seed in the Ufa district arrived too late to be sown.

The Soviet famine committee determined that overall 65 percent of the seed was distributed in time for the planting, a statement that, whatever its accuracy, leaves unaddressed the question of what percentage of that seed may have ended up in the peasants' stomachs.[37]

As it turned out, the concerns aroused in the United States by the prospect of American corn confounding the starving Russians had been exaggerated. Where milling was available at the distribution points, most village representatives requested that their allotment be ground—which makes sense, the peasants being familiar with flour and not with corn. But since there was only a limited number of mills in the villages, many peasants received their share as whole corn. As far as the relief workers could tell, the Russians improvised its preparation more or less successfully. Shafroth says that in one peasant home he visited the corn was chopped very fine and boiled for a long time, producing a "very palatable" meal.

Buckley in Orenburg said that as a general rule the recipients of whole corn had a tendency to undercook it, which might raise havoc with their digestive systems. He noted a few instances of death caused by the consumption of raw corn, which had been one of the nightmare scenarios discussed in the United States the previous December. The Saratov ARA history records that "many families," upon receipt of their first corn ration, "mixed it with water and a little salt and ate as much as they could hold becoming violently ill." In Novorossisk, Hutchinson saw a man sitting on a roadside munching an apronful of raw corn, like a horse. The normally inquisitive professor apparently did not wait around to study the effect.[38]

All told, the corn campaign, which would continue past the crisis through the summer of 1922, was a success. "Corn is King" in Russia, American newspapers proclaimed, though in fact it never became truly popular with the Russians, who would take to complaining about its taste once the worst was over.[39] Yet the central fact is that American corn secured the harvest of 1922, and this was the supreme achievement of the ARA in Russia. The corn accomplished this not merely by preventing the consumption of seed and nourishing the tillers of the soil. The ARA was itself the agent for the import and distribution of the seed, and the push to deliver the corn was the driving force behind the revival of the ports and railways, which enabled a critical mass of seed to get through in time for the planting. According to Russian and American testimony, numerous peasants used the ARA corn itself to expand the seeded area, planting their rations while they continued to survive on food substitutes.

Other effects of the corn, aside from its direct nutritive value, were immediately palpable, most significantly its role in turning back the tide of the refugee movement. Actually, the coming of the corn initially exacerbated the problem by accelerating the flight of refugees toward the cities and other distribution points. But upon arrival there, all refugees were told to return to their villages where their own food committees would issue them corn—although desperate cases were supplied with rations sufficient to sustain them for the journey back home. Within a short time a countercurrent of refugees had been set in motion.[40]

In local marketplaces the announcement of the corn's arrival triggered reductions in food prices and resulted in an even greater increase in the general food supply since hidden stocks now emerged and were often put up for sale.

An unforeseen application of the corn was as remuneration in spring-cleaning campaigns sponsored in the districts by the ARA. Corn rations served as wages for "corn gangs," mobilized to clean city streets of the filth that had accumulated over the previous five years and was now laid bare by the melting of the snow. Typically composed of refugees, corn gangs were employed for a variety of projects, including the repair of railways, roads, and buildings, and the construction of bridges and dams. These protopublic works projects were organized in the provincial capitals and subdistrict cities and towns. The corn gangs of Orenburg city gave employment, at peak, to some one thousand refugees.

This particular use of corn was not inspired by a central directive from Moscow headquarters; rather, several district supervisors hit upon the idea independently at roughly the same time. The chief purpose was to promote sanitation and thereby prevent epidemic disease, but the end result was also an improvement in psychological health.

All of this came under the umbrella of the ARA's corn campaign, a job "put over in big shape," in the parlance of the relief workers. They were proud of its role in reviving the Russian economy, but they derived more satisfaction from noting its influence on the spirit of the people. In mid-August 1922, Buckley took in the scene in Orsk, his bailiwick in the district of Orenburg, and considered the transformation brought about by America's gift.

The effects of the corn have been to change Orsk from a dead city, and one with a distant mourning appearance, to a city of happy people who live in the natural way of natural people, who sing as they stroll in the evening in little groups through the streets, who dance in the park on the nights when the band plays, who, in short, do everything they did in better days.[41]

Tsar Famine had been vanquished by King Corn, not to return for another decade.

CHAPTER 9

THE GIFT HORSE

Frank Golder's journey from Moscow to the Caucasus brought him to Novorossisk late in the evening of February 6, 1922, just a few hours after the docking of the first corn ship, the *Winnebago*, which he learned had been "met by a brass band, saluted by a military company, and greeted by the leading citizens with speeches." On the 7th he watched the unloading of the grain, which drew to the dock a number of Greeks eager to help themselves and indignant to learn that this was not permitted. "They are not the only people who demand the grain": the railway employees all along Golder's route were assuming that they would get a share, "and the list of others who think they are entitled to some is endless." The thought of it was enough to drive him to despair.

The ARA has tackled the biggest and hardest job of its existence and I shall breathe a sigh of relief when our organization has left this country. It is working against almost insurmountable obstacles, against a government that is suspicious, against railway officials and employees who are thinking how to steal most for themselves, against a transportation system that is on its last legs, against dishonesty, trickery, demoralization, incompetence, apathy, famine, typhus etc. God help us all.[1]

The question of how long the ARA would remain in Russia had been left open at the outset of the mission. Hoover had long been eager to get a relief expedition inside the country, and at the moment that this became possible it seemed that an American presence might well serve as a catalyst in a transition to a post-Bolshevik Russia, so vulnerable did Lenin's government appear to be. Once Haskell and the Russian unit informed Washington of the durability of Bolshevik power, however, and after a few months of dealing with Soviet officials on the famine front and with left-wing critics at home, the question became how long it would be before the ARA could reasonably withdraw from Russia.

By the time the corn and seed campaign was underway the thinking among Hoover and his men in Washington and New York was that once the back of the famine had been broken and the 1922 harvest secured, the relief workers could quickly and cleanly evacuate. The termination of such a large and complex operation required considerable advance planning, and so as early as March when the corn delivery was as yet in its early stages, the chiefs began to deliberate about getting out. Rickard cabled Brown on March 15 that New York headquarters was working with "definite determination" toward a September 1 "liquidation," an

ARA term borrowed from the U.S. Army. According to this timetable, the sale of food remittances would have to end by April 30 and all medical supplies would have to reach Russian ports no later than June 15.

Brown seems to have been caught short by Rickard's message, responding that no matter how successful the harvest, if not the ARA then *some* relief organization ought to be operating in Russia through the winter of 1922–23 for the purpose of carrying over three million children. Of course the thought of the ARA staying on another year was "a hard thing to contemplate and a question of policy and resources for the Chief to pass upon, and on which I do not wish to recommend. I simply wish to make clear that, in the interests of humanity, *a competent organization* ought to be prepared for another year's intensive work for children in Russia on a big scale."[2] Even with all the diplomatic tiptoeing around, Brown was arguing forcefully against an ARA withdrawal.

The very idea that the ARA would simply pull out of Russia after meeting the emergency was not in keeping with the organization's own philosophy of relief. Every one of its European operations included a significant phase of "reconstruction," which looked beyond the immediate task of relieving hunger to promoting the economic revival of the beneficiary country. Nowhere was the case for such assistance more compelling than in Soviet Russia, but Russia was different in being ruled by an ideologically repugnant government, which Hoover had no desire to aid economically. Better to disengage from the enemy and return to a pure policy of waiting him out. Yet political considerations could not be made to serve as a rationale for ending relief to Russia; on humanitarian grounds alone, quick termination was going to be difficult to justify to the American public.

At Spiridonovka 30, as word began to filter through in early April that New York was seriously considering closing down the show upon completion of the corn program, publicity man Lupton Wilkinson found the prospect scandalous, protesting to Baker that such a precipitate withdrawal "would be an astounding act. In all our consideration of the Russian problem it must be remembered that we have to create a new set of mental values and standards." The appropriate model for Russia, Wilkinson thought, was Poland, where the ARA's reconstruction program had been essential to the final success of the mission.

An abrupt cut-off of our work in Russia this fall would be in absolute contravention of the principle of gradual easement to self-support, exemplified by our operations in other countries of Europe. From the standpoint of sheer humanity the proposed cutting off of the sale of food remittances at the end of this month, for instance, is no less than staggering to one who has seen the incredible and heart-breaking value placed upon these packages in even so prosperous a place as Petrograd.[3]

The ARA might depart in September, but "misery and suffering on a large scale and the tremendous, pitiful tragedy of Russia's undernourished children will most certainly not have been terminated."

Others in the Russian unit, especially among those in the field, felt less of a sense of obligation to stay beyond the harvest. Their number would increase with the approach of summer, as corn rolled back the famine, bread prices fell, and hopes for the autumn crop rose. They assumed that there would be hunger in Russia in the coming year, even starvation in places. But Russia being Russia, there would be always be hunger. The ARA was not designed to address a permanent condition, and one had to draw a line somewhere.

The inclination to withdraw was fed by the outspoken optimism of the Soviet government, which in spring was quick to declare victory over the famine and in summer to exude confidence about the harvest. Official enthusiasm was fueled by a desire to impress Western opinion, most directly the diplomats at the Hague Conference, the successor to Genoa, which opened on June 15 and continued through July. More anxious than ever to attract foreign trade and capital investment, the Bolsheviks wished to make it understood that the famine was completely behind them and that Russia was well on its way to full economic recovery.

Considering their source, such hopeful prognostications would seem to have offered Hoover sufficient protective cover to justify closing down the Russian mission at the harvest. Yet liberal-to-radical opinion in the United States urged a continuation of American relief for another year, with Hoover's critics accusing him of purposely underestimating the need.[4] Rosy Soviet forecasts did nothing to dampen such sentiment, which was occasionally inflamed by dire predictions given to the press by independent American "observers" after flying visits through the former famine zone. Of course, to any first-time Yankee visitor to Russia the Volga countryside even in its postfamine recovery stage might evoke one or another of Dante's circles. Yet even Nansen, who should have known better, made alarmist public remarks about an impending catastrophe, announcing on July 20 that the harvest was a failure—eleven days after *Pravda* had proclaimed it a success.

The ARA had to make its own estimate of the size of the crop and the outlook for hunger beyond the harvest. To this end, Haskell summoned the district supervisors to Moscow for a mid-June conference to discuss the future of the mission. Some of these men had not seen the capital since their arrival in Russia the previous autumn, and Haskell's invitation now afforded them the opportunity to witness the remarkable revival that had taken place in the intervening months. Actually, already by January 1922 there had been a dramatic improvement, to judge by the testimony of Childs, who had been serving in Kazan since September. To him the Moscow street scene now compared favorably with that of London or Paris: the roads much traveled, the people well dressed, the stores well stocked. "It was such a sight as to make one rub one's eyes and to wonder how otherwise than in the rubbing of the genie's lamp by an Aladdin this transformation had been so suddenly effected."[5]

Shafroth passed through town in May as he was retiring from the mission. His father had died the previous winter, and with the corn campaign over he was going to meet his mother, who was traveling in Europe. After nine months in Samara, he found Moscow radically different from the city he had explored with the members of the advance guard the previous August. "The dull, weary, hopeless look had gone, and in its place there was the bustle of a busy metropolis. Sidewalks thronged with people, stores with actually something to see, a comparatively small number of unoccupied shops, many automobiles hooting along at a rapid pace, much fewer people carrying sacks, many more well dressed." Of course the metamorphosis had to do with nothing so otherworldly as a genie's lamp. "Commerce had restored a dying trading place and made it again into a community of our own day and time."[6]

The district supervisors, arriving now in the middle of June, had the same fascinated reactions, and subconsciously this may well have inspired them to offer sunnier assessments than otherwise of their own regions' economic health. They were joined from the United States by Rickard, Goodrich, and Christian Herter, Hoover's assistant, and from London by Brown. Haskell chaired the two-day conference.[7]

On June 16 the eight supervisors present were each asked to make a report. Most complained of a lack of government cooperation. Fatigue and the letdown after the great campaign were clearly in evidence and not only among the men serving in the field. Golder wrote to a Stanford colleague on June 10: "Our men have lost interest in the work and the best men are quitting. Colonel Haskell does not wish to remain, Quinn intends to resign, in fact our most dependable men have had enough and do not care to stay on the job in order to wind it up."[8]

The four Volga supervisors on hand—Tsaritsyn's could not attend—confirmed that the famine in their districts was over and that the outlook for the harvest was good, while Bell of Ufa and Coleman of Orenburg, districts where the seed program had largely failed, warned that famine would return to their regions in the coming winter. Coleman, however, was so fed up with his treatment at the hands of the Orenburg Bolos that he favored early withdrawal anyway. When Haskell put the question to them, all the supervisors except for the indefatigable Bell voted to discontinue relief by September 1.

When asked, however, about continuing beyond September with a reduced program, four of the eight supervisors expressed support for the idea. All were against attempting to set a deadline of January 1, by which time regional food shortages would begin to occur and make withdrawal politically infeasible. The colonel, who seems to have been the most determined of anyone to get out of Russia, then expressed the opinion that if it could be shown that European Russia could feed itself, the ARA ought to pull out as soon as possible. The record indicates that all the supervisors agreed with this ambiguous statement.

On the following day, the discussion turned to the future of the food remittance program. The value of the food package was falling steadily, and in some places already approached the sum of the market prices of its component commodities. Haskell proposed to halt shipments immediately so that deliveries could be completed by September 1. All the district men agreed except for Renshaw of Moscow, whose food remittance department could barely keep up with business and who urged that the program be continued for as long as the ARA remained in Russia.

The floor was then turned over to Hutchinson, who presented his economic forecast for the coming year, based mainly on central and local official Soviet statistics and thus involving, he allowed, considerable "guess work." He estimated that the 1922 crop would exceed that of the previous year by anywhere from 333 to 480 million poods—a pood being the equivalent of about forty pounds—and noted that all foreign relief for the previous year had amounted to about 120 million poods. He concluded that while there would no doubt be hard times ahead, by and large the former famishing regions would be able to take care of themselves.

Guesswork or not, this was good enough for Haskell, although as he then explained to the gathering, it was up to the Chief to make the final decision and that meant a further conference in the United States. Still, the district men came away thinking that the end was near. Haskell, Goodrich, Rickard, Herter, Brown, and Quinn then met in a separate session, and following that, Haskell cabled Hoover his report.

This curious document reflected the tension between the colonel's resolve to wind up the show by the harvest and his inability to vouch for the sufficiency of Russia's food supply beyond that point. Haskell conveyed what he said was the consensus of the ARA officers present in Moscow, that the harvest would provide enough food to last only until about February, after which the provinces of Kazan, Ufa, Orenburg, possibly Samara, and isolated spots elsewhere would experience localized famine unless supplies arrived from the southern parts of Russia or from abroad. What information this prognosis was based on is not clear, but it was a good deal less optimistic than Hutchinson's assessment.

This would appear to have made the case for a continuation of American relief, but Haskell was more impressed by a different set of considerations. He advised Hoover that the ARA's situation would become unbearable in postfamine Russia, especially if it carried on with a reduced program. Extending the mission, Haskell predicted, would involve the Americans in "a constant struggle to retain control." He was also convinced that after the harvest the government would, through taxation, remove an amount of food from the countryside roughly equivalent to the quantity of food brought in by the ARA.

It would be impossible, Haskell advised Hoover, to withdraw in midwinter, when food shortages would have broken out, and so the choice was between getting out at the coming harvest or remaining on through to the next. Given all this, and especially in light of the "excellent" crop in the fields and the fact that any incidences of local famine during the winter would be directly attributable to inefficient Soviet administration, Haskell recommended termination as of the harvest. This, he added, was the unanimous conclusion of the chiefs assembled in Moscow. The timetable appended to his report came close to undercutting its own recommendation: cessation of all relief activities by October 15 followed by six weeks for liquidation and then final withdrawal by December 1.[9]

In any case, a schizophrenic telegram was not going to decide the issue, and Haskell, Rickard, Brown, and Herter departed Moscow for New York to be joined later by Goodrich. In the meantime, other foreign, especially American, relief organizations were announcing their intentions to stay on in Russia for another year, which heightened the anticipation of Hoover's impending decision because a total ARA withdrawal, it was felt, would make it especially difficult for these agencies to conduct successful fund-raising appeals. The staffs in Moscow and New York were cautioned to remain tight-lipped until the matter was settled in conference with the Chief.

Goodrich, being something of a free agent and having become accustomed to the spotlight, was not so easily restrained, and this threatened to become a problem. Rickard and Brown cabled ahead from London to New York to advise that the governor was making public statements far too optimistic about Russia's recovery, which might end up embarrassing the ARA, depending on its ultimate decision. After the Moscow conference Goodrich had headed to Kazan to have a look around. Hutchinson's report had estimated that the region would bring in a crop sufficient to last, on the most optimistic end, ten and a half months. The Tatar authorities told Goodrich that the district would have enough to eat for eight months. But the governor's optimism was unbounded: "My own judgment after driving thru the worst canton in the republic is that they will raise enough to last thru the entire year and have an actual surplus."

After a further excursion to Samara he made his way out of Russia and on to Washington, where he issued a statement on July 15 that read in part, "If the grain on hand and the coming harvest are properly distributed there will be no famine in Russia this winter."[10]

As Goodrich must have understood by now, in Russia the conditional phrase "if properly distributed" left ample room for a devastating famine. Few relief workers in the field were feeling so sanguine. Childs, for one, was not prepared to declare the end of the famine in Kazan; maybe in the Tatar Republic, the district's largest territory, but "we have only begun to scratch the surface of it in Perm and Votskaya." He worried that in the coming winter Kazan would see conditions as bad as those of the previous year. Barringer, based in Ekaterinoslav, relates that the Americans there read "with strange emotions the statements of Gov. Goodrich that the famine is over and all's well in the Ukraine," when in fact Ekaterinoslav's food supply was insufficient to last beyond December.[11]

Goodrich arrived in New York in time to attend an extraordinary meeting of the ARA's executive committee and officers, which Hoover convened on July 30 for the purpose of deciding the future of the Russian mission. Fisher's book gives no hint of it, but in fact right up to the final moment Hoover was seeking a politically acceptable way of shutting down operations at the harvest. Two days prior to the conference he wrote a letter to Hughes following up on their recent conversation concerning Hoover's suggestion that the American Red Cross assume responsibility for the conduct of all further "charitable activities" in Russia. Such a handoff made perfect sense. "The American Relief Administration in its whole inception, character of its organization and personnel, is a famine fighting organization. The great famine in Russia is over with the present harvest."

True, Hoover allowed, the Russian unit had been carrying on a substantial medical relief program, but medical and sanitary work was foreign to the ARA; a typical Red Cross mission would be far better suited to mount the large-scale operation necessary to fight contagious disease. The Red Cross could also administer a supplemental program to provide food to the many thousands of waif children that had survived the famine. Moreover, it had an organizational network throughout the United States capable at any time of conducting a special appeal for funds. This would help prevent Americans from being preyed upon by relief organizations of "communistic inspiration."

Such an arrangement would not only be reasonable but just: "The American Relief Administration being a voluntary body grown out of the war, composed of professional and business men who have given many years of voluntary service, has a right now of laying down its burden, having dealt at one time or another with upwards of two hundred millions of people."[12]

The proposed Red Cross solution, whatever its actual promise, was nullified two days later by the decision of the New York conference to commit the ARA to remain in Russia with a reduced program until the harvest of 1923. There being no

record of the deliberations, it is impossible to say for certain what it was in particular that persuaded Hoover to opt for continuation. The announcement issued at
the end of the session, on July 30, cited the need for medical relief to fight disease
and for further food relief for waifs and for urban children generally, and stressed
the importance of continuing the food remittance program as a way of safeguard-
ing the future of Russian culture. These considerations alone would have justified
extending the mission, but the statement indicated two further, negative induce-
ments: "If the A.R.A. retired, it would create a great shock of abandonment and a
loss of the high appreciation of American ideals that has been bred in the Russian
people during the past year and it would open the field to the prey of dishonest,
inexperienced, and propaganda organizations in appeals for relief funds from the
American public."[13]

Thus, there was no hint of what was perhaps the most crucial factor behind
the decision to keep the ARA in the field, which had to do with opinion on the
home front. Given all the talk, not to mention the actual possibility of a return of
widespread hunger, even famine, in the coming winter, evacuating Russia at that
moment would have raised no small amount of controversy—and a considerable
scandal in the event that the most dire predictions came to pass.

Hoover, in other words, having succeeded in getting into Russia, now found
he had no politically acceptable way of getting out.

THIS WAS NOT GOING to be welcome news to a good many relief workers inside Russia, who had been getting used to the idea of going home. Fisher, who
was in Moscow on August 3, 1922, before the outcome of the New York conference was known, relates that a rumor was in the air that operations would continue for another year, which if true, would deliver a "hard blow to some of the
boys who are all set to clear out as soon as possible." Two days later, Barringer
wrote from Ekaterinoslav: "The American personnel is a wee bit 'fed up' with the
whole show but if the A.R.A. wishes will be willing to carry on until the end of
our operations." And on August 10, after the rumor had been confirmed as fact,
Golder reported that it was "a great disappointment to the men here and in the
field." Nonetheless, being "loyal to the Chief and to the organization," they would
remain at their posts "until the whistle blows."[14]

The announcement was made just as the ARA reached the peak of its activity, with 199 Americans administering the feeding of 10.5 million adults and children, the adults receiving daily rations of corn grits, the children being served
their balanced daily meals.

The food remittance program also attained its high point that summer as
measured by the number of individual food packages delivered and also by the distribution of "general," or "special," relief packages. General relief was slow in getting started because the Soviet government, which never warmed to the entire
food remittance enterprise, understood that among its primary beneficiaries would
be individuals it had at one or another time labeled enemies of the people. Thus,
when in autumn 1921 the ARA forwarded to the authorities a proposal by the
Harkness Fund to provide $250,000 in food packages for intelligentsia relief, sus-
picion got the upper hand and the government rejected the offer.

A more protracted negotiation began the following March, when the Commonwealth Fund of New York offered to provide $50,000 per month for general relief targeted at university professors and students. The fund wanted written assurance of ARA control over the distribution of the packages. The Soviet government equivocated, which served to exacerbate tensions during the spring transport crisis. At the April 11 showdown, Kamenev instructed Haskell that there were two classes of students in the new Russia: one consisting of the sons and daughters of "former people" and the other of the children of peasants and workers. There would have to be an equitable distribution between the two groups, he told the colonel, something that could be achieved only through the formation of an ARA-Soviet committee to identify the particular beneficiaries. Haskell could not accept such an arrangement, and the matter continued to hang fire until July, at which point the project was abandoned.

This setback did not greatly hinder intelligentsia relief, however, as the ARA decided simply to proceed without written agreements with the government. In December 1922 the Laura Spelman Rockefeller Memorial Fund donated $230,000 for intelligentsia relief, which was distributed without interference from the authorities. In February 1923 the Rockefeller Fund made a further gift of $600,000, most of it for relief to secondary school teachers, an especially needy, and worthy, lot. This necessitated making a special agreement with the government, which with the famine behind it and ARA influence at a low ebb was able to negotiate an arrangement that gave it the majority voice in the selection of beneficiaries. In the end the Rockefeller fund would donate over $1.1 million in support of such relief. Among the individual donors the largest contributor was William Bingham, Jr., whose $95,000 gift supplied food packages to Russian physicians. Other beneficiaries of general relief packages were nurses, professors, school inspectors, notaries, judges, artists, musicians, writers, ballet schools, religious bodies, and unclassifiables such as families of priests in prison and other unfortunates.

The testimony of numerous relief workers confirms Ellingston's assertion that nothing in the entire operation gave them so much satisfaction as the distribution of these discretionary packages, which could not but have a profound impact on the lives of the recipients. An American in Rostov relates how the local Russian in charge of overseeing general relief, a woman of French background, often wept when making her verbal reports on individual cases. "The American donor, through whose generosity this assistance was made possible, will never really know —never can imagine—the immense relief he afforded these people, their worthiness, and their gratitude."[15]

Throughout the summer the corn-powered "spring cleaning" campaigns continued, focused chiefly on the repair and reconstruction of public facilities. Among the many projects undertaken was the construction of a road from Odessa to Nikolaev, the rehabilitation of an agricultural experiment station in Samara, and the renovation and equipment of a hospital in Kiev, which became a home for waifs. As before, a major emphasis of these campaigns was on sanitation, which dovetailed with the purposes of the ARA's medical program.

Disease prevention was a high priority and toward that end the ARA conducted an aggressive inoculation program. The vaccine employed was designed to immunize against cholera, typhoid, paratyphoid, and dysentery. Predictably, this "invention of the devil," as some peasants in Ufa called it, aroused popular suspicions and, where defiance led to the issuance of a corn ration being made contingent on getting a shot, resentment.

The medical program afforded the districts the freedom to improvise. In Orenburg in March 1922 the ARA opened a drug store, where the needy could obtain drugs free of charge. This establishment turned out to be terrifically popular, the crush of overzealous customers sometimes making it impossible to get in the door. In August, when it was operating seven days a week, the Orenburg drug store served some 320 customers a day. The Kazan district opened a free venereal clinic and on the banks of the Volga a large sanatorium for tubercular children.[16]

Several districts began to sponsor free baths, a service subsidized with corn rations. Those Russians willing to submit were provided with soap and had their clothes sterilized while they bathed. A bonus here, much remarked upon by the Americans, anyway, was the noticeable atmospheric improvement at the theater, where the collective odor of the spectators was said to have grown tolerable.

THE RUSSIAN MISSION in its second year was bound to be a far less adventurous errand of mercy. In the words of the ARA's July 30 announcement, "the great famine battle is over and the problem is now one of re-adjustment of the aftermath of famine." The sharply reduced program for the second year went into effect on September 1. The focus of relief now shifted from the villages to urban areas, with special attention to be given to the waif children roaming the cities in packs like wild animals, a problem so acute that it would persist throughout the decade.

The plan was for the ARA to provide relief for up to one million children, the original target at the outset of the mission, while adult feeding was to be dropped almost entirely except for a limited number of hospital patients. In fact, the ARA's feeding rolls were cut from 10.5 million in August to somewhat less than a million in September, although this figure would begin to rise again steeply beginning in late autumn. The distribution of medical supplies, which had earlier been accelerated in anticipation of an autumn withdrawal, was now slowed inasmuch as the medical program was to be extended through the second year, as was the sale of food remittances.

Just as radical as the steep drop in feeding figures was the change in the mission's modus operandi. In keeping with the "time-honored policy of the A.R.A. of building up local institutions," as the July 30 statement put it, the relief workers would continue to operate American kitchens only to the extent that home-grown institutions such as hospitals and orphanages were unable to receive and serve the American food, until eventually all feeding was administered through such government-run establishments. As part of the new arrangement, the American ration was reduced in size in order to feed as many children as possible.[17]

To the degree that there was to be a gradual shift of operations from ARA-run "open" kitchens to Soviet, or "closed," institutions, it was unavoidable that the relief workers would have less influence over the selection of beneficiaries. Increasingly, their job was to ensure that these Soviet establishments were properly managed, using American food as leverage to enforce ARA standards of sanitation.

The new emphasis on inspection and control led to the creation at Spiridonovka 30 of an administrative division bearing that title. This was to be the only such expansion after September 1922, the intention being to decrease the number of American personnel in accordance with the reduced program. The goal was to retain sixty relief workers through the winter, though on December 31—as the feeding totals rose to meet the upwardly revised target of three million children—there would still be 124 ARA men on the job in Russia.

There was as well a reduction in the geographical size of the ARA mission: in order to avoid spreading the diminished relief supplies too thin, Moscow closed the Orenburg district and momentarily considered shutting down Ufa, the largest ARA district, before concluding that the need there was simply too great. On the Volga the Tsaritsyn district was merged with the food remittance station at Rostov, which became the headquarters of this new Rostov-Tsaritsyn district.

In Ukraine, a spring 1922 plan to place American operations under the authority of the Jewish Joint Distribution Committee, which would then maintain a mission there after the ARA's autumn departure, was aborted after Hoover's decision to stay on. The troubled ARA-JDC marriage was thus fated to continue through another trying year. The setup remained as before, with six Ukrainian districts, each reporting separately to Moscow. Relations between the ARA and the JDC, a rich subplot of the relief story, were strained by the thorny issue of how much administrative control the ARA should retain over an affiliated organization that in the end would contribute nearly $5 million to the Russian mission; by tensions between the ARA's nonsectarian principles and the JDC's sectarian purpose; by feelings of antisemitism—both of the local population and, allegedly, of some of the ARA Americans; and, inevitably, by clashes of personalities, most pointedly with Haskell's.

A key personnel change that ensured that relations with the government would be less unpleasant during the second year was the replacement, on June 27, of Eiduk by Karl Lander. Like Eiduk, Lander was a Lett with a background in the Cheka. Unlike Eiduk, he was not one of the Party's leather jackets, having entered pre-1917 revolutionary politics through the intelligentsia door. He was a former professor of folklore at the University of Riga and a onetime disciple of Tolstoy, with whom he exchanged correspondence on one occasion.[18] Lander was no Tolstoy, but the new chief plenipotentiary was certainly a more cultivated man than his predecessor, and this would help keep the lid from blowing off in the months ahead. It also did not hurt matters that unlike his prying predecessor, he maintained his office separate from Spiridonovka 30.

Things got off to a reasonably good start. The day after his appointment, Lander issued instructions to all his representatives in the districts, outlining their responsibilities and delimiting their authority.[19] Such an order had been promised by Kamenev back during the April crisis, and, also as promised, Haskell's office was invited to make editorial suggestions during its drafting. This gesture of cooperation seemed to herald a new era of harmony in ARA-Soviet relations, but its significance was vastly outweighed by the essential fact that with the famine conquered and the harvest secured, the Bolsheviks no longer needed the ARA.

To complicate matters, the Bolshevik leadership was in a foul mood in the wake of Soviet diplomatic failures at the Genoa and Hague conferences. This inspired the Party to launch a propaganda counterstrike against NEP, a backlash that manifested itself not in the realm of economic policy but of politics. The summer witnessed the noisy trial of the Socialist Revolutionaries in Moscow, though this bit of political theater had been in the works for several months. More telling was the exile abroad, in August and September, of several dozen *intelligenty*—principally professors, engineers, and non-Bolshevik former political activists.

This anti-NEP surge, manifest in a harder line taken in Soviet newspaper articles, took place just as the struggle to succeed the ailing Lenin was getting into full swing. The "Old Man," as he was known among the Party elite, was an active force in Kremlin politics only fitfully now. In March 1923 partial paralysis and loss of speech would end his political career; a final stroke in January 1924 would send the father of bolshevism off to commune with Marx and Engels.

On July 24, with the machinery of relief still going strong, ARA inspector Arthur Ruhl observed that the psychology that had accompanied the period of acute famine had passed, that "the gift horse is being subjected to a rather determined dental gaze, and the powers are looking forward to a time when they will again be running their own show without interference." The harvest was upon them, and already "the authorities are beginning, figuratively and literally, to feel their oats."

Two days earlier, Gregg at Saratov had remarked that the ARA's "greatest weapon," its food supplies, had become "considerably blunted" because of the forecast of an abundant harvest. And two weeks after that, Quinn informed London that the relief workers were experiencing increasing difficulties in their relations with the authorities, notably in those regions where the crop was starting to come in, which had the effect of placing the ARA's "heavy weapon" hors de combat. Quinn nonetheless speculated that relations with the government would not substantially deteriorate because the Soviets still wished to court the ARA in order to win political recognition from the United States.[20]

This leverage would from now on have to serve as the mission's principal weapon as the districts radically reduced their programs. In Simbirsk, for example, on September 1, child-feeding allocations dropped from 445,000 to 50,000, while all of the 400,000 adults who had been enjoying a daily corn ration since early April were cut off. Thus, Somerville reports, overnight the ARA had become in the eyes of local citizens and officials "just a plain ordinary relief organization." He interpreted the new perception of the ARA as an interesting commentary on the ability of the human mind to accustom itself to anything: whereas in November 1921 feeding 50,000 Simbirsk residents was regarded as a remarkable accomplishment, in September 1922 it was considered "almost niggardly." By December the total would rise sharply, to 265,000, but never again would the American relief workers be able to recover their status as idols in Bololand.

Accustomed to holding in their hands the power of life and death for whole territories of people; to being able to deal with the local governments with tremendous prestige and bargaining power which this fact gave—it was just a little difficult at first to become accustomed to the new idea of an organization relieving only fifty thousand people, instead of eight hundred thousand and to dealing with a local government that was—or pretended to be—much more impressed with the number of rubles which it was paying out on expenses of the A.R.A than it was with the value of the food and medicines of the A.R.A. It knew that most of the fifty thousand would probably not actually be starving without A.R.A. relief; and as for the few that might starve, they were not important. The American giant, saving a whole population, had become an everyday man, helping needy people—needy individuals. And under some theories of society, the individual does not count.[21]

Getting used to an existence as mere mortals was distressing enough, but the relief workers also had to adjust to the new practice of turning over American foodstuffs to government institutions. For a full year they had steadily fought to retain complete ARA control over relief supplies, but now they were supposed to release their grip. It was expected that the Soviet authorities, especially local officials, desperately hard-up for cash, would be pleased with the change in policy because it would relieve them of the expense of running American kitchens. This assumption was correct, but the anticipated windfall from it—namely, better government cooperation—proved to be illusory because the Bolsheviks were disposed to turn the ARA's retreat into a rout.

On September 8, Kamenev informed Haskell that in view of the revisions made to the ARA program it would be necessary to draw up a new written agreement. The colonel could not have been completely surprised by this bid. Back in the second week of May, when the two men had first sat down to discuss the question of continuation, Kamenev had called for amending the Riga accord. On that occasion Haskell shot back that the ARA was "only too anxious too quit," and that if it were to remain in Russia beyond the summer, it would be under the same conditions or not at all. Kamenev persisted, voicing concern that insofar as a smaller program would have food remittance as its largest component, it would ruffle the Party's left wing because the bourgeoisie supposedly benefited far more than the laboring classes from the distribution of food packages. Haskell refused to budge, however, and Kamenev let the matter drop. Now, in their September 8 meeting, Haskell once again held firm and Kamenev backed off, claiming that he had only sought to ascertain the colonel's opinion.[22]

So the issue seemed to have been put to rest, but this was only how it seemed. On October 1 Haskell received a memorandum from Lander's office introducing certain changes in Soviet government policy with regard to all foreign relief organizations in light of the improved food situation. The famine having been defeated, the document announced, foreign agencies would now be required to pay those costs of their operations formerly borne by the government. In the specific case of the ARA, its open kitchens would have to be shut down—not gradually, but all at once—and its food supplies handed over to Soviet institutions as dry rations. As well, the ARA would have to assume responsibility for the import and transportation fees of its food package program and distribute all packages in close consultation with the trade union organizations—conditions that, if agreed to, would have gutted the food remittance agreement. A similar stipulation addressed the distribution of ARA medical supplies. Lander requested a prompt and favorable reply.

Haskell immediately passed the document on to London, editorializing for Brown, "You can see at once that this is an effort on the part of the Communist Party to thoroughly Nansenize the A. R. A." He vowed to stand firm, believing that any retreat from the fundamentals of the Riga Agreement would be "a fatal mistake." The analysis at Moscow headquarters was that Lander's thrust was part of the stepped-up Soviet press campaign against "bourgeois ideology" and reflected the related rise in influence and militancy of the trade unions, now rebounding from the initial shock of NEP.[23]

On the following day Haskell fired off a stiff reply to Lander, declaring that either the Riga accord be allowed to stand or the ARA would withdraw from Russia. The Russian unit had always strived to keep the expenses of the Soviet government at a minimum, the colonel contended, and had since September 1 sharply reduced the number of its open kitchens as it made the transition to institutional feeding. Altogether, since August the operating funds required of the government by the ARA had been cut by over two-thirds. Apparently, though, this was not good enough. "I can quite realize that the time may have arrived when the Soviet government no longer requires the assistance of the American Relief Administration. If this time has arrived, I should be officially advised in order that I may cancel orders abroad and commence liquidating."

Haskell requested a definite reply within two days: by high noon on Wednesday, October 4. Five hours later Lander sent over a response, which was an attempt to stand by his directive while insisting that it did not signify a revision of the Riga Agreement. Haskell decided to ignore this message, and at 11:00 A.M. on the morning of October 4, one hour before the deadline, Lander appeared in person at Spiridonovka 30, embarrassed and unhappy—in fact, "very humble," according to the colonel. He brought with him a document prepared after a conference with Kamenev, Dzerzhinskii, and Krassin, which maintained that no one in the government had raised the question of repudiating the Riga principles, and explained that the new conditions set out in the October 1 memo were directed primarily at other foreign relief organizations.

This was the climb-down Haskell had been holding out for. He boasted to Brown, "When the show-down came and we stood pat, the Government decided that it was better to have us in Russia and to turn down the unions and satisfy them some other way rather than to have us withdraw entirely." The only carrot Haskell offered was a willingness to compromise on the payment of freight charges for food packages. Otherwise, "We have definitely exploded their balloonful of ideas that the various professional unions of Russia are going to be directors of our policy and absorb the administration of the American Relief Administration." The colonel declared complete victory.[24]

But the celebration was premature, as reports from his commanders in the field shortly made plain. At the beginning of November the district supervisors all at once began to pepper Moscow headquarters with queries about an alleged new ARA-Soviet agreement transferring control over American kitchens to the government. The source of the problem was the Committee for the Struggle Against the Consequences of the Famine—or, in the Russian acronym, the Posledgol—the recent successor to the Pomgol. It turned out that on September 25, five days before Lander issued his memorandum, the Posledgol, assuming that the ARA would yield to the government, issued a circular letter to its local affiliates announcing the new order as fact. Then, evidently unimpressed by Haskell's diplomatic triumph, the Posledgol issued another circular on October 31 confirming the revised arrangement. Armed with this authority, local Soviet officials and Lander's plenipotentiaries made it their purpose to close all American kitchens.

Childs of Kazan, normally generous in his praise of local cooperation, wrote bitterly to Haskell: "Of course, we all expected the attitude of the Government to change so soon as our operations were reduced but I was hardly prepared for the almost brutal haste of this change of attitude from one of 'apparent' gratefulness to one of scarcely concealed annoyance." Although only four open kitchens remained in operation, the local plenipotentiary was not satisfied and insisted on further closures. Childs complained of the "waste of nervous energy in constant wrangling and dispute in the delivery of successive ultimatums." Meanwhile, local Posledgol officials were demanding the authority to select the children to be fed in the remaining open kitchens.[25]

The relief workers assumed that a major incentive behind the drive to funnel all ARA food into Soviet institutions was the opportunity it would afford the government to exercise political discrimination in the selection of beneficiaries, though officials defended their actions by pleading tight budgets. Indeed, during the second year of NEP, as Moscow pressed on with the task of putting Russia's fiscal house in order, local governments, cut loose financially by the center, operated on the verge if not in a state of bankruptcy. John Gregg of Saratov reported in spring 1923: "It is not an uncommon sight to see a sign in front of a bureau informing the employees thereof that the January pay will be issued on May 15th. And the back pay is never made up." Government departments now demanded payment up front for services. "Money, money, is the cry everywhere," Golder recorded.[26]

As long as Tsar Famine ruled Russia and American food was saving lives, local authorities in most places usually managed somehow to scrounge up the necessary cash to keep relief operations running, though not without constant pressure applied by the ARA. The Orenburg Americans, cursed with the company of obstructive apparatchiks, were especially caught in the money squeeze, even as the corn was making its way into their district. Yet even in Simbirsk, a district blessed with a generally cooperative local government, shortages of funds dogged the ARA throughout the famine year. The Tsaritsyn records indicate that already by November 1921 the government's tightfistedness had become a regular source of anxiety to the relief workers there. Supervisor Bowden, never timid about offering advice to Moscow, wrote Haskell on March 10, 1922, urging him to confront Eiduk about the Tsaritsyn district's financial straits, which he called a violation of the Riga Agreement.

Moscow counseled understanding and patience, but Bowden and his successor, Dorsey Stephens, refused to believe that this was simply a case of government insolvency. Stephens, who was at Oxford with Bowden in 1915 and belonged to the same school of upward management, unburdened himself to Quinn on July 21:

I cannot agree with you that the question of finance is not one on which we can go to the bat with the government. My brain is, perhaps, becoming soft, but I am absolutely convinced that an attempt is being made to demoralize and discredit our organization (we have daily proof of it here) and evidently one of the best methods is to shut down or cut down on the pay of our employees, in order to cause the best of them to leave our employ and to spread dissatisfaction among the rest. . . . With the new crop coming in fast and the famine temporarily arrested, we have been able to note a decided stiffening in the antagonistic attitude of the authorities towards us (as I say, I consider the refusal to pay our employees adequately indicative of this attitude).

Stephens was writing after the corn rush had already performed its miracle work, liberating local authorities from their dependence on the ARA and making them that much less inclined to expend precious rubles to support the activities of a foreign relief organization, least of all one of bourgeois-American type. The successful harvest and the steep reduction in the ARA program served to harden such resistance. Then in October came an official declaration of the end of the famine and with it a sharp curtailment of the size of central government appropriations set aside for foreign relief operations.

James Hodgson found the well going dry in September upon his arrival in Rostov to open the headquarters of the newly merged Rostov-Tsaritsyn district. Procuring funds from the Rostov soviet, he informed Moscow on September 22, was "like finding water in the Sahara, only worse." When he reminded local officials that they were three months behind in paying the salaries of his Russian staff, he was told that if these people had been able to sustain themselves for that length of time without government assistance, then such rations must not be needed and would therefore no longer be issued. "Life in Rostov since the writer arrived here has consisted of just one damned ultimatum after another."[27]

Hodgson's lament was echoed by other men in the field throughout the second year of the mission. In themselves, none of the individual district confrontations, however grave they may have seemed at the time to the Americans directly involved, could have led to a serious crisis in ARA-Soviet relations. Given the high stakes involved and the ARA's weakened bargaining position, only an objectionable initiative openly undertaken by the Kremlin itself would have been capable of casting a shadow over the future of the mission. As it happened, such a threat arose in autumn, when the Soviet government began to export grain.

AS EARLY AS JULY, Soviet officials were predicting that the harvest would be plentiful enough to make possible the sale of grain abroad. Some of this optimism was calculated, part of the orchestrated effort to convince the world of Russia's full economic recovery, in particular its return to an influential position in the world grain market. Nonetheless, even mention of the possibility of grain exports had the effect of undercutting the position of foreign relief organizations planning to bring food into Russia after the harvest. The official Soviet posture tried to have it both ways, asserting either that the amount of exports would be very limited or that the government would sell abroad only that grain that the as-yet frail internal transportation system prevented from being distributed to the needy at home.

In September Moscow headquarters began receiving reports from men in the field that Volga rye was being shipped out of Petrograd, Ukrainian wheat and barley out of Odessa, and Kuban wheat and barley from Novorossisk—three of the ports the ARA was using to import food for needy Russians. It is true that aside from flour to make bread the products the ARA used for its rations did not duplicate the items the Soviets were said to be exporting. But it was at this very time, in mid-September, that Haskell had begun to explore with the Soviet authorities the possibility of the ARA resuming the daily feeding of as many as 2.5 million adults. The most suitable grains for this purpose, as the Americans saw it, were wheat and rye, two of the cereals the government had reportedly begun to sell abroad. This fact would make it next to impossible for the ARA to raise the money necessary to support a return to adult relief.[28]

Hoover was said to have been considering an appeal to the American public for funds until he was deterred by reports of the abundant harvest and rumors of Soviet grain exports. Instead, he drew up a letter addressed to former ARA contributors asking them to donate to the Russian mission to the best of their abilities. The distribution of this letter awaited a clarification of the Kremlin's grain export policy, which was the central topic on the agenda of a further Haskell-Kamenev conference held on October 20.

At this meeting, Kamenev estimated that by November 1 there would be 4.3 million Russians in need of food relief; by January 1 over eight million. The government would be able to support four million, and other foreign relief organizations could be counted on to look after one million, thus leaving three million to the charity of the ARA. Informed of these calculations, Hoover demurred. He found it curious that while the Soviets' present estimate of the crop was four hundred million poods larger than their forecast of July, when their tone was unconditionally optimistic, they now claimed that eight million Russians would go hungry without foreign assistance. And although they had tempered their public enthusiasm, they nonetheless continued to profess an ability to export food.

Hoover wired Haskell that Kamenev's story did not hold up—worse, it aroused suspicion that the Soviets "wish to secure charitable imports, in order to realize an export business." He directed the colonel to inform Kamenev that the ARA would expand its program to adult feeding only if the Kremlin pledged to halt its grain exports. The American people could not rightly be asked to donate funds for Russian relief if the Soviet government refused to make every effort to assist its own people.

At subsequent sessions between Haskell and Kamenev, on November 6 and 8, a clearer picture of the Soviet outlook emerged. The grain the government was exporting, Kamenev explained, had been acquired from peasants through the food tax and other standard practices, much of it on credit from peasant cooperatives. This grain was expected to be sold abroad for at least ten to fifteen million dollars, money which was to be used to acquire badly needed agricultural implements and industrial machinery unavailable in Russia. Grain was the only resource available to the Soviet government to enable it to make such purchases. Kamenev told Haskell that only if it could secure a foreign loan of ten to twelve million dollars would the government be in a position to prohibit the export of all cereals for the coming year.

In other words the Soviet government was saying, as Fisher formulates it, either we must export grain and leave four million of our people dependent on foreign charity, or the ARA or some other agency must help us arrange a foreign loan, which we have up to now been unable to secure through direct negotiations with foreign governments.

This fuller explanation at least had the advantage of plausibility, but it appears to have sent Hoover into a genuine fit of outrage, which he expressed to Haskell in a cable of November 18:

[T]he A.R.A. being a charitable organization devoted to saving human life from starvation must protest against the inhumanity of a government policy of exporting food from starving people in order that through such exports it may secure machinery and raw materials for the economic improvement of the survivors. Any such action imposes the direct responsibility for the death of millions of people upon the government authorities.

The Soviet government's view of these matters was, needless to say, radically different. Its chief priority in 1922 was the revival of heavy industry, without which there could be no talk of building socialism in Russia. Lenin told the delegates to the Fourth Congress of the Communist International in Moscow in November 1922 that the recovery of industry was "indispensable" to Soviet Russia. "Heavy industry needs state subsidies. Unless we find them we are lost as a civilized state—let alone, as a socialist state." Most any Russian government would have set such a priority, but ideological imperatives made the Bolshevik cause an urgent one. Ideology was at the same time the chief obstacle to its success. Having tried and failed to win trade agreements, loans, and credits at Genoa and The Hague, the Kremlin's sole recourse, other than acceding to Western economic and political demands, was to export grain.

Hoover, on his part, wanted nothing to do with subsidizing Soviet industrial reconstruction. In any case, his thinking on these matters was not circumscribed by adherence to Marxist precepts, let alone by feelings of Russian nationalism. He believed, as he wrote in a private letter in March 1923, that Russia should abandon heavy industry and establish a "low-grade agricultural state dependent upon exchange of food to other countries for manufactured necessities."[29]

Hoover may have been surprised to learn that most of the American relief workers in Russia, Haskell included, eventually came around to accepting the Soviet position on grain exports. Among them was Ellingston in Moscow. After an initial outburst of Hoover-style indignation, he became the most coherent defender of the Soviet export policy inside the mission. In a memorandum to Quinn of January 23, 1923, he dismissed the notion that there could be no need for foreign food relief in a country exporting grain and also the argument that the ARA had no business unloading a cargo of American flour on one dock while Russian grain was being loaded for shipment at an adjacent dock.

This argument is not sound. The grain does not belong to the Government; it is the surplus of the rich peasant; it may be in the Government's hands, but they have paid for it on credit or by promises and must export and sell in order to repay those promises. Export is inevitable, and would probably take place to the utter damnation of the Soviet Government if there wasn't an ounce of feeding going on in the country.

To Fisher's objection that because the exported grain belonged to the rich peasant, he alone would reap the returns on it, Ellingston countered:

It isn't a question of individual benefit; it's a question of national economic rehabilitation. If the rich and enterprising peasant plants twice as much grain as he did last year, the national wealth of the country will be just as much increased as if three poor peasants planted the same increase. Also the poor will benefit because of the need for labor that increased planting will mean. The more he plants the more help the rich peasant will need. Not Communistic but sound business.[30]

Not Communistic, indeed. Ellingston's brief on behalf of the Soviet government underscored a feature of NEP that struck the relief workers with special force: the Bolsheviks' almost complete abandonment of the so-called poor peasants, whom they had championed after Red October as the Party's "vanguard" in the countryside. In those heroic days they were cast as the village "proletariat," allies of Soviet power in the class war against the "capitalist" peasants, or kulaks—that elastic label, applied as convenient to any and all prosperous or recalcitrant peasants. With the introduction of NEP, Bolshevik agrarian policy shifted to a tacit wager on these very kulaks, seen now as the best hope for reviving agriculture.

The practical consequences of the new conservatism first became evident to the relief workers during the spring 1922 seed distribution when Moscow instructed that the seed be supplied to the well-off peasants, who could be counted on to plant it. As Somerville observed from Simbirsk, "Even a communistic State finds itself forced, at last, to bring back to life the truth once spoken: 'To him that hath, it shall be given.'" Somerville noted that the peasants who had come through the famine intact were those who before the Revolution had been of the thrifty, hardworking sort. "This lesson has not been wholly lost on that less substantial class who had taken the Revolution as a heaven-sent opportunity to live without working, and becoming the backbone of government support in the villages had spent their time attending meetings, plundering landlords' houses, and making requisitions of the better-to-do peasants."

Despite the severe shortage of draught animals, the authorities refused to press better-off peasants to make their horses available to transport corn and other food supplies into the villages. Nor was the government inclined to use grain in its possession to pay for such services, even though those who stood to benefit most were peasant "proletarians" who had only recently served in Bolshevik requisition squads. As a result, the delivery of food was often delayed, giving rise to what one relief worker called the "strange anomaly" of the "bourgeois" ARA taking the side of the village "proletariat" against the Bolsheviks. The Americans urged government officials to squeeze the rich again, while Communist officials defended their right to build up a class of strong peasants.

Fisher remarked in May 1923 that "the poor devils that were first gathered in by the Communists to do their dirty work have now been left high and dry and of course cannot do anything about it. The Kulaks have always said that the poor peasants were a worthless lot who were better dead and now it seems that the Communists have come around to the same point of view."

Somerville captured the new spirit of the times: "The word has gone out: 'Every man for himself, and the devil get the hindmost.'"[31]

THE OUTCOME of the ARA-Soviet dispute over grain exports was that Hoover decided to abandon any idea of an appeal for funds and forgo an expansion to adult relief. Based on Haskell's recommendation, however, the Russian unit was authorized to increase its feeding rolls through the winter to three million children and sick adults. This resolution removed an obstacle that had threatened to derail the entire mission, but it was not the end of trouble.

Though Haskell had successfully rebuffed Lander's October 1922 attempt to Nansenize the ARA, "the Bolos are not so easily beaten," as Ellingston phrased it. Soviet meddling markedly intensified after Haskell left Moscow at the end of

November for an extended visit in the United States. What they had failed to achieve preemptively in October, the Bolsheviks now sought to win by means of what acting director Quinn called "indirect action." It began with Lander informing Quinn that the number of railroad cars at the personal disposal of the Americans would be cut from thirteen to five, that the ARA would have to pay for the use of its Moscow personnel houses, and that the government would no longer pay the salaries of the Russian employees engaged in inspection work. Quinn invoked the Riga Agreement, but Lander stated flatly that there was not enough money available to pay for relief operations. Why could the ARA not simply turn over its supplies to the government for distribution?

In reporting this on December 28 to the New York office—to which Brown and the London headquarters had been relocated the previous month—Quinn maintained that the Bolsheviks were merely using the plea of bankruptcy as a ploy to attain control over ARA operations. He recommended standing firmly by the Riga Agreement. Granting concessions, he asserted, would be "a very unsatisfactory policy."

On December 31 at a combined meeting of the Posledgol and of delegates to the Tenth All-Russian Congress of Soviets much was made of the fact that the value of American relief was not worth the cost to the government of ARA operations. As reported in *Pravda* on January 3, this gathering recommended that an effort be made to close American kitchens and that the Riga Agreement be appropriately revised. On the following day, Quinn cabled New York in regard to this mounting pressure: "we forced conclusion Government using economy as weapon control our feeding."[32]

Quinn sat down with Lander and explained to him that 31 percent of ARA food was already being distributed in hospitals and other government institutions and that the ongoing expansion of American relief could only be carried out through open kitchens since the neediest villages typically had no established institutions to serve the purpose. Quinn pointed out also that the amount of the funds the ARA received from the central government was less than half of what the Russian unit itself had disbursed to its own local employees, whose wages, according to the Riga Agreement, were supposed to be paid entirely by the Soviet authorities. He then produced figures to prove that the total ARA-related expenses of the Kazan government for the previous year—minus transportation costs, which would have been the same regardless of which agency had brought in the food—amounted to a mere 3 percent of the value of American relief. In Simbirsk in the month of September 1922 it was 2.3 percent. On what, Quinn wondered, had the Soviet government based its recent finding that its share of the cost of American relief was inordinate?

Reaching right for the source, Lander produced Roman Weller, formerly one of Eiduk's finest in Simbirsk, now an assistant in the Posledgol. Weller determined that the cost to the Samara provincial government of American relief operations added up to 33 percent of the value of the actual relief itself. It was based on this figure that the joint session of the Posledgol and Congress of Soviets had called for the rollback of the Riga Agreement.

Quinn informed the promising Soviet statistician that he had somewhere made a mistake. Together they worked through the math and, lo and behold, arrived at the figure 3.3 percent, Weller's own 33 percent having resulted from a misplaced decimal point.[33]

Weller is said to have "apologized profusely," but the entire exercise hardly mattered in any case: as Quinn understood, the latest Bolo drive was about attitude, not arithmetic. On January 6 Hoover notified New York that since the Russian unit would withdraw in April or May, the best thing for the ARA was to avoid a conflict over money and thus to assume a larger share of the overhead costs. Hoover cabled Quinn on January 8 to advise him that, providing that the Moscow government agreed that the Riga Agreement was to remain in full force, he was authorized to take on some of the expenses hitherto the responsibility of local governments, including the salaries of office staff and inspectors, though not of kitchen, warehouse, or transportation personnel.

Hoover wished to emphasize that this modest adjustment did not contravene the Riga principles: "It is nothing more than a liberal interpretation of minor clauses to meet changing conditions as we enter the liquidation period of A.R.A. efforts." Thus the ARA had committed itself to pay some $10,000 per month in order to avoid a fight and to retain control over some seven or eight million dollars in foodstuffs until the close of operations.[34]

That this step would not magically set matters aright between the government and the ARA was to be assumed. Still, having gone some way toward satisfying the Soviet demand to pay the wages of the Russian personnel, the Americans in Moscow appear to have been counting on a measure of gratitude from the Bolos; instead they got more demands.

The central and local governments now began to insist that the Americans pay for their own housing, automobiles, and fuel and pressured the ARA to sign a collective agreement with the increasingly assertive Soviet trade unions. The ARA's courier pouches, meanwhile, were subject to aggravating delays—and on one occasion seized and the contents disclosed, with scandalous results publicly revealed in the Soviet press—while a supply of incoming medical alcohol confiscated by customs agents was held up for several months until Haskell gave up and ordered its return shipment. A member of the liaison division whom the Soviets found politically odious and who had gone out on leave was for several weeks stranded in Riga, denied permission to reenter the country. These and other such annoyances lent ARA-Soviet relations during the second year the feel of a running feud.

Shortly after Haskell returned to Moscow at the start of February he had a rather curious encounter with Mikhail Kalinin, the former peasant and now figurehead Soviet president, who offered the colonel what he claimed was the view of ARA relief from the village. He said that the peasant was grateful for the lifesaving food of the previous year, but that with the famine over he had lost all enthusiasm for American relief. Raised on a diet of black bread and some meat and fish, he did not appreciate having his children consuming white bread, cocoa, corn grits, rice, and so on. Kalinin said that in the peasant's eyes this balanced ration was "altogether too fancy and unnecessary," in fact comparable to a "box of candy," and that he resented having to pay taxes in order to cover the cost of its delivery.[35]

It was only a matter of time before the next financial crisis led to a further Haskell-Kamenev tête-à-tête, this one on February 27, when the colonel delivered another of his by now well-rehearsed threats to withdraw the mission. Haskell had been appointed high commissioner for Greece by the American Red Cross in December 1922 and charged with alleviating the refugee problem caused by the war with Turkey. Regardless of how eager he may have been to devote time to his new assignment, he was by now itching to be out of Russia. Thus, while he yet again declared that the Soviet government ought to honor its financial obligations under the Riga Agreement, on the other hand, "If the Government cannot see its way clear to meet the minimum responsibilities and expenses still borne by them and will tell us so frankly, asking us to withdraw, we can divert food-stuffs now coming forward to Greece, Germany or Turkey and can get out of Russia without any hard feelings whatsoever."[36]

As on previous such occasions, Kamenev managed to say the right words—or perhaps by now from the colonel's perspective the wrong ones—which meant that the show had to go on.

WITH THE AIM of deterring smaller-fry Bolos from causing an incident during the final phase of the mission, Moscow headquarters decided it had better enforce a kid-glove approach to relations with local officials. The new policy, christened "samovar diplomacy," was inaugurated in a January 22 memo from Quinn to the district supervisors, which advised the men in the field to exercise tact and restraint in going about their business and to stifle any urge to arrogance, a quality known to exist in abundant supply among these congenitally cocksure Americans. They were to conduct their relations with local officials in "a spirit of fairness and courtesy—if for no other reason than that we owe it to our own self-respect. We have found that a certain amount of 'samovar diplomacy' helps much, and that periodical informal discussions of our plans, fears, and even hopes, has helped in avoiding the many difficulties that are due in large part to misunderstanding and lack of sympathy." The purpose of the new line was to facilitate a clean-cut "liquidation" of ARA operations. "This is a difficult task and will require the enthusiasm and hard work of everyone in the show."

Inspection chief Phil Baldwin coached the supervisors in the fine points of samovar diplomacy through circular and personal letters. Much of this instruction came down to jollying the men along, as in this passage from his February 19 missive to the Ekaterinoslav supervisor: "'Samovar diplomacy' is not always easy or pleasant when the representative is not endowed with personal attraction. However, we know that you clearly understand our point of view, and where government relations can be improved by sacrificing yourself by hobnobbing with a bewhiskered boor, for instance, you will gladly offer yourself as a martyr to the cause."[37]

Hoover himself had effectively set the new tone in January 1923 when he agreed to have the Russian unit assume more of its own overhead costs. The point was that the ARA should by all means avoid being drawn into a fight as it turned toward the home stretch. Haskell understood perfectly well what was at stake, advising Brown on February 28, "If, for any reason, we should break off between now and the conclusion of our task, I am sure that we would be accused of having forced the fight at the last moment." Like Hoover, Haskell was concerned ultimately with making the proper impression on the American audience. "I feel that we are so near a successful conclusion of our work that we can stand almost anything for the few remaining months, rather than have a break with these people and give the radicals in America the opportunity to attack us for deserting these people and forcing a fight with them."

In the event, samovar diplomacy did indeed help to keep the peace in Russia, but this did not keep the ARA out of controversy in America. Beginning in January, Hoover came under some pressure, mostly from "pinks and reds," as he colored them, to organize an appeal for Russian relief in order to finance the adult feeding that the ARA had months earlier considered taking up. Privately, Hoover now reasoned that his hands were tied in this matter by the failure of the negotiations with Kamenev the previous November to resolve the grain export issue in the ARA's favor. Mulling over ways to undercut the position of his critics, he briefly contemplated publishing the telegraphic and other correspondence between Haskell and himself on the export question, which, he hyperbolized, would be "equivalent to accusing the Soviet government of being a wholesale murderer." Accusing and, to his mind, convicting. The risk with taking that step, as he undoubtedly understood and as Haskell was quick to point out, was that it would likely make the ARA's situation in Russia untenable. Instead, Moscow headquarters was advised to encourage the American correspondents to file stories optimistic about the coming Soviet harvest.[38]

The issue would not have entered the realm of controversy, let alone scandal, but for a misstep at 42 Broadway. The source of the trouble was a March 6 telegram from Haskell to Hoover which stated the unarguable fact that, there being no more starvation in Russia, what that country required was not food relief but credit or investment in order to rebuild the economy.

Realize reconstruction outside province ARA but we should give public correct situation so any assistance can hereafter be directed proper purposes.

Decision Soviets export grain based effort accomplish above but upbuilding without foreign financial help slow and ineffective and sure entail misery and suffering by millions over long period years.

Kamenev has read above and concurs.

By this time Haskell had become an advocate of official American relations with Soviet Russia, which seems improbable given all the unpleasantness he experienced as director of the mission. Yet the colonel was by no means an exceptional case: most of the principal ARA staff members in Moscow sooner or later came around to urging some form of U.S. recognition of Lenin's government—not out of love for the Bolos but rather as a way to move them in the direction of further economic and political moderation and eventually, in the best possible world, unwitting political self-extinction.

Regardless, in making an unambiguous statement in favor of American economic assistance to Russia, Haskell was exceeding his charge as an official of the ARA. His telegram arrived in Washington in the midst of a new round of public debate over the prospects for U.S. recognition, including, on March 21, Secretary Hughes's first official statement on Russia in two years: an uncompromising affirmation of the administration's nonrecognition policy, though with a new emphasis on the evils of Soviet propaganda.[39]

Other ARA advocates of recognition argued the point privately, but Haskell became publicly associated with the prorecognitionists when on March 19 *Izvestiia* published an article signed by Lander, identifying the colonel and Senator William Borah as the American champions of American-Russian friendship. This was overdone, but as Haskell was living among the Russians and regularly negotiating face-to-face with the Bolsheviks, his name lent the prorecognition camp the kind of hard-bitten credibility it otherwise lacked. What is more, he was a Hoover man. On March 6 Haskell wrote to Herter in Washington:

The question of politics is entirely eliminated in my feelings—the form of their Government or its efficiency, is also quite immaterial to me and, while I realize that those may be controlling factors, still I know that one hundred million people are never going to be dragged out of the mud until some such action is taken. When one contemplates day after day the constant deterioration of farms, transportation and industries, and when one sees the appalling lack of education, and the horrible living conditions under which this great mass of people exist, it is impossible not to wish to see the day come when something which promises a permanent improvement will come.[40]

On March 8 Hoover issued a statement to the press that quoted Haskell's March 6 telegram, though not the passage justifying Soviet grain exports and pleading for outside assistance in the reconstruction of Russia. Unfortunately for Hoover, someone at New York headquarters, responding to a request from the editors of the *Nation*, inadvertently turned over the complete, unedited text of Haskell's communication, and the journal went to press with it on March 21 under the headline "Mr. Hoover Stabs Russia."[41] Beyond making public the suppressed passages of the telegram, the *Nation* revealed that Hoover, in his recent statement, had attributed to Haskell a sentence that was not in fact his own: "Economic reconstruction is outside the province of the A.R.A. which is purely an emergency charitable organization for amelioration of famine conditions." The editors condemned Hoover for the cover-up and insisted that he stop using Soviet grain exports as an argument against an extension of American relief.

Now this was certainly a cause for embarrassment. It was, however, completely obscured ten days later by a colossal blunder committed in Moscow, where the Soviet government, having chosen this most inopportune moment to stage a trial of the Catholic clergy, put to death Polish Monsignor Constantine Butkevitch. It was an act that outraged opinion in the West and set back the cause of American recognition of the Soviet Union by a decade. Hoover may have stabbed Soviet Russia, but once again the Kremlin had shot itself in the foot.

AS IT HAPPENED, the ARA had not been able to expand its program according to schedule and remain on course for a spring termination. The low mark of relief during the second year came in November 1922, when American rations fed 743,453 children and 62,050 infirm adults. Thereafter the totals increased steadily until June 1923, when 2,767,598 children and 142,227 adults were on the ARA's feeding rolls.[42] In the process, the Orenburg district was reopened, and operations were spread to the Republic of Daghestan, on the Caspian, where in a unique arrangement the local authorities were allowed to distribute American supplies after having signed an agreement on the principles of their distribution.

This expansion took place principally in American-run open kitchens, which was bound to complicate the process of phasing out the mission. This time, though, nothing was going to get in the way of an American withdrawal from Russia before the next harvest. Once again Hoover sent in Goodrich to confirm that the danger of recurring starvation had passed. Hutchinson produced another optimistic assessment of Russia's food prospects, and the district supervisors all pitched in accordingly. The outlook for the harvest was good, some noted, thanks in part to the continued presence of the ARA: with American food there to serve as a safety net, peasants were emboldened to plant more of their grain or to use it to buy horses, carrying on with much smaller reserves than usual.[43]

All was not well in the former famine zone, of course, but the worst fears of renewed starvation in 1923 had not materialized, and for the hardened relief workers of the ARA it was a matter of starvation having given way to mere hunger and want—of the sort that had been common in Russia for as long as there had been a Russia. It was time to go home.

Despite Kalinin's admonition about a box of candy, most peasants did not wish to see the ARA withdraw. Not every supplicant was what he appeared, though, as Samara's Richard Bonnevalle learned during an inspection trip in the first half of April. There he heard peasants cry, "We are starving," "We will die." The "starvation" victim presented to him as an omen of the coming disaster, however, turned out to be the same one that had been trotted out for Harold Fleming two months earlier. Further along, Bonnevalle encountered a Tatar who "swears to me by the bones of Islam" that he was without bread, but after a bit of poking around, the skeptical American discovered four or five poods of whole millet and half a pood of white flour in the zealous Tatar's possession.[44]

Things were bad, but they were no longer unusually bad. Around 25 percent of the people in the region, Bonnevalle found, were living on food substitutes, but these were far more nutritious than those of the previous year. Hunger-related deaths would from now on be isolated.

On March 1 Haskell outlined for Brown his plan for the liquidation of the mission, an undertaking which the colonel conceived like a military withdrawal. The ARA would wait as late as possible to announce its departure date, in order not to give the Soviet government an opportunity to launch an offensive against the retreating Americans. First, the distribution of medical supplies would be halted, then the delivery of food packages would wind down. Unlike the previous year, there could be no argument in favor of prolonging the sale of food remittances. By this time the value of a food package had fallen below the combined price of its individual products in the United States, meaning that the potential buyer could better aid the intended beneficiary by sending ten dollars than by spending the same amount on a package.

Following this, all feeding at open kitchens would be terminated, at which point Moscow headquarters would be transferred as expeditiously as possible to 42 Broadway.

Haskell requested New York's approval up front for such an operation "because it is like a mobilization, if once underway in one direction it will be a most difficult thing to turn around or to stop." The Moscow staff was informed, confidentially, of the liquidation timetable on March 13. Food and clothing remittance sales were discontinued in the United States as of March 15 and in Europe as of April 1, on which date the ARA offices in Warsaw, Vienna, Paris, Constantinople, Prague, and Hamburg—whose sole activity was food remittance transactions for Russia—were closed. The intention was to be out of Russia by June 1, though in fact the final withdrawal would be delayed until mid-July.[45]

Soviet provincial officials, sensing an opportunity, became less willing to help the ARA ship its supplies out to the subdistricts, figuring that if they stalled long enough there would be more American food to confiscate once the relief workers departed. In order to hasten the liquidation, the ARA decided in May to distribute to each Soviet "closed" institution its prorated share of the remaining food products. The idea was to supply these establishments with an amount sufficient to carry them on a program of approximately three million people through the harvest. The government's postfamine committee, however, took the position that all undistributed food ought to revert to it, and this ensured that ARA-Soviet relations were marked by the usual unpleasantries right to the end.

On June 4 Haskell wrote to Kamenev formally announcing the discontinuation of the ARA mission with the harvest. On June 13 the last food shipment from America arrived at Riga; on June 15 the food remittance division ceased operations, and on that same date Haskell and Kamenev signed a simplified liquidation agreement waiving all potential American and Soviet claims and counter-claims.

BY THE TIME it was over, the ARA, following its standard practice, had gathered a mass of statistical data documenting the types and quantities of food and medical supplies it had distributed in Russia over nearly two years. An appendix in Fisher's book conveys many of the details in the form of meticulously crafted statistical tables. Here American food relief, as measured in metric tons, is broken down by commodity, by district, and by numbers of persons fed daily per month per district; the distribution of medical supplies is specified in numbers of bales, boxes, and barrels, cases and cars, by month and by type of institution supplied.

Fisher calculates that in the end ARA relief to Russia totalled $61,566,231.53, though this sum includes over $11 million spent by Russia and Ukraine, mostly to purchase seed. The ARA sold $9,305,300 in food remittances to individuals, which means 930,530 individual packages, of which 99 percent were said to have been successfully delivered. When combined with the amount of remittance supplies sold in bulk to other relief organizations in Russia, the total comes to $13,680,193, representing seventy-five thousand tons of foodstuffs. From these sales the ARA earned a profit for its child-feeding operation of approximately $3,600,000, a sum sufficient to support the feeding of 3,600,000 children for one month.

Dedicated as it was to the practice of sound business principles, the ARA prided itself on keeping a close accounting of the movement and dispensation of its relief supplies, and except for the troubling anecdotal evidence of widespread theft of American products there is no reason to question the general accuracy of its statistical data. Some facts about the famine, however, were indeterminable. How many lives did the ARA save in Russia through its food and medical relief? Here precise measurement lay beyond the reach of even the statistical whizzes of the ARA.

Of course the ultimate famine statistic is the number of famine-related deaths.

For any large-scale famine the range of estimates is usually considerable. The substantial discrepancies in the tallies of the victims of Russia's Great Famine—of both the eyewitness and the expert variety—can be partly explained by the fact that some observers concern themselves exclusively with the famine year, 1921–22, while others take into account the "postfamine" year, 1922–23; that some count deaths from starvation only while others figure in deaths caused by famine-related disease, primarily cholera and typhus; and that some restrict their inquiries to the Volga and trans-Volga regions while others include Ukraine and the southeastern borderlands.

Yet, not surprisingly, even those examining the same geographic regions for the same time period and using the same basic criteria can reach widely diverging totals—from many hundreds of thousands to many millions. The American relief workers themselves arrived at figures scattered up and down the scale. At the high end, Kelley, who served in Ufa, estimated that between September 1921 and September 1922 famine and disease combined may have claimed as many as ten million lives, while his supervisor, Colonel Bell, concluded in summer 1923 that the ARA had saved from death by starvation "easily over a million children and adults" in Ufa alone. Ellingston, who sat mostly in Moscow but had served for several months in Saratov, also came up with the figure of ten million deaths. At the other end, Shafroth, having left Russia for good in the summer of 1922, counted for all of Russia not more than a million total famine victims, "probably considerably less."

Most relief workers had access to statistical data only for the famine in their own particular districts, and the estimates of men in the field like Kelley, Bell, and Shafroth were the product of a collection of visual images of starvation that had been seared into their memories and that they then projected across the entire famine zone. Among those in Moscow with a view of the big picture, at least on paper, was Harold Fleming, who had studied economics at Harvard and as a Rhodes Scholar at Oxford, which expertise he would later bring to Wall Street as a securities analyst, stockbroker, and correspondent for the *Christian Science Monitor*. He figured that "Hunger probably swept off a million and a half, and but for the timely arrival of the American corn would have taken double this number."

Fleming joined the mission only in summer 1922, and his absence during the catastrophic year might account for his relatively conservative figure. In any case, one is inclined to trust the extrapolated ten million of an eyewitness over the million and a half of a Moscow-based economist. Yet Professor Hutchinson, who personally witnessed the worst of it, endorsed the calculation of the ARA's medical division that the total number of deaths from starvation and related disease over the period from 1921 to 1923 was about two million.

An official Soviet publication of the early 1920s, basing its assessment on a comparison of a partial census of autumn 1920 with another of June 1922, concluded that about five million deaths occurred in 1921–22 from famine and related disease, a figure with which the 1927 edition of the *Great Soviet Encyclopedia* concurred.[46]

Post–World War II Western literature has tended to prefer the monumental figure of ten million deaths even when no credible source is cited to back up the claim. Whatever its general accuracy, such a number hardly seems extravagant after the many tens of millions of victims of war, famine, and terror in the twentieth century. Some would credit the ARA with having saved ten million lives, though not even the most swell-headed relief worker would have thought to make such a claim. One easily arrives at such a figure by taking the ARA's peak feeding total, of August 1922, and assuming that a meal eaten is a life saved. This kind of thinking was evidently what inspired Gorky, in a letter he wrote to Hoover from Berlin on August 7, 1922, to declare that the ARA had rescued three and a half million children and five and a half million adults from starvation. Of course Gorky knew better, but he was urging Hoover to keep the ARA in Russia for another year, and flattery suited his purpose.

In July 1922 the *New Republic* generously credited Hoover's mission with having saved between five and ten million lives. This may have been what prompted the ARA chiefs in New York at around that time to request that Moscow headquarters provide them with a rough estimate of the number of famine-related deaths. Quinn fretted over this assignment, citing the fuzziness of the term "famine deaths" and pointing out that for many remote regions of Russia there was simply no information regarding causes of deaths, let alone mortality rates. Still, he took a stab, of a sort, in a telegraphic reply of July 20: "Our best guess based on other guesses famine deaths in all Russia, including Ukraine, from 1,000,000 to 1,250,000."[47]

Arriving at such a "best guess" required familiarizing oneself with official government data, even though the relief workers found Soviet economic statistics to be highly unreliable and routinely dismissed them as "practically useless," "notoriously worthless," and so on. Kelley called them "a joke." At the Moscow conference of ARA chiefs and district supervisors in June, where his job was to project Russia's food supply for the coming year, Hutchinson preached to the converted: "I have a great variety of figures, none of which are accurate. The best of them are very poor. Even under the old regime, statistics lied a good deal as they do everywhere so that we won't place too much reliance on the figures. The best that we can do is to gather all and make as intelligent a guess as is possible in the circumstances."

"Lies, damned lies, and Soviet statistics," it would appear. Even Fleming observed that "Statistics in Russia are all compiled on the intuitional system." Despite his hearty appetite for the economic data, both ARA and Soviet, that crossed his desk, he conceded that he could establish "truth unadulterated by statistics" only by leaving Moscow and journeying out to the Volga and trans-Volga regions, where one could actually observe the individual daily dramas of famine and relief, take in the unquantifiables.

Mowe Mitchell heartily concurred. Although based in London, he spent enough time with the men in the famine zone during his extended visit in the winter of 1922 to understand that a faithful history of the ARA in Russia would have to be steeped in the anecdotal, "i.e., a side separate and distinct from the cold, hard facts, figures, tonnages, etc., which will not tell the real story by any means."[48]

Harold Fisher's account is of course far more than a collection of statistical tables. Yet as the ARA's official historian writing in the immediate wake of the events he described, Fisher was constrained by the need for circumspection in political and personal matters. In any case, he completed his work without the benefit of some essential documentation, notably the personal letters, diaries, and memoirs of most of those who served. These limitations, among others, precluded him from chronicling the American experience in Russia's Great Famine from the perspective of the relief workers stationed at the famine front. His book reveals little about their particular triumphs and tragedies, their moments of epiphany and absurdity, their individual acts of heroism, generosity, romance, arrogance, stupidity, and lunacy. Nor could Fisher do justice to the unprecedented American-Russian cultural encounter occasioned by the relief mission.

Only by slipping the narrative confines of famine-and-relief can a history of the ARA in Russia hope to realize Mitchell's vision of "a most excellent, human history of the show . . . which would serve as a record when all we who now have the details at our finger-tips will have forgotten them or will be dead."

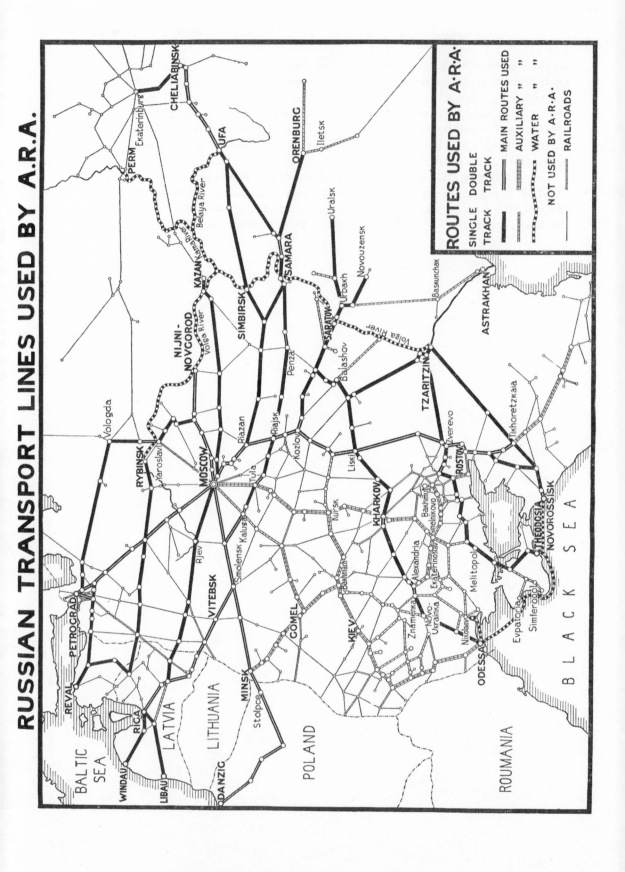

RUSSIAN TRANSPORT LINES USED BY A.R.A.

ROUTES USED BY A·R·A·

| SINGLE | DOUBLE | |
| TRACK | TRACK | |

▬	▬	MAIN ROUTES USED
		AUXILIARY " "
		WATER " "
		NOT USED BY A·R·A·
		RAILROADS

Opposite: Russian transport
lines used by the ARA.
Original ARA map.

Left: Herbert Hoover:
Chairman of the ARA.

Below: ARA kitchen, Tsaritsyn.

Right: Walter Lyman Brown.
Below: ARA food package.

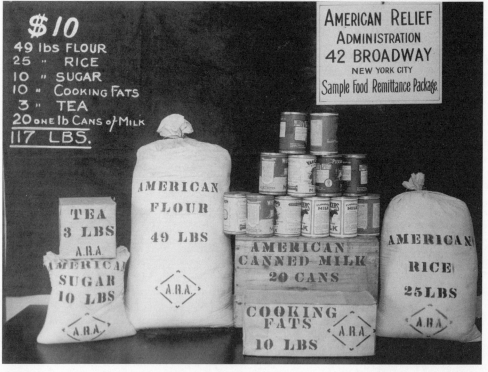

Above: At a children's home, Tsaritsyn district.

Left: Will Shafroth.

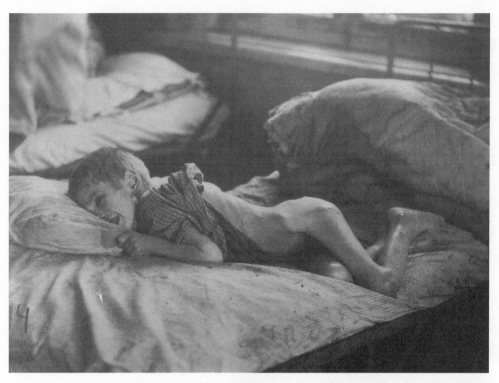

Above: Starvation victim.
Right: Col. William N. Haskell,
1922.

Left: Philip Carroll.

Below: Vernon Kellogg encounters two refugees on a Moscow street, September 1921. Courtesy of the family of Elmer G. Burland.

Above: ARA village kitchen, Tsaritsyn.
Right: Refugee girl, Melitopol.

Left: Aleksandr Eiduk.

Below: ARA headquarters at
Spiridonovka 30, Moscow.

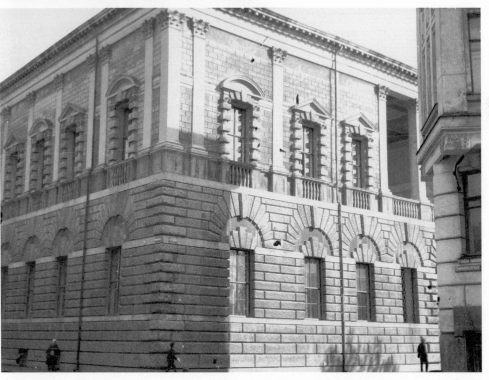

Right: Col. Thomas Lonergan.
Below: Arrival of ARA corn train, Simbirsk.

Above: Haskell at Moscow headquarters.

Left: Carlton Bowden.

MOVEMENT OF SUPPLIES A.R.A. 1921 - 1922.

LEGEND

Steamer Routes.
Ports of Final Discharge.
Overland Shipments to Principal Points.
Central or District Warehouses.
General Relief & Food Remittance.
Sub-District Warehouses.
Food Remittance Warehouses.
Transportation Control Stations.

Opposite: Movement of ARA supplies, 1921–1922. Original ARA map.

Left: Gov. James P. Goodrich.

Below: A "railroad graveyard."

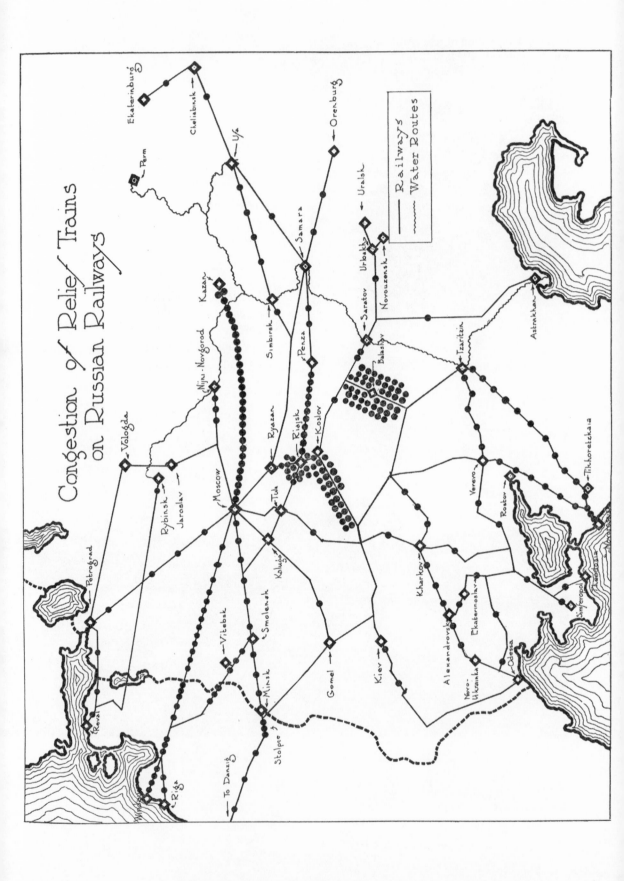

Congestion of Relief Trains on Russian Railways

Railways
Water Routes

Ekaterinburg
Perm
Cheliabinsk
Ufa
Orenburg
Uralsk
Urbakh
Samara
Novouzensk
Saratov
Balashov
Kazan
Simbirsk
Nijni-Novgorod
Penza
Vologda
Riajsk
Koslov
Rybinsk
Jaroslav
Moscow
Tula
Astrakhan
Tzaritzin
Verevo
Rostov
Tikhoretskaia
Petrograd
Kaluga
Smolensk
Vitebsk
Kharkov
Reval
Minsk
Gomel
Kiev
Alexandrovsk
Ekaterinoslav
Novo-Ukrainka
Odessa
Simferopol
Sevastopol
Stolpce
To Danzig
Riga

Opposite: Congestion of relief trains on Russian railroads, April 1922. Each block represents a single shipment, usually a trainload. Original ARA map.

Below, top: Caravan of ARA supplies on the frozen Volga, Saratov.

Below, bottom: Loading ARA supplies, Kazan.

Opposite, top: ARA caravan on the frozen Volga, Tsaritsyn.

Opposite, bottom: Loading ARA supplies, Orenburg, 1922.

Left: Karl Lander.

Below: ARA transport column on the frozen Volga, Tsaritsyn.

Above: ARA chiefs gather in Moscow, June 1922. *Left to right*: Edgar Rickard, Walter Lyman Brown, William Haskell, William Grove, Christian Herter, Cyril Quinn, and John Mangan.

Opposite, top: Waifs, Ekaterinoslav, 1922.

Opposite, bottom: Haskell and Quinn, Moscow.

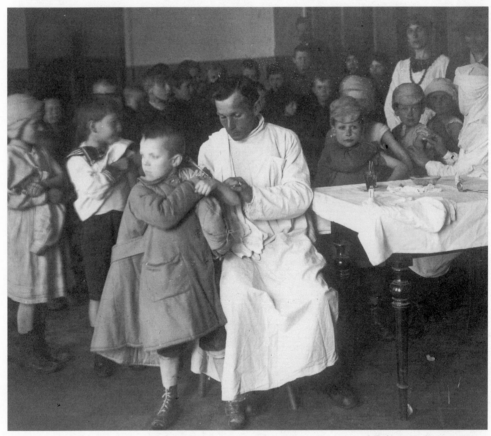

ARA inoculation point.

PART TWO

LOVE AND DEATH ON THE VOLGA

Dramas and Distractions at the Famine Front

[I]f the personal lives of ARA men in the districts ever came to the knowledge
of the large mass of people who contributed small sums to child-feeding
purposes it would have a disastrous effect upon their willingness to further
contribute. Drunkenness on a large scale and relations with women, which
have made a reputation none too savory even in lax Russia, have been kept
under everybody's hat, but if anybody ever wrote an unabridged "Personal
Reminiscences in ARA Work in Russia" it would certainly prove a bomb-shell.
                        —Harold Fleming, Moscow, January 1923

Incidentally, *The New York Times* correspondent has yet to meet any American
who does not say at least once weekly he wishes he had died before he came to
this infernal country, and that if he has to stay here he will blow his head off.
                        —Walter Duranty, *New York Times*, October 23, 1922

THEATERS OF ACTION

In the Great Famine of 1921 starvation was said to threaten the existence of millions of people in Soviet Russia. The nearly three hundred famine relief workers associated with the American Relief Administration were, strictly speaking, not among those millions. They could perform their duties with the knowledge that, barring some catastrophic human miscalculation, they would not starve. In all likelihood they could count on going home again when their mission was completed.

The Americans stationed in the famine zone, in and beyond the Volga valley and in Ukraine, were especially conscious of their relative immunity from the physical sufferings endured by their beneficiaries. Even if many felt a moral obligation to remain in Russia "for the duration," their participation in the ARA mission was voluntary and at any time they could choose to pick up and return to "civilization." For most it was only this sense of insulation from the surrounding environment that made their Russian sojourn tolerable.

To what extent the American relievers mentally leaned upon their special status is revealed in the personal correspondence and diaries they left behind. Frank Golder wrote home to his Stanford colleagues that, "In all these wanderings and through all the discomforts there is one blessed thought, that I have another land to go to. You have no idea how comforting it is."

Edwin Vail, a former Stanford student from Pasadena, was an American Quaker posted in one of the worst famine areas in the province of Samara. In a letter from Russia in which he remarks upon the sense of detachment essential to the mental balance of every famine relief worker, Vail points up the benefits enjoyed by the Americans—not only the physical comforts but "above all the knowledge that we can leave this awful land and return to comfortable homes and friends." He illustrates his point by employing a couple of vivid analogies: "It is like seeing a great tragedy on the stage while sitting on soft upholstered seats with a box of chocolates in your lap and a limousine waiting outside to take you home. It would not be very unpleasant to watch the operations down in hell if you had a railing to hold on to, and a pass on an elevator to the celestial realms controlled by St. Peter."

Striking imagery, but neither analogy is apt. The notion of the famine reliever as a spectator seated among an audience in a darkened theater is one that occurred to other ARA men in Russia. But it is appropriate only if the script of the drama allows for the participation of members of the audience, for during the two-year mission, many American relief workers would climb the stage and assume the roles of saviors, victims, and villains, thus writing themselves into Russia's great tragedy.

The trouble with likening starvation in the Volga valley to the "operations down in hell" is that in Soviet Russia in 1921 innocents were suffering, millions of them, and this made the viewing most unpleasant; in fact, it often took a severe emotional and mental toll on those forced to watch for too long. An American doctor named Eversole, not associated with the ARA but sent to Russia to evaluate its operations, was struck by this. Looking into the faces of the American relief workers stationed in the city of Orenburg, he could see what the men had been through.

I took the liberty of asking a big strong American why he showed such signs of suffering when there was no doubt in my mind that he had had good food, a warm place to sleep and a good bed. . . . Among other things he said . . . How in hell can a real man eat or sleep in comfort when he knows that in the morning the first thing that will greet his eyes when he looks out the window will be corpses along the street[?][1]

Such hazards aside, Edwin Vail forgets that although the relief workers were secure from starvation, there were genuine physical dangers involved in the work, to which no one, not even a big, strong American, was invulnerable. That elevator ride to the "celestial realms" was in no way guaranteed.

ONE OF THE FIRST AMERICANS to arrive in the Volga valley in the autumn of 1921 was assigned the task of counting the corpses in a barn. It is reported that this barn contained hundreds of corpses in piles; this cannot be verified, but it must have held at least several dozen. The American, whose identity is uncertain, counted only as far as the number forty-eight, at which point something in his head must have snapped because he could count no further. As the story was told, "The ARA man went crazy," repeating aloud the number forty-eight "for the rest of the day," although by the next morning he is said to have come to his senses and been able to return to work.

While the tone of official ARA reports and press releases is typically phlegmatic, emphasizing cool American energy and efficiency in "putting the job over in fine shape," elsewhere, especially throughout the personal writings of the ARA men, nerves are vibrating: they are "strained" and "frayed," and the danger of "nervous breakdown" seems always imminent. As one American put it, "practically everything that we accomplished took more nervous energy and pep from us than would have been required for ten times the size of the job in any other country." Another wrote that "Nothing but a saving sense of humor kept the nerve of the personnel." Golder felt that his work was "exceedingly interesting" but "painful and it takes all the nervous force out of a person." On a later date he observes that "Quinn is running the show pretty well but is working hard and I am afraid that he might break down."[2]

When the horrors of the famine and the challenges of the mission were first revealed to an arriving American, there was no telling how he might react. The district supervisor of the Zaporozhiia, in Ukraine, suffered what was said to be a "nervous breakdown" shortly after he opened up ARA headquarters. In Samara province in the autumn of 1921, as the Americans went about establishing a relief program with what one of them called "quiet American energy," an American and several Russian inspectors reportedly "broke down under the nervous strain."

Even the participants in the ARA mission who would prove to be among the most durable might early on display an unsteady hand. A Russian professor of history living in Simbirsk recalls in a memoir how Dr. Mark Godfrey, after his first day of making the rounds to local hospitals and children's homes, wept "like a sentimental girl." The professor recalls this with evident satisfaction: it confirmed for him that these businesslike Americans were human beings after all. And there were other instances when American emotion appears to have helped establish the credibility of the ARA. The president of the Bashkir Republic told a relief worker that any doubt he had as to the humanitarian intentions of the ARA was removed when he witnessed Golder break down and sob at the suffering of the starvation victims.[3]

It is impossible to assess the cost of the mission in strained, frayed, and broken American nerves. It is not even clear how many ARA men were sent home prematurely as a consequence. Haskell states in his unpublished 1932 memoir that "[M]any clever young Americans had to be sent out of Russia with nerves completely wrecked or on the verge of insanity due not only to the horrible suffering which they were forced to witness but to the interference and annoyance to which they were unnecessarily subjected by the very Soviet officials who should have been their helpers." Haskell might also have mentioned what the Americans perceived to be the passivity, fatalism, and innate inefficiency of the people they had come to save—this too taxed the confounded and exasperated American relief workers.

The nervous strain of the Russian relief mission was not confined to the men working in the famine districts. This was made clear to ARA publicity chief Baker during his February 1922 visit to Moscow. He was surprised at, and seems to have been a bit disturbed by, the reaction among the Americans stationed in Moscow when it became known that he was in position to distribute five hundred food packages at his own discretion. Several of the men pleaded outright for permission to distribute a portion of these packages to Russian acquaintances. To Baker it became evident that "each of our men seem to have their particular shocks, some better, some worse, mostly worse." The issue was decided, he later recalled, when Haskell ordered that none of these food packages could be distributed to people in Moscow. "He said that our American men in the famine districts, during every one of their waking hours faced situations so much more desperate than these in Moscow, that the strain was more apt to break them than it was to break the men in Moscow, who at least had American associations, warm rooms and warm water."[4]

In fact one month before Baker's Moscow visit it began to come to the attention of the ARA chiefs in London and New York just how great was the strain on the men in the famine zone. This gave rise to a concern that if some of these clever Americans were to remain in the field for too long, the quality of their work would suffer. Thomas Dickinson was the first to turn the organization's attention to this upon his return to the United States from Russia in January 1922. In his telegraphically composed, internally circulated "Notes on the Russian Famine" he wrote: "One factor to be considered in relief administration never before present in like measure is psychological factor of relief workers among de-pressing conditions. This worth as serious consideration as in arctic exploration or in tours through jungle."

At ARA headquarters in New York City, Director General Edgar Rickard, among others, was becoming especially concerned about the kinds of stories re-garding the Russian mission that were finding their way into the hometown American newspapers. The source for many of these articles was the correspon-dence of the relief workers to family and friends back home, the tone of which was not always suited to the ARA image of businesslike efficiency. How many tons of this or that product were hauled over Russia's railways, how many of the starving were fed, the smiling faces of the grateful children—these were the ele-ments of the ideal newspaper story. But the letters home from the famine front seldom fit this formula.

In April 1922, Rickard sent a telegram to London headquarters warning that "Individual letters to families and friends without exception record excessive strain and tone of letters invariably hysterical." It is unclear from this precisely what he means by "hysterical," and he does not elaborate. Nor could he have, re-ally, for when he composed this telegram his first and only trip to Soviet Russia was still three months away. He went on to recommend shorter shifts and longer holidays in Europe for the American personnel; otherwise, he feared, ARA stan-dards would slip. In this communication, Rickard introduced a new phrase into the ARA vocabulary: "This Russian job to judge from semiofficial personal nar-ratives has developed among workers quote famine shock unquote such as we have not experienced in any other operations and which apparently renders oth-erwise superior individuals insufficient."[5]

"Famine shock," adapted from the Great War's "shell shock," came into rather liberal use in ARA parlance during the first year of the mission. No one appears to have attempted to define the term, and in fact in the spring of 1922 it even came to be used as a term of disparagement, to discredit the statements of some returning Americans whose "hysterical" starvation stories threatened to under-mine the ARA's self-projected image as an organization methodically bringing the Russian famine under control.

When Dr. Francis Rollins, Ufa's district physician, departed Russia in the summer of 1922, he gave an interview to the *Rigasche Rundschau* in which he por-trayed the famine zone as a land of horrors and lawlessness. The ARA informed the State Department that Rollins was suffering from "famine shock" and that he should be ignored. And when in the spring of 1922 journalist Nellie Gardner, who did publicity work for the ARA, submitted several articles that played up the danger of a continuing Russian famine at a time when the organization was claiming to have broken its back, she was said to be a victim of "famine shock."

Similar use was made of the word "neurasthenic." The Russian employees of the ARA, particularly those representatives of the old bourgeoisie and aristocracy whose nerves had been strained by years of hardship, frequently had their ineffi-ciency attributed, whether they knew it or not, to "neurasthenia," as in: my secre-tary is "so damn neurasthenic."

After the mission, an ARA publication stated that "five or six" Americans had suffered from "famine shock," but this can only mean in a very narrow sense of the term—perhaps those whose condition had forced them to quit Russia prematurely. There were many more still who displayed symptoms of a kind of "famine shock" and yet remained on the job. Testimony comes from Dr. Eversole, who witnessed relief operations in the autumn of 1922 when the worst of the suffering was over. He found that "the boys of the ARA were in a really hyper nervous condition from hard work and memories of the horrors that they worked night and day to alleviate last winter." The doctor had observed these symptoms before. "It was not in the least necessary for those American boys to tell me what they had been through: I read it in their eyes before they had spoken a word. That same blank, mirthless smile, in which the eyes took no part, that I found among the prisoners of war after five years of prison hell, typhus, cholera, smallpox, starvation and freezing."

There is a similar passage in the journal of Evelyn Sharp, a British Quaker, who wrote upon arriving in the village of Buzuluk in Samara province: "At once we knew we had reached the real thing—you could tell from the faces of the workers what horrors they had looked upon, though they showed no signs of it in overwrought manner or speech."[6]

There can be little doubt that the excessive drinking by the ARA men is in some cases attributable to the psychological stress of their work. There are several open references in the ARA literature to drinking in order to relieve nervous tension. It is not for the historian to attempt to explain what caused District Supervisor David Kinne to drink himself nearly to death while on duty in Saratov in the winter of 1921, but the pressures of his job could well have been a major immediate factor. The cold eye of one of his Russian employees, Alexis Babine, observed Kinne's self-destruction day by day. Babine records Kinne's denouement with clinical detachment in a diary entry of February 27, 1922: "Kinne sent in his resignation yesterday by wire. His nerves are badly shattered. His heart gave out, and a doctor had to be sent for last night to pull him through."

Naturally, the men stationed in the famine districts served under the greatest strain. Here American man power was spread thin, and the responsibilities placed upon the shoulders of individual relief workers were considerable. The same circumstances that gave many of the Americans a sometimes intoxicating sense of power—their personal responsibility for the life and death of hundreds of thousands of Russians—were simultaneously a source of tremendous anxiety. Everywhere there was death and ruin, transportation and communications were crippled, local officials were often inefficient and outright obstructionist, and the Russian people seemed incapable of helping themselves; meanwhile Moscow headquarters was waiting on statistical reports and surveys documenting your district's feeding operations and detailing its future needs. Surely this might be enough, as the saying goes, to drive a man to drink.

IN SOME FAMINE REGIONS, especially in some of the more remote subdistricts, the American relief worker had to go about the job with the knowledge that so desperate was the situation, no matter how supremely efficient his operation, no matter how appropriate each of his individual decisions, many thousands of people within his area of administration were going to die.

The American Quakers, who worked as a unit within one of the hardest hit regions in Samara province, had to struggle every day with the thought that in feeding some, as one put it, you effectively give the rest a "death sentence." Another Quaker wrote back to the States: "It is not easy, I assure you, for an American to deliberately turn his back upon an emaciated human being, probably a child, with glorious beseeching, patient eyes, asking for a small piece of bread, but we did it, hundreds and hundreds of times." Nor was it any easier for the British Quaker working just across the Volga River who wrote, "It is no light matter to be in the midst of a starving population and to be only able to feed about 10% of them."

The testimony of yet another Quaker, Murray Kentworthy, the head of the American Friends Service Committee in Russia, points to the most logical recourse available to the relief worker: "I have seen sights which make me sob, but I will have to harden to it for it's going to be death over and over again all year and no way to help it."[7]

To "harden." If the ARA man wanted to endure, to see the mission through to the end, he would have to become desensitized to all the suffering; otherwise the job would fast become impossible. The Americans were quite conscious of their own internal metamorphosis. A few tracked it week by week, with no little fascination, documenting it in diaries and letters home.

George Cornick, a medical doctor from San Angelo, Texas, on duty in Tsaritsyn, wrote to his parents that "if it were not for the fact that we have all become hardened to the sights I am sure that we would be able to do nothing in the way of work for thinking of the poor wretches." Russell Cobb, John Kinne's deputy in Saratov, confided to his parents, "I feel that I am getting to be hard and heartless—Kinne feels the same. . . . One has to be pretty rough and ready and almost cruel. One preacher was shocked at Kinne, and said we must sympathize with the people—Kinne said yes, and let them starve."

This comment from Kinne was probably not intended to be flippant. Several Americans record how going about their job and watching people die "like flies" or "like rats," they came to wonder at the point of prolonging the agony by feeding people who in the end could not be saved anyway. Why not concentrate on the few with the best chance to make it, and let the remainder move on to an eternal, and peaceful, resting place? Alvin Blomquist in Simbirsk stated this quite directly in an interesting little memoir he pulled together in the final days of the ARA mission:

Frankly, despite his belief in the sacredness of human life, and the Administration's avowed purpose of feeding the famine-stricken without regard to race, creed, color—or economic value—one was often tempted to wonder at the purpose of saving the lives of the many people who were and would be only a burden to themselves and to the State, and whose most merciful relief would be at the hands of Death.[8]

This line of thought recurs in the letters of William Kelley, the ARA's supply chief in the district of Ufa. Kelley had studied journalism at the Pulitzer School at Columbia University before spending two years at Harvard, where he received his B.A. in 1917. He was commissioned in August of that year, and the following January joined the AEF as an intelligence officer, in which capacity he authored reports on the German military and food situation and, during the armistice, on the attitudes of Germans in the occupied zone toward the American army. After his return to the States he worked for a time as a reporter for the Associated Press in Washington and eventually, in August 1921, landed at 42 Broadway where he did publicity work for the ARA as Baker's assistant. So Kelley knew something about writing, and his correspondence from Ufa, relentlessly cynical, seems to have performed the therapeutic function normally reserved for the personal diary.

On January 21, 1922, he is in the city of Cheliabinsk, beyond the Urals and one of the easternmost points of ARA operations. Together with the ARA physician Francis Rollins of later "famine shock" notoriety, he inspects a local hospital.

I would not try to describe what these hospitals look like. You will never see anything like them or the people in them. No blankets nor bedclothes, no clothes, wretched food, little heat, improvised buildings, everything worse than you can imagine. It would be much better to put them all out of their misery at once. In all this district with more than 2,000,000 inhabitants, there are only 56 doctors. Never have I seen such frightful looking specimens of humanity as I saw yesterday in these hospitals. Only the children look human. Dr. Rollins was so disgusted at the sight that he objected to walking through the wards.

On January 26, Kelley is on his way back to Ufa by train and ponders the scale of the tragedy he is witnessing: "I often think now of how people in New York told me how they envied me the opportunity of seeing so many interesting things. Yes, interesting, that's the word. Yes, it's very interesting to move among people who a glance tells you would be better off dead than alive." On February 23 he writes: "When twenty or thirty or forty million people have died there may be an improvement." In mid-March he contemplates the impact of the Russian environment on his own personality:

In recent days I find myself inquiring: "Is it really true that I am a conscientious cuss?" I couldn't tell you why I have worked as I have these last few days. I don't expect any credit—no one except possibly my interpreter will know what the strain has been. I am utterly void of enthusiasm, as I know we are only prolonging the lives of people whose doom is sealed. I care nothing for the opinion or gratitude of the Russians. Theodore [the interpreter] has orders not to read me any letters of thanks from persons to whom I have allocated food packages. And yet there is something driving me to give everything I have to my job. I wonder if I imbibed more of the idea of military discipline in the army than I suspected.

In April, as the corn is being distributed, he senses that he has passed the test. "To be callous," he writes on the 5th, "is to be efficient in this work."

On April 12 he is on an inspection trip in the town of Sterlitamak, where he visits two children's homes: "I go merely to report that I have been for I have lost all of my interest in the details of misery." Later in the day he observes: "My immunization is progressing. Today I passed two corpses lying on the street. I scarcely gave them a second glance." One week later he reflects further on his internal transformation: "What, think you, will be the effect of this experience on me? One thing I notice, I am growing dictatorial as the very devil. No one presumes an acquaintance with me. I think I have a reputation for being hard."

Later in the month, he writes to "G.L.H.," describing how he has distanced himself from the suffering and cut himself off from all personal relations with members of the ARA Russian staff, who he says steal food supplies, and with local Soviet officials, who conspire to gain control over American operations.

Ordinarily neither the general misery nor particular cases of suffering touch my emotions. If I did not check my sympathies, my work and my health would suffer. The staff finds me hard and distant, difficult to convince that an exception should be made to our rules in some individual's case.

I am constantly called on to protect the interests of the 300,000 children who don't come to my office against the hungry adults that do. . . . Having no friends and no interest in the country and counting the weeks until someone else can take my place, I can be as conscientious as a Prussian functionary.

I am well; I am harder than I thought, mentally and physically.

In the middle of May, during one of the busiest periods for the Americans in Ufa, Kelley closes a letter thus: "I am working smoothly without fatigue or nervous strain. Theodore, who was on the verge of a nervous breakdown when he greeted me on my return from Sterlitamak, now credits me for restoring his self control. I told him to imitate my demeanor and he would acquire the same mental attitude I have toward the work."

In June, Kelley is in Perm, the northeastern outpost of the ARA at the mouth of the Kama River, some two hundred miles from Ufa headquarters. Here he visits a shelter for refugees and finds the experience thoroughly depressing.

The refugee is a horrible sight when you see him in the open air and with a few normal beings within range to rest the eye; but imagine what they are like in a close and dark building with nothing suggestive of normal humanity within sight! As I entered one large corridor lined with bunks, I observed a patient who had rolled off on the floor dead, since the last tour of the attendant. Women and men indiscriminately were lying about on the bunks, without bedcovers or any facilities whatever. Having no clothes to give them, delousing was a waste of time, so the man in charge told me. A bowl of greasy water was the only sign of food I noticed. They told me they had three grains of aspirin a month to meet the needs of the inmates.

They asked me for nothing and I promised nothing. We have a special allocation for feeding refugees, but I cannot bring myself to issuing good children's food to condemned wretches such as these. Nothing can save them now.[9]

IN HIS HARDNOSED LETTERS from Russia, Kelley frequently vents his impatience with one of his American colleagues in Ufa, Harold Blandy. Blandy was born and raised in Manhattan, the son of a well-known New York attorney. He was educated at St. Paul's School in Garden City, at Pawling, and then at Yale. In 1916 he enlisted in the British Royal Flying Corps in Toronto and went off to England to fight the air war. After the fighting stopped, he went into business in London, where, when the ARA mission to Russia got under way, he wrote to his mother requesting her permission to sign on. In doing so, he is said to have told her of the effect on him of the misery and heartbreak he had seen during the war: he could not be happy, he wrote, while others suffered.

That is what the newspapers wrote after his death. In fact, Mitchell tells us that Blandy turned up at the ARA's London offices "absolutely down and out. His clothes, his jewellery, in fact practically all his personal effects, were in hock and he was just one jump ahead of the bailiffs, who were put on his trail by numerous creditors." He was "very fond of night life in a mild parlour sort of way, and had a rather large acquaintance in the dancing set here in London," but his funds had run out and he came begging for a job with the ARA. Mitchell took him on. Within weeks of his joining the Russian unit, the Moscow chiefs decided that Blandy and Moscow were a bad mix and sent him out to Ufa.[10]

There, big-hearted Blandy came to be loved by his Russian interpreters and by his many beneficiaries. Kelley, on the other hand, professed indifference to their attentions. The faces of the two men as captured in photographs reflect the contrast in their temperaments. Kelley has a penetrating gaze, and with the aid of a thick, dark mustache he scowls for the camera in the approved manner of the day. Blandy, who at thirty-three was six years Kelley's elder, has soft features and eyes that exude sensitivity and a hint of melancholy in every pose. To a present-day observer he has the tragic visage of a silent-film star.

In Kelley's letters, "poor Blandy" cuts a pathetic figure. He is often in a state of near hysteria, frantically attempting to save lives with "haphazard hand outs" and "individual charity," for which purpose he kept a stock of food in his room at the personnel house. On February 15, 1922, Kelley was eating dinner at the residence when, as he describes it, he got a telephone call from Blandy at the railway station:

It developed that he had seen six children about to be shipped on a four day journey. He had examined their rations and assured me in a semi-hysterical tone that all would be dead before they reached their destination. He wanted all the loose food there was in the house. I feel very keenly the futility of haphazard relief, but consented, and he held the train while I sent down three loaves of bread and some gift cookies which was practically all the cooked food in the house. May it do them some good.

Kelley deemed this and other such gestures "pathetic in their futility," and repeatedly dismissed Blandy as "useless" to the ARA.[11]

It is unclear to what extent Blandy's soft touch may have detracted from his performance on the job, or if the very fact of it simply prejudiced Kelley against him outright. The ARA ethos associated the idea of "individual relief"—and all that this expression implied about allowing emotional engagement with the victim to get the upper hand—with inefficiency. Most newcomers to the ARA who might have entertained a different notion of famine relief work quickly made the adjustment. As Blomquist relates,

Many members of the ARA, on entering Russia, doubtless had the same vague conception of methods of procedure as did I. They pictured, possibly, an existence in barracks, or tents, or draughty houses; of feeding from rolling kitchens; of a wiping of little noses, and of a patting of little heads. It was only upon reaching Moscow that any such illusions were dispelled, and that there became apparent the impersonal but wholly-efficient Administration methods.

Still, he recalls, soon after his arrival in Simbirsk, he attempted his own "venture into the field of more or less individual relief," when he and the ARA physician brought some articles of clothing to "some refugee points of concentration" near the Simbirsk railway station. "In one twenty-by-thirty foot windowless barrack we found about eighty refugees, emaciated, diseased, and freezing; whole families huddled on top of one another, with their worthless bundles of rags serving as beds; several of the refugees delirious with typhus; one little girl blind; pregnant women; recent mothers: a perfect Hell of human misery and despair."[12] It was Blomquist's last such undertaking.

At Ufa, certain of Blandy's "methods of procedure" set him further apart from the ARA staff. A Russian colleague, whose written English is thick with the slang of his American chiefs, claims that Blandy never rose before noon, was always complaining of feeling ill, and was "a dead weight in the organization," and that the only things that motivated him were his "instinct for publicity" and his prodigious appetite for the opposite sex. "Blandy had but one interest in the A.R.A. show and that was the distribution of General relief food packages to recipients mostly of the female sex whom he met in his horsey peregrinations." Blandy's sensitivity to the suffering of the famine victims goes undisputed, yet it is not to be confused with squeamishness about the dead: in one of Kelley's letters we read about Blandy descending into a mass grave to pose for ARA photographer and motion picture man Floyd Traynham, who turned away in disgust.[13]

IN THE ARA LITERATURE, where corpses are everywhere strewn, death means deliverance from suffering, and as such it is frequently a welcome sight. Blomquist, still at the Simbirsk railroad station, records how, when a Russian Red Cross train pulled into town, one of the freight cars yielded the corpses of five children, "naked, and thin, and frozen stiff, but happily beyond the travails of the Russian generation-to-come."

The larger the number of corpses, the easier it was mentally to distance oneself from thoughts of the suffering of individual victims. A large pile of them might be reduced to a mere curiosity. There are not a few descriptions of "stacks" of corpses in the documentation of the mission. Most of the dead have been stripped of all clothing, revealing them to be mere skeletons covered with skin. Sometimes the bodies are whole, sometimes they have been partially devoured by dogs, wolves, or crows. Infrequently they are reported to be of a bluish color; most often they are a deathly white.

In the ARA archive there is a series of photographs of famine victims in Tsaritsyn—children's corpses loaded every which way into some kind of open transport vehicle waiting to be hauled away. Several of the corpses have eyes wide open in horrifying stares, which is initially unsettling because it seems to indicate a continuation of suffering in death. Only after repeated viewing do they become nothing more than corpses with their eyes open. It is not unlikely that it is these photographs Russell Cobb had in mind when he informed his parents that he was in possession of "terrible pictures of car loads of naked bodies. I have seen many, many such. In some towns they are piled up near the cemetery as the ground is too hard and no one has the strength to bury them."[14] At the cemetery it was not unusual to press into service one of the deceased to stand guard over his fellow corpses as a human scarecrow.

For tales of the unburied dead no place surpasses the city of Odessa. Here they are on view in various poses and states of dress, sitting, lying, or standing, alone or in pairs, in groups small or large, with families or without. In the cold of winter it was possible to leave the dead where they fell or store them away while the living struggled to survive. But the spring thaw threatened to spread disease, and mass burials had to be carried out. If warming temperatures were not signal enough, the odor of a putrefying corpse would serve as a warning.

The commanding officer of the U.S.S. *Williamson*, docked at Odessa, recorded in the ship's diary for April 13 how two professors at the university reported to him that "in the basements of several hospitals in Odessa the dead are piled up like cordwood." The following day, he was able to see this for himself:

In one of the large University hospitals we inspected a room in the basement where there were about 200 corpses in various stages of decomposition piled haphazard into this room. Of the few which were clothed the clothing consisted of only one garment. In another basement room of this same hospital there were 600 bodies. Upon leaving this hospital I noticed a pile of bodies abreast a door leading into the room we had just inspected and a cart piled with dead bodies standing on the street. It is easier to haul bodies to the hospital than to carry them to the cemetery, so this is what is done. Were I to try for hours I could not paint a picture as gruesome as I saw conditions this morning.

In Odessa in the spring of 1922 a law was passed that a person had to be buried on the day of expiration. If the cemetery or the hospital were not close enough, the local church would do. One day a priest walked into ARA headquarters to complain about the six hundred corpses that had accumulated in front of his door and to ask if the Americans would do anything about this.

With spring the streets of Odessa were filled with the crude two-wheeled carts —wooden wheelbarrows, really—normally used to transport food or supplies, now employed as makeshift hearses. These enabled even those severely weakened by hunger to transport their loads all the way to the cemetery. The commanding officer of the *Williamson* described the street scene:

While driving through the streets about a dozen funeral processions—if they can be called such—were observed. One consisted of a man, with a child's corpse on his shoulders, followed by a woman, but the majority of these processions were made up of a two-wheeled cart being pulled by two or three people and followed by several others. The most pretentious one consisted of a horse cart followed by about 20 people. Three dead bodies (one a child about 6) were seen on the side-walk and at the entrance to a large cemetery there were about 20 bodies heaped in one pile. The latter had been stripped of all clothing. All must have died of starvation as they were very much emaciated.

At the cemetery the officer saw bodies partially eaten by dogs, some almost completely devoured. He noticed blood dripping from the wound of one of the victims as it was being removed from a cart and upon inquiry was told by Dr. McElroy of the ARA that this was not yet a corpse. "From what I have gathered while here from personal observation and talking with others," he wrote," I consider that such things are not very unusual, if at all."

Grave diggers do not seem to have been in short supply, perhaps because American food was used as wages. H. L. Pence, the commanding officer of the U.S.S. *MacFarland*, docked in Odessa around this time, made note in the ship's diary of a visit to a mass gravesite where the men doing the digging seemed unaffected by the work. They only occasionally asked the Russian doctor for a bit of cognac, which he never refused them.

Perhaps this same burial site is the setting where Pence posed for photographs with a fellow U.S. naval officer and two ARA men. In one of these the men are in the foreground; behind them the small pile of naked corpses against the barren landscape appears as if painted on a canvas backdrop in a photographer's studio. In other words, the scene looks unreal. This brings to mind something Thomas Dickinson jotted in his Russian notes as he contemplated an especially picturesque pile of corpses: "All terribly emaciated and contorted into all shapes of grotesque agony. As one sees the lopsided houses of the Russian villages, the gnarled, skin clad bones of the famine corpses, one seizes the dominant motifs of the new Russian art. An unreality about these corpses that made it seem appropriate to discuss anything in their presence, cabarets, soda water and futurist verse."

In British Quaker Muriel Payne's description of a barn full of corpses, death seems to imitate art: "They were not just heaped up, but were rather carefully arranged like waxwork figures—some standing, some sitting, and some had tumbled down as the thaw had set in. In the hand of each was a piece of paper with the name of the person and a recommendation from the priest to St. Peter to allow them through when he had time to attend it."

So ubiquitous were these corpses, so prone were they to appear in the most unexpected places, that they were bound to become a source of dark humor among the Americans. In John Driscoll's description of his search for living quarters in the town of Nikolaevsk, near Tsaritsyn, the introduction of a corpse to the story turns it into farce. Driscoll has set off with a local official to inspect a private home:

On our way to the place he told me that if there was anything about the room I did not like he would have same removed. When he entered the house and said "this is the sitting room" he had forgotten to tell me that the man of the house had died the evening before, and I was a bit shocked to find the body set out in the sitting room. We passed through to the bed room and I casually inquired if the bed was the one in which the lately departed had expired, and he smilingly said it was, as though that were a strong recommendation for the bed.[15]

Of course, a worse shock for Driscoll would have been for the corpse to come back to life. This is not as absurd as it sounds; several of the relief workers had such an experience. The observer sees before him what can only be a corpse—nothing that looks like this could be alive—but the eyes deceive, the corpse stirs, and Lazarus rises. This is not merely death but living death. The most haunting of such encounters are those involving children, those with the faces of shrunken old men and women, cheeks and eyeballs sunken, skin stretched tautly over scalp and face. Mercifully, one of them appears to have been put out of its horrid misery. As the American visitor ponders this specimen, suddenly, without warning, its eyes open and meet his own, gripping him with terror. The face contorts into a smile, and the picture of perfect horror is complete.

No matter how "hardened" one might think oneself, a visit to the living hell of a children's home—overcrowded with skeletal children, some with the swollen "hunger belly," all smelling of death—might break through anybody's protective shell. Several American visitors remarked upon the eerie silence within, not the wailing cries one expects from children in this condition; they merely stare silently.

It does not seem to make the visit any less unpleasant, however. Dickinson recalls the "Swollen bellies of children so common as no longer to excite remark. The characteristic expression of childhood in provincial Russia is that of a person 'sore at life.' I have learned to dread going into a room full of children. They all look up at me accusingly, bitterly, as if I had done it. They were born with resentment at their hearts." The *MacFarland* diarist was haunted by children who "just look at you in an absent sort of way as if nothing mattered and they realize the end was near." A plea for bread—"*Khleb, khleb*"—might have been preferable.

Even Kelley was not thoroughly immune. Three weeks before his departure from Russia, in June 1922, he was in the town of Troitsk, on the boundary between Europe and Asia, traveling with new American arrival Conway Howard. The two visited a children's home, and Conway, for whom it was his first such experience, "sickened of it very early." Kelley confesses that an image from this visit "stayed with me"—the sight of a three-year-old boy lying on the floor:

He was obviously dying but no one was giving him any attention as the women about the place didn't know what to do for him. The doctor makes his regular visits and it is not the custom to bother him between times. It occurred to me that someone might undertake to keep the flies off the kid's face while he was dying, but doubtless they had their hands full with the care of the living.

Even those children who could be saved could not have their suffering noticeably eased with a single feeding. More than one American recorded his frustration at the blank looks, the apathy, and the passivity of the children even after they were washed and fed. Dr. Eversole was told about this in his interviews with American relievers:

One A R A man told me that the thing that "got his goat" last winter when he first arrived was the thousands of children piled into filthy buildings, practically no clothes, dirty, full of vermin, no heat, starving. That didn't bother him so much, but after they were cleaned up, fed and at least partially clothed, to see them sit on the edge of the beds with their face in their hands, inanimate for hours, days at a time, no spirit, not enough life left to notice or play . . . That was too much.

Most of the ARA men at the famine front documented at least one utterly gut-wrenching scene. Will Shafroth recorded several, including one he came upon during his initial tour of the Volga, in a "Tartar settlement" in Simbirsk province, where he was taken to a "small one-room cabin":

On one side of the room was a sort of platform which served as a bed. On it were standing three children, so thin and white and emaciated looking, that one almost wondered how they could stand. They had the swollen bellies of grass eaters, and when the peasant woman showed us the "flour" from which she made her bread, it was green. Those children were dying of starvation. They would hold out ten days, two weeks, maybe longer. But if food with some nourishment in it did not come soon, they would all die. As their mother looked at us, we could see that she knew it. She dropped to her knees and began to pray to us, sobbing. We turned away sick of heart. Thousands of little children dying like that. It was unthinkable.

Downriver at Samara, Shafroth entered a children's home in which 283 children were living in three rooms, each about twenty-five by forty feet.

They were sitting on the floor, and when I asked the brave little lady superintendent, who was doing her best to struggle against overwhelming odds, where they slept, she pointed to the floor and said: "There. We have no other place for them." And then she had those little hungry, homeless waifs sing for me. I had to turn away. It was more than I could stand.[16]

Among the most moving stories were those involving mothers and their children, with neither party necessarily still among the living. A recurring image is that of the desperate mother, unable to feed her children, abandoning them at the marketplace or drowning them in the Volga so as not to have to witness their slow death by starvation. An ARA Russian inspector arrived at a peasant household where the children were so undernourished they had slipped into unconsciousness. For seven days they had howled in agony, but now they were quiet, nearly senseless. Their mother had tied them up and put them in separate corners because they had begun to bite each others' hands. Near hysteria, she begged that they not be revived into a state of suffering—for who would feed them tomorrow or in a week? She pleaded with the inspector, "Go away and let them die in peace."

A Russian doctor who heard this story from a different source observed that the famine intertwined what seemed to be the "polar opposite feelings of the highest love and the most extreme brutality, the height of compassion—and the limit of heartlessness." In such an atmosphere evidence of human dignity under siege could be terribly affecting. Dickinson records his reaction to a horrendous mass grave of children's corpses, but continues: "Coming away I saw a sight that affected me more. A young woman done up in shawls was pulling a sled with a little wooden coffin on it. It was windy and the way was very rough. The sled would strike a frozen obstacle and the coffin would come off, and she would place it on again, trying to hold it as she pulled as if it were a child."[17]

The widespread incidence of child abandonment made a deep impression on the Americans, who knew firsthand the dreadful conditions in the children's homes: for parents to deliver their children over to this fate was the strongest testimony to their desperate state of mind. It sometimes happened that a lone child would appear at an ARA kitchen. Questioned by the management as to who and where its parents are, the child repeats through tears the words it has been told to say as a matter of its own life and death: "I don't know." "The misery of a peasant people who love their little ones," wrote the English writer Philip Gibbs, "may be reckoned by the frightful desertion."

Other accounts are more ambiguous, such as the time George Cornick came across a small boy asking for food and claiming to be an orphan. Cornick was so taken with the child that he had just about decided to bring him home to live at ARA headquarters as a "mascot," when the boy let it slip that his parents were living in the nearby train station. He had been instructed to return with food or be beaten.[18]

Golder looked upon this nightmarish landscape and mused, "it would be so nice to lie out on the green grass and play with children who are clean and well fed and happy. I keep telling myself that they do exist."

Yet while they might often contemplate a more comfortable existence at home, and were perhaps at times tempted to request an easier assignment, most of the relief workers who served at the famine front could not have been torn away. Shortly after his arrival in Ufa, after he witnessed a mother of two children twice drop to her knees and try to kiss Colonel Bell's feet, cold-blooded Kelley was moved to write, "Do you wonder that I am becoming so attached to this work that I would revolt if they tried to pull me back to Moscow to do headquarters work?"

Paul Clapp, at the end of another long, exhausting day of administering relief to the starving in Saratov's German colony, told his diary: "I need rest badly. Sometimes I am afraid I will break down. The load is not easy but the intense human element of the work keeps a man going."[19]

Hardly the words of mere spectators in the audience at Russia's great tragedy.

CHAPTER II

FUNERALS

Probably the greatest single threat to the physical well-being of the ARA man in Russia was typhus. For protection against other forms of infectious disease, such as cholera, which was epidemic in the summer of 1922, the relief worker could be vaccinated; but typhus was the great equalizer.

Many ARA men had already made the acquaintance of the typhus louse, dubbed "cootie," during the Great War, but they had seen nothing like what the Russian setting had to offer. An ARA feeding instruction manual stated the danger plainly, calling the louse the "greatest enemy to mankind today in Russia." There are numerous depictions of refugees at train stations engaged in mutual delousing, an activity described by more than one American as "the favorite indoor and outdoor sport in Russia."

Although the Americans of the ARA were not nearly as exposed to the danger as were their beneficiaries or even their employees, among them the fear of infection was a continuous source of anxiety. This did not prevent the louse from becoming, as it had been among the doughboys in recent years, an object of black humor. The weekly ARA newsletter produced in Moscow, the "Russian Unit Record," brought to light a good-natured difference of opinion among the personnel as to the most effective preventive measures for stopping the cootie in his tracks: some, dubbed "smooth roaders," advocated the wearing of silk underwear; the rest of the crowd were "rough roaders."

When Baker returned from his February visit to Soviet Russia, he released a statement to the press on the mode of operations of the Russian louse. As reported in the ARA "New York News Letter," Mr. Louse was said to take three working days to accomplish his deadly mission. "On the first day, he takes up his position on the human frame and devotes himself to exquisite and diabolical meditation; on the second day, he discharges his cargo of fatal juices and retires to his thoughts until the third, his day of days, when he buries his obnoxious cargo beneath the epidermis of his victim." Soap and water were said to be the "pet abominations" of Sir Louse, and it was found that frequent revolving of one's underwear hampered his progress. "First allow him to work his way through the strands of your balbriggan; then turn the garment inside out forcing him to repeat the digging-in process. By constantly reversing the garment, M. Louse will become utterly exhausted." Evidently Baker was a "rough roader."

That the cootie had penetrated the consciousness of everyday life even in Moscow is illustrated in Fleming's description of a ride on a streetcar, a means of transportation that doubles as an institution designed to spread typhus. The scene Fleming recounts involves a car typically overcrowded with passengers, not all of them of the human variety.

Now having gotten all the dirty ones into this means of common intercourse, you push them up against each other as far as they can go till they hang on the outer doors, and compel them to rub themselves against each other as much as possible. Having gotten them well rubbed, you then require them to leave the car by the forward door, instead of the rear door by which they came in, and when they hesitate, you push them on and say, "Go on up there and get infected!"[1]

The Americans stationed in the capital could better afford such levity, for as compared with their colleagues in the famine districts they were hardly at all in danger of infection. But as soon as they climbed on board that train departing Moscow for the provinces they left behind their relative invulnerability. The Russians who worked for the ARA as couriers and whose job involved nearly continuous train travel fell victim in large numbers, with nearly one-third of their number becoming infected during the first year of the mission. New American arrivals to Moscow had the danger impressed upon them and anticipated their rail journey into the famine zone with considerable trepidation. Cornick, the Texas medical doctor, setting out from Moscow by train for Tsaritsyn on Christmas Eve 1921, confided to his diary that he was "trusting to insect powders, luck and the Lord on high to protect me from Typhus or recurrent fever this trip." Kelley left Moscow for the Volga the following day, and he shared in the paranoia: "Last night I refused to take off a single garment. I stretched out with the flannel lining of my trench coat on me and the coat itself as a cover. The equipment of the wagon-lit is limited to a mattress and a pillow, both under suspicion. I was not aware that I was sleeping for very long intervals but morning came soon enough."

Shortly after Freddie Lyon arrived in Orenburg to open up ARA headquarters there, he dashed off a letter to a Moscow colleague describing the "trials and tribulations of a homesick childfeeder in the wilds of the Asiatic frontier." Lyon's train pulled into Orenburg, which he calls "this horrible village," at 1:30 A.M., with no one to meet the train and nowhere to go, "'cold, tired, hungry, and nobody loves me,' as little Eva said." He bunked down in the train station hoping to get some shut-eye, but as he tells it, the local citizens kept him occupied by walking on his feet and spitting the shucks of sunflower seeds in his face. All of which left him convinced that

the Russian peasant or Kirghis cossack has a very clever sense of humor and is quite a comedian. At any rate they kept me amused all night long with their tubercular coughs and their wild, speedy, and I believe accurate lunges after what I took to be the typhus louse. Any desire that I may have had for sleep was taken away after witnessing the wild gesticulations of my fellow travellers in their pursuit of the ever present insect, the flea or louse.

At Lyon's outpost in Orenburg the threat was substantial: at one time as many as a quarter of the ARA's local Russian employees across the district were stricken.

It is remarkable that out of three hundred Americans in the mission only ten relief workers contracted typhus or relapsing fever while in Russia, and of them
there was only one fatality.[2]

This was a result not simply of the preventive measures taken by individuals
but was partly a reflection of the ARA's modus operandi. An American's con-
tracting typhus in the famine region was considered a serious affair, with consequences extending beyond the health of the particular individual. American man
power was spread thin in the famine districts, and the loss of one relief worker for
several weeks, especially a district supervisor, increased the already enormous
burden on his colleagues and threatened the efficiency of ARA operations. Still,
beyond that, there was something more at work. An American laid low by typhus
was regarded within the organization as a threat to its reputation as a smooth-
running machine. It was the American's duty to take all preventive measures in
order to keep himself in good health and on the job. To be outwitted by Mr.
Louse was to fall short of being a clever and efficient relief worker.

It is likely that the precautionary measures they took against typhus contributed to the Americans' reputation for being cold and aloof. "We never think
of picking up the kids or even patting them on the head for fear of infection."
This is Kelley writing about Ufa, but the statement could well have come from
almost any of the Americans in the famine zone. Cornick wrote to his parents on
January 19, 1922, describing the outdoor ceremonies in Tsaritsyn marking "one of
the big Church holidays," where "the crowd got too thick and we like to avoid
crowds on account of the filth and vermin." He relates that on this religious holiday the waters of the Volga River were said to have "healing properties" and that
"every man woman and child had a bucket or pail with which they dipped some
of the water from this common bathing hole and drank. Instead of healing them
I of course feel that this will help to further spread the Typhoid, cholera, and
dysentery, but religious customs can not be changed."

During Easter, Cornick was surprised to find that the Soviet government "saw
fit to proclaim it as an official holiday," beginning Friday at noon and extending
until Tuesday morning, "but the ARA is not abiding strictly by the decree as our
work has to go on." He tells his father, also a medical doctor, that he and his colleagues expect to join up at the great cathedral with "all good Russians," who "after saying 'Christ is Risen' will proceed to kiss all of their companions three
times. If you could see most of the Russians you would realize that this doesn't
sound extremely interesting, but we are going to brave the dangers anyway and
trust that we will be exempt from all the formalities."[3]

In Odessa, once those wooden carts had delivered their cadaverous loads to
the grave digger, they were subsequently often seen in the city streets transporting living children or an ARA food package, with no thought to sanitation.

CHILDS BECAME THE FIRST well-known ARA typhus case when the Associated Press reported it in the American newspapers in January 1922, which he says
made his parents "desperate with anxiety." A special prayer service for him was
held in a Kazan church. Only after five weeks was he able to rise from his bed and
begin to learn how to walk again before making his way out to Berlin for convalescence. Bell was unlucky enough to contract typhus a full three days' sleigh ride

away from Ufa headquarters and was said to have been "out of his head" on the journey back.

The high fever of the typhus patient lasted at least several days, with most of that time spent unconscious. The delirium induced in some the most creative kinds of hallucinations, not all of which seem to have been unpleasant.

Childs was left "fully convinced that my parents had died during the Christmas holidays and it was not until I had actually received letters from them dated in the month of January that I could be assured that they were alive."

Another victim, Joseph Brown, was stationed in the Crimean port of Theodosia, where there was no American physician within hundreds of miles. When the Soviet doctor gave a preliminary diagnosis of spotted typhus, Brown felt "like a person who had received his death sentence." Local doctors informed him that there were "absolutely no drugs of any kind in the Crimea." A U.S. Navy destroyer was sent from Odessa with an American doctor on board. It is unclear if Brown was made aware of this before he slipped into unconsciousness, burning up with a 105-degree temperature. Sixteen days later he became conscious again. "There was a terrible buzzing sound in my ears and my head was full of boiler-shop noises. I discovered I was unable to move my right leg and when I spoke it was hardly above a whisper."

True to the peripatetic spirit of the ARA personnel, Brown did not spend these two weeks idly. "I was under the impression that I had fallen from an airship, and that was the reason I was in bed; for during my period of unconsciousness I had made regular trips around the world in a big Zeppelin and discharged passengers at such places as Shanghai, San Francisco, Chicago, New York and Paris."

Anna Louise Strong, who worked with the American Quakers, also made productive use of her period of unconsciousness, "escaping from Samara in a soft, warm airplane." For years she traveled the world, visiting London, Chicago, crossing the Arctic Circle, until finally, seven days later, she landed safely back in Samara.[4]

Harold Blandy's bout with typhus lasted only one week, for that was all his heart could take. He died in Ufa on May 17, 1922. In Moscow he was given the equivalent of a state funeral by the Soviet government. Of this latter event there are several journalists' accounts, numerous photographs, and motion picture film as well.

Blandy's body lay in state at Spiridonovka 17. The casket, provided by the Moscow soviet, was draped with a large American flag and a blanket of blue forget-me-nots and wreaths. The American Lutheran minister Dr. J. A. Morehead performed the service, during which he read aloud from a telegram Blandy had sent his mother a few days before his death, telling her he could not come home "till my work is finished." In his eulogy Morehead told the congregation that Blandy had performed his work not only with efficiency but with sympathy. We know that the second part of this is true from Kelley's unsympathetic portrait, but it is noteworthy that in the ARA context this needed to be pointed out. Perhaps, ultimately, it was Blandy's undoing.

The formal ceremony was followed by a grand procession, seven miles in length, two hours in duration, through the sun-drenched streets of Moscow to the train station. Participants included the ARA's local American and Russian personnel as well as a good number of curious Muscovites. The casket, escorted by ushers in white formal attire, was borne on an open white hearse led by eight impressive horses. "Moscow must have been searched to find them," wrote a foreign journalist. The ARA was forbidden to fly Old Glory in Russia and the appearance of the stars and stripes on the casket lends a further disorienting note to the surviving images of the occasion.

At the railway station the casket was loaded onto a special train destined for Riga. Motion picture man Floyd Traynham accompanied Blandy's body out of Soviet Russia.

The Blandy funeral was the occasion for a bit of sentimental editorializing in the U.S. newspapers. To the editors of the New York *World* the event demonstrated "the vitality of the one touch of human nature which makes even the Soviet world kin with the rest. . . . Those Russians, even the Bolshevisk part of them, reveal themselves as human beings after all." The U.S. press reported that an illiterate workman from Zlatoust, a remote village in the Ural Mountains, had designed a sculpture for Blandy's mother depicting a blacksmith at his anvil, with a Russian inscription rendered thus by the ARA translator: "Dedicated to the mother of Blandy in memory of her son who met an untimely death on the field of combat against famine in the granite-gray Urals. This tribute of the workers and the local government."

After Blandy's body arrived in the States, another funeral service was held, on the morning of June 14, in New York City at the Church of the Beloved Disciple on East Eighty-ninth Street, with Blandy's relatives and old friends in attendance. The litanies were sung without accompaniment by the Ukrainian choir from the Russian Cathedral and the Buketoff Quartet.

In September, American newspapers reported the founding in Ufa city of the Harold Blandy Memorial Hospital, a former surgical hospital recently repaired by Russian workmen receiving ARA corn rations. There was also an announcement of the intention to erect a Blandy Memorial Monument in Ufa's central square.

Hoover sent a telegram of condolence to Blandy's mother, assuring her that her son had made the supreme sacrifice for a gallant cause "on the battlefield of famine." President Harding wrote to her: "He has died in the service of America."[5]

HOW DIFFERENT THE VIEW from Ufa. When Blandy died, District Supervisor Bell was en route from Ekaterinburg, having cut short a tour of inspection in order to rush back to Ufa. He was writing a letter to Moscow headquarters expressing his concern for Blandy's condition when a telegram arrived from Kelley with the news. Perhaps Bell felt guilty for having departed Ufa after Blandy had come down with a fever, which at that time appeared to be, but had not yet been diagnosed as, typhus.

Or maybe there was an even deeper sense of guilt at work. Blandy contracted typhus while on a trip to unhappy Sterlitamak, capital of the Bashkir Republic. As Kelley tells it, Blandy had been sent out of Ufa "in disgrace . . . to get him out of the way," for he was "utterly useless to the A. R. A., in fact worse." If Kelley has this right, maybe Bell's conscience ate at him as he sat in his railway car on the way back to Ufa.

In any case, the news of Blandy's death seems to have genuinely moved Bell. "While I greatly feared this," he continued his letter, "it is a great shock, and I cannot sufficiently express my intense regret."

Bell eulogized Blandy, recalling his "intense sympathetic nature," for which he was beloved by the ARA Russian personnel and Russian citizens throughout the district. This is confirmed by the letters received by the ARA in Ufa in the subsequent days. The Russian staff members wrote of Blandy that they had "learned to love him for his sensitive heart always ready to respond to human affliction." A letter signed by "Beeshev" observed that Blandy had worked "not for fear, but for love, not even caring for his life," and that "the memory of him will live for a long time in the hearts of the Bashkir people." A letter written by Blandy's interpreter, Gorin, told of Blandy's "great sympathy" for the starving people, whom he "sincerely and greatheartedly" assisted. Gorin recalled how Blandy visited the sick, "never thinking of the possibility of getting the infection"—in fact, he "often laughed at the danger of death from typhus."

When he fell ill, Blandy was fully aware of the seriousness of his case and may have sensed—indeed, welcomed—what was coming. A highly unflattering sketch of Blandy written by one of the Russian staff remarks, "The moment Blandy knew that he had typhus he lost all heart and decided that he was bound to die." A year later, Bell looked back and concluded, "There is no doubt that Blandy was doomed. The nervous strain had been too great for him," and he stood no chance against *typhus exanthimaticus*: "Collapse followed collapse and it was inevitable that the result would be fatal."

With Bell away, it fell to Kelley to make the arrangements for the disposition of Blandy's body. His account of these difficult days is, as one might expect, devoid of all romance.[6]

Kelley probably went about his task with a good deal more concern for his own health than he chose to reveal to his correspondent. Before Blandy was diagnosed as having typhus, Kelley had had physical contact with him, and so for several days, during the period of incubation, he had to live with the uncertainty of himself having contracted the dreaded disease, although he later admitted to experiencing only "slight fears." Kelley's concern would have been made still more acute if his conscience was troubled by his having ridiculed his doomed colleague, which may not have been confined to third-party correspondence.

These were difficult days for the ARA in Ufa. At the time of Blandy's death, sixteen of the city's Russian staff were infected with typhus. "Its ravages have been terrific here lately," Kelley reported. When Blandy fell ill, Piet Hofstra was just coming around after his own bout with the disease. Hofstra came down with it shortly after his return in the first week of April from the Ufa outback. It was thought that he contracted it in a peasant hut where he and his interpreter, Willig, were forced to stay overnight. Willig developed typhus at the same time as Hofstra and died early in his illness.

Hofstra's case was severe, and the ARA physician, Raymond Sloan, had his hands full. A wire was sent to Samara to have its district physician come east to assist Sloan. According to Bell, Hofstra was "coming back to earth" when Blandy became ill. Sloan had the assistance of two of the best local doctors, but nothing could help Blandy. Kelley tells us that Sloan was "much cut up about the loss of his patient," while Hofstra "received quite a shock from Blandy's death. His recovery may be retarded."

Ufa ranks as one of the true ARA hardship posts. Later in the year, two

American secretaries in the Ufa unit would have to be sent out of Russia with preliminary diagnoses of tuberculosis.[7]

Blandy's death was the occasion for some uncharacteristic inefficiency on the part of the ARA publicity department. Or maybe it was just poor luck. The Associated Press broke the Blandy story the day after he died, and it made the U.S. newspapers the following day. The A.P. item consisted of only several lines; the *New York Times* printed it along with an addendum, on page seventeen:

H. F. BLANDY DIES IN RUSSIA

American Relief Administration
Worker Was a New Yorker.

Moscow, May 18 (Associated Press)

—Harold F. Blandy, an American Relief Administration worker of 221 West 121st Street, New York City, died of typhus at Ufa yesterday, according to word reaching Moscow today. He is the first Relief Administration worker to die in Russia.

His body will be embalmed and held until further directions are received from his relatives.

At the 121st Street address the janitor said last night that Mr. Blandy was not known there.

This notice appeared before the ARA in London—and thus in New York— ever got word of Blandy's death. The ARA chiefs appear to have been furious when they picked up the newspapers. Hoover himself cabled Brown in London on May 20, characterizing the situation as "extremely embarrassing" and demanding an immediate explanation.[8]

ARA London attributed the problem to "unfortunate chance," a technical failure in the transmission of the message from Moscow to London, but in fact it seems that there were more general transmission problems at Spiridonovka 30. Otherwise it is impossible to explain why Kelley's initial telegram to Moscow from Ufa on May 17 reporting Blandy's death and asking for instructions went unacknowledged and unanswered for two days. This annoyed Kelley, as he wondered what kind of arrangements he should make: "The Government shop is working overtime on the production of a metal casket which is promised for tomorrow. I hesitate to proceed further in the matter of transportation until Moscow replies to my query. After all, they may want him buried here . . . a horrible thought to me."

The matter of the coffin was no mere detail. Out in Ufa, where the numbers of corpses were high and the material resources few, a genuine casket was something of a luxury item. A "last remnant of tin" was used to make an airtight case, and this was placed inside a wooden container—"the best we could get," Kelley says, "but shockingly crude by American standards." Nor was the Ufa undertaker equal to the demands of the occasion, and Blandy's body would have to be re-embalmed in Moscow and again in New York before being turned over to the family.[9]

The pathetic state of the coffin, the absence of a formal funeral service, and the rather businesslike way the Ufa relief workers continued to perform their duties— although the ARA office was officially closed for one day—all of this elicited critical comment from the Russian personnel as to the casual manner in which the Americans were behaving under the circumstances. Kelley became aware of this but claimed that he never did "give a hang" what the local citizenry thought of the ARA's doings. "For one who craves a ceremonious funeral," he observed, "Ufa is no place to die. With us it is necessarily a case of let the dead bury the dead."

In fact the removal of Blandy's body from ARA headquarters to the train station did constitute a kind of funeral service. Kelley's uncompromisingly realistic account offers a striking contrast to the descriptions of the dignified funeral ceremony staged a few days later in Moscow.[10]

We moved Blandy to the station without mishap. Only the American personnel escorted the truck from the Red House to the filthy station. During the ride I noticed a swarm of kids running along beside the truck. I thought they were the usual crowd of street urchins but learned afterwards that they were from a school which Blandy had visited several times and in which he performed tricks for the children. The station was a sorry sight. Directly in front of the entrance lay two corpses, a mother and a baby. Refugees were lying about the clearing in front of the building engaged in the task of self-delousing. One patriarchial gentleman was standing stark naked in full view bathing with the aid of his wife who poured from a tea cup. We hastened through this mess with the flag draped coffin, bore it across a few tracks, and placed it in a box-car. A large crowd of our employees were at the station, standing in the way, and gaping at us as we tugged to get the coffin into the box in which it is to make its long journey. We hastened to mount the guard and close the car door to shut off the view of the motley aggregation that had gathered.

Almost seamlessly, with only a paragraph indentation, Kelley takes us to the site of a mass grave. The effect is to drain every last trace of dignity and individuality from his account of Blandy's death:

By chance we wandered into another funeral, if I might use that word to describe primitive burial, as we were out for an airing in the Dodge tonight. Our road led into an open field where we noticed a number of fresh mounds. A man and a boy were moving among them evidently preparing to unload bodies from a wagon that stood near. We approached and stood on the edge of a large grave while they proceeded to uncover the wagon and dump six of the most horrible corpses into the ground. Five were men and one a child. All were dead of hunger and blue from time. Unlike those in the postcard I sent you, they were clothed in a few rags, but not so as to conceal the wasted condition of their bodies. Fancy a fourteen year old boy engaged in this kind of work for his living!

Then Blandy is, in effect, lowered in: "This was probably the same dumping place that I recall Blandy picturing with horror last March after a day spent with Traynam, the movie man. To get the picture he climbed down into the grave and posed the corpses while Traynam stood off in horror unwilling to take a picture."

CHAPTER 12

TRAVELERS

It was thought that Blandy might have become infected during his return trip by boat from Sterlitamak. Childs contracted typhus on the train from Moscow to Kazan. Although the men of the ARA were especially vulnerable to disease while on the road, the organization and inspection of relief required frequent travel. The Americans made use of diverse means of transport: railroad, sleigh, boat, automobile, and occasionally camel.

One of the provisions of the Riga Agreement was that the Soviet authorities were to provide special railway cars for the exclusive use of the ARA, the idea being to protect the relief workers from disease, filth, and cold. But the principle proved difficult to put into regular practice, and ARA access to special cars was erratic. During the first months of the mission, the Americans, especially those departing Moscow, stood a decent chance of securing a first-class car, usually an International Wagon-Lit, which meant a ride in privacy and relative comfort. The alternative, which as time went by increasingly became the rule, was the Russian third-class car. Of the phantom second-class car there is barely a mention in the ARA documentation.

The infamous third-class car was usually unlit and unheated. Its compartments were said by one American to resemble "a series of pantry shelves"—"three tiers of wooden benches on which the passengers roost like so many chickens" in the words of the *Chicago Tribune*'s Larry Rue. In the year of the famine, relief workers might find themselves sharing such a car with a crush of people, mostly refugees of the most uninviting type, themselves transporting many other unpaying and undesirable passengers. This was especially the case with American inspectors journeying throughout the famine zone. "The very nature of their work," elaborates one of their number, speaking from experience,

brought them into contact with vermin infested, starving people, and in plain English the Americans were very often cold, lousy, and hungry themselves. Russians of the better class, doctors and others, have often come up to box-cars in which American inspectors were travelling, and offered them their sincere regrets that the authorities could not find it possible to give them, the Americans, more decent accommodations. As a matter of fact the Americans did not mind it such a great deal, and very often probably would not have noticed that they were getting a "raw deal" were it not for the evident concern which some of the Russians themselves spoke of the matter. All this time Russian officials, of high and low degree, were rolling about the country in comfortable cars.

In Simbirsk, early in the mission the American personnel had a special car to themselves "when the Government representative did not need the car himself," but this arrangement "died a natural death" when "The car went to Moscow, and, like the cat, never came back." A "fusillade" of letters and telegrams brought no results and the Simbirsk Americans, in Somerville's words, "gave the thing up as a bad job, and finally began to trust their lives to the terrors of Russian Soviet third-class."

Travel "with the natives," though, did keep things interesting. Freddie Lyon was not able to make his journey from the capital to distant Orenburg quite the way he had imagined, and upon his arrival he let his Moscow colleague Donald Renshaw know about this in a most emphatic tone:

After having been assured of a double coupé on the train I was informed by the porter that the three of us—"Doc" Davenport, myself and interpreter and our five-ton truck load of luggage—had been assigned three seats in the car. Can you imagine that, damn it all Don, if I could have laid my hands on the party who made the reservations for us I'd have choked him until he looked like one of these Mongolian committee-men of mine. After much "pozhalista-ing, spasibooaing, tavarishing," etc., we finally pushed ourselves into a small coupé and locked the door—three of us and baggage occupied one small coupé on a wagon-lit. Oh! such a pleasant trip. After such an expedition, Don, I feel that I can journey back to America as a steerage passenger on a cattleship and enjoy myself.[1]

In the records of the ARA mission there are numerous accounts—far too many, in fact—of abortive efforts by Americans to set off on a journey by rail. The attempt is foiled because either the promised railroad car does not appear or it turns up but is unfit to occupy. Golder tells the story of going to the railway station in Moscow and finding that the car assigned to him had within the previous few days been used to transport typhus patients and had not since been fumigated. It happened that these false starts, with attendant farewells, were repeated nightly for as long as two weeks.

Notably jinxed in this regard was the Moscow-Tsaritsyn run. Dorsey Stephens experienced over a week of "fruitless farewells" before he decided to beat the system by taking the train to Samara and from there float down river to Tsaritsyn. He got away on schedule, but the train broke down in Riazan, about a hundred versts—some sixty-five miles—outside Moscow, leaving Stephens and two ARA colleagues to await repairs. This delighted the editors of the "Russian Unit Record," who reported that telegrams received from the stranded Americans "convey the impression that they do not recommend Riazan as a place to spend one's vacation."

Progress was usually slow, sometimes at a crawl. Stops were frequent and could last for many hours at a time. There were long delays spent immobile on sidings— waiting for engine repairs, for the cutting of wood fuel, for a refugee train to pass, for who-knows-what. As to the specific reason for a particular delay, passengers were often left in the dark, and in the literal sense as well. One had to pack one's food supplies accordingly, which did not always happen. The most extreme case involved Lonergan and Henry Beeuwkes, who set out from Samara for Orenburg—at that time, in February 1922, a four-day journey—in the company of the publicist Eleanor Eagan. Due to someone's oversight, they departed Samara without any food at all. According to the "Russian Unit Record," at a local market along the way they purchased twenty pounds of lamb, which they proceeded to consume "in every culinary disguise that human ingenuity could invent."[2]

Written accounts of the frustrations endured by the American train traveler in Russia are themselves victimized by the tedium. The peripatetic Golder meticulously recorded the frustrating details of most of his false starts and delays en route—how many hours the journey took, how many it used to take before the Revolution, and so on. Thus, while Golder's diary is often engrossing, it lapses into lengthy sections as interesting as a railroad timetable. The point is quickly gotten.

If a train came to a halt somewhere short of no-man's-land, the passengers were subject to the desperate pleas of those "poor hungry devils outside who are looking in." After dark the traveler had to listen to the starving, "tapping at the window all night with that piteous wail for food." During one of his inspection trips, Kelley laments that there is "no escape, even in this car, for men and women come to the door begging for bread and children can be heard whining beneath the car window whenever the light is showing."

An American's slow roll across Russia might generate anxious interest back at headquarters. "Three of the ARA men are lost," wrote Golder in January 1922. "They departed for their destinations days ago and no word has been heard from them. Life in Russia is not dull." It is not unlikely that as Golder was writing those words, the three men in question were gathered rather comfortably in a coupé, well into their supply of whiskey and absorbed in a candlelight game of poker, with stakes running into the tens of millions of rubles.

The ubiquitous complaint of the ARA train traveler in Soviet Russia was the wretched odor of the cars. The American mind could not fathom the Russian preference for keeping all train windows shut tight, even in warm weather—especially, given the fact that many of the Russian trains were wood burners, which meant that an open window would produce no unpleasant consequences in the way of coal fumes. Instead, the American passenger often found himself nearly overcome by the fumes trapped inside, notably the "toilet smell so characteristic of Russian cars." This could spoil a ride even in the most special car, as Tom Barringer discovered: "Here we are in one of the finest sleeping cars to be imagined— one that Mr. Pullman would envy, but no self respecting negro porter would put his foot in it. The air vents are polished up but have not been opened in four years. One can't open the windows and the toilet arrangements are unspeakable." Blomquist recalled his inaugural trip from Moscow to Simbirsk on the "Swine Special," a car "with an atmosphere sufficient to make the roof rise in protest."[3]

THE ESCAPE FROM the foul air was, for inspecting Americans, a big attraction of travel by sleigh, which was in any case an indispensable mode of wintertime expeditions to remote towns and villages. The vehicles themselves were not nearly the splendid troikas seen gliding over magnificent snowy landscapes in paintings from old-regime Russia; in fact the typical sleigh at the disposal of the relief worker was little more than a "crude wooden box on runners" with braces projecting from each side to prevent it from tipping over. The ride was correspondingly rough, but it was a clean ride in fresh air, free from unwanted fellow travelers like the lice and the bed bug.

The primary hazard of sleigh travel was exposure to the elements. Blizzard conditions aside, cold temperatures could make for an uncomfortable journey. For protection the Americans outfitted themselves with bulky Russian fur coats and hats, which they purchased locally. In the exterior winter photographs of the mission, the ARA men, bundled up against the snow and cold and squinting at the photographer between shaggy ear flaps, often resemble arctic explorers. The alternative might be a frozen nose, ear, cheek, or much worse. One did not have to be stationed in a famine outpost in order to share in the experience. George Townsend, personal secretary to Colonel Haskell, experienced a brief moment of terror, which he recalled forty years after the mission. He and a group of ARA men had taken a sleigh ride to the outskirts of Moscow to hear a gypsy performance. "Answering a call to nature," Townsend went out into the back yard.

A few short steps from the house and I was promptly lost. The light in the window disappeared. The sounds of revelry were cut off with the closing of the door. Only the darkness, the howling of the wind and the cold death blast from the Arctic. I rushed back towards the house. Turbulent darkness in every direction. Total bewilderment. I was hopelessly lost. Cold. Terrified. Obviously, I had gone in the wrong direction. . . . I turned left and barged blindly ahead in a new direction. A few strides and a blurred mass appeared before me, then the faint light in the window. I burst through the door into the warmth, light and noise inside. It seemed I had been away an eternity. My colleagues yelled: "Shut the door!"

Which leaves open the question of whether Townsend did indeed get to answer his call to nature.

Out on the treeless landscape of the Volga valley navigation by sleigh could be hazardous. Should a blizzard come up, the danger of losing one's way was considerable. Louis Landy set out in a sleigh from the Volga town of Pugachev for Erzhov, some sixty miles away. He and his party took along food provisions for two days of traveling, but a storm kept them from their destination for five days, during which time, according to a Russian colleague, "they were nearly starved." Stephen Martindale was on a sleigh journey when he also became caught up in a blizzard. Fifteen hours after departing, he arrived in a village that turned out to be only five miles from where he had started out.[4]

Another challenge of sleigh travel was finding suitable quarters in which to overnight. With the precise schedule of the journey impossible to fix beforehand, the traveling American and his interpreter usually resorted to knocking on the door of a peasant hut, perhaps in the middle of the night. Sometimes the process was drawn out: the peasant on the inside, unconvinced that the person on the other side of the door was an American from the ARA, might refuse to open it. On the other hand, a quick inspection of the hut might convince the travelers that it was worth their while to press on with their journey.

One of the Kazan Americans had better luck than most when he entered a village and was hosted by a peasant family. The head of the household triumphantly presented him with a single egg, which he said he had been saving for some weeks in order to give it to the first American to visit his village. This information may not have favorably influenced the American's appetite, but to refuse this prize might have upset the host. So he proceeded to consume the precious egg, and as he did, the man and his entire family—his wife, six kids, a rooster, a hen, and a goat—looked on with admiration. When the American then offered to share his sugar for tea, "their wonder and delight was manifested by howls of glee, this being their first sight of sugar for four years."

Childs had a different story to tell in this vein. To pass a few hours while waiting for a change of horses for his sleigh, he was conducted into a peasant hut, which he describes as "one of the filthiest homes into which it has ever been my lot to be introduced. . . . I was worn out and I desired to lie down, but when I saw bugs crawling about the floor, I changed my mind.

"I took my seat on a bench alongside the wall and was about to put down my coats and lie upon these on the bench, when I took one look at the wall and felt my skin creep at the sight of the hundreds of bugs which were disporting themselves behind me."

Some travelers brought along a folding cot, thus solving one problem, although it could do nothing to improve the air. After his frustrating day's journey, Martindale's only refuge for the night was a cottage that was so filthy and malodorous that he retreated outside into the sleigh and, under two fur coats, went to sleep. In the morning, his interpreter found him half-frozen and had to apply a snow massage to thaw him out. While Martindale's experience was not unusual, more typically, with the temperature outside dipping to thirty and forty degrees below zero, the decision to retire to the sleigh was arrived at only after a few fitful hours spent in the close air of the peasant's hut conjuring up terrifying images of the invisible typhus carrier within.

While underway, the sleigh traveler's nemesis was not the cootie but the wolf. Apparently the Russian wolf also was feeling the effects of the famine, for the locals found him to be far more aggressive than in previous years. Kelley describes setting out on a sleigh that was equipped with bells, which jangled loudly over the otherwise snow-hushed landscape. This, he says, made him nervous, for he feared that the noise would attract the attention of bandits, but he was told that wolves would be frightened by it. Not on this occasion, however, as he reports that several stalked his sleigh and that he "fingered my Colt whenever one drew near."

The only genuine close call with a wolf was had by the district physician in Kazan, John Cox. Traveling by sleigh on a tour of inspection, Cox and his guide were pursued by a pack of scrawny wolves, who, an American colleague later embellished, occasionally paused to deliver a "long tremulous howl of unadulterated delight at the prospect of a feast on a nice juicy American." So certain was Cox that his end was near that he scratched out his last will and testament on the back of a tin mess kit, which happily for the young doctor he was able to bring out of Soviet Russia as a souvenir.[5]

CHAPTER 13

GUNMEN

One might ask why Dr. Cox had not packed a rod for such an occasion. Childs, in his diary from November 1921, recounts undertaking a sleigh journey and quite incidentally remarks: "Of course we all had our revolvers and were prepared for any eventuality in the shape of wolves, but during the entire trip we saw none."

In Moscow the Americans did not feel the need to arm themselves, though they expended a good deal of mental energy on matters of self-protection. An American correspondent reported that the Russian capital in those days was one of the most crime-free cities in Europe—"Life is safer for the pedestrian on the streets of Moscow after midnight than on the streets of New York"—though some ARA testimony from the first year of the mission disputes this. There were no wolves in the center of city, but there were a good many thieves. The men at Spiridonovka 30 are frequently heard discussing how best to defend against the holdup man. George Townsend recalls that, for a time anyway, the practice of the Moscow relief workers was to travel at night in groups of *droshkies* through the city streets: strength in numbers. "We all carried canes. Mine was a stout stick with a regulation white billiard ball on top. I never had to use it as a weapon. It certainly made my defense posture unassailable."

New American arrivals to Russia were routinely warned to be vigilant. The message apparently got through to two Massachusetts boys out for their first Saturday night in Moscow. As they were returning to the personnel house at a late hour, they saw the droshki ahead of them come to a halt and its occupants throw their hands up in the air. It is not clear if in reacting as they did they were heeding some ARA veteran's advice, but the two men leaped out of their droshki and made a run for it. Bullets whizzed by them and one American went down with a flesh wound in the foot. It turned out that the "thieves" were in fact Moscow policemen making routine inquiries on the street; when they saw the two men fleeing, they felt this was sufficient cause to begin firing.

James Callahan of Fall River would remain ignorant of these circumstances until noon the next day. Unable to find his way back to his residence, which he was able to identify only as "the Brown House," in the middle of the night Callahan wandered into a Red Army barracks. Here some of Trotsky's soldiers took him in and revealed to him the mysteries of Russian vodka. When he reached home the next afternoon, he was said to be "tight as a tick."

Out in the districts, frontier conditions made the matter of a proper defense much more of a life-and-death affair, and in some places carrying a gun was an absolute requirement. Several of the men, especially those who entered Soviet Russia early in the mission, brought along their own revolvers: after all, this was the land of the Bolos, and no one knew what to expect. In his 1929 memoir, *You Can't Print That!*, the American newspaperman George Seldes wrote that "Haskell's agents" got their relief trains through Russia "at the point of revolvers." An arresting image, but Seldes is at most generalizing from an isolated incident or two, now long forgotten.

It was sometimes the case that local officials took it upon themselves to supply the Americans with arms. Alexis Babine's diary entry for February 23, 1922, includes this sentence: "To protect Americans against attacks, the Pugachev Soviets have issued revolvers to them with 25 shells apiece." This was in Saratov province.

In the city of Orenburg, according to an ARA report, the "first act upon the arrival of a new man was to produce him a permit to carry a revolver. . . . [N]o one ventured out on the streets of Orenburg at night without carrying his loaded revolver in his right hand, no matter how cold the weather. . . . Men meeting in the street circled around each other."

In Ufa over two successive nights twelve people were murdered within a stone's throw of ARA headquarters, which prompted Col. Bell to demand firearms from the local authorities, who, admitting they could not control the city's crime, brought out a "wealth of armaments." Ufa appears to be the extreme case; here, at least in Kelley's account, revolvers are continually being drawn. His instructive dissertation on the daily routine of the American relief worker in Ufa ends as the ARA man rises from his desk, "pats his coat pocket to make sure that his revolver is still there, and retires to his house." Himself preparing to go out for the evening, Kelley closes a private letter with a little local color:

I shall keep my right hand firmly on my Colt 45 during the entire stroll. Ufa may once have had street lights, but I see no evidence of them. The moon and the snow provide such illumination as there is at present. Reports of holdups are so unpleasantly frequent that I strongly favor the middle of the street where no citizen, no matter how empty his cupboards, can head my way without courting a serious shock. If he survives, someone else may ask him in his own lingo what it was that he wanted. I must admit that so far the few pedestrians I have passed in the night seemed desirous of keeping as far away from me as possible. Doubtless they were not prepared for trouble or did not carry the comforting immunity from all molestation and arrest that reposes in my pocket.

On a later occasion he remarks, "I don't want to shoot any poor wretch who only meant to ask his way." A long enough stretch spent at the edge of Siberia might instill certain frontier habits. It is no wonder that the visit of one of these gun-toting "provincial" ARA boys to the Russian capital could serve as a source of considerable amusement to the Moscow Americans.[1]

THE ROBBERY VICTIM in the Russia of 1922 was less likely to lose his large wad of devalued rubles than his clothes.

During the Revolution and Civil War, when the class war raged in Russia, the old aristocracy and the middle classes in the capitals and in the provincial cities and towns shed the clothing that had attested to their social status in tsarist Russia. Sometimes clothes were hidden away; more often they were exchanged for food, and in this fashion entire wardrobes were bartered away. Many borrowed or took the clothes of their servants in an attempt to fit in with the crowd of workers and peasants, the new nominal governing classes of Russia.

In Golder's documentation of the fate of the intelligentsia in the Russian Revolution, clothes are never far out of mind, beginning especially during the Civil War when the night searches of the secret police meant that, "For weeks at a time families went to bed with their clothes on and laid there hourly expecting the dreaded knock and search." This was nearly two decades before Stalin's Great Terror.

By 1921 quality clothing was hard to come by in Soviet Russia. The pedestrian walking the city streets might be wearing his only set of clothes, perhaps the only clothing he had possessed for a few years. Now with the coming of NEP and the uncertain truce in the class war, "former people" could begin again at least to think about dressing like their former selves. Variety and taste in clothing, however modest, began to matter again. Childs recalls seeing in Petrograd in 1922, alongside the "richly and overdressed new bourgeoisie," men and women "attired in clothes of pre-revolutionary style. With what care they had been preserved, one could judge from the little marks of attention which were paid to their apparel by their possessors." He observed the "magical," if momentary, transformation of one of the ARA Russian employees in Moscow:

Five years ago she had danced with officers of the Imperial Guard and had worn a pearl necklace about her neck where now was a chain of simple beads. And one Sunday afternoon when she appeared in a dress of black silk ornaments and tull[e] and beautiful lace one might have visualized the courtly mien which had characterized her person but a little while before if there had not been such a weariness about her eyes and such a pitiful droop about her mouth.[2]

It is fair to say that post–Civil War Russia's obsession with clothing was surpassed only by its fixation on food. It did not take long for the American relief workers to become conscious of this and of the need to keep a weather eye on their own articles of clothing. Townsend recalls how upon arrival in Moscow in autumn and winter 1921, all the Americans were "warned of hold-ups where victims were stripped of their clothes and their nude bodies left to freeze in the snow." One imagines the schoolboy glee with which veterans of the unit delivered such admonitions to the newcomers.

That such things transpired in the wilds of the Volga valley was of course entirely imaginable. Babine's diary for February 11, 1922, offers one example: "People have been undressed by footpads in this frost right in the streets, and without clothes and shoes, in their underwear alone, forced to speed home the best they could. A lady friend of mine got pneumonia under this maltreatment."

But why would a thief stop at underwear, which in postrevolutionary Russia had become a luxury item? Pat Verdon estimated that fully half of the residents of the city of Rostov had to make do without underclothing.

Ten years after the mission, Haskell recalled that "On a number of occasions small groups of Americans returning to Moscow HQ late at night were waylaid by groups of hoodlums and their every article of clothing was stripped from them." Maybe Haskell truly believed he was reporting fact, but there is no hard evidence that anything of the kind was ever inflicted upon any ARA member. It seems likely that any incident in which an American had all his clothes taken from his person, especially in the middle of Moscow, would have been the subject of considerable ARA chatter, and would have rated at least an oblique and satirical reference in the "Russian Unit Record."

One has only to consider the amount of excitement occasioned by the simple theft of articles of clothing from ARA men—as opposed to their removal from their persons. This, it can be confirmed, occurred quite frequently. James Walsh awoke in his third-class railway car to find that his bed roll containing all his best clothes was missing. The "Russian Unit Record" for August 27, 1922, estimated the loss at $150, or 630,000,000 rubles: "The brand new pair of shoes which Jim thought too good to wear in Russia, will be worn here but not by Jim." In the subsequent issue of the "Record" we learn that "sneak thieves" had made a raid on the Brown House, carrying off "some half dozen suits of men's clothing." Among the victims was Walsh, who was said to be "waxing mildly indignant over these repeated assaults upon his trousseau."

Above all, one had to mind one's trousers. Golder tells us that in Civil-War Petrograd, many men sold the pants of their dress suits to sailors, who wore them as part of their uniforms. Frock coats were more difficult to dispose of, and so in 1922 Petrograd "former people" and the "red bourgeoisie" might have stylish jackets but ill-suited trousers to accompany them.

So the American relief workers had to make sure they kept their pants on. Feeding their paranoia, the "Police Court News" section of the "Russian Unit Record" reveled in reporting cases of ARA men being "divested of raiment." For example, on July 9, 1922, there appeared the following report out of Samara: "Dr. Caffey on the night of July 3rd went to bed after placing a loaded gun, his watch and all his roubles under his pillow and carefully locking up his coats and vests. During the night thieves entered and carried off all his trousers, and since then the Doctor has been appearing at work in a pair of Red Cross pajamas."

A later issue revealed that "Samara's Professor Moriarty" had extracted Henry Wolfe's trousers from his room while he slept.

The relief workers were especially vulnerable to clothes snatchers when traveling in the dreaded third-class railroad car. Here the intrepid Russian thief displayed a remarkable talent for entering a sleeping American's quarters and, undetected, stealing the clothing the ARA man had removed before retiring. Perhaps these Americans just slept soundly: it was said that Walsh's snoring covered up the noise of his robbers.

The amount of fear that the reporting of a few such cases could induce in the traveling American is evident in Golder's account of a rail journey he took with Harold Fisher in late summer 1922 through Ukraine, a land legendary for its pantaloon pirates. Golder describes how he and Fisher settle in for a night of sleep in their coupé: "The fate of McSweeney and his trousers was before our minds, as well as the story of how Bogen lost his pants and Rosen his trousers. We therefore concluded not to take off the only pantaloons we had on so as not to lose them and we did not."

Emboldened by this uneventful night, Golder and Fisher dared to remove their pants for bed the next evening; when they awoke the next morning, "our trousers were still with us and soon on us." They may not have slept all that peacefully, however, for the following night they "put off going to bed as long as possible" before finally deciding to erect a barrier to the entrance of the coupé. Despite these precautions they spent a restless night. Nonetheless, as Golder wrote to Quinn in Moscow in mock triumph, "thanks to our vigilance and foresight, we have our pants on today."

Golder's remark about the "fate of McSweeney and his trousers" refers to the most celebrated of the ARA trouser incidents. No doubt this has to do with the popularity within the unit of the roguish Denis McSweeney, proudly Irish and at fifty years old one of the ARA's senior citizens in Russia. The actual facts of the McSweeney case are forever lost beneath layers of ARA tomfoolery. What we know is that on July 8, 1922, the editor of the "Russian Unit Record," Farmer Murphy, reported receiving the following special dispatch from ARA Kiev: "McSweeney passed hurriedly through Kiev last night after dark enroute Moscow with all clothes gone. Please meet at station with barrel."

The "Record" dispatched its "crime reporter"—undoubtedly the editor himself—to meet the train, "with a closed vehicle," and found McSweeney clad in a three-piece suit of three different patterns. The able reporter managed to induce McSweeney to disclose the chilling details of his story. "Every expression of sympathy warmed him to greater eloquence and the tale grew and grew in luxuriance and color till it would have put to shame the most imaginative Russian famine sufferer who ever piteously cried, 'Khlieb, khlieb.'" If McSweeney's story can be believed, after waking in his coupé and discovering the theft, he again lay down to sleep attired in the only clothing he had left, when he was awakened once more, this time by someone trying to remove the shoes from his feet.

Trousers were at the center of an ARA scandal in which an American was said to have made himself the "laughing stock of Petrograd." According to Sam Keeny of the YMCA, who recalled the incident sixty years after the fact, this particular ARA man, whom he does not name, was fond of the night locales in the former capital, which he usually patronized in the company of his bulldog. Early one morning, this young American returned to his apartment after a night on the town to find that his landlady had locked the door. Before climbing in through a side window through which he first placed the dog, he removed his white slacks so as not soil them—this in full view of a "big crowd" of amused Petrograd citizens waiting for a streetcar. As Keeny recalls, "some wag wrote it up in the newspaper. . . . The Russians roared with laughter and we were humiliated."[3]

MORE SERIOUS A THREAT to the welfare of the ARA men than run-of-the-mill thieves were "bandits." This is the term the Bolsheviks used as a label for the anti-Communist peasant armies in the heartland that rose up against Bolshevik power in 1920–21. Non-Bolsheviks used the term "Greens," but this destroyed the tidy symmetry of Red versus White and implied a movement with some organizational and, perhaps, ideological coherence and legitimacy, which the government was unwilling to concede. Although the last of the fighting in the Russian Civil War is commonly said to have ended by the winter of 1920–21, the activities

of these partisan armies in effect kept the authorities preoccupied into the following summer.[4]

In Russian history the most famous peasant rebellions are associated with the
names of their leaders: Pugachev, Razin, Bolotnikov, Bulavin. In 1920–21, new
names were added to the pantheon of Russian rebels. In Ukraine "banditism" was
associated with the figures of Petliura and especially Makhno. The bloodiest of the
Green uprisings, in Tambov province, only a few hundred miles southeast of Moscow, was led by Antonov. What the Soviets derisively called the *Antonovshchina*
began in August 1920 and was brought to a violent end in the spring of 1921.

There was no large single force on the scale of Antonov's in the Volga valley but
rather a number of smaller outfits. This might explain why they were able to hold
out so long after the defeat of Antonov, even undergoing something of a revival
early in 1922. Well into that year, Communist and Soviet offices and Red Army
men in the smaller Volga towns and villages were vulnerable to "bandit" attack.

Of course some of these gangs were little more than groups of glorified highwaymen—in other words, genuine bandits—but it was not always easy to tell
them apart from Green soldiers since their appearance and their methods, namely
robbery and murder, were quite similar. Nonetheless, there were some "bandits"
who appeared to behave as latter-day Robin Hoods, taking from the Communist
—usually envisioned as a Jew—and giving to the Russian peasant. The ARA men
recognized differences among them but used the term "bandits" indiscriminately
and with a certain satisfaction: to the American ear it evoked romantic images of
the wild West. Among the relief workers the more high-minded outlaws enjoyed
a reputation, which appears to have been generally accurate, for respecting the
name of the ARA and leaving its supplies untouched, or at most taking them out
of the hands of Communists.

American relievers had several opportunities to witness this ARA immunity
first hand. In November 1921, Carl Floete of San Francisco was in the Volga town
of Pugachev—named after the eighteenth-century peasant who incited an enormous rebellion against Catherine the Great's Moscow—when a group of eight
hundred Cossacks descended on horseback upon the town and a fierce battle ensued. When it was over, it was reported that thirty Red Army soldiers and several
Cossacks lay dead in the street and that the Communist Party offices were left
ransacked, but that ARA supplies and headquarters, in which Floete had barri-
caded himself, had not been violated.

Floete's "close call" became legendary in ARA circles. The "Russian Unit
Record" called him "Hairbrea[d]th Harry, King of the Bandits." Floete himself,
though, was in no condition to appreciate such levity. Within days he was on a
train heading toward Riga. Kelley, who encountered him there, says he was suffering from a "nervous breakdown," and according to another witness, though
Floete had come through unscathed, he was "pretty well shot to pieces."[5]

In Ukraine, in the vicinity of Ekaterinoslav, the "bandits" associated with Petliura were notorious for ambushing trains, in order, it was said, "to shoot the
Commissars and rob the rich Jews." However, a local ARA man testified, "They
never molested the ARA shipments and once even gave us a receipt for the
money taken from one of our warehouse managers."

Mayer Kowalsky may have come the closest to ruining the ARA's perfect record with bandits and highwaymen. Returning by automobile to headquarters in the Ukrainian town of Volhynia in July 1922, Kowalsky and his driver were overtaken by five armed men. For a Jew, even an American Jew working for the ARA, to be held up by bandits of whatever variety in Ukraine was a very serious matter. Kowalsky knew at once that he was up against it, as his attackers made clear their decision to have done with him and to commandeer his auto and chauffeur. His state of terror must have been almost unbearable: he later recalled "long begging for my life" and confesses, "I was unconscious for some time after the accident happened"—which sounds like a nervous collapse. It was Kowalsky's knowledge of Russian—he knew just enough but in this case not too much—that appears to have saved his life. Attempting to invoke his immunity as a member of the ARA, he informed his would-be executioners that he was a famine relief worker who "eats little children." The bandits were said to have found this simply hilarious, and, the tone of the proceedings having been considerably lightened, they took the American's money, gold watch and Browning, but let him go unharmed.[6]

The most famous ARA "close call" with bandits is told in the "thrilling tale" of Marshall Tuthill's encounter with the infamous Ivanov gang. Tuthill was returning from Novouzensk to the city of Saratov in June 1922. This stretch of steppe to the southeast of Saratov was a territory where bandits roamed freely, and their attacks continually disrupted transportation and communication. On the lone railroad line Soviet officials traveled only in an armored train, said by Tuthill to be "bristling with machine guns and rifles."

On the day of his encounter with Ivanov, Tuthill was riding in an open Ford with his chauffeur and interpreter. In a memorandum to Col. Haskell he described what then took place:

We were passing through a small village by the name of Novo Yama with everything nice and quiet (except the Ford) when I was jarred out of a peaceful doze by the slamming on of our much worn brakes, accompanied by the startling yells from several ferocious looking fellows bearing down on our starboard beam in a cloud of dust. They were leaning low over the necks of their mounts in a most picturesque attitude, pointing efficient looking rifles in a very business-like manner at our respective Adam's apples. It was not necessary for my interpreter to translate their snappy order to "get out damn quick and throw up your hands." We obeyed tout de suite.

One of the bandits, having discovered Tuthill's Colt .38, let out a "true Cossack whoop of delight and swung it around the atmosphere without any regard at all for the precautions one usually takes with a loaded gun with the safety open." While this "Jesse James stunt" was being performed, Tuthill's interpreter explained that they were representatives of the ARA, which the bandits appeared not to believe. At that moment, Ivanov himself galloped along, "to supervise the execution." "They were a very picturesque lot—especially the chief. His costume was the old Cossack outfit—Persian lamb hat and long and wide skirted maroon overcoat with the usual silver tipped cartridge belts crossed on his chest. All were armed to the teeth and extremely well mounted—that is for this country where practically all one sees is camel power."

Soon the matter was cleared up as a case of mistaken identity. Ivanov explained that his men were hiding behind the walls of the town's roofless mud huts—"vacated," Tuthill offered, "by order of the old gentleman with the scythe"—waiting to ambush a group of Bolsheviks due to pass in an automobile. At this point Tuthill says he glanced back along Main Street and saw "half a hundred" gun barrels protruding through doorways and windows, a scene worthy of a Hollywood Western.

According to Tuthill, the man who had taken his gun then asked Ivanov if he should return it. With a "proper bandit chieftain scowl" Ivanov replied, "Of course, you poor fool; you can't handle a gun anyhow."

One report of this incident, which must have been informed by Tuthill, has Ivanov riding up and offering him a cigar. Tuthill's letter to Haskell does not mention this detail, though it does indicate that the atmosphere became friendly: "We had a short chat with Ivanoff and his lieutenant during which we were heartily assured that all of the bandits had the greatest admiration for America and Americans and their relief work in Russia."

Ivanov made a point of showing Tuthill stocks of ARA food stashed in the house of a local Communist leader. They swore that in the home of practically every Communist they came across they found abundant ARA child-feeding supplies, which, Ivanov explained, was a good enough reason to kill all these Bolsheviks, "because they stole American food intended for the children of the peasants."

With an expression of mock concern that perhaps the discussion would appear to Haskell to have strayed into the forbidden realm of politics, Tuthill assures his chief, "I am merely giving you the story as the plot unraveled, and of course am expressing no political opinion—in accordance with the Riga Agreement." He closes with a gratuitous addendum, tongue now placed firmly in cheek:

There is one bandit gang I hope to be captured by one of these days. The chief is a remarkably pretty, young, black-eyed she-devil by the name of Marriene, reported to be the daughter of a former general in the Czar's Army. My interpreter was fortunate enough to be caught by her sometime ago and he verifies the stories of her beauty, horsemanship and daring. While he was in her fair young hands he witnessed the execution of two Communist leaders of the town—by her orders, after a tribunal of villagers had explained to her how the aforesaid leaders had applied the theories of Carl Marx in their village.[7]

Tuthill had along an interpreter, so there was no problem communicating with Ivanov and Company. When Eddie Fox encountered two holdup men a few miles outside Simferopol, in the Crimea, the temporary absence of his interpreter left him some room for maneuver but not as much as he thought.

Fox was making a final tour of inspection in the closing weeks of the mission, in May 1923, when a tire blew out. The chauffeur went to work on the tire, the interpreter wandered off to gather some flowers, and Fox and an American companion sat down to rest by the side of the road. Suddenly from out of the brush there appeared two bandits of the plain empty-your-wallet variety—although not quite, as these two proved themselves to be accomplished linguists as well. Fox later reported the ensuing give-and-take to the ARA publicity department in Moscow, which reproduced it as follows:

"Daite dengy," quoth bandit number one. "Give me your money."

"I don't understand," said Fox in his worst Russian. The bandit repeated his demand.

"But I don't speak Russian," answered Fox, accenting the Russian as badly as possible.

"Parlez vous Français?" asked the accomplished gentleman of the highway. This required some tact, Fox reflected.

"I don't understand," he mumbled again, in Russian.

"Argent," growled the exasperated bandit. Again Fox appeared to be at a total loss as far as linguistic ability was concerned.

"Sprechen Sie Deutsch?" demanded the bandit, this time with a touch of irritation.

"Geldt," shouted the other.

"I don't understand," said Fox for the sixth time.

At last the interpreter appeared, dropping an armful of flowers at his feet and making it impossible for Fox to continue his act. At this point the American smiled and produced his ARA identification, which had no effect, however, for all his money was taken. When he protested that he was an American relief worker, one of the robbers "grumbled something about the feeding of communist children."[8]

Charlie Veil had the opposite problem when in the autumn of 1921 he came upon a group of bandits in the area of Novouzensk, the same region where Tuthill would later cross paths with Ivanov. Veil, a truly unconventional individual even by ARA standards, tells the story of how he was riding atop his camel, Pike's Peak, when he wandered into a bandit camp of horsehide lean-tos, populated by "men and women, grimy, wild-looking creatures, inhuman in aspect. . . . " Veil's arrival caused quite a stir, and a big crowd gathered around him. He dismounted Pike's Peak and pronounced the Russian equivalent of "Where is the chief?"—the ARA variant of "Take me to your leader." Apparently he had made himself understood and was, as he tells it,

led down a ravine where another horsehide lean-to, pinned against the rocks, debouched a tall slender fellow, handsome of face, graceful of physique. My two dozen words of Russian were soon exhausted but the fellow was just as intelligent as I was dumb. I strove to remedy the fault by talking in German. He shook his head, then surprisingly he asked slowly, laboriously in English, "What do you want?"

In English I answered him but again he shook his head. He had used up *his* four words. A few French words slipped into the conglomeration and at [the] sound of them his face lighted. He spoke French easily; at mutual realization that we had overcome the terrible obstacle of language we almost threw our arms around each other in joy.[9]

As the bandit Ivanov's statements imply, and despite the official ARA version of events, the degree of theft of ARA supplies, ranging from minor pilferage from the occasional torn sack of flour to large-scale warehouse robberies, was not trivial. The thievery began at the Russian seaports with the local stevedores unloading ARA supply ships. Railway cars stocked with American supplies were vandalized, although never in the wholesale fashion imagined in the ARA's worst nightmares at the start of the mission, which probably explains why the organization was only moderately disturbed by the theft that actually did take place.

Considering the frequency with which acts of theft of ARA food and medical supplies were attempted right under the noses of the Americans in Moscow, one can imagine that in the subdistricts, beyond the direct supervision of the American personnel, mishandling of ARA products by Bolshevik and Soviet officials and by local ARA employees was considerable.

On numerous occasions the Americans themselves stumbled upon thieves in the act and then took part in the capture, sometimes employing physical violence. It was thought that something along these lines occurred—and went terribly wrong—in the case of Philip Sheild, who walked out of ARA headquarters in Simbirsk on Sunday evening, October 15, 1922, and disappeared forever, "as though the earth had swallowed him up."

SHEILD WAS a twenty-six-year-old Richmond, Virginia, man, who in 1917 quit the University of Virginia to join the American Ambulance Service with the French army, in which he served for two years and was twice cited, once with the Croix de Guerre. He returned after the war to finish his education at UVA, graduating in June 1921. In December he "felt the call" to go to Russia and arrived for duty in Simbirsk on February 5, 1922.

The public ARA theory about the fate of Phil Sheild is that he was murdered, probably in connection with a robbery from the ARA warehouse in Simbirsk. Two days prior to Sheild's disappearance it was discovered that four tons of sugar had been stolen from the ARA supply depot. The catch was valued at about $500, a veritable fortune on the Russian market, easily worth $5,000, or at that time six billion rubles. The thieves, among whom was the ARA's Russian warehouse manager, were apprehended just at about the time that Sheild was made head of the supply division, replacing Denis McSweeney. In fact, Sheild took an active part in the investigation.

Speculation had it that the thieves and their at-large accomplices believed that Sheild's promotion was somehow connected with the arrests, and sought revenge. The fact that those in custody faced a possible death sentence, some thought, pointed to an additional motive, namely eliminating the "principal witness for the prosecution." The thinking is that when Sheild left the ARA personnel house that Sunday evening, these conspirators were waiting for him.

Some believed that he may have simply gotten into a "brawl." If the assault had not been planned beforehand, one report stated, "it could easily be attributed to his temper, which though he controlled it ordinarily, sometimes went beyond all bounds, during which periods, according to those who knew him best, he was liable to do anything." Elsewhere, Sheild was said to be "the sort that, when real angry, will fight a buzz saw, and recognizes no superior forces." We know from another source that Sheild did not carry a gun.[10]

Back home, the case of the "lost Virginian"—whose name was most often rendered as "Shields," sometimes "Sheilds" or "Shield"—attracted nationwide attention. It was reported in the newspapers that at the request of Sheild's parents, his college friend Tom Barringer had left his ARA post in Ukraine to join in the investigation. Still, concerned Virginians worried that the ARA was not doing enough. The president of the First National Bank of Richmond wrote to Hoover to complain that the $500 reward money put up by the ARA in Simbirsk for information on Sheild's whereabouts was "entirely disproportionate to the seriousness of the situation." Another cabled that the total was "utterly inadequate." Hoover's office replied, quite correctly, that $500 was a considerable sum of money in currency-starved Russia.

An editorialist in Memphis made perverse use of the occasion to lash out at

Senator Borah, who "would have us shake hands with those who are biting the hand that feeds them." Newspaper readers could follow the unfolding of the Sheild murder mystery as day after day there came to light new details of the case: how, two days after he disappeared, Sheild's hat was found on the Volga riverbank, a few miles above Simbirsk; how a man was terribly beaten in a brick pit near to where the hat had been discovered; how three other men, reputable residents of Simbirsk, went hunting on the same day Sheild disappeared and themselves vanished without a trace; how a woman had stepped forward to claim that on the day in question she had through the darkness glimpsed two men carrying a large sack with legs protruding, whose feet wore "tan oxfords of American make"—though no doubt she had a different way of saying it.[11]

There was a new twist on October 17, when a brutal murder took place on the same street as ARA headquarters—one hundred yards away, according to a relief worker; less than fifty yards, according to Walter Duranty, reporting in the *New York Times*. The manager of a bathhouse was returning home with his wife late at night when they were confronted by a holdup man who fired a pistol into the husband's face, at such close range that the skin was charred. Duranty wrote that this gave rise to fears within Simbirsk that "a gang of desperate bandits" was on the loose.

Among his Simbirsk colleagues Sheild appears to have been well liked, and his disappearance was said to have caused a "great deal of sorrow and anxiety" in the ranks. District Supervisor Joe Dalton, an army captain from Winston-Salem and a graduate of the Virginia Military Institute, was reported to be "taking it all to heart," though in fact he had only recently arrived in Simbirsk. His burden would have been lightened by some timely instruction or encouragement from Moscow. As it happened, his first six telegrams to Spiridonovka 30 on the Sheild case, sent over a four-day period, went unacknowledged: "It would relieve our minds a good deal if we could get word from Moscow that our telegrams are being received."

Dalton conducted an initial inquiry then brought Sheild's disappearance to the attention of the local authorities, who mounted an investigation. Once contact with Moscow was established, Dalton was kept busy apprising the chiefs of the latest developments if not actual progress. In one of his first letters to Haskell, he complained that although local officials were doing "a great deal of running around, much of it in our Ford," they were "unable to cope" and "absolutely incapable" of solving the case. He found he had to go through "endless red-tape channels" in order to have the reward posters printed up, an idea that had met with a "decided disinclination on the part of the Government."

Apparently the Sheild case had set off some serious infighting among the local authorities. Dalton reviewed the petty intrigues at work among the provincial and town militia and the Department of Criminal Investigation. He thought the local police would never get to the bottom of the case and requested in strong terms that Haskell send down "thoroughly qualified" men from Moscow, including a member of the colonel's staff. Within days, 150 of Moscow's "best detectives" were reported, implausibly, to be on the job in Simbirsk. On October 27, Haskell himself arrived to conduct his own investigation, vowing, it was said, to "turn Simbirsk upside down" in order to find the missing American.

What followed was a slow and, at least for the Americans, frustrating investigation. There developed a considerable tension between the Simbirsk relievers and the ever elusive Soviet investigators, who preferred to divulge none of their findings. The Americans became resentful and at times suspected government complicity in the affair, though this was never demonstrated. Several Russians were arrested, but in a country whose government had only recently measured progress in numbers of arrests, this alone could mean very little.

The chauffeur and his wife were arrested but soon let go. Then on November 14, formal indictments for murder were issued against a local man and woman: he, according to police, a former bandit who went by the name of "Vaska"; she known to "run with a bad crowd." No evidence was ever found to convict anyone and all arrested parties were eventually released.

Sheild's hat was indeed found, on October 17, washed up on the riverbank some four miles above Simbirsk, although this was reported to the ARA only on the 23rd, a few days after the reward posters had gone up. Thereafter the search for the body focused on the river, which was dragged daily. Soon blizzard conditions hampered the search, and the Volga began to freeze up; after only another week the search for Sheild had to be called off.

Duranty accompanied Haskell to Simbirsk and the stories he filed for the *Times* were given nationwide circulation in the States. His dispatch of October 29, describing the dragging of the Volga, was meant to tug at the heart:

From the bank and from another boat forty yards upstream they are throwing five-pronged grappling irons attached to a long rope. The iron from one boat catches and the tension grows as the sturdy fishermen strain at the rope. Slowly, regretfully, the river gives up its prey—no, it is but a piece of waterlogged tree, and as the men heave it to the bottom of the boat you realize suddenly that it is dusk and very cold.

The fishermen call it a day, and Duranty watches them "gulp greedily the special allowances of strong spirits permitted—sparingly it appears—for such work." In the deepening darkness the Ford drives off over snow-packed roads. "At last it halts and a moment later you are in a clean, cheerful room before a roaring fire, with honest American talk and honest American faces around. The contrast is staggering and brings home to the full the extent of the sacrifice they are making, these sons of fortunate America, to bring the food that is life to the people of the unhappy Volga."

Among the things Duranty reported was that the Sheild mystery had caused a "prodigious sensation" in Simbirsk, which was exactly wrong. In fact, underlying the American frustration at the slow progress of the Sheild investigation was dismay that the affair had not "taken hold of the public imagination as we thought it would or in the way a similar occurrence would have in America." Dalton saw the cause of this in recent Russian experience: "All of these people are intensely interested in self-preservation, and in making both ends meet from day to day; disappearances such as this, also murders, suicides, and imprisonments among Russians, are not unusual." The local police official heading up the investigation was said to be "very much surprised" that the fate of a single relief worker was creating such a stir in America. He asked for newspaper clippings on the Sheild case.[12]

When the reward posters went up, Dalton says, people came forward with small bits of information that led nowhere. It was said that actual witnesses would be terrified to speak up for fear of being implicated in the affair. These fears were probably justified. The woman who reported spying those "tan oxfords" protruding from a sack was subsequently charged with Sheild's murder and placed under arrest, though she was later released for lack of evidence.

In Moscow a speech by Soviet President Kalinin linked Sheild's name to that of Blandy and of others who had "perished on the famine front." In Simbirsk in April 1923 a school for orphans dedicated to the memory of Philip Sheild was established. To finance the repair of the building, the ARA sold empty condensed milk cans, flour sacks, barrels, and "other junk incidental to operations."

In the spring, as the Volga thawed, it disgorged numerous corpses, as it had been doing every spring for several years now. In mid-May a good deal of excitement was generated among the Americans when a body surfaced that was thought to be Sheild's: it checked out in every respect except that there was no scar in the appendix region. This brought renewed calls to the War Department to send Sheild's dental chart, which, however, could not be located in Washington.[13]

The ARA was still waiting for the release of the official Soviet police report. As things stood, the American public was under the assumption that Phil Sheild was the victim of a theft-related murder.

CHAPTER 14

TALES OF CANNIBALISM

As the Sheild mystery unfolded, Haskell complained that the American newspaper correspondents were reporting inaccurate information. This was true, and yet a review of the clippings shows that none of the correspondents, or their editors, chose to speculate that the "lost Virginian" might have been killed, cooked, and eaten. The famine having been broken during the previous spring, cannibalism could safely be excluded as a possible explanation for the Sheild disappearance.

When the famine raged, there were many reports of what was called "cannibalism." The term was applied loosely both to genuine cases of cannibalism, or anthropophagy—which implied an act of barbarous murder—and to the much more common incidences of corpse eating. In Russian the terminology was also somewhat ambiguously used although the language provides two neatly descriptive words: *liudoedstvo*, literally "people eating," and *trupoedstvo*, or "corpse eating." There is also *kanibal'stvo*, which means "cannibalism" but was used indiscriminately as a label for all acts of corpse eating. "Cannibalism" is usually associated with some form of religious ritual, but there was nothing of the kind in the Russian context.

Back home in the States tales of cannibalism on the Volga confirmed for Americans that Hoover's boys were indeed on assignment beyond "civilization." That there were numerous cases of cannibalism and corpse eating in the Russian famine zone is beyond any doubt. Trying to gauge the extent of the phenomenon even approximately is impossible as undoubtedly many incidences went undiscovered, while it often happened that genuine evidence was grossly exaggerated. In the telling and retelling, stories of corpse snatching, of man eating man, became sensationalized, thereby placing the whole nasty business under a cloud of skepticism.

In the spring of 1922, two Russian physicians produced serious studies of the subject. One is a pamphlet published in Ufa called *The Dreadful Chronicle of Famine (Suicide and Anthropophagy)*, the other a chapter in a book manuscript titled "Horrors of Famine and Cannibalism in Russia, 1921–1922," written by a doctor in Kazan enlisted by the ARA.[1] The authors aspired to "scientific" analysis, and each appears to have worked carefully with the available evidence, which consists largely of second hand anecdotes of the most horrific kind, "surpassing all limits of the imagination," in the words of one of them.

The Ufa study, authored by Dr. L. M. Vasilevskii, examines several dozen episodes of "cannibalism" described in the Soviet press and speculates that in the remote countryside there were many dozens, if not hundreds, more cases left unreported. The author of the Kazan study, Dr. I. A. Violin, agrees that the incidences documented in the press were only a small number of the actual total. Based on press accounts and his own observation and investigations, Violin provides estimated totals for several famishing regions. For the Tartar Republic, for example, he counts 72 cases of corpse eating and 223 incidences of cannibalism; for the Bashkir Republic the proportions are reversed, with 220 cases of corpse eating and 58 cases of cannibalism; for Samara province the respective numbers are 200, and 60.

Violin believes that the number of witnessed cases was much higher than the number reported, but that so desensitized had people become by repeated exposure to the ghastly deed—"we read [about it] with a cool indifference"—they no longer considered it worth bringing to the attention of the authorities. This was especially true of the more common practice of corpse eating.

Vasilevskii says the worst affected areas were Ufa province and two notorious Volga regions, Pugachev and Buzuluk. There is nothing in the ARA documentation that would contradict this assertion. Vasilevskii compares conditions in the 1921 famine with those of the previous major Russian famine, that of 1891–92, when reported cases of cannibalism and corpse eating were few. The difference in 1921 was not only that the famine was larger, both geographically and as measured by the number of people affected, but also that it came after years of suffering and brutality in Russia had brought about a "coarsening" of the people, a numbness to "bloodletting," and consequently a cheapening of the value placed upon human life.

A third author, Yurii Smel'nitskii from Kazan, wrote an introduction to a planned second edition of his 1909 book *On the Volga*, devoting it almost exclusively to the subject of "cannibalism." He, too, contrasted the two great famines of recent Russian history:

In 1891 when human beings, domestic animals and beasts were suffering from hunger, people died quietly . . . continuing to be human up to the very last.
In 1921–22, when parents killed their children, and children killed their little brothers and sisters, eating the flesh raw and salted, they proved to have gone mad and become beasts.[2]

Most of the analysis in the Vasilevskii and Violin studies involves their ruminations on the mental state of those committing these unspeakable acts. Vasilevskii writes of the "extreme insanity" and "extreme psychosis" of the "corpse-eater" and advises the courts to act with due deliberation. The "cannibal" he considers a different case entirely, though he fails to make a convincing argument for the clinical sanity and thus legal culpability of this type of offender.

Violin is a bit more thoughtful on this point. Generally, he writes, people who commit such acts are in a "state of alienation" and cannot in all cases be held accountable for their actions. The "terrible distress" produced by starvation severely affects the activity of the brain such that the "mental state of a human being who is almost on the verge of death cannot be considered normal." Violin, too, advised the authorities to use discrimination in prosecuting individuals accused of cannibalism and corpse eating. Even cases involving mothers devouring children might not be what they appeared. While it seemed that the very "instinct of mother-hood," this "holy feeling," has been crushed by a stronger instinctive urge, yet

Very frequently the deed is promoted by a deep, inborn feeling of motherhood. We know of a case that had been observed in the Pugachev district of Samara Province, where a mother, wishing to save her children from starvation, fed three of her remaining infants with the corpse of her daughter aged 13, who had died.

We are also reminded of the case when the tears of her hungry children led the mother to feed them on the corpse of her baby of 2 months of age.

There were also instances where the evidence indicated that a form of insanity was at work: when people began by eating the intestines of the corpses, for example, and in the case of the woman who cooked the head of the corpse first. And what should be done with the man in Ufa province who turned to the local authorities with a request for permission to kill his own children for food?

Another point of discussion is the particular behavior of the cannibal and corpse eater when confronted with the evidence of his or her crime. Violin claims that most corpse eaters "deeply repent their action," though in fact much of the anecdotal ARA evidence portrays the perpetrators as unremorseful. Moreover, while Violin rejects the notion that there is anything habit-forming about the act, there is testimony in the ARA records, unscientifically gathered though it is, that supports the opposite conclusion. In any case, the two doctors noted that corpse eating tended to be engaged in by entire families.

Violin concludes his study by recommending that the cannibal, as opposed to the more mentally fit corpse eater, be considered insane and kept isolated temporarily in a hospital rather than be severely punished. However, "drastic punishment" is called for in cases of clear criminality; for instance, the man who commits the deed "for the dreadful purpose of speculation"—that is, with the intention of making a profit from the sale of the flesh.

DESPITE THEIR DESIRE to attract foreign economic assistance, not to mention famine relief, the Bolshevik authorities would not have been eager to give currency to such tales. At a time when they were trying to impress the world that they should be welcomed once again into the community of great nations, the image of Russian peasants eating each other was not likely to help the cause. Moreover, as Russians—or Ukrainians, or Bashkirs, or whatever—they would naturally have been sensitive, their avowed internationalism notwithstanding, to how the outside world looked upon their culture.

Nonetheless, the topic was not taboo in the official Soviet press. In March 1922, Golder picked up the Moscow newspapers and read what he called, "tragic stories of hunger, deprivation and general demoralization. Parts of Russia are returning not only to a primitive but to an animal state. Decency, self respect, cleanliness and the finer feelings for which the human race has fought for so long are disappearing and the purely animal instincts are reasserting themselves and taking control." At about the time Golder wrote this, the people's commissar of health complained in the pages of *Izvestiia* that the Soviet newspapers were treating cannibalism as a "boulevard sensation."

The ARA literature contains numerous second- and third-hand tales of cannibalism and corpse eating. Some of the same ones reverberate through the documentation, undergoing whatever alterations are necessary to suit local circumstances and the particular taste of the teller.

Babine's Saratov diary for February–March 1922 is a rather rich source in this regard. On February 14 he repeats a story he has heard of how a woman was discovered using her husband's dead body for food. When the local authorities tried to remove it, she went into a frenzy, screaming, "We won't give him up, we will eat him ourselves, he is ours." On February 20 he writes, "At Pugachev kegs of salt human flesh are brought in every day from outlying districts—and confiscated by the Soviet authorities." Two days later he reports that the corpse of a country feldsher, a doctor's apprentice, has been devoured by starving peasants: "He was a big, portly man, and his patients did not want him to go to waste when he died from some cause or other." In the same entry he relates that a medical colleague of a local doctor "has had an occasion to taste human flesh." He became caught in a blizzard near Novouzensk and, driven to the point of starvation, was forced to consume parts of human corpses in order to stay alive. "The doctor stated that the worst part of that experience was the insuperable and uncomfortable craving he and his companion had acquired from human flesh."

On the next day, Babine remarks on this "peculiar craving," how people will "stop before nothing" to get another taste of human flesh. Anna Louise Strong heard someone quote someone else who, when asked how he liked the flavor of human flesh, responded, "Quite well: you don't need much salt."

There are several stories told of the authorities having to deter corpse eaters, especially at cemeteries. Among the corpses piled up in the graveyards, inevitably some had been partially devoured. Usually this could be attributed to the activities of wolves—or dogs, until they had all been consumed. In the worst famine areas, though, human beings were sometimes the culprits. Dr. Violin describes a scene at a cemetery where twelve people had dug up the corpse of a man who had recently died of an infectious disease and were eating the flesh "quite raw on the spot."

Babine tells his diary that at Pugachev a Communist official was showing an American relief worker a barn in which seventy-five bodies lay frozen stiff: "He cried ('a Communist cried,' repeated my informant) when he said that villagers had come and begged him on their knees, and kissed his hands, to let them have the corpses—to be used for food."

To the north at Simbirsk, there were fewer verified cases of cannibalism, but the unconfirmed reports that circulated were just as gruesome. A Russian university professor working for the ARA recalls that, beginning in November 1921,

we heard stories of cannibalism; in December such stories became frequent and proved to be true. Families were killing and devouring fathers, grandfathers and children. Ghastly rumours about sausages prepared with human corpses (the technical expression was "ground to sausages") though officially contradicted (gaol for repeating them publicly) were common. In the market among rough huckstresses swearing at each other one heard threats to make sausages of a person unfortunate enough to elicit anger in her interlocutor.[3]

The sausage motif was quite common. It features in a story that became widely circulated within the ARA—namely, the one about the Persian. Most often this takes place in Orenburg and begins at the ruins of the fire-gutted post office, where in December 1921 a severed human head is found. The police inquiry leads to the arrest of the murderer, who explains that he had killed his friend and was hauling the body away in a sack, but finding the load too heavy, decided to relieve his burden of its head. The rest of the corpse he sold at the market to the proprietor of a small restaurant, a Persian. Following the arrest of the two men, the local board of health posts a notice throughout town forbidding the sale of "meatballs, cutlets and all forms of hashed meats."

Fleming, who was for a time stationed in Samara, told a very similar story in a memoir written shortly after the mission. In this version, told to him by a "Dr. Ivanoff," the physician in charge of ARA medical supplies in the village of Syzran, the detail is almost the same except that the restaurant owner is not identified as a Persian and the board of health ends up forbidding the sale of veal cutlets. Veal cutlets? Either an important piece of the story has been left out or someone was putting young Fleming on.

When a similar story went around Saratov province in the autumn of 1921, Charlie Veil recalls that "Suddenly we became good vegetarians unless we could find a scrawny cow or even a horse on the hoof."

From the diary of one of the Orenburg Americans comes this bit of information: in cases of corpse eating, "the punishment meted to offenders was to imprison and then forget them until they died of starvation."[4]

THE ARA WAS UNCERTAIN as to how to deal with so novel and awkward a subject. It was careful to disassociate itself from the scattered rumors of cannibalism that began to appear in Western newspapers in the autumn of 1921. As winter set in and cases were reported as fact in the Soviet press, the ARA refused to verify any of them. On February 4, 1922, Lupton Wilkinson, who handled publicity out of Spiridonovka 30, cabled the London office that Moscow headquarters had "no direct evidence from American investigators of cannibalism, and I should think that if this material be given to the press, it should be offered to them for what the stories are worth on their face." That is to say, "any implication that the American Relief Administration vouches for the existence of cannibalism should be carefully avoided." The Russian unit did not want to be accused of sensationalizing the cannibalism story. Non-American eyewitnesses, no matter how reliable, were inadequate.

So Wilkinson's publicity men, Bill Garner and Harry Gilchriese, were told to be on the lookout for the real thing. In Ufa, Kelley found Garner's quest for cannibal stories amusing: "We have 'em but they won't talk for publication." In any case, Gilchriese struck first. Traveling through the Kazan district, he obtained circumstantial evidence of corpse eating. In one of his cables to Moscow he related an interview he had with a man who had eaten his child and, in the presence of his dying wife, said, "I shall eat her tomorrow she is too weak for any protest and could only grumble." Wilkinson cabled New York: "Gilchriese hears cannibal stories without end is 4th responsible American to be thoroughly convinced in field condition exists still no direct American proof."

Wilkinson later maintained that the New York and London headquarters of the ARA and the Moscow-based newspaper correspondents, with whom he held discussions on the subject in February, were "all agreed that the subject was so gruesome and so untypical of general conditions in the Volga that it was misleading to issue releases about it. We therefore confined ourself to the plain statement that so far as we could learn cannibalism did exist in widely separated instances."

As a result, there was a kind of delayed reaction, and the cannibalism "story" picked up momentum outside Russia in the spring of 1922 when the number of actual cases was probably on the decline. In April a Reuters dispatch out of Reval reported starvation riots in Samara and suggested that an ARA staff member had been the victim of cannibals; so, on April 21, all the Paris newspapers carried the story that the American chief in Samara, the unnamed Will Shafroth, had been killed and his corpse cooked and eaten by cannibals, a sensation the ARA dismissed as "absolutely ludicrous."

After the *New York Times* ran a further item on Russian cannibalism in May, Wilkinson wrote a letter to Baker in New York admitting that it had been a mistake to downplay the matter the previous winter. Had the ARA chosen to engage the reporters on the story from the beginning, he now realized, by spring it would have played itself out. "The old inexorable law that news can not be suppressed, and that news temporarily suppressed gains in interest when it finally breaks out is something which we should remember. I myself take the blame for aiding in soft-pedalling the cannibal news last winter, and I do not think the damage very great from the present pop-up of old news."

In this memo Wilkinson surmised that the Bolsheviks had been using reports of cannibalism in order to draw sympathetic attention in the West to Russia's plight. He voiced the suspicion that the recent outbreak of new stories was part of Moscow's attempt to build pressure on the ARA to stay on in Russia for another year.

Baker, meanwhile, sent a memorandum to the press department at 42 Broadway containing guidelines for preventive publicity. Baker justified the ARA's handling of the "sporadic," "occasional" instances of cannibalism that had occurred in Russia during the previous winter. The ARA had not given out its evidence "because every report indicated that the local populations were shocked and that persons practicing cannibalism were of a weak order of intellect and were punished or completely ostracized." And besides, the arrival of American corn "would seem to have eliminated the shocking scenes."

With the aim of blunting any Soviet effort to make political use of the matter, Baker pointed out that the present situation could not in fact be so dire if the Soviets had expended, in the period of the reported incidences, none of their gold reserves for outside food purchases, nor chosen to spend any of the nearly $100,000,000 in precious metals and stones they had apparently removed from Russia's churches: "This treasure is piled up in the Kremlin or is being piled up as rapidly as possible."[5]

When Kelley arrived back in the United States after leaving the ARA mission in the summer of 1922, he too realized that some of the responsibility for the way the cannibalism story refused to quit lay with the ARA. He indicated this in a newspaper article published at the time, in which he wrote that "The A.R.A. made it a policy to soft-pedal 'horror stuff' in its publicity for fear of being accused of exaggeration." Yet although "Stories of cannibalism strain the credulity of the modern ear," there were many cases in starving Russia. Referring to a police photograph he once saw of a boiled human head, Kelley informed readers that the phenomenon was "common in sparsely settled regions, remote from any railway, where Government and police control did not extend. Children were quite common victims, I heard, being killed and eaten by mothers who had gone insane from hunger." As one who had been stationed in faraway Ufa and had logged considerable travel time throughout this district, Kelley could claim to speak with some authority: "Personally, I have no doubt that thousands of cases of cannibalism occurred last winter and spring. The Soviet Government dealt out very summary punishment to those caught at this abomination. They said very little about it to Americans, feeling that it was a reflection upon their civilization."

In the ill-fated Pugachev region, one American reported that cannibalism was "getting to be more or less of a pest for the authorities." Another American brought his tales of horror from Pugachev to headquarters in Saratov, where Russell Cobb had just sat down to eat his dinner and instead had his ears filled with a description of children's skulls, their tops removed and the brains missing. Cobb reacted violently: "I know it could be true, but I got up and called him every name in the world. Anyone that has been here any length of time lets each American learn these stories for themselves. We ought to talk to each other about something different."

Some of the most convincing ARA testimony regarding cannibalism and corpse eating came out of Samara, where Shafroth saw enough indirect evidence to conclude that its occurrence in the province was "frequent." In January 1922 he cabled Moscow that a Russian who recently died from typhus had his body dug up and eaten by "some starving persons." Shafroth used the episode to taunt the supply division: "We urge you to take all possible measures to prevent our warehouse in Pugachov Uyezd where this town is situated from again running out of products."

In Samara city itself, ten butcher shops were closed for selling human flesh. Shafroth relates that he personally interviewed admitted cannibals in Samara jails. With proof such as this available to Western reporters, Shafroth found it "a curious reflection on human credulity that papers refusing to print the actual facts about cannibalism . . . for the reason that they considered them unbelievable, yet gave full display to ridiculous rumors"—meaning of the greatly exaggerated kind that reported his death at the hands of cannibals.

Henry Wolfe spent several weeks on the trail of the cannibal. He was on an inspection tour in Samara province in March 1922 when the authorities in the subdistrict of Melekes provided him with what he called "definite information concerning cannibalism." It seems a father had killed and eaten his two small children; afterward, Wolfe was told, he confessed that the "children's flesh tasted sweeter than pork." But Wolfe's "definite information" apparently did not include any hard physical evidence. He pressed on, promising his chiefs to try to inspect a partially intact corpse he had been told had been discovered in a nearby town: "If it can be seen, perhaps it would be valuable information to the ARA."[6]

Eventually Wolfe found what he was looking for. In the ARA archive there is a posed photograph of him standing among a row of five local citizens, cultivated in appearance and dressed in Russian winter wear. Before them, set out on a wooden plank, lies the grim evidence, which appears to consist of at least two human heads and a hand.

After one has looked through dozens of ARA photographs of grotesque corpses twisted into every shape and, worse, of barely living skeletons, the Wolfe photograph fails to shock. Curiously, what attracts the eye is the figure of the lone American himself, outfitted in trench coat and brimmed hat, hands clasped before him in leather gloves. He looks as if he has walked onto the set of a horror film. His face is expressionless; his incongruous presence alone conveys the idea that something terribly significant has taken place.

It is not clear whether the perpetrators of this particular deed were apprehended—or in fact photographed, the way some offenders were made to sit before the camera in the presence of what was left of their victims. In one such image a local official, poised with pen and paper in hand and assuming a severe countenance, sits among a half-dozen culprits, affecting to take a statement for the record. In the foreground lie various parts of human corpses, and one of the accused is made to sit with a severed something in her lap. This scene is shot against a canvas backdrop painted like a cloudscape. The subjects' gaze is fixed on the camera, probably the first they have ever faced. They appear to cower before it. Perhaps they think they are about to be executed for their crime, and that this strange contraption before them has been brought in to accomplish the task. Or maybe they are simply unaware of the gravity of their situation: looking into their faces, one has no problem agreeing with those who argue the insanity of corpse eaters.

THERE WERE NO cannibals in Moscow, but this did not prevent the relief workers stationed there from entertaining each other with anecdotes involving cannibalism. The most recited of them all is perhaps not entirely apocryphal. It involves a young doctor of foreign origin—usually an American—who escorts a Russian ballerina home from the Bolshoi theater late one night. A blizzard having come up and the doctor having been abandoned by his droshki, he is invited by the ballerina and her mother to spend the night. He retires to the spare room and closes the door behind him, at which point he hears the lock click and suspects trouble. By the light of a lamp he sees that there is a corpse in his closet. He attempts escape but discovers his room has a false window. Realizing what is afoot, and having no wish to be ground into sausage meat by some crafty restaurateur, the clever American places the corpse under the covers, and hides himself under the bed.

In the middle of the night ballerina and mother steal into the room and deliver a "death" blow to what they think is the young American lying asleep on the bed. After exchanging verbal expressions of satisfaction at having bagged yet another one, the two call it a night, leaving the door unlocked, which enables the would-be victim to make his escape.

Haskell rehearses this tale in his memoir, although in his version the motive is not cannibalism, but simple robbery. He introduces it as merely the most entertaining of yarns, "the prize story." In the telling, however, he warms to his subject, and by story's end we read that the "swift and summary punishment by death" of the ballerina and her mother "must be chalked up on the credit side of the Soviet ledger."

In this same memoir Haskell recalls another ARA favorite: the canard that in Orenburg after dark pedestrians walk only in the middle of the road, for in that city the cannibals lasso their victims from second-story windows. This must have tingled the spine of some young American preparing to set out for his assignment in Orenburg.

Father Edmund Walsh, head of the ARA-affiliated National Catholic Welfare Council, had been in Moscow but three weeks when he listed in his journal on April 16, 1922, a "Resume of things heard and seen." Among the things he had heard were

5. The ballet girl inviting the American to escort her home—mother—room—false window—closet—& bodies—escape.

6. Orenburg—the lassoo trick!

They did not lasso victims in Simbirsk, so this possibility was never considered in the case of Phil Sheild. In fact by the time Sheild disappeared, in October 1922, the famine was history, and rumors of cannibalism had dried up months before. During the second year of the mission, the ARA could afford to adopt a far more relaxed attitude toward the once forbidden topic, as in a press release on Louis Landy, fresh from service in Pugachev. Landy, described as having a portly build, is quoted as saying, "Gee! When I used to walk the streets of Pugatchev it seemed to me I could hear the cannibals smacking their lips."

The fascination persisted to the end. In Simbirsk in the spring of 1923, as the Americans prepared to leave Russia and went about the business of getting their paperwork in order, a letter went out from district headquarters to the subdistrict chiefs with the instruction to preserve all written documents "of historical importance, such as proven cases of cannibalism, etc."[7]

CHAPTER 15

FLIGHT OF THE FLIVVER

Contemplating this landscape of ruin, suffering, typhus, banditry, and canni-balism, the men of the ARA might fantasize about mastering their hostile sur-roundings while reading about great explorers or fearless warriors. Or they might turn to the "Russian Unit Record" and follow the daring exploits of their very own John Foy.

Within the Russian mission Foy was renowned for his extraordinary expedi-tions into the famine zone, undertaken in his homemade "flivver." For once the freely flowing superlatives of the ARA press releases and the imaginative report-ing of the "Record" seem to come near to being matched by reality.

Foy's background precisely fits the ARA adventurer mold. Said to be from Washington and Connecticut—one place of origin would not have sufficed—in the early weeks of the Great War he joined the Foreign Legion as an aviator. He was shot down several times, was heavily decorated, and ended the war a lieu-tenant. Afterward Foy worked for a time in Armenia with the Near East Re-lief—where he probably first came to Haskell's attention—and subsequently served in the U.S. consul's office at Constantinople. He was hired for the Rus-sian unit as a "chauffeur mechanic," two talents he would continue to rely upon mightily after his promotion and posting to the Tsaritsyn district as a roaming inspector.[1]

It was not long before Foy was making a name for himself across the district through his derring-do, motoring by Ford into isolated regions where only the camel roamed, singlehandedly engaging bandits and highwaymen, and time and again drawing upon his remarkable resourcefulness to bring his trademark flivver back to life. A colleague wrote, quite in earnest, that "a volume could be written" about Foy's adventures.

Foy was already becoming the object of missionwide attention when in De-cember 1921 he set out, in subzero temperatures, on a whirlwind organizational tour of the lower regions of the district. His colleagues informed the "Russian Unit Record" that "Mr. Foy is roaming over the Steppes to the south with the battered Ford which Moscow sent us. We expect Mr. Foy to return in a few days but we do not expect the Ford." In fact, more than the Ford almost failed to return.

Foy set out on the trip without an interpreter, and it is not difficult to imagine why eligible candidates would have been unwilling to offer their services. A volunteer, however, was found en route, a young man who had learned his English in the stockyards of Chicago and who for some reason insisted on calling Foy "Steve," which was said to be a "severe blow to Foy's dignity."

The journey proved to be eventful. The "Record" reports of Foy that "forty five bandits tried to ambush him, but the Ford was too nimble, and he eluded them by crossing a bit of country where the horses could not follow." On the trip down, a group of Red Army soldiers fired on him, and this salute he returned with his Colt .45.

The flivver, a former army camionette in Coblenz that Foy called "Henry," broke down in an area of desert, and Foy and his companion were left for two days without water except that which they could extract from the radiator. An unfortunate *tovarishch* on camel approached, and Foy convinced him, at gunpoint, to haul the vehicle to the nearest village. On his return trip, with the Ford evidently coughing and wheezing in full fury, Foy was halted by a group of Red Army soldiers whose senior officer accused him of harboring a machine gun in his engine.

Some valuable lessons having been learned from this trip, upon his return Foy began to outfit the flivver for desert work, the goal being total self-sufficiency. By this time Foy's reputation as a master fixer was already solidly intact. On one occasion he was given the assignment of traveling by rail to Novorossisk, the Black Sea port from which Tsaritsyn received its supplies, and escorting two trains of ARA foodstuffs back to the district. On the way down, the engine hauling Foy's train gave out, the engineer determining that a broken valve and a burned bearing could not be fixed until the next train for Novorossisk came along. Not so, however, for Foy showed this man how to make the appropriate repairs, and a little while later the train was able to resume its advance.

The return trip also presented its challenges, as officials at every station naturally looked with suspicion on two freight trains under the authority of an American bearing no papers: Foy had left Tsaritsyn empty-handed, not caring to wait around to secure the appropriate government orders. Not only did he manage to talk his way past every such checkpoint—if an interpreter was present, this is not mentioned—but along the route he collected several railway cars of ARA supplies that had been left on sidings.

Foy's Novorossisk feat made him the envy of every relief worker who ever had to idle away long hours in some cold, vile-smelling railroad car, left to the mercy of hapless or suspicious government officials.

The chief remodeling of the flivver, executed with only a monkey wrench and a hatchet, was the fashioning of a large torpedo-shaped body, whose entire rear half served as a gas tank with a capacity of eleven poods, or 440 pounds. In theory this enabled the vehicle to travel eight hundred miles without refueling. In the front Foy mounted a wooden imitation of a machine gun, a modification perhaps inspired by his earlier encounters with the Red Army. Visually the effect was said to be "devastating," especially on camels.

The refashioned flivver, it turns out, was almost swallowed up by the mighty Volga. In the cold and snowy March of 1922, Foy was making use of the frozen river in motoring about on inspection trips. One day he rolled into Tsaritsyn headquarters on one of his stopovers for fuel and supplies. According to a fellow reliever, such visits were infrequent: "He lives with the peasants up the river. We rarely see him. Now and then he comes in for some food, more gasoline, a few cigarettes and he is off again."

Off yet again, but this time not for long. The ARA staff members who stepped outside to witness another flight of the flivver were startled to see Foy, interpreter, and "tin Lizzie" disappear halfway across the river. The men and their machine had fallen through a large fishing hole, and only the flivver's outsized body kept it from sinking under the ice. Foy rescued his interpreter, who is said to have "almost drowned," and then "began to swear in his best Russian." As the story is told, nearly a hundred oxen were recruited to haul the flivver to shore and drag it back into town.

Foy's machine appeared to be on death's door. All the cylinders were cracked as was the gasoline tank, and the radiator had fallen off. An official report out of Tsaritsyn says that "The engine froze up and burst immediately." This was truly a job for Foy. He had the engine "patched up" in no time, and according to the "Russian Unit Record," "A few hours' work with chicken wire, clay and some miscellaneous parts put the machine back to its feet again." Foy was ready to resume the journey. Not so his thoroughly terrified interpreter, who absolutely refused to travel with "Meester Foi" again. "So Foy went without him, back on the Volga and into the night."

With the approach of summer, our hero, now Chief Inspector Foy, was ready for his greatest challenge: passage of the flivver across the Kalmyk steppe, southeastward in the direction of the Caspian Sea, a land "where no car had been before." The distance across the steppe was over six hundred miles. Previous motorists had declared travel by motor across this "sea of land" impossible because of the quicksand-like salt marshes and also because of the bandits who preyed on camel trains. But there was a report of a crop failure in the region, which required an inspection trip, so in May "Mr. Foy decided to attempt the impossible."

The journey took six days to complete. An ARA press release states that at one point the flivver became stuck in a salt marsh and had to be towed out by camels. Foy is said to have encountered "a large band of political bandits, who had proved entirely friendly to all Americans, and who on one occasion had loaned Mr. Foy machinery to repair his automobile." When a small group of holdup men approached, he attempted to bluff them with his imitation machine gun, and when that failed, he sped away. And he worked the usual miracles with his "hand-made Lizzie":

Its front spring had broken, and Mr. Foy had to buy a Russian vehicle to get another. Its main bearings disappeared, and he made others for it from a lead pipe he got in the sink of an old house. Its rear tires were punctured, and he ran the last 250 versts, with tires filled with sand, an excellent substitute, according to Mr. Foy. The clutch band broke, and he put a marine belt in its place. At last, his grease all gone, he came the last few miles with lard in the engine.

The flivver entered Tsaritsyn, "gave a faint apologetic cough, and stood still. The trip was made."[2]

Undeterred by bandits or Bolos or soldiers, undaunted by lice or wolves or the elements, and unimpeded by the complexities of the Russian language, this "rather weird person," as Quinn called him, was the ultimate ARA individualist. What is more, it could never be said that John Foy feared for his pants.

Along the way, he inspected some fifteen hundred kitchens and in the process, according to his Tsaritsyn chief, through his ingenuity and enterprise "succeeded in impressing upon those receiving relief the American nature of our enterprise."

Yet even as the "Russian Unit Record" was relating tales of Foy's exploits, his doctor in Tsaritsyn, George Cornick, was recording the physical toll exacted by his reckless adventures. After the celebrated flight across the Kalmyk steppe, Cornick saw that the game was up.

In July he wrote to the chief of the medical division in Moscow about his patient. He characterized Foy as a "person who stops at nothing, no matter how great the hardship, and I feel safe in saying that he has covered territory which few others would have had the hardihood or grit to tackle." But Cornick had observed in the previous several weeks that Foy had acquired a persistent cough, had lost weight, and seemed "very much subdued in spirit." Since the Kalmyk steppe expedition he was "definitely worse," complaining of "lassitude, loss of weight, night sweats, and a chronic cough." "Physical examination showed no definite pathology in chest, but there is the suggestion of increased vocal and tactile fremitas, with slight whispered pectoriloq[u]y at both apices, more marked on left in supra scapular and infraclavicular regions."

The "fearless flivverist of Tsaritsyn" was human after all.

Cornick described the nervous stress involved in Foy's line of work and advised an immediate leave of absence; otherwise a "very definite and serious breakdown" was probable: "I do not feel justified in further sanctioning his being submitted to these hardships."

Foy himself had had enough. On his way back from Astrakhan he dispatched a report to District Supervisor Dorsey Stephens, which he ended on a sober note:

Well, Chief, I am well fed up on this Russki Travel and trying to run a Ford on wire and nails. Please wire Moscow for four inner tubes, one jump and one new connecting rod complete.

Nothing funny to report only I have a bad head and need a trip to Paris.

Elsewhere Cornick reveals that Foy had fractured his right hand in an automobile accident in January, leaving him with "both disagreeable deformity and marked impairment of function." The bone would have to be surgically refractured and reset, an operation "not deemed wise under the conditions existing in Russia." In any case it was nothing that could be set right with a monkey wrench and hatchet, and spare parts could not be improvised.

Stephens pronounced him "in very bad shape." To the very end, though, the "Russian Unit Record" played the game, reporting that Foy could find no takers for his bet that he could outrace the Riga express, giving the train an hour's handicap.[3]

CHAPTER 16

ENTERTAINMENTS

The men of the ARA were fond of repeating chief Cyril Quinn's line that life in the Russian mission was not all "skittles and beer." But despite the long, arduous days of famine relief work, the documentation makes clear that there was opportunity for leisure activity of one kind or another. Just as with the organization of relief, how an American entertained himself varied considerably depending on where he was stationed. For sheer variety no place could surpass Moscow, though the first Americans to arrive there in August 1921 were hardly enthusiastic about the social possibilities. When the ARA came on the scene, the social life of the capital was as yet still emerging from its War Communist stupor. Hoover's boys tended to measure every European capital against Paris, and Moscow was no Paris. Nor did it live up to the romantic images of old Russia that some of the men seem to have brought in with them despite the lurid tales they had been hearing for years about daily life in the land of the Bolos.

Alvin Blomquist is one example. At mission's end he gave thoughtful expression to his own picture-postcard expectations going in and what he encountered upon arrival in autumn 1921:

Who, unknowing, has not pictured Moscow as did I, from the knowledge gained from novels, and from woodcuts in primary-school geographies: a City of fur-clad ladies and gentlemen, riding gainly in sleighs drawn by bell-bedecked thoroughbreds; a City of laughter and mirth, of native dances, and pleasing costumes—of much that life and wealth have given? But it was through another Moscow that I was driven— a City of dirty slush, of ruined houses, deserted byways, despoiled stores, match vendors, sunflower-seed vendors, herring-and-bread peddlers; scarcely-moving streetcars, rags, and misery.

Russian and foreign witnesses record with remarkable unanimity the sudden appearance in the spring and summer of 1921 of pastry shops, as if on every block, catering to the formidable Russian sweet tooth. No doubt had Blomquist been able to see the condition of Moscow only a few months earlier, he would have noted a marked change by August. The various peddlers and vendors might have seemed not as weeds but as the blossoms of early spring. It was all a matter of one's point of reference. Even a year later, newly arrived Americans would describe Moscow to the folks back home as a city of squalor.

Nonetheless, it was a fact that in late summer 1921 the majority of Moscow's storefronts were still boarded up. For "entertainment" there was but one restaurant—the first to be opened since the beginning of NEP—located on the Arbat near ARA headquarters. Childs, passing through on his way to Kazan, likened it to "an oasis in this city of dead souls." With the autumn came an expansion of economic freedom, and as Muscovites became convinced that NEP was not in fact some new Bolshevik ruse, the streets of Moscow were transformed with a rapidity that startled all who absented themselves from it for but a few weeks. It happened elsewhere, too, notably in Petrograd, but in most other places the revival occurred less dramatically.

Stores began to open; markets and bazaars, having led a tenuous existence through the black years, were now reanimated with the bustle of buying and selling; restaurants and *cafés chantants* proliferated and soon were serving wine and, illegally but quite openly, vodka; theaters reopened to packed houses. Everywhere there was reconstruction. Edouard Herriot, then mayor of Lyons, paid a visit and called Moscow a "city of scaffolding." To the ear of an American reporter, "The sound of the hammer drowned the cracking of the executioner's rifles."

Blomquist remained away from the capital for over a year, and upon his return he barely recognized the place:

At the end of December, 1921, Moscow impressed me as a City dying; in February, 1923, when next I visited it, as a metropolis gone crazy—hysterical, hurrying God knows where, artificial—striving only to keep ahead of some unseen pursuing and destructive force. In 1921, Ivan Citizen's life was linked closely with black bread; in 1923, Isaac Citizen's with Corona cigars, French champagnes, Westphalian hams, Packard automobiles, and like luxuries—if one had the price.[1]

This was to be NEP's most extreme phase, one that would last only for several months and end once the Soviet leadership had had time to catch its collective breath and put a stop to the retreat. That its lifespan roughly corresponded to the stay of the ARA in Soviet Russia was mostly coincidence, though afterward the American presence would in the Russian mind be associated with this, NEP's orgiastic beginnings.

Some of the associations were quite tangible. In Petrograd it was a casino called "Splendid Palace," described by Golder as the Monte Carlo of the former Russian capital. The locals dubbed it the "ARA Palace" since a percentage of the winnings was used to pay off the obligations of the local government to the ARA.

Splendid Palace was not an anomaly. Starved of cash necessary to pay its bills, the Soviet state got involved in gambling operations in Petrograd and Moscow, running casinos and raking in a large percentage of the profit. This association led to one of the most titillating Moscow scandals to occur while the ARA was in Russia, all the more so as it involved the head of the Soviet famine committee, Madame Kameneva, who happened to be the sister of Trotsky and the wife of Lev Kamenev. In addition to his Politburo responsibilities, Kamenev administered Moscow. As the story is told by the American journalist Sam Spewack, Kameneva, whom he calls a "second Catherine the Great," took under her wing a certain Mikhail Razumnyi, described as a "handsome young actor with polished manners and keen wit." Razumnyi had left Russia at the Revolution. Returning after the introduction of NEP, he took over the cellar theater that had once housed Baliev's Chauve Souris and established there the Krivoi Jimmy, a cabaret for the newly rich.

Razumnyi came to the attention of Kameneva, who seems to have fashioned herself a kind of patron of the popular arts. He suggested to her that her famine relief activity could benefit from the establishment in Moscow of several gambling casinos, which he offered to take it upon himself to manage. According to Spewack, Kameneva sold her husband on the idea, and soon three casinos were opened up. One of these was the Monaco, where the attendants wore blue pants and red coats with gold buttons; another was called the Hermitage, where the croupiers were attired in frock coats of the ancien régime. Guests drank wine and vodka and tried their luck at chemin de fer and roulette. Spewak describes the clientele as "speculators, pickpockets, fallen bourgeoisie, drug fiends, prostitutes and ex-Countesses."

Thus did the old and new regimes find common ground in the urban underworld of unfettered speculation. The game ended for Razumnyi when the Cheka discovered that he had quietly skimmed off for himself some ten trillion rubles, or about $100,000, some of it in foreign currency. He was jailed and Kameneva was scandalized.

Spewack informs us that in Petrograd the "Red underworld" was even more extensive, at least in the beginning, which one would expect of the old imperial capital. What went on in the cradle of Soviet Communism, Spewack reports, "made our Tenderloin seem a sanctuary by comparison. All the Petrograd Soviet did was to take over the Czarist underworld and run it, just as the Soviets took over the Czarist Ochrana and made it a Tcheka."

The Petrograd soviet's monopoly on vice—its "Wine, Women and Song Trust" —was centered in three casinos and twice as many restaurants, which in addition to serving food, staged musical and other entertainments. The head of one casino described its patrons as "the scum of the earth," though he added, "the Government needs the money." On the other hand, the establishments themselves would not have passed muster in prerevolutionary Russia. Childs testifies, based on several weeks spent in Petrograd, that attempts to recapture the "magnificence and luxury" of imperial times were "feeble and pathetic. . . . Fantastically colored carpets were put down from heaven knew whither and servants were liveried in such a variety of costumes as would have done credit to a comic opera."[2]

THE YOUNG MEN of the ARA brought with them to Russia their tastes for *cafés chantants*, cabarets, and casinos, tastes these mostly small-town boys had acquired only recently in places like Paris and London. There are several accounts of American relief workers "painting the town red." Fleming left behind a rich retelling, in his letter to "Doris" of December 3, 1922, of an all-night romp through the capital's seamy side with his ARA friend Tracy Kohl. The evening begins with, and is punctuated by, dickering with the droshki drivers, who deliver their American occupants to establishments with distinctly un-proletarian names: "Domino," "Empire," "Grotesque," "Riche Café," and "Casino." A long night of chemin de fer, faro, and beer and vodka lubricants comes to an end near 5:00 A.M.

Fleming might have given his correspondent the impression that the ARA men all but came to own the capital. In fact, although as "bourgeois" Americans they could open many doors in Moscow, in essential ways they never really came to feel at home there. For one, especially during the first year of the mission, few Muscovites had the means to play host to them. Most of the relief workers, strangers in a strange land, would in any case have made awkward guests in the homes of local residents, but even Golder and Coolidge, both at ease with the language and culture, were frustrated by the lack of social opportunities. "Nobody is in a position to entertain," Coolidge wrote to his father on November 13, 1921. "Most of those who used to do so in old times are now living in one room and suffering from the bitterest poverty."

Beyond this, locals had to consider the fact that an American visitor would attract the attention of the Cheka. Nor would every Muscovite, Coolidge notes, accept an invitation to the ARA personnel houses: "I have been told that the secret police note whoever comes to the house in which a dozen or so of the chief members of our mission (including myself) are staying. This may be mere rumor, but I do know that people are afraid to come to it for fear of bringing the authorities down on them."

Quite naturally, then, the personnel houses—color-coded Blue, Brown, Pink, Green and White—all spacious former residences of wealthy prerevolutionary families and all located within walking distance of each other in the center of Moscow, became the chief venues of ARA social activity. With their support staffs of cooks, maids, housekeepers, and doormen they were by most accounts comfortable, in Golder's words "very, very comfortable" with "an abundance of food and no shortage of drinks."[3]

The Pink House, where the chiefs lived, was understood by the Americans to be "formerly the finest residence in Moscow." One of the building's fixtures was its doorman, who came to be known as Pazhalsta. This is a rough transliteration of the Russian equivalent for "please" or "you're welcome," an expression he would have used routinely when opening the front door or when offering the many services he is credited with having provided, such as hanging up your coat, drawing your bath, lighting up your smoke, cleaning your shoes, and sounding morning reveille without a bugle.

Pazhalsta, whose real name was Grigorii, or Gregory, is described in an item in the "Russian Unit Record" as "shrivelled and bent from years of service. He has a scrubby, gray beard and always wears a black Astrakhan cap, indoors and out. He wears spectacles with big round glasses which give to his eyes the appearance of a wide stare. Altogether he suggests a plucked chicken or a half-fledged bird." One Pink House resident thought to teach him a few English phrases, which he pronounced with great deliberation—"I . . . am . . . an . . . old . . . guy. I . . . am . . . a . . . good . . . sport"—and broke into a broad grin. One can guess that Pazhalsta was not in the habit of performing this linguistic exercise upon being stirred from his slumbers in the wee hours of the morning by ARA nighthawks.[4]

Thus, the Moscow Americans—some fifty in all by summer 1922, not counting journalists and occasional visitors from abroad—were well positioned to entertain. And, it turned out, to be entertained. Indeed, some of Moscow's most illustrious artistic talent came to perform for, and in turn to be charmed and fed by, the relief workers, with more formal occasions usually reserved for the grand ballroom of the Pink House. Typically, the Americans held dinner parties attended by local Russians, mostly female, mostly ARA clerks, accountants, and translators, all hungry for a well-prepared meal and for the chance to rekindle memories of the good old days.

In the accounts of two American journalists these evenings are rather tamely called "dance-parties" and "small dances." Dance, in fact, was an essential feature. The American journalist Hullinger observed that the blockade had kept the latest dances out of Russia, although word of them had gotten through so that by 1921 "every girl in Moscow has one great social ambition—to learn the fox-trot." Thus when the ARA came to town

with its staff of some fifty fox-trotting college boys . . . [t]hey found an entire city waiting to receive it. And during their spare hours these young philanthropists could easily have kept themselves occupied (and many did) introducing ballet dancers or princesses, as the case might be, to the mystic steps and rhythm of Broadway. In the space of a year, the fox-trot became the big feature of the slowly reviving pleasure life in Moscow.

This benign description could have appeared in the society pages back home, unlike much of the testimony of the high-stepping philanthropists themselves.

There seems to have been a kind of tacit competition among the personnel houses for throwing the best parties. Just what particular mix of women, alcohol, dance, and live talent made for a successful evening is difficult to gauge from the ARA morning-after descriptions, which suffered from the effects of the alcohol. In these hazy recollections, alcohol and women usually blend together. Ellingston, in one of his several contributions to the genre, describes a "glorious Bluehouse Blow, which was very wet and very exhilarating and—come nine months—very prolific in all probability. . . . I fully intended to devote the next day to the office but there wasn't a next day, only a next night. If you wish to know how three nights come together in a week, come to Moscow." It is this occasion that Fleming was anticipating when, with the precise intention of scandalizing his parents, he wrote, "Christmas will be rather tame here; probably a blow-out at the Blue House, with most everybody tight, shocking as it may seem."[5]

Looking back, it is difficult to determine which of the two largest personnel houses, the Blue or the Brown, deserved top honors in this rivalry. Several years later the ARA alumni newsletter, in its "Non-Statistical Notes of the A.R.A.," skirted controversy: it credited the Blue House with introducing the "jazz age for the chrysalis of the Russian flapper" yet recalled "Wild nights at the Brown House."

OUT IN THE FAMINE DISTRICTS, of course, the daily life of the American relief worker was radically different, and it could vary dramatically according to whether he was stationed at district headquarters, placed in command of a subdistrict, or made an inspector, in which case most of his time would be spent on the road. No matter what the individual assignment, in the districts there were far fewer fellow Americans on whom to unload one's mental and emotional burdens or with whom to pass the leisure time. This fact of life was more tolerable to the "district guy" that had only briefly passed through the capital on his way to his initial posting in the field. But for those who had served long enough in Moscow to get a taste of a "glorious Bluehouse Blow," the plunge into the provinces delivered a distinct shock.

Freddie Lyon experienced it. After working at Spiridonovka 30 for several weeks, he was reassigned to remote Orenburg, the place where entertainment was orchestrated by the man with the lasso. His first letter back to a colleague in Moscow contained a homesick lament for the camaraderie and civilization of Moscow and the Blue House:

I dreamed of beautiful, gay, wonderful Moscow, with its ballets, operas and cabarets— of the good old steam-heated barracks at #7 Granatnyi pereyoolok—of my real American comrades gathered around the poker-table, comrade Dodge madly counting out a boost of 30,000 roubles, Langworthy proudly displaying an inlaid cigarette case. "Get down, you son-of-a-gun McSweeney" with his whole hearted and good natured laugh. . . . Oh! I tell you, Don, joking aside, in Moscow you are well fixed.

Lyon was, at that moment, as yet on his own, but once a district show was up and running, the provincial capital was home to several Americans at any one time. Not so in the subdistricts. Paul Clapp was the lone American organizing and administering relief in Russia's German colony, in southeastern Saratov province. A fluent speaker of German, Clapp was not inhibited by the barrier of language; still, as his diary and correspondence make plain, his existence was one of lonely isolation. In a report to Saratov headquarters written in January 1922, he states that he is "very busy but that is a good thing because there is absolutely no social life and a man would go crazy if not intent on his work." The sole compensation for all the effort, Clapp wrote, is that which "a man gets from within himself in the knowledge that he is saving human lives."[6]

Kelley got to experience the feeling of utter isolation after he set out by sleigh in March 1922 from Ufa headquarters for Sterlitamak. He figured that he and his interpreter could complete their inspection trip before the breakup of the Belaya River, but this turned out to be a misjudgment. A thaw came on and the river rose, flooding roads and making the return trip impossible. For three weeks Kelley was stuck in the Bashkir capital, a "prisoner of mud," which essentially meant confinement to the ARA office. Each day a dozen or so fresh corpses had to be cleared from the roads, and there were "numerous candidates for the dead wagon that still walk the street." These, Kelley testified, "take from an American any desire he might have to stroll about for pleasure or exercise."

Though he did not mention it, Kelley surely missed the warm atmosphere of the American personnel house in Ufa, which like all ARA district residences was regarded as a place for relaxation and retreat, a shelter from an alien, often hostile environment. Kelley got his first taste of the provincial ARA lifestyle on his way from Moscow to his Ufa assignment when he stopped off at Samara: "In such a town as this the A.R.A. men have no inclination to go outside their house after darkness. The five of us gathered around the piano where Shafroth, the district supervisor, dispensed ragtime. The conversation centered about three subjects, lice, wolves, and bandits—the three most interesting features on the landscape."

The personnel houses in the districts were usually among the finest residences in town, as Kelley observed after reaching his destination: "We have one of the best houses in Ufa, well heated and lit by electricity. The Americans have succeeded in fitting out their rooms with curtains, Turkestan rugs, and odd bric-a-brac. There is a grand piano and a victrola to complete the household equipment."

The Simbirsk ARA men lived in a large two-story structure with five bedrooms, a dining room, and a kitchen. The support staff, according to one of the Americans, was efficient. "The personal inventory included: one housekeeper, one chef, one maid, one laundress, one charwoman, one man to build fires in the huge Russian stoves, and an old lady to darn socks and affix patches. Add a parlor with an open fire-place, a piano, and a gramophone, and you have the basic setting for the ups and downs of American bachelor homelife on the Volga."

Just as in Moscow, the personnel houses in the districts were the settings for various social occasions, to which selected ARA Russian employees and others, mostly females, were often invited. For residents of the provincial capitals, much more than for Muscovites, the American presence was a novelty. Haskell had sufficient opportunity to be entertained while on his tours of inspection in the famine zone to be able to confirm that "American cigarettes and table delicacies attained a tremendous vogue in the districts, and no invitation was more eagerly sought than one to be present at a soirée chez les Américains."

The American kitchen was well stocked and of necessity, for even in the provincial capitals there was no such thing as a decent restaurant. The establishment just downstairs from ARA headquarters in Kiev featured a single item on the menu, "sausage and chops," which did not prevent the waiter from inquiring every time: "What will you have?"[7]

The relief workers were able to afford the offerings of the local markets in the way of fresh meat, milk, fruit, and vegetables, and these were supplemented with American foods and delicacies from the ARA commissary in Moscow, such as canned vegetables, pickles, olives, cheeses, corned beef hash, various sauces and syrups, and coffee—and, of course, liquor. While the "Russian Unit Record" and the "New York Newsletter" reported on the trials of life in America in the grip of the Volstead Act, the ARA courier was making regular runs of whiskey from Moscow to the districts. When the supply ran dry, the thirsty American could sample the local products, mostly home-brew vodka of wildly unpredictable ingredients, flavor, and potency. In Dr. Mark Godfrey's verse "The Ship-Shape Simbirsk Show" printed in the "Record," the spirits are as ill concealed as at a big city speakeasy back in the States.

> Now when workin' hours are over—
> Its another story now—
> We're all right at your service,
> With a scrape, dig and bow;
> Just name your chief diversion,
> No matter how sublime,
> And we'll slip it over to you,
> And you can not spend a dime.

With all due respect to the good doctor, the best that can be said about the quality of this and his other verse is that it may well serve as testimony to an abundant supply of alcohol at the Simbirsk personnel house.

All in all, the Americans were able to lay out a good spread even though there was a major famine on. In Simbirsk the ARA dinner table was frequently set for ten or twelve people in addition to the Americans. In Tsaritsyn on January 6, 1922, Cornick told his diary, "Although we are in the famine district, life is not without its frivolity even here, and during this holiday season at any rate, parties seem to be quite the thing." Cornick might have thought to give partial credit for this to the Bolsheviks for having abandoned the old-style Russian calendar, which was thirteen days behind that used most everywhere else. Centuries of custom die hard, however, and some rituals continued to be dictated by the old calendar, including the observance of religious and other holidays. One result of this was that after the Americans had marked their own Christmas and New Year, they had the benefit of a Russian Christmas, celebrated New Style January 7, and a Russian New Year on January 13. This helps explain all the giddy references by American relief workers to the Russian "holiday season."

When the 1921–22 season was over, Cornick reported to his father that he had gained weight: "I don't know just how much I have gained but certainly I must have put on at least ten pounds, as my ribs are now better covered with fat than in a great while."

No doubt some found all this American banqueting unseemly in the midst of widespread starvation. Babine's diary says of the ARA New Year's party in Saratov that "the table was inappropriately, almost indecently sumptuous. My friends said they had not seen a table so served and provisioned for many years."

After the meal, jazz was king. At the time, the word "jazz" was still a novelty—frequently placed between quotation marks—and often when the Americans pronounced or wrote it, they were mindful of one of its other connotations: for example, Simbirsk's Eddie Fox is described as "an exponent of jazz in his work and his music too." In his previous life, Fox had been a somewhat successful performer on the concert and vaudeville stages in his home state of Pennsylvania and had entertained in various East Coast cities as well. He had served in France during the war and later with the Near East Relief, but the ARA publicity department preferred to emphasize his musical experience. He was said to have been well known in Erie, where he appeared as a concert pianist with violinist Miss Autumn Hall, though he favored "rag and jazz tunes and old home ballads."

Fox was a small-time musician, really. But in postrevolutionary Russia there was plenty of room at the top, and Fox managed to find time away from his duties as district supervisor to expose the locals to "the American brand of pep-and-paprika melody." His fellow relief workers called him an "inimitable entertainer," in fact "the topnotch 'jazz' piano player of all Russia."[8]

In Samara Shafroth did the honors. Upriver in Kazan, Childs resisted the trend, chiding his colleagues for their lack of taste. Childs preferred the classical symphony and opera, which, mercifully for him, still prevailed in Russia's music halls and theaters. "Here in Socialist Russia [is] to be heard a better music than anywhere in a public park of a city similar in size in America, where some clangy ragtime, if such might be called music, was beaten out upon the helpless winds."

After he attends a Soviet party where music was played on the victrola, he writes, "thank God, no jazz! What with the 'jazz' given the Russian people by the Soviet Government, I doubt whether a taste for this so-called American music could be developed with any success in Russia."

In fact there was a good deal of more traditional music to be heard in the provincial ARA personnel houses, often performed by the best local artistic talent, however modest the offerings in comparison with those of Moscow and Petrograd. After one such occasion, Cornick wrote to his parents from Tsaritsyn of a "most excellent musical evening," a further manifestation of the fact that "we have a very pleasant and congenial home life." These provincial gatherings seem, more often than similar events in the capitals, to have local Party and Soviet officials included on the guest list, which probably says something about the available pool of invitees. The ever sardonic Kelley, guiding his correspondent through the Ufa ARA's New Year's festivities, manages to make the affair sound pleasant enough until the action moves onto the dance floor:

There was a pretense of dancing on the floor waxed with candles, music furnished by two American records on a feeble machine of a nondescript make. Hofstra taught the girls a kind of two step which is all they know. I tried a foxtrot with the Bolo officer's wife but broke down completely. It was after two before everyone had left so you can imagine how bored the American personnel was.

The social contacts of the Americans in the districts were almost exclusively from among the native staff members, who in some ways had more in common with their foreign employers than with their starving fellow countrymen in the villages. On the one hand, the Americans' greater sense of isolation and thus the stronger feelings of mutual dependence between the relief workers and their staffs appear to have lent their relations a particular intensity absent in Moscow and Petrograd. On the other hand, the same factors that inhibited social intercourse between relief workers and locals in the capital cities—the absolute poverty of the formerly well-off, if not well-to-do; the fear of police scrutiny—operated to a greater degree in the provinces.

Blomquist of Simbirsk gave thoughtful consideration to the matter of Russian companionship as the mission neared its end. Looking back, he saw that "our circle of personal friends did not extend far beyond the limits of our Russian employees." These he characterizes as a "medley of types and classes": "Young men and women of former high social standing in the community, teachers, professors of mathematics, a judge of instruction, a baron, a princess (though not of the "blood r'yal"), the wife of a former provincial governor, engineers—these were the persecuted intelligentzia, our friends, and our assistants."

Although these Russians were educated people and spoke foreign languages, Blomquist observes, "we had but little with them in common. . . . Especially was this true of the young Russian men of our own ages—twenty four to thirty five. Of these latter, I cannot recall a single one with whom we developed the slightest degree of intimacy. One must realize, however, that the flower of Russia's young manhood has been either killed off or has fled the country." Those who stayed behind had for six years been cut off from information about the outside world. "To them the radio, The Ruhr, the development of flight through air and in the water, and the trend of thought in America and Europe were as remote as the moon."

Although most of the socializing took place at the ARA personnel house, "There were two or three homes which stood always open to us, and at which we could be sure of a pleasant few hours, with music and tea, and talk of glories past, miseries present, and prospects for the future." That such invitations were few was not due to any lack of hospitality but to the fact that "our friends, most of whom were but little better off than those people whom we were feeding, hesitated to expose to our eyes their pitiful quarters, their penury, and their trampled hearths."[9]

CHAPTER 17

ENTR'ACTE

One leisure-time diversion more or less available to most of the American relief workers was the theater. With all that had happened, the theater in Soviet Russia, including opera and ballet, had managed somehow to maintain its pre-revolutionary standards. This was the case despite shortages of funds, hunger, and a significant loss to emigration of dancers, singers, and actors. Chaliapin, the world's greatest opera singer, was gone; the dancers Balashova and Pavlova no longer graced the Bolshoi stage; Baliev, Moscow's most famous impresario, had removed his popular revue company, La Chauve-Souris, to Paris and from there in January 1922 to New York City.

With the coming of NEP and the restoration of ordinary accounting, state support for the performing arts dwindled. The threat to remove all state funding from the ballet and opera in 1921–22 caused genuine concern among residents of Moscow and Petrograd that the theaters would be forced to close down. To raise income, theater companies took advantage of the new permissiveness to open "midnight cabarets," where, one critic wrote, fabulous prices were charged for the "privilege of watching celebrated artists off their dignity." But despite the shadow this cast over the world of the performing arts, the show usually went on and the 1922–23 theater season was said to be the best throughout Russia since the Revolution. A Western theater critic wrote at the time that although "dazed," the theater was still the "most normal and the most vital of all the social institutions of Russia."[1]

Experimental theater lived on, especially in the capital cities, although the new financial stringency meant that drawing an audience was becoming increasingly important. As the state cut theaters loose, they had to sink or swim on ticket sales, and more conservative offerings, especially opera and ballet, were liable to do better at the box office. Meyerhold's "proletarian" theater was well attended but, it was said, only because workers were supplied with cheap or free tickets. They would rather have been at Stanislavsky's conservative Art Theater or, better yet, at the State Opera.

A good number of the Americans of the ARA were quite avid theatergoers. Of course the contingents living in Moscow and Petrograd had a much richer theater fare from which to choose, although even here there were limitations. For one thing the obstacle of language prevented most of them from taking in plays, so the Art Theater was out. Most desirable were the opera and the ballet—as it happens, the two forms most favored by the Russian public.

The matter of language aside, in their taste in theater the relief workers were decidedly not in the avant-garde. No, these Americans, whom a quirk of fate had cast in the role of popular-cultural mavericks in Russia, "dispensing ragtime" and performing a Broadway two-step in Moscow and on the Volga—these same men liked their Russian theater served straight up and traditional. Above all they were drawn to ballet at the Bolshoi Theater. There is hardly an ARA diarist or correspondent that fails to provide a wide-eyed account of a trip to the Bolshoi. Forty years after the mission, George Townsend reminisced about the power it exerted over him and his colleagues: "We discovered the ballet at the Bolshoi Theatre and became addicts to its loveliness—the most beautiful thing in all Russia."

Fleming was "[q]uite staggered" by the "entrancing" beauty and color of the spectacle and confessed to his parents to feeling "like a college girl visiting Paris for the first time when I start to describe the ballet at the Bolshoi." Several more performances, Fleming declared, and "pretty soon I shall be able to tell the difference between art and legs." Although conceding that "art and theater are not in my mental beat," he did not hesitate to play the critic in letters back home, and a conservative one at that. He seems to have approached experimental theater with an open mind, describing with boyish enthusiasm a "Russian comedy of most striking stage-settings and costumes—what we call futurists in the states."[2]

For such fare in the capital one could visit the Kamernyi, known as Moscow's "revolutionary" theater. Here one got a taste of the avant-garde even before they raised the curtain, which was of a most striking cubist design characterized approvingly by a Western critic as a "bold study in the grotesque." The Kamernyi was notable for its geometric stage designs, dramatic lighting, cubist costumes and props, and the distinctive gestures of its actors. Its signature production was its *Salome*, Wilde's erotic tragedy in one act. In fact, the Kamernyi specialized in the erotic, with *Salome* in the vanguard. A Western critic at the time, Oliver Sayler, called it "frank and unashamed" and "vivid," which means it was easily accessible to the non–Russian speaker. Sayler describes Salome's "maddeningly sensuous" dance for Herod, the "quick, sinuous movements and angular, passionate poses" of the "erotic princess." The music pulses louder and faster as she removes, one by one, the veils from around her breast until, at the moment of climax, the seventh veil is torn away and the stage is instantly plunged into darkness and silence. Her part of the bargain having been fulfilled, Salome then demands and is granted her wish: the severed head of John the Baptist. This she takes into her hands and kisses, and as it drips blood on her, she performs another, more subdued dance movement.

Sayler felt that this kind of production was possible only in Russia, where they staged their art "frankly and openly, stepping over and beyond the half-mood, middle ground of the *double entendre* of the French and other Europeans. . . . It may be due to the primitive nature of the Russian, still unspoiled by contact with Western civilization. It may be due to the Eastern strain in his blood and his own civilization."

Fleming was less taken with the Kamernyi, though he seems to have been seduced by *Salome*. In a letter addressed to "Harry," he wrote that what they put on at the Kamernyi "strikes all worldly-wise Americans as the product of pure nuts let loose": it "definitely repudiates anything verging on reality." Following a recent performance—which began thirty-five minutes late "in true Russian artistic style"—the theater's management approached Fleming and his colleagues in attendance in order to inquire as to how the theater's productions might be received in America. "We told him we thought Salome would go, but that the rest would need considerable polishing up with pretty girls and things appealing to the vulgar American taste before it could be put across in New York, especially in view of the inability of the company to present it in English."

A performance of an experimental ballet one week later leaves Fleming thoroughly numb. He finds it to be "the most futuristic thing in the most futuristic town in the world, and while it was striking, let me go on record that I am not sophisticated enough to properly enjoy those things. It requires people who have seen everything there is—for whom there is nothing more—just a faint hope, a flickering light of imagination. I personally would rather see Charlie Chaplin."

Sometimes the experimental would turn up in unexpected places. Golder describes going to a symphony performed by an orchestra without a conductor, a "Bolshevik innovation here." The orchestra had a five-man "soviet," which decided how a certain composition was to be played. The comedy in the thing was that as soon as the performance began, the chairman of the soviet, sitting in a prominent seat, made all kinds of facial distortions and unsubtle signals to influence the playing, which nonetheless, Golder found, was not enjoyable.[3]

IN THE ACCOUNTS of theatergoing left behind by the American relief workers in Russia—not just in Moscow—the performance is very often upstaged by the spectacle of the audience, those many thousands of bit players on the stage of history. At a March 1922 performance in Petrograd of the opera *The Queen of Spades*, based on Pushkin's tale of life among the St. Petersburg nobility in the early nineteenth century, Childs looked around the theater and detected remnants of the old aristocracy and bourgeoisie, "beaten into insensibility"—their "spirit is crushed"; their "morale is broken." There in the audience Childs discovered "the real drama and to me it overshadowed that stage upon which the professional actors were strutting. Within the box itself in which I was seated there was more of tragedy and dramatic interest than was to be seen on all the artificial stages of Petrograd." It was the audience too that Fleming had in mind when he wrote that "The theater in Russia can show many things about her mental state and nervous situation."

Golder, whose observations are all the more interesting because of his familiarity with prerevolutionary theater, came up with a rough generalization about the social composition of audiences attending the various performing arts: only at the symphony did one run into any genuine former aristocracy; the opera audiences were mostly impoverished bourgeoisie; while the ballet crowd consisted of "mostly tovarishchi." Above all, it was the behavior of the "tovarishchi"—the "comrades," here meaning both officials and workers—that drew fascinated and amused comment from American observers, especially first-time theatergoers in Soviet Russia, who were struck by the incongruity between the proletarian dress and manners of the audience and the opulence of the setting. The contrast was particularly stark at the Bolshoi Theater, as Charlie Veil found: "Revolution hadn't ruined the ballet but the Czar's box was filled with tovarishchi in old blouses, caps pulled over their eyes, smoking pipes. Everywhere the Imperial Eagle had been replaced by the hammer and sickle." Philip Gibbs was similarly impressed by the scene inside Petrograd's Marinskii Theater, where he attended an opera that he found to be

magnificently staged, and well played, but . . . the audience was of more interest than the performance. The immense and splendid theatre was packed with "the proletariat." . . . In the Imperial box sat a group of men with black hair over their foreheads, like women's "fringes," and grimy hands. Above their heads the Imperial Eagle had been covered with the Red Flag of Revolution.

Dickinson, having once been an expert on the theater by profession, disappoints, as he has little to say about the performances he attended during his three months in Moscow. Perhaps he was distracted. "During the action of the play," he later generalized, "the people cough a great deal. Sometimes it is impossible to hear the words or the music for the storm of coughing that passes over the audience."

The entr'actes afforded the Americans the opportunity to observe members of this supporting cast close up, either promenading in the reception halls or, depending on the season, stamping their feet in the foyers, attempting to generate some heat.

As the weeks passed, the relief workers in the capitals noted more and more jewelry, more and more ostentatiously displayed by members of the audience—a sign, they thought, that things were getting back to "normal." The abundance of furs, they quickly learned, meant nothing: virtually anyone could get one. During his February 1922 visit from New York, Baker either was coached on this or perceived it himself. He describes a Bolshoi ballet crowd made up mostly of workers, "all very badly dressed, excepting that they wore good furs in every case that we could observe. However, as furs are almost universal in Russia, there was nothing to be argued from this." Then he turns to inspect the artists: "The appearance of the performers on the stage might be expected to delight the eyes of Mr. Ziegfeld, if report is true that he spends much of his time seeking slender people. There was not meat enough on any of them to be discoverable with opera glasses."

It was in the theater that Russians and foreign visitors as well had the chance to observe the manners of the new bourgeois, who came to the theater to put on individual performances of their own. Sayler, in his informative 1922 book *The Russian Theater*, could not leave the subject undiscussed: "In the theatre life of Moscow today, a strange new figure is discernible—the unlettered, unrefined peace-profiteer, or NEP-man. . . . Even in the serious theatres, he and his kept and bejewelled women appear as a minor stratum, but he is most at home in the music halls, at the opera or the ballet."

If "all Moscow" were reported seen at a theater performance, this meant the Moscow of the nouveaux riches. Although this might be the surest sign of the defeat of communism, to most people, including the American relief workers, the NEP man was never a benign figure. Journalist Spewack summed up the sentiment of many who were, to be sure, not favorably inclined toward the Bolos:

The new economic policy produced a new bourgeoisie. There can be a legitimate difference of opinion on the calibre of the Communists, but none on the capitalists they produced. Almost without exception the new bourgeoisie combines all the vices of crooked business men without a tinge of the virtue of legitimate business. Comparatively few were traders before. Most were market hangers-on, pickpockets, con men, gamblers and renegade radicals.

Inside a theater, the NEP man could play the role only of the villain. After a visit to the Bolshoi, Fleming informed the folks back home that "Moscow is getting back to good old capitalist ways, you see; wine and women;—and out in the refreshment room before the show began, we counted at least a half a dozen fat Jews sitting eating and drinking in good bourgeois fashion."

Golder described in his diary on January 19, 1922, "one of the finest displays of parvenueism that I have ever seen." In a Bolshoi audience sprinkled with "speculators," a couple in a neighboring box opened a container of sweets and then ostentatiously peeled an orange, a rare and coveted item. During the entr'acte they left the orange on display, peeled and unguarded, and at the end of the evening they made a point of leaving behind some of the sweets. Golder could only shake his head and record an ironic "Hurrah for the Red Rich!"[4]

A FEW OF THE AMERICANS stationed in the capital cities had the opportunity to sample theatrical performances of a different type, in the form of Soviet government conferences. As the ARA was considered the equivalent of a foreign government legation, it was issued a limited number of passes to selected state-run events, such as special sessions of the annual Soviet national congress, which brought together representatives from around the country. For some of these delegates it was a long, long way from the darkness of the village to the awesome brightness of the Bolshoi, their gathering place. "It fills them with the power of Moscow," wrote Hullinger, who understood the intended effect of such political theater:

That scene in the Bolshoi Theater, no one could forget—thousands of electric lights, a vast room furnished in gold and trimmed in red plush curtains, four tiers of crowded galleries, a stage banked against a courtyard scene from an opera, the stage three-fourths filled with officers, in their uniforms of red and khaki, Red Guards, with their helmets and long rifles, and in front, near the footlights, the table of commissars, with the gentle Kallinin, Kamenev, and a few others. It has an excuse for existence, if only as a spectacle.[5]

The performance Hullinger describes must have been the Ninth Congress of Soviets in December 1921. It was back in November 1917 at the Second Congress of Soviets that Lenin and Trotsky had announced the Bolshevik seizure of power. Now, four years later, they were still the main act in the eyes of the delegates, though this was about to change. Lenin was already a very sick man, and this would be his last Soviet congress; Trotsky, never particularly popular among the Bolshevik leadership, was about to find himself being crowded off the stage. But in December 1921 both men still commanded the spotlight and used the occasion to justify their New Economic Policy before their troubled comrades.

Coolidge and Golder attended several sessions of the Ninth Congress, which they described in reports and private correspondence back to the States. Their observations of the leading players sound much like those of other contemporary foreign eyewitnesses. Lenin surprises at first. He is physically unimpressive and has a high-pitched, squeaky voice, not at all what one expects to issue forth from the severe countenance so familiar from the ubiquitous photographs. But Lenin knows his audience. He drives home his points through the repetition of simple phrases and achieves the desired effect.

Trotsky, on the other hand, instantly lives up to his reputation as the greatest Bolshevik orator. Physically erect, even military, he harangues his audience, gesturing dramatically—although with Bolshevism now in retreat it is becoming difficult to sustain this act. Trotsky is best at whipping up enthusiasm, stirring the masses to action, but the times have become decidedly unromantic.

Though Lenin and Trotsky certainly must have held their attention, Coolidge and Golder were at times preoccupied by the ill manners of the assembled delegates. Coolidge wondered why, with the theater sufficiently heated, many chose not to remove their fur coats and caps. Golder thought that the meeting "suggested a bit a Hobo Convention. People were there in all kinds of clothing, hats on, hats off, coats on and off, people sat everywhere." Farmer Murphy was drawn to the faces in the crowd:

One thing I thought was this, that here was a congress of reformers, men who were professing the highest ideals, who said that their purpose was to make the lot of the masses easier, to bring content and comfort to all mankind. So I searched with a glass every face for some trace of sympathy and kindness, for lines about the eyes and mouth that would indicate frequent laughter, for a benevolent eye, but nowhere—not in a single countenance in all that throng did I find anything but hardness and insolence. Either every jaw was set in hate or on the face was a sneer.

On New Year's Eve 1921 the Petrograd soviet put on a celebration at the opera house, and Golder managed to get an invitation. Looking down on the proceedings below, he fell to reminiscing about a different Russia.

The first time I was in this opera was early in 1914, that is before the war. One of the semi-oriental ballets was played and to the color of the staging, the soft oriental music was added the brilliance of the audience, the military uniforms, the gorgeously dressed women in their beautiful evening gowns displaying beautiful necks and arms. The whole scene was a page from the Arabian nights and I remember being greatly moved by it all.

Today, at the door of the opera house stood Red Army soldiers in the uniform of the old imperial guard. "The uniform hung on these poor peasant soldiers and they behaved like farmers, smoking cigarettes on duty, but the uniform was there." As for the audience, Golder recognized the usual "short-haired women and long nosed men, dressed in proletariat clothes and thinking how much superior they are to the rest of the world." He and an ARA colleague were invited to sit in the loge of the tsar. "I thought at first how unfit for such plebeians as we two to sit there until I looked around and saw the communists our companions. After all we were bourgeois and in that respect more closely related to the tsar than any of the others."

Petrograd was ruled, absolutely, by Bolshevik Party chief Zinoviev, who was said to have a charismatic personality and by most accounts was a brilliant public speaker. He was also known to be a man with a monumental ego. Perhaps this influenced Golder's thinking as he contemplated the scene on the stage at the Petrograd opera house that New Year's Eve, where a long rectangular table was besat on three sides, with Comrade Zinoviev in the center. "It seems sacrilege to say it," Golder wrote, "but the scene recalled to me an Italian picture of the Last Supper."[6]

THERE WAS CERTAINLY nothing in the provincial capitals to compare to the Bolshoi Theater, but there was legitimate theater—though not in the frontier city of Orenburg, according to one American there, who decided that "Amusements such as the theater were impossible; the atmosphere of the latter so resembled a refugee camp that the merits, if there were any, of the show were lost sight of." The relief workers in Samara evidently had it better. One of them wrote of the opera that "After getting used to the 'unwashed' odor of the spectators, which filled the place, the productions were not bad."

Kelley attended a performance of *Rigoletto* in that city during his brief stopover there. "Tout Samara was present," he relates. "From the aspect of the people promenading between the acts, we would never suspect that anything was wrong in this district." He said that the Samara opera house was "the only social center of any sort unless one counts the railroad station with morgue attached."

Cornick, who was no expert in these matters, thought that the theatrical offerings in Tsaritsyn were nothing to boast about, though he found during a summer 1922 visit to Astrakhan, on the Caspian Sea, a "very fair Opera": "We went one night and enjoyed a performance of the 'Barber of Seville (?)' It was probably very poor in comparison to real grand opera, but I have heard a lot of music in America that would not come up to it." The young Texan goes on to reveal his real passion:

But the opera was not the only interesting place that I visited. On the day of my arrival I saw advertisements of horse races, and even though it was Sunday I went out to the track.—I wish you could have seen the races. The horses are only about half as big as our Texas cow ponies, and although they are quite pretty to look at they move at about the same rate as everything else in Russia. . . . But the people seemed to find it exciting and were betting their millions of rubles quite excitedly.[7]

How fortunate for Childs, the ARA's cultural snob, that he ended up in Kazan, a city with a rich prerevolutionary theatrical tradition. There one could attend an opera or a play virtually every evening, and the ARA was regularly given passes to both. "The Russians might be starving," he wrote, "but they could not forego their theatre and opera."

One evening during the height of the famine, Childs attended a performance of the American play *Potash and Perlmutter* in the company of a local opera singer. "There were probably not ten people in the audience who were not hungry," he observed. When the curtain rose his companion let out a gasp, for there on the stage was her furniture, recently requisitioned by the government. She retained her composure, though, and even seemed to be amused by it all. Recalling this incident much later, after World War II, Childs sees in the woman's reaction an illustration of the Russians' "fatalistic resignation" and "simple dignity of spirit," which he says in 1941 left him with "no doubts of their ability to withstand the Hitler invasion."

On this particular evening, Childs found the Kazan audience rather unimpressive in appearance: "If bourgeois were ever present they were at pains to conceal their identity for men and women were alike shabbily dressed although their attire never appeared to detract from their enjoyment of the music."

In fact Kazan theater audiences were supposed to be more prosperous, as well as more sophisticated, than those elsewhere on the Volga. Given the city's large Tatar population, they were certainly more variegated. Goodrich was struck by this during a visit there in October 1921. Between acts of a theater performance he joined the spectators in the lobby for a closer look: "I stood and watched them with much interest. All plainly but cleanly dressed. Tartar, Semitic, Mongolian and Caucasian all mixed, they impressed me as a strong clean sort of folks, so much like the average American crowd in one of our cities that it was rather startling." This might be dismissed as yet another naive just-folks-like-us statement from the former governor of Indiana, who was prone to that sort of thing, but he was not alone in this impression: "I said to Sir Phillip Gibbs 'what does this crowd remind you of' and he answered 'of an English or American audience' and the same thought was in both our minds."

Gibbs too had a tendency to romanticize, but he was all in all a reliable observer of the ARA mission and of the Russian scene. In his autobiographical novel *The Middle of the Road*, he attends a performance in Kazan of the opera *Boris Godunov* in the company of Haskell and Quinn, each given a fictitious name. A disagreement arises among the three men over what conclusion should be drawn from the appearance of the audience. Looking down at the crowd, Haskell confesses his bafflement: millions of Russians are starving, yet the people inside the theater appear to be well fed. He can only conclude that this indicates the rise of a new bourgeoisie. Quinn, however, looks out over the audience and sees hungry people who "come to the opera as the one little gleam of light and joy and colour in the monotony of misery." The Gibbs character does not know what to think at that moment, but after spending more time in Kazan he comes to the conclusion that "the glamour and glitter of the opera only concealed the sharp tooth of hunger."

In Odessa, on the other hand, very little was concealed. The Americans stationed there made few references to the theater, and these tend to reinforce the general picture of the place as a city of the dead. In the March 9, 1922, entry in the ship's diary of the U.S.S. *Fox*, the commanding officer wrote: "The Odessa opera is now open and there is a performance nearly every evening. A member of the A.R.A. who attended last evening said it was very good but that the effect was rather spoiled when he stumbled over a corpse lying on the sidewalk just outside." The captain of the U.S.S. *MacFarland*, meanwhile, found that the scene inside the opera house reminded him of a "morgue": "The odor from the audience was almost nauseating."

The defeat of the famine, it seems, did not completely clear the atmosphere. When the commander of the *Fox* returned to Odessa in October 1922, he found that "At the opera 'Carmen' the air seemed to be permeated with sorrow." This got him thinking about the general state of affairs in Russia, though he had seen only a few square miles of it: "One gathers the impression that this government could not last overnight except for the seeming impossibility of overthrowing the present government."[8]

A MOSCOW INTELLECTUAL at this time maintained that of all forms of theater opera was the most attractive to the proletarian audience because of its "strange emotional atmosphere, . . . [s]trange events, costumes and music [which] take him far away from his everyday life and labor." Of all operatic offerings, *Carmen*, with its tragic tale of seduction, passion, and murder in a faraway land and with its undercurrent of class struggle, seems to have had a special appeal to Russian theatergoers.

It certainly left its mark on the American relief workers, to judge from its recurrent mention in letters, diaries, and memoirs. Forty-two years after the mission, George Townsend still recalled how he and his American companions broke into "acute hysterics when the gypsy in 'Carmen' weighed in at 250 pounds for her dance—although, he adds contritely, "she had a wonderful voice."

On the stage in Kiev, where references to the ARA—not always of the friendly sort—occasionally found their way into the script, there occurred one such instance, perhaps unintentional, during a production of *Carmen*. Sidney Brooks recalls what happened: "During the smuggling scene one of the boxes carried by a smuggler was turned sideways toward the front of the stage on which appeared in large letters across the box 'Van Camp's Evaporated Milk,' which met with a roar of laughter and shouts of 'Ara,' 'Call the GPU,' and other witty remarks from the audience."

In Kazan, the old opera house having been gutted by fire before the ARA arrived, performances were staged in the former light opera theater, at that time called the Palace of Red Army Soldiers. It was here on the night of November 12, 1921, during a performance of *Carmen*, that Van Arsdale Turner rushed into the ARA box with the news of the Cheka's arrest of an ARA Russian employee. This detail comes from Childs, who was enthralled with the idea of a drama within a drama. On the evening of October 15, 1922, attending a performance of *Carmen*, Childs is under the spell of the Persian diva Mukhtarova. "[T]hough I have heard Farrar and Caruso from beneath that ultra-conventional diamond horseshoe in the Metropolitan and though I have heard it on more than one occasion at the Opera Comique in Paris, I must confess that I have never enjoyed a performance of it such as I witnessed given by a mediocre company on the shabby stage of Kazan in the Russian Socialist Republic." It inspires the idealistic young American to new melodramatic heights:

I could not but think of that greater drama of which all of us who were present in the Palace of Red Army Soldiers formed a part. There before us was a little make-believe tragedy which was being produced in the midst of a great living tragedy but, while the former was enacted upon a few boards, the latter commanded a stage extending from the White to the Black and Caspian Seas. Principals of the greater tragedy were pressing as spectators into the lesser one to forget, in the tragedy of the other, their own. It recalled to my mind old German romantic plays of the early eighteenth century in which spectators of plays within plays themselves were placed upon the stage to take mimic parts before other spectators.

He leaves the theater "moved as I had never been before by a performance of *Carmen*," but moved not by the quality of the singing or acting: "It was the dramatic performance of the spectators which had so deeply impressed me!"[9]

CHAPTER 18

BACKSTAGE

Among the many descriptions by the American relief workers of the Russian theater audience there are disappointingly few recorded statements as to the impression made upon the Russians by the ARA theatergoers. They usually occupied seats reserved for dignitaries, though they would have stood out distinctly in the crowd anyway. Rare testimony comes from a university professor employed by the ARA in Simbirsk:

It was amusing to observe Americans in the theatre or in a concert. The distinguished foreigners attracted no less attention than the artists and had to stand a hail of observations and appreciations on the part of the public gathered in the hall. Their clean shaven faces, clearly cut features, contrasting with the semi-Mongolian type of the Russian population, their half-military dress all were objects of many a good humoured remark on the part of the crowd.[1]

In other ways, too, when it came to local theater, these Americans were no ordinary spectators. As part of its program to assist the Russian intelligentsia, the ARA supported, through food and clothing relief, the work of individual theaters and their artists, notably in the two capital cities. That theater directors and staffs were aware of such patronage had something to do with the ARA's easy access to artistic performances and the choice seating the men were given inside the theater.

When Baker visited Russia in February 1922, among his purposes was to arrange such relief. Between acts of a ballet performance at the Bolshoi, he and Haskell went backstage to invite the assistant director to ARA headquarters in order to discuss American support for the theater's artists. The following day this official arrived at Spiridonovka 30 for an interview accompanied by his Communist superior, "a laboring man type in a frayed blue denim shirt with turn down collar and no necktie."

After the parties agreed that the ARA would begin providing food packages to Bolshoi performers, the talk turned to the children associated with a high school run by the theater. Would the ARA take upon itself the feeding of some of these boys and girls? Upon request the two Russians produced a list of some six hundred needy children. "Arrangements were set on foot," Baker says, "for the immediate establishment of a kitchen for supplying these children one daily meal. . . . This was too much for the Communist; he remained for some time

looking at us quite unbelievingly. The silence was as though they were both waiting to catch their breath."

These privileged Americans often found themselves invited backstage to meet
and be met by the artists, which typically resulted in invitations to an ARA personnel house for a meal and entertainment. The Russian guests tended to be female; many were from the ballet. It seems fitting that the American baby-feeder
and the Russian ballerina, representing the benign image of their respective countries in the world, found themselves so often in each other's company during the
Great Famine. The combination proved to be stimulating to both parties. Fleming described for Harry back home a "big dinner" at an ARA residence, where

two sisters from the Bolshoi danced for us in the big parlor of the house. *That* was
enough to make you dream dreams; they cavorted about the floor, but they were developing the theme, and you didn't have to think hard to recognize it as the ancient
one of woman's attractiveness. Cambridge or Beverly would certainly have run them
out of town on a single rail; but they were quite innocent young ladies, taught to
dance that way since they were knee-high to a grass-hopper.

Ellington wrote to Fisher in New York of a "very gay, swank, expensive and
highly successful party." It was February 1923, and Ellington had just set himself
up in a private apartment with Phil Baldwin, which event the occasion was
meant to celebrate. Among the Russian artists present were Mmes. Abramova,
Iliushenka, Koudriazeva, and Kurdiumova, of whom Ellington remarked, "there
are no more famous names in the Ballet." He was able to report that the party
was a "tremendous success, for which of course one must pay. I am paying now.
That is why it was a strain to tear through the foregoing."

From the viewpoint of the Russian guests these encounters held out the prospect of decent food, the company of charming young men, and a warm, cozy environment. Above all, food. At the end of an opera performance in Kazan, Childs
invited Mukhtarova—the black-eyed Persian diva whose performance that night
seemed to cast a spell over him—along with several other female players back to
the personnel house. There the spell was abruptly broken by "the ravenous way
they threw themselves on the food."

Gibbs attended a performance in the same city of *Boris Godunov*. He tells the
story of how, afterward, the opera's stars showed up at ARA headquarters expressing a "desire to know if they might invite themselves to supper with *Messieurs
les Américains*." The answer was obvious: "How could a party of young Americans, six thousand miles from home, refuse to share their bully beef with art in
distress?" Among the callers was a "Prima Donna, a Persian lady with a wonderful voice, enormous black eyes, and a ferocious appetite"—who could only have
been Mukhtarova. The Americans break out their tinned beef and biscuits, cheese
and butter, and hot cocoa. In Gibbs's description, the performance turns into
camp: "They fell upon [the food] like harpies, and it was the beautiful Persian girl
who devoured the last of a Dutch cheese with her big black eyes raised in ecstasy."

This is followed by the inevitable maneuvers on the dance floor: "One of the
Americans produced a gramophone, and turned on a jazz tune, and initiated the
Persian lady into the mysteries of the fox-trot, while she screamed with laughter.
The others, still roving round for stray biscuits, laughed up and down the scale."

To Gibbs, "Those dancers . . . were like the merry ladies of the Decameron, surrounded by plague."[2]

This was Kazan. In Moscow, the cast of extravagant characters featured the American dancer Isadora Duncan. No stranger to Russia, Duncan had danced there on three separate visits before the Revolution. She arrived in Soviet Russia in July 1921, condemning Western capitalism and announcing her intention to found her own dance school—a "big school of a new type," in the words of Lunacharsky, the commissar of enlightenment.

Lunacharsky, who was Isadora's patron within the Soviet establishment and had issued her the invitation to Moscow, was among the first to realize that she had arrived in Bolshevik Russia a year too late. Her idea for a government-supported school for dance large enough to take in a thousand students ran up against the new financial realities of NEP—in other words, the very capitalist principles she thought she had left behind. Mortified by the decline of revolutionary enthusiasm, "tovarishch" Duncan, as she insisted on being called, openly condemned the "bourgeois" ways of the Soviet Communists. Lunacharsky was a gentle critic: "At present, Duncan is going through a phase of rather militant communism that sometimes, involuntarily, makes us smile."

Isadora had also come to dance. She composed two new works to études of Scriabin, said to be "charged with pity and terror" and inspired by the famine. She performed her controversial "Marche Slav," which in the words of a Western critic used "the allegory of the Russian workman struggling to free himself from his chains and the Tsar's heel as accompaniment to Tchaikovsky's Sixth Symphony." She thus made a hymn to the monarchy sound revolutionary, and the Bolshevik faithful watching her on the Bolshoi stage seemed to like it. Among the many unverifiable, and implausible, stories associated with Isadora's Russian sojourn there is one that places Lenin at this performance, rising in his loge in applause, crying out, "Brava, brava, Miss Duncan"—apparently unapprised of the unbending orthodoxy of "tovarishch Duncan."

She was forty-four years old in 1921, and in the photographs she looks quite full in the face as well as in other places. Although Duncan was past her physical prime, she still preferred to perform in minimal dress. Maxim Gorky watched Isadora dance at a dinner party at the apartment of Alexei Tolstoi in Berlin in 1922, after she had eaten and drunk vodka. Perhaps on this occasion too her movements were meant to represent the struggle of the forces of good against evil, but to Gorky they seemed "to depict the struggle between the weight of Duncan's age and the constraint of her body, spoilt by fame and love."

During her brief time in Russia, Isadora made her presence felt on the Moscow social scene. Her home was a refuge to a "motley crew of Russian bohemians" and was frequented by foreign journalists like Walter Duranty. This milieu was already thriving when Isadora fell in love with Sergei Esenin, the mercurial twenty-six-year-old peasant poet who ran with the crowd of imagist and other avant-garde artists of the time. Wherever he went, the proceedings were always lively and often scandalous. Esenin spoke not a word of a foreign language, and Isadora knew very little Russian. But as is often said to happen to such people, they spoke each other's language. Their time together, in and out of Soviet Russia, was tempestuous. Drink made Esenin violent, and he drank deeply and often, which was probably a factor in his violent end: in 1925 he committed suicide in the Leningrad Hotel Angleterre, today part of the Hotel Astoria.[3]

Duncan and Esenin married in May 1922 and flew to Berlin, touring Europe and then the United States, where the misunderstood poet behaved remarkably like a latter-day rock musician on the road, destroying hotel rooms and engaging in angry confrontations with the press. Isadora scandalized in her own way, on the stage, where during her performances she made short speeches expressing her support for Bolshevism in Russia. She also advocated free art. At Boston's Symphony Hall she was quoted as saying: "I would rather dance completely nude than strut in half-clothed suggestiveness as so many women do today on the streets of America. Nudity is truth, it is beauty, it is art."

According to one newspaper account, Isadora then "tore her tunic down to bare one of her breasts." Other versions said that she stripped naked, which is unbelievable. Whatever she exposed, it was said that "proper" Bostonians abandoned the hall while Harvard students cheered. Mayor Curley banned Duncan from Boston for "as long as I am Mayor."

Such details were faithfully reported by the "Russian Unit Record," including the "bad black eye" Esenin allegedly gave her before leaving America. The "Record" justified its coverage by noting that while she had been in Moscow, Duncan had been an "acquaintance of many of the American personnel." Not surprisingly, the association was founded on ARA food.

When Isadora's Moscow school opened in October 1921, despite the fact that it was a far more modest undertaking than originally planned, it immediately ran into funding problems. There was no heat for the building and little nourishment for the dancers. Government support was minimal and drying up. In a memoir, Lunacharsky recalled Isadora's plight and expressed his regret that "We could only platonically thank her, give her paltry aid, and in the end, sadly shrug our shoulders, to tell her that our time was too harsh for such problems."

In November, though, Isadora was able to announce in the pages of *Izvestiia* the promise of the ARA to provide food and clothing for her students. Perhaps it is not a coincidence that right around this time, at Thanksgiving, Isadora danced in the ballroom of the Pink House. Alvin Blomquist came out of Simbirsk to get a breather in Moscow and was surprised to find "our own Isadora, who flouted the Adamses in Boston," performing the "Dance of the Enraged Proletariat" and the "Dance of the Descent of Reason" for the American personnel. One of those Boston Brahmins, Coolidge, wrote to his father that even before Thanksgiving he found Isadora "rather too much in evidence"—a neat, if unintended, double entendre.

One American later remembered the holiday as a "hilarious night of celebration." The only running account comes from Golder, next to Goodrich the most prudish ARA diarist. As he sits in his room in the Pink House not far from the main center of the festivities, pen firmly in hand, he seems unable to decide whether he is a part of the frivolity or a disapproving spectator.

Our ARA army officer crowd decided to give a Thanksgiving party and we have a lot of ballet dancers and other females of that kind and all the men and women are more than half full of booze and we are having a happy time. I hear the music going now and I wish I were quietly asleep. The prize guest is Isadora Duncan and the woman is either drunk or crazy, perhaps both. She is half dressed and calls the boys to pull down her chimies, I think that is the way they are called. The poor ballet dancers have eaten and drank everything in sight and they are still hungry. We are a happy crowd, particularly Professor Hutchinson and Coolidge and I. They have just gone into my neighbor's room asking for cognac, I mean the ballet dancers. What may happen before morning I do not know. The pitiful part of it all is that we are housed in a museum where there are many rare and beautiful things, finest furniture and the pigs are crawling all over it, throwing cigarettes around and more like that. But enough of this.

This is not to say that Golder was not capable of letting go; just that his idea of fun was joining Professors Hutchinson and Coolidge in a rendition of "Down in the Heart of the Gas House District" and "Little Tommy Murphy." In his mid-forties, Golder was one of the elder statesmen of the Russian unit. As a faithful diarist and correspondent he served as its conscience. He could see all too well that American bounty had placed the American relief workers in an unnaturally favorable position vis-à-vis the young women of Russia. It led to absurd situations like that which occurred in a Petrograd theater, where he was joined by two local ARA men:

After the first part the director or assistant director came into our box, there were three of us Americans there, to invite us behind the scenes and to offer us any other honor or courtesy in his power. I was in the same opera house just eight years ago and then it was the grand dukes, the young military officers of noble birth who were invited behind the scenes to chuckle the girls under the chins, to take them out to champagne suppers, and today, three plebeian Americans of no importance at home but looming up big here because they are feeding hungry people have the place of honor. I pointed out to our men that we could not accept these honors without obligating ourselves very deeply and young America spoke up "then we will invite the girls home and give them a square [meal]." I am sure that you will see with me the comedy and tragedy of the whole thing.[4]

FOR MOST OF THESE AMERICANS, experience with women was part of their wartime and postwar adventure in Europe—experience and women of the kind that were impossible to find in small-town America. European morals, already loose by American standards, had been further relaxed by the war. And these young, cigarette-toting American males were certainly a novelty for European women. Such factors seemed to operate in spades in Russia, where many native observers noted a marked decline in moral standards after years of death and destruction. A Russian history professor in Simbirsk stated it plainly: "Relations with women have become coarse and cynical, and on the other hand the moral level of the young women has likewise considerably fallen." American physicians reported an enormous increase in venereal disease during the previous three or four years, which prompted several ARA districts to establish venereal clinics.

Golder, who may not have been influenced in the discussion of such matters by an attraction to the opposite sex, took up the case of Russia's young women— usually having in mind the daughters of better families—with an acute sensitivity. To him their fate was "tragic." So many young men between the ages of twenty and thirty-five had been killed off in the wars or had fled the country, while those who had survived were "demoralized. There are few marriageable men for decent girls and even if there were there is nothing of home life to look forward to." Enter the ARA: "Our men here are under the impression that Russian women are most immoral, but it is not that at all. The poor girls want to live, they want to taste some of the joys of life, before they are too old, but all legitimate doors are closed."

Prostitution did not enter the picture, for in the Soviet Russia of 1921 there was little demand for such a specialization. Fleming reported that in Moscow the prostitute's business was poor, "owing to the large number of what the social tabulators like to call 'casuals,' and the lack of that form of Christian morality so evident in the reign of the late queen of England." Fleming wrote to his brother of the "one commodity in this country that is—well not hard to find," and one ARA man told Golder, "You can get any girl for a square meal."

Given this ready availability, one would not expect the Americans in Moscow to have made such a fuss over the naked bodies of the female bathers on the shores of the Moscow River. It seems to have made quite an impression on Fleming. In the same breath in which he notes the absence in Russia of Victorian morals, he writes:

Men, women, and children go in bathing completely naked in the river in the very heart of the city under the walls of the Kremlin; the only concession to a prurient world being that the women jump in as soon as they have undressed, and then pull a shirt on before they come out of the water. I know because I watched them. There weren't many spectators, tho; only a few Americans.

A week later he informs a correspondent that "bathing suits are not the fashion in Russia" and again describes the scene along the river, noting that "the Russkies are used to it and never bat a lash, but we go for it like flies round a honey-pot or kids at a circus."

Alexis Babine, the Russian-American in Saratov whose diary documents his frequent perturbation with what he considers to be the bad, even crude manners of his American employers, describes how during his stay in Moscow the ARA automobile made a special trip to the beach, where "some of our men stopped on the bank and studied women's anatomy through a field glass, to the wonderment of the uncouth Russian passers-by." The fascination was hard to kick. Six years afterward, the ARA alumni newsletter made reference to the "Bathing beauties of a Moskva River summer evening." When that was written, visitors to Moscow who so desired could still witness this spectacle in the shadow of the Kremlin. By the mid-1930s, though, as with so much else, things had changed: bathing suits had become de rigueur, which gives present-day Muscovites something else to blame Stalin for.[5]

So much for the beach. The disrobing, so to speak, had actually begun with the arrival of spring, when Russians shed their winter clothing. Townsend, recalling Easter 1922 in Moscow, remembers the effect this had on the Americans: "Gone were the shapeless, heavy garments of winter and, behold, we youngsters discovered that Russian girls had legs after all and not all by any means were heavy-boned truck horses."

Not a few relief workers had made this discovery much earlier. Judging from the abundance of anecdotal evidence, a good deal of fraternizing was going on at the ARA personnel houses in all the districts, which means that John Saunders must have been extremely indiscreet because his association with a woman was largely the cause of his expulsion from the mission in December 1921. Perhaps it was really his fondness for alcohol that did him in. The particular facts of the case are obscure, though the general thrust of the indictment against him is clear enough. Golder says that Saunders had "turned his back on all decent people red and white and has been busy chasing women and booze. When you stop to consider that the ARA is the most important foreign organization in Russia, that in Petrograd the two or three Americans are the only foreigners here you can picture to yourself the impression we are making." Golder says that Saunders—"this representative of the Army and protege of our Russian chief"—had brought "his girl" home and that she spent the night at the ARA personnel house, hardly scandalous behavior by ARA standards but clearly upsetting to Golder: "Think how low the old ARA has fallen and how it hurts the men who have stood by the organization for years and who have been loyal to it and to the Chief."

Goodrich painted the Saunders affair in darker tones. He informed London that when Saunders wanted a "prostitute"—a term the governor might have chosen for its moral weight rather than as an occupational description—he would send his Russian chauffeur out to fetch one and bring her to the ARA house. Goodrich vented his outrage in a rather excited sentence:

Saunders was not only intoxicated time after time, but that he brought prostitutes to the ARA headquarters, which were very luxuriously furnished, and maintained and kept them there to such an extent and his conduct became so well known that the Russians in Petrograd freely discussed the matter and expressed surprise that the ARA would permit the continuance of a man of that character in such an important work.

Charlie Veil also would have his association with the ARA terminated prematurely, though not over a woman. One would have predicted otherwise had one been familiar with his prior exploits in Europe, at least as alleged in his swaggering 1932 autobiography, *Adventure's a Wench*, which opens with the statement, "Adventure is a red-hot little female devil longing to be raped." Veil portrays himself in postwar Europe as "forever chasing that whore, Adventure, when I should have been living in matrimonial respectability." What seems to have kept him on comparatively good behavior in Russia was his assignment to a relatively isolated subdistrict, Novouzensk, where suitable female material must have been scarce. For in this new environment, he concedes, he "didn't sleep with the girls—that is, not very often."

Babine expressed his disgust at the fact that his American chief in Saratov would consort with a "street-walker," but this was as nothing compared to what he witnessed during his few weeks' stay in the capital. His diary entry for June 14, 1922, takes us inside the Brown House. It is nighttime.

Searles [Surles] and I were already in bed when Farraher entered our room hardly able to stand on his feet. Leaning on Searles's table, he explained to us that they had four women in their room and only three men—that he had so-and-so, and could not we come and help them, etc., etc., of the most disgusting character. We suggested his trying our neighbors, which he did.

As one who had lived in both Russia and America, Babine seems to have been especially sensitive to the idea that all this carnal activity might blacken America's reputation among the Russians. One day a relief worker at a personnel house asked him to translate for a female caller who did not speak English. "She wondered if all Americans were like those who came with the ARA to Moscow. 'Our Russian young men are not much on morals—I mean about women—but they are angels in comparison with you Americans.'"

A Russian who worked at the ARA's medical warehouse in Moscow recounted for Babine how from the street he looked up through a window of one of the American residences and saw several relief workers, "hog-drunk," with naked women in their company. The offended Muscovite remarked; "Of course, Americans have helped us very much, but we might have a soberer lot sent here."[6]

CHAPTER 19

ENTANGLEMENTS

In his letters home, Fleming devoted ample space to his amorous experiences in Russia. This correspondence reveals that Oxford had not imparted to young Harold every last bit of knowledge about engaging the opposite sex.

Fleming arrived in Moscow in June 1922 and immediately sank into self-pity out of loneliness and homesickness. In his first letter to his parents he laments, "It would make me melancholy to tell you how moribund Moscow is so I will avoid it." This is how it was with Moscow, it was never love at first sight.

In his second letter, dated June 30, where he catalogs all the cherished things absent from his life in the Russian capital, he complains that there are "not even two to gather together for the Holy Ghost to rest upon." On July 7, in a letter to "Bill," he is more straightforward about the problem: "My evenings are a source of constant perplexity and dissatisfaction, after supper I think of going to the office, and then begin to wonder why I haven't found a Russian girl yet."

Quite suddenly, only two weeks later, everything is looking up. Harold is exuberant, for he has found his Russian girl, and he is not shy about telling his parents:

Just to let you know first off that I am having the time of my life; feel happy as the day is long; in the best of health and seem to be always feeling ready to start something, plenty of energy, etc; my work is interesting and engrossing during the day; and I have found a very pretty dictionary who can't speak anything but Russian and, I think, likes me as much as I like her, which is quite a bit, now I tell you.

Fleming has fallen for his Russian language teacher, Paulina Zhirnova, and all at once Moscow has become magically transformed into a city of unlimited social possibilities. He asks his parents to send him one and another suit and coat.

By August 9, after a few weeks of picnicking and long walks, Harold is thoroughly smitten, although at times he expresses himself in a way that might mislead the uninitiated as to the true object of his affection: "I am getting so fond of Moscow that I shall be most heart-broken when the time comes to leave; I should be content to stay here in Russia for a couple of years, I believe."

What happened to Fleming happened to quite a few other ARA Americans: they fell in love with their language teachers. This is understandable given that most of the relievers were single, young males, initially disoriented in an alien environment and completely at a loss in the Russian language; whereas their teachers were usually young females, single or widowed, desirous of male attention and companionship, and ready to be pitied. It seems there were quite a few cases—Paulina was one of them—where the teacher did not speak any English at all, a circumstance that seems only to have strengthened the appeal. The point of combustion might arrive at the moment the instructor widened her eyes, pursed her lips, and introduced the avid student to the mysteries of the Russian soft sign—then, kaboom!

After that there was no telling how things might develop. In Fleming's case we have a pretty good idea because of his lifelong love affair with the written word.

In November Paulina enters a Moscow hospital to have her appendix and a kidney removed, no light matter in Soviet Russia in 1922. "She looks even prettier in the gray uniform bath robe they put on her at the hospital and when I get over to the hospital after work I see her with her nose glued against the window watching for me." She pulls through just fine, and Harold is flying high: "Paulina is a queen figuratively, being the prettiest little woman I have seen in Moscow—hhhmmm—hhhmmm—hhhmmm. Literally she is only a common ordinary specimen of the garden-variety bourgeoisie (petit) of which we are members in the states."

He begins to spend some of his nights away from the Blue House. He tells his parents that because Pauline speaks only Russian, she would make a difficult daughter-in-law—a statement calculated to enliven the dinner conversation back home in Beverly.

It is not long, however, before different winds begin to blow. In December, with Paulina now fully recovered from her operation, Harold begins seeing other women: one evening he attends a ballet with a cabaret singer; on another evening another ballet, this time in the company of "my chief clerk, who once was a countess and can't seem to get over it, which is her principal fault. If Paulina hears of all these goings on it sure will be a blow-up for me." Having sampled "garden-variety bourgeoisie" and former aristocracy and having observed his fellow Americans in action, Fleming feels qualified to draw some general conclusions about matters of the heart in Russia. In a December 1922 letter to "Bert," he writes:

I have been acquiring a different attitude toward women since I came to Europe than that in which I was brought up. Particularly here in Russia, a woman is a play-thing that changes hands. They are not made for partners but for play-mates. But it is the women themselves who bring it upon themselves. Far from being in Russia the Supermen that Shaw has them, they are the things to be pitied."

Most pathetic and hopeless are the "Madame Butterflies," who "seem to be everywhere Americans go." "I met recently a 'Madame Butterfly' in the flesh. When the first Americans came in a certain X made love to her. She left her husband for him, believing that he loved her. He was then released from the Russian unit and left Russia, promising to try and get her out to be his wife. Since then she received a few letters; old story."

Then another ARA man enters this woman's life—and soon exits it in similar fashion. Still, her heart remains open. What could make Russian women act this way? "They are a riddle to me. Maybe some day I shall learn to know them but I shall never learn to understand them. I have a couple of friends in the Unit who always clean up a perfect score on such cases. I never make out as villain at all."

Fleming attests to the "wicked instability of American affections" and the "ephemeral brittleness of their words of love." He makes this case to a "Butterfly" whose acquaintance he has recently made, but she seems impervious to his warnings about insidious American charm: "Those mellifluous and sweet words which are spoken in tones and strains that would make an American girl show you the hat-rack have dulcet and soothing effect upon this young lady, which quite for the time effaces the memory of past despairs." Not that he himself is capable of thus capturing a "Butterfly": "Honeyed words come to my lips like molasses flowing up hill on a cold January morning."

Apparently, the strain of carrying on a steady relationship with Paulina while trying to unravel the mysteries of the Russian female proved to be too much for Harold. "I am fed up," he writes to Bert on December 14, indicating that he walked out on her, retreating to the Blue House. "Maybe she is as tired of me as I am of her. I want to work; and I am fed up. Nothing more. I think a breathing spell is in order. I don't know for how long."

He declares himself tired of "the whole sex" yet reveals that the woman who has "played through already two Madame Butterfly episodes with Americans" is in fact the cabaret singer he has been seeing. She even "looks Japanese." He insists, however, that he is only in it for "the spirit of the chase." Clearly influenced by the physical appearance of this particular specimen, he finds that Russian women "have a ravishing sensuous bearing when they are beautiful that the Anglo-Saxon likes to have about him in his leisure hours, but hates to have around during business—the kind that go big on the American stage, but mighty small in the American home."

In January 1923, Fleming is transferred to Samara, a reassignment he seems to welcome with relief though Paulina "is a bit weepy about it." Predictably, though, when he arrives at his new post, he finds he misses her, and the Bolshoi ballet, but he consoles himself with the fact that "The girls here are pretty good looking and just adore Americans, according to rumor, which sounds good." Before long he has taken up with a new girl, a local actress. He receives a letter from Paulina describing Christmas without Harold as "long and weary," which leads him to conclude that "These Russian women are enchanting, though one must not take them too seriously."

At mission's end he finds himself in Peking, dating a Chinese but with his mind on Moscow: "I spend a lot of time thinking about Paulina nowadays, sometimes almost wishing I had married her and brought her out to Peking with me."[1]

THERE WERE NO ARA RULES against marrying a Russian, and by mission's end as many as thirty American relief workers, nearly one in ten, had taken Soviet brides—"succumbed to feminine charms in Russia" is how the ARA alumni review put it. Moscow's Sidney Brooks rated this a "pretty good batting average!"

In this the ARA men merely carried on a tradition begun by the American doughboys who returned home after the war with European wives. Or they returned without them. Veil's, here again, is a caricaturized version of the serviceman's experience. His adventure began at home in 1916 when his "adolescent love affair" with the daughter of a manufacturer in a small Connecticut town put him in a spot: "it became a question of a shotgun marriage or flight." To escape, the nineteen-year old Veil went off to fight the air war over France, thus signing his "covenant with Adventure." When the war ended, Veil wooed and married a French girl on the Côte d'Azur, but she failed to hold his interest and soon he was in flight once again.

Golder probably never met Veil, but such details about the adventurer's exploits would hardly have surprised him. When Golder expressed his qualms about the relief workers' easy sexual conquests, he did so in the context of the American soldier's unnaturally elevated position in Europe after the close of hostilities. Back then it was "war brides"; now it was "famine brides." Looking at the personnel of the Russian unit in September 1922, Golder saw that not a few among them were "the equivalent of the squaw men, and some of our men are not gentlemen. They have knocked about in Europe during the last six years and have picked a wife in one or more of the countries and they are now playing the same game here. One does not have to pay much for women who are starving and some of our boys are making the most of the market."

One wonders what Golder would have thought had he read John Ellingston's announcement of his marriage to a Russian staff member, which he made in a letter to Fisher in New York: "This is a very profound secret and I hold you to keep it so. I am married. God knows why and how. I have a few vague ideas re the latter but am blank in regard to the former." Hardly the stuff of great romance, though this is perhaps merely Ellingston's embarrassed way of breaking the news.

On the other hand, one might speculate as to the true motivations of his future bride in entering matrimony with an American relief worker. The "Russian Unit Record" distributed a questionnaire to the female employees at Moscow headquarters in May 1922 under the title "Why I would never marry an American." The spirit of the questionnaire must have been as obviously tongue-in-cheek as the editors' analysis of the results because only one of the ladies in question took the trouble to reply, and she was a married woman. The sole respondent seems to have given the matter some serious thought. The "Record" printed her response in full:

> I would never marry an American.
> Because I should not like to feel myself in the position of an Indian girl married to an Englishman. It is all very well to be treated as a "native" in the office.
> Because Americans are thick-skinned. They would never know the right thing to do or not to do. It's the surest way to ruin marriage.
> Because they are too normal—it is tiring.
> Because they are too realistic. Their only fancy is their decided weakness for the Russian ballet.
> Because they are too business-like. They would talk business when I would talk dresses.

Although these shortcomings might have been generally shared, they were apparently not insurmountable: the editors were informed verbally by several female staff members that they would indeed marry an American "because they wanted to go to America."[2] The prospect of a honeymoon in Paris was also enticing. This is not to question the integrity of every ARA famine bride. But it is only fair to point out that just as Soviet Russia had its Paulina Zhirnovas, it also had its Elena Riazantsevas.

Riazantseva lived in the city of Ufa, where she worked as a housekeeper for the ARA. She was the daughter of a landowner, who at one time owned the Ufa house in which the Americans were headquartered on Pushkin Street. During the Civil War her family fled to Siberia, where Riazantseva married a Bolshevik commissar, only to divorce him and return to Ufa when the war ended. She is described as "energetic, interesting, and vivacious," qualities which evidently more than made up for her plain looks.

A relief worker in the Ufa unit, Simon Baird, courted Riazantseva and eventually asked for her hand in marriage, which she refused to give, though apparently not before playing out the game for all it was worth. As Kelley tells it, Baird became thoroughly lovesick, which turned him into a hopelessly inefficient relief worker. Baird, he says, was "diagnosed as a pronounced neurasthenic," although it is most unlikely that this was a professional diagnosis. Elsewhere he identifies Baird's affliction as a "disease brought on by Ufa and a Russian woman who teases him." The Ufa Americans were almost certainly unaware that Baird was already married to a woman in Belgium.

In his evaluations of the American personnel in Ufa written after Baird's departure, Bell called him "absolutely useless": he had been "on the verge of a complete nervous breakdown practically ever since arriving in Ufa late in December." Eventually he had to be "invalided to Moscow." Bell does not mention the involvement of a woman. It was Baird who accompanied Blandy's body to Moscow, where he clearly ought to have been put on the Riga Express; yet for some reason he was sent back out to Ufa. There he once again fell victim to the curse of the Russian housekeeper, with the result that Haskell finally interceded, ordering Baird to Moscow for reassignment—a move that put his Ufa colleagues on notice against entering into "entangling alliances."

Riazantseva, too, eventually made it out of Ufa. After the departure of the ARA, she went to work as an interpreter for Intourist in Moscow. There she met an American engineer from Detroit and accepted his marriage proposal. Shortly after the couple arrived in the United States, she broke off the relationship. Her last reported whereabouts was the household of Governor and Mrs. Goodrich in Indianapolis.[3]

Housekeepers were one thing, but to wed a former princess had a certain appeal to the untitled relief worker, even after he had adjusted to the idea that some of the former "grandes dames" of imperial Russia—Tatishchevas, Bobrinskaias, Golitsyns, and the like—were on the ARA payroll as clerks, secretaries, and interpreters. Some of the allure was no doubt subconscious, though one ARA press release on marriages within the ranks took open delight in the idea of our boys domesticating those highfalutin titles: "Some Russian princesses have solved their problems by becoming plain Mrs. Blank of the U.S.A. . . . . [P]robably ninety percent of them gave up rank, high-sounding still if somewhat hollow, in the process of becoming American wives."

The tone of these press releases about the "Russian cupid aiming his bow" is typically playful, as when "the little Bolshevik felled Dr. Patrick Kennedy."[4] But not every story of ARA courtship and marriage suited this formula—for example, that of William J. Casey of Utica, New York. Casey was stationed in Simferopol in the Crimea, where he fell in love with a Russian on the ARA staff, a widow by the name of Elizaveta Voikina, who was a former aristocrat from Petrograd. A marriage proposal followed and was accepted. Nothing out of the ordinary so far, until the day an anonymous letter in Russian script, dated March 26, 1923, and penned by a self-described representative of the "suffering Russian intelligenzia," arrived at ARA headquarters in Moscow.

The writer claimed that the lady in question was in fact not a widow: that her husband, a former colonel on the general staff, was abroad, having been forced to leave the country two years earlier. In another place and time this piece of information might have caused some degree of trouble for the betrothed couple, but in the Russia of 1922 it could hardly raise an eyebrow. The writer knew this and so proceeded to raise other objections, in language translated by someone at ARA headquarters:

The case is very indecent. Mr. Casey is 23 - 24 years old, Mrs. Voikina is 36 years old. This difference of age (Madam could be his mother) shows that they both are mad. Not speaking about the fact that they are speaking different languages and are professing different religions (Mr. Casey does not know Russian and Madam knows only Russian), you must note that Madam has a husband and a child.

This "false romance," this "crime against the laws of morality . . . can end with blood in America." Worse yet, the husband might return to Russia and "raise a scandal" for the ARA. The anonymous writer asked that the ARA "Make haste to protect the reputation of Americans as gentlemen and benefactors" and ended with a plea that Casey be reassigned out of Simferopol.

Soon after this, ARA headquarters in Moscow received another such letter—this one signed by the bride-to-be's mother, Maria Durneva—protesting "this degrading and criminal marriage," insisting that "Love between parties of twenty-three and thirty-six can not have but a base object," and begging the ARA to avert this "catastrophe."

Cyril Quinn read these prophecies of doom and passed them on to Simferopol to the attention of District Supervisor Eddie Fox, the erstwhile Simbirsk jazz man, now dispensing ragtime on the shores of the Black Sea. Quinn told Fox that while anonymous letters to the ARA were usually relegated to the waste basket, if this Casey situation was what it seemed, "someone ought to step in."

In fact Quinn already had some practice in offering advice to the ARA love-struck and not only in Moscow. The district supervisor in Odessa, Harry Harris, wrote to him in January 1923 to ask whether he should marry "a wonderful little Russian lady" with whom he had fallen in love. In his reply, Quinn reminded Harris that his future bride would face great difficulty adjusting to life in America. "There are so many factors which militate against successful marriages that it is flying in the face of Providence to bring in additional ones." Quinn was skeptical of the ARA marriage proposition: "I cannot help feeling that the epidemic of marriages in the A. R. A. has been largely a question of propinquity and the psychological moment and I am not sure that this is a fundamentally sound basis." Quinn was being perfectly reasonable, but nonetheless Harry Harris departed Soviet Russia a married man.

Back in the Crimea, meanwhile, Fox admitted to Quinn that he had tried to talk Casey out of what he, Fox, felt was a mésalliance, "in spite of the fact that I was treading on dangerous ground when handing out advice to the lovelorn." Curiously, Fox never mentions the absent first husband, whether deceased or alive. Perhaps Casey had convinced him that Mrs. Voikina was in fact a widow. In a letter to Fox defending his actions, Casey stated that "The lady in question is quite free to marry"—which does not really settle the question.

Fox was concerned that Voikina was not a "good match" for Casey, whom he considered a "darn fine chap." She was, after all, ten years' Casey's senior, had a four-year-old son, and was in poor health as a result of all of the hardships she had experienced. "I would hate to see him do something, he may regret later on. Personally, I think it is more a case of sympathy with Casey than real love & after a few days in Paris he would begin to realize his error."

Fox asked Quinn to offer Casey "a little fatherly advice," and Quinn agreed to send him a note, but there is no evidence that he ever did so. Rather, the matter was put to rest when Voikina arrived one day at Quinn's office with a written statement from her mother confessing to an attempt to thwart the marriage in order to keep her daughter in Russia. Voikina asked Quinn for an official letter from the ARA declaring that the organization had no objection to Casey marrying her, but Quinn refused, telling her that it was not an official matter.

Casey, on his part, assured his chiefs that he had no intention of "in any way 'outraging the Russian intelligentsia.'"[5]

THUS FAR, the prenuptial maneuverings. The wedding ceremonies of the relief workers almost always went off without a hitch, though there were the inevitable peculiarities. Usually, for example, there was need for an additional participant: the descriptions of several ARA weddings note the presence of an interpreter, there to assist the bride and groom in taking their vows.

Among the most detailed of these accounts is Childs's description—printed in the "Russian Unit Record" under the title "How to Marry a Russian"—of the very first ARA wedding, that of John Norris of Kazan and Mrs. Pankratova, his Russian language teacher. Norris was said to be the first native-born American to contract a marriage with a Russian woman under the laws of the Soviet government. The ceremony—the first of them, that is—took place in Kazan's Russian Orthodox church, into which more than a thousand people crowded in order to witness the "unusual spectacle."

The only awkward moment occurred when the groom entered reeking of petrol. He is said to have drunk half a bottle of gasoline just before departing for the church, the fuel ingested by mistake from a container used for mineral water—"at least, that is the explanation which he made when confronted by the excited bride." It appears that Norris had imbibed the kerosene-and-vodka concoction that some of the Americans called a "k-v cocktail." If so, in this particular case the mix would appear to have strongly favored the kerosene. "According to Norris' friends the gasoline must have contained elements for the fortification of the courage for despite the handicap of the language in which the ceremony was performed there was not another hitch, the bridegroom preserving his bravery and composure to the bitter end."

Later in the day there was another service, this one in the Roman Catholic ritual, the religion of the groom. A few weeks earlier, Norris and his bride-to-be had gone through the Soviet civil ceremony, an exercise in paperwork that he found shockingly impersonal: "You might have been filling in an income tax return."[6]

Once the newlyweds left Russia, there remained one last ceremonial hurdle. Because the American government did not recognize marriages concluded by American citizens in Russia, in order for Mrs. Norris to obtain an American passport it was necessary for the couple to formalize the arrangement in the presence of an American consul. This took place, as it did for most of the other ARA couples, in Riga.

Beginning in autumn 1922, there arose a further obstacle. In October the United States government passed a law stating that a foreign national did not automatically acquire American citizenship by marrying a U.S. citizen. This meant that the non-American spouse had to enter the country as an immigrant, and that meant making the yearly immigration quota, which was broken down by country. This became a real concern near the end of the mission, in summer 1923, when there was a rush of ARA weddings. Those who could not make the quota for Russia found their European honeymoon extended until the new fiscal year began on August 1.

This is where Casey miscalculated. He arrived in New York on July 18 with his new bride, only to find that the quota for Russia had been filled. Mrs. Casey had to remain in detention on Ellis Island for two weeks.[7] Thus did William J. Casey leave himself open to the charge of having outraged the suffering Russian intelligentsia.

Despite the conspicuous presence of a large number of former nobility and bourgeoisie among the Russian spouses, it appears there were few problems getting the new brides out of the country. Somerville wed in Simbirsk in September 1923 shortly after the departure of the Russian unit, which might explain why, in order for the couple to leave together, they had to obtain a document from the Simbirsk GPU certifying as to the "absence of counter-revolutionary activities on the part of my wife."[8]

The only case where the Soviet government stood in the way of the departure of an ARA spouse involved another Kazan American, District Supervisor Ivar Wahren. Born of a well-to-do family in Finland, Wahren ran away to America, learning his English in the U.S. Army, in which he rose to the rank of captain. His new wife, the Princess Chegodaeva of Petrograd, would never be allowed to leave Soviet Russia. The particular reasons for this are not clear, as perhaps they were not to the unfortunate couple, though the problem undoubtedly stemmed from the nature of her family's opposition to Bolshevism during the Revolution. Anyway, after holding out for a few years, Wahren was forced to divorce his princess. When the Great Depression came, he fell upon hard times, and, according to Childs, "heavy drinking caused his death." To what extent the unhappy ending to his Russian love story contributed to his demise is of course a matter of conjecture. Childs tells us that even in Kazan Wahren "would often remark wistfully to me: 'You need have no concern about the future, but everything looks dark for me.'"

Wahren's fate contrasts most sharply with that of his Kazan colleague, whose amorous pursuit of Georgina Klokacheva of Petrograd is the stuff of Victorian romance novels. One arrives at this conclusion after a visit to the Alderman Library at the University of Virginia, in Charlottesville, which houses Childs's papers, including the couple's courtship correspondence: Georgina writing from Petrograd, Rives from Kazan.

When they met, Georgina was twenty-nine years old, one year older than Childs. She was from a cultivated and formerly wealthy family—her mother was French, the widow of a Russian naval officer—and she had seen much of Europe before the war. Georgina's previous marriage, which seems to have lasted only three weeks, was to a man who was killed by Bolshevik forces in Ukraine during the Civil War.

Georgina had her portrait painted by Nikolai Feshin in 1922 after she had moved to Kazan. Feshin had made the acquaintance of the relief workers there, some of whom commissioned him to paint their portraits at a price of 250,000,000 rubles, or about $50, each. Among them was Childs, who says he endured eighteen sittings. Feshin had studied under Repin, the great Russian realist painter, and the master's influence is discernible in the student's work, which at this time also owed something to the late impressionists. With the help of the ARA, Childs in particular, Feshin was able emigrate to the United States in 1923, eventually settling in Taos, where, his name permanently mistransliterated as "Fechin," he would reinvent himself as one of the premier painters of the American Southwest.

Fechin's Georgina is a slight woman of exceptional beauty, distinctive for her large, almost bulging eyes. From this it is not difficult to understand the physical dimension of Childs's attraction, although Georgina found the likeness unflattering.

Childs had stopped briefly in Petrograd in March 1922 on his return from Europe, where he had spent several weeks convalescing after his bout with typhus. He was introduced to Georgina at the ARA office, where she was employed on the clerical staff. It was, at least for him, a case of love at first sight. "I had no time for protracted maneuvers," he later remembered, "since I was obliged to return to Kazan after three or four days."[9]

Childs was the son of an exceptionally possessive mother, a trait that is perhaps partly explained by the death of his older brother. She meddled fiercely in Rives's romances, seeing any woman who entered his life as a potential rival for his love. Childs, a future U.S. ambassador to Saudi Arabia, Yemen, and Ethiopia, bore up reasonably well under the burden, though his mind was preoccupied by the intricate diplomacy required to demonstrate to his mother his undying devotion to her as well as to Georgina. To his father, who cuts an indistinct figure here, he was never close.

Now in the spring and summer of 1922, Childs's mother, in Richmond, became something like the third corner of a love triangle with Rives and Georgina. She is today a mute participant, her letters to her son in Kazan having apparently been lost. Nonetheless, his missives to her, with their emotional entreaties for her understanding, support, and love, suggest her manner of resistance.

In March, after first laying eyes upon Georgina, "one of the most attractive girls I have ever met," Childs, in faithfully reporting his discovery, seeks to reassure his mother, telling her, "never fear. Kazan is 1200 miles from Petrograd and I suppose this means the end of perhaps a potential romance."

One month later, with spring in full bloom and Georgina responding from Petrograd to his epistolary overtures, Childs decides he must make his feelings clear. He begins, perhaps subconsciously, by indirection: "I have reached the point where I do not think I would ever be satisfied with living anywhere except in Russia. Old timers say the Russian bug is a disease and that when it gets into your veins you are hopeless; that there is nothing like the Russian nostalgia."

Having thus prepared the ground, he openly confesses his love for Georgina; then, no doubt anticipating a future line of argument, he generalizes about her kind: "I suppose you think Russian women must have some extraordinary attractions and I will answer by saying that they have. To me they have all the virtues of the French and none of their vices: cultured and extremely artistic and I believe the most highly developed in idealism of any people in the world." This, from the most idealistic of the American relief workers in Russia.

In June, after much agonizing, he reveals that Georgina has accepted his offer of marriage. Mrs. Childs naturally disapproves of the match, not least because her permission was not asked. Consumed with guilt, Rives implores his mother to be reasonable, to honor his wishes. He is by turns beseeching and defiant when he senses she is giving him the silent treatment. He sends her the letters he has received from Georgina, sends her Georgina's photograph, and has Georgina write to his mother. Her letter of June 25 sets him off: "Some day I shall make you sorry you wrote me that letter." Eventually Mrs. Childs releases her grip, and the couple is able to enter into matrimony with the full blessing of the groom's mother.

On Sunday, August 13, 1922, at 2:00 P.M., Rives and Georgina were wed at St. Isaac's Cathedral in Petrograd. The service was performed in the Russian Orthodox ritual, with minor alterations because Childs was not of that faith. Farmer Murphy left behind an irreverent description of the ceremony, at which the priest read from "epistles of the Apostle Paul wherein he gives instructions to wives and enjoins them to fear their husbands. The Apostle Paul never married."[10]

Forty-two years later, fellow ARA man John Boyd stood by Childs's side in Nice when Georgina was laid to rest there. Childs would outlive her by twenty years.

It turned out otherwise for Bill Casey, whose marital fortunes were not as predicted. He died in Utica at thirty years of age. His widow explained that his nervous system had been impaired during his service in France. She and her ten-year-old son turned to the ARA in New York City for help. She was broke and unable to understand or speak English, and it was December 1929.

CHAPTER 20

DENOUEMENT

On February 21, 1923, a former Russian employee of the ARA living in Kharkov, who signed his name M. Stepanoff, was composing a letter to send to a relief worker in Moscow when he received "a dredfull news": in Kazan, Nina Niliubin, a young woman known to both men, had taken her own life. More shocking still, she had "shot herself in the room of an American."[1]

Suicide seemed to be epidemic in Soviet Russia in the early 1920s. No class of people was exempt. Peasants took their own lives rather than face the excruciating final days or weeks of death by starvation. The relief workers would wonder, contemplating a pile of corpses, how many of the deceased had themselves put a stop to their suffering—and perhaps that of loved ones as well. Stories went around about starving people lying down among typhus victims in order to become infected and thereby speed their exit. In other cases, entire families secured themselves inside their homes, having sealed all exits with clay, and set fire to the structures. Dr. Vasilevskii sees in such behavior "many elements of psychosis, very probably, even collective, massive psychosis."

The dispossessed classes, broken though generally not starving, also lost their share to suicide—"former people" becoming so in the literal sense. One ARA Russian employee in Odessa stated that there were "numerous" such incidents, "not only due to privation, but to hopelessness and deep moral depression caused by utter isolation." Here the evidence is more tangible, for the identities of individual victims were usually known to a larger circle of people.

Another kind of suicide that left its mark on Soviet Russia in the early 1920s was that of the young Bolshevik true believer psychologically devastated by the sudden retreat from War Communism. Whatever the extent of this phenomenon, the wide currency given this image of the death of youthful idealism says a great deal about the spiritual crisis of Bolshevism in 1921.

Childs records in his diary the case of a young, enthusiastic Communist in Kazan whose "room was adjoining that of a friend of mine, one of the employees in our office, and she said she heard the shot fired by him from a revolver and then the scream of his mother." The deceased was said to have been "in despair over the difficulties confronting the forward movement of communism which, in this moment, had been forced to make a retreat. So he blew his brains out from being disillusioned over an idea." The romance in this clearly appeals to the romantic in Childs.[2]

When Phil Sheild disappeared in Simbirsk in October 1922, it seemed at first that the ARA might have a case of suicide on its hands. In the aftermath, in the absence of conclusive proof, the chiefs attempted to suppress the relevant circumstantial evidence by deleting information from ARA reports, even some of those labeled "confidential." Apparently, the main concern was to put the foreign correspondents off the scent. And no wonder: the Americans in Simbirsk suspected suicide from the first, citing Sheild's troubled state of mind—due in no small part, it was said, to his affair with a married woman.

In District Supervisor Joe Dalton's first memorandum to Haskell concerning the disappearance, written on October 17, he describes Sheild as "a man who keeps his own counsel." He is "high tempered, although, except on rare occasions, has always been able to control that temper. Those who know him best say that he is subject to periods of depression, contrasted by periods of cheerfulness." Sheild's father was known to be dying of cancer—he would succumb within a few weeks—which distressed young Sheild, as did the discovery of the sugar thefts at the warehouse, although he was in no way responsible.

Dalton was new to Simbirsk and had to rely for such detail on his ARA colleagues, among them Dr. Mark Godfrey. Writing to the head of the medical division in Moscow, Dr. Beeuwkes, Godfrey stated that Sheild "has always been a little eccentric and is said to have had marked melancholy periods." Godfrey declared himself "inclined to think that he has committed suicide by jumping into the river, as it is reported that he has been rather despondent at times for several days. Confidentially I think he has had a love affair of some sort."

None of this would remain confidential for long, however. Godfrey's letter somehow ended up in the hands of Duranty in Moscow, who quoted it at length in a dispatch on the case, and the suicide theory made headlines in the *New York Times*. It was a real scoop, and Godfrey's reconstruction of Sheild's final hours packed a melodramatic punch: "On Saturday he told a girl friend that he wished to tell her 'Good-bye' as he was tired of this place. On questioning by the girl she states that he said to her 'I wish I had never been born, every body hates me.'" This was good, but Duranty must have felt it needed a little touching up. He reproduces Sheild's last words as: "I want to say good-bye to you. You won't see me again in Simbirsk. Every one hates me here and I am sick of the whole business."

On the other hand, this same *Times* story quotes Sheild's "buddy" in Simbirsk, James Somerville, who had written to someone in Moscow describing the missing American as a "quiet, sober-minded sort of chap. But not sufficiently different from the average run of our fellows for them to think him queer."

Duranty was also allowed to read Dalton's "confidential" October 17 memorandum to Haskell, which enabled him to report that after canvassing the men in Simbirsk as to Sheild's behavior—"drinking, night-life, women, etc."—Dalton had determined that "his habits, whereas not those of a prude, was not such as to lead anyone to believe that he had been a debauch. In fact, no one could recall Shield ever having spent a night out of his own quarters." This was enough for Duranty, too, who wrote, "This proves pretty conclusively he was not deeply involved in any love affair." Duranty attributed the speculation about suicide to an attempt to blacken the memory of Sheild, though it is unclear whom he could have had in mind. In a story filed on October 29, after he had accompanied Haskell on his brief investigative visit to Simbirsk, he affirmed that "Shield was in no way involved in a discreditable liaison."

It is possible that Duranty was simply hewing to the ARA's line. In any case, it is almost certain that he was given access to only the expurgated versions of Dalton's reports. The originals tell a more complicated story and not just about Sheild's private life.

In his October 17 report, Dalton discloses that his initial investigation reached into the darker side of town:

Having exhausted all possibilities among his friends whose characters are known to be good, I obtained the addresses of the usual several resorts in a town of this size, thinking that he had, perhaps, taken "a night off." These places were all visited quietly by one of us Americans, but nowhere could we find a trace of him, although we did find that he had, on rare occasions, visited certain of these places.

In fact, Dalton initially hesitated even to bring the matter to the attention of the Soviet authorities for fear that the explanation for Sheild's absence would bring "notoriety" upon the ARA. When he did notify the government plenipotentiary, this man had the same hunch. He was, Dalton reports, "inclined to believe that Shield had merely taken a 'flyer' and would turn up before dark."

Further along in this same memorandum Dalton reveals that Sheild had at one time been involved with a local woman, perhaps two:

A thorough search of his personal effects reveals nothing which would indicate that he contemplated suicide, although we have found out from one woman here with whom he is known to have been more or less intimate some months ago that Shield recently told her he was very much discouraged on account of the illness of his father and his (Shield's) work, and that unless he got out of Russia pretty soon, he would "throw up the sponge." He also told the same woman that he had been drinking very heavily, although we have seen no indications of this. . . . As to this conversation, we are rather inclined to think that Shield wished to break off certain relations which he had previously had with this woman. The woman insists that she has seen nothing of Shield, except in a casual way, for nearly two months.

Sheild's disappearance, Dalton concludes, "will eventually be traced to his connection with one of two women here."

Two days later Dalton speculates on three possibilities. First, Sheild may have "left Simbirsk voluntarily, either for the outside world, or without any definite destination in view"—this, the result of "extreme depression, or possible mental derangement resulting from worry over the warehouse thefts, or over some woman, or both." One piece of evidence in support of this theory was Sheild's remark to a fellow relief worker on the day before his disappearance: "How would you like to take charge of Supply[?] I may be leaving Simbirsk." Furthermore, the local wharf authorities reported that an American had telephoned on Saturday afternoon requesting that a cabin be reserved for him on the next boat "going up-stream." If he had in fact departed Simbirsk, he did so with only the clothes on his back.

A second possibility is that Sheild was assaulted either in a spontaneous "brawl" or in a premeditated attack. If foul play was involved, it might be related to the warehouse thefts, though here Dalton expresses strong doubt the thieves would have waylaid Sheild in order to avoid detection, "as the method of investigation, so far as I have seen it in Russia, would not cause any guilty parties to be very apprehensive."

Or Sheild may have met a violent end as a result of "his attentions to some woman": a man had come forward to say that he had seen Sheild with an unidentified Russian female the night of his disappearance, as late as midnight, at a theater.

The third possibility is that Sheild committed suicide, again, because of matters weighing on his mind, which may have included the fact that he "anticipated complications resulting from intimacy with some woman." Dalton then offers this clarification:

He is known to have been on very intimate terms with one Russian woman here, whose husband suddenly returned last spring after an absence of five years or more. Whether the attentions that Shield had paid to this woman was the cause, or whether there were other reasons—at any rate, this woman has had absolutely nothing to do with her husband, according to our best information, since his return.

This would seem to preempt that line of inquiry, but Dalton is not finished: "The husband . . . at present lives in the same house with the wife, and naturally has shown [*sic*], and apparently has not objected to the frequent visits made by Shield." About six weeks before his disappearance, Sheild had stopped seeing the woman, although he visited her on the afternoon before his disappearance, at which time he is alleged to have made his desperate statements. Although alone in his opinion, Dalton believed it was entirely possible that the husband, "being denied his legal rights and privileges, and goaded by seeing someone else constantly in his house, has taken, or instigated criminal recourse."

All things considered though, the Simbirsk Americans believed that Sheild had taken his own life and suspected that it was his relationship with his married lover that had pushed him over the edge. Elaborating on this theory, Dalton gingerly enters the perilous realm of psychology: "Shield is a University of Virginia man, and a native of that State; and we are all agreed that he held woman, as such, in very high regard. I do not believe that he had 'fooled around' to any appreciable extent before he came to Russia." Words to warm the heart of every UVA coed's parents, but Dalton is trying to establish a motive for suicide:

His affair with this married woman had caused him a great deal of worry, and he had made himself believe that he was responsible for the breaking up of her home. According to the statements of this woman, and also from an undelivered letter which she wrote to him prior to his disappearance, and which we found, it appears that she had repeatedly tried to show him that her estrangement from her husband was not caused by Shield. Nevertheless, the woman was, and, we believe, still is in love with Shield. Also, it is known that Shield was practically in love with her. In fact, we can find no record of his promiscuous running around prior to the time he broke off relations with her.

What is more, there were among Sheild's effects "many poems which he had copied, all of which were in a more or less despondent strain." There was also an old diary, which recorded some of his thoughts in France during the war and later in Richmond; these showed "a very decided tendency toward mental dejection and depressed sentimentality." Dalton reproduced for Haskell some jottings Sheild had made on a scrap of paper:

Out with house
  God (or "gov," meaning Government)
  Office
  Town
Past Irrevocable
Advice not followed

Good friends
Doc ——
weakness
Good friends
Now must leave Simbirsk
I will give you up, you call me selfish. You must say:
  I will give you up.

Dalton then provides an explication de texte.

The "Doc" mentioned above is Godfrey, with whom, it turns out, Sheild had become "intensely angry" over a remark the doctor had made concerning the above-mentioned woman. Later Sheild patched things up with his colleague, but "it is believed he never quite recovered from this prejudice."

As for "Out with God," if this should actually read "Out with gov," it refers merely to the fact that Sheild was unpopular with government officials, probably because he refused to allow certain Soviet officials to use ARA automobiles when he was in charge of transportation. If Sheild really wrote "Out with God," however, "we know nothing about it, of course."

As for "Out with Office," "We can find no ground for the remark." "Out with Town" probably refers to a period of local criticism of the ARA in the wake of a "party." "We assume that in 'past irrevocable', he refers to his 'past' in general and in particular to his relations with this married woman."

Had Duranty been privy to such unfiltered testimony, he would undoubtedly have made the most of it in his 1935 memoir, *I Write As I Please*, where instead he offered up this choice bit of fantasy:

Shields' personal secretary, a haggard dark girl in her early thirties, was convinced that it was a *crime passionnel* and hinted darkly of an affair between the lost boy and the blonde wife of the head of the Simbirsk Gay-pay-oo [GPU], a man of notoriously jealous habits. For this hypothesis there was no confirmation beyond the fact that Shields and the lady in question had danced together at one of the A.R.A. parties and that the husband had remarked audibly that Communist women should be ashamed to dance *bourgeois* foxtrots.

The ARA chiefs in Moscow were persuaded by Dalton's evidence. On October 28 they cabled New York: "Though not convinced feel inclined suicide."

As it happened, after the detectives from Moscow descended on Simbirsk and got down to work, and after other murders and attacks and disappearances in the area were reported, and the tan oxfords were spotted, and Sheild's hat was found, and arrests and indictments were made, there were enough unanswered questions to sustain a credible theory of murder in connection with the warehouse thefts, which suited the purposes of the ARA.

After the death of Sheild's father in December, the ARA was concerned to reverse the damage done by the *Times* and protect his widow from further talk about her late son's mental health and amorous liaisons in Russia. The New York office wired Barringer, Sheild's close and lifelong friend, who had been transferred to Simbirsk to take part in the investigation, that they had convinced the family that Sheild had "died in the line of duty. . . . There has been no intimation connection entanglement and suicide theory has never been hinted at to family."

Barringer was informed that as a precaution, his letters to Mrs. Sheild were being held up in New York, and as it would be "criminal" to trouble her with the speculations about her son's love and death, he was asked to write the family along the lines of the official story. Barringer played along, though he firmly believed that his fellow Virginian was a suicide: "A study of his personal effects clearly indicates such a move was premeditated."[3]

ONCE THE AMERICANS in Simbirsk realized that Sheild's absence was indeed a serious matter, they contacted ARA Kazan headquarters on the open wire in order to talk to Pat Murray. On the day of Sheild's disappearance Murray was in Simbirsk, making a brief stopover on a river journey from Samara to Kazan, his new post. It seems obvious that Murray should have been immediately presumed to be the mysterious American who had telephoned the wharf to book passage on a boat going upriver, but evidently something about the particular circumstances of the call excluded this possibility. Anyway, Murray had been accompanied to the wharf by Sheild, and the Simbirsk Americans wondered if he might not recall any noteworthy statements or behavior on the part of the lost Virginian in the hours before he vanished.

Murray himself was to make news while in Russia, though not the kind that was fit to print. Originally from Brooklyn, Columba Murray was working at the U.S. consulate in Kovno when he signed on to the ARA, accompanying Carroll's advance party into Russia in August 1921. He served in Moscow, originally as a stenographer, before being transferred in the summer of 1922 to the Crimea, and from there to Kiev, and then in the autumn to Kazan. It is difficult to determine what kind of impression Murray made on his superiors and colleagues at Spiridonovka 30. Quinn described his work as "on the whole . . . satisfactory," a statement that may be taken at face value. The ARA alumni newsletter's ironical "Non-Statistical Notes of the A.R.A." honored him by citing "The heavy executive responsibilities of Columba P. Murray"—which seems to imply that the twenty-three-year-old stenographer had a rather inflated opinion of himself.

The picture becomes clearer after his move to Kazan, but only because it was there that he was struck by tragedy. Childs, who must be considered a hostile witness, would later recall that the arrival of Murray—that "brash, egocentric young man to whom we all took instant dislike"—destroyed the special chemistry at district headquarters. According to Childs, Murray was married to an American living in Europe and awaiting his return. Yet soon after taking up his duties in Kazan, he entered into—or continued, it is unclear—a relationship with twenty-year-old Nina Gavrilovna Nikitina, an attractive blonde who at one time had managed an ARA kitchen and seems to have remained a favorite, in a most innocent sense, of the Kazan Americans.

To what extent Murray bears responsibility for the unhappy turn of events is a matter of conjecture. What is beyond doubt is that on the evening of January 28, 1923, Nina Nikitina committed suicide in Murray's room at the Kazan personnel house; that she blew her head off, as they say, with Murray's pistol; and that subsequently Murray was on a train heading toward Moscow, having become the latest ARA victim of a "nervous breakdown."

The details of the story are impossible to establish with any certainty because of the existence of several conflicting versions of what transpired. Childs himself left behind three separate accounts, which together might have qualified as a kind of mono-Rashomon-style investigation of the episode were it not for the fact that Childs was no longer in Russia at the time it occurred. He learned about it only after the ARA mission from his Kazan colleagues.

Childs's first description appeared in an anonymously authored, docu-fictional 1932 memoir, *Before the Curtain Falls*. Here Nina is the golden-haired Hilda while a nameless Murray is cast as the "insignificant, irreverent individual with no respect for others." Not only does he seduce Hilda but "vaunts his conquest," treating her as a mere "instrument for his sexual gratification." In this version, when the vulgar American returns from an inspection trip, a depressed Hilda uses his revolver to kill herself.

In Childs's undated manuscript "Thirty Years in the Near East," written probably in the 1950s, Nina is called "Veronica." She is a "lovely unspoiled child" of "barely eighteen," strikingly beautiful with the wavy blonde hair of a Viking and embraced as a sister by all the Kazan Americans. Enter the villain, again unnamed. Veronica meets him and "of course she fell in love with him. There is never any accounting for a woman's taste." She becomes pregnant, and his indifference to this circumstance makes her distraught. One day he returns from an inspection trip, and Veronica, following him into his room, pleads with him only to be brushed aside as he walks into the bathroom. She grabs his revolver and shoots herself in the temple.

Childs's 1969 memoir, *Foreign Service Farewell*, altered the script somewhat. Here after Murray, again unidentified, seduces Veronica, the Kazan Americans are so outraged that they have him recalled to Moscow. But too late, for "the damage had been done; she was unable to forget him." One day Nina turns to John Boyd and says, "John, you must never forget me." In walks Van Arsdale Turner from an inspection trip and makes his way into the bathroom for a shave. Nina takes his unholstered gun and puts a bullet in her brain.

It is not clear what inspired Childs to produce this last account, which is, as he must at one time have understood, the furthest from the truth. His earlier, 1950s' effort to reconstruct the episode had been motivated, he says, by the need to rebut the version put out in the 1930s by Duranty in *I Write As I Please*, which he called "a miserable travesty of the facts." Indeed, if Childs's premature departure from the scene left him room to invent—and reinvent—particular details of the story, Duranty's remove five hundred miles away in Moscow and his mere passing acquaintance with the principals in the tragedy left him free to write pretty much as he pleased.

Duranty even inserts himself into the drama's first act. When the curtain rises, "Nina Nikolaevna" has journeyed to Moscow—from where it is not clear—in search of Murray, here given the name "Joe Parrott." Apparently Nina had met

Parrott on a previous visit to Moscow. Her search has led her to Duranty's apartment, which Parrott had rented in the spring while the reporter was out of the country. Duranty is clearly quite taken with this young innocent: "She had the combination of sweetness and dumbness and youth which appeals to men like me, who earn their bread with their brains and are glad of relaxation."

Duranty informs Nina that Parrott has been transferred to the Crimea. The girl is plainly obsessed, in the manner of one of Fleming's "Butterflies." "She used to drop in quite often to see me and sat curled up in a big chair eating candy and babbling about Mister Parrott, as she always called him, and how marvelous he was." They subsequently learn that Parrott has been reassigned to Kazan. Much to his later regret, he suggests to Nina that she move in with her relatives in Kazan and get a job there with the ARA—and so off she went. "She was fantastically jealous in a morbid Russian way," Duranty observed of her attachment to Parrott. "Russians are like that; they are either what seems to us shockingly casual and promiscuous about sex or so intensely devoted to a single person as to be an infernal nuisance."

Act Two begins in Kazan with Nina in a jealous rage after discovering that Parrott has acquired a lover while serving in the Crimea. Now, Duranty submits, if Parrott had "only ended up by smacking her, everything would have been all right." Instead, he devises a little scheme in order to tease her. He composes a phony telegram of affection to his Crimean belle and leaves a carbon for Nina to find. When she does, she is driven to desperation and in Parrott's absence shoots herself with his revolver in his room. He arrives home from work and in the darkness stumbles over the body. Duranty reports that Nina "had made a thorough job of it, blew the back of her head right off; the floor was flooded with blood and mush of brains." The body was very cold, he assures his readers, so Parrott was beyond suspicion.

Up to this point all versions are at least in agreement that Nina has shot herself in the head and lies dead on the floor of the ARA personnel house. What happens next reads like cheap fiction no matter whose account of events one chooses to believe.

In Duranty's telling, District Supervisor John Boyd executes a clever act of deception. He and another ARA man collect Nina together as best they can, put on her hat and coat, and escort her out the front door to the ARA car. It is all made to look as though the young lady has merely had far too much to drink. She is driven to her uncle's house, where her relatives, working in cahoots with the Americans, call the police to report that Nina has committed suicide at their home. Thus is the ARA saved from scandal.

All of this could be written off to Duranty's fertile imagination if not for the fact that two of Childs's three versions—one published before Duranty's—are so similar. In "Thirty Years in the Near East," Boyd, the "calm, phlegmatic Mississippian," hears the fatal shot and finds Nina dead on the floor, alone. "Get me a car and chauffeur," he orders, "and someone come help me." Boyd and another American walk the corpse out to the ARA car and transport it to the home of Nina's parents, not her uncle. From there, Boyd approaches the local authorities, explains the entire incident, and asks that it not be divulged to the local press, which assurance he receives. Again, an ARA scandal is avoided.

Childs brought the scene to vivid life in his earlier, novelistic *Before the Curtain Falls*, where he took the liberty of giving himself a lead role in the drama, assisting Boyd and Turner—here called Baird and Prescott—in carrying out their ruse.

John Baird and I lifted her up as tenderly as we would have lifted a living child, this late comrade of ours, with the same reverent touch we had always used with her when she was alive and we had skated hand-in-hand together. And we washed her shattered bloody face and adjusted the old tam-o'-shanter over her head to conceal the bullet's ravages and pulled her coat collar about her neck and head and walked with her between us slowly out of the house and past the Soviet guard by the door outside while Prescott brought a motor-car from the garage and helped us seat her within.

They arrive at the home of Nina's father, who "received the news calmly, as far as outward appearance went, with only a slight, almost imperceptible sagging of the head and shoulders." Childs then directs his wrath at the villain in the piece: "Although we would have all desired to deliver her betrayer to the Cheka, which would have meted out to him the punishment decreed by Russian law for seduction, we contented ourselves with giving him twenty-four hours to leave Kazan."

Duranty and Childs, though their respective narrations of events may seem improbable, never venture into the realm of the absurd. This cannot be said of Boyd, the man on the spot, who provides the most bizarre account of the postmortem proceedings in a report written for Moscow headquarters on the day after the events which sounds like something out of Ionesco.

As Boyd tells it, at seven in the evening on the day in question he was in his room getting ready for an evening at the theater when in rushed Murray in a panic to say that a "lady with whom he had gone out three or four times had shot herself, with a small calibre (25) revolver." No doubt Murray said something less cluttered, but Boyd was aiming for concision. He immediately went in to inspect and found Nina being examined by Dr. Cox, who determined that she had no chance to live.

Although the "calm, phlegmatic Mississippian" appears indeed to have kept his head throughout, he must have been shaken by the sight before him and apprehensive of the trouble it might cause the ARA. Boyd states that he went straight to the authorities to report the incident. Strangely, he could not seem to find an official who shared his opinion of the gravity of the matter. What, they wondered, was the big deal? "Naturally I was quite excited and after explaining the matter to . . . them they stated not to take the matter so seriously as such things happened five or six a day and Mr. Sabiroff (President of the Tartar Republic) informed me that a woman shot herself with his revolver in his room less than a year ago." When it came to phlegm, Boyd was no match for these hard-bitten Russians.

Sabiroff contacted the local Cheka chief and assured Boyd that the matter would be kept "absolutely quiet, not even a notice would appear in the paper." The Cheka man brought three of his agents and a doctor to the personnel house, where after an "investigation lasting approximately five minutes," they emerged with a suicide note they had found on a table in the room. Its simple text was something on the order of, "Forgive me, I am tired of life. Nina."

Boyd and Murray then gave statements to the authorities. Under questioning,

Murray revealed that he had first met Nina at a concert at the Palace of Red Army Soldiers about four weeks earlier; that she had been tutoring him in the Russian language; that his revolver had gone missing four days earlier and that Nina, when confronted, admitted to having taken it and promised yet failed to return it; that three days prior to shooting herself, she had asked Murray to procure for her five grams of cocaine, which he refused to do; and that in making this request she stated two or three times, through laughter, that there was nothing to live for.

At this point, close to midnight, Nina's father was sent for. He received the news with no visible emotion, identified the body, and confirmed that the handwriting of the note was his daughter's. The policeman declared that Nina had been a "fool" of a girl and after writing up a few protocols, closed the investigation.

The father, a forty-two-year-old schoolteacher, told Boyd that he tried to give his nine children "the best in life that was possible on his scanty means of 400 million per month"—rubles, that is—but without apparent success: "an older daughter also committed suicide several months ago on account of economic conditions." He described Nina as being "of a very nervous temperament and that several times she had threatened to end all as she was tired of living." Her condition seemed to become worse after a bout with typhus in 1921. According to Boyd, this stoical man then turned to him and delivered these lines of apology: "Oh how sorry I am that you have been inconvenienced in this manner but please remember that we hold absolutely nothing against you and that you will always remain in our eyes the same as before, one of those Samaritans that came to give help to Russia."

He said he could not afford to bury his daughter, so Boyd handed him a billion rubles and offered to help out in the future, realizing of course "what a burden nine children were when a person's salary was only four hundred million per month."

Nina's body was then transported home—horizontally, it would seem. On the day after the suicide a letter signed by Nina's mother was delivered to ARA headquarters. It was then translated into English, though poorly because Boyd felt compelled to assign the task to his most trustworthy interpreter, whose skills were distinctly limited:

HIGHLY ESTIMABLE FRIENDS OF RUSSIAN PEOPLE:

A great sorrow has come once more on our parents heads. There is no more our dear gay Nina. Grief not one could stand even Nina who had good judgment on everything. It brought her down through she strugled against it; tried to forget but could not stand it. In the morning when wasing her body they have found Mr. Hillman's picture on her breast. I also knew how deeply her heart was wounded by him. I have my best to concole her but failed. If you are going to write to him let him know about our great loss. She has been a good daughter and had a wonderfully tender heart.

Mother of the dead T. Nikitina

Hillman is Arthur Hillman, a YMCA man who had been transferred from Kazan to Moscow several months earlier. His sole appearance in the documentation here, as a photographic image on Nina's breast, is completely unexpected. Perhaps it is merely another exercise in deception, the parent's pathetic contribution to the exoneration of Murray. But if Nina's suicide was the result of a broken heart, as her mother maintained and as Childs and Duranty assumed, and if Hillman had indeed done the honors, it turns out that Murray is the wrong man.

Boyd must have decided that this text needed touching up for the Moscow chiefs. He reports having received a letter signed by both parents addressed "To the American Saviour of the Russian People," whose text he quotes as follows: "It is with regret that I announce to you the death of my daughter Nina last night caused by heart failure. The funeral will take place today etc. We found on her body next to her heart the picture of Mr. Hillman, will you please write him that she loved Mr. Hillman very much. Signed _____"

The reference to Hillman passes without comment, but of course here it hardly matters because heart failure has replaced heartbreak as the cause of death.

Boyd informed Moscow that Murray was "in a very high state of nervousness" and that Dr. Cox had advised that it was "absolutely necessary that he leave at once." Only days before the tragic episode, Boyd claimed, Murray had visited a local doctor who informed him that he was, as Boyd puts it, "in a very nervous state" and who recommended that he leave Kazan as soon as possible. Murray passed the night after the suicide "under an awful strain mumbling and singing and acting in a very peculiar manner" and had since had to be kept under constant supervision. Moreover, he was "very much inclined to talk" about what had happened. Boyd's point was clear: he wanted Murray out of Kazan "for good." Without waiting for instructions, on the following day he put the shattered American on a train to Moscow in the company of an ARA escort.[4]

His stay in the capital was by necessity brief. The "Russian Unit Record" reported without elaboration that Murray had arrived in town "suffering a nervous breakdown," which by then was an old story, indeed: he might just as well have required the services of a good dentist. An internal ARA memorandum confirms that the Kazan business had "rather broke him up both physically and mentally." For some reason, Murray exited Soviet Russia through the south, departing Odessa for Constantinople. Within a few weeks he was threatening to return to Russia, which prompted an urgent cable from Moscow to London insisting, "we do not want him back." He showed up at Spiridonovka 30 anyway, where Quinn pronounced him "temperamentally unfit for further service in Russia. . . . He was the central figure in what might have developed into a scandal most unfortunate for the A.R.A. and we are not sure his remaining in Russia might not precipitate another."

Eventually Murray was convinced to go quietly. The ARA went out of its way to effect a peaceful separation, accepting his resignation "owing to your need of a well-earned rest."[5]

On January 29 a modest funeral, without a church ceremony, was held for Nina Nikitina in Kazan. At the service several ARA employees expressed their understanding that the cause of death was heart failure, proof of "how completely everything was covered up by both the government and the parents of the girl," Boyd assured Moscow. Fortunately for the Americans, when the incident took place, their Russian employees had already gone home for the day, and so none of them, it was believed, learned what had really happened. Boyd credited the authorities and the Kazan ARA's "high relations" with them for the fact that, as he states, fewer than ten people in the whole city of Kazan knew of the "terrible affair." The matter was said to have been "squashed completely here."

Maybe so, but two weeks later a Russian living in Kharkov would learn from someone in Kazan the "dredfull news" that Nina Niliubin—a fitting misnomer that might be rendered in English as "Unloved"—had "shot herself in the room of an American."

On February 9 Boyd confidently declared, "The matter is history and no one even speaks of her death now."[6] Thus did the curtain fall on another drama-within-a-drama in the Russian theater of action.

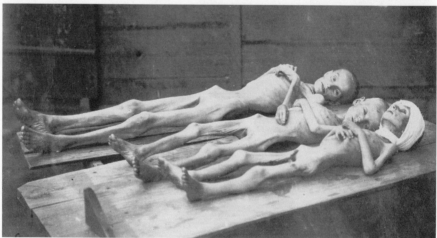

Top: At the Odessa cemetery.
Left to right: Randolph Clement and Harry Harris of the ARA, and Commander H. L. Pence and an unidentified officer of the U.S.S. *MacFarland*.

Bottom: At the Ufa morgue.

Left: Harold Blandy.

Below: Removal of corpses from a children's home, Tsaritsyn.

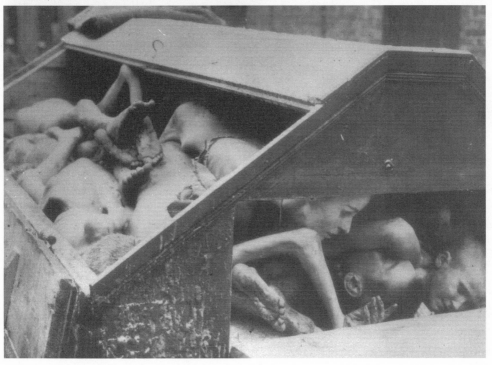

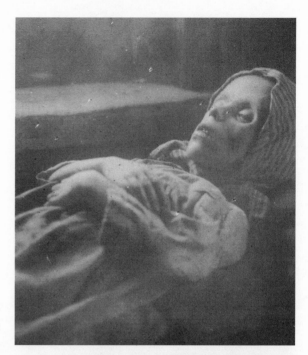

Right: Awaiting death.

Below: At a children's home
on the Volga.

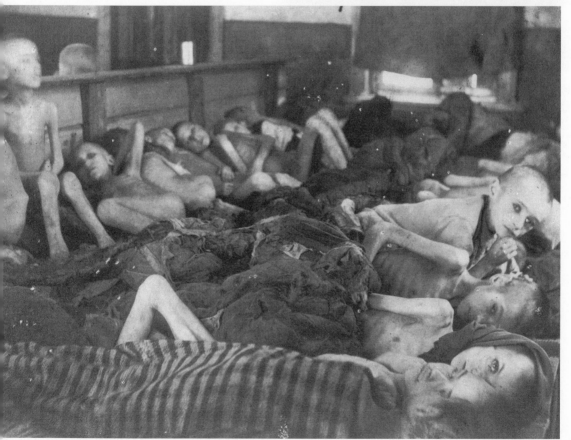

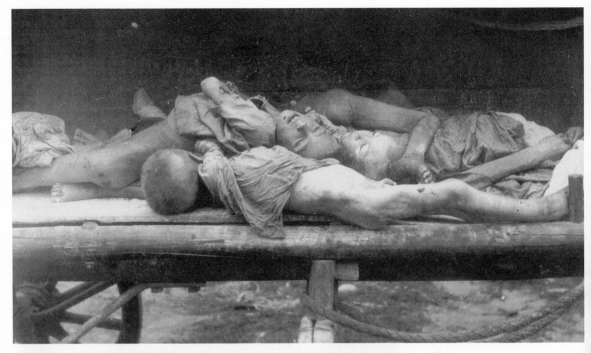

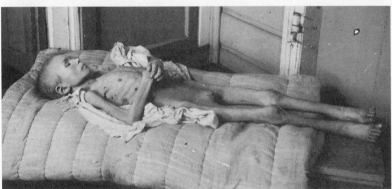

Top: Children's corpses removed
from an orphanage.

Bottom: Famine victim, Tsaritsyn.

Top: Harold Fleming.

Below: Blandy, *standing third from left*, among
abandoned children in Sterlitamak;
Gorin stands to his left.

Left: Coffin of Harold Blandy.

Below: Funeral of Harold Blandy, Moscow, May 1922.

Above: Elmer Burland, *second from right, arms akimbo*, looks on as an ARA private sleeper car is outfitted with signs that read "American Relief Administration, Russian Unit." Courtesy of the family of Elmer G. Burland.

Right: Philip Sheild, Simbirsk, 1922.

Left: John Foy behind the wheel of his flivver.

Below: Samara, 1922. *Seated, left to right*: Frederick Foucar (in fur hood), Oscar Anderson, Will Shafroth, and Gov. Goodrich.

Right and below:
Corpse-eaters and
the remains of
their victims.

PART THREE

SAY IT AIN'T SO, COMRADE

American Adventures in the Communist Utopia

Just before I came into Russia in September I had the pleasure of rereading, after many years, Alice's Adventures in Wonderland; and throughout my experiences of the last six months in this topsy-turvy land, I have had the constant feeling that I have been accompanying Alice in her bizarre adventures. Nothing happens as one feels it should in a normal world. Things start in one direction but are suddenly discovered to be moving in quite another; you sit down at a tea table and wake up to find that you are being crammed into the teapot with the dormouse; you ring a bell for a servant and the piano begins to turn somersaults.

—Lincoln Hutchinson, Moscow, March 1922

One of the boys says this is a trick country; the men wear their shirts outside their trousers, and they write a P for an R; but it really is a rather strange place; they call each other "Tovarish" and secretly suspect each other of being either members of the "Cheka" or counter-revolutionaries.

—Harold Fleming, Moscow, June 1922

CHAPTER 21

RED DAYS IN RUSSIA

On March 4, 1921, ill and exhausted, Woodrow Wilson stood down as president of the United States. His vision of a new international order, embodied in the League of Nations, had been rejected by the citizens of his own country, and he left the White House a man broken in body and spirit.

On that day, one of the most idealistic presidents in U.S. history gave way to that quintessential product of American machine politics, Warren G. Harding. Wilson was too ill to attend the inaugural and so after a brief ceremony at the Capitol the ex-President and Mrs. Wilson were driven to their new home on S Street in northwest Washington, where a crowd of well-wishers had gathered outside. Inside, the Wilsons greeted friends and supporters; among the first in the receiving line were the half-dozen White House correspondents. When it came the turn of the Associated Press reporter, Wilson said to him, "Childs, I've writ you a line."

To James Rives Childs this was a tragic day in American history. Woodrow Wilson, "my great leader," had been forsaken by his own countrymen.

Childs had witnessed the carnage of the world war in 1915 as a volunteer with the American Ambulance Field Service in France. He had thrilled at Wilson's challenge to the governments of the world to bring moral principles to bear on international politics, his vision of a single code of ethics for nations and men, and his call for American self-sacrifice and service to mankind.

It had seemed to Childs that Wilson's ideals were beginning to take root among the nations of Europe. He was present in Paris in December 1918 when the American president rode in a triumphal procession down the Champs-Elysées to the "thunderous cries of men and women alike in welcoming him; most of them were weeping uncontrollably, overcome by emotion, in one of the greatest displays of reverence I had ever witnessed." Childs says he had to slip away from the delirious crowd in order to get a grip on himself.

But back home the initial enthusiasm of the American people for Wilsonian idealism fast evaporated: "Wilson had conducted them to the mountain tops," Childs recalled nearly half a century later, "but what they were longing for was a more tranquil existence in the valley."

As he observed the final act of Wilson's political destruction, he was deeply bitter. On March 3 he wrote to his mother in Richmond: "Tonight on the eve of his leavetaking of the White House I am very sad as I think his going a great tragedy for the American people. A ponderous piece of flesh known as Harding takes his place, that is to say he succeeds to his office for there is no one to take his place nor will there be for many a long year to come."

Childs saw Wilson as a Christ figure who had attempted to apply "the great social principles of the Sermon on the Mount" to national and international institutions. But the American public that had once hailed him as a savior put him on the cross. "This is a sad and inglorious day for America for it was America who crucified Wilson."

A sad day for America, but for Childs, at least as he recounted it, it was not without its personal rewards. A few days earlier he had written Wilson a letter of appreciation, which included the standard journalist's request for an interview. Now in the receiving line on the second floor in the house on S Street, Wilson politely turned aside the proposal but thanked Childs for his missive. "The President appreciated your letter very much," added Mrs. Wilson. Joseph Tumulty, Wilson's secretary, told Childs that the President's reply was among the final four letters he had dictated during his last night in the White House.[1]

Six months later Childs was posted to Kazan on the Volga River, from which vantage point the March events in Washington, the final encounter with Wilson, all seemed to him like a dream, even a "dream within a dream." On a late September evening he attended a masquerade ball at the University of Kazan. He arrived to find the guests, most in some form of disguise, dancing to the music of a military band. He does not tell us how he was attired, but he does report that the costume that attracted the most attention was a caricature of the Entente powers.

Masquerades were popular in Soviet Russia in 1921 under the truce in the class war called NEP. After four years of masquerading as members of the lower classes in order to deflect hostile attention, former bourgeois and aristocrats could use these occasions to dress as in the old days—that is, if they had managed during the years of deprivation to hide away some prewar finery rather than sell it for bread. There was a frenzied activity of mazurkas and polkas as people seemed in a hurry to make up for lost time, to live again. Under the partial cover of a masquerade, life in Soviet Russia was beginning to return to something approaching normal.

As Childs paused to consider the moment, his eyes gazed up to the portraits on the wall above the festive dancers where the severe countenances of Lenin and other Soviet leaders seemed to look disapprovingly upon the merrymakers. He described his thoughts in his first letter to his mother, dated October 1:

I do not know that I have ever witnessed any scene which struck me as being so much of the nature of a dream as this; the varied uniforms of the red army, the quaint masquerade costumes, the incongruous apparel of most of the men and women, the red posters and portraits plastered about the walls to remind me of the singular form of government of the land in which I found myself and the music—which accentuated the imaginative impulses. I was in the heart of Russia, Red Russia. . . . It is a strange world and I doubt if there is a stranger spot in the many weird places of this old planet than Red Russia at present.[2]

Childs was in the heart of a country where most of the old ruling elite—the aging men he so despised for having sent hundreds of thousands of young men to their deaths in a world war and, in the United States, for leading the charge against the ideals of Wilson—were either in foreign exile or in hiding, or had been killed or otherwise repressed. The Revolution had put in their place a new breed of leader, many of whom were of humble origin and most of whom had had no prior administrative experience. Many had spent a considerable amount of time before the revolution in prison and exile and were far better trained in the art of conspiracy than that of government; a good number had risen to their present positions through service as military commissars during the Civil War, and some were genuine war heroes.

New decrees issued in Moscow ordering one or another radical reform were to many a hardened Communist official incomprehensible and, through summer and autumn, were frequently ignored or merely paid lip service. The moderating winds of NEP would take months to penetrate into the provinces and in fact would never succeed in penetrating the ideological armor of many die-hard Bolsheviks.

In September 1921 the suspicions of provincial Bolshevik officials toward this detour from the direct road to communism were heightened by the arrival in their respective domains of representatives of the foreign imperialist powers calling themselves famine relief workers.

Colonel Haskell, on his part, did not like what he saw. After his first tour through the famine zone he wired Hoover on October 20: "Central Government shrewd but provincial and local Soviets hopelessly inefficient and composed ignorant representatives proletariat."[3]

In fact the Americans assigned to the provinces—or "districts" as the ARA called its territorial subdivisions—were, with a few outstanding exceptions, appalled at the caliber of Soviet and Party officials, which fell far short of the standards they were used to in Central and Eastern Europe. They were struck above all by the lowly appearance and lack of education and experience of the Soviet representatives, who seemed eager to compensate for this with a surplus of arrogance. Many of the Americans would have agreed, at least initially, with the commanding officer of the U.S.S. *MacLeish*, who wrote after an August 1922 visit to the Black Sea port of Novorossisk that the "typical Soviet representative" was "without education, without much intelligence and with an exalted idea of his importance."[4]

Still, there were marked differences in the quality of the local leadership from district to district, and it soon became common knowledge among the Americans that the ARA Kazan district was in this respect exceptionally blessed. Just why this was so, it was generally assumed, had to do with an absence of Russians.

THE KAZAN REGION was populated largely by Tatars, a Turkic people who were descendants—just how directly is a subject of longstanding dispute—of Genghis Khan and the Tatars of the Golden Horde, who ruled over Russia for nearly 250 years, from the thirteenth to the fifteenth centuries. As the Mongol influence waned, the khanate of Kazan, one of the last successor states to the Golden Horde, fell to Russia and Ivan the Terrible in 1552. Thus did the Volga Tatars, who were Sunni Muslims, become the first Islamic subjects of Muscovy.

Over the centuries the Volga Tatars managed to resist the forces of Russification—either outright repression or more subtle economic and educational measures—and maintain a distinct cultural and religious identity. So successful were they that the temporary disintegration of the Russian empire in 1917 gave immediate rise to aspirations in Kazan for the formation of a large state encompassing all peoples of Turkic language and ethnic origin, in and out of Russia. Indeed, shortly after the October Revolution a national assembly of Russian and Siberian Muslims called for the establishment of just such an entity. A more modest proposal discussed at the same time, as a kind of minimum program, envisioned a state uniting the Volga Tatars and their Sunni Muslim brethren to the east, the Bashkirs, who had come under Russian rule soon after the Tatars, with whom they enjoyed close historical and cultural ties. The territory of this hypothetical political-administrative unit was to extend from Kazan south through the Middle Volga and east to the southern Urals.

The Bolsheviks came to power riding the waves of nationalism throughout the empire and at first cautiously and selectively encouraging them. They allowed the formation of Islamic government institutions in the various Muslim regions and even for a brief time an independent Muslim Communist Party. But they had no desire to see the establishment of a huge Islamic state in the heart of old Russia, and at the beginning of 1918 they began to intervene politically. They walked a cautious line, seeking to improve their reputation and appease local nationalisms with gestures of national autonomy yet keep the Russian empire from flying totally apart. Despite all the talk about freeing the oppressed nationalities from the Russian and other yokes, and for all the short-term political advantages it may have given the Party in taking and holding onto power, such rhetoric ran counter to the unmistakable Great Russian flavor of Russian Bolshevism. Moreover, as was soon to become apparent, the greatest of the Party's Great Russian chauvinists was the people's commissar of nationalities, the Georgian-born Joseph Stalin.

Yet as Lenin's government began to apply the brakes to local nationalisms in the spring of 1918, the Civil War was getting under way. In order not to create enemies, the Kremlin needed to accommodate national aspirations. In March 1918 it passed a decree proclaiming the formation of the Tatar-Bashkir Soviet Republic of the Russian Soviet Federation, which was apparently intended to be, or appear to be, a republic on an equal footing in federation with Russia. These plans were placed on hold several months later when the Tatar and Bashkir territories were occupied by the White Armies. This gave the Bolsheviks a necessary breathing space.

As the area was cleared of the White forces in spring 1919, the Kremlin engaged in a strategy of divide and rule, characteristic of its nationalities policy for the next seventy years. The idea was to create smaller and politically less powerful Muslim republics. A decree of March 1919 formed the Bashkir Autonomous Soviet Socialist Republic, or Bashkiria, which effectively doomed aspirations for a larger Turkic state. As an "autonomous" republic, Bashkiria was to be an administrative subdivision of the Russian republic, not a federative republic equal to it, and all Bashkir government bodies were to be subordinated to those in Moscow.

In May 1920 another Soviet decree created the Tatar Autonomous Soviet Socialist Republic, or Tatarstan, with the capital at Kazan. Bashkiria and Tatarstan were the largest of the autonomous republics, strategically separated by a strip of territory belonging to the Russian Republic. Tatarstan's total territory was 68,000 square kilometers as opposed to the 220,000 square kilometers of the prospective single Turkic state. Politics outweighed ethnic considerations in the geographical delineation of the Tatar republic. Only 1.5 million of the 4.2 million Tatars living in the Middle Volga area were included in Tatarstan, and Tatars represented only 51 percent of the population of the republic, about 39 percent being Russian. Moreover the new republic did not encompass the Ufa region, where the Tatars were in a majority. Meanwhile the Tatars were an ethnic majority in Bashkiria, where Bashkirs constituted 25 percent.

This arrangement led by design to a certain amount of tension between the Tatars and the culturally inferior Bashkirs, whom Moscow now encouraged to develop their own literary language. It also meant steady friction between Moscow and the "national communist" leaderships of the autonomous republics. The constitution forming the Union of Soviet Socialist Republics in 1922 technically gave equal representation and the right of secession to all union republics, such as Russia and Ukraine, and autonomous republics—although by then, with Soviet power unrivaled, no one took this right seriously. Rather the real gains were made in the area of national culture, which here and there was allowed to flourish under the selectively tolerant NEP regime.[5]

AS COMPLICATED AS this might seem on the printed page, it must have been especially perplexing to the newly-arrived American relief workers, who were barely coping with the strain of, among many other tasks, hiring local staffs, organizing food committees, establishing kitchens, and locating warehouse and office space and personnel quarters, all the while trying to answer the impatient telegraphic requests of the chiefs in Moscow for statistical information on the extent of the famine in their regions.

The ARA did not set up its administrative districts in Soviet Russia to correspond precisely to Soviet political-administrative units. The most important factors had to do with railroad and river networks and the locations of warehouses —everything else was subordinate to this. The ARA Kazan district did not comprise the Tatar Autonomous Republic although the latter made up the largest part of the district, whose population, like that of Tatarstan, was about one-half Tatar. It also included the adjacent Chuvash and Marinskii autonomous regions. Kazan was the northernmost Volga district, and for most of the first year of the mission it was the largest geographically: at its peak in summer 1922 it covered a territory of 81,550 square miles—about the size of New England, New York, and New Jersey combined.

The city of Kazan, situated at the confluence of the Volga and Kama Rivers, was a significant commercial center and the obvious location for local ARA headquarters. Kazan had a world-famous university, founded in 1804, among whose most renowned students were the mathematician Lobachevsky, Tolstoy, and Lenin, the latter two also the most famous to have been expelled. The city's population of between 150,000 and 200,000 was about one-third Tatar, most of whom were segregated in one neighborhood. The Tatars had managed to preserve the partial official use of their language and its Arabic script—though they were soon to give in to official Soviet pressure to adopt the Latin alphabet—and most public signs were written in both Tatar and Russian.

The ARA men formed a highly favorable opinion of these Tatars. Unlike the local Russians, most of whom were peasant descendants of the serfs who moved into the area after its absorption by Russia, the Tatars traditionally were traders and were typically the shopkeepers in the towns and villages. Childs found them to be a "naturally thrifty" people who before the Revolution had accumulated considerable wealth. He and his colleagues noted the higher percentage of literacy among the Tatars as compared to Kazan's Russians—a characteristic the Americans understandably found appealing.

The Tatar presence gave the district an exotic flavor. Tatar towns, where the local mullah commanded considerable authority, were distinguished by wooden mosques with minarets from which the muezzin called the faithful to prayer. The Americans were struck by the physical appearance of the Tatars: the "copper-colored" skin, the "Mongolian" cheek bones, dark black eyes and hair, and their eastern dress, notably the black skull cap.

At the initial ARA meeting with the leading officials of the Tatar republic—including "President" Rauf Sabirov and "Prime Minister" Keshaf Mukhtarov—Childs was especially taken by the appearance of Sabirov, whom he describes as "of an almost olive complexion and jet black hair and high cheek bones." These were features familiar to him from an American context: "Placed in the vicinity of an Indian reservation in America and one would have identified him as an Indian. Actually he was a Tartar, as were most of those composing the assembly." He would not have guessed this from their family names, which had been Russianized with an "-ov" suffix, according to custom. But physical appearance left no doubt. To his mother Childs wrote that Sabirov had "much the features of a semi-civilized Indian chief."

The American Indian connection had been made several weeks earlier by Hoover's special investigator Vernon Kellogg, a native of Kansas. Kellogg kept one of those handwritten diaries, which despite—or maybe because of—the fact that it is irregular, telegraphic, sometimes cryptic, and occasionally indecipherable, is treasured by the historian for its apparent spontaneity and authenticity, unlike more polished typewritten diaries such as the one Childs left behind. After the first of Kellogg's powwows with the local Tatar chiefs, he wrote in his notebook: "The conference in govt house and especially in the saloon car—Muchtarov, Validov and Sabirov—by dim light of candles—low soft voices—quiet—black hair—dark faces—B the checker—the interpreters and endless *cigarettes*—like a conference with N[orth] A[merican] Indians."

Although Sabirov was chairman of the council of people's commissars and therefore, as the Americans understood it, "president," they quickly discovered that he was not the real power in Kazan. Childs describes him as a "lumbering Newfoundland dog. He was painfully conscious of his inadequacies and never pretended to be other than the simple peasant he was." Mukhtarov, as chairman of the central executive committee of the soviet, had the real power and the physical presence to match. He was, wrote Childs, the "driving force" of the government in Kazan—"slim, dynamic, deeply earnest, utterly honest and entirely consecrated to the Revolution."

Kellogg's diary describes him as "young, slight, looking like a student—soft, white shirt open at neck band—white hands—intelligent—quick quiet—'He is speaking slowly but acting quickly.'" Of the local officials generally he writes that "passed on the street they would be anybody of the general population—except Muchtarov—who is quickly distinguished in Auto."

Childs found Mukhtarov's manner "very brisk and business-like"; he acted "with the assurance of a field marshal."

Keen piercing black eyes betrayed a strong resolute will which received confirmation in the direct and forceful manner in which he spoke and gave his orders. It was his youth which was of really the greatest interest for he could not have been more than thirty years of age; yet there was nothing lacking in his air of authority nor yet was there any assumption of arrogance in his demeanour. He was attired in a faded blue shirt and wore no cravat. During the course of the conference, which lasted approximately an hour, I do not believe that he gave utterance to one superfluous word. It was the more remarkable since the Russian seems to like nothing better than to talk endlessly about nothing.

This was the first of many unflattering comparisons drawn by ARA men between the "efficient" Tatars and the more deliberate Russians. The Americans stationed among the Tatars felt compelled to write about it as did the traveling inspectors and casual visitors to the region. Farmer Murphy visited Kazan in October with an ARA delegation from Moscow and immediately fell for Mukhtarov.

He received the party in a direct, simple, unaffected manner and said a few words of welcome which, in the courtesy of their form and content, would have done credit to any trained diplomat. In the matters which were discussed he was clear-headed and business-like. He made notes on a pad on his desk of the things that were to be done and there were no words wasted in elaboration or explanation. When the audience was over he took leave of our party in the same easy, straightforward way with which he had greeted them. We went away feeling that there was a man who was not only efficient but who could be relied on. They say the Tartars are like that.

After a few weeks on the job, Childs's enthusiasm for the performance of Mukhtarov and company was undiminished: "They are very plain and simple in manner, of an earnest and forceful disposition and they seem to be working very hard to whip things into shape."

ARA first impressions of the local leadership were rarely so positive. Yet it was frequently the case that after the Americans had recovered from the shock of the first encounter and had a look around, they realized that the local men in charge were among the most effective individuals left in the entire province. In order to rise to the top of the local soviet administration they had to be energetic, and this energy was often sufficient to compensate for what they lacked in brain power or experience.

After his first tour through the cantons of the Tatar republic, Childs concluded that "with very few exceptions the chairman of the local soviet is the strongest and most capable man in the community." Above all, the "honesty and force" of these men was their strongest asset, and "what is lacking in education and refinement is more than made up by a strong and fearless will." It is only when one penetrates "a little deeper into the soviet organization and when one encounters the sub-chiefs of bureaus that incompetency becomes manifest. The leaders are here but they are grievously lacking in competent subordinates to undertake the execution of the tasks conceived by them."[6]

In many ARA districts, then, the American relievers found in these energetic soviet chiefs, most of them Russians, natural allies in the struggle against the notorious Russian inertia and inefficiency.

Not all the credit for the good relations between the Kazan ARA and the local government was given to Mukhtarov or to the superior skills of the Tatars. The Americans, led by district supervisor Ivar Wahren with Childs as his assistant, earned Haskell's praise early on for their diplomatic handling of "government relations." And the Kazan Americans were not shy about accepting such praise.

Childs reported to his mother on November 6 that Wahren had just returned from Moscow where he had found Col. Haskell "delighted" with Kazan's performance: "no one could understand in Moscow how we had been able to accomplish so much in such a short time. It looks as if we are in a fair way to become the especial fair-haired child of the Russian mission." As Kazan's good government relations continued through the winter, its reputation spread throughout the mission so that in July 1922 Childs was able to boast to his mother: "We have of course the largest of the ARA districts in Russia and I do not need to tell you, the best. That is admitted even by the other districts."

The famous American war correspondent Arthur Ruhl, who served as a traveling inspector for the ARA in the summer of 1922, reinforced Kazan's reputation in a report to Moscow: "All things considered, Kazan impressed me more favorably than any of the district headquarters I have seen. . . . Kazan does give a very distinct notion of knowing what it is about and doing it intelligently and thoroughly. Wahren has been fortunate in his personnel and the local government has certainly been more helpful here than in many other places."

Working in the Kazan district was so agreeable that in November 1921 when Haskell wanted to make Childs district supervisor of the newly opened Orenburg district, with Wahren's assistance Childs eluded the unwanted promotion. This was rather unusual behavior for a man of the ARA, and most ARA men would have found it un-American. Not John Boyd, who, a year later with the help of now district supervisor Childs, himself avoided promotion to district supervisor of Simbirsk. He later succeeded Childs as ARA chief in Kazan. Such was the appeal of relief work among the Tatars.[7]

Childs's guilt about his decision is indicated by a defensive line in a letter to his mother, who was as ambitious for her son as she was possessive of him: "I would much rather be second in the most successful and most important mission in Russia than first in a second rate mission. Don't you agree with me?"

Meanwhile Childs continued to fill his diary and correspondence with references to the achievements of the Kazan district, especially as measured by the "most cordial" relations it enjoyed with the local officials. Childs's summer 1922 journey down the Volga to the ARA headquarters at Simbirsk and Samara only reinforced his feelings of self-satisfaction. The contrast with Kazan was stark: "It was as if one had set a great smoothly running and highly organized shop on Fifth Avenue over alongside a dowdy ramshackle store of Sixth or Seventh Avenue."

In both cities he heard the Americans blame most of their difficulties on unenlightened local officials, but he was not persuaded: "When I thought of the cordial relations which had always subsisted between the Kazan district of the ARA and the Government I wondered whether the fault lay altogether on the side of the

Government, that Samara and Simbirsk were not equally fortunate in the degree of cooperation which they had succeeded in obtaining."

By the time of his visit to Samara in July 1922, the most difficult phase of the relief work was over. Will Shafroth, having served as district supervisor until the American corn drive ended in April, pronounced himself "fed up on" Russia. He made it plain that government mistrust and obstruction were responsible for most of the Samara ARA's considerable difficulties. He recalled that at one point during the winter the Samara ARA was so frustrated at the lack of cooperation by Soviet officials that "only Col. Haskell's visit kept our morale from going to pieces."

Shafroth's place in Samara was taken by Ronald Allen, Harvard Class of 1914, who lacked Shafroth's experience and was felt by some of the Americans to be a bit young for the job of district supervisor. Ruhl remarked generally on the youthfulness of the Samara relievers: "There is not, at Samara, the same 'grown-up' atmosphere that one feels at Kazan, for instance. They are more like a lot of boys, but a nice lot of boys, and in so far as their cheerfulness, willingness, and family-harmony goes, their 'morale' is very good, indeed."

He indicated that the district's difficult relations with the government might stem from youth and inexperience. Still, even "a lot of boys" could have legitimate grievances against the local authorities. This was readily apparent to William Kelley, Harvard Class of 1917, when he visited Samara from Ufa earlier in the summer. "Allen's load of worries was so evident that I begin to think that we in Ufa have worked along more smoothly with the Government than in any other district."

For Childs, however, the visit to Samara and Simbirsk reaffirmed his belief in the superior diplomatic skills of the Kazan Americans. The critical difference as he saw it was that the Kazan ARA had successfully resisted making distrust the basis of their relations with the local soviet. By not automatically assuming that all Soviet officials were dishonest and incapable, they managed to sow the "seeds of confidence and trust." "We avoided assuming any superior airs or a blustering attitude toward men drawn for the most part from humble strata, who would have been the first to take offense at any display of arrogance. We proceeded, moreover, on the assumption they could be trusted. There is no more infallible breeder of misunderstanding than suspicion."

"Happily," he wrote in an unpublished memoir in the 1970s, "we were not living in the America of McCarthy of 1953–1958."[8]

IT WAS A TRIUMPH of Wilsonian diplomacy that not even Wilson could achieve. Childs's attraction to Lenin and the new Russia was probably inevitable. It was fed by and in turn fed his distaste for the American political system, indeed for capitalism in general. He saved the most forceful expressions of his self-consciously unorthodox political views for his mother. It is striking, in reading his letters to her, how cautiously he had to tread when the subject was his romantic life yet how openly and eagerly he confessed to her his most radical political beliefs. It seems it should have been the other way around, especially for the future international authority on Casanova and future U.S. ambassador. But Childs knew that portraying himself to his mother as a political iconoclast would not only not shock her, as he openly professed to fear, but would win him her approval, which he desired above all else. After all, nonconformity ran in the family.

Childs grew up in a Virginia household steeped in defiant Confederate politics. His father had been a messenger for General Lee, and the idea of the Lost Cause had been indelibly marked upon the young Rives. There was, he later recalled, only one thing his father had ever asked him to do in life: never to vote Republican. Childs *père* could forgive the North the war, even forgive it his own disfranchisement after the guns fell silent. But he could never forgive the fact that Lee died without having had his citizenship restored. "It was in this atmosphere that I was raised, from my birth in 1893. There had been a laying down of arms but the bitterness remained." Until World War I he saw only the Confederate flag fly. On the Fourth of July local businesses might close, but there was no holiday spirit.

In every one of his memoirs Childs maintains that race relations were not at the heart of the division between the North and the South. But the examples he provides of Southern racial tolerance have to do exclusively with members of his own family and underscore their exceptional nature. He is proud of the fact that his mother became the first white teacher of Negroes in Lynchburg, despite warnings from friends that her reputation would suffer as a consequence. He recalls his stunned reaction the day his father tipped his cap to a Negro they passed on the street.

Here, it seems, lie the roots of Child's contrariness on matters political and his ostentatious championing of ethnic minorities. He was always on the lookout for suspect stereotypes, be they of Old Dominion or Bolshevik Russia, and he brought his Confederate spirit with him into the Volga valley.

In a letter to his mother from Kazan, dated December 8, 1921, after three months in Red Russia, he wrote:

As you know I have never been an extremist in my attitude toward the Russian government and I think the tolerant views which I have expressed to you have been to an extent justified. I would never say that this is the best of all possible governments but I will say that I believe there is a sincerer desire to serve the people on the part of the ruling class of Russia today than there is in America.

In a way I have greater faith that the true principles of democracy will be obtained in Russia than I have that they will be preserved in America. . . .

Now personally I believe that capitalism is at the root of the wrong and I think that Wilson perceived this and was doing his best to educate America to the inevitable change which must take place in our principle of government.

In the United States the government was in the hands of senile politicians, with rare exceptions like Herbert Hoover. In Russia, youth was on the move, building a new world. To Childs, whose father had lost his wealth in a bank failure and who had grown up "on the borderline of poverty," the humble origins and limited experience of the Soviet leaders were testimony to their purity and bode well for their success.

After a year on the job in Russia—more than enough time to sour the most ardent American admirer of the Soviet experiment—he was not disenchanted: "If nothing interferes with the program of practical socialism which Russia is today working out I believe her recovery will be much more accelerated than that of many other European nations." He suggested to his mother that she read H. G. Wells's *New Worlds for Old*, and if that doesn't convince you of the efficacy and desirability of a socialist program then I give up. The trouble is that in America there is so much hysteria about social-ism that it is difficult to separate the ugly connotation which the word has come to convey to the average citizen from what the word actually means. Have you ever stopped to think of what the word actually means? Suppose you look it up in a good dictionary. I have never done so but I think you will find that the word will be defined somewhat as follows: anything that promotes the general welfare, that contributes to the greater good of the greater number.

Abraham Lincoln himself was a "great socialist" who stressed the necessity of maintaining government "of the people, by the people and for the people"—that is to say, a government in the interest of no particular class. That the Bolsheviks professed to rule as a "dictatorship of the proletariat" did not trouble Childs, who felt it was a necessary corrective to centuries of domination by the wealthy. The important thing, he felt, was for the West to approach the Bolshevik government with an open mind, to show respect for the ideals of its young leaders, such as Mukhtarov and Sabirov. This would lead to genuine understanding and a better world. The success of the Kazan ARA in its relations with the local government was the proof.

It is hard to believe that Childs would have been so forthright about his parlor socialism with his fiancée, Georgina, a widowed Russian aristocrat whose husband fell to the Reds in the Civil War. We get no indication from their courtship cor-respondence between Petrograd and Kazan in the spring of 1922, which is devoted to mutual expressions of affection and anticipation. Yet in his final letter to his mother from Kazan, dated December 20, 1922, he wrote: "As I leave here Georgie says that I leave more of a Bolshevik than ever. That is not strictly true as I have never professed myself a communist or any other than a socialist of the English Fabians. But I have never wavered from my socialism and after this experience in Russia it is never likely that I shall."[9]

Certainly he must have restrained himself in the presence of his aristocratic mother-in-law, who seems to have been a fierce anti-Bolshevik. He needed ap-proval from her as well, but of a different kind.

CHAPTER 22

COMRADE EIDUK

The near idyllic state of government relations in the Kazan district was placed in doubt one day in November 1921 by what Wahren called an "unpleasant occurrence." A man arrived from Moscow calling himself a "plenipotentiary" of the central government and carrying instructions to assist the ARA in all aspects of its operations. This was Comrade Muskatt, whose physical appearance and suspicious "mandate" won him no instant friends at ARA headquarters. Wahren dispatched an urgent letter to Haskell in Moscow about the unwelcome outsider: "Wholly aside from my personal feeling of repulsion when I see the man, his oily face and grin, I object to having a man come to my office and tell me that he will share the responsibility of the work of the A.R.A. in the Tartar Republic. I object to it and what is more I have no intention of standing for it."[1]

The arrival of Comrade Muskatt and others like him in all districts was the result of the decision by the Soviet leaders in Moscow that they could not afford to leave to local officials the job of government relations with the ARA. Instead they established a liaison system under Eiduk in Moscow, who appointed subordinates to the individual ARA districts, who in turn assigned their agents to the subdistricts, forming a very roughly pyramidal structure.

As with Eiduk at the center, the official title given to these men was "plenipotentiary representative of the RSFSR attached to all foreign relief organizations," but the ARA was far and away their primary responsibility. The American relievers took to calling them "government representatives," by which they meant the *central* government in Moscow as distinct from the local soviet governments. The ostensible role of these "liaisonites" was to simplify the work of the ARA by acting as its agent in all dealings with the various government departments. Instead of having to identify and negotiate with an array of government agencies and officials, most of whom were unused to working with foreigners, the ARA could take all of its requests, complaints, suggestions, and so on to the plenipotentiary, who would take over from there. The Simbirsk ARA history says that theirs was "the familiar role of the political commissar. The ordinary *raison d'être* for the commissar is suspicion. Doubtless, there was also the aim of establishing over the ARA the usual 'invisible' but effective control of the commissar."[2]

Naturally Eiduk drew his team heavily from the Cheka. And this meant just as naturally that they included a great many non-Russians. The founding head of the Cheka, Feliks Dzerzhinskii, was a Pole; many of his subordinates in the top ranks of the Cheka were non-Russians, and of these a remarkably high number were Letts, like Eiduk, former residents of the Baltic province of Latvia, which as a result of the revolution had won independence from the Russian empire. According to one source, three-fourths of the central Cheka staff of two thousand were Letts. There is a certain irony in this: before the revolution the Baltic Germans—the landowning class and political elite in the provinces of Latvia, Lithuania, and Estonia—played a disproportionately large role in policing tsarist Russia.

These Letts of the Cheka came to their position of prominence and numerical predominance through service in an unusual military corps formed during the world war. In 1915, with the German army advancing into the Baltic provinces, the tsarist government took the extraordinary step of allowing the formation of Latvian light infantry regiments, the only such homegrown military units in the Baltics. These so-called Latvian Riflemen, who were under the command of their own officers, had an important influence on the rise of the Latvian national identity. By 1917 they consisted of eight regular regiments—thirty-eight thousand soldiers and one thousand officers—and a reserve regiment of ten thousand men.

Most of the Riflemen were of worker and peasant background, thus adding a class element to their contempt for the Baltic German barons. They were also none too fond of the Russian high command, who led them to slaughter in battle on the Riga front. After the fall of Nicholas II in March 1917, they formed their own soviet and, receptive to Bolshevik propaganda, set themselves in opposition to the Provisional Government. With the fall of Riga to the Germans in August, the Latvian regiments retreated into unoccupied Latvia and then into Russia. After the Bolsheviks took power in November, Lenin brought Latvian units into Petrograd to act as a kind of praetorian guard at Bolshevik headquarters at Smolny, and later, when the Soviet government moved to Moscow in March 1918, at the Kremlin.

It was widely believed at the time that the loyalty of the Latvian regiments to Lenin's government was secured by the provisioning, or promise, of large sums of money. Whatever the case, they performed an invaluable service to the Bolsheviks during that uncertain period between the October Revolution and the formation in summer 1918 of the Red Army, of which they were the nucleus. In April they were called upon to wipe out anarchist strongholds in Moscow, and in July they were instrumental in suppressing revolts staged by the Left Socialist Revolutionaries in the capital and the Right Socialist Revolutionaries in Yaroslavl, to the north.

During the Civil War they fought in the Red Army in decisive battles on the Volga, in the Urals, on the southern front, and in the defense of Petrograd. In August 1918 the Fifth Latvian Infantry Regiment was the first military unit to receive the Order of the Red Banner for its defense of the city of Kazan. The Latvians fought in heroic fashion, and they were known as disciplined and tenacious, even ferocious, fighters. Walter Duranty called them "loyal as steel, and damn tough."[3]

Eiduk served with them as a machine-gunner, which is how he acquired his reputation for brutality, achieving a special notoriety for executing tsarist officers with his own hand. Fisher says that while on patrol on the Riga-Moscow railroad, Eiduk's detachment was overtaken by White cavalry forces and he was severely wounded and left for dead.[4] That was not his only close call.

An American named Roger E. Simmons, a Department of Commerce trade

commissioner in Russia in 1917–18, got a close-up look at Eiduk and left an interesting account in his testimony during a Senate subcommittee's hearings on
"Bolshevik propaganda" in February–March 1919. The senators on the committee were clearly intrigued by the prominence of Letts in the Bolshevik police and
by this character Eiduk.

Simmons was surveying the forests around Vologda, a city some 350 miles
north of Moscow at the junction of the Trans-Siberian and Archangel-Moscow
railroad lines, in the spring of 1918. At that time, the Allied embassies and lega-
tions were situated in Vologda, having recently relocated there from Petrograd instead of following the Soviet government in its transfer to Moscow. Simmons
came down with pneumonia and was left behind in July when, as the military situation grew ominous, the American embassy officials evacuated Vologda, either
managing to exit Russia via Archangel with the American ambassador, or having
to go to Moscow.

Now recovered and eager to get out of Vologda, Simmons applied to the Cheka
man in charge, Eiduk, whom he describes as "a Lettish Jew, a man of a very irasci-
ble nature, and, on account of his experience in the uprising in Yaroslav[1], where
the protest against the Bolshevik regime had become quite formidable, he had the
reputation of being the cruelest and the most bloodthirsty Bolshevik leader of the
revolution."

Eiduk did not like the fact that Simmons's passport had been issued by the
American embassy in Petrograd. This was a serious situation. After all, Eiduk
had a reputation for taking extreme measures all out of proportion to the apparent "crime." But on this particular day Simmons was lucky: Eiduk decided to imprison him and send him under guard to Moscow for trial.

While they were discussing the details in Eiduk's railroad car office, two Kronstadt sailors entered. They represented some four hundred sailors who were on
their way to the White Sea front but now refused to go any farther unless given
larger bread rations—that is, more than their current 1.25 lbs. per day. Eiduk ar-
rogantly waved them off, ordering them to leave. They, with equal arrogance, invited him to Kronstadt in order to learn a bit of efficiency so he could properly
ration bread to his units. Simmons testified that this so enraged Eiduk that he
told the guards nearby, "Put these men under ground in 20 minutes." He meant
this order literally, and it was carried out.

When the rest of the four hundred learned what had happened, they went on
a rampage, riddling Eiduk's railroad car with bullets "so that it looked like a tin
can that had been shot at a hundred times, and I tell you their action was quick."
Eiduk may have been forewarned because he was not in the car at the time. He
called in a company of Lettish troops to put down the mutiny.[5]

The stories of Eiduk's civil war exploits circulated at ARA headquarters, probably with his encouragement. His physical appearance acted as supporting evidence. Haskell described him as a "squareheaded Latvian with one of the cruelest
faces I have ever seen."

The disproportionately large number of Letts in the Cheka was widely assumed to have a basis in ethnic antagonism. Mackenzie of the *Chicago Daily News*
wrote in 1922: "Between Letts and Russians there has long been bitter hatred. . . .
The Lett has a reputation for being hard and unforgiving." He traced this situa-

tion back to the early years of the century during the agrarian risings in Latvia, when the tsarist police brutalized local peasants. On their part, Russians were said to look down upon the Letts for their lack of culture, of which their poor facility with the Russian language was considered a symptom. Whatever the reason, by the time the ARA arrived the Russian mind associated the Lett with some of the worst excesses of Bolshevik rule.[6]

All of these extraordinary measures of the Extraordinary Commission could be rationalized in extraordinary times: after all, there was a great revolution going on. But when the Civil War came to an end and the retreat to a limited market economy began, Lenin and some other clear-headed Soviet leaders saw that in order for the reforms to work, the activities of the political police would have to be curbed. Already when the ARA arrived in late summer 1921 there was talk in the air about an impending reform of the secret police. Dzerzhinskii himself was heard to say that the Cheka was about to be "Scotland-Yardized." By February 1922 came new laws guaranteeing every arrested person the right to a written statement of his alleged crimes within two weeks of arrest and the right to a trial within two months.[7]

The big step was taken on February 6, 1922, when the Cheka was formally abolished and replaced by the State Political Administration under the People's Commissariat of Internal Affairs. It became known by the Russian pronunciation of its initials, GPU—"GAY-PAY-OO"—or, to denote its "All-Russian" scope, the OGPU.

The new arrangement removed, legally speaking, much of the Cheka's independence, placing the police organs firmly in the hands of the state. The GPU, unlike its predecessor, had no judicial authority, and new NEP decrees established a formally independent judiciary to enforce new legal and criminal codes.

At the time most Russians dismissed the changes and claimed that the new laws existed only on paper, intended mostly for a foreign audience, and that the GPU was really the Cheka with a new name. Did it not after all occupy the same premises and employ the same people? The name "Cheka" endured in popular parlance well beyond its official demise. According to Mackenzie, "One rarely attended a party where there were not some recently released from the Che-ka prison. 'I must not stay out late, or my wife will think the Che-ka have taken me,' was a common excuse when a man left early."

The Americans of the ARA would not stay in Soviet Russia long enough to get used to the initials GPU, which most of them dismissed anyway as little more than a change of letterhead. Besides, "Cheka" had a real bite to it, unlike the delicate "GAY-PAY-OO." It is not clear that more than a few foreigners understood that the term stood for "Extraordinary Commission." They certainly found various ways to spell it: Chekka, Chechka, Checka, Tchekka, Tchecka, Che-Ka. The English writer Philip Gibbs wrote it "Cheka" and assumed that "each letter of that dreaded word formed the initial of the full Russian title for this organization." That adjective "dreaded" was well worn in this context.

Many of the Americans relief workers, probably following the lead of the local citizens, used the word to denote a person or a prison. For example, Eiduk was referred to as a "big 'cheka'"; Tom Barringer wrote after the arrests of some of his ARA Russian staff in Ekaterinoslav that he was "going around trying to get them out of the dreaded 'chekka.'"[8]

It did not take the Americans long to recognize what Childs called the "psychological endowment of fear" left by the Cheka, which "passes its judgements and executes its decrees with the dispatch and unobtrusiveness of the Ku Klux Klan. When one speaks of the Checka the voice is lowered and the tones of the syllables are hushed." When his first translator, a former White officer named Antonov who had served with the British and American intervention forces in Archangel, received word of his arrest, Childs asked him what he was going to do about it. Do about it? "It's the Extraordinary Commission, sir, and there's really nothing to be done. I must go."

The Cheka's well-known ability to cut through red tape was still very much intact in the autumn of 1921, and the Americans learned that they could make use of it to promote their relief effort. During his Moscow layover in September, Childs observed a Cheka man named Bublikov—"who I am told is a Lett"—order a first-class cooking car for an ARA party over the telephone, his voice sounding like the "rat-a-tat-tat of a machine gun" and leaving no doubt that his command would be obeyed.

In the spring of 1922, at the critical moment in the delivery of American corn to the countryside, the spur track between the Kazan railroad station and the wharf was damaged, a result of the spring floods. The ARA made an urgent request of the provincial people's commissar of transportation that the spur be repaired. When told it would take a week, the Americans turned to the local Cheka chief, Comrade Schwartz—said by some to be a Lett—who telephoned the transportation commissar and ordered him to make the necessary repairs within forty-eight hours. The commissar apparently balked at this, for Comrade Schwartz said into the telephone: "I tell you that if it is not done you will be arrested as an enemy of the state and shot for sabotage." The commissar then pleaded a lack of man power, and Schwartz promised him two hundred men. Within thirty-six hours the first train had moved over the spur.[9]

Just how many genuine Letts were in their midst was difficult for the ARA men to determine. They expended quite a bit of mental energy trying to penetrate a pseudonym in order to determine if one or another Bolshevik was a Lett or a Jew or perhaps both. They got so used to having Lettish Cheka agents turn up among the Soviet establishment that they tended to refer indiscriminately to government representatives and agents of the Cheka, or Bolsheviks generally, as "Letts." It was the same as calling someone a "Cheka," a "commissar," or a "Bolo"—it was not always meant literally but rather to denote a general type.

Or they might say a "Jew," falling back on the generalization that *all* Bolsheviks were Jews. In fact a disproportionately large number of the leading Bolshevik Party officials were Jews, a people the tsarist government had given much more than its share of reasons to become involved in revolutionary politics before 1917. At the very top, Trotsky, Kamenev, and Zinoviev—Bronstein, Rosenfeld, and Apfelbaum—were the most high-profile examples. Only in the waning days of the Soviet Union would confirmation emerge that Lenin's maternal grandfather was Jewish. The many ARA anecdotes about Litvinov, from the Riga negotiations through the final Moscow banquet, make frequent allusions to his Semitism though there is not one reference to his original name, Finkelstein.[10]

Russians typically exaggerated both the number and influence of Jews on Rus-

sian Bolshevism, and many blamed the Jews for the Revolution itself or for its unfortunate outcome. These sentiments fed upon a well-known tradition of Russian
anti-Semitism. The American relief workers entered Soviet Russia with enough
of their own evident prejudices, as well as preconceived ideas about the state of affairs in Russia, so that generally speaking they were vulnerable to infection from
some of the darkest postrevolutionary Russian attitudes about Jews.

The American relief workers came into contact with an unusually large number
of Jewish Bolsheviks, who were assigned to the ARA because of their English-
language skills. A fair number had only recently been residents of Manhattan's
East Side—former refugees from the tsarist pogroms who returned to Russia after the Revolution. In the United States they may have been involved in radical
politics of one or another flavor. When the Romanov dynasty fell, Trotsky himself
was living among them.

The ARA men knew that Eiduk was a Lett, but unlike Simmons before them,
they do not seem to have guessed him to be a Jewish Lett. His Latvian origin was
clearly spelled out in his family name whereas many other real or suspected Letts
had Russian names. There were other evidently Latvian Chekists whose names
were known to the ARA—Peters, Lander, Latsis, Pelshe—but none more notorious, next to Eiduk, than Penis. Actually this name was pronounced "PEE-noos"
and the Americans spelled it variously as "Penus," "Penas," "Pinez," "Pinous," or
"Pinus," the last of which would today be recognized as the correct transliteration
from the Russian.

Said person was chief of Eiduk's transportation department and was at the
center of the railroad controversy in winter 1922, when it appeared that the Russian railways would collapse under the weight of American corn. Haskell demanded and won the release of this "obstructionist," who was one of the most
disliked of all Soviet officials in the American relief story. This fact together with
the self-conscious references to his name in the official ARA documentation suggest the extent and brand of humor he inspired at Moscow headquarters, right
through his "removal," or "withdrawal."

In a later day someone might have been inspired to muse on the Freudian ap-
propriateness of having a man called Penis in charge of keeping the trains moving. But in those days a train was usually just a train. Quinn expressed relief at his
dismissal, calling him a "conversational embarrassment to us."[11]

THE AMERICANS NEVER referred to him on paper as "Comrade" Pinus—but
they almost certainly did so verbally, unless somehow in this particular case they
felt the designation to be redundant. By 1921 the use of the word "comrade," "*tovarishch*," was on the wane, as if to mark the passing of the revolutionary era.
Frank Golder had been in Russia in the heady days of March 1917 when the Romanov dynasty collapsed without bloodshed and the residents of Petrograd took
to the streets in a jubilant mood, astounded that the thing had come off so peacefully while blissfully ignorant of the tragedy that lay ahead. Golder was swept up
by this enthusiasm, and he wrote to a friend in the States: "People congratulate
each other and call each other 'Comrade.'"

Since then much water—and blood—had passed under the bridge, and the
general optimism of 1917 had long before dried up. In the process the word "com-

rade" lost its idealistic allure, especially outside the Party. The loss of enthusiasm that marked the coming of NEP made the salutation seem especially inappropriate. Still, some tried to uphold revolutionary standards. Golder and Fisher were sitting in a train in a Moscow station in August 1922 when the ticket takers discovered a problem with their ticket. The conductor brought it to the attention of the station's Cheka agent, explaining that the mistake was not the fault of these two "gentlemen." Golder tells us that the Cheka man could barely contain himself: "Gentlemen! They are no more gentlemen than you and I, they are tovarischi."

Most people had simply grown tired of it. Philip Gibbs quotes a Russian woman's exasperated remark: "Do not use that word comrade! It has been debased. *Tavarish! Tavarish! Tavarish!* I am sick of it." One Moscow intellectual reports with evident satisfaction that by 1921 if someone were addressed as "Comrade," the likely reply would be, "Go to hell."

Charlie Veil recalls a Riga-Moscow train ride in September 1921 in the company of some American socialists going into Russia "to be tovarischi, or comrades, . . . but already they were almost as sick of that word as I became later." A chapter in Veil's autobiography is entitled "Tovarisch Tolstoi." This referred to one of writer Lev Tolstoy's daughters, the Countess Nadia Tolstoy, who worked as a housekeeper at one of the American personnel houses. The title is intended to set a tone of intrigue for Veil's macho musings as to whether the countess had in fact been a Bolshevik agent and what implications this may have had for their supposedly mutual physical attraction.[12]

Most often the ARA men used the word ironically, as in "Comrade Eiduk," although they certainly would never have used it this way in his presence. It meant that he was one of *them* and implied no feelings of camaraderie. Eiduk's replacement at midmission, Karl Lander, was also a Lett, but he was a Social Democrat of the intelligentsia type, quite distinct from Eiduk's leather-jackets. The ARA Moscow staff vastly preferred Lander as a chief plenipotentiary and as a human being, realizing that most of the time he was doing his best for his country under extraordinarily difficult circumstances. They would never have belittled him by calling him "comrade."

IN THE BEGINNING the ARA district supervisors were much more aggressive in resisting the encroachments of Eiduk's agents than were their chiefs in Moscow in dealing with Eiduk himself. In this they were often assisted by the local soviet officials, who were none too thrilled at having a man from the center pitch his tent in their territory, interposing himself between them and the ARA. They were eager to take for themselves the credit for American famine relief and resented having a third force winning the glory for Moscow. It sometimes happened that the ARA men and the local soviet officials found themselves conspiring against Eiduk's plenipotentiaries.

This triangular struggle for control played itself out in a variety of ways in the various districts. It is difficult to generalize. In Kazan the ARA had managed to establish a smooth working relationship with the local officials during the initial weeks of the mission. This is why Wahren was so displeased when the unattractive Comrade Muskatt strolled into the ARA office that November day with his mandate from Comrade Eiduk to engage in the struggle against ARA "parallelism." Wahren wrote to Haskell that the ARA was getting fine cooperation from the local government and did not need any "assistance" from the center, especially from a man who knew nothing about relief work: "I told Mr. Muskat upon his arriving here exactly what I thought of him and his Mission, in other words that I understood perfectly well that his Mission here was not one of assistance to me but much more to keep a vigilant eye on the activities of the A.R.A. and its representatives here."

Wahren told him he would recognize only those orders of Eiduk that had been countersigned by Haskell, which set Muskatt off to Moscow to get the situation clarified. Wahren wrote ahead and asked Haskell if Eiduk might not at least be persuaded to send down a different plenipotentiary, but Muskatt soon returned with his original mandate intact.

Few details about Comrade Muskatt are to be found in the ARA documentation. In one report he is called a "Lett." He was certainly not a Tatar. Wahren's use of the adjective "oily" in his letter to Haskell was probably meant to imply "Semitic," and indeed Childs says he was "an English Jew."

What is unusual about the Kazan story is that after Wahren's initial appeal to Haskell, Muskatt, whose tenure in Kazan lasted over a year, is for long stretches invisible in the ARA documentation. In most of the other districts Eiduk's agents dominate the "government relations" sections of the official reports and histories. Apparently ARA relations with Mukhtarov and Sabirov were so smooth that Muskatt was kept at bay. Most of the time he was, in Wahren's words, "easily led and easily bullied."

Perhaps Muskatt had orders to tread lightly so as not to appear to encroach upon the independence of the Tatar nationalist leadership, just as the Kremlin tried to be sensitive in its dealings with Tatarstan's officials. It was only after Stalin's rise to supremacy toward the end of the 1920s that Moscow moved to suppress "national Bolshevism" and went over to the outright Russification of the Tatars. It was then that Sabirov and Mukhtarov along with other "right-bourgeois Tatar nationalists," to quote the Stalinist charges, were arrested and expelled from the Party for "plotting against the dictatorship of the proletariat."

In April 1922 Wahren wrote to Haskell again to complain about Muskatt but primarily for being a "bag of hot air." He reported that the ARA men were dealing "more or less" directly with the local government, that there was not a single issue on which Eiduk's man had proven to be "of any earthly use." However, his presence alone made him a nuisance. "If it were possible for you I would like to ask you Colonel, please to influence Mr. Eiduck so as to change this man. I would much rather have a man, red-eyed and rabid, but one who could do things when you asked him to, than one who can do nothing but talk."[13]

But all was not what it seemed in the district of Kazan.

CHAPTER 23

COMRADE SKVORTSOV

The Kazan ARA's record for good government relations may have had something to do with the presence in that district of a man named Skvortsov, one of the most curious figures in the ARA story.

His full name was Mikhail Ilarionovich Skvortsov, and he was at that time one of the leading Bolsheviks in the Tatar Autonomous Republic. During the world war he had served as a noncommissioned officer at the front before being taken prisoner and shipped to Belgium; after that his history is unclear. Childs describes him as "young, alert, with keen eyes and almost a handsome face and apparently a sincere and devoted disciple of the doctrines of Karl Marx."

Skvortsov and Childs, both around thirty years old, became fast friends. "I have known few more selfless individuals," Childs wrote, praising his "keen sense of humanity and dedication, with complete disinterestedness, to the ideals of the Revolution." As Skvortsov told it, his devotion to Marxism had come between him and his father, an Orthodox priest. This was the kind of idealism that attracted Childs, who found Skvortsov's company so enjoyable and helpful that he invited him along on his journeys into the interior "as often as I could entice him from his pressing duties."

It was unusual for a Bolshevik Party official to be so openly involved in ARA activities. Childs's diary records the episode that sealed their relationship. They were in a town called Elabuga arranging the selection, by popular vote, of the local ARA committee. The town meeting where the balloting took place was held in a saloon. When Skvortsov finished reporting the election results, a "swarthy faced and uncouthly appearing individual" stood up and began to protest the presence of non-Communists on the committee. While the man was emitting a rapid stream of Russian syllables, Childs noticed that Skvortsov "had begun the nervous tapping of the table with the point of a pencil" when suddenly he brought the instrument down with a series of "incisive raps . . . held up his hand with a significantly authoritative gesture" and delivered "a few brief but emphatic phrases" that silenced the protester. "This incident established my confidence in Skvartzov and I resolved that whenever I should have occasion to go into the cantons again I would make special application of the Government for his services that he might accompany me as Government representative."

Skvortsov came to perform on a part-time basis duties not unlike those of Eiduk's plenipotentiaries, though it does not appear that he was ever so designated, at least not openly. But in view of subsequent events and Childs's general innocence about such matters, it seems likely that there was more to Comrade Skvortsov's ARA involvement than met Childs's eye. In a memoir written several decades later, when he was eager to compensate for his earlier naïveté, Childs explained that Skvortsov had been attached to the ARA because of suspicion "until the government gained confidence in us." But during the mission he did not even hint at this. In May 1922, after seven months of working alongside Skvortsov on ARA operations, he described him as a "very warm friend of mine."

Considering all the unpleasantness that this man was to cause the ARA in the coming months, it is strange that in Childs's voluminous writings there is no sign of the trouble to come. None of the other Kazan ARA men appears to have fallen under Skvortsov's spell; in fact none even mentions the man. The only other American testimony out of Kazan is that of journalist Edwin Hullinger, who traveled by sleigh with Childs and Skvortsov through the Tatar republic in December 1921. In his 1923 *The Reforging of Russia*, Hullinger's Skvortsov is a dramatic character, a "splendid type of man, straight-forward, courageous, strong. He would have made a wonderful central figure for a novel."

While on one of their expeditions, on December 20, the feast of St. Nikolai, Skvortsov and his fellow traveler entered a church in the town of Lenino, where a service was underway. During the singing of a hymn Skvortsov approached the priests and asked to be allowed to conduct one of the readings. According to Childs, he put them at ease by adding his "very excellent bass" to the choir. "For a moment as he was making his way forward through the crowd to present his request I was thrown almost into consternation as to his purpose, fearing that he was projecting as a communist some mimicry of the service. But he was formerly a choir singer and his father before him was a priest and he participated in the service with all the solemnity which was due it."[1]

Childs did document Skvortsov's later-infamous temper, which displayed itself in ways other than the thwack of a pencil. One of their journeys into the subdistricts brought them to the train station in the town of Viatskaia Poliana, where Childs attempted to send a telegram. All such communications by the ARA were supposed to be free of charge, but the local telegraph official demanded payment and dismissed appeals to the Riga Agreement. This sent Skvortsov into a rage, and his verbal threats produced the desired effect, for Childs was allowed to send his telegram free of charge.

The problem for Skvortsov was that Viatskaia Poliana, while situated within the ARA Kazan district, was located outside the Tatar Autonomous Republic and thus outside his jurisdiction as a Tatar Party official. The telegraph agent was answerable to the authorities in Moscow, not Kazan. Skvortsov may have been aware of this, but these inspection trips through the famine zone put nerves on edge and at that moment it must have seemed like a tremendously irritating detail. When the telegraph official protested the incident, however, it was deemed serious enough to bring to the attention of the "Examiner of Important Matters" of the People's Commissariat of Justice in Kazan, where a hearing was held at the end of May 1922 on the "improper activities of M. I. Skvortsov."

Skvortsov was not present for the hearing, having recently been transferred out of Kazan, apparently for unrelated reasons. Among other things, he was charged with having used "abusive language" in dealing with the telegraph official. On the appointed day Childs, accompanied by his translator, Simson, walked into the hearing room, a small, bare office, where at tables in opposite corners of the room sat the examiners of important matters. One of these magistrates, an unshaven worker wearing a cap, told Childs to take a seat. During routine preliminary questioning the interrogator asked him about his political background. The frustrated novelist and former journalist gave three versions of the exchange that followed. In a letter written on May 18 to his mother, he described it this way:

> "Tell him I'm a socialist," I said to Simson.
> That translated, the judge himself could not conceal a start of surprise since the Americans here seem generally to be regarded by the officials of the government as most confirmed bourgeois in spirit and in political faith.
> "What kind of socialist?" was the next inquiry directed of me when the magistrate had regained his self-possession. "Menshevik, bolshevik, social revolutionary or what?"
> Again I smiled indulgently. I remembered that in the past, communists with whom I had discussed politics and to whom I had expressed my political faith, had described me as a menshevik.
> "Tell him we haven't any such political divisions in America," I replied, and the magistrate duly and solemnly recorded my answer.

The Mensheviks had been the archrivals of the Bolsheviks since the split of the Russian Social Democratic Party into two factions in 1903. Despite growing Bolshevik political intolerance after 1917 and the dwindling of the active Menshevik ranks through emigration and exile, the party managed to maintain a limited presence in Russia through successive waves of repression. As late as July 1921 the Menshevik Central Committee continued to operate inside Soviet Russia, but the introduction of NEP brought with it another political crackdown, and by early 1922 most of the party's leadership had found its way abroad.

Had Childs not enjoyed the immunity granted him by his American citizenship, the judge would have been in a position to wipe that indulgent smile off his face by tossing him into the Leninist slammer.

In the May 16 entry in his diary, a document Childs intended for eventual publication under the title "Red Days in Russia" and whose language is therefore somewhat circumspect, he described the exchange with the judge as follows:

> "What is your political faith?"
> "Tell him I'm a progressive-democrat, if there's such a thing," I said to Simson.
> The examiner screwed his eyes up and puckered his forehead.
> "Into what category does a progressive-democrat fall?" was the next query directed of me: "Menshevik, Bolshevik, Social Revolutionary or what?"
> Again I smiled. I remembered that in the past, communists with whom I had discussed politics and to whom I had expressed my political faith, had described me as a Social Revolutionary.
> "Tell him we haven't such political divisions in America," I replied, and the magistrate duly and solemnly recorded my answer.

By "Social Revolutionary" Childs means the Social*ist* Revolutionaries. For a long time after the Revolution in English-language accounts they were referred to by this mistranslated name, as if to distinguish them from the general run of antisocial revolutionaries. The SRs, as they were also called, were a non-Marxist agrarian party, which in the political pressure cooker of 1917 underwent its own split into radical and moderate wings. It was the Left SRs who formed a short-lived coalition government with the Bolsheviks after the October Revolution and who, when this fell apart in the spring of 1918 after the Soviet government signed a separate peace with Germany, clashed with the Bolsheviks and became the first target of the Red Terror.

By 1921 most SR leaders had fled abroad, but former party members were still in Russia in sufficient numbers to make the Bolshevik Party, now retreating toward moderate agrarian policies, uneasy. As Childs addressed this proletarian investigative body, the GPU was rounding up SRs across Russia in preparation for a show trial, which was held in Moscow in June with much international publicity. The thirty-four defendants were charged with counterrevolution and terrorism, including the attempt on Lenin's life in 1918. Most were found guilty, and fifteen were condemned to death, though these sentences were later commuted. Under different circumstances Childs might have found himself sitting in the dock among the condemned.

In an article he published after the mission in 1923, in the *Christian Science Monitor*, Childs thought it wise to tread lightly. He reported that in answer to the query regarding his political faith, "I replied that I was so-and-so." In none of these accounts does he tell us the outcome of the hearings.

AT THE TIME Childs was giving his testimony, ARA operations in the Ukrainian city of Ekaterinoslav were just getting into running order under district supervisor Tom Barringer, a Charlottesville native whose father was chairman of the medical faculty at the University of Virginia. Nowhere is there a detectable trace of Confederate spirit in him. He attended UVA, but after three years the war cut short his work on the Bachelor of Sciences degree.

Ekaterinoslav, which means "Catherine's Glory," was founded in 1776 by Prince Potemkin, Catherine the Great's adviser and lover, perhaps best known outside of Russia for his alleged construction of phony villages in southern Russia along the route of the visiting monarch. It is said that he hired scene designers and carpenters from the Imperial Theater to do the job. The idea was to create for her the impression of thriving development in these recently colonized territories—thus the expression "Potemkin village." Actually, the "e" in "Potemkin" carries an umlaut, which means its correct pronunciation is "Pa-TYOM-kin," but by now it is too late to repair the damage. The original town was built on the Kilchen' River, but the site proved to be unhealthy, and in 1784 Catherine's Glory was moved, Potemkin-village-style, ten kilometers east to the Dnepr River.

When Barringer arrived in February 1922, there was no attempt to impress the American visitor with false appearances. At the train station he came upon a "never to be forgotten sight, my first introduction to human misery on a mass scale." This consisted of the usual crowd of lice-infested refugees, most of them desperate to hop a train out of town, others too weak to lift themselves off the station floor, and a few having already gone West.

Traveling by automobile over the gap-toothed cobblestone of Catherine Boulevard, he noted that every second house was destroyed and that those still standing bore the scars of machine gun fire. The Civil War in the Ukraine had been particularly fierce, and the widespread destruction and leftover barbed wire kept the memories fresh. Barringer compared the scene to the most devastated cities he had seen in wartime France.

Novodrianskaia Street, where the ARA office and personnel house were located, was once lined with the city's finest houses. Most of the buildings were now empty, filled with broken glass and fallen plaster; many of these ruins had been stripped for firewood. "All showed the signs of former occupancy by some 'Soviet institution,' the finest house wrecking organization in the world."

The condition of the local officialdom was comparable in Barringer's eyes. "The scarcity of good and courageous executive material was appalling. The intensity of the political and civil wars had completely wiped out of every community the best element." At his first meeting with the authorities he followed the standard procedure of reading the Riga Agreement and explaining the ARA system of operation, laying special emphasis on the fact that the ARA would choose its own independent committees to select the children to be fed and that it would retain full control over American kitchens. This elicited looks of absolute incredulity on the faces of the assembled, for whom such concepts as "nonpartisan" and "independent" had long since ceased to have any meaning, if they ever had at all.

"The wires were hot that evening" between Ekaterinoslav and the Ukrainian capital, Kharkov, as the local authorities protested to their superiors this American insolence. All they could get out of Ukrainian President Christian Rakovsky was the terse reply, "Give the Americans every assistance."

Barringer's relations with the local government could not be called cordial; certainly they did not approach the standard of ARA-Soviet cooperation set in Kazan. On June 15 he expressed his exasperation to ARA chief Frank Page in New York City: "In all my dealings with the authorities here I find that they are only interested in the welfare of the people politically—starvation and countless deaths mean nothing to them and it is on this account only that so many of the American personnel get fed up."

After several weeks on the job he managed to establish tolerable relations with officials in several local government departments. Operations were settling down into a routine when "One bright day in the last week in May a rather genial looking man wearing an English cape came into my office with a strong letter of recommendation from Childs of Kazan." This was Skvortsov, now the former party official of the Tatar republic. This has to be checked and rechecked to verify that it is in fact the same individual because Childs's Skvortsov is barely recognizable in the Comrade Skvortsov who surfaced in Ekaterinoslav.

Barringer describes the new arrival, Eiduk's plenipotentiary, as a "product of the Cheka," though it is impossible to say if this was meant literally; certainly Childs never indicated a Cheka background. Barringer also refers to him as a Lett, which if true is another detail Childs seems to have missed. By now a shadow looms over the entire body of Childs's testimony. Perhaps Barringer pinned this ethnic identification on him as a kind of plenipotentiary's badge. He also reports that Skvortsov's male secretary was an "inoffensive Lett."

Childs's recommendation letter, which praised Skvortsov as an "able and devoted worker," misled Barringer as to the reason for his transfer to Ekaterinoslav.

He had come to be the government representative to the ARA, but Barringer assumed he was merely looking for work. On the strength of the letter, Barringer offered him a position as an inspector, which Skvortsov, possibly aware of the misunderstanding, turned down after some hesitation. Once the true nature of his mission had been cleared up, he offered the ARA the services of his wife, who turned out to be an excellent employee.

Barringer, for the moment oblivious to the game of Eiduk's liaisonites, initially did not regard this agent from the center as an intruder but rather as someone who might light a fire under the local officials and expedite the relief work. He gave Skvortsov an office in the ARA building so as to familiarize him with operations as quickly as possible and to get a close look at his methods.

On his part Skvortsov set about doing what most of the government representatives had been instructed to do: he established his own organization parallel to that of the ARA throughout the district, forbade local authorities to have any direct contact with the Americans, and politely but firmly informed Barringer that the ARA could deal with the departments of the local soviet only through him. Furthermore, all ARA telegrams and telephone calls out of Ekaterinoslav had to have his prior approval.

The soviet officials, who are faceless in Barringer's account, were even less well disposed to Skvortsov than were the Americans. When Barringer encountered their resistance to his selection of particular candidates for an ARA committee, "Mr Skvarzoff assured me that he could arrange everything, that when his stamp was upon the committee it would be 'official' and that was all there was to it. No local government would dare disobey his authority. Events proved that Mr Skvarzoff, a Russian Lett, had never encountered a Ukrainian bandit before."

It took Skvortsov only several weeks to get his bearings and begin a drive to stack the ARA committees with loyal comrades. He managed to spoil the good relations between the ARA and the Ekaterinoslav railroad authorities, which Barringer had worked hard to cultivate. He proved especially adept at projecting to the local population the appearance of supreme authority over the ARA.

From May until August, when an open break in relations occurred, "life was made interesting by the tactics we had to pursue to out-wit the fellow and keep the childfeeding going as well."

Skvortsov becomes in the Ekaterinoslav documentation a perfect monster. The contrast to Childs's well-behaved choirboy is remarkable. While Childs had favored his companionship in their travels through Tatarstan, the Ekaterinoslav relief workers went to elaborate lengths to avoid him. This was not easy, as the Ekaterinoslav ARA had only one automobile, and the Americans were forced to travel in the same car with Skvortsov and his secretary. "We always longed for a second auto to arrive for then our freedom of action would have been unlimited."

Among a string of minor Skvortsov scandals was an incident involving the ARA's child-feeding maps. Barringer returned one day from an inspection trip to find everyone at headquarters "in a tremendous state of excitement." Skvortsov had walked into his office and seized the ARA maps, performing this feat with his characteristic dramatic flair, making a "loud proclamation" to the Ukrainian employees.

These maps were typically annotated with up-to-date demographic and economic statistics—often better than anything in the possession of the local soviet. Although they contained information not strictly related to famine relief, they were a fixture of every ARA headquarters.

Skvortsov seized them as proof that the Americans were engaged in "economic espionage." The ARA appealed to Skvortsov's superiors in Kharkov, who promptly informed him that he was in the wrong and ordered him to return the maps forthwith. Barringer somehow learned of this message ahead of time and, when Skvortsov walked into the ARA office, let him off the hook with a casual request that he return the "borrowed" maps, which he did with apparent relief.

The question is, how did Skvortsov the angel of Kazan turn into the devil of Ekaterinoslav? Barringer was certain that Skvortsov had always been Comrade Skvortsov, that the explanation for the mystery was Childs. He wrote to Page at the moment of greatest crisis on August 5:

One is confronted with the question as to whether the distinction should be made between a famine on account of economics or a famine by an Act of God, as the people die, just the same, particularly when the Govt gives literally not a happy darn, as long as there is anything left politically to dabble with. Its maddening to deal with these people and its this that makes the Americans so "fed up" at times. The "Polit Commissar" so to speak that is sent down to me as the representative of the Central Govt [is] an extremely able man from the standpoint of the Party and an Apportunist of the first water. He practically killed his wife, one of my employees, with the butt of his revolver for the lack of nothing else to do. To be a relief worker in Russia one must be a diplomat first and a babyfeeder next. The above mentioned gentleman came from Kazan and was very highly recommended by Rives Childs. A most glowing tribute to my ex-Chekka, but since I have heard from Mr. Johnson that Childs is a Socialist (parlour). I realize now what a dupe he has been.

Johnson was Kazan's Charles Johnson, Harvard Class of 1902 and former deputy warden at Sing Sing prison. He was spreading the word that Childs was so-and-so.

Still, there has to be more to the Skvortsov mystery than just Childs's political inclinations. It is possible that the circumstances of Skvortov's transfer to Ekaterinoslav induced him to show a tougher face to the ARA. Maybe his cooperation with Childs had cost him his Party position. Who knows, maybe someone in that little church in Lenino had reported his most un-Leninist behavior in the choir that day. It is possible that the dramatic change in Skvortsov's behavior can be explained simply by his change of assignment: as plenipotentiary it was now his duty to strive for control over the Ekaterinoslav ARA. The attitude came with the job.

After the mission John Ellingston wrote of government relations in the districts that "the worst crises and the most severe friction could trace their origin to the personal ill-will or deficiencies of individuals, and the removal of these individuals proved the good will of Government and ARA alike." Ellingston was not excluding the individuals of the ARA, but in the case of Barringer and Skvortsov it is difficult to see how the American could have been the chief offender. He was regarded within the organization as a good man, and he certainly seems to have had a long fuse. Still the situation in Ekaterinoslav deteriorated to the point where Barringer almost used physical violence against Skvortsov.

The decisive moment came in early August when Skvortsov is said to have gone "on a rampage," arresting an ARA traffic agent and giving orders to the native personnel, which was forbidden. When he persisted and threatened to make more arrests, Barringer says, "it brought us nearly to blows."

The situation was saved by the dispatch from Moscow of Comrade Volodin, formerly Eiduk's and now Lander's principal assistant. It seems that Lander had been made aware of the Skvortsov problem and sent Volodin down to straighten him out. One evening at dinner, in the presence of several Americans, he openly reprimanded Skvortsov for his uncooperative behavior. From that moment until October, when Barringer left for Simbirsk to join in the search for Phil Sheild and then to remain on as district supervisor, Skvortsov "gave no further trouble and was always willing to do what was requested. He was indeed a changed man." "[A]s meek as a lamb" is how Barringer described him in a letter to Haskell.

In Simbirsk Barringer received a letter from his ex-Cheka expressing great regret at the American's transfer and sending him a "Russian 'spassibo'" for his "self-denial" and "humanly feelings." The flame of goodwill flickers as Skvortsov closes with a request that Barringer provide assistance to his in-laws, who live ten miles outside of Simbirsk city.

After the mission, in 1924, he sent Barringer a letter in Virginia, remembering him as "a friend with whom I once worked on the famine front."[2]

It may be that the warm sentiments expressed in these letters were genuine. Nonetheless, Barringer's successor, George Harrington, arrived to find that Skvortsov had spread the story that Barringer had been removed at Skvortsov's request. It did not take long for government relations in Ekaterinoslav to degenerate once again and then, in the spring of 1923, to reel out of control.

THE PRINCIPAL AMERICAN figure in the next round of action with Skvortsov was William J. Murphy, a thirty-year-old native of Portland, Maine, whom Harrington remembered fifty years after these events as having been "somewhat impulsive and hot-tempered"—which sounds like a good match for Skvortsov. It also played to one of the ARA men's favorite stereotypes, the hotheaded Irishman. This is probably in part why, after their showdown, Murphy was so readily credited with having struck down Skvortsov.

The record shows that there was trouble brewing between these two men even before their first encounter. Murphy was stationed in the Ukrainian town of Aleksandrovsk, seventy-five miles south of Ekaterinoslav, where as head of the food remittance division he was in charge of dispersing ARA food packages. In the first week of January 1923 he closed down an ARA warehouse for several hours because the local authorities—possibly one of Skvortsov's direct subordinates—failed to supply the ARA with fuel for the personnel house. It appears to have been a minor affair as these things went and was shortly resolved.

Soon afterward Murphy was reassigned to Ekaterinoslav city, where he was to head up the food and clothing remittance program. He arrived in the afternoon by automobile, accompanied by two young ladies, an ARA clerk and typist, who had been transferred with him. Skvortsov happened to be on the street when Murphy motored into town, and he did not like what he saw. Perhaps he was already prejudiced against the American for the Aleksandrovsk warehouse episode. Whatever the case, he asked one of the ARA employees to find out for him the identity of

Murphy's female companions and stated that Murphy had traveled to Ekaterinoslav "with a regular harem."

This was not a good beginning and serious trouble was not long in coming. Friday, January 19, was a religious holiday, the feast of the Epiphany, the day the local Orthodox priests went in procession to the Dnepr to bless the waters. Harrington told his employees to come to work anyway in view of the ARA's heavy work load. When word of this reached Skvortsov, alienated son of a priest and devotee of the teachings of Karl Marx, he drove over to headquarters and, finding Murphy on duty, ordered him to close the office in observance of the feast of the Epiphany. This Murphy gladly refused to do, and Skvortsov vowed to report him.

One week later, out of the blue, Harrington received a letter from Skvortsov demanding that Murphy be removed from the ARA because of his behavior at Aleksandrovsk. Harrington would not hear of this, and in his reply he stated that Murphy was much too valuable a worker to be let go for no legitimate reason. Subsequent events would bear out that he was sincere in this assessment of Murphy. The local soviet authorities then entered the picture, also demanding Murphy's ouster, but Harrington stood firm: "Mr. Murphy will not be moved."

Eventually the tension subsided and all seemed to be back on track until, at the end of March, Lander in Moscow informed Cyril Quinn, standing in for Haskell, that he was receiving negative reports out of Ekaterinoslav about Murphy. One of the principal accusations against the American was that he favored the Russian intelligentsia with food packages while sending "Jews and the shabbily dressed" to the Jewish Joint Distribution Committee, the JDC. He was also charged with giving food packages exclusively to "ex-bourgeois intellectuals" and with soliciting sex from a woman in exchange for a food package, reportedly telling her that he would oblige her "only after he had paid her a visit at home." Generally, it was said that the ARA employees, especially the women, complained of his rough treatment. Lander closed his letter to Quinn with a demand for Murphy's immediate recall, declaring that the local authorities and the general population demanded it.

Coming from the chief plenipotentiary, these were serious charges. At a time when ARA-Soviet relations were on the mend and with the mission only a few months from completion the ARA wished to keep friction with the central government to a minimum. Quinn informed Harrington that since Murphy's case had "assumed more and more difficult proportions," the accused should come at once to Moscow for a hearing. But he also wrote, "It seems to me the main source of the trouble is the Government representative at Ekaterinoslav on whom it would also be a good idea to send me complete data."

Harrington sent Murphy to Moscow, followed on April 13 by a point-by-point written refutation of Lander's charges, which he labeled "absurd" and "cooked up." With regard to the recipients of ARA food packages, Harrington confirmed that many were indeed from the dispossessed classes, citing as examples the princesses Golitsyna and Meshcherskaia, but he maintained that this was after all the point of this kind of relief, which was precisely why the Soviets were so hostile to it from the first. About one-half of the packages were distributed to Jews while the remainder of the Jewish applicants were directed to the JDC by arrangement with this ARA-affiliated organization.

As to the charge that Murphy tried to buy a girl with a food package, first of all, Murphy always had an interpreter with him in his office. "And in the second place, if we had to worry about every girl or woman who leaves his office or mine, after being refused a food package, in tears we would have time for nothing else."

The idea that the local population was clamoring for Murphy's removal Harrington dismissed as "too ridiculous." Murphy, he said, was the most popular ARA man in town because local citizens believed that he was personally responsible for distributing them food packages. The whole affair, Harrington claimed, was the result of a "pure case of spleen" on Skvortsov's part.

Attached to this letter was a lengthy counterindictment of Skvortsov, which among other things accused him of actively working to discredit the ARA. It described a flagrant case that had occurred only a few days before, on Easter Sunday, which found the ARA men in church, "a most natural thing." On the following day a priest from the church came to the ARA personnel house to thank the relief workers and the American people for their generosity. Later in the day the church choir, uninvited, came to the house to show appreciation in song to the Americans, who then served the party what Harrington calls "a little refreshment."

On the next day Skvortsov came to Harrington and in his very excellent bass accused the ARA of breaking the Riga Agreement by spreading political and religious propaganda against the Soviet government. "He also claimed that we invited the choir to our house, made them all drunk and promised them all packages. As there were thirty people in all, and as fully a third were children under fifteen, this was rather startling. This story has now spread all over Ekaterinoslav, especially among government circles."

On another occasion, after the theft of cocaine from the ARA medical warehouse, Skvortsov sent a militiaman to the train station with orders to intercept and search a departing ARA man and his baggage for the stolen stuff. This was said to have been done ostentatiously with the intent of creating maximum scandal.

One of Skvortsov's most annoying habits was his repeated demand to be given copies of the lists of food and clothing package recipients. And so on.

Harrington concluded with the observation that as Skvortsov was suffering from tuberculosis "it has occurred to me that his health might improve in another climate. . . . At all events, I am sure that the effectiveness of our program will increase in inverse ratio to proximity of the present representative."

Whether or not this report helped his defense, Murphy was able to satisfy the ARA chiefs that he was innocent of all charges. Haskell wrote to Lander informing him that Murphy was clean and, turning the tables, demanded that Skvortsov be removed from his post. How seriously he intended to pursue this is unclear. At any rate, at Moscow headquarters the controversy appeared to have been laid to rest—until May 5, when an urgent telegram arrived from Harrington stating that Murphy had been arrested and imprisoned by order of Skvortsov and that he was to be sent under guard to Kharkov.

The ARA Americans enjoyed immunity from arrest under the Riga Agreement so this message must have caused quite a jolt. Harrington asked that Moscow send someone down "with full authority to define our rights."

Both Haskell and Quinn were out of Moscow when this communication arrived, but acting chief Tommy Burland moved swiftly and decisively. He delivered a note to Lander protesting this "flagrant violation" of the Riga Agreement

and issuing an ultimatum: at 6:00 P.M. he would send Harrington a cable ordering that all feeding in the Ekaterinoslav district be stopped unless Murphy were
released and Skvortsov removed and left with "no connection whatsoever with
the operation of the A. R. A. in any of its branches."

Lander's response was equally swift. Gilchriese in Moscow said that he was
"genuinely distressed and jumped on the wire with more speed than any Russian
has displayed since the inception of work here." His reply was remarkably conciliatory, offering apologies to Burland, Harrington, and Murphy. At the same time he
claimed that he had received information that Murphy had "beaten" one of Skvortsov's men, and he requested that the American be urgently recalled to Moscow.[3]

Just what did happen in Ekaterinoslav?

On Friday morning, May 4, Skvortsov's representative at the food remittance
station, a man named Levine, was questioning recipients of ARA clothing packages. He had earlier demanded and been denied a list of the recipients, so he was
standing outside the office taking down their names and addresses as well as the
names of the benefactors outside of Soviet Russia who had paid for the packages.
This was at minimum a form of intimidation. Harrington ordered him to stop
and Levine went away.

At about 1:00 P.M. Murphy came by and found Levine standing in the same
place engaged in the same activity. He snatched the paper out of his hand and
told him to step into his office. Murphy was evidently quite hot because although
Levine followed him to the door he refused to enter. Ellingston, sitting in Moscow, thought that this demonstrated "a good Jewish wariness when dealing with
an Irishman, certainly."

Murphy continues the narrative:

Thinking that he intended to make a scene before the employees I put my hand upon
his shoulder to urge him to come in but as he still resisted I slipped my hand to the
back of his neck, drew him in and closed the door. I then turned to him and with my
fist closed and my arm raised I told him in English that he must not continue to
bother either the persons who were receiving packages nor any of our employees.

Why he bothers to add the detail about speaking in English is curious since his
Russian was known to be minimal, and whatever Levine's competence in English, Murphy's body language must have gotten the point across.

Levine fled to Skvortsov's office and, pointing to a scratch on his hand, claimed
that Murphy had roughed him up. We know this because Callahan happened to
be in the same office and witnessed the scene. How significant was this "scratch"
is impossible to say, but it was all that Skvortsov needed to take action.

At about 3:00 P.M. he arrived by auto at the ARA office accompanied by two
armed men from the GPU. They flung open the door to Murphy's office as Skvortsov, who may have been wearing his signature cape at the time, strode in and in
his dramatic style pointed at Murphy and declared in Russian, "Arrest that man!"

At least they must have been words similar to these. Ellingston's mind's eye
envisioned the balloon above the caped crusader's head containing the words,
"There's the man." He also imagined that the "bayonet carrying" GPU men
"looked menacing."

Murphy himself does not tell us what Skvortsov said, possibly because he could not understand the Russian words. He wrote in his report, "I arose and called an interpreter."

The interpreter told him that he was under arrest for assaulting a government representative. Skvortsov ordered him to get his hat and coat and come along to the GPU prison. Murphy refused to budge and ordered the interpreter to stop translating Skvortsov's words. At this point Harrington arrived, and Skvortsov told him that he had orders from his superiors at Kharkov to transport Murphy to prison there under guard. He told Harrington outright that he had orders to arrest Murphy at the first opportunity, which the Levine incident presented. To Harrington it was clear that they were "just laying for a chance to start something against him."

Harrington invoked the American personnel's immunity from arrest and, showing the guards Murphy's ARA identification, asked them if they would recognize it, which they answered in the negative. At GPU headquarters he appealed to the chief, who also refused to acknowledge ARA immunity. Desperate to buy time he hit upon a diplomatic maneuver that in retrospect probably saved all parties much grief.

Harrington got Skvortsov to agree to place Murphy under house arrest and not put him on the train to Kharkov until Sunday. That Skvortsov went along with this may indicate that his violent temper had by then subsided and that he was beginning to apply some rational thought to the possible consequences of his actions. Had Murphy been put on that train, the affair would automatically have escalated and almost certainly become the subject of sensational publicity by the American correspondents—"Bolshevists Arrest Portland, ME, Famine Worker," and so on— which would have complicated the search for a diplomatic solution in Moscow.

Relieved to get away with this arrangement, Harrington thought he would humor the guards at GPU headquarters, assuring them that by confining Murphy to the ARA personnel house they had indeed placed him under arrest. "Oh, no," one of them laughed. "If he were arrested, he would be put in one of these rooms back here." That night GPU guards were stationed around the ARA house.[4]

Then, as they say, the wires began to burn between Ekaterinoslav and Moscow as Harrington sent his urgent telegram. The next day Skvortsov began to question the ARA employees about what they had seen the day before. He decided to detain five of them, telling Harrington that they would not be released until he handed over the list of clothing package recipients. All five were young women, whom Harrington did not wish to put through any further mental suffering, so he gave up the list.

At 10:00 P.M. Skvortsov came by to report that a telegram had arrived from Lander ordering him to release Murphy. There is no description of Skvortsov's comportment as he delivered the news, but he may well have felt relieved.

There could no longer be any question that the town of Ekaterinoslav was not big enough for both Murphy and Skvortsov. The question was, which should go? Burland wrote to Harrington that since word had it that Murphy had physically assaulted someone and since the ARA was so taken with the "admirable way" that Lander had handled the matter, Murphy should be sent to Moscow. Since the mission was winding down anyway, Murphy's release could neatly be attributed to the general cutback in personnel.

Meanwhile ARA Moscow headquarters was all abuzz at these goings-on. Ellingston wrote that it was the "Bolshoi scandale of the week," though no one had any clear information about what precisely had transpired. This was because the ARA chiefs tried to keep the story under wraps in order to prevent it from appearing in the newspapers. So the facts spread by rumor, with the inevitable distortion.

Harry Gilchriese, head of ARA publicity, got wind of the incident and confronted the chiefs so that they had to let him in on it. But in doing so they appear intentionally to have distorted the facts. Writing on May 7, before he could have interviewed Murphy and with all the enthusiasm of a gossip columnist, Gilchriese passed on the exciting details to the New York office. Of course, "the offensive Mr. Skvartsov" had caused the ARA "no end of trouble" in Ekaterinoslav. Nonetheless, it was Murphy who had been in the wrong because he "was inviting trouble when he let fly" and "punched the govt. representative in the vicinity of the jaw."

Evidently the ARA chiefs decided that this version of events would be easier to keep out of the American newspapers. It had no clear-cut commissar-villain; an American reliever shared the blame. And they knew that it would do Murphy's reputation within the organization no harm to have it thought that he laid out a plenipotentiary, especially Skvortsov.

The strategy worked. Gilchriese took Duranty into his confidence and managed to convince him that it would not be in the interests of the ARA to put out the story now that Murphy had been set free and "especially as he had been in the wrong." Burland records that there was some difficulty in getting the correspondents to agree to keep it quiet—they said that if it hit the local papers, they would have to file their own stories. Here Lander promised to keep the business out of the Soviet newspapers; thus it remained "air tight."

Back in Ekaterinoslav Harrington pleaded with Moscow to let Murphy stay on, so valuable was he to operations. He declared that he would almost be willing to agree to have Skvortsov retain his position if it meant that Murphy could keep his. Skvortsov, he noted incidentally, was "still on the job. . . . and is functioning as if nothing ever happened albeit he seems a bit subdued."[5]

In the end Murphy was sacrificed, but the order for Skvortsov's removal never came. He stayed on through the remaining weeks of the mission, with one more surprise up his sleeve.

CHAPTER 24

THE PROFESSOR AND THE SAILOR

Three weeks after the arrival of Skvortsov in Ekaterinoslav, on June 15, 1922, Barringer wrote to Page in New York:

The various [ARA] officials that visit us from time to time all say that each District Supervisor believes that he has less help, more trouble, worst govt. authorities to deal with, and the hardest job after all, than anyone else, so all we can do after that is to rest our case, but when this show is over I want to meet the fellow who conceived the idea that 250 Americans could feed the 8,000,000 Russians, amongst as many bandits in a milder sense.

Barringer was convinced that his ARA colleagues serving in the Volga region were far better off than he in his Ukrainian backwater and that the stories he was hearing about their fierce battles with Eiduk's plenipotentiaries were much exaggerated. "We who were in the Ukraine show felt with a certain amount of pride that our program was then more difficult on account of the quickness of the political life and we had moments of intense envy of the 'fellows on the Volga' who, we were lead to believe, were having everything there way."

He was given the opportunity to judge this for himself four months later when Phil Sheild's disappearance led to his transfer to Simbirsk as district supervisor. Six months on the job changed his opinion about the life of the fellows on the Volga:

It would be a great pity if some District Supervisor who is really gifted with the art of writing does not sit down now and write of his experiences. The true history of the ARA will never be until such experiences which have confronted the responsible men in the Districts has been recorded.

In many respects the relationships with the Government officials have been very much the same thru out Russia. . . .

In fact from what I have heard since I have been at Simbirsk and my experience here to date, it appears that I am dealing with the same old Bolo in all respects, except here the men in charge are hopefully enlightened.[1]

By the time Barringer arrived in Simbirsk the worst period of government relations in the district had passed. The first year of relief work, under the direction of Eddie Fox, had witnessed one storm after another. These were documented in considerable detail by James Somerville, Fox's second-in-command.

Somerville had more Russian experience than most ARA men. Born in 1892 in Vaiden, Mississippi, he received his B.A. and M.A. in economics from Washington and Lee University. Disqualified from the military draft because of defective vision in one eye, he served with the YMCA in Russia for five months in 1917–18 as a relief worker at hospitals for returning POWs. In 1918–19 he worked in a similar capacity for eleven months in north Russia with the Allied intervention forces and then with the YMCA in Germany and Poland. He could speak Russian, apparently quite well.

The Soviet authorities in Simbirsk were apparently not a bad lot. The first ARA party to the Volga in September 1921 found that while the Simbirsk officials did not measure up to those of Kazan, their attitudes were "excellent." Actually these initial reports spoke highly of the energy and ability of the top official in the province, Richard Rein, chairman of the *gubispolkom*—that is, of the executive committee of the provincial soviet. The Americans used this word—oftentimes misspelling it "gubispolkum"—to denote not only the committee but its chairman and the capitol building as well.

Rein was a genuine ethnic Lett. Somerville describes him in the Simbirsk history as "energetic, capable, and practical-minded." He was an experienced revolutionary of proletarian background. Imprisoned for his role in the 1905 revolution, he was kept in a jail cell for eleven years until the next revolution sprung him. Over a decade gritting it out behind bars in a tsarist prison, he was now himself something of a tsar in Simbirsk province.

His ARA counterpart was Eddie Fox, the jazzman from Erie who had endured years of confinement to a piano stool in order to share the concert stage with Miss Autumn Hall.

The Americans fell in with Rein from the start. They appreciated his "immense executive ability," a talent in short supply in revolutionary Russia. They also found his personality agreeable. "Rein has the temperament of a good American 'politician'—the hail-fellow-well-met type—and therefore there were no disagreements over trifles, and the atmosphere was in general favorable to agreement." Here was one Lett the Americans could work with. Of course, as Somerville observed, he was "a man whose forte was more in action than in logic," but they expected this from someone of his background.

Rein's assistants were said to be "the usual run," but he had the authority to make them run. This is not to imply that the Simbirsk ARA did not encounter the usual difficulties in starting up operations, especially in choosing local personnel satisfactory to Rein. And there was the perennial problem of securing money from the soviet to fund ARA operations. Yet the Simbirsk history presents the early period as one of relative calm; in fact looking back through the turbulence that followed, it seemed positively idyllic. Wrote Somerville, "Unfortunately such a state of affairs was too close an approach to the millennium to be allowed to continue."

It ended in early November 1921 when there arrived on the scene, without warning, a plenipotentiary representative from Moscow, a certain Lev Tarasov, or Leo Tarassoff in the anglicized ARA version. A "queer type," according to Somerville, although neither he nor his colleagues has left us a physical description of the man, nor are there any ARA photographs. Tarasov was one of those truly special characters tossed up by the tumult of the Russian Revolution. Under the old regime a professor of Latin at Moscow University, on this side of the looking glass he had been transformed—as incredible as it seemed—into a political commissar in the Red Army on the southern front during the struggle against Kolchak.

As the Americans figured it, during this period he must have come into the favor of Eiduk, which led to his present appointment. That was merely the provincial ARA man's guess, but how else could one explain it? Somerville wrote that Tarasov possessed a "poetic temperament and an unquenchable thirst for alcohol," which left him "without balance, and with not one iota of business capacity"—in other words, he was "quite unfit to cope with the job assigned to him."

His arrival in Simbirsk was greeted less like Muskatt's in Kazan, more like Skvortsov's in Ekaterinoslav. Fox was initially pleased that Moscow had sent down a troubleshooter who would help remedy the ARA's cash shortage, someone who spoke good English besides. Tarasov himself fed this fantasy. "From the profuse assurances of Tarassoff," wrote Somerville, "the District Supervisor had visions of special couriers with sackfuls of rubles, hurrying from Moscow." But soon enough he showed his true colors: "Instead of helping, Tarassoff only contrived to muddle things up."

He sought to block all communications between the ARA and soviet officials and insisted on signing off on even the most insignificant ARA request to the government. His impertinent behavior around the ARA office produced the intended result of intimidating local personnel and obstructing the work. Fox called him "a *professor* and if there is such a thing a *perfect* ass."

Not surprisingly, Rein regarded Tarasov as an interloper. When he discovered the nature of the plenipotentiary's mandate, he refused to accept it and wired Moscow for clarification. Beyond the institutional dimension to their rivalry, Rein's proletarian roots predisposed him to a special resentment of the bourgeois Tarasov, whom he is said to have regarded with "supreme contempt" and to whom he referred derisively in Russian as "the Professor"—phonetically close to Fox's "perfect ass."

Rein told Fox that he had ordered the "demagogue" Tarasov never to enter his office except on official business, and these two sometimes conspired to keep the plenipotentiary from exerting his influence over relief operations. Only one time did his meddling threaten the unity of the Simbirsk ARA. The incident involved Lenin himself.

Early in the operations, Fox hired a former Moscow University history professor by the name of Aleksei Yakovlev to be his office manager. He was a native of Simbirsk, where he and Lenin had been childhood friends. They somehow maintained a thread of contact over the years—or rather renewed it after Lenin's 1917 return from European exile—and on several occasions during the Civil War Yakovlev interceded with the Bolshevik leader on behalf of friends or acquaintances imprisoned by the Cheka. In 1920, to escape hunger in the capital, he returned to Simbirsk. By then famine in the provinces was only a year away.

It seems that Yakovlev, a specialist on seventeenth-century Russia, was unsuited for his ARA assignment, and after he committed what Fox regarded as an indiscretion, he was let go. He had in the meantime become friends with Somerville, who on his part had had his own disagreements with Fox, although these were apparently minor and now behind them. As Somerville put it, the first few days of operations had been rough and "not every spoken word of us three Americans was buttered with honey."

Somehow Tarasov became aware of this past friction, perhaps through Yakovlev, whose acquaintance he may have made at Moscow University. Exactly what he was told is unknown, but it was enough to inspire him to a bit of intrigue. He sent a telegram in original English to Haskell in Moscow, reporting serious personnel problems within the Simbirsk ARA. He felt in duty bound, he wrote, to bring to the colonel's attention the "tactless and rough conduct of M. Fox in his relations with the Russian people . . . his full ignorance of Russian life and language," and his "few intelligence."

In contrast to the wicked M. Fox there was M. Somerville, with his "high personal qualities," his "acquaintance of Russian language and life," and the obvious "public sympathy to him in local society." Surely it was evident to all that this man would be a "more convenient and usefull chief of local A R A section than M. Fox." Knowing that Colonel Haskell would desire to have the best possible organization in Simbirsk and in view of the "persistent disconscensions between two gentlemen," Tarasov advised him to remove M. Fox.

Tarasov closed this audacious communication on a warm note: "Please and my hearty filiditations to you of holy day 24 November. Your obedient servant Leo Tarassow."

Even by the standards for impudence set by Eiduk's satellites this was brazen behavior. Something must have possessed Tarasov to bypass Eiduk and approach Haskell directly. We know he had an aching ambition to return to Moscow. Perhaps it was Yakovlev's connection to Lenin. It may have inspired his poetic imagination with a vision of a summons to the Kremlin where the Great Leader praises his deft outmaneuvering of the sly M. Fox and other American imperialists: "Good work, Comrade Tarasov. We've decided that your talents will be put to better use here in the capital." Whatever his dreams of glory they soon turned to nightmares.

The Tarasov telegram, with its report of "disconscensions" between Fox and Somerville, was taken very seriously at ARA headquarters, where it was handled by Haskell's chief of staff, Colonel Tom Lonergan, a longtime acquaintance of Fox. Lonergan and Somerville had not gotten on well during their brief encounter in Moscow the previous September. The documentation is short on specifics, but Somerville's YMCA background and failure to serve in the army would have been two strikes against him with Lonergan, who may now have anticipated calling strike three. Was Somerville behind the Tarasov telegram?

The ARA men in Simbirsk, meanwhile, had no idea of Tarasov's doing until word of it arrived by post from Moscow, producing the effect of a "bombshell." Lonergan wanted details.

Fox's response cleared the air. He admitted that the two men had indeed had their differences in the beginning but had reached an understanding. Somerville was very definitely "playing the game"; Tarasov was playing a different kind of game.

Soon after Fox's letter reached Lonergan, Tarasov received a telegram from Moscow. It was not from Lenin. Eiduk was ordering him to Moscow for a "consultation."

Before Tarasov's departure Fox was invited to meet with him. He walked into the plenipotentiary's office surprised to find a table covered with a large selection of food and bottles of vodka, cognac, and wine—the sumptuousness of the spread a measure of Tarasov's concern for his job. He now wished to mend fences with Fox and admitted to the district supervisor that he had recommended to Haskell his replacement by Somerville, "an older man."

Tarasov begged Fox to have a drink with him.

He loves his liquor and it did not take long for him to begin to talk. He began by telling me that [he] felt he could do his country more good in the capacity of a professor than his present duties which was signing papers written by me.

I said I thought it was a shame that his Government should send such an intelligent man, a former professor of the University of Moscow, to do such inferior work. He said he was disgusted with his duties and would not return from Moscow unless he had to.

Fox quotes Tarasov as saying, "You see, Mr. Fox, my Government suspects the A.R.A. of having political motives back of relief work, and Mr. Eiduck's orders must be carried out as he is a strong man in the Chechka." He also warned Fox that if he did not return from Moscow, the American should be considerate of Professor Yakovlev, who was "very friendly with certain powers in Moscow."

Tarasov survived his consultation with Eiduk and kept his job, which meant that he was forced to return from Moscow. He came back in a much more conciliatory mood—that is, until the desk incident in December.

As the story is told, Tarasov walked into the supply department at ARA headquarters and simply took over the desk of a Russian employee, who was absent at the time. Just why he suddenly became obsessed with this particular desk is not clear, but supply chief Evan Renshaw resisted. Tarasov protested, declaring that he was in absolute control of the ARA and that this was a Russian, not an American office. When Renshaw still refused to give way, Tarasov demanded the dismissal of the inconvenient employee, but as he had no authority over Russian personnel this was an empty gesture.

Fox's letter to Haskell recounting this incident closed with an expression of impatience echoed by other district supervisors in the final months of 1921: "As I have not received any information from Hqdrs outlining the work of Mr. Eiduck's representative in connection with the work of this office, I should like to have his duties defined."

The outcome of the desk episode deflated Tarasov's pride and diminished his authority, and he seemed despondent. In fact he lost interest in the work, remaining out of town for long stretches. Somerville wrote in the Simbirsk history:

Toward the end Mr Tarassoff quite lost his belligerency, and became what he himself styled a "super-diplomat," which, as it seemed to us, consisted chiefly in his becoming excessively convivial as a result of continuous imbibings from an apparently inexhaustible supply of alcohol. In such moments he was apt to become very confiding, and would tell how he really had been sent to Simbirsk by Mr Eiduk with a commission to spy on the activities of the Americans—a job which he himself hated, etc., etc.[2]

After departing Simbirsk for good in early March 1922, Tarasov resurfaced a few weeks later in Ufa. The ARA Ufa mission enjoyed a glowing reputation for its handling of government relations, second only to Kazan's. Its success was at-tributed to the genius of the district supervisor, Colonel Walter Bell, who had an extraordinary way with people, even comrades. Reading through the Ufa docu-mentation, one comes away with the feeling that the job of relief in that district was so huge that there was simply no time for the petty disputes that marked government relations elsewhere, such as fighting over a desk.

Bell held regular conferences with the plenipotentiaries and local officials on all important questions, making them feel a part of the operation even as he al-lowed them little input into final decisions. The idea, Bell says, was to intimidate them by showing up their ignorance in famine relief matters. Tarasov seems to have been thoroughly cowed upon his arrival in the district. Or perhaps his Sim-birsk experiences had humbled him. Whatever the reason, the Tarasov of Ufa was no longer the troublemaker he had been in Simbirsk.

In one of the several histories of the ARA Ufa mission there is a paragraph about him that reads like something out of the *Lives of the Saints*:

Professor L. Tarasov, possessing a great spirit of humanity and desirous of doing all possible to relieve the misery, joining us as representative in the late winter of 1921–22, was the first of these [plenipotentiaries] to realize the real spirit of the work of the A.R.A. and on his part carried out to the fullest extent possible every reasonable re-quest made through him to the various local authorities. With a good knowledge of the English language our liaison became much closer and all in all much credit and thanks are due to Mr Tarasov.

This sounds like propaganda composed by Bell for the ARA publicity depart-ment. In another document Bell describes him on a human scale: "strongly com-munistic, formerly professor of dead languages." He had, writes the colonel, one idea in mind: to get control of ARA operations, which of course was "hopeless from the start and never had a chance, in fact [it] became quite a joke, at least on our part."

Bell probably never learned of Bill Kelley's contribution to the taming of Tara-sov. On Saturday, April 1, there was a party at the ARA personnel house, among the invitees being some members of the government and the newly arrived plenipotentiary. Kelley guessed what was on Tarasov's mind and could barely re-strain himself from setting the professor straight on how little his mandate meant in Ufa.

Well, some wicked person gave me a couple of vodkas. Whereupon I buttonholed the genial Professor and gave him the strongest talk on the sanctity of the Riga Agree-ment and the duty of the Soviet Government that I fancy any of their plenipoten-tiaries have ever taken. He swallowed it all and when he left at three A.M. he insisted that he went only on condition that I promise to continue the discussion at our next opportunity. Had Bell heard what I said he would have been disturbed I know, but I am sure that it did no harm and if he took my words to heart one-tenth as much as he seemed to, it will do some good. Personally the old boy is well disposed toward me. He expressed the fear that I am too "idealistic."

Whatever Kelley's buttonholing had to do with it, Bell reports that in time Tarasov became "most friendly," and as far as the Americans at Ufa could tell, he did his best to aid the relief work although "he never really grasped what the whole thing was about." In the end, the ARA men "admired his large-hearted desire to do all possible to help the ones in such great need."

In June, Tarasov moved on, apparently called away by a serious illness in his family. His successors in Ufa appear to have been well liked, although they make no major splash in the Ufa documentation; in fact, barely a ripple. First came Tarasov's secretary, Charles Mayer, a veteran of the Latvian aviation service. The generous Bell calls him a "large-hearted chap" and the "largest asset we had." Before long Mayer was called to Moscow to take over the boot-making industry, so it was said, and was replaced by Bernhard Hermann, a Latvian cavalry veteran with whom the Americans built a "strong friendship" and who "enjoyed the spirit of American hospitality that dominated our private life."[3] Thus did the Ufa district of the ARA lead a relatively charmed life of government relations.

MEANWHILE, back in Simbirsk the departure of Tarasov in March 1922 marked the beginning of a time of troubles that would make the Americans long for the "lame duck days" of the professor of Latin. His successor was Stephen Chernikh, who had once been a sailor with the Baltic fleet before becoming a Red Army commissar. Somerville described him as a "big, rough fellow of peasant extraction, of rather dominant personality . . . not, however, a particularly brainy individual"; in fact he was "a peasant type with less than his due share of brains, but making up for this deficiency by a certain decisiveness and self confidence."

The brains to Chernikh's brawn was his assistant, Roman Weller, a former Russian émigré not long from the United States, who was later to gain mission-wide notoriety for a missing decimal point. The Americans attributed his qualifications for the job largely to his Semitic heritage. Somerville, who says they dubbed him "Samuel," refers to him as "an alert energetic little Jew" with a good command of English, French, and German and with a "leaning toward diplomacy, and a consuming ambition to go higher in the world."

When Chernikh arrived on March 6, the Americans in Simbirsk were feeding one-half the population of the district. "Surely, if ever, they had reason to expect good will and confidence," reads the district history. "Instead they got a commissar." He came to town with the air of a conqueror, certain that these bourgeois American boys would be as "putty in his hands. What could a few youngsters, ignorant of Russia, do against his authority and his skilled experience in working the hidden wires of that instrument of control that enables three hundred thousand Communists to be the masters of one hundred million Russians?"

One Chernikh satellite after another surfaced in the subdistricts as he launched a drive to gain control over the ARA. In Simbirsk city he assembled a team of office assistants, four or five inspectors, and a corps of traveling inspectors, creating a buzz of activity intended to give the impression that the ARA was a Soviet government operation.

Chernikh parked his desk in a room situated between that of the district supervisor, Fox, and the general office, "an excellent look-out station," according to Somerville. There the former sailor held important conferences and carried out his heavy load of duties, always with a pretense of supreme authority. Still, there must have been idle moments even for Chernikh, since it is reported that he had the habit of wandering over to an American's desk and "carelessly fingering such of your papers as were in reach." One such occasion provoked a lecture from Fox on office ethics.

Unlike Tarasov, Chernikh was able to establish good relations with Rein, which made it far more difficult to keep Chernikh at bay.

Three weeks after the coming of Chernikh and Weller, one of the Simbirsk Americans drew up some notes on their "campaign for credit and control." Chernikh's strong point was that he was a "military man of action, who knows what he wants, and the way to get it." He had a special ability to "instill a certain 'fear of God' into the hearts of the ARA Russian personnel. . . . For such work his experience as a political commissar in the Red army comes in handy. I suspect he could teach the old Ku Klux Klan quite a few tricks in the art of invisible control." In any case, he made life at ARA headquarters more interesting than in the "burlesque days of Tarassoff."

The Americans did find that in specific areas they could harness Chernikh's raw energy to further the relief work. He and Weller proved to be adept at digging up the scarce funds to support day-to-day ARA operations; they were especially helpful when it came to the district's transportation problems. And it was rewarding for the ARA man, fed up on Soviet bureaucratic paralysis and inefficiency, to watch the mighty Chernikh in action, rolling the heads of obstructionist bureaucrats content to put off action on critical matters until *zaftra*, tomorrow. Particularly effective was

his favorite knock-em-down-and-drag-em-out gesture with a bared arm, closed fist, and prize-fighter grin, in response to all requests for some quick action from some government department. It was quite effective. You could fairly see "zaftra"-minded officials being bowled over, and picking themselves up in frantic haste to get that job done for the A.R.A. But he did it too much; and one soon learned that it was only a gesture.

Chernikh's manner was not amusing to the Simbirsk Russian personnel, who were subject to his methods of intimidation. Having failed to insinuate himself into the personnel selection process, he sought to establish himself as a kind of father-confessor to the native employees. This usually entailed inviting one or more of them into his office for a little chat, an invitation they had no choice but to accept although Fox had strictly forbidden direct contact between the government representative and local staff.

When the door closed, Chernikh would gently remind them that they were not in America and that one day the ARA would leave Simbirsk. These words, Somerville reminds his reader, were delivered by a "fierce-looking former political commissar with a smiling, oily little Jew at his elbow to complete the picture of future vengeance."

The Simbirsk ARA's two-front war—hunger and disease on the one hand, Chernikh and Weller on the other—continued without letup until April, when the Americans got a lucky break. Chernikh, apparently with the collaboration of Rein, had conspired to divert an ARA corn car in the railroad yard and distribute from it six sacks of American corn to government employees. By Russian standards a matter of a few sacks of corn was strictly small-time, but in the new NEP era, with the Cheka aiming its sights on official graft, it was for Chernikh potentially disastrous. With comrades like these, who needed enemies of the people?

Fox somehow picked up the scent of this dirty deed, and by means of a series of cleverly written communications to a suddenly unnerved Chernikh he succeeded in cornering the commissar. It ended with a reprimand from Eiduk and a falling-out with Rein: "Tchernik never quite recovered from this humiliation and in fact became a meeker and wiser man."

The final victory came in June when Lander replaced Eiduk and sent down word to his plenipotentiaries that in fact they had no rights beyond those set forth in their written mandates—a concept that might have come as a rude shock to Chernikh. After this, he mellowed considerably and turned into a "pretty decent representative" until his removal in late summer.

He found much solace in his favorite sport of drinking somebody else under the table. His vodka supply was equal to Tarassoff's. It also made him equally affectionate; and at such times he would bring his rich breath within two inches of one's ear and whisper interminably—about future best excursions on the Volga, numerous private passenger cars that he expected soon to receive from Moscow, or beautiful ladies in The Crimea, or nearer home. And when he finally departed for The Crimea—as he thought—very happy over the prospect of living in the best vineyard in Russia, and properly primed in advance for coming delights, he astounded two Americans who happened to be at the station by kissing them with impulsive affection (they had left their revolvers at home).

It is unclear whether he made it to his Crimean paradise, but by the spring of 1923 he could be found clenching his fists and raising havoc in the ARA district of Rostov on the lower Volga. His successor in Simbirsk, a man named Lipatov, was by comparison a "hopeless jellyfish."

As for the ambitious Weller, he was rewarded with the post of secretary to Madame Kameneva, head of the Soviet famine committee, although one would be hard-pressed to attribute this promotion to any particular achievements in Simbirsk. A few years later he decided that he had had enough of Soviet political life and made his way out of Russia to New York City, where an ARA man helped get him a job at Macy's.[4]

CHAPTER 25

AND THE SHOW WHIRLED MERRILY ON

Government relations in Ekaterinoslav and Simbirsk never descended to the depths of incivility mined in the ARA district of Orenburg. All things considered, this state of affairs seems to have been due in part to the utter remoteness of the district, most of which lay in Asia.

Orenburg was the capital of the Kirghiz Autonomous Soviet Socialist Republic, yet another Soviet Muslim political entity, situated at the southeast extremity of European Russia along the southern ranges of the Ural Mountains and extending southeast into the steppe. Orenburg city is located on the right bank of the Ural River, the dividing line between two continents. As the ARA Orenburg history states: "a stroll from the office in the evening brings one to the ferry over the Ural River where one can cross from Europe to Asia for a few thousand roubles."

Orenburg was not included in the ARA relief picture in the initial stages of the mission when it was assumed that the "famine zone" constituted primarily the Volga valley. But once the territories east of the Volga—and in the southern Ukraine as well—were inspected and discovered to have famine conditions on a comparable scale, the ARA made plans to move in.

In November 1921 Moscow headquarters sent out Freddie Lyon, along with Dr. Walter Davenport and an interpreter, to set up operations in what was considered No-Man's-Land. Lyon was a twenty-four-year-old University of Michigan graduate from Cleveland who signed on with the ARA from the Graves Registration Service, generally considered the source of the lowest-caliber ARA recruits. This did not prevent him from becoming one of the best-liked men in the Russian unit.

That an inexperienced Graves man was sent out virtually alone—a mere boy among the "half-savage" Kirghiz—says something about the priority the chiefs in Moscow assigned to Orenburg, especially in the early months. They had their hands full trying to staff the Volga missions from a limited supply of seasoned baby feeders. Lyon was made acting district supervisor until one of the Volga men could be freed up to relieve him.

His unpleasant journey by boxcar to Orenburg, followed upon arrival by his sleepless night in a filthy train station fending off the airborne shucks of sunflower seeds, must have eaten away at his spirit. In town he found an appalling lack of even the most basic facilities for his work. There was no typewriter available, and paper and pencils could be had only with great difficulty.

Orenburg city had been occupied by the Reds and Whites three times each and heavily shelled during the Civil War; its state of near-complete dilapidation discouraged Lyon from searching for a separate ARA headquarters building. Instead he accepted the offer of the local soviet officials to use a room in their building until appropriate office space could be found; for living quarters he checked into the Soviet Hotel. This was reserved for distinguished guests, as he wrote to Don Renshaw in Moscow.

With the aid of the candle I could distinguish my bed—the room resembled one in a fraternity house the "morning after" a real "collegy" soirée—"now when I was in college." Actually Don, I did not know whether to laugh or cry—the result was that I flew into a rage and told them that if they wanted me to feed children here that they would have to "snap out of their hops" and give me a clean room. They immediately turned me into the supposedly best room in the house—a hell of a place but I was too tired to complain further.

Lyon's arrangement for the ARA office was highly irregular and would almost certainly have been overruled by the chiefs had they been aware of it: it would have seemed like a virtual invitation to the government to meddle in the relief work. But Lyon may have been eager to avoid a fuss with the local soviet crowd, who apparently had been given no advance notice about his arrival and had great difficulty making sense of all the "whereases" and "therefores" in his copy of the Riga Agreement. Besides it was thirty-five degrees below zero, cold enough to make the soviet office building seem positively cozy to a young American in a strange land.

As Orenburg was already in the dead of winter, this made a visual assessment of famine conditions in the city nearly impossible. Frozen corpses could be seen along the streets, but many more were said to be buried underneath the snow.

On November 12 the first ARA food shipment arrived by rail—quantities of flour, cocoa, beans, sugar, milk, rice, and corn—the initial shipment toward the feeding of fifty thousand children. Lyon wired a request to Moscow that this total be doubled, and he went about the business of building a staff, organizing kitchens, creating local ARA committees, finding warehouse space, and arranging for the transportation of food supplies to the interior.

Overwhelmed by the enormity of his assignment and discouraged by the dearth of qualified personnel in his midst, Lyon knew he would have to count on the support of the local authorities if he had any hope of putting his show over. And so he requested a meeting with the highest authority in the land, the president of the Kirghiz republic.

I had been thrilled at the thought of seeing a president of a republic on official business—this thrill made me forget temporarily that I was in the Land of the Proletariat. Therefore I was quite startled at my first glimpse of him—I thought for a minute they had led me into the janitor's quarters. But not so—this individual before me was actually the President of the Republic, a small yellow-skinned, slit-eyed man who sat in the ruler's chair with his legs curled under him like a little child, and crudely called out to me as I entered—"Greetings Comrade."

The president said all the appropriate things about giving full cooperation to the ARA, but more generous promises of assistance were soon forthcoming from another quarter: because of the late date there was no lag time between the opening of ARA operations in Orenburg and the arrival of Eiduk's plenipotentiary.

Barely had I made a survey of my new home when the door opened and in bounced a thin, pimply faced little Jew. He introduced himself as the government representative with the A.R.A. and produced numerous stamped mandates to prove it—he was Comrade Moroz. His appearance was very strongly against him and I knew that he and I were to have our troubles. I later learned that previous to the revolution he had been a tailor's helper and was at this time the head of the Cheka of the whole republic, and his word was law.[1]

This was Grigorii Semenovich Moroz, collegium member of the Cheka and since December 1920 Cheka representative in Kirghizia. It was unusual to have the local head of the secret police present himself as the plenipotentiary to the ARA, but this was not to be the last unusual occurrence in Orenburg.

Moroz has been rather widely quoted by historians, as Cheka officials go, largely because he wrote newspaper articles. In one of these, in the pages of *Izvestiia* in 1918, he wrote, "There is no sphere of our life where the Cheka does not have its eagle eye." This was the spirit of an article he published in the local Orenburg daily shortly after Lyon's arrival, which called for vigilance over the ARA and had a chilling effect on its nascent native staff.

Comrade Moroz was not the only caller claiming to be the plenipotentiary to the ARA. Soon there came knocking a second such individual. Then a third. Then another. "By the 1st of December I was completely hemmed in by so-called government representatives—there were six of them and each one had stamped mandates to prove that he was the legitimate representative. They took turns bouncing in and out of my office." Lyon put up with this Marx Brothers routine for a few weeks and then hired "the biggest man in Orenburg" to guard his door and let no one in without his permission.

At the time of Lyon's arrival it was estimated that there were 150 deaths per day in the city and over 800 in the district. The city was swarming with refugees fleeing the villages on foot and by wagon, camel, and rail. Fifty thousand rations were not going to save the situation. Even to execute this plan he faced a thousand and one obstacles to do with personnel, transportation, warehouse space, and the elements.

His problems were compounded by the difficulty of communicating with Moscow, which increased his sense of isolation. During these first weeks the average time elapsing between the dispatch of a telegram from Moscow and its arrival in Orenburg—"including transmission, translation, re-translation, re-transmission, wires down, etc."—was two weeks.

Despite the spirited tone of his letters, whose sardonic humor was a great hit at Moscow headquarters, he must have been under an enormous strain. Duranty met him when he returned to Moscow in February 1922 and wrote that upon his "cheerful American youth the experience of the last three months has stamped an indelible impression."[2] In late November, working alone under siege for long hours, his health gave out.

AT ABOUT THIS SAME TIME, some two hundred miles to the southwest as the vulture flies, in the town of Uralsk in the Saratov district, Walter H. Coleman received word that he was to proceed to Orenburg to serve as district supervisor. Uralsk was located at the eastern dead-end of the railway extension beyond the Volga, and so Coleman would have to backtrack west to Saratov city, about two hundred miles in all, and then circle around along a northeastern route by way of Samara, then east to Orenburg—a difficult winter journey on the Russian railway.

News of his reassignment reached Coleman on November 25, and he left that day, traveling first by train to Pokrovsk then by icebreaker and boxcar to Saratov. From there he had to travel by boxcar even though he claims to have seen in the Saratov train station "at least fifty splendid class wagons standing idle." At Samara, although he had secured an International Sleeping Car ticket, he had to ask the help of the Cheka to get a seat in a third-class car, which when located was found to be so overcrowded with refugees that he needed the assistance of armed guards to get to his seat.

One of the main problems for the Orenburg ARA was transportation. The main railway line from Moscow to Tashkent ran straight through the district, but it was a single track, and in winter it was frequently blocked with snow for weeks at a time. In fact during the winter of 1921–22 it was impassable for six straight weeks, which created tremendous difficulties, holding up supplies and preventing couriers from coming and going.

But that was still several weeks away. Coleman's problem on the trip from Samara to Orenburg was not the snow. His train was unheated, and although the WC was but four feet away, he says it was "impossible" to reach, so tightly packed were the passengers. If it was literally impossible, this may have made it terribly uncomfortable for him as the trip took thirty-six hours. He arrived "alive with vermin" in Orenburg on December 13, eighteen days after setting out from Uralsk.

Orenburg was under five feet of snow, and the temperature stood at forty below zero. The city was under martial law. Frozen corpses were lying about. Freddie Lyon was flat on his back, and the ARA staff and supplies were securely in the hands of the local government.

Coleman essentially shut down operations and rebuilt them from scratch. In a letter to Moscow he expressed amazement that headquarters had charged an inexperienced kid like Lyon with the responsibility for administering relief to what in Central Europe would amount to an entire country. Coleman's outspokenness and irreverent tone marked all of his correspondence and did not endear him to his ARA chiefs.

He informed Moscow that the Orenburg train station was jammed with four thousand refugees and that near the station there were four trains, filled with would-be passengers, going nowhere. Every day the doors of the cars would be opened and the dead removed.

Coleman monitored this situation. On January 13 he reported to Moscow that another eighty refugees had "cashed in" the day before and another thirty up until noon that day.

One of his first acts was to demand office space outside of the soviet building, and he was able to secure the top floor of the old Siberian Bank building; in time, room by room, the ARA occupied the entire structure. He also issued the first of his numerous warnings to local officials to give up their attempts to dominate the ARA.

Among his most immediate tasks was to sort through the mandates of the various pretenders to the post of government representative. There was Comrade Moroz. There was also a certain Rowden, said to be "ex-president" of the local

Cheka and a former resident of England. There were also Karlin, Ivanov, Serajedz, and a man named London, who had apparently never lived in England. London's "mandate" was the most objectionable: it empowered him outright to direct and control ARA operations in Orenburg.

The most interesting candidate was Anna Karlin, who spoke perfect English, the result of years of residence in Detroit, where she had run unsuccessfully for chief of the board of education on the Socialist ticket and from where she had recently been deported. She said she had left behind a daughter.[3]

The plenipotentiary question gave Coleman his introduction to the mix of national and political-administrative entities that composed the ARA Orenburg district. Typically the territorial parameters of a district took shape over the course of several months as ARA traveling inspectors assessed the need for and feasibility of relief in one and then another region.

The Orenburg district came to consist of two provinces of the Kirghiz republic—Orenburg and Aktiubinsk—part of a third, Kustanai, and five cantons of the southern fringe of the Bashkir republic in the Ural Mountains. The greater part of the Bashkir republic was under the administration of the ARA Ufa district. On August 1, 1922, the Orenburg district constituted 63,320 square miles, about the size of North Dakota.

Kirghizia, like Tatarstan and Bashkiria, was an administrative subdivision of the Russian republic, another product of Moscow's divide-and-rule strategy for dealing with Soviet Russia's Muslims. It was one of the five Muslim republics of Soviet Central Asia—Tatarstan and Bashkiria were considered the Volga-Urals region.

The populations of both the Bashkir and Kirghiz republics had sided heavily with the Whites in the Civil War, and as a consequence Moscow exerted more rigid control there than in Tatarstan, keeping an even sharper eye on local political affairs. At least this was how the Americans stationed in these territories viewed it. As they saw it, Moscow ruled over the area with a "rod of iron." Coleman stated it crudely: "The Kirghis Republic is supposed to have autonomy. It has to the extent that the Kirghis are outnumbered on the Soviet by the henchmen of Moscow, a splendid jewish crowd of gentlemen who all wear guns and terrorize the town. Not openly, but their secret methods so well known keep everyone in a complete turmoil of fear."

Relations between the Khirgiz and the Bashkirs were complicated as well, in part due to dissatisfaction with the geographical delineations of the two republics, which the Americans concluded had been designed in Moscow with this result in mind. Coleman referred to a "continual series of banana wars," which was interfering with the relief work. The Orenburg district history speaks of "more or less jealousy" prevailing between the Bashkirs and the Kirghiz, marked by charges and countercharges of being shortchanged in the ARA feeding: each republic thought it was getting less than its fair share.

The situation was further confused by a lack of adequate maps. The Orenburg Americans discovered that none of the maps at hand agreed on the parameters of the Kirghiz republic. The only authentic one belonged to the president of the republic, and he loaned it to the ARA to copy. It had to be amended within a few months. On July 1, 1922, Orenburg province was moved out of Kirghizia and brought into the Russian republic—part of the fine-tuning leading up to the formation of the Union of Soviet Socialist Republics at the end of the year.

So the Orenburg district was a mix of Kirghiz, Bashkirs, Tatars, Russians, and Jews. A large majority were Russians, by far most of them peasants. Regarding the upper classes Coleman wrote that "the best have flown or are dead with very few exceptions, and the few that remain are gradually being hounded to death."

Like the Tatars and Bashkirs, the Kirghiz are Turkic peoples of Sunni Muslim faith. The Bashkirs were the least religious of the three, their Muslim clergy being almost exclusively Tatar. At the time of the Revolution their chief livelihood was cattle breeding. They had been a main source of recruits for the Cossacks, which inspired Coleman to classify "the Bash" as a "tribe of legal outlaws maintained by the Czar for odd jobs here and there." He called the Bashkirs "good soldiers" who excelled at fighting on ski, yet the Orenburg district history describes them as "careless and lazy."

The Kirghiz were a nomadic people, also cattle breeders. Coleman found them to be "enterprising" but had little else good to say about them. The Tatars in the district he characterized as "temperate, industrious and capable," which squares with the impressions of the ARA men in Kazan and Ufa.

The Orenburg Americans found the Bashkirs and Tatars to be extremely clean, the Kirghiz just the opposite. Coleman sized up all three peoples as "short and stocky. Wear beards and keep their heads shaved in summer and winter." In a letter to Harold Fisher in New York City he characterized all three peoples in his blunt shorthand.

The Bashkirs are honest and splendid to deal with. They are 97% illiterate. The Kirghis have the same distinction. They are not so honest. Really they do not understand honor and justice. Tartars are also here and are honest, intelligent and hard workers. All three worship Allah in a slightly different way. Mosques and minarets pierce the skies and the Moulah shouts from the steeple at sun up and sun down the prayer beginning "ALLAH EL AC BAHR." Extremely picturesque and all that.

Orenburg city was located near the confluence of the Ural and Sakmarskaia Rivers. In prerevolutionary times the population of the city was somewhere around 125,000 to 150,000, but now, with the influx of refugees, it was up near 200,000. Russians predominated, followed by Tatars, Jews, and Kirghiz.

Coleman described the city as "low squat and dingy," and above all filthy. "The people live like rats. As many as eight in one room." Spring and summer were extremely hot with high humidity.

Fleming came to Orenburg in September 1922 when the worst of the famine had passed. He was struck by the "frontier-like appearance of the town," which with its dusty main street of one-and-a-half-story buildings "reminds one forcibly of the scenes of Mark Twain's 'Roughing It' and Bret Harte's 'The Luck of Roaring Camp.'"[4]

The city had one paved avenue, Soviet Street, which neglect had made more hazardous than the dirt roads. The town was somewhat hilly, though the Ural Mountains, despite their proximity, were not visible from the city. Coleman wrote, "From dawn until dark the wails of camels are heard as they haul loads behind them." As with horses, these four-legged imports from Central Asia had become emaciated and died off in large numbers during the winter, although with the warmer weather the survivors returned to better health. "They still bellow with zest."

In his July 1922 letter to Fisher, Coleman wrote about the town's bazaar, where "stuff of ages old is sold and resold" and where one could now purchase fresh vegetables. Before the revolution the bazaar had been Orenburg's central attraction. Was it still the main center of activity in Orenburg?

NO! NO! NO! We are blessed with two Checka's. One for the whole Kirghis Republic and one for the State of Orenburg. The former is known as the KIRCHECKA and the latter GUBCHEKA. These two organizations, which are existing no longer as far as the outside world is informed are more busy now than ever before. They were petering out and many of the worthies would have been released only that the ARA appeared on the scene when many of the plankowners saw a seemingly splendid subject appear on the scene. They have been going forced draught ever since, having changed the name to the Orenburg Gubernie (state) Political Administration.

Such overlapping jurisdictions help to explain the presence of six government representatives in Orenburg in the early going: the Russian, Bashkir, and Kirghiz republics had one each, and Orenburg province had at least one. When Coleman arrived, he found them acting in a "sort of rotation," and despite their number it was difficult to get action from any one of them.

He appealed to Moscow for assistance in clarifying which of these candidates really was Eiduk's plenipotentiary. Personally he favored Karlin, who he said was behaving satisfactorily and was the only one of the lot who understood the Riga Agreement. In fact Karlin, a Lett, was the only plenipotentiary to have been sent out from the center, but her credentials and probably her gender did not impress the local powers; twice she returned to Moscow and obtained stronger mandates from Eiduk, but to no avail.

THE MATTER WAS RESOLVED with the arrival from Moscow of Comrade Klimov—actually Commander Klimov—who had a mandate from Eiduk to supersede that of all other contenders and a commissar's authority to back it up. To leave no doubt in anyone's mind as to his status, he printed his own letterhead: "Plenipotentiary Representative of the RSFSR to all Foreign Relief Organizations."

The Orenburg files shed little light on Klimov's background other than that he had been a general in the Red Army and, according to Coleman, could "write nothing but his name." From the ARA documentation it can only be reasonably assumed that he could write his family name. In fact there is not a trace of his first name, typed or handwritten. Often he, or his secretary, simply signed his communications to the ARA with the initial "K." Eiduk, in justifying his choice of Klimov, informed Haskell that the general knew French, which cannot be verified and certainly invites skepticism. For English he definitely needed an interpreter.

After a while the illiteracy of Red officials would cease to elicit comment from the Americans, so true to type did it turn out to be. But it did take getting used to. Most of the district supervisors had attended college, though Coleman was not among their number. Born in 1892 in Philadelphia, he went to work straight out of high school as an engineer for the Pennsylvania Railroad. An autobiographical statement says that he and another man constructed a by-product coke oven, one of the first in the United States. His training as a railroad man made him painfully sensitive to the ruin of Russia's railways, and the engineer in him could not help looking beyond strict famine relief to the repair of Orenburg's bridges, the initiation of irrigation projects, and the cleaning of the city's sewage system, which he undertook using his personal copy of the Metcalf and Eddy handbook on *American Sewage Practice*.

During the war he served in the destroyer flotilla of the U.S. Navy based in Queenstown. After the armistice and until his going into Russia with the ARA he filled a minor post at the American Embassy in London. Of this experience he wrote to Fisher, "You know of the diplomacy of Russia and this might be a good contrast."

That is about all that the Orenburg files reveal about Coleman's background. There are no personal letters to help penetrate the thick crust of cynicism offered up in his more or less official communications, which includes his missive to Fisher where he concedes, "I have played football and baseball but not worth mentioning."

With this letter he enclosed a photograph of himself taken out-of-doors in Orenburg. Coleman, the lone figure, is some twenty feet distant, slightly bent over under the weight of his fur coat and dog-eared *shapka*. He stands against an almost perfectly snow-white background; only a sliver of a slanted roof on a one-story building visible through the snow drifts behind him indicates the presence of civilization.[5]

Coleman and Klimov proved to be the most incendiary matchup between a district supervisor and a government representative of any in the mission. The local Orenburg officials did not like Klimov, and they may have engineered his removal in the summer of 1922, but they were no friends of the ARA. "As far as the soviets are concerned there is not one of them who is truthful," wrote Coleman. In the end, for all of the ARA's objections to Klimov, it would be the lack of cooperation shown by the local authorities that decided Moscow headquarters to close down the Orenburg district.

With the ARA and soviet officials at odds, Klimov was at an advantage. Coleman lamented: "I can go direct to no one or speak officially to no one except through him. He does not know enough to come in out of the rain with the exception of obstruction." Besides having to importune Klimov on matters of famine relief—warehouses, railroad cars, kitchen staffs, and the like—Coleman was kept busy by the continual need to badger him for action on mundane matters. For example, on January 31: "May I call your attention to the fact that the cesspool into which empties the refuse from the house occupied by the American personnel in Orenburg is again full, and ask that immediate steps be taken to have it emptied."

The dirt and filth of Orenburg city were a preoccupation of the Americans. Coleman writes of "feces, refuse from houses, fires, and kitchens" that had been piling up in streets and courtyards for five years. "Garbage cans were unknown." The spring thaw and the onset of cholera turned filth into something of an obsession. The ARA Sanitary Report for March 1922 reads in part as follows:

The streets of Orenburg are in a horrible condition. They are the repository for every description of human filth. . . . Lacking the means for their proper disposal it is a common practice to throw all the kitchen refuse into the streets. Similarly the contents of cesspools are frequently poured into the public streets. . . . The streets are rapidly thawing out at the present time and rivers of filth are running everywhere. Children are playing in these filthy streams while men in the market place have been observed washing their hands in it. . . . Approximately six inches of filth covers the stratum of every street.

Warming temperatures uncovered other kinds of filth: "Carcasses of cattle, cats and dogs. The dogs were few however, for they feasted galore on the dead." In April, after an inspection trip into the subdistricts, Coleman reported to Moscow that at Aktiubinsk, about two hundred miles southeast of Orenburg city at a hairpin turn in the Iletsk River, the spring floods had washed ashore numerous human corpses. Aktiubinsk was inhabited primarily by Kirghiz. The city had only about ten thousand residents, but the ARA figured that it had suffered about forty thousand starvation casualties, most of them refugees who had wandered in from the steppe.

Coleman said that on the shore at this hairpin turn lay about ten thousand corpses. This figure seems unimaginable. He himself was not there to make the count although he arrived in time to witness the leftover clothing and boots that "still lay waiting to be buried" and perhaps he based his estimate on this evidence. Most of the corpses were buried en masse in an abandoned coal shaft.

On the same day, April 22, that he wrote his report on this scene of horror, he addressed to Klimov a letter complaining about the disrepair of the ARA office furniture, which he claimed was "not fit for a stable."

Uroff's Mill, which has been turned over to the A.R.A. for use as a warehouse, is found by me to contain two desks, two chairs, one divan, one small roll-top typewriter desk and two sectional book-cases.

This furniture has been lying in that office unused since this mill has been in our possession, and I request that you immediately consult with the proper authorities and procure this furniture for the use of the A.R.A. during its activities in Orenburg.

I trust that it will not be necessary to go through the regular routine of weeks and weeks of waiting before this result is achieved.

Klimov responded that "notwithstanding all my effort" he had not been able to procure this furniture for the ARA, the local food committee having categorically refused to give it up. Someone in the office wrote at the bottom of the translation copy of this letter in blue pencil, "AND THE SHOW WHIRLS MERRILY ON," a favorite phrase of the Orenburg Americans whose origin is unclear, but which they may have picked up in the American Expeditionary Force. If so, it must have been long out of date back in the civilized world because it does not appear even in the writings of the boys on the Volga.

A few weeks later Klimov wrote to Coleman requesting that the district supervisor notify all ARA employees who were former officers, wartime officials, students at military schools, and military volunteers to report to the OGPU. The American sniffed at this, replying that he knew of no such people. He told Klimov to figure out for himself who were the "culprits" and then to "furnish me with a list of their names, when I will instruct these men to appear or, if necessary, will fall them in in two ranks, in Enginersnaia Street, and march them in squad formation to the O.G.P.A."

By now Coleman and Klimov were using every available occasion to snipe at each other. One such effort by Klimov, through his interpreter, took aim in original English in a handwritten message in pencil, dated May 12, 1922. It was a misfire.

Supervisor, A.R.A.
I should be much obliged to you if you will advise me either had you bought from anyone or sold to somebody peas.
Waiting your reply at earliest date,
Government Representative

Something happened over the course of the subsequent eleven days to prompt Coleman to inform Klimov that "hereafter, when we converse, you furnish your own interpreter. I will also have an interpreter and will arrange to have a written record made of each conversation."

In their battles with government representatives the ARA men often fell back upon the Riga Agreement. The official Orenburg history calls it the "Gibraltar" upon which the district supervisor always stood, yet in no other district did it seem to have so little influence over the behavior of the plenipotentiary or the local soviet officials. In fact the same document says of these men that the Riga Agreement "meant nothing in their young lives . . . and the show whirled dizzily on."

Klimov did not even pretend to observe it. He once approached Coleman with a request to feed local detachments of the Red Army, reasoning that "They are no longer really an army." Coleman replied that this was strictly forbidden by the Riga Agreement, which moved Klimov to remark that that was "only paper and could be disregarded." So Coleman tells us.

It might seem that all of this frustration and Coleman's obvious disgust with it would have made him welcome, even lobby for, a reassignment to another district, perhaps even a comfortable position at Moscow headquarters. In fact the opposite was the case. In April he learned that when Lyon had been transferred to Moscow in February, he had told Haskell that so adverse were conditions in Orenburg that no American should be stationed there for longer than three months. By then there were six Americans in the district: three in Orenburg city —Coleman, L'Engel Hartridge, and Fred Wells—and three in the subdistricts. Haskell had reportedly expressed agreement with Lyon and may have been contemplating a change of personnel once the corn drive was over.

It was apparently this that led Coleman to write a curious appeal to Quinn, which was an attempt to preempt his reassignment. Yes, he admits, the job is huge, but he assures Quinn that he is not cracking under the pressure: "I request that you do not consider that I am weakening, either in physique or nerve, and permit me to stay here and see this thing through."

He praises his staff and the "splendid" work they are carrying out despite the many obstacles thrown up by the government.

The conditions are most difficult, but I have a thorough understanding of them and revel in the fact that I can put this job across. I do not mean to infer that there is more than normal intelligence to cope with on the surface, but the intrigue and espionage are amusing, exciting, ridiculous and annoying in turn. Not one of my employees has been arrested either during the winter or the spring.

At this point he assumes the tone of a frontier sheriff at High Noon: "Nothing would please some better than to have me shanghaied out of Orenburg, and there is no secret of this, but in so many words my retort has reached them that they will never be able to run me out of town."

What fate would have befallen Childs had he been unable to resist Haskell's promotion to chief of the Orenburg mission is of course impossible to say for sure, but the imagination is able to summon up only images of disaster. In any event, he was a luckier man than he probably knew.

Coleman closed by thanking Quinn for his interest and thoughtfulness: "it is good to know that someone realizes there is an Orenburg."[6]

He then braced himself for another round with Klimov. On May 20 he fired off another missive:

Dear Sir:
Referring to the illegible note you sent me this date, scratched over a letter written by someone else to someone else, I have to inform you that in the future, when you require anything of this office, you write your letters on a clean sheet of paper and sign your name in full, rather than "K", for my past experience has been to have everything in writing, particularly in dealing with you.
Very truly yours,

On July 6 he complained to the commander that the ARA headquarters was "reeking with the smell of fish." Klimov must have carried some fish into the office, and Coleman was not about to let pass an opportunity to let him know that "this is an office and not a fish warehouse and I do not want it used as such." On the same day he instructed Klimov, "Hereafter you will under no condition enter the ARA warehouses without my permission or without my presence."

There are very few descriptions of actual encounters between the two warriors—unlike the Simbirsk accounts of Tarasov and Chernikh—so much is left to the imagination to fill in the background of these hostile communications. Klimov shot back that he had the authority to enter freely all ARA premises.

Besides that, I consider it necessary to point out to you that neither you nor I can order each other to do anything.
So long as I remain a Government Representative to a relief organization, I am of the same rank as you. The only difference is that you are a representative of one of the largest philanthropic firms in the world and I am a plenipotentiary representative of the First World Socialist Federative Republic.

It gets worse. One week later Coleman again fired at the Red General: "If you will permit me to say so, you have been so accustomed in the past to write divisional general orders etc., just the big things, you know, that your requests to me often lack details." The ARA is not the Red Army, he wrote, ordering Klimov to get specific.

On the following day Coleman, responding to a letter from Klimov about his investigation into the local consumer cooperative, wished him luck and expressed the hope that when the investigation ended, "you will be able to use one of your thoroughly disciplined firing squads."

Meanwhile there was a backup of requests to the local government for transport, funds to pay ARA employees, warehouse labor and guards, and the usual arguments over violations of the sanctity of the ARA courier and delays in sending ARA telegrams. The most frequent cause for complaint was intimidation of the native personnel. One of Klimov's aides reminded Coleman's principal Russian assistant, "we could shoot pretty straight in 1918 and we can do it again."

Of course Klimov had hatched a number of junior Klimovs in the subdistricts, and they kept things interesting for the likes of Harold Buckley, who spent most of his time on inspection tours through the district. On June 15 he wrote to Baker in New York: "Our friends the 'Bolos' are not helping us very much; on the contrary, it seems actually as if they were trying to hinder us. This is difficult to understand; nevertheless I can believe nothing else. I presume it is hard for them not to have their own way; apparently that is what hurts most; they never cease trying to get their fingers in the pie."[7]

PERIODICALLY Buckley and the other roaming ARA men would return to headquarters with their tales of adventure and intrigue involving Klimov's satellites. The most curious of these were compiled together with anecdotes from headquarters into a document called the "Orenburg diary." It appears to have had a collective authorship, but its originator and primary contributor was probably Fred Wells, the ARA secretary.

The diary's chief source of material was the running battles with Commander Klimov. Its literary style was heavily American-colloquial and featured expressions that had been all the rage in the States a few years earlier but were by now fashionable only among a handful of Americans whom time had left behind on the Khirgiz steppe. It was also sprinkled with mistranslated Russian-to-English expressions that had found their way into the conversational English of the Orenburg Americans.

A favorite expression of the Orenburg Americans was "to throw [someone] out into the street." It is hard to say how literally this was meant to be understood; in some contexts it seems to denote laughing someone out of the ARA office. It may have its origins in some lowbrow American fiction, possibly of the frontier variety, because it evokes the swinging doors of a saloon in the Old West. Or it might have been coined right there at headquarters.

The Orenburg diary was kept in several copies. Barringer, who never traveled east of the Volga, somehow acquired one in Simbirsk, where all the Americans were able to enjoy its many amusements. The Simbirsk district history refers to having someone "finally disposed of (or 'thrown out into the street', in the vernacular of the Orenburg diary)."

The Soviet authorities also got hold of a copy: as Wells was departing Russia in February 1923, his was confiscated at the border. No ordinary border guard could have penetrated its linguistic mysteries, but it must have had the appearance of an important document, and so it was sent back to Moscow probably for analysis by a team of code breakers from the Foreign Affairs Commissariat.

By this time, Coleman had left Orenburg and was district supervisor in the Ukrainian city of Elizavetgrad. Quinn wrote him a stiff letter describing Wells's border problems and identifying the diary as Coleman's, calling it "not only a record of incidents, but personal observations and comments on the Soviet Government and its officials." Quinn put Coleman on notice that the seizure of this sensitive material might move the Soviets to require his expulsion from the ARA mission; judging from the tone of this letter, Quinn would not have tried to stand in the way of this.

Quinn does not appear to have actually seen the diary but rather was told of its contents by the Soviets, and this may have aroused his curiosity. He told Coleman to send to him the original copy. In his reply Coleman stood his ground, maintaining that every man in the district had contributed to the document, which anyway was nothing more than a recounting of what had actually taken place. Perhaps the "truthfulness" of its observations made it seem so "scathing." He told Quinn that he had left his copy in London during his recent vacation. With that the Orenburg diary incident was laid to rest.

After the mission, Barringer's copy was sent to the ARA in New York for safe-keeping and consulted by Fisher in writing his ARA history. Ten years later Fleming made tempting reference in the "A.R.A. Association Review" to the "celebrated Orenburg diary," claiming that it had been "concealed from the curious" and then "hidden in the vaults by Fisher." In 1942 Perry Galpin came across this copy in the New York office—not in a vault, for it had been chewed by rats—and sent it along to Fisher, who was then teaching history at Stanford. Page advised him to handle the document with caution as "it might be subject to a good deal of misinterpretation. On the other hand, there is a lot of pretty good stuff there, I think."[8] After that the trail runs dry.

Quinn was willing to accept at face value the Soviet assessment of the diary's contents because he had gotten a taste of Coleman's unsubtle style from correspondence the previous summer. An ARA district supervisor was expected to uphold certain standards of diplomacy and tact in his relations with government officials, no matter how strained these might become. But Coleman in his embattled isolation lost sight of all such limits with the result that the go-to-hell spirit of the Orenburg diary seeped into his correspondence with Moscow headquarters.

In a July 13 letter to Quinn, Coleman referred to the Orenburg soviet officials as "local henchmen of Moscow." Two days later he sent Quinn recent examples of typically caustic communications with Klimov. In his cover letter he wrote, "While I am waiting instructions to straighten this fellow out from Moscow I will adopt the gentle and tactful method of taking his side arms from him and throwing him into the street." This was not the way a district supervisor addressed the chiefs in Moscow. Coleman was losing touch.

Quinn answered with a letter upbraiding Coleman for the "curt, belligerent and sarcastic" tone of his correspondence with Klimov. It was enough, he wrote, to make Moscow wonder if the sorry state of government relations in Orenburg was not at least in part the American's fault. Certainly Klimov is a difficult character, but after all, Coleman had it no worse than any other district supervisor. In any case, "whatever may be your opinion of the Government Representative and whatever his actions may be, it is not going to help the situation to adopt other than a dignified attitude toward him."

But Coleman was not alone in finding it impossible to work with Klimov, and even as Quinn's letter was on its way a change of command in Orenburg was in the works. The plenipotentiary had in some particularly egregious way over-stepped his bounds with the local authorities—at least this was Coleman's un-derstanding of why Klimov was now being squeezed out. He says that the gen-eral was to be ejected from the Party and prosecuted, but that part sounds like wishful thinking. Perhaps Eiduk's replacement by Lander spelled the end for Klimov. Or it may have had something to do with a controversy surrounding two hundred cars of ARA supplies that had been left unloaded in a freight yard in the town of Orsk, but the details of this episode and the evidence, if any, that it played a role in Klimov's demise are not in the Orenburg files.

Whatever the case, on July 17 Klimov submitted to Coleman a kind of resig-nation letter. In it he accused the district supervisor of insulting not only him personally but the Red Army and the Soviet government as well. He professed himself "extremely surprised" that an official ARA representative and a "gentle-man from America" could sink so low as to write such insulting lines. Klimov sounds so sincerely offended that it is enough to give an outsider pause. Cole-man, however, was unfazed: he annotated the Russian version of this letter with the words, "File with a sigh."

As it happened Klimov was not to be run out of town so easily. On the 17th, the same day the commander had supposedly fired off his last round, Coleman cabled Haskell to report that although Klimov was supposed to have been re-lieved, in fact he had not given up his office and was still threatening the ARA personnel. For some reason, Coleman's tone was urgent, even desperate. He wrote that if Klimov were not removed from Orenburg immediately, it might be necessary to shut down ARA operations in Orenburg. "I mean this literally and must have immediate action."

Whether the chiefs took up the matter with Lander is uncertain. Klimov lin-gered a while longer, finally departing Orenburg in mid-August. His withdrawal did not change the ARA's decision to close down the district in September when the size of the entire mission was scaled down. This was the only district thus put out of action. Moscow had had enough of official Orenburg hospitality and or-dered Coleman to wrap up his show "with all possible speed."

In the waning days of the Orenburg operations, during the first week of Sep-tember, a new plenipotentiary, A. K. Karpov, arrived from the Crimea. He is said to have "speedily ingratiated himself with the American personnel," complying with all their wishes. As Coleman was about to depart Orenburg, Karpov eulo-gized him in gushing terms, citing his "tremendous energy and great hearted-ness," acknowledged by all citizens throughout the land.

I am sure that the name of Walter Coleman will not be forgotten but will find its place in the history of the titanic struggle against the famine which threatened to en-gulf the immense territory of Soviet Russia. . . . Once more permit me to shake your hand, the hand of an honest citizen of the Starry Republic and to tell you that I re-gret that I have worked with you for so short a time.

Karpov assured Coleman that his achievement would place him "in the ranks of the prominent persons of the new world." This encomium, which sounds like a product of the ARA publicity department, was indeed tidied up and turned into an press release. One can only imagine what Quinn would have made of it.[9]

The new era of good feeling was short lived. The last Americans pulled out of Orenburg on the "Knickerbocker Express" on September 30.

BUT THIS WAS NOT the end. In the autumn the central authorities in the person of Lander made several appeals to the ARA to reopen the Orenburg district, promising a new brand of cooperation from the local government and the plenipotentiary. The ARA did not go along easily and insisted on the signing of a special agreement involving the central and Orenburg governments. Its principles were little different from what the ARA required in other districts according to the Riga Agreement, but the idea was to emphasize the need for improved cooperation.

A final understanding was reached in Moscow on January 2, 1923, at a meeting attended at the ARA's insistence by the head of the Orenburg soviet and the new Moscow plenipotentiary to the district, Rudminsky, who had first surfaced during the final weeks of Klimov's reign and would not likely have been Coleman's first choice for the job.

The agreement called for the ARA to begin its operations immediately, at one hundred thousand rations. The Soviets promised to make ready for the ARA's arrival, setting up headquarters, personnel house, warehouses, and so on. Hartridge was made district supervisor, and he and a reliever named Smith made the journey by rail, arriving in Orenburg on January 19. They drove into the center of town at 11:00 A.M. and pulled up to their old personnel house, which they found occupied by Rudminsky. He opened the door in his pajamas and pleaded total ignorance about the timing of the ARA's return, for which he had made no preparations.

The temperature was thirty-five below zero, and with no place to go except the railroad car Hartridge demanded action, but Rudminsky said that as it was a holiday—the feast of the Epiphany—he could arrange nothing for at least a few days.

Eventually Hartridge and Smith reclaimed the former residence, although when Rudminsky abandoned it he removed the telephone, the electric lights, and all beds; the rooms were filled with trash and there was a half-inch of ice on the kitchen floor.

It did not take long for Hartridge to realize that luring them back to Orenburg was the doing of the local officials who were anxious to erase popular suspicions of their responsibility for the ARA's withdrawal. Now that the Americans had returned, everything reverted to the old form. Hartridge's first written communications to Rudminsky, dated February 3, read as follows: "The toilet in the A.R.A. office is out of order. Will you please take immediate steps to remedy this condition."

On February 11 Hartridge reported the unsatisfactory situation to Moscow and pleaded with the chiefs to have Rudminsky replaced. "Mr. Rudminsky is a mere boy, of but slight intelligence and has no weight. Personally, as you know, he is a Jew and is detested in this community. His official position permits him to bark and snap at practically any one who has to deal with him and he takes full advantage of this power." Hartridge also called him "small, mean, vindictive and contemptible."

Nine days later, possibly at Moscow's request, Hartridge sent along a more complete report. High on the list of complaints, among the expected objections to Rudminsky's intimidation of ARA personnel, his indifference, incompetence, interference with ARA telegrams, and so on, is a reference to the "disgusting condition" of the ARA office toilet. Hartridge then describes his uncomradely manner: "He regards me as his enemy and treats me as such. In all dealings with him he is curt to an insulting degree, his tone is acid, and he manifests his venom in every possible way."

According to Hartridge, Rudminsky threatened to send an ARA employee to jail and "to throw his family into the street in twenty four hours. . . . The position which he holds in Orenburg has affected him like strong wine, and all his efforts are directed toward impressing the realization of his power and might upon those who have to deal with him, to the criminal neglect of his duties he was sent here to fulfill. He is like a cur, barking and snapping at a mastiff, strongly and safely held in leash." On his own part Hartridge claimed to have remained "abstemiously polite and courteous" in his conduct toward Rudminsky.

At Moscow headquarters there were no doubts that Rudminsky was behaving intolerably. Ellingston said he was "several kinds of a bastard." But the chiefs were in a cautious mood. As the ARA entered the so-called liquidation period, what they wanted most of all was a peaceful winding up of the mission to cap their success and protect Hoover's reputation at home. To the entreaties of the district supervisors for the cover of heavy artillery fire out of Moscow in their government relations battles, headquarters responded by preaching further practice of "samovar diplomacy"—which increasingly meant to turn the other cheek. They certainly were not eager to kick up any dust in distant Orenburg.

Despite Hartridge's best efforts, Rudminsky remained at his post until the end of the mission, so somehow there was room enough in that town for both of them. As fate would have it, they were destined to endure more than simple co-existence. In April the two were returning together from Moscow to Orenburg—at least they were on the same train, if they did not share a coupé—a journey that turned into something of an adventure, which Hartridge related in a letter to Phil Baldwin in Moscow.[10]

All was well until they reached Samara and were told that over twenty-five miles of track and two bridges had been washed out between Samara and Orenburg and that it would be four weeks before rail service was resumed. "Rudminsky was on the train with me and of course we were both in the same boat."

They decided to circle north and go by way of Simbirsk and Ufa, where they arrived on April 22 and were welcomed at the ARA personnel house: "Can you imagine it? Rudminsky and myself hobnobbing together."

This part was easy, but the rest of the way was nightmarish. Traveling by wagon and in the company of local guides, with great difficulty they worked their way southeast toward Orsk in order to make an indirect approach to their destination. Spring thaw was well underway, and the roads to Orsk were mostly impassable, which forced their guides to improvise. Their carts frequently became stuck in the mud, and several times they were lost out on the steppe. At Orsk they were forced to swim across the Uralsk River, Hartridge holding the precious ARA mailbags above water.

In all they were a total of fifteen days en route from Samara and used twenty-eight horses. Hartridge says he wore the same clothes for ten days and averaged three hours of sleep per night in mud huts or in the carts. Jostled around for hours on end, in the journey's final stages they had to be helped to get in and out of the wagons. These vehicles were uncovered, and as protection from the driving rains they wrapped themselves in blankets, which they wore day and night like robes. Near the end their food supply of bread, eggs, milk, and onions was running out.

Hartridge records not a single word of dialogue between the two men; he does not even indicate that they conversed, although they must have. Still, as his account draws to a close, expectations build: surely this extraordinary ordeal will have drawn these two defiant ones together in mutual understanding, perhaps even respect. It seems unimaginable, after such an experience, that they will ever again exchange sharp words over such matters as a disgusting toilet.

But there is no uplifting ending. Instead we learn that Hartridge has physically recovered and is ready to resume his duties as district supervisor. "I am pretty well fed up and rested now and the show is whirling merrily on to the grand finale."

CHAPTER 26

FOOD AS A WEAPON

It may be that what finally provoked the ARA chiefs to shut down Orenburg operations was their interview in Moscow with Grigorii Sakharov, Coleman's right-hand man. Sakharov was an engineer; in fact for two years prior to the arrival of the ARA he was the chief engineer of Orenburg, sent there from Moscow by the Bolshevik leader Leonid Krassin to repair bridges along the Tashkent railroad line destroyed in the Civil War.

This meant that he was one of the "bourgeois specialists," resented but yet indispensable to the new Soviet establishment in its struggle to keep the wheels of government and the economy rolling, though only until enough Red specialists could be trained to take their place.

When Coleman arrived in Orenburg, the two engineers joined forces, and the American had found for himself the person most district supervisors found to be vital to operations: a chief Russian executive. Coleman was a bit unusual in leaning so heavily on his assistant, making Sakharov his agent in many official dealings with Klimov, thereby pitting two class and political enemies against each other. How this affected government relations in the Orenburg district is impossible to say for sure, but it could not have helped.

In July 1922, with Klimov's exit imminent, he seemed to be preparing the ground for Sakharov's arrest. In one of his last letters to Coleman he attributed the hostile tone of the American's communications with him to the influence of Sakharov, who he said had twice applied for Party membership and had twice been rejected and was now using his position with the ARA to avenge this rejection. This explanation sounds improbable, but that does not mean Klimov did not believe it.

Further, Klimov accused Sakharov of having stolen two sacks of flour from the ARA warehouse, and he said that Sakharov had challenged him to a duel. "I do not accept his challenge" because an engineer would be no match for "an experienced frontline rifleman." Instead the fair-minded general suggested "a more honest duel, a duel of justice—the Tribunal." Here he promised certain conviction, with heavy consequences for Sakharov and the ARA. The Orenburg history relates obscurely that Klimov had personally told Coleman of "his desire to get this man in jail if he was shot for it," which sounds ominous whatever it was supposed to mean.

Steppe pravda of July 16—the day before Klimov's "resignation"—published a letter to the editor, signed "N," that accused Sakharov's son of having thrown "puff-paste pies" to his dog. These pies were said to be made of white flour, which could only mean ARA flour. The writer, who professed to be horrified at such behavior, referred to Sakharov as the "Merchant of Orenburg City." On the translation copy one of the Americans scrawled, "Old Boy Klinoff—Aha!!" "Klinoff" was apparently an ARA nickname for the commander.

Coleman interpreted the letter as a sign that Klimov was about to arrest Sakharov, and this probably motivated his urgent telegram to Haskell the next day warning about the possible necessity to close down the Orenburg mission. Coleman was so rattled that he put Sakharov, without his family, on a train for Moscow. Upon his arrival he was promptly arrested by the GPU and put in jail. He was shortly released, probably thanks to the intercession of the ARA. Quinn wrote to Coleman, "We were very much impressed with him in our talks with him and will do our utmost to see that no harm comes to him because of the efficient work he did for our organization."[1]

Sakharov must have told headquarters in detail about the Orenburg mission's difficulties with Klimov and the local Soviet authorities, which probably shored up Coleman's credibility with his chiefs. This was to be the last piece of work he did for the ARA.

It must have been difficult for someone like Klimov to have to restrain himself from simply locking up Sakharov, a leftover bourgeois—or *burzhui*, in derogatory Russian—or having him shot outright, as was done with class enemies in the recent good old days of the Civil War. Spies, saboteurs, speculators—they could be dealt with in summary fashion without the need to cook up puff-paste pies. Nowadays it was not so simple, and the frustration was exacerbated by the fact that the class enemies were enjoying the protection of representatives of foreign imperialism posing as famine relief workers.

Bill Casey gained some insight into the problem on New Year's night 1923 in the port city of Theodosia in the Crimea. He had decided to drop in for a few minutes on a masquerade ball and was waiting for his chauffeur to fetch him when a Red Army officer, very drunk, entered the hall and "bumped up against me knocking me about three feet. He said afterward that he thought I was a Russian; I wasn't." Given the officer's state of inebriation and the occasion of a masquerade, the mistake may be forgiven.

Casey described the ensuing exchange:

I faced him and wanted to know what he meant by it. He drew his sword instead of his pistol and slashed at me. He cut one of my fingers and that was rather irritating. I just backed him up against the wall and held him by the throat with one hand, while I used the other on his face. His nose was broken and one eye blackened and the rest of his face badly bruised.

When Casey released his grip the Russian again lashed at him with the sword but "did no damage," which must mean that he was indeed in a bad way or else that his weapon was only a masquerade prop.

This scene was said to have been witnessed by five "friendly" policemen. They suggested that the two disputants go outside since they seemed to be dampening the enthusiasm of the partygoers. Casey's car had arrived so they all piled in for the

ride to police headquarters where they could sort it all out. "On the way to the police station one of the policemen pinched my wrist watch, which I later recovered."

When we got to the station the officers on duty were all drunk and were unable to
write out the protocol. The fellow who had attacked me still had his sword and gun
and kicked me in the stomach. The others tried to restrain him and he began to weep.

"I killed 5,000 bourjooie in the revolution," he said, "and it touches my honor that
you will not let me kill this American bourjooie."

According to Casey, the officer was eventually tried, reprimanded, and deprived
of a considerable portion of his pay. When he had sobered, he pleaded his innocence by insisting that he had mistaken Casey for a Russian.[2]

The Riga Agreement spelled out in black and white that the ARA Americans
were immune from arrest in Russia. The Soviet government at the center honored this clause. It understood very well that to act otherwise would jeopardize
the entire Hoover mission, and it knew what the consequences would be for its
already tarnished international reputation if the Western newspapers printed sensational headlines about the jailing of American relief workers.

Even in the districts ARA immunity was generally upheld, which is remarkable considering the explosive potential built into the situation, not to mention
incendiary personalities like Murphy and Skvortsov.

The only other potentially scandalous case of the "arrest" of an ARA American occurred in Odessa in June 1922. District supervisor John Hynes boarded the
American steamer *Norlina* on ARA business without a pass, which led a port official to arrest him—or at least to refuse to allow him to come ashore, one of the
two. The facts are obscure and not likely to become the subject of learned academic dispute.

When two other Americans, Kernan and Brown, learned of Hynes's predicament, they went immediately to the government representative, a Red Army
general named Studenikin, and demanded their chief's release. According to the
general, the two "excited" Americans insulted him, which seems a fair bet.

After this the facts grow murkier. Hynes later reported in a telegram to Moscow that Studenikin placed the two Americans under arrest, which he called "incompatible with dignity of ARA and clearly exceeding authority vested in him
by central authorities."

Studenikin cabled Eiduk that "the insolent behavior of Brown and Kernan
made me warn them that if they persisted in their impertinent conduct, I would
forbid them to go in the automobile"—as if Brown and Kernan could be admon-
ished like a couple of eight-year-olds. Hynes, he said, misinterpreted this as a
threat to arrest them.

Studenikin used the opportunity to air other complaints about the ARA.
Hynes, he wrote, fails to recognize Eiduk's instructions to his plenipotentiaries,
which, after all, are approved by Colonel Haskell. Furthermore, Hynes has rebuffed his perfectly legitimate demands to examine the ARA account books,
calling this interference. Moreover the ARA selects its local personnel "through
certain social functionaries without our approval." Studenikin requested Hynes's
immediate recall.

This minor episode might have joined dozens of others like it in eternal obscurity had not word of the "arrests" of the Odessa Americans reached Moscow at a moment when Governor Goodrich, as emissary of President Harding, and several leading Bolsheviks, notably Lev Kamenev, were holding discussions on the future of America's relations with Soviet Russia. Goodrich raised the Odessa incident, which Kamenev assured him would have already been set aright but for poor lines of communication between the Kremlin and the periphery. That was the last word on the matter.[3]

There were other "arrests" of ARA Americans, but these were more on the order of curiosities and do not come under the heading of "government relations." There was, for example, the case of Stephen Venear, a thirty-four-year-old veteran relief worker with experience in the American Red Cross. He had served as an ARC special investigator in the Crimea in 1920 when General Wrangel made his abortive final bid against Soviet power. Childs says that in the retreat Venear had escaped capture by the Bolsheviks only "by the skin of his teeth." Had he been caught, he might have been among the American prisoners in Moscow whose release Hoover made a precondition for the ARA to begin feeding in Russia in 1921. Childs says also that Venear had been born in Russia, which explains his fluent command of the language.

In spring 1922 Venear was stationed in Kazan. One of the distinctive features of that ARA district was its limited railway network. In fact there was only one rail line, which came from Moscow and cut horizontally across the extreme northern portion of the district, extending about a hundred miles to the east of Kazan city. Because of this, relief operations in Kazan relied heavily on water transportation on the Volga and Kama Rivers and their tributaries. In order to facilitate boat inspection trips—especially when the spring thaw flooded the roads—the ARA commissioned the passenger steamer S.S. *Varland.*

District physician William Dear tells us that when the ship was handed over to the ARA in the first days of May, an inspection revealed that the first-class staterooms were infested with bedbugs, which the doctor imagined "awaiting anxiously an opportunity to feast on the well nourished Americans who were to inhabit their domain." The nature and extent of the problem having been determined, the rooms were emptied and arrangements made for their fumigation with sulphur. Venear, as Dear's assistant, was given the assignment.

On the appointed day, all windows, doors, and ventilators were sealed and seventeen sulphur pots were arranged throughout the rooms. Dear took obvious pleasure in recounting the story: "The setting of the scene in the final note of the sanitary drama now about to be unfolded was complete. The hearthfires were carefully lighted, the sulphur ignited cheerfully and commenced its work of annihilating the remaining bedbugs. The doors were closed and the deadly fumes proceeded to do their work."

Venear decided to remain on hand to make sure there were no mishaps. He noticed that the ship's captain was very uneasy about these proceedings, the point of which he did not seem to comprehend: why all this fuss about a few invisible bugs? Apparently no one took the trouble to explain to him the actual procedure, for when he spied a thin spiral of smoke drifting from a crack in one of the imperfectly sealed rooms, he assumed the worst and sounded the *Varland*'s alarm bells. Then all hell broke loose.

The families of the crew rushed toward the shore; the sentry on the dock fired his rifle several times in rapid succession; the workers loading the ship with corn immediately threw the operation into reverse. A bystander, seeing his chance, made a move to steal a sack of corn only to have the sentry bring the butt end of a revolver down on his head, the would-be thief collapsing in a heap on the gangplank. Three sailing vessels approached the *Varland* with whistles blowing. The fire department arrived and attacked the ship with fire hoses, breaking windows to get at the sulphur pots. The captain ordered a fireman to carry a hose into the cloud of smoke, and this man was overcome and had to be carried off.

Then the Cheka arrived. "Its chief had caught Mr. Venear red handed in the act and had taken him into custody without further ado. Mr. Venear's fluent knowledge of Russian combined with the fact that he had in his possession no papers certifying to his A.R.A. identity, confirmed the charge of arson against him."

Venear was dripping wet, poisoned by sulphur fumes, and in the hands of the dreaded Cheka. The misunderstanding was cleared up before long but had presented the local police with a "big job" to tackle. "Such excitement has not been seen in Kazan since the days of the Chech invasion. The protokol is still being written. And thus ended ignominiously the first practical demonstration of sanitation attempted by the A.R.A."[4]

There is not a trace of humor to be found in the documentation of the case of John Ward of the Moscow staff. One afternoon during the first week of April 1922 he rushed into ARA headquarters and declared that he absolutely had to leave that night for Paris. Ward was from Knoxville, Iowa, but he made his residence in Paris.

This was, to state the obvious, an extraordinary request. A visa would have to be processed, and this normally took a few days. There was no apparent emergency, no urgent telegrams from Paris, which made Ward's sudden, urgent demand appear unwarranted. When this was pointed out to him, he became quite agitated, declaring, "You can't keep me. You can't keep me." According to Haskell, Ward claimed that the reason for his request to leave Russia was "so highly personal that he could not reveal it to anyone."

Ward had served efficiently as secretary to Quinn and was in very good standing with all the chiefs, and this probably saved him a good deal of embarrassment, if not much worse. Haskell took extraordinary steps to get him a passport and a seat on a train leaving Russia with Governor Goodrich that same night. However, at the train station Ward's passport failed to arrive. It was then arranged that he would take the train anyway and that Eiduk would telegraph the border authorities so that Ward would be able to exit Russia using only his ARA identity card. Haskell wired the American consul at Riga to have an emergency passport ready for him on the other side. All of this was done without Ward having offered any explanation, so he must indeed have been on good terms with Haskell.

After the train left the station there was a further hitch. Eiduk was prevented from sending the necessary wires to the border by the same authorities who were holding up Ward's passport. It was at this point that Eiduk learned, and then informed Haskell, that Ward was wanted by the Moscow police for "criminal relations with small boys." This, says Haskell, struck "like a crash out of a clear sky." He asked Eiduk if Ward were merely under suspicion, but was told that it was a "clearly established case." Eiduk said that he had no desire to make a scandal for the ARA and would let Haskell handle the matter as he pleased.

Now what was Haskell to do? Ward was on his way to the border, but the Moscow police had the goods on him for criminal behavior. The colonel later mused that had the United States had diplomatic relations with Soviet Russia, he would readily have turned him over to the Soviet courts for trial. On second thought he figured that the American public would not believe that Ward could get a fair trial in the land of the Bolsheviks. Anyway, the ARA did not need another scandal.

Eiduk agreed to arrange for Ward to exit the country and to provide Haskell with the police evidence although both men realized that Ward would probably go "scotfree."

One wonders what words passed between Ward and the governor during their train ride out of Russia, if they spoke at all. Goodrich must have sensed something was amiss behind Ward's frantic departure; his suspicion must have been heightened when the young man was briefly detained and questioned at the border. Ward knew that he had nothing to gain by confiding in the governor. In fact, had Goodrich learned of the scandal back of all this fuss, he might well have tried to have Ward put off the train and returned to Moscow.

Probably they traveled in separate compartments: Goodrich, pen in hand, drafting another report for President Harding on his quiet negotiations with the Kremlin over U.S. recognition of Soviet Russia; Ward, his fingers crossed, unaware of how fortunate he might have been that Secretary of State Hughes was so stubbornly opposed to recognition.

Ward's case was heard before the Moscow Revolutionary Tribunal the following month. The evidence was handed over to Haskell, who passed it on to London; after that it disappeared.[5]

THE ARA'S NATIVE STAFF members did not enjoy the immunity granted to their American employers, and their arrests were one of the biggest sources of controversy in ARA-Soviet relations.

Paragraph 12 of the Riga Agreement stipulated that "the A.R.A. shall be allowed to set up the necessary organizations for carrying on its relief work free from governmental or other interference." The Soviet authorities reserved the right to block the appointments of specific native personnel, but they had to demonstrate sufficient cause. This question had been a sticking point during the Riga negotiations, and its final wording was left purposely vague. The bottom line for the Soviet side was that the ARA recognized that its local employees remained citizens of Soviet Russia and thus subject to its laws.

Among so many citizens employed by the ARA—in all they numbered around 120,000—there were bound to be a fair number whom the Soviet authorities would find objectionable, especially as so many were recruited from yesterday's better-off classes, today's "former people." If counterrevolutionaries happened to be working for the ARA, went the Soviet thinking, this was unfortunate, but their arrests were unavoidable and none of the ARA's business.

The Americans interpreted the situation differently, regarding their local employees—whatever the wording of paragraph 12—as being under ARA jurisdiction and protection, just like their staffs in Central Europe in previous years. Moreover, the ARA tended automatically to view every arrest of one of its employees as the direct result of that individual's association with it and, therefore, as another attempt to hamper relief operations. This went well beyond concern for the loss of the services of particular individuals: if it was thought that a person could be arrested because of his or her affiliation with the ARA, this would strike fear in the ranks of all the native staff and frighten off potential recruits from among the limited pool of available qualified personnel, thereby threatening the ARA's signature efficiency.

The most frequent charge brought by the government against an ARA employee—whether or not a recent specific misdeed might serve as the trigger for arrest—had to do with an anti-Bolshevik past. Most often this meant some kind of association with or demonstrated sympathy for the Whites, but it might simply imply membership or past membership in a non-Bolshevik—therefore anti-Bolshevik—political party, most commonly the Socialist Revolutionaries and the Mensheviks. The Civil War was over, but there were still plenty of old scores to settle.

The ARA Americans were, on the whole, baffled by all this activity, which they placed under the pejorative heading "politics." Just what had come between the Bolsheviks and their socialist opponents before and since 1917 was beyond the ARA men's range of interests, and anyway they couldn't get the straight dope from the antagonists, who told conflicting tales. Suddenly thrust into the cross fire, it seemed to them to make as much sense as a feud between the Hatfields and the McCoys. And with millions of people starving to death it seemed positively criminal. They could not fathom the depths of the animosities fueling Russian political life, and so they tended to assume that each arrest of one of their staff was an attack on them.

On the other hand there were instances when the primary goal of an arrest was to remove someone from the service of the ARA, in which case the individual's alleged political past was merely the pretext for taking action. It is a matter of fact that quite a number of these people had managed through their ARA position to accumulate a certain amount of power. This aroused resentment in Soviet officials unused to having to tolerate independent authority in their midst and galled to see it assumed by class enemies thought to have been relegated to history's dustbin. Oftentimes personalities were the engines of confrontation, but the circumstance of rival bases of power was in itself a prescription for trouble: several ARA reports note that even employees chosen with the full approval, indeed at times at the recommendation, of Soviet officials could in a short amount of time come to be seen as intolerable.

At the subdistrict level things could get even stickier. There, qualified personnel were especially scarce, and an official might be enlisted to work for the ARA as, say, a kitchen manager. Suppose, then, that this kitchen manager made a mess of things and a traveling ARA inspector from the provincial capital—perhaps a former aristocrat with a tsarist or White Army past—decided to relieve him of his duties. Such cases were routine, and they were a drain on the energies of the American sent to break the ensuing stalemate. More often it was an ARA inspector and a Soviet official in conflict over the hiring or firing of a third party.

And a former tsarist officer was not above wielding his new ARA club for no legitimate reason.

On Thanksgiving Day, 1921, Farmer Murphy entered Moscow headquarters and noticed that Miss Strashkevich, an ARA office clerk, was not at her desk. The young lady was of once-respectable background, highly educated, and in Murphy's eyes "good looking and in every way attractive," which probably made him especially aware of her absence. What is more, she was usually on time for work, "a decidedly un-Russian quality."

As time passed he became increasingly uneasy, until another female employee informed him that Miss Strashkevich had been arrested the night before on what Murphy calls the "loose charge of 'espionage.'" This personal encounter with the burning embers of the Red Terror inspired Murphy to enlighten the folks back home about the Cheka method of arrest, which, he reported, usually happened at night—"anywhere from 11 to 4." The Chekists arrived at Strashkevich's home, searched the place, then packed her and her sister into a car and drove them to Lubianka No. 2, a prison for political offenders. It was like so many stories Murphy had heard since his arrival but to have it happen to someone he had been associating with every day was a "distinct shock." "I cannot tell you how deeply and strangely this has affected me. It is as if some powerful, invisible hand had reached out of the dark, quietly plucked some one from beside you and drawn her back into the dark."

For many of the ARA's native staff this had been the normal way of life since 1917. Many had served time in jail—or "sat," as the Russians say—for some period of time. "Most people are rather proud of having been in prison in those days because it gives them a cachet—a stamp of quality. These young ladies are always prefacing their remarks with, 'When I was sitting in prison . . .'"

The Strashkevich case was the first ARA arrest of any consequence, and the conflict that resulted set a pattern for the ones that followed. The Americans protested, insisting upon the woman's innocence. Eiduk replied that the arrest was totally unrelated to the fact of Strashkevich's employment with the ARA and that in fact the Cheka made the arrest before her affiliation became known to it.

This seems farfetched, but Eiduk wanted to make the point that this was not an ARA-related affair. He suggested that the Americans cross her name off their staff list and reminded them that the Riga Agreement did not provide immunity for Russian employees, who, he pointed out, had been "picked up in haste and it is not surprising that there are criminal as well as political offenders among them."

The ARA response was a letter to Eiduk, dated December 6, over Haskell's signature. The colonel admitted that some ARA employees had been hastily chosen and that there might indeed be "offenders" among them. But he asked Eiduk to consider the "moral effect" of the arrest, which would strike fear in the hearts of other personnel.

Haskell's letter also warned that Strashkevich's arrest would generate bad publicity, which might affect future funding for the ARA, thereby resulting in needless deaths. What will the American public think when it reads in the newspapers that the "Russian employees of the A.R.A., women as well as men, were living in constant terror of being arrested at night and carried off to indefinite imprisonment on the charge of 'espionage'"? Haskell professed to believe Eiduk's claim that the Cheka had planned the Strashkevich arrest before knowing that she was working for the ARA. However,

we should have been gratified by an expression of regret on the part of the Cheka for their ignorance of that fact and also for the inconvenience to which they put Mr. Murphy in suddenly depriving him of his assistant, and for the disturbing effects of their action upon the morale of our force. We had even hoped that in view of the disagreeable and disturbing character of this incident, it would be found possible to overlook such fault as Miss Strashkievich may have committed and to release her as a manifestation of friendliness towards this mission.

This carefully worded comme il faut diplomatic note was almost certainly dictated by Archibald Cary Coolidge as head of the ARA's liaison division. Eighty years later it seems painfully inappropriate, though Eiduk may have been entertained by its quaintness.

The Strashkevich story did have a happy ending, apparently entirely unconnected to ARA intercession. On Easter Sunday 1922, the long-lost secretary appeared at the office, as if risen from the dead. She said she had been treated well except for long periods in solitary confinement. She told Murphy stories of the prisoners' method of communication through tapping in code on the walls of their cells and how they sneaked information to and from the outside world—all standard features of tsarist prison memoirs. How the Bolsheviks with all of their combined years of experience behind bars could have been such lax jailers is a mystery.

When the prisoners learned in February that the Cheka had been scrapped for the GPU, they demanded immediate trials. When this brought no results, they threatened a hunger strike. When this failed to work, they began screaming in a continuous howl in unison from their cells, which lasted, she said, from dawn until dusk. This collective cry was heard out in the street, and crowds gathered outside the prison. This got the judicial gears turning and led to the release of many of the prisoners, our young heroine among them.

As for the wailing, Strashkevich told Murphy: "I was so *happy*. It was so much *fun*. I screamed and screamed until I lost my voice."[6]

IN MAKING ITS no doubt sincere argument about the potential effect on the ARA native staff of the Strashkevich arrest, never did the Haskell-Coolidge letter say or imply that her absence in itself would disrupt ARA operations, only that it would "inconvenience" Mr. Murphy. After all, Strashkevich was but an office secretary among two dozen at Moscow headquarters and finding a suitable replacement would not be difficult in the capital city. Out in the districts it was a different story; there each qualified employee was a precious resource. This meant that the arrest of any one of them might do considerable harm to the relief work, aside from whatever fear it might inspire in others.

Freddie Lyon complained to Moscow shortly after he started up the Orenburg show that no sooner would he break in a new staff member than this person would land in jail, paralyzing some aspect of the work until a replacement could be found and trained. Lyon assumed that the main purpose of such arrests was to throw a monkey wrench into the ARA machinery.

Dudley Hale, who spent most of his time inspecting the Samara subdistricts, saw it in less narrowly ARA terms:

The Red Terror of two years ago makes counter-revolution a very dangerous sport in the minds of most people, and I am convinced that the political arrests both among our Russian personnel and outside of it are largely for the purpose of showing the people that the workers and peasants mean business in that one particular, even if they are not able to show themselves overcapable of business in many others.

The typical immediate reaction of a district supervisor was to interpret an arrest as a challenge to his personal authority, especially when the victim was a key assistant, which happened often. Barringer, for example, says that "time and again" a district supervisor's "right-hand man" would be arrested or exiled "for no apparent reason except that it was part of a political program." By this he means a plan devised in Moscow to intimidate the ARA and check its influence by periodically reminding the Americans and the local population who was in charge.[7]

To defend the integrity of the ARA, the district supervisor often felt he had to stand up for staff members, no matter in whose army they had fought. The results were contests of power, some of them protracted and bitter.

The first such case occurred in November 1921 in of all places Kazan, which had already acquired its reputation for harmonious coexistence with the local authorities. The incident, which occurred at about the same time as the Strashkevich arrest, afterward came to be viewed as merely a "false start" in the district's government relations. At the time, however, it seemed that the entire Kazan show might come to a close.

The spark was the arrest of an ARA kitchen inspector, Mrs. Depould, a French name sometimes transliterated back from its Russian equivalent as Tippold. This occurred on the evening of November 12 as several of the Americans were at the Palace of Red Army Soldiers enjoying a performance of *Carmen*. Childs's diary introduces the scene with characteristic melodrama: "The first act had been completed and we were settling ourselves down to an evening of enjoyment from the nervous cares of our position as bourgeois in a communistic society, when Turner appeared, the excited bearer of momentous news."

Van Arsdale Turner's report of the arrests may have provided a shock, yet the Kazan Americans must have anticipated some such trouble. The previous entry in Childs's diary cites a report from Moscow about the supposed escape from prison of many Socialist Revolutionaries and the Kremlin's proclamation of a "RED TERROR" against them. He states that more than one hundred people had recently been arrested in Kazan, including on the previous day the ARA office manager, Mr. Salomine.

Why exactly the arrest of the office manager did not elicit from the Americans nearly the level of outrage as did that of the kitchen inspector is hard to determine. Perhaps Salomine's anti-Bolshevik past was so unambiguous that it seemed hopeless to intervene. Or maybe it was the fact that Depould was a woman, or that she was especially liked or so obviously innocent. Anyway, it was her arrest that was the start of serious trouble.

Details of her alleged crimes are found in a report from Kazan officials that found its way to Eiduk, who interpreted them for Haskell. The "ex-baroness" supposedly appeared in ARA kitchens "in diamond rings and bracelets, and dé-coulleté [*sic*], and by her external aspect alone evoked the protest and indignation of the hungry crowd of children and their mothers." But she didn't stop there. She also "expressed herself in a most emphatically anti-Soviet spirit," which moved the local proletariat to take matters into its own hands and inform the local authorities, who detained her.

In the course of an investigation it was established that the husband of the former baroness had at one time fought with Kolchak against the Red Army. According to Soviet law, the wives of hostile officers were supposed to be detained in a "labor house." The only reason that Depould had not been so treated is that she had not exhibited anti-Soviet behavior—that is, until now.

As for Salomine, Eiduk wrote that he was a man with an "undoubtedly counter-revolutionary past," who had been "kept on a special list as an outspoken enemy of the Workers' Government" and who was using his position with the ARA to carry out anti-government propaganda.

Whatever the actual or imagined transgressions of the two employees and the true motivations behind their arrests, the Kazan Americans feared the worst. As Childs wrote, the incident "seemed to portend the dreaded general arrest of our employees which had been our chief concern since arriving to take up our work."

In their box at the Palace of Red Army Soldiers, Childs tells us, the Americans were "projected to a high pitch of excitement as we did not know what might eventuate but we were determined that it would be a showdown." In a letter to his mother he wrote that the Americans simply rose and left the theater "immediately." However, in the diary account, after Turner rushed in with the news, the tension mounted:

We stood a little excited group of four Americans in the forefront of the theatre, filled with workers and peasants and Red Army soldiers, a hundred representatives of that power which had challenged that of the one we represented.

As we looked into the stolid alien faces, which hedged us about on every side, I think there must have come into us one and all the same feeling simultaneously of inexpressible isolation.

It was Wahren who spoke first after a few moments of silence brought about by the surprising news.

"Let's get out of here", he said.

And we trooped out in single file, with faces so set and determined that the attention of the audience must have been attracted, judging from the stares which were directed toward us.

Outside the theater the Americans huddled in a "little council of war." Turner spoke first. He recommended that they close down operations and leave as a group for Moscow before their inevitable arrest.

Turner's words held weight with these men, for he was a veteran of crisis confrontations with the Bolsheviks. Born in Maryland in 1888, the son of a preacher, he was a graduate of Mercersburg Academy and studied for one and a half years at George Washington University Law School. He had never been a doughboy, but he fit the mold of the ARA wanderer.

Childs called him "the impractical idealistic type" and an "incorrigible romance seeker," which seems like a fair assessment. Only such an individual would have signed onto Henry Ford's Peace Ship, which sailed for Europe from Hoboken in December 1915. Ford, declaring himself horrified by the world war, financed an unofficial peace mission to Scandinavia in the hope of inspiring one of the neutral governments there to propose an armistice. The undertaking ended in failure, and in May 1916 Turner left Stockholm for Petrograd, where he went to work as a courier for the American Embassy and got a close-up view of the Russian Revolution. He remained on the embassy staff during the tense winter months through May 1918 when he made his way out of Russia through Siberia and on to Washington.

After working at the State Department for six months, he was assigned to the American Embassy in Paris, where he served during the first half of 1919 before joining the ARA. His relief work took him again in the direction of Petrograd, this time with the advancing Northwest Army of Yudenich. The ARA was supposed to be feeding exclusively among the civilian population behind White lines in the summer of 1919; that was the official story then and afterward. On his personnel questionnaire for the Russian mission Turner described his past ARA service: "In charge of food distribution to the Yudenich Army on Russian front." Under the section "Most interesting experience in relief work," he wrote: "The supervisor of 400 Bolshevik prisoners engaged in unloading American flour for the Yudenich Army was of extreme interest. The work of arranging for the transportation of supplies for an army of 40,000 men possessing only one motor car and one lorry was as interesting as it was difficult."

Some years after the ARA Russian mission Turner could be found managing his own little bookshop inside the entrance to the subway at Times Square.

More than the other Americans standing outside the Red Army Theater, then, Turner could claim to know something about how to deal with the Bolsheviks when the going got rough. "In his opinion," Childs relates, "it was the old treacherous soviet game all over again which he had witnessed in 1917 and in 1918 in Petrograd." The only course of action was for the Americans to depart for Moscow as soon as possible without waiting for instructions from headquarters—it would be futile to try to cable Moscow as the authorities would block all communication.

District supervisor Wahren maintained a cooler head and decided simply to halt all movement of American foodstuffs within the Kazan district, without closing ARA kitchens. He took this step without first consulting Moscow. All agreed that there was too little time for that, what with the capriciousness of telegraphic communication in Russia, even if the local authorities decided not to prevent it. Apparently Wahren did draft a telegram to Haskell requesting that all food supplies from Moscow to Kazan be suspended, but he decided not to send it after entreaties from Kazan officials.

A key assumption informing the Americans' course of action was that the Cheka, not the local government, was behind the affair. They knew that Mukhtarov had more than once crossed swords with the local Cheka chief, and they were guessing that he would silently welcome a hard-line response from them.

On the day following Depould's arrest the Kazan ARA issued a formal ultimatum to the head of the government of the Tatar Autonomous Republic. This document, written by Wahren and Childs, claimed that the arrests violated not only paragraph 12 of the Riga Agreement but a "verbal understanding" with the government that no ARA employee would be arrested without notification and explanation given to the district supervisor. It announced that all movements of American food within the district were suspended until the ARA had been furnished with "exhaustive and satisfactory explanations."

This verbal understanding did not entail *prior* notification of an arrest. As Wahren later explained it to Haskell, the agreement was that in the event of an arrest Wahren would be notified "instantly," which had not happened in either of these two cases. Of course, if the arrests had been the work of the Cheka, the local officials themselves might not have been made aware of them "instantly," which meant that Mukhtarov had not broken the agreement. If the Americans considered this angle, they decided nonetheless that the best course of action was to turn up the heat on the local government.

Childs's letters and diary lead us to believe that all discussions with government officials during these tension-filled hours were cordial. But in his several memoirs he included a scene of a different flavor, in the process adding a third arrest. Mukhtarov received the Americans' ultimatum and sent for them at once.

It was in the evening, the electricity had failed, and we were received in the shadows of flickering oil lamps. His associates, gaunt figures, pinched with hunger, regarded us with ill-concealed hostility. Apart from Muktarov they were largely uneducated, unskilled workers. In their eyes we were members of the capitalist class, their mortal enemies. In view of the coldness of their greeting we speculated as to whether we might not join our three employees in prison before the evening was over.

In this version the soviet officials denounced the ARA ultimatum "in bitter terms." How could they let innocent children starve simply to protect these insignificant bourgeois?

This seems like another product of Childs's imagination. In fact Wahren's statement to Haskell is more believable: "I can assure you that no friction has occurred and that the whole unpleasant incident was carried on in a most amiable way."

The period of crisis lasted only a short time. On the following afternoon, Salomine walked into the ARA office. Childs describes him as "a very pale and haggard figure, his hair and clothes disarranged."

As his slender short figure presented itself in motion across the room, I thought he resembled nothing so much as a terrified rat terrier dog who, upon being frightened, scurries to safety with his head directed constantly this way and that in observation.

He sat down and commenced a hurried narrative of the events which had taken place from the moment of his arrest until his release a few minutes previously. He had come directly from prison and as he spoke he kept rubbing his hands together and wetting his lips with his tongue under the stress of the nervous excitement from which he was suffering.

Salomine said that during the interrogation he had signed, out of fear, a statement acknowledging his anti-Soviet sympathies. Depould was released the same day. Both asked to be let go from the service of the ARA, and their resignations were accepted.

As much as Mukhtarov may have been annoyed by the meddling of the Cheka, he could not have been enthusiastic about having to give in to an ultimatum from foreign relief workers. His formal written reply to Wahren made plain his misgivings about whether the ARA had been justified in stopping the movement of famine relief supplies over the arrest of two Soviet citizens under Soviet law.

The ARA's position was that it had no choice but to defend its employees. According to Childs, "The arrests struck terror in their ranks and threatened the disorganization of our work," making a firm response absolutely necessary. But since Depould and Salomine resigned in terror anyway, this was a questionable victory.

The episode had been played out without any communication between Kazan and Moscow headquarters. This must have made Wahren uneasy, and indeed in his written report to Haskell he struck a defensive note: "I trust that the action has met with your approval. I know it was harsh but I could not see my way clear to act in any other way."

Wahren was one of the "old ARA" men with baby-feeding experience in the European theater, men who were accustomed to a decentralized organization and a considerable amount of leeway in handling local crises. But he must have been wary because he knew that the colonel ran a tight ship and did not take well to independent action by subordinates. In fact Haskell was beside himself with anger when he discovered what had transpired in Kazan. Childs says that he and his colleagues were "severely taken to task" for their "draconian" action.

Word that the director of the mission had not backed his men in a confrontation with the Cheka spread along the line, feeding the enmity of the "old ARA" men against their army officer chiefs.

Eiduk, too, was outraged. He complained bitterly to Haskell, wondering why Wahren had chosen to direct his ultimatum to the local government and not to the plenipotentiary from Moscow, Comrade Muskatt, "who knows the English language well." He said he found it difficult to believe that the great American people would approve of jeopardizing its extraordinary act of beneficence over the fate of two obvious class enemies of the workers' government. Besides, as Haskell well knew, the Riga Agreement provided no guarantees for Russian employees, who remained subject to Soviet law.

What especially disturbed Eiduk was the ARA's use of the threat to halt relief operations in order to achieve a "political" goal. He probably sensed a danger of establishing a precedent, clearing the way for future ARA threats to secure ever greater political demands. Perhaps he saw it as a confirmation of the worst Soviet fears about the ARA's true intentions, summed up in Litvinov's signature line during the Riga negotiations. This was certainly on the minds of the Kazan Americans. Childs wrote to his mother: "We had won our first battle and naturally were very much elated. Some one recalled what Maxim Litvinof had said at the Riga Conference. 'Food is a veapon' he is reported to have stated."[8]

THE KAZAN AFFAIR was not the last time the ARA would threaten to close or scale down operations in the face of what it considered unacceptable official conduct. In the districts and subdistricts the threat was employed on a routine basis, though usually with little fanfare and only occasionally creating controversy. The ultimate example was Haskell's April 1922 *en clair* telegram to Washington advising a halt to all further food shipments bound for Russia unless the Soviet authorities took emergency measures to deal with the railroad transportation crisis.

Haskell's bluff worked: it mobilized the Soviet leadership and was critical to the success of the American corn drive.

Somerville used the threat in Kurmish, a small town in Simbirsk situated some thirty-five miles from the nearest railway line and the site of repeated ARA troubles. He went there in January 1922 to investigate reports that the authorities were trying to remove the local ARA director, chosen by the Americans, and install their own man. When he discovered that the local officials were engaging in foul play, the Mississippian told them directly that in the next round of food distribution Kurmish might just find its allocations trimmed; after all, there were thousands of other children in need, and the ARA would have no trouble finding another place for the Kurmish rations.

Apparently he delivered his words with some heat. As he spoke, one of the assembled passed another a note, later found, which read, "A hot man, evidently from the south." Eventually Somerville had his way, although the local soviet president professed himself horrified at this cold-blooded willingness to "sacrifice the welfare of the hungry children" of Kurmish for the sake of a "*déclassé*" individual.

Marshall Tuthill of Saratov was in the town of Novouzensk in July 1922 just before his encounter with the bandit Ivanov. There he became embroiled in a fierce conflict with Eiduk's local agent, a man named Gubin, who refused to send one or more of Tuthill's telegrams to Saratov city. Then he told him not to leave Novouzensk under threat of arrest, although he later explained that he was only trying to save the American from bandits. Tuthill threatened to stop ARA feeding, which Gubin called "inhuman." He succeeded in reporting his difficulties by wire to district supervisor John Gregg, who passed on the information to Moscow where Lander had only just replaced Eiduk. Word soon came back down the line that Gubin had been ordered removed by the center; the feeding at Novouzensk was never interrupted.[9]

The Kurmish and Novouzensk episodes and the others like them did not create nearly as much fuss as the standoff that occurred in the city of Tsaritsyn, beginning in late winter 1922 at the height of the corn campaign. By that time Haskell and the other chiefs were a good deal more fed up on their treatment at the hands of the Bolsheviks than they had been in November during the Kazan incident.

The Tsaritsyn affair began in February when the principal Russian assistant to district supervisor Carlton Bowden, a man named Arzamasov, was arrested on the charge of promoting counterrevolution. It was said that as a schoolteacher in 1919 he had actively collaborated with the White forces in Tsaritsyn. It was also charged that since taking up employment with the ARA he had again become engaged in counterrevolutionary activities.

Bowden swore up and down to Haskell that Arzamasov was clean and that the government representative was simply out to get him. However, he was not in a position to defend Arzamasov regarding events that had taken place three years earlier, with which Eiduk himself claimed to be familiar. The chief plenipotentiary ordered the Tsaritsyn authorities to send the accused to Moscow so that he personally could testify against him before the revolutionary tribunal. Evidently these two men had crossed paths during the Civil War.

Haskell found Eiduk's behavior unacceptable and told him why in a letter dated February 25: "The most intelligent workers in Tzaritzin, in view of the danger involved, refuse to accept responsible positions with the American Relief Administration." In a further letter he explained that when the "principal employees live in terror of threatened arrests which are liable to take place at any time of day or night," this prevents the ARA from functioning "in a businesslike manner" and "efficiently."

This was not a good time to enter into a fight with Haskell, who had recently come under a cloud within the ARA organization for failing to stand up to the Bolos. He told Eiduk that Arzamasov's release and reinstatement with the ARA were "quite essential to our freedom of action as guaranteed by the Riga Agreement." To show he was serious, he gave Eiduk a copy of his telegram to Bowden stating that unless there was satisfactory evidence of guilt, the ARA would halt relief activities in the city of Tsaritsyn, there being plenty of other places in Russia in need of food supplies. Haskell told Bowden to "use his judgement"—a neat reversal of his stand in the Kazan episode.

In this exchange with Eiduk, Haskell accused the Tsaritsyn officials of "injecting political matters into the relief work there," and from his tone it is clear that he regarded "politics" in this context as entirely frivolous, tantamount to a sporting activity.

The blunt language Haskell used to address Eiduk was not in the diplomatic vocabulary of Coolidge, who had left the mission at the New Year. It may well have been inspired by Mitchell, visiting from London, who wrote to Brown approvingly of Haskell's tough stance: "It will be more or less a test of power."

Eiduk was infuriated and may have been surprised at Haskell's hard line. He insisted that Arzamasov was engaging in "provocatory work" and was an "unreliable element," whose guilt or innocence would be determined by the legal authorities of the Soviet government and had nothing to do with Bowden or the ARA. But he retreated from his unwise insistence on having the accused sent to Moscow and announced instead that he was sending a special agent to the scene to investigate. His exasperation at this American impertinence is evident: "I am sure, my dear Colonel, that you will report the content of my letter to Mr. Bowden and impress upon him the impermissability of dooming to death 30,000 children . . . on account of the arrest of Mr. Arzamasov, even if the latter were not guilty."[10]

While this case simmered, in mid-March there came news of the arrests of seven ARA employees in Samara city, and four more in the Samara subdistrict of Pugachev, all on political charges. Among the accused was the new Russian executive assistant of district supervisor Will Shafroth, Andrei Borodin.

There had been trouble involving Borodin earlier in the mission. He had been arrested in November 1921 and released three weeks later after an ARA protest, but had caught typhus in prison and was unable to return to work for two months. Shafroth says he was a "former inspector in the government co-operative organization" and "a man of most unusual ability and judgement."

Also among those arrested was the ARA office manager, Rothstein. According to a wholly untrustworthy Soviet article published in the 1960s, Rothstein had formerly been assistant to the chief of staff of the Volga military district under the Whites. This source claims that after his arrest a search of his apartment revealed that he had hidden away over fifty secret decrees and other military documents, which added up to a charge of espionage for American military intelligence via the ARA.

Shafroth surmised that this was purely a Cheka job, since even Eiduk's agent—Karklin, a Lett—seemed caught off guard by the arrests. He assured his mother in a letter of March 20, "I am going to give them a couple of days more to release the whole bunch, and if they don't do it I am going to hop a train for Moscow and take it up with the central authorities." He used the occasion to enlighten her on the Soviet judicial process, describing a recent trial he had been invited to witness at the City Theater. Shafroth, who received his J.D. from the University of California in 1916, cast an expert eye on the proceedings.

The three judges sat at a table in the middle of the stage and were flanked by tables for the lawyers. The accused, a band of thieves, sat in the orchestra pit, "and there were enough to have made a very loud noise if they had all had instruments." "Soldiers of the Red Army were everywhere in evidence acting as guards, ushers, pages, witnesses and spectators. It gave me quite a shock to see that the head of the department of Justice was also the prosecuting attorney; especially when I remembered that the appointment of all the judges in the gubernia including those who were trying this case, must be confirmed by him."

This glimpse of rough justice in Soviet Russia hardened Shafroth's determination not to allow his ARA staff to end up in the dock, or the orchestra pit, and certainly not on trumped-up charges intended to compromise the ARA.

Four months earlier, when the authorities had released Borodin from prison but refused to let him return to work for the ARA, Shafroth had protested to the local government that "in America" nobody who had been released from prison, even had he served time for committing a crime, would be denied the right to work where he pleased. The official reply reminded Shafroth that he was not in America: "the Soviet republic directs its work according to the class principle of the proletariat." The author of the 1949 Soviet article that published this exchange mocked Shafroth's appeal to law and order in America, "the country where they lynch Negroes."

Dudley Hale, still touring the subdistricts, assumed that the arrests were the result of a Cheka "crise de nerfs"—that rumors of trouble at the frontier had prompted the arrests of potential troublemakers of old-regime stamp. He said that one of the arrested Pugachev employees was accused of turning away an applicant for employment with the ARA on the grounds that she was insufficiently intelligent.

The Moscow chiefs were convinced that the men in question had been arrested, as Quinn put it, for their "fearless adherence to our regulations," that it was purely an attempt to "terrorize" the local personnel. The time had come, Quinn wrote London, to "take a firm stand in the matter and to insist that they treat us with a little less suspicion and a little more cooperation."

Haskell wrote Eiduk on March 30 that the charges against Arzamasov in Tsaritsyn were "more or less imaginary" and, taking a questionable leap, expressed his conviction that the Russian had engaged in no counterrevolutionary activity in 1919. There was, he wrote, "sufficient proof of the existence of an unbearable attitude on the part of some of the government officials at Tzaritzin" toward the ARA and its employees.

But there was more to this case than a campaign against the ARA. At the time preparations were underway for the June trial of the Socialist Revolutionaries, and at least some of the arrested ARA personnel appear to have been caught in this web. In fact, Eiduk admitted it. Eager to disprove Haskell's interpretation of events, he made what Quinn called a "most amazing statement": all "active members" of the SRs were presently being rounded up. Quinn informed London, "As the members of this party are in a great many cases intelligent and energetic men, this action on the part of the government is naturally going to have some effect on us."

Eiduk was telling the truth, but probably only a part of it. A secret GPU resolution of February 11, five days after the abolition of the Cheka, ordered its agents to "Take all measures to purge the ARA organization of undesirable elements." This was not exclusively directed at SRs, nor was a further resolution of March 28 calling for an intensified monitoring of the ARA and its native personnel.[11]

In any case, in Samara the ARA was not able to get satisfaction, and when Shafroth departed Russia in July, Borodin, Rothstein, and their colleagues were sitting in a Moscow prison awaiting trial, while two of their number had reportedly been sentenced without trial to exile in Archangel.

In Tsaritsyn, however, despite Eiduk's ominous threats in the initial period, Bowden and company won the day. In April Arzamasov was freed and returned to work, while Eiduk's plenipotentiary was replaced. George Cornick wrote home on April 24 in a victorious mood:

It has been a fight all along to get their co-operation in the work, but at present we have them working very well in this district. In fact only today the chief of the Gub-Checka most humbly apologized to Mr. Bowden for arresting one of our Russian workers in the district, and stated that hereafter none of our employees would be arrested for any cause without at first getting his permission. To appreciate what a real victory this is for us you must realize that formerly this same Checka was the most powerful section of the entire government, and arrested and condemned to death whosoever they pleased without trial. Also you must realize that about one half of our employees were formerly "White soldiers" so there are many reasons why the Reds might want to arrest them from time to time.

This arrangement of prior notification of arrests was extraordinary but not unique. In Simbirsk at about this same time, after Comrade Chernikh had been caught diverting an ARA corn car, he received an order from Moscow that no Russian employee of the ARA could be arrested without the district supervisor having first been notified and his consent obtained. This meant that the Russian personnel actually came to share, in the words of Somerville, "a sort of extra-territoriality—some compensation for the fright which Mr. Tchernik had given them on his arrival."

Curiously, though, there is no reference to the Tsaritsyn or Simbirsk understandings—which seem to have been only verbal—in any of the Haskell-Eiduk correspondence nor in the ARA Moscow communications with London and New York. It seems natural that Haskell or Quinn would have notified New York and London of this victory and even attempted to put it in force in other districts. The extent of Eiduk's concession to Haskell in April 1922 was merely the verbal promise that "no one will be arrested in the districts without my consent."[12]

Whatever the particulars, the resolution of these disputes helped to clear the air, and with ARA corn now pouring into the districts the number of arrests dropped off. More than this, in places the Soviet authorities went out of their way to avoid arresting ARA native personnel. The furthest lengths to which this was taken occurred during the arrest in May of the Simbirsk Engineering Society during its convention. Somerville called the act "just one of the periodic reminders to people that despite its being called the 'G.P.U.' . . . the old 'Cheka' (Extraordinary Commission) machine was still working at the old stand, and Russian citizens had better conduct themselves accordingly."

But this was a mass arrest with a difference. When the militia entered, the first words uttered by a policeman were, "Is there anyone here employed by the ARA?" One imagines sighs of relief emanating from among the suddenly reassured engineers, some silently congratulating themselves for having resisted the lure of ARA employment. "The uninitiated might have imagined that a St. Bartholomew's Eve for ARA employees was being staged," wrote Somerville. "It was whispered among the employees, occasionally, that there were some people who would enjoy such a thing."

One of those present, realizing that it was useless to try to conceal his guilt, arose and confessed. "Very well; leave the room," he was told. The rest were led off to jail.

CHAPTER 27

SHOOT THE INTERPRETER

Defending one of his subordinates charged with slandering the ARA, Comrade Muskatt explained to Childs that it was all a "misunderstanding": "You are certainly aware that our interpreters frequently garble the sense of personal discourses, especially as regards political addresses."

Blaming the interpreter was a common practice in ARA-Soviet diplomacy. There can be no doubt that government relations were made far more complicated—and interesting—by the presence of ARA and other interpreters and translators, few of whom had been professionally trained for the job.

To read through a random stack of ARA telegrams with all their technical detail and specialized jargon, it is a wonder that the translators managed to make sense of the original Russian, let alone turn it into comprehensible English. The Riga Agreement itself was a major challenge to make intelligible to a Russian speaker.

Most of the Americans knew no Russian, forcing them to rely heavily on interpreters. This meant that when they engaged even in delicate negotiations or discussions of sensitive political issues, their words were not their own.

George F. Kennan was especially sensitive to the danger of diplomats relying on interpreters. In his two-volume study of the United States and the Russian Revolution he included a passage about the predicament of the Americans in Petrograd in 1917, which can be applied to the men of the ARA:

[O]n how many . . . occasions were these American representatives—ignorant as most of them were of the language in which the political life around them was transpiring—betrayed in this manner by their interpreters, and how much was added, in this way, to the confusion and misunderstandings of the time? The exact answer to this question we shall never know; but that a considerable measure of distortion was occasioned generally in the presentation of the American position by the dependence of the leading American representatives on Russian interpreters, each of whom had some ax of his own to grind, is scarcely open to doubt.

On the eve of the mission in the summer of 1921, when the ARA chiefs in New York and London discussed the language problem, it was first thought that the best plan would be to attach to the mission expert Russian émigré interpreters hired in the United States and Europe. After further consideration they rejected this idea as dangerous, their assumption being that such people would likely be hostile to Bolshevism and might jeopardize relations with the Soviet government. Then too there might turn out to be among them Bolshevik sympathizers who might wish to harm ARA interests.

Brown in London cabled New York on August 5 of a decision not to hire émigrés, "owing certain strong affiliations one or other side." Besides, from all that the London staff had heard, there would be no shortage of English speakers inside Soviet Russia, at least in the principal cities.

But the real situation was different. Of the several rude shocks administered to the Americans during the opening weeks of the mission one was the realization that during the previous seven years many of the English-speaking Russians had been killed, had emigrated, or were in hiding. And genuine trained interpreters were a rare species indeed. Among those the ARA resorted to hiring, many claimed to have forgotten much of their English as a result of disuse since 1917. Unworthy applicants used this excuse to help them win a plum ARA interpreter job. The Simbirsk history states flatly that there were no capable English speakers to be found in the entire district. Yet,

There were any number of people who claimed to have spoken English in "the good old days," to have forgotten it in the four years of the Revolution during which they had been cutting wood and scrubbing floors, but who were sure that it would come back to them. It will never be known how many mistakes and misunderstanding had their origin purely in the mistakes of "reliable" interpreters.

The ARA's administrative division sent out instructions that interpreters be chosen only with extreme care: "Better to have none at all than bad ones." But the need was extreme as the Americans in the districts scrambled to get lifesaving operations under way, so there was no time to fuss about quality control.

As it happened, in attempting to avoid the potential pitfalls of hiring émigré interpreters, the ARA found itself having to rely upon an even more suspect group: *former* émigrés. These were largely men who had left, or had been exiled from, Russia before the Revolution, settled in the United States or England, and then returned to Russia after the Revolution in search of a better life. Of these a good number had been political radicals in the United States. Some came expecting to enter the much-celebrated workers' paradise and instead landed in the Bolshevik utopia. Still others returned in 1921 when word of famine reached the West, in order to come to the aid of relatives.

The American relievers, oblivious to divisions on the political left, commonly referred to these former radicals as "anarchists" and fully expected them to sympathize with the Bolos when in fact they could be as antagonistic as the dispossessed classes. A number of them had arrived in Russia in 1920 in the wave of radicals deported from the United States, which included Emma Goldman, soon to become disillusioned and then further disillusioned with Bolshevik power. On its part the Soviet government was not enthusiastic about taking in these outcasts and potential troublemakers, but it could not well turn them away.

Anyway, it did not take long to become apparent that most ARA interpreters were anti-Bolshevik. And not only interpreters: in Moscow and Petrograd, where the talent pool was much larger, the Americans favored the foreign-language speaker for any job. It made giving orders and making themselves understood so much easier.

Driscoll of Tsaritysn judged that the interpreters he employed were "not otherwise desirable citizens" of Soviet Russia and that "their conduct at times would justify the suspicion that they were helped out of America as undesirable."

Few applicants for interpreter or other positions with the ARA cared to be very forthcoming with details about their personal backgrounds, especially their political affiliations. But in order to prove one's qualifications there was an advantage to be gained by emphasizing work experience in the United States and naming an American hometown. Preston Kumler's interpreter was a "German Lett" who learned his English as a mechanic in Chicago. Charlie Veil had Pete, who had worked for eight years as a baker in Akron. And so on.

John Mangan, chief of the administrative division, recalled that in the beginning this situation was a source of some amusement. He could not get the hang of the pronunciation of Russian names, so he addressed his staff members by the cities they had lived in: Detroit, Cincinnati, Chicago, and so on. "But then we got three 'Chicagos' and that killed it."[1]

The other main source of ARA interpreters were the former well-to-do classes, mostly aristocratic widows. When their English fell short, usually they could switch to French or German, two languages with which many of the American relievers after their years of wandering across Europe had become familiar, and were quite proficient. This European common denominator was one of the strongest bonds between them.

Of course neither anarchists nor aristocrats were the first choice of the Bolsheviks, who offered the ARA their own candidates for the interpreter posts, some of whom were taken on. Many Old Bolsheviks had mastered foreign languages, including English, during their lengthy European exile, and they too drew upon returned Russian émigrés to staff their offices in Moscow, especially departments dealing with foreign affairs.

And so, when the ARA Americans in Moscow confronted Soviet officials, they frequently found themselves engaging in that timeless practice of guessing, while the interpreter went about his work, how much English their Russian counterparts actually comprehended on their own. It was commonly assumed that one or more of the Russians present at a conference understood English but feigned ignorance and a reliance on an interpreter in order to gain some advantage. This deception has figured in many travelers' and journalists' accounts from long before and since the Revolution. Of course it was by no means exclusive to Russia, but the widely traveled ARA chiefs felt that the Bolos excelled in it. Several ARA men attributed this to a Russian obsession with intrigue.

Two members of the ARA Poland mission, Maurice Pate and Herschel Walker, got a taste of it during the Russo-Polish War in the summer of 1920. They remained at their posts as the Red Army swept westward in its march on Warsaw. Hoover personally had given them permission to allow themselves to be "captured" and escorted to Moscow, where they could sit down among the Bolo chiefs and discuss the possibility of establishing ARA relief operations in Russia. This authority had not been granted lightly. At the time the Bolsheviks were believed to be rounding up and imprisoning Americans for use as hostages to blackmail the United States into granting Soviet Russia official recognition.

So Pate and Walker were taking a risk. They succeeded in being captured and taken to Minsk, where they were attended by a guard and a waiter, both of whom "gave the impression of being more or less stupid types, and were present on a number of occasions when we had great difficulty in making ourselves understood by persons whom we met. A few days after our arrival in Moscow we were surprised to see both of them in the Foreign Office, well dressed and talking perfect English."

This left the two Americans to search their memories for possible verbal indiscretions of a compromising nature—that is, beyond expressions of ridicule at the feeble mental powers of the guard and the waiter.

Yes, you had to have your wits about you in this "trick country." On the other hand it was possible to overreact and attribute to an official's unwillingness to use English some sinister motive when in fact he may simply have wished to avoid projecting an appearance of weakness by using accented, ungrammatical, even incomprehensible English—perhaps even emitting a schoolboy howler. The Bolos already had enough working against them at the international negotiating table without looking like fools.

The ARA men were always on the lookout for subtle signs of comprehension: a premature nod of the head, a poorly suppressed smile before the interpreter caught up to the punch line. Eiduk came under this kind of scrutiny. He always used an interpreter, although one ARA relief worker claimed that he spoke "quite fluent English." Proof of his alleged ability came by accident when this same American accompanied him to Petrograd in February 1922. With no interpreter along, he is said to have handled himself quite well in English. Naturally this story spread throughout the mission, and Eiduk's linguistic abilities—and thus his talent for deception—became quite legendary. Once his secret was discovered it amused the Moscow Americans to observe him during the daily ARA conference, in Ellingston's words, "always immune from the excitement of the discussion, like a rock on a ruffled beach, shifting his eyes from the American speaker to the interpreter and back again."

Whatever was Eiduk's actual proficiency in English when he became chief plenipotentiary in October 1921, it is safe to assume that he at least increased his listening comprehension during his tenure with the ARA. And his vocabulary must have been spiced up with a number of the colorful curse words that Colonel Haskell had once used to inspire his Fighting Irish regiment during the war with Mexico.

ALTHOUGH THE AMERICAN personnel's exposure to other European languages, some of them Slavic, gave them a psychological boost, when it came to Russian they found the going tough. Joseph Driscoll wrote, "The average American is not a linguistic marvel, and the ARA workers found the language a trying handicap."[2] A number of the relief workers undertook to study Russian with private tutors, although their own testimony indicates they may have made more progress with their young female instructors than with the declension of Russian nouns. In any case, as it usually happens, most of the actual learning took place in the course of the work day.

Childs took the study of Russian seriously. He seems to have put in a good deal of effort to develop some basic speaking and comprehension skills. He had learned the importance of knowing a foreign language several years earlier as a masters student at Harvard. It was his first exposure to the English of New Englanders. "In the beginning I was made to feel very much an outsider. When I entered a store to make a purchase it was difficult for me to make myself understood. The loneliness at first was almost unbearable."

During meals in the dining room at Memorial Hall his classmates took great pleasure in making fun of his Virginia accent. This seems to have gone on for some time until he was rescued by an unlikely savior: T. V. Soong, brother of Madame Sun Yat-sen and future finance minister in the Sun government. As Childs recalled it, "after hearing me badgered more or less regularly by the New Englanders for my accent, he broke out, to everyone's amazement, with the protesting exclamation: 'Stop picking on Childs.'"

The general reaction was that it was none of his business, as it was an affair between students of two traditionally antagonistic sections of the country.

"Oh, but it *is* my affair," Soon protested. "My father attended Vanderbilt University and became a southern sympathizer, and he taught me to be one."

Everyone was dumbfounded; after that, I was left relatively in peace.

The Cyrillic alphabet presented a challenge not entirely novel to the Virginian, who as a military intelligence officer at GHQ in Chaumont in 1918 had solved two key German ciphers—this despite the fact that he was a novice at cryptography and that his ignorance of German was near-total, "save for that instinctive feel for the mechanics of it which the cryptographer acquires from such intimate daily contact with it as I had had."

Anyway, Childs seems to have mastered Cyrillic with little difficulty, and his confidence picked up. In January 1922 he sent his mother a progress report: "I can read it now although I don't know always what I am reading and I can speak a sort of pigeon Russian which, however, seems to improve day by day."

In April he writes that he is about to set out on an inspection trip without Simson, his interpreter, but he feels confident he can get by. At journey's end he reports that he has done just fine, though only the Russians and Tatars he encountered along the way knew for sure. Childs made this trip in the company of Skvortsov, who must have had at least some small command of English for the two to have so effortlessly become friends. This is not certain, but it seems to make sense, which may mean that by the time of Skvortsov's transfer to Ekaterinoslav his English was flavored with a Virginia accent. If so, it was not nearly enough to facilitate understanding between him and Barringer, the Charlottesville native.

The Simbirsk district was fortunate to have a Russian-speaking American in Somerville. This enabled him to conduct ARA business in Russian and allowed him to go off on inspection trips by himself, freeing up an interpreter for another American. "To me it seems a tremendous advantage not to be at the mercy of an interpreter, for even the most capable ones we have occasionally make important mistakes, and more often 'use their own heads' in putting twists on one's language."

In his travels through the district, Somerville observed that if the local ARA Russian employees had something of a sensitive or confidential nature to report, they were far less willing to do so through a third party. "Talking directly to an

American, a Russian will almost always talk freely about questions on which his lips are sealed if he has to talk through another Russian."

In Samara it was said that Ronald Allen, who was later promoted to district supervisor, could get along pretty well in Russian, though it is impossible to verify this from the ARA documentation or to discover how he had acquired this skill. To judge from a letter he wrote in March 1922, whatever his ability in Russian, he had come by it only since arriving in Soviet Russia five months earlier.

It is documented that he did a bit of singing with the Harvard Glee Club. This sidelight comes courtesy of Dudley Hale, Class of 1914, who also was assigned to the Samara district. Hale wrote of his classmate that he "handles his foreign languages, French, German and Russian very well." His French he mastered during his service in the American ambulance corps with the French Army, which he joined directly after graduation.

As for Hale himself, he informed Christian Herter, Hoover's assistant in Washington and the future U.S. Secretary of State, that his current interpreter was a "funny little shaved-headed (ex-typhus) girl of seventeen, named Borisofskaia, [who] prefers to talk French, though she also knows English, and so I am getting very proficient in that tongue. When she isn't around, I am obliged to rely on Russian, which is a swell language, Chris, provided you find Chinese easy."

Three times a week at 8:30 A.M. he took Russian lessons like bitter medicine. He recommended to Herter in the strongest terms that all further ARA recruits come over with some background in the language. "The old fiction about all Russians being linguists is all very well for those who are now dead or out of the country, but in this work you don't run across many train guards or starving children reading Moliere or E.A. Poe in the original."[3]

The native personnel could be equally impatient with the language barrier. One employee in Kiev dwelled on it in a brief memoir of the ARA mission, which is in the ARA archive in English translation. In a section called "The Dumb," he lamented the inability of the American staff to communicate properly in Russian. He remembered one occasion when district supervisor Kenneth Macpherson attempted to bring order to the chaos of the food package delivery room. Would-be beneficiaries, some hysterical, pressed forward to claim packages they understood, or imagined, had been paid for by relatives abroad and were waiting to be picked up. This was a typical scene at Kiev headquarters. Three times during the mission the door to the delivery room was broken down by the crush of anxious supplicants.

The American entered the room and demanded quiet but could not make himself heard above the wail of the crowd. One well-meaning citizen came to his assistance, echoing the plea for quiet in Russian: "*Tishe!*" Mac could not have understood this correctly because it provoked him to throw the man out into the street, quite literally. "All this seems to be funny, comical," wrote the Kiev memoirist. "We call it curiosities, but in reality? In reality—how much suffering and tears did it cause the poor consignees."

Some of the Americans found that ignorance of the language, or feigning it, had its advantages. Fleming begins his lengthy account of his "Trip Through the Volga in September 1922" with the scene at the train station in Moscow, where "after a considerable delay [we] passed through the gate to the train. Even then the gatemen started to stop us, but we brushed through with an air of 'ne poni-maiou russki' and they let us past. God takes care of foreigners and drunkards in their travels in Russia."

Ordinarily, though, the advantage did not go to the ignorant. On a snowy night in December 1922 an ARA man walked out of the Blue House and came upon Tommy Burland in a heated negotiation with a local *izvoshchik* over the proposed fare: the obstinate American waving off the driver's proposal of four million rubles and insisting on paying "only" five million.

On his Volga journey Fleming brought along his regular interpreter, George, a "short, jolly little Jew" of about twenty-five. Fleming admired his powers of perception as applied to the opposite sex. He served not only as the American's interpreter and batman but as "social ring master . . . a position he fulfilled throughout the trip as nobly as he did that of interpreter."

More than most interpreters, George was called upon to refine as well as translate Fleming's words, allowing the American considerable diplomatic latitude in his discussions with Soviet officials. On one occasion, in the town of Suizran, Fleming and his Man Friday called upon the local soviet authorities, who had been complaining that American relief was costing them too much. By now this was a familiar ploy to induce the ARA to foot the entire bill for its operations.

Fleming, who knew his way around with statistics, produced figures to demonstrate that American relief had in fact amounted to over two trillion rubles more than the value of all expenses incurred through it by the government. He allowed a moment for this to sink in. "I now felt that the proper effect had been produced and came in with a clincher. My little speech was spiced, I fear, with diverse strong, but profane terms. The profanity did not get across, as I knew, but the speech, properly edited and delivered in Russian by George, was to the effect that the ARA . . . should only be too glad to clear out of Suizran, shut our office, and send our supplies elsewhere."

This elicited equally familiar profuse apologies and promises of future cooperation. "Two thumps on the floor at once brought the conference to an end, and hot tea was served from the steaming samovar brought from the lower depths."[4]

THE KAZAN DISTRICT seems to have gotten by without great difficulty. Childs had Simson, whose services were offered by the local government. Despite having been an officer in the Red Army, he had been in and out of Bolshevik prisons before being exiled to Kazan, another wanderer in the grey zone of Soviet life.

Kazan also had John F. de Jacobs, a Lett who had been a student of diplomacy in St. Petersburg before the war and later entered the Imperial Guard Cavalry. When the Revolution came, he escaped from Petrograd, avoiding German-occupied Latvia and ending up in London where he obtained a commission in the British Army in 1918 and was sent to fight with the intervention army in Archangel. There he was captured by the Bolsheviks and placed in a prison camp with some two thousand other White officers.

As he tells it, he luckily fell sick and was transferred to a hospital, which spared him from sharing the fate of his fellow officers. These unfortunates were placed in confinement on a barge on the Neva River and bombarded with artillery fire.

He spent almost a year in a Petrograd prison, then was sent to Kazan where, like Simson, he went to work as a translator of foreign news received over the wireless. He landed with the ARA, but Childs had to get special authorization to take him along on trips outside of Kazan city.

The ARA proved to be his salvation, although not before a further period of adventure. After the Soviet and Latvian governments signed a state treaty in autumn 1921, he decided to attempt a legal exit of the country. So he made his way to Moscow and was arrested as an ARA spy.

The Kazan Americans had no knowledge of this and, not having heard from him, assumed that he had made his way out of Russia. Then in April 1922 a letter from de Jacobs arrived relating his story of hard luck.

After his arrest he was jailed for a short time and released. Without a job he was forced to live in a Moscow refugee center, which was extremely unpleasant but kept him out of prison. Apparently his pride prevented him from appealing for help to the ARA in Moscow, although after drifting to Vitebsk on the western frontier of Soviet Russia he ended up going to work for the local ARA. There he caught spotted typhus, recovered, and after a few failed attempts, he secured with ARA assistance the necessary papers to leave Soviet Russia. Shorn of all possessions, he eventually landed in New York City.

In Tsaritsyn finding adequate interpreters was a perennial problem. Bowden complained to Moscow in January 1922 that his written instructions for employees had to be dictated in French, then translated into Russian, and then, for the benefit of the Moscow record-keepers, translated from this Russian into an English that was said to be so convoluted as to be nearly incomprehensible.

This sounds like the problem of the Americans at the Soviet ports attempting to send telegrams to Moscow headquarters. At the start of operations this was attempted in English, but what came out at the other end was a mess: "it is questionable if there is a better collection of nonsense syllables extant than is contained in these telegrams." So they switched to Russian, but the process of translating the original English to Russian and then back into English at destination made a different mess, although a more tolerable one.

Shortly after arriving at Saratov, Kinne sent a touchy letter to Moscow requesting male interpreters under the age of thirty-five. He complained that he had to work with women and old men. Kinne may not have realized how lucky he was to have Alexis Babine on his staff, the "chief Russian assistant" of the Saratov mission.

Babine's was an unusual story even by ARA standards. Born the son of a builder in central Russia in 1866, he was a language student in St. Petersburg in the 1880s. His life was dramatically changed one day in 1890 and only by a matter of inches. His closest friend dared him to shoot a pine cone off his head with a revolver, a challenge the young Babine took up with fateful consequences: the bullet ended his friend's life. Fearing a murder charge, he fled Russia for the West. It all sounds like something out of Turgenev.

The would-be fugitive made his way to the United States. He had once read in a Russian newspaper that Cornell University would offer a job to anyone willing to work his way through college, so he moved to Ithaca and completed his B.A. and M.A. in American history before moving on to Indiana University, then to Stanford, then back east to a job at the Library of Congress. In 1910 he went to work for the Associated Press and was assigned to its St. Petersburg bureau. Two years later in the Russian capital he published a two-volume history of the United States.

Babine decided to remain in Russia and became a public school inspector in Kharkov province, then in 1916 in Vologda province. The Revolution set him in motion again, and he ended up in Saratov, where he taught English and worked at the university library. Then came the famine.

He was an extraordinary asset for the Saratov district, and the ARA paid him back in autumn 1922 by arranging his exit from Soviet Russia as well as the safe passage of his private papers. He returned to Cornell and eventually to the Library of Congress.

By the time John Gregg became district supervisor in Saratov, Babine had left. None of his American staff spoke Russian, and most ARA work had to be done through interpreters when these could be found. On one occasion the absence of an interpreter had forced him to cancel a planned inspection trip, trapping him at headquarters.

He asked the chiefs to send down qualified interpreters. Certainly they could do better than their most recent offering, "a young lady from Petrograd, sixteen years old, who neither speaks, writes, nor reads English well, who has no business experience, and is utterly incompetent for the difficult and delicate interpretation necessary with the government representative, as well as the complicated explanations necessary reference commodity reporting and the functions of the Supply Division."[5]

The Ufa Americans had no Russian speakers among them. The native personnel of the district numbered, at peak, thirty thousand, and Bell says that the Americans could speak directly with only a few of them, essentially the interpreters. Reading through the documentation reveals that the Ufa mission was stretched so thin that the principal interpreters were by necessity forced to perform duties far more important than the translation of words.

Boris Elperin was practically considered one of the American staff, so vital was his role. Elperin joined the ARA Moscow staff in autumn 1921 and in November accompanied Bell to Ufa to set up the district; he stayed on until it closed in June 1923. Bell's right-hand man was born in Russia and educated in Belgium, returning only after 1917. He could speak English, German, and French, as well as Russian, with ease. He was refined, intelligent, and was an attractive character; Bell and Kelley repeatedly praised his diplomatic skill in dealing with delicate ARA business and gave him generous credit for Ufa's good record of government relations.

Elperin loved to travel, and Kelley found him to be a "charming companion" on the road, an essential quality for the successful ARA interpreter. "Boris alone of all the Russians I came to regard as a friend." After the mission, from his home in Vermont, Bell took up a collection of funds from the ARA Ufa alumni, which enabled Elperin to get out of Russia and go to New York City.[6]

Ufa had a considerable German colony, and this gave Piet Hofstra an advantage over the other Americans because his German was excellent. By the end of the mission he was also said to have acquired "considerable Russian," though it is hard to say what this means since he had come into Russia with little or none.

Shortly after he arrived in Ufa Hofstra wrote to Shafroth in Samara of the unsatisfactory interpreters in his hire. These included a "Moscow-Polish-Jewish Doctor"; a professor; and his real language "shark," an Austrian prisoner of war who was a cook by training and who knew only a little English and less Russian. The cook, Hofstra soon discovered, either took his translation work to the professor or had it translated from English to German and then asked his friends to produce a Russian equivalent. Hofstra decided to put him to work in the ARA warehouse alongside a Russian who spoke German.

Another English-speaking "native" staffer in Ufa was Eugene Willig, whose name is also spelled Villig, Willich, and Velig. He was Estonian-born and, like Elperin, educated in Belgium. Before the revolution he had worked for European manufacturing concerns with branches in Moscow and Petrograd. He is described as a fine "older" gentleman, older than the ARA men, anyway, who came to respect and admire him. Kelley wrote, "He has saved a frock coat from the wreckage somehow and is very imposing about the office." He served as chief of various ARA departments but was also called upon to double as an interpreter.

Kelley worked him hard in discussions with the staff of the ARA supply department. On February 23 he reported that his "Teutonic interpreter" was weakening: "Three hours of discussion on the supply problems with my Tartar Col. last night was too much for him. He gave out before the end of the argument and had to quit." He gave out again the next night, so Kelley gave him the following day off. "Without him I can do nothing and I fear he is on the verge of a nervous breakdown. It is too much to expect of these middle aged Russians weakened by the living conditions of the last five years, that they exert as much energy as we youngsters."

Willig's absence made for a quiet February 26. The supply department men came in, had a look around, and, not seeing the interpreter, left without so much as a grunt for Kelley, who found this amusing. "I am here, but then again I am not here so far as they are concerned." Willig's weak constitution left him vulnerable to the typhus that took his life several weeks later.

Kelley seemed to revel in the alphabet soup of languages used for ARA business in Ufa. And for pleasure as well: about to dress for a dinner party he closed a letter with a reference to the evening ahead: "It will be a fine mess of Russian, English, French and German conversation." He was well equipped to hold his own, having a good command of French and German.

Kelley's correspondence is the best source of information about two other ARA interpreters in Ufa. In his opinion, the best of them from a strictly linguistic point of view was Theodore, to whom he does not give a last name. A man in his early twenties, Theodore's past was a mystery to most of the ARA men, who were satisfied to leave it that way.

One of the Russian staff says his full name was Theodore Kushnarev and that his Russian-Jewish parents had emigrated to New York City before the war. The Revolution had brought him back to the Old Country.

"In America," Kelley wrote with a self-conscious nod to President Harding, "I fancy he ran with the extreme radical group, but since coming to Russia he has drifted back to normalcy. Whether he is Jewish or Russian I can't yet make out." His experience with Bolshevism was not a happy one. "Theodore has been a communist, turned against them, and served time in prison for it."

I know he has been under death sentence several times in the past two years. I believe I have converted him into an enthusiast for the A. R. A. by a few "inspiring" talks about Hoover and our organization. He retains much of that form of idealism so common among American collegians in spite of all the hard knocks he has had to take. My own pessimism over the future of Russia, based on arguments he cannot controvert, is a source of great worry to him because the kid loves Russia deeply. Nor is he sour on America so far as I have found out.

Elsewhere Kelley notes that Soviet officials in Ufa did not trust Theodore, possibly because he was "youthful and too indiscreet," but no doubt in part due to his past. On one of his inspection trips Kelley had intended to take him along, but the Ufa officials raised such a fuss that he decided instead to bring Elperin, a "violent anti-Red," but who nonetheless "seems to have the respect and confidence of all the government officials. He is a model of discretion I am sure."

THEN THERE WAS young Alexander Sukharev. Kelley and Bell were walking through the streets of the Ural mining town Zlatoust in the winter of 1921, when a young boy about thirteen years old approached. His appearance was no different from the thousands of other street urchins that had been pestering them in their travels, but this one addressed them in unaccented American English. So incongruous was the sound of the language with the appearance of the boy that it must have stopped them dead in their tracks. Alex said he was from Chicago.

Kelley took him back to Ufa, making him "my personal body-guard" and thereby saving, or at least prolonging, his life. Doctor Sloan confined him to bed, and it was two months before he was up and about. Alex had been born in Saratov and taken to America by his parents at the age of six. Kelley says that the family lived in Chicago for five years, Alex passing through the fifth grade. Life in America could not have been joyful for the Sukharevs because after the October Revolution Alex's father took him back to Russia, via San Francisco and Vladivostok. It was 1919 and the Civil War was still underway, so they only got as far as Ufa. Two years later, Alex's father died in the famine. At this point, in Kelley's cynical words, "A Russian family that had only eight children of their own took him in to share their various substitutes for food." He credits Alex's "Chicago instincts" for leading him to the ARA kitchen in Zlatoust, where an ARA Russian inspector adopted him; then Bell and Kelley arrived.

Alex's English was a bit rusty after three years of disuse, but he picked it up again quickly. "He is very intelligent, with a grave manner that you might expect after his hard life." He was a bit young to be an interpreter, but Kelley found him to be "very useful for minor communications." His personal property consisted of "a mail order typewriter, value $1.00, two geography books, and an American history. I believe he also owns a towel, a toothbrush, and a bar of soap."

Alex had an older brother—Ivan in Russia, John in America—who had stayed behind in Chicago to finish school. He was concerned to try to make contact with him and with his help get a passport out of Russia. One day "Little Alex" entered Kelley's room and asked for the address of "President Hoover" so that he could write to him for the necessary papers to get to America.

If Kelley was moved by this, he was not the kind to let on to his correspondent. Instead he changed the subject to Alex's frail health and the fact that a Russian doctor had said he had a weak heart and one bad lung. "It would cost thousands of dollars in America to give him the treatment necessary to restore his health. All told, I see little that can be done for him."

Harold Blandy had a bigger heart, so big it blurred his vision of reality. In his farewell letter to his mother, which is a last will and testament even though it was written before he was diagnosed with the typhus that killed him, he closed with these words:

My body is to be sent back to America by the A.R.A. all expenses being paid by them. The body is to be placed as near my Father as possible. I have taken a great liking to a small Russian Boy who Mr. Kelley and Col. Walter Bell, A.R.A. men, found in Slatuse Russia. If possible please take care of him and try and educate him as you have all your sons. He was kind to me in all my unhappy days of sickness and I want to help him to lead his life as I have tried to lead mine.

Alex signed his name to the letter as witness.

There is no happy ending with Alex living in the comfort and safety of the Blandy household in Virginia. Told of Alex's medical condition and the burden, financial and otherwise, it would place on Mrs. Blandy, the ARA chiefs in New York talked her out of honoring her son's last wish. It might seem heartless not to have gotten Alex out under this or another pretext, but Bell himself was against it, and Bell, too, was a man with a big heart. It turns out that it was more than Alex's frail health that troubled him. Alex was suspected of disloyalty to the ARA, Bell wrote confidentially to New York in February 1923; specifically, of leaking "private information" from the office and the residence, though it is not clear to whom.

In the meantime, it was discovered that Alex's brother also had returned to Russia and was working for the ARA in Saratov. The boys were reunited in Ufa, and from there they went to live with an uncle in Tashkent. The only source on Alex's fate after the mission is another young ARA "interpreter," Alexis Lapteff, a boy in his late teens who spoke a smattering of English enabling him to perform odd jobs for the Americans. According to Lapteff, after many unsuccessful attempts to get permission, the brothers tried to cross the border illegally into either China or Persia. In this attempt John was shot and killed. Alex's fate was unknown.

Lapteff was luckier. After the ARA's departure he gravitated to Moscow with the hope of emigrating to Detroit, where he had a cousin. It took a few years, but his passport came through. He sold his brand-new Underwood typewriter, a gift from Bell, for $175.00 and used the money to buy passage from Moscow to Cuba, then made his way to Detroit where he went to work in the design section at General Motors.

In the 1930s at New York's Russian Tea Room, at the cashier, Lapteff ran into Elperin, who now went by the name Perry and worked for a U.S.S.R. import company out of Sweden. He recalled this encounter in a telephone conversation from Flushing, New York, in February 1991, which he asked to conduct in Russian.

In Ufa the ARA interpreters faced an additional challenge. Aside from Russians and Germans there was also a large Bashkir population that spoke Russian as a second language. This probably complicated Kelley's assignment in the Bashkir town of Argayash, which he describes as a "mere village of a hundred or so wooden huts set down beside the railway tracks on this tractless plain." Alex was along, but the job of translating went to a man named Tossman, "my 'kike' interpreter."

The principal men of the town had gathered in the office of the A.R.A. inspector to meet me, the first American they had ever seen. An endless pow-wow ensued in which it developed that considerable friction existed between our Russian inspector and the Baskir committees with which he has to work. Our work is progressing slowly. Only about 26 kitchens feeding 2,200 children have been opened up to the present, although food is on hand for 5,000 and the canton's allocation is 10,500. My position is a delicate one. My slightest suggestion was law, my ignorance of local conditions complete, and my means of understanding or communicating with them, oh so weak! You can imagine what a nervous strain it must be to have to deal so directly with matters of life and death through the medium of any interpreter to say nothing of a Jewish tailor whose knowledge of Russian and English are both faulty. As best I could I tried to sense the situation and made a speech in part conciliatory and in part threatening. God knows how it sounded when it was put into Russian![7]

Kelley would otherwise have been totally in the dark about the soundness of the translation except for Alex's presence, which offered at least some measure of quality control. Had Tossman's Russian translation been seriously off the mark, Alex was there to alert Kelley.

MOST OF THE TIME there was no sure way for an ARA man to determine the quality of the translation. For Farmer Murphy this reality was lit up in a flash. He was standing on a railroad station platform in a Volga town with his interpreter, "a young Jewish man" whom he describes as "always accommodating," when he noticed several peasant women in sheepskin coats with babies in their arms and desperate looks in their eyes. He asked his companion to tell the women that he wished to buy them a bottle of milk for their babies. "To my surprise he made no move to do so. I urged him again and then he went over to one of them and mumbled something which I could not hear, but the woman showed no sign of understanding. I asked him what the woman had said but he did not reply." Murphy went ahead and bought the milk for them.

It then came out that the interpreter could not speak Russian. He had been born of Russian Jewish parents in London but had never been in Russia until the Revolution. "Then he hurried there to find the new paradise. There are thousands of cases like his."

Incompetence was not the only thing that could leave an interpreter speechless. Fear could have the same effect. It frequently happened that an interpreter would refuse to translate the words of an American, or to convey their meaning accurately, for fear of bringing down upon himself the anger of the official to whom they were directed. How often an American's words were purposely mistranslated, or softened, for this reason is impossible to know, but it could not have been unusual. Driscoll underscored the problem: "At times, in the course of conversation or argument with local authorities, it would become necessary to stress a point, and always it lacked its kick in the interpretation. Aside from real ignorance the interpreters were themselves handicapped by fear, so that remarks which Americans wished to put across for the good of the soul of the party addressed were gentled considerably by the interpreters."

The interpreters had good reason to be wary. As Driscoll saw it, "The officials resented the idea of a Russian pointing out an unpleasant fact to them, even though aware that the interpreter was merely acting as the mouthpiece of the American."

But not all were so aware, as Coleman pointed out: "The position of the interpreter is extremely precarious for in voicing the thoughts of the American the local officials do not consider them our mouthpiece, but individuals who are not permitting the authorities to do as they choose, as they do in all instances with the exception of the ARA operation."

Whatever went through the heads of the officials, their kill-the-messenger mentality could inhibit even the most faithful translator. Walter Duranty wrote in his 1943 memoir, *Search for a Key*, "I'd go so far as to say that the value and success of any foreigner in Russia, from American relief workers to engineers, technical advisors, diplomats, and reporters, has been in direct ratio to the accuracy, *and courage*, of their interpreters."

Duranty illustrates the point with an anecdote, of the purely fictional variety, about ARA relief worker "Bill Jones"—recognizable as Charlie Veil—who told his interpreter, Sergei, to prepare a sleigh for a journey to a Volga village said to be held by the bandit Serov, who had been looting ARA food supplies. Jones wanted to confront him. Sergei promptly balked at this idea. "No less promptly Jones stuck a Colt automatic in his ribs and said, 'Sirov may kill us both, that is the chance we take; but I shall certainly kill you unless you get into the sleigh.'" In the subsequent encounter between Jones and Serov, the American threatens to shoot the interpreter unless he translates his words exactly.

There is testimony of a different kind. An ARA Kiev employee suggested that the ARA interpreter—some "evil genius"—might purposely mistranslate a communication between an American and a Soviet official in order to stir up trouble. He found the interpreters generally to be a "great evil in the life of the ARA."

The Americans did have enjoyable moments behind the language barrier. It allowed them to have their little jokes at the expense of their Russian audience.

A delegation of ARA chiefs from New York, London, and Moscow got to witness this during a tour of the Volga in the summer of 1922 when they were toasted at a series of banquets at each district headquarters. At the dinner table in Simbirsk, once the diplomatic protocol of toasting had passed down along the Soviet and American lines of authority and had reached the district Americans, one of these rose, glass in hand, to address the assembled dignitaries. Perhaps inspired by alcoholic spirits he spoke glowing words about the attractions of Simbirsk city. Turning to Haskell he capped his tribute with the words, "It's a hell of a hole, Colonel."

John Lehrs of Moscow's liaison division and a former American diplomat had the wherewithal and self-control to translate this into Russian as: "I shall always remember with deep affection this city, and its people who are my friends." Or something to that effect; it sounds a bit long, but that is how Somerville remembered it. He called the moment the "high water point in Russia of A. R. A. oratory and diplomacy." Whatever it was, it must surely have been a supreme challenge to hold in the laughter.

The Americans also got uncounted cheap laughs out of the many English mistranslations and mispronunciations by Russian speakers, which were bound to occur in the daily routine of an American relief organization with a huge native staff.

In the Moscow office a former countess whose job it was to translate items from the Russian press came up with a list of theater performances that included "The Shaver of Seville" and "How Important It Is to Be Serious." This kind of innocent error would be printed in the "Russian Unit Record" and then reverberate through the documentation of other districts. Later readers of the "Record" would add "The Lake of the Swans" to the list of malapropisms, but this was a standard English translation back then.

Columba Murray told a story, repeated with evident delight in the "Record," of the visit to the ARA personnel house in Kiev of an Armenian who spoke no English. As this man was leaving, he heard one of the Americans say something to another about the keys to the office. The Armenian was eager to bid the Americans goodbye in their native tongue, and believing that he had heard the magic words, smiled and bowed deeply as he backed out, repeating the phrase, "Keys to the office! Keys to the office!"[8]

In no district did the hazards of language occupy such a central place in the daily life of the ARA man as in Orenburg, where the show whirled merrily on. In this as in other ways, Orenburg was like a cartoon version of the rest of the ARA mission.

Fleming understood this right away when he arrived there during his excursion through the districts in September 1922, a moment when in most places the harvest was in and the famine had been declared ended. As his train pulled into town, he had the sensation of having gone back in time. Here, in a scene familiar from a year earlier, he found the railroad station packed with miserable refugees. "It is said that whatever Russia suffers from afflicts Orenburg worst of all, and certainly the first impressions of the city would lead one to believe that it deserved it."

The town itself was "frontier-like" in appearance, with its one-and-a-half-story buildings and its dusty main street full of horse and camel traffic. "A more morbidly depressing place than Orenburg can hardly be imagined."

Of course, it was much worse the previous November when Freddie Lyon arrived. Among all the other challenges he faced, the shortage of capable local assistance, particularly interpreters, was acute. He hired what he claimed were the only two English speakers within thousands of miles and placed them in responsible positions. One of them was a local Party official whom he made head of the supply division and who proceeded to staff the office with politically acceptable subordinates. This man essentially built the initial ARA structure that Coleman later had to dismantle.

The quality of the Orenburg translators can be judged by perusing the translations of Klimov's letters to Coleman and comparing these to the original Russian. The ARA translators, intentionally or not, produced a crude, broken English that exaggerated the hostility of Klimov's tone and at times makes him seem utterly stupid. The fact that he could not read or write must have made it seem natural to the Americans for him to "think" in such illiterate English sentences. It must have encouraged Coleman's imperious attitude toward the commander.

In the subdistricts it was worse. Anna Karlin, the former socialist candidate for the school board in Detroit and one-time pretender to the post of Moscow plenipotentiary to the Orenburg ARA, was stationed in a distant village on the staff of the Russian Red Cross. She wrote a letter on June 25, 1922, to Coleman's adjutant, Sakharov, with whom she seems to have had decent relations. In it she described a confrontation that had taken place between Joseph Fitzgerald of the ARA and the local authorities over the issuance of some kerosene.

Karlin blamed the whole affair on Fitzgerald's translator, Ivan, whom Sakharov apparently had met. You remember, "the stupid man with the long legs." To her the matter of blame was clear: "Of course if there had been a reasonable interpreter, the matter would have turned out differently, but with such a buffoon, it is impossible to expect anything else."

During his stay in Orenburg, Fleming assumed the task of writing the history of the first year of the district, and as part of his research he made a thorough study of the Orenburg diary. His history tries to convey a sense of the loony atmosphere at headquarters and includes a description of what is supposed to pass as a typical morning at the office. Coleman is at his desk wrestling with matters of supply, transport, office space, and so on, while across from him sits Fred Wells, "filling out form I-6 for Moscow's statistical fiends." In walks a staff member with a translation of an important news item fresh from the morning newspaper, *Steppe pravda*:

A fearful danger menaces the sowing of fields in the Orenburg and Aktubinsk Gubernias and drive away them can only the railway employees.

Right of that sentense is shown by a very clear and intelligible to everybody evidence. It can be fearlessly said that the sowing of the spring corn and salvation from the starvation of this two gubernias depends of railway employees. The countrymen waiting sowing corn loose the hope to receive it. The doubt slinks in, could the destined to delivery be received seen the delivery be detained from day to day.

This was the morning of March 30, 1922, and as the novelty of this kind of interruption had not as yet worn off, the two Americans had a bit of fun trying to decipher the nature of the "fearful danger." But there was so much of this kind of thing coming at them every day that at some point it must have run dry as a source of humorous distraction.

Sometimes the evidence of a translator having gone astray is less direct. In a moment of exasperation at the shenanigans of the local officials, Coleman wrote to Haskell: "Mr. Lenin's statement in a recent speech in Moscow 'we must cease our communistic lies,' has not been effected in Orenburg to date." This sounds suspiciously like an inspired translation from the local newspaper.

The English vocabulary of the Orenburg Americans, already rich in outdated American slang, steadily accumulated new words and phrases of mistranslated Russian. For example, the starving became the "hungries." In an even worse plight were the "wanting of work hungries." Three of the Orenburg Americans were assigned to the subdistricts for several months in a stretch, during which time the only conversations they could conduct were with their interpreters, who operated on this level of pidgin English.

Harold Buckley was stationed in the town of Iletsk, where one day he was awaiting detailed orders by telegram from Coleman in Orenburg regarding the distribution of a cargo of ARA supplies. His interpreter was "a little short old man named Jacob," a returned émigré who had once been a tailor in Manchester, but whose busy work schedule there had left him little time to learn English. Even the names of common vegetables proved too much for the former tailor, who rendered them as "long green ones," "little red ones," and so on. It was Jacob who provided the Orenburg Americans with much of their new "English" vocabulary.

Coleman's telegram finally arrived. In over one hundred Russian words it spelled out for Buckley the details concerning distribution, allocation, and all other necessary instructions. Spotlight on the interpreter: "Jacob carefully adjusted his spectacles and read the telegram through and through for about ten minutes; then he looked up and announced, 'He says, "You must give out the food!"'"

On another occasion, a washed-out bridge interrupted shipments from Orenburg city and Coleman wired Buckley the news, which Jacob announced: "He says, 'The floor is broke.'" A further telegram from Coleman mentioned nursing mothers, which Jacob rendered graphically as "women who feed children at the chest"—which is certainly unambiguous.

Curiously, the matter of a Russian-English dictionary is never once raised—not in Orenburg, not anywhere.

After several months spent conversing with Jacob, Buckley returned to Orenburg city fluent in his companion's English and hard-pressed to break its hold on his mental processes—much to the amusement of his ARA colleagues, who took great delight in incorporating elements of this mysterious tongue into their daily conversation.

But when it comes to anecdotes about interpreters, no one can top the yarns spun by Charlie Veil. He was in Novouzensk in autumn 1921 when the arrival of a cargo of ARA supplies inspired local officials to declare a week of holidays. But things did not proceed all that smoothly, at least as Veil tells it. In his autobiography he describes a town meeting where speakers informed the peasants that the carloads of American food were a gift of the International Workers of the World.

He was getting a rough simultaneous translation from Pete, and he did not like what he was hearing. "There in Novo Uzensk my rage mounted as the speakers' misrepresentation increased." He stepped forward and got the attention of the crowd. "Demanding that Pete translate my exact words, I told the assembled townspeople that their leaders were lying to them and that the food had been sent by the citizens of America. Fearful that Pete would not dare the dreaded Cheka by repeating my remarks exactly I found another interpreter who could understand French and he, supposedly, also translated."

God knows what the locals made of this performance in many tongues. Veil had the suspicion that his two interpreters may have "tempered" his message, "for the Communists showed no rancor; instead, as soon as the meeting was over they invited me to their private party, which consisted of the proper combination of vodka and pretty women. The Communists seem to have a corner on both."[9]

This is the way most of Veil's stories turn out: a happy ending for our hero, his interpreter, and the devil-may-care Russians. Without Duranty there's no gun; still it sounds like what Twain would call a "fancy sketch," but there it is.

CHAPTER 28

VODKA AS A WEAPON

Charlie Veil's tales from the famine zone, however far-fetched, were generally on the mark in their depiction of the central role of alcoholic spirits in ARA-Soviet relations in the districts. Like typhus and the elements, alcohol was part of the adventure of fighting famine in Russia.

The men of the ARA knew long before their mission of the Russian reputation for strong drink, especially the consumption of vodka, the scourge of Russia. When the world war broke out Tsar Nicholas II introduced prohibition because "he knew that otherwise the Russian propensity for drunkenness would paralyze every military effort," according to journalist Louis Fischer.

In the already heady days of the October Revolution, fearing that looting and drunkenness would lead to anarchy in Petrograd, soldiers loyal to the Bolsheviks destroyed some nine hundred thousand bottles of wine in the royal cellars at the Winter Palace.

The Bolsheviks had good reason to retain the Tsar's ban on alcohol, not alone because it squared with their condemnation of the Russian state's traditional vodka monopoly—which was a considerable revenue source—as a form of exploitation of the masses. But the increased production of moonshine—*samogon*, another Russian tradition—took up much of the slack. Unlike in the United States under Prohibition, there was no equivalent to a Canadian outpost, no rum runners; this was genuine home brew. Russian hooch was traditionally made from wheat, but increasingly in these times of want it was abstracted from potatoes.

The Bolsheviks waged war on *samogon* but without success, and when the Americans arrived it was raging out of control. One ARA Russian employee from the Volga wrote: "The principal distraction of the villages (grown wild as they are) is generally drink, which fills up all the hours of all the holidays and festivals. No idea can be formed of the huge extension of secret vodka-distilling; it has pervaded Russian life throughout and is a calamity both for the national morals and the national health."

This sounds like the reports of life in tsarist Russia, such as that of Hullinger, who wrote of those days: "The stockyard saloon district in Chicago at its balmiest was not worse. In the villages the peasants gulped down vodka in tumblers, like beer. 'Drunken Russia' was an international byword." As he looked around him in 1922, he noted a marked contrast to life under the old regime. He claims that during his eight months in Soviet Russia he saw only one intoxicated person on the streets—even in the tiniest villages everyone was sober in public.

This last remark is hard to believe given the abundant testimony as to the ubiquity of alcohol in the land of the Bolos. Yet Soviet laws regarding public displays of drunkenness were severe, and most of the drinking bouts and drunken celebrations recounted in the ARA documentation take place behind closed doors. Still, one does not simply leave one's state of inebriation at the door, and it is difficult to imagine having lived through the famine winter of 1921–22 and not having encountered a single intoxicated individual on the street.

The testimony of another Western visitor, Charles Sarolea, regarding Russia's "drink problem" in 1922 supports Hullinger's account. He too claims that there were very few intoxicated people to be found in the streets of Moscow despite "the enormous number of public houses. I am told that there are more than two thousand of them in Moscow. In some streets every other house was a 'pivnaia,' or beer-house."

"Opening of Moscow Peevnyas" earned a place in the postmission "Non-Statistical Notes of the A.R.A.," although Russians traditionally were not beer drinkers. These establishments opened in the autumn of 1921 with the first inroads into prohibition. Sarolea overcame his repugnance to their nauseating atmosphere and became a frequent visitor, "as nowhere else could one have a better opportunity of observing the Russian proletariat. I never saw so much drunkenness in my life. Only the drunkards are wise enough to stay in the beer-house until they have worked off the effects of drink and until they can face the policeman with impunity. That is the reason why one sees so little drunkenness in the streets."

All observers agree that the Soviet authorities were merciless with bootleggers, who were often passed over when pardons spared others from death by firing squad.

Soviet Russia was still officially dry in the summer of 1921, but the Bolshevik economic retreat soon spread to the prohibition front. In the NEP era of balanced budgets and legitimate accounting practices the Soviet government was desperate for income and began to give in to the temptation to conduct its own monopoly sale of alcoholic spirits. Timidly and with much public handwringing and controversy on display in the press, the Kremlin retreated from full prohibition. In autumn 1921 came a decree lifting the ban on the sale of light wines and beer, at first allowing 16 percent alcohol content. The immediate benefit to the state was its ability to sell off the thousands of bottles of choice wines left over from the royal cellars.

The people's commissar of health, Semashko, had a sick feeling about all of this, which he made known in the national press. He expressed his misgivings to Hullinger in a personal interview, in which he insisted that lifting the ban was only a temporary revenue measure and that prohibition would be back. But he must have sensed that as with so many of the "temporary" retreats during this period, this one would prove difficult to reverse.

Officially the sale of vodka was forbidden in the winter of 1921–22, but most wine shops had a supply hidden away for those who could pay the high price; so did the cafés and cabarets of Moscow and Petrograd. Hullinger says that even the price of wine was beyond the reach of all but the newly rich and foreigners. Maybe so, but there were usually long queues outside the wine shops.

In January 1922 rumors began to circulate about the legalization of vodka at 38 percent alcohol. How this 38 percent figure was arrived at may have had to do with a desire to preserve the idea, even if largely symbolic, of a break in continuity with old-regime Russia, when 40 percent was the limit. This was the subject of a popular 1922 cartoon. Nicholas II, a glass of 40 percent in hand, shares a table with Lenin, who sips his 38 percent. Says the last Romanov to the father of Bolshevism, "Do you really think it was worth turning Russia upside down for 2 percent?"

Rumors of 38 percent vodka had evaporated by spring, then were succeeded by another wave of rumors in July with more doomsday warnings about its potential effects on the Russian people. Frank Golder wrote, "It is feared that the already demoralized Russian masses will go to pieces under it, now that all moral restraints, external and internal, have broken down."

In August came the official announcement that the state monopoly on vodka was to be restored, followed a few weeks later by a reversal and published attacks against the proposal. Finally, in February 1923 the Council of People's Commissars issued a decree permitting the sale of liquors of up to 20 percent alcohol—only halfway down the tsarist road.[1]

THERE WERE of course no limits on the alcohol content of local moonshine, as the ARA Americans discovered for themselves. Somerville testifies that "'samogonka' stories of Russian village life would put to shame anything in the line of 'boot-legging' stories that Prohibition has ever brought out of Main Street." Judging the situation from his Simbirsk outpost, he estimated that drunkenness reached a height in the autumn of 1922, although there was no Anti-Saloon League in Russia to collect the statistics.

The Americans' frame of reference for Soviet prohibition policies was their own Volstead Act of 1919, which outlawed all intoxicating liquor, defined as any beverage containing more than one-half of one percent alcohol. Of course many in the ARA mission had not had the opportunity to feel Prohibition's sobering effects, not having been in the United States since 1917. In any case it did not apply to them in Russia, nor did the prohibition laws of the first socialist state.

During the Riga negotiations the Americans informally raised the subject of alcohol with Litvinov, who told Brown he did not object to the ARA bringing its own supplies of alcoholic beverages into Russia. Of course, there was not a hint of the Brown-Litvinov understanding in the Riga Agreement. In fact paragraph 27 stated that the ARA "will import no alcohol in its relief supplies," but this was not applied to shipments of ARA commissary supplies in Moscow. It is impossible to say in what quantity the commissary was stocked with whiskey, gin, and other American favorites since the ARA kept these items off the books, but the anecdotal evidence indicates it was substantial.

It was certainly not in Eiduk's interest to protest the practice, as he was one of its beneficiaries. And it was said of him that he drank "like a fish."

The only alcohol accounted for in the ARA records was medical alcohol—that is, pure alcohol used primarily for slides—most of which was brought in during the second year of the mission. Strangely enough, the ARA had repeated difficulties with the Soviet authorities over its medical alcohol, starting with the first large shipment in June 1922.

The pattern was that officials would seize the shipments, hold onto them for a couple of months while the ARA protested, then release them. The final shipment was confiscated and held for so long that Haskell had it sent back out. Ellingston informed New York that the Soviet government had expressed concern that the ARA medical alcohol would find its way to the market and thus affect the price of spirits and threaten the state's monopoly. This is difficult to take seriously, though Ellingston was faithfully reporting what he understood to be the government's position.

The ARA imported this alcohol solely for medical use, but this does not mean that it did not fulfill other needs in a pinch. The alumni newsletter's "Non-Statistical Notes of the A.R.A." includes this tantalizing item: "Accounting form for medical alcohol."

Duranty, in *I Write As I Please*, recalls his encounter in one of the Volga districts with an ARA man, "a confirmed alcoholic" who "drank all the medical alcohol, or maybe methylated spirit, belonging to the A.R.A. sanitary outfit in Simbirsk. He didn't die of it but got delirium tremens and had to be sent home."

Russian moonshine could be as devastating. The consumer could only guess at the contents of the bottle in hand, and the first sips were usually taken with no little apprehension. Back in the United States the newspapers occasionally reported cases of blindness or death caused by the consumption of drinks made with antifreeze or chafing-dish fuel. God knows how many such incidents went unreported in Russia, where hooch was highly regarded as a substitute for auto fuel. Tuthill told Duranty that Volga bandit chief Serov was able to drink "a bucket of pure vodka, which Americans more than once have used as fuel for their autos successfully." Thus the term "k-v cocktail," for kerosene and vodka.

Fleming described in one of his letters out of Russia a wedding scene where the host handed out drinking cups made from ARA milk cans "containing the foulest liquid I had ever (up to that time) tasted—samogonka, or Russian hooch. . . . May I never have a disease such as will call for such a combination of fuel-oil, benzine, and kerosine, as that liquor was." Fleming groaned, but like most of his fellow relief workers he saw drink as part of his Russian adventure, another test of his American manhood.

Veil told Duranty that Serov could drink "a half bucket of vodka without pausing for breath. The other half bucket was drunk by his horse, a ferocious black stallion named Koshchei." Serov had no automobile. In Duranty's telling, Serov and Veil have a drinking match, in which the much larger Serov fails to drink the American under the table. "I can drink interminably," Veil boasted in his autobiography.[2]

IN RUSSIA drink implied excess and although not all of the Americans could have lived up to the fictional standards set by Veil, there were many occasions in ARA dealings with local officials where the ability to hold one's liquor was of critical importance. For the cause of ARA diplomacy the Americans often felt obligated to accept invitations to dinners and banquets sponsored by local officials, where the eating and drinking lasted into the early morning hours.

It would be inaccurate to say that the primary motivation behind such affairs was to compromise the Americans. Often the idea was to express goodwill and to satisfy a considerable curiosity about the foreigners and their distant homeland. Yet in places, official hospitality became a kind of banquet campaign whose purpose was to employ alcohol to induce the Americans to talk about "forbidden" subjects, mainly politics—or simply to catch them with their guard down, maybe even their trousers.

The Americans were wise to the game, and some enjoyed taking up the challenge, but many grew wary of its physical toll. An evening with the local soviet was anticipated like a boxing match, with rounds of toasts into the night until a winner was left standing or conscious, if there was a winner. Compounding the challenge was the fact that most of the Soviet hosts were night owls and could easily outlast their guests. When Haskell returned to Moscow from New York in September 1922 to begin the second year of the mission, he found on his desk an invitation from Lander to attend a banquet in honor of the ARA. This did not delight the colonel. "I don't know what kind of banquet we are going to have but I bet it won't start at ten o'clock, it will be nearer twelve when they get at it."

By September 1922 the Americans had at least gotten used to the phenomenon. In the beginning the very idea of tables spread with abundant food and drink in a time of famine struck them as highly inappropriate. Alvin Blomquist in Simbirsk found it a "curious contradiction" that such Bolo banquets—three or four in the summer of 1922—were staged while hunger was still widespread and with the apocalyptical scenes of famine only just receding into the background.

Just as incongruous was the fact that the sponsors of these events were representatives of the dictatorship of the proletariat, who it might have been thought would have banished banqueting to the irretrievable past. Instead, the proletariat's parvenu vanguard seemed intent upon outdoing the defeated class enemy even in the social sphere, as if to demonstrate its suitability to rule the country.

Barringer remembers the official gatherings as "no mean affairs": "The confiscated services of the former nobility, the cellars of the former wine merchant, and last but not least, the services of the chefs who were out of a job since their former lord went up the lamp post, all combined to show that 'proletarians,' after all, are very human and thoroughly enjoy 'bourgeois' dinners."

In Odessa, the commanding officer of the U.S.S. *Fox* recorded in the ship's log his arrival ashore and the welcome offered by a certain Admiral Maximov. Together they had "the usual cup of tea which consisted of vodka and something to eat."

The log entry does not mention toasts, though it is a safe bet that Maximov offered at least one to Russian-American friendship. Second in importance to holding one's alcohol was a mastery of the art of toasting. For the Americans this was more delicate than it might sound. Often the native host would use a toast as the occasion to introduce a political topic—usually without mischievous intent—and the ARA men, forbidden to discuss "politics," would start to squirm.

A common toast expressed a desire for official U.S. recognition of Soviet Russia, a subject about which the Americans had strict instructions to pronounce no opinions. Blomquist says that every Simbirsk banquet featured "sincere expressions, on the Russians' part, of the hope that America would soon recognize the Soviet Government, and extend the sympathy of a sister republic, as well as tractors and other agricultural implements. And so on and on."

Barringer says that the relief worker in the districts was "often put to wit's end to find a way out of an embarrassing toast." He recalls an occasion at an ARA-sponsored banquet in Ekaterinoslav where the senior Soviet official made a "long, rambling speech about the 'great island of America'; had Washington and Roosevelt contemporary in history; included passionate protests against the cruelties of American boxing as a sport; and then proposed a toast 'to the day America recognizes Russia!' We did not respond, when it was interpreted for us, but responded with a toast 'to the day that Russia would balance her budget,' and everybody was happy."

Fleming took great pride in his toasting abilities, which seems to have depended a good deal on the clever translating of George. During their journey through the valley they visited Gorodishche, in the Samara district, where after a day of inspecting work there was an evening of food, drink, and dance. First came the fried fish course, then the ham and egg course washed down with some kind of alcohol concoction. At one point, through a thick mental haze Fleming became aware that he was being asked to deliver a speech about Russian women.

His recollection of this moment, written months later, may actually approximate what actually transpired, who can tell. If so, he could not have been too drunk since, encouraged by the cheers of the crowd, he was able without assistance to stand on a chair in order to deliver his address. When the applause died down, young Harold—who in ARA photographs bears a resemblance to Alfalfa of *Our Gang*—began to speak:

George, tell them I cannot express the timidity with which I approach the subject of Russian women.

The American inspector says that he cannot express the charm which Russian women have for him.

Tell 'em they're humdingers.

The American inspector says that though he comes from a land of fair women, he cannot compare them with the Russian women for beauty.

Take these present for instance, George. While I wish to mention no names, there are no social possibilities here for you, my boy. The two fair sisters are both mine. Also I like our Bolo friend here with the nursing bottle under his arm. I think he's a good scout. But I think you'll find, George, that this is a hell of a town, just like the last one.

The American inspector takes those present as examples. While he mentions no names, the party is one of the most pleasant, and the ladies amongst the most charming he has ever met. His stay in Russia is not long, but he hopes to come back many times to Gorodische which has made an excellent impression upon him.

Tell 'em, George, that I'm forced to observe that Russia has gone dry like the United States.

The American inspector says that America welcomes Russia as a sister nation in the democratic ideals of prohibition.

Tell 'em, George, that I think their home brew is only a little worse than ours.

The American inspector welcomes the friendly rivalry of Russia and America in producing the best drinks in the world.

Tell 'em, George, that when it comes to capitalism and communism we may differ, but on prohibition there is only one answer, and that is, down with it.

The American inspector says that if you will drink to capitalism he will drink to communism and then we'll all have a drink to prohibition.

Tell 'em that's all I can think of just now, George.

The American inspector thanks you all for your kind attention.

The only one not amused by Fleming's performance was the Bolo with the "nursing bottle," who poured cold water on the warm atmosphere with a counter-toast, in which he predicted a revolution in the United States and offered to harbor the bourgeois American when it happened. He probably wanted to shoot George.[3]

IN UFA, more than anywhere else, vodka was the supreme test of good government relations. Ellingston returned to Moscow from an autumn 1922 visit singing the praises of Colonel Bell, idol of the Bashkirs.

You should see the bunch of cut throats, with whom he has had to deal for the last year in Ufa, worship at his feet. He has perfect control of his show—even in back country villages where [neither] he nor his assistants had ever been. I saw that myself. Whenever he goes into the districts the local Ispolkoms turn out en masse to receive him and the banquets they spread will kill him eventually. It only took a week to crack my liver and he's been at it for over a year.

Bell's physical constitution served him well in his drinking bouts with the first plenipotentiary, Savelev, a former telegraph operator who rose to the rank of regimental commander in the Red Army during the Civil War. Aside from his ARA duties he was local party chief and chairman of the Ufa famine relief committee. Savelev behaved like many other plenipotentiaries: Elperin says that in public he would knock Bell and the ARA "in the best approved political style." But on a personal level he became quite fond of the colonel, and with a few drinks in him his affection for Bell got the better of him and "he insists upon kissing him."

Savelev was a Russian, but the Ufa Americans were feeding a mix of peoples in their district, which at the height of the mission was composed of Ufa province and nine cantons of the Bashkir republic—the other three were in the domain of the Orenburg ARA—along with the Russian provinces of Cheliabinsk, Kustanai, and Ekaterinburg, and the canton of Perm. By the summer of 1922 Ufa was geographically the largest ARA district at 160,000 square miles and 8,900,000 inhabitants. As it grew to include the heart of the southern Urals, its name was changed to the Ufa-Urals district.

This was one of the most beautiful areas in Russia, with a multitude of rivers, lakes, and rushing streams through its many ridges and valleys. It was a contrast of thick forest and steppe, where herds of wild horses used to roam. The Ural Mountains, dividing Europe from Asia, were rich in minerals and natural resources, not to mention precious metals, which before the Revolution had attracted mining concerns from around the world, including that of Herbert Hoover. As for their elevation, however, the Urals are a disappointment. Kelley wrote, "They are the most insignificant mountains to have such fame in geographies."

Anyway, Bell was idolized across a vast area. "Our territory," he wrote, "is larger than all of France and the work in this district greater than the entire relief in Poland."[4]

The population of the Ufa-Urals district was largely Russian, but in Bashkiria as well as in parts of Cheliabinsk and Ekaterinburg there were many entirely Bashkir villages. There were Kirghiz as well in Kustanai, part of the Kirghiz republic.

This cutting across political-administrative and ethnic lines made for compli-cations. For one, relations between Bashkiria and Moscow were somewhat deli-cate. The Bashkirs had signed on in large numbers with Kolchak's army when it occupied the territory in 1919. The Kremlin was attempting to placate the Bash-kirs' desire for autonomy by granting them autonomous republic status, all the while keeping a tight rein on them.

In the beginning Eiduk wanted the ARA to establish its local headquarters not at Ufa city, which was located some twenty-three miles from the border of Bashkiria, but at Sterlitamak, the capital of the Bashkir republic, eighty miles south of Ufa along the Belaya River. There was politics behind this, the idea be-ing to mollify the Bashkirs.

Kelley notes that the ARA chiefs rejected this proposal as "preposterous," Sterlitamak being sixty miles from the nearest warehouse. In fact, he says that the only reason the ARA set up kitchens in the Bashkir republic at all was because of Soviet government pressure: the ARA policy was to feed only in regions accessi-ble by rail, which Sterlitamak was not, whereas Ufa—founded in 1586 and with a population of eighty thousand—was situated on the Trans-Siberian line.

Eventually the Kremlin would redraw the map: on August 1, 1922, the bound-aries of the Bashkir republic were enlarged to include most of the former Ufa province, and the capital was moved from Sterlitamak to Ufa, the new entity called Greater Bashkiria.

For much of the first year of the mission the political atmosphere in the re-gion was tense. When Bell and Elperin arrived in Ufa city in November 1921, they were met by Bashkir officials who tried to convince Bell to distribute all of his fifty thousand rations in the Bashkir republic. Bell had to be quick on his feet. The instructions he carried from Moscow headquarters ordered him to "proceed to Ufa, in the Bashkir Republic, the capital of which is Orenburg"—wrong on both counts. He surveyed the scene and, finding severe starvation in more-accessible Ufa province but sensitive to local politics, decided to divide the rations equally between it and the Bashkir territories.

Meanwhile, Eiduk's representative set up his headquarters in Sterlitamak, sent down word that he expected the ARA to do the same, and dismissed an Ameri-can request that he move to Ufa. Piet Hofstra was sent to Sterlitamak to negoti-ate with the plenipotentiary. "I told him we sympathized with the autonomy and independence of the Bashkirs, but that we could not let nationality stand in the way of the effective relief work, and further that for the number of portions we were distributing in Ufa and Bashkir we were not entitled to ask for two distinct A.R.A. district organizations." After putting up stubborn resistance for several weeks, Eiduk's man relented and moved to Ufa.

This was only the first of such political complications. Bell wrote of his dis-trict, "The diplomatic entanglements involved make the Peace Conference seem like a well conducted private school."

Just as in Orenburg, the Americans at Ufa came to like and respect the Bash-kirs—"the Bash" for short—preferring to deal with them than with the local Rus-sians. Kelley was surprised to find them there: "Has anyone ever heard of Baskiria? I hadn't." But he got used to them quickly enough. "These Baskirs are an altogether different race from the Russians and it seems to us much more mentally alert."

The Revolution had not brought the same sweeping social revolution to the Bashkir population. Still the ARA saw ethnicity as the heart of the matter. Elperin, the Estonian, explained in his imperfect English: "These Bashkirs were naturally intelligent type of people. Many of them were not communists; they had much native intelligence and represented fairly educated type. They were intelligently interested in the whole situation of the Bashkir Repub. rather than of their own little corner."

Bell and Elperin were struck by the difference in reception they got, first in Ufa city, then in Sterlitamak. In Ufa the Russian officials were reserved and suspicious, and apparently attempted to downplay the extent of the famine conditions in their region. In Sterlitamak, an "overgrown village" of about twenty thousand inhabitants, the Bashkir leaders offered a cordial welcome, which Bell later recalled was the start of "strong friendships." They stated quite openly, as Elperin recalled, "that they didn't have a damn thing in the way of food."

During this initial visit, Bell put into action an emergency plan intended to stem the tide of refugees pouring into Sterlitamak, setting up temporary kitchens along the roads leading into town. The effect was immediate, and there was said to be "wild enthusiasm" among the people. More success followed when Bell managed to drink the president of the Bashkir republic under the table, "to the glory of the Americans and the A.R.A.," says Elperin who witnessed the spectacle. He says that Bell had a "long and hard struggle," but that victory came into sight when the president began to sing Bashkir love songs.

The Bashkir officials drank vodka and wine requisitioned from the local commissariat of health, whose chief had been a veterinarian before the Revolution. The stomach was fortified with a kind of local piroshki the Americans called "Bashkir oysters."

Whatever ill effects Bell may have suffered the next day, from a distance of several months he had fond recollections of those early days, and ARA relations with the Bashkirs were consistently good.

The Bashkirs were most likable, keenly interested in their own people and with a great thirst for knowledge of affairs of the outside world, especially along educational lines. They were extremely hospitable and intensely appreciative of everything done for them. This feeling has existed throughout the entire operation and without exception every visit to Sterlitamak by any American of the A.R.A. has been most pleasant.[5]

THE "GREAT THIRST" of the Bashkirs is thoroughly documented in the ARA archive, but Bell knew better than to characterize every American visit to Sterlitamak as "most pleasant." William Kelley's entire Russian experience was deeply marked by his spring 1922 misadventure in the Bashkir capital.

Kelley's mission was to investigate official accusations of a misuse of funds by the local ARA, which was staffed heavily with Germans and said to be strongly anti-Soviet. Bell suspected that the charges were justified. Kelley wrote in a personal letter that the local ARA employees had "run wild," that "anything is possible," and feared that word of it might get back to Moscow headquarters. "I depart on a secret mission with plenipotentiary powers to clean house and conciliate the government. If I am successful, Moscow will never hear a breath of scandal."

He reassured his correspondent: "Sterlitamak is a sizeable city even if not on a railroad. You must not think that I will be living on horse meat or human flesh. While there I shall be the government's official guest."

There was nothing in Kelley's background that would have prepared him for this kind of diplomatic undertaking. What he possessed in abundant supply was plainspokenness, some of which he unloaded the night before his departure on Tarasov, who had just been transferred from Simbirsk. "We suspect all representatives of the Center as being sent here to throw monkey wrenches in our works; they are equally unwelcome with the local Soviet Government which wishes to deal with us direct, and they are anathema to the Baskir Government which hates Moscow and awaits the hour to spring a war of independence. It may come any month, so the rumor goes."

A few weeks later, in the middle of his Sterlitamak ordeal, he took out his frustrations on the Bashkir republic, describing it as an "absurd little state, having no reason for existence except Moscow's desire to placate the nascent Tatar nationalist movement, a gesture pure and simple as it has no real independence." As he saw it, there was a "deep political game" being played between the center and the Bashkirs, who wanted to form a pan-Islamic state that would include several Islamic republics; the ARA, as "the controller of most of the food in this part of the world," could not help but get caught up in the game.

Bashkir officials encouraged the ARA men to publicize Bashkiria in the United States and urge American political recognition of the new republic. To this end they went out of their way to ingratiate themselves with the Americans, Kelley not the least. "As they have absolutely no foreign connections that gives me a significance apart from that which is derived from my position as Bell's envoy. Don't you find all this amusing?"

Traveling ahead of Kelley as an advance man was a Bashkir named Churnishev, who had until recently served as the ARA plenipotentiary of the Bashkir government, as distinct from Tarasov who represented the center. Kelley called him "my good friend" without irony; he and the other Americans were genuinely fond of the man. "Although a government representative he is less of a Communist than I am. He would like to come to America to study but has only 10 gold roubles to his name."

When Churnishev resigned as Bashkir envoy, Bell decided to make him the ARA's chief inspector for several Bashkir districts, including Sterlitamak. So Kelley's mission had a second purpose. "Bell and I have so much confidence in Churnishev's integrity that we feel he can step from the one position into the other without complications. We are gambling and I am going down to cut the cards. Churnishev precedes me but is to lie low until I arrive and install him."

The day before his departure he sounded confident: "I will stay longer than any American who has preceded me. There will be nothing unpleasant about the mission." In fact his stay would be much longer than intended and thoroughly unpleasant.

Kelley, in the company of Elperin together with their drivers, guides, and supplies occupying three sleighs, made the two-day journey, which he described as "memorable. No one can make it and remain a tender foot." The sleigh was equipped with side braces to prevent it from tipping over, and "would have turned over countless times" without them. And there were wolves and thoughts of bandits to keep the mind occupied. "Among my other worries was the fact that I had on my person about 200,000,000 roubles, a tidy sum in this country. I remembered how three months ago the Baskir Government had been unwilling to transfer 50,000,000 roubles from Ufa to Sterlitamak for fear of robbers."

On April 7 Kelley and Elperin arrived at destination. "Already I sigh for the flesh pots of Ufa! May you never know this queer feeling of being at the edge of the world."

The spring thaw, which had made some of the roads on their route nearly impassable, had turned Sterlitamak into a "sea of mud," and shortly after their arrival they realized that their departure would have to wait for navigation to open on the Belaya River.

Kelley was able within a short time to set ARA affairs right, defusing the potential scandal and smoothing the way for Churnishev, and now there was nothing for the international diplomat to do but "engage in the not unusual Russian pastime of waiting." Thus did William Kelley become one in a long line of foreigners, friendly and hostile, to learn the hard way that the only thing more formidable than the notorious Russian winter was the Russian spring.

In the weeks it took him to acquire this knowledge he was cutting wisdom teeth. "I slept or tried to sleep with my mouth stuffed full of cotton, dreaming of the nearest trustworthy dentist. He probably resides in Berlin and might as well be on Mars for all the good he does me."

Boredom drove him to write lengthy letters. Except for one, they all seem to have been written to Frank Page of the New York office, whom Kelley would have known from his brief stint there in autumn 1921 as Baker's assistant in the publicity department before packing off to Ufa. In one of these letters he discoursed on the social life of the Bashkir capital: "This town is unspeakably dreary. There is no iota of interest in it. All is mud and squalor. I cannot imagine an American residing here permanently. Ufa is a veritable metropolis by comparison."

The ARA envoy was lodged in a cottage once occupied by the manager of an adjacent alcohol factory, which stood idle. There was a telephone, which Kelley left off the hook when he heard that he was to be invited to "a social" on Saturday, April 8. Somehow he could not decline the invitation to a banquet the following evening, possibly because the guest list included the chairman of the Council of People's Commissars, the head of the executive committee of the soviet, the people's commissar of health, and the government representative to the ARA from the Bashkir republic.

"It was a scream and I confess a scandal," he wrote on the day after. "My intentions were the best, but little did I guess the potency of Baskir hooch. Tonight twenty hours later I am as good as new. In fact my tooth aches less than before the debauch." The menu was standard fare: Bashkir oysters in soup, brown bread, cake, and tea. As for the liquor,

It makes my head spin to think of it. Call it by any name it was virtually straight alcohol. They toasted me, I toasted them, they toasted the American people, I toasted the Baskir Republic, and so it went. While none of us ever have drunk to the health of the Soviet Government we do propose toasts to the Baskir Republic. I don't know if they have ever noted this distinction or not. One very fervent toast was to the health of Herbert Hoover.

Kelley regretted not having a stenographic report of what he said to the Bashkir "statesmen," though he could remember certain critical moments. "I was very emphatic and rattled the dishes by striking the table. I told them what the American people thought of the Soviet Government." Essentially he told them it was not representative of the Soviet people, which prompted the Bashkir president to object and explain the democratic basis of Soviet power, but "his case was so weak that the others laughed at him."

When Kelley pointed out the economic shortcomings of the Soviet system, he felt that everyone agreed with him since they listened to his speech in silence, "And I must have talked two hours." He claims to have been able to attest that Elperin had translated his words exactly, holding back nothing. Boris, in fact, "enjoyed the evening immensely. He is contemptuous of this crowd of ragamuffins and took delight in passing on my caustic remarks." The spirited and open discussion seemed to clear the air.

We parted the best of friends. Boris tells me they are delighted with me. Perhaps. My memory is not a good guide to the last part of the evening. I am charged with singing, but I don't remember it. I do remember falling out of the cart. I also remember firing my automatic once in the market place and again outside my door. I had some reasons but I don't remember what they were.

The days of Sterlitamak exile dragged on and the tone of this "prisoner of mud" grew morose. On April 10 he went by cart to the local outdoor market, but as the mud was so deep and he was without rubber boots, he did not get out. An old Tatar man "swam" out to him and sold him "another eight foot Baskir towel. It is so dirty and worn that I doubt if it is worth the 300,000 roubles I paid."

More official dinner invitations arrived, including one from the people's commissar of transportation, all of which Kelley declined until he felt obliged to attend a party at the house of the government representative, Bishoff. It turned out that Bishoff lived at the house of the transportation commissar, Achmadullah— Ach, for short—who seemed especially eager to entertain the American.

The evening began with the playing of "scratchy records on a vile horn phonograph." On this occasion there were four women in attendance. "Achmadullah entered, garbed in a Caucasian or Circassian costume, I don't know which he said it was. He was already tight, so perhaps he didn't know himself." Kelley knew the object of the game: "to get me intoxicated at supper and rob me of my dignified reserve."

When all were present and seated, a gallon bottle of imitation vodka was carried in, which Elperin found to be the "vilest liquor in all his experience." Bishoff, the host, had arrived an hour late with this brew, leading Kelley to speculate that there had been a "hitch in the negotiations with the bootlegger." Drinks were poured all around.

With the first toast the fight was on, they fighting to get me drunk and I determined to stay on deck. Instead of emptying my glass with each toast, as is the inviolable custom here, I merely sipped my liquor.

I did not expect to find good manners in this crowd but the howl that went up when they saw my tactics was even louder than I expected. The two women at my sides so exasperated me that I insulted them outright. That is to say, I insulted them in English; what Boris may have said in translation is another matter.

Bishoff started to apply the pressure with such toasts as "Bottoms Up," etc., but I let him down with some heat. The sarcasm that the women poured out was lost on me. Boris only interpreted what he thought was "important."

When it was over, Kelley surveyed the battlefield of this "wretched mess of an evening." "Midnight found the bottle empty. The Commissar of Transport was oozing vodka at every port, but still cheerful and peaceful. Bishoff was sick and very quiet. Churnishev was unperturbed. Lady No. 4 had been led away to bed. Nos. 2 and 3 were plainly drunk. The hostess, I must say, was well mannered and well poised throughout. I caught her eye once and we toasted each other quietly across the table." Boris had overindulged and began to "pour honeyed words into the drooping ears of Miss No. 4," presumably at her bedside. Kelley conversed in German with a Red Army officer, who told him that he would soon be off to fight France, Poland, or Romania—he wasn't certain which.

Kelley found the evening an edifying experience, illuminating the social life of the "governing class" of the country. "I came through unscathed. My head was clear, my tongue under control, and my gait steady. . . . If I don't look out for myself in this country, no one else will. It's a fine school in self reliance." He figured that having won the battle he had won the war and that his hosts would be discouraged from further attempts to get him drunk and to "introduce women for my benefit."

The next morning, his head aching, he made his way to the ARA office. Along the road he passed the body of a soldier who had been killed during the night—through the crowd of onlookers he could see a "mass of human brains in the mud." Half a block down the road he came upon a group of children playing hopscotch at a place where the entire previous day had lain the corpse of a child, its clothing and flesh chewed up by dogs. It had been removed, but nearby lay an apparent successor, a woman lying on a doorstep.

The trial by boredom continued. On April 15 he spent the evening peacefully reading the *Saturday Evening Post* of the previous December 11. On April 22 he wrote, "The days pass, the rain pours, and still no boat from Ufa."

He slept as late as he could and took occasional walks with Boris "to retain the use of our limbs." He exhausted his reading material: "I have read every advertisement in the American and the Saturday Evening Post. . . . so many of them deal with delicious foods and impair my morale." The only positive note to report was that "No more parties are on the program and I have hopes of escaping without having the lining of my stomach further damaged. It's fortunate for me that my stomach has never shown any symptoms of delicacy. This Russian adventure is a severe test."

On the 24th, "the seventeenth day of my sentence," it began to snow, "a most discouraging performance for the end of April," he wrote, unaware that this blast of cold weather had ensured the success of the ARA corn drive.

On the 29th he wrote that the idea of trying to make the trek to Ufa by power boat had fallen through because the only available motor was in disrepair. By now he felt in a "state of coma," telling his correspondent: "I don't know what to say. Reduced to the verge of insanity by the tedium of this enforced stay, I am unfit to associate with you even so indirectly as by mail."

Perhaps to escape boredom he accepted an invitation to another of Bishoff's parties, but to his amusement no one came to fetch him. "The affair was given in the house of the Minister of Transport, and yet he was unable to transport me from my house to his. Such is his discipline over his drivers.

"I heard the next day that it was a terrible stew party with a half dozen of the lowest females of the town present."

On Sunday, April 30, Kelley decided to make a go of it. The ARA corn was by now arriving in the district. In Ufa Hofstra was convalescing from typhus, Willig had succumbed to it, and Bell was desperate for Kelley's and Elperin's help. Traveling by troika along near impassable roads, they made it to Ufa in thirty-six hours, the last segment by ferry across the Belaya River. "A brand new White truck met me at the pier and in grand style, frightened horses bolting at every block, I rode through the city to the house, where the Colonel fell on my neck."

Kelley and Elperin measured all subsequent personal hardships against the adversities of their Sterlitamak misadventure. In June they were with their Celtic companion, Patrick Verdon, in Ekaterinburg, where they were invited to dinner in a cooperative restaurant. Kelley enjoyed himself thoroughly. "Anything seems like Heaven to me after my days in Sterlitamak last April." The dinner consisted of hors d'oeuvres of fish, eggs, and cucumbers, followed by a soup course, and roast veal with potatoes, ice cream, cake, and tea. "The tea is always the cue to the end, thank Heaven."

The spirits consisted only of a moderate amount of weak wine, which did not inhibit Kelley's powers of imagination. Turning to his female host, "I toasted the lady in extravagant phrases that almost choked in Boris's throat. It went against his grain to lie so glibly about her intelligence. She was much touched. I gave a cue to Verdon, a lawyer by profession, and he toasted the co-operatives of Russia in suitable words, first asking me what the 'ell they were."

One of the dinner guests entertained the ARA men with an account of the execution of the Romanov family, which had taken place in Ekaterinburg on August 19, 1918. Earlier the ARA party had been shown the building where the infamous deed had transpired—a structure razed by order of local Party chief Boris Yeltsin in 1971, when the city was called Sverdlovsk. The executions were announced from the stage of the State Theater two nights afterward. The man did not claim to have been an eyewitness but said he had been a member of the court that had decided upon the execution. Perhaps he and Verdon discussed some obscure point of Soviet legal procedure that attended the dispatch of the royal family.

Two weeks later, back in Ufa, Kelley was awakened by Theodore who asked if he wanted to witness a Tatar wedding. "It smacked of strong drink to me so I repudiated the invitation. Boris did the same, averring that it was bad enough to have to drink their liquor on official business."[6]

KELLEY'S ACCOUNT of his struggles on the vodka front are nothing like the story of Major David Kinne, district supervisor of Saratov. Kinne—whose name was often misspelled "Kinney," indicating its pronunciation—a Dartmouth College graduate, Class of 1915, was one of Colonel Haskell's "army officer crowd" who had served under him in the Near East Relief in 1919–20. Veil describes him as "tall, dark, severe as an army M.P.," which is how he appears in photographs.

As a district supervisor on the Volga, Kinne's nerves were under a severe strain;

that much is clear. We also know that in Armenia two years earlier Haskell had served him warning about his excessive intake of alcohol and its effect on his performance as a relief worker. To judge from the testimony of those working with him in Saratov, especially that of Alexis Babine, Kinne stood up to the stress well enough during the first few months of operations; it was around Christmas time that he lost control.

Babine records him getting drunk on ARA Christmas liquor but leaves the impression that it was not the first time. Kinne, he wrote, "has not will power enough to fight the devil. The relief work suffers badly." On January 2 Babine tells his diary that Kinne was "dead drunk" and had to miss the ARA New Year's supper party.

The entry for January 6 describes a children's Christmas party—observed according to the Russian calendar—in the town of Pokrovsk across the Volga. "Before the feast prepared for Americans began, they were all invited to a little dark closet, where a demijohn of some strong concoction was produced. Kinne swallowed three tumblers of the stuff, liked it, but looked dazed at the table. I found out afterwards that the mixture consisted of pure alcohol with some aromatic spirits of ammonia in it."

He knocked back two more "tumblers," which left him unable to stand in order to give the obligatory toast. So he remained seated as Babine stood straining to give meaning in Russian to his "incoherent sentences." The Pokrovsk children were probably unaware of the problem, but the local famine committee members knew exactly what they were doing in keeping Kinne's glass full. There was beer, champagne, wine, and more pure alcohol. Evening's end found him in a "pitiful state."

Kinne's loyal second-in-command at Saratov, Russell Cobb, swallowed only one glass of holiday punch and kept his head. Cobb was from New York City, Harvard Class of 1919. Chris Herter describes him as the "heavyweight champion of Harvard." Whether or not this was meant as a literal boxing title, he was a big man who could handle his liquor. As Kinne's health began to fail, Cobb took on the responsibilities of the district supervisor.

On January 9 the ARA courier arrived with more whiskey and gin; on the following day Kinne could not come to work. Babine quotes Cobb as saying: "I'm getting tired of the damned thing . . . I'll either have all of it or none of it"—meaning the district supervisor's duties.

January dragged on and the situation deteriorated, with Kinne unable to work most of the time. Considering how hard up for qualified man power and hardpressed for time were the Americans in the valley, the virtual absence of the district supervisor was catastrophic for Saratov operations.

On January 14 Babine reports the discovery that the ARA chauffeur has been supplying Kinne with booze, which on this occasion had incapacitated him by midday. Cobb called Babine into his office and shut the door behind him. "'Tell this man,' said he pointing to Kinne's chauffeur, 'that I will kill him if he dares to get another drop of spirits for Kinne, will just kill him.' I saw it was hard for him to keep his hands from the man's throat, all six-feet-two of him trembling with emotion. 'I am not trying to scare him—I will actually kill him.'"

Cobb wrote to his parents in New York City about the strain upon the Americans in the district: "I have done enough of Kinne's job to appreciate what has made him a nervous wreck. We must keep a tight hold and no one can imagine what a job it is."

Babine tells us that in mid-January the district physician, Dr. Jesse McElroy, wired Moscow about Kinne, treading cautiously but concluding bluntly: "Condition hopeless. Do you understand[?]" This was not a piece of gossip but an urgent medical report from an American physician. Yet it went unheeded.

At the other end of the wire in Moscow sat chief of staff Lonergan. As Babine knew from firsthand observation, Lonergan himself was a heavy drinker. Within one month it would cause his dismissal from the Russian mission. He happened also to be a good friend of Kinne from the Near East Relief days and, like him, had been warned by Haskell about excessive drinking. It may well be, then, that with Lonergan as a filter the full facts of the case were not brought to Haskell's attention early on. This would explain the colonel's inaccurate account to London and New York regarding the timetable of Kinne's downfall as the result of ignorance, not misrepresentation.

Having received no response to his telegram, McElroy traveled to Moscow to make the point in person. Amazingly, even this failed to impress the chiefs. He wired back to Saratov on February 9 that Haskell and Lonergan were standing by Kinne, "the best man they have." And so the horror story continued to unfold.

The point of so much detail is not to document Kinne's Lost Weekend per se but as the reason behind the Soviet takeover of the ARA's Saratov operations. At least in part, Kinne was a victim of government relations. The local representative of Eiduk, a man named Poretskii, took advantage of the American's condition—indeed contributed to it—in order to gain control over American relief.

Poretskii was instrumental in keeping Kinne off his feet, which is how he was on February 20 when Babine reported him absent from his post. The night before, Kinne, Poretskii, and a man named Perlov—whom Babine characterizes as a "Jewish Soviet spy"—visited a local "dive." Kinne "managed to tank Poretskii up," which inspired Eiduk's emissary to telephone for women. Came the morning, Poretskii could not be found, and his wife was out looking for him, inquiring at all the police stations—this "to Kinne's joy and amusement."

On February 24 Babine records that Kinne was not eating and was in such a weakened condition that a half-bottle of weak wine was all it took to put him on his back. All the while, Poretskii kept him supplied because, as Babine wrote, "It certainly is to the Soviets' advantage to keep Kinne drunk and out of their way as much as possible."

He managed to lose a check for 1.3 trillion rubles and a confidential letter he had written to Haskell on matters in Saratov. Poretskii was under suspicion.

On February 26 came the denouement as Kinne, a physical wreck, submitted his resignation by wire. Alas, Moscow still could not comprehend the situation and rejected the resignation. Cobb wrote to his parents bitterly:

Kinne is done now. Last week he sent in his resignation, they not knowing his real condition since last December asked him to wait. He agreed, but to-day had a second bad turn, unconscious for ten minutes, and I have told him that unless he left I would take him to Moscow. The Doctor says there is real danger of his dying, so he is going, but is a broken man, and all because he worked himself to death and is very sensitive to suffering and hatred all around.

Finally, in the first week of March Haskell came to Saratov. Kinne was unable to stay sober, and on March 8 the colonel ordered Moscow to send down a new district supervisor. Accompanying Haskell was Mowatt Mitchell, assistant director of the London office, who wrote to Brown that Kinne had "busted into little bits" and had a "bad case of nerves"; he "came very clean and admitted that he had fallen for the stuff." Haskell told Mitchell that he had been aware of Kinne's and Lonergan's weakness and had made them pledge to "keep off for six months," though just when this pledge had been taken is unclear.

It was Haskell's understanding—at least this is what he reported to his superiors—that Kinne had tendered his resignation early in February but that he could not be released until a qualified replacement had been found. Haskell explained Kinne's condition as the result of the "strain" of the relief work, specifically that "the straffing he took from the Bolsheviks got more and more on his nerves until about February he broke down." He tried to get by on "alcoholic stimulants," which unfortunately only "hastened his breakdown." Of course he should have been sent out of Russia for a month-long rest, but there had been no one who could replace him, and in Moscow "we did not quite realize his actual condition."

Two men, Ellingston and Charles Gaskill, were reassigned from Moscow to put the district in order, but the repair job was monumental. As Babine wrote, "The Soviets have certainly turned to their advantage Kinne's drunkenness."

The new arrivals discovered that Poretskii—who evidently survived the interrogations of his wife—had established a "complete and detailed organization of inspection and control" over the ARA in Saratov. The Russian personnel did not understand how ARA operations were supposed to be run. In order to break government control, district supervisor Gaskill fired much of the native staff and started over again.

The loss to the ARA can be measured by the large gap in the Saratov files in the ARA archive: for a period of several months there are no commodity reports, no weekly letters, and few statistical reports, not even the notorious Form I-6. Meanwhile the Americans in the subdistricts had been ignored. In Uralsk, John Clapp wrote to Gaskill in March thanking him for his first courier shipment since December.

The ARA Saratov history states that Soviet control was broken by April 1922, but as late as August, Quinn informed London that "owing to the unfortunate situation during Mr. Kinne's regime, the Government has secured practical control of our feeding, and it is almost too late now to break." Not until the autumn, under John Gregg, did the Saratov ARA get a handle on its own operations.[7]

EIDUK'S SATELLITES and local officials were not all bent on introducing alcohol only to outdrink and compromise ARA relief workers. Made to feel inferior in so many ways to the men of the ARA with their glorious efficiency and speedy automobiles, they looked for occasions to demonstrate their superior grasp of political topics and to make these Americans understand that their days in the driver's seat were numbered.

This is not to say that all of the officials in question—most being post-1917 converts to the Communist faith—had a genuine grasp of the gospels of Marx and Lenin. And the NEP retreat to capitalism had sown further ideological confusion in their ranks. But for the most part they retained a belief that history was on their side, that the class they claimed to represent, the proletariat, was bound to prevail, and that the Americans, while temporarily enjoying a position of superiority over them, were mere remnants of the old older destined to be swept away in the coming world revolution—though coming not as quickly as once thought.

Not that all the Bolos condescended to talk to the ignorant Americans. Hale wrote from Samara that it was difficult to find a "really earnest communist, who will explain his views in a calm and sensible manner. The general run of them either fly into a rage every time you ask a question or two, or else shrug the shoulders good naturedly and refuse to talk, on the ground that you are so unused to questions of capital and labor as to be unable to appreciate the merits of the question."

When it came to Marxism, the Americans were almost totally in the dark, and the Bolos were eager to flaunt their advantage. But they sometimes found it difficult to get a response out of the Americans, who were forbidden to talk politics.

Crossing the Atlantic on his way to Russia, on September 6 at 11:30 A.M., Haskell called a meeting of his party of fourteen ARA men. Clapp's diary summarizes his remarks: "Talk little; express no political opinions; moral conduct must be above criticism. Wants clean group of men. If any man is not willing to submerge his personality in this, wants to know as he can go home on same boat."

At Riga, the American side sought to calm the fears of the Soviet representatives that the American relief workers would work to spread propaganda. According to paragraph 25 of the Riga Agreement the ARA men were to "confine themselves strictly to the ministration of relief and will engage in no political or commercial activity whatever. . . . [A]ny personnel contravening this will be withdrawn or discharged on the request of the Central Soviet Authorities. The Central Soviet Authorities will submit to the chief officer of the A.R.A. the reasons for this request and the evidence in their possession."

"Political activity," as Haskell interpreted it, included all discussions of politics with Soviet citizens and officials. The Americans were supposed to decline, for example, Bolo invitations to compare the American and Russian political systems. This is where vodka came in: it corroded the Americans' armor.

The ARA men followed Haskell's instructions with varying degrees of compliance. At one extreme was Childs, who observed the letter of paragraph 25. In his diary he describes a sleigh journey with translator de Jacobs in October 1921, during which he fell into conversation with a once-prosperous peasant who asked him what the American people thought of the Russian Revolution: "Speak honestly and tell me whether or not they think us lunatics here in Russia."

Childs portrays the moment as a delicate one, claiming that it was the first time that he had been confronted with a "political" question. He professed himself to be "not merely puzzled, I was almost shocked. I glanced stealthily at our driver to observe whether he was showing any agitation for I was disturbed that my inquirer had not dropped his voice in putting to me such compromising queries."

He begged off, telling the curious peasant in whispers—probably through de Jacob's whispers—that he could not speak for the American people. The Russian persisted, but Childs fended him off. "The truth is I had left my politics at home when I came to Russia."

Childs would have needed ARA approval to publish his diary, and this may have influenced his account of this scene, which reads like something out of a doughboy pamphlet on venereal disease prevention. Yet it would barely have satisfied Baker in New York, who wrote to one of his Moscow publicity department subordinates in January 1922 that the ARA man was forbidden even "to seek or let himself be drawn into *social relations* with Russian people" as this might lead to expressions of opinion on political, racial, or religious matters and thus be grounds for dismissal.

Baker might have been shocked to learn about the behavior of most Americans in the districts. Fleming described in a private letter the daily routine at district headquarters in Samara in the winter of 1922.

Here the business of the day consists in going through the feeding plan of the inspector, looking over the book-keeping work of the office, getting some economic information, talking with the local government representative, etc, etc; the evening's business consists in drinking vodka and other baneful compounds and discussing Russian-American relations—some of the government representatives are real good scouts, and some are real sons of bitches.

Perhaps relations between Coleman and Klimov would have benefited from an injection of vodka. In the Orenburg documentation not a drop is spilled between them.

Of course, even Fleming had to pick his spots. Several months earlier, at the end of his tour of inspection through the famine zone, he was traveling by rail from Kazan to Moscow in a third-class sleeper car. He shared a coupé with two women and a man who were reading from a newspaper Fleming calls "Kommunista." They offered him some tea; he contributed some Dairy Farm Pure Cow's Milk Evaporated. The atmosphere having become sufficiently relaxed, Fleming asked if they were Communists, which they were.

They asked me how the working class fared in the United States and I told them, adding a teaser, however, that they fared much better than they do in Russia. He then asked me what I thought about Russia, and I said that as a member of the A R A I didn't think anything about it except that it ought to be fed and clothed, and then asked him what he thought about the United States. He told me we were going to have a revolution in the next twenty-five years at most. I told him I would ship my money out to Russia when that happened. Sort of religious people.

The Americans felt most comfortable comparing the economic performances of the United States and Soviet Russia, Fleming especially so since he always carried around with him a headful of economic statistics. During his inspection tour, near Kazan he and some ARA colleagues encountered a group of people eager to know more about economic life in America. Fleming reports that he and his mates

spun them some long yarns about the cheapness of bread in the states, and the high prices of agricultural labor during the harvesting season in the west; also the number of motor-cars turned out by Henry Ford to the minute, and the number of cars owned by the farmers of the United States and by the population generally. We didn't tell them how they were divided up, or the low [wages] that miners get in the United States, as we ought to have.

One of the Americans inquired what the Russians thought of the ARA and received "the politically excellent answer, that it depended entirely upon which party the interrogated person belonged to. I replied that the A R A had no interest whatsoever in parties, but no answer was forthcoming."

George Cornick in Tsaritsyn wrote to his father on September 3, 1922, that the Americans had entertained the new government representative at dinner. "He is of course an ardent communist, and something of the dreamer type, but has some practical ideas too. The nice thing however is that he really enjoys argument and discussion of the failure of communism as we have found it here. The fellow was a good sport throughout however and I believe really enjoyed the evening quite as much as we did, notwithstanding the fact that everyone talked straight from the shoulder."

Straight from the shoulder was how Bill Kelley preferred it, even on a stomach full of fermented mare's milk. During a visit to Kustanai, the head of the *gubispolkom* suggested a trip into the countryside, in Kelley's words, "to see the Kirghiz in their lairs." This particular "goob" Kelley found to be

an interesting type. He had been an exile in Siberia under the Czar, and just prior to becoming Gubispolkum he had been in an insane asylum. He was dignified but taciturn. During the stroll he loosened up a bit to remark that he had heard much of the Americans and had not known what to expect from them. Now that he had met us he knew we were just like other folk and not nearly as "stuck up" as the old Russian aristocracy. Shades of my immigrant ancestors! Boris thinks he did not expect me to call on him, to shake his hand, and to converse like an equal with him.

Kelley's party included the local government representative, Berkovsky, a "young Jew of the student type." They ventured by wagon onto the steppe, "this appalling stretch of unbroken plain. No trees, bushes, hills, crops, or anything but level earth of brown or green hue extending to the horizon."

Finally the horizon was broken by a Kirghiz village, an "owoul," consisting of about a dozen cone-shaped teepees and around them scores of "Mongolian typed natives." The party was escorted to the abode of the richest man in the owoul. From the outside this tent looked like all the others, but inside they found the floor and wall covered with handmade rugs. There were also a table and chairs, "a most unkhirghizlike innovation." The guests took the chairs; the host preferred the floor.

By the time I had examined all of the rugs and hangings, noted the Singer sewing machine and the great heap of silk comforts stacked against the wall, the meal was ready. KUMISS! Do you know what it is? The dictionary calls it fermented mare's milk. Perhaps it is. With intense suffering I disposed of a third of the bowl placed before me while the Russians tossed off two or three pints of the stuff.

There followed the obligatory picture-taking session with the natives, including the milking of a camel "and other weird things." Then tea was served.

Berkovsky was full of questions about political and economic conditions in America, and while Kelley held forth the Khirgiz listened with interest. "They brought out a Russian paper and quizzed me about an item there in which told of a lynching in Texas. Which stirred the Gubispolkum to remark that lately they buried a man alive in Kustanai for horse stealing."

Kelley's readiness to mix it up with local officials in discussions of what the ARA would call politics had no detrimental effect on government relations in Ufa. The only ruffle occurred when Blandy attended a meeting of mullahs in Belebei. He and his interpreter assumed mullah garb, which was said to have delighted the natives, but set off alarm bells with the Bolshevik authorities in Ufa who may have had visions of an ARA-inspired insurrection.[8]

IN THE END there was only one clear-cut case of an ARA man being expelled from Soviet Russia for expressing his political views. This was the affair of Malcolm Grant.

Grant was assigned to Simferopol in the Crimea, where he was in charge of the food remittance division. In the summer of 1922 he began to cross swords with Eiduk's agent, General A. K. Karpov. John Hynes arrived in Simferopol in July and found Grant "in a very agitated condition," chiefly due to bad blood with Karpov.

Just how the situation had reached this stage is not clear, but by the time Hynes arrived, Karpov had it in for Grant. According to a local official friendly to the ARA, Karpov had learned during a trip to Moscow that Grant had complained about him, and he told the official he was set on revenge. He also told this informant that he expected to be treated like a general of the Red Army and that he wanted to make a few personnel changes at the ARA. In fact it is said that when he first arrived in the district, he announced himself as "first, a general of the Red Army; second, a member of the Communist Party; and third, a relief official." Fisher wrote of him that, while he could not read or write, "words gushed from him like water from a hydrant."

Karpov asked the same local official to write a statement declaring that Grant had hit the man with a stick, but he refused to do this. Karpov then drew up a bill of particulars against Grant, which included charges that the American purchased rugs from the museums and palaces of the Crimea for purposes of speculation, used the ARA mail service to contact relatives of Russian citizens living outside Soviet Russia, and spread anti-Soviet propaganda. The local ARA maintained Grant's innocence. John Hynes had been sent down from Moscow to investigate.

Hynes says that Grant was "absolutely rabid on the question of Government representatives and it appeared was practically not on speaking terms with the local Soviet authorities." He spoke bitterly of Karpov's obstruction of the ARA work: all business had to be transacted through the general, yet he was often out of town and thus the work was held up.

Grant may have been guilty of small-time speculation, but it is doubtful that he would have been expelled for this, so common was the practice within the ARA. As for the other two charges, there was clear evidence to back them up in his private correspondence, which fell into the hands of the military censor—"accidentally," according to the authorities. The contents of these letters were so incriminating that the censor demanded Grant's immediate removal.

We know exactly what Grant wrote because there are copies in the archives— copies not only of Grant's original English but also of the military censor's Russian translations, which for some reason were then translated back into English. Any version would have been grounds for dismissal.

The chief piece of evidence was a letter he wrote on June 11, 1922, to his mother in Birmingham, Alabama. He told her of a conversation he had had that afternoon with the prerevolutionary mayor of Simferopol, now barely able to keep his family and himself alive. "It gives one a thrill to talk to the FEW—'old people'—the true, stern, polished, educated people left from the old regime."

Leaving the former mayor, he paid a visit to the president of the Crimean government and "gave him hell" for not cooperating with the ARA. "He looks like a Cohaba River dirt eater and with very little more intelligence." The forth-and-back Soviet translation of this sentence reads: "He looks like a resident of the rever Cahaba, feeding on filth, and has not more sence."

More pleasantries follow: "I never quite realised what it meant to have an American passport in my pocket—than when cursing some of these filthy animals. I feel sure when I talk to them that their souls are of a dirty brown color and that they stink." Then comes the loaded finale: "Must close and send this by Mr. Karpoff to Moscow. (He is the Bolo general—the target of most of my cursing for the last month). We are dining together tonight (he does steal good wine from the Royal cellars). . . . We had some 85 year old port the other day—wish you could have tasted it."

This kind of invective targeted at officials was rare in the private letters of ARA men, but it was not unique. It is hard to imagine anyone topping the stream of abuse in Russ Cobb's letters to his parents. In these he calls the Bolos "ignorant dishonest jealous swine," a "filthy sneaking ignorant crowd of cut throats," a "bunch of embittered, revengeful Jews, absolutely heartless and cruel, selfish and domineering." He also uses the word "devils." His opinion of the "damned Russians," that "filthy race," is no better. "They must always have been a rotten crowd —no country could lose all honesty and decency so quickly unless it had always been rotten. The men all look like animals, cruel snarling faces." It is "fight, fight, curse, curse day and night."

None of Cobb's letters was intercepted by the authorities, but they did come to the attention of Chris Herter in Washington. Cobb's father, a New York City architect, was a friend of Herter and sent him excerpts of Russ's letters. In his cover letter, Cobb senior felt he should make it absolutely clear that young Russ was not pro-Bolshevik, that he regarded the Bolsheviks as a "miserable, worthless, selfish, ignorant, heartless and hopelessly incompetent gang." Herter does not appear to have been alarmed by any of this correspondence.

Cobb never got into trouble, but Grant never had a chance. Whatever the charges against him, the fact that he entrusted such compromising correspondence to Karpov left him open to the charge of stupidity, which might in itself have done him in with the ARA chiefs. As it happened, his fate was sealed when his correspondence was passed up the ladder to Kamenev, who personally requested Grant's removal.

Quinn justified the severe action taken in the Grant case in a report to London. When the ARA came into Russia, it agreed "to take no sides in the political struggle," but the evidence revealed that Grant had taken "violent sides against the Government." What is more, he had been "extremely indiscreet" and had proved himself "temperamentally unfitted for the job" and had to be let go. "[W]e feel that Mr. Grant has proved too young and too unbalanced to stand the gaff." He was exiled to the Cohaba River.

Quinn informed London that the one positive outcome of the episode was that Comrade Karpov had also been removed, "more or less in disgrace."[9] He had long been the object of ARA protests, but it is tempting to speculate that his undoing was the line in Grant's letter about his theft of wine from the imperial cellars. Ironically, it was probably Karpov that turned over Grant's letters to the censor. The illiterate general was unable on his own to decipher their contents.

Karpov's place of exile was Orenburg province, where he replaced General Klimov as government representative during the final weeks before the premature closing of that mission. His arrival marked a dramatic improvement in government relations there, and reports of his excellent cooperation must have been a source of wonder at Moscow headquarters.

This is the same Karpov whose letter showered unctuous praise on the departing Coleman, placing him "in the ranks of the prominent persons of the new world." If he was not a changed man, he had certainly learned something about the importance of the written word.

CHAPTER 29

MACHINE POLITICS

Besides Grant's letter to his mother, there was a second piece of correspondence intercepted by the military censor and used in the case against him. Addressed to "My wild Celtic Rose," it adds an interesting detail to the picture of his relations with the local authorities: "Up until now my work has consisted chiefly in cursing Soviet Officials. Yesterday I took on the President of the Crimean Govt. I get a Henry Ford tomorrow and then I can cause the traffic cop a little annoyance."

The mention of driving a Henry Ford in the same breath as cursing out a president is by no means fortuitous. In Russia, perhaps to a greater extent than in the more advanced West, the automobile was a coveted symbol of authority, and as such it came to play a superficially important role in daily ARA-Soviet affairs. In fact from the very first days of the mission the automobile and the peculiarities of motoring in Russia featured prominently in the writings of the ARA men.

Childs arrived in Moscow on August 31, four days after Carroll's advance party, and motored from the train station to ARA headquarters in a freshly painted ARA Cadillac limousine. He anticipated the stares of pedestrians and was surprised at how little attention they paid him and his colleagues. "This lack of interest in even new automobiles was not to be wondered at when one viewed the number of old and new automobiles which were rushing past us in every direction."

What caught his eye were the passengers in these machines, "containing as they did, not beautifully attired ladies and gentlemen in the most correctly tailored clothes but men in the plain rough clothes of workers, many of them with unshaven faces and most of them with very tired countenances—all of them, different grades of officials of the Soviet Government." In this way Childs, like a number of his fellow relievers, gained his first insights into the social consequences of the Russian Revolution by observing automobile passengers on Moscow streets from the back seat of a Cadillac.

Golder, sitting beside Childs, recorded a somewhat different impression in his diary: "There were very few vehicles about, and these kicked up clouds of dust as they zig-zagged along to escape the ruts and holes."

Shafroth journeyed to Moscow with Carroll's party, reaching the capital on Saturday evening, August 27. "We passed more than a dozen automobiles on our way, and a number of people, evidently natives riding in droskies."

Haskell and his party from Riga, numbering twenty-one, arrived on Wednesday, September 21. The colonel described the capital as a "deserted city." Like the others he was struck by the closed storefronts, but in his description even the streets themselves are deserted: "It was rare to see even a droshky, and except for an occasional hurrying motor car bearing a Communist official from one part of the city to another, there was hardly any vehicular traffic in evidence."

Virtually every ARA man's, indeed foreigner's, description of Moscow at this time mentions the near-comic velocity of the street traffic, which today evokes images of autos from early silent films, their movements accelerated by the unnatural speed of the 35 mm film. And just as in those silent-era films, life for pedestrians was hazardous.

In the ARA archives there is a short memoir about daily life in Moscow, probably in the year 1920, translated into English with the title "How a Soviet Slave Spends Her Day." In this bitter narrative, the automobile is a symbol of a heartless, ruthless, impersonal Soviet government. The "slave" begins her day dodging traffic on the city streets: "Empty motors, puffing out malodorous soot, run like mad in all directions in order to bring the administrative personnel. If you do not pay attention, if you stand gaping and do not give way, the chauffeur is sure to knock you down, maybe he will crush you dead, as a useless creature, and will hurry further with an oath." When the work day ends and the slaves are let out, "Numerous motors hurry past them conveying home contented and well-fed chiefs."

Farmer Murphy observed how the women whose job it was to sweep the snow from the trolley tracks resented having to get out of the way of passing automobiles that preferred the cleared tracks to the snow-covered streets. "It has frequently happened when one of them has had to step reluctantly off the tracks to avoid our car that she has spit at us as we went past."

One week earlier, he ruminated in a private letter about how the new ruling class of Russia was conducting itself much like the old regime, "aping the manners and doings of the old favored classes as best they can. The Soviet automobiles shriek through the streets in insolent disregard of pedestrians, commissars give expensive parties to their friends at cabarets or dinner parties with wines taken from the cellars of the Kremlin, their women attend the theaters and opera swathed in sables which their former owners had to sell for food. Everything will soon be the same." On the basis of such evidence did so many outsiders come to believe that NEP meant the death of communism in Russia.

When ARA historian Thomas Dickinson returned to the States early in 1922, he wrote a series of fifteen newspaper articles for the *New York Herald Tribune*. Like their author they were acidly anti-Bolshevik. His first impressions of Moscow in September 1921 were dominated by "automobiles, travelling usually at a very great speed, splattering dirty water over the crowds." These include a commissar's car, "cutting a quick swath through crowded streets, as it shrieks a continual siren note, forty miles an hour toward the Kremlin."

The Americans seemed surprised that the otherwise slow-moving Russians chose to roll about Moscow at such high speeds and were even more amazed that the autos could accomplish this feat over the city's pitiful streets. To illustrate the point Dickinson takes us behind the wheel:

We are in a rattling flivver without headlights, electric bulbs having disappeared some time ago. The driver avoids collision by the rattle of his engine and by shrill whistles in the dark. The pavement always of rough cobblestones, is now broken into great holes several feet wide and a foot or so in depth. These are full of water. A mist is over the city. But the dark and the mist do not hamper the speed of the car.

Speed above all, until—"A long whistle, a scrape of jangled gears. A woman with a heavy bundle over her shoulder jumps in one direction; a girl carrying a log as large as herself drops it in the mud and scurries to the side of the road. They are saved to the joy of another day in Bolshevist Moscow."

Dickinson interpreted the vulnerability of the Moscow pedestrian in the context of what he felt to be the low value placed on human life in Soviet Russia. Edwin Vail saw it the same way: "Life is cheap here as evidenced by the careless way everybody drives. There are evidently no traffic rules, and you think every minute some poor soul who is not quite quick enough will be caught. It would be merciful if some of the poor beggars were killed, but not in that way."

Curiously, there are only a few first hand accounts by ARA men of auto accidents involving pedestrians, although the journalist McCullagh says that there were "innumerable" such mishaps. "I never saw so many legless people, especially young boys and girls, and reckless driving is largely responsible for this condition."

The plight of the Moscow pedestrian was not improved during the 1920s by the moderating influences of NEP. Satirists Il'f and Petrov began their 1931 classic satire of NEP Russia, *The Golden Calf*, with a memorable description of the dangers of Moscow's streets. The opening words of the book constitute its first paragraph: "Pedestrians should be loved." Yet, "In our enormous country the ordinary motor car, which the pedestrians intended to be used for peaceful purposes, has taken on the menacing aspect of a fratricidal missile."

In provincial Russia, they relate, "pedestrians are still loved and respected," but in Moscow the motorist rules. Just how did this come about? The authors remind the reader that "Pedestrians created the world," documenting the great inventions in history they have contributed to mankind. "It should be noted that the motor car was also invented by pedestrians. But for some reason the motorists soon forgot about that. They began to run over the meek and mild, clever pedestrians. The streets built by the pedestrians passed into the hands of the motorists. . . . In a large city, pedestrians lead the life of martyrs, just as though they were in a traffic-run ghetto."

One such martyr is a hypothetical hobo: "He's a hiker who left Vladivostok as a young man and who, in his old age, will be run over at the very gates of Moscow by a large truck, the number of which no one will have a chance to catch."

The main problem in 1921, especially in Moscow, was a lack of regulations, not to mention traffic control, which spelled anarchy on the streets. Bill Kearney, chief of the ARA motor transportation division, wrote in autumn 1921 that "Traffic regulations and road discipline mean nothing to Russian drivers." One of his colleagues observed that the ARA was forced to operate "in a country almost without traffic regulations of any kind or if they have them on their books, they are not enforced."

This situation began to change with the return to some semblance of law and order under NEP so that by the time Tom Barringer arrived in Moscow in the first weeks of 1922 there were traffic cops in place, although the one he describes wore "a sheepskin hat, sporting a sabre, rifle and automatic pistol to augment his decisions."

By the time Barringer left the country this "revolutionary" type of traffic cop had given way to the traditional policeman in olive drab armed only with a billy and a badge. Duranty reported at the end of the ARA mission that genuine traffic control had finally returned to Moscow. He himself motored about the capital in 1922 in a "little T-model Ford" and for reasons of personal safety hired a chauffeur who was "not too Russian."[1]

THE ARA BROUGHT its own automobiles into Soviet Russia. Carroll's party arrived with a Cadillac and a Ford camionette. These first Americans realized right away that the ARA would have to import a large fleet of cars for the mission. Several autos would be needed to cover the expanse of Moscow alone. In the provinces ARA autos would be critical for keeping the American staff mobile for tours of inspection within the cities and throughout the districts. In short, the automobile would be vital to maintaining American control.

In January 1922 the Russian unit created a motor transportation division to handle the large fleet of incoming trucks and automobiles, including maintenance work. Kearney, its chief, was the typical ARA wanderer. His records tell us that he hailed from Edwardsville, Illinois, and that in 1918 the war took him to Europe as a lieutenant attached to the general staff of the First Army. When the fighting ended, he resigned from the army in Germany with the rank of captain, managed to stay in Europe, and in 1921 worked in some minor capacity on the Inter-Allied High Commission. When the Russian mission began, he was serving in France as chief of motor transportation for the American Graves Registration Service. He went to work in Russia for the ARA in January 1922, having spent a total of only thirty days in the United States since 1918.

Kearney's department supplied itself with automobiles from a number of sources, the most important being the surplus motor transportation of the various American relief organizations operating in Europe. The American Red Cross in Riga donated seven Ford camionettes, three Ford touring cars, nine Liberty trucks, and one White truck. The American YMCA in Paris turned over two Cadillac touring cars, two Ford touring cars, six Ford camionettes, two Ford trucks, and eight Pierce-Arrow trucks. The American YMCA at Coblenz contributed two Ford touring cars, three Ford camionettes, and three Ford trucks. In all some fifty-three vehicles were delivered between September 15 and November 1, 1921, and were distributed among the districts.

Other motor vehicles came from various ARA headquarters in the European capitals; still others were purchased. All told, the ARA brought in 149 vehicles during the mission. In Moscow the ARA garage was a major hub of activity, with twenty-five to thirty-five people on its staff. One of the American statistical wizards estimated at mission's end that ARA automobiles and trucks had traveled in Russia some 1.4 million miles.

Among Kearney's concerns were motor accidents involving the ARA fleet, but these appear to have been few. The final report of the administration division claims that there were "absolutely no smash-ups of cars or trucks and this may be considered extraordinary in view of the conditions under which the transportation had to operate." By "smash-ups" the writer must mean accidents in which a vehicle was incapacitated—or what in a later day would be called "totaled."

There was also the problem of the elements, what with temperatures in the winter of 1921–22 down well below zero degrees Fahrenheit. Kearney reported that many radiators in ARA cars froze—twenty of these during January and February 1922, some of them while the motors were running. Aside from this, the constant driving and the poor grade of gasoline and oil furnished by the Soviet government necessitated numerous motor overhauls.

He claimed that his "chief worry" was finding suitable chauffeurs. The lot that drove Soviet officials around Moscow were not up to ARA standards. For one, they were far too preoccupied with using their vehicles to exhibit their manhood. When Moscow drivers approached from opposite directions on the streetcar tracks, neither would give the right-of-way for fearing to appear the weaker. The challenge was to find chauffeurs who would submit to ARA discipline, if not Moscow's nascent traffic regulations.

An early ARA memorandum on the subject of traffic violations makes clear that the primary concern was not the defenseless pedestrians but its automobiles, which called for the "utmost care and economy." "No reason nor necessity exists for driving about at excessive speeds and risking the destruction of the transportation." The ARA Americans were made personally responsible for the driving behavior of their chauffeurs and the conditions of their automobiles.

They were required also to observe a speed limit of thirty versts—or about twenty miles—an hour. But trying to enforce this would have been like trying to apply the Volstead Act to the ARA Americans.

If the search for suitable chauffeurs was indeed Kearney's "chief worry," then it must have been a considerable one. He was forced to retire from the Russian mission in December 1922, suffering from what was described as a "bad case of nerves," though he had apparently never set foot in the famine zone.

Reckless driving was not what motivated H. Alexander Smith to assault the ARA chauffeur in Minsk, a man named Podberezka. This happened on November 22, 1922, and caused the local trade union committee to declare a strike of ARA workers. The union demanded Smith's "delivery into the hands of Justice." It seems that the chauffeur had provoked the violence by spreading false rumors about Smith. Lander called them "libellous reports" and says Podberezka would be charged by the Russian courts. "Assault, however, is considered absolutely impermissible. I request you therefore to have Mr. Smith recalled from Russia."

Lander wrote to Quinn that he had it on good information that Smith's action had been "premeditated and deliberate." The union was somehow satisfied and the strike ended, but Smith's fate hung in the air through the month of December. Finally Quinn seemed to hit upon a solution. In conversation he told Lander that Smith was "an energetic, conscientious and valuable worker and that his services were urgently needed in view of our proposed reopening of our work in Orenburg District."[2] Message: If you want the ARA to return to Orenburg, drop the Smith matter. Lander saw the light, perhaps figuring that a posting to Orenburg was tantamount to exile from Russia.

IN PETROGRAD, a city spread out over an area of about one hundred square miles, automobiles were essential for daily ARA inspections of ports, warehouses, food depots, feeding stations, kitchens, and the bakery. When the Americans arrived, the telephone exchange had been destroyed by fire, and repairs were said to be a long way off. There were streetcars, of course, but these were inconveniently laid out and anyway were often terribly overcrowded and unreliable.

That was the former capital, where in prerevolutionary times the automobile had become a familiar sight. In many provincial cities and towns in 1921 it was still something of a novelty. Of course even in Moscow the automobile was heavily outnumbered by the *droshki,* the horse-drawn carriage. This was also called an "izvoshchik," which meant "cabby" but had come to denote the entire conveyance.

Barringer found upon his arrival in February 1922 at the Ekaterinoslav train station that a man-powered pushcart for hire, used to haul baggage, was called a "Trotsky," a play on "droshki." That was for a one-man cart; the two-man was called a "Lenin & Trotsky." The locals informed him that conditions were now such that there were no more horses to pull the droshkies so these had given way to man-powered pushcarts and that "the new vehicles are named after the sponsors of such conditions."

There were also automobiles in these towns, and if the ARA men are to be believed, their appearance and erratic movements over the streets were even more cartoonlike than in Moscow. Golder paused to dwell upon this in a diary entry of October 30, 1921, by which time he had passed through numerous Volga towns. To him the provincial automobiles were like aging veterans of the Russian Civil War.

Moscow still sports good automobiles, some new; but the provinces use cars that have seen military service on various fronts—English, French, Denikin, Kolchak, and Wrangel—and by all military regulations should be demobilized. But this is not done, and they continue in service, coughing and sneezing. Their food is kerosene, their shelter a leaky garage or the open sky, the drivers Russian chauffeurs who mistreat them as the *isvozchiks* (cab drivers) mistreat their nags. In another year these veterans of many campaigns will be no more and the only people to weep for them will be the commissars, for they, like the other members of the proletariat, will be obliged to walk or take cheap cabs.

Perhaps it was because they sensed that the end was not far off that the local officials cast envious eyes on the ARA's automobiles.

Dudley Hale was surprised to find high-class motors in Samara—Locomobile, Benz, Mercedes, Peugot. Their human cargo impressed him less favorably: "The stupidity and officiousness written on the faces of the leather coated commissars to be seen riding about in the tonneaus of their powerful automobiles, makes a rather shocking contrast with the looks of some of the automobiles."

Barringer remarked after the mission that most of the cars he had encountered in Russia were American-made and enjoyed the highest reputation with the local citizens. His understanding was that the American trucks "in various stages of service in every Russian town of any size" had been left behind by Kolchak's retreating army in 1919, having earlier been abandoned by the American intervention forces in Siberia. As for their appearance,

No funny paper can describe, adequately, the patched up "official cars" that we have seen around small towns, amidst smoke and back-fires, and always painted in brilliant colors, the sickle and hammer as the coat-of-arms. Peasants with a grievance and a rifle were not adverse to taking pot shots from the hillsides at any automobile, as nothing but a higher official or his crowd ever travelled in one. So we were just as glad that ours were distinctive by not having so glaring a coat-of-arms.

This may explain why in Elizavetgrad the government officials traveled about the district only in autos armed with machine guns. The ARA district history says that this was so and that "Semites do not travel in the village at all." This led to friction when the local officials insisted on borrowing the ARA car for trips into the countryside: the one time the Americans relented, the automobile was returned with a machine gun mounted on the front hood.

In most places it was not so easy for bandits to differentiate between ARA and Soviet autos, if they cared to. When Marshal Tuthill had his encounter with the bandit leader Ivanov he was traveling in a Ford, and Ivanov told him he was lucky because the Bolo commissar they were intending to ambush was supposed to pass along the same route in a Ford.

As for the caliber of driving in the districts, Moscow's chauffeurs appear to have had nothing on their provincial counterparts for speed and recklessness—at least this is the conclusion drawn by Fleming, who had a chance to sample both. He began his September 1922 grand inspection tour in Samara, where he got his first taste of provincial Russian motoring. Upon arrival at the train station he found his way to the ARA personnel house and from there was driven to the office in the back seat of a Cadillac.

The driver of this car had a very strange and alarming manner of driving us, though our hosts seemed to pay no attention to his vagaries. First he drove on one side of the street; then on the other; he then concentrated his attention on the telephone pole, and running the car full force at it, changed his mind at the last moment and dodged it by a quarter of an inch. Then he ran up on the sidewalk with two wheels and then off again, just flicking a stone post set in the curb with the mudguard, but not touching it; he then proceeded to the middle of the street again, and decided to stop; changed his mind at the last moment again, eased the car over a rolling bump, and repeat the reel. Once or twice he drew up beside a large building and all but stopped; I thought we had arrived, but we had not and kept going. For variety and curiosity it certainly was a star performance; but in the few days that I stayed in Samara I found that the chauffeur had it all learned by heart, and did the same tricks in the same place every time.

After a few more stops on his journey he realized that the Samara performance was typical.

It turned out that all the chauffeurs in all the districts have their little song and dance memorized for every street in town. It is a remarkable example of adaptation. Why repair the streets, now, argue the local street departments, when the droshkies, our sea-going hacks, do not mind the difference, and all the chauffeurs of the foreign organizations have already learned where our mud puddles lie and where our cobblestones have been removed for street-warfare?

Petrograd too was notorious for the condition of its streets. Mackenzie wrote that when he arrived there in summer 1922, he learned that a week or two earlier a motorcar waiting on the Nevsky Prospect had "literally disappeared. The street caved in under it, and it sank right down." This may not have been an exaggeration. The story appears to have spread throughout the city, and a well-known line of a Petrograd comic had it that in the former capital you disappear when you drive and the streetcar fares rise while you ride.

Fleming continued his journey northward to Simbirsk, where he witnessed the chauffeurs "careen about the streets in the same drunken manner as the chauffeurs do in Samara." The difference was the amount of street traffic. "The main street of Simbirsk on Saturday night hasn't got the traffic that Brattle Street, Cambridge, has on Sunday morning."

Outside the provincial capitals the arrival of an automobile could be the cause of great excitement. American relievers were frequently told that theirs was the first car ever seen in a particular locale. Childs's report of an "excited mob" of children and adults greeting the arrival of an ARA automobile is echoed throughout the documentation. It happened all the time to John Foy, although this may have been due in part to the otherworldly appearance of his flivver.

At Sterlitamak, after the local officials had transported Kelley from a business meeting back to his living quarters in the only automobile in town, he expressed a preference for a droshki, "because it is surer and infinitely less conspicuous. The natives ran from all directions to see who was in the car."

Mackenzie rode in what he says was the first automobile in Cheliabinsk since Kolchak had paid an extended visit. "It was like travelling in a car in England twenty years ago. Horses took fright and bolted madly as we approached. Everyone watched us."

Governor Goodrich wrote in his diary on October 20, 1921, of his arrival in Markstadt in the Saratov district, a city that had until recently been called Ekaterinstadt after Catherine the Great. For his visit he was provided with the only machine in town, a rarely used Cadillac captured from Denikin's army. As he was chauffeured along through the streets, the Cadillac turned a corner and came face to face with a camel and a horse, both hitched to a wagon loaded with potatoes. Atop the pile of potatoes, sitting cross-legged, was the owner. Goodrich describes the action: "It must have been the first Auto the camel ever saw for as soon as he spied this devil coming in his direction with smoke belching from the exhaust, he gave a hoarse moaning cry and turning about, bolted down the street dragging the horse with him and spilling the Mujac and his potatoes on the ground."

When the owner set out after his panicked team, a group of delighted children saw its chance and began to gather up the spilled potatoes, which brought the peasant frantically running back to the upset cart—like something out of Chaplin or Keaton. Camel and horse finally halted some distance down the road, "the camel gazing with wondering eyes at the strange monster." Goodrich gave the man two hundred thousand rubles for his lost potatoes and his troubles, and continued on his way.

This aversion to the automobile was not exclusive to the animal world: in Ufa it was reported that when an ARA truck arrived in a small village, "the people all turned out and wanted to manhandle the chauffeur, claiming that he had brought a 'devil machine' to their midst."[3]

IN TIME THE ARA succeeded in creating in the minds of local citizens a positive association with the automobile, which had earlier been connected only with the occupation Whites or the oppressive Reds. Russ Cobb wrote back to Saratov headquarters during an inspection tour in the interior: "When we arrived and stopped in a village the automobile would be surrounded by everyone in town, the only other automobiles that they had seen were the ones in which the communists came to shoot them up and take grain."

Cobb once left his "dirty ole flivver" standing in a street in the town of Kamenka and returned to find that peasants had decorated it with flowers.

All through the ARA documentation in photographic or written form there is the recurring image of children running to greet the ARA car or truck. Among the ARA publicity posters made by Russian hands there is one depicting a group of ragged orphans hailing a delivery truck bearing the words "American Relief Administration." The artist would not have had to look far for inspiration.

An ARA report out of Odessa in July 1922 makes reference to the "lively youngsters playing and shouting and crying 'Arah' whenever an ARA automobile would pass. It is from the children that we get the spontaneous recognition of relief work, as they know nothing of politics and no amount of propaganda can convince them that their best friend is not the one that feeds them."

Another American eyewitness in Odessa noted the impression made upon the local populace by ARA relief, which had been carried out so rapidly "as to beggar comprehension, and it is doubtful if there ever existed an organization that gained the sympathy and respect of the population so thoroughly and quickly as the A.R.A. One need only ride the streets of city, town or village in the A.R.A. automobile and listen to the shouts of welcome that greet him to be convinced of the popularity of the A.R.A."[4]

At the end of the mission there were hundreds of letters of thanks to the ARA written by children and adults, many decorated with drawings and watercolors. It is the image of the festively greeted ARA automobile that predominates. It had become a symbol of American beneficence.

In Ufa the celebrated Colonel Bell used to drive around the city in the company of a cub bear. This was a gift to Bell from the appreciative local townsfolk. One of the Ufa staff members remembered that the bear rode with Bell "on every occasion" and was a kind of ARA mascot. It is reported that once it spilled a large jar of honey on the back seat of the Ford. Bell is quoted as saying that this animal "nearly frightened a woman to death one day and scared the life out of several others."

Bell was the recipient of all kinds of gifts from local citizens, including a brace of six-week-old wolves. When these began to torment the bear, he had to give them all away.

Shafroth tells the story of traveling by motor outside of Samara city on May 1, 1922, in a Ford camionette, "with which to make a bourgeois impression." Behind the wheel of the car sat Shafroth's chauffeur, a machine-gunner during the war. On this particular journey the Ford became stuck in mud and could not be budged. In the distance Shafroth could make out a church and surrounding peasant huts, so he set out on foot for what turned out to be the Tatar village of Lopatino. There he located the chairman of the ARA committee, the head of the village soviet, and four or five "husky" peasants who volunteered to attempt a rescue of the Ford. Their eagerness to help might be explained by the arrival a few days before of American corn in the village.

Once the Ford had been extracted from the mud, the soviet chief insisted that

Shafroth spend the night in the village. There was the obstacle of a stream sepa-
rating them from the village, but this enthusiastic official declared that he would,
if need be, bring out the entire village and have the Ford carried across. They
hopped aboard and drove up to the bank of the stream, on the opposite side of
which rose a Tatar mosque. "Before many minutes, men, women and children
came swarming to the bank from all directions. A rope was fastened to the front
of the car, trousers were rolled up, and a guard of honor of about thirty waded in
and pulled us across, amidst the shouts and delight of the children on the bank."

Unlike Charlie Veil, Shafroth did not feel a need to drown this scene in a vodka
celebration. He survived the episode with his pride intact because the culprit was
not the performance of the ARA automobile but the almighty spring mud.

The Russian winter provided different challenges. Shafroth's successor at Samara, Ron Allen, said that a December 1922 inspection trip south into Stavropol
had caused him and the ARA a good deal of embarrassment even though he
claimed that the elements were mostly to blame. He advised Moscow to abandon
all motor transportation in winter. "The snow brings into existence an entirely
new system of roads connecting interior points, and they are roads which spell
impossibility to automobiles." Horse and sledge, he wrote, would greatly extend
ARA control.

To say nothing of prestige. If I should drive through Kurmutch with a fine span of
Arabs—or even Buguruslans ginger in their heels, snorts in their nostrils and bells, it
would go a long way toward making the people forget I once broke down in Bolshoi
Ulitza when Ford 114 lost animation. The Ford tried nobly to do its bit, but after am-
bling for the Army on the Rhine, and rustling for the Red Cross in Riga, there is a
very little bit left for A.R.A.

The ARA's pride became tied to the performance of its automobiles, which
reflected on its efficiency. Golder arrived in Moscow on November 5, 1921, after
an extensive inspection tour of the famine zone, during which he had to suffer
through the vagaries of travel by Russian automobile. Now at the Moscow station he and a government plenipotentiary named Wolf, whom he called Tovarisch, were met by the ARA car. "I told Tovarisch, 'Now we will have a ride in
a real car that does not break down.' We rode ten minutes and then got a flat,
there being no other tire we had to wait for more than half an hour for another
car. The ARA is becoming Russianized quickly."

In Ekaterinoslav Barringer said that when the ARA operations opened there
on February 7, 1922, the local newspapers heralded the arrival of the ARA, the
Amerikanskaia rabochaia administratsiia, or "American Workers Administration."
Here the arrival of the ARA automobile served to clarify matters: "When the
Dodge Sedan appeared on the streets of Ekaterinoslav all doubts as to the proletarian composition of our organization vanished and from that day on we were
known as a 'bourgeois' organization in the minds of the 'sovetnics.'"

In the ARA files there is a crude translation of a stenographic report taken at
an August 1922 meeting of ARA inspectors in Tsaritsyn. This document is loaded
with straight talk. The assembled employees were in agreement that the condition
of many of the ARA Russian inspectors was pitiful, some of them having to get
about on foot, dressed all in tatters, "often as ridiculous as Don Kikhot [Quixote]."

What kind of respect could such people command? One speaker declared that nothing less than an automobile was required for every inspector.

A representative of the Powers will only have authority then when he will arrive in a motor-car. There have been cases when one has said: "Yes, we will see that this one is a representative of the Power because he has arrived in a motor-car. . . . " It has all a great deal to do with the psychologie of the crowd. . . . In the long run the great American Relief Administration makes the impression that it creeps along on cows.

For the Americans at headquarters it had to be the right kind of car. In Kiev, as George Harrington relates, during the first few months of operations the sole means of transportation was an old Ford delivery wagon.

When it was necessary to call upon the president—which was very often in the early days—the district supervisor climbed into his delivery wagon, and rattled and bounced along to the Sovnarkom. While he was in the building, the worn out Ford stood in front of the door between the presidential Rolls-Royce and Packard, the chauffeur suffering, as only chauffeurs can, at the jibes of his fellow drivers. In February a new Dodge arrived, and the morale of the district was saved.

In Kharkov the chief of the Jewish Joint Distribution Committee wrote to Haskell in the autumn of 1922 to complain that his ARA car was inadequate for his standing in the community. So Haskell sent down one of the ARA's best Cadillacs and his reputation was saved.

BY THE SECOND YEAR of the mission the Cadillac had become a purely prestige vehicle in the ARA. At the outset every district wanted a Cadillac, of course, until it became clear that its weight and size made it unsuitable for the Russian roads. Phil Carroll realized this shortly after his arrival and wrote London with a request to send only Dodges and Fords, as "the streets in Moscow cause excessive wear and tear on Cadillacs." Still, one could not sniff at donated Cadillacs, and so they began to appear in the districts.

Most of the men soon came to share Carroll's opinion. Allen did so on the roads of Samara. He conveyed to the Moscow chiefs his suggestions on motor transportation, which he says were in part informed by his experience in the automobile industry. Among his recommendations: "Abandon the Cadillac habit which reacts pleasantly enough on the man that gets one, but leaves someone else just where Adam was when he started the apartment problem by eating the forbidden fruit. The same investment, if spread over the purchase of Dodges, Chevrolets or Maxwells, must give everybody a ride, and personally I think A.R.A. inspectors should ride."

Well before then Moscow headquarters had come to regard Cadillacs as "white elephants," but no one tried to dissuade Edgar Rickard, the ARA director general from New York, from bringing in a Cadillac limousine for his summer 1922 visit to Soviet Russia. Kelley got a look at it when he passed through the capital in July and declared it to be "about the 'swellest' thing in the R.S.F.S.R."[5]

There was a lot of boastful talk by ARA men about their "swelling around" Bololand, and to those who found the Americans cold and aloof—and there were not a few Russians who did—the automobile became a symbol of ARA arrogance.

The Petrograd writer Kornei Chukovskii, a friend of the ARA, wrote that there were residents of the former capital who came to think of the relief workers not as benevolent saviors but as "proud, hurrying Americans flying about in auto cars."

It was this negative association that was at the center of a controversy involving an early Soviet feature film. This took place in December 1922 after Ivar Wahren had moved from Kazan to become district supervisor in Petrograd. The film was called *There Is No Happiness on Earth*, and when Wahren heard rumors that it portrayed the ARA in an unflattering light, he asked the state film authorities for permission to view it. They obliged, although after the lights went up he was told by the filmmakers that the version he had screened had had certain anti-ARA references edited out.

The plot had to do with a Soviet state employee and his wife, who is seduced by an ARA man—at least that was the insinuation. In the critical scene, which Wahren described in his report to Moscow, the villain exits the ARA office building in Petrograd, "driving off in his private automobile." At another point the victim agonizes, "I must go and finish with this foreigner."

Wahren informed Moscow that he had succeeded in having the film authorities cut the offensive material. Quinn nonetheless protested to Lander, sending him a copy of the report. Wahren may indeed have influenced the film's editing, because Lander sent a representative to Petrograd to investigate and the version he saw did not contain the scene with the ARA office and automobile. This enabled Lander to fire back a note to Quinn speculating that Wahren had been hallucinating.

Word of this imbroglio may have reached Baker in New York and helped inspire his January 1923 memo to the ARA publicity department, which instructed "leaving out from all articles written by men over there references to their moving about in private cars or by motor car. This seems a little thing, but we have been criticized in the past by people who knew nothing about it, but who accused us of 'swelling around' in automobiles. Sen. Watson was one of these."

Baker may also have had on his desk in front of him some clippings from the Soviet press critical of ARA driving. There was an incident in the city of Vitebsk, as one of the relievers tells it, where the ARA car jumped a curb: "Nobody was hit, but right the next day the official paper wrote that we should abandon these capitalistic habits of riding the proletariat to death, and that we should remember that we were in a free country and not in the U.S.A."

Despite all the American "swelling around" the only serious accidents involving ARA autos and pedestrians were clustered in Odessa, which the "Russian Unit Record" called "the Hoboken of the Ukraine" and where things always seemed to go to extremes: "The streets are wide and straight, the telegraph poles set well apart and with this civic virtue one can give credit for the fact that Mr. Hynes' new tin Lizzy is still as new and undamaged as when it arrived from the Bosphorus."

Nothing in the ARA documentation indicates that driving in Odessa was any more hazardous than it was in the rest of Soviet Russia; one report speaks of government automobiles "going as fast as was mechanically possible." What is surprising, however, in looking through the accident reports, is that none of them involved Randolph Clement, one of the most accident-prone of the ARA relief workers. Clement was born in 1898 in Charleston. In the war he served as a fighter pilot—which usually implied a certain amount of audacity—and apparently after the war he continued to fly pretty high, or at least that is the impression he gave from the stories he told.

Barringer made his acquaintance on his way into Russia on the Riga-Moscow run in January 1922. The Virginian wrote home that Clement was "a member of the Old Guard of Moultine St., S.C. and has had more hairbrea[d]th accidents than Harry him self. Is always-there-when-it-happens-guy from the lynching of Leo Frank to the Bolo outbreak in Seattle. A champion second class storyteller, but we all have hopes of him."

Clement's first assignment was Odessa, where a few weeks into the work he made an appearance in the ship's diary of the U.S.S. *MacFarland*. The commander wrote that Clement "had a brick thrown into his automobile this morning on his way to the dock. He seems to have most of the wild experiences in Odessa. He has a reputation in the A.R.A. of doing very well every job except his own. He is a likeable sort of person but rather irresponsible."

Clement was forced to quit the Russian mission after only four months because of illness. He had gone into Russia with a case of syphilis, for which he was treated in Odessa by Dr. Caffey with injections of Neo-Salvarsan. After his departure he passed through London where he told Brown that Caffey had botched one of these injections, causing leakage into his arm muscle, which left him partially paralyzed. Brown thought it prudent to have the ARA pay for part of his medical bills, although Quinn swore that Clement was telling another of his stories.[6]

The Bolos had been used to having the exclusive privilege of swelling around the roads of Soviet Russia, and they were resentful of this intrusion by the Americans. Most ARA men assumed that the Bolo obsession with motorcars was simply an imitation, to typical excess, of the behavior of the old-regime ruling classes, much like their weakness for elaborate banquets. The Americans could tell how much it meant to Soviet officials, especially those in the provincial towns, to be seen being driven about in an automobile. Hale wrote from Samara, "I have never seen a lone commisar riding in the front seat with the chauffer, which rather gets my goat."

For the Americans this Bolshevik attraction to automobiles served as evidence of the insincerity of their ideals. The ARA men were not the first Americans to think this way. Three years earlier in the Senate hearings on Bolshevik propaganda, one Senator saw as incriminating evidence against the Bolsheviks the fact that "many of the people who had been in comfortable circumstances in the past were forced to work on the street, carry bundles, act as porters, and so on, whereas the Bolsheviki leaders were living in palaces, riding around in automobiles and generally enjoying the kind of life which the very rich in the rest of the world are able to enjoy."

Later the senator added that the palaces were "beautiful" and the automobiles Pierce-Arrows. One of the witnesses, a YMCA official, said of the Bolsheviks, "They all have Peerless automobiles, those who have not Packards."

After the ARA mission Phil Matthews publicly condemned the Bolo leaders by pointing out that Trotsky, Kamenev, and Dzerzhinskii were chauffeured around the streets of Moscow in Rolls-Royces while Russia starved—as if they rolled along with no particular destination in mind, or their going on foot would have fed the hungry. Carl Floete, when he came out of Russia in November 1921, was quoted as saying that "Lenin rode around in a luxurious automobile," which in itself was supposed to indicate that there was nothing proletarian about him.

Of course Floete was still suffering from "famine shock" after his narrow escape from Volga bandits, which may explain his nervous obsession at the time with automobiles. In Pugachev, on November 18, 1921, when he realized that the bandit attack was imminent and his life in danger, he sent a desperate telegram to Shafroth in Samara, begging him for help, "as an American to an American. . . . In the name of humanity send the automobile today."

Shafroth did just that, dispatching a lone ARA Russian chauffeur, who arrived on the outskirts of town, probably about six hours later just as the attack was beginning. To his query as to what all the noise was about he was told, "Cossacks have come." According to Shafroth, "Without pausing for further enlightenment, he stepped on the accelerator, completely forgetting his mission, and arrived in Samara the same evening, with three flat tires, after traveling over 120 miles of bumpy road."

Floete's life-and-death telegram obviously made an impression on Shafroth: he kept the Russian original for himself. Seventy years later, in a retirement home outside of Raleigh, North Carolina, he squinted at it, searching his mind to recall what significance could have earned it a place in his scrapbook so long ago.

There was more to Soviet swelling around than simple parvenu posturing. For the Bolsheviks the automobile was an important symbol of technological progress. Russia was a backward country and despite the Revolution could not become industrialized overnight—this was the major theme of Lenin's new message of patience. But the automobile offered the commissar a taste of the future in the here and now. And when he got behind the wheel, he acted as though the faster he drove, the sooner he might arrive at the communist utopia—or at least it might help him to forget that Lenin had recently thrown the gears of the Revolution into reverse.

Part of the allure was the automobile's association with America, and the Bolsheviks were lately swept up in something of a craze over American technology and work methods. In Russia Henry Ford was considered to be the archetypical American. What better way then to become "Americanized" than to drive a Henry Ford. McCullagh put his finger exactly on this point: "This wild caricature of American activity—speeding through the streets—is regarded by the Reds as evidence of progress and is characteristic of the whole Bolshevist experiment on a kindly leisurely people who needed waking up but are not benefited by being run over."[7]

THE AUTOMOBILE BECAME another "arena" of the ARA-Soviet competition for authority and popularity. Sometimes it involved important matters of control over scarce automobiles and petrol. Often it operated on the level of who would get to ride in which model car or even sit in which seat. It sounds silly, but it does make sense out of Comrade Studenikin's threat to forbid Brown and Kernan from riding in the Odessa automobile.

Paragraph 13 of the Riga Agreement stated that the Soviet government was obligated to supply such motor transportation as the ARA needed "to efficiently control relief operations." In practice the government complied about as well as it fulfilled its obligation to provide the ARA with first-class railroad cars.

When Coleman requested an auto from the Orenburg authorities, the transportation department sent a man to his office who said that he had been instructed to turn over to the ARA one automobile for temporary use at a cost of about fifty thousand rubles per mile, at a minimum of forty miles per day. Coleman protested to the head of the local famine committee, reminding him of the Soviet obligation under paragraph 13: "In so far as Orenburg is concerned the Riga Agreement may just as well have not been written, but it is still the medium under which we are working here and although it is not complied with, I shall take the liberty of calling your attention to it from time to time."

Expecting no satisfaction, he appealed to Quinn, saying that the district had only a "dilapidated and useless Ford Camionette" and wondering about the status of two Dodge touring cars he had been promised. The ARA's efficiency was reduced by all the time wasted getting around town on foot. The local officials had promised a car, but "not a ripple to date." If Quinn could help out, wrote Coleman, unable to restrain himself, "I will not ask for anything but those three revolvers and sufficient ammunition about which I have wired and written you."

In July Coleman informed Fisher that the local authorities were providing the ARA with one motor truck for fifteen minutes each month, which sounds like Coleman letting off steam. He also declared to Fisher: "I'd rather ride the Irish Sea in winter any time than try to get two gallons of petrol from the soviet government representative . . . regardless of the fact that they signed an article known as the Riga Agreement which promised all an ARA man asks for."

In many of the district supervisors' monthly reports to Moscow the struggle to procure auto fuel was prominently mentioned under the "government relations" heading. In the provinces fuel was as much fought over as automobiles. In a September 1922 report Eddie Fox complained that the Simbirsk ARA's motor transportation was "almost at a stand still" and living "from 'tank to carburetter,' so to speak."

The Americans tended to assume harmful intent: that in denying them fuel the local officials were out to hamper ARA operations or to curb the American relievers' independence. But the provincial authorities were themselves hard up for fuel, which in the NEP cash-paying economy drained their precious money supply. They had little incentive to hand over the scarce commodity to the Americans so that they could roam around like foreign conquerors.

To keep the motors turning, periodically Moscow headquarters would allow the districts to purchase fuel on the local market at astronomically high prices. A spring purchase by Fox's successor, Barringer, brought a long dry spell to an end and "the ARA Motor Transportation burst forth upon the surprised citizens of Simbirsk after 3 months hibernation."

Then there was the problem of quality. At the ARA garage in Moscow Kearney could count on an adequate supply of decent fuel. However, in the districts, where it was said to double as a beverage, standards were notoriously low. Kelley was amazed watching the autos in Ufa: "It is a complete mystery to me how they operate on the alcohol mixture over these streets."

In Veil's Russia the ARA man on the road could be faced with the difficult choice of filling up his car or his stomach. In the winter of 1922, after putting affairs in order in Novouzensk, he decided to inspect "the hinterland." He asked the local soviet chief's permission to borrow his Ford, vintage 1910. "Da, he would loan it to me for the trip through the back areas. Fuel? No gasoline of course, but a mixture two-thirds vodka and one-third kerosene made the dilapidated steel steed agilely traverse trails which had frozen hard in the past few days."

He and Pete were motoring along on the barren steppe when his car quit, its radiator frozen and cracked. He walked several miles to a railroad station, where he found a piece of pipe, which he heated and worked into a coil to create a new radiator. "It was almost as funny as using tractor bearings for my airplane back in the Alps, but it worked for many miles, worked until a con rod broke and went through the motor block. With a rattle and a bang the old Ford expired. We were still miles from anywhere.

"We decided not to waste that vodka and kerosene in the gasoline tank; it represented so many calories of heat." So they drained the precious liquid into a pigskin and waited at the scene until a peasant in a horse-drawn cart came along and offered to drive them to a nearby town.

Veil goes typically heavy on the swagger, complaining that his only nourishment for several days were "those awful kerosene-vodka cocktails." Still there are enough references to using moonshine as "motor spirits" to believe that there were occasions when it went the other way.

In Moscow Eiduk was allowed to have an ARA Cadillac for his personal use. This was Haskell's decision, and it was about as popular among the Americans as allowing the chief plenipotentiary to occupy an office in the ARA building. It did not take long for the word to get around that Eiduk was giving the Cadillac a typical Russian workout; that is to say, he was abusing it. Kearney became so distressed by this that he wrote a memo listing the mechanical problems with the car—Cadillac No. 4—when it was brought in for repairs on February 23, 1922. His indictment of Eiduk reads as follows:

1st — Distributor has been neglected,—
  no oil, screws missing from cover—
  Resistance unit broken—had piece of wire to make
  connection, which could have burnt out coil.

2nd — Carburator Control rod screw missing.

3rd — Front and Rear universal dry—no grease—evidently
  has been operating in this condition some time.

4th — Oil in clutch—contrary to instructions.

5th — No grease in clutch thrust bearing.

6th — 3 Grease cups missing—spring shackle bolts dry.

7th — Drive shaft Pinion bearing dry and worn.

8th — Car in general, very dirty, has never been washed—
  shows plainly lack of proper care.
  The valves have been burnt and will have to be
  ground in; also brakes will have to be adjusted.

The odometer showed that the car had traveled 5,159 miles, this in 561 trips within Moscow over five months. The car had three different chauffeurs, and the ARA never saw it except every other day when it was filled with gas and oil.

Unfortunately for Eiduk, Kearney's memo arrived on Haskell's desk at a time when the colonel was feeling some heat for not standing up tall enough to the Soviets. He wrote a stiff note to the chief plenipotentiary, stating that the Cadillac had not been properly cared for and that from then on the car would have to be kept in the ARA garage and driven by an ARA chauffeur under Kearney's direction. Eiduk was to inform the ARA when he desired to use it. There was excited anticipation at headquarters that he might choose to fight this new arrangement, but apparently he did not.[8]

As the mission was nearing completion, the Soviet authorities must have felt that they were finally going to come into possession of the prize American automobiles. You can sense the anticipation. In mid-May Volodin, Lander's assistant, asked Phil Matthews to intercede on his behalf with Haskell in order that he might acquire the ARA Cadillac sedan "as a gift for his services to the A.R.A."

"Of course, I know there's not much chance of my getting it, but take it up with the Colonel anyway, kidding like," importuned the ex-resident of Boston.

Matthews raised the matter in joking fashion with Haskell, who cursed the idea. A few days later Volodin telephoned Matthews, who told him he was not about to inherit the Cadillac sedan.

Volodin kept probing: "Well, I thought he would like to give me a car so that when he comes to Moscow again he will always have a car to ride around in. I will keep it for him." This was but a taste of things to come.

The ARA had other plans for disposing of its property, which the Riga Agreement stipulated could be transported out of Russia at no cost. As part of its "liquidation" plans, in May 1923 Moscow headquarters ordered the districts to sell off ARA motor vehicles to the highest bidders, government or private, setting minimum prices for each model.

As if according to a plan, Lander's plenipotentiaries took measures to block private sales in their districts by intimidating potential buyers, prompting a number of district supervisors to complain to Haskell. Among them was Harrington in Ekaterinoslav, where Skvortsov was also holding up the sale of ARA typewriters to local banks and government institutions. To Moscow headquarters all the evidence pointed to a campaign directed from Lander's office.

Particularly flagrant behavior was reported out of Samara, where the government representative Karklin had refused to provide the ARA rail service for shipping out its motorcars. In Moscow Ellingston said that Karklin was "practically confiscating A.R.A. automobile transportation." After the matter was taken up with Lander, a letter came back from one of his assistants—Reichman, a Lett—supporting Karklin's action. "This called for fight, of course, and the Colonel had a show down with Lander."

"Have we or have we not the right to sell our motor transportation as we please?" he asked.

"You have," said Lander.

"Have we or have we not the right to sell any typewriter, chair, pencil or anything else we bought with our own money in Russia or outside Russia as we please?"

"You have," repeated Lander.

"Have you or have you not sent out to your districts any instructions to the effect that we have not this right and that they should see that we didn't use it?"

"I have not," said Lander.

The colonel asked the last question three times, and each time Lander said it wasn't so.

On the next day came a thunderbolt: a messenger hurried from Simbirsk with a copy of Lander's confidential instructions to his plenipotentiaries to prevent the sale of ARA automobiles. The Simbirsk ARA had come upon a copy—probably the work of a friendly spy—and dashed it off to Moscow.

Ellingston said it exemplified Soviet "lack of honesty" and "underhandedness" and hoped that the colonel might use it in an official letter to Kamenev to "arraign" the government. For the moment Haskell was unsure of whether to confront Lander with it; he did not, and in the end the Soviet government never learned that it had come into ARA hands.

In the face of ARA resistance Lander decided to try a different tack. He wrote to Haskell asking the ARA to consider donating its motor transport to the Soviet committee for dealing with the consequences of the famine, the Posledgol. So important was the matter that he asked Haskell to submit the request to Hoover. Apparently the thought of having to go about on foot had sown panic around Lander's office. He fawningly appealed to the ARA's "interests in preserving the popularity which you at present enjoy among the population."

I presume that this is not difficult, since the ARA's motor transport has seen a great deal of service, is much worn and its sale would hardly fetch much money; in any case the money would not be in any way commensurate with the proportion of the contributions and donations which have been made. . . .

You will understand, dear Colonel Haskell, that I shall await with impatience Mr. Hoover's reply.

Haskell was having none of this but was agreeable to selling the ARA fleet exclusively to the Posledgol at the right price. However, his mind was made up that there would be no charity for Samara, where Karklin had been a constant headache since autumn 1921.

Haskell wrote to Lander that "no matter what might be done in other districts no special consideration will be extended in Samara where we have constantly failed to obtain the cooperation guaranteed by the Riga Agreement, and where a spirit of friendly co-operation has never been apparent. Mr. Karkline's attitude from the beginning to the end of our operation in Samara has been hostile and obstructive."

In the end virtually all the remaining motor transportation was sold to the Posledgol—$100,000 for ninety-five vehicles, "an excellent price," according to Ellingston. "The Colonel finally proved to Lander and Volodin that he meant business in the sale of these machines and they came through on the dot and most meekly."

When Haskell went to collect payment, Lander and Volodin thanked him in the name of the Posledgol for selling the autos at such a reasonable price. Six cars were still in use in Moscow and had not been sold, though the ARA had set a price for their purchase. Lander asked if Haskell wouldn't consider simply throwing in the unsold six vehicles. Haskell replied he would not. "Whereupon Lander pulled his hand out from under the desk and handed over a check for the sum in question to the Colonel."[9]

CHAPTER 30

PLAYING THE GAME

The ARA Americans could not escape the entanglements of politics in Soviet Russia, not even on holidays. In fact, Bolshevik holiday celebrations proved to be occasions for heightened tension in the mission, especially the two main political holidays, November 7 and May 1.

On both November 7, the anniversary of the Bolshevik seizure of power, and May Day across Soviet Russia there were parades and demonstrations in cities and towns, with banners and speeches heralding the extraordinary achievements of the Revolution and rallying the population to the heroic tasks still ahead in the building of socialism. A good deal of energy was devoted during these celebrations to preaching vigilance against the foreign exploiters and imperialists, who would use any means to attempt to turn back the clock of history and overthrow the world's first proletarian government.

Childs was in Kazan for the November 7, 1921, festivities. On the eve of the sacred day he and his ARA colleagues sat in the opera house listening to the speeches of the local leaders who were singing the praises of Soviet power. "It seemed strange that I should be present at a meeting where the war in which I [had] engaged should be characterized as one of imperialism and that the American government as well as those of France and Great Britain should be described as bourgeois governments united to oppress workers."

One of the speakers was the local Party chief, Karpov, who admitted, following Lenin's line, that the Soviet government had made many mistakes since 1917 but said that this was understandable for the first attempt to build socialism and that the road ahead appeared promising. When the curtain came down, Childs and his fellow Americans were left shaking their heads. "As one of us was led to remark after leaving the theatre it gave one a strange feeling to be attending a meeting in an official capacity which the police back home would have pinched in an instant after it had begun. This is one of the novelties of our position which I am enjoying immensely."

The Bolshevik holiday orator was naturally tempted to place the American Relief Administration in the context of the Soviet struggle to outduel the encircling imperialists. Here and there the ARA name was raised directly, but more often speakers condemned it by guilt through association. This provoked expressions of bitterness from the relief workers in their diaries and letters, but the irony of the situation was a source of amusement: while the Bolos decried the evil intentions of the foreign bourgeoisie, its American representatives were saving the starving in the land of proletarian dictatorship.

In the districts it happened that ARA relievers were invited as special guests of the local government to attend holiday celebrations, at which the Soviet hosts would launch into anticapitalist diatribes, seemingly unaware that the Americans might take their words as an insult. Some Bolsheviks had repeated the slogans so often since 1917 that they had clearly lost sight of their content. Generally the Americans learned to avoid such affairs.

George Cornick in Tsaritsyn wrote to his sister Elsie that he and his colleagues in the district had been invited to be present as "guests of honor" at the city's 1922 May Day celebrations, which they knew would include speeches "lambasting capitalism, etc." Instead they went on a motor boat cruise on the Volga and had a picnic lunch.

I was very much amused at one thing that I did see however. Children were present from all of the children's homes in the parade, and each home had its big red banner. I saw one of them the next day and it was quite interesting. On this large satin banner, red of course, was an inscription to the effect that there was no hunger at Children's Home No 78. But the interesting thing is that none of the people seemed to realize that if there really was no hunger here, it was largely due to the gifts from capitalistic America. But such is life in Russia.

In Theodosia two officers and eight sailors of the U.S.S. *Barry* felt duty-bound to attend meetings organized to celebrate the 1922 anniversary of the Revolution. One of these was a banquet at the International Seaman's Club, where the Americans found themselves listening to "Red propaganda" and to numerous renditions of the "International," during the playing of which they were obliged to stand. The tension was only partly relieved when the pianist broke into "Hail Columbia" and everyone rose, "evidently believing it to be our National Anthem."

The entire affair, down to the small talk, was awkward. A union official approached Ensign M. Van Cleave and asked through an interpreter whether the majority of Americans were Communists or "Maximillianists"—he no doubt said "Maximalists," but that is how the bewildered Van Cleave understood it or heard it translated. The same man asked about an American named "Gardine," who, after several quizzical backs and forths through a translator, turned out to be President Harding.

At one point the Americans were asked to address the meeting. Ensign W. C. Bobbitt reported that in their remarks they tried to avoid giving approval to the Soviet form of government but were helpless to control the interpreter's translation of their remarks. Bobbitt dismissed the whole thing as a great propaganda hoax: "it impressed me as a seething den of radicalisse."

Back home in the States the issue of Bolshevik propaganda was still red hot, and even in Soviet Russia there were several occasions when the ARA was moved to protest the treatment it received from Soviet speakers and journalists. There appears to have been no such controversy surrounding holiday celebrations. Still, the observance of official and other holidays did become a point of contention between the ARA and the Soviet authorities and gave rise to several incidents that came under the rubric of "government relations." The usual source of conflict was the ARA's determination to keep its offices running on holidays and the inclination of the Soviet government, central and local, to regard this as a challenge to its authority.

Caught in the middle were the ARA native personnel, most of whom were not sympathetic to Bolshevik power and were dedicated to the ARA, but all the same were not averse to observing a state holiday in order to have a day off. Murphy records that on November 7, 1921, although few of his office staff sympathized with Soviet power, "they are always willing to take a holiday just the same—'to mend our stockings,' one of the young ladies said." Kelley found that on March 18, 1922, the anniversary of the Paris Commune, "a Bolo holiday," the ARA Ufa office was nearly empty: "Most of my work force, although not devoted to the principles of Lenin and Trotsky, took advantage of the law to obtain a rest."

The Russians were used to observing an inordinate number of traditional holidays, chiefly religious. Before the Revolution they numbered 128—over a third of the year away from the workplace. No wonder a Russian proverb counseled, "Marry a wife who can read, and she will find all the holidays in the calendar." There seemed to be no good reason to pass up observance of the holy days of the new Communist religion, especially when the chief employer was Lenin's government. And the ARA native staff members, despite their loyalty, were on the whole not willing to sacrifice the celebration of traditional religious holidays, especially Christmas and Easter, each of which took up several days of the work calendar. Like most Russians they insisted on observing these holidays according to the old Russian calendar, no matter that they had already taken advantage of the official Soviet observance of the same holiday thirteen days before. A few years hence the Bolsheviks would give up on trying to enforce observance of religious holidays according to the new calendar. For now, though, the dual observance of an already large number of holidays ate further into the work schedule.

Murphy observed that "Almost every week there is some church holiday or a day which is connected with some superstition of the people." He was most intrigued by Elijah's Day, July 20, when a great thunderstorm was supposed to take place. Elijah had been taken to heaven in a chariot, and it was believed that he used it to roll around the heavens; every July 20 he was supposed to ride at a particularly furious clip, causing a violent thunder. Murphy records that on Elijah's Day 1922, a Wednesday, there was good weather, although there had been a thunderstorm the day before and a severe one on the previous Friday night. "No doubt the missing of the exact date can be satisfactorily explained by the faithful, for a matter of only two days delay is a trifle in Russia."

He tells us that on January 7, 1922, Russian Christmas, the employees at Moscow headquarters were not required to come to work. When he arrived at the office, he discovered that not everyone had taken advantage of the opportunity. For some, coming to work was an escape from a cold, empty home—"the pleasantest hours for them are when they are in our office." "One of these I told last night that she did not need to come around today, but she said she would be very glad to come if there was anything to do. 'It is more agreeable here than at home', she said, 'for I am quite alone and my room is cold. All of my family are dead—or shot.'"

By contrast, Easter 1922 found life returning to normal, and warmer temperatures helped to lift the mood. Easter is the grandest of Russian religious holidays, and the ARA men found it curious that the atheistic Bolsheviks made such a big fuss about it. All employees were let out of work for the observance, beginning officially Friday noon and lasting through Sunday but in practice beginning at midweek and extending well into the next.

Easter 1922, April 16, was an especially hectic moment in the ARA mission, and there was a good deal of American frustration that so few native personnel were willing to work. As Quinn informed London, "Hardly a single Russian could be induced to come to work, even those of Jewish faith."

The ARA went out of its way to show respect to religious observances, despite the hunger, but it had less patience for official Soviet holidays in troubled times. May Day 1922 witnessed ARA-Soviet tensions. Barringer was chief in Ekaterinoslav at the time. His local personnel there remembered that the May Day celebrations of the previous year had been quite elaborate, mainly because the Bolsheviks were still in the Civil War habit of enforcing enthusiasm. In 1921 all Soviet offices were closed for the day, and every citizen in a city or town where a demonstration was to take place had to participate. "Failure to be present to march in the parade brought imprisonment, fines, and even death," Barringer was told.

By 1922 the enthusiasm, official and otherwise, had faded, and Bolshevism was in ideological turmoil. Besides, there was a famine going on, and most ARA offices kept working. Still the Ekaterinoslav soviet ordered the ARA to close its offices for the day. Barringer told them that "if they could declare a holiday for the starving, we would declare a holiday for the famine relief workers." The work went on "in spite of lots of idle talk and threats by the Bolos."

A year later on May Day Barringer was stationed in Simbirsk. Again he declared that the ARA office would stay open, though with the ARA phasing out its operations he was not in a position to be so insistent about it. Besides, the occasion was marked by considerable international tension, and war talk was rife. A Soviet diplomat had just been murdered in Lausanne, and the British government had recently delivered an ultimatum note to the Kremlin over its perceived meddling in British politics. The Soviet labor unions called a demonstration for May 1, and the ARA native personnel were threatened with discipline if they failed to take part. In this atmosphere, Barringer kept the office open but advised his Russian staff not to come to work. Still, when the day came, he observed that the demonstrations were mostly confined to Party members, "while the ordinary citizen looked on amusedly from the sidewalks."[1]

There were similar minor confrontations in other ARA districts, but the only incident of potential consequence surrounding the observance of May Day 1922 occurred at the Moscow district, as opposed to mission, headquarters, where Raymond Tourtillot directed the food remittance division. Tourtillot had studied for two years at Stanford until the war came and landed him with the American Expeditionary Force in France. Exactly what he did after the war to enable him to avoid returning home is not known, but he did take a wife, who was waiting for him in Coblenz.

The Moscow district had fallen behind in its food package deliveries, and Tourtillot felt he could not afford to give the local staff the day off on May 1. Instead he gave the order to come to work, which not all employees obeyed, and this led to some disaccord at the office. It proved to be inspiring material for a hack journalist who wrote it up for *Pravda* on May 11 under the ironic title "Gift of the American People."

The author claimed that the decision of the ARA to ignore the international proletarian holiday had been intended as an insult to the Russian people. He also wrote that those employees who had decided not to appear at work that day had to face "the terrible judgement of the exploiters in the person of Captain Tourtillot and Mr. Renshaw." The Russian manager of the food remittance division, referred to as "comrade German," with a hard "g," was fired—this, because he failed not only to show up for work but to see to it that the other employees did as well. *Pravda*, the organ of the vanguard of the proletariat, came to the rescue of these unfortunate former ARA employees.

The article quotes Tourtillot telling his staff: "First, I want you to understand that I am the boss around here, and not you. Secondly, I recognize no groups and no collective protests and none of your collective decisions. I ordered you to work May 1st, and it was your business to work, for I am not used to having my orders disobeyed." These were probably not his precise words, but the general drift sounds authentic.

Mr. German wished to take the floor to thank the employees for their solidarity with him, but the Americans were accused of having prevented this, as well as having discharged him without the two weeks of wages to which he was entitled.

Let this be exemplary proof of the fact that the American, same as other European capitalists, came to Russia not in order to save the starving or to improve the workers' conditions. Oh, no! They weld chains for the working class, they are preparing the noose for him.

And, therefore, workers, be on your guard! If, due to economic conditions, due to our state of ruin, you should be forced to work together with the bourgeoisie of Europe and America, we must be on guard, and at their first attempt to throw the chains and noose upon us, we must do that very thing to them.

At the time that this sterling piece of Soviet journalism appeared in print, thousands of tons of American corn were making their way into the Volga valley. This was, if anything, bad timing. Only two days later, in an attempt to patch things up, *Izvestiia* printed an article over Eiduk's name, which served up glowing praise of American relief and was quoted in numerous subsequent ARA press releases. The ARA publicity department chose to ignore Eiduk's fervent expression of hope that the ARA's presence might pave the way for the establishment of official U.S.-Soviet relations. His closing paragraph referred to the Tourtillot incident as a "minor case" caused by a "misunderstanding." Comrade German came in for criticism for his lack of tact and for stirring up trouble.

Case closed—until June 8, when Tourtillot was back in the pages of *Pravda*, this time accused of firing two soviet employees at the ARA warehouse where he had been reassigned from the food remittance division, possibly as a result of the May Day incident. This second article accused him of letting these employees go because one was pregnant and the other recovering from an illness. The writer reminded Tourtillot that in Soviet Russia a woman was entitled to eight weeks of leave before and after childbirth. Why, he wondered, were these violations of Soviet law allowed to stand?

The ARA was permitted to respond with a rebuttal in the pages of *Pravda*, pointing out that the dismissals in question were the result of a general reduction of native personnel underway now that the famine had been defeated. Neither this article nor the internal ARA correspondence about it demonstrated a ringing ARA endorsement of Tourtillot.

In July the Bolos were finally able to score one on him. The Americans working at the ARA warehouse were usually authorized by the Moscow authorities to carry firearms, but Tourtillot's request for permission to pack a Colt .45 while on duty was turned down. No one at ARA headquarters seemed motivated to go to bat for Tourtillot. On a piece of paper attached to the Soviet rejection notice one of the American staff wrote, "Guess they figure him dangerous enough *without* a gun!"[2]

THE NOVEMBER 7 HOLIDAY was also less festive during NEP than in years past. The fourth anniversary of the Revolution came during an especially bleak period for the Bolsheviks, with the economy in ruin and the threat of famine hanging over tens of millions. They did not object when the ARA proposed to keep operations running through the holiday.

November 7, 1921, found Charlie Veil in Novouzensk, the heart of the famine zone. He arrived there in the morning with the task of opening ARA kitchens and commencing the feeding of thirty thousand children. What really transpired that day will never be known because the story we have was passed down by two champion storytellers: Veil told his tale to Duranty, who published it in the *New York Times*. Which of them deserves more credit for powers of imagination is impossible to tell. Duranty might have bought the product as is. One American observer of Russia, Professor Edward Alsworth Ross, said of him at this time that "as a swallower [he] puts Jonah's whale to blush."

In Duranty's article, Veil—whose name he spells "Weill"—and his interpreter, Pete—whom he calls Andy—arrived at 6:00 A.M. on an ARA food train. They were met at the station by the president of the soviet, who explained that the only automobile in the canton was out "scouting after bandits," but that horse and camel were available to assist with the work. Veil was then escorted into town where he was greeted by other officials, each wearing a "large red rosette" in honor of the holiday.

Once a suitable warehouse was located, a camel and horse train was organized to transport the food from train to warehouse, a distance of about four miles. By 10:00 A.M. a caravan several miles in length was proceeding toward the train. We are expected to believe that these beasts of burden, rounded up from neighboring towns, numbered two or three hundred camels and several scores of horses, so already the story takes on fairy-tale proportions.

The station was all confusion, with crowds of people and animals milling about and the situation on the verge of anarchy. That's when Veil took control. He climbed atop a fifteen-foot pole and shouted out commands in English, French, and German to the assembled multitudes. Both man and beast obeyed his instructions and proceeded to organize themselves accordingly. It sounds like a scene from the Bible.

By about 3:00 in the afternoon the caravan was loaded up and began the march back. All went well until about one mile out of town at a deep gully.

Here a veritable disaster occurred. Camel after camel toiled laboriously up the steep slope, but before reaching the top the strength of the underfed beasts gave out and with appalling groans they came sliding down again, all four feet outspread like skis.

It was excruciatingly funny to see the camels thus tobogganing, but at the bottom of the gully they met in a kicking, grunting, fighting mass, mingled pell-mell with carts, upset loads, tangled harness and cursing drivers.

A dozen camels and several horses are reported to have died from "sheer exhaustion," but the life-saving food was gotten through and unloaded at the warehouse. The end of the day found Veil and Pete exhausted and expecting to head back to their hotel,

but almost before they knew it they found themselves bound for the local theatre, where they were ushered to a seat on the stage amid beaming dignitaries with red rosettes.

The curtain went up to loud strains of the "Internationale" and with great applause from a crowded house.

Weill replied suitably through the interpreter, and the applause which greeted both speeches became deafening when the President announced that in honor of the distinguished guest from across the sea there would be a public holiday for a week and a fancy dress ball in the theatre every night for the benefit of the famine fund.

Chairs were cleared out, and everyone began to dance, garbed in their "picturesque Tartar, Spanish, Polish, Ukrainian and Russian peasant costumes." "When the weary American left the scene an hour or two later, the people were enjoying themselves with Russian enthusiasm, as if such a calamity as the famine had never entered their experience."

Thousands of miles away reassured *Times* readers could turn the page, smiling and shaking their heads in wonder at the carefree spirit of these mysterious peoples of the East—although a skeptic or two might have pondered the source of Spanish influence on the Volga.

One year later Fleming was in Moscow taking in the celebrations, which he described in a letter to Bert Wallis. Fleming had worked in Wallis's garage in Beverly, Massachusetts, on and off between 1917 and 1919. He told Wallis of the "endless parade" he had witnessed earlier in the day: a "motley crowd of people, tied up like immigrants to keep the cold out of their ears, parading under futuristic banners depicting the proletariat of England, France, Germany, and the United States, all on one banner, stretching out their hands from their native land toward Russia, where the united hosts of the redeemed are moving toward the Kingdom of Heaven—on the banner." But he saw something there that inspired him to suspend the smart-alecky tone:

There is, however, something admirable about the new independence of these people, in spite of their stupidity, their slip-shod methods, and their exasperating patience. I looked hard to find the workmen whom both we, and the Soviet government, have so much talked about, and found them, in the parade; a small number, but bony, hard, admirable looking men. The revolution has very much thinned their numbers; both by death in the civil war, and by the melting away of the working class to the country during the period when food was the first thought of every man. . . . I believe that the revolution has worked a distinct broadening in the life of most of them. I don't know, but simply state that from a guess, and from what I have heard and inferred. They feel rather like supers in the play that is being enacted in their behalf, but nevertheless they have the sense if not the reality of controlling their own destinies.

For the twenty-two-year-old relief worker from Beverly this is an admirable bit of writing.

By the fifth anniversary of the Revolution the famine had been conquered, and the ARA mission, much reduced in size, no longer wielded the same authority. The Soviet government, no longer feeling the need to handle the ARA so gingerly, in most places demanded that ARA offices close for the day. The Americans did not attempt to resist, and the only noteworthy ARA-related incident surrounding the observance of the holiday occurred in Petrograd.

District supervisor Wahren objected to the city soviet decorating the ARA building on Herzen Street with a red banner. He called this "propaganda" and refused to have the ARA be associated with it. It did not matter to him that every building on the street was to be outfitted in the same fashion and that the ARA, which did not after all own the building, was not being singled out. Possibly his sour relations with the local plenipotentiary, Z. Z. Zhukov, got the better of his common sense. Zhukov is described in one ARA document as a "rugged old sailor—big leader of Revolution," and he seems to have made a formidable government representative. After the ARA mission he became head of a factory for making playing cards, so it was said.

Apparently for a time the decoration of ARA headquarters was delayed, because George Seldes wrote that the building produced the effect of "a gap in the street like a missing tooth."

Zhukov described the decorations on each building as follows:

A red star illuminated by electric globes was fastened to the upper cornice of the building; the balustrades of the balconies were trimmed with red cloth and a garland of leaves, which was also drawn through the space between the balconies; finally a crest, representing a white shield in the form of an ellipse bearing the emblem of a hammer and a scythe and with the inscription "RSFSR" and "Workers of all countries, unite," was hung over the front entrance. The shield was surmounted by an illuminated red star.

Wahren wanted nothing more adorning the building than an ARA sign. Zhukov countered that his office was also in the building and that he worked for a government agency. Besides, he reasoned, the inscriptions and emblems on the decorations were part of the state coat of arms and "can be regarded as propaganda only in so far as one regards the fact of the Soviet Government's existence as propaganda." Which gets right to the heart of the matter.

Something similar had occurred a year earlier in Moscow when the local government representative walked into an ARA kitchen and discovered that the photographs of Marx, Lenin, Trotsky, and Zinoviev had been removed from the walls of the dining room and stacked in a corner. The liaison man asked the Russian kitchen manager about this, and she told him that an ARA Russian inspector had come around and ordered the photographs taken down, saying, "You are again engaging in propaganda." This set Bolo chief Eiduk on a regular war dance. He accused the ARA inspector of "deeply wounding the civil sentiments of the

population of the RSFSR" and threatened him with arrest. The portraits were
soon back in place.

In Petrograd the flap about the Red decorations was brought to the attention
of the central authorities in Moscow who complained to the ARA, and Wahren
was quietly advised to give way. And so the missing tooth was restored in time for
the big event.

Seldes says that these red banners, a yard wide, were flying all over the city
from end to end. The contrast with the recently fallen snow was quite striking.

But on November 6, with all the decorations in place, the weather took a turn
for the worse. The temperature rose, the skies grew dark, and, writes Seldes, "suddenly I saw drops of blood beginning to fall on Petrograd." Not blood, of course,
but Red war paint raining down on Trotsky's military parade.

There were red spots in the snow, then splashes of red showing the whip of the wind,
and then large areas of the snow became bloody red, as the wind ripped through the
banners and bunting converting the rain into splashes and sheets of blood. The grand-
stand in which we stood ran blood from top to bottom, and the Winter Palace was
red, and all the houses we could see were streaked, and all the snow nearby started to
melt in red pools. The new Soviet dyes were not waterproof.

Three hundred delegates of the Communist International, representing forty-
five countries looked on from under cover as through the red rain and red snow
marched the Red Army. Red propaganda, indeed.[3]

THE ARA AMERICANS marked their own national holidays, of course. They observed Thanksgiving Day 1921 with a wild ARA celebration at the Pink House.
On the morning after, Golder, who was probably the first American to rise, was
greeted downstairs by Pazhalsta, the doorman, who was scratching his head trying to figure out which American holiday had laid his boys out flat. "It can not be
Christmas, because that comes in December. Some say it is the anniversary of the
day when you became independent of France, and others tell me that it is in
memory of the time when you threw off the yoke of Spain. But it can not be the
latter because that happened about twenty years ago."[4]

The American holiday equivalent to the Russian November 7 was the Fourth
of July, of which there was to be only one ARA celebration in Soviet Russia. The
ARA observance of Independence Day 1922 had the usual noise and bombast
here and there, although in Odessa, where the Americans had access to fireworks,
there was less of it than had been hoped for because the American Navy sky-
rockets turned out to be mostly duds.

The Fourth of July offered an opportunity for the American personnel from
various districts to come together in celebration. The biggest part of their job
was behind them, and the ARA chiefs, having just completed their grand inspection tour of the districts, were having a powwow in Washington to decide the future of the mission; all signs pointed to an August departure. It was a good time
to celebrate.

On the Volga big doings were planned. Haskell had given his approval for a
major rendezvous in Samara of the American personnel from six ARA districts.

On July 2 six Americans set out from Kazan southward on the Volga aboard their private steamer, the *Pecherets*. They brought along the ARA Cadillac for land excursions, as well as a chef and plenty of food and drink. Childs says that the *Pecherets* was better appointed than most sailing vessels on the Volga, "for the berths of the state-rooms are upholstered in leather and the first class saloon is as well furnished and as comfortable as any of the passenger boats which are to be found in the coastwise service of the United States." In a letter to his mother he compared the ship to a yacht, about the size of those running between Norfolk and Richmond, only the *Pecherets* was better appointed.

The scenery along this particular stretch of the Volga was unexceptional. Vernon Kellogg traveled it during his pioneering ARA inspection trip in August 1921. A few penciled lines in his notebook record his observations: "broad sluggish—dirty water—sand bars. Cowhills or bluffs on west side—no lift on East side—*much*—*much* like the Colorado between Needles & Yuma except lack of the occasional cañon & real desert."

On the morning of July 3 the *Pecherets* arrived in Simbirsk, whose population was about two hundred thousand. Childs's diary notes that the city was "perched upon the high bluffs overlooking the right bank of the Volga," where the gilded domes of its churches and the towers of the old buildings rose "with some little majesty to greet the eye." He was impressed with the city, calling it one of the cleanest in all of Soviet Russia. Other ARA testimony confirms this feature of Simbirsk, which was also called the "city on the hill" and the "city of princes." Gregg visited in September 1921 and found it "surprisingly clean and pretty." Goodrich attributed its clean appearance to the presence of a university.

At the ARA personnel house on 12 Kirpichnaia, or Brick, Street, which Childs describes as a "large white stone building with Corinthian pillars which give it the appearance of an American courthouse," the Kazan delegation was greeted by Eddie Fox, who gave them the ARA tour. Childs says that he and his Kazan colleagues saw nothing to change their view as to the superiority of their own mission. Although he admitted that theirs was merely a "superficial inspection" of Simbirsk operations, still it "did not give us any cause to feel that our own work suffered in any way by comparison." He wrote proudly to his mother that unlike the men of the Kazan district the Simbirsk Americans had no idea about how to live in comfort.

The *Pecherets* set sail late in the day, counting among its passengers three of the Simbirsk mission, the remaining five having stayed behind to keep the wheels of relief turning.

The stretch of the Volga between Simbirsk and Samara was in those days the most beautiful of all. In later years the Soviet government erected a series of dams along the Volga, submerging riverside villages and turning much of the river, including this section, into a series of lakes. In the summer of 1922 riverboat passengers along this route looked out at rich vegetation along steep banks. Childs told his diary how "we sat up until late into the night to view the lovely colors cast upon the water and the shores by the rising moon."

One of the Simbirsk contingent, Alvin Blomquist, regarded this holiday trip as one of the highlights of his Russian experience, recalling the "splendid boat, a full-fledged steamer which we had all to ourselves." It was an occasion to block out the famine and all the difficulties with the government and enjoy "the camaraderie, the lolling on the decks to the strains of the latest 'jazz' records, the lubricants, and the freedom from all care," making it "a trip to be long remembered."

Someone on board, possibly Blomquist himself, preserved the moment in a photograph taken on the deck of the *Pecherets*. There half in the sunshine sits Childs in white Russian tunic; behind him stands Dr. Dear; to his left sits Henry Wolfe of the Samara district, which means that the photo was probably taken at Samara and probably on the Fourth. To Childs's right is a phonograph. It is impossible to detect if it was functioning at that moment, but if so, it was probably playing one of those jazz records that so inspired Blomquist. Perhaps this explains why Childs, with his strong distaste for jazz, wears a look of disgust on his face, which is turned away from the camera. Or it may just have been his natural shyness from which, he says in his 1983 memoir, *Let the Credit Go*, he suffered terribly and did not overcome until he was in his fifties.

On the morning of July 4 the sailing party reached the rendezvous point. Childs's diary reads: "Fourth of July in Samara of Soviet Russia! It is certainly the strangest Fourth I have ever celebrated."

The *Pecherets* passengers arrived to find eight—or was it nine?—Samara Americans, who reported the news that the Americans at Ufa, Orenburg, and Saratov had sent word that they found it impossible to get away from the office for the holiday.

Samara was a city of 175,000, like Kazan, but this was one of the few similarities. It was but a railroad junction on the Volga with little of Kazan's rich cultural tradition and none of the fine architecture or signs of former grandeur present in Simbirsk. The contrast struck all American visitors to the city, among them Childs, who remarked upon the "terrible filth and uncleanliness of the streets and of indeed the entire city." It was as remarkably dirty as Simbirsk was clean. "There are heaps of dirt and garbage on every hand so that one wonders whether the city has been cleaned since the Revolution."

The first Americans to the Volga in late summer 1921 had all noted the same thing. Mackenzie traveled through the valley at that time, and he found Samara to be the most depressing and poverty-stricken city on the Volga. He also called it "the Chicago of Russia."

Farmer Murphy added his voice to the chorus one month later, summing up his impressions of the place in one word: "Filth." "I am sure that during all my life Samara will remain with me as a synonym of dirty people, dirty streets, mud, slime, refuse. Walking through the public market was worse than traversing an ill-kept barnyard in wet weather. A children's home, where waifs are taken in, which I visited was more unclean than any pig sty I ever saw."

On the Fourth, Dr. Dear was upset that the Samara Americans seemed to be descending to Samara standards of cleanliness. For one, there were flies all through the personnel house, and he suggested that screens be placed on the windows. Arthur Ruhl was distracted by the flies in the Americans' quarters during his visit the month before: "saucers of dead flies decorated the dining-room table." When Ruhl returned in September, he noticed that the flies were gone because the boys had properly screened themselves in—possibly the result of Dear's July 4 prescription.

All of the Americans who could participate were now assembled, and there was no question that the day's activities had to include the national pastime. Wrote Childs, unrestrained by any Confederate bitterness, "it was necessary to complete the faithful performance of the Fourth by a game of baseball." Baseball on Independence Day was a certain thing—more so than any Marxist law of history.

Equipment was not wanting. Kelley says that when the ARA chiefs made their June swing through the districts, they distributed baseball equipment and tennis racquets provided courtesy of the YMCA. Harry Hand used them to propagandize the sport among the Kirghiz, who demonstrated a "lively interest" in the game. "Give the Russians enough baseballs and bats and the whole country would go mad over the sport."

In Kiev, according to a local resident, in the beginning of August 1922 the ARA men, whom he calls "fond of sport," began to organize baseball games. "They proved to be very skillful and threw the ball with great energy; if the ball hit somebody he remembered the fact for a long time. They moved and turned round with such swiftness that all other players lost their wits and forgot what to do." It fit the image of superior American speed, energy, and efficiency.

The Kiev rookie recalls how district supervisor MacPherson threw him the ball, which he dropped, prompting Mac to call him a "poor catcher": "I knew it, but could not help it, and it is impossible to expect us to play base-ball as well as did the Supervisor, who probably began to play it while he was yet a baby. Generally it seems to me that we, Russians, do not have a great aptitude for sports."

Of course, not all Americans are naturals. Not even Herbert Hoover had the touch. In his memoirs he recalls that he had been the shortstop on the Stanford baseball team during the 1897–98 academic year but did not stand out. Instead he became the team manager. As he remembered it, "The job of manager consisted of arranging games, collecting the gate money and otherwise finding cash for equipment and uniforms." This was the Chief's best role: he was the consummate general manager, fielding teams of famine relievers across Europe.[5]

Hoover stood alongside Warren Harding at Griffiths Stadium in Washington, D.C., as the president threw out the first ball on opening day of the 1922 baseball season. These were the kinds of details the men in the Russian mission could read in the pages of the "Russian Unit Record," which printed baseball scores and standings. They followed Babe Ruth's tumultuous season: on September 17 the "Record" reported that the Babe had been suspended for a third time for making unkind remarks about the umpires, bringing the total number of games he was forced to sit out to 49 out of a season total of 170.

In the World Series the following month, Ruth had a dreadful time of it, going three for seventeen as the Yankees were swept by the New York Giants. It took the Giants five games to accomplish this best-of-seven sweep, since Game Two had to be called on account of darkness and ended in a 3-3 tie, never to be resumed.

SITTING IN THE STANDS for this all-New York series was Harry J. Fink, possibly the most widely known ARA man within the mission. Fink was a former sportswriter for the *New York American* and a member of the Baseball Writers Association. The war took him from his beat on the Polo Grounds, and somehow he ended up going to work for the ARA as a courier between Riga and Moscow. This was about the distance between New York and Cleveland, a fifteen-hour

trip in the States, twenty-two in Russia before the Revolution. But in 1921 it usually took at least five days to make the five-hundred-mile rail journey between
the two cities.

Fink's principal duty was supervising the transport of ARA documents and supplies. One report says that it was not unusual for the courier to have in his charge
as many as twenty boxes of first- and second-class matter, some of which occupied
a separate car on the train and all of which had to be watched around the clock.
The job required "resourcefulness and energy," which Fink had in abundance.

Over the year-long period he served with the ARA Fink made the Riga-
Moscow round trip over fifty times. It was said that the thirty-five-year-old sportswriter, who stood six feet two inches and weighed 225 lbs., had been selected for
his well-known endurance. He acquired this reputation during the war when his
ship, the *Westover*, was torpedoed by a German U-boat in July 1918 on the Bay of
Biscay. It seems that Fink was taken aboard the attacking submarine for a brief
time and then transferred to a lifeboat. Somehow in making the leap from U-boat
to lifeboat he tore off two fingers from one hand; he was adrift with other survivors for ninety-two hours before being rescued. So Fink had endurance.

His name could be regularly found in the pages of the "Russian Unit Record,"
often in the context of his avidity for baseball. His prominence in the "Record"
was due to his role as courier. Despite all the references to the camaraderie of the
ARA men in Russia, in fact most of the Americans would never meet personally
until the ARA reunions in the 1920s, when they could finally match faces to the
names they had heard about during the mission from other colleagues or had
read about in the "Record." The Fourth of July gathering on the Volga could have
put a big dent in this had the Orenburg, Ufa, and Saratov teams been able to
come to bat.

But virtually all of the Americans entered Russia through Riga, and it was on
this, usually their first, trip that many met the giant, bear-like Fink, who escorted
them to Moscow. The uninitiated ARA man, full of trepidation about journeying into the heart of Bololand, looked to Fink as a kind of shepherd. He played
the role masterfully, procuring food and drink and other comforts for his charges.
To the green recruits Fink's performance seemed like miracle work and made a
deep impression on them.

George Seldes recalled in *Tell the Truth and Run* how he made the journey
into Russia in a so-called sleeper car, one with bare wooden compartments for
beds. "There was no bedding, no heat, no water, no food, no service. By great
good fortune an American courier named Fink was on my train. He bought huge
shrimps one day, a roasted chicken another; he cooked tea and coffee on his
stove, got the water for shaving and for washing. In Moscow, where I would have
been lost, he took me in his official car to the Hotel Savoy."

There are many accounts of Fink's legendary resourcefulness. When spirits
lagged, he entertained the Americans with stories and led them in song. Of all
the great ARA storytellers Fink was the greatest, no doubt taking advantage of
the impressionability of his tenderfoot audience.

George Cornick sized up Fink in a diary entry for December 19, 1921, when he
was en route from Riga: "Travelled in charge of Fink—a veritable giant, former
Bronx sport editor—now courier. Much breezy B.S., but with it all a very inter-

esting fellow. Had been torpedoed in war and was in boat with other survivors 4 days and 5 nights." That particular tale had two missing fingers to back it up.

Donald Grant associated Fink with an uplifting introduction to Russia. In his first letter from Moscow he described the activities aboard the train, where the Americans "sang some choruses and jazzes there, all to pass the time and kept ourselves cheerful, and all led of course by the chief bluffer, Fink." He describes Fink as "a large man, like a white Jack Johnson, . . . who has an inveterate habit of 'kidding'"—which is another expression for it. "He makes a good courier in one way because he can bluff his way through almost any situation, if all that matters is the mere getting through."

Even when he accompanied the ARA advance party to Moscow, his first exposure to Soviet Russia, Fink acted as if he owned the place. He went in a droshki to the Kremlin with several of the men, among them Shafroth, who wrote to his mother, "The guards refused to let us in even tho Fink, our happy-go-lucky fat boy and convoy officer, said he wanted to drop in on Trotski."

Haskell was strictly a straight-shooter and had no patience with bluffers like Fink. When the colonel made his entrance into Russia in September 1921, Fink was his escort. In his first general report to London on conditions inside Russia, in the middle of a long dissertation on famine conditions and the problems of ARA staffing, he felt compelled to say something about the Great Provider. "We met Fink . . . on our way to Moscow. He is a courier operating between Riga and Moscow. He told us with great glee that while in Riga this time he would take himself a wife who had agreed to marry him because 'he had gone into Russia.' The logic in this is too deep for me."

The colonel may have been further flummoxed, six months later, by an item in the "Russian Unit Record" announcing the birth in Riga on February 28 of "the Fink baby," weighing 9 lbs.

Reference to his marriage is made in the ARA alumni newsletter's 1929 "Non-Statistical Notes of the A.R.A.," where under the Riga heading we read: "Harry Jay Fink . . . Best courier in Europe . . . In the world . . . Treat 'em rough . . . Only man in world married three times to same woman . . . Advice . . . More advice . . . Innocents abroad."

Just how Fink bluffed his way through has been preserved for the ages by Philip Gibbs in his docu-fictional *The Middle of the Road*. The Englishman was quite taken with this minor character in the famine epic and seems to have regarded him as somehow typically American. Here Fink is called "Cherry," doing his "courier stunt" on the Riga to Moscow run. "I also boss this train, and make it move. When it stops, I make it move again. Sometimes. If I get out and push. I inspire terror among Tavarishes. When they play tricks I treat 'em rough. When they play straight I'm full of loving-kindness. It's the only way to get anything done by these lousy Tavarishes." What's a Tavarish? he is asked. "A Comrade. It's a nice way of saying Bolshevik. Call them Tavarish all the time. It makes them feel good. Human equality and all that punk. Have you brought any bug-powder?"

Fink shares his bully beef, pork and beans, tinned butter, and fresh bread with his human cargo. At each station he procures steaming hot water. At the Soviet border town of Sebesh, in no-man's-land, the Bolo officials approach, and Gibbs notices that they greet Fink with "a kind of forced amusement" in which there is detectable "a hint of fear"—they have encountered him before. "Perhaps it was due to the vice-like grip with which he insisted upon shaking hands with them; and the bear-like way in which he thumped them on the back." Gibbs must have sanitized his words for the reading audience:

"*Dobra den, Tavarish*! How goes it, old face-fungus? *Kraseeva*, eh? Fine and dandy, what? Well, *dos vidanya*, your darned old hypocrite, and don't you come poking your nose into my car. *Niet*! *No pannamayo*?"

He fondled the head Bolshevik's beard, patted him playfully on both cheeks, gave him a mighty dig in the ribs which took his breath away.

"That's how I treat 'em. . . . A touch of good humour works wonders with them. Look at those two young murderers! Laughing like hell! It's the first time they've laughed since I came this way before."

Gibbs looks over toward two young Red Army soldiers watching Fink "with eyes of wonder and admiration, between guffaws of laughter." Soon Fink is surrounded by a group of Russian porters and peasants, and he works the crowd like an American politician.

With time to kill at the border he takes Gibbs for a walk and gives him his first look at the famine's horrors in the form of refugees lying near the station, waiting to die.

Then it's time to move on.

The Americans on the train begin singing "negro choruses in harmony, and queer rag-time songs from the Winter Garden, New York." Fink leads them in the choruses and in college yells, exhorting them with his huge hands.

The train slows to a halt. There is no more fuel. The conductor and other officials begin the hunt for wood near the tracks, and Fink is out there urging them on with "shouts and curses and roars of laughter, and back-thumpings and general noises of encouragement to make them 'get a move on.'" From the train come the strains of Americans singing more "nigger melodies":

"Just hear that whistle blow!
I want you all to know
That train is taking my sweet man away
From me today
Don't know the reason why,
I must just sit and cry—"

An ARA press release from the winter of 1921–22 has Fink half-joking that although he can put his job over, "when spring sets in and the Giants and Yankees are trotting out again—gosh, I'll be homesick." He was spared some of the pain: when the ARA reduced its American staff in September 1922, he did not make the cut, so he was able to reach the Polo Grounds by the time the hometown teams squared off in the World Series. Perhaps he wrote up the games for one of the New York papers. You could look it up.[6]

BACK AT SAMARA on the Fourth of July, after lunch the Volga ARA men gathered on a vacant lot on the outskirts of town for their game of baseball, though they did not play a full nine innings. Childs says that "the duty was religiously executed of playing four innings or enough to legitimize the proceedings."

The teams were Kazan-Simbirsk versus Samara. Childs pitched—for the first time his life, he says—and his team won by a score of 12-7. The "Record" of July 9 reported a final score of 12-8. "The task for which we were there had been accomplished and the great American professional sport had been introduced upon the Russian steppes and within the shadows of the Urals in the Soviet Republic of Russia. Assuredly we had given proof of our patriotism!"

Childs boasted to his mother of his pitching prowess, never mentioning that he had given up seven runs in four innings. The former journalist, with his characteristic carelessness with facts, helped to obscure a potentially significant detail about the Samara ball game. He wrote in his diary that there had been eighteen Americans present—"enough to fill out two nines." The teams consisted of six Kazan and three Simbirsk Americans against nine "Samaratans." But this contradicts an earlier diary entry and a letter to his mother, in which he says that there were only eight Americans present in Samara.

In the larger scheme of things this is a minor point, but there are serious historians of baseball who will want to know if this was possibly the first game ever played in Russia by two teams made up entirely of Americans.

The answer seems to be no and is explained by the absence of the ARA Samara physician Frederick Foucar. Foucar was by all accounts a moody individual who did not make much of an effort to get along with others. Ruhl described him as "the only member of the group with whom there is any weakness on the personal side. His touchiness and disinclination for meeting people seem at times to amount almost to a sort of neuresthenia." District supervisor Allen told Ruhl that he had great respect for Foucar's medical work, with which his "personal eccentricities" did not interfere. Enough ARA men passing through Samara made note of it so that the "Non-Statistical Notes of the A.R.A." honored him with "Loss of temper of Foucar." His decision to sit out the July 4 festivities upset Dear, whose opinion of the doctor could not have been helped by the presence in the personnel house of several dozen flies.

Anyway, without Foucar the Samaratans numbered only eight. So who was the ninth player? It was the habit of the Samara ARA to have an "open seat" at their table for every social occasion, and usually a Russian was invited to occupy the place of honor, as was the case on the Fourth. This might have been some Harvard tradition carried on by Allen. It is possible that the Russian guest also filled in for Foucar on the baseball field.

In any case, Childs has it wrong. The shadows of the Urals do not reach Samara, and the ARA boys of summer on the Volga were one shy of filling out two nines.

This is a smaller matter than it otherwise might have been because at the same time, on the outskirts of Moscow, there was also a celebration of the Fourth with a picnic and a ball game, and there the benches were filled to overflowing with Americans.

The great event was reported with much fanfare in the "Russian Unit Record," probably by editor Farmer Murphy. The site of the big game was Kuzminsky Park, the former estate of the prominent Golitsyn family, located about a forty-five-minute automobile drive east of Moscow. The estate was thickly wooded and had a lake, but there was an open space "fairly suitable for a ball game."

The Americans and their Russian staff and friends arrived at the park in the late morning, and at once baseball practice began, after which a picnic lunch was eaten under the trees. By accident, literally, Kelley was in the lineup that day. He was on his way out of Russia for good, passing through Moscow, and he had expected to be on a train to Riga on the morning of the Fourth, but a wreck on the railway delayed his departure. After his ten days in a boxcar on the inbound journey the previous December, he could not have been looking forward to the trip, and the image of a wreck may have further unsettled him.

He offers a few characteristically dry observations on the festivities, which he described as an "old fashioned picnic. . . . A number of Russian girls of English speech were brought along to make it natural. We did the usual thing, picked wild flowers, ate sandwiches on the ground, and poked about the ruins of the nobleman's castle."

Then came the call to play ball. Teams were designated "Blue House" and "Outlaws." Automobile transportation had been provided for those Russian personnel who might wish to witness a genuine baseball game. According to the "Record" account, "scores came and the Americans were busy explaining all the different points of the game and the jargon of the coachers." The principles of historical materialism could not have seemed more arcane.

As the Blue House boys took the field to start the game, there came from among the spectators the crackling sounds of splintering husks. This sound, but for the venue, might have been mistaken for the breaking of peanut shells, but in this case it was sunflower seeds. No one who was at the game actually mentions this noise, but this might only mean that no one found it worth mentioning, so ubiquitous in the Russia of those days was the consumption of sunflower seeds. Russians were wild about them.

The American Quaker Edwin Vail called it Russia's "universal pastime." Millions and millions of them were shelled and consumed every day. "Eating sunflower seeds is an institution for which I can think of no parallel in America unless it be peanuts at a ballgame."

Kellogg's diary records his fascination with the mechanical process of the shelling: "Everywhere, everybody eating sunflower seeds—with constant cracking sound—putting the seeds into the mouth *quickly* one after another—manipulated by tongue and teeth alone—the seed cracked side to side, the hull removed in two pieces and blown out of the mouth. Some food value = starch and oil."

Not a few American relief workers mastered the technique and sooner or later grew disgusted at their own addiction. Murphy had read about this Russian practice before the mission, so he was not surprised by what he saw:

It is completely true about the lower classes munching sunflower seeds. The streets are littered with the hulls. The eaters are quite expert, being able to break the hull with their front teeth, extract the kernel with the tongue and spit out the hull with one quick motion. Vendors squatting against buildings or standing at corners sell the seeds by the glass. The streets are lined, you might say, with women and girls and old men selling all sorts of edibles from sunflower seeds to poppy seed cakes and disgusting looking candies.

On a dock in Samara in September 1922, Fleming watched the stevedores unloading these seeds, reaching into torn sacks and grabbing them by the handful, leaving some sacks as much as half empty. He compared the Russian sunflower seed craze to the popularity of chewing gum in America.

At Novouzensk, when Veil heard the local soviet chief announce a week of holidays in honor of his delivery of ARA child-feeding supplies, he assumed that in celebration of the arrival of food for the children the adults could "chew the eternal black sunflower seeds."

The Moscow authorities grew so alarmed at the quantity of husks in public places that in the autumn of 1924 they passed a decree forbidding the chewing of sunflower seeds on the streets. An Englishmen who was there at the time wrote a few years later: "The effect was almost magical; the streets became at once, and still remain, more free from litter than anywhere I know and the sellers of sunflower seeds almost disappeared."[7]

As for the ball game at Kuzminsky Park, it seems to have come off well enough and even included a kill-the-umpire scene, described by the "Record" reporter: "The game almost broke up in a row when the Bluehousers got peeved at a decision of the umpire, Mr. Porter, threw down their gloves on the ground in approved style and threatened to quit. After growling around a while, however, they decided to continue."

The mood even infected Kelley, who confessed to "cavorting about second base with much fun." He left before game's end, returning to the city in the expectation of catching the 7 P.M. train for Riga, but when he got to headquarters, he learned that there would be no train.

His place was taken by John Mangan, who had problems of a different kind that day. A false rumor led him to the wrong picnic site, and he spent several hours driving around the outskirts of Moscow with some office boys and a pet bear in search of the celebration. "He arrived only after the ball game was half over, hungry and in no mood for jokes."

The final score was 13-12 in favor of the Outlaws. The box score was lost, and there is no record of how many innings were played. There were no parades, no banners, no speeches or slogans, other than the usual exhortations and some infield chatter.

ONE YEAR EARLIER, the Bolshevik leaders could not have imagined this. They were braced for an onslaught of bourgeois propagandists who would preach the wonders of the capitalist system and, using the weapon of food, try to turn their beneficiaries against Soviet power. The most paranoid Bolsheviks feared that the Americans would even try to smuggle in machine guns among the relief supplies. But over the course of several months they came to realize that the American relief workers were not interested in politics and that they were playing the game squarely.

This did not spell the end of trouble, though. The Americans could not avoid trouble because "politics" unavoidably infused the entire mission. It crept into every aspect of the American relief workers' daily lives: from whom they hired to whom they fed and clothed to how they toasted, even to what and how they drove. Every day was a struggle to maintain independent control over their operations, which in Soviet Russia meant a "political struggle."

Barringer wrote thoughtfully about this at the end of the mission: "The curse of the present ruling 'opportunists' is that they convert everything, yes, even life itself, into politics. That we were not interested in the country politically was beyond their understanding." He assumes the point of view of an ARA Russian employee, though the voice is unmistakably American:

What is to be done with the American who is not only politically impartial, but who dislikes politics to the extent of not knowing more about them than is good for any ordinary mortal? During the course of a day's work, this American will, in his innocence, say and do things which, if he were a Russian, would cause him to be fired in more than one sense. How is one to keep out of politics if the first thing in the morning, full of vim and go, he meets a Russian official, who is also full of vim and go, and who being a healthy animal with natural fighting instincts would like to show the American what he can do? Here are two men rearing to go at each other out of what is called mere "joie de vivre." The American is burning to impress the Russian with the latter's lack of efficiency, to call him down from the clouds and to inspire some common sense into him, whilst the Russian is all afire to point out to the American that his political education is sadly neglected and that he is only a member of a miserable, humanitarian, bourgeois old show. The ensuing fight is a most interesting sight to witness, though generally the only witnesses are a couple of clerks, or boys, and the interpreter. Never mind the boys, but God have mercy on the interpreter!

Childs was arguably the most politically self-conscious of all the ARA Americans, but his self-styled Wilsonian idealism, far from getting him into trouble with Soviet power, seems merely to have blurred his vision of its realities. In fact his political orientation seems to have had less to do with faith in the ideals of Woodrow Wilson than with his own personal idiosyncrasies. He used Lee and Wilson and Lenin to set himself apart and to rationalize his nonconformity.

In an unpublished memoir from the 1970s called "Behind the Scenes of History," he quotes a remark made to him many years after these events by an old childhood playmate: "You were never really one of us as a boy; you were apart from us and never merged your identity with the group." Childs agreed: "My reserve and introspection have plagued me all my life." In Russia Childs served with the ARA, but he was never one of the boys.

His exit from the mission in December 1922 saved his reputation within the ARA, for he was not in Kazan when a bombshell dropped the following June.

As operations drew to a close, Moscow headquarters detected irregularities in the way John Boyd was wrapping up the Kazan show. Among these was the generous deal he made with the government for the sale of the ARA motor transport, a fact which, Moscow headquarters informed him, was a cause of "grave concern." So executive assistant Phil Matthews and a team of Americans was sent from Moscow to investigate.

What they discovered far exceeded Moscow's worst fears: the local government was in complete control of Kazan operations. The three successive district supervisors, Wahren, Childs, and Boyd had been, according to Matthews's report, "three weak sisters who hadn't guts enough to tell the truth to either the Government or to us in Moscow." Muskatt's successor as plenipotentiary, Zeidner, a Lett educated in England, ran the show, dominating Boyd and the ARA office.

Worse for Boyd, he was dominated by a woman. This was Zina Galitch, his secretary, "a woman with whom his social relations were intimate to say the least."

She was found to have "exerted undue influence on Mr. Boyd and the A.R.A. in Kazan to such an extent that the A.R.A. was referred to in Kazan as Galitch & Company."

Other findings included insufficient American inspection in the district; improper use of ARA food packages, such as awarding them to Zeidner's men, and also to a shoemaker and a tailor in return for special services; and falsifying reports to Moscow. Kazan headquarters was said to be "honeycombed with informers or government agents," among them Simson, Childs's former interpreter, who is called a "spy."

Boyd was judged to have "not conducted the work of this District efficiently nor to the best interests of the A.R.A." It was noted, however, that in many instances he was simply continuing practices established by his predecessors, Wahren and Childs. The gaff had been blown on the "fair-haired child" of the ARA.

Barringer, Fox, Shafroth, Coleman, Allen, Kelley, Bell, and so on—these were the ARA "boys." Even the high-flying Charlie Veil, whose outrageous personal behavior eventually got him expelled from the mission, was, despite all his excesses, more typical of the general run of ARA reliever than Childs. Veil wanted nothing to do with the game of politics and preferred to drink the vodka cup of peace with the Bolo chiefs.

In his autobiography, *Adventure's a Wench*, he recounts a scene from his Novouzensk sojourn when he went door-to-door inspecting peasant huts and observing the pitiful conditions within. Tovarishch Chaparov, the government representative, became uneasy at this and would protest, through Pete, every time Veil entered one of these sorry dwellings that the inspection was unnecessary and try to "lure us back to his home and his vodka." Chaparov, said Veil, did not want the "black side of Communism" shown to a visiting American. "'Tell him to shut up or go to hell!' I told Pete. 'After we have fed these starving children I'll play politics with him, or chess or polo or anything else he wants. But I won't play politics when these kids are dying in front of my eyes.'"

The venerable Coolidge, who did not belong to this new breed of efficiency expert, was very conscious of Russian-American contrasts. When he stepped down as head of the ARA's liaison division in February 1922, he wrote a final report that documented the Kremlin's slowly melting suspicions toward the ARA. "One thing that as time went on helped to strengthen our position was the obviousness of the fact that we were not carrying on any political game." In fact most of the ARA men "knew and cared surprisingly little about the political conditions around them. To be sure they had scant sympathy for communist theories, but they were not bothering about such matters but only about food relief."

Actually there were a number of things that could divert the ARA man's attention from food relief, but politics was not one of them.

Two months after Coolidge's departure from Russia came the great corn drive that saved many thousands of lives and gave the autumn harvest a fighting chance. The ARA had delivered on its promise, putting beyond any doubt that its primary purpose was indeed famine relief. By the time of the Fourth of July 1922 the Bolsheviks were hardly surprised to see an entirely nonpolitical holiday celebration. To be sure, the Americans did gather at the former estate of a Russian aristocrat, but when they got there the only demonstration they organized was a curious ritual involving oversized gloves, a wooden club, and a white spherical object. It may have been the opium of the people in the United States, but it did not threaten Soviet power.

The Americanist Dixon Wecter wrote of the returning doughboy: "Statesmanship he did not understand; domestic politics was apt to bore him. . . . He preferred baseball." The boys of the ARA were typical of their generation. And when the corn got through in the nick of time and against considerable odds in that spring of 1922, they could say that they had put their show over in big shape. The success of their mission was assured, and this gave them a profound sense of satisfaction. Eddie Fox echoed the sentiments of his fellow relievers across Soviet Russia:

[T]he deathly former silence of the villages has been broken by the laughter of children, people who lay formerly at death's door are now being pulled through and while there may be no joy in Mudville since the Mighty Casey struck out, a happiness and content reigns in the many Mudvilles scattered throughout Simbirsk.[8]

Left: James Rives Childs.

Below: Murphy and his "harem": the food remittance division, Ekaterinoslav.

Right: Eddie Fox, flanked by, *left*, Richard Rein and Stephen Chernikh, Simbirsk, 1922.

Below: American relief workers at Simbirsk. *Left to right*: Thomas Barringer, Alvin Blomquist, Mark Godfrey, James Somerville, and William Otis.

Above: Corpses in transit to the morgue.

Left: Walter Coleman, Moscow, June 1922.

Above: Small village between Ufa and Sterlitamak.

Right: William Kelley, *center*, enjoying the company of Bolo chief Savelev, *right*, and an unidentified official, Ufa.

Left: Achmadullah, garbed in a Caucasian (or Circassian) costume, Sterlitamak.

Below: The ARA garage, Moscow.

Above: A main street in
Kazan, spring 1923.

Right: U.S. sailor and
Red Army soldier,
Novorossisk, 1922.

Left: Harry J. Fink, Moscow.

Below: A main street in Simbirsk.

Top: Moscow *droshki*.

Bottom: William Kearney,
alongside Haskell's machine.

PART FOUR

MASTERS OF EFFICIENCY

Youthful America Confronts Eternal Russia

Our objective was to establish a rush business organization on American
lines,—the terrain was the tortuous one of bureaucracy, with commissars,
military law, red ink, visas, stamps and bitter poverty thrown in.
—Kenneth Macpherson, Kiev, 1923

The Slavs were a people entirely unknown to us; and as such, their methods
of reasoning; their channels of thought; their social, economic, and business
policies; their religion, and their manner of life—and death—revealed a new
chapter in the lives of all of us.
—Alvin Blomquist, Simbirsk, 1923

CHAPTER 31

A TASTE OF POWER

During his pioneering ARA inspection tour of the Volga valley in September 1921, Vernon Kellogg examined a number of children's homes. He spoke about one of them in a talk he gave at New York headquarters the following month. His lecture notes recount his entering a "very bare room—all around on the floor, against the walls and out in the middle of the floor but mostly against the walls, were tiny little children with shaved heads." Most of the children had the swollen "hunger belly" from eating grass.

"What do the children do here? Do they sleep here?" he asked the two female administrators, also with shaved heads, who answered in the affirmative. "You mean you bring in mattresses for them to sleep on?" "No, we have no mattresses. They sleep on the floor leaning against each other."

Nothing in Kellogg's description—certainly not the sleeping arrangements—comes close to equaling the horrors of these children's death homes as described by countless other witnesses or even elsewhere in Kellogg's own testimony. Still, something about this place, something not spelled out in his notes, distressed him, made him feel that it was "almost impossible that the thing can go on." As a representative of the American Relief Administration he had it in his power to see that it did not. He informed the two women that relief was on the way, that "the next day or certainly by the day after that they would have some meal, rice, flour, etc., for all these children." Upon hearing these words, the women "simply broke down and cried hysterically. Could not believe that as they had gone so long in this situation that somewhere out of a clear sky had come the kind of food to keep the children alive. . . . Could hardly believe that this food was to begin day after tomorrow because two or three Americans had come out of the sky. It was simply too much."

Such scenes were repeated hundreds of times across the Russian famine zone during the subsequent eight months. After years of war and deprivation, fear and suffering, the famine made death appear imminent, indeed preferable to further horrific dying. But then suddenly, as if from on high, there appeared these strangers bringing word of salvation.

Bill Kelley rolled into Soviet Russia in an ordinary freight car, then secured a private car for the trip to Ufa, where he arrived on New Year's Eve 1921. A few days after his arrival he joined district supervisor Walter Bell on an inspection tour, through the city's snowbound streets, of the American kitchens. Making the rounds for the first time was an eye-opener for every tenderfoot relief worker, and Kelley was, as usual, all eyes. "In the first kitchen I saw a tot who had been deserted by its mother. It was standing beside the stove sticking out its tiny hands to warm them and whimpering in a soft voice. I swear the kid could not have been two and a half years old. As I stopped to look, it tottered over and clung to my coat." Kelley was fascinated by the behavior of the children caught up in this great calamity. Himself loath to express emotion to his correspondent, he wondered at the impassiveness of the little ones, such as those he observed at the next destination:

When we entered the kitchen there was immediate silence, just as when the school superintendent used to visit our classroom. I walked down the long line of 200 kids looking at each one closely. Not a one smiled or showed any feeling whatever. You can't imagine how stolid these kids have come to be—very, very few are heard to cry. They stand in line for their cards, move past the counter, take their food to a bench and eat every grain of it without uttering a sound.

During Kelley's inaugural weeks in Ufa, an item appeared in a local newspaper about a woman and four children in especially dire straits. "This is only one case in thousands that happened to come to our attention," but something about this one moved Bell. He ordered that five rations be sent to the family and some time later took Kelley along to investigate.

They found mother and children living in one small room of a small building, which may once have been a servants' quarters set back behind the main house. Three of the four children were under four years of age; the only girl Kelley guessed to be about ten. "They were pretty kids, but oh, so white and expressionless—not a move from them while we were there. They simply stared at us." Their father was in the hospital, probably a typhus victim. To most Russians even in nonfamine times a hospital was where you went to die, so his return would not have been expected. The mother, "in tears, apparently on the verge of a collapse," stood before the Americans dressed in rags, having sold her clothing for food. She told them that for some days her family had been without food and without wood for the fire, the furniture having since been exhausted as a source of fuel.

When all hope was gone, they had prayed, as the little girl had assured her that God would hear their prayers. Then the American food had come with the promise that it would continue until the children were well enough to come to the Kitchen. We comforted her as best we could and tonight have sent down sweaters, blankets and socks from our small stock of Red nCross supplies as a Xmas gift.

God had indeed heard their prayers. "The poor woman twice dropped to her knees and tried to kiss Bell's feet."

Bell and Kelley as God's instruments, as "messengers from heaven"—it was imagery used by many Russians, to whom the unheralded American relief workers seemed to have come down from the sky. The historian Yakovlev of Simbirsk wrote that American relief was "as unexpected as if it were coming directly from Heaven." "As if by a Higher command," in the words of another memoirist. Possessions, friends, family, and finally hope had all been lost, "And then, as if by the stroke of a magic hand things suddenly changed," recalled Dr. Babayeff of the ARA Odessa staff, choosing an unholy image.

It was much more common to hear of a "miracle." To a deeply superstitious people struggling to survive a prolonged time of troubles and staring death in the face this word "miracle" must have carried more genuinely religious, or supernatural, significance than it does for people of a later day, who are ready to attach it to every improbable felicitous turn of events. One who beheld this miracle was the writer Kornei Chukovskii. In order to escape starvation, he and his family fled Petrograd for the countryside early in 1921 only to discover that the hunger in the village had by then grown worse than in the city. The peasants were eating "clay and mice and the bark from trees. They knew death even better than we and in three months time I returned with my family to Petrograd and to die."

Nearing the station, the writer, best known for his children's stories, came upon "what I took to be a miracle": two children standing on the doorstep of a building laughing. "I would not, could not believe my eyes. For three years I had seen no laughing children. Boys and girls I had been wont to meet looked like old men and women: wrinkled, gray and cross. But these children were standing up and laughing as if all the youngsters of Petrograd were reincarnated."

What could explain this? "Everyone was saying that from very far off, from some sort of America, a strange and not to be understood people had arrived."[1]

This was written by an *intelligent* in the former capital, where before the Revolution the presence of foreigners, even Americans, would hardly have been a cause for such excitement. To a great many peasants in the heartland, most of whom had never seen foreigners in the flesh, their coming at the apocalyptic moment could only mean that they had been "sent by God," an expression the American relief worker heard frequently during his travels in the districts. "Sent by God" because they were able to find even the smallest villages. For Russ Cobb this was the greatest reward of the relief work: hearing people say, after describing their tragic fate in recent years, "Then the Americans came."

"Out of the sky" might mean a place less ethereal than God's kingdom. "They seemed to us to come from another planet," recalled a Russian in Kazan, while Golder's reading of it was quite specific: "To many people here I seem to be a man from Mars."

Salvation had come to the Russians collectively, but at the individual level not all were blessed. You might receive a life-saving ARA food package while your apparently equally needy and worthy neighbor would have to go without. For some reason God had chosen to spare you. To the Petrograd artist Alexander Benoit the gift of a food package "seemed like a miraculous manifestation of Providence." Harrington at Ekaterinoslav wrote that "The delivery of A.R.A. food packages came as the Manna of biblical days." Barringer said that the receipt of one in Simbirsk was "nothing short of a gift from Heaven." This explains the absolute frenzy at the food remittance stations, described by Ellingston, where people frantically tried to push their way to the front: "If they could only reach the desk! It became for these people, half crazed by starvation and suffering, an altar of miracles."

After his return to America Arthur Ruhl wrote an article for the *New Republic* titled "What the Russians Think of Us," in which he quoted a newspaper in a remote Volga town discussing the speculation that had surrounded the Americans since the day "Kitchens appeared as if by magic." However mysterious the circumstances of their coming, there was no doubt that everyone would cooperate with them: "We Russians love miracles, believe in them and expect them. A.R.A. is miraculous. To interfere with it would be a sin."

Haskell had heard so much of this kind of talk over two years that it inevitably figured in his final "mission accomplished" message to Hoover in October 1923: "To the mind of the Russian common people," he wrote with needless qualification, "the American Relief Administration was a miracle of God which came to them in their darkest hour under the stars and stripes."[2]

WORDS ASIDE, it was the sight of Russians kneeling before them that made the American relief workers feel like the saviors sent from heaven they were proclaimed to be. Upon receiving their food package, a mother in Kazan commanded her children, "Kneel down, Kneel down and ask God to bless the Americans who have given us this food." To Childs it was a scene worth a hundred acknowledgment cards.

This image of prostrate Russia made heartwarming reading to those back home who liked to think of their relief workers as agents of "civilization" bringing light to the benighted Russian masses. "America is a holy name in Russia and Americans are regarded as super-beings," Will Shafroth told the Associated Press in June 1922 just after he had left the mission. "People fall on their knees and kiss the earth upon which the relief workers walk. The United States can have a solemn feeling of pride in saving the Russian race from extinction."

Shafroth's own serialized account of what he saw, published in the *New York Evening World*, dwelled upon his standing as an American idol in Bololand:

The simple peasant who would have died if he had not been fed by America, the mother whose children ate at an ARA kitchen—these are the people for whom we brought in the food, and they are the ones who will never forget. To them American inspectors were almost gods. I have seen them crowd around and fall on their knees trying to kiss my feet, because I symbolized to them the nation which was saving them from death. And I believe that they will always feel unceasing gratitude to the American people.

The Americans as God's emissaries, the Americans as gods—the two notions seem to have become blurred together in the minds of the ARA men. The Russians declare their intent to go to church to pray *for* the ARA or for its individual representatives, but just as often they are said to pray *to* it. The writer Philip Gibbs wrote that "the Russians spoke of 'Ara' as though it were God." When one of his docu-fictional relief workers ordered sleighs and horses from some small-town officials, "He spoke in the name of the A.R.A., to which they bowed their heads as at the name of God." Whatever was the actual significance of such reverential behavior—which was rendered still more ambiguous by the unintelligibility of the Russian words that accompanied it—it must have been difficult for these young Americans to resist its seductive power.

Henry Wolfe was no stranger to its temptations. In March 1922 while he was on an inspection trip from Samara to Melekes, the ARA committee in one village told him that the people who came to the kitchen "worship America as they do at church." Elsewhere he visited what he says was a Ukrainian kitchen where they were serving a fish soup that "only people in a very bad condition could swallow and which had the appearance of the paste used to stick up show bills back in the States." The arrival of the American corn intended to relieve this situation was still a few anxious weeks away.

Later the same day Wolfe was having dinner at the house of one of the ARA committee members when he was called upon by a delegation of women, who told him between sobs that without American relief everyone in the village would die before winter. Somehow he managed to calm them and send them on their way. This was followed by the visit of another delegation, this one of old men. Actually, "visit" cannot be the correct word: they "forced their way into the room where we were and fell on their knees making signs of the cross. They began to cry too and touched their foreheads on the floor. They wanted to worship the representative of the A.R.A. which they look upon as something all powerful and the only thing that can save them." All their savior could tell them was that the much-anticipated American corn was on its way.

Unlike the arrival of the relief workers the previous autumn, there was nothing sudden about the advent of the corn, which had been foretold in January and promised for late March. Dickinson was one of the ARA prophets sent out from Moscow to spread the word among the starving multitudes. He later claimed to have entered "more than three hundred villages," where he was welcomed by reverential local officials. "To them we were as the representatives of Joseph, sent ahead to herald the coming of corn."

And when the corn finally did appear—after a nearly catastrophic delay had threatened to cast Dickinson and the others in the role of false prophets—the scenes of rapture, or at least the depictions of them, had an almost biblical quality about them. In the words of Ruhl, "One could tell of whole villages which fell on their knees and bowed their heads in the snow when the first American corn arrived." And they did tell of such scenes—not only the Americans but very many Russians. An ARA Russian inspector narrated the story of the coming of the corn to a Simbirsk village in words translated for his American chiefs: "But then the long awaited day 27 April came, there arrived 5 cars of corn, but here there was not feverish celebration, but only one prayerful ecstasy, among skeletons standing on the edge of the grave they prayed, crossed themselves, and said Praise be to God, there has come a rescue from death by starvation for us and our children."[3]

There are perhaps hundreds of similar moments documented in the ARA records, but one that stands out from the rest took place in the village of Vasil'evka in the Samara district on the morning of April 11, 1922. Like the others it involved a moving display of collective thanksgiving by ecstatic villagers. The Vasil'evka story was well known within the ARA and preserved for the ages because it was "captured" on film by Floyd Traynham, the ARA motion picture man. He and his traveling companion, Harry Gilchriese of the communications division, had been assigned to compile visual documentation of the corn drama and were on the prowl for compelling deliverance material—which should at the outset make one suspicious about what they actually found in Vasil'evka.

Also along were George McClintock of Samara and the Rev. Edmund A. Walsh, a Jesuit priest and the head of the National Catholic Welfare Council. Walsh kept a good telegraphic diary, which indicates that on April 10, when the party of Americans arrived in its private railroad car at a nearby village, there were

"People on knees on ground waiting for us—tears—cries—prayers for the Americans." The next day they reached their destination, the "famine village of Basileivska": "We arrived about noon. Village waiting—all on knees—'You are our Saviours—We perish if you did not come.' Kissed our feet—hands—and touched foreheads to ground before us."

Walsh did not record the size of this congregation. Dudley Hale of the Samara district, not an eyewitness, wrote to Herter in Washington that there had been two hundred overwrought peasants in Vasil'evka. Perhaps McClintock told him this. If the figure was near accurate, it was insufficient for the purposes of Gilchriese, who relayed his account to New York in the form of a press release titled "A Tribute to American Benevolence."

In this telling, Gilchriese and Traynham are the sole Americans. They are met at the train station by a delegation of villagers who doff their hats and bow in greeting and then escort the visitors in wagons to the village, one mile away.

Upon their arrival at Bassilievka, Gilchriese and Traynham were stunned by the sight which met their eyes. Five hundred peasants, the majority of whom were women and children, were kneeling in a large open space in front of a church facing the road, and with outstretched arms in gestures of supplication, and with tears streaming down their faces they cried as they approached "You are our Saviours. We would die if you did not come. May God bless you and America."

The A.R.A. representatives begged the people to rise and refrain from this emotional demonstration, but they were so overwhelmed that they persisted in remaining on their knees, bowing their heads to the ground and crying out their thanks to America and Americans.

At some point the delirious villagers remembered why they had assembled there and rose to save themselves by lining up for corn. Still, "At frequent intervals one could see a group here and there leave their places on the line to come and kneel in front of the Americans to again express their gratitude.

"After they received the corn the recipients lost no time in hurrying to the windmill to have it ground while others rushed to grind it in their own hand mill."

Meanwhile Traynham's motion-picture camera was turning, and his Vasil'evka sequence ended up featured in the ARA's 1922 two-reeler, "America's Gift to Famine-Stricken Russia." Whatever impact this particular segment had on the film's contemporary American audience, for those who live in an age more skeptical about the moving image, the effect is deflating.

Those were not the days of as-it-happened journalism, and Traynham could not have had his camera rolling as the wagon pulled into town. With all the time he would have needed to set up his cumbersome apparatus it is unlikely that he and his colleagues begged the assembled to rise from their knees. No doubt the demonstration the Americans came upon was something like what Walsh and Gilchriese described, and it may even have been somewhat spontaneous. But the scenes in Traynham's film are stiff and stagy. A title reads, "Entire remaining population of the village found on their knees in thanks as first food is brought by the A.R.A." The camera pans slowly from left to right, and, sure enough, there are the residents of Vasil'evka, kneeling, hands held out in supplication, some bowing their heads to the ground. But it has the feel of a reenactment of the actual event with hundreds of extras, though fewer than Gilchriese's five hundred.

McClintock is seen weighing the corn allotments in the large tray of a scale suspended from a wooden tripod some eight feet high, measuring out a two-week supply for each in the long line of waiting peasants. Walsh wrote: "many people barely able to totter up to scales." On film an elderly woman standing at the scale holds the opening of her sack over the mouth of the tray as she and Mc-Clintock and everyone else apparently wait for a cue from Traynham before finishing the procedure. Clearly straining, the woman puts up with the delay for at least the few seconds from the point we see her until she visibly loses patience. Curiously, these awkward frames ended up in the finished film.

Walsh's diary tells of "children diving into mud to get grains that fell and eat them!" On film the children on the ground reach for grains dropped intentionally from the scales for the benefit of the motion-picture man.

This is followed by the most artificial moment in the film: a self-congratulatory exercise with one of the Americans, presumably the publicity man himself, working a crowd of beneficiaries with a toothy smile, violently shaking the hands of the mostly sick and elderly women. "Accepting the thanks" reads the movie title, but the American is positively grabbing for it while his weak and fragile subjects are obviously confused and agitated by his indelicate pumping of the hands. In a later day, Gilchriese would have been the one to plunge into the crowd with microphone in hand and subject his victims to the inevitable query, "How do you feel?"

Traynham's celluloid sucked the emotional content out of an episode that appears to have genuinely moved its American eyewitnesses. Gilchriese's melodramatic copy, with its Second Coming atmospherics, doubtless served the purposes of his publicity chiefs in New York. But for the ring of authenticity and a sense of immediacy to the event neither the film nor the press release can compare with the pencil jottings in Walsh's little journal.

For all of the surface cinematic appeal of Vasil'evka, the most affecting scenes in the culmination of the corn drama were more intimate and did not require the Russians to get on their knees. One of these can be found in the letters of Paul Clapp. At about the time of the rescue of Vasil'evka, Clapp was working what passed for miracles in the town of Uralsk in the eastern extreme of the Saratov district. On Sunday, April 9, at noon he was invited to the city hall to meet with a gathering of more than two hundred representatives from children's homes, kitchens, worker organizations, and the local government.

The selected delegates one after another thanked the American people for having saved their lives. A little girl only eight years old was the first to speak, and then followed several boys and girls. By the time the first grown persons spoke the whole group was crying like babies. Grey-haired men and women, little children, Russians, Tartars, Kirghis, all, from doctors and leaders to farmers, simply broke down. When you realize the suffering these people have endured, it is surprising that they are so touched by the appeals of these children. I believe the feelings I saw and heard expressed Sunday are the real feelings of these poor people toward us. It seems to me now that we have pulled them over the highest hill.[4]

AFTER THE SHOCK of autumn 1921 when the Americans came out of the sky, and beyond the emotional climax of spring 1922 when American corn delivered

Russians from death's embrace, there was the more enduring phenomenon of ARA celebrity inside Russia. It was sustained until the end of the mission, although it appears to have peaked in summer 1922 at the time of maximum American activity. By then it was associated less with the raw corn of spring than with the items on the menus at ARA kitchens, as well as with food and clothing packages, medical relief, and the personal activities of the relief workers.

It was in the cities and larger towns, where the organization's presence was especially conspicuous and American relief workers were usually in evidence, that the ARA produced the biggest buzz of excitement. Even here, just as in the smallest village, the ARA had little competition for the attention of local residents. Joseph Driscoll cited some particulars of its visibility in Tsaritsyn, including

hospital patients parading in small parks on fine afternoons, wearing ARA pajamas—boys comparing their ARA clothing with others—people lined up before ARA vaccine stations waiting for a "shot" of anti-typhoid or anti-cholera dope—refugees being fed in barracks, railroad yards, everywhere—and incidentally being introduced to a bath and a "shot." There's no doubt about it—ARA was the biggest thing in southeast Russia—the most talked of—and, taken by and large—the most popular institution in Russia.

Dr. Babayeff of the Odessa ARA staff observed that "the word 'American' has acquired a fascination and a weight in all classes of the population"; he was certain that "the remembrance of the work of the American Relief Administration will live for a long time in everybody's mind."

In cities like Odessa, the Americans became the objects of sometimes obsessive attention on the part of residents who had for too long been preoccupied with talk about politics and food—namely the surplus of the former and the scarcity of the latter. Now they could marvel at ARA energy and efficiency or gossip about the strange behavior of the individual Americans—how they dressed, drank, smoked, drove, spoke, relaxed, romanced—and it helped to take the mind off darker subjects and painful memories. Driscoll, in considering the local Tsaritsyn "conjectures and speculations" about the ARA, believed that these were

in themselves an indirect blessing to a people who had too long been brooding over their own particular troubles. Old women blessed ARA and ascribed the most fantastic reasons for its being among them—children yelled ARA whenever they saw an American—or an automobile of the ARA—old men formed themselves into groups and told each other all about the ARA—young women and men were interested also.

It was generally the children, once their hunger had been relieved, who demonstrated the most unrestrained enthusiasm. Harrington on several occasions passed little ragged kids on the street in Ekaterinoslav who, on seeing him, held one foot in air to show off their new "bootinkies" and let out a cry of "Ara. Spassibo!" Chukovskii, his Russian prose filtered through an ARA translation, recorded the impact on Petrograd's youngsters:

Soon in the children's language there cropped out a new word "Americanitza" meaning stuffed full. Children returning home panted "I am stuffed full by the Americans to-day". When they had thoroughly mastered their lessons they would say "We know our lessons the American way". One lad marvelling at the muscle of his play fellow, described it as "a real American wrist". . . . Is it a wonder that hungry fathers grew envious of quickly fattening children? We were proletariats but our offspring were becoming bourgeois, who would return home and boast "You munch cucumbers and potatoes but to-day we had hot macaroni and cocoa". Is it a wonder that every child wanted to take to its mother just one bit of macaroni?

Instead of "hoorah," children in Petrograd's streets yelled "Ahra." In fact the enunciation of the initials A.R.A. as a word, with a festive ring, was universal in Russia. The new noun spawned other grammatical forms, Chukovskii lists "Aravtsy; Ariitsy; Aravskii; Arskii." The latter two entries are variations of an adjectival form of "Ara"; the first two are nouns used to denote the people working in the organization. A *Pravda* article suggested that the Americans were called "arovtsy" while their Russian personnel were "ariitsy." Golder made note of a different classification: "Some wag has recently divided the population of Russia into: Ara-ites, Semites, and Anti-semites."[5]

This sounds like something that might have originated in Kiev, where the Americans decided toward mission's end to hold a contest for the best essay about the ARA, the purpose being to inspire local residents to document the organization's activities. The deadline for submission was May 15, 1923, and the prize was three food packages, an alluring trophy even in those postfamine days. It is impossible to guess the total number of essays turned in; the ARA archive contains a couple of dozen, most by current and former employees, some in their original Russian or German, others in rough translation, and all signed in code names like "Mushroom," "Crest," "Homo Sapiens," and "Non-American."

Considering the circumstances of their authorship, the essays are surprisingly critical of the behavior of the relief workers—as individuals, though not identified by name—for their arrogance, ignorance, insensitivity, and coldness. Such candor strengthens the credibility of the pro-ARA sentiments expressed in the essays, whose outstanding common theme is the absolute mania for the ARA in Kiev.

"Old Maid" wrote, "The word 'ARA' became the fashion and was on everybody's lips."

"Friend of America" remarked "that the ARA became the 'Idée fixe' of everybody, especially of the intelligencia."

"May Bug" thought that the effect was strongest on Kiev's children, for whom it was once fashionable to play "execution" or "shooting" but who were now heard to say, "Let's play Americans."

The essays convey a sense of the gossip-filled, rumor-fueled conversation at ARA headquarters, where the activities of district supervisor Kenneth Macpherson, known to all as "Mac," were the object of intense public scrutiny, from his alleged pugilistic prowess around the office to his rabbit hunts and other shooting parties. An ARA wedding—Kiev had five in all—was the talk of the town. "Without being aware of the fact, the Americans influenced the fashion," according to "Brun," who tells what happened when one of the Americans ordered a new suit at a tailor's, providing some of his old clothes to serve as a model. After filling the order, the tailor boasted that he was making suits for the ARA, which brought all the "swells" of the city to his shop to order their own suits. "All that was 'American' became the fashion of the day," wrote another contestant, "some shops even selling 'American herring,' which in reality the Americans never sent to Russia."

American influence extended even to the local theater, as "Brun" testified: "The A.R.A. occupied too much the imagination of the population and the enterprising theatre managers availed themselves of this fact and tried to suit the tastes of the public by having witty and humourous plays put on stage." The "Intimate Theater" staged a production called *ARA Packages*, whose plot might accurately reflect a new fact of the social life of Kiev in 1922: a daughter with no dowry cannot attract a husband until, unexpectedly, ARA food packages arrive and she is considered rich, is courted, and marries. The story line of a drama with the uninviting title *ARA Inoculation Point* sounds baldly didactic, having something to do with the need to be inoculated in order to be able to claim the last button in town. Another practice was the insertion of references to the ARA into standard works, such as Puccini's *Turandot*.

Music too was enlisted in the cause. A local composer wrote a solemn march in honor of the ARA. One Paul Herman came up with a musical tribute on the motif of the operetta *Silva*. It tells the story of how the ARA, "our idol . . . sweeter than an aunt, than a sister . . . undertook to warm the unlucky bourjois," supplied a dowry for every fiancée, provided work for "elegant girls," and gave the people rice, cocoa, and milk.

Herman's song drew upon the most familiar images and symbols of American relief, though it leaves out a favorite analogy: the ARA as the life-giving sun. "All at once, as a bright sun among the clouds, as a bright ray in a dark kingdom, shone to us the fairy 'ARA,'" wrote a Kiev *intelligent*. A more cosmic variation was suggested by the writer Mikhail Bulgakov, whose brother worked for the ARA in Kiev: "'Ara' is the sun, around which, like the earth, revolves Kiev."

Bulgakov divided the local population into three categories: those lucky ones working for the ARA and drinking cocoa, those lucky ones who had received flour and pants from America, and the rabble with no connection at all to the ARA. Cocoa was emblematic of the ARA throughout Soviet Russia. On cocoa days in Moscow eager students lined up at ARA kitchens, tin cups in hands, a scene that one American thought "would make a very good advertisement for Bakers."

These students were served lunch, and it was their principal meal of the day, as mornings and evenings they had to get by on tea with saccharine and black bread. Of course the main fare at lunch was not cocoa but the more nourishing, though far less tantalizing, corn grit kasha. Rice and bread were also staples of the ARA student menu, but it was the kasha that most often stuck to the ribs and, as the months went by, in the mind. The limits of its appeal were on display at a benefit concert put on by Moscow medical students, who performed their own composition, "ARAfskaya kasha," using their utensils and tin soup plates to mark the beat of the chorus:

> We sing to thee, oh ARA gruel,
> Our joy, our life, our daily fuel.
> *ARAfskaya, ARAfskaya, ARAfskaya* kasha.
>
> If lectures do not let us free,
> We leave them joyfully for thee.
> *Refrain*
>
> Oh, give us help in heaven's name!
> For one whole year we eat the same!

We sing to thee, oh ARA gruel,
Our joy, our life, our daily fuel.
ARAfskaya, *ARAfskaya*, *ARAfskaya* kasha,
ARAfskaya, *ARAfskaya*, *ARAfskaya* kasha.

To relieve the monotony, during the second year the menu incorporated local products, including potatoes, cabbage, onions, fish, and occasionally meat. And on December 25, 1922, when the Americans observed Christmas, the students were served a special dinner of meat cutlets, macaroni, tea, and—"a real luxury" —a chocolate bar.

For a people that dreamed of its bread as black, the American white roll was another distinctive feature of the ARA kitchen. As a boy in his native Kiev, the writer Viktor Nekrasov was a beneficiary of "Hoover's organization" in the summer of 1922. Forty years later he could still recall reading in *Proletarian pravda* about the war between Greece and Turkey and about the Washington Conference, and he also remembered the ARA's "snow white bread, soft as a cotton ball."[6]

Nekrasov mentioned the milk as well. Of all the symbols of American beneficence—corn, kasha, white bread, cocoa—it was milk and its associations with maternal nurturing that seemed to strike the deepest emotional chord. In Paul Herman's song the ARA provides milk better than a cow, an expression used by others who often had more than strictly physical nourishment in mind, as "Brun" articulates: "Russian children fed with American milk will have in their blood the germ of natural love to America."

Milk had another advantage over its alimentary rivals. Condensed milk in tins was part of the standard ARA food package. The labels read "Evaporated Milk"— words Bulgakov wrote in English in his essay. They were said to have sparked a sudden interest in Minsk in learning English. Accompanying the foreign script were wonderfully strange images to excite the imaginations of the children: Nekrasov never forgot "the labels on the cans with Indians and buffalos, which we avidly collected."

The concept of evaporated milk was new to the Russians, who were understandably suspicious as to its true composition. One rumor in Kiev had it prepared chemically from nuts. The Americans seem to have gotten much enjoyment from revealing this wonder of technology to the unenlightened natives. Hullinger wrote about such an experience in the Kazan district, where he visited the home of a peasant family: "They laughed with childish delight when I exhibited my can of condensed milk. They had never heard of condensed milk." They thought he was joking when he told them it would keep for an entire year. One imagines that had Kellogg sprung a few cans on his bedazed Russians at the moment when he came out of the sky in September 1921, the effect might have been fatal.

The cans made the milk mobile and extended its reach as a symbol, both geographically and temporally, even beyond the duration of the actual liquid itself. The tins were sold around, and as a way to draw business, enterprising store owners put them in display windows, usually stacked in a pyramid, often already drained of their contents. This was not a practice exclusive to food stores. An American in Ekaterinoslav reported in the autumn of 1922 that "In every window are cans of American milk. It is sold in jewelry shops and locksmiths' shops. It is stacked in the open market, and the price is very low."

By the time Fleming made his Volga inspection tour that autumn the milk cans were inescapable. In Samara he attended a wedding where they were used as cups for drinking punch, and he found that the labels were serving the Russians as "excellent writing paper." On the train from Samara to Orenburg he told his traveling companions bragging stories about life in America, boasting about "traffic jams" in New York City and "how the subway trains at 42nd street run on a headway of a minute and a half with five cars to a train"—an observation almost certainly inspired by the more deliberate pace of his present means of conveyance. Whatever his listeners chose to believe, they had already seen one thing they liked: "They were outspoken in praise of American condensed milk, with which everyone in these parts is evidently familiar, and gave yeoman assistance in emptying a couple of my cans."

However long the lives of the cans and labels and no matter how enduring the memory of ARA milk, the genuine article had to run out with the end of the mission. Not even the American cow could provide forever. Most places were going dry before the Americans had left the country and as operations wound down, just as the cocoa and the white buns and the kasha were being phased out. The loss was felt mostly by the children. One of these, a boy from Kiev by the name of Vania Serechin, wrote some verse on the back of a photograph of a children's home. It tells of how boring it had become to eat at the home without "Ara" feeding him: the kasha did not taste the same, rice had been replaced by millet, the noodle soup was no longer served with milk, and most depressingly, the cocoa was all gone. His closing lament is as much from the heart as from the stomach:

> *A kakao, a kakao!*
> *Gde ty, miloe moe?*
> *Ty sovsem, sovsem ushlo!*

> Oh, cocoa; oh, cocoa!
> Where have you gone, my dear?
> You've completely, completely disappeared![7]

FOR MANY OF THE AMERICANS in the Russian mission, having only recently served in the countries of Central Europe with the ARA or in the Caucasus with the Near East Relief under Colonel Haskell, this was not a first experience being the object of adoring attention. Harold Fisher's history of the ARA mission to Poland contains a sentence that could be adapted to suit any of these other operations: "The words Missia Amerikansky (American Mission) were a password anywhere,—at the front, through any line of guards, or even past the sentinels at the Palace of the Polish Chief of State." A relief official posted in Vienna remarked about the ARA's Gardner Richardson, "I have no doubt that if he were available for election to the presidency of Austria, he would poll a tremendous vote." Haskell says he was greeted as "a messiah" by the Armenians he had come to save from hunger.

A few years after the Russian mission, the ARA's last, at a time when these American ex-idols were still struggling to come to terms with life as ordinary mortals in the United States, Ellingston reminisced about their good old days of 1919 to 1922, when "they suddenly found themselves the one vital essential factor in the life of a continent. They found themselves the key pin which held the driving wheel of many a state's economy in place. Old men and masters deferred to them, governments rose and stood supported by them, trains moved for them, they broke laws and ignored revolutions, and above all whole nations of children thanked and blessed them."

The Russian unit being by far the largest of all the missions, the American staff of necessity included a good number of recruits with no background in relief work and therefore no previous experience at being treated as gods. It was more often the men of this background who proved unable to handle the sudden acquisition of power. Yet even the ARA veterans found that when it came to being a savior, there was nothing quite like the Russian show. It was unsurpassed in size—including the geographic spread, the number of beneficiaries, the total tonnage, and so on—and setting, with the climatic extremes, the ethnic variety, and the exotica. On top of that it offered an excellent villain in the Bolshevik regime. It was, in short, every bit the adventure the ARA veterans had dreamed about up to summer 1921.

Russia was the forbidden country, the subject of endless speculation in the outside world since the Revolution of 1917; then, quite abruptly, these young American men were allowed not simply to peek inside but to enjoy what Fleming called "the privilege of being able to talk with all classes of provincial society and all political persuasions before the feelings of the revolution had yet cooled off." Ellingston called it an opportunity "to watch the great Russian Revolution from the Emperor's box"—in fact literally so on numerous occasions in the theaters of Petrograd and Moscow, where they were entertained in the manner of the grand dukes of old.

Other circumstances made the Americans feel like royalty. They directed a Russian staff whose senior positions were filled by the best society of the old regime, counts and countesses numerous among them, even a Countess Tolstoy serving as housekeeper at one of the Moscow personnel houses. Pishkin, once the chef for Tsar Nicholas, now boiled rice and beans and prepared cocoa at the ARA kitchen in the former imperial summer palace at Tsarskoe selo. Some of Russia's great and once-great artists gave private performances for the Americans and sought to make their acquaintance—and not always with the primary goal of filling up on their food.

The men of the ARA stood above Soviet law and could live, as very few Russians could, without fear of the Cheka. As long as famine threatened, they could demand of government officials the best warehouses and other facilities. If anyone tried to stand in the way, simply losing one's temper or pretending to do so was often enough to remove the obstacle, leading more than one unhappy Soviet official to refer contemptuously to the ARA as "a state within a state." Ellingston called it "the most important single factor in Russia of 1922," and quite a few Russians would have agreed.

Low-level functionaries—ferrymen, postal and railway officials, and the like—generally stood in awe of "our friends from America" and were ready to offer "anything the Americans wished." The ARA name could be a remarkably effective calling card, as Horsley Gantt learned from experience in Petrograd: "Personally I was admitted to inspect practically all places that I desired, even prisons—the holy of holies of Soviet Russia where even Bolshevik officials cannot go without passes. 'ARA' (arrah) was usually the 'open Sesame' to any door."[8]

Despite the many difficulties of "government relations," the Americans in the districts felt that their personal treatment at the hands of local officials—as distinct from those sent in by Moscow—was generally friendly and courteous. Barringer rated his "excellent."

A Gubispolcom President, or State Governor, often took upon himself strange duties upon the advent of the Americans. If you wanted a bed or a pillow-case, you took the matter up with the President who often brought them around personally. It seemed ridiculous that a man whose word was law among four million Russian citizens would have to worry a lot to find a suitable building and necessary comforts, such as were required by our mission.

For all the dangers and discomforts of being a relief worker, life at district headquarters offered selective comforts that would have passed for luxuries in any country. Childs boasted to his mother about the good life in Kazan: "With a Cadillac, two Dodges, two Fords, a summer home, a private steamboat and my own special railroad car I could hardly be any better off, do you think? Why even Harding can't manage to take his own automobile out with him when he goes out on the Mayflower as I am able to do. I hope such a life doesn't spoil me but I am afraid it is apt to do so." His new wife Georgina, who had lived in aristocratic comfort in St. Petersburg until 1917, one day surprised him by asking if they would enjoy a comparable existence in the States. "Twenty four years elapsed before we even approached that standard," he recalled many years later.

For the feeling of power and responsibility, few ARA jobs—certainly none outside Moscow headquarters—surpassed the position of district supervisor. Moscow determined each district's total food allocation—though each lobbied fiercely to have its allotment increased—but within his realm the supervisor decided on most matters of distribution, based on the reports of Russian and American inspectors, transport conditions, warehouse space, and other factors, including on occasion the whim of the moment. As the population of the typical district numbered in the several millions while allocations could support only hundreds of thousands, these were decisions over life and death. Opening kitchens or a warehouse in one subdistrict necessarily meant dooming residents in another. Usually this was as impersonal a matter as the repositioning of straight pins, with their round color-coded heads, on the district map in the supervisor's office, so the doomed did not present themselves before his mind's eye, remaining but a name on a map. Of course, the arrival of an emissary petitioning for relief and telling tales of woe complicated the decision: now that name had a face.

Most of the petitioners at the door of the supervisor's office were from among the city's residents, come to appeal an individual case or on behalf of a group— artists, professors, teachers, doctors, priests, and others. Often the object of their visit was relief in the form of food packages, especially in those locations with large food remittance programs such as Kharkov, as that district's history relates:

Undoubtedly, each district supervisor's office has been the scene of anxious longing, of unexpected joy, of tearful and heartfelt gratitude and this has been no exception.

The elderly widow without friends or kin with a starving family, the broken widower who has lost his wife from typhus and who is left with four small children, the aged and the blind, the highly educated grande dame of other days, now dressed in rags and broken in health, the professor of a discarded science looking like a beggar and struggling under the heavy burden of tuberculosis—they all come to the ARA head-quarters, receive their gift of food and depart with enduring thanks to the generosity of the American people.

Unless the packages had been funded by a foreign donor and designated for a particular beneficiary or professional group, the decision on their distribution was left up to the Americans, and there was no rule book to guide them in passing judgment on the worthiness of a case. Sometimes the difference between yes and no came down to an intangible something. Kelley was present when a committee of Ufa priests called to ask the ARA for corn rations. "They have received food packages through the ARA and have come to feel that the ARA exists to aid them." Bell explained that he had no say over who could receive corn as this was the decision of the local ARA committee, which was only technically true.

"On the heels of the priests a Red Officer is shown in." He is convalescing from typhus, and his regiment has gone on to Omsk. The army system does not provide for him, and he asks Bell for assistance. "He makes a good appearance and the Supervisor is probably a bit flattered that the officer should be so guile-less as to turn to the ARA for help in his distress. He surprises the interpreter by writing an order for the Chief of the Food Remittance Division to issue a general relief food package to the applicant. It will cause much gossip among the staff and further confuse their ideas about Americans."[9]

Not a few of these petitioners, excluding the bluffers, had somehow come to believe that they were being denied their fair share of the ARA's largess—"Surely there must be a mistake somewhere"—and some of these half-mad, hunger-crazed individuals were turned away with no little difficulty. Others, perhaps mis-led by all the talk of the ARA "miracle," overestimated the earthly powers of their American saviors. Freddie Lyon was struggling to get the Orenburg show under way in the frozen November of 1921 when a "huge woman" entered his office and requested that he bring "relief" into her household. Her husband refused to work, and she wanted a divorce. Having heard of the celebrated "efficiency" of the ARA, she was appealing to its representative to bring her immediate relief by granting her wish. Lyon, highly amused, explained that as yet the work of the great ARA was limited to feeding children; divorce courts were for another day.

Babine, the interpreter in Saratov, tells of a more typical bit of confusion in his diary entry of December 12, 1921. An old German peasant from Gnadentau called that morning at the ARA office and inquired on behalf of his neighbors "if Kinne could not do something to deliver their neighborhood from bandits. Suppressing a smile and having cautioned Kinne, I translated the German's request. But the obtuse Yankee did not appreciate the humour of the situation." Worse still, he sent for the government representative, Poretskii, and

told him to transmit the old man's application to the head State commissar. The German had barely time to say that there were good men among those bandits who wished to give up their raids but would not trust the Soviet amnesty proclamation—that indeed they would surrender if Americans had vouched for the Soviets, that there were "White bandits" and "Red bandits," and that both took away their cattle and horses—when Poretski hurriedly spirited him away.

This was not an isolated case, as Barringer reported from Ekaterinoslav in August 1922: "The demand that the Americans be asked to rule them is becoming daily more frequent the talk of the peasant. I have had many amusing and embarrassing moments in my travels about the district and run across these demands of the Moujik, who for the past winter has had his belly full of talk and nothing else."

Other relief workers were more receptive to such submissiveness. One of them must have been Harry Harris, whom the ARA alumni review honored as "Czar of Odessa," though formally he had been merely district supervisor. Also among the less inhibited was James Robinson, the lone American in Nizhnii Novgorod. His responsibility was to monitor the transfer point where the railway line from Moscow dead-ended at the Volga River, but this hardly accounts for his standing in the local community. Ruhl paid a call at Nizhnii and found Robinson more than equal to his assignment. He had picked up "quite a bit of Russian" without study and

he seems to know how to get along with Russians. He goes down the street distributing salutes as if he were reviewing his own troops, and the Chief of Police had been so won over by him that he came round to the house while I was there with a passport which he had made out for Robinson's interpreter—an ex-White officer—and which would permit him to travel in Russia without the likelihood, which was previously his, of being shot if he ventured outside the Nizhni government.

At district headquarters the position of executive assistant commanded considerable authority and was supreme when the supervisor was traveling or laid flat by typhus. Third down the chain came the district supply officer, and as Kelley testified from personal experience, "within his domain his power was absolute. Trains and boats moved and stopped at his orders. The Supervisor and the Executive outranked him but he had no cause to complain of lack of responsibility. Nor would ten American assistants if they had been available." Kelley's correspondence is punctuated by expressions of wonder at his elevated status in Russia. When he first arrives, he notes that there are three million people in the district and that "We four Americans are the only contact they have with the rest of the world. . . . Certainly no Grand Duke under the Czar ever held the position which we hold here. Our slightest word is law at home and in the office. The government is thoroughly tamed."

Kelley was not one to flaunt his power, but he did allow himself an occasional outburst of harmless epistolary swagger, as when he contemplated a visit to Sterlitamak: "These Baskirs are most friendly to us and when I go to their capital I expect to be given the country. Maybe we will compromise on a few of their quaint hand towels, full of colors and strange designs." Stopping in the town of Perm to consider an appeal from the chairman of the local relief committee, Kelley is in the compartment of a railroad car waiting for the arrival of the petitioner, who is late: "I have it in my power to feed a few thousand of his children but if the gentleman doesn't put in his appearance shortly he shall find me in a sour humor."

Only a few weeks later, after departing Russia, he sits at ARA headquarters at

42 Broadway, composing a report on the daily operations of the Ufa district and weighing the pluses and minuses of being a relief worker in Russia.

Did the Americans like the work? Certainly once they get into the work few seem to want to stop, but I doubt if many find it enjoyable. The power and prestige that go with any job in the district are very stimulating to young men. Such scope of action in the normal course of events is given to few until well into middle life. It offsets the discomforts of life and travel, the dangers of infection, and the almost total absence of recreation. But one hesitates long before calling work enjoyable that brings one into contact only with unhappy people. . . . I should never call the work "enjoyable" or even "interesting" but it was immense experience that none who came through unimpaired will ever regret. And yet very few, I imagine, would care to go through it again.[10]

At about this time, on August 20, 1922, Barringer was reflecting on these same matters at his post in Ekaterinoslav, where the residents' devotion to him was expressed by one of them in a few simple words: "You are a god to us." It was enough to make one giddy, as Barringer wrote to his father:

I realize what it is to have had a taste of power. Today our names are known over the entire Guberniia and the people know that the only hope they have of surviving this winter will be "the Americans" so you can imagine with what regard our position has put us. "Food King" even in Russia will spoil a [damned] good man for life except that the work keeps you so busy you lose sight entirely of the personal side of it.

Fleming tried on this shoe and found he liked the fit just fine. Initially he was based in Moscow, where his powers were limited to supervising the small Russian staff of the historical division and exhibiting the carefree, conquering air of the American relief worker on the streets of Moscow. In September 1922 his horizons were expanded when he became a "district guy" in Samara. Preparing for his first inspection trip into the interior, he pauses to consider the moment:

My travel orders and official duties, I was informed, were a carte blanche to every part of provincial life in Russia, without fear of the government nor favor of the old bourgeoisie. I had an open sesame to all doors and all classes. In the same day I might threaten the chairman of a county ispolkom, the biggest man in the county, with closing all the kitchens in his county if he did not come to order; I could then talk with a former well-to-do merchant now proscribed and ostracised by the government, and finish the day by attending a peasant wedding where the most violent liquor ever concocted was poured out for the guests.
    The richest man in two counties, I was also the only man in two counties who could afford to laugh at the name of the Government Political Department. I was privileged to talk on equal terms with heads of provincial departments, to open or close kitchens feeding thousands of children, and to give carpet talks to small-town officials for negligence in the discharge of their duties. These were among the powers I found in my hands as I started out on my first trip to Suizran and Gorodische.

Six months later his appetite is undiminished: "my career now in cruising about our district, which is a thousand versts long, is one of combined ambition and lust."
    Fleming was as anxious as any other relief worker that family and friends back home be made to understand that the ARA was much more than some "association of babyfeeders." It was a heroic crusade of rescue deserving of commensurate glory. In a letter to his parents he called it "the biggest job in mass famine fight-

ing ever done in the history of man, not excluding the job Joseph put across, and we do it free, while Joseph mortgaged the whole nation to the crown into the bargain." The light touch notwithstanding, Fleming shared the belief of his fellow famine fighters that their Russian mission was an historic event by any standard, not just within the domain of humanitarian assistance.

"When one stops to think it over," as did Bell, "the work of the ARA in Russia has certainly been a most remarkable undertaking and probably in many ways one of the greatest operations in history." Blomquist wrote of "seeing history made before my eyes, and of taking part in the greatest relief operation in the history of mankind." The "Russian Unit Record" called it "the greatest single feeding job—famine or military—in the history of the world." Cornick was even less inhibited: "Certainly there has never been anything like it before in history of the world." A year later, Haskell said of his mission, "It turned the corner for civilization in Russia."[11]

In 1922 the Norwegian explorer and humanitarian Fridtjof Nansen called ARA relief to Russia "the beau geste of the Twentieth Century," though that century was not yet a quarter old. Nansen's tribute inspired Ellingston to expand upon the topic of the mission's place in history:

People have told themselves—because it sounded well and flattered them indirectly—that American Relief to Soviet Russia in 1921 was the finest act of the 20th century. Superlatives have an inherent weakness to the cautious ear, but that superlative will bear believing. I can think of no act, no international act, of modern history, let alone the 20th century, which compares with ARA relief to Russia. . . . We probably saved from death not less than 5,000,000 people and even Russia, lavish as she is of lives, could hardly have stood up under the moral shock of the destruction of so many more human beings by so terrible a weapon as starvation.

As Moscow chief of the historical division it was Ellingston's job to see that the story of this monumental achievement was thoroughly documented so it could be told to future generations. On January 31, 1923, he wrote a memo to the division, a kind of pep talk to himself and his staff not to lose sight of the significance of their work during its final months:

The history of the A.R.A. operation is . . . not an account whose interest is confined to an "association of veteran babysitters." It is the great constructive fact of the century just as the war was the great destructive fact of the century. That history must therefore be written by a genius as the story of the landing at Gallipoli was written by Masefield. The business of the Historical Division is therefore to prepare the material for that genius.

One week later he drew up a circular letter to the division chiefs, pressing them to see to the writing of their department histories, an unpopular pastime for the overextended personnel. To sweeten the medicine he appealed to their sense of pride: this was a tale of American heroism, no "ordinary charity job," and deserved a proper telling.

Russia has fallen far enough behind the world as it is; think of what an irreparable moral blow the death by the horrible agent of starvation of ten million more people would have meant to her; could she have recovered? That is what I mean by saying that our relief by its very immensity was prevented from being transient or temporary. Whether the Russian or anyone else realizes it or not, we have saved a nation.[12]

This is how the American relief workers—miracle workers in the eyes of millions they rescued—thought of their mission while it was yet unfolding and before subsequent great destructive facts of a turbulent century caused it to slip into obscurity, as if Kellogg and the others had never come out of the sky.

CHAPTER 32

CONQUERING NEW WORLDS

"If ever there was an epic of relief work it is the story of Colonel Bell of Ufa, the man who saved from starvation hundreds of thousands of half-savage Bashkir Tatars, away out on the desolate steppes between European Russia and Siberia." Walter Duranty wrote these words in the waning days of the Russian mission in July 1923. He never made the trek out to those desolate steppes, instead basing his report on an interview with the colonel, who was passing through Moscow on his way out of Soviet Russia. Like most of his fellow Moscow-based correspondents, Duranty now and then let a baroque expression get in the way of journalistic accuracy: he probably knew better than to write "Bashkir Tatars." But seventy-five years later it is hard to argue with his choice of the word "epic" to characterize Bell's story in Ufa.

The epic quality was in part a product of the outsized dimensions of the Ufa mission: territorially it was to become the largest ARA district, extending the farthest east, into Asiatic Russia, which lent it the aura of the frontier. As ranked by number of beneficiaries it was also unsurpassed, eventually totaling over 1.6 million a day.

The figure of Bell measured up to the magnitude of the Ufa show. He was the only American to command a single district from start to finish. He was as well the only supervisor to fall victim to typhus. Near death, he was saved from an untimely end by the local inhabitants, who stayed the hand of the Reaper and nurtured their beloved leader back to health. Actually, reasonable reports give most of the credit to ARA physician Walter Davenport, but other chroniclers, even Bell himself on occasion, could not resist this romantic touch.

The ARA alumni newsletter called him "idol of the Bashkirs," an epithet supported by surviving photographs presenting him in various poses among the half-savages. They show a lanky, fifty-ish man with thinning hair and large eyes and ears set in a long, creased face. He wears an easy smile even with his pipe clenched between his teeth. This is what his indoor and summer attire reveals; in the exterior winter shots he is outfitted like an Arctic explorer and is barely distinguishable from any other relief worker. There are photographs of Bell holding in his arms a fattened bear cub, which seems appropriate to his image as a colonial master "out here in the wilds of Russia," as he once phrased it.

Little in the personal background of this ARA legend portends the stature he achieved in Russia. Walter Lincoln Bell was born in 1874 in Brooklyn, where he studied at the Polytechnic Institute before attending McGill University. His military experience began with the outbreak of the Spanish-American War, at which time he enlisted in the army, where he served for fifteen years in the cavalry service, attaining the rank of captain. He returned to active duty in 1914 to join the campaign in Mexico, and subsequently the Great War took him to France, where he saw action as a lieutenant colonel in the Fifty-second Artillery Regiment in the Verdun and Meuse-Argonne campaigns. He was later placed in command of the ammunition train of the Twenty-seventh Division, which was attached to the Second and Fourth British Armies during their operations in Belgium and northern France. Back home, which was now Syracuse, in 1921 he was promoted to full colonel, a rank he held until he retired in 1937 from the New York National Guard.

Bell had no background in food relief, strictly speaking, although among his papers there is a clipping from the *Philadelphia Record* of September 1, 1930, where reference is made to his "experience in the army in feeding soldiers on the transport Mt. Vernon, where 5000 were fed in 45 minutes in two small dining rooms." Still this is small potatoes compared to what was to come.

Boris Elperin, Bell's interpreter and Man Friday, confirms that his chief entered upon his ARA assignment totally unfamiliar with the machinery of food relief but that, compensating for this, "he had an instinct for administration and he knew that he could not give anything out without accounting for it."

The fact that a man with no experience in relief work ended up commanding the largest district in the greatest expeditionary relief operation of all time indicates the extent to which the ARA was forced to recruit beyond the ranks of its veterans in order to staff its most extensive mission. Though he was a complete outsider to the ARA, Bell's outstanding military credentials gave him an advantage over most of the other applicants hoping to get past the door. When Haskell's appointment to head up the unit was announced in August 1921, he was deluged with letters of application and recommendation. Among these was one that was impossible for this army colonel to ignore, a letter of support for Bell signed by the secretary of war, John F. O'Ryan, who was forceful in his praise: "I commend him to you strongly. He is an indefatigable worker; he is resourceful and handles men in exceptionally efficient manner." The course of events in Russia would show that the secretary had not exaggerated these qualities of the colonel, whom he characterized also as "a very live wire (he is known as 'Ginger' Bell)."

So the ARA chiefs enlisted this career soldier in the fight against what was at first believed to be the "Volga famine." They reserved the running of the higher-profile Volga districts for the veteran relievers and dispatched into the abyss of the unknown this total newcomer to the ways of relief administration. There beyond the valley he would need to summon up all of his celebrated resourcefulness in order to emerge victorious in the struggle with starvation.

The saga was nearly cut short in November 1921 when Bell contracted typhus. He developed a chill and fever in the town of Belyi Bey and was rushed back in a delirious state to Ufa, where the diagnosis was made by a local doctor, who the next day was himself laid low by the disease. The outlook was bleak until spirits were lifted three or four days later by the arrival of Dr. Davenport. Elperin says that he dropped in by chance, making it sound as if he happened to be sledding along on the snowy steppe with a different destination in mind. "This was a blessing from the Gods for Bell's condition was so serious that none of the Russians held out any hope for him."

Reporter Mackenzie, arriving in Ufa at this juncture, also seemed to hold out no hope for the colonel. His book *Russia Before Dawn*, which did not go to press until a full year later, leaves the impression that Bell had given up the ghost: "The list of deaths among relief workers was soon to grow." In fact while members of other foreign relief organizations had recently succumbed, Bell was the first ARA man to be stricken. Although he held on, it was three weeks before he regained consciousness.

In January "Ginger" Bell was back on the trail of the famine. Haskell had ordered him to the Riviera for a rest, but he refused. Elperin says that he had so much energy now that it was difficult to keep up with him during a run from Ufa to Sterlitamak. When the drivers of the sled team lagged, Bell perked them up with a "nervous jag," meaning liberal servings of coffee. This was prepared in the dwellings of inhabitants, usually peasants, along the route. They too were presumably given the benefit of a jag, in addition to the one they had received moments before upon discovering their idol standing outside their door.

Word of Bell's "miraculous" recovery had preceded him. Elperin says that "At one of these houses which the local teacher inhabited, the Col. found that his reputation had spread and that the whole story of his illness was known. The teacher presented him two beautiful bashkir towels in token of gratitude." Elperin might have said two *more* Bashkir towels as these were by far the most popular souvenir for a thousand miles. But here his memory was drawn to a distracting detail: "A propos of peasants houses, the Colonel once stopped in one, part of the main room of which was given over to the calf. When this animal required to relieve its bladder the owner of the household caught the piss in a can."

Bell's travels fueled the wildfire territorial expansion of the Ufa district in the first half of 1922. The Americans journeyed by sleigh and by rail, which Bell rated "even more primitive than when our pioneers went to California in '49. Railroads in shocking condition, positively no wagon roads such as we know of and draft animals down to less than 25 per cent of pre revolution times." Native ARA inspectors crossed the Urals on horse or camel.

The enlargement of the Ufa district, mainly eastward and northward, was not part of a new American Gold Rush—a drive to take control of the precious metals and gems of the Urals—as local opinion at first suspected. The fact was that famine conditions extended in all directions seemingly without end. To the west and south respectively were the neighboring Kazan and Orenburg districts, but otherwise there was nothing to limit the horizons of the Ufa Americans, who felt at liberty, in fact duty-bound, to respond to the many calls for relief. The urge to lay claim to virgin territory must have fed on the frontier atmosphere of the district, where "we all have to go about dressed like [Bret] Harte, with a six gun on the hip," as Bell put it. "France in 1918 was a summer resort, compared with our present assignment."

Moscow headquarters was too preoccupied to offer resistance. "The district was practically autonomous," wrote Kelley, who as supply chief had figured on close coordination with Moscow. Initially he was frustrated by the lack of communication regarding the specific details about incoming supplies and their allocation, but soon he came to realize that it was not worth worrying about Moscow if Moscow was not going to worry about you: "They simply don't reply to our inquiries. In the last ten weeks we haven't sent any."

Word of the December 1921 congressional appropriation of $20 million for Russian relief reached the Ufa district on January 4 in the form of a telegram with a vague message about the forthcoming delivery of twenty million bushels of wheat and milk. This caused much head scratching in Kelley's supply division: "We have no details. We are only told to 'prepare for big things.'" Information trickled in from Moscow until Bell paid a visit to the capital in February and was told the general outlines of the program. Still, Kelley says that up to a few days before the arrival of the first train on March 7 it was not clear to the Ufa staff whether they should prepare for maize or wheat, whether it was to be in sacks or bulk, whether the ARA was to grind it, or how it was to be accounted for. Once the "corn shower" began, Kelley was amused at how Moscow's instructions on corn matters typically arrived once decisions had already been taken on the ground in Ufa. After a while their timely arrival was not allowed to influence matters. This state of affairs suited Bell, who was not complaining when he called his team the "American Exiles in Ufa."

The feeling of isolation was intensified by the absence of proper maps, even before the great expansion unfolded. The available maps were limited to either the European or the Asiatic parts of Russia, and as the Ufa district sat astride two continents, Bell and company were forced to go into the mapmaking business in order to delineate their territory, an exercise that could only have intensified the spirit of Manifest Destiny that seemed to animate the Ufa Americans in the early going. The famine was out there, and it had to be conquered. Why? Because it was there. So the pins on the homemade district map began to multiply eastward to Kustanai and Cheliabinsk, northeast to Ekaterinburg, and north to Perm.

The initial enthusiasm for the enterprise is palpable in Kelley's correspondence, as in a letter of January 12 where he anticipates his first journey out of Ufa city, to be undertaken in the company of the colonel: "We are both eager to get away and conquer new worlds. You know, we shall be the first A. R. A. men that have entered Asia." Actually, no: he was forced to withdraw this claim after the mission when he learned that a ferryboat ride across the Ural River brought the Orenburg Americans into Asia most any day they desired. But at the time he had the pleasure of believing otherwise, which increased his anticipation of the coming adventure.

As it turned out, less than two weeks on the road was enough to satisfy Kelley's appetite for conquering new worlds. This conqueror returned pretty thoroughly demoralized:

I have been to Argayash and back. The discomfort of the trip, the makeshift meals, the extreme cold, and above all the constant presence of human misery, worse than which I cannot imagine, has wearied me. I am heartily glad that Bell has thought it best to send me direct to Ufa while he and the Doctor branch off and go down a narrow gauge road into another Bashkir canton. I have lost all curiosity to explore further in this region. I can tell in advance what I would see if I went down into Baskiria. There seems to be no boundaries to the famine area. Were we to travel as far as China, I doubt if we should see any great difference in the condition of the people.

The absurdity of the term "Volga famine" became perfectly apparent when starvation appeared to reach north to the Arctic Circle and east to Harbin. "Journey to the end of the railroad at Kustanai and inquire about the tribes inhabiting the steppes for a thousand miles toward India and it was the same story of famine and disease. Neither the Soviet Government nor the ARA by proclamation could limit the famine to the zone of the accessible."

On February 2, Bell returned to Ufa with reports of conditions worse than those witnessed by Kelley, who records that the colonel brought back a sample of "fried skin"—presumably human—which was being consumed in a Bashkir canton.

I believe the most unusual story I have heard is his tale of how a priest came to him in a town and begged him for enough bread to make hosts for Communion to the dying. Out of his pocket, he bought forty pounds of flour and gave them to the priest for the purpose. You can imagine what the situation must be when there isn't even enough bread for Communion purposes.

In the subsequent weeks and especially with the arrival of the corn, appeals for relief inundated headquarters, and as it was not in Bell's nature to say no, his empire grew larger. Kelley looked on with a mixture of exhilaration and horror: "we are asked to extend our operations into Kustanai, a district in Siberia belonging to the Khirghiz Republic! And Bell said: 'All right.'" And so Kustanai was "annexed."

The expansion overstretched the Ufa Americans, who numbered seven in March 1922, and the incoming corn threatened to bury them completely. "Frantic appeals to Moscow for additional personnel have brought no response," which by then should hardly have surprised Kelley. The feeding figures before him rose in great leaps as in the space of eight months the Ufa mission expanded from a program of fifty thousand children to one of five hundred thousand children and over a million adults. "Had need alone been the controlling factor we might have easily doubled these figures." In September the total would peak at 1.6 million fed in 2,750 kitchens.

The primary motivation that drove Bell to assume the responsibility for feeding so many people was, it seems plain, humanitarian. He considered the issue in the grimmest terms of the very survival of the Bashkir nation: "As we are the only relief organization these latter people have ever seen and their economic condition is so extremely bad, the A.R.A. is the only hope they have to save them from complete extinction." At the same time, Bell made no secret of his satisfaction at the growth of what he once satisfyingly referred to as "this rather rambling district," which became so large it was renamed the Ufa-Urals district. In June he headlined a letter to an ARA New York colleague: "Ufa-Bashkir-Cheliabinsk-Ekaterinburg-Koustanai District":

We are now by far the largest of all the A.R.A. districts in Russia as concerns territory and pretty well up near the head as concerns allocation. The heading of this letter will give you some idea of the scope of the work ahead of us. Our territory is larger than all of France and the work in this district greater than the entire relief of Poland.

At the time Ufa's only competitor in number of allocations was the more densely populated Kazan district, which was on Bell's mind: he wondered how his numbers compared with those of "our friend 'Childs.'"

Nor was Bell at all reluctant to exercise the authority that came with his exalted position. In the midst of the corn drive he learned that the local Soviet authorities were planning to transfer the capital of the Bashkir republic from Sterlitamak to Ufa as part of the absorption of most of Ufa province by Bashkiria, thus creating Greater Bashkiria. Moving the government would require the expenditure of a considerable sum of money on the part of the cash-strapped Bashkir government, thereby threatening the funding it used to support ARA operations. Bell claimed that it would disrupt the transport of food products and necessitate the removal of ninety thousand people from the feeding rolls. This may indeed have been the case, though perhaps an additional consideration was the unappealing prospect of a large force of Soviet officials descending on Ufa and hovering around ARA headquarters at a critical time—better to keep them out of the way in Sterlitamak.

Anyway, the plan to move the government was unacceptable to Bell, who took forceful action. He raised the Sterlitamak soviet chief on the direct wire from Ufa and informed him that if the capital were to be moved, the ARA would be forced to close down a principal warehouse and ship the products to some other part of the district, presumably implying outside Bashkiria. The colonel wished to know if the transfer of the capital could not be postponed; he required an immediate answer. This is the story as Bell relates it. There is probably no way to discover what calculations exercised the mind of the man at the other end of the wire, but he must have realized that there was only one hardheaded response. The transfer of the capital would take place but only on August 1. For now the requirements of Greater Bashkiria had to give way to those of the Big Ufa Show.[1]

IN HIS REALM Bell was supreme, but to the Moscow division heads he was just another worrisome district supervisor importuning them for increased allocations, personnel, and firearms. After the corn had been delivered the attitude at headquarters was that the men in the districts exaggerated the threat of persistent famine, tending too readily to believe the hair-raising stories about the man with the scythe dreamed up by peasants fearful of losing their ARA nanny. Only the cooler heads in Moscow, sufficiently removed from the famine front, could be trusted to maintain a focus on the big picture of Russian operations and keep clearly in mind that the ARA was an emergency famine relief organization and not a charity outfit.

So when a conference of all district supervisors was convened in Moscow in June 1922 to discuss the future of the mission, the idol of the Bashkirs took a seat at the table as just another district guy. The New York and Moscow chiefs intended to recommend to Hoover that the ARA close down the Russian unit by the autumn harvest, and they were not receptive to reports that famine conditions would reappear the following winter. They could not have been cheered by Bell's gloomy outlook for the following winter in Ufa. Although his was not the only pessimistic forecast, he seemed perhaps a bit too settled into his job. At a moment when the idea was to build a case for withdrawal, the colonel's big talk about the enormity of his expanding empire struck a discordant note. It appears to have created some ill feeling toward him. Allen of Samara, for one, claimed to be unimpressed:

About all the conference got out of Bell was "Well we are now operating in five gubernees and three republics". It sounded big, but I happened to bust in on a conference he was having with Haskell, and I heard Haskell saying that there were certain limits to conquering these new worlds and it would be inconvenient for him some time to have to go to Vladivostock for Bell, if such occasion should arise that he was needed.

Haskell had a nose particularly sensitive to the scent of swagger, and he may already have gotten an occasional whiff from Bell's monthly reports and correspondence, which here and there do indicate a weakness for self-congratulation: "I do not think that any of us Americans can really tell how we managed to put the job over."

Ellingston tended to think of Bell as merely another whining supervisor obsessed with the importance of his own show and certain his accomplishments went unappreciated in Moscow. This opinion was completely transformed, however, when Ellingston journeyed beyond the valley to the Bashkir outlands in summer 1922. When he had returned to relative civilization in Moscow, he wrote an excited letter to Fisher in New York to say that he had found an epic of relief for the ARA history: Bell was nothing short of "a genius."

You've no idea what a magnificent job the Colonel has done out there on the edge of Siberia—nor what enormous obstacles, human and other, he had to overcome. As I say, he is a genius and I hope to do something towards making that fact known before I get through. I travelled and ate and slept and drank with him for two weeks and watched him work and I think I gathered together enough material during that time to do him some justice.

Fisher might have imagined that Bell was living among apes, but then Ellingston becomes more specific: "His outstanding characteristic, of course, is his genius for reading and handling men, the extraordinary kindliness and humanity of his judgements combined with his unmovable hard headedness in matters of business." It sounds like a description of the model American relief administrator.

There is one factor that may have worked to Bell's considerable advantage in his role, although no one documented it: at forty-eight he was the oldest district supervisor by at least a decade, and twenty years older than the average reliever. Operating in cultures where age merited respect, Bell's years probably entitled him to a degree of automatic authority not given to the ARA boys. Otherwise, the secret of his technique is elusive. On occasion his diplomatic skills were augmented by his ability to hold his liquor, but no amount of alcohol could alone explain the fact that Ufa had a model record of government relations, even considering that he was dealing with a "bunch of cutthroats," as Ellingston characterized the local authorities.

Ufa never has to complain to headquarters about lack of cooperation; as a matter of fact, Ufa could teach headquarters a good deal about how to get cooperation. Madame Kameneva officially asked that Colonel Bell be thanked for his splendid work in the district, saying that it was the best in Russia. He gets all the local money, all the transportation, all everything else he needs. They worship him out there and have asked him to stay on after the ARA leaves to help them.

Ellingston thought he detected the secret of Bell's success: "He doesn't wheedle these people; he out thinks them and wins them by his courtesy." As a general rule, courtesy would win you very little in confrontations with Eiduk's satellites, but Bell's particular brand seemed to cast a strange spell, as Ellingston related to Fisher: "Just as an incident of what he can do with these Bolos, with whom every other district in Russia is at war to the hilt, let me tell you the Karklin story." Karklin was Eiduk's man in Samara, a "hard boiled Communist who leads Samara district a dog's life—as you know, by the way."

In February 1922, as Bell prepared to travel to Moscow to appeal in person for increased allocations, man power, and so on, he naturally desired to avoid undertaking the journey in the purgatorial third-class car and to secure the much-coveted and ever-elusive private car. Bell managed to depart Ufa so accommodated, but because the particular car belonged to the Ufa-Urals railroad, he was not to be allowed to take it beyond Samara. The challenge was to procure a successor en route.

At Samara the boys told the colonel not to waste his time with Karklin, who had only recently requisitioned their own private car, but Bell was undaunted. Elperin picks up the narrative in his lush English prose: "To understand what happened one must understand that Colonel Bell is a master handler of men, that he has a personality made superlatively charming by the real sincerity of his geniality." Calling upon Karklin, Bell worked his magic, with the result that this hard-boiled Communist at once placed at his disposal "the best private car in the region."

Thus did Bell journey in relative luxury to Moscow, where he was immediately confronted with a greater challenge when one of Eiduk's assistants, unable to restrain himself, requisitioned the car. Lesser men might have been intimidated by the big Bolos in the big city, but Bell was intrepid. First, he made an urgent appeal to ARA transportation chief Charles Gaskill: "They've taken my car, Gaskill, and I've got to have it to get back to Ufa. I'm loaded up with supplies which I can't trust to the baggage car, besides my personal stuff. God knows what sort of accommodation I'll get without a private car nor when. I've got to have that car."

Gaskill threw up his hands, so Bell went up the ladder to chief of staff Lonergan, who gave him permission to approach Eiduk personally. It may have been that Lonergan took fiendish delight in clearing the way for this encounter, perhaps figuring that when Eiduk was finished with him, the big-talking, pipe-smoking man from Ufa would have a better understanding of the breed of Bolo the Moscow chiefs were up against. Bell brought along Gaskill, who together with Elperin watched as the master handler of men enchanted the Bolo chief, causing him to behave as if spellbound. "Eiduc said it was an outrage, declared that he knew nothing of it, picked up the phone and called his man at the station who had taken the car away, informed him that if he ever did such a thing again he would be turned over to the Chekka for good, and ordered him to return Colonel Bell's car immediately."

By now Elperin was accustomed to the colonel getting his way and was unsurprised by this outcome, whereas "Gaskill followed the Colonel out of Eiduc's office stupefied."

Perhaps Bell and Elperin shared a quiet laugh about the expression on Gaskill's face as they rolled along in their luxury car back to Ufa, where they retained its use for another six months. Wrote Ellingston of the colonel's performance: "He bearded the lion."[2]

REPORTERS AND ARA PUBLICISTS had no difficulty finding local color in Ufa, so great was the ethnic and religious variety among the human inhabitants. The adjective "picturesque" was probably more frequently applied to the residents of this district than to any other. One would not guess from reading the American newspaper stories that Bell's kingdom was populated largely by ethnic Russians. It was the non-Russian peoples—Bashkirs, Tatars, Khirgiz, Chuvash, Mordva, Meshcheriaki, and others—with their more alien physical features, language, dress, and customs who won most of the attention.

Ufa was the headquarters of Russia's fourteen million Muslims, whose representatives convened there in the summer of 1922 to discuss ways to achieve the closer unity of all Soviet citizens of Muslim faith and to select a new mufti to guide them in this endeavor.

"When the Prophet speaks mountains move and the entire East listens" are the opening words of an ARA press release about this momentous gathering—though on this occasion the prophet in question was not Col. Bell. He was, however, invited to attend the proceedings, thus making him, if one believes Duranty, "the only foreigner and only non-Mohammedan so honored in Russian or Tatar history from the days of Genghis Khan and Tamerlane until today." There are photographs of Bell in a skullcap posing among Asiatic-looking men in Eastern garb, which may have been taken on this occasion. The body of religious men delivered thanks to him on behalf of all the Muslims of Russia.

The ARA report was accompanied by a photograph of the new spiritual leader, Kiraeddin ben Fakreddin, shown sitting among twenty-nine Muslim leaders in the presence of one of seven original Korans said to have been inscribed in the sacred blood of the first successor to Mohammed himself. "This is one of the few photos of the Koran in existence." Here Duranty attributes to Bell another first: "Never before had infidel eyes looked upon this holy relic; but at Colonel Bell's request the Muslim clerics brought it out into the open air for young Traynham, the official A.R.A. photographer, to photograph it, while their holy men were turning its sacred pages."

In fact Duranty telescoped two events quite distinct in time. Bell was almost certainly invited to examine the Koran in June, but Kelley had cast his own infidel eyes upon it some four months earlier. Of course Kelley wrote about his experience, so we have the pleasure of watching the graduate of the Pulitzer School of Journalism lay waste to Duranty's sand-castle reporting.

On Wednesday night, February 15, while Bell was on his Moscow sojourn and with Kelley serving as acting district supervisor, ARA publicity man William Garner and Traynham arrived in town. On Thursday morning Kelley escorted them around the city, visiting kitchens, hospitals, and children's homes. "They sought local color and found it, I think. One poor wretch dropped at their feet and had to be hauled off to a hospital in our Ford. Later we passed two frozen corpses in a sleigh. The sights in the refugee home were too much for the photographer. He fled from the building.

"Well, at any rate, they saw the worst and got some pictures including one of me talking to a picturesque Soviet official."

Friday was even more interesting:

About noon, ARA office visited by a delegation of three Tartar priests in ecclesiastical robes. They had the inevitable petition, as to the contents of which I am still in the dark. The accompanying speech was passed from Tartar to Russian to German, but got no further. Traynam, the movie man, blew into the office and was right on the job. Interiors were taken of the priests, Hofstra and me. Eager for more shots, Traynam and I pursued them to their house and spent the entire afternoon taking pictures, both stills and movies. In one, Baird and I were shot meeting and exchanging badinage with the mufti in his back yard. These priests possess a venerable Koran, born I believe about 1300 years or so ago. We had it out in the snow, and filmed them reading it.

This scene made the final cut of the ARA's two-reeler. It indeed shows Kelley and friends out in the snow. The priests stand before an opened glass casing containing the Koran; they self-consciously turn the pages and read from it, one tracing his fingers along the sacred blood script, all the while exposing the ancient holy document to the sunlight and moisture. It is a scene out of an archivist's nightmare.

A title reads: "Mohammedan priests, of the Tartar race. The A.R.A. distributes relief without regard to race, politics or creed," and we see the three religious men in an unconvincing show of engaging in small talk. Actually, in the finished film this sequence is preceded by one more visually impressive, filmed one week later, also with Kelley in a leading role:

Again this morning I posed for the movies. Blandy arranged a scene with about fifty Russian priests as actors. When the stage was set I abandoned my desk long enough to go out into the courtyard and be "shot" distributing food remittances and talking to the priests. They actually received their part of the food bought by the Russian clergy in America several days ago, and returned today specially to pose for the movies.

With their long beards and black robes and *shapkas* these aging Orthodox holy men seem the personification of old Russia. They certainly yield nothing to their Muslim counterparts in picturesqueness. What is remarkable is that the two scenes were filmed in the same city. Absent the continuity provided by the snowy landscape and the appearance of Kelley, they would seem spliced together from different worlds.

Kelley enjoyed playing a relief worker in Traynham's movies, yet he could never lose himself in his role. The bigger part of him remained in the audience, scrutinizing his own and others' performances with the skeptical eye of the hardened critic. He could never have taken himself as seriously as Bell, who seemed to own his part. In other ways the two personalities were fundamentally different: Bell brought out the best in people and pushed everyone, even suspected traitors and saboteurs, along with him toward a goal; Kelley, with his cynical view of human nature, was the perfect adjutant to the soft-hearted colonel, whom he once described as typical of those "easy-going persons who dislike to reprimand anyone."

While Kelley reveled, in his own self-deprecating way, in his status as American savior, he did not aspire to head his own district. Other Ufa Americans—Hofstra, Howard, and Verdon—sought and achieved this rank, but it was not for

Kelley. He had signed on to the mission resolved upon staying in Russia only six months. In May 1922 the district was still expanding, the job ahead still enormous, but already he was thinking about pulling up stakes and returning to a career in advertising and publicity, and told Bell of his intentions. "Of course, as I expected, he won't consent to my talking of leaving in June. As he put it, 'We are all alone, Kel, and the job must be done.'"

Replacing an ARA man in any district was no small matter. The tasks of even the ordinary reliever were so elaborate that to train a newcomer—at least to do it properly in Ufa—took two to three months. But Kelley was no ordinary relief worker. In letters written to the Moscow and New York chiefs after Kelley's departure, Bell rolled out the superlatives, calling him "a great development" with "wonderful capabilities," "a most capable youngster" who did "brilliant work"; he was "in every way as clever a youngster as I have ever known and certainly did a big job here"; "he has been a life saver for me."

So there were good reasons for Bell to try to convince his executive assistant to change his mind and stay, and he must have thrown his considerable persuasive powers into the effort because Kelley hints that he may have hesitated: "I thought it over and then solemnly told him that I must leave here not later than June 20th (six months from the day I entered Russia) and that he must press Moscow for replacements." A couple of weeks later, on May 20, his tone is confident as he can see the end in sight: "On June 20th I shall down tools and turn my face toward the West." On the same day, he wrote his resignation letter to Haskell, explaining that he had "contracted an engagement," that he was "bound by a prior obligation," and that he had set himself to leave Russia "six months from the day I climbed out of a freight car in the Moscow yards."

Kelley told Haskell that Bell understood his decision despite the twenty years' difference in their ages. Bell may have understood it, but he could not have identified with the temperament behind it. Kelley, at age twenty-six, was thinking about a career, whereas Bell, at forty-eight, had found one. He must have felt that there could be no higher purpose than this responsibility for the welfare of over a million people. He had reached his personal summit. He was animated neither by the diamonds in the Ufa hills nor by the adoration of the Ufa masses, but by the satisfaction of putting his show over: "We are all alone, Kel, and the job must be done."

THE SHOW WENT ON without Kelley, and as in other districts, after the harvest of 1922 the Ufa mission engaged in "reconstruction" activities. Duranty's encomium to Bell held this particular phase up for special praise, and the various accounts of the district's operations make it clear that the American exiles in Ufa were especially proud of their postfamine enterprise.

One community that turned it to good account was the factory town of Beloretsk in the Bashkir canton Taman-Kataiskii, an iron works where during the war sixteen thousand men had been employed producing shells for the tsarist army. The works had since been converted to the production of ornamental swords, damascened metalwork, and the like, but in the sink-or-swim conditions of NEP the town was in danger of going under. Bell kept things afloat with ARA food supplies and in spring 1923 as a way to generate employment he provided corn to support the construction of a narrow-gauge railroad to cover the twenty versts between the factory and the coal and iron mines at Lapishtinskii. Why they had not managed to construct such an artery in the old days is not clear.

In the town of Zlatoust Bell arranged the employment of 2,142 refugees to engage in various cleaning and construction projects in return for one meal a day in regular kitchens or in mobile "military" kitchens when the work site was out of town. In this way 270 road bridges were built and 160 repaired, ninety-four drinking fountains were constructed, and two large schools completely restored. The flower of this enterprise was the construction of a drainage canal nearly eight hundred meters long and one and three-quarters meters wide and deep. It seems that such a canal had been discussed for over seventy years, but only the extraordinary circumstance of American famine relief could bring the idea to life.

Bell mentions as well the reopening of an Ufa glass factory of five hundred workers and the repair of the city's hospitals. Duranty credits him with the construction of two pontoon bridges across the Belaya River.

In a kind of farewell article to the ARA, a Moscow Bolshevik writing in *Pravda* on July 1, 1923, stated that the workers of the Urals heartily thanked Mr. Bell, "who actively assisted the unemployed and, it seems, against the instructions of the ARA, contributed to the provisioning and operation of two factories."

Pravda was instinctively fixated on the proletariat, whereas Duranty's mind's eye saw a uniform mass of half-savage natives: "The Bashkirs could not make Bell out: Why did he do it? So they offered him concessions—the mountains of Solomon's mines of gold, platinum deposits that once produced hundreds of tons yearly. Colonel Bell refused, and gradually they came to understand this strange American who liked his job for its own sake."

On May 4, 1923, James F. La Salle wrote a report on his recent inspection trip through Cheliabinsk and Ekaterinburg provinces: "In every place visited inquiries were made for Polkovnik BELL and when he was going to spend a few days with them for hunting etc. Our work has been made easy by Col. Bell and now all we have to do is express that it is the wish of Col. Bell and they immediately do all they can for the ARA. Very little credit if any should go to us."

Bell apparently liked being addressed by the Russian word for "colonel": he signed a personal note to Ellingston simply "Polkovnik." Other titles were bestowed on him toward the end, including honorary mayor of Ufa, honorary chairman of the Ufa city council, and honorary life member of the Voluntary Fire Department of the town of Meass. This last was awarded in thanks for a donation of ARA medical supplies, which allowed the Meass firemen to continue to put themselves in harm's way. At around the same time the town experienced a "flurry of excitement" caused by the discovery of gold deposits beneath the city streets during a reconstruction campaign. This was not a rare occurrence in Meass, a town at the foot of the famously rich Ilmen mountain. Yet an ARA publicist maintained that it was "sufficient to throw the community into an uproar"; then, serving to "cap the climax," came Bell's invitation to join the fire department. "Meass is working the streets now in feverish anticipation of extracting therefrom enough gold to pay its taxes for the next ten centuries, and between this and the A.R.A. the natives of the town have conversation a-plenty."

The honors and accolades proliferated in the final stage, and, according to

Bell, "Our last three days at Ufa were just successions of banquets and farewells."
Among the gifts presented to Polkovnik were beautifully engraved gold watches,
a chest of precious stones and metals from the Urals, locally crafted shawls, rugs
and tapestries with Bell's name fashioned into the fabric, gold and silver ornaments, parchments with tributes inscribed on them, boxes containing complete
sets of articles of local industry, and albums of photographs of Ufa operations.

"They even brought six young wolves around to the house the day we left,"
Bell is quoted as saying. "We had had some experience with wolves, and bears, on
our staff, so we politely, but firmly rejected this gift."

The item Bell was said to have prized most was what an artfully ingenuous
ARA publicity writer called a "native Bashkir costume, presented to him with
great ceremony by a Bashkir chieftain. This costume, in blue and red with gold
embroidery, is a mark of distinction among the Bashkirs and is only given to
those whom this picturesque people wish to honor. In former days it was conferred much the same as a high decoration is conferred for a great work accomplished, or a battle won." In this case it served for both.

Naturally those bidding farewell wished to know if their paleface hero would
return and naturally the answer had to be some form of yes: "Colonel Bell is determined to return to Ufa in the near future to lend his services to this quaint
people whom he has learned to like very much during the two years he has lived
among them." Indeed, he is made to sound resolute:

I feel as though I were a part of them. I have lived with them through the worst period of suffering and hardship they have ever endured. I have traveled into every corner of their republic, slept under their roofs, broken their bread and listened to their
tales of woe and happiness. They nursed me through typhus. I feel as though I am a
part of their new existence, and as they want me to come back and help them, I am
determined to do so.

Duranty says that were the United States ever to recognize Soviet Russia and
the Bashkir republic be allowed a foreign representative—a prospect for which
the local chieftains were still holding out hope in the early 1920s—the Bashkirs
would certainly request that Bell represent them in Washington.

A number of the tributes to Bell and the Ufa Americans ended up in the man-
uscript boxes of the ARA collections at Stanford and in West Branch. Among the
Stanford materials there is a very different kind of document, a letter dated Octo-
ber 26, 1921, from Mrs. Evelyn Bell, Brooklyn, New York, to Herbert Hoover.
Mrs. Bell had read in the newspapers that her husband, or former husband, was in
Russia doing "releif" work. She found this situation curious, since

He has utterly failed to comply with his agreement to contribute to my support. Last
Winter I was obliged to apply to the Court of Domestic Relations for assistance and
he was ordered to make monthly payments to me. These payments have not been
made. At that time I surrendered an insurance policy on his life on which I had paid
premiums and he took half the cash received claiming that he was in need.

She claimed that his business, which is not specified in his personnel records,
had been extremely profitable from the beginning of the world war until he went
to Camp Wadsworth and that the army paid him well. For months she had been

looking for work but lacked the training and experience to land a job. She had pawned everything of value she possessed and was at the end of her rope: "Not having the means to engage legal assistance am relying on your sense of fairness to see that I receive some releif from my present condition."[3]

Of course this appeal never reached Hoover's desk. It was answered by New York headquarters, which promised Mrs. Bell an investigation but advised her that her husband had a solid reference file, including letters from the secretary of war and "many other prominent men." It is unclear if the matter was pursued beyond that.

Perhaps there is nothing more to say about this, or maybe saying so little says too much since the colonel's side of the story is unknown. But it is interesting to consider that for the man who saved the Bashkirs from extinction and turned down Solomon's mines, charity may have begun only at the edge of Siberia.

CHAPTER 33

FROM THE BELL TOWER

Among the documentation of Bell's adventures in Bololand there is a scene recalled by Elperin that took place during one of the colonel's shuttles between Ufa city and Sterlitamak in autumn 1921. The party stopped for a respite in a village along the route. Most of the ARA relievers in the districts had occasion to make such house calls in the villages, providing them with a firsthand look at peasant domestic life and a chance to put questions to their remotest beneficiaries about the severity of the famine. Elperin noted that for most of the peasants in the region the situation was desperate. Winter was upon them, and most were surviving on food substitutes—grass, leaves, twigs, bark, and other, even less appetizing, improvisations. Yet there was no panic. "The peasants were stolid and resigned to their fate."

"What do you think of your situation?" asked the Colonel of one old peasant.
"I don't know. All I do know is that when Nicholas (the czar) was around we had all we wanted to eat. Now we have nothing."
"Well, what are you going to do about it?"
"I expect we'll die," was the stolid response.

The American relief workers had to accustom themselves to unfamiliar attitudes and behavior while they were stationed in Soviet Russia, but they never managed to become reconciled to the resignation to death they encountered at every turn during the famine year 1921–22. The men of the ARA had come to do battle with a famine, and they expected its victims to join as best they could in the struggle to save themselves. Instead what they discovered was that great numbers of peasants—who had recently seen their crops destroyed by drought or go up in flames in the field, their livestock disappear, their families succumb to hunger and disease—these peasants behaved as though their destiny was now entirely out of their hands.

This fatalism was not exclusive to the countryside, manifesting itself among the town and city residents as well. To the American relievers it was at first an object of extreme curiosity and later of frustration, even exasperation. The extent to which it exercised them is made apparent by the pervasiveness of the subject in their diaries, letters, and reports.

In the very beginning, evidence of the lethargy and passivity of the broad masses was welcomed by the ARA. One of the biggest fears going in was that hunger-crazed mobs would storm the American food trains and attack the relief workers. The reality was that the victims, even when in the safety of large numbers, made no attempt to save themselves by forcibly taking possession of the food in their midst. Yet even the initial relief at such behavior was mixed with a feeling of mystification.

Floyd Gibbons of the *Chicago Tribune* brought this strange conduct to the attention of his readers. In an unnamed town on the Volga, there on the water's edge, some two hundred feet away from a group of several hundred starving peasants, was gathered a smaller number of "more fortunate peasants" selling bread, butter, eggs, melons, tomatoes, and one roasted chicken. They did this with no apparent uneasiness about the less fortunate lot looking on.

Nearby Gibbons walked past a lone soldier guarding an indeterminate mound obscured by tarpaulin. Upon inquiry he was told that it harbored 17,000 poods, or 680,000 pounds, of seed for the next harvest. "And these people dying here without eating it—one solitary soldier surely couldn't keep 400 hungry humans away from food within their reach—why haven't they rushed it?" he asked a local official. "You don't know Russia," came the reply. "The seed for next year's harvest is sacred." According to his *Tribune* colleague Seldes, Gibbons then approached the starving peasants and asked them why they did not rush the guard and try to save themselves, "but although they understood him, no one would defy authority. Mr. Gibbons thought they did not act like real Americans would."

Gregg and Shafroth, among the first ARA men to enter the Volga valley, were quick to calm Moscow headquarters concerning rumors of mob violence. Gregg wrote from Kazan on September 6: "The attitude of the peasant is one of resignation to the situation and to death if necessary, they are illy prepared to meet this famine. . . . They are still hopeful of help coming from the government, and show no present tendency to riot or to move on the towns en masse in search of food."

Shafroth wrote from Samara two weeks later that the American newspaper stories were "bunk": the peasants were "too weak to be infuriated. . . . Their attitude is mostly one of resignation to what fate has brot on them, and to death if necessary."

Nor did the tens of thousands of refugees fleeing the famine behave as expected. Kellogg was flabbergasted by the signs of their passivity. As he recorded in his journal in September 1921, they seemed to be sleepwalking: "The potato patches along the railway—open unprotected—the refugees who walk along the railway line have them before their eyes—they walk along almost through them—moving from place to place to find food *and they do not touch these potatoes!!* In one patch several miles from any town and far away from the hut of the owner I saw just 3 (out of 300) hills dug into & the potatoes taken."

Weeks passed; the situation grew worse; the ranks of the starving swelled. Still this odd self-control prevailed, as Spratt reported from Kazan on February 28, 1922: "A curious phase of the present catastrophy is shown in the absolute lack of panic through this district. The subject is discussed every where calmly and dispassionately, and the fact that it is manifest that only a small percentage of the population can survive is accepted with stoicism that is pathetic."

Also in Kazan, Childs observed the same phenomenon, though typically he viewed it through a different lens. Behavior others considered pitiful he saw as evidence of the "heroism" of the "Russian people." He traveled hundreds of miles through the district, usually with relief supplies in tow, but nowhere did the hungry attempt to take ARA food or bring harm to him. "Resignation to their fate was their most striking characteristic. In other countries under similar circumstances I would have risked having my throat cut."

More than this, Childs says that in none of the famine-stricken villages he visited was he even once solicited for food; no one begged. This seems unbelievable. Whatever the case, Childs attributed the resignation and passivity he witnessed not to the influence of the traumatic events of recent Russian history or to the effects of starvation but to the "racial" features of the Russians, or more generally the Slavs. In the town of Bogorodsk in October 1921 from the wharf he watches refugees digging shallow graves in the mud. Nearby are the ARA foodstuffs and one guard holding a gun which, he figures, would not fire and has only symbolic value. Even that appears unnecessary because the dying are preparing for death. "And each day they look longingly at the food which is piled and stacked so neatly beside them, but they make no movement other than to cross themselves devoutly and to clutch a little stronger at the fatalistic shadows and conceptions of life inbred through long centuries in the Slavic nature." Childs was aware that the Tatars, who constituted a large minority of the district's population, were not Slavs, but he must have assumed that Russians and non-Russians in the land had evolved under the same shadows.

Kelley also took it for granted that the passive behavior he was witnessing was not the result of the Revolution and its disastrous aftermath but was an inherent characteristic of the people. He spelled this out in an article he wrote after his return to the States in the *New York Evening Post* of October 5, 1922, in which he informed Americans:

The Bolsheviki have given Russia a name for violence. And yet there is no more peaceable, harmless people than the peasants, who make up nine-tenths of the population. Themselves starving, they would stand by and watch others eat without a murmur. I never saw or heard of a food riot or demonstration in a Russian city. Uncomplaining, they bore their lot, reasoning little as to the causes of their plight and feeling no great resentment against anybody. But all I spoke with recalled that "times were better under the Czar."

Of course, Kelley had not been around a few years earlier when food riots and other manner of uprising involving those same "peaceable, harmless" peasants had helped to bring an end to the good old days under the tsar. And 1917 was hardly the first such occasion.

A more credible authority on peasant behavior was Pitirim Sorokin, the Russian sociologist, who after being exiled from Russia in 1922 moved to the United States and founded the department of sociology at Harvard. Before his departure he completed a scientific study on hunger, which was prepared for publication and then suppressed. In it he argues that the fundamental cause of the riots, revolts, and rebellions in Russian history going back to ancient times was hunger. In the early modern period, the Time of Troubles was rooted in "catastrophic crop failures" in the years 1601 and 1602. The periodic mass violence of the rest of the seventeenth century was hunger related, including the great peasant rebellion led by Stenka Razin. Sorokin cites the historians Platonov and Solovev in making the case that the Razin episode had a "nutritional foundation," that a "deficiency of calories played a role."

Later, under Catherine the Great, crop failures occurred in 1766, 1772, 1774, 1776, 1783, 1784, 1785, 1787, and 1788—all accompanied by riots and uprisings of various proportions, the greatest being the Pugachev rebellion, which reached its peak during the famine of autumn 1774.

Sorokin sees crop failure as a major cause of the revolution of 1905; "the factor of hunger was also at the base of the 1917 revolution"; and later, hunger was the critical factor in February–March 1921 when workers and peasants turned to mass violence against Soviet power and the Kronstadt sailors rebelled.

So history demonstrates that Russians, especially Russian peasants, were capable of considerable violence when faced with hunger. But it was at the point in time Sorokin was writing—six and a half years since the beginning of the Great War and four years since the fall of the Romanovs—that the energy for rebellion had run out, the result of "long and severe deficiency starvation." The large-scale peasant insurrections of the winter and spring of 1920–21—from the black-earth provinces to western Siberia—were a kind of last gasp. When the Great Famine began in the summer, a dazed population responded with apathy because it was physically incapable of action on account of prolonged hunger.[1]

Enter the American relief workers. Seeing so many submissive figures all around, these strangers assumed that things had always been this way. Barringer was quite certain of it: "In Russia, relief would be possible that could never be in America under the same conditions. With millions of people starving, where a sack of flour meant life to oneself and all those dear to him, our ARA food trains rolled over Russia, thru villages, with amazing little molestation."

"A crude passive race that has been disciplined is the only reason."

"The Russian people, ever patient, are dying quietly, but they are dying." So wrote Duranty, who observed firsthand the "despairing fatalism" of the Samara peasants, their "amazing docility and uncomplainingness." He too assumed that the explanation for such conduct lay in the Russian national character—namely, the fatalism of "this Mongolian race." Yet he made allowance for the effects of the famine, which had brought about "a degree of hopeless acceptance of fate's cruelty hardly to be paralleled even in this Russia, where passive suffering is such a universal rule." The famine had thus intensified an inbred feature of the Russian character.

In one place Duranty described the peasants as "helpless like sheep." Elsewhere he wrote, "Like cattle in a drought they waited apathetic for death." Analogies from the animal kingdom were quite common. Among the ARA records there is a report written by an American identified only as "N," who remarks about the Russian peasant: "He looks out with a kind of bovine inquiry, adapting himself to the wind, wondering what he has done to make circumstances so untoward. He is likely to blame events on himself rather than to search for the reason in himself." Although elsewhere in the same report the same peasants are said to be "highly endowed with horse sense."

Governor Goodrich was instantly fascinated by the ways of these peasants. As an Indianan he considered himself something of a natural expert on farming matters, although in famine matters he was a tenderfoot. His ARA colleagues marveled at how the starving peasants did not *take* food; Goodrich wondered why those peasants who possessed stores of food did not *share* it. In autumn 1921 he came to the village of Norga in the Saratov district, which he called the richest settlement in the Volga valley. Here there was enough food to feed everyone, yet some were starving. He wrote in his journal that he did not understand this, "for it seemed to me that I would share my last crust with another who was hungry and both of us live or die together." Americans, who were not "imbued with that certain something we call oriental fatalism," found it difficult to accept how little value the Russians placed on human life.

The governor confronted a group of peasants in possession of a grain surplus of at least four months and asked why they allowed their neighbors to die. A tense silence followed, until one dared to speak up: "You Americans, living in a land of plenty, don't understand. It cannot be helped, there is not enough to feed us all, it is necessary that some should die that others might live." Or, in the less parochial formulation of an old Russian proverb, "They don't cry in Riazan about a crop failure in Pskov."

One year later, after two more visits to Soviet Russia, Goodrich believed himself to be a minor authority on the Russian peasants, whom he called "The True Communists of Russia," the title of an article he published in *Current History* in September 1922. Like a long line of foreign visitors to Russia before him, he was intrigued by the village self-administration—the commune, or *mir*—which he called a "thoroughly democratic, self-governing body." Russian intellectuals in the nineteenth century expended a great deal of energy in thinking, talking, and writing about it. From across the ideological spectrum many saw in its rough-and-ready system of democracy, egalitarianism, and justice a unique institution that might allow Russia to avoid capitalism and build its own distinct social order.

The traditional peasant commune was fundamentally distinct from the Soviet collective farm or commune, *kommuna*, which the Bolsheviks promoted only tentatively in the early years of the Revolution and which, as the *kolkhoz*, would transform the countryside only later, under Stalin. That Soviet "commune" was predicated on the collective tenure of the land, whereas in the traditional commune the soil was tilled individually. Peasants were allotted land in separate and sometimes numerous strips, with the total size of the holding determined by the number of "eaters" in a family. As this was a variable condition, the land was subject to periodic redistribution by collective decision of the *mir*, although this practice had largely fallen into disuse by the time of the Revolution.

It was a wastefully inefficient arrangement, which promoted overpopulation while perpetuating primitive production methods. After the Revolution of 1905 the tsarist government sought with mixed success to break the *mir*'s hold over agriculture, and by the time of the war fewer than half of all peasant households belonged to a commune—though many of the breakaway householders had yet to consolidate their separate strips of land into a single farm.

Notwithstanding the collectivist features of the peasant commune, the Russian peasant was a firm believer in farming his own land. This appealed to Goodrich, whose play on words may have confused his American readers: "In this respect the communist is a strict individualist." But it explains why Stalin's 1929 "collectivization" of the peasantry—their organization into collective farms where the land was to be worked in common—far from corresponding to the Russian spirit, cut against its grain. Millions died in the resistance.

As for the *mir*, the communal gathering where the peasants managed their affairs, Governor Goodrich thought this was a fine institution, like "the old New England town meeting." His enthusiasm carried him away and inspired him to draw broad comparisons between the peasants and "our own folks." "I visited many of these communes; I slept in the homes of their people and ate at their tables. They are a simple, kindhearted, honest people, very much like the American farmer in many ways, and I like them much." In a letter to his friend President Harding on March 24, 1922, he wrote of the Russians generally: "They are a fine, open-faced, honest, industrious sort of people, and you would like them if you could see them and get in touch with them as I have during my two trips." Just two trips, but it was nonetheless self-evident: "Inherently, the Russian, like the American, is not a militarist but a man of peace."

At such moments he sounds like the teddy-bear version of Khrushchev holding forth in the Iowa cornfields about the basic similarities between Russians and Americans—their broad, open nature, their desire for peace—looking for anything that might throw a bridge over the profound ideological divide that lay between the two countries.

Goodrich could not sustain his wishful thinking. Taking the entire body of his Russian observations, it is the many Russian-American contrasts that prevail. In his article on the peasants he has not forgotten the residents of Norga and their behavior in the face of starvation: "With true Oriental fatalism they accept it stoically. Famine has occurred before, and will occur again. When food is scarce, some in the communes must perish in order that others may live. 'It is fate,' these patient Russians will tell you, and they do not complain because some of their neighbors may be a little better provided with food than they."

Here he is a tolerant observer, but even the governor allowed himself private moments of exasperation, as when he wrote to Hoover, "It is difficult to understand the Russian mind, and how patiently they endure hardships, injustices and oppression that would bring a revolution in twenty-four hours in our own country." Hardly like our own folks after all.

Goodrich liked to think that he had come to know these Russians, although he did not have nearly the exposure of the typical ARA man. As special investigator he made a couple of flying trips through the countryside to assess the famine and then the relief and report back to Hoover. The ARA alumni newsletter recalled "The meteoric passage of Gov. Goodrich."

The regular relief workers were planted in the heartland for months on end. They had far more time for observation and contemplation. In the substantial written record they left behind rarely do they point to similarities between Russian peasants and American farmers. These young men, most of them like Goodrich complete novices in Russian affairs, indulged in a great deal of speculation about the Russian "character" or "temperament"—the later popular expression "Russian soul" was not in their vocabulary. This tendency, shared by the governor, is understandable. A great revolution had only recently taken place, and a great famine was now raging; those arriving on the scene could not help but wonder why things in

Russia had turned out so tragically. The answer seemed to lie in the nature of the people, especially the overwhelmingly predominant social class, the peasantry.

Images of darkness and light permeate the descriptions of the peasants and the countryside. During a sleigh circuit through the Kazan district in December 1921 Childs met with local ARA committees in the villages, one in the town of Umatova:

> By the light of a flickering oil lamp they were presently assembled and with them a cu-rious crowd of onlookers, of old and young and of both sexes. The members of the committee were sturdy, Godfearing honest appearing peasants with dark brown skins and beards which seemed to have been washed in the soil. When one asked them a question so simple as how the children were selected to receive the American food they screwed up their eyes and wrinkled their foreheads in an effort to arrive in their minds at the answer. To other questions they would lift up their direct frank glances and with the innocence of a child reply, "Comrade, how can one say?" To the question concern-ing the percentage of the population which might live through the winter on their present resources there was no hesitation in replying: "Not more than three percent".[2]

One might call these the peasants of Tolstoy: God-fearing, simple, innocent, like children. In 1891, in the early stage of the largest previous Russian famine, Tolstoy walked among them in Tula province. They were already reduced to eat-ing *lebeda*, though with enough supplemental rye to last for maybe another month. He asked them how it had come to this:

> There was an instant chorus of replies:
> "What are you going to do? Last summer half of the village burned, as if a cow had licked off the earth. And this summer there are no crops and it's getting worse all the time!"
> "But what are you going to do?"
> "Just as God wills. We'll sell what we can, and then just live. . . . "
> But it is perfectly apparent that these peasants will not be able to live through the coming winter unless they do something to help themselves. . . . Scarcely one of them seems to understand the situation.

In 1921 the difference was that the Volga peasants appeared to understand what lay ahead.

FARMER MURPHY sensed that the landscape and the climate were crucial in-fluences on the peasants' mentality. Murphy was based in Moscow in 1921 and made his only tour of the famine zone in late autumn, which in Russia often counts as winter. In order to understand the "brooding and gloomy spirit of the people," he wrote upon his return to the capital, one had only to visit a Russian village in winter.

> I saw many on my recent trip and the effect was always a feeling of a contraction of the heart, a sensation of stifling. The landscape, as far as the eye can reach, is covered with snow. Nothing disturbs the monotony of this white expanse and the leaden gray of the low hanging clouds except an occasional flock of black and dun crows which only add to the mournful general aspect. The silence is deep and unbroken. It is as if all the senses except that of sight were paralyzed and even that was dimmed. Then at a dis-tance you note a dark purple spot amidst the white. It is a cluster of houses or izbas.

*Izba*s were typically arranged in clusters. Because the peasant commune system had traditionally provided for a periodic redistribution of the land, it did not make sense to build your home on land you might someday cede to another. So dwellings were concentrated in the villages. Gorky saw nothing in the arrangement to recommend itself: "The boundless flatness on which wooden, straw-thatched villages are bunched together has a poisonous quality which devastates a man and drains him of all desires. If a peasant goes beyond the boundaries of his village he looks out into the emptiness around him and in a short time feels that this emptiness has poured into his soul." Escape is impossible; the peasant is reduced to an "insignificant, little man cast upon this boring earth for hard labor."

Professor I. I. Mossoloff, a historian at Moscow University, in an essay solicited and translated into English by the ARA, wrote more inclusively of the decisive influence of nature in shaping the peasant's outlook on life:

A primitive system of farming carried on amidst an unstable nature not yet mastered by man—makes of the Russian peasant a helpless fatalist. Not knowing how to fight with frost and heat, with drought and rain, which all in turn can become a danger for the stubborn work he has carried on for a whole year—he endeavours to save his handiwork by humility and by submission to Nature. His life is limited by strictest traditions that pass from father to son and grandson—only on certain days does he begin his sowing, ploughing, mowing and harvesting; he has no initiative of his own, no ability to take the best advantage of nature and to adapt her to his needs.

This timidity and this slave's psychology are features that the natural conditions of the country have imprinted upon his mind and that history has subsequently helped to render still more salient.

Gorky allowed that summer could be quite wonderful, but with the arrival of autumn the land demanded of the peasant backbreaking labor. "Then comes the severe, six-month winter, the earth is covered with a blindingly white shroud, angrily and threateningly the snowstorms rage and a person suffocates from inactivity and melancholy in a cramped, dirty izba. Out of everything that he does, all that remains on the earth are his straw and a straw-thatched izba—which three times in the life of every generation is destroyed by fire."

Actually, in the famine of 1921 it happened that in order to stay alive peasants were driven to eat the straw thatch on the roofs of these *izba*s, leaving only the walls in place. Thus the survivor's recurrent lament, "I ate my house." Murphy takes us inside an uneaten *izba*:

If it is dull without it is necessarily darker within for the tiny windows admit only a little of the already muddied light, and in the winter there are only five or six hours of day. During the long evenings there can be only the dim light of candle or small oil lamps. So it is in this twilight that millions of peasants dwell for more than half of every year of their lives. Generations of this kind of existence must have had a profound influence on the temper of the people.

Mossoloff attributes to the long, severe winter, which imposed months of idleness on the peasant after the excruciating labors of autumn, responsibility for one of the distinctive features of the Russian, and not just the Russian peasant: namely, a lack of steadfastness in matters of labor. Mossoloff was by no means the first to draw this connection, and observers after him would see in the practice of "storming" by Soviet workers and collective farmers—the frantic push near the end of each month to achieve planned production targets set by the state—the natural rhythm of peasant Russia.

Here also was one explanation for the large number of holidays on the Russian calendar: with little to do in winter, the peasant needed some diversion to punctuate daily life and help pass the time. In its own way drink served the same purpose. It all added up to a cartoon version of Marx's "idiocy of rural life," one that seemed to have gone on with little change over the centuries. Consider the opportunities this presented to the Russian historian specializing in the social history of the medieval period. He need not have restricted his inquiry to the study of written sources but could engage in something like field research simply by wandering far enough away from the railway lines into the peasant darkness. Though he risked having the dogs set on him or being stoned to death.

Gorky relates a story involving the ceremonies marking the three hundredth anniversary of the Romanov dynasty, which began with Tsar Michael in 1613. The Grand Duke Nikolai Mikhailovich, author of a number of historical works, was standing alongside Tsar Nicholas before a crowd of peasants in the town of Kostroma, situated northeast of Moscow on the Volga. Looking out at their subjects, the Grand Duke said to the Tsar: "You see, they are absolutely the same as they were in the 17th century, when they put Michael on the throne, the same; that is bad, don't you think?"

Kostroma was part of the more industrialized north, the "consuming" provinces where the seeds of capitalism had taken root. The peasants in the north were more dependent on handicraft industries and were generally more enterprising than the peasants in the "producing" black soil region to the south. So if the story of what the Grand Duke said is true, he had engaged in more than his due share of exaggeration. Still he had a point as he stared into the collective face of Russian backwardness. Though the country had taken mighty strides forward along the path of modernization since the industrialization drive begun in the 1890s, peasant Russia was vast and resistant to change. Was there not some way to accelerate its development?

Murphy emerged from the twilight of the *izba* and declared that the solution was "more and better artificial light. If electricity were everywhere made available or if even good kerosene lamps were put into general use would not this added light put cheer into the lives of the people and in time affect their character? An economic enterprise might thus give a different direction to the minds of a race."

This was the approximate spirit of Lenin's utopian scheme for the electrification of the countryside, which became all the rage in 1920, at least among certain Bolsheviks in the Kremlin. Lenin, whose mind worked overtime on ways to leap over stages of development, seized upon the electric lamp as the means to penetrate the peasant darkness and, thereby, darkness of mind. The coming of light would make it possible for the peasant to put aside the bottle for the book with all that this implied for promoting literacy and overcoming backwardness, not to mention the new vistas it would open up for Bolshevik propaganda. The spirit of the campaign was captured in Lenin's exhortative equation: "Communism is Soviet power plus the electrification of the whole country." At the time he thought this could take place in ten years.

Electrification turned out to be the last utopian hurrah of the revolutionary period. Then came the turbulent events of the winter of 1920–21 and the turn to realism in economic policy. In purely economic terms the electrification plan was now seen to be totally impractical. When the famine began, the struggle was to get seed, not light bulbs, to the countryside.

After having deluded themselves into believing that they were making a leap over Russian backwardness, the Bolsheviks were brought to their senses by circumstances, which made them realize that in actual fact their revolution was in danger of being smothered by Russian backwardness. Russia was after all still overwhelmingly a peasant country. The "dictatorship of the proletariat" was an island in a sea of peasants—and now many of them were angry peasants. The turning point was the Tenth Party Congress in March 1921, where Lenin led the way, placing before the assembled delegates some unpleasant facts about the country in which they had made their socialist revolution:

Take a look at a map of the R.S.F.S.R. To the north from Vologda, to the southeast from Rostov-on-the-Don and from Saratov, to the south from Orenburg and from Omsk, to the north from Tomsk there are enormous distances, along which there are room for dozens of tremendous cultured states. And along all these stretches there rules patriarchalism, half-savagery, and the most real savagery. And in the peasant backwaters of the rest of Russia? Everywhere where there are dozens of versts of country roads—better: dozens of versts of no roads—the village is separated from the railroads, that is, from the material ties with culture, with capitalism, with heavy industry, with a big town. Do you not think that in those places as well predominate patriarchalism, oblomovism, half-savagery?

"Oblomovism"—or *oblomovshchina* in the unambiguously derogatory Russian— is a reference to Oblomov, the eponymous protagonist of Ivan Goncharov's 1859 novel, who in the words of Professor Riasanovsky, "snored his way to fame as one of the most unforgettable as well as most 'superfluous' heroes of Russian literature." The fictional young nobleman became a ubiquitous symbol of the Russian gentry's inertia and lethargy. But the Bolsheviks discovered that getting rid of the nobility did not rid Russia of oblomovism. Alas, it turned out that there was also a particular peasant strain of the disease.

The Bolshevik economist Preobrazhenskii, in a July 28, 1923, *Pravda* article, called it a "democratic, peasant *oblomovshchina*." Its sources lay in the backwardness and structure of Russian agriculture, notably those huge stretches of idle time caused by seasonal inactivity due to the climate. Comrade Preobrazhenskii, meet Professor Mossoloff.

What is more, the disease had spread to the factory since there was no clear dividing line between peasants and workers: every Russian worker was either the son, grandson, or great-grandson of a peasant serf. Factory life had not had time to recast the mentality of those who had been uprooted from the countryside, especially when they remained regular visitors to their native villages, chiefly at harvest time. This explained the Russian proletarian's shoddy work habits, lack of punctuality, and general carelessness with time. Preobrazhenskii thought that this peasant *oblomovshchina* had been largely overcome in the northern industrial provinces where the peasants had been more "Europeanized" by capitalism. The way to surmount it elsewhere, in his view, was to initiate a cultural revolution, conduct a "struggle against our old national character," and create a "new type of Soviet man." In fact this is roughly the story of the Soviet experiment during the subsequent decade and beyond.

In 1921 not only the Bolsheviks saw a threat in the ascendancy of the peasantry. Gorky regarded the situation as ominous. He told a visiting French journalist that summer:

Up to now the workers have been the masters, but they are only a tiny minority in our country: they represent at most a few millions. The peasants are legion. In the struggle between the two classes that has been going on since the beginning of the revolution, the peasants have every chance of coming out victorious. . . . The urban proletariat has been declining incessantly for four years. . . . The immense peasant tide will end by engulfing everything. . . . The peasant will become master of Russia, since he represents numbers, and it will be terrible for our future.

Soon after speaking these words and shortly after the ARA arrived, Gorky left Soviet Russia, choosing the life of the émigré exile in Berlin. He would return to Moscow before the decade was out, just in time to witness Stalin's solution to the "immense peasant tide." In Berlin in 1922 he published an infamous little book, *On the Russian Peasant*, which is replete with shocking anecdotes illustrating the savagery of the Russian peasant, a condition which, he revealed, "my whole life has astounded and tormented me."

Gorky had come to the conclusion that the Russians were by nature a cruel people; in fact a "sense of exceptional cruelty" was as peculiar to the Russian character as was a sense of humor to the British. This was no ordinary cruelty but a special brand, one bent on "testing the limits of human endurance." It had acquired over the centuries a "devilish refinement," surpassing that of all other peoples. In order to back up these extreme assertions, he raised the curtain on a gruesome gallery depicting the "collective amusements of human torture."

In Siberia some peasants dig a large hole into which they lower captured Red Army soldiers head first, then fill in the hole, leaving above ground only the prisoners' legs at the knee—then they observe from the spasms of these free limbs which victim holds out the longest.

In Tambovsk they round up some Communists and use railroad spikes to nail their left hands and left feet to trees, a meter off the ground, and then watch the suffering of these human beings, "intentionally incorrectly crucified."

Cutting open their prisoner's stomach, they remove one end of his small intestine and, nailing it to a tree, chase him with blows 'round and 'round to see how the intestine unravels out of him.

They carve from the shoulder of a Red Army officer a piece of skin in the shape of an epaulet; in place of a star they hammer in a nail.

Gorky selected most of his examples from the recent period, and indeed he recognized that the world war, the Revolution, and especially the Civil War had shattered Russia's moral standards. To illustrate this he cites the report of a scientific expedition to the Urals in 1921, which tells the story of a man who has killed a Bashkir and taken his cow. Now the man is worried that he may be punished for stealing the cow; the death of the Bashkir, however, does not trouble him: "that's nothing—a human being is cheap." The barbarity of the Civil War had made murder commonplace, yet Gorky saw this as merely an amplification of something already present in the Russian character: "The cruelty of the forms of the revolution I explain by the extraordinary cruelty of the Russian people." As to the question of which side, Red or White, had been crueler in the Civil War, Gorky guessed that probably they were equally cruel because both were Russian.

Mossoloff was less of a pessimist than Gorky. He was encouraged to note that since 1917 the peasants were striving to enrich themselves, freeing themselves from the commune and setting up independent farms—a process he called a "new colonization by the Russians of their own country." Nonetheless, he admitted, this was overshadowed by behavior worthy of "wild beasts."

Mossoloff placed great weight on the influence of the Mongol domination of Russia in the thirteenth and fourteenth centuries, which brought "much cruelty and savageness into the life and customs of the Russian people." In emphasizing this historical phase, Mossoloff was in good company. There is a large and long-standing literature, both Russian and non-Russian, disputing the impact of Mongol rule over Russia. For some, especially the nonscholars, it has served as the all-purpose explanation for why the Russians turned out so differently from other Europeans, despite the westernizing efforts of Peter the Great: beneath the veneer of Western culture they are actually "Asiatic." Napoleon set the standard for conciseness with his oft-repeated dictum, "Scratch a Russian and you'll find a Tatar."

Mossoloff was not so deterministic. He maintained that during the centuries following Mongol domination, the Russian peasant established admirable values and customs based upon the patriarchal family. He blamed the urbanization at the end of the nineteenth century for undermining these traditions, and the turn of the century saw "the old primitive uncultured beast of prey reappear in the Russians." Things became especially bad with the revolution of 1905, when hooliganism became rampant and morality declined. Much animosity was directed at the towns, and the visit to the countryside of a townsman often served as the occasion for "insolent mischief," though not as yet of the wicked forms documented by Gorky.

In the cities and larger towns the educated classes had become far removed from all this savagery. Sustained isolation made it possible for them during the mid to late nineteenth century to entertain the idea that the peasant possessed certain exceptional virtues. His nearness to the soil, his relative insulation from the urban environment, his ties to that uniquely Russian institution, the commune—all this made him appear a figure purely Russian, unspoiled by modern, primarily Western, influences. "In the eyes of the Russian 'intelligentzia,'" Mossoloff testified, "the peasants were sufferers, martyrs, they were the bearers of the supreme truth and of high moral ideals."

The peasant, in other words, as noble savage. Mossoloff saw a parallel to the way Europeans of the eighteenth and nineteenth centuries from their safe distance "idealized the life of the American savages." In the United States it was nineteenth century New Englanders who ennobled the American Indian. This could take place, of course, only after they had elbowed and otherwise dislodged his ignoble ancestor westward. Only then could they afford hypocritically to extol the Indian's virtues. Only then were they free to thrill to the romanticized images of Indian warriors and maidens in the novels of James Fenimore Cooper.

The homesteaders advancing "civilization" out on the frontier saw the more complex reality, some losing their scalps if they did not pay close enough attention.

Russia's writers promoted the peasant myth. Gorky was perplexed by this. "But where, after all," he asked in 1922, "is that good-natured, thoughtful Russian peasant, the tireless seeker of truth and justice, about whom 19th century Russian literature wrote so convincingly and beautifully?" He went to meet this peasant but instead discovered a "stern realist and cunning person" who knew how to pose as a simpleton. True, toward the end of the nineteenth century the writers began to portray the peasant with more realism, beginning with the stories of Chekhov. But it was not nearly enough to prepare the town for the unspeakable behavior of the countryside in the Revolution.

In 1917–18, before the outbreak of civil war, peasants pillaged the manors and farms of the gentry, destroying libraries and works of art, carrying away furniture, slaughtering livestock, and cutting down forests. In the north, where class animosity was not so acute, the plunder was given a legal appearance as the gentry's manors and possessions were auctioned off.

There was also at that time a contest *among* the peasants for possession of the land. To an extent this was inevitable, and it was naturally exacerbated as peasants in uniform rushed from the front to claim their share while others in the factories also returned to the land. But the Bolsheviks further poisoned the atmosphere by setting the have-nots against the haves in a "class war"—an attempt to split the peasantry and win the allegiance of putatively "poor" or "proletarian" peasants. It is this that Mossoloff had in mind when he wrote that "envy of one's neighbor became all of a sudden a thing ideologically admissible." This class-war policy had to be abandoned once the Civil War began, but the damage had been done.

Over the next two years the ties between the cities and the countryside weakened. As more and more railroad lines were severed, wrote Mossoloff, "The peasants were left to themselves." In 1919 and 1920 starvation and disease ravaged the urban population, cut off from its food supply. "The country began to rule the town."

Gorky wrote bitterly of this nightmarish period: "It is difficult to speak about the crudely mocking, vindictive scorn with which the countryside met the starving people of the city." He recalled pathetic scenes of townspeople struggling to stay alive by bartering possessions—clothes, furniture, gramophones, mirrors—in exchange for bread, butter, milk, meat, and potatoes. "In 1919 the meekest village inhabitant calmly removed the townsman's shoes, stripped him of his clothes, and altogether robbed him, bartering from him for bread and potatoes everything necessary and unnecessary to the countryside."

The peasants made no little effort to give their bartering with the former well-to-do the "humiliating character of alms." While the worker was treated more cautiously because of his connection to the government, the *intelligent* was subject to "moral torment": after arguing long and hard over the terms of an exchange, the *muzhik* or *baba* calculatingly tells the pitiful exile with children at home to feed, "No, go on your way. We changed our minds, we won't give potatoes."

Gorky and Mossoloff neglect to mention another feature of the Civil War countryside, one essential for understanding later developments. In order to feed the Red Army and to keep industry running, the Bolshevik government requisitioned grain by force of arms. The peasant resisted, sometimes violently but more commonly through passive resistance by concealing grain and cutting back on planting so as to produce only enough to feed his family. This left him, however, with minimal reserves of grain and thus dangerously vulnerable. When the drought occurred in the summer of 1920, famine was unavoidable.

So when Gorky was writing his exposé of the cruel and cunning Russian peasants, tens of millions of them were threatened with starvation. Yes, they had forced the Bolsheviks to halt the requisitions, and they had won the right to trade their surpluses; yes, they were rid of the landlord, and they owned the land. But at their supposed moment of triumph they—at least those in the famine zone—were hardly feeling like the masters of Russia of Gorky's nightmare. Their stomachs were empty, and their land was unsown. They looked to the *vlast'*, the government, and wondered what it would now do to help them. They knew that God was punishing them for their sins. Meek as children they slipped into passivity and submissiveness. Gorky's peasants were gone; Tolstoy's peasants had returned.[3]

THE BOLSHEVIK WHOSE JOB it was to explain to the peasants what the government could and could not do to assist them was one of their own, Mikhail Kalinin, the titular president of the country, whose official title was chairman of the All-Russian Central Executive Committee. Kalinin was born in 1875 in Tver province northwest of Moscow. In 1889 he moved to St. Petersburg and the enormous Putilov plant, where he worked as a lathe operator and electrician, among other trades. There he fell into radical politics and in the period up to 1917 this Bolshevik chalked up fourteen arrests. After the October Revolution he served in the administration of Petrograd until the premature death of a leading Bolshevik cleared the way for him to be appointed figurehead president in March 1919, at a time when the Party was looking to mend fences with the peasantry.

Kalinin served an important symbolic purpose. He was not, as were most of the leading Bolsheviks, of bourgeois background. William Henry Chamberlin called him "a shrewd muzhik, with no influence on affairs of state, but with a certain decorative value for the regime because everything about him, his blue eyes, straw-colored beard, wrinkled face, clumsy manners, proclaimed his peasant origin." Actually, his more vital connection had long since been to the factory, though he maintained his personal ties to the land through his family in Tver. So he was able to serve as the dual embodiment of workers' and peasants' power.

Kellogg sat in with the president in late September 1921. In his diary he spells the name "Kalenin," a common error of English speakers in the early years, which made it seem like a diminutive of "Lenin." Kellogg called him "the present pleasant peasant President" and was charmed by his simple dress and straightforward manner: "no form, no fluff—the intelligent political peasant with impression of openness & no make-up or glad hand manner."

After the meeting, Kellogg's interpreter told him that Kalinin's words were difficult to translate because he used an "unliterate and peasant Russian. *K.* also spoke for 6 or 7 minutes or even longer at a time, verging occasionally on an almost speechmaking manner."

Kalinin's tendency to peasantize his spoken Russian must have been reinforced by the fact that most of the visitors he received were peasants. They were petitioners from all over the country, upholding the time-honored tradition of the *khodok* —meaning "envoy" but literally "walker," since in past times these ambassadors from the villages had to go on foot, often across considerable distances, in order to present their petitions to the "little father," the tsar. Kalinin, the Soviet "little father," listened to and pronounced judgment on their requests. He sat behind a simple wooden table in his office, which was located outside the Kremlin opposite its main gate, making him more available to the common people than the average tsar.

Kalinin's unofficial title was "All-Russian *starosta*," or elder, the term used to denote the senior authority figure in the village. During the Civil War he traveled extensively in his private agitprop train "October Revolution," whistle-stopping across whatever at the moment constituted the country and addressing gatherings of peasants and soldiers. In the villages he listened to the peasants' many complaints and promised to intercede for them in Moscow, thereby sparing some the long journey to the capital.

On August 16, 1921, Kalinin addressed a gathering, *skhodka*, of peasants in the village of Viazovaya-Gai on the Moch River in the Pugachev district of Samara province—in other words, ground zero of the Great Famine. The published record of this meeting could hardly be the stenographic report it purports to be, but it does nevertheless document the peasants' anguished state of mind, and it illuminates Kalinin's unusual role and methods. At times the All-Russian *starosta* sounds as if he is quoting from a book of traditional peasant proverbs as he tries to reason with his audience about matters of life and death. His manner thickens the atmosphere of apocalyptic foreboding that hangs over the gathering.

Kalinin had two points to make. The first was intended to slow the exodus from the Volga, both westward into northern Ukraine and eastward into Siberia and Turkestan. To accomplish this he had to convince his listeners that refugees suffered a worse fate than those who remained at home. His argument was based in part on an assurance that the government would do all it could to help the peasants who stayed in place to fight the famine. In view of this, he was remarkably honest about the limits to what the government could in fact contribute: actual food relief would be negligible; as for winter seed, there would be enough to cover only one-tenth of the needs of Samara province.

The thinness of this pledge placed a great deal of weight on his second message: a call on the peasants to use *every* possible means to survive on the meager reserve they possessed. Above all, don't take to the road, for that means certain death.

Voice: Staying here also means death.
Kalinin: If you slaughter a horse, then you will have 15 puds of meat and you can get by with grass and hay.
Voice: And if there's no horse?
Kalinin: Comrades, if there is no horse, no cow, no wife, then there is no use hanging around here. I am speaking, comrades, of the majority of the people. I don't doubt that many people will die. It all depends on know-how: you have to know how to fight famine.
Voice: We all will die.
Kalinin: It is a question of time when we will die. We prefer that people do not die. In Samara province the population numbers 3 million and the more who survive the better, but some of these people, of course, will die. Why, today you had one per-

son die of starvation—that's the best example, but you have to use all your efforts. The government of course, will do everything possible.

But it was up to the peasants to husband their resources. They had to preserve grain, said Kalinin, "as a husband protects his wife during the first month, when he loves her." Here his choice of phrase seems a conscious effort to reinforce with his listeners his salt-of-the-earth credentials, of which he also reminded them directly: "I myself am a peasant and know how to thresh rye no worse than you." He also knew, he said, that there were numerous ways to stretch out two poods of grain.

To demonstrate that he was not simply some commissar whose interest was in plunder, he told the gathering that even though he was president he still owned two cows and three *dessiatinas*, about eight acres, of land. This was in his native village of Kimry in Tver province where his mother was forever moaning to him about how "your people robbed us." He mentioned that he had a cow requisitioned before he became president: "And my mother does not forget, every day she recalls that the cow was a good one."

Yes, Kalinin admitted, the government took from you—it did this in order to feed the army, save the factories and the railroads, in order to seed the land in the north. But the government did not take as much as you think; it only seemed like more than it really was. That, he said, was human nature, especially peasant nature.

Maybe so, but in the Pugachev district there were heavy government requisitions as late as July 1921, which meant that the peasants he was addressing were left stripped of their defenses in the struggle against the famine.

Voice: The government knows how to take, but doesn't know how to give.

Kalinin: . . . And if we had not taken a single pood from you in 1919, do you think you would not now be starving? You would be starving magnificently. Well, of course, maybe 5 people in the entire village would not be starving, but the rest would still be starving.

Voice: No, we would not all be starving, on our own we would be satisfied.

He reminded them that famine was not an unusual occurrence in recent Russian history:

Kalinin: I know how in '11 you lived on your own. I know how you were dying in '91; the old men certainly remember how many people died.

Voice: That was from cholera.

Kalinin: It's always like that: either famine or cholera, typhus or war.

(Noise)

In other words, that's the life of the peasant: "today you are rich, but tomorrow you are poor. So it is in the countryside: today the countryside is rich, but tomorrow there's a crop failure."

One of the voices asked Kalinin, "our leader," to give just a little encouragement. He refused to indulge them, telling them to stop feeling sorry for themselves. He rejected the entire basis for their self-pity and offered a positive assessment of their situation, emphasizing their victories since 1917:

The peasants are always saying: we are poor, we are poor. But I must say that the peasantry has never lived so well as under Soviet power. And the peasants have never had such a privileged situation as at the present moment. [Voice: "We can see better."] But I think you don't see better; you see only your own village, but I am now standing in the bell tower and from there I see all of Russia, the whole population—I see former generals, former representatives of the bourgeois class, former landlords, teachers, and I see doctors, engineers, commissars, and all workers and peasants. . . . And as I look from above, I see that no one lives better than the peasants.

A voice in the crowd objected that Kalinin was criticizing them for complaining, yet "We are only crying because the government has thrown us on the mercy of fate." Kalinin would not stand for talk of "fate": "a famine obliges you to fight back."

Don't worry, you have lived through the magnificent school of famine. When you ate all kinds of garbage, potato peels—all of that took place, all of that you experienced. But you cannot lose heart. It's the same as on cold days, when you are walking in a blizzard, when you are caught in a winter snowstorm, you have the desire to lie down. He who lies down dies, but he who walks on, exhausted, will survive.

Kellogg was not yet in Russia at the time of this *skhodka* of August 16, but when he arrived shortly afterward he came across an English translation of the record of its proceedings. It must have made an impression on him because he copied part of it into his diary. Several weeks later in New York he could not remember its source and turned for guidance to Samuel Harper, America's foremost Russianist, who remembered seeing a published account of it, probably in *Izvestiia*.

Whatever meaning it had for Harper, Kellogg read Kalinin's message to the peasants as a quintessential example of Russian fatalism. According to notes Kellogg made in New York based upon his diary, Kalinin had gone to the village to deliver a death sentence:

When he was appealed to by the people and asked what the government was going to do to cope with the situation, tried to tell them—in a speech—what the government was trying to do—"But it won't be enough. Many of you will have to die, but better to die here now making a little fight to live than to take to the road and die along the roadway like the refugees who spent months before getting to Siberia. Men, women and children crowded in cars for days, nights, weeks. No windows—long visits at stations." Many of you will have to die.—An extraordinary statement—Think of Pres. Harding standing up in front of the people here and saying "Many of you will have to die. Better to die making a fight than along the roadways."

In fact judging from the published Soviet account—presumably the source for Kellogg's translation—what is remarkable is the contrast between Kalinin's peasantized manner of speech and his very unpeasantlike call on his audience to stand and fight in the face of death. He is supposed to have said that the government hoped that only 5 percent of the peasants would die. But the ARA image of the brutal, Asiatic, long-suffering, fatalistic Russians found a better match in Kellogg's diary version, which has Russia's president telling a group of its citizens: "Many of you will die. But you can die fighting. It is better to suffer and die here than to try and flee and die by the road side."

The ARA's New York office passed on an abridged text of the diary version to the *New York Times* as "extracts from a stenographic report of a speech by Ka-

lenin," which the *Times* published on November 14 on its editorial page, unat-
tributed to the ARA. The editors remarked, "No more vivid or hopeless picture
of the attitude of the Soviet Government toward its own people has come out of
Russia than is revealed in the following extracts from a stenographic report of a
speech by Kalinin."

The British writer Gibbs, who had a weakness for the melodramatic, depicted
Kalinin asking a peasant his age; "Fifty" was the reply. "'Then you are old enough
to die,' said Kalinin brutally. 'The old must die that the young may live.'"[4]

IN HIS EXTRAORDINARY DIARY of the Russian Revolution, the historian Iurii
Got'e describes spending a Sunday in May 1919 on the outskirts of the capital
with a party of some fifteen Russians of bourgeois background "who had escaped
from horrible and revolting Moscow, forgetting for several hours the woe and
sufferings they were experiencing." He felt pity for these "poor bourgeois and
bourgeoises" when they had to catch the night train back to the city in order to
return to their government jobs. "The Russian intellectual bourgeois is amazingly
meek and submissive to fate; in this company there were very rich men and very
rich women, and all of them have accepted their fate with amazing simplicity; I
don't know whether to praise them for their philosophical worldview or to de-
spise them for their lack of character."

As Got'e testifies, Russian fatalism was not exclusive to the peasantry. Childs
had in mind especially the dispossessed classes when he praised the Russians for
their quiet heroism in the face of adversity. For him, as for so many other foreign
visitors before and since, this aspect of the Russian character was epitomized by
the Russian expression "*nichevo.*" He called it "the perfect summation of the attitude of the Russian masses to life." It can be rendered in English a number of
ways, including "no matter" and "all right." "*Nitchevo.* No word so perfectly reflects the philosophic resignation of the Slav confronted by adversity, however severe. The Russian has been uttering it during centuries of suffering, faced by one
of the severest climates in the world, under the tyranny of the czars and the oppression of such Soviet leaders as Stalin."

But again, how does one explain 1917? Had not the Russians—or a good number of them, anyway—in that year taken matters into their own hands, poured
into the streets, and brought down the tsar and later the Provisional Government?
Did this not represent a different, active side of the Russians? One American eyewitness to the Revolution, the theater critic Oliver Sayler, thought not. He was in
Moscow during the Bolshevik coup d'état, which he called in his 1919 book, *Russia White or Red*, "my baptism of fire into the Russian scene." The many demonstrations he observed in those October days he interpreted as merely more evidence of Russian passivity. The demonstrators he talks about might just as well
have been standing in a queue, that abiding symbol of Russian patience.

In the *demonstratsia*, too, there is a sense of helplessness. Impotence knows no other
outlet. Fatalism is written all over its face. Russia is, indeed, helpless to-day but she
has that curious Oriental strain of resignation in her character partly to thank for her
prostration. In the *demonstratsia*, also, emerges that most Russian of all characteristics, the endless patience which has enabled these people to endure a thousand years

and which will carry them through whatever the Revolution still has in store to add to their already grievous burdens.

Even Sayler, with his acute powers of imagination, probably could not have anticipated what was in store for Russia during the next few years. And if by "the Revolution" one includes the brutality of the Stalin period—the forced collectivization, the famine of 1932, the Great Terror—these were "grievous burdens" beyond anything conceivable to anyone writing in 1918. Still, others who came after him would make pronouncements on the 1930s in words similar to those he used to judge the events of 1917:

Unless we know the Russian, unless we know the Russian in Russia, we find it almost impossible to conceive of this spirit of resignation and long-suffering. Why will he tolerate the Russia of to-day? Why doesn't he do something to change it? There is only one answer. His will to action has been dulled by the process of centuries. "Time is long. *Nietchevo*—it doesn't matter! Russia will find herself some day."

Nichevo, spelled several ways, became part of the everyday vocabulary of the American relief workers, even as its habitual use by Russians tried their patience. They encountered it in every setting, from the peasant hut to the Kremlin. An American at Moscow headquarters, categorizing the attitudes of the former nobility toward Bolshevik power based upon observation of representatives of this social class at work in the office, distinguished between three main groupings: the irreconcilables; the my-country-right-or-wrong set, willing to accept the government in the Kremlin however distasteful its members and practices; and by far the largest group, those who "have accepted their fate with true Slav philosophy. They shrug their shoulders over old times and, when asked how they feel, say calmly: "'Nichevo.'"

Duranty felt that the word represented both a positive and a negative side of the Russians. After listening to a discussion among several NEP businessmen regarding moneymaking schemes, he observed:

No one seemed to bother about the hardships of the past or have any anxiety for the future. They were Russians, you see, whose racial quality it is to live intensely in the present and dismiss doubts or fears or horrid memories with the easy insouciance of children. "*Nichevo*"—"what of it" or "no matter"—has been for centuries the Russian national watchword, and the general spirit of indifference to which it bears witness is an element both of strength and of weakness.

The word appears in the official and personal communications among the ARA men, where it doubled as an expression of professed indifference and of irony. In wrapping up an official report from a Volga town detailing the magnitude of the job ahead and the many physical, climatic, bureaucratic, political, and other obstacles standing in the way of its completion, the American might well close with a "*Nichevo*." It was a kind of "What the hell" or "What, me worry?"—ironic because it mimicked the voice of the greatest psychological hindrance he faced.

The relief workers, like the reporters, liked to place "*Nichevo*" on the lips of their Russian everyman as he was confronted with a fate worse than death. Had there been a prize for the most effective use of this literary device, the journalist Mackenzie would have walked away with the honors. He might have come up with the ultimate symbol of prostrate Russia—even though this may not have been what he had in mind—in June 1922 when he visited a famous Nizhnii Novgorod surgical hospital run by the Red Cross and noted for its abdominal work. Professional dedication, curiosity, or something else led him into the operating room to observe a patient undergo major abdominal surgery. The procedure lasted one hour and forty minutes. The surgeons could administer only local anaesthetics. In fact the hospital had no sedatives, no stimulants, no rubber sheeting, no rubber gloves, very few swabs, and only dull surgical knives.

The fully conscious patient was bound upon the operating table. He was a brave man. His limbs moved at first in uncontrollable shudders. But at the height of the operation, with his very vitals drawn out and rejected, he whispered, when asked how he felt, "*Nichevo! Nichevo!*"

"Suffering, misfortune and torture had accustomed them to tolerate every extremity with supine indifference," wrote Shafroth, who like just about all of his fellow relief workers had never set foot in Russia before 1921, yet was ready to believe that this behavior was ingrained in the national character. "Absolute inertness," "natural inertia," "oriental fatalism," "phlegmatic fatalism"—the Americans used various combinations of words to characterize the "Slav nature" or "Slav race." Dickinson called them a "race of cave men."

The Russian people are a peculiar people, answering to few of the tests of the Western democracies. They are lethargic except when driven to bay, philosophic, acquiescent to the arbitrary decrees of chance or selfishness as if these were the laws of fate.

They are for all the world like a finely ordered electric motor for which the current is wanting, of little value of themselves, functioning when the power is given.[5]

Dickinson was well read, in fact a specialist in English literature, yet neither he nor any of his ARA colleagues, for all their easy generalizing about the Russian character, refer to actual books on Russian history. Few seem to have read the works of nineteenth-century Russian literature, which would have provided them with an extensive literary record of this fatalism. They would have learned that Oblomov was only one in a remarkable succession of passive Russian fictional characters.

Charles Sarolea, professor of French literature at the University of Edinburgh, who was in Moscow in 1923, his first visit since the revolution of 1905, considered Russian letters an ideal window on the Russian character, notably its hallmark "paralysis of the will." It was, he wrote, a feature of every masterpiece of Russian literature, beginning with Pushkin's *Eugene Onegin* to Lermontov's *Hero of Our Time*, Goncharov's *Oblomov*, every novel of Turgenev, every short story of Chekhov, and the main protagonists of Tolstoy's *War and Peace* and Dostoevsky's *Crime and Punishment*. Somehow he overlooked Gogol and his famously shrinking "little man" in frantic search of his overcoat. "The Russian hero is never a hero in the European sense of the word. He does not challenge destiny, he is generally its passive victim."

This "paralysis of the will," Sarolea believed, is "the key which unlocks mysteries of the Russian character which otherwise would appear insoluble." It explains why the Russian is "capable of savage energy and sacrifice, but he is incapable of patient systematic effort, of self-restraint and self control. . . . Like the savage or the child he will yield to his impulses and instincts; he has no staying power. He is erratic and unstable and incalculable. With him it is the unexpected that always happens." He is also "prone to extremes," "lacks balanced judgment," "has no sense of measure and proportion," and is "incapable of compromise." "The Russian character is like the Russian climate, subject to the most abrupt and most violent variations. The Russian is either a drunkard or a total abstainer. He is either superstitious or atheist. He is either an ascet or a sensualist. He is either greedy or disinterested, meek or violent, a loyal subject or a base traitor."

But if paralysis of the will is behind all this, then what is behind it? "I do not believe that the explanation of the mystery is a racial or physical one, rather is it a moral and religious one. It is rooted in the very essence of the Greek Orthodox Church." Here he put his finger on an explanation accepted by many past and present students of Russian culture.

Those who emphasize the effect of religion on the cultural development of Russia have in mind one or both of two determinants. One has to do with the history of ideas. When in 1054 Christianity split into Eastern and Western branches, Russia's allegiance was to Byzantium. Its separation from the Roman Catholic Church fundamentally affected the subsequent course of Russia's intellectual development by cutting it off from Europe's Latin influences. The fall of Constantinople, "the second Rome" to the Turks in 1453 further isolated Moscow, elevating it in the minds of some thinking Russians to the status of "the third Rome," with all that this implied about a separate path for Russia.

The second, related element—and the one that preoccupies Sarolea—is the theological doctrine of Orthodoxy, which seems to hold the answers to the mystery of Russian passivity and fatalism, as Sarolea explains:

Christianity in the Catholic Church or in the Calvinistic Church is a stern discipline of the will, it is a constant training in self-government. On the contrary, Christianity in the Russian Church has only developed the negative, the passive and the contemplative virtues. Greek Orthodoxy teaches mainly obedience to authority, submission and resignation to the will of God and to the will of the Tsar, who is the representative of God. It preaches the "way of Mary" rather than the "way of Martha." The Russian knows how to die for his faith, he does not know how to live for it and still less how to live up to it.[6]

Such erudition was beyond the American relief workers, who generally did not invoke the teachings of Orthodoxy to explain the behavior of their Russians. Here and there, though, these instant Russia experts, aiming to make an impression with the folks back home, gave evidence of having absorbed the general drift of the case for religion. After serving up for his father one of his regular diatribes against Bolshevik power, Cornick seems to realize that something needs explaining: "Naturally we all wonder, as you must when you read this, why do the people stand for this? I must admit that I can not explain it, unless it is all the result of their religion which has made them all fatalists and causes them to submit to anything on the grounds that they themselves can do nothing to change the course of events."

Horsley Gantt arrived at a different conclusion, perhaps guided to it by Pavlov's dog. Gantt served as district physician for the Petrograd ARA, then returned after the mission in January 1925 to work at the Institute of Experimental

Medicine under the physiologist Ivan Pavlov, who was conducting research into the nature of conditioned reflexes and the inheritability of acquired characteristics, among other things. Much of the work involved experimentation on animals, mostly on their digestive glands, and entailed analyzing prodigious amounts of saliva of various consistencies.

Gantt would spend much of the next fifty-six years in the laboratory performing experiments on conditioned reflexes. In January 1928, after three years of intensive research in the Leningrad laboratory, Gantt came out for a breather, passing through Helsingfors where he had an interview with the American consul, James R. Wilkinson, who informed the State Department of the substance of their discussion. The usual fare of these routine reports was the subject's opinions on recent political and economic developments, but something inspired Gantt to address the more general topic of the Russian character:

The great writers have attempted to account for Russian temperament by studying the Russian mind and have thought they have succeeded. But they have failed. Russian temperament is explained by the Russian stomach where not enough food is put to keep the Russian mind and the Russian body going.

The listlessness, the fatalism, the lack of backbone, and the general worthlessness of the Russian are attributable to the fact that for generation after generation he has starved his body. He eats black bread and drinks weak tea, and then sits around and wonders why he does not feel like doing anything.

He does a great deal of vague thinking, but his fundamental ideas are so devoid of intelligence that his outbursts which are intended to give them expressions are vapid and meaningless.

It would appear that his work with Pavlov had influenced his thinking, although in the interview he does not seem to have compared the Russians to animals. Rather, he said, "Living among the Russians today is like living among silly children." They are mesmerized by even the simplest modern device. "They behave like the Red Indians did when the white men brought them beads." They walk about in a daze instead of overthrowing the government.

Gantt must have rambled on a bit. Wilkinson grew uneasy listening to "his curiously inconsistent pity for the Russians." He found Gantt to be a "good Virginian," but Russia had left its mark on him: "he took almost childish pleasure in little blessings."

Gantt had already begun his professional relationship with Pavlov during the relief mission. They met after Gantt's interpreter offered an introduction to the great scientist, which surprised Gantt because he had read Pavlov's obituary in the *Encyclopaedia Britannica*. Their association originated in October 1922 when Gantt began working in the laboratory after hours. Perhaps this is what was meant by the item in the ARA newsletter's "Non-Statistical Notes"—"Various adventures of Horsley Gantt"—because there were no tales to tell about boozing or women that would account for it. It is possible that it refers to the practical jokes he endured at the hands of the Petrograd relief workers, which may have been inspired by stories he told them about his scientific activities. Otherwise their repeated exercise of moving all the clocks in the personnel house ahead by several hours in order to observe the punctilious Virginian become seized with panic thinking he had overslept—otherwise that entire experiment amounted to no more than a childish prank.

Gantt noted that in the previous few years food was in such short supply that there was not enough to feed the animals, and regular nourishment was essential for the experiments on conditioned reflexes and digestion. But other activities were less dependent on food, as Gantt revealed in one of his ARA medical reports, summarizing a personal interview with the great scientist:

Now Dr. Pavlov is studying the state of hypnotism in animals. This he considers an analogous physiological state to sleep. It is caused by weak or by very strong irritation. He has succeeded in hypnotising dogs by extreme and very peculiar stimuli, such as by bringing rapidly before the dog the brilliant light of burning magnesium, an excessively shrill and peculiar whistle, and finally some person dressed in a fantastic and gaudy costume. After this the dog is thrown into a sleepy and half dazed condition which corresponds to the hypnotic trance.

Nichevo.

Among Gantt papers at Johns Hopkins there is documentation of Pavlov's anti-Bolshevism, including his defiant letter of June 25, 1928, "To the Soviet of People's Commissars: Including Stalin, etc.," in which he protested that "we are ordered to elect as members of the highest scientific institution people we can not conscientiously recognize as scientists." In 1935, however, near the end of his life, he was heard toasting Stalin at a state dinner: "I raise my goblet and drink to the only government in the world that . . . values science so highly and supports it so fervently—to the government of my country." Whether such altered states were induced by a form of hypnosis or were a conditioned reflex or whatever will long remain the subject of scientific and unscientific speculation.[7]

Sorokin, a colleague of Pavlov at the Institute of the Brain, writing during the famine, also pondered the effect of the peasant's diet on his behavior, specifically the fact that he ate so little meat, which made him "far more placid than the masses of other peoples. Perhaps because of the almost exclusively vegetarian diet of the population of Russia during these years of starvation they became excessively passive, lacking in volition. If this is so, then those rulers who wish to dominate their people should eat meat and keep the population on a vegetarian diet."

Gorky also considered the stomach. He wondered whether the Russian bent for cruelty was caused by excessive consumption of alcohol. But he had lived in the West and did not think that the Russian was any more "poisoned" by alcohol than other European peoples, even taking into account the moonshine explosion since the war. However, he allowed that the poison might have a greater effect on the stomach of the Russian peasant, given his poor diet.

THE STOMACH MIGHT HAVE BEEN a cause of the Russians' lethargy and passivity, but it does not explain their veritable obsession with suffering and repentance in 1921. It was simply inescapable. Its most common expression was the belief that the famine was God's punishment for Russia's sins, especially those of the past several years.

The British journalist Roberts recorded this certitude among a group of Volga peasants when he inquired as to the causes of the famine: "We are suffering for our sins. We've no longer any respect for God or for friend. We've become like beasts." These peasants made a direct connection between the plundering of the gentry's estates and manors in 1917–18 and the drought of 1920. "Our landlord was a good man. He built us schools and gave us flour when anyone was hungry. We didn't want to sack his house; but the peasants from the next village came along and started to sack it, so we couldn't stand by and let them take all. Ah, the peasant's a fool! But we're being punished now."

Roberts countered that a drought was a drought, but these peasants knew better: "We've sinned. We've sinned. Ah, peasants, peasants!"

This wail of woe has about it the ring of the distant past. In fact the Russian notion of famine as God's retribution is as old as Russian history. It is a thread running through the *Chronicle of Novgorod*, the medieval Russian capital that was vulnerable to periodic famine on account of frosts.

In the year 1128 "corpses were in the streets, in the market place, and on the roads, and everywhere . . . woe and misery on all!" Parents gave their children up to merchants as slaves in exchange for bread, or they put them to death. "Thus did our country perish on account of our sins." In the year 1215, "O, there was trouble! corpses in the market-place, corpses in the street, corpses in the field; the dogs could not eat up the men! . . . And thus for our sins our power and our town went asunder." And so on.[8]

Of course, man's attribution of famine to divine punishment is a phenomenon much older than Russia. But what struck the Western visitor in 1921 was its persistence into the twentieth century among the population of a great European power. Yet nowhere else in modern Europe did famine occur with such tragic regularity as in Russia, where on average every seven years people were starving in one or another region of the country, sometimes in prodigious numbers as in the general famines of 1891 and 1921.

In 1921 peasants were burdened with guilt over having reduced their planting in response to government requisitions during the Civil War. In their minds they had violated the sanctity of the land and the seed and were now being justly punished for it, whatever the culpability of the Bolsheviks. The ARA's Corcoran testified to the existence of this thinking among Tsaritsyn's peasants:

If you don't plough in the spring, you don't eat in the fall, and so why not die now and be done with it? Leaving land lie idle, then, that could be sown is a sin. Whose sin, doesn't matter. The heavens will punish the peasants for it. That's one explanation of last year's famine, if you question some peasants closely. God just simply turned his back on a bad country. He had often half turned it before, for famines are not rare in Russia, though only once at a date no one now remembers the Hunger almost assumed the proportions of last year.

This was probably a reference to the year 1891.

Golder, who was inspecting the famine zone with Shafroth and Gregg, recorded in his diary on September 10, 1921, that at about one o'clock in the afternoon their train came to a standstill in the Simbirsk freight yard, two or three miles from town. Along for the ride were the still numerous "sackers," peasants loaded down with sacks of grain or potatoes or other food items, riding on the roofs of the railroad cars.

Hoping that our car and platform would be moved nearer the city, all the sackers from the other parts of the train climbed on our front platform car. Some of them, bent double under their heavy loads, kept repeating, "*Vot nam svoboda!*" ("This is freedom!") "We cheered, we clapped our hands," some continued, "and here we are dying of hunger and going hundreds of versts for a sack of potatoes and carrying it on our backs. We drove off the *pomeschik* (landlord), we plundered his house, putting his pictures and mirrors into our cow barns, we divided his land; and what is the result? We are famishing, the land is untilled, and the country is becoming a graveyard. Fools, we Russians are; we are not fit for freedom. God has turned his face from us, and the civilized world regards us as unclean, as the children of the devil. It is a good thing we are dying. We get what we deserve. Svoboda! Svoboda!"

It sounds like dialogue from a Romantic play. Shafroth's account was very similar. He published it in a newspaper article shortly after the mission, using it to demonstrate that the peasants blamed themselves for their ordeal. A few paragraphs later he comes upon a peasant who points an accusing finger at the Bolsheviks, which leads Shafroth to contradict himself: "This was typical of the attitude we found among the peasants. They blamed the government for their condition, and pointed back to 'the good old days.' But most of them didn't want the old government back, and didn't know what kind of government they did want."

So who did the peasants think was responsible, the Bolsheviks or themselves? Both, no doubt. Most peasants were ready to blame the Soviet government for the food requisitions; they blamed themselves for responding to the requisitions by planting only enough to feed themselves. Both these moments, the requisitions and the peasants' response to them, depleted the supply of grain and other food in the countryside and set the stage for the disaster to come. Here is where God intervened. The drought of summer 1920 was His judgment in retribution for leaving the land untilled and, more generally, for lawless behavior during the Revolution. So on one level the peasants blamed the government while on a deeper level they blamed themselves.

Maybe, maybe not. It is a hazardous practice to make generalizations about "the Russian peasants," let alone "the Russians." Some things remain obscure even from the bell tower. Yet Kalinin's method of dealing with peasants might seem to support such an interpretation. When forced to defend the government from the charge of having brought on the famine, he countered by playing on the peasants' own sense of guilt. It seems to have worked at Viazovaya-Gai, where he told the crowd to dispense with the teary-eyed speeches, that they were getting what they deserved: "I was among you in '19, you abused us and said: 'Just you wait: God will punish you.' And I said: Don't you scream about God; you yourselves are behaving godlessly."

Kalinin reminded his audience that the priests too were starving, those not already dead, thanks to the peasants' seizure of their land during the Revolution. Golder paid a visit in January 1923 to the Troitse-Sergieva monastery about forty miles north of Moscow, where he inquired of one of the monks why he thought such grief had come to the Church. "My son," was the reply, "we have put to ourselves the same question." He explained that the older monks saw the persecution of the Church as a sign that the world was coming to an end. But he and others did not think it could be the coming of the anti-Christ, for if that were so, the Church would be repressed everywhere, not just in Russia. "Whatever the explanation may be, we know it is God's will, it is in expiation for our sins, and for our good."

While visiting the monastery, Golder stayed at the house of a local tailor. In the evening, around the samovar, someone made mention of the suffering of the peasants, which provoked the host to a violent reaction. "Let the rascals be miserable! It is their turn now!" he roared.

They deserve to suffer as they made us suffer. Two or three years ago they rode into town with a [pood] of flour or a can of milk and acted as if they owned the world. In exchange for their bit of food they picked out the finest furniture, the costliest jewels, the best clothing. They got my warm overcoat. I used to wander from village to village in search of work and in payment for several days of hard work to fit them into their finery they gave me a few pounds of flour. Don't you waste any pity on them. Go to the bazaar and note who buys sugar and expensive cloth and you will see it is the peasants. Let them suffer, the scoundrels. They got my overcoat.

Golder wanders among all types of people, listening to their tales of woe and suffering. Occasionally the moral of the story he hears is not readily apparent. Arriving in the railway yard in Samara in autumn 1921, he struck up a conversation with the switchmen. They were not inclined to blame themselves for their present condition and were unrestrained in their condemnation of the Bolsheviks, "the crocodiles who steal our food." They began to recite the many sins of Soviet officials and seemed especially upset with the idea of commissars getting drunk. Golder asked if tsarist officials too had not in their time gotten drunk. This prompted a spirited response:

Yes, not only the officials but the Tsar himself, but when in that condition they did not show themselves in public. Those were good days before we had svoboda. When a *prazdnik* [holiday] came on, a workman went to his boss, took off his hat, and asked for two or three rubles, and with that he had a real *prazdnik*. He got drunk, to be sure; he smashed windows, yes; but when he sobered up and was brought before the *nachalnik* [boss] he took off his hat and explained that it was a *prazdnik* and got off. Look at it now. These crocodiles do not even know what a *prazdnik* is, and when a decent man gets drunk or lays off a few days he is arrested. This is what they call svoboda.

Bring back the good old tsarist days, when the common man could have himself a holiday and get drunk: "When the Tsar comes back every child will climb on a telephone pole to cheer, and each and every muzhik and *baba* (peasant woman) will kneel down and thank God. To the devil with svoboda and hunger!"

Duranty arrived in Samara not long afterward, though he seems to have eluded the switchmen. He described a nightmarish scene in a children's home where most of the three or four hundred occupants were "past hunger; one child of seven with fingers no thicker than matches refused the chocolate and biscuits I offered him and just turned his head away without a sound. The inside of the house was dreadful, children in all stages of a dozen different diseases huddled together anyhow in the most noxious atmosphere I have ever known."

He interviewed the woman and three girls responsible for running the home. They told him that without food, soap, or medicine there was nothing they could do for the children. At this, Duranty admits he got upset, even indignant. He urged them to build fires in order to heat water and wash the children, to apply to the city soviet for food rations—but do *something*.

The matron shrugged her shoulders, "What is the use?" she said. "They would die anyway."

At first she had tried to do something, she said, and the city had tried, but now there were too many. She suddenly stiffened into protest. "God has hid his face from Russia," she cried. "We are being punished for our sins. In one month there will not be a soul alive along the Volga. I tell you and I know." She slumped into her chair and buried her face in her hands.

These words were not spoken by a simple *baba* but by a schoolteacher. The educated, too, were prone to believe that the famine was retribution for Russia's sins and therefore useless to fight. Even men of science were susceptible.

Sorokin, a peasant by origin, was already working on the effects of hunger on the human organism when starvation descended upon the countryside. He had been studying famine in the cities with himself as one of the subjects, "but now I had a very great laboratory in the starving villages of Russia." This was in summer 1921 before the arrival of the ARA. His scientific enthusiasm quickly evaporated. After a brief period of observation he was forced to admit to professional failure: "My nervous system, accustomed to many horrors in the years of the Revolution, broke down completely before the spectacle of the actual starvation of millions in my ravaged country."

"Who or what was to blame for this terrible famine?" he asked rhetorically. "We have a proverb which says: 'A bad crop is from God, a famine is from the people.'" There had been a drought, yes, but this alone had not caused the famine. By "the people" Sorokin meant certain people: "the monsters who were devouring Russia"—that is, the Bolsheviks with their policy of "plundering the peasantry."

In his travels he came upon three peasants dragging a sledge, upon which lay a dead body. The three collapsed exhausted in the snow. "'God help you,' we addressed them. Simply because it was necessary to say something. The lips of one man and the woman moved but nothing but a mumbling sound came from them. The third peasant, who seemed a little more alive, said: 'God? We forgot God and He forgot us.'"

Farther on, a madman insisted on ringing the church bells, thinking the world would hear and come to help. "But nobody will hear," the local policeman said to Sorokin, "not even God." After repeated exposure to this way of thinking, the scientist falls under its influence and begins to sound unscientific. He ends this account of his famine observations, in *Leaves from a Russian Diary*, with the text of an ancient curse, which he says had filled his mind during his wanderings and after his return to Petrograd, implying that he had at some point previous committed its two hundred or so words to memory. The curse is a curse on the famine victims, who have brought their calamity upon themselves. "And thou shalt eat the fruit of thine own body, the flesh of thy sons and of thy daughters."

But Sorokin closes on a hopeful note: "Many and great have been the sins of the Russian people, but in these years of famine suffering and death, through all the punishments of God, the nation has paid in full for all its offenses." Perhaps he started going to church again, if he had ever stopped. One of Golder's monks told him that even the educated were embracing religion in this time of troubles: "You have no idea how many of the intelligentsia who formerly reviled God are now turning to Him in prayer, 'Have mercy on me, a sinner.'"[9]

There is striking testimony to the Russian intelligentsia's preoccupation with the redemptive powers of suffering in a conversation Golder had in Moscow in summer 1922 with Sergei Oldenburg, permanent secretary of the Russian Academy of Sciences. At the time Professor Oldenburg was in ill health, and Golder doubted he would be long for this world. He told Golder that he regarded the pervasive suffering of his countrymen as a process of purification that would lead to a better future for Russia. Golder raised the possibility of U.S. recognition of Soviet power and asked whether the coming of American investment capital would not bring about that better future sooner.

No, it will not. Our salvation can not come from without but must come from within, and we, as a government and to some extent as a nation have not yet confessed and repented our sins. . . . Let us recover slowly, let us suffer some more the cruel pangs of hunger because it is the only way to get well and strong. . . . All the suffering, all the misery we have endured and are enduring is teaching us Russians to think clearly and that is a great step in the line of progress.

It recalls Kalinin exhorting his peasants, "Well, *nichevo*, this is a school, you have to get used to it all." And in return they moaned, "A very severe school."

What Oldenburg and Kalinin were saying was not merely that suffering was a healing force, a means of erasing one's past sins; more than making possible a return to the status quo ante, it could serve to make one a superior person, beyond any previously attained level. Perhaps this is why some Russians wore their suffering like a badge. Golder found one former aristocrat "glowing in her martyrdom." Gibbs devoted a chapter to "The Martyrdom of Russia," for which he found his most compelling material among the former well-to-do: "On the whole they showed great courage and a wonderful spirit of resignation, with some pride in their suffering, like soldiers in the front-line trenches." He quotes the remark of a member of the old aristocracy about her kind: "Now . . . they have learned how to work and how to suffer. It is by suffering that one learns most."

This belief in the meliorative powers of suffering seemed to rub off on some outsiders exposed to it for prolonged periods. After reporting on Russia during the famine, Hullinger, in his *Reforging of Russia*, had good things to say about the culture of the peasants, their handicrafts, their songs. True, some of their behavior had not been so attractive during the Revolution, and the folk songs had been stilled, but the peasants would one day sing again, "and in notes all the richer for the suffering they have gone through.

"'It is suffering that makes a man noble; until he has suffered he is hardly better than a beast,' runs a Russian proverb. Thus Russia's ordeal in the end will enrich her art."[10]

The belief that salvation is attained through suffering is central to Russian Orthodoxy, and it is long thought to have been an important influence on the development of the Russian mind. Its lineage is traced back to the time shortly after Prince Vladimir converted Kiev to Christianity in the year 988. In the fratricidal struggle for power after his death, two of his sons, Boris and Gleb, are said to have accepted death willingly, in the words of James Billington, "in order to redeem their people through innocent, Christ-like suffering." Thus, Boris and Gleb, who voluntarily shared in the Passion of Christ, became the first Russian Orthodox saints.

After that the motif of Russia imitating Christ reverberates through the centuries. Professor Billington has described the persistence in the Muscovite ideology of a "cult of humility and self-abnegation: the attempt to be 'very like' the Lord in the outpouring of love and the acceptance of suffering in the kenotic manner of Russia's first national saints: Boris and Gleb."

Max Weber is never far out of mind when the subject is the role of Orthodoxy in shaping the Russian mind. In his sociology of religion he distinguished between two views of salvation among the world's religions: the ascetic-ecstatic, or world-rejecting, and the ascetic-ethical, or world-involved and rationalist. Among the religions in the second category were mainstream Judaism, Catholicism, and Protestantism, especially Calvinism. The first included, among a diverse group of mostly eastern religions, Russian Orthodoxy with its mystical traditions of *hesychasm*, which emphasizes flight from the world, and *kenoticism*, or quietist submission. Hugh Ragsdale extracts the essential difference between the two: "In Western religion moral edification comes from moral striving. In Russian Orthodoxy, it comes from innocent suffering. The first saints, Boris and Gleb, are classic examples."[11]

The sticking point in applying this analysis to the postrevolutionary period is the fact of so many Russians carrying around so much *guilty* suffering: paying for the sins of the Revolution and all that. Yet other voices in 1921—perhaps some of these very same ones—spoke of "the misery of a nation which had suffered innocently for years and years," to cite the words of one Tsaritsyn *intelligent*. In this view, the Great Famine was just another in a long line of tribulations, which persecuted Russia was forced to endure. Once again Russia was up on the cross.

Actually, the imagery varies. Sometimes Russia is still yet on the road to Calvary. Then God intervenes: He sends in the Americans.

Near the end of the relief mission, the ARA employees in the Koshskii subdistrict of Simbirsk wrote a tribute to America, to the ARA, and to district supervisor Barringer. Like several other such documents among Barringer's papers its artwork is unrefined, in the style of a homemade greeting card. On the cover is a pencilled drawing of a ragged old man and a child making their way barefoot through a driving snow; they are pursued by Death, depicted as a skeleton with a scythe, leaning into the picture at the right. Beneath the scene are two lines taken from Nekrasov's poem published in 1864, "The Railroad," which told of the suffering and starvation of the peasants recruited to construct the railroads, built literally on their bones:

> There is a tsar in the world: this tsar is merciless,
> Famine is his name

The appreciation inside states that "At the time when thousand-year-old Russia, submissively and courageously as always, was going to its Golgotha, wearing a crown of thorns," only the "sympathetic hearts of the American people" were touched by its calls of distress. The arrival of the Americans had meant that Russia's cup had been taken from it, that God had stopped turning away his face—though a good number of these world-rejecting Russians would need time to become convinced of this.

It just so happened that the men who had come to their rescue were intensely world-involved. They were Americans, crusaders of the Protestant ethic. They showed no outward concern as to whether heaven held a reward for them. They had a job to do on earth, in the here and now. The collision of these two radically different mentalities produced many of the comedies and tragedies of the relief story and for a time made of famine Russia the kind of great laboratory that might have occupied Weber's dreams.

One who clearly grasped this was Corcoran, serving with the ARA but himself a Briton and as such regarding himself as culturally distinct enough from his "get-out-and-get-it" American colleagues to describe them in action among the eternal Russians from the perspective of a third party:

[I]f you take a walk with an A.R.A. man in some district, as often as not it will lead to a peasant's hut. You go in and find a gloomy family sitting in silence around the plain but wholesome American food, which they got by gift of the U.S. Congress. I've watched the faces of such a family after the American's entry. I've seen an old man whose features were lined with seemingly indelible traces of suffering, with an expression so sad that the sadness seemed ineffaceable, become almost human, as some youngster from Coshocton, O., greeted him with his best Russian equivalent for: "Well, how's the old man to-day?"

It is a contrast between youth and old age, health and ill health, vigor and languor, wealth and poverty. Then Corcoran assumes the voice of the old peasant as he marvels at his American savior:

You explain that God just hates Russia for its iniquities and that is why he sent the famine; and the mad young fellow laughs and shouts something that might be interpreted as profanity or a defense of the Deity, depending on your point of view. . . . You really did believe God had deserted you and He sent them—them above all people, wealthy, confident and kindly. He couldn't hate you and send you such a friend!

It is not that these Americans were godless, only that they were less reliant on their God. Journeying through the former valley of death in June 1922, Goodrich came upon a little village of some twenty-five houses, which had been spared by the famine.

We saw three peasant girls pulling weeds in a field and asked them how the crops were, they said "all right." We inquired if anyone in that village had died of starvation, they said "none at all." We asked them if they would have enough food to go through the next year; they said "we have planted and are now caring for our crops, the result is now in the hands of God who alone knows."

But the governor knew better: "From the appearance of the crops and the number of people at work in the fields hoeing and pulling weeds I am certain that God's answer will be an abundant crop and again no one will starve in this little commune. God still helps those who help themselves."[12]

CHAPTER 34

TIME MEANT NOTHING

The American relief workers spent far less time in peasant dwellings than in their own offices, and it was there that they had most frequent occasion to observe the Russians go about their daily lives.

Ellingston, whose duties in the historical division left him plenty of intellectual room to wander, came to consider himself something of an expert on the office mentality of the Russians, a subject to which he devoted some thoughtful writing. He was fascinated by the different psychologies of Americans and Russians as revealed by their distinctly different work habits. Toward mission's end, he looked back on the initial stages of the mission, recalling that the "Russian business psychology" had presented "an intensely interesting and very important obstruction to the earlier ARA operations." At the outset, just finding someone who could communicate and type in English was regarded as a great victory.

But it is one thing to be fluent in the English of the drawing rooms of the aristocracy and quite another to be fluent in the English of an office. Not that the two vocabularies are so widely different; it is the habits of mind and training that go with them which are unlike. With the best will in the world it is rather difficult for an ex-princess to do cross-filing.

Subject, alphabetical, chronological filing, accounting—the average Russian employee seemed unable to get the hang of it. And anyway, many wondered, what was the point of it all? More disturbing to the ARA chiefs than this lack of business training was the fact that the Russians they hired seemed to have little notion of what the Americans called "work rhythm." To begin with, they had difficulty keeping a regular schedule. Ellingston refers to the "characteristic Russian inability to keep an appointment," a finding of most of the Americans who served in Russia.

Some of the mystery is removed when one realizes that not a few of those engaged from among the former well-to-do had before 1917 never seen the inside of an office, let alone worked in one. But what especially bewildered the Americans was that even those they had hired as "experienced" workers—who had been employed in a Russian, or more typically a Soviet, office—appeared to have no concept of regular hours or intensive and detailed work assignments. What could explain this? After all, these were not peasants whose irregular behavior could be attributed to the climate, the landscape, or a lack of electric light.

Farmer Murphy sat down to tea in June 1922 with some Russian friends who got to talking about the goings-on in Soviet offices in Moscow during the Civil War. Officially, hours were from ten to four, with an hour for lunch; however, "The idea of arriving on time in the morning was repugnant and never observed." After arrival there was no thought given to actual work but a lot of sitting around, reading or talking, and the smoking of many, many cigarettes. At half past three it was time to get ready to go home. The system of the sign-up sheet was easily circumvented in the timeworn tradition of having one designated person arrive on time and sign in for the whole force, who would then drift into "work" at leisure—if they bothered to show up at all; everyone took off at least a full day each week.

It does not appear that the New Economic Policy introduced a profound change in the Soviet office regime. But for those Russians fortunate enough to gain employment with the ARA—which opened up the prospects of receiving American food and tobacco, not to mention the prestige attached to such a position—for them the permissive days came to an abrupt end. Mackenzie reported on the rude awakening at ARA headquarters in the capital:

Workers are expected to work. Some Russian girls who joined the office staff at Moscow found that. "You might as well be in an ordinary office," one of them grumbled. "You have to come in time in the morning. If you stop for a talk with a friend, or an extra cup of tea, you are sent back to work. Now, when I was in a Government office, it was not like that." The girl forgot to add that the Americans paid and fed her well, while the Government rewards were on a minimum scale.

So taken aback were the American chiefs by what passed for work habits among their native employees that it stayed with some of them late into their lives. In the final issue of the ARA alumni newsletter in May 1965, George Townsend, who served as Col. Haskell's secretary, reminisced about how his Russian staffers "busied themselves on A.R.A. paper work, briefly, between 'tea breaks.'" Tea drinking played a big role in Russian office life and life in general. Ellingston identified the positive, medicinal effect of the drinking of large quantities of boiled water, though he knew from direct observation that this was hardly ever the main motivation behind an activity that acted as a drag on operations and exasperated the coffee-driven, full-steam-ahead American staff. But Townsend's memories were troubled by more than time wasted at the samovar: "I was fiercely convinced at the time that there was nothing more stupid, s-t-u-p-i-d, than a Russian female clerk who thought she knew a little English. When one of the sweet young bundled-up-for-the-winter heavyboned fillies would be remonstrated with for an atrocious error, the answer would be invariably, and so brightly: 'It iss a misteck? Yiss?'"

Confrontations over this or that "misteck" might lead to unpleasantness, even threats to terminate employment, at which point the ultimate weapon of the female clerk was an appeal to pedigree. Why, Mr. Townsend, do you know who my family is? Do you realize that my father was a friend of Tsar Nicholas? This was not the kind of argument to move a young, self-made, hardheaded American individualist; in fact it might just provoke him further. An ARA report quotes the reply of an American at Moscow headquarters who might well have been Townsend: "Sure I believe you, kid. I believe every word you say, but honey, don't waste it on me. I'm just an American, I hardly know a countess from a cook. Save it for the Russkies. All I want from you is hard work."

A report called "The Problem of the Russian Personnel" says of the local employees that at the beginning "their methods were not ours. We had temperament to contend with and a psychology entirely foreign to us." The Moscow chiefs decided that the only way to achieve efficiency was to train its staff, providing intensive instruction in typing, filing, bookkeeping, and accounting. These ARA-trained personnel are said to have gone on to perform their duties in a satisfactory manner once they had caught on to American methods and the ARA system. But that took several months, and in the meantime the solution was to hire a very large work force, which did not sit well with the efficiency-minded Americans.[1]

One of the local habits that the ARA training course apparently did not attempt to change was the use of the abacus. The Americans were surprised to discover it in wide use in Moscow. It served them as a symbol of Russian primitiveness and slowness. Haskell contrasted the American ARA accountant, armed with modern business equipment and timesaving methods, tackling a problem straightaway, with the ARA's Russian bookkeepers, engaged in "an endless shifting back and forth of the colored beads of the abacus."

He identifies the abacus as well by its American epithet, the "Chinese laundry machine"—its common association in the United States. The "Chinese" connection must have seemed appropriate for these "Asiatic" Russians. The abacus was also a popular American children's toy. In Russia this toy was employed in most establishments, including the large banks, which left the Americans shaking their heads. Wrote Murphy, "A westerner is inclined to be amused at this, especially when he sees a dignified man with evident education and intelligence operating one of these frames and pushing the buttons back and forth like a child at play. The first impulse is to smile condescendingly at such an archaic device."

It may have looked out of place, but in the proper hands it was certainly not slow—apparently not slow enough anyway to decide the Americans to try to wean their Russians off the instrument. Haskell implies as much when he says that the employees preferred their "click-clack" methods and never mastered the "peaks and valleys" of the modern statistical chart. Murphy recounts a moment at Moscow headquarters when one of the office girls declared that she could solve a certain mathematical problem if only she had an abacus. "I jokingly taunted her a little on the mental backwardness of Russians who had to have a primitive machine to do their adding for them." She shot back that Murphy needed a little perspective: the abacus had been in use in Russia for hundreds of years and therefore had to be superior to the comparatively new calculating machine. Murphy must have become disoriented by this logic, because he thought she had a point.

In the districts there was less talent to draw upon and no time to organize secretarial minicourses. This meant a need for still larger local staffs, something that had to be continually justified to Moscow, which kept a sharp eye on the bottom line. Kelley said that in Ufa, as everywhere else in Russia, the ARA had no competition as an employer, that the best talent was drawn to it: "But the best in this part of the country is woefully ignorant and inefficient. The deprivations suffered in the last five years have made them sluggish. To the American, with his ideas of office efficiency, every district office seemed greatly overstaffed; but the inspectors, who think in terms of current Russian labor standards, were always pressing for permission to take on more clerks and assistants."

Kelley understood that contributing to the Russians' poor work performance in 1921 was the physical toll of the years of war and revolution, a factor perhaps underappreciated by many of the relief workers. A farewell letter to Shafroth from his Samara staff members in summer 1922 asked him, "as a sensitive person," to "understand our fatigue and nervous weariness which have considerably diminished our ability for work."

Hale was for a time in charge of the Samara district's traffic division. He praised the Russians under him as "very good" workers who "take a great interest in the work and never seem to mind staying after hours or coming on holidays." He did not find their energy wanting, but criticized their lack of efficiency, their being "rather inclined to go in for detail at the expense of the general view of any particular matter." Also, "such a thing as inventing a means of saving themselves work is rare."

When I came here, the Russian who had been doing Traffic work had a system of looking after shipments enroute which would have taken a veritable army of workers to keep going. Shafroth and I fixed up a very simple system by which we figured that two men or three at the most could account for four thousand cars enroute, and forced them to take it on against their will. Today when we actually have all those cars to look after, they are very glad that they jumped the league and took on the simplified system, but it went in with weeping and gnashing of teeth.

Clapp, stationed out in remote Uralsk, wrote in his journal, "The people are extremely ignorant and it takes patience to the limit to teach them how to do the most simple work." By "the people" he meant more than merely the local talent; he used his Uralsk observations to generalize about an entire people: "The Russians surely cannot organize—they have no sense of order and coordination."

BASED UPON what he saw of the relatively advanced state of affairs in Moscow, Ellingston wrote sweepingly of "the Russian inability to get things done." An official of the Joint Distribution Committee concluded that "the Slav temperament works more slowly than the American, and less according to programme." Gantt agreed: "Whereas the American thinks straight and as it appears to the Russian, ruthlessly, to the thing he wants to do, the Russian thinks of the simplest thing as insuperable obstacles. He finds a Mt. Everest at every street corner. Frequently you could do something yourself quicker than you could explain to a Russian what you wanted and how he could do it."

Here, famous American impatience ran up against the famously endless patience of the Russians, who had an entirely different mental concept of time. The evidence, the Americans were quick to point out, was right there on the streets in the form of well-attended queues where the Russians demonstrated their patience by the hour. "Wherever you go in Moscow you see lines and more lines of men and women, standing, waiting," Samuel Spewack informed readers of the New York *World*. "In the Government offices, outside of the co-operative stores, at the theatres. It seems to be the most popular outdoor sport—this manifestation of the Oriental. It explains a good deal of Russia, politically and economically."[2]

The Americans thought speed; the Russians did not, particularly. They had, in the American idiom of the day, no jazz. Their obliviousness to the importance of time, to punctuality, was—as it to an extent still is—illustrated by their use of two time words, both of which achieved a certain notoriety with the ARA Americans.

When a Russian promised, in Russian, to do something "right away," it might actually mean he would not get to it until much later in the day, or maybe, if the order came late enough in the day, he would not get around to it until the next day, if then. The Russian word *seichas* has over time become rather elastic and can imply substantially different timetables depending on the context, though its literal meaning is "this hour" and it carries the sense of "immediately." Imagine then what a rude surprise it was for the newly arrived American relief worker, eager to go out and conquer a famine, to discover that the *seichas* he had earlier in the day received from a Russian employee in reply to his instructions had actually meant "any old time," which it turned out was not in time to accomplish the required task. Childs wrote in his diary that it actually meant "an indefinite period of time." Kellogg's diary aims at greater precision:

utter disregard for time—"si-chass" = "right away" or "in a little while" or "pretty soon"—means anything from a minute to a day—almost impossible to make the Russian understand "getting action." However he is willing & if somebody will be responsible as it were for speed he will fit in—that is he will accept the situation as he accepts acts of Providence as all in the day's happening.

So the American relief workers, allegedly sent by Providence, had to go about enforcing a new kind of *seichas*, as Ellingston explains: "'Sichas' is the Russian word for presently, and shares the vague indefiniteness of the Spanish 'manana.' Soon after the arrival of the Americans, Russians began differentiating between the unqualified 'sichas' and the 'Amerikanskii sichas' which meant literally 'at once.' That symbolized the activity of the American everywhere."

This new phrase gained currency in ARA offices across Russia, and even outside those offices. Elperin says that in Ufa Colonel Bell succeeded so well in delivering on his promises "that American faithfulness to the given word has become a byword in Ufa district. Now when a Russian gives a promise and says he will fulfill it 'Sichas' he is asked whether he means the Russky sichas or Americansky sichas."[3]

Still more threatening to the American ear was the Russian word for "tomorrow," *zavtra*. It took but a day for the relief workers to realize that a pledge to fulfill an assignment *zavtra* was not to be taken literally.

Cornick, the doctor from San Angelo, Texas, who was district physician in Tsaritsyn and who could get himself really worked up about Russian fuzziness with time and numbers, wrote to his sister Elsie on January 19, 1922: "I am beginning to learn that the Russians are worse than the Mexicans in putting things off until tomorrow. They have promised me faithfully time and again that they would have certain necessary equipment that I need 'By the next day' but that day seems never to come." Six months later it still has not come:

Honestly, I don't believe that I have ever had such a profound contempt for the mentality of any group of people as I have for the Russians who are trying to work here with me at present. I really believe that their intentions are good, but they can't follow simple instructions to save their lives, and can't count ten bottles on a shelf and get the same result three times straight along.

Driscoll, also based in Tsaritsyn, made a trip to Astrakhan on the Caspian Sea in spring 1923, mainly to discuss with the local Soviet leader the then-delicate issue of when the authorities would hand over the money to pay the local ARA personnel. He arrived on April 30 and, realizing that the next day, May 1, was "the big Red holiday," knew he would have to wait it out. On the second of May the Astrakhan president had some Moscow officials visiting, which looked like an excuse for further delay, but Driscoll was determined to pin him down. "He rang me up several times apologizing for his unability to get away and suggested about eight p.m. that perhaps tomorrow would be a better time. But I had learned to hate the Russian 'Zavtra' and said I'd see him that evening—no matter how late. It was one a.m. when I did see him, and we talked shop from that hour until five a.m." So it was *zavtra* after all but only in the strictly literal sense.

Driscoll was fortunate to get action from the Astrakhan chief and thereby make good on his promise to the local employees to win the release of their wages. In Orenburg, when the local government repeatedly failed to provide the ARA with the funds to pay its staff, the Americans found that the only way to face their employees was with "a liberal use of the word 'zaftra.'"

In their exasperation with the Russians' indifference to time, the ARA men sound like the Bolsheviks, who could lately be heard complaining about the prevalence of this characteristic among their own beloved proletariat, a distinctly peasantized lot which had become even more so during the course of the Civil War. The numbers on the clock meant nothing in the life of the peasant, who measured time according to when the sun went up and down and by the cycle of the seasons—any attempt at further precision in rural life was meaningless. In traditional societies like Russia where nature ruled, haste was no virtue but rather signified excessive ambitiousness and a loss of dignity. For the Russian, time was long—and it certainly was not money.

This hardly suited the plans of the Bolsheviks, who in the summer of 1923 endorsed the launching of the League of Time, an enterprise intended to teach Russians to value time and to overcome "seichasism" and "nichevoism." In deploring the Russians' lack of punctuality, Lenin and his colleagues found their performance especially depressing when contrasted with the German sensitivity to time. Goodrich endorsed this judgment, attributing the cleanliness and general coherence of Saratov city to the influence of the Volga Germans, "who seem to have retained some of that efficiency and orderly habits for which the Germans are noted," while "the genuine Russian is apt to be more careless in most things than his neighbor of Teutonic extraction."[4]

BY 'GENUINE' RUSSIANS, Goodrich here means ethnic Russians—*russkie*—as opposed to the citizens of Soviet Russia—*rossiiane*—who included dozens of distinct ethnic groups. Among these the relief workers had their favorites. The Volga Germans were well regarded. The general ARA consensus was that the Tatars of Russia were also markedly superior to ethnic Russians in energy and organizational ability.

Standing above all the rest on this scale were the Jews, "the only class of native

Russians with much real 'push,'" according to Hullinger. This had been a widely held, if hardly always benignly expressed, opinion before the Revolution. It became more popular still after 1917 with the presence of so many Jews within the upper reaches of the Soviet leadership. Their number was not nearly so great as many current rumors had it, but exaggerated estimates of their influence were readily believed by the citizens of Soviet Russia, who assumed that these Bolsheviks simply *had* to be Jews: no small group of mere *Russians* could have had the energy, initiative, and cleverness necessary to pull off the feat of bringing to heel 150 million people.

Thus, the historian Got'e recorded in his diary a joke circulating in Moscow in January 1920: "On what is soviet power based? On Jewish brains, Lettish riflemen, and Russian fools." In 1921, with the coming of free trade, there was no doubt who was first out of the starting gate: the phrase "Jew-Bolshevik" now had to make room for "Jew-Speculator."

Others attributed the unhappy outcome of the Revolution to the Russianness of the Bolsheviks. One of these was Emma Goldman, America's most famous anarchist, who was deported from the United States in 1920 and landed in Soviet Russia during the final months of War Communism. She speculated that the unhappy outcome of the Revolution might have something to do with the character of the Russian people—between *russkie* or *rossiiane* she made no distinction: "A peculiar people, these Russians, saint and devil in one, manifesting the highest as well as the most brutal impulses, capable of almost anything except sustained effort. I have often wondered whether this lack did not to some extent explain the disorganization of the country and the tragic condition of the Revolution."

Big Bill Haywood was another American political exile having difficulty adjusting to his new life in the land of the Bolos. Haywood was one of a group of former members of the International Workers of the World who had been sentenced to long prison terms in the Red Scare of 1919–1920 and who had "skipped" to Russia when released on bail during an appeal of their convictions. Haywood felt entirely out of his element in the capital of the socialist utopia. Talking to Duranty, he sounded frustrated. "The trouble with us old Wobblies is that we all know how to sock scabs and mine-guards and policemen or make tough fighting speeches to a crowd of strikers but we aren't so long on this *ideological* theory stuff as the Russians."

Duranty suggested that the difference might be that Wobblies had been trying to destroy whereas the Bolsheviks had come to power and were now trying to build. "There's something in that," said Big Bill, "but it goes far deeper. These Russians attach the hell of a lot to *ideological* theory, and mark my words, if they're not careful they'll come to blows about it one of these days. Don't you know yet that most of them would sooner talk than work, or even eat?"

Lenin would have been quick to second Haywood on this point. One of his most frequent complaints in 1921 was with the long-winded speeches and endless discussion at countless Party and government meetings—a phenomenon he called *mitingovanie*, which the poet Mayakovsky ridiculed in verse as did Lenin in prose. It is easy to imagine that the Bolsheviks had refined, if not acquired, this characteristic during their long years of European exile, when philosophical discussion and ideological sparring in speech and print were among the principal activities of the professional revolutionary. But so much talk was ill suited to the purposes of a ruling party.

Golder remarked in December 1921, "It is as if two doctors stood before the bed of a very sick man and argued while he was dying, knowing full well that some of the remedies might save his life." "It is getting my goat, as the boys say. The country is in ruins and I wish I could see sunshine ahead. So much suffering, so much talking, so much arresting, so much stealing, so much demoralization one finds nowhere else and while Rome burns the leaders fiddle."

The testimony of the American relief workers was nearly unanimous in depicting Bolshevik volubility as being typically Russian. Childs expressed admiration for the "business-like" manner of Mukhtarov, the Tatar prime minister in Kazan, but attributed this quality in part to his Tatar origin: "the Russian seems to like nothing better than to talk endlessly about nothing."

Ellingston remarked that "a love of harangue and procrastination are so deep-seated in the Russian character as to exasperate the quick-deciding American for whom time in Russia was not only money, but life."

In the ARA offices, the Americans marveled at how their otherwise low-energy Russian employees would come alive at an opportunity to palaver. Any excuse to put aside a piece of work would do. Already on September 7, 1921, Bowden made note of it: "A remarkable thing about Russia, and one which would remind a doughboy very much of the American army, is the number of men for every job, and the number of loungers who gather round and ask foolish questions every time anything out of the ordinary occurs. Only those who were busy were allowed to be in the kitchen."[5]

The Russian propensity for idle talk was often on the mind of Harold Fleming, who spent his first months in Moscow in summer 1922 working under Ellingston in the historical division. Perhaps influenced by the proclivities of his chief, he fancied himself an expert on Russian office psychology—"the Russkies are not strong on what we Americans enjoy—organized facts"—which became a regular topic of his weekly letters home. On August 1 he had been in Moscow only six weeks:

Am going to install new methods of checking up on my typists now; of all the slow, dawdling, poking, meandering, mooning crews they are the worst. Somebody comes in the door, and every machine stops; you start to give one of them a mild hauling over the coals, or describe some new work you want her to do, and every machine in the whole outfit stops automatically till you have finished.

Part of the problem with the arrangement at Moscow headquarters was that there were few private offices and the Russian staff of each division worked in one big room with no partitions between desks. Everyone could monitor everyone else's activities.

Honestly they give me the willies. I go out of the room and when I come back they are talking about their paiok (ration) or likely as not chewing the fat about me in Russian, and what a hard-boiled American capitalist exploiter I am. One of them doesn't come down to work in the morning, and another wants to go down and see her and find out if she is sick; they seem to think the office is a family and office hours a picnic. Then the bunch of typewriters we have musta been transported in the Ark, and on top of that there isn't one of the whole crew that can hit more than fifteen words a minute if you offered them a barrel of flour to do it. They come from the Russian so-called "intelligentsia" but believe me, it doesn't mean what it sounds like. I'd like to import an American typist for about half a day to show them how the job ought to be done—it wouldn't budge them, though; their skulls are solid lead. Leave it to me, tho, kid, I'll train 'em American methods before I get through [with] them, if I have to offer sticks of candy to the girl that works the fastest, or fire the whole lot of them.

SEVEN MONTHS LATER, after wintering in the districts and observing dozens of ARA employees on the job, Fleming is more than ever convinced that "the Russians are terrible office workers. . . . I'm no Emerson efficiency expert, but I find a day or two in a district office can point out several important changes provided one has time to stop for the purely office personnel questions."

Kelley was another who regularly commented on the ARA office scene in his correspondence. One of his pet grievances was that the few Americans at Ufa headquarters were constantly being called upon by the local staff for guidance on even the most minor matters. "Every once in a while I lapse into melancholy from which Boris or someone pulls me with the inevitable request for a decision on some question or other. It is always: 'Well, how shall this be done?' There is no word for 'initiative' in the Russian tongue. I must find an answer to every 'How.'"

Shifting of responsibility onto someone else seemed to be the chief concern. "No Russian nowadays covets responsibility. A safe clerkship with a regular ration attached is his highest ambition." Kelley surveys a gathering of the Ufa ARA's local department heads summoned by Bell:

If he permitted them, they would bring every little question to him for decision. Tired, timid men they are, the best that the country affords, but woefully inadequate for the jobs they hold. The size of the ARA operation stuns them. No one but who would gladly exchange his position for that of one of his clerks if he could do it without antagonising the Americans. Utterly without ambition, they are not however without fear that after the ARA leaves the enemies they have made in the performance of their duties will do them harm. In all things their motto is "Safety First." . . . We needed no wall motto to teach us that if we wanted a thing done well we should do it ourselves. It was a case of doing all that you could keep awake to do and delegating the rest with misgiving.

Kelley was inclined to attribute this lack of initiative more to the inhibiting influences of Soviet politics and to fatigue than to anything inherent in the Russian national character, though his analysis of Russian inefficiency begins with the clean sweep of the Revolution:

My impression is that the Imperial functionaries were more competent than the present occupants of official positions. Otherwise I cannot explain the existence of the cities, the buildings, the property, and other evidences of civilization I find here. I have never seen in this region a building or a public work that does not antedate the Soviet regime. They are carrying on with the overhead they found, and ever falling behind for inability to effect repairs.

He allowed that the score of men running the Kremlin might be ruthlessly efficient, but that was beside the point, really: "Were they all Hoovers they could do little to improve the general situation working through the existing personnel in the districts." To bring the matter alive for his correspondent, he employs American points of reference:

Is the government conducted efficiently? The Board of Aldermen of any Dakota town could be counted on to administer the Gubernias I have come in contact with or this Baskir Republic better than their present executives. I have tested their knowledge of their own districts, of their institutions, of their resources, and avow that with rare exceptions they are incompetent to conduct the affairs of a small town grocery store.

Take the leading officials in Bashkiria, "a country much larger than Kentucky."

The President is a peasant and nothing more. He is without experience in any legislative or executive capacity. He is genial enough, probably has the gift of making friends in this Tartar country and doubtless has a following in the party. His education, I infer, is about that of a boy who has passed the fifth grade. The president of the People's Commissars, corresponding in this republic to Lenin at Moscow, was a teacher in a Tartar village school—and nothing else. His training was about that of a grammar school grade in the States. And so it goes. The best educated is the Minister of Health, as he is a graduate doctor. In Ufa this position is held by a veterinarian and in Cheliabinsk by a male nurse. I have yet to meet an important commissar whose education and mentality was above that of a Russian village teacher.

To be fair, these men were up against enormous obstacles, not least an appalling lack of material equipment; and yet, "Personally I would place my bet on the aldermen, if a competition could be arranged."

Anyway, Kelley saw the circumstances of recent history—not least the "Reign of Terror"—as the explanation for the passivity of his local staff, but he was in a minority on this, and not only among the Americans. An employee of the Kiev district saw it as a more deeply ingrained feature of his fellow countrymen:

The principles of Russian and American work are quite different. The worst in the Russian work is the fear of responsibility. Everybody wants to take any responsibility off himself by securing the signature of a superior official. Therefore when something happens such a man is sure he will not account for it.

The American principle is, so far as I understand, just the opposite. The person who acts has full initiative, but when things go wrong—he alone is responsible for it.

Fleming sided with the Kiev staffer on these matters. In his sketches of local Soviet officialdom he can sound remarkably like Kelley, and yet unlike Kelley he refuses to credit the pernicious effects of the Revolution. Writing from Samara on April 22, 1923, he is typically direct:

The shortage of good men out here is remarkable. The government in power suffers particularly from this. It has been my good fortune in the past two months to become acquainted with several "good fellows" in this government—honest and conscientious men, including the government representatives in Buguruslan and Gorodische, the head of the Posledgol in Samara, and the head of the Zemotdel in Penza. Not one of these men, however, would ever reach much higher than the owner of a hardware store back home; not one of them would last long in conflict with a South Boston or Tenth Avenue ward boss.

A mere few minutes spent in a government office inclined an American to Fleming's point of view. In Moscow the ARA man's first exposure to the atmosphere—here meant literally as well—of a Soviet office took place inside ARA headquarters, where the chief plenipotentiary and his several assistants were encamped. In the very early days, before the coming of Eiduk in October made government relations so terribly interesting, the government team consisted of Palmer and his earnest underlings, who conducted their business in the presence of Coolidge and Murphy of the ARA liaison division.

Shortly after Murphy arrived, on September 29, he was eagerly assuring the folks back home that contrary to all reports, the Russians were no less efficient than other peoples. "It is no harder to get things done than it was in France, for instance, and as for the delays of government bureaus and postponed promises, they are not a whit worse than are to be found in Poland, Czecho-Slovakia or even Germany—perhaps even America." Well, perhaps on a good day, but already on the following day Murphy's enthusiasm was fast deflating:

It is perfect bedlam in the office where I am writing. I have my desk in the same room with a Soviet official. He has his heelers coming in all the time and running back and forth. They stand around and jabber and smoke cigarettes. Some times there are as many as six or eight persons talking at the top of their voices at the same time. Then at lunch time food for half a dozen or more people is brought in and is eaten here. The result is that all the afternoon there is a fine mixture of odors of tobacco, food and bolsheviki.

It begins to sound like a Soviet version of *Room Service*: "They have just now carried in two bags of potatoes and deposited them in the corner of the room. It looks as if more were coming."

A day later, October 1, it was Coolidge's turn, although this veteran student of Russia bypassed the stage of gung-ho optimism. He wrote to his father:

You can imagine how easy it is to work in a room about the size of the library in town with eight or ten people, several of them talking loudly in Russian, frequent use of the telephone, people rushing in and out etc. As for the air—the door of the room is kept shut, most of the people smoke most of the time (we won't go into the question of how much any of them bathe) and when I get back from my lunch downstairs the Russians are usually beginning theirs, which is served in the room and lasts an hour or so.

Day in, day out, the ARA took the measure of Soviet ineptitude by observing the performance of the various government representatives and their retainers. There was appreciation of the occasional burst of raw energy from the likes of Eiduk, but he was hardly up to American standards of efficiency. Brooks, in his history of the ARA and the Russian railroads, wrote of Eiduk that he was "always ready with excuses and justifications, generous with promises and assurances, and failing absolutely in action," which reads like an ARA handbook description of a Soviet plenipotentiary. "He met urgent requests for cars or for the clearing up of some difficult transport question with vague promises that 'everything would be all right' and then apparently made no effort to do that which had to be done." In his history of the food package program, Ellingston could not resist taking another jab at one of his favorite targets:

Whatever his qualities as a leader of machine gunners, Mr. Eiduk was a most inefficient businessman. The ordinary merits of promptness, reliability, orderliness and energy, he and his subordinates lacked entirely. "It will be done at once," was a favorite
phrase used prodigally but rarely fulfilled. When the irritated American officials became too exasperated and too insistent, Eiduk would begin failing to keep appointments to avoid their wrath. Against this wall of lethargy and irresponsibility the
A.R.A. and the Food Remittance Division battered their heads with an uncomprehending violence made all the more futile by their own contrasting energy and deft-
ness in practical things. Henry Adams said that Europe feels about the American as
a pine forest feels about a buzz saw. So the Russian official through whom the Americans had to get things done felt about the A.R.A. In his turn the American regarded
the Russian official as a buzzsaw regards a stone wall. The American cuts into it, but
only ineffectively and after fearful self-punishment.[6]

Haskell had frequent occasion to play the American buzzsaw to the Russian
stone wall. He met his first resistance at the very start as he and his force arrived
in the Soviet capital ready to save the lives of millions of Russians, only to find
that the Bolsheviks had not yet managed to locate living accommodations for the
American saviors. Time was of the essence, but as he recalled in his memoir,
"Time meant absolutely nothing to the Soviet Government."

In one of his first letters to the States, on September 28, he informed Edgar
Rickard that "it takes about ten times as long to do anything, of course, as it does
in the United States." Looking around, he saw a great deal of "passing the buck."
To Walter Lyman Brown in London he complained of interminable delays: "This
is partly due to the old time Russian method of business, to which the Soviet government is gradually reverting." In this point of view he was consistent, even into
the early 1930s when he wrote in his memoir that Soviet inefficiency was attributable to "Russian methods of doing things, and to Russian procrastination and
undependability." To illustrate this behavior he recounted the story of the Battle
of the Firebrick.

At the start of the mission, the ARA headquarters at Spiridonovka 30 was
without heat, the firebrick for the furnace having melted away. Haskell turned to
Eiduk's deputy and requested new firebrick: "This was promised for immediate
delivery—*si chass* by one Volodin, an ex-Red of Boston who had been an agitator
there, and who had been deported from the United States some years before."

Though promised, it was still not delivered after three days, at which point
and under growing pressure, Volodin had to admit that there was in fact no firebrick to be had in all of Moscow. He was able to assure the colonel, however, that
the brick had been ordered from Nizhni Novgorod with delivery guaranteed
within three days. After those three days had been used up, Volodin bought himself more time by explaining that the brick had in fact arrived in Moscow but
that the car in which it had been shipped had unfortunately become lost in the
Moscow railway yards. "When asked for the number of the car in order that the
members of my organization might try to locate it, the promising ex-Red of
Boston stalled me off for yet another day while he attempted to procure it, and
then finally told me that the car had been located, and that even as we spoke the
brick was being loaded into lorries for delivery at 30 Spiridonovka the next day."

By now *seichas* had turned into *zavtra*. "The next day came—but the firebrick did not. I summoned Volodin. He was distressed that delivery had not actually been made; he could not understand it; but he said that the precious brick was actually moving across the city of Moscow towards us." It had to have been moving very slowly because on the next day there was still no firebrick.

By this time I had reached the end of my patience. I sent once more for Volodin, and, aided and abetted by several other enraged Americans, I demanded a show-down on the subject of the firebrick. The unhappy Volodin, by this time at the end of his resourcefulness, had to admit, under threat of personal and immediate punishment for his continued deception, that his serial story about the ordering and movement of the brick had been a complete fabrication from beginning to end. I asked him what possible justification he had for his deception.

"Well, I'll tell you, Colonel," he replied, wiping his forehead, "the truth is that there was not and is not any firebrick to be had. But you wouldn't have been satisfied with that for an answer, and so I *had* to tell you something."

Haskell understood that Volodin was putting off "the day of final reckoning, hoping that meanwhile some happy circumstance would enable him to obtain the firebrick and thus put an end to our insistent and annoying demands upon him."

Coolidge came to the same conclusion. Possibly Haskell meant to include him among the Americans "enraged" about the firebrick, yet Coolidge never seemed to get ruffled when reflecting on "certain defects both in the Russian character and in the ingrained official habits," which led to confrontations like the firebrick episode.

Of course more was promised us than has been fulfilled. This is human nature and especially Russian nature. When we ask whether a thing can be guaranteed we can always get an affirmative answer if we press hard enough. Rather than run the risk of having us reduce our assistance, the Russians at this moment would guarantee us the moon, not perhaps entirely dishonestly but with a happy-go-lucky hope that by some chance or miracle they might be able to get it or something like it.

Haskell was less able to contain his anger: "Plain and fancy lying was Volodin's chief ability, and I never saw him around our headquarters building in the two years we occupied without calling to mind the long and complicated tissues of lies which he had spun so deftly while the Battle of the Firebrick was raging." Despite such prickliness, Haskell came to believe that oftentimes what appeared at first to be Soviet indifference and uncooperativeness toward the ARA effort was in fact ascribable to old-fashioned Russian incompetence.

This was Goodrich's point, in a diary entry of November 12, 1921, written in Moscow after his return from a tour of the famine zone: "I find the same complaint that all the work is dragging and children are starving because of the dilatoriousness of the soviet government in getting the work done. The truth of the matter is they are doing their best, but they are inefficient and are too much afflicted with the proverbial slowness of the Asiatic."

An employee of the Kiev district felt that the Americans in that city were too quick to accuse local officials of apathy when in fact "This was not a matter of negligence but of our Russian inability to work rapidly and systematically." The local government in Kiev had tried to meet the ARA halfway, but came up short because of "our Russian inability to work with an American rapidity."

Volodin, being Eiduk's second-in-command, was in a relatively advantageous position to deliver on promises, his unproductive performance with the firebrick notwithstanding. As one descended the ladder of authority, an official's ability to live up to his words seemed to deteriorate correspondingly. In the supply division, Lyon's nemesis was a Soviet food supply official who could not, or would not, meet the most modest requests: "to procure from him even a rough broom was like trying to get thru an amendment to the Volstead Act." At other times ARA and Soviet officials had different notions of what constituted "getting action," as in the following exchange prompted by the delayed departure of an American supply train.

"What's the trouble about this engine?" the Traffic Chief asked in laconic American.

"Oh, we have straightened that all out," the government official replied. "We have put the railroad man responsible for this in jail."

"But has the train left?"

"No, we are getting another railroad man to get the engine, but everything will be all right—we have the first man who failed to get the engine in arrest."[7]

WHATEVER LYON'S DIFFICULTIES in obtaining rough brooms and other implements as supply division chief in Moscow, he would have remembered from his Orenburg days that it was far more challenging to outfit an office in the districts. Ellingston, who had served for several months in the Saratov district, figured "It took twice as long in the districts as in Moscow to have a window pane fixed or a telephone installed, simply because of the inefficiency of the local officials through whom such things had to be done." He was another who came to the conclusion that the problem was "not so much ill-will as inefficiency and inertia."

The most effective American course of action was relentless pestering, as the Kiev district history relates: "By experience we had learned that the only way to get anything from the government was to bother them until they had produced action in order to get rid of us, so part of our daily routine consisted in going to the Gubispolkom to ask for offices, warehouses and other equipment." The Vitebsk district supervisor employed a martial analogy: "Every advance step is a fight and nothing is accomplished unless an American follows it through inch by inch."

Kelley remarked that in Ufa an American encountered "difficulties, which no one who has not actually worked in Russia can hope to visualize. To disinfect and equip an office alone required an immense expenditure of time and patience. . . . To secure desks, a telephone, Russian typewriters, paper, printed forms, stoves, etc., called for incessant negotiations with a demoralized government whose invariable answer was 'Zaftra', tomorrow."

Complicating matters was the fact that an American's idea of the proper office environment was markedly different from that of a Russian. His first exposure to a Soviet government office made this apparent to Kelley: "No American could conceivably work amid the litter and discomforts that seem not to bother a Russian Soviet department." He joined Bell and Boris in paying a formal call upon the new local chief of the executive committee of the soviet, the *gubispolkom*:

We droshkied to the Government headquarters and were shown in at once to his office. Various "comrades" were hollering about the sanctum as though it were a salon. Soon the gentleman came in and we held forth with him for a half hour. We hear he has a black reputation gained during the days of the executions. To me he seemed a pleasant but warped enthusiast with plenty of force and intensity.

This last comment corresponds with many American descriptions of provincial Bolshevik and Soviet officials. In other ways as well was he typical: "Being a communist the Gubispolkum affects extreme simplicity of manner and in his surroundings. Lenin's picture and a statue of Karl Marx were the sole ornaments in his office. He paid us the compliment of calling us 'Tavarishe' which is the communist salutation, 'comrade'."

Kelley got much enjoyment out of describing such moments, but it was Fleming who truly reveled in detailing what today would go by the name of Soviet office "culture." In March 1923 he paid a visit to the headquarters of the Soviet famine relief committee in Penza, a city about one hundred miles directly west of Samara. Here he had the opportunity to take in the scene at what he considered to be a representative Soviet office, or at least "a pretty good example. George (interpreter) and I walked in one morning at half-past nine—the chief had not come yet, and the two machinists were just tuning up their machines preparatory to getting into low gear."

The chief arrived and Fleming proceeded to query him about statistical data. Fleming, who later became a Wall Street economist, had the reputation in the Russian unit of being a voracious consumer of statistics, which he evidently aspired to work into some grand prescription for Soviet Russia's economic recovery. The ARA's "Non-Statistical Notes" remembered him with, "Fleming searches [for] the master formula of economic reintegration." On this particular day in Penza he was curious about general population figures, the numbers of children in local detention homes, and the extent of government feeding—that is, matters of famine relief. Unfortunately for young Harold, this local official in charge of famine relief did not share his enthusiasm for such data—or at least he seems not to have had the figures handy—so "the conversation lagged, until he got out a little chart of a device of his for walking on water by means of water skis, which he showed me in great detail until the arrival of the two gubs."

The chief had summoned them to his office by means of a "telephonogram," which provided Fleming with the biggest thrill of his visit: "To watch one of these telephonograms being sent over the phone is an indescribable but unforgettable experience." Indeed, he made no attempt to describe it.

Everybody works in overcoats, the men with hats on; nobody has anything on their desks except scattered papers and occasionally a chinese laundryman's counting machine; though this is a mark of lower caste; and the papers they do business with are badly exploited. Over the original request, memorandum, or order, is scratched the remarks of everyone through whose hands it has gone. Such memos in our Moscow office start out with one slip, and end up where they started trailing clouds of memo slips and papers attached with a clip; but the Soviet offices save paper and write all their remarks on the same sheet. No sheet is valid without a stamp of some department, and the ink used is always of an unchanging cheap velvet color that I hope never to see again when I leave the soil of Russia.[8]

He does not remark on the exceptionally poor quality of Russian paper by 1922, which enhanced the cheapness of the velvet color, but he does seem to make the connection between the degree of exploitation of the paper and its severely short supply: "There are no waste-baskets, primarily because nobody ever gets through with a paper once it is started on its existence, but also because if by chance a sheet of paper succeeds in finishing and concluding its mission in life, it goes for cigarette paper. The Russian cigarette in New York and the Russian cigarette in Russia are different things."

Of all the distinctive features of the Soviet office—indeed, of Soviet life—perhaps the most remarked upon in the letters and diaries of the American relief workers was the smell of Russian tobacco, which often went by the name *makhorka*. It was the bête noire of every ARA man, and it lends a claustrophobic quality to many of the interior settings they describe.

On a train journey in the Volga region Fleming shared a coupé with three comrades, who "smoked quantities of cigarettes, which filled the top of the room with a dense smoke and an odor I shall never forget and one which will never fail to bring back the most vivid dreams of Russian life,—the smell of mahorka. Mahorka is a weed the Russians use for tobacco. While its scent is distinctive, it is not fragrant."

Blomquist's brief memoir written at the end of the mission recalled the inside of the Simbirsk railway station "choking with the stench of 'mahorka' (a species of raw, uncured, substitute tobacco)." Golder, who alone transliterated the word properly, said that in the Volga region *makhorka* was made into cigarettes using newspaper.

The steady disappearance since the Revolution of Western brands of tobacco and cigarettes and the general descent into the use of *makhorka* meant that for the ARA man access to American tobacco was of vital importance. The records of the ARA Moscow commissary contain lists of which brand was ordered in which quantity by which American: among the most requested tobacco labels were Bull Durham, Prince Albert, Tuxedo, and Velvet; of cigarettes, the most popular were Fatimas, Chesterfields, and Gold Flakes. In the districts, the irregular arrivals of these products stand out like exclamation points in the documentation. They were perhaps more coveted than whiskey and gin; apparently, having to imbibe Russian hooch was considered less of a trial than having to inhale *makhorka*.

Kelley, in a letter of January 10, 1922, makes clear his priorities: "We are all cheered to learn by mail that commissary supplies of food, tobacco, and liquor are en route. I would like to send you some of the execrable Soviet cigarettes which we are now reduced to. All cigarettes in Russia have the monogram of the Soviet Government."

Although there are occasional indications that some Russians preferred the Soviet brand or to roll their own *makhorka*, most of the locals were extremely fond of American tobacco and this meant that the commissary supplies could be used to serve the relief worker beyond his own direct personal enjoyment. Just as in a later, post-Stalinist Marlboro era, so in the Fatima days of 1921, cigarettes could open doors, grease wheels, turn a *seichas* into an *amerikanskii seichas*. When government relations improved in the Tsaritsyn district, Cornick noted in his diary a nondiplomatic factor behind the new cooperation: "I give much credit at present to my good American tobacco (Tuxedo & Velvet)."

In Soviet Russia tobacco and cigarettes were a fixture of government offices beyond the immoderate amount of smoking that went on inside them. As economic conditions deteriorated during the Civil War and as the ruble sank in value and barter replaced monetary transactions, tobacco became a standard substitute for money wages and for food rations. Some of this tobacco was of high quality until stocks ran low.

Many rationed cigarettes ended up for sale at the outdoor markets, which were tolerated even during the severest days of War Communism, though with sporadic crackdowns that kept everyone on edge. In 1921 this petty trade became legal, and one of the images of the early NEP days preserved in photos and news-reels is the cigarette girl peddling her merchandise at the markets. In Moscow Fleming observed "a whole row of them, standing elbow to elbow, with a little box suspended at the waist containing twenty boxes or so of cigarettes apiece."

By that point in time Russian tobacco—*makhorka* or a cousin to it—was about all that was left to Soviet bureaucrats to smoke, and its aroma penetrated the ARA offices through various agents, including the government plenipotentiaries. Murphy and Coolidge complained openly about it in their correspondence as did numerous other ARA men, who also made it the subject of repeated cynical asides, indicating that the product and the practice had burned a hole in their consciousness. Ellingston's history of the food remittance work relates that Eiduk was so suspicious of the ARA's intentions with its food package program that he assigned to the division a subplenipotentiary, a certain Popoff. "He was given a desk in Mr. Burland's office, ornamented with all the paraphernalia of candle sticks, pen holders, and mid-Victorian blotters without which the business man seems unable to do business. Mr. Popoff's most useful bit of equipment for the time being was undoubtedly his ash tray."

Just what kind of tobacco Popoff puffed to pass the time is not known, but it is a good bet that it did not take long for his American office mates to supply him with American brands—not out of any particular fondness for Popoff but rather in order to keep him from fouling the office with the stench from an inferior type. Actually, there was a third option: an American chief might choose to outlaw Russian tobacco. But this might raise a scandal, as Harvey Holden discovered when he introduced such a ban in the Moscow district office. This and other sins earned him a fuming attack in the April 11, 1922, issue of *Laboring Moscow* with the sarcastic title "'Democratic Habits.'"

The writer accused Holden of mocking his Russian employees. To one of them, who had committed some blunder, Holden read "an entire lecture about the incapacity for work of the Slavs in general and the Russians in particular." That was bad enough, but then "one fine day" this American bully declared to the staff: "I can't stand the smell of Russian tobacco. Anyone who wants to smoke, let him smoke only American cigarettes [*tsigarety*], from now on it is strictly forbidden to smoke Russian cigarettes [*papirosy*]." A *papirosa* was distinctive for its cardboard mouthpiece, though it was the quality of its tobacco that the Americans found objectionable. According to the writer, Holden knew very well that none of his employees had access to American cigarettes, nor was he offering. "This is how 'democratic' America treats its employees in Soviet Russia."

It is not clear that Holden really attempted to enforce his prohibition. As for his alleged remark about the abilities of the Slavs, certainly just about every American relief worker harbored such thoughts and in the heat of the moment would have been capable of uttering them. If Holden indeed made the statement attributed to him, it may have been merely a bad day at the office. His final letter to his family from Russia in July 1923 indicates a more sensitive soul than one would guess from reading *Laboring Moscow*. Of his Russian employees he wrote: "They are a good people, and like the French, the women who are given to idealism and clean living far out number the men with the same view-point." About either sex's smoking habits he made no remark.[9]

Meanwhile, in Soviet offices it was no holds barred, and Fleming, zeroing in on the intricacies of Russian smoking etiquette as demonstrated by the staff of the government relief committee in Penza, brings his treatise on the Soviet office regime to a breathless climax:

To make a Russian cigarette a la Russe you take a piece of note- or wrapping paper about 1 1/2 inches by 2 1/2 and roll it out into a narrow cone; then elongate it by pulling out the ends carefully; wet the small end and role it tight. You then bend it in the middle, and drop sawdust (called mahorka in Russian) into the larger end of the cone; then carefully fold the protruding tips over the sawdust, and ignite. Down on the general scene of blank desks, blank floor, blank walls, and Russian cigarettes, beams from one side of the room the ever-smiling face of Lenin, and from the other side the ever militant Trotsky; a salutation to the world's proletariat and the communist party painted on the wall completes the scene—and one of the Sovbars (sovietsky bareshnias —offices misses) sending a telephonogram adds the piece de resistance.

ACTUALLY, Lenin found little to smile about when it came to the doings in Soviet offices, especially now in the new hardheaded NEP days of living within budgets and strict accounting procedures. It was time to move away from utopian schemes for walking on water and to plant one's feet firmly on the ground.

One of Lenin's greatest concerns in these, his final years was the mammoth bureaucracy that was the Soviet government. When the Bolsheviks took power, they were a tiny organization and were forced to rely on the tsarist bureaucracy to maintain the big Russian state and keep them in power. The tsarist administration had a well-deserved reputation for inefficiency; in the words of an ARA Kiev employee: "Burocratism and red tape had ever been one of the striking particularities of the Russian administrative life."

This situation grew worse after 1917 as the state progressively assumed authority over virtually the entire economy. The result was the growth of a bureaucracy and of bureaucratism more onerous and oppressive than anything Russia had known before the Revolution. "Officialism has always been the curse of Russia," wrote Mackenzie; nonetheless, "officialism under the Commune has reached a point that it never touched in the worst Czarist days. The officials of one department play up against those in another. So many permits have to be obtained that the most ordinary and necessary business is blocked. Overworked officials, often inexpert in routine work, helped by ignorant subordinates, muddle and delay." The Red Revolution was strangling in its own red tape.

The onset of NEP meant that the people's commissariats had to introduce legitimate bookkeeping and operate on a cash-paying basis, and that entailed reducing their bloated staffs. According to Mackenzie, in numerical terms Soviet bureaucratism reached its height in October 1921 when the number of people directly employed by the central government was 7,481,000; by spring 1922 it had been reduced to 4,571,000. Yet bureaucratic habits could not be similarly cut away, and in 1923 his fellow reporter Hullinger could still write that "There is no government in the world more deeply enmeshed in red tape." Naturally, this complicated the job of famine relief. An American in Tsaritsyn recounts how a green reliever returned from the interior to the provincial capital totally disheartened: "'Russia is the hardest _____ _____ country to give away things in that I ever saw.' The other Americans who had been there for some time merely grinned dourly—it was old stuff for them."

"Delays are enough to make a saint swear," wrote Goodrich, who tried to convey to Hoover a sense of the difficulties standing in the way of accomplishing even the simplest tasks in Russia. "The bureaucracy of the Czar was bad enough, but the Communist Government finds itself entangled in a mass of bureaucratic organizations through which it is impossible to penetrate and out of which there can come no efficiency." Coming from an American, this was a most damning assessment.

Coolidge, one of the few ARA men to have been in Russia before the Revolution, made the case for continuity. He thought that a good many of the present difficulties were "inevitable" due in large measure to the "slackness, irresponsibility, habits of prevarication and other faults inherent to the Russian character; likewise to bureaucratic traditions and lack of capacity for team play. All of this existed under the old regime, as I can remember myself, indeed I sometimes wonder if the obstacles we encounter would not have been as great then as now, in spite of the disorder and demoralization consequent to the present revolution."

William Henry Chamberlin of the *Christian Science Monitor* disagreed. Though he had not visited Russia before 1921, he had seen and heard enough of the "endless red tape which surrounded the simplest operation, such as buying a railway ticket, the number of stamps which had to be affixed to all sorts of documents," and so on, to conclude that the quantitative enlargement of the bureaucracy since the tsarist period had produced a qualitative degeneration of Russian bureaucratism. "Moreover, the Tsarist bureaucrats were at least tolerably educated— which could not be said of many of their Soviet successors."

Lenin was especially concerned that Soviet bureaucratic practices threatened the growth of foreign trade and business concessions considered essential to the rehabilitation of the economy, especially to the revival of heavy industry. Indeed, as it happened, the Soviet government's campaign in the early 1920s to attract foreign business investment and international trade produced disappointing results. It did not help matters that the Bolsheviks, after much agonizing, decided to retain the state monopoly on foreign trade, but this was only a symptom of a deeper problem underlined by Mackenzie, namely, "Russian business methods. The Russian, in Czarist and Bolshevist days alike, has always hated giving any control over his natural resources to foreigners. When he does business, he surrounds it with endless formalities and delays." The result was that foreign concessions were "wrapped up in red tape beyond anything known before."

Individual projects might start well: the would-be concessionaire meets in London with Leonid Krassin, the enlightened Soviet foreign trade minister, with whom he comes to a handshake agreement about the details of his proposed business venture. Believing he has a deal nearly in hand, he then goes to Moscow to clinch it only to discover that he must renegotiate everything from the beginning. And not with the likes of Krassin, as Mackenzie explains:

Officials take their own time for seeing the applicants. The time may be now or next week, or maybe next month. What does time matter? The official makes amiable promises which he forgets or never intends to keep. Fresh conditions are sprung up at the last moment. . . . This is typically Russian. Bolshevism has not brought business efficiency. The foreigner who wants to do business in Russia has to reckon with this. It is useless to kick against the pricks.

The old hands recognized the game from an earlier day. Fleming encountered a group of American and English businessmen in Harbin, Manchuria, as he was exiting Russia in June 1923.

They have been in here before the war, are acquainted with the difficulties of working with the old Russian government and realize that 98% of the difficulties, the inconveniences, the rudenesses and crudenesses, the obstructions and obliquenesses which they have to put up with in dealing with Soviet officials are not due to the fact that they are Soviet, but to the fact that they are Russian government officials. So it was, so it is, and so it ever will be.[10]

Among the Americans there was much comment on the Russian addiction to paperwork. Considering the scarcity of paper, this was an expensive habit. Tracy Kohl wrote in the ARA Crimea history: "It was early apparent that the Russians wanted an abundance of detailed written instructions and that they were used to making out reports and handling blank forms. That is, what some might call 'red tape' was to these Russians quite a natural means if not a necessary part of the operation."

To the ARA man, nothing symbolized the prodigious Russian appetite for written matter like the *protokol*, the record of the proceedings of an official gathering. It sometimes appeared that Soviet officials were more interested in the written summary of the meeting than in the meeting itself: somehow the piece of paper seemed to carry more significance than the event it described. During his time in Soviet Russia Shafroth sampled his share of them, and when he reached the United States, he expressed a definite opinion as to their usefulness:

The protocol is the chief indoor sport of Soviet officialdom, and consists of a secretary's written report of what any two or more people said, might have said, or ought to have said, when they had a conference. When drawn up, it is signed by the parties at the conference and constitutes an admission that they did say what the secretary says they said.

If all the protocols written in Russia in the last year were piled together and turned into food, there would soon be more deaths from gout than from starvation.

Actually, it is a reasonable bet that a fair number of protocols were used to roll *makhorka*, thereby contributing to deaths from causes other than gout.

The lower the level of the official, the greater seemed his dependency on written formalities. At Odessa, when the first clothing consignments arrived, they were taken to the customs warehouse for inspection. Several days went by, and district supervisor Joseph Brown got curious and went with a colleague to make his own inspection.

To our great surprise we found only two cases had been examined, for the method of the examination was elaborate and would make a horse laugh. The procedure was as follows:

1. The case was opened.
2. The packages in each case were counted.
3. The small boxes in each package were counted.
4. The buttons in each box were counted.
5. Then every button was put in its place in every box and every box in its place in every package and every package in its place in every case, and the lid nailed down.

Brown asked if this procedure would be repeated with each case and was assured it would be. "An interview was held with the Manager of the Customs, and he was told it would be impossible for him to examine all the cases in this fashion. He asked why and was told that neither he nor his employees would live long enough. He saw the point and immediately dispensed with the red tape procedure."

More typically, small-time officials met reasoned argument against their procedures with stiff resistance. American relievers in the districts could relate individual tales of tragedy produced by bullheaded petty officials in a time of famine. For Dr. Godfrey in Simbirsk it was the story of the wolf of Alatyr. It was November 1922 when "A wolf bounded into a village in the Alatyr Ouezd in broad day light and bit an 11 year old boy quite severely about the head, face and neck. There being no guns in the town, the wolf was finally killed with clubs and stones."

There was no physician in the village, not even a feldsher, so one was called in from a neighboring village. It very soon became apparent that the danger to the boy went beyond the severity of his wounds. "On questioning about the accident it was learned that the wolf acted very strangely, carried his tail between his legs, acted as if he were partially blind and was frothing at his mouth. This together with the fact that wolves do not frequent villages at this time of the year alone and in daylight led the felsher to suspect RABIES." The nearest Pasteur cure was in Kazan, where the boy was immediately sent. In Godfrey's professional opinion, "Time meant everything." But at the station the ticket agent would not sell them a ticket because their documents were not "technically correct."

Godfrey says that the feldsher had had great difficulty overcoming the "superstition" of the family and getting them to agree to the treatment to save the boy's life. There is no detail about the parents' misgivings, but perhaps they assumed, in the Russian tradition, that a hospital was a place where people died, and that therefore by giving their son over to the feldsher they would automatically condemn him to death. Whatever was the case, they did not seem to grasp the urgency of the matter, and it was only after considerable pleading that they gave way. The ticket agent, however, was immovable. The feldsher insisted that the boy's life was at stake, but rules being rules, "The agent was obstinate; the train pulled out and left the patient behind."

The next triweekly train, which arrived a day late, took the boy to Kazan, where he received his treatment but not in time to prevent his death by hydrophobia.

It was bureaucratic creatures like the Alatyr ticket agent that could set Chamberlin off: "As a general rule my temper is rather phlegmatic and placid; but nothing is so calculated to make me depart from this general rule as the puffed-up arrogance of the small official, in any country, taking a sadistic pleasure in his power to delay, obstruct, and annoy. There was an enormous amount of this sort of thing in Soviet Russia."

Vasilyi Rozanov, the Russian literary critic, wrote shortly before his death in 1919 after retreating to a monastery and declaring the Russian Revolution to be the "Apocalypse of Our Time"—the title of an unfinished manuscript—that the Russians were "made for ideas and feelings, for prayer and music, but not to rule over people."

Few American relief workers would have taken exception to Rozanov's statement. As they went about their duties, making mental and written notes of the behavior of Russians at work, including the habits of those who administered Soviet Russia—the absence of punctuality, the procrastination, the garrulousness, the buck-passing, the fear of responsibility, the use of the abacus, the abuse of *makhorka*, the cheap velvet-colored ink—they contrasted the resulting portrait of the Russians with the already Olympian estimation they held of their own administrative abilities as Americans. None of them spelled out the conclusion they drew from this comparison as bluntly as Fleming: "The longer out here the more one gets the feeling of belonging to a superior race; we all get it—we believe it, and it stays with us."[11]

CHAPTER 35

THE BUSINESS OF RELIEF

John Ellingston ran the historical division in Moscow, but his chief in New York City, Harold Fisher, was designated to write the official history of the mission. Ellingston's responsibility was to gather the documentation, and in the winter and spring of 1923 this entailed seeing to it that the individual division and district histories were written before the ARA left Soviet Russia. This exercise had been done before, in summer 1922, when it appeared that the ARA show was about to close down, but the time had come to write sequels. Most of these were to be authored by the respective chiefs, but not to be left out, Ellingston chose to chronicle the story of the food remittance program himself. As with most things he undertook, he made the most of it.

A native of Butte, Montana, Ellingston attended high school in Hollywood, then spent the years 1914–15 at the University of California before transferring to Yale. The war interrupted his education—by his own choice—as he enlisted with an American ambulance unit in the service of the French Army, earning a French Croix de Guerre, with palm, for services in Serbia and Albania. He then joined the British Army, with a commission as a second lieutenant in the Machine Gun Corps. After the war he returned to Yale and graduated summa cum laude in 1919, then went back to Europe as a fellow of Hoover's Commission for the Relief of Belgium Education Foundation, which had an exchange program with the Universities of Brussels and Ghent. From the CRB it was only a short hop to the ARA and to Moscow.

The product of Ellingston's labors as chronicler of the ARA food package program was "The Carriage of Philanthropy," a 156-page survey credited to "One Who Served," which roamed freely over the story of the ARA in Soviet Russia.

The dominant theme of Ellingston's history is the clash of American and Russian cultures. This took various forms, but its mainspring, as he saw it, was the contrast between American "native energy" and Russian "racial inertia": "Aside from the abnormal stagnation and decay resulting from the revolution and the famine, a Russian characteristic is a proneness to inactivity and to an easy going attitude foreign to the American." He offered as the embodiment of American energy in action the veteran reliever Tommy Burland, about to present to the Soviet government the ARA proposal to establish a food remittance program in Russia:

He was young and energetic America charged with a great idea. To him the essential was action. He represented a people whose hero is the man who breaks records, whether on the running track, or on the stock exchange. Accustomed to direct and speedy dealing and conscious of the straightforwardness of his cause, he anticipated immediate agreement. Technical objections he could meet with the quickness of one whose mind is in the possession of all the facts. He didn't expect to meet any other. To him the discussion was to be merely a discussion of terms. . . . The Russian negotiator required but little time to disillusion him. . . . Mr. Eiduk met the proposal as if it were a criminal on trial before him, and as if he were a French court, which considers the accused guilty until proven innocent.

That encounter set the tone of exceptional Bolshevik suspicion toward the remittance operation, which was inevitable considering that most of the food packages were intended to relieve the country's "brainworkers," most of whom had come out on the losing end of the Revolution. Yet as Ellingston demonstrated, the greatest obstacle facing the food remittance program—more, the entire relief mission—was not the obstruction of Soviet officials but the behavior of the Russian population. The suspicions of commissars could be overcome much more easily than could the lethargy and inefficiency of an entire people.

As the biggest non-ARA cheerleader of the organization, Duranty, who showcased these Russian-American contrasts in his newspaper stories, remarked at the outset on the "sore need of American system and 'pep' to galvanize the whole work." Pep—short for pepper and usually not placed between quotation marks—was a favorite expression of the ARA men, especially as applied to their own energy and quickness.

The supreme achievement of the American relief workers, as Ellingston saw it, was their ability to transform the Russians in their midst by breathing into them a remarkable energy: "as administrators of an emergency relief operation effective in proportion to the speed with which it was applied they increased that energy manyfold. . . . They imparted their own energy to everything with which they came in contact, and in the spring of 1922 they came into contact with practically everything in Russia." Actually the choice of wording is a bit misleading because to instill this energy required a considerable expenditure of it:

At every point along the line of the relief operation the Americans worked under pressure and forced the Russians to follow suit. At the ports they pushed the stevedores to halve their unloading time; they hammered the railroads to keep empties rolling in and loaded trains rolling out; they hounded the local governments to supply equipment and warehouses; they gave their personnel a time limit for every job.

In Ellingston's telling, all the drive and push brought about a remarkable, if not quite "miraculous," metamorphosis:

The activity, the spirit of reconstruction which the A.R.A. inspired in the national utilities and in the individuals with whom it came in contact, bred a new spirit of life in the stagnant land, which spread to everyone. And with the new stirring, came new hope, new desire. The A.R.A. represented an enormous concrete aid, but it also symbolized the efficacy of work. Wherever the Administration went in 1921 and 22 it found an inert despondency, a listlessness without hope, or an indifferent inefficiency. Within six months these characteristics had changed; there was life in the air, bustle, a very definite struggle against famine and disease. The moral recuperation of the country was marvelous; without it physical recuperation would have been impossible.

Ellingston gives a nod to the role of the New Economic Policy and the good harvest of 1922 in Russia's revival, "But the connection between the A.R.A. and this recuperation stands out too clearly, too definitely, to permit of doubt that the Administration began it and kept it alive."

And this was not all. After the ARA departed Russia this life-giving American stimulus would continue to make itself felt, especially in the methods of efficiency the ARA had taught the Russians. Such thoughts inspired "One Who Served" to speculate on the role of the American relief workers in "Influencing the National Character," as he titled the section:

It is, of course, too much to suppose that the American Relief operation permanently influenced a change in the national character; it would be presumptuous to suppose that it is desirable. We are an efficient people, but are we any better for that? Perhaps the efficacy and magnitude of our relief to Russia proves that we are. However, it is quite probable that Russian business has taken a lesson from the American Relief operation which will bear fruit, at least during the lifetime of the 120,000 Russians who worked directly for the A.R.A. These people received a training in business efficiency, which, though they resented it at times, they eventually recognized as justifiable. . . .

It may very well be that these people will forget the strictness of the personal relations, but they will not forget the thousand and one hints in improved office management which they learned from the A.R.A. They will not forget that they were part of an organization which achieved the supposedly impossible in Russia, nor the means by which it did so.

Ellingston had a head full of ideas and a desire to put them on paper, and the nature of his ARA duties allowed him this luxury. The other chiefs, even if so inclined, worked in conditions less favorable to the writing of thoughtful prose, especially the district supervisors, and Ellingston knew they would have to be "hounded to death" to write their histories.

He began an aggressive cheerleading drive that included a memorandum to the division chiefs, dated February 6. Appealing to their pride, he reminded them of their acts of heroism, of the gripping drama of their mission. Perhaps they were so preoccupied with the "gnats of petty difficulties and minor details" that they had lost sight of the epic proportions of their story. To guide them in recounting it, he reviewed the subjects their histories should include, urging them to give special attention to the ultimate hero of the tale: American work methods. "We are a scientific organization working on hard business principles, with a very highly perfected business organization. . . . There is something intensely dramatic in the contrast between the humanity of our motives and the bloodless impersonality of our methods. The cold story of that organization, of how we actually worked, is therefore of intense interest."

True, but it was nonetheless difficult for a mightily overextended district supervisor to work up an intense interest in passing several hours at the typewriter, and it was only after some importuning and some improvising—such as sending in Fleming to write the Orenburg history—that the much anticipated oeuvres began to arrive on Ellingston's desk in late spring. On the whole, he was pleased. The district historians and their division counterparts eagerly adopted as the theme of their narratives the triumph of American energy and organization over Russian inertia and disorganization.

Somerville opened his spirited account of government relations in the Simbirsk district with a dramatic touch:

An organization with a personnel of thirteen thousand workers in one Gubernia alone; directed by business men of the straitest capitalistic convictions, run on business principles purely capitalistic; working in the midst of a Communistic and Sovietized State; brought into daily contact with anti-capitalistic government officials in the seats of the local governments and in hundreds of villages—surely there has not been in history a more interesting adventure in relief than this, of the A.R.A. in Russia.

Yet this juxtaposition is not the best fit for the story he goes on to tell, which is less about a struggle between capitalism and communism, and more about a collision of American and Russian ways. The chronicler of the administrative division gives a typically ARA assessment to the outcome of the struggle: "Enough to say that we believe this institution was a lesson of considerable value in efficiency, order, cleanliness, punctuality and absence of red tape."

The lesson was absorbed principally by the ARA's own local personnel, but a number of Americans implied or stated directly that its effects extended beyond their organization. The mere example of excellence set by the ARA had an impact on Soviet institutions. Administrative chief John Mangan boasted that the government departments had copied the ARA's "series system, with the result that we have contributed to the permanent efficiency of at least one Russian public service."

Driscoll wrote in the Rostov-Tsaritsyn history: "anyone who knows the Russians can well imagine what a struggle the Americans had to get things moving, and to keep them moving." Here his Russians are the ones working for the ARA. His colleague Pat Verdon elaborates: "To break them all in in their various lines of work was a heartbreaking task in itself, for it was felt that the work must be done on strictly American lines if it was to be made as effective as possible." The Americans had to learn and take into account Russian methods of business, the more quickly to be able to supplant them with superior American methods. On the whole it was an unpleasant transition, "and the rapidity and frequency with which inefficient employees were let out was in itself a revelation to the average Russian." In time, though, the effect on the local personnel was, as Bowden describes it, profound: "As happened in other countries where the A.R.A. has operated, the native personnel have become inbred with the 'Hoover spirit,' and are sparing neither time nor energy to perfect our organization."

The Ekaterinoslav history expressed a similarly hopeful outlook: "Many came into the office untrained and lacking in the simple rules of office detail and routine. They will leave with a good knowledge of business methods and an experience which will make them valuable assets for Russian offices. The effects of the training which they have received should be noticeable for many years in the various positions to which they may go."

The Saratov history underscored the high standards set by the "drive and impatience of the young Americans." Raskin in Nikolaev gave great weight to "our example of efficiency and push."[1] And so on and on.

Brooks, in his account of the ARA and the railroads, wrote in the same vein, though his assessment of the mission as "a triumph of American efficiency and

Russian sacrifice and stamina" implies that the Americans left the Russians exactly as they found them, the human equivalent of draft animals. No influencing the national character here. This is consistent with a passage in his summing-up, where he points to an ARA influence of a less tangible kind:

When the last Americans left Moscow for home, their job finished, it was at least with pardonable satisfaction that America had left in the memory of Russians not only heartfelt gratitude, but a reputation for excellence of organization and efficiency of accomplishment. The one has brought the people of Russia perhaps closer in spirit to those of our own country than ever before to any foreign nation. The other has left American prestige and respect that should have much bearing on the course of future relations between the two countries.

They may have had varying opinions as to the effects of their work on the Russians, but the relief workers were unanimous in the conviction that their work methods were archetypically American. Most thought of themselves as efficient, hardheaded businessmen and could be quite sensitive about their image outside the organization. They were "relief workers," but not in a conventional sense. Ellingston liked to say that most people tended to think of the ARA as a kind of "Association of Veteran Babyfeeders." "Babyfeeder" was a label the ARA men liked to apply to themselves for ironic effect; it conveyed a closeness to the individual beneficiary that belied the much-vaunted "bloodless impersonality" of their operation. They were keen to set themselves apart from relief workers like those of the Red Cross, the YMCA, and the Quakers whose emotional attachment to the beneficiary, in the ARA view, took precedence over matters of organization and management and who were, in a word, inefficient.

The correctness of the ARA's cold, "scientific" methods, Ellingston believed, had never been given a clearer demonstration than in the vast Russian operation: "had we worked on the intimate personal lines which obtain among Settlement House Workers, our stocks would have rotted on the tracks while we were futilely saving hundreds."

Haskell says that when he arrived in Armenia in 1920 he encountered foreign, including American, relief workers "of the missionary type": they were doing what they could "but doing it in a very unbusinesslike manner." He writes patronizingly of "the sincere but futile efforts of these well-meaning missionaries and inexperienced relief workers." Haskell would have been very pleased to read how an officer with American military intelligence visiting Odessa on a U.S. destroyer in summer 1922 evaluated the work of the local ARA:

Mr. Hodgson and his assistants are extremely able and efficient. Sentiment does not enter into their work. They regard it as purely a business proposition, so many people to be fed, so many bales of clothing to be distributed where they will do the most good. There is nothing of the missionary atmosphere about the organization at all. There is no attempt at propaganda, and the whole organization operates with an almost mechanical regularity.

Yet the men of the ARA were indeed missionaries of a kind. They preached the superiority of the American way; their propaganda was their own example of efficiency, a word they repeated like a mantra. They promoted it, the idea of it, and the idea of their own mastery of it with a kind of messianic zeal. As they were saving lives, they were also bringing light to the uncivilized masses, they liked to think, winning many thousands of converts to their faith in salvation through efficiency, thereby permanently altering the Russian national character. "It may be that the influence of American business methods as exemplified by the A.R.A. will be traced in Russian economic life long after the lives the Administration saved have gone out of memory." Ellingston seemed to believe that it would be, despite his cautious wording.

In trumpeting their efficient ways, the Americans set themselves apart from all Europeans; the Russians were only the worst case. Corcoran, the ARA's rare non-American, in discussing the Russian view of Hoover's men, seemed to identify himself with it: "Of course from a purely Russian pre-war standpoint the Americans are slightly crazy. You tell them for example, that something is impossible—something that your centuries-old European mind knows to be impossible through its centuries-old experience, and all they say is some Russian jargon, which translated freely means:

"'Forget it.'"

This American distinctiveness is strikingly evident in the writings of the Englishman Philip Gibbs, whose enthusiastic accounts of Russian relief in his non- and docu-fictional works inspired an item in the ARA's "Non-Statistical Notes": "Immortality of the A.R.A. personalities via Philip Gibbs." But more than honoring individuals, he celebrated the organization as "a model of efficiency and zeal." His pronouncement on the Russian mission could easily have been spoken by Ellingston: "A new hope dawned in Russia, which learnt something from American methods of efficiency."[2]

THE IMAGE AND SELF-IMAGE of America as a land of youth, vigor, and efficiency was at least as old as the republic. Benjamin Franklin—"the prototype of Max Weber's ethical Protestant," in Daniel Bell's words—was considered "The Father of Efficiency." Number six on his list of virtues reads, "Lose no time; be always employed in something useful; cut off all unnecessary action." Franklin is also associated with that quintessentially American aphorism, "Time is money."

Such eminent lineage notwithstanding, America's national fixation on efficiency was a more recent and transitory phenomenon elevated to something of a movement during the Progressive Era in the early years of the century. It became a national craze around 1910 when calls for "efficiency" and "scientific management" generated popular excitement, and there circulated unlikely new vogue words like "management," "control," and "regulation."

In his classic study of the period, *The End of American Innocence*, Henry May characterized this movement as "an unsuccessful effort to add the word 'efficiency' to the national watchwords, to make room for it by throwing out 'culture,' and to put a little less emphasis on 'morality.'" The life span of the efficiency mania was bound to be short, but historian Samuel Haber attests to its momentary potency: "Efficient and good came closer to meaning the same thing in these years than in any other period of American history. . . . An efficient person was an effective person, and that characterization brought with it a long shadow of latent associations and predispositions; a turning toward hard work and away from feeling, toward discipline and away from sympathy, toward masculinity and away from femininity."

Already during the Great War enthusiasm began to wane, in particular for the idea of efficiency as a surrogate morality. The strain that proved to be the most durable was scientific, or industrial, management. It went also by the name of Taylorism after Frederick Winslow Taylor, its most important theorist and champion until his death in 1915. Taylor advocated rationalizing the production process by breaking it down into component parts, with workers performing particular tasks at predefined speeds. The human body was likened to a machine. Through the application of time-motion studies, Taylorism sought to organize production in such a way that the body performed no superfluous movements. The result, in theory, would be maximum efficiency, although labor leaders called it maximum exploitation.

"In the 1920s the Taylorites were in the vanguard of American business thought," Haber writes, and no less a figure than the secretary of commerce seemed to endorse their program. Hoover himself was not a Taylorist, but much of what he stood for made him appear sympathetic to the principles of scientific management. The way he engineered food relief to Belgians under the German occupation earned him a worldwide reputation for innovation and efficiency. The American journal the *Independent* wrote admiringly of his performance: "If there ever was an efficient job done, it is that of carrying relief to the wretched millions of Belgium. Herbert C. Hoover, the young American engineer who has managed this job, has established beyond a peradventure his right to the title Master of Efficiency."

Belgian relief brought Hoover to the attention of President Wilson, who asked him to come to Washington in 1917 to head up the wartime Food Administration, where his aggressive campaigns for voluntary rationing put him very much on the minds of a "Hooverizing" American public. Then came his statesmanship at Versailles and the tremendously complex food relief operations across Europe and in the Near East.

On November 23, 1918, with so many of his accomplishments still ahead, the *Bellman* rhapsodized that Hoover had become "virtually the Food Administrator of the World, occupying a position unique in history." Five years earlier he had been unknown outside the engineering profession; now "kings and rulers delight to honour him, and nations justly acclaim him as their preserver from hunger." Hoover had become "the embodiment of the efficient American in his achievements" with his "genius for organization, his inexhaustible capacity for work, his extraordinary grasp of perplexing and intricate problems and his magnetic leadership of men."

Behind all these rare qualities, and beneath a taciturn and reserved attitude, there is a generous soul and a kindly heart from which springs the desire to expend all he has of energy, strength, endowments and talents in the service of his fellows. This is the exceptional combination of attributes which make[s] him one of the greatest men of his age, whose name, when the history of this period is written, will stand out among the world's elect.

Unfortunately for Hoover, today his name is inseparable from the history of a subsequent period: the Great Depression, like a Great Eclipse, has obscured his earlier reputation in the popular American mind. Only those aware of what came before, who know of the extraordinary rise before the tragic fall, recognize in the figure of Hoover the ultimate American unmade man.

As he arrived in Washington in 1917 to manage wartime food supply, the newspapers took to calling him "Food Dictator" and "Food Czar." In order to head off this kind of labeling he assigned himself the title food administrator. It is a revealing choice. The word "administration" was especially fashionable with Americans at this time, particularly in Washington. Enthusiasts like Walter Lippmann spoke of administration as a budding science. Politics, it was thought, could be removed from pure administration: just get the politicians out of the way and leave matters to the administrators, and through this will come the highest efficiency.

Hoover was widely considered to be the consummate administrator. Historian David Kennedy characterizes the image of Hoover and Bernard Baruch during those years as "self-styled classless men who would skillfully administer the apparatus of an active but disinterested state that somehow stood above its constituent parts." Some predicted that administration would become a fourth branch of government, and in fact the administrative arm of the U.S. government grew significantly during the war, which was also when the term "white collar" came into use.

So the name American Relief *Administration* was appropriate for the times and especially for Hoover. And it served to distinguish his businesslike relief operations from those of conventional humanitarian agencies. Over the years historians and others have regularly mislabeled it the American Relief *Association*, which often betrays a misconception of the ARA as a charitable organization of the very missionary type its members disdained.

The job of the ARA men was to "administer" relief, using the most sophisticated methods of efficiency while standing above sentiment and politics. This was the image the organization sought to project throughout postwar Europe, although it later became blurred by charges that in fact Hoover had used ARA food as a political weapon, most sensationally to engineer the reversal of a bolshevik revolution in Hungary in March 1919. Still the popular American estimation of Hoover's work in Europe was close in spirit to that presented by Thomas Dickinson in his unpublished official history of the ARA's European operations: "Hoover applied to the problems of world statecraft the methods used by the engineer in breaking a way through the wilderness, or in bringing order again after an outbreak of nature. He applied the philosophy of the engineer to statecraft."[3]

The men of the ARA, generally speaking, saw themselves as "practical idealists" in the Hoover mold: they were engineer-administrators who prided themselves on an efficient and hardheaded dispensation of relief using strict accounting practices. Most professed to be animated by a strong sense of loyalty to the man who had sent them, as Kazan's Van Arsdale Turner recalled over forty years later: "During the difficult and frequently dangerous days of the A.R.A. Mission to the Baltic, and later the Russian Mission, it was only necessary to say 'The Chief wants it done, and in this particular way.' That was that, not only for me but for all the men I knew who served in those missions. A singularly undivided loyalty."

In fact few of them had ever met the man, but they knew what he personified, and many were intensely loyal to that ideal. "There is a saying among the old ARA men that 'once you tie up with Hoover you can never quite shake him off,'" wrote Golder in Moscow in 1922 as he himself was feeling the tug. When the frustrations of their Russian show seemed about to overwhelm them, the relief workers told themselves to "Do it for Hoover," and pressed on.

Reporter Mackenzie, observing the operation at the ground level, saw for himself that all the talk of the Hoover system was more than mere public relations:

Mr. Hoover's organization is intensely practical. It deals with the question of relief as a business proposition. There is so much money available. The work is to translate that money into as many meals for hungry children as you can, and to give these meals where they are needed most. Herbert Hoover hates inefficiency and waste. The men under him hate it too.

The ARA does not deal in sentiment, at least not in the famine area

The peculiarities of the Russian environment seem to have amplified the crusading spirit of the American relief workers. Their zeal for spreading their particular idea of civilization grew more fervent in proportion to the level of inefficiency and waste they came up against in Russia. Looking back on them now, listening to them talk about themselves and their mission, we find them almost cartoonlike. As they self-righteously contrast their can-do, energetic, efficient selves with the Asiatic, fatalistic, long-suffering Russians, they often sound programmed. It is as if they are reading their lines from a story authored by Herbert Hoover as told to Walter Duranty, based on an original concept by Max Weber.

It was the matter of the efficiency of the Russian operation that was at the heart of the bad feeling between the "old ARA" veterans and the army newcomers, which threatened to tear the mission apart during its first six months. That the Russian unit did not perform as efficiently as its ARA predecessors most of the old hands privately agreed, despite all the public self-congratulations. They attributed this in part to the unprecedented challenges of the Russian situation, physical, political, and human. But those who had served in the European theater placed much of the blame on the large presence at Moscow headquarters of U.S. Army officers at the expense of men experienced in Hoover-style relief work.

There were several related sources of the friction between the two camps, but underlying all of them was the "old ARA" complaint that the army-led Russian mission was not up to traditional ARA standards of efficiency. When Dickinson wrote his explosive January 1922 memo attacking Haskell's leadership and bringing the confrontation to a head, the most damning charge he could make was this: "For efficiency the Russian Unit belongs with the Red Cross and the Y.M.C.A. in war days."

Haskell maintained Hoover's confidence and survived this challenge, but his victory became final only in March when he found cause to dismiss from the mission the most senior of the "old ARA" men, Phil Carroll, who then fired off his own Dickinsonian parting shot. Its portrait of Moscow operations reads like a page from Soviet officialism:

In Headquarters office paper work and shifting of responsibility (buck-passing) were the principal time consumers. The amount of paper consumed would horrify a business enterprise. Ten to twelve copies of each telegram, two duplicating machines always behind, scores of busy typists, dozens of specially typed memoranda from stenographic notes, all spell paper consumption and time wasted. Shifting of responsibility was a logical resultant in an organization where no-one cared nor dared to make a final decision, and where paper work obliterated the real objective of office procedure. Incoming telegrams took hours to reach the division concerned and in some cases days. Letters took days to reach Mr. Eiduck's office in the same building, and weeks elapsed before receipt of many replies. The files all too frequently failed to disclose requisite information.

The whole thing smells strongly of *makhorka*.

The army's reputation had preceded it. "Passing the buck" was an army expression, the "buck" referring to the buckhorn handle of the knife used to mark the dealer in a poker game. Those Americans who had joined the American Expeditionary Force and served only for the duration came to view the army as untypically American for its inefficiency. Sarcastic asides on the subject came easily to them, no doubt nourished by unpleasant memories of army hierarchy and discipline.

The fallout from Dickinson's bombshell was still in the air in February 1922 when London chief Walter Lyman Brown dispatched Mowatt Mitchell to Moscow to assess the damage. Mitchell spent several weeks in the capital and accompanied Haskell on a trip to Saratov. In a series of detailed letters he reassured Brown that on the whole the situation at headquarters was stable and that the colonel was doing a satisfactory job. "But his inspection trips are hardly such as we are used to—in the first place he doesn't know what to look for or how to inspect as we understand the word, and in the second place he is very impatient of delays, detailed explanation, or studies of conditions or problems. He wants instantaneous glimpses and likes to give equally rapid answers and makes equally rapid decisions." In other words, Mitchell had found in Haskell just the army man he had expected.

His idea of seeing a kitchen is to drive up in front, stand at the door, ask how many are fed, look in the door a moment and then say that it's dirty, or crowded, or all right, and drive off again. We saw six or eight kitchens, and after the second one I managed to drive him in, and he stood around impatiently on one foot or the other and looked bored. He, of course, had no idea until it was called to his attention that the rice and milk and sugar was too thin in one place and too stodgy in another, or that the bread was stale or that the medical certificates on which some of the food was being taken home by adults for sick children were a month old. When three cases of the latter had been called to his attention he was all for issuing peremptory orders that no food at all could be taken out of kitchens, sick children or no sick children—the army way of going to one extreme or the other.

The colonel was open to the advice of those of his rank or intelligence, but all others he considered his subordinates and expected them to obey his orders. This was not at all the ARA way, Mitchell wrote, and Haskell's performance did not meet ARA standards. "The job as a whole, Walter, will go—not because of Haskell, but in spite of him, and I am convinced that it will add materially to the fame of the ARA and the world will rate it a huge success, and only those of us on the inside will know that it has not been a thoroughly ARA success, such as it could have been made."

Whatever the colonel's abilities as an inspector of kitchens and a manager of men, the overall plan he had settled on for Russian operations—relatively centralized, with no real authority granted to committees of local citizens—though it departed from ARA tradition, was probably the only feasible one given the un-usual circumstances of the Russian and Soviet environment: nowhere in Europe had the ARA operated under a Bolshevik government; nowhere had starvation and disease been so rife; nowhere had the relief effort been so vast.

Over time the general method of Haskell's administration of the Russian unit came to be accepted by the ARA veterans, even if grudgingly. Holden wrote to a former colleague of the Poland unit living in California, on November 3, 1922: "You have heard, of course, that the Russia show is not the same as the Old A.R.A. That is quite true; and probably it could not be." Still the nostalgia for the old-time efficiency was strong. He goes on to say that Burland with his three or four "old ARA" assistants in the food remittance division was able to do an im-mense amount of work per man in comparison with the army-run child-feeding side of the operation. "I will say that I like to think of the way we used to work; and the stimulation of being on our toes all the time."[4]

THE RUSSIANS, of course, had no "old ARA" point of reference. The lavish praise they heaped upon the organization as an example of American energy and organizing ability served to validate for the American relievers the superiority of their nation. Burland offered a typically self-satisfied assessment of the Russian perspective:

Put together, as it was, by men who were experienced in the business of relief, and be-ing thus, in large part, a duplication of similar organizations created in other parts of Europe, the organization of the ARA in Russia was considered a model of efficiency by the multitude of Russians with whom it came in contact. Whatever may have been its shortcomings the Russian people were glad to overlook faults and to accept it as a symbol of American energy and capacity.

The numerous essays they solicited from Russians on the famine and Ameri-can relief confirmed the ARA men's view of themselves as much more than kind-hearted brothers of mercy: they were masters of efficiency.

The Petrograd artist Aleksandr Benoit remarked, "I know of other people from whom nothing but the delicate way your service was organized brought forth tears of emotion." The historian Yakovlev of the Simbirsk staff wrote, "One could not help wondering at the technical skill and excellent working of all that complicated machinery."

Russians had long heard and read about America's ingenuity, about discover-ies like electricity and inventions like the steam engine. The Russian Imperial Academy of Sciences elected Benjamin Franklin to membership in 1789. But Russians had always been at least equally fascinated by stories of American style and method, and it was this part of their American dream, the trademark of Hoover relief, that the ARA made a reality across European Russia.

Once they recovered from the initial shock at the ARA's scale and effective-ness, not a few Russians wished to imitate its ways. In the words of Dr. Babayeff of the Odessa staff, "The work of the American Relief Administration in Russia shows a striking example of how strong and manifold the influence of a great, ra-tionally planned and cleverly organized institution can be on the mind and life of a nation." Babayeff's testimony was undoubtedly influenced by his contact with his American chiefs, for he expresses the Russian-American contrast in terms that could have been theirs, though the English is his own:

What a bright and lasting impression has this efficient, quick and energetic work made upon people tired of idleness and of useless bustle! There were two diametrically opposed systems confronted for the first time, expressing the ideology of two nations! The Russians with their traditional "The slower the better" and the Americans advocating productive utilization of time. The contrast was strikingly eloquent and it has proved the advantage of the American system, guaranteeing productiveness of work and concrete results. It is not astonishing therefore that large circles felt induced to copy the American method. This has become a fashion among young people and it is to be hoped that it will be adopted permanently and give satisfactory results.

The Russian perception of *Amerika* as the land of great size, speed, and efficiency long preceded the ARA's arrival in Russia. Among literate Russians it reached well back into the nineteenth century. In the popular press, in travelers' accounts, and in high- to low-brow fiction Russians viewed America with a simultaneous mixture of awe and revulsion. They were thrilled by tales of America's vastness, technological prowess, economic success, equality, and freedom yet repulsed by depictions of poverty, racism, inequality, and excessive freedom.[5] Forceful evocations of the magical hold on Russians of the idea of *Amerika* can be found in the pseudonymously signed essays submitted by the local Kiev personnel, one of them attributed to "Across the Ocean":

We do not know America, but we love her. We have read much about her, but we fear her. We are indignant about the horrible exploitation in America, but we respect her.
Already as children we "ran away to America." We stored up the essential products for the road and . . . ran away. "Just get to America—there you'll find plenty of everything."
And in these childhood thoughts is our entire opinion about America.
There you'll find abundance. There you'll find America, and with this word everything is said.

With such visions of America setting the standard, American-Russian comparisons were bound to be unflattering to the Russians, some devastatingly so, as in this passage from the translated essay by "Libbis":

Russia as well as America is a country of wide spaces, and these immense spaces—by way of a certain psychological process—have influence over the people inhabiting them. At the first glance it appears that this psychological influence of vast, fertile fields, of richest forests and the priceless depths of Russia and America should bring up nations spiritually analogical; but in reality it is otherwise: the vast and rich America calls forth the boiling activity of her sons—descendants of the energetic Anglo-Saxon, their energetic permanent labour; but Russia—as vast and rich—has created a careless in his nature Slavonian—half-lazy, half-phylosopher. This is the reason of their mutual misunderstanding: in America, the colossal towns are growing like mushrooms after a rain; in Russia scores of years are needed for building a barrack for a garrizon detachment.

ARA operations in Ukraine began only in December 1921, so that whereas Russians on and beyond the Volga might have believed that their American saviors had come out of the sky so sudden was their arrival, by the time the relief workers were on the job in Kiev, anticipation of their coming among the city's residents had been building for a few months. Expectations were great, according to "Friend of America": "The fact that the relief would be organized by Americans guaranteed, especially in the opinion of the intelligencia, its efficiency and scope. In this circle there was since ever a definite opinion of the practical sense of the 'yankees' on one side, and the grandiosity of all their undertakings on the other." Certainly the Americans would bring to Russia one quality in severely short supply: "practical common sense."

Another recalled that in their youth Russians had always associated America with something "extraordinary, omnipotent, and distinctive" and that upon hearing that aid would come from America, "everyone expects a miracle, convinced of the omnipotence of an American institution."

How far down the social ladder such thinking extended is hard to say. Clapp reported in autumn 1921 that when he asked the mostly peasant refugees fleeing the German Commune near Saratov where they were going, they responded, "To America": "I was continually asked whether it was possible to go to America." Goodrich encountered the same phenomenon while assessing the famine in this region: "Here we met the question that always comes everywhere in Russia— 'How can I get to America?'" But what did this *Amerika* mean to such people? Ruhl answered that to the peasants "America is scarcely more than a name—a mythical place, as far away as Mars, filled with sky-scrapers, whirring machinery and millionaires." The fact is that not all peasants had even heard of Mars or skyscrapers. That America was at least to some peasants indeed "scarcely more than a name" is best illustrated by an exchange overheard between two villagers in Ukraine anticipating the ARA's arrival:

"'Everything American has to be the best.'

'Why? How do you know that?'

'Because it's American it's the best, and it's the best because it's American.'"

The Kiev essays, along with many other Russian statements from the period, make it clear that in important ways these tremendous expectations were fulfilled. The ARA lived up to the American reputation for energy and efficiency. Already in prerevolutionary times Russians had used the expression *"po-amerikanski"*—"in an American fashion"—to express the idea that something was accomplished with speed and precision. Now in January 1922 the newspaper *Poor Peasants* (*Bednota*) could declare of the relief workers, "The Americans are acting quickly, really *po-amerikanski."*

Some Russian employees were ready to bear witness that yet another, unanticipated miracle had taken place before their eyes: the Americans had somehow been able to Americanize their indigenous personnel. "Across the Ocean" takes this notion further than even Ellingston might have dared. It would have warmed his heart to read, but it was not translated into English so he probably never saw it. The author claimed that soon after the Americans had established themselves in Kiev, "They began to inculcate the tempo of American life. To give RHYTHM, which up to now had not been characteristic of us, but that rhythm toward which we constantly strove.

"The Americans trained us in the rhythm of work." More valuable than their gifts of food and clothing they instilled in their local staffs a "trace of their en-

ergy, enterprise, perseverance, and all that which characterizes an American."
The thought of it launches him into his furthest inspirational orbit:

"We are trying to perfect our life, give it mechanicalness, we are establishing a
rhythm of steel, electricity and airplanes. We are setting production records. We
are strengthening and increasing them.

"WE ARE AMERICANIZING."

So extraordinary was this American influence that it extended to the machine
world. ARA automobiles and trucks operated with characteristic American push
and impatience, moving along city streets with speeds beyond the power of the
ordinary Russian vehicle. ARA trucks exerted a direct influence over the local
economy: when they drove past the bazaar from the train station on their way to
the warehouse, buyers and sellers realized that American products had arrived,
and prices immediately began to fall. When it happened that American machines were in short supply, the ARA hired Russian motors, "And these automobiles adopt the tempo of ARA work. They become infected with it. And on those
days when the rented automobile works for the ARA—especially if it is made to
work several days in a row—the rented auto is imbued with the mechanicalness
of ARA work and other than in its exterior appearance is no different from the
other ARA autos. Such is the strength of American influence."

As for the human specimens behind the wheel, they all had to be of a superior
stamp: "Ara does not take on the weak for such work—at the head of Ara are
Americans, and in America there is not and should not be compassion and pity.
The weak—step side, the strong—step forward."

Some Russians actually had "run away" to America, though not as children.
Some of these eventually returned home and became known as "our Americans,"
as opposed to "genuine Americans." Naturally they brought back a mixed bag of
stories about that distant land. One returned émigré told the author of "Across
the Ocean" that he would never go back:

"'I was afraid and am afraid of that tempo. It's not for me. It is very difficult to
become an American; you have to be born one.'

"This is true. There are among us businessmen who have had a headspinning
career in the shortest period of time, but all the same they are not Americans.
They are surrogates."

There usually being one in every crowd, the Kiev observers had among their
number a skeptic, who was not willing to grant all of the Americans the status of
supermen:

I was impressed by their extreme punctuality, amused by their efforts to awake the
initiative of the employees and their impatience when they failed. . . . I saw in the office the living illustration of the equality of the classes in America, when the chief being abused by the worker ran after him with the words "come and fight" and many
other examples illustrating the lack of reflection and readiness of action. Here I met
also the tendency to the "efficiency" in business and the morbid fright of an American to be suspected of its lack. Though to tell the truth only two Americans of all I
met could claim to be near the standart.

THE KIEV AMERICANS must have been aware that since a prize of three food
packages awaited the winner of the best essay, some of the praise directed at

them was inspired as much by the stomach as by the heart and mind. Yet, as it happened, the writers did express criticism of the relief workers, though not for failing to meet American standards of efficiency. Several of the very essayists who flatter the Americans for their efficient ways rebuke them for taking a good thing too far: the Americans tended to be unfeeling and thoughtless, even at times rude and crude, and could be merciless toward those who could not keep pace with them. This too was perceived as *po-amerikanski*: the relief workers were merely living up to other, negative images of *Amerika* lodged in the popular Russian mind.

Among the Kiev writers those with the highest praise for the ARA were the most reproachful of the Americans for their coldness, remoteness, and arrogance in their relations both with their beneficiaries and their own employees. Some were diplomatic, like the unidentified author who quoted a line of Russian poetry to make the point:

So far away, across the Pacific Ocean, in the country of speed and justice, several people, Titans who vigilantly followed our distresses, took close to heart our sufferings and hurried to us, as hurry true brothers of mercy to a wounded person, in order the sooner to ease his suffering.

The name of these brothers of mercy is the "American people," in the form of the "American Relief Administration."

... [T]he Russian people will not forget those who "under a mask of outward coldness hid an endless love," will not forget its transatlantic brothers, who greatly assisted them in slaying the dragon of terrible trials.

The mask analogy was employed by Russians in all the districts with striking consistency, though few thought of poetry when the subject was American insensibility to the human dimension of famine relief. "How did the Americans understand the psychology of the masses they met in their relief work?" asked the author of "What I Saw and What I Know." "From the start it was a tragedy and a comedy at the same time. I am sorry to state that the ARA representatives did not pay enough attention to a question of such a cardinal importance.... For a philanthropical organization the psychological understanding of the unfortunate, but not hopeless, a delicate study of his feelings, is itself a valuable part of noble work."

To illustrate his point he described the scene in Kiev's food package receiving room. All reports agree that it was usually a "madhouse," where every variety of emotion was on display. This was the case at all the food remittance stations, but Kiev seems to have specialized in extremes of agony and ecstasy.

Most of those receiving packages in Kiev were Jews, which added another dimension to the problem of the psychology of the beneficiary. The writer of "What I Saw" lamented that the Americans "did not study the specific circumstances of that extraordinary after revolution pogrom periods and bitter experiences of those masses." In this vein he criticizes the ARA for not giving enough care to how it selected its employees: the staff in the receiving room was made up primarily of Russian-speaking, ex-bourgeois Gentiles from Kiev, while most of the recipients were poor and illiterate Jews from remote areas of the district who spoke only Yiddish. So even setting aside the poisonous effects of anti-Semitism, the language barrier and other cultural and social differences would anyway have complicated relations between giver and receiver. The result: "very often we had to witness such scenes as wild laughing on one side of the counter, and on the other helpless and crying consignees."[6]

The writer did not directly implicate the Americans in such vulgar behavior, but he meant to say that their general insensitivity was behind it. The relief workers are absent as well from the "indescribable scenes of happiness" in the receiving room when the disbelieving beneficiaries, overcome with emotion, embrace their lifesaving food packages. This is not at all surprising given the Americans' acute sensitivity to time. This point is made reflexively by the district historian in Gomel, White Russia, where the main activity was also the delivery of food packages: "The first work was also hampered greatly by people kneeling in the entrance of the warehouse to give thanks . . . clutching wildly at the hands and clothing of the men working on delivery and showering them with kisses."

Even absent the danger of the typhus-bearing louse, one can think of several good reasons that most relief workers would not have cared to place themselves in this line of fire. But the men of the ARA liked to think of themselves as a hardened bunch, and whatever were their actual reactions and feelings when confronted with demonstrative gratitude *à la Russe*, as storytellers they preferred to uphold their reputation as cold-blooded administrators. So receiving thanks was best portrayed as a potential hindrance to their beloved efficiency.

On entering a children's home in the Nikolaevsk region of Tsaritsyn, Joe Driscoll nearly stumbled over the corpse of a child. The young woman in charge explained that the home had been opened about five days earlier with twenty children and that six had since died, the sixth being the obstacle in the doorway awaiting the wagon to come and take it away. She had appealed to the ARA for help, and Driscoll had come to make an inspection, issuing her supplies at once.

It was useless to try to describe the gratitude of this poor woman. Appreciation is a fine thing, but by this time it was getting on my nerves a bit. I felt rather that I should try and express to her just what I thought of the wonderfully fine work she had done—scrubbing the whole place—taking care of her charges—with at least one death each day—and all by herself.

Later he supplied four country doctors with blankets, linens, and other supplies for hospitals and homes. "Was it appreciated? I'll say it was—so much so in fact that I wish some thousands of other Americans could have been there to help me bear the brunt of it."

This may have been only feigned impatience in the best-approved ARA style. Or it may have been a less conscious form of self-defense, part of the internal hardening necessary to protect one's nerves in the presence of so much suffering —and in order to achieve maximum efficiency. Whatever it was, it made an impression, because this reputation for callous efficiency stuck to the ARA men. It occasionally made it easier for the Soviet press to depict Bolshevik officials as defenders of the hungry Russians against the imperious Americans, those monsters of efficiency.

On September 2, 1922, *Izvestiia* printed an article signed by K. Richter about an alleged incident in Dergatchi in the Saratov district, involving Paul Clapp. It provides a generous description of the beneficence of ARA kitchens only to stand it in contrast to the unbenevolent relief workers, who "don't always measure up to their job; many of them are too power-hungry, vain and cruel toward the hungry."

In Dergatchi, for example, there was Clapp, whom the writer calls Colonel Clapp, perhaps to make him appear more despotic. In fact Clapp, from Perry, Iowa, and a graduate of Iowa State College, Class of 1913, had been commissioned a first lieutenant in 1917 and was later a captain in the Signal Corps, but that's as high in rank as he rose. He went on to work for the ARA in Paris, Trieste, Belgrade, Bucharest, Prague, and Vienna before taking up his post in the wilds of Saratov province. He had a stellar record as a reliever, and after the Russian mission he went to Washington to serve as Hoover's personal assistant.

As K. Richter told the story, one day, over some trifle, Clapp closed down an ARA kitchen, shutting out a crowd of tearful mothers and hungry children. To their assistance came Comrade Rumiantsev to upbraid the heartless colonel, who brushed him off as a "Russian rascal." This exchange was witnessed by a hungry crowd waiting outside the kitchen, provoking one of them to toss her ration card at Clapp, declaring that she did not need American food. Others followed her example until the gathering had dispersed.

Like a caricature villain, Clapp is supposed to have panicked and reopened the kitchen and when no one would come, gone door-to-door begging parents to bring their children. But of course, better to go hungry than to subject oneself to the exploitation of an arrogant American. Normally Moscow headquarters would have paid attention to such prominently placed criticism of an American reliever. But this was, after all, Paul Clapp, and after perfunctory inquiries the chiefs dismissed the story as an instance of bad casting.

For *Izvestiia*, however, it was but the tip of the iceberg: "Many such examples from the ARA could be cited." Perhaps there were many, but only a few made it into print. The editors of the Minsk newspaper *Zvezda* on April 10, 1923, objected when the ARA chauffeur was fired because he used an American automobile to transport wood to his wife at home: "The ARA is run on business ways according to American standards. And it is doing great work in White Russia. But the young grey-haired American should know by this time that this is a workers' government, and that wives of workers will not be allowed to freeze because formalities as in America are necessary. Russia is not America."

The image of the overbearing American relief worker was reinforced by all his boozing and reckless driving as well as by his occasional employment of pugilistic solutions to red tape and other obstructions. Murphy's rough handling of Comrade Skvortsov in Ekaterinoslav was only the most famous case. Willoughby and Macpherson seem to have used their fists to settle affairs with their own employees. And there must have been others. In Simbirsk Yakovlev quoted one Russian saying to another: "Be careful with the big American. I saw him boxing the other day." Cobb of Saratov was the former heavyweight boxing champion at Harvard, and he may well have let fly in the famine zone.

When John Aicher roughed up Eiduk's agent in Vitebsk, a local paper ran a story on the American art of boxing. The altercation took place in January 1922, and the Bolshevik in question was one Sergei Trevas—a Latvian and, perhaps not incidentally, a Jew. The paper stated that Aicher had pushed Trevas out of the ARA office—a feat which in those days did not qualify as boxing—although the

Vitebsk history uses the words "fist fight." This was not Aicher's only bout. Two days later the local *Izvestiia* reported another incident, which was apparently sparked by a frenzied crowd trying to enter the receiving room to claim food packages. For reasons not made clear, Aicher is alleged to have gotten into another fistfight and to have shouted "Bloody Jews." Vitebsk city at the time was said to be as much as 90 percent Jewish, so this was the sort of utterance that would have supplied him no end of potential challengers. The Vitebsk *Izvestiia*, perhaps sensing the tide, called for Aicher's head.

The controversy floated along for a while. In May Eiduk wrote to Haskell, reminding him of the matter and calling Aicher an anti-Semite. In June the presidium of the Vitebsk *gubispolkom* telegraphed Eiduk requesting the American's removal. In the same month the Vitebsk Department of Justice had a hearing on the affair, at which the evidence included a letter of support for the accused signed by his employees, though how many it is not known. Whatever was the effect of this petition at the hearing, it was not enough for Haskell, who in mid-July withdrew Aicher from Vitebsk, but not from the mission.

Apparently Moscow headquarters thought that the great fuss surrounding Aicher, whatever his actual wrongdoing, had made it impossible for him to remain in Vitebsk. But the chiefs evidently were not persuaded that he was an anti-Semite, otherwise it would not have made good sense to reassign him to Ukraine. Whatever Aicher was, he sounds like an unsteady character. In May 1923 when he was supposed to be in the Ukrainian capital, Kharkov, one of the chiefs paid a call to the city and discovered that he was AWOL in the Crimea. He was booted from the mission.[7] In all these ways, too, the men of the ARA distinguished themselves from Settlement House Workers.

As for the bloodhounds of the Soviet press, it took much less than the scent of an Aicher to set them howling. Besides, they had pegged Hoover's men as an arrogant lot even as they arrived in Russia. In the September 21, 1921, issue of *Pravda*, Mikhail Kol'tsov described the activity at the docks as the U.S. cargo ship *Phoenix*, arriving in Petrograd from Hamburg, began to discharge its life-giving cargo under the direction of Bowden and Noyes: "Shaven gentlemen with badges of the 'American Relief Administration' are supervising the work.

"America is acting quickly." He reports accurately that "Mister Bowden" was supervising the feeding of fifty thousand children, that in a very brief time the Americans had surveyed the entire city, hustling about in their automobiles, and had managed to set up fifty kitchens. There was no doubt that these were already great accomplishments. "True, Hoover's envoys behave with a splendid arrogance, in the style of a duke visiting the hut of a coal burner, plus the manners of a merchant educated in the Sundays schools of the 'Young Men's Christian Association.'"

Bowden, in passing this item along to London, took issue with the charge of "splendid arrogance," "especially in view of the fact that we very often found it necessary to lend a hand with the unloading. I can hardly imagine a duke, even a present-day duke, staggering down the gangplank embracing a sack of flour."

But Kol'tsov must have spotted something that Bowden could not see, because during the subsequent two years the ARA men could not shake their reputation for haughtiness, not only in the Soviet press but even among some of their best Russian friends. The Petrograd writer Chukovskii, a beneficiary of

ARA food packages and an ardent Americanophile, saw the problem. Many Russians thought of the relief workers as "proud, hurrying Americans flying about in auto cars."

Foremost in Russian eyes is that these people do not appear kind. They are ever preoccupied, even in a hurry. They are always official and seem to look down from a self-created superior position. . . .
    I have frequently noted that after personal contact with Americans, the Russians seem offended. They would like to have the Americans not only feed them but show sympathetic interest in their personal life. The Americans are reserved to a fault. As a consequence, it is said the Americans are insensitive and stiffly formal.

Chukovskii knew better but only because he spent time with the Americans and was able to see beneath their cool exterior. The ARA's employees had the same opportunity, but not its beneficiaries. Of course, a people so obsessed with its own suffering as the Russians were in 1921 would have been especially sensitive to another's undemonstrativeness. Yet these were Americans of the ARA, for whom emotion and sympathy were not, to use a later-day term, standard operating procedure in the business of relief.
    It may not have been coincidental that their Chief, while celebrated as the greatest humanitarian of the age, was also regarded in certain quarters as detached and *too* business minded. Among his biggest critics were the Quakers of the American Friends Service Committee. The Friends viewed Hoover as much too concerned with having the ARA dominate Russian relief and with putting American economic interests ahead of philanthropy, notably by opting to send corn and not wheat to Russia.
    These were among the charges of a nasty letter Anna Haines of the Friends wrote to Hoover on January 19, 1922, in which she criticized him as well for requiring the Soviet government to put up $10 million in gold rubles against the appropriation of $20 million from the American Congress. In a sharp reply Hoover came to the heart of their differences: "If I were to make a summary as to my judgement of your state of mind, I should say it is due to a visualization of relief problems in the terms of individual givers and of individual sufferers instead of in terms of our political institutions, our public sentiment, and the needs and means of saving the lives of millions."
    It was such considerations that Walter Lippmann took into account when he wrote of Hoover in May 1922 in the New York *World*: "probably no other living man could have done nearly so much."[8]
    As for the American relief workers their dichotomous image as insensitive humanitarians was not a product of some subsequent rewriting of history. It was puzzled over at the time by their most intimate Russian associates, among them Ellingston's secretary in a report written in her own English called "Americans As I See (or Understand) Them." She did not stint on praise for the extraordinary native talents of the relief workers: "A trait which all the Russians greatly admire in the Americans, is their business mind, the efficiency of their work and the ability to arrange everything in the most perfect way." But she proceeded to undermine the point by reducing her Americans to so many young men in a hurry:

Mostly rushing in, stating facts, joking on something (the American sense of humor a Russian can seldom understand) and rushing out after getting all information they can from the chief. They always seem to understand from half-words and sentences, all their mind is concentrated on business and it is difficult to see the "person" in these machines. Even joking they don't loose the thread of their business talk and after peals of rather wild and loud laughter they continue in the same "rushing" way to pile figures, facts, etc till both (the chief and the guest) understand or make believe that they understand each other perfectly well. Then the guest departs greatly delighted with himself and his listner, with a parting joke which nobody hears, or understands, but everybody answers with another uproar of laughter.

It is true, she wrote, that for the intelligent classes of Russia after years of isolation it is a breath of fresh air to come into contact with these Americans, informed as they are about events and cultures around the world.

But later on, getting better acquainted with them one begins to realize that most of them have only a very brief and superficial knowledge of things but which they have the ability of always remembering. I should call it a "universal mind" and couldn't say that it lacks a certain interest, but a superficial mind can't be appreciated by Russians which are mostly slow-thinking but very deep. The general impression is that the Russians always walk deeply in the soil and the Americans are floating several yards above the ground.

Americans are "very matter of fact, terre-à-terre people, with utter lack of imagination all their minds deep in business. This type is very narrow-minded, from my point of view, and very uninteresting and shallow. Such a man one can know in length and breadth after an hour's talk with him.

"Of course, this is an opinion of one who sees business men of A.R.A. in office hours."

At this point, as if suddenly aware of the negative portrait she had created— or perhaps by design—she reverses direction and begins to soften the image, remarking that "some Americans have a very poetical and even sentimental frame of mind, and are endowed with very human characters. They are 'real men' (in the Russian sense of word, which means that they are really human, open for the most unpracticable movements of kindness, generosity, etc.)." But they perform their good deeds in secret, "As if they are ashamed before their fellow-men to show that they are human. . . . Such a combination of business-mind and great soul is very remarkable and beautiful."

She had seen behind the mask. An ARA housekeeper in Moscow was more succinct: "Americans have a misleading manner, also a misleading reputation. They are abrupt, efficient. They say, Yes and No, like drill sergeants. But underneath they are more idealistic than any other people." "My boys," she called them.[9]

The drill sergeant tag was better suited to some Americans than to others. Macpherson wore it like a badge, according to the Kiev personnel. One accused him of running the office like a "well organized business establishment." Another wrote of the "iron discipline" at headquarters, of the "almost mysterious fear of the Supervisor. No negligence or neglect in regard to one's duties, so common even in old times in Russia, were to be noted in A.R.A. The smallest breach of duty could result in being dismissed."

There were many complaints at the way Macpherson and the other Kiev Americans placed themselves above their employees, creating, as one phrased it, "a kind of caste distinction between 'us' and 'them.' 'We are white negroes for them,' many used to say." The general public remarked upon the American chief's inaccessibility. "To receive an audience from the Supervisor," people would say, "is as difficult as to get an audience from the Tsar." His way of dealing with applicants called to mind the attitude of a "crowned conqueror to a vanquished or inferior race." Macpherson's well-known temper rounded out the picture of American arbitrariness:

A certain exterritoriality which the A.R.A. enjoyed in Soviet Russia, contributed to maintain this halo of other world grandeur which in the eyes of public surrounded the Supervisor, as well as his orders. . . . It is true that the character of the public itself, the absence of discipline, stupidity, rudeness and insolence, made it necessary to recur sometimes to measures which at first sight seemed not quite suitable, such as kicking out of the doors, etc.

Yet come to think of it, Macpherson's authoritarian way was after all only "a method of maintaining business discipline and necessary submission." By now the pattern is familiar as the reader is allowed a glimpse behind the mask of coldness: "Not once together with inaccessible haughtyness the employees saw thoughtfulness and sympathy to their needs on the part of the Supervisor, and support when in critical circumstances."[10]

Being made to feel inferior to the American chiefs, like "white negroes," made the Russian personnel touchy, according to Farmer Murphy. "Americans are probably the worst offenders. Crude or merely thoughtless they often distinguish Russians from Americans by calling the former 'native'. It makes the sensitive, delicately reared Russian wince for no matter how kindly it may be said it smacks of condescension or contempt." This word "native" clearly rubbed Russians the wrong way, not exclusively the employees. In Petrograd Chukovskii wrote in his diary for March 22, 1922: "I was at Eikhval'd's. She works for the Americans. She relates that they call us, Russians: 'Natives.'" From the lack of further comment we can presume his disapproval.

There was also an informal style about these Americans, which some considered a lack of manners. Ellingston's secretary wrote that one of the things that "shocks the Russian women" was the way the Americans addressed them: "Hello girls," or "Hey, you people." She professed to be "astonished at the lack of courtesy." Murphy, who worked with her in the same office, extended the catalog of American habits that mystified the Russians:

They don't understand the manly habit of putting the feet on top of a table or desk in the office. And they don't understand why all (as they say) Americans say "Yeh", or "Yuh", or "Yah" instead of yes, which they have been taught is the correct word for affirmation or assent. They are astonished too by the American habit at the telephone, when a proper name is mentioned of always asking how it is spelled. To them this seems strange for they say the Russian language is so perfectly phonetic that to pronounce a name is to know how to spell it.

There is contrary testimony on this point out of Kiev, where an employee recalled that the personnel "fell under the influence of the Americans at once. We all wished to imitate them. We began to show more dignity in our relations to other persons, and became more polite and cordial. It may be said that the A.R.A. was a school of good manners." This did not escape the attention of Macpherson, who found it amusing that "everyone began addressing their co-workers as 'Mr.' or 'Miss,' even though they spoke in Russian. The manager of the warehouse would politely say: 'Mr. Dubrovsky,' then in Russian, 'put that sack in the corner.'"

Even some of the Americans recognized that their struggle for efficiency was sometimes taken to absurd lengths, as Haskell admitted afterward:

The Americans took with them into the districts their own ideas of efficiency and management. Occasionally the American idea of efficiency went to extremes, as was instanced when the supervisor of one district forbade the kissing of the hands of the women among the Russian employees in his office. This touching of the lips to the hand of a woman has been a graceful custom among Europeans for generations past, and it was observed by the cultured but impoverished male employees of the district office I have in mind. The American supervisor's interdict against this custom was pronounced not because he was hostile to the ex-bourgeoisie, or because he was pro-Soviet, but because he considered that time was wasted in the observance of what seemed to him an unnecessary gesture.

This may have been in the proper Taylorist spirit, but Ben Franklin would certainly not have approved. Nor did Archibald Cary Coolidge, the closest thing to an old-European bourgeois among the ARA men. Coolidge felt that a big reason for the ARA's government relations problems was that the Americans were too full of themselves. He wrote to Secretary of State Hughes on December 30, 1921, "as you will have surmised our men are not all distinguished for tact in their dealings with officials whom they suspect of interference or obstruction." Yes, Soviet officials could be high-handed and meddlesome, he informed his father, but the young Americans on the scene in Moscow were not without blame. "Our people belong to the efficiency type whose main idea is to get things done and done at once, regardless of the habits and susceptibilities of others."[11]

TOM BARRINGER MAY NOT have been a typical ARA man, but he is proof that it was possible for an American master of efficiency to be a man of open compassion as well, without the need to conceal it behind a mask.

Barringer enjoyed the devotion and respect of his staff in Ekaterinoslav where he served as district supervisor. Most would have said that they worshipped him, though he did not cut the benevolent tsar figure of Bell in Ufa; rather he earned the affection of his staff on an individual basis through close personal relationships. Or perhaps it only seems that way from this distance because of an unusual kind of evidence left behind in the form of a couple of dozen letters to Barringer from his Ekaterinoslav employees. It has been reduced to a one-way correspondence, as Barringer evidently did not make duplicates of his own letters.

The existence of this unusual documentation is partly due to the fact of Barringer's unexpected transfer to the Simbirsk district after the disappearance of his friend Phil Sheild. He was supposed to be away from Ekaterinoslav for only as long as it took to complete the investigation, but he ended up staying on in Simbirsk, never having said proper goodbyes. So farewell and follow-up letters were sent interdistrict. Usually when a district supervisor left his post, he retired from the mission, so personal appreciations were final and mostly spoken in person. Barringer's devotees expressed their thanks, and much more, in writing.

Of his staff he wrote shortly after departing Russia: "That this collection of former nobles, princesses, generals, professors, bookkeepers, teachers, and a fair share of intelligent people of more humble origin, was most interesting would be putting it mildly. It was our privilege to have around us a few men of outstanding character, men who for intellect and integrity could qualify as citizens anywhere in the world except Russia."

At the peak of operations the number of local personnel at headquarters might run to as high as two hundred, depending on the size of the district. Then came the scaling down of the program in the second year, and the local staffs were reduced accordingly, with a steep drop in autumn 1922. Letting go of employees was an unpleasant duty for the district supervisor, who knew that for such people ARA employment meant the difference between hope and despair, in some cases between life and death.

Barringer was spared much of the agony by his transfer out of his district at the critical moment. This meant that the Ekaterinoslav staff associated his replacement with the coming of hard times, which made them see their former chief in an even rosier light. One could deduce this, but it is also explicitly stated in their correspondence.

After word came through to Ekaterinoslav that he would in fact not be returning, Mrs. C. Krantz, known as the "town mother," wrote to "Dear, dear Mr Barringer" on November 16, 1922, telling him in her animated English what a "blow" it was to find out he would be staying on in Simbirsk: "When the news of your appointment reached us, it raised a terrible clamour, everybody was dumbfounded and you cannot imagine how sorry, how awfully sorry everybody was! Do you know hard woman as I am even I thought it is worth while to be so loved as you are. Nina Yerlitzina she simply hurt and crying and I could not console her with anything."

Two day earlier, she writes, Nina had been "reduced," but the new district supervisor, Lester Prager, promised to continue providing her with a monthly food package. Despite the gesture, Mrs. Krantz was bitter about the new atmosphere at headquarters: "After you have left I was very miserable at ARA, you have spoiled me so much and I could not adapt myself to the new regime, which is a hard one I can tell you; I have asked Mr Prager once to release me." She says she was talked out of it but insisted to Prager that she would resign by December.

P. Riabchenko described for Barringer some of Mrs. Krantz's problems. Mr. Howard had asked her to get him a cup of coffee downstairs, giving her two minutes to complete the task. Downstairs meant two floors down, and just the thought of having to make the round trip in two minutes reduced her to tears. According to Riabchenko, when Howard asked what was the matter, Mrs. Krantz replied that she was too big to move so quickly. Howard is said to have barked, "Time worth money!" Riabchenko was not surprised by this response—"That is the American way!"—and yet he knew that Barringer would have gotten his coffee himself rather than put her to the test.

Mrs. Krantz wrote several letters, each filled with local news—Princess Yusupov did not go to Italy after all, because her mother fell ill; she is eager to return you the money you lent her, and so on—which must have held some interest for Barringer although one imagines that he was able to enjoy it more from his safe distance. There are details regarding local petty squabbles among the former and current employees, and the implication is that Barringer used to mediate some of them. Several writers request his photograph.

Barringer apparently indicated in a letter to Mrs. Krantz that she would be welcome in Simbirsk; she writes that she is "threatening" to take him up on his offer and is assuming that Barringer would be willing to advance her traveling expenses. Perhaps the prospect of the town mother actually moving to Simbirsk struck terror in him, but there is no way of knowing.

Olga Karetsky, who addressed him as "Thomas Pavlovich," declared: "Mr. Barringer you are a stranger but you have a Russian soul, I like you as my brother, and always I wish you only good."

Mr. Umansky of the food remittance station in Aleksandrovsk thanked Barringer for saving his life: "You were like a father to me."

Nicholas Podassinnikov wrote on December 14, 1922, that the ARA was firing people on the 1st and 15th of every month. "The work there is very little; daily delivery is no more, than 100 packages. Yes! your absence Mr Barringer, sensates very much. When you were here amongst us, the work boiled; but now it is a little, little warm; it was so pleasant to work with you."

Olga Frangzilova spoke for the entire staff: "Since you have left us the soul of the office has much changed. We have lost in you not only a good chief, but a real man and a kind friend."

V. Galkova, now a former ARA employee, decided to make a fight of it, blasting Prager for his treatment of employees. Her husband had been a man of considerable reputation before the Revolution, yet Prager made her beg for a food package.

I am sending one copy of this letter to the Moscow Headquarters for circulation among the American personnel and another to Colonel Haskell in order that he be aware of the situation. If he is an American proud of his nation, of Herbert Hoover, his chief, and of the name of the American Relief Administration he will surely see that more attention is paid to the psychology of the White Negroes and that people who know a little more about social work are placed at the head of district Headquarters.

Not only Prager suffered by comparison. One of Barringer's Simbirsk employees, Nicholas Davidoff, after returning to his home in Petrograd, where he then went to work in the ARA medical department, wrote to his former chief on April 28, 1923, that Renshaw and Gantt were not very personable. They interacted with their employees only on business matters, "and I even wonder if they know them by their names or even by faces. I did not hear them go to anybody of the employees or call anybody of them to their house. Mr. Renshaw himself holds an attitude of a little king. . . . The doctor, who is my immediate chief pays very few attention to the work."

Reading through this correspondence gives a sense of what a burden these people must have been for Barringer. They press him for his charity and his sympathy, clinging to him, and like most relievers he pitied them. But this was not a sound basis for friendship: they called him god, father, brother, chief, even friend, but probably few of them were his genuine friends. If he had grown tired of all the intrigues and the pettiness he had left behind in Ekaterinoslav, of the many demands on his attention and personal diplomatic skills, there is no indication of this anywhere in the written record, not a single note of cynicism. He dealt with all of it with great patience and, to judge by the words of his correspondents, a generous heart. Yet his chiefs never had cause to single him out for inefficiency.

Barringer's generous ways continued in Simbirsk. In spring 1923 he wrote to Richard Rein, president of the *gubispolkom*, on behalf of a Madame Orlova, protesting the confiscation of her property in the Revolution. In his reply Rein sounds incredulous, instructing the ingenuous American that, after all, expropriation was what the Revolution was all about: Mme. Orlova's property had been passed into the hands of the Russian people "according to the will of the workers and peasants."[12]

Next to actual employment the most important link between the district supervisor and the Russian employees was their food ration, or *paiok*, which often served as a partial wage. Originally the employees were not to be paid in food, but because the local governments were hard up for cash and the personnel were hungry and weak, the food package arrangement could be justified in the name of greater efficiency.

It is hard to overestimate the importance of food packages to their recipients, both those on and off the ARA staff, especially during the first year of relief. The moment of impact was captured in the diary of Moscow historian Got'e, who wrote on December 26, 1921: "A Christmas present from the Americans, Coolidge and Golder: a *food packet* with a very kind letter, which I append here. One [pood] of the finest wheat flour, twenty-five pounds of rice, fifteen pounds of sugar, three pounds of tea, a tub of lard, twenty jars of condensed milk. I admit I was touched, and contented, and a little upset."

Ecstatic was how Chukovskii felt:

Do you know what these three ARA packages meant to me, my dear Rockefeller? Do you realize how thankful I am to Columbus that he one day discovered America? Thank you old mariner. Thank you old vagabond. Those three packages meant more to me than simply a reprieve from death. They made possible a return to my literary work. I felt myself again a writer. . . . I doubt if any American will ever understand our poetical happiness on the great day when, dusted with flour, my whole family dragged home the cart with the long awaited ARA packages and carried them up to our lodgings on the third floor.

On their side, the Americans took great pleasure in succoring Soviet Russia's brain workers. After reviewing a report on the situation of the intelligentsia in the Tatar republic, Ellingston shot a note over to Burland: "Great Christ, Tommy, that cold list of Professors from Kazan is more bitter than the news of the death of a million peasants." Burland commented on this outburst: "I think it expresses in a very pat way, what we all feel, after thoughtful consideration of the plight of the thinkers and culture bearers of Russia. More successful than all its land and industrial programs has been the determined will of the Bolsheviks to exterminate courageous and honest Russian intelligence."

How hard it must have been for district supervisors to strike from their own food package lists the names of employees they had come to know so well at the office, but who were now being reduced. A measure of the difficulty was the apparently widespread practice of continuing to provide former employees with food packages—keeping them on the payroll, for all practical purposes.

Not all were so fortunate, and when Barringer's Ekaterinoslav correspondents complain about the loss of their privilege to receive food or clothing packages, they seem to hope that he will intercede for them. One of these, "S.B.," a sixty-six-year-old woman who had been let go by Barringer before he left for Simbirsk, wrote to him there in October before his transfer had been made permanent: "I hear that A.R.A.'s collaborators have all of them received *warm underwear* and *don't you consider me as one any longer*? Am I to be the *only one* to stay without it?"

Even after learning of Barringer's new status, "S.B." continued to petition him, as in a letter dated December 4, 1922. Her name had recently been struck from the food package list, and now for the first time she was without: "you not having signed an order for me as you did before." Prager had offered her employment with the Jewish Joint Distribution Committee, "But I really don't understand *why*, having worked for the *American* Relief Administration, I should be *remunerated* for my services by the *Jews*? Is it possible there are no Americans, no Christians left in America? Is America then the twin sister of Russia, the thrall of Judah?"

G. I. Issaak, of Nicopol, in the Ekaterinoslav district, wrote to his former chief, in Russian, just after his release from the ARA, after putting "all my heart" into the job: "Your philanthropy exceeds the philanthropy of your successor in our district." He appealed to Barringer for relief: "If only I would be authorized to receive monthly an ARA food ration." Although he has lost that privilege, Issaak could not have been in desperate straits since, as he told Barringer, he occupied the position of "responsible secretary" in the Nicopol ARA office. But it was not like the good old days. "Remembering our old friendship I press your bountiful hand."

Many district supervisors were quite susceptible to such appeals, and there were many bountiful hands among them—too many, according to Moscow headquarters, which kept warning the districts that they were cutting their staffs too slowly and their food package allowances more slowly still. Among Barringer's papers is a circular letter over Haskell's signature to all district supervisors, dated November 13, 1922, accusing them collectively of conducting "relief through employment." The idea behind the policy announced in September was "that the number of Russian employees would be reduced to common sense business heads," yet in several districts the number of local personnel was 100 percent greater than necessary.

Also unacceptable was the unauthorized distribution of food packages to employees—former employees go unmentioned. "The paiok, which was given as a bonus for high type and necessary employees, apparently has become a right which is demanded by every Tom, Dick and Harry connected with the American Relief Administration." Whether or not he actually authored the memo, its recipients would have recognized in this last remark the unmistakable voice of Haskell.

There was a third problem: waste. The district supervisors had to understand that it was "incumbent upon them as the business managers of a business operation to see to it that there is no waste anywhere within their jurisdiction."

It is not alone sufficient to distribute food, any irresponsible and unbusinesslike person could do that, but it is highly commendable when a man can distribute food stuffs properly and, at the same time, do it economically and give proof that he has done it by proper accounting. . . .

We will, of course, always keep in mind that our main object is to feed the starving and to provide medical relief, but in doing so let our charity be administered with some businesslike methods of economy and accounting.

This was the voice of efficiency speaking into one ear of the relief workers. In the other they heard voices of despair, like those in Barringer's letters. This was the voice that made it impossible for the district Americans to think about staff size as simply an accounting problem. They had before them individual tales of tragedy, not mere numbers on a sheet. A dramatic counterpoint to Haskell's memorandum is a letter to Barringer from Princess Meshcherskaia—before her marriage a Princess Golitsina—in Ekaterinoslav. Tellingly, she dated it in both old- and new-style calendars, December 6/19, 1922, closing with these words:

I shall never forget that you admitted me at once into your office when I applied to you for work and that, *thanks to your being Supervisor of the A.R.A. at the time I could dine every day,* and could make for myself a warm dress (out of the cloth we got then).

May Heaven shower all possible blessings on you and those dear to you at home, such is the sincere and heartiest wish of

Yours gratefully,

E. Meschersky

By the time Barringer received this she had taken her own life. He wrote a note beneath her signature: "When I saw her last I felt that she would not face another winter without employment and had a premonition she would kill herself. I sent some one to find her next day but it was too late."

Fisher wrote that the ARA had given such people, "the middle classes," who had been terrorized and oppressed and left without meaningful work, "an opportunity to do something of service to their country, as well as offering a decent kind of employment which assured stability and fairness of treatment. . . . People who had been discouraged and helpless and who felt that Russia had been forgotten by the world took a new interest in life and began to see that it was worth while to work for the regeneration of their country."

Ekaterinoslav's Riabchenko, who served as an ARA traffic agent, is a case in point. Before the Revolution he had emigrated to the United States, where he was employed for ten and a half years as an engineer, returning with this experience to Russia after 1917 to lend a hand in its revival—but "all I get is a commissar laughing at me." The ARA had given him the opportunity to feel useful again, though now he was waiting for word about an exit visa.

For some, their ARA connection allowed them to put to use one or more of the foreign languages they had long cherished. Professors with European names were able once again to feel connected to their society by working for the ARA. A Moscow *intelligent* remarked that merely "the appearance of Americans was often important simply as the live symbol of the existence of that great world from which Russians had been radically cut off." For the intelligentsia in particular, the sense of "moral isolation" since 1917 had been acute:

Russian intellectual classes had always been very cosmopolitan and lived a life connected in a much nearer way with the life of foreign nations, than can be imagined by Europeans or Americans who are much more shut up in their own interests and their own culture. This resulted from the fact that in order to be cultivated a Russian had to read foreign books, to follow foreign science, to study foreign conditions, and as a rule most educated Russians lived in very close touch with the general trend of foreign life. The war and the revolution dealt a great blow to this state of things and created the situation of isolation we have spoken of. Trampled and rejected at home, vowed to destruction as "parasitical elements" the intellectual classes of Russia thought they had been proclaimed pariahs also abroad and were left absolutely to their sad fate.

Olga Yakountchakov, one of the privileged of the old regime and now a housekeeper for the ARA, was more fatalistic: "We are like the pyramids of Egypt. Historically we are interesting but we have no vital significance. No one is to blame for this but ourselves. . . . We were educated as foreigners. So we grew like delicate, exotic plants in hot-houses, avoiding contact with the rough open soil, so Russia has rejected us and rightly."

Nonetheless, the sudden presence of a large contingent of Americans, more than giving her a job, must have sparked in her, as in so many others, hope for a new life. It did in Grigorii Sobolev, a former colonel in the Imperial Army who served with the ARA in Simbirsk: "At this nightmarish time destiny saw fit to send us a bright, warm sun in the person of you, unforgettable Mr. Barringer. You took a close interest in my sufferings and the sufferings of my unhappy wife, both moral and material."

The warm ARA sun had rejuvenated these delicate plants, but when Sobolev was writing, on May 27, 1923, the ARA mission was coming to a close. "And now our sun is sinking once more. You are going away to your dear America."[13]

CHAPTER 36

WE ARE ALL THIEVES

It was near midnight on Thursday, September 1, 1921, when the first American cargo ship, the S.S. *Phoenix*, docked in Petrograd carrying seven hundred tons of ARA rations. Early the next morning the first American relief workers—Noyes and Lowrie, soon followed by Bowden—started supervising the unloading of the ship. Noyes describes an unanticipated development:

The work proceeded smoothly until the men commenced the handling of sacks. They all had hooks and proceeded to use them on the sacks so that by the time the sack was in the warehouse it had from eight to ten holes, depending on the amount of handling it had to undergo. I took the hooks away from some of the men explaining to them that they could use them on the cases, but not on the sacks, and it was here that the fun commenced. The men from whom I had taken the hooks ran to the ship and told all the workmen in the hold what had happened and they all decided that unless they could use the hooks they would not work. I appealed to the man in charge of the men and soon learned that although he might have the very best intentions his control was only a myth. We did, however, succeed in getting the men to go back to work and to use the hooks more carefully. From then on the work proceeded very well until it came time for the second shift to relieve; at this time the men started to fill their pockets, hats, trousers, legs and even the seats of their trousers with flour, sugar, milk, in fact all of the commodities that they possibly had room for.

Other sources report more discreet methods of pilfering used by Russian stevedores. Ellingston mentions their "curious Dutch trousers, the legs of which would hold almost a sack of flour." He says they were masters at dropping a crate of milk in a way that split it open just enough to remove one or two cans. The workers unloading the *Phoenix*, however, did not bother to conceal their activity. They

deliberately and methodically proceeded to rip open a sack or case with their hooks and before the eyes of the soldiers on guard and all present helped themselves, in one or two cases passing some to the guards. To all our protests, they merely replied, "we are hungry and have got to eat." Upon leaving the yard the men are supposed to be searched but in case of these workmen the search was made by slapping the pockets of the men and letting them go on; some of the men had so much in their trousers legs that they could hardly walk and yet they got by with a "slap."

The humor and pathos created by the attitude of the workmen in this sort of pilfering was indeed striking to the most unobservant.

On the second day, a determined Lowrie had the police arrest one of the most unrestrained pilferers in order to make an example of him.

In about two minutes the men had stopped work and all crowded around protesting against the arrest. They said, "Why arrest this man? We are all thieves, look here! and here!" and all showed that they had also stuff stored in their clothes. The situation was decidedly ticklish and the man was finally released on the joint request of all the other workmen and their promise that they would each watch the other fellow to see that there was no more pilfering, but as it lacked only an hour before knocking off time the men decided that they would not go back to work and they didn't.

In several instances arrests were made by members of the Extraordinary Committee who were present but the men were led out of sight and then released after he divided with the guard. The chief of the stevedores told me himself that the guards could do nothing and would do nothing as they received their portion from the workmen. He admitted that he had absolutely no control of the men and that he could only request the men to do certain things but not command.

The chief stevedore told Noyes to compare the situation of the *Phoenix* with that of a nearby coal ship, where the work proceeded slowly because there was nothing for the men to steal. Sure enough, when the *Phoenix* crew began unloading containers of lard, too difficult even for Russian stevedores to transport in their trousers, the work proceeded "at a snail's pace."

Noyes calculated that in the end the pilfering of the *Phoenix* was "petty," amounting to only one-seventh of one percent of the cargo—which may indicate that the ship carried a large proportion of lard.

Thus were the American relief workers rudely introduced to the pervasiveness of thievery in Soviet Russia. It was not a phenomenon of recent origin. Toward the end of the eighteenth century the Russian historian Nicholas Karamzin remarked that if he would have to answer in one word the question, "What goes on in Russia?" he would respond, "Thieving." Yet even by Russia's extraordinary standards the amount of thieving going on in Soviet Russia was extraordinary. This was partly attributable to the deprivations of the revolutionary and civil war periods when starvation in the cities brought into the ranks of thieves new legions of formerly guiltless citizens. As Brooks observed, "A starving man thinks not of the Seventh Commandment."

A Moscow historian, no doubt writing from experience, left behind a vivid description of how the transformation of the Russian *intelligent*'s physical environment brought an inevitable disintegration of his moral world:

[Y]our apartment has been peopled with manual workmen to whom your furniture has been transferred; you are packed with your family in one dingy room; your property and money have been confiscated; you have to dress in rags; you have sold your books and cannot read; your whole time is occupied by hard physical work; you have to chop wood, cook, wash, light the stove, carry weights for yourself and your family. And as your hands gradually become coarse and are covered with a brown crust, your inner soul also gives way and, getting hardened in this fight for existence, little by little throws off all its previous elevated and delicate aspirations. The voice of famine really, every day, menacing his children drives a man to expedients, makes him forget everything except the question of everyday bread.

More than hard times were to blame. The moral atmosphere had been clouded by the Bolshevik abolition of private property and the confiscation of the property of the aristocracy, the bourgeoisie, and the Church, which further emboldened the already criminally minded, demoralized the workers and peasants, and in Ellingston's words, "gave that class of the population which is generally considered the guardian of public morals a sense of injury which overrode the precepts of conscience." Historian Mossoloff wrote of the new "confusion in the notion of property": "People that would have been blameless in former years take now part in thefts of governmental property."

And as the Soviet government came to "own" more and more property as its nationalization program expanded to include most industry, stealing increasingly could be rationalized as stealing from the Bolsheviks—that is to say, expropriating from the expropriators. This provided desperate people with a further incentive to help themselves. Best situated of all to rob from the state were its own officials. Graft had long been "a profitable sideline of the Czarist bureaucrats," as Fisher wrote, but under Bolshevik rule it had become by the end of the Civil War "almost the only remunerative activity."

Nor did matters improve perceptibly upon the introduction of NEP. Cornick at Tsaritsyn wrote in a letter dated August 15, 1922, that the previous night one of his colleagues had gone to a local theater to see a comedy called *ARA*, presuming that it would satirize American relief. Instead, before the curtain rose a statement was read out from the stage to the effect that no ridicule of the ARA was intended, as the actors did not feel themselves worthy to criticize that organization. "Then they deliberately poked fun at every local government department, showing how poorly they functioned, and laughing at the graft that goes on everywhere." So in 1921 thievery in Russia was an all-pervading activity, and Golder echoed Karamzin: "Stealing, stealing, everybody is stealing in one form or another."[1]

NOW INTO THIS hazardous setting the ARA was transporting hundreds of thousands of tons of food, clothing, and medical supplies—an irresistible target for the tens of thousands of Russians who were to handle, hook, or otherwise help distribute it. Kellogg got a sense of the dimensions of the problem during his Volga scouting expedition in September 1921. In his diary he recorded a representative case of theft, to which he gave the title "Our car cook and the Moral Debacle":

Caught our car cook selling some of our commissary supplies and putting some more away in bags and knotted shirt sleeves to bring home. Confessed & explained that *everybody* did it—it was necessary to keep from starving.

The combination of the inculcation of the doctrine of no right to private property—that those who had property had it because they had stolen it from the poor—and the economic breakdown and drouth—has morally debased the whole Russian people. Some men genuinely believe in the communistic doctrine but in applying & carrying it out they have developed a *sauve qui peut* situation—everyone for himself—robbery no crime.

The worst initial fears of the ARA chiefs of outright large-scale theft or Bolshevik confiscation of ARA supplies never materialized. The thievery that the ARA men confronted day-to-day, though widespread, was of a small-scale and more devious kind. This made it difficult to assess its magnitude. Paragraph 11 of the Riga Agreement committed the Soviet authorities to undertake to reimburse the ARA in dollars for, or replace in kind, any misused or stolen relief supplies. Quinn wrote to London headquarters in March 1923—in other words, with the huge majority of the aid already delivered—that as of that point the Russian mission had submitted claims to the Soviet government totaling $286,000 for pilferage and other losses—which is substantial, though not scandalously so, and might even have been an accurate measure of the losses for which the central government was demonstrably responsible and could therefore be held accountable.

But of the considerable amount of petty theft only a portion could be documented and little of it charged to the government. The ARA's accounting whizzes may have taken a stab at estimating its scope, but there was no incentive to do so publicly. Edgar Rickard, director general of the ARA, who had not as yet set foot in Soviet Russia, gave the American public the official ARA view in a May 1922 article in *Our World*: "Although nearly everyone in Russia is hungry, our losses from pilferage have been negligible and have not exceeded losses from the same cause in other countries." This was consistent with the ARA's reputation for excellence in management, accounting, and efficiency, but it does not hold up very well in the face of the abundant anecdotal evidence of the resourcefulness of the Russian thief. Rickard made his reassuring statement from the safe distance of New York City. In the famine zone the relief workers had a harder time looking past the problem: living in fear of having your trousers stolen has a way of focusing the mind.

The journey of the ARA's food supplies as they made their way from Russian port to hearth was a dangerous one. Hungry stevedores were only the first challenge. The threat increased on the railroads. All freight cars were sealed with Soviet railway seals as well as those of the ARA. Shipments of medical and hospital supplies and motor transport equipment enjoyed the special protection of convoys of soldier guards from a special ARA regiment formed by the Red Army for this purpose. Yet trainmen and refugees found ways to get into the cars en route; when a hot box forced a transshipment of food between trains, there was bound to be losses.

For the contents of the ARA food packages the first stop was the Moscow repacking room where, Ellingston wrote, there appeared "a new order of dangers; in making up postal parcels, for instance, the laborers developed a talent for substituting three pounds of tin foil for three pounds of tea, sand for sugar, and even of emptying milk cans and refilling them with water. The ingenuity of the food thief knew no bounds."

Once the food package reached the intended district headquarters there was a further set of dangers, such as theft of notification cards by postal workers, misdeliveries of packages due to forged documents of identification, and other forms of subtle graft by the office workers at the food remittance delivery stations, who knew the identity of the consignees, which of them could not be located, "and such other information as cried to be used." It often was: several districts reported widespread speculation in food packages within the ARA warehouse involving the sale of delivery orders to outsiders.

It was this kind of theft—the inside jobs—that caused the biggest headaches for the relief workers once the food had arrived at district headquarters. The lo-

cal personnel may have held coveted positions, but most were not entitled to receive regular ARA food packages, and with hungry families at home temptation
was strong. In any case the thieving habit was by now difficult to kick, even if its
target was a famine relief organization feeding mostly children. Better to think of
the act as something other than theft—like the cashier in Ufa who after an accounting discrepancy was discovered and an investigation exposed him, insisted
that Soviet law allowed him a certain percentage of error.

All the districts had to combat the thieving epidemic, and none appears to have
been harder hit than others, though there are indications that Odessa lived up to
its reputation for exceptional excess. Haskell noted the statement of John Lange,
the ARA port officer there, that "he had seen a good deal of pilfering in his life
but that all pilferers should be sent to Odessa to take a post-graduate course."

Much of the petty theft was the doing of kitchen managers, who were well
placed to serve themselves. In his *Russia Before Dawn*, Mackenzie recounted his
participation in the exposure of what was probably a typical incidence of this
kind of graft, when he accompanied three ARA men on an inspection tour of
subdistrict kitchens in Samara. Naturally the party arrived on the scene unannounced. The chief, probably Shafroth, opened the lid of one of the copper pots
containing the children's dinner, reached in with a big wooden spoon, stirred up
the contents, and then drew out a ladleful. "There should have been a fairly thick
mass of rice. He found a thin liquid, in which a few scattered grains of rice appeared." He turned to Mackenzie: "'Look at this,' he said, as he poured the watery mixture back into the pot. 'You see what this means, don't you? Someone has
stolen the children's rice. There should be thirty pounds of rice in this; there are
not seven.'"

The head of the local committee was a priest; a woman tending the dung fires
told the Americans that he was in church, gone to pray for more famine relief.
Had he known what was cooking back at the kitchen, he would have been able
to pray for relief of a different kind.

The local chief of the A.R.A. was a big man, with big body and big head. He had the
direct manner of a soldier who has been accustomed to work in the front lines. He
came up to the boiler and glanced at its contents. "Give me a bowl," he commanded.
Carefully stirring the dish up from the bottom, he gathered and weighed a bowl full.
He knew how much this ought to weigh. The scales showed that two-thirds of the
rice had been stolen.

The chief's brows gathered thunder. "Send for the committee," he said curtly.
"Send for the priest."

It was very cold in the room, and the visitors, not yet thawed out from their
journey, kept their heavy coats on and probably did a bit of pacing to take the
edge off their impatience. When the committee had assembled, the chief confronted them with the evidence and demanded an explanation. Mackenzie's narrative turns melodramatic:

At once the priest burst into a torrent of talk. He was a little oily man, with long black
hair, slightly curling at the ends, the usual style affected by priests of the Greek
Church in Russia. He tried to laugh the matter off. A mere accident! Such things were
unavoidable sometimes! Some stupid person had measured wrongly! He laughed. The

other committee-men, gaunt peasants, who stood twiddling their leather caps, joined nervously in the laugh. An accident!

The administrator's brow grew blacker. "They think it a damned laughing matter, do they!" he muttered. He flung one sentence at them, so low that I could not catch the words. They jumped. It was as though each of them felt the hand of the agent of the Che-ka at his collar.

Predictably at this point, the accused began pointing fingers at one another. The committee was dissolved and its stores taken away; a new one would have to be selected. The fate of the unstrung priest and his peasant collaborators is unclear, though not the state of mind of their accusers:

One could see from the administrator's face how he felt; but we knew his feelings from our own. Had we been a court martial, we would have sentenced the thieves to death, and I, for one, would, if needs be, have taken part in executing the sentence. For most crimes there is forgiveness. Ordinary theft one palliates; under certain circumstances murder can be pardoned; there are even cases of cowardice that we agree to forget. But the men who steal food sent from their own starving children do not deserve to live.[2]

This was a morally principled position but an entirely unrealistic one in famine Russia, where all theft was ordinary. The relief worker was forced to make a difficult adjustment to this reality and learn to live within its many shades of grey, as Ellingston observed: "In his eyes a thief was a thief and it took considerable association with the tragedies of the Russian famine before he could bring himself to judge pilfering of food and fraudulent dealing with that leniency to which in Soviet Russia it was entitled."

But there were degrees of accommodation, and Kelley, for one, never allowed himself to descend to Soviet Russian standards of leniency, although he was under no illusions about the "enormous amount" of graft taking place at Ufa headquarters.

Not much is likely to be heard of graft in the distribution of ARA supplies, and yet no ARA field worker doubts but that the distributive system is honeycombed with it. In a famine country, especially in a country with such traditions of graft as Russia, it was inevitable. The Soviet Government is implicated in it to such an extent that they are not likely to air the subject in Russia.

Mackenzie's depiction of the relief workers as traveling kitchen inspectors, handling ladles and exposing corrupt committees, might be misleading. As Kelley makes clear—and it seems to apply to all districts—more typically, American inspections of kitchens amounted to acknowledging the thanks of the committee and relying on the vigilance of the ARA's Russian personnel: "If the Russian instructors could not prevent irregularities and graft, it was certain that the American personnel couldn't."

Open sales of ARA products were rare in Ufa; on the other hand, the appropriation by employees of small amounts of child-feeding products for their own needs or that of family or friends was, "we felt confident, practically universal." When the American corn arrived in the district, tolls in corn were taken by drivers of convoys, river transport workers, and almost everyone else who handled it.

When Kelley arrived back at New York headquarters in summer 1922 and was asked to write up an overview of Russian operations, he dismissed the figures on theft supplied by Haskell's staff: they did not include "losses incurred below the District base warehouse, of which there was practically no record. Warehouse managers may short change ignorant committeemen and receive a full receipt. . . . Local committees might steal from the village kitchen warehouse and 'fix it up' with the instructor." And so on.

The Russian department chiefs knew there was graft, accepted the fact, and seldom went out of their way to investigate it. "Whenever a definite complaint was filed with an American he took action, usually lopping off a few heads in the vicinity of the alleged crime on general suspicion; but for the Americans to have made any systematic effort to eradicate graft would have required their resigning the helm of the ship to Russians while devoting themselves to prying about the engine room." Kelley surmised that the only effective check on such graft was the fear of exposure by a whistle-blower and the resultant loss of position. "To be discharged by the ARA meant to fall from the top rung of prosperity's ladder into the class of famine subjects."

Kelley's awareness of the ubiquity of the practice did nothing to soften his reaction to the case of Linhart, the central warehouse manager who was arrested in March 1922 by the Cheka on his way home with "a few poods of ARA products in his sleigh." Not a major offense by current Russian standards, but it was the end of the line for Linhart, whom Kelley discharged and who was "deeply pained at the severity of our prosecution. It was such a small amount!"

On the evening of March 15 Linhart came by the personnel house to plead his case. It was not the most favorable moment, since Kelley's emerging wisdom teeth were causing him acute pain, and he had just settled down to distract himself with a February edition of the *New York Times*. "He came into my bedroom as I was reading. There were tears and excuses to which I was even less than coolly indifferent." Kelley turned him away, telling him that if Bell wished to see him he'd be sent for. "The man expects us to condone his taking 'small' amounts of food for his own use. Little sympathy he got from me, although I suspect the esteemed Cheka were trying to put themselves in a position of doing us a favor."

Linhart persisted. On March 18 he showed up at the office, hoping to collect his February ration.

Needless to say, I dismissed him very sharply sans payok. His explanation that he took only what he needed for his own use, as though that exonerated him, so irritated me that I have no compassion on him. The police (Cheka) confiscated everything of value they could find in his home. I don't doubt that he is starving, but starve he may before I authorize any payok to him. To show mercy to a confessed thief would be to condone his act and encourage further theft of food destined for starving children. There is no system which can protect us from dishonest warehouse men. His life or his wife's life are nothing to me when I stack them against the lives of a score of children that might have been saved, or prolonged, with the food he stole. Bell has more sentiment than I and weakened in the face of the man's pleas to the point of passing the decision on to me. What would you do? . . . The man makes a personal appeal, the children don't. They are huddled in the corner of an orphan's home . . . dumb.

Linhart asserts that he can reveal many instances of graft, but this has no effect on Kelley.

I am ready to believe that every Russian that has anything to do with our food grafts a little on his own. In a famine country I suppose it can't be otherwise. But it is clear as day that every bit of graft means less food for children. From now on I trust no one. I am going to devise every possible check, and make myself the most cordially hated American in the district. I will have no personal nor social relations with any of the Russian personnel, so that I can be free to discharge any offender without a moment's hesitation.

Kelley was only stating forcefully what is implicit in the documentation of other districts: that graft by employees "raised a barrier" between them and their American chiefs. Ufa was almost certainly an extreme case, probably due to Kelley's personal influence, especially if one accepts his statement that

we practically ceased social intercourse with our employees, suspicious of everyone, and wishing to be free to direct the discharge or arrest of anyone at any time for the good of the service. Frequent shifting of the staff was found to be excellent for the discipline. No one was allowed to feel secure in his post with the ARA. Intimidation of this kind was our only practicable substitute for that close inspection that our limited numbers and handicap of language made impossible.

Kelley himself assumed direct control over the distribution of employees' food rations, up to then a source of much petty graft. Revising the ration list, he crossed off the names of persons such as the house cook and maid, reasoning that they already took as much food from the kitchen as did the Americans. "The people I put in were workers in the field, while those I cut out were office employees in Ufa, so you can imagine how popular I must be. As the Russians say so often, 'nichevo.'"[3]

IT IS FITTING THAT, for all the attention Kelley gave to the problem of theft in his correspondence, his only flesh-and-blood thief was a warehouse manager. The position was at once coveted and cursed. Revealing is the reaction of the Simbirsk Americans when the police arrested their warehouse manager in connection with the disappearance of Phil Sheild. They were not at all upset by this, evidently regarding him as capable of even the worst sort of foul play: in famine-stricken Russia the warehouse manager stood in for the butler as the stereotypical prime suspect.

Simbirsk's streak of bad luck with warehouses and their managers may have been a bit unusual. At about 7 o'clock on the evening of January 16, 1923, as Blomquist and Otis emerged from the ARA food remittance warehouse, shooting erupted. The shots were directed at the warehouse entrance. The ARA guards emerged from within, and there was an exchange of gunfire. Some unlucky fellow named Fadeev was found hiding in the bushes nearby, and though unarmed, because he could not account for his presence there, he was arrested, his supposed accomplices assumed to have escaped. Some considered it a case of attempted robbery. Others thought it was an attempted assassination, which certainly sounds more plausible than the first. Why would anybody begin shooting at the ARA warehouse at closing time when two Americans and all the guards were present?

One month later there was a suspicious fire at another of the Simbirsk warehouses resulting in a considerable loss of ARA property. Barringer reported to

Moscow that the fire had started so soon after closing that the local police were suspicious and moved to arrest, "with our consent," the warehouse manager and his assistant and the chief of the ARA guard. The theory of the police was that the fire was a diversion for theft, but Barringer said the Americans believed that the real culprit was a spent cigarette—the warehouse manager smoked in his office. So the charge probably should have been criminal negligence, but Barringer did not bother to object to the arrest of the warehouse manager on a more serious charge, for by then he was resigned to the practice.

The arrest of the W.H. Mgr. and Assistant is the usual consequence of warehouse trouble in Russia regardless the evidence, so we have not protested, giving the authorities every facility to run down the cause and purpose if any. Incidently I believe this is the sixth W.H. Mgr out of seven employed since beginning operations September 1921, whose career with the ARA has ended in jail. Its a hoodoo job.

There were several occasions when the relief workers did come to the defense of their personnel accused of stealing. One such episode, involving the sale of American corn by Saratov employees in the summer of 1922, brought a minor scandal down on the ARA.

The matter came to Moscow's urgent attention only after the trial had ended and the verdicts had been pronounced: the chief defendant, an ARA employee, was sentenced to execution within forty-eight hours. District supervisor John Gregg cabled Haskell, requesting that he attempt to obtain a stay of execution. The severity of the sentences, he felt, was meant to discredit the ARA: "Verdict not in line with facts." The wire was delivered to Haskell as he sat in a meeting with Lander when only twenty-four hours remained until the sentence was to be carried out. Lander arranged a postponement.

Gregg did not deny that the four ARA employees in question had illegally sold ARA corn—in fact an entire carload of it. He himself had ordered them to sell the corn, presumed to be spoiled, and to hand over the proceeds to the ARA. It turned out that most of the corn was good, but they sold it anyway and pocketed most of the returns.

According to Ruhl, who arrived in Saratov just after the trial, the main defendant, a man named Bogoslavskii, was pronounced "virtually guilty of treason." Specifically, he was charged with having violated section 110 of the Criminal Code, having to do with administrators who convert to their own use government property placed in their custody. There was some basis to this charge since, according to the Riga Agreement, the government had to reimburse the ARA in gold for all stolen American products. Bogoslavskii's lawyer, while admitting his client's guilt, argued that he should not be tried as a government administrator but merely as an employee who had stolen his employer's money.

Gregg was in a fix. He felt that the verdict was too harsh, and he wished to come forward to testify in order to get Bogoslavskii a milder sentence, yet he knew that this risked compromising the ARA. He decided to write a letter to the authorities, requesting detailed information about the case and inquiring as to whether there would be any bail for the defendants. Even this apparently innocent query got him into trouble. In his letter Gregg wrote that the ARA itself had brought no charges against the men and that it had no intention of demanding compensation for the stolen corn—that in fact the corn had been sold per order of the ARA. In making this statement he was only trying to be helpful, and, as Ruhl wrote to Moscow, "This was also legally correct, but a stranger, reading it, would have thought that the men had committed no offense and the A.R.A. was backing them up completely."

Local officials made the most of Gregg's letter, quoting it out of context in the press alongside their own professions of bafflement as to why the Americans were so interested in the fate of a few thieves and why they appeared to be upset that the guilty had been brought to justice. An editorial declared that bourgeois elements like Bogoslavskii were attracted to the ARA because of the immunity it provided its associates: it had created "a sort of state within a state." The Americans were objecting to the punishment of the offenders only because of the threat it posed to their organization's extraterritoriality.

In fact it was the way justice had been carried out that troubled the Saratov Americans. The president of the court had been an employee of Bogoslavskii before the Revolution and evidently was gunning for his former boss. Before and throughout the trial the local press heaped venom on the chief defendant, while Gregg's requests to testify had been refused. "In short," wrote Ruhl, "the trial was plainly unfair, however guilty Bogoslavsky may have been."

The ARA's protests led to a retrial in November. Ellingston, who had been stationed in Saratov at the time the crime was committed, was allowed to come from Moscow to testify. Whatever was the influence of this American intervention, Bogoslavskii's life was spared.[4]

THE ARA HAD GOOD REASON to believe that the Saratov Bolsheviks would carry out Bogoslavskii's execution. Every day the newspapers ran stories about robberies in which the culprit, or at least the suspect, was caught and shot by the Cheka. In their own struggle against theft, the Americans on occasion sought to tap into fear of the ultimate punishment by calling upon the assistance of the Cheka.

In Saratov, Goodrich witnessed what he called "a striking example of the efficiency of the *Checka* in settling a strike," and it serves as a contrast to the ARA's inability to put a stop to the pilferage of the *Phoenix* cargo. An ARA food ship docked at Saratov and began unloading. At the end of the day, the stevedores tried to walk off with a portion of the food in their pockets. When district supervisor Kinne reclaimed these rations, the workers struck. The ARA then hired university students to replace the workers, but this provoked an angry demonstration causing the students to withdraw.

Kinne turned to the Cheka, which sent an official to talk things over with the workers, who refused to continue unloading the vessel unless they received a food ration in addition to their wages. The Cheka man took a look at his watch: "I will give you thirty minutes to get to work. If you refuse, I will have some of you shot." He also said that if Kinne gave him the name of workers pilfering ARA food, they too would be shot. The word "trial" probably did not pass his lips. The unloading recommenced, reportedly without the pilfering.

More commonly, the Cheka was employed by the ARA to help combat theft at the central warehouses. All warehouses and stock rooms were kept under continuous guard and under lock and seal when closed. There were few robberies of great significance, and these usually turned out to be the work of well-organized gangs. In one case, cars were arriving in Moscow from Petrograd with their seals intact but with some of their contents missing. It was later discovered that a gang working the Petrograd yards was able to raise the roofs of the cars and help themselves.

In Moscow the ARA's central warehouse at the Boinaia railway yards was the scene of constant theft and attempted theft of American supplies. A gang of Chinese laborers was caught using an instrument that enabled them to open the lead seals sufficiently to extract the wire and then replace it without leaving signs of tampering. Another gang working the Boinaia yards was fully manned for the theft and disposal of goods, composed as it was of laborers, guards, and merchants. When this team of thieves was exposed, according to an ARA document, "Their trial was given much publicity and excited considerable comment, some of the leaders being sentenced to be shot and others getting ten years solitary confinement."

That kind of story made headlines, yet as was the case elsewhere, the most worrisome theft at the Moscow central warehouse was of the petty variety. The man who lost the most sleep over it was Freddie Lyon, who was shifted from Orenburg in the winter of 1921–22 to the post of assistant chief of Boinaia. He was a witness to both crime and punishment—or at least the evidence of it—as in the incident involving a shipment of three railroad cars filled with food packages, which were left standing for a couple of weeks under guard, awaiting the arrival of locomotives. Inspecting these cars one day, Lyon discovered some empty milk cans and other containers in their vicinity, and went right to the Cheka.

The bloodhounds were brought in, and it took only a short time to discover the thieves hiding inside one of the cars: they were the men who were supposed to be guarding the cars. The Cheka was pleased with this catch—if that is what it really was—and arranged an execution. Lyon was invited to be a spectator at the event the following morning at the scene of the crime. He declined the offer, though when he visited the spot the next day, he was shown bullet holes in the sides of one of the cars and assured that justice had been served. Maybe so. Lyon did not ask for further proof. "It is said that the method employed in these al fresco executions is to line up the condemned, or perhaps more accurately the doomed, and put a revolver at the head of each of one after another until the job is done."

It turns out that this was only the most notorious of the Cheka's methods. It used other, less straightforward procedures as well, as Haskell discovered after an apparent overnight break-in at the ARA commissary. Nothing of significance was stolen, only a few cartons of American cigarettes, nonetheless the matter had to be investigated. Haskell figured that there was only one thing to do: "I directed the American in charge of the commissary to notify the Tcheka of whose prowess we had heard so much."

Three black leather jackets appeared, accompanied by a droopy-eared bloodhound. They made a cursory examination of the premises and pronounced the matter an "inside job." The next step was to interview the three Russians employed in the commissary. They were lined up before the chief Chekist, who looked each of them fiercely in the eye as he held their hands firmly in his own, this process lasting about thirty seconds for each suspect. Not a word was spoken.

When this exercise was completed, the Chekist turned to Haskell and said, "The man in the middle is the thief."

Haskell was not about to let pass this unorthodox form of interrogation and said he would need more proof than a "mysterious laying on of the hands." So the bloodhound was brought forward. It sniffed all three men, "nosed around the window and the floor, and then with an eager whine, made straight for the unfortunate wretch who stood accused and leaped upon him."

Haskell, who might anyway have come from Missouri, was still not satisfied, and this moved the Cheka chief to state that for the previous two weeks his men had been on the alert for a gang planning to rob the commissary. So they had stationed agents at a second-story window across the street, and these men had seen the accused enter through a window on the previous night. Haskell did not doubt the presence of the Cheka agents, though he called the explanation about what they were up to "the merest moonshine." In the end the thief was released almost immediately, "which was as we would have wished it."

Haskell had another story to tell concerning the Cheka, a dog, and a thief. It happened at midpoint in the mission when his bull terrier, Nevsky, was stolen from the personnel house. In his memoir, Haskell recalls that he "sought the advice of the Cheka," which suggested that he post a reward. This he did, setting the amount at five billion rubles, which he later recalled being the equivalent, at par, of two and a half billion dollars, though it was actually worth only about ten dollars. Still, in Soviet Russia "This astronomical figure represented in a way, what was probably the largest reward ever offered for a mongrel's return." Haskell inquired if the Cheka thought that this was a reasonable sum. He was told that it did not matter since whoever showed up to claim the reward would be arrested and put in prison. Now the colonel worried that some innocent person might be made to suffer, and he says he was pleased that little Nevsky was never returned.[5]

When Haskell turned to the Cheka after the break-in at the ARA commissary, he did this, as he later recalled, "more for the sake of its moral effect upon other employees who might be tempted to steal from us than for my conviction that the Soviet sleuths would be able to accomplish anything." It was this "moral effect" that the Kazan Americans had in mind when they called in the Cheka in a much bigger way in December 1921.

Childs described their motivation in a diary entry for January 5. He wrote that in the final days of December it had been decided at a conference with the government representative, presumably Muskatt, that because of the ARA's "inability to control petty thievery among the employees in the kitchens" in Kazan city, the ARA would "make use of the Extraordinary Commission." In effect, what was proposed was a Cheka raid on the ARA's own employees. Of course, wrote Childs, the Kazan Americans never really thought they would apprehend anyone, "but it was proposed to enlist the aid of the special secret police of the government for the moral effect which would be produced more than for anything else." It must have been difficult for Comrade Muskatt to suppress his glee: the Cheka was to be given the run of the place.

It was arranged that on December 31 each of the city's kitchens would be "visited" by Cheka agents, who would, as Childs put it, "make a search of the premises, subject the employees to a cross-examination and if necessary even visit their homes for the purpose of prosecuting the investigation." Childs, who could be shockingly naive about the realities of Soviet power, could not have truly understood what a Cheka "visit" would mean to its victims.

Usually the ARA men put up a struggle to keep the Cheka out of the lives of their employees. This was a continual cause of friction in Orenburg between Coleman and his archenemy, Comrade Klimov. In April 1922 Eiduk ordered that one of Coleman's Russian personnel, Smirnoff-Nikiforoff, said to be a Left-SR with several arrests on his record, be dismissed from the ARA. Before the matter was cleared up, the Cheka searched Smirnoff's house one morning, and later in the day he was dead. Judging from Coleman's reaction, the cause was probably a heart attack. He was not about to let Klimov off the hook: "Although Mr. Smearnoff has departed this earth, I must request that you treat this matter in the same way as if he were still here. In other words, I ask that you write me advising me of the conditions."

No one would die during the Cheka searches in Kazan, but the result of the investigation, which Childs himself calls "Cheka raids," was a near catastrophe—for individual employees but also for district operations.

Childs noted that the Cheka's methods, which he said were typical of the period of the Red Terror, "certainly could not be criticised for any lack of thoroughness." As had been anticipated, no one was discovered to be a thief, and yet "the moral effect which it was sought to produce was of such a nature as to have nearly caused the ARA the loss of its most capable and conscientious employees."

Turner's official report on this strange business makes uncomfortable reading. At least fourteen ARA kitchens were investigated.

At kitchen no. 1 the manager, Mrs. Shliapnikova, was asked for the keys to the storeroom, but she refused to hand them over unless an American were present. This was as she had been instructed. When she refused to cooperate, a Cheka agent asked her whom she trusted more, the Americans or the Cheka. She replied that she was working for the Americans and therefore trusted them. "If that is the case," said the Chekist, "you are arrested." During her first hearing before the Revolutionary Tribunal the judge asked Mrs. Shliapnikova why she had refused to obey Soviet power, saying, "You are living in Soviet Russia, not in the United States."

A similar thing happened at kitchen no. 3, where the manager, another woman, was marched through the streets, a soldier at each side, to her home, where nine agents conducted a search. Turner records that the woman was "completely upset by the experience, unusually so because of the fact that her father, a priest, was shot a year or two ago after a similar raid."

The father of the manager of kitchen no. 9 was so incensed by the indignity done him by his house being searched that he made his daughter resign immediately from the ARA.

At kitchen no. 14 four soldiers entered the room of the kitchen manager where she was changing clothes to go out for the evening. She was made to finish dressing in their presence. After a search of the kitchen, they each ate two rolls and two dishes of beans—rations of the manager and her assistant. Their stomachs filled, they sat back and put questions to her as to what she thought the Americans were doing in Kazan, if she thought they had really come to feed children.

Turner noted that the Cheka had forgotten to leave "protocols" at kitchens nos. 1, 5, 6, and 14. But he had read enough. He concluded his report by recommending that in view of the "slight results" of the raids as compared to the "mental distress and mortification" caused so many innocent people, he be allowed to assure the employees that such a thing would never happen again.

An account of this affair, complete with Turner's report, is in Childs's diary. It contains not a hint of remorse. The fact that he intended to publish it seems further proof that he was blind to how unfavorably it reflected on his judgment.

The Americans might on occasion enlist the Cheka to combat theft of various kinds, but they generally tended to think of individual Chekists as thieves with firearms and attitude. Charles Morris reached this conclusion as he struggled to control the theft of ARA products by the railway authorities in Tsaritsyn. In one incident, eighty-five sacks of ARA corn were stolen from the railway warehouse in a manner suggesting that it was an inside job. An investigation by the ARA revealed that the Cheka guards themselves had been involved in the theft, and they were apprehended, presumably by other Cheka guards.

Following another case of theft at the same warehouse, the ARA called in the City Detective Service, which discovered that entry to the warehouse had been made by cutting out a plank in the side of the building, which could readily be removed and replaced. The detectives found a considerable quantity of sugar, some flour, and a large supply of American shoes in the homes of the Cheka guards and of other railway employees. These were confiscated. Soon afterward, Morris sent one of his Russian employees to the Railway Cheka to retrieve the stolen items. New American shoes would have stood out boldly in a place like Tsaritysn—or anywhere else in Soviet Russia—and so it did not take Morris's emissary long to notice that the entire staff was sporting the stolen shoes. An inquiry revealed that the head of the Railway Cheka had himself given permission for these shoes to be distributed to his personnel. Which Cheka was called in to deal with the Railway Cheka is not recorded.

At a time when Kelley was investigating four attempted thefts of the Ufa Americans' personal items within a week, one of which involved an attempt to set fire to the personnel house, he wondered where to turn: "We could get a military guard but they would be as likely to steal as anyone else."

In Moscow, after individual ARA men requested that the authorities recover their stolen personal property—which the Americans regularly had reason to do—there often ensued a long period during which the investigation was supposed to be taking place. In the meantime, it sometimes happened that a third party would approach the American in question and offer to see to the recovery of his property in return for a small consideration, with the assurance that the guilty party would be punished. More often the Americans were told that the goods had not been found but that the thief had been shot.

Lyon probably collected more interesting anecdotes on theft during his Boinaia days than any other ARA man. Their cumulative effect was to leave him doubtful that anyone in Russia still stood on the right side of the law. One day a Chekist dragged in a scrubwoman who had been found eating a handful of sugar. Caught red-handed and now in the clutches of the Cheka. Lyon appealed for leniency.

After I had made my plea in behalf of this wretched creature our chief cheka broke out with a most wonderful line of talk and he bitterly condemned these people who would stoop so low as to steal from an organization that was feeding their starving children. As he talked on he became quite eloquent and he warmed up to his subject with wild gestures—as he threw his arms around I noticed a tin of ARA milk up his sleeve.

Lyon called a halt to the sermon, demanded the tin of milk, and ordered the guard to leave, resolving that "henceforth no Chekkist would be allowed to step inside the warehouse. All of this goes to prove that in Russia one must have a watchman to look after the watchman."[6]

CHAPTER 37

THE MASK OF MAMMON

The ARA may have been left even more exposed to the thieving epidemic by the fact that a good many Russians were not entirely convinced that its purpose was strictly humanitarian: they suspected that it had an ulterior commercial motive. The Bolsheviks, of course, were supposed to assume this because their ideology informed them that there was no such thing as bourgeois philanthropy. But it frustrated the relief workers to find the suspicion voiced by a broad segment of the Russian people. Over time the doubts tended to fade, but in places they lingered until the end of the mission.

In the initial months especially, fantastic rumors went around as to the real reason that the ARA had come to Soviet Russia. One American heard some railroad workers in the famine zone wondering aloud if it was true that as payment for the relief, Russia would have to give up Kamchatka.

Residents of Simbirsk city scratched their heads and tried to guess the true explanation: "Wasn't it to make an investigation about the Russian factories and industries to buy them for the Americans? Interest for Volga shipping? For blackland?" In the port cities some assumed that American destroyers were investigating port conditions for future commercial shipping prospects.

The Ufa history records that in the beginning, locals suspected that "concealed somewhere in the plan was a scheme to get hold of some of the valuable metal or mineral wealth so freely found here, concessions for gold and platinum mines, etc. At least there must be some commercial scheme that would yield a good financial return."

After months of trying to set the record straight in Kiev, Macpherson threw up his hands and decided that the idea of a humanitarian enterprise was "not at present within the scope of understanding of the Russian mind, which has just traversed four years of social and economic upheaval."

Certainly what the Russians had lived through in the preceding seven years—for the brutalization had begun with the world war—was enough to make any people doubt the sincerity of another's charity. But as Macpherson learned, there were additional reasons for their skepticism about the ARA. For one, the relief workers were Americans, and their organization was in many ways typically American; Americans being by nature commercially minded, this thinking went, the ARA simply had to be driven by commerce. A Russian employee in the Tsaritsyn district put the matter this way:

Most of the people of Tzaritzin knew the Americans only as people who were always inventing something new,—wonderful apparatus and machines, building factories and workshops, carrying on a tremendous commerce, rushing about from place to place without rest. It was even said of them that they never slept. Everybody was interested to know under what conditions they would organize the feeding of the starving. It was said that at any rate, the help would not be gratis; that the Americans would take over the Volga shipping and the railways. Others said, "What do they want with these? Haven't they sufficient at home?"

A Moscow *intelligent* noted that after the initial shock, the residents of the capital looked upon the Americans with a certain ambivalence: "Next to the feeling of gratefulness there was at the same time a feeling of astonishment and even of suspicion." The suspicion derived from Russian preconceptions about their saviors: "[T]he general opinion concerning Americans in Russia is that they are very practical and few people consented to believe that there could be no egoistical commercial motive to their help. As a rule Russians know very little of the idealistic tendencies in foreign and especially anglo-saxon countries and always identify foreigners with business men."

This and other reports out of Moscow testify to an eventual clearing of the air, as "suspicion for the greater part vanished, and Russians understood the disinterested aim of the relief work." Elsewhere suspicion endured.

The Americans in Petrograd seem to have been especially frustrated by the persistence of such doubts. One remarked that it was a widely held opinion among the city's residents that the ARA was "nothing else but a good banking business house, and that many people abroad are profiting very nicely in that 'commercial enterprise.'" Another wrote in the district history that "There are very many people still in the belief that the ARA is a commercial concern, sacrificing a certain amount of their profits for charity purposes." Gantt thought, nonetheless, that most were not bothered by the probability that the ARA was actually a commercial organization since "they knew it gave them what they wanted and when they wanted it. The question of its ultimate purpose was to them a remote one. . . . It was to them as a mother to a child."

Chukovskii knew that in his own circle it was more complicated than that. He was disappointed to hear sophisticated people in Petrograd question the motives of the ARA—"It is not sincere, there must be some trickery"—but he considered it unsurprising when viewed in the context of late-Imperial Russian perceptions of Americans as seekers of money and success. This was especially the case after the turn of the century, when the social justice fiction and muckraking journalism of Upton Sinclair, the American author most extensively translated into Russian, enjoyed a wide readership. Chukovskii himself had come to share these perceptions, as he revealed in describing his reaction to the ARA's beneficence: "Is it not a miracle that from the other side of the world some sort of Yankees whom I had heard referred to all my life as hard hearted worshippers of Mammon and people vowed to commercialism should come thousands of miles to feed and make ME happy?"

Chukovskii blamed the aloofness of the relief workers for reinforcing the skepticism about their motives. One of Renshaw's local staff said that the ARA's "bloodless impersonality of method" led people to believe that it was a commercial operation, and he wondered why the Americans did not take action to correct this misperception.[1]

Many other Russians echoed the point that the ARA's modus operandi fueled the suspicion. Its representatives certainly did not behave like relief workers. All their loud talk about business methods and all that elaborate accounting and record-keeping raised questions: If the ARA really did have only philanthropy in mind, then why did it put such an effort into collecting an enormous amount of statistics about all aspects of the Russian economy? And why did it need receipts for everything? Why not simply give the food away? No, someone in Chicago must be waiting for the profits. This apparent incongruity between its actual methods and its stated purpose created something of an image problem for the ARA. The Americans took it into account, and Macpherson later included it as a contributing factor in his revised explanation for Russian wariness: "the conception and the working of the ARA has in it something sublimely humanitarian, which, carried out on the strictly business basis under which the ARA operates, is not comprehensible to the average Russian mind."

Russians were puzzled in particular by the fact that the Soviet government had to pay for the operating costs of American relief—that is, the wages of the local employees, internal transportation and communication, warehouses, living quarters, and other facilities. Like the elaborate collection of economic statistics, this had been a standard feature of ARA operations in other countries, but it was not an arrangement usually associated with a charity. It became very unpopular with local Soviet officials. Thus the Odessa trade union newspaper, *Sovrabotnik*, on November 3, 1922, complained that, while the ARA had done much good, it had saddled the local government with too many financial burdens: "Something like that was to be expected from the practical, business-like Yankees."

During the second year of the mission, when American relief was less essential, local governments were able to force the district supervisors to assume much of the burden. As Somerville observed, what hardened the resistance of every local official was the businesslike character of the ARA: "Why should his Government pay the operating expenses of such an organization, or deal with it otherwise than one deals with a commercial firm trying to drive with him a hard bargain?"

Popular opinion must have been influenced by the coincidence of the coming of Hoover's men—who were eager to have it understood that they represented a *private* American relief organization—and NEP's lifting of restrictions on trade and private enterprise, the second only firmly established by government decrees in August 1921 just before the Americans came on the scene. Some relief workers, such as Ellingston, convinced themselves that the ARA's activities had made the successful transition to NEP possible. Burland was more modest: "It is not unlikely that these two events are not completely dissociated in some Russian minds and that America may enjoy an undue measure of credit." He did believe, however, that the ARA had served as an important catalyst in the transition, helping to create an atmosphere of political and economic security and by its example encouraging the new traders to a more energetic pursuit of their affairs— which sounds entirely plausible.

Burland's own food remittance program, constantly hailed by the relief workers as the most businesslike component of their operation, was probably most responsible for the Russian perception of the entire relief mission as a commercially inspired enterprise.

What Russians found curious about this system was its built-in profit mechanism. The donor paid ten dollars for each food package, but until well into the mission the actual value of an individual package amounted to a few dollars less than that. The difference was contributed to the child-feeding side of operations. By mission's end the food remittance division had made a profit of $3,600,000, which was used to feed 3,600,000 people for one month. Here was the clearest example of that marriage of the spirits of capitalism and philanthropy—Hoover himself having administered the oath—in which the men of the ARA took special pride.

To Ellingston this carriage of philanthropy was also a business success story: "As a gauge of business possibilities in Soviet Russia, the Food Remittance operation definitely proved that a foreign business concern could carry on under something approaching acceptable conditions in Russia." Although in critical ways it was in fact not a typical commercial concern, still "it forced the new rulers of Russia, central and local, to accustom themselves to the free operation of a foreign business organization." Ellingston intended his characterizations of the food remittance program to apply by extension to the relief mission as a whole: "Though it wore the mask of Mammon, it came to symbolize straightforward dealing and tangible effective sympathy. It was a truly American operation in every sense of the word, bloodlessly impersonal in operation yet noble and human in its purposes and accomplishments. In it were constantly contrasted the most hard-headed commercial methods with the most delicate and kindly benevolence."

But not all Russians found it so easy to distinguish methods from motives, and when it came to food packages, even the ARA's employees, who were properly informed that the "profit" generated by their sale was being used to pay for further philanthropy, had skeptics among their ranks. It seemed that the ARA was in truth nothing more than a reconnaissance mission, scoping out future business opportunities in Russia: why, it was already doing business right now!

Soviet officials were naturally inclined to think along these lines, but just in case, there was helpful instruction from the center. Lander sent a confidential memorandum to his plenipotentiaries regarding the parallel program of clothing remittances, in which he noted under the heading "What the ARA Gets" the word "profit," with no mention of its purpose. He added that clothing packages aided the bourgeoisie and harmed the domestic textile industry. In a report to the Politburo he wrote, "The ARA's work is divided into two parts: the philanthropic and the food package program."[2]

When ARA representatives held a meeting with Kiev officials in December 1921 to brief them on the food remittance scheme, the reaction of those in the room was divided, according to an American who was present: "The representatives of [Soviet] relief organizations exclaimed with horror at the commerciality of Food remittances, while those with Uncles in America smiled in patient anticipation." At first the ARA in Kiev was engaged exclusively in the delivery of food packages and only later supplemented this with a modest child-feeding operation. This explains what one of the local Kiev staff meant when he wrote that at first the ARA was "of a commercial character, but with time it developed into a very wide philanthropic organization." Many friends of the ARA in Kiev assumed to the end that food remittance was, as one of its employees put it, "the commercial part of the business."

Food package delivery was the chief activity in Ukraine and White Russia, and in both places the notion of the commerciality of the ARA was complicated by the predominance of Jewish beneficiaries. One Kiev employee wrote that upon hearing of the coming of the ARA and of the nature of its program, many suspected that the mission would not be staffed by "real" Americans but by Jews, and that the head of the ARA would be an "elderly, honorable, small sized, with-two-long-wiskers Jew!" Although this did not turn out to be the case, when the first packages went to Jews, some called American relief "Yidrelief," "*Zhidopomoshch*."

Another account out of Kiev quotes someone in an angry crowd chastising the impatient Americans: "You, idols! You arrive from America, and wish to make an America here! The Jews can wait for their packages."

One of the Kiev employees cites a local rumor that the organization was called "ARA" so that its name could be read from the left or the right in order to make it as easy for a Jew to read as for a Russian. This same writer tells how one of the office girls thought that "General Relief"—the term used to designate food packages distributed at the discretion of the district supervisor—was a person, and she could not figure out why the Americans favored this particular individual: "Again a package to General Relief."[3]

Further reinforcing the suspicions that the ARA was not all it appeared was the fact that it put up with so much rough handling by the Bolsheviks when it could instead have simply picked up and gone home. Carroll thought that the Bolsheviks themselves were especially being misled in this way, a point he made while attacking Haskell's leadership: "By our weak policy in Russia, we have lowered American prestige and by tolerating unwarranted interference on the part of the Soviets, we have, I believe, helped to confirm their suspicions, that behind our relief work there still lurks some mysterious and hidden and ulterior motive." Turrou encountered this reasoning among the Moscow personnel: "The intelligent part of the Russian employees approached me many times with the question why we remained in Russia when the aggressiveness was so marked? They could not understand that we had no ulterior motive that was making us stand the treatment we were getting."

Certainly Bolshevik propaganda of the previous four years—a relentless barrage of newspaper stories about bloodthirsty imperialists and greedy foreign capitalists—influenced popular perceptions of the ARA. As Chukovskii testified, "Stories are constantly being printed that the American is stingy and crafty; that the only good Americans are the negroes and the laborers, the others being swindlers."

The plight of the American Negro was a favorite topic of the Soviet press. In an article called "What the Russians Think of Us," which appeared in the *New Republic* shortly after the mission, Ruhl described how a Moscow comic paper in summer 1922 had printed a front-page cartoon juxtaposing two scenes: one, titled "In Barbarous Africa," showed a group of African cannibals seated around a fire roasting a white man; the other, "In Cultured America," depicted a Negro burning at the stake surrounded by mob of gleeful whites. Years of exposure to such images, Ruhl felt, could not have but shaped Russian views of America. Even absent this negative influence the Russians would have tended to think that "There must be a joker somewhere," that the Americans were expecting a return on their investment of famine relief. But Bolshevik propaganda had contributed to the atmosphere of suspicion: "You cannot teach a people for several years that foreigners are devils and then all at once receive them with open arms."

Although as far as devils go, these young American relief workers in olive drab and in a hurry were not a good match for the crude Soviet poster image of the corpulent bourgeois in tails and top hat. Nor did they fit the prerevolutionary stereotype of the "typical Yankee millionaire, a whimsical spendthrift such as we knew from the boulevard-novels," as Yakovlev wrote in recalling, with intentional hyperbole, his reaction upon first catching sight of the American relief workers. "Really they do not look like real American Yankee millionaires, indulging in their extravagant fancies, like those we have met on the continent and of whom (rastacouères!) we have read in many a European novel. Surely there is some hoax in the whole business—look how plainly they are dressed, some in simple khaki or canvass." They carry their own loads, fix their own lights—and there is Dr. Godfrey, putting on the stockings for the children who are to receive ARA shoes: "It was again not like an American millionaire of a fairy tale."

As Dr. Gantt testified of Petrograd's residents, those Russians who suspected commercial designs behind the famine relief did not sound terribly alarmed by this. After all, the ARA was run by Americans, and Americans had in mind nothing more than business, whereas the Europeans, it was assumed, eyed Russia with visions of political domination. Russia had nothing to fear from America. In fact as the mission unfolded and the presumed commercial aspirations of the ARA seemed to remain largely implicit, some began to worry that humanitarian relief might indeed be all the Americans had in mind. A concerned Muscovite wrote that although philanthropy was a noble act,

There remained however an idea that it would be important for us too if the ARA could prepare the ground for future economical relations as Russia severely wants coming back to normal commercial relations with other nations and in that respect the help of America would be of the utmost importance. If they help us physically and morally they will help us too economically, thought many Russians, seeing that in the relief work not only a philanthropical action but also the first link renewing economical connection of Russia with the world.[4]

For all their proud talk about having shown the Russians an example of America's superior business methods and efficiency, and despite the occasional claim to having blazed a trail for Western business concerns, the relief workers preferred not to think of their mission as the vanguard of American business. That businessmen might follow in their footsteps they assumed to be in the natural order of things, an essential element in the next stage of Russia's economic recovery. But that was entirely separate from their own roles as actors in the most extraordinary humanitarian undertaking of all time—extraordinary in part because of the very purity of its humanitarianism. Typical of their thinking was a statement Burland made in response to the Bolshevik charge that the ARA had a hidden agenda:

Relief to foreign countries by official and semi-official government agencies is as old as civilization, but it has almost never been purely humanitarian. Instead it has been coupled with some sort of commercial preference or political advantage. Consequently the ARA has met a natural suspicion in official circles in every country where it has distributed American help. Every such country has learned, in due time, of America's disinterested position, and Russian officials might have known this, too, had they not supposed that the ARA's price was secretly exacted from the other countries.

LIKE MANY OF THEIR fellow Americans at the time and since—and in harmony with the opinion of most Russians in 1922—the ARA men contrasted the innocence of their motives with the underhanded scheming of the corrupt Europeans. This made it even more galling that those same Europeans refused to accept the Russian mission for what it was. Mitchell wrote that they could not conceive that it was in fact a 100 percent humanitarian operation; to them "the Hoover crowd" was simply "too damned efficient and business like." Yet listening to Mitchell and the rest of the ARA chiefs as they discuss, even publicly, the goals of their mission, the picture seldom adds up to 100 percent humanitarianism.

Since the Revolution, Washington's Russian policy had been shaped in part by a concern to maintain the integrity of the Russian empire, which was thought to be under threat from the "colonial" ambitions of the European governments—most worrisomely in the specific forms of a latent German revanchism and an uncompromising French insistence that the Bolsheviks be made to repay tsarist Russian debts. By 1920 perhaps the only positive thing that the Wilson administration could say, sotto voce, about Bolshevik power was that it had been able to restore most of the old empire. Now if only the Bolsheviks would do what had long been predicted and fall from power, a "normal" Russian government could set things aright in Moscow and be able to resist European encroachments.

One of the hopes Washington placed on the American relief mission was that it would ease Russia's passage to a safer shore and in the meantime safeguard it from outside interference. Such assistance could be included under the umbrella of humanitarianism. In an April 1922 article in the *New York Herald Tribune*, Dickinson put forward two possible policies toward Russia: the interventionist approach of the Europeans, which meant carving up the country, dividing up its resources and territories, and thereby "solving" the debt problem; and the American way, "the policy of moral trusteeship during the period of Russia's agony, a policy which would respect the integrity of a great nation, and would conserve it for great uses in the future."

One of the greatest users, of course, would be the United States, and it was obvious to all that the ARA mission, in creating an extraordinary amount of goodwill among the Russian people, would put the U.S. government and American business in the best position to take advantage of trade and investment opportunities in Russia, especially if the Bolsheviks fell from power. But the connection between the idealism of ongoing philanthropy and the self-interest of future commerce was tenuous enough in the minds of Americans like Dickinson that they were able to place the two in entirely separate spheres. In other words, the possibility of someday reaping benefits from American relief did not at all dilute its pure humanitarianism.

Europeans tended to take a more old-world view of the matter. Haskell liked to tell a story from his days heading up American relief in the Caucasus in 1920, when a French officer in Bucharest wondered aloud about the true intentions behind his mission: "Is it that the Standard Oil wants to obtain control of the Ploeste oilfields?" The colonel responded that in fact the sole purpose was to get the Romanians back on their feet, which got a laugh out of the Frenchman: "Our general opinion about your relief work here can be summed up as follows: you are either trying to work a Yankee trick, which is too deep for us to understand—or else you are a pack of the world's greatest fools." Haskell repeated this story to Kamenev in September 1922 in arguing the case for American disinterestedness in Russia, adding: "As the oil fields and ports are still in Roumania's possession they must now think that we are fools. The big men in America have no desire to exploit Russia and they are not concession hunters."

When Gov. Goodrich told the head of the Soviet State Bank that America was giving Russia $50 million in famine relief solely out of its duty as a Christian nation, with no ulterior purpose whatsoever, "the expression upon his face indicated that he wondered if I thought he was foolish enough to believe or understood that sort of thing." Goodrich stood his ground, yet his own perspective as elaborated in *Current History* in September 1922 indicates the presence of other considerations lurking deep in the background. The foreground is occupied by American benevolence:

The generous impulses which this magnificent gift to a starving people will awaken in ourselves, the gratifying national feeling we will have because of a good deed well done, will be worth more than it has cost us in dollars and cents. If we received nothing more than the satisfaction of having performed a duty to humanity, we could account ourselves well paid.

This is the way Americans then and now have preferred to think of themselves, as "an exceptionally altruistic nation," in the words of historian David Kennedy. President Harding expressed this sentiment while the Riga negotiations were underway: "I know that the entrance of America into the problem of Russia through the full heart of charity is one that will appeal to the whole American people."[5]

Goodrich did not leave it at that, however. He speculated that with this generosity as a foundation, "we are building better than we know."

We are again proving to all the world that in America human sympathy outweighs material achievement, and in the heart of a giant nation, which is about to awaken from a long sleep, we are planting seeds of affection, of common understanding, that some day will flourish and stand us in good stead, materially as well as sentimentally or morally. Let there be no mistake about it: in the not distant future the Russian giant will awaken, throw off the shackles of inefficiency and, no longer hampered by the tyranny of the autocrat, will become a driving force in the affairs of the world.

So material interests happened to coincide with America's native philanthropic instincts. Goodrich strongly believed that the advancement of American economic relations with Russia offered the fastest and most favorable means of reviving that country, and behind the scenes in Washington he aggressively, though unsuccessfully, lobbied for a U.S.-Soviet commercial treaty.

Being one of the chiefs, Goodrich did not have to deal with a problem that confronted the men in the districts planting those seeds of affection, who found that their status as ordinary relievers undermined their defense of the ARA.

A frustrated Hale wrote that there was no talking Russian friends of the ARA in Samara out of their belief that its ultimate business was business, and if an American made a convincing case for the sincerity of his own humanitarianism, the doubting Fomas still knew better: "Ah, that is all that *you* who are actually doing the work know of, but those who sent you had something different in mind."

What Hoover actually had in mind in sending these men to Russia has been the subject of speculation, then and since. Hoover's outspoken antibolshevism has always carried great weight with the skeptics, among whom the most unimaginative have charged that American relief was aimed at bringing down the Bolsheviks by giving sustenance to their political enemies. More commonly, Hoover's antibolshevism has been used to make the case for what the Russian mission was *not*—namely, straightforward philanthropy—while the search for its true, or ancillary, purpose has focused on alleged commercial motives. Suspicion has centered on three related sets of circumstances.

The first has to do with Hoover's personal business interests: specifically, that he was using the ARA as a means to recover his prerevolutionary mining interests at Kishtim in the Urals. In fact the only demonstrable use made of the ARA in this regard was the quiet delivery by Bell and Kelley of several food packages to Hoover's former Russian business colleagues and employees, but at the time the idea that personal gain was a factor was advanced by Hoover's political enemies—mostly radical groups but even a U.S. Senator. They found support for their charge in the way Hoover conducted his relief operations. Rickard, the ARA's director-general and himself a mining engineer by profession, told an audience of mining engineers that the administration's governing principles were "the same as those successful in American engineering enterprises and particularly those controlled in foreign countries by Mr. Hoover." Statements like this may have given the theory a shred of credibility, but few Americans seriously entertained the idea that the Master of Efficiency, already a man of enormous personal wealth, was a mere instrument of mammon.

Another, more credible basis for questioning Hoover's motives relates to his role as secretary of commerce. Russia offered a vast, unconquered market, and it was Hoover's job to ensure that the United States was well positioned to take advantage of it. He was perfectly aware that although the ARA's mission was to fight famine, its presence in Russia promised to give the United States a jump on the European competition by greasing the wheels for American trade and investment. His thinking is documented in a December 1921 response he wrote to Secretary of State Hughes's proposal that Germany act as the intermediary for future American trade with Russia. Hoover reacted sharply to this, declaring that Americans were "infinitely more popular in Russia and our Government more deeply respected by even the Bolsheviks than any other. The relief measures already initiated are greatly increasing the status and kindliness of relations and their continuation will build a situation which, combined with other factors[,] will enable the Americans to undertake the leadership in the reconstruction of Russia when the proper moment arrives."

Since it was declassified in the 1940s, this letter has become a standard feature of the argument against Hoover as Great Humanitarian. Yet it is not as if there had been a contradiction between the private and the public Hoover waiting to be exposed by correspondence from the archives. While he was certainly cautious in his public statements when it came to questions of potential U.S.-Soviet official and trade relations, Hoover was not at all reticent about his satisfaction that the ARA was carrying the American flag, figuratively speaking, and spreading the good name of America across Europe and into Russia. He would have agreed wholeheartedly with Meyer Bloomfield, the lawyer and banker who visited Moscow in 1922, when he said that "the A.R.A. represents in Russia the flower of our American spirit." It was only natural that it would, by spreading goodwill, serve to promote U.S. economic interests.

The shadow over Hoover's motives is darkened by a further, related accusation against him: that he used the Russian mission to ease the postwar depression by disposing of surpluses of American corn, for which he as food administrator during the war had been largely responsible. One reason this charge stands up so well is that Hoover himself publicly acknowledged it—"embraced" might be a better word when one considers his affirmation of it during testimony before the Senate Foreign Relations Committee in December 1921: "The food supplies that we wish to take to Russia are all in surplus in the United States, and are without a market in any quarter of the globe. . . . We are today feeding milk to our hogs; burning corn under our boilers."

The frank appeal to self-interest unsettled one Senator on the committee, who preferred his altruism straight up: "Let us not dilute our generosity with any selfish purposes. Is it a fact that it would have an appreciable effect, or affect the market on corn? Let us not put it on the basis of helping ourselves by giving away the $20,000,000 to Russia." The message in Hoover's enigmatic response, at least as it was printed in the transcript, seems to be that one could have it both ways: "I have a feeling we are dealing to-day with a situation of a great deal of depression and have a proper right to inquire not only whether we are doing an act of great humanity, but whether we are doing an act of economic soundness. To me, after assessing our ability to give, no other argument is needed beyond the sheer humanity."

Hoover biographer David Burner, commenting on this exchange, concludes that Hoover, who "in a philosophical way liked to perceive concurrences of morality and self-interest and in practice knew something about managing people, did indeed use the fact of the surplus to obtain Congressional approval of funds for the ARA. But it is not easy to say whether his own thoughts were on unloading the surplus, or on manipulating Congress for the sake of the hungry or both." In the end, "the simplest explanation for Hoover's response to the famine is that he had been, for several years, an administrator of world relief; his conscience, compassion, workmanship, and pride were now fully committed to this task."

Hoover seldom kept it simple. As he was lining up support for the congressional appropriation bill, he pressured the Soviet government behind the scenes to spend $10 million of its gold reserve to purchase seed from American farmers— just as, a few months later, he persuaded the Ukrainian republic to contribute $2 million as part of its own separate agreement with the ARA. In making his case to Moscow, he wired that it was imperative that the Soviet government "make strong demonstration self-help." Or was it? It is not well known that in 1919, when he was attempting to arrange an Allied plan for a cease-fire in the Russian Civil

War and arrange food relief to Russia, Hoover intended to have the Bolshevik government pay for everything with tsarist gold.

During these same years the name of this politically alert, business-minded humanitarian was associated in the public mind with the concept of "service," a word that possessed near-religious significance for Americans, especially at the time the United States entered the war. According to historian Kennedy, "it is a matter of some importance that the term was incorporated into the official title of the draft agency. 'Service' was a kind of rhetorical vessel into which were being poured the often contradictory emotional and political impulses of the day. . . . Everywhere Americans agreed that a commitment to 'service' was an attribute of the national soul that the war had quickened." In 1922 Hoover held aloft the torch of "the ideal of service," which he called "a great spiritual force poured out by our people as never before in the history of the world." It took the forms of "service to those with whom we come in contact, service to the nation, and service to the world itself."[6]

When all was said and done, this was the context in which by far most contemporary Americans viewed the ARA, even those who anticipated its indirect commercial benefits: it was a vehicle for serving the peoples of Europe and Russia.

TROTSKY NATURALLY saw it as a vehicle of a different type. "Of course, help to the starving is spontaneous philanthropy," he is quoted as saying in a Soviet publication just prior to the arrival of the ARA, "but there are few real philanthropists—even among the Quakers. Philanthropy is tied to business, to enterprises, to interests—if not today, then tomorrow." Relief workers were like the missionaries of old, preparing the way for the merchants. Nothing about the operations of the ARA in Russia changed his mind. In a subsequent *Pravda* interview he called the Hoover mission a "highly skillful feeler projected by the ruling elements of America into the very depths of Russia."

This interpretation was simply good Leninism, and it came reflexively to Bolshevik officials all down the line. But some relief workers found that in unguarded moments individual Bolsheviks might make appreciative comments about the spirit of the ARA enterprise. Herschel Walker believed that officials in Petrograd understood that the primary motive behind American relief was humanitarian but that politics prevented them from acknowledging this fact openly:

The government appreciation of the ARA work is very difficult to describe; it is undoubtedly true that should one have a personal talk with a government official in an intimate manner, the official would undoubtedly express his true mind and say that the ARA is doing a great deal of good and saving many children that would otherwise have died of starvation. However, the minute he thinks of his government or the present ruling party, his attitude towards the ARA changes and he says that the bringing in of food is only a cloak to hide other desires, either commercial or political, and that the amount of food brought in, expressed monetarily, is nothing for so rich a country as the United States, etc.

The pro- and anti-ARA sentiments Walker lays out here are not mutually exclusive, but his point is clear.

Somerville saw the middle- and lower-level Bolsheviks as true-believers, for whom there could only be one reason that any capitalist country would mount a famine relief effort:

Taught as an A-B-C principle that all human conduct is guided purely by motives of self interest, how can the good Communistic Soviet government official be expected to think that such a thing as a relief organization animated by philanthropic motives is possible—the more so when that organization is from the most capitalistic of all states, and headed by a man who has been the kind of capitalist they most dislike and fear—through his having proved in practice that Capitalism is not incompatible with a square deal.

Undoubtedly the ARA had come to Russia as a "commercial-diplomatic organization hiding its true colors under the banner of relief, but with a long-distance eye on the gold-bearing concessions with which every loyal Soviet adherent fondly imagines that Russia teems, and toward which he pictures in his mind's eye the capitalists of all the world to be rushing in feverish haste."

Barringer too was amused by the cocksureness of the ordinary Bolshevik that the outside world was drunk with dreams of Russia's natural treasures:

[T]he Bolsheviks, having read in geographies of the world for years about the vast resources and unlimited wealth of their country, will think the world is wild to exploit their country and will make any concessions of principle in time to any offer of recognition for concessions. It's hard for a Bolo official to realize that our relief work was in the interest of suffering humanity and not a clever Yankee scheme for coming into a ripe Russian field some day on a "grand scale". Having nothing except control they talk in the language of a dictator instead of that of a bankrupt.[7]

And when a Bolshevik challenged the honor of the ARA in the crudely mechanistic terms of his ideology, the true-believer relief worker was likely to offer an all-out defense of the ARA's humanitarianism, which in turn might inspire that Bolo to a more forceful insistence that he could detect the face of mammon behind the mask of humanitarianism.

It is odd that such a combustible mix produced only one noticeable explosion: an incident at Sarapol, a canton in the subdistrict of Perm, in the Kazan district. The ARA expanded its operations there quite late—on June 14, 1922, to be precise, when Ralph Pearson arrived, accompanying the first boatload of ARA food and medical supplies. That evening there was a "mass meeting" of some three hundred people in the Palace of Labor, at which Pearson got up and explained that the food would be sufficient to supply eighteen thousand children and hospital patients with one daily ration for one month. He also told them that this shipment would be followed by a cargo of corn rations for the same number of adults, and that they could depend on the ARA to feed thirty-six thousand people altogether until at least September 1.

Pearson's words were met with warm applause: for the residents of Sarapol this was good news, indeed. Walter Davenport, the ARA physician, had made the journey with Pearson. He turned over to the local famine committee enough tetravaccine to inoculate thirty thousand people, several barrels of cod liver oil to help combat scurvy, as well as thermometers, rubber goods, blankets, soap, hypodermic syringes, and other medical items.

The mass meeting was going along just fine until the secretary of the local trade union, one Yakunin, stood up to deliver a speech. Precisely what Comrade Yakunin said was later the subject of some dispute, but it is certain that he did not have kind words for the ARA. Pearson and Davenport could not understand Russian, which explains why Pearson later confessed that the two of them had "failed to catch the drift of the discourse." But they could tell from Yakunin's manner that it was an "impassioned speech."

They learned afterward from their interpreter that Yakunin had minimized the contribution of the ARA, stating that America was such a rich country that it was no sacrifice for it to feed so many. He was also reported to have said that the present American government wanted nothing to do with the Soviet government, and that it had been the only one of the great powers to stay away from the recent Genoa Conference. In this last particular he could not be disputed. The absence of the U.S. government from Genoa set back Soviet hopes for a breakthrough at the conference in the form of trade agreements and official recognition, and this provoked a wave of condemnation from the Moscow Bolsheviks directed primarily at the U.S. State Department.

As was the standard practice, instructions went out from Moscow down the chain to the officials in the provinces, even those of minor stature like Yakunin, to generate an equal amount of outrage among the people, even those in relatively remote places like Sarapol. It is easy to imagine that Yakunin's audience was annoyed that he had chosen this occasion to work himself into such a lather over a failed diplomatic conference in a faraway land—"When do we eat?" was the burning question of the Sarapol masses—but everyone recognized the cue to applaud wildly. Yakunin then reminded the gathering that there was reason for hope, that the day was coming when the American proletariat would overthrow its government and extend its hand to the Russian proletariat.

Thus far Yakunin had served up nothing more than familiar anticapitalist propaganda and had avoided specific reference to the ARA. In view of the circumstances, it still does not speak well of his sense of tact, but after five years of practicing such demagoguery, it had become second nature to him. Having gotten started, however, he was unable to contain himself as he turned his sights on the two Americans at his side. Pearson paraphrased his interpreter's rendition of what came out next: "I am not, he said, going to characterize the representatives of the American people who came to feed Sarapol. By looking at them anyone could say whom they represent. We know that they are not so much interested in relief as in Russian gold mines. We know that they will try to knock out all the gold they can."

The ARA was fighting the famine in Russia only because America's workers had demanded it, so that if anyone deserved thanks it was the heroic American proletariat. Pearson and Davenport listened to this flurry of Russian syllables, which was met by a "burst of applause."

When the meeting ended and the two Americans were made aware of what had transpired, Pearson requested and received from the chairman of the Sarapol soviet a "protocol" deprecating Yakunin's remarks. The affair might have ended there except that word of it reached Kazan, where Childs felt that Yakunin's attack could not be allowed to go unchallenged. It was one thing to speak in vague Marxist generalities; it was quite another to impugn the motives of the ARA and of individual ARA men. Childs protested to Comrade Muskatt, calling Yakunin's speech a "direct insult to a representative of the American Relief Administration in the charge—not a mere imputation—that the chief interest of the Americans in this district is one of gold rather than relief."

What especially disturbed Childs was the report that Yakunin's "defamations of our character" had been "generously applauded." To make matters worse, they had been published in the local newspaper. No, this could not be allowed to stand. The apology Pearson had received from the Sarapol soviet, wrote Childs, was "too private for so public an insult." He informed Muskat that he was sending documentation on the affair to Moscow.

In his reply to Childs, Muskat tried to finesse the problem, arguing that "a few cheers on the part of a small audience" could hardly be said to represent Russian public opinion. The real voice of the people in Russia was the local soviets, and the fact that the chairman of the Sarapol soviet had signed a protocol repudiating Yakunin's speech should lay the issue to rest. As he continued, he contradicted himself, expressing regret that the mass meeting had taken place out in a remote region where the fine work of the ARA was so little known. "Much to our regret I must add that it often happens that our public, especially in the provinces, judges the speaker's abilities more by his dialectical and oratorical effects than by the ideas expressed in his speech." If Childs were to investigate this "vexatious incident," he would find that it was nothing but a "pure misunderstanding."

Whatever it was, it struck Haskell as serious enough to advise Childs to suspend ARA feeding in Sarapol until Yakunin was recalled to Moscow. Haskell complained to Lander that this was not the deed of some private individual but a trade union official. In order to show good faith, Haskell thought, the press in Sarapol should denounce the speech and Yakunin should be punished.

The Sarapol incident was a microcosm of the U.S.-Soviet dispute over Bolshevik propaganda. Since the Revolution, official Washington had been concerned, at times obsessed, with the subject of propaganda, and Hughes's State Department was no exception. Moscow was taken at its word that it was seeking the overthrow of all "capitalist" governments, even though since 1921 and NEP's search for respectability, Soviet officials were quietly advising U.S. and ARA officials not to take such talk seriously. It was only for domestic consumption, meant to appease the Party's die-hards.

One of them was the unfortunate Comrade Yakunin, who now issued a statement explaining his behavior. It began with the predictable claim that his words had been mistranslated: in fact he had not referred to the ARA, the aim of which is of course the salvation of the starving, but to the United States government. As for that zinger about the gold mines, "I must say that every capitalistic Government is interested in the increasing of its riches, therefore I simply meant all the Bourgeois Governments and not only the American." Regarding his prediction about the American proletariat overthrowing its bourgeois government, Yakunin admitted saying it but explained that he meant only that, generally speaking, the reign of capitalism was inevitably giving way to that of socialism. Nothing personal, you understand, just the laws of history. Surely, he finished on a note of exasperation, a person was allowed to express his personal opinions on his own territory.

In the end, Yakunin had to be sacrificed. He was sent to Moscow for "disciplining," and the local famine committee drew up a statement condemning his behavior, which the local *Red Kama Valley* published, watering down its effect by printing supportive supplementary material including an editorial that criticized the ARA for threatening to shut down the feeding. The editors were protective of their fallen comrade: Comrade Yakunin, the great champion of the working class, while he realized the importance of the ARA, had not felt it necessary to conceal his attitude toward the "remainder of the American bourgeoisie."[8]

The trouble was that the Bolsheviks were trying to learn to coexist with capitalists at this time, both their own and those in the West—temporarily, of course, until that glorious day when they could safely be deposited in the dustbin of history. But it was hard to suspend the old propaganda habits. The qualities that had made Yakunin a good revolutionary did not serve him well as a government official—a statement that says much about Bolshevism in general at this time.

CHAPTER 38

STEALING THE THUNDER

The Sarapol incident stands out only because Yakunin was so indelicate as to stand up before a public audience and abuse the ARA in the presence of its representatives. There were many second-hand reports of officials belittling the American mission out of earshot of the relief workers, as when the Kiev Americans were told that the president of the Union of Medical Workers had made the following statement: "Where there is fire dirty water is good enough to extinguish it. The A.R.A. relief is for us as dirty water is for the fire."

Harold Buckley reported from Orsk that "There is not an atom of doubt that the G[overnment] R[epresentative] got up before a gathering of six or seven hundred parents of children [fed by the ARA] and said that there was no reason to thank the American people"—in other words, that the Soviet government deserved the thanks. Buckley spoke to many witnesses, but none was willing to confirm the incident in writing, and an interview with the G.R. elicited only denials. So Buckley could not justify closing the ARA's kitchens, but he did halt the distribution of supplies for ten days in order to send a message.

Typically the alleged offenders sought to discount the importance of the American relief effort and to disclaim the professed altruism behind it, much as Yakunin had done. Some insisted that the ARA mission had come about as a result of pressure applied to the U.S. government by the American proletariat out of its concern for the starving workers and peasants of Russia. Others claimed that the U.S. government was sending food to Russia because its inability to dispose of its surplus crops had caused economic discontent, which some interpreted as a sign of an imminent American revolution.

The Saratov Americans reported that government officials carried on a "steady and pernicious propaganda" to the effect that the ARA had been sent by the American working class. In fact this line was not entirely insincere. Prominent Bolsheviks of course knew better, but those of a lower order, who had never been abroad and had been introduced to Marxism by the Leninists in power, would have been inclined to accept the propaganda of the Bolo high priests about the fierceness of the class struggle in that distant land.

Charlie Veil, working the subdistricts of Saratov, felt that the rank-and-file Bolsheviks he encountered genuinely believed that the American proletariat was behind the ARA. In Novouzensk he found the local population was divided over the question. Local officials and their supporters maintained that the ARA food was the gift of American Communists, while those opposed to Soviet power were certain that it came from America's "capitalists." Veil, noting that both beliefs were based upon "sincere ignorance," preached the word that the ARA food was in fact from the American people.

It is not hard to imagine how ordinary Russians, and not only those sympathetic to the Bolsheviks, might presume a role for the American proletariat. It made it easier to grasp why the Americans had come to the rescue of the Soviet government, which many understood to be an important consequence of relief to Russia. Who else in America but the laboring classes would want to bail out the Bolsheviks?

The story is told of some bewildered Russian workers finally hitting upon the meaning of the initials "ARA," in Russian, as "American Workers Association." Another had it that in Kiev, when the first relief shipment arrived at a freight station accompanied by a document in Russian referring to "A.R.A." supplies, the handlers scratched their heads: A.R.A.? What on earth could this stand for? Someone's best guess was *Arestansko-rabochaia assotsiatsiia*, Prisoners-Workers Association. So they shrugged their shoulders and proceeded to requisition it.

An April 1922 article in *Izvestiia* referred to the American corn pouring into the villages as a gift of the American farmer. When this issue reached Coleman out on the steppe in Orenburg, he had already become quite touchy on the question of giving the ARA proper credit, the result of his ongoing struggle with his Bolo nemesis, Comrade Klimov. The *Izvestiia* item prompted him to shoot off a letter to Moscow headquarters on the subject. In a technical sense, he wrote, the *Izvestiia* interpretation was defensible, because some of the sacks of ARA corn bore the inscription "Gift of the American Farmers"; but clearly the authorities were playing on people's ignorance and attempting to associate American relief in the popular mind with America's toiling masses, led by the proletariat.

In Orenburg he came upon a poster consisting of a series of six drawings depicting Uncle Sam arriving in Russia and bringing food to "well-dressed, corpulent bourgeoisie and speculators," while peasants starved. This was posted in the window of the library on the city's main street. Further inspection revealed that it had been lithographed in Moscow, which is odd as there are no other references to such a poster by any Americans in Moscow or anywhere else in Russia. Coleman says he tried to swipe it but was unsuccessful.

Later, when he was reassigned to Elizavetgrad in Ukraine, he found the place to be a hotbed of rumors "methodically circulated" by the authorities, most to the effect the ARA was an organization of commercial spies sent to Soviet Russia in the guise of relief workers to locate mines, oil wells, and so on. One decidedly un-Marxist interpretation was that the American government, having come into the largest share of "Denikin's loot," was conscience stricken and by means of food relief was trying to relieve its guilt for having supporting the White Army campaigns, which had brought on the famine.[1]

COLEMAN'S DARKEST SUSPICIONS notwithstanding, the Bolsheviks were not the source of every outlandish rumor about the ARA. Popular imagination did well enough on its own. Besides, a charge of Bolshevik disinformation was usually impossible to prove. It was much easier to make the case that the Soviet authorities had failed to take action to enlighten the public about the purpose of the ARA. For this there was a ready instrument at hand in the form of paragraph 21 of the Riga Agreement, which obligated the Soviet authorities to "acquaint the Russian people with the aims and methods of the relief work of the A.R.A. in order to facilitate the rapid development of its efficiency." Efficiency aside, the idea was to make sure that the word got out that this lifesaving food was coming from America.

Naturally the Soviet authorities had little incentive to publicize the fact that their so-called class enemies had answered their call for help. Clapp wrote in his diary, "it is a dose of Castor Oil for the Communists when they are called upon to openly admit they have made a bad mess of affairs." But the ARA was simply too big to ignore. The central and local press did occasionally print articles accurately depicting the extent of the relief and expressing gratefulness for it, although in the Moscow papers the high-profile items were often intended to promote the establishment of official U.S.-Soviet relations. Otherwise what made it into print contained a great deal of distortion, seldom of the subtle variety.

In Moscow there was an effort to create the impression that the Soviet authorities were playing a leading role in the ARA mission: the important thing was to maintain the image of undiminished authority at the center. Hoover's July 1921 telegraphed replies to Gorky's appeals for help were published in a way that made the Bolsheviks appear to be their recipient.

When Moscow headquarters received a telegram from Hoover on December 29 informing it about the passage of the $20 million congressional appropriation, Eiduk was very keen to get a copy of this telegram and one was provided. On the following day its text appeared in *Izvestiia*, presented as a message from Herbert Hoover to Eiduk: "Comrade A. Eiduk has received a telegram, in which Hoover (the head of the ARA) informs . . . " Why Eiduk? When asked about it, the chief plenipotentiary said it was a mistake. Golder wrote, "The impression they are trying to give is that the Soviet is running the ARA."

The next night, New Year's Eve, Golder was in Petrograd and attended a local soviet celebration at the opera house. Zinoviev gave a speech in which he pointed out that the congressional appropriation had been passed while the Congress of Soviets in Moscow was in session, "intimating that our Congress planned it as a Sovet greeting for the occasion and the offer was accepted."

He then went on to say that the year 1921 will be memorable in history because in that year in capitalistic countries grain was being burned as fuel (Sovet papers had it announced some time ago that in the U.S. the farmers were using grain as fuel) while millions of the Russian proletariat are dying of hunger. It is the crumbs that the bourgeois give to the proletariat. There was not a word of gratitude and appreciation, nothing to show that we did it out of purely human kindness, nothing like that. No matter what we do we are nothing more than capitalists who are trying to crush the life out of the proletariat.

So the example was set by the leading Bolsheviks and followed down the line, although after four years most Party members behaved this way instinctively. The Soviet effort to take the credit entered a new phase in summer 1922, when the ARA's popularity with the Russians was at its height but after the delivery of the corn had deprived the Americans of their greatest instrument of leverage with the government.

The Odessa Americans found that the local government at first was eager to have them fight the famine but that after a while "The officials felt that the A.R.A. was getting too popular, and that it was hurting them politically." In Ufa, where the ARA had an exemplary record of government relations, Bell complained of "the constant effort of the ones in control of affairs here to discredit and belittle the general operation," although he admitted that the Ufa Americans had not had to put up with so much of this "propaganda," probably, he guessed, due to its remoteness from the "Center."[2]

Coleman would have taken issue with this last point: Orenburg was as far from Moscow as was Ufa, yet it was the scene of a continual struggle between the ARA and the authorities to take the credit for American relief. Being an aggressive-minded engineer, Coleman was eager to go beyond straightforward famine relief and take the lead in initiating a number of reconstruction projects. As the spring 1922 thaw set in and the melting snows began to disclose the dozens of human corpses and the carcasses of cattle, cats, and dogs that had been buried during the winter, he proposed a citywide cleanup operation, which included purifying the water supply by reconstructing a filtration plant at the city's main pumping station. He used the ARA's chloride of lime to clean the sewage pipes. He claims also to have had fifty thousand trees planted in the city. And he had other ideas in mind, such as constructing a brick factory, building bridges, repairing roads, and improving irrigation. But his enthusiasm for these projects was sapped by the behavior of Orenburg officials. "I have been stumped by the government at every move. They do not want the ARA to have a look in. The great scheme is to get the thunder. It is not good practice to tell them of any anticipated move for they will take the idea and work it out in a blundering way themselves."

The worst villains were the government representatives sent from Moscow. "They all not only interfered but obstructed both actively and passively. Their instructions are to give the ARA credit for nothing and divert the thunder to the Royal Holy Soviet Government. They have attempted to do this but I think they did not accomplish great success."

Coleman was frustrated that the local newspapers would not publish even purely statistical information about the ARA's work in Orenburg: "I have tried to get honest publicity as to the number I have fed and all that but nothing doing unless it is framed up in their style." This was a common complaint in the districts, where the Americans assumed that the silence was imposed by the center. The Orenburg Americans, though, believed that their own Comrade Klimov was an exceptionally strict enforcer. Buckley related that Klimov's agent in the subdistrict of Orsk "frankly admitted" that he was, in Buckley's words, "forbidden to allow the A.R.A. any but the most ordinary publicity." Buckley observed in August 1922:

The attitude of the people generally is one of bewildered thanks. This does not include the government officials. They are just bewildered, but have no thanks and look upon all our actions with suspicion. The local press has been quiet because it was told to be so, although I believe that had they been left to follow their own inclinations they would have been very friendly to us in so far as Orsk is concerned.

Coleman's running indictment of Klimov's inhibitive influence included an anecdote whose point is clear, even though with Coleman fact was usually dressed up in imaginative sarcasm. After a brief inspection tour of the district, Haskell's chief of staff, Tom Lonergan, departed Orenburg for Samara, a journey which at the time could be long and unpleasant. All went smoothly, however, and upon his arrival Lonergan wired Coleman, asking him to thank the railroad officials for their promptness and courtesy, which Coleman did by letter. The chief of the Tashkent Railway line, as Coleman tells the story, forwarded his missive to the "traction division" with this notation: "Accept these thanks and communicate them to the participant agents." The Traction Division passed the letter on to the "Exploitation Division" with a notation: "Expressing hopes that in the future the Exploitation Division will show the same zeal and conscientiousness in the fulfillment of its official duties." It then came to the attention of the railway newspaper, which published it—on the last page, "just to fill the space," as Coleman put it. As soon as this issue appeared, "the Editor of the newspaper was placed on the rack for giving publicity to the A.R.A., and was immediately dismissed."

Coleman decided to take matters into his own hands. Outside headquarters he posted a homemade bulletin board showing a breakdown of ARA feeding by subdistrict, which was regularly updated. He was pleased to report that "During the first few days after these were posted up they were almost as much stared at as the baseball bulletins in the United States." As well, he had a stamp made up with the message "A.R.A. FREE" in Russian, and this was used on all kinds of ARA paperwork and packaging. The stamp idea was employed also in Saratov. In Tsaritsyn and Simbirsk the ARA distributed signs with the Russian equivalent of "Free Gift of the American People."[3]

In Moscow Haskell initiated his own ARA propaganda campaign, which he recalled with obvious satisfaction several years later. He held a competition among Moscow artists for the best poster design. The winning entry depicts an enormous American cargo ship approaching a wharf on which is congregated a crowd of ragged, starving refugees—unmistakably Russian in appearance—some with hands outstretched in supplication toward the ship. The primary colors are red, white, and blue, with a row of ears of corn as a bottom border. The Russian text reads: "America to the Starving People of Russia."

More striking is another ARA poster, perhaps the runner-up in the contest. It shows Dame Columbia, draped in the American flag, doling out porridge to four small Russian peasant children in a tiny village. The Russian text reads "Gift of the American People"; some copies identify, in both Russian and English, Herbert Hoover as ARA chairman. Its stark simplicity and maternal imagery made it a more effective messenger than its rival, proof of which is evident even today: examining archival photographs of ARA kitchens, where the display of one or both of these posters was added to the regulations, the eye automatically locks on to the figure of Columbia.

Copies of the winning poster were lithographed in the hundreds of thousands and pasted onto both doors of every freight car leaving the ports. Aside from providing free publicity, this was also supposed to give these cars preference along the railway lines. When a train of these cars was thus outfitted, it must have attracted attention. It was not a spectacle many had the chance to witness. Most of the posters were torn down very soon after leaving port. Haskell blames the authorities for this, accusing them of having the offensive ornaments removed at the first railroad junction. When the ARA learned of this practice, he says, it distributed more posters to all junction points along the line.

Ellingston wrote of the copies posted in Moscow that "Very few of them enjoyed more than a day or two of glory." Some were taken as souvenirs, some to be used as cigarette paper, and others just out of the "general spirit of destruction."

In Saratov, Clapp—of the castor oil analogy—said that the Bolos found them "distasteful." He reported that during the seventy-two continuous days he was lodged in a railway car they were torn down almost every night, so "irked" were officials at the sight of them.

In the end, though, the surest publicity was the ARA food itself. As Kelley said, "There was no disguising white flour, condensed milk and cocoa."[4]

ONE OF THE WAYS that the Soviet press was able to obscure the importance of the ARA was to publish its feeding figures as part of the aggregate total of all foreign relief organizations, thereby putting the ARA on an equal footing with the British Quakers, the International Red Cross, the International Workers Relief, and so on. Alongside such an item there might appear a feature article about the relief work of the Soviet government.

Even more notorious with the Americans was the Soviet practice of giving the ARA second billing to the epic figure of Fridtjof Nansen, the great Norwegian scientist, arctic explorer, and humanitarian, who led the relief mission of the League of Nations. The story of this mission is instructive.

Nansen's achievements as a scientist and explorer are a matter of record; opinion of his humanitarian accomplishments, however, is mixed. His first major undertaking began in April 1920, when the League appointed him high commissioner for the repatriation from Russia of about 425,000 mostly German and Austrian prisoners of war. Reports as to his own abilities and personal input while serving in this position are not universally favorable, but his prestige and reputation for fair-mindedness attracted world attention and support to his effort, which contributed to its decided success. Subsequently, in August 1921, he became the League's high commissioner for Russian refugees abroad and in 1922 was assigned responsibility for the relocation of Greek and Turkish refugees.

Nansen's association with food relief dated back to the Paris Peace Conference in 1919, when his name, together with Hoover's, was associated with an unrealized Allied proposal for feeding in Soviet Russia. In August 1921, at a conference in Geneva of national relief associations, he was named high commissioner of the International Committee for Russian Relief. After the ARA signed its Riga Agreement, the way was clear for Nansen, in the name of the League, to negotiate his own contract with the Soviet government, which was finalized on August 27. The so-called Nansen mission, then, represented various governments and various political and humanitarian organizations, including the national Red Cross societies.

The Nansen agreement is a peculiar document, which appears even more so when compared with the arrangement worked out by the ARA one week earlier. It left ultimate control over its relief supplies in the hands of the Soviet government with no stipulation that this food not be distributed to the Red Army or government employees. The most curious clause in the agreement obligated Nansen to act as an intermediary between the Soviet and European governments in order to secure for Russia a food loan in the amount of ten million pounds, repayable in ten years at an annual interest of 6 percent. In view of the fact that these same European governments were still indignant over the Bolshevik refusal to repay them their loans to pre-Revolutionary Russia, and that this was the principal obstacle standing in the way of a normalization of relations between Russia and the West, it was a bizarre proposition indeed. Now here was someone the Bolsheviks could do business with.

Needless to say, the loan was never secured. When this part of his agreement was made public, subscriptions to Nansen's mission virtually dried up. Even Nansen's friends considered it unacceptable. The U.S. trade commissioner in London wrote in November 1921 that the food loan idea had "caused great surprise to those who had sent out Nansen." The commissioner found this a suitable occasion to register his disapproval of Nansen, who, he wrote, "does not convey the impression of a big man with a brilliant mind." Rather, "He is a man in 'blinkers.' Thanks to these 'blinkers' Nansen obstinately refuses to see the horror and the business impracticability of the Bolshevist experiment in Russia. In spite of his age and apparent fatigue he is not devoid of ambition which all the more weakens his ability to discriminate in his surroundings."

And as for Nansen's much-acclaimed work with Russian POWs, his personal role in the matter was said to be insignificant, others covering for him because he "exhibited no talent either for organization or for administration." What is more, the people around him—who included one Captain Vidkun Quisling—were of questionable integrity. Nansen was no quisling *avant la lettre*, but the Bolsheviks found him to be a useful propaganda tool in their dealings with the West and in particular with the ARA. And of course they readily accepted whatever famine relief he had to offer, though its actual amount did not come close to matching the fanfare that surrounded it, for which they were in large part responsible. The commissioner called the Nansen mission a "pure advertising campaign."

The feeling in Russia that Nansen was in the Soviet pocket gathered force over time and was not exclusive to ARA circles. An American Quaker observed in October 1922 that Nansen was "not in as good favor with the other Relief Organizations as he has been. It seems that he has been playing with the Soviet officials rather more than some of them thought was wise, and so they have sort of withdrawn their support from him."[5]

It is no wonder then that Nansen turned out to be the darling of the Soviet press. This was not simply because he had signed such a generous agreement but also because he led a mission sponsored by no single country, which made it a more acceptable object of gratitude. Nansen himself was an internationalist, to the Bolsheviks the only tolerable form of non-Communist. On top of this, he had long been a well-known figure among educated Russians—he was since 1898 an honorary member of the Russian Academy of Sciences—a fact that lent a measure of authenticity to his enthusiastic treatment in the Soviet press, where the Nansen mission towered over that of the ARA.

In the end, Nansen's contribution to Russian relief added up to a few million dollars. The ARA men stationed in those places where his mission was operating testified to its failure to live up to its ambitious promises, succumbing to "anemia of products"—with the notable exception of Samara, where the Americans worked effectively in a joint effort with his team of Swedish relief workers. Haskell had Nansen in mind when he wrote to Brown in London on December 14, 1921: "It is perfectly apparent that as usual all the relief other than American being done is so thoroughly deluted [*sic*] with hot air that it is fairly thin."

Haskell was writing during the first of Nansen's two extended tours of Russia—the second came in January 1923—which were made the object of great official fuss. He reports that Nansen's first visit to the famine zone, in early December 1921, was marked by a public celebration in Samara, where he was "received with brass bands and a great demonstration, made many speeches during the day and was given a banquet. I don't know how much Nansen is actually accomplishing but he certainly is popular in Russia and they expect great things of him. I cannot give him very much for permitting them to banquet him in a starving community like Samara."

Word of the festivity reached Ufa, where Davenport paused to consider the significance of Nansen's clamorous reception on the Volga: "brass band, automobile parade, public banquet, speeches, etc. with our cars hauling Bolo officials, thunderous applause and much acclaim for Nansen who, so far as I know, has done nothing but make speeches. It's rather tragic to think—no brass bands for the ARA."

Farmer Murphy was an eyewitness to this first act of the "booming of Nansen." He was in the audience one evening at the Bolshoi Theater waiting for the performance to begin, when someone rose and pointed to Nansen in the tsar's box in the rear. The audience began to clap, and Nansen stood and acknowledged the applause, which went on for a minute or two. Murphy felt that the moment had been prearranged, although he did acknowledge that Nansen was a recognized figure and would have been cheered anyway. Alongside Nansen sat Eiduk. Haskell looked on from a box near the stage, unapplauded.

Murphy says that shortly after the start of the ARA mission *Pravda* published an article that stated that the Americans had not accomplished much and that the more valuable work was being done by Nansen's relief. In his capacity as an ARA publicity man, Murphy went about inquiring of Bolshevik officials how such a statement got into print: "the best opinion I could get was that it was only a stupidity."

Near the end of December Nansen was paid tribute by the All-Russian Congress of Soviets and made an honorary member of the Moscow soviet. These events were given full play in the newspapers at the same time that the ARA was virtually ignored—this on the eve of the vote in the U.S. Congress to appropriate $20 million to Russian relief. Golder could barely contain his frustration:

In some corner of the papers something was said about a vote of thanks to us. Yet Nansen does hardly anything and the ARA does very much. Of course Nansen works through the Sovet and we do not. . . . I dare say that nowhere in Europe have our people suffered so many humiliations and have been appreciated so little as here. Were it not for the fact that all realize that the honor of the ARA and of Hoover are mixed up with this work many of our men would not remain here.

Nansen rose from the banquet table and departed Russia, and things quieted down. At least they did until March 12, 1922, when Trotsky addressed a gathering of the Moscow soviet. Mitchell passed on to London the gist of a key moment of the speech as it was interpreted for him. Trotsky is reported to have declared: "We are grateful to the ARA who have done and are doing twenty times as much for the famine as is anyone else, but we are even more grateful to Nansen, and why is this? It is because Nansen expects to gain out of Russia—nothing! But we do not know what the ARA wants to make out of Russia."

To judge from a transcript of the speech published in the 1990s, Trotsky expressed his ambivalence toward the generosity of "the Great Republic Across the Ocean" rather more reflectively, but to Gov. Goodrich, who was seated in the audience as Trotsky spoke, the speech was "an insult to every decent American." Golder, who heard about it from Goodrich, felt the same way:

For some reason or other it seems to be the official policy of the government to pull the feathers out of the American eagle, perhaps in the hopes of making him say something. The ARA is praised by one man while the other questions and suspects its motives. Whenever a good word is said for the ARA the name of Nansen is mentioned alongside and the ARA looks cheap. The ARA is doing good work nevertheless and will manage the hunger and keep it down.

Two weeks later something provoked Golder to throw up his hands again over "the insinuations that the welfare work which the ARA is doing is prompted by selfish motives, the praise which is everlastingly showered on Nansen, who does hardly anything, and the damned praise which the ARA receives."

Nansen's January 1923 visit to Russia prompted another wave of official celebrations and further grumbling within the ARA. It seemed to the Americans at Moscow headquarters that this time the Soviets were going to great lengths to rub it in. Golder protested to Karl Radek the "invidious comparisons" being drawn between Nansen and the ARA, which he said were a direct insult to the American relief workers.[6]

It is not that the ARA men disliked Nansen personally. As an individual he was, according to all who encountered him in Russia, an impressive figure. At sixty, he had a striking physical appearance—tall and rugged, with white hair and a thick, flowing grey moustache, his broad-brimmed hat worn angled to the right. This and his extraordinary personal charisma complete the contrast with Hoover, this time to Nansen's advantage. Mackenzie saw him as one of those men who conveys a "dominating impression of strength, courage and sincerity immediately [when] one meets them."

Quinn wrote, "We don't think much of his organization but we do like Mr. Nansen personally." Even Haskell called him "a very attractive personality," though no one was more upset by all of the attention paid to Nansen than the neglected man seated in the theater box. After surviving the second Nansen wave, he wrote to Herter in Washington that the Soviets had overplayed the Nansen card:

It is a funny thing that at the banquet they gave for Nansen just before my arrival, no representative of the A. R. A. was invited, but they had the nerve to send to the A. R. A. to borrow some forty or fifty chairs marked "A. R. A." on the back to seat the guests, and asked Quinn if he could loan them several motor cars to transport their principal guests to the feast. Of course, we have maintained an absolutely indifferent attitude throughout the matter and even granted their requests.

Despite the tone of imperturbability, the matter had definitely gotten under the colonel's skin. One week later he reminded Brown that "the Nansen Mission is doing practically nothing at all" and called it the "Nansen Promissary Relief Operation."

Several years later, Haskell had still not put it behind him. In his memoir he criticized the European governments and press, and also H. G. Wells and his *Outline of History* for ignoring the ARA and making Nansen the hero of Russian relief. Haskell conceded that Nansen was merely a figurehead and not the instigator of "this grand misrepresentation"; still, "What Nansen did not know about the first principles of a relief operation was appalling, notwithstanding his great scientific achievements and his reputation as a great explorer."[7]

Yet it was his humanitarian relief activities that brought Nansen the 1922 Nobel Peace Prize.

CHAPTER 39

MAD MONKS AND HOLY FOOLS

Among the contradictory rumors swirling around the ARA, the one that best served the immediate political purposes of the Bolsheviks—and one they certainly made no effort to discredit—alleged that the Soviet government was impelled to requisition the treasures of the Russian Orthodox Church by the need to pay for American famine relief.

It might seem surprising that the Bolsheviks were getting around to acting against the Church only now, more than four years after the Revolution. The Orthodox Church had been an obvious target for Soviet government repression since 1917. Marxism condemned religion as the "opium of the people," and Russian revolutionaries had long portrayed Orthodoxy as the handmaiden of tsarist autocracy. Yet once in power, Lenin's government did not attempt to make a clean sweep of the Church. Although many monasteries and convents near the major urban centers were seized, most in rural areas were left undisturbed—though this can be explained by the fact that Soviet power had not as yet penetrated the countryside.

During the Civil War there was much looting of churches, yet there was no centrally directed government action to expropriate the Church's gold, silver, and diamonds. And for good reason: Bolshevik food requisitions were doing enough to antagonize the peasants, and with a civil war underway, it made no sense to risk further alienating the countryside through an all-out offensive against the Church. So from 1918 to 1922 the Bolsheviks attacked Russian Orthodoxy chiefly by means of propaganda, which came in waves of varying intensities depending on the needs and mood of the moment.

The idea was to destroy the credibility of the Church, and the initial thrust was directed at revealing its mysteries to be a fraud. The most devastating way to accomplish this, it was thought, was to expose the relics of the saints to the people and thereby demonstrate in the most sensational manner that these supposedly sacred remains were fakes. In fact, often when the coffins were opened, those gathered there as witnesses saw with their own eyes that they contained not the perfectly preserved relics of legend but life-sized dolls of papier-maché, fabric, and straw, or simply dust. Word of such revelations spread across the land, though it hardly had the intended effect of shattering the credibility of the Church.

Marguerite Harrison, who was in Moscow in 1920, says that despite the sensationalistic publicity the government gave to such disclosures, the results were marginal because most believers were illiterate peasants who were not able to read all about it. And when word of mouth got the news across, it still had to pass through the peasant's interpretive filter, from which it sometimes emerged in unexpected forms. Not uncommon was the reaction of one peasant cited by Harrison: "our holy saints disappeared to heaven and substituted rags and straw for their relics when they found that their tombs were to be desecrated by nonbelievers. It was a great miracle."

This was a conviction Gorky heard expressed by some of those who had seen firsthand the evidence that the imperishable bodies of the saints were actually dolls or dust. Others believed that the priests had carried out a deception but of an innocent kind: upon learning of the impending desecrations, they removed the holy relics and substituted the fakes. These reactions, Gorky found, were mostly those of older, illiterate peasants.

The younger ones tended to agree with the Bolsheviks that the Church had been engaged in a great and long-standing hoax, and that now, thank God, there was one hoax fewer. But why stop there? Some thought that it would be a good idea to continue the process and expose the humbuggery of doctors and scholars. One warned of the dangers of the coming of electric light. Gorky says that his conversations with peasants convinced him that the desecrations had only served to strengthen the suspicions of the countryside toward the town.

In more general terms, Gorky believed that the Revolution had exposed the religiosity of the Russian peasants as a myth. The shocking manner in which the very relics of their saints were treated did not provoke them to resistance, nor had they put up a fight when the Bolsheviks destroyed monasteries long professed to be sacred. It was as if these holy objects and places all of a sudden had lost their magical powers. On the other hand, these same peasants risked their lives to guard their precious poods of grain from the requisition squads.

Such evidence notwithstanding, the Bolsheviks had reason to temper their repression of the Church until the end of the Civil War. While the core of the retreat to NEP was a painful, even traumatic, and certainly dangerous accommodation with capitalism on the economic "front," the Party felt it had to secure its positions, and even to advance at several points, along the political "front." Thus the transition to NEP was marked by the show trial of the SRs, the exile of political opponents and "bourgeois" specialists, and to ensure a closing of the ranks during the retreat, the ban on factions within the Party.

The Church was arguably the last independent organization in Russia and as such could be portrayed as a potential rallying point for political opposition. Of course it was no such thing, but at a moment when the Bolshevik faith was severely shaken, an attack on the Church was another way to help restore a sense of purpose among the Party faithful, especially the recent recruits who knew only how to struggle against enemies and were utterly confused and demoralized by the abandonment of "communism." So as things stood, it was an ideal time to pick a fight with a thoroughly routed enemy.

Along the way, the Bolsheviks would enlist allies from within the Church, as a group of "progressive" clergy, with official blessing, established an alternative, so-called Living Church, whose name announced the death of the original, but which itself was destined to be short-lived. The founders of the Living Church—also called Renewal but popularly known as the Red Church—declared that

Christianity and socialism were not incompatible. But although politics was at the heart of the matter, the split from the mainstream was presented as the product of a dispute over reforming the Church hierarchy and ritual, and so it had the surface texture of another classic schism in the history of Russian Orthodoxy. Indeed, there seems to have been enough genuine internal disaffection with the status quo to rally a measure of clerical support for the Living Church in 1922, though once Bolshevik interest in the project waned the following year, it died a quick death.[1]

But all of this was merely a sideshow to the main attraction, which was the Bolsheviks' frontal assault on the Church, and it was the famine that provided them with a pretext. On March 19, 1922, Lenin addressed a secret letter to the Politburo ordering that the Cheka be instructed to exploit the famine in order to crush Russian Orthodoxy once and for all, using the confiscation of its assets as the opening wedge.

It is precisely now and only now, when in the starving regions people are eating human flesh, and hundreds if not thousands of corpses are littering the roads, that we can (and therefore must) carry out the confiscation of church valuables with the most savage and merciless energy. . . . We must teach these people a lesson right now, so that they will not dare even to think of any resistance for several decades.

Resistance by the Church establishment to the confiscations was anticipated, even welcomed, because it would provide the opportunity to intensify the repression. The strike began in February 1922 with a decree calling for the removal from the churches of all "objects of value." This document was quite soberly worded; it declared that nothing should be taken that would disrupt the Orthodox service. This meant, for example, that the gold borders of icons could be removed, these having no inherent religious value, while the icons themselves were to be left behind. This was how it looked on paper, but the operation itself was by design a thoroughly intemperate affair. To create the proper atmosphere, young Communists were sent out to organize another round of mock-religious ceremonies and processions and to put up anti-Church posters, these displaying the by now familiar images of priests engaging in drinking bouts with capitalists and Tsar Nicholas—dead but still hauled out for special occasions—and carrying out other unspeakable acts while the peasants starve.

The requisition campaign itself seems to have aroused more popular resistance, especially among urban residents, than had been anticipated. Only a few weeks into the operation, on March 11, Trotsky sent a memo to his fellow Politburo members saying that it had been "extremely muddled up." If so, it may have been due in part to Patriarch Tikhon's appeal to the faithful on February 28, which though apparently not intended to inflame passions—and even conceding to the government all valuables not actually required for religious ceremony—nonetheless could be read as a call for passive resistance. Naturally this is precisely how it was interpreted by the Bolsheviks, who used it as the pretext for Tikhon's arrest.

It is not easy to make a judgment about popular attitudes at this time concerning the Russian Orthodox Church—which is a separate, if not easily separable, matter from that of the strength of the Russians' religiousness. Hullinger believed that the Church was in fact popular and that the Bolsheviks' decision to attack it at that moment was a sign of how secure they themselves were feeling about their own political situation. Most contemporary testimony agreed that church attendance since 1917 had remained high or had even risen, but church-going is not in itself a measure of loyalty to a church establishment. Worshippers too were heard to complain about the traditional corruption in the Church and its well-known failure to stand up to the autocracy. Some of the faithful felt that the Church's treasures should indeed be used to raise money for famine relief, but few seemed to think it was a good idea to entrust this task to the Bolsheviks.

Nor is it a simple matter to estimate the amount of actual physical resistance to the confiscations. There were incidences of violence in the cities and towns, notably in Moscow and Petrograd. In places people surrounded churches and re-fused to let the commissars in; it happened that soldiers fired into crowds, killing and wounding; here and there soldiers and commissars were killed. In Smolensk there was a stand-off as thousands of people defended the cathedral and the sol-diers refused to fire on them. The Soviet newspapers gave publicity to such inci-dents, framing them as evidence of the treachery of Church officials, who were inciting people to violence.

Reading such reports and listening to the eyewitness accounts of friends and acquaintances, Golder concluded that the government had "raised a hornets' nest about its ears." Heard amidst the buzz were the inevitable comments about Bol-shevik Jews trying to smother the Russians' religion. In a village outside Moscow Golder inquired of an old peasant to which Church, Orthodox or Living, his vil-lage was loyal, and received the reply: "They tried to get us to accept the New Church, but we told them that if the Jews wanted a new Church we would not raise any objections, but as for us we did not want a new Church and did not want a new God, and they have left us alone."

Mackenzie witnessed a crowd outside a Moscow church attempt to deter a requisition squad with stones. Evidently epithets were hurled as well: "Make no doubt on one point. The taking of the Church treasures has enormously deep-ened the hatred entertained by large masses against the Jews. . . . One of the first things that would happen in many parts of Russia were the Soviet Government to lose its power would be a massacre of Jews on a scale that would make all pre-vious pogroms look insignificant."

Standing outside a Moscow church as its riches were removed, Farmer Murphy heard voices in the crowd shout "thieves" and "dirty Jews." He tells how his house-keeper came to him trembling and in tears over the requisitions at the church on their very street. She told him that earlier in the day at the service, the priest had denounced the government and had dared the authorities to touch him. She was certain that he would be arrested and shot.

Duranty, who did some of his best reporting on this story, asserted that the Bolsheviks were on the whole surprised by how little popular resistance they met. This, he believed, encouraged them to proceed in 1922–23 with the public trials of clergy accused of inspiring public opposition to the campaign, which led to the executions of several Moscow and Petrograd priests, including Archbishop Ben-jamin and the Metropolitan of Petrograd. The trial of Tikhon was several times postponed, and he was released in June 1923 after confessing his guilt and vowing his loyalty to the Soviet government. The Russian Orthodox Church was still alive, but it was a living corpse.[2]

ALTHOUGH IT HOPED to steer clear of involvement in Soviet domestic politics, the ARA was unable to insulate itself from these developments. Because the church treasures were being expropriated ostensibly in order to pay for famine relief, and because the ARA led by far the largest foreign relief effort, it was probably inevitable that a connection would be drawn in the popular, especially peasant, mind between the requisitions and American relief. For the most part this occurred spontaneously, but where assistance was needed, the Bolsheviks were ready to connect the dots.

From the very outset the American relief workers were made aware of Soviet sensitivity to the Church question, which they could judge by the hostility of the authorities to their selection of priests to sit on the ARA food committees. This was a routine procedure in earlier missions. The priest, like the local doctor, was considered a natural choice for the assignment since he could be assumed to be personally familiar with most people in the community. But in Bolshevik Russia some of the old routines had changed, as officials were quick to explain to the obtuse Yankees.

The Simbirsk history, as one example of many, noted that appointment of a priest to an ARA committee in that city in October 1921 "stirred the hornets' nest." Rein, the local soviet chief, forbade the selection and would not be moved on the matter, declaring that his government objected, "by reason of the moral and political character thereof, to any ecclesiastical representative in these committees. This the more so as by the laws of our Constitution, the said element, being harmful to the young generation, are deprived of all active or passive participation in our work." The usual practice of the district ARA men was to yield to such protests in keeping with their instructions to avoid politics.

Considerations of efficiency aside, official hostility to the enlistment of priests did not especially exercise the relief workers, whose evident compassion for the Revolution's losers did not extend to the Orthodox clergy as a group. Most of the Americans spoke of being moved by the mysterious beauty of the Orthodox churches and the service: the ornate vestments, the supplicating worshippers, the haunting intonations, the burning incense, and ultimately the distressing length. Childs wrote: "One could fancy as he stood there with these peasants with the hearts of children who were crossing themselves and prostrating themselves before graven images that one had stepped from the 20th century into premedieval times."

But when it came to the question of theology, the Americans tended to believe that the religious faith of the Russians extended no further than an unthinking observance of ritual, that they were not so much religious as superstitious. In this the relief workers were only the latest in a long line of foreign observers to arrive at such a conclusion. Had these Americans been students of Russian history, they could have, like some of their predecessors, supported their personal observations with citations of historical documents such as the Primary Chronicle. There it is written that in the year 988 Prince Vladimir of Kiev chose for his people the Greek Orthodox faith because his emissaries returned with reports of the stunning beauty of Constantinople—"we knew not whether we were in heaven or on earth"—and its places and forms of worship. That is to say, from the beginning, aesthetics seemed to take priority over theological substance.

The Russian fixation on religious ritual was standard fare in travelers' accounts, continuing into the postrevolutionary period, when circumstances lifted it to new heights of absurdity in a story first widely reported in the West by the journalist Arthur Ransome in 1919. Ransome watched as Russians genuflected and crossed themselves before a sign affixed to a wall of a building adjacent to the Moscow city duma. The sign read, "Religion is the opium of the people." The French journalist André Morizet said he had read Ransome's description of this scene but had not believed it until he saw it with his own eyes in the summer of 1921. No ARA man seems to have remarked on it though several in Moscow watched as men and women regularly stopped to cross themselves before the sign "American Dining Hall."[3]

In Lenin's Russia, when it came to sacred articles, sometimes you had to take what you could get. Spewack tells of two peasants who ended their visit with Kalinin by wandering about the reception room apparently in search of something. "What do you seek?" asked the Soviet Little Father. "An icon," came the reply. "We must talk to God before we are done." Kalinin's secretary told them that the icons had been removed. "Both peasants shook their heads mournfully. They waited. Finally they scraped out. Organized religion as a power is dead in Russia. But the forms remain."

The forms may have remained, but what about the content? Duranty's answer was that to such peasants and most other Russians the Orthodox faith was merely a "superstitious ritual," "a ceremony they went through at stated periods without it greatly affecting their lives." But the Bolsheviks were becoming less tolerant of such habits, and even after the drive to expropriate the Church treasures had run its course in 1922, the propaganda campaign against religion was maintained. The most intense attack came at Russian Christmas, January 7, 1923, which saw large demonstrations in the major cities mocking the deities of a variety of religions. Moscow was the site of the most elaborate activity, which correspondent Mackenzie called a "carnival against religion." "Processions formed in different districts at noon and paraded the streets until dark, bearing grotesque dummies of sacred characters." These included Jesus, Buddha, Confucius, Mohammed, and the Virgin Mary. Seldes says that "The Jewish prophets were caricatured by men with long paper noses, dressed in the Hebrew praying cloths and wearing phylacteries between their legs and on their backsides."

It was like a circus parade which had broken up on the tent grounds, with all the clowns, acrobats, magicians, and mountebanks continuing to do their acts here and there to admiring columns of marchers and little groups of applauding people. Only these clowns and mountebanks were imitating priests and rabbis, mimicking the Orthodox prayers and chants, parodying religion and ritual.

Mackenzie learned that the performers were mostly students from the Communist Workers' University and the University of the Far East.

The lads and lassies marched along with linked arms, many of them drunk with excitement or with other stimulants, laughing, reeling and scoffing. Horsemen bearing anti-religious banners led the way. Trucks carried groups of men in grotesque fancy

dress, symbolizing God, Christ, and deities of other faiths. One favourite design, repeated by different processions, showed God holding the naked figure of a woman in
His hands. There were dummies of rabbis and priests, strung like marionettes.

There were also parodies of chants and a send-up of the Lord's Prayer addressed to "Lord Capital." Mackenzie, like his fellow reporters, noted that the
event drew comparatively few spectators, and he felt that the main result of the
exercise was to advertise the enormous hold religion still had on the mass of the
people. Moscow's churches were more crowded that Christmas than in tsarist
days, he was told, and he was surprised at the number of Red Army soldiers to be
seen among the worshippers. "At dark, bonfires were lit on an open space and the
effigies were thrown on them, the young people joining hands and dancing
around the flames."

Golder called it the "burning of the gods." He asked Russians of the Right
and Left why the Bolshevik government would do something so "stupid" and was
told that in order to keep the "communist fire of enthusiasm burning" it was "always necessary to have some stunt." Golder was more sympathetic toward the
Orthodox Church than were most ARA men, but this may have been a reflection
of his age—he was then in his mid-forties—and his many years studying Russian culture. More characteristic of the thinking of the ARA men was a cold-
blooded passage in a letter Fleming wrote home at Easter 1923:

I have one thing in common with the Communists—I cannot take this church seriously. The service is very impressive, but it is a slave's service; the deep vaults of the
church and the moving sound of the distant singing, the soundless movements of the
priest and the magnificent bass voice of the attendant who leads the singing—the
worshippers all standing, and crossing themselves, make altogether a very deep effect;
but I have noticed that effect to be very slight outside the church. I visited also on the
same evening the hall of the Society of Communist Youth, where a crowd of roughs
were singing parodies of the church ceremonies, and issuing forth to stamp irreverently into the churches, stand a few moments, sniff, and stamp out of the churches.
Between the two of them is hard to choose.

Actually Fleming takes this a bit too far, yet many of his colleagues shared his
indifference toward Orthodoxy even though they discussed the fate of the clergy
with more compassion. Barringer, who witnessed the repression of the Church
in Ekaterinoslav in 1922, described the culmination of the trial of the Archbishop
of Ekaterinoslav for anti-Soviet activities:

[W]hen the time came to pronounce the sentence after three days' trial, the Bishop
was ordered to stand up, the two soldiers presented their bayonets against him and the
"commandant," or sheriff, pointed his revolver in his face. Then the president of the
Tribunal pronounced the death sentence, which he, a few minutes later, changed to
five years' imprisonment, and a week later, the Archbishop was about preaching to be
good at his old church. He had agreed, however, on the side, to support the Living
Church movement which is aided and sponsored by the Soviet Government. If the local governments of Russia are inefficient it is not from lack of power.

He dismissed the Living Church as being "full of Soviet political chicanery" and
in general considered the anti-Church crusade to be a fruitless exercise: "The pres-

ent campaign by the Bolos to destroy the last vestige of prestige of the Church and to put over the atheistical idea is making about as much impression now on the peasants as a Republican candidate would in South Carolina 30 years ago."

He did not mean by this, however, that the Russian faith was in fine working order. He too took a dim view of the obsession with ritual—the "innumerable crossings before the ikons"—and observed that although "record breaking crowds" turned out in Ekaterinoslav to resist the requisitions, this was purely the emotion of the moment: "during the week and in one's life there is very little rational Christianity."

As troubling was the fact that the Church establishment had for centuries proven itself to be "absolutely oblivious" to the sentiments of the people. "The priests are not leaders as a rule only the exception and with their peculiar garb, long hair and family clanishness, they have become a race set apart." What these Russians needed, he believed, was a ritualistic yet more "rational" religion like Catholicism: "unless the Catholics take over the finances and furnishing of new blood into this shell shocked and despoiled Church, its life is doomed, and Russia will have lost her last hold in civilization."[4]

The story going around that the expropriation of the Church treasures was necessary to finance American relief seems to have been based on five parts public suspicion and one part Bolshevik disinformation. To many peasants it was simply logical: if something comes in, something has to go out. Saratov district supervisor John Gregg wrote to Moscow headquarters in August 1922 that there was no question that "a large part of the ignorant peasantry of this district" believed that the treasures were taken to pay for ARA corn. In the towns, where there was less ignorance, the authorities offered guidance. Saratov residents were enlightened by a propaganda poster depicting church treasures going out of and relief supplies going into the famine zone, with some of the food labeled "corn." To the east at Uralsk, Clapp reported that as the churches were being stripped of gold and silver, the local Bolsheviks were openly telling people that the Americans had demanded this as payment for its relief supplies.

Godfrey visited a convent in a small village in the Simbirsk district and was asked by its occupants "what the Americans expected to do with the gold and silver removed from the churches. I was dumbfounded at such a question and could hardly make them believe that we had nothing to do with it whatsoever." By the end of his excursion in the district, Godfrey realized that the story was widely believed.

Yakovlev, the Simbirsk historian, says that those Russians who had from the beginning doubted the pure humanitarianism of the ARA sensed that they had found the proof when the Bolsheviks began to confiscate the church treasures: "the Americans brought their condensed milk and sugar to receive as pay for them the ikons of the Russian churches." Yet curiously, "the Americans did not load their empty box-cars with ikons and chalices to carry them away to some Chicago market!"

Of course it was the Bolsheviks who carried them off—at least the gold, silver, and jewels—though the value of their plunder did not nearly match the hopes they had placed on it. Early on there was speculation in government circles that the Church loot would bring in as much as a half billion dollars. That sounds extreme; still, Duranty found the Bolsheviks' initial expectations were "enormously exaggerated" and figured that they took in a total of only one or two million dollars, perhaps as many as five million. Although the Russian Church's wealth had long been legendary, he wrote, in fact most of it was in the form of landed property, land stocks, and bonds; much had been looted in the Revolution and much hidden away; and a portion of the Church's "treasures" was of a kind that was unmarketable.

Col. Haskell had watched the entire process with a wary eye, mindful that it threatened to bring the good name of the ARA under a shadow. He was under no illusions about the ultimate purpose of the requisitions, confirming to Hoover in a coded cable in August that "we well know that no considerable amount if any has actually been expended for foodstuffs." He estimated the value of the confiscated items to be about $50 million but was demanding figures from the government.

These were supplied by Lander in October 1922, after the storm had died down. The source of his information was the People's Commissariat of Finance, which provided a breakdown of the worth of the treasures by specific item: gold, silver, diamonds, pearls, gold and silver coins, and so on. The appraisal process being necessarily inexact—due to the approximate nature of the weight assessments and the need to translate values across rubles, gold rubles, U.S. dollars, and British shillings—the Finance Commissariat's rough estimate of the total Soviet government take was nearly $4 million, of which a little short of a million had so far been turned over to the Soviet famine relief committee, most of that having supposedly been used to purchase flour from Finland.

However approximate were these figures, four million was not even close to Haskell's fifty million and light years away from someone's half-billion. Lander admitted to Haskell that "the hopes put upon this source have been greatly exaggerated."[5] The document he gave the colonel indicates that the articles of silver were of such an inferior quality that they were estimated to contain only about one-third pure silver. Also, it appears that what people had been saying was true: many of the stones bordering the icons were imitation, having been substituted a few years—or was it centuries?—earlier by farsighted—or was it corrupt?—clergy. Or maybe the deception was another miracle brought off at the last moment by departing saints. Whatever the case, those who had so recently orchestrated the disclosure of the counterfeit relics should have expected as much.

IN HIS LUDICROUS 1985 "memoir" of the Cheka "struggle" against the forces of the ARA, *Diversion Under the Flag of Aid*, aging ex-Chekist Aleksandr Poliakov dispensed completely with innuendo and simply had the American relief workers themselves walk in and rob the church treasures. In a most bizarre twist, Haskell is portrayed meeting surreptitiously with Tikhon, and the two conspire to plunder Russia's churches. Perhaps this was the stuff of a young Chekist's dreams in 1922, but the fact is that the only occasion when the names of Haskell and Tikhon came up together was when the colonel, under instructions from New York, proposed to provide food packages to the Church and give Tikhon responsibility for their distribution, a proposal rejected by the Soviets.

Had he looked further, Poliakov would have found much richer material on which to base his conspiratorial fantasies, for the relief workers did have a direct connection to a most sinister figure in the Church, a figure far more dangerous than Tikhon—at least in an earlier day. This was Iliodor, the self-styled "Mad Monk of Russia."

Iliodor was born Sergei Mikhailovich Trufanov, a Don Cossack and the son of a peasant, who became a protégé and later the archenemy of Rasputin. He was known as a fierce and rabidly xenophobic reactionary, which were not bad credentials in late imperial Russia, though in the years preceding the world war he became something of a problem for the monarchy when he turned his fire on government ministers and figures close to the tsar for not dealing severely enough with the Duma, with the intelligentsia, increasingly with the aristocracy, and of course with the Jews. In his autobiography he wrote: "I demanded that the Government should treat the revolutionists without mercy. The Jews I hated with every fiber in my soul." Ultimately, he defied everyone, from the Holy Synod to Rasputin to the royal family.

Iliodor had been tending to the needs of the faithful along the lower Volga since 1907 when the Tsar had sent him to Tsaritsyn because his Slavophile populism had been causing no end of trouble at monasteries in the north. The more southerly location, adjacent to his native Don region, seemed to suit him just fine. He established himself in a fortress-monastery built with the help of his flock, said to number in the tens of thousands, and he found the time to organize local chapters of the reactionary Union of Russian People.

Part of the secret to his success was his ability as a speaker. He loved to address large crowds. It was said that during his sermons a huge guard stood beside him holding a standard in one hand and brandishing a gun in the other. His motto, as reported in the *New York Times*, was "We must pray to God noisily." The *Times* believed that this appealed to the emotional Russian temperament. "Noisily" seems like a poor translation, yet he was also known as the Great Curser.

On one occasion he is supposed to have declared: "Till now, we have only menaced. Henceforth we shall begin to shoot. It is war to the death. Arise, orthodox people! Arise for the defense of holy faith, of aristocracy and of Russian brotherhood. Look out, Jews and Russian fools! Holy Russia is marching." This kind of demagoguery led some to see in him a potential second Pugachev. In 1909 he traveled to St. Petersburg, where Rasputin arranged for an interview with the Tsarina, who tried to convince him to be less noisy. This had little effect, and after he returned to Tsaritsyn Prime Minister Stolypin tried to remove him, but Rasputin supposedly thwarted this action.

Matters reached such a state that at the end of 1910 the Tsar personally ordered Iliodor to a monastery in Tula. He went but after a short time fled in disguise back to Tsaritsyn, where in the spring of 1911, he and his followers held out in their little Kremlin, resisting an armed siege by Stolypin's Cossacks for twenty days, at which point Rasputin again intervened on Iliodor's behalf.

Iliodor's faithful were described by the local governor as "a fanatical mob of howling hysterical women, and men, tough barefoot peasants, who shook their fists and swore to kill anybody who tried to touch him." The steadfastness of their loyalty was attributed in part to a "widespread belief" that Iliodor was the illegitimate brother of Nicholas II by a father of pure Russian blood. It begins to sound like something out of *Monty Python*, but it is not at all ridiculous in the context of modern, not to mention medieval, Russian history.

After the siege was lifted, the Tsar received Iliodor at Tsarskoe selo, the summer palace, and the two seemed to have patched things up. But it was at this point that relations between Iliodor and Rasputin went sour. Rasputin's influence at court, as has been told many times, derived from his supposed ability to stop the bleeding of the hemophiliac Tsarevich. Iliodor apparently came to have doubts about this; he was also repelled by his mentor's boastful tales of his sexual exploits, an especially infamous aspect of Rasputin's biography. It was said that many of Iliodor's fanatical followers were women who had been wronged by Rasputin.

It came to a showdown between these two robed warriors in December 1911, when Rasputin visited Tsaritsyn; Iliodor confronted him about his personal behavior and accused him of poisoning the Tsarevich with a "harmful yellow powder" in order to be able then to "cure" him. This may have been a very close call for Rasputin: it is said that in the mayhem Misha the Blissful tried to castrate him. Somehow he managed to flee and return to St. Petersburg, where he told the Tsar of his narrow escape, and the Holy Synod promptly exiled Iliodor to a monastery in Vladimir. In December 1912 he was defrocked.

But Iliodor could not sit still. He returned to the Don region, in civilian dress, and plotted a revolution. In his thoroughly unreliable memoir he claimed that he intended to start his revolution in 1913, on October 6, the Tsar's name day, by exploding a bomb in St. Isaac's Cathedral, where the leading lights of the aristocracy and the Holy Synod were gathered in celebration. Whatever was on his mind, it was criminal enough to earn him in June 1914 a prison sentence in the Peter and Paul Fortress, though for some reason he was released after a short time.

He claims that he then approved a plan of one of his female followers to assassinate Rasputin. Knowing that he would be held responsible for the murder, he fled the country disguised as a woman. He landed in Finland, where, he says, he met Gorky, who "took a warm, brotherly interest in me." After living in Norway for almost two years, he made his way to the United States, arriving in New York City in June 1916, six months before Rasputin was assassinated by a notable aristocrat—so he could not possibly take the credit for that preposterously protracted affair.

Nor could he be credited with the fall of the Romanovs in March 1917, although his name did figure into events in a distinctly minor way. Golder was in Petrograd in those days and recorded how a revolutionary orator ended an eloquent speech to a gathering of Russian soldiers with the message that "from now on Russia will have but one monarch, the revolutionary proletariat." The soldiers were puzzled: what was a "revolutionary proletariat"? They also misunderstood the word "monarch," hearing instead "*monakh*," monk.

They therefore concluded that it was planned to put a monk on the throne, and an argument arose whether they would have a monk or not. Some were in favor and others opposed. By the time it got to the next regiment the question was whether they would have the monk Iliodor as their ruler. It was no longer a question whether Russia was to have a tsar but whether the tsar should be a monk or not, and whether it should be Iliodor or some other one.[6]

Meanwhile back in New York, Iliodor was at the center of another bit of confusion, this involving the rights to his book manuscript about Rasputin, which was published in Moscow and Petrograd in 1917 as *Sviatoi chort, The Holy Devil.* Two Yiddish newspapers claimed to own the material, both having signed the author to contracts. However their dispute was settled, Iliodor's pray-and-tell inside story of Rasputin was serialized in three hundred American newspapers. In February 1918 it was revised and published as a memoir, *The Mad Monk of Russia: Iliodor. Life, Memoirs, and Confessions of Sergei Michailovich Trufanoff (Iliodor).* It contains all kinds of interesting insights into the man and the monk, including an explanation for his recently recanted anti-Semitism:

All I had been taught about the Jews was this: the Jew drinks human blood, the Jew regards it as a pious deed to kill a Christian, the anti-Christ will spring from Jewish stock, the Jew is accursed by God, the Jew is the source of all the evil in the world. My hatred of Jews was thus based wholly on religious fanaticism. The Jew in private life I did not know, and the first Jews I actually met were here in America.

A book publication in New York City would have been the sky for most new immigrants, but Iliodor was no ordinary immigrant. He was quickly signed to a motion picture contract by filmmaker Lewis J. Selznick, né Zelenik, a Ukrainian Jew and the father of future Hollywood titan David O. Selznick. And so it came to be that in 1917 Iliodor starred in the feature film *The Fall of the Romanoffs,* which premiered in New York on September 6.

The screenplay was based on Iliodor's book manuscript. Its central characters were not Nicholas and Alexandra but the "Holy Devil" Rasputin and the "Sinful Angel" Iliodor, played by himself. The opening title read "The Fall of the Romanoffs" accompanied by the words "with Iliodor." Film historian Kevin Brownlow says that as part of his agreement to make his first film Iliodor formed his own motion picture company, the "Iliodor Corporation." Clearly when it came to self-promotion, the Mad Monk knew his way around.

Whatever the artistic merits of the film, its script allowed Iliodor to settle an old score: the film itself has been lost, but a surviving still photograph shows the Sinful Angel in full priestly regalia grabbing hold of a cowering, wide-eyed Rasputin while a company of Orthodox priests looks on. For its time this might have been a satisfying big-screen showdown, but in a later day Hollywood would have brought in Misha the Blissful and let him do his work; and in a still later day the entire film would have been rewritten in order that Misha could be set loose on the empire as a serial castrator.

It seems that the reviewers of the film did not care for Iliodor's performance as himself. Perhaps this soured him on his nascent movie career. In any case, toward the end of 1917 he returned to Russia, evidently intending to initiate a religious uprising against the Soviet government with Trotsky cast in the role of the anti-Christ. Something about the Bolsheviks won him over, however, and he was soon back at his fortress-monastery preaching a pro-Soviet line. In 1922 he became an advocate of the Living Church.

The American relief workers in Tsaritsyn caught up with him at Christmas 1921. He told them that he had been Rasputin's best friend and adviser, and with his unfaltering instinct for self-publicity insisted on being called "the Mad

Monk." Two of the Americans attended his Christmas service and were deeply impressed. It must have had some exceptional appeal because it lasted for three hours with the entire congregation on its feet the entire time, in accordance with Orthodox practice. The service was followed by a "really good" banquet, and maybe that and the wonderful sensation of sitting down after three hours had left the most lasting impression.

The ARA motion picture man, Floyd Traynham, passed through Tsaritsyn in early 1922, and he filmed Iliodor, his first performance before the camera since *The Fall of the Romanoffs*. The ARA's two-reeler about the Russian mission, which was edited from Traynham's material and shown in theaters in the States, includes a sequence featuring Iliodor, played by Iliodor. It shows exterior shots of him together with his beautiful wife and two children. The Mad Monk appears quite harmless, except for the fact that he behaves like a man who is no stranger to the camera, unlike all of Traynham's other Russian subjects. He had not lost his boyish good looks or shaven his goatee and moustache, though his shoulder-length hair had been shorn long before the Revolution. A wide shot shows him standing among some of his flock—none looking especially threatening—together with a few masticating camels just outside the monastery wall. The accompanying title respectfully calls him the Mad Monk and his monastery the Commune of Eternal Peace. Indeed it all seems rather tame compared to the old fire-and-brimstone days.

Cornick wrote to his father to say that Iliodor's faithful consisted of about three hundred peasants and that his monastery was run entirely "on a communistic plan" and seemed to function very well—though perhaps not all that well, since Iliodor "hopes someday to take his whole flock with him and go to America and settle in New Jersey."[7] As it happened, only Iliodor and his immediate family made the journey to America, by way of Riga, where he paused long enough in spring 1922 to become a Baptist. This was not such an extraordinary development: since the Revolution the Baptists had made considerable headway in winning converts in southeastern Russia.

After being briefly detained because his papers were not in order, Iliodor set sail for New York on November 15. The *New York Times* wrote: "It is hard to say what he will do; but whatever it is, it will be picturesque and unexpected and well worth watching." The ARA's own "Russian Unit Record" informed the inquiring minds among the relief workers on March 18, 1923: "Iliodor, the 'Mad Monk' of Russia, has announced his intention to become a citizen of the U.S."

Historian Brownlow says that Iliodor preached regularly at the Russian Baptist Church in New York City. But not for the Sinful Angel the tranquil ecclesiastical life: he was a daily visitor at the office of the city's district attorney, seeking redress against one Al Gilbert and the Sunrise Picture Company for failing to honor a contract to star him in a motion picture called *Five Days in Hell*.

CHAPTER 40

DANGEROUS MEN IN RUSSIA

The reputation of the ARA in Soviet Russia came under its greatest threat as a result of an incident that occurred in December 1922, when Soviet customs officials intercepted the ARA's mail pouch. Several relief workers were caught using their courier privileges to smuggle out of the country treasures they had been accumulating at famine prices—diamonds, objets d'art, antique rugs, furs, and so on—in addition to politically sensitive correspondence and other documents. The episode unmasked at least one famine relief worker as a devout worshipper of mammon.

This was only the most scandalous of several so-called frontier incidents, which involved the best and the worst representatives of the ARA. The first American to encounter trouble was that rogue reliever and self-described soldier of fortune, Charlie Veil, who had gone off to war with the Lafayette Escadrille before joining the American Flying Corps. Whatever glory he won as a fighter pilot, in his personal life he managed to acquire a reputation as a "high-flyer"—which means he was always looking to pull off some stunt—as on November 17, 1918, during the celebration of Alsace-Lorraine Day in Paris when, flying in a squadron down the Champs Elysées, he steered his plane through the Arc du Triomphe. So he claims.

During and after the peace negotiations he worked for the American Embassy in Paris as an aerial courier between Paris, Berlin, and Warsaw. Then he wandered in search of further adventure. He claims to have joined the Pulaski Squadron during the 1920 Russo-Polish War, but his autobiography speaks mostly of boozing, fornicating, smoking hashish, touring southern France with a jazz band, and spending considerable sums of other people's money.

In his ARA application letter, Veil summed up his motivation for wanting to join the mission: "It has been my desire for some time to go to Russia as soon as it opens and now is the chance." He was that direct: no Hoover-like phrases about service to mankind, no lip service to the attractions of a Hoover-run mission. It was the great adventure, and he wanted a piece of the action. Whether or not he spoke the appropriate lines during his interview at London headquarters, Mitchell decided to sign him on. "Immediately," Veil wrote, "I was one of the boys."

It was decided to have Veil serve as the Riga-Moscow train courier, an assignment that must have left him with some free time in Moscow because he says he made friends among the American correspondents: "They took me on their interviews with the big Bolos." One of these was Trotsky, whom Veil claims to have met several times, an honor given to no other ARA man or indeed to any of Veil's reporter friends. The chief of staff of the October Revolution could not sit still; he was "always sputtering like a fire cracker and jerking around as if he had ants in his pants; he was willing to fight the whole damn' world at any second and he'd slay capitalistic nations with one blast of threat and oratory."

Stalin was not known to grant interviews to foreign visitors; nonetheless, he is supposed to have sat down for Veil, impressing him as a "hard hombre, just naturally tough in word and action; he was swarthy, arrogant, scheming, much as I imagine a Chicago gunman." Of course in 1921 Veil had no idea who Stalin was, but when he was writing his self-serving memoir in the early 1930s, the idea of a face-to-face encounter with the future Great Dictator was too good to pass up.

He even tried to leave the impression that he had hobnobbed with the intelligentsia crowd: "At parties we met Maxim Gorky, whose convictions did not seem sincere because he overplayed them so constantly."[1]

Somehow during all of this he managed to find time to fulfill his courier duties, making several trips back and forth across the border, until Fink was given the Riga-Moscow line at the end of September and Veil was tapped to inaugurate a Moscow-Petrograd-Reval route. The idea was abandoned after its near-disastrous first run.

In recalling the episode in his autobiography, Veil sets the stage for high drama, saying that at the last moment before his departure from Moscow Haskell handed him two sealed envelopes with instructions to guard them with his life. Nothing in the documentation corroborates this, though it is conceivable that Haskell indeed spoke such words without intending them to carry the gravity implied in their literal meaning, the way people often speak.

Veil departed Moscow, and at 10:30 on the evening of October 2 his train reached Yamborg on the Russian-Estonian border. He was traveling in the company of *Chicago Tribune* reporter Larry Rue, who may have been ill—Veil said he had stomach and bladder problems and an infection in his leg.

What happened at Yamborg that evening is the subject of conflicting testimony. Of the three versions of events, two by Veil and another by Soviet customs officials, the Soviet one is almost certainly closest to the truth, although the account in Veil's memoir is the hands-down winner for action and adventure, with the narrator singlehandedly taking on a customs agent and a handful of border guards. The trouble began when these officials seized his suitcase and the ARA mail pouch and began to rummage through it:

They uncovered a Mauser, a police revolver which had been given me by Captain Miller in Riga. It was one of a pair and I had sold the other but the Russians didn't know that and glanced at me quickly. I thrust my hand into my coat pocket, grabbed my pipe. They saw the bulge and rose from my suitcase. Slowly they closed in on me and I backed to the wall. One of them made a sudden grab and I kicked again. With a yell of surprise he doubled up. I jerked my hand from my pocket, hurled my can of tobacco at the torch which was just over head. The darkness was greeted with a roar; slow-witted Russians groped for me but I had already grabbed the suitcase and what little remained in it and ducked for the door, leaving behind me a howling mob, each expecting his neighbor to shoot.

The mob then chased after him. He grabbed the gun of an unsuspecting soldier and used it to hold off his pursuers as he locked himself in his coupé. The soldiers pounded on the door, and a voice declared that the train would not depart unless he submitted himself to a search. At that moment he recalled the two envelopes and Haskell's instructions. Thinking fast he opened the door and quickly yanked the conductor inside, locking the door again behind them. Pressing the gun against his hostage, he said to him, "The train will go on or I'll kill you! Give the order!" The train moved across the border with the Soviets in pursuit, and when it stopped again, the Soviet and Estonian border guards confronted each other "in real comedy style with the Soviets running down the track and the Esthonians following them, firing imprecations but nothing more serious."

Veil says that though he and Rue lost some personal items, they came through with Haskell's two envelopes, which they now realized were the reason they had been given all this unwanted attention. They tried to guess at their contents: "Probably the secret code, Lenin's confessions or plans of a Czarist plot." Probably not.

The Soviet border guards had a completely different recollection of the Veil incident. The Yamborg Custom House issued an "Indictment," dated October 3, accusing Veil of being "in an intoxicated condition" and resisting an inspection of his baggage. After a time he relented, and the guards went about their business, finding a few bottles of alcohol and a Mauser with twenty bullets, for which Veil had no permit to carry beyond Soviet borders, so it was confiscated. He was also in possession of sixteen private letters without a seal; these were taken for the military censor. At this, Citizen Veil is said to have thrown his papers and identification on the table and "demonstratively left the Custom House." These documents were passed on to Moscow together with the indictment. In a separate letter, a customs officer claimed that the inspection of his unsealed baggage was carried out very politely but that it was rough going because "VEIL was drunk."

Veil's own report of his troubles, written in Moscow and dated October 9, contains little of the melodrama of the memoir version. Here he tells Haskell that before the trouble started he and Rue had been settling down for a peaceful evening: "neither of us felt inclined to use any stimulants, but were satisfied to sleep." But it was not to be, as the customs officials and Chekists arrived and began to turn the place upside-down. In this account, the documents that Veil protects are merely "a bundle of army papers which I was carrying and which were wrapped around some toilet articles." So much for codes, confessions, and plots. "I kept one hand in my pocket at all times on a can of tobacco with which I could put out the light in case trouble started." Only in his autobiography, it seems, did he let it fly.

Veil assumed that the whole affair had been "premeditated and carefully planned." Rue was so angry about what had happened that there was nothing to be done to stop him from publishing a sensational story about it in his newspaper. As Veil continued, he began to protest too much: "Neither Mr. Rue nor myself were using any undue supply of alcohol, insomuch as Mr. Rue was very sick and I was kept busy helping him by heating compresses."

For the time being, Veil survived the incident, and the Soviet government offered an apology, but there must have been a cloud hanging over the matter because he was relieved of his courier duties and sent to the famine zone—"banished to the steppes," as he put it. There, in the Saratov district, Veil had plenty of new adventures, real and imagined, but his days as "one of the boys" were now numbered.

In late October, London headquarters learned that while he was in England Veil had sold an airplane to the Russian Red Cross. The ARA had strict rules forbidding its relief workers from benefiting from a charitable organization operating in the same country in which they were working. London informed Haskell of the situation, but by the time word reached him in mid-November, something had already made up his mind that Veil was a walking time bomb. He wrote in reply: "In so far as Veil himself is concerned, I am of the firm opinion that it would be well if you would recall him to London and let him go, or transfer him elsewhere, as in my opinion he is a dangerous man in Russia." In fact, wrote the colonel, his prompt release would "clear the atmosphere a lot in Russia."

Somehow the word had gotten out about Veil—perhaps it was his behavior in Saratov, but more likely it was the result of new information or second thoughts about the Yamborg episode. In the last week of November he was relieved of further duty in Saratov and told to proceed immediately to Moscow with all his baggage. Once at headquarters, he later recalled, Lonergan gave him the straight dope:

You're still in wrong as hell about that Yamborg mess. If you had been killed, as you should have been, we would have had serious international trouble. You know our orders from Hoover perfectly: "Keep out of trouble!" You disobeyed them as courier; what's more, although you did a fine piece of work out in your district, you kept things stirred up against the local authorities. For your own good you better get out of here as fast as you can.

This all sounds rather self-serving. The decision to yank Veil from the mission may well have been made at New York headquarters in reaction to the unwelcome publicity Rue seems to have given the Yamborg incident in the *Tribune*, as he had threatened to do. This would explain the substance and tone of ARA public relations chief George Barr Baker's statement on the matter: "The courier incident need never have occurred had not a bottle on the hip and something in the belly influenced these gentlemen to feel that they were born sovereigns in America and took their ex-territorial rights and privileges with them to Russia."

There were things they took with them out of Russia as well, for Baker missed the third leg of the triad: something in the hand. Fink escorted Veil as he made his way from Moscow to Riga for the last time. "Quite obviously Fink couldn't know that my baggage consisted largely of jewels, sables, white and silver fox furs, two Bokhara rugs, scores of other articles which would serve to finance a certain little Turkish expedition I already had in mind. This was not loot but carefully garnered treasure selected with the aid and expert advice of the newspaper men and their interpreters."[2]

Actually Fink would have assumed no less. The American relief workers and correspondents he had been accompanying out of Russia over the previous two months had boasted to him of their treasure, and they counted on him to help ensure its safe passage to Riga.

THE ARA MEN HAD ARRIVED in Russia to find that the spoils of the Revolution were available to them at ridiculously low prices, making large-scale purchases irresistible. Adding to the temptation was the fact that the relief workers were paid relatively well and had virtually no personal expenses while on the job. Their salaries were determined according to a scale, with the most qualified personnel receiving the highest wage of $200 per month plus $6 per day for a subsistence allowance. During the first year of the mission, London carried the personal accounts of the American personnel, most of whom had their salaries deposited directly into a bank account or turned over to a relative in the United States. Salaries could be paid out in Moscow but only with London's approval. The subsistence accounts were maintained in Moscow and drawn in rubles. It was difficult to spend as much as $6 a day on basic needs in 1921 Soviet Russia, especially for those relievers stationed in the districts.

So the Americans had the financial means to purchase valuables that had been hidden away over the previous four years. Since the introduction of NEP, some of these articles—lace and fineries, furs, and so on—could be bought openly at the markets, though much was still traded in private, especially articles of exceptional value. The Americans used both routes, though their biggest purchases resulted from personal connections since they were frequently sought out by small- and big-time speculators. The bargains they struck made their hearts race, and they could not resist telling friends and relatives back home about their acquisitions.

Soon enough, evidence of the volume of this activity set off alarm bells in the New York and London headquarters. Rickard in New York wrote to Brown in London on November 28, 1921, that the private correspondence sent to the States by the personnel in Russia—whose recipients included the staff at 42 Broadway—indicated that "these men are purchasing furs, diamonds and other things, evidently with an idea that they will personally profit by these investments." Brown responded on December 16: "This has already come to our attention through various rumors, and Quinn, who has just arrived today from Warsaw, tells me that both the 'Izvestia' and 'Pravda' Moscow papers which had arrived in Warsaw before his departure carried stories to the same effect, intimating that we were more interested in the purchasing of valuables than in the feeding of babies."

Quinn was at that time still head of the Polish mission, so Moscow had yet to be contacted about the problem. On December 19 Brown conveyed to Haskell the substance of Rickard's letter and indicated that the London staff had heard "certain echos" of it, and indeed that the continental press had made reference to the large-scale purchasing by the Russian unit personnel: "All this is, or can be, very damaging to the organization." Brown urged that the men be limited to "reasonable personal requirements": necessary wearing apparel, a trinket for personal use, "fur for direct use in one's own family"—all that was fine, but "bargain-hunting in general with the idea of personal profit is intolerable to the ARA and should be strongly handled." He added a postscript: "Rumor has mentioned McSweeney. If true or not I have no means of knowing."

On the following day Brown learned of a disturbing report by Floete, who had arrived in London after retiring from the Russian mission as a result of his near-fatal encounter with Volga bandits. It seems that on his way through Moscow Floete had gotten an earful. He learned that there was a number of ARA men in Moscow accumulating large stores of rugs, furs, art objects, and diamonds, which they planned to transport out of Russia. He named McSweeney and Telford as the key figures. This was the last mention of McSweeney's name in connection with this business; on the other hand, Major Charles Telford, chief of finance and accounting, turned out to be a bad penny.

The first head to roll in connection with these matters was that of Telford's assistant, Adolph Tordy. This occurred in February 1922, when Mitchell was visiting Moscow from London. He wrote to Brown that Tordy proved to be a "washout"; he was "constantly in difficulty with his accounts even though he is now acting only as cashier," seemed "utterly unable to let the exchange alone," and was "constantly turning deals for outsiders." As a result they counted the cash in the Moscow unit for the first time since the mission opened and discovered a shortage of 520 million rubles, about $660: "the Colonel was furious, but it had never occurred to him to have it counted before."

Tordy was born in Bohemia in 1875 and was a banker by trade. He had served with U.S. Military Intelligence during the war before signing on with the ARA in Paris—the finance and accounting division, naturally—and then transferring to Moscow. It was Eiduk who blew the whistle on Tordy, confronting Haskell with the evidence that the ARA cashier was mixed up with a group of Russians who had stolen alcoholic beverages from a warehouse. Haskell said of Tordy: "He appeared to me to be a confirmed money lender or money changer, or some sort of an animal and could not get those ideas out of his head." In any event, the Soviets "have the goods" on him.

When told he was being let go, Tordy seemed to snap. He got abusive with his chiefs. He accused Haskell of plotting to kill him on the train out of Moscow. "I really believe the poor old man is losing his mind," the colonel wrote. Tordy went to the Cheka and made a statement against Carroll, Burland, and Telford, accusing them of speculating in money and goods.[3]

It is almost certain that Tordy was not the only ARA man to pass the word to the Cheka. In the ARA files there is a copy of a "strictly secret" telegram, dated May 10, signed by Eiduk's assistant Volodin and addressed to the GPU: "According to information received by us from the leaders of the American Relief Administration in Russia, the members of this administration: Booman, Dodge and Burland are speculating here in Moscow. We request that you take note of this and take appropriate measures. With Communist regards."

Oscar Booman was a Latvian citizen who had worked under Haskell in the Transcaucasian mission, serving in the finance department, and had followed him to Russia.

As for Dodge, as early as March there were rumors about his dealing, enough so that Gov. Goodrich told him he was under suspicion as a speculator and to watch out or he would be released from the ARA—and the same went for Telford unless he cut his liquor. Mitchell wrote satisfyingly to Brown that Dodge and Telford were "a couple of badly scared young men."

This was only the first of several unheeded warnings given to Captain Earl J. Dodge, the man who was to be the central figure in the brewing scandal. Dodge's several duties included auditing the individual charge accounts of the American personnel and running the mess at the Blue House. But after the mission he was recalled only in the context of an epithet printed in the ARA's alumni newsletter: "Dodge's Diamonds."

Dodge hailed from Darien, Wisconsin. His professional experience before World War I was mostly in advertising and life insurance. He began his army career in Missoula, Montana, where he enlisted as a private and was given command of the army canteen—in which position he presumably either learned or refined some of the creative accounting techniques he would put to use in Moscow. During the war he saw action in France, then served in Germany with the Army of Occupation until he joined Haskell's mission in the Transcaucasus. There he functioned as finance officer with Booman as his assistant. Subsequently he was called in to audit the final accounts at ARA headquarters in Constantinople and Paris, before being transferred to the New York office. Haskell specifically requested his services for the Russian mission from the War Department.

The storm clouds were gathering over Dodge long before the storm actually broke. There were unmistakable signs of trouble in July 1922 when he sent out of Russia ten antique rugs and a sable stole of thirty-two skins, said to be a present for his fiancée. More disturbing was that he had passed these items off as official baggage and used the ARA courier. Officials in the museum section of the scientific department of the People's Commissariat of Enlightenment declared that the rugs were of "great antiquarian value," but that in view of the extraordinary services performed in Russia by the ARA it would make an exception and allow them to be shipped out of the country. The officials had been led to believe that the rugs were being sent out by Haskell under official ARA auspices.

Quinn, now temporarily at the helm in Moscow, was surprised when told of this, but he did not make a move against Dodge because Haskell was out of the country, and Dodge was Haskell's man. He did inform Lander, however, that the shipment was entirely Dodge's doing.

In August came another warning, this time from London. Mitchell wrote to Quinn that the cases of certain ARA men "give one to think." One was Dodge, whose handling of both his own and of the Russian unit's money was unsettling: his account book was "entirely too 'active' for a man who has his mind on nothing but our work"; two out of three men coming out of Russia had talked about his transactions in furs and diamonds; he was making numerous cash transfers from the accounts of other relief workers; and more disquieting, during the month of May he withdrew $900 as an advance. Telford, his chief, should be informed about this activity and put a stop to it. Other cases mentioned were those of Morris, Barret, Burnett, Musa, Bowden, Clement, Cochrane, Spratt, and Thompson. Mitchell found the conduct of these men, Dodge in particular, to be "worrying."

Quinn replied that while it was a bit unorthodox for Dodge to be acting as private banker for the rest of the organization, "technically" he was in the clear. Once again Haskell was out of the country, and once again Quinn thought it best to wait for his return.

Shortly after the colonel arrived back in Moscow the following month, he received a letter from Brown reminding him that "you have always felt certain slight misgivings as to Dodge" and appending a copy of an anonymous letter, dated August 31, received in London a few days earlier and written by an ARA man in Moscow. The writer wished to bring to the attention of the London chiefs the "infamous debauchery which is rampant in the Finance Section of this office," the "pernicious crimes" of Dodge and Booman, and the "terrible disgrace" of their "criminal speculation." He alleged that the two Americans were furnishing tens of billions of rubles to professional speculators for the operation of their own private business activities: Moscow speculators were made to pay heavy interest, which money went to the purchase of rugs and diamonds that were then shipped to Riga. It was an open secret that Dodge had already sent out no fewer than twenty highly priced rugs and many precious stones and furs. Speculation in foreign currency, the particular specialty of Booman, was conducted on a large scale. What is more, these same two men took part in "uninterrupted drinking bouts" that were "the talk of the city."

The anonymous accuser suggested that an inspection be carried out in the middle of the month when scores of billions of rubles were distributed among the speculators. Brown, fearing an "outburst in the press," advised Haskell to seal the safe with the cash and books, make a complete investigation, and count the cash.

On the morning of September 21—the day after he received this communication but already past the middle of the month—Haskell acted on Brown's recommendation. He discovered everything to be in good order and so informed Brown by letter that day. Dodge and Booman were both "perfectly reliable, although it is true that Dodge has some personal characteristics which are not particularly likeable or inspiring." The charge regarding the rugs and diamonds was greatly magnified. That regarding speculation was "absolutely ridiculous" as there were no transactions in foreign exchange going on in Moscow; besides, "Dodge will not even give two ten dollar bills for a twenty."

As for the drinking bouts, Haskell dismissed the charge as "ridiculous." In fact, the entire body of accusations was "pure unadulterated bunk and a fabrication on the part of some disgruntled man who is a coward." Dodge was "absolutely OK."[4] Two months would pass, and the colonel would have to eat these words.

There is no question that Moscow was the site of the most major purchasing and speculating activity involving ARA personnel, but the Americans in the districts also were kept busy in this way. Yet until the December crash there was only one ARA casualty on account of this: in Odessa Arthur Gill got caught speculating in silver and was released in September 1922.

That is to say, there is only one clearly documented case. Duranty tells the story of a baby feeder on the Volga, "a Southerner of good family" who was delighted to find that the money changers there accepted the twenty-dollar Confederate bills he carried around to remind himself of the South's glory days. Duranty says the young man became so enthusiastic that he wired home via Moscow headquarters to ask that an old trunk of Confederate bills in the attic be sent to him. When his telegram was read by the chiefs, he was summoned to Moscow, fired, and ordered to reimburse the speculators he had cheated. "To him, it was a cruel echo of the guns of Grant and Sherman, and a final injustice to the South."

Most of what went on in the districts was straightforward purchasing. By reputation Kazan had the best furs. Childs wrote to his mother on October 16, 1921: "You need not worry about my bringing you back plenty of furs. Just write me what you want in particular and you will have a trunk full for a mere song." In a memoir he recalled buying a fur coat for $35 and later discovering that the lining was silver fox. He had it removed and made into a jacket for his mother, which a

Berlin furrier valued at $1,500. At the time of his purchase, in Petrograd his future wife, Georgina, was bartering a sable cape for a pound of butter.

Ufa held out different prospects, which Kelley described in January 1922: "Our shopping instincts are whetted by tales of fancy metal work to be found in Zlatoust and other points close to the mining centers of the Urals." Zlatoust means "gold mouth," but here the reality did not live up to the promise, at least to judge from the subdued tone of Kelley's subsequent correspondence: "Inform all concerned that I undertake no purchasing orders in Russia. I have but two small trunks, neither of which I can carry in my pocket. My chances of getting them safely out of Russia are about even. I should hate to lose many of the trinkets I have bought, but I am stoical about them."

In June 1922, near the end of his tour of duty, he says he has spent a bit less than two hundred dollars for purchases of "my collection of junk." He does not reveal what kind of junk he had acquired; the only indication is contained in a letter he wrote in March referring to the purchase of "a Japanese vase of carved steel and a strip of Chinese hand silk embroidery. The two didn't cost as much as a dollar. Bashkiria is the land of 8 foot towels and I go in with a voracious appetite for them."

These Bashkir towels show up in various places in the documentation and not only in the letters of the Ufa Americans. The unsurpassed collector was the ill-starred Harold Blandy, who accumulated them by the dozens before going over to the Great Beyond. Elperin says that the hapless Blandy was kept out of Ufa and on the road "in the hope that he wouldn't break too much glass." To the towns he intended to visit he would send ahead word of his coming and direct that meetings of local officials and ARA committees be arranged to mark the occasion. He is said by his ARA colleagues to have understood little about the relief operation, never having read the instructions issued to local inspectors. "His interpreter would advise the local ARA staffs of this and encourage them to make Blandy a present of some Bashkir towels so that he would write a good report about them. When Blandy eventually returned to Ufa he had over 200 Bashkir towels."

It was during one of these tours, in May 1922, that he caught the typhus that killed him. In Sterlitamak he became very ill, and even before his condition was diagnosed, sensing that the end was near, he composed a final will and testament in the form of a letter to "My darling sweet Mother." After dealing with the dispensation of his $5000 life insurance policy, he takes up the most vital issue: the apportionment of the two hundred Bashkir towels. One is to go to Hoover, one to Harding, another to Secretary Hughes, and one to each of the forty-eight states in the Union. He describes them as gifts received in appreciation for having risked his life in the famine zone. "I don't feel that I deserve all these gifts, on the other hand I was only doing my duty. The American people have given the money and they should get these beautiful gifts of the Bashkir people."

He then runs through the list of other items, including a painting depicting a meeting of two blind men, three rugs, sable furs for his mother, laces for his sister-in-law, a silver belt, and a silver dining set. Apparently his feverish state had made him forget that he was still in debt forty-five pounds sterling to Mitchell for having rescued him from the clutches of his London creditors.

Mrs. Blandy fulfilled her son's dying wish regarding the Bashkir towels, sending one to each governor of every state, a gesture that in October 1922 generated local press headlines such as the one in the Springfield, Illinois, *Register*:

GOVERNOR SMALL RECEIVES LARGE RUSSIAN TOWEL

The Illinois governor was reported to be in receipt of a Russian "bath towel": "The towel is 8 feet in length and 16 inches in width. It is of brown linen with a heavy border in red, the border being worked by hand. The towel was made by peasants in Russia."

Virginia Governor Trinkle's gift was described as being "about the size of the average American bath towel." Governor Baxter of Maine decided that the best place for his towel was at the state museum in Augusta, where curator Thomas A. James was reported to have "placed the donation in a conspicuous place in the museum," presumably meaning outside the washroom.

Had more American relief workers restricted their purchases to harmless souvenirs like Bashkir towels, there would have been far less grumbling among the Russian public about ARA plunder. Anna Louise Strong, though she must be considered a hostile witness, was relatively restrained when considering the purchasing habits of the relief workers:

I knew of men among them who bought a diamond a week out of their salaries. Their income in dollars enabled them to buy at famine prices quantities of jewelry, gold ornaments, paintings and art treasures which their diplomatic immunity allowed them to ship out of the country. I disapproved of those acts but I was unwilling to class the whole Relief Administration by them, even when a well-informed Russian communist said to me: "It is becoming a question whether the millions of loot they are taking out of the country isn't more than their relief."[5]

Whatever the magnitude of this "loot," it was sufficient to enable the Soviet authorities to build a convincing case—as they could not for the charge that the ARA was an organization of commercial spies and advance men—that individual relief workers were, deep down, mere worshippers of mammon. All that was needed was an expedient moment to unveil the evidence; that moment presented itself in the form of the December 1922 courier incident, which Strong aptly characterized as a move to reveal to the Russian people "the wolf of capitalism under the sheepskin of charity."

IT WOULD LATER BE SAID that the Soviets had waited to strike until well into the second year of the mission when American relief had become no longer indispensable. But that only partly explains the timing, which had more to do with specific circumstances. And there had already been a frontier incident involving American "loot" in February 1922, during a critical phase of the mission.

That earlier episode occurred at the border town of Sebesh, on the Moscow-Riga line, and involved two relief workers of solid reputation, Donald Renshaw and Jesse McElroy, who were going out on leave. They would probably have passed through without difficulty but for the fact that they were traveling in the company of a third American, Ariel Varges, the motion picture man with the International Newsreel Corporation and one of the treasure-hunting correspondents of Veil's acquaintance. Varges, who was departing Russia for good, was almost certainly the intended target of the raid, though the border guards treated all three Americans with equal indignity.

Renshaw was carrying the ARA courier mandate, and when the trouble started he presented it as a laissez-passer, which the customs officials ignored. They seized the ARA mail bag, cut off the seal, and attempted to open the bag, but Renshaw had the key and refused to surrender it. The bag was then carried out of the coupé, but Renshaw grabbed it and brought it back in, whereupon it was again seized and taken away.

Perhaps with the Veil incident in mind, Renshaw and McElroy later wrote at the top of their report: "We are pleased to state that during the duration of the entire incident, we used no profane nor abusive language. Neither did we conduct ourselves in a way calculated to show disrespect to government officials." The behavior of those officials, however, was "insolent and offensive, and it appeared as though a studied attempt was being made to humiliate us."

The train was held up for a day until the customs authorities returned the mail bag, which had not been opened but now carried a Soviet seal, and the passengers were allowed to proceed but minus certain personal property, which had been confiscated.

All three Americans sent statements on the affair to Haskell from Riga on February 11.[6] Renshaw declared that the customs agents had taken from him two enameled silver goblets bought for a million rubles each—about six dollars at the time of purchase—which he intended to send to his father as a souvenir. He says he made no attempt to hide them in his luggage, and yet, he wrote, "I am now made to appear as an attempted smuggler."

McElroy's big loss was a fur cape intended for his wife and a Browning automatic he had brought with him into Russia. He sounds more upset than Renshaw: "I am sure that I do not care to be humiliated and treated like a Jew smuggler another time and would therefore be pleased to receive assurances that there will be no reoccurance of any such incident."

Varges was a different story entirely. He had come into Russia with the pioneer ARA crew led by Phil Carroll so he had been on the inside long enough to have gathered quite a few possessions—and the word in Moscow was that he had indeed. In his testimony he adds journalistic spice to Renshaw's rather bland description of the incident, calling it a "Hold Up." He quoted a Cheka official as saying to Renshaw, "We want you and your loot." The search was humiliating as it was conducted in the "open DIPLOMATIC CAR" before all the passengers and the crowd on the station platform. He praised Renshaw for his "most noble fight," waged "without using insulting language." Now, "with reference to my personal purchases I beg to inform you that all were for my personal use and the furs were for my Mother. The furs were purchased from the Soviet Fur Shop. However, insomuch as I had been in Russia for six months and shared an apartment with Mr. Duranty I naturally purchased a supply of bric a brac." Here he was hinting at Duranty's well-known habits along these lines, as if an association with Duranty should be considered an extenuating circumstance.

Aware that this would not provide him enough cover, he employed some barely veiled threats. He had always been friendly to the Soviet government, he wrote, and as far as the ARA was concerned he had "always pushed American propaganda." Although he had already wired home the courier story since it was anyway bound to leak out, he could cause a much bigger explosion if he did not get satisfaction:

I have been to the Soviet Bureau here and presented the incident and asked that they communicate with Moscow and guarantee my property or I will have to take the initiative and launch an Anti-Bolshevick programme which on the eve of the Genoa Conference will be most unpleasant. I have been in Russia six months and have played fair but I still have collected a lot of useful information of conditions. I speak frankly as I have been neutral to date.

Varges was seeking the return of his "bric a brac." Unfortunately for him, it was already known around Moscow headquarters that he was carrying out a "considerable plunder," as Haskell phrased it. A week later the Soviets apologized for the treatment given Renshaw and McElroy, but they had hit the jackpot with Varges, who reportedly had been transporting nineteen kilos of gold and platinum and twenty-six carats of diamonds. He had lost a small fortune, a fact that would have absolutely no bearing on Bolshevik diplomacy at Genoa.

That was in February. In the autumn, difficulties began to pile up at the border crossings. One of the problems for the Americans was that the Soviet famine relief organization, the Pomgol, of which Kamenev was the official head, had been superseded in September 1922 by a committee to deal with the "aftermath" of the famine, the Posledgol. This meant that the documents carried by the ARA men, certificates issued by Pomgol, had become "absolutely worthless," according to Leon Turrou, writing to his chiefs in Moscow on November 2 after his arrival in Warsaw. "They do not pay a bit of attention to our identity books signed by Kameneff."

Haskell expressed his concern to Lander on November 10, citing the behavior of the small-time officials who seemed to enjoy discriminating against ARA men at the frontiers. At Sebesh they minutely examined all ARA personal baggage, confiscated the Americans' currency, and had lately grown especially fond of these passengers' revolvers. At Stolpce, on the frontier with Poland, the officials laughed when the Americans presented their Soviet-issued mandates, then proceeded to seize cameras, glasses, and typewriters, claiming that there was no permission to export these items from Russia. Haskell called such "inconsiderate treatment" a "very serious condition" and told Lander he could only conclude that it was a "matter of policy."

A week later, Golder and Quinn were traveling into Russia from Riga. At the frontier the customs officials entered the coupé and, examining the space over the corridor, found a broken screw, which made them suspicious, so they began "unscrewing everything in sight," Golder wrote in a private letter. They came upon some kind of contraband, leading them to unscrew panels in the other coupés, from which they ended up "hauling out much loot, estimated by them to be worth 300,000,000,000 rubles. Figure out the value on dollars if you like, I am too tired. The crowd of customs officials danced a regular war dance for they will get a good share of the stuff."

In late November Haskell departed Russia for an extended break during the holiday season. Upon reaching London he must have had a conversation with the chiefs about money matters because he wrote to Quinn that there was too much transmission of currency through the ARA courier pouch to the personnel in Russia. Haskell says he encouraged the London office to open personal mail if it was evident that there was money inside, and he directed Quinn to impose "strict censorship" on all mail going out of Moscow, though his concern here was apparently that certain Americans were sending information to government departments in Washington, perhaps to Military Intelligence. How censorship was to be imposed on outgoing American mail is unclear, but Haskell thought Quinn could make examples of two or three ARA men to get the point across.[7] As it turned out, it was too late: while Haskell's letter was en route to Moscow, the Soviets had already decided to make their own ARA examples.

The courier to Riga left Moscow on Monday, November 27. On board the train were four bags of ARA mail and one marked man: Captain Earl J. Dodge was going out on leave; with him was Joe Dalton, who was departing the mission. Between them they had five personal trunks sealed with the ARA seal, which was against regulations. The plan was for the courier to pass the trunks through as official baggage, but at Sebesh both the mail and the trunks were seized and returned to Moscow, where they were held in a customs warehouse. Dodge and Dalton, no doubt grim-faced, continued on to Riga.

On Friday, December 1, Lander sent a note to Quinn asking if he could take advantage of a personal promise made to him by Haskell that at any time he could go through the ARA mail pouches to satisfy himself that there was no abuse of the courier privileges. Quinn obliged, unaware of what this search was about to reveal; as for the customs officials, "Apparently they had information of what was leaving and were pretty sure of their ground in holding up the mail."

Perhaps even Lander and company were surprised at what the courier pouches disclosed, for it brought scandal down not only on Dodge but on Childs, Wahren, and Turner. Childs was sending out valuables from Petrograd belonging to his mother-in-law, and politically sensitive correspondence. Wahren's case was particularly offensive to the Soviets: he had enclosed private correspondence and photographs of the royal family—items that at one time belonged to Russians living in Kazan who had since emigrated. Turner's transgression was far less serious: two paintings for which he had paid twenty dollars; nonetheless he was passing it through as official ARA mail. These last three men, the core of the original ARA Kazan staff, would now have to leave the mission.

Dodge's contribution to the ARA mail pouch was one envelope containing diamonds. Later he would claim he was sending these diamonds to Gov. Goodrich—which is a variation of the plea of buying furs for mother. Quinn realized he would have to go, but not forgetting that Dodge was Haskell's man, he wrote to the colonel in New York, passing on the decision to him: "I personally feel rather strongly on the subject in view of the fact that you had spoken to Dodge on several occasions about the reputation he had secured. . . . What will be discovered in his trunks the Lord only knows, but it cannot add much to our embarrassment."[8]

Meanwhile, there was a second incident at Sebesh, this one involving the chief of the medical division, Henry Beeuwkes, liaison chief John Lehrs, plus Tracy Kohl and Arthur Daley. This group had departed Moscow on December 3 carrying the ARA mail bags, which were seized and sent back to Moscow. At the same time, the Americans' personal baggage was searched and particular articles were confiscated. Beeuwkes called it "a disgrace and an insult to the Administration." He was outraged not because of his own material loss, since nothing had been taken from him, but "from the point of view of decency and efficiency."

The American who came through the worst, according to Beeuwkes, was "poor old Kohl," who had "everything except the kitchen stove in his luggage: personal letters, photographs, paintings, Bashkir towels, candle sticks; stuff he brought in from Austria and also Russian accumulations." They read his letters, looked through his photos, and took away his film, but only the blank rolls, "evidently thinking there was something mysterious about them." They removed and examined each item, and with each Kohl would say: "You can have it. I'm glad to get rid of it." They even pulled the feathers from his pillow. "It really was amusing but Kohl was up most of the night attempting to make his things fit back into their places."

Daley found Kohl's plight less amusing: "His baggage was scattered over the entire car, and they subjected him to extreme mental torture for one hour and a half." In the end, though, except for the blank film and a map, Kohl got everything back but thirty thousand German marks—which in a few months' time would become absolutely worthless.[9]

Back in Moscow, on December 8 Soviet and ARA officials assembled at the Moscow customs office for the much-anticipated opening of the Dodge and Dalton trunks. Each article was carefully noted and weighed. Trunk no. 1 contained seven antique woolen rugs. Trunk no. 2 contained, among other things, nine Gobelin tapestries, more antique rugs, shawls, apparel, tablecloths, a silk embroidered kimono, and, it appears, one Bashkir towel. Trunk no. 3 contained three antique woolen rugs. Trunk no. 4 contained nine antique woolen rugs and one antique silk rug. Trunk no. 5 contained miscellaneous items, including various European currencies, fourteen sable skins, a squirrel fur, a vase, a lamp, and a silk rug.

Lander had been handed an early Christmas present and could not help but get into the spirit of the occasion, writing to Quinn on the same day to reflect on the "evil things" that had been done by his men. The contents of the mail bags demonstrated that the courier service was regularly used by ARA men "to keep up a relation between the enemies of the Russian Government, between those living in Russia and those outside. What makes the case look even worse is that the letters which went through Mr. Childs, the head of the Kazan District, indicate that this correspondence has been carried on systematically."

Childs had already had a close call earlier in the year. He had built up a coin collection in Russia amounting to some twenty-six hundred pieces, which he called the greatest collection of Russian coins in the world outside of the Hermitage. When he went abroad for convalescence in spring 1922, he brought along a large portion of it to keep in Berlin, but this was taken from him at the Lithuanian-German border. A year later, however, after he returned to Berlin, it was delivered to him intact. The rest of his coins he mailed out in small packets through the ARA courier during the course of 1922. He was so encouraged by how easy this was that he told his new wife's mother that he would send out all her valuables in this way. Among these treasures was a priceless collection of some sixty eighteenth-century gold snuffboxes.

Looking back on this disaster years later, he claimed to have made two grave errors: first, he did not heed the warning given him in a dream about a seizure by customs agents. This is impossible to verify, but his second error is a matter of record: he attempted to send out nearly all of his mother-in-law's fortune in one load. All was lost.

The ARA did the proper thing for Childs. The Kazan district physician, Dr. John E. Cox, wrote To Whom It May Concern that Childs was "in a generally run down condition, very nervous, and in great need of a prolonged rest." Russia in winter was no place for a man in his condition. Childs was equally candid with his mother, informing her in a letter that because his mother-in-law's nerves were shot, he had decided to resign from the ARA in order to get her out of Russia.

Lander's list of the damned was more extensive than Quinn's. Dalton had already called it quits, and Dodge, Childs, Wahren, and Turner were let go. Lander's net had also hauled in Hynes, Dunham, and Fox, whose names had been connected indirectly with the mail pouch contraband and who therefore, he maintained, also had violated paragraph 25 of the Riga Agreement, forbidding the relief workers from engaging in commercial activity. And because those responsible for the ARA courier service had to have been involved in the matter, liaison chief Lehrs and postal chief Shuckman should be dismissed—and not to forget whoever is in charge of the lead seals. For good measure he closed with a reference to the "abuse of the confidence of Colonel Haskell"—a phrase Quinn took to be a slap at himself.[10]

In the end, only the four Americans had to be sacrificed. On the rest Quinn stood his ground, although he did ask for any documentation the Soviets might have on Booman, Dodge's sidekick, who may well have been an anonymous victim of the trunk seizures. Later, Lander demanded that the ARA pay a fine of 23,511.95 gold rubles, or about $11,000—a demand Quinn rejected.

Meanwhile the courier leaving Moscow December 7 and carrying all the returned mail from the first two episodes was held up at Sebesh. Then on the night of December 12 at Kharkov there occurred the "rifling" of seven ARA mail pouches. At that point Quinn threatened that unless a halt was put to such activity, he would advise Haskell to stop all further increases in ARA feeding.

The scene of the trouble now shifted to Moscow. On December 16 *Izvestiia* ran an article on the courier affair under the title "How They Help." It was only a brief item printed on page four, yet it had all the effects of a front-page headline. It told readers that since the beginning of the mission there had been rumors that the American relief workers were storing up jewels, rugs, and furs, worth trillions of rubles. Now, thanks to the vigilance of the Soviet authorities, these rumors had been confirmed. "This is how they help the starving. This is how the representatives of 'civilized' America behave in 'barbarous' Russia. This is how 'rich' America exploits 'poor' Russia."

Despite Kamenev's insistence that the article was not official, Quinn felt that the government considered the affair "too good a chance to weaken our prestige to let pass." It was at this point that Haskell intervened from New York with a message to Kamenev via Quinn. Before his departure, Haskell had met privately with Lenin, and the two had discussed how they might bring about the establishment of U.S.-Soviet relations and what role Hoover might play in this. The colonel had promised Lenin to raise the matter with Hoover when he was in Washington. His message for Kamenev cautioned that "insignificant details of operation not be exaggerated and heralded to America at this time as it makes more difficult task accomplishing more important matters." Kamenev said he understood and promised a follow-up article giving a fairer treatment of the episode, and such an item did appear, over Lander's name, but only six days later in order, it was felt, to give the negative story time to settle in.

Now Quinn had another problem on his hands. Once the *Izvestiia* coverage appeared, the American correspondents—who had learned some of the facts about the incident but had not been inclined to write it up—felt that they had no choice but to file their own stories. Since the beginning of the mission they had honored the ARA's request not to publicize details about its various troubles with Soviet officials. The fear within the ARA was that such publicity would jeopardize the mission. Now that *Izvestiia* had struck in this fashion, however, the reporters—themselves fervent treasure hunters by reputation—wished to fire back. Quinn called them together in his office and, without naming names, laid out the "bare facts" of the case.

So the correspondents were set loose. Seldes of the *Chicago Tribune* appears to have completely lost his head over the matter. Until recently, he and his fellow reporters had been able to send censorable material out of the country through the ARA courier bag, thinly disguising it as personal correspondence. The ARA winked at this, but the December courier scandal forced Quinn to put a stop to it. Seldes was so worked up by the *Izvestiia* attack that he went over to the Hotel Savoy and attempted to send to his newspaper over the wireless a direct blast against the Bolsheviks: that they had always harbored "severest suspicion" of the ARA and showed "frequently directest antagonism." "These facts hitherto not presented American public because relief agencies feared should American support cease account these difficulties twould mean digging another five million graves along Volga."

Seldes mentioned Haskell's recent meeting with Lenin, at which the ailing Soviet leader told the colonel that he hated the Soviet bureaucracy and all the many ways it was hindering the ARA, and promised better cooperation. Seldes must have been hoping that by thus invoking Lenin's name he would disarm the censor, otherwise it is a mystery why he even tried to send the story. As for the scandal itself, he reduced it to a matter of a few articles of jewelry, some cheap prints, Russian letters, and Christmas toys. "Upon this minor incident involving couple hundred dollars public press bases attack Americans."

As a result of this outburst, Seldes became another casualty of the courier incident: he was told that he could not get a visa to return to Russia, only to depart. Quinn expressed his relief to Haskell that Seldes's story had not passed the censor: "We have, as you know, always kept to ourselves the various difficulties had with the government, for, on the whole, they are very small in consideration of the size and extent of the operation, and irritating as they may be, we do not want to herald them to America."

Duranty, who was cleverer and had better connections than Seldes, was able to get his story on the courier affair cleared through the censor and sent to the *Times* by wireless on the same day the *Izvestiia* article appeared. Unlike Seldes,

Duranty conceded that there had been a legitimate reason for the Soviet action. The authorities had never objected to Americans taking carpets and a fur or two as souvenirs but "drew the line at anything that looked like a business deal"—and one relief worker had crossed this line. "Indeed, there is reason to believe that the whole incident arose from what the Russians knew about purchases by this particular individual." The Soviets had crossed a different kind of line, however, when they used the incident to condemn the ARA:

It is a pitiable commentary on the Russian state of mind that during the whole period of eighteen months for which the association has been working here the Russian press has not published a single article honestly appreciative of the services of these young Americans, who, for relatively small salaries, risk their lives—any one who has travelled in the typhus area in Winter will bear me out—and undergo many hardships for the benefit of Russia's famine victims.

Unlike Seldes, Duranty took careful aim at a specific target. The problem was not the Bolshevik leadership, but a noisy and influential group of die-hard radicals within the Party:

[T]he trouble with this country is that there is a whole mass of Communists so fanatical in their revolutionary ideals that they will not admit that any good thing can come out of Nazareth. Like all people long enslaved and suddenly freed, they retain the servile trait of acute suspicion. To some of them the relief administration from the outset has been a capitalist plot. They do not represent Russia, but unfortunately they appear to have enough influence to get misleading articles printed in one of the official Russian newspapers.

This story appeared in the *New York Times* on December 18 and inspired Baker to wire a comment on it to Moscow: "Duranty's article today splendid."[11]

It took a while longer for things to settle down, and until they did, the ARA postponed the expansion of its operations, as Quinn had threatened, and put on hold the reopening of the Orenburg district. From this distance, the entire affair appears to be little more than a passing public relations problem for the ARA, but Ellingston claimed that until late in December Quinn was "somewhat obsessed with the danger of the show's going on the rocks all together."

In the aftermath there were further courier problems but on a lesser scale. The last week of February 1923 was a period of high tension for the ARA, as officials began to seize and open the ingoing and outgoing ARA mail pouches. "Every single damn letter as far as we could make out had been opened, and clumsily resealed," Ellingston complained. "A letter to Gregg from the war department on some old routine stuff was resealed in an envelope addressed to Miller of the Mennonites." And there were "daubs of paste and dirty finger marks everywhere."

Haskell was in Russia on this occasion and took his complaint directly to Litvinov, who naturally pleaded complete ignorance. Ellingston, who positively reveled in reporting Haskell's occasional outbursts at the Bolo chiefs, records that the colonel then said to the deputy foreign minister:

Now look here, Litvinoff, I'm no child; you know and I know damn well that our bags were opened, all our mail read and perhaps some of it held out. Who ordered it done and why? Is the Soviet Government trying to show us that they don't want us here anymore? I want a definite statement that this sort of thing won't happen again or a definite request that we get out.

Litvinov did the only thing he could do, which was to shrug his shoulders and blame the Party's die-hards.

The February standoff cleared the air on the question of ARA mail, but the harassment of relief workers at the frontier would occur sporadically until the end. In May 1923 Quinn himself, passing through Stolpce, was subjected to "a most thorough and embarrassing search."

But there were in any case fewer diamonds, furs, and rugs to be discovered. This was mostly due to the fact that the best bargains had dried up during the first year of the mission, partly as a result of the economic stability achieved under NEP. But perhaps a contributing factor was a certain kind of fatigue that had set in among the relief workers, best captured in the last letter home written by Holden from Moscow in July 1923, addressed to his "Dear Folks" in Berkeley.

I am glad that I am coming home. I have been away from the States too long, and I need to come up for air. I may decide to go off again, sometime, but I expect that I will be home for a while. . . . It is all right to have a view point that will not place too great importance upon things which are minor; but it is well to be alive to all the things about you. Last night one of the men who has just come in from the Ural district was talking to me. He brought out a small test-tube filled with rubies and gave me ten of them. He was not drunk. I actually thanked him for the stones. Granted that they are reconstructed, and that all but one of them is very small, yet they have a value, and that value amounts to something. I expect that most of them will go into a ring for Edith. We will see. But at least I should be home for a while where people give dough-nuts and not rubies. A dough-nut is a much more wildly exciting gift to me now.[12]

WHEN THE DODGE-DALTON TRUNKS were opened on December 8, Leon Turrou was present as a witness, and he signed the Soviet government's "Act" as its translator. The shadow of Turrou falls ominously over the December courier incident.

Four years later Burland remembered the "gossip" in Moscow about Turrou: that "he was acting spy for the Bolos and gave away the Dodge trunk episode." It is unclear why it was thought that the Soviets would have needed the services of a spy to unmask Dodge, whose reputation had long preceded the train that was carrying him and his plunder out of Russia. Still this does not necessarily mean that Turrou did not spy for the Bolos. The career path he followed after leaving the ARA indicates a proclivity for the espionage game. And the remarkably nomadic existence of his pre-adult years might suggest long experience in changing allegiances, although for the details of his early biography one must rely on Turrou's own testimony, delivered under oath in United States District Court in New York in 1938.

Turrou—who pronounced his name to rhyme with "Ferow"—was born in Cracow on September 14, 1895, several months after his father had died in Paris. Three months after his birth his mother died, and he was adopted by neighbors, who took him to Cairo and Alexandria, and later, at age seven, to China. After his foster mother died, his foster father took him to Odessa and then to Warsaw, and after serving with the Imperial Russian Army during the Russo-Japanese War, returned with the boy to China, working there as an importer until his death a few years later. Turrou, by then a teenager, was sent back to Poland, wandered to Berlin, then London, and then came to the United States, where he earned a living washing dishes and translating, for by then he had acquired a proficiency in several languages.

In 1915 he left for Paris, seeking opportunity in the war, and ended up joining the Russian Imperial Army. He saw action on the eastern front and was twice wounded. After the war he was briefly in Shanghai; in 1919 he returned to the United States and supported himself on his translating skills, working for the Russian-language newspaper *Slovo* until he joined the marines in 1920. He then picked up and moved to Paris, where he worked as a translator and somehow got connected with the ARA. In September 1921 he signed on with the Russian unit, for which his knowledge of languages and his Russian background must have made him seem an attractive candidate. He felt right at home in Moscow; he himself said that he had the "typical high-cheekboned oval face of a Russian."

Turrou had been hired as an interpreter, and he continued to serve in that capacity throughout his time in the mission, but he had a knack for insinuating himself into more responsible positions. Early on he was placed in charge of clothing manufacture at Moscow headquarters, which meant supervising the assembly of clothing packages. Several weeks later he was transferred to the administrative division, where he served as special assistant to its chief. In April 1922, Haskell raved about Turrou's talents and spirited performance in a variety of roles: he was "swinging one of the most trying and difficult positions at these headquarters and he is at present the only man filling a position with responsibility beyond that which he was engaged." These words would later take on an entirely different meaning from that intended. Haskell was hooked, and once he was hooked, he stubbornly resisted being unhooked in the face of adverse evidence.

The first complaints about Turrou came from Soviet officials who were upset about the quality of his interpreting during ARA-Soviet meetings, charging that he distorted their own words and delivered the American message with an excessively hostile slant. If the quality of his translations of newspaper articles and official texts is any indication, the Soviets had a legitimate gripe. Turrou had a creative imagination, which he put to liberal use as a translator.

The more serious problem with Turrou, however, was not his translations but his transactions, those of the monetary variety. His record is an assortment of odds and ends.

On November 1, 1922, the London office informed Moscow that Turrou had been complaining that he was losing money because London was depositing his pay checks in dollars in a Paris bank; since it was impossible to have a checking account in dollars with a Paris bank, they had no idea what he was talking about.

In January 1923, after reliever Joseph Janicki had left the mission and was living in Riga, he was told by a succession of Americans traveling from Moscow that he had left some unpaid bills there at the Empire casino. This did not make any sense to him until someone told him that his visiting cards had been left at the Empire with an IOU signed by Turrou, and that it was Turrou who was telling people about Janicki's alleged unpaid bills. Janicki wrote to Quinn of this dirty "trick" and asked for help in clearing his name; if Quinn had any doubts, he could just ask Freddie Lyon.

This question could not have been resolved to Janicki's satisfaction because a year after the mission he wrote to the New York office and asked to be remembered to all his ARA friends—all, that is, "EXCEPT TURROU. You can forget him for me, if you please. I will convey my best wishes to him personally when I arrive and he should yet survive."

Others would readily have joined in such well-wishing. One was Michael Banetski, a Soviet citizen who turned to Haskell at mission's end and asked to be taken to the United States He was worried that his contribution as an ARA employee might have been obscured from the colonel by Turrou, with whom he had worked for nine months: "He always try to keep me down never did give me a credit for important work but always did take credit for it to himself."

Turrou was connected with an unhappy story involving the renting of an apartment in Moscow by three ARA men. The cost was about forty-five dollars per man per month, and each American put down two months rent in advance and moved in. Their joy at having graduated from life at the personnel house was cut short, however, when the Cheka showed up one evening to take possession of the place, which it had previously requisitioned for office space. The landlord had vanished. It seems that Turrou had brokered the arrangements.

All this came to light while Turrou was serving in Moscow, but it did nothing to dampen the enthusiasm of Haskell, who in February 1923, as Turrou was departing Russia, wrote a glowing letter thanking him for his "efficient service," especially his excellent interpreting at the many conferences with the Soviets.[13]

Turrou's difficulties began only after he crossed the Soviet border. In early March there were questions about a case of needles, worth $60, that he had taken from the Boinaia warehouse without a proper receipt. London headquarters was trying to track him down for a proper explanation. At this very time, Turrou was in Warsaw writing to Haskell about another troubling development. Before his departure from Russia he had purchased four diamonds and a platinum watch for $2,500, but on arrival in Warsaw he discovered that the diamonds were merely Ural sapphires—in other words, he had been conned. He was about to depart for the States but asked Haskell's permission to send the fake stones by ARA courier to Russia addressed to Booman and with a request that his Latvian friend do something about this. Haskell was out on leave, so Quinn wired London to advise that if Turrou were to surface there on his way to the States, he be informed that his request was denied.

A week later it was revealed that Turrou, who had paid the Moscow diamond seller with a check on the Banker's Trust in Paris, had stopped payment on the check—a fact he neglected to mention in his letter to Haskell—and that now the seller was in debt to the Soviet State Bank for the money. Quinn characterized this individual as being "one of the particularly undesirable types," though he thought the diamonds were probably genuine and that Turrou himself was the con. Quinn then learned from a separate source that Turrou had stopped payment by claiming that the check had been stolen and that the signature was a forgery. "On the whole it is a pretty shady deal and we are glad that Turrou is out of Russia."

But where was he? Mitchell in London wrote to New York that they could not track him down in Warsaw and that he had avoided the London offices, apparently "doing a will-o'-wisp stunt." He had set sail from Le Havre for New York, and the plan was to intercept him there. Mitchell characterized his behavior "an example of perfect nerve. The young man can speak thirteen different languages and I think has apparently been doing a bit of business in each."

By March 26 Turrou had arrived in New York and had somehow been lured to ARA headquarters. There he explained that he no longer was in possession of the diamonds in question, that he had given them to a man named Nachimoff in Warsaw, who was to return to Moscow and deliver them to Volodin in Lander's office. He was also to carry a letter from Turrou explaining to Volodin that the stones were worth only about seventy dollars and requesting him to return the jewelry to the seller. As for the missing needles, Turrou claimed that these had been given to a Catholic institution in Moscow as agreed to by Burland.

This information was cabled to Quinn, who wired back on March 31 that no such Nachimoff had appeared in Moscow and that the needles story was plainly untrue. He felt that Turrou should be forced to make good on the canceled check.

On April 4, Brown wrote to Haskell, now back in Moscow, that Turrou had come clean on the diamonds question, and had signed a sworn affidavit. It is unclear what he confessed to because the affidavit is lost, but somewhere along the line Turrou may in fact have been suckered because the chiefs characterized his statement as "a long sad story of what purports to be his attempt to enter into the 'get rich quick game.'" As for the needles question, he stood by his story, and there was no evidence to contradict it.[14] Nowhere in the documentation is there any indication of what Haskell thought about these matters.

This should have been the end of the Turrou story; he should have disappeared from the scene like those other ARA operators, Veil and Dodge. But Turrou was a confidence man of a higher breed.

In late April, only three weeks after developments that would have left a normal man with his head lowered, he addressed a rather brash letter to Hoover. He told the Chief that the day he had been hired to interpret for Haskell had been the happiest of his life because it had put him in an ideal position to discover "the real truth" about Russia. His ARA role and his facility with languages had enabled him "to penetrate into untoward situations." He had succeeded in gaining the confidence of the Soviet leaders and had thus been able to learn the inside story about Bolo affairs. After a while he had decided to leave Russia because "I was tired of being followed and being spied upon and I felt that I had done as much as I could with enough time left to get away safely." He felt that Hoover would benefit from hearing the "detailed facts" of his "personal continuous investigations."

But just in case the Chief might not see it that way, Turrou dropped an unsubtle hint. The newspapers were all asking him for his story, he said, but he thought he should get Hoover's approval before making any of his findings public. These findings had mostly to do with official Soviet obstructionism. Why, hardly a paragraph of the Riga Agreement had not been violated. He was in possession of confidential information that Lander's agents had been ordered to disseminate anti-ARA propaganda. Haskell's meeting with Lenin had raised Soviet expectations of a deal with Washington, but "Colonel Haskell came back empty handed and they never got over the disappointment." And so on.

With only a few months remaining in the mission and with the ARA wishing to avoid controversy, Turrou could raise quite a fuss. In order to prevent this, Hoover would have to agree to see him, which was Turrou's calculation. This was decided in the New York office, where the discussion must have been accompanied by much gritting of teeth. There is no record of the Hoover-Turrou encounter, but it happened on or before May 14 when Page wrote to Herter that Turrou was "not a genuine ARA man"—Quinn's words—and that he was not to be allowed to see the Chief again.

Turrou dropped out of sight for about two years, until he wrote another letter to Hoover, this one regarding a supposed six-week business trip he had just taken to Russia. His most sensational news was that scores of former ARA Russian employees were languishing in GPU prisons on charges of espionage. He seems to have been obsessed with the details of Soviet spying, citing a popular saying in Russia that whenever two people are together talking, one is an informer; and that in Russia all the walls have ears.

A year later Turrou applied for membership in the ARA Association. Burland weighed the costs and benefits. Although Turrou was clearly an undesirable element, it was thought wise not to antagonize him: "He himself could tell many interesting tales if he put his mind to it. Turrou could make out a case for himself if he decided to fight."[15]

Turrou took a job as a foreign correspondence clerk in a New York City department store, then as a post office clerk in the Bronx. On April 1, 1929, he went to work for the other Hoover, joining the FBI. Turrou was now a G-man; his new motto, "For God, for country, and for J. Edgar Hoover." To this day he remains one of the most controversial agents in the bureau's history.

His first big case came when he was assigned in 1932 as a member of the "Lindbergh squad" in New York, charged with tracking down the kidnapped Lindbergh baby. A colleague on the squad was former ARA man John Seykora.

But what brought Turrou national fame was his work uncovering Nazi spies in America in the late 1930s. As he later put it, Hoover had appointed him to "direct the FBI's counterattack against the Nazi spy ring." This step had been taken after evidence of such a ring came to light in Scotland, prompting the British War Office to contact the American General Staff in Washington. There the matter was turned over to Major Joseph Dalton of Military Intelligence in the Second Corps Area on Governor's Island and former trunk mate of Earl Dodge. Dalton thought the report serious enough to call in the FBI, and Turrou got the nod.

His investigation led to the arrest of eighteen members of an alleged Nazi spy ring, three of whom came up for trial in autumn 1938. The defendants, German immigrants with limited abilities in English, claimed that Turrou had framed them, tricking them into endorsing false confessions: he had drawn up the documents and then browbeaten them into signing.

The spy trial created a huge sensation, and Turrou was at its center. Photos of his high-cheekboned oval face appeared in newspapers across the country. But the main reason for all this attention was that before the case had even come to trial, Turrou had resigned from the bureau in order to write a series of newspaper articles on his spy roundup. He told his editor at the *New York Post* that he had been planning to retire anyway because of ill health and wanted to publish his story in order to awaken the country to the dangers of foreign espionage activity.

The FBI refused to accept his resignation and instead dismissed him with prejudice, depriving him of his retirement benefits and of three months' pay for accumulated leave. According to the *New York Times*, he had committed a "breach of the G-man oath which binds all agents of the bureau not to disclose service information either during or after their service." It seems that for an FBI agent to resign before seeing a case through to completion was unprecedented. J. Edgar Hoover refused to discuss Turrou. President Roosevelt condemned him.

The trial turned out to be, for a while anyway, as much about Turrou's character as that of the alleged spies. One of the defense lawyers, George C. Dix, went after Turrou with particular zeal. The high point came when the counsel called to the witness stand a man who would destroy former special agent Turrou's credibility—none other than Major General William N. Haskell, commander of the New York National Guard. He would testify that Turrou was unreliable and disloyal, thereby completely undermining the prosecution's case—at least that was the script in Dix's head, but it did not play out that way.

Upon questioning, Haskell denied that he had ever had reason for doubting Turrou's loyalty during the ARA mission.

"Didn't you receive reports from members of your staff that Turrou was suspected of being disloyal?" asked Dix in a clear reference to Turrou's alleged role as spy for the Bolos in the courier incident.

"Oh, I heard some gossip," Haskell sniffed, "but I paid no attention to it." Dix must have felt the room start spinning around him, but he pressed on gamely: "Didn't you tell me last July that you used an interpreter named Lears [Lehrs] whenever you could instead of Mr. Turrou?"

"Yes, but I also told you why. I said Lears didn't have as much brains as Turrou, and anybody who has used interpreters a lot knows that the less brains they have the better they are apt to be, so long as they know the language."

This stopped Dix right in his tracks. You can almost hear the shuffle of feet as the reporters scramble for the exits. The New York *Sun* called Haskell's testimony a "boomerang."

The FBI won its case against the spy ring, and Turrou moved on, though without leave and retirement benefits. The following year, his book *Nazi Spies in America* was published; it sold well and was turned into the Warner Bros. film *Confessions of a Nazi Spy*, starring Edward G. Robinson. Also in 1939 Turrou coauthored the instructional *How To Be a G-Man*, which informed readers about the kinds of techniques used by agents, such as shadowing and disguise. It had this to say on the vital subject of personal integrity: "You must not associate with bad companions and must pay your bills promptly. The F. B. I. is proud of its splendid reputation and you must not do anything to bring shame to the name G-man."

Turrou went into private investigating with two former G-men but also found time for the lecture circuit. In March 1941 he spoke at the Yale Club in New York and was announced as "Leon G. Turrou, Former Ace G-Man of America, the man who exposed the Nazi Spy Ring in America: Asked not to talk until the Spy Trials were over—and who now is ABLE TO TELL ALL." He was also doing a series of dramatic broadcasts for radio station WHN in New York, perhaps recreating his counterespionage exploits.

In 1949 he published a memoir with the *noiriste* title *Where My Shadow Falls: Two Decades of Crime Detection*, in which he told of his "Twenty years as a sort of straight shooting knight errant, riding the white charger of the avenging Law on the merry-go-round of Crime."

This book recounted his further adventures after leaving the bureau. Lying about his age, he joined the army in World War II and went off to fight as Private Turrou; in 1950 he was discharged as a lieutenant colonel.

Toward the end of his memoir he demonstrated that he had not lost his powers of imagination or his taste for conspiracy theories. He posited that Hitler was alive and living in Moscow as part of a Soviet plot. "It should not surprise us too much to see the spectacle of a Marxian-indoctrinated Hitler popping out one day like a communist jack-in-the-box to unite an ever adoring Germany with totalitarian Russia in a common assault on Western democracy."

The last word on Turrou came in the final issue of the *A.R.A. Association Review*, in 1965, which printed his letter to the editor. He reported that his permanent residence was Monte Carlo, that he had "never worked so hard in my life as I do now." His place of employment was the Getty Oil Company, where since 1950 he had been serving as special consultant to J. Paul Getty.[16]

CHAPTER 41

THE WIND AND THE SUN

A man with a passion for espionage like Turrou would have found himself among kindred spirits at ARA Moscow headquarters, which by most accounts was honeycombed with Cheka agents. This term "agents" was often applied indiscriminately, not only to full-time secret police personnel who had "penetrated" the ARA but as well to those ARA employees pressed into service, often unwillingly, as informants. The distinction was not always evident to the relief workers, yet it seems that in most districts the men were able with little difficulty to identify at least one or two of their hires who had been sent to observe them and otherwise gather information about the ARA. Quinn is quoted by Seldes as saying that every wastebasket in the Moscow office had its contents taken to Cheka headquarters every night. "Yes, and they have done a thousand other dirty tricks on us."

Haskell professed to be completely indifferent to such behavior. He told reporter Hullinger that the Cheka's spies were free to come and go: "I don't mind. I have nothing to conceal from them. I spotted a couple the other day in one of my departments. I decided to give them a good look, so I shifted them about from one department to another. One of them is now in my telegraph room where he sees every message coming into this office or leaving it!" Haskell liked to assume the air of a tolerant master putting up with predictable schoolboy antics: Bolos will be Bolos. He wrote to New York in December 1921: "The situation is quite delicate here due to the Russian failure to comprehend that anybody could be in Russia without some ulterior motive of a political or commercial nature. We run the show wide open, have purposely put the most rabid Russians we can find in our file rooms so as to show our indifference as to what they see."

The most celebrated Cheka spy to operate within the ARA—assuming the innocence of Turrou—was Helen Balin, who was almost certainly the "Bolo spy girl" referred to in the 1929 "Non-Statistical Notes of the A.R.A." During the first eight months of the mission she served in a number of capacities, including interpreter for Gov. Goodrich. She is brought to life in Hullinger's 1925 *The Reforging of Russia* in a section where he describes how he was railroaded out of Russia by the Cheka. The ARA alumni newsletter reviewer wrote that the scenes with Balin, "Cheka Vamp and Agent Provocateur," were worth the price of the book.

In spring 1922 Hullinger was ordered to leave the country as punishment for a number of sins, the most serious of which appears to have been his attack on Soviet censorship published at about the time of the Genoa Conference in April. As he scurried around to various government offices trying to get his expulsion order reversed, Balin, now an ex-ARA employee, emerged from the shadows. He vaguely remembered her from the ARA's Thanksgiving dance. Her current assignment was to enlist him in the cause of the Cheka, by then officially the GPU. She told Hullinger: "As you know, the Soviet government does not like Colonel Haskell and the A. R. A. They are suspicious of the Americans. They want information about them. Perhaps you can help in that way." Hoping to weaken his resistance, she told him that three American relief workers were already working for the secret police; he recognized one of the names.

As the drama unfolded to a climax in the final tension-filled hours in Moscow, Hullinger was dogged by his Cheka shadow, Tomson—"an earnest but not overly clever Lett"—and trailed to the railway station by Eiduk, then handed off to an agent on the train who, in an unconvincing performance as an innocent passenger, accompanied him out of Russia. To Hullinger all the surveillance was a manifestation not of Bolshevism but of the Russian mentality: "Espionage has always been a large factor in Russian national life. The Russian mind thrives on intrigue."

It was more of the same out in the famine zone. In Samara, according to Dudley Hale, "the secret police (Chekka) are so anxious to find out that we are all a crowd of Czarists that they over step the limits of secrecy in their efforts to be secret, so that we usually know just who [of] the people in our employ are supposed to report on our activities." At Kazan headquarters, ARA interpreter John de Jacobs kept a mental scorecard of who was playing on whose side, and it bothered him that his American chiefs paid little attention to such matters. In 1925, after emigrating to the United States, he wrote a report that was quite harsh on the Kazan Americans for being insensitive to the significance of having so many spies operating within the ARA:

They came as watchmen, cooks, chauffeurs etc. Most of these were connected with the Cheka, men and women alike. Every word and gesture of the "bourgeois element" were being watched. Our American office, perhaps unknown to the Americans themselves, became the playground of suspicions, denunciations, accusations. . . . They even went so far as to suggest to the American District Supervisor to put the desks of a couple of them in his private office. As in all other instances he smilingly agreed.

The American recalled here was probably Childs, who shared Haskell's the-more-the-better attitude toward the espionage activity. In a letter from Kazan of November 6, 1921, he referred to a conversation he had had with the government representative, who assured him that there were no Cheka agents among the employees. Childs was quick to inform this official that "we had nothing to conceal and that therefore the presence of such agents was a matter of indifference to us."

It was hardly a matter of indifference, however, to the "bourgeois element" among the staff, who came under as much scrutiny as the Americans. To judge from a diary entry of late September 1921, Childs did not understand the implications of this. One of the ARA employees had come to him in fear, telling him that the office was filled with agents of the Cheka and that she was concerned for her future and that of her fellow employees if their ARA protector were to leave after only a few months, as was the current rumor. Childs's response was not quite to the point:

As well as I could I attempted to calm her fears and also found the occasion an excellent one for expressing my entire indifference to the surveillance of the Checka. Since we had nothing to conceal about our work, I said, we welcomed the placing of as many agents in our organization as the Extraordinary Commission desired. I represented it as a very desirable action since nothing would more quickly gain us the confidence of the government than the presence in our midst of such secret agents.

This makes perfect sense from an ARA American's point of view, but it disregards the precarious situation of those employees whose loyal service to the ARA—no matter how "innocent" that organization was found to be—was by no means innocent in the eyes of Chekists looking for excuses to round up more class enemies. The fact that Childs apparently remained oblivious to such considerations until the end is made even more curious by the fact that along the way he married a Russian woman who had worked for the ARA in Petrograd.

The starting point of Childs's insensibility was his incognizance of the Chekists in his own office, beginning with his own interpreter. Decades afterward, in his various memoirs, he attempted to compensate for what he came to realize had been his utter ignorance of the extent of the Cheka's activities. It was a phenomenon typical of the Stalin period when people projected the features of High Stalinism back onto Lenin's rule. And it was typical of a onetime Bolshevik sympathizer like Childs to leap to the opposite extreme and attribute to Lenin's Cheka near-supernatural powers:

Our organization of Russian employees was swarming with spies and informers. Every bit of paper which was filed was read surreptitiously by Soviet agents, and even our most secret reports were subject in some mysterious way to their scrutiny. Those of our employees who were not hand-picked Soviet agents, and who came in close contact with us, were called periodically before the Soviet authorities for questioning as to our activities. This, however, was seldom necessary as those of our Russian employees, the closest to us in positions of the greatest confidence, were carefully selected Soviet agents.[1]

A substantially different picture emerges from the Cheka's own records, where the ARA is portrayed, in the words of one internal document, as a "very important nerve center of espionage activity," though here of course meaning of the imperialist and White Guard variety. In Samara the Cheka held a two-week course for its agents in the spring of 1922 called "Leading the fight against the inimical activities of the ARA." Cheka resolutions in the winter of 1921–22 preached vigilance with regard to the ARA, whose staff was said to consist mostly of former White officers, police officials, aristocrats, intelligentsia, and priests—which for all the paranoia behind it, is a more accurate profile of the ARA staff than the near-perfect collection of Soviet spies and informers Childs later imagined for himself.

Among the rare items of Soviet historiography devoted to the American relief story is a 1968 article with the alluring title "A Little-Known Page in the Activities of the ARA in Soviet Russia," written by what in those days passed for a professional historian in that strange land, a certain N. F. Gorodnichii. Based upon apparently authentic Cheka sources, it describes how the heroic Chekists fearlessly and brilliantly exposed the many U.S. intelligence agents disguised as relief workers with the ARA. Those uncovered are all identified by name and, most fantastically, include among their number the pathetic Harold Blandy.

One of the heroes of the struggle against the inimical ARA was Poliakov, author of the 1985 *Diversion Under the Flag of Aid*. The book's title page announces it as an "artistic-documentary story." In fact the documentary sections were new and useful at the time of publication; the rest makes it perfectly evident what kind of artist the author deserved to be called. He takes his reader behind the scenes of the "American Relief Show," revealing how the Cheka was able to enlist from among the ARA's Russian employees, most of them SRs and *kulak*s, several well-placed figures as Cheka operatives in order to foil the intrigues of the American imperialists. Along the way, nearly every one of the two dozen American relief workers mentioned by name is shown to have had a counterrevolutionary past and to be an active agent of American military intelligence inside Soviet Russia. It is in short an old-fashioned Cheka shoot-'em-up with "Iron Felix" Dzerzhinskii leading the struggle.

IT IS INTERESTING that Soviet authors would cast Dzerzhinskii in the role of ARA opponent because this is not at all the Dzerzhinskii of the ARA's version of the story: in a completely different context he became the Bolshevik hero of the American relief mission.

By the time the ARA came on the scene, the head of the Cheka was already getting out of the terror business, but his dark reputation was by then legendary and indelible. Before the Revolution Dzerzhinskii had spent only a brief time in European exile, unlike the other Bolshevik revolutionaries, instead remaining in the Party underground inside Russia. "Nothing could be more perilous," correspondent Mackenzie wrote. "Dzerzhinsky was chosen for this lot. He was often in prison, often a secret fugitive. Between 1897 and 1917 he spent eleven years in prison, nine of them at hard labour in chains. Many tales are told by his old friends of his doings in prison, how whenever possible he took the hardest tasks on himself, and how he defied his gaolers in every way possible."

He brought all this experience to the job of secret police chief after the Revolution. It was his direction of the Red Terror, begun in spring 1918, that established his image—or images: to opponents of the Bolshevik regime he was evil incarnate, whereas the Soviets depicted him in romantic-heroic terms, a kind of Soviet St. George slaying the class-enemy dragon. In his day, one of the several honorifics conferred on him was "Knight of the Revolution."

To friend and foe alike Dzerzhinskii stood apart from the other Bolsheviks. There was something about the man's delicate physical appearance that made him seem at once saintly and slightly insane—specifically his "deathmask face," which took the unacquainted by surprise because it was not the face of a killer. Yet those with a background in modern history needed only a few moments to find an appropriate context for it. Marguerite Harrison, who encountered him in 1920, was one such person: "'Where have I seen a face like that?' I reflected, for there was something vaguely familiar about his appearance. Then I remembered the pictures of Robespierre. . . . There was the same air of frailty and refinement about him." Many Western observers were put in mind of the Jacobin leaders: Robespierre, Marat, St. Just, and now Dzerzhinskii, the "Slavic St. Just"—they were a special brand of fanatical, incorruptible revolutionary.

Dzerzhinskii was understandably a favorite subject of the Western correspondents in Moscow. "Mild-mannered, blue-eyed and quiet-spoken, the real man is an amazing contrast to the usual idea of him," Mackenzie reported. "He is an idealist with the relentlessness of the high-purposed fanatic." In a May 1923 story he elaborated:

He is the type of man from which martyrs are made, gentle in his personal relations, remorselessly severe in his official life. I am quite sure that personally he could not inflict needless pain on the humblest of God's creatures. He loves children and can be roused to anger by any tale of childish wrong. His friends call him the "man with the golden heart." And yet this man is the overlord and directing spirit of the most terrible political police in the world.

Goodrich and Golder met with him on April 1, 1922. When Goodrich asked him about the Cheka and all those executions he had heard about, Dzerzhinskii "laughed very heartily" and said that many tall tales had been told about its activities. In fact, he assured the Governor, the Cheka had kept a very careful record of the cases it had tried and the penalties it had handed out, and he promised to furnish a statement. Having heard of the man's reputation, Goodrich expected "to see a bluebeard. As it was I met as 'kindly mannered a man as ever scuttled a ship.'" Here before him sat "a slight built, intellectual looking gentleman with a kindly blue eye, mustache and goatee, and the general appearance of a man more adapted to the study or the class room than to the operation of a railroad."[2]

It was only now, in April 1922, as Dzerzhinskii stepped forward to help the ARA overcome its transport crisis, that the relief workers began to encounter him in the flesh and reacted to his unexpectedly mild appearance and manner in the context of his fitness to manage Russia's railroads. The ARA men seem never to have realized that Dzerzhinskii had been named people's commissar of transportation—meaning, for the most part, railroads—already a year earlier. It was an assignment he took on in addition to his duties as secret police chief and people's commissar of internal affairs, and it was not a completely unrelated line of work: the Cheka since 1918 had its own railroad department and was on occasion called in for economic troubleshooting.

In January and February 1922 Dzerzhinskii wore all three official hats in undertaking an expedition to Siberia intended to clear the way for grain to European Russia obstructed by "bandit" raids and, more generally, to restore the disrupted rail links to the east. But despite the ARA's constant difficulties with rail transport, it was only in early spring, when the shipments of American corn were jammed up at junctions west of the Volga, that Dzerzhinskii entered the picture as the solution to the crisis. This prompted his conference with Goodrich and Golder.

Golder sized him up as "a thoroughly honest, conscientious fanatic who has formed his ideas during the ten years that he has spent in Siberia. He is about as fitted to run a railway as I am, but he is better qualified merely because he is a

Communist. He is like an inquisitor of old; he regards Communism as a religion and those who disagree with him are heretics to be rooted out."

Golder was not the only American to remark on Dzerzhinskii's apparently unorthodox qualifications for his new assignment, though they were ignorant of his hands-on experience. As Fisher later remembered: "As far as was known, Djerjinsky's acquaintance with the administrative and operative technique of railways was limited to that of a casual passenger. He was neither an engineer, like Krassin, nor a man of affairs." Appearances also were not encouraging:

The A.R.A. found this legendary figure mild mannered, courteous, and soft-spoken. He lacked all the bluster and aggressive mannerisms which had deceived some of the A.R.A. men into believing that Eiduk was a man who could get results. Djerjinsky was apparently the antithesis of the traditional go-getter. Except for a calm imperturbability, there was nothing in his bearing to suggest the capable executive. What would have happened had this man been introduced to the officers and directors of the principal railways in America or Great Britain, as chosen to take over complete control of their administration, baffles the imagination.

Yet word that Iron Felix was going to help tackle the railroad crisis lifted the spirits of the Americans. For "this was Russia, and Russia of the Revolution, and hence the members of the A.R.A. most concerned with the transportation question found it satisfying to think that where others had failed, the man who had stamped out anarchy and disorder by terror might be able to terrorize the railways into greater usefulness."

Brooks's account of the ARA and the Russian railways placed a blunt emphasis on this last point: "There could be no doubt of his efficiency as the exterminator of all those who stood in the path of the Communistic advance. The members of the A.R.A. found it better to hope his force of character would succeed in untangling the railway snarl than to speculate on his renowned activities as chief of the secret police."

He arrived on the scene at the eleventh hour. With hundreds of cars of corn bottlenecked at the western edge of the Volga valley and railroad workers diverting cars and seizing corn, Haskell forced a showdown by threatening to cancel all further corn shipments into Russia. This brought about the decisive April 12 conference of the ARA chiefs and Kamenev, Dzerzhinskii, Eiduk, and several railroad officials.

The most interesting testimony concerning this meeting comes from Haskell, who was most curious to have a look at the legendary Cheka chief. "At first sight Djerjinski rather surprised me," the colonel told Duranty. "He seemed so gentle with his mild blue eyes." After a while these reports of first-time Dzerzhinskii sightings assume a monotonous regularity, like all those accounts of near-death experiences. The description Haskell left behind in his memoir was more original. He recalled that the meeting took place in Dzerzhinskii's office and that a number of railroad officials were present. "Their dreaded chief sat at the head of the table—a tall, thin, serious-miened individual, with an Oriental case of features, and a long, scraggly beard which gave him the appearance of a Chinese."

At his side was Eiduk. By now the ferocious Latvian had become, in the eyes of Haskell and company, a force for obstruction. One reason that the April conference was so memorable for the Americans and forever endeared Dzerzhinskii to them was that on this occasion he removed that obstruction, humiliating Eiduk in the process.

As he recounted it to Duranty in 1923, Haskell began the meeting with a review of the severity of the railroad car shortage and a statement of how many cars were needed to put the show over. Eiduk then responded, but not to the satisfaction of Dzerzhinskii, who cut him short: "I want you to be quite sure of your facts and figures, comrade, because you will have to account for them to me personally, and if they are wrong—."

"His eyes were not mild then," Haskell noticed. "I began to understand what sort of man this was. Eyduk subsided and we did not hear another squeak from him but once, when Kamenief silenced him with a wave of the hand."

Dzerzhinskii then turned to Haskell: "You have told me your minimum requirements. Well, now, I will see they are met."

In his memoir, Haskell laid it on a bit thicker. He remembered Dzerzhinskii chastising Eiduk "in a tone of voice that I had never heard before and with a look in his eyes calculated to inspire terror." Dzerzhinskii directly accused Eiduk of deceiving him, and he, realizing that his boss was "on the point of taking drastic action against him, . . . sat frozen in his chair unable to talk."

Here the colonel saw fit to use the moment to finish off his square-headed nemesis: he reported that within a week of the conference Eiduk was removed as chief plenipotentiary, and that "it is rumored that he took a hurried trip to the White Sea region. In any event, no member of the American Mission in Russia, nor any of its one hundred twenty-five thousand employees, ever saw or heard of Eiduk again during the year which followed, or until our departure from Russia." The implication, of course, is that Eiduk had been sent into exile. In fact he remained on the job as chief plenipotentiary through the corn drive and until the summer. That Haskell chose to make Eiduk thus disappear probably indicates the extent to which Dzerzhinskii had reduced the man in his eyes.

Haskell's major accomplishment at the conference was an agreement that the ARA could now have direct dealings with railroad officials, something Eiduk had up to then been able to prevent. Subsequently, on every Wednesday until the transportation crisis was resolved, ARA officials met with Dzerzhinskii and his railroad staff to discuss ongoing problems.

Several days after the April 12 meeting, executive assistant Mathews led the first such session. In the course of the discussion Dzerzhinskii asked one of his men, Zhukov, what he could deliver to the ARA in numbers of railroad cars. Mathews found the response excessively optimistic and said so. Dzerzhinskii turned to Zhukov: "Don't promise a single car that you cannot deliver, for every car you promise must be absolutely delivered. Say exactly how many you can deliver, and deliver them. Then later if you find you can supply more, give more, but your promise must be only what you are sure you can get. How many can you really deliver?" Zhukov redid his calculations and came up with an estimate about half the size of the first. Thus, right before the Americans' eyes Dzerzhinskii was breaking the Russians of their notorious habit of promising more than one could give.

Dzerzhinskii led by example, Brooks wrote, and the force of his leadership effected a turning point in the railway crisis: "Soon, his vigorous measures for raising the efficiency of the railways began to bear fruit and the required number of cars at last began to be received at ports."

It was no secret that Dzerzhinskii was able to deliver on his promises and save the day in part by bringing the force of iron discipline to bear on the railroad workers and, in Fisher's words, "by methods so severe that they would never be employed by the most ruthless of those whom the Bolsheviks are fond of describing as 'capitalistic exploiters of labor.'"

Haskell had no doubt that Dzerzhinskii ordered the imprisonment and even execution of obstructionist railroad officials: "This may be considered by western standards as horrible, but it was also horrible to think of the millions of helpless, starving human beings beyond the Volga who would certainly have died in large numbers had it not been for the ability of Dzerzhinsky to move the trains." The important thing to the ARA was that Dzerzhinskii had been able to put his job over, however draconian his methods.

But Haskell, Fisher, and others realized as well that Dzerzhinskii's administration of the railroads was not all blood and iron; that one reason for his success was his willingness and ability to enlist the cooperation of the railroad technical experts, who had been trained under the old regime and stayed on the job through the Revolution and Civil War. Several ARA men made a special point of expressing their admiration for the contribution of Russia's railway men to the relief effort. Ruhl noted the large number of "old minor officials who are still at their posts—men with a habit of work, technical knowledge, and a certain *esprit de corps* as railroaders. . . . The impossible was sometimes done simply because of the pride of the railway personnel in getting the train through, whatever the cost." Barringer called them

the most efficient body of steady workmen in Russia. With only a few engines and cars out of every hundred they had in normal times, these men, free from all political hindrances carried our thousands of tons of supplies all over European Russia safely quickly and with most careful accounting. No other institution of the government could approach these fellows. It was a great pleasure to deal with them after milling around for hours with a civil official, as, in many respects, both in character and "ways of doing business", they were not unlike our own splendid railwaymen. Fortunately for Russia, "the Center" made them, early in the game, free from all political control by local governments, so that they were able to tackle their problem of keeping the wheels moving and their organization together without a local Bolo official trying to apply his half-baked interpretation of how Karl Marx said it should be done.

Fisher concluded that the amazing revival of the railroads "would not have been possible without the splendid efforts of the non-Communist experts who are inspired unquestionably by a loyalty to Russia rather than loyalty to the present government. The fact remains, however, that they have given this service under a Soviet Commissar who is undoubtedly in complete control of the transportation system."[3]

And so it happened that the man who personified the Red Terror became a hero to the American Relief Administration. "I don't care about his past record," Haskell declared. "Djerjinski is all right in this country—he gets things done." Mackenzie wrote: "Dzerzhinsky is efficiency personified"; he was "one of the two really great organizers the Russian Revolution has produced."

Brooks's monographic essay, "Russian Railroads in the National Crisis," printed as a special issue of the *A.R.A. Bulletin* in November 1923, had as its frontispiece a sketch of Dzerzhinskii with the caption "Commissar of Transport of Soviet Russia whose management of Russia's broken down railways saved a broken down nation." He even earned a place in the ARA's "Non-Statistical Notes": "Djerjinsky fires the railroads." He was the Bolo Master of Efficiency.

Important though Dzerzhinskii's contribution was, the fact is that the key to the revival of Russia's railroads in 1922 was the stimulus provided by the American Relief Administration. Dzerzhinskii had already been railway commissar for a full year before the corn crisis without having achieved dramatic results. It was the sudden prospect of a catastrophe in March-April that forced a breakthrough. Yes, Dzerzhinskii's leadership was crucial, an ARA employee in Rostov observed, "But it is just as evident that had not the ARA promised Russia such splendid help and had there not been the absolute necessity to realize these promises by ways of improving the railroad service, the abilities of the Commisariate for Communication would have remained latent for some time still to come and Russian railroads would not be what they now are."

The relief simply had to be put through or millions more might have starved. Moreover, failure in such circumstances would have been, as Duranty wrote before these events, in October 1921, a "tragic confession of impotence to the world." The extreme urgency of the moment energized the entire railway administration, from the commissar himself down to his lowest subordinates. The Rostov observer agreed: "The Russian railroader, submerged in lethargy and despair was roused, and learned that the life of his children was dependant [*sic*] upon his ability to expedite trains and cars containing foodstuffs and medicines to be distributed 'to the poor and afflicted' by the A.R.A. All these facts were mighty stimula, and a transport put in shape meant indeed much in the economical life of Russia." This is about how Fisher presented it in the official ARA history:

For the first time since the Revolution here was an organization, with a difficult task to perform, with a definite plan of doing it, and with a dogged insistence that the plan be carried out. Gradually the railways were forced, by the hounding of the A.R.A., and later by the insistence of Djerjinsky, to establish *poriadok*—a systematic and orderly way of doing things, which, as Russians were fond of saying, had been banished by the Revolution.[4]

Arguably this statement does an injustice to Trotsky's Red Army, but Fisher rightly emphasizes the vitalizing importance of the ARA's injection into the Russian setting.

FOR THE SOVIET GOVERNMENT the days of attempting to solve economic problems through terror, ruthlessness, and enthusiasm—hallmarks of the military-style storming campaigns of War Communism—were now over. The corn crisis of spring 1922 was a last hurrah for Dzerzhinskii's direct-action methods—that is, until Stalin revived them in more monstrous form at the end of the decade. For the rehabilitation of the Soviet economy was now to be brought about by a partial reliance on orthodox economics in the form of the limited market ushered in by NEP.

Here the Bolsheviks placed their hopes on the prospect of adopting American work methods. Lenin and some of his colleagues had expressed interest in applying such methods to Soviet Russia ever since taking power; now, with the transition to NEP and especially once the ARA got to work and offered a living example of American efficiency, their interest was redoubled. The most conspicuous evidence of this was a renewed attention to Taylorism. The Bolshevik attraction to the theories of scientific management predated the world war, but the Bolsheviks in power, with Lenin leading the way, took a special interest in it despite its association with advanced capitalism.

Some Bolsheviks were not comfortable with the idea of Soviet power openly employing the tools of capitalism. Lenin himself wrote in spring 1918 that Taylorism represented the "last word of the most reckless capitalist exploitation," that it was understandable that it had been greeted by the laboring masses with such hatred. On the other hand, he argued, Taylorism represented the latest advance of science and, with its use of piece-rates and other incentives, made possible a huge increase in the productivity of human labor. Soviet power should take advantage of this and promote the systematic study and testing of Taylorism in Russia.

Of course a strict Marxist analysis would assert that since Russia had reached merely the earliest stages of capitalism, its success in importing the exploitative methods of advanced capitalism would signify a big step forward along the developmental path in the direction of socialism. But typically and understandably, Lenin framed the matter in more acceptably undeterministic terms: Taylorism in the hands of the capitalists was a force of evil, but the dictatorship of the proletariat could minimize its exploitative features and maximize the benefits it brought to workers, such as shorter work days.

Such a system was what Russia especially needed, Lenin wrote, because "Russians are bad workers compared to those of the leading nations," especially Germany and America. This was an unavoidable result of the deadening effects of tsarist rule and the remains of serfdom. Taylorism seemed to offer a way to leap over Russian backwardness because it did not require a highly skilled work force in a conventional sense. It produced efficiency by simplifying the tasks of the individual worker, removing all superfluous movement, and subjecting everything to strict accounting and control. Superior organization was seen as the answer to the inferior skills of the Russian worker.

Lenin's interest in Taylorism became best known from his April 1918 essay, "Current Tasks of Soviet Power," published in the United States as "Soviets at Work." It struck some American readers as surprisingly commonsensical, one newspaper commenting: "Lenine's advice to the Bolsheviki in the pamphlet 'Soviets at Work,' might be published in any of our efficiency magazines with some changes of phraseology, for it is devoted to urging increase of production, speeding up processes, iron discipline during work, careful accounting, business devices, the Taylor system of scientific management, and the like."

Lenin's enthusiasm waned as his attention was diverted by the outbreak of the Civil War, when the movements of armies, more than workers, preoccupied him. The concomitant rise of War Communism deluded him and his colleagues into believing that they could build communism directly, skipping stages of economic development in other ways. Then with the war over, at the end of 1920 Lenin was temporarily blinded by the utopian possibilities of electrification, in which again, he thought he perceived a scheme for leaping over Russian backwardness.

But the return to relative sobriety under NEP brought Taylorism back to the forefront—and this seemed to make doubly good sense, since Lenin and company now rationalized the retreat as merely a return to their more moderate policies of the winter of 1917–18, before civil war had forced them to adopt radical measures. Once the War Communist illusions of a great leap forward had been stripped away and with little hope held out for rescue by a revolution in the West, it was time once again to deal with the problem of the primitiveness of Russian labor.

The first conference on Soviet Taylorism was held in 1921. In part as a way to make it more palatable to the skeptical Bolsheviks within the Party the movement was given the name Scientific Organization of Labor. The conference led to the establishment of a network of institutes and schools and of a number of journals concerned with questions of efficiency and productivity.

During the time the ARA was in Russia, Soviet interest in Taylorism grew. Golder wrote in January 1923: "One hears a good deal of talk of the Taylor system, and I am told that it has been put into operation in certain shops. But it is not likely that anything is coming out of it. The efficiency needed here is freedom in selecting directors, managers, etc. There is a beginning that way, too."[5]

Taylorism was only one piece of a larger Bolshevik—as distinguished though not distinct from the Russian—preoccupation with *Amerika*. For the Bolsheviks had their own American dream. Theirs, like the more general Russian one, was a simultaneous mixture of attraction and repulsion: simply put, it was an attraction to American means and a repulsion from capitalist ends.

The Bolsheviks were drawn to the work ethic, efficiency, and awesome energy of the Americans and could be quite uninhibited about expressing this in the Soviet press, especially since 1921. Efficient Russians were called "Russian Americans." Here again, just as with Taylorism, there was a bit of a balancing act to be performed, as Soviet officials had to be careful not to portray capitalist America itself as an economic model. Praise for Americans was confined to the cultural-anthropological sphere. For political reasons public praise for the ARA in this context was muted.

The Russian term used to designate those desirable features of Americans, above all their energy and efficiency, was *amerikanizm*. In September 1923 Trotsky had a conversation with a visiting U.S. senator, during which he spoke optimistically about the prospects for U.S.-Soviet relations, mentioning that "there is also a very important moral and by no means sentimental factor easing our cooperation with the United States of America. The words *amerikanizm* and *amerikanizatsiia* are used in our newspapers and technical journals in an altogether sympathetic way, and by no means in the sense of reproach." True enough, though Trotsky was putting the most idealistic face on this for the benefit of his American visitor. Among their own, the Bolsheviks stressed that they intended to harness the best American methods to the cause of Soviet socialism. Thus Trotsky declared in August 1924, "Americanized Bolshevism will triumph and smash imperialist Americanism."

Historian Hans Rogger argues that in Soviet Russia in the 1920s the Bolsheviks saw in Americanism a supplement to Marxism as an ideology of development and industrialization. It represented a tacit admission that Marxism—"hard to grasp, resisted, and nowhere realized"—was an inadequate explanatory device of modernization for the Russian people. Americanism, American efficiency, was not a far-off promised land; it existed in the present and, significantly, had already for some time held a fascination for Russians of all classes. "It was used to demonstrate the promises and benefits that would accompany Russia's economic transformation, to justify and to make more bearable its costs and consequences, and to be a tangible goal and a goad for mobilizing a people who needed to be convinced of the desirability of modernity."

The matter was stated most bluntly by the Party's chief ideologist, Bukharin, in a February 1923 speech: "We need Marxism plus Americanism."

Yet strictly speaking, they could not have it both ways. In appealing to *amerikanizm*, the Bolsheviks were in effect suspending their Marxism, temporarily shelving their dialectical materialism in order to detach American national character from the American political economy. Or to state it in the most basic terms of Marxist theory, they were detaching part of the American superstructure from its economic base. Or—since such maneuvers often passed for good Leninism—to state it in pointedly blasphemous terms, they were siding with Weber or Tocqueville over Marx.

As a consequence, the Bolsheviks could sound very much like ordinary Russians talking about Americans. What Rogger writes about general Russian attitudes regarding the two countries can be applied to many Bolshevik leaders as well in 1922: that they saw

frequent, if superficial, parallels and affinities between the two nations; both were young and unencumbered by the burdens of the past; both occupied vast territories with rich natural and human resources; both lacked rigid hierarchies and customs that inhibited bold undertakings and innovation. Real or imagined similarities of climate, size, national character or temperament, problems and prospects, made the ingenious, energetic, open Yankee a more welcome teacher or model than the stiff class-conscious Englishman or the deliberate and pompous German.

All this was in tune with the new expressions of nationalism by the Soviet leaders, which were no doubt part of the strategy to attract foreign trade and recognition by appearing as members of a legitimate, even conventional, government. These expressions were also to some extent the sincere product of the Bolsheviks having won a civil war and now settling down to govern the country.

In the Soviet press matters were increasingly framed not as conflicts between capitalists and communists but as contrasts between Americans and Russians. Thus the Kazan *Izvestiia* in May 1923 observed: "The name of America has come to be synonymous in Kazan with speed and efficiency in the discharge of a task. The name of Russia is synonymous with drone. Our job now is to make both names equal in value, to raise the Russian to the American level."

Typically, the ARA went unmentioned, but readers made the connection. It is in this context of the Soviet fascination with American effectiveness, including the more specific focus on Taylorism, that the reputation of the ARA in Soviet Russia must be viewed. While the ARA did not plant the seeds of the Soviet Taylorism movement or of the general interest in American work methods, its conspicuous presence and popularity inside the country clearly catalyzed the interest in America. Hoover's organization seemed to offer a combination of the organizational-technical aspects of Taylorism and the speed and efficiency of *amerikanizm*. Even though most did not declare it openly, Soviet leaders considered the ARA a model of efficiency: this lean staff of American boys overcoming formidable obstacles, even the Russian winter, to accomplish a monumental undertaking.

In this respect, for Lenin the ARA was a godsend, serving as a living, breathing example of a system that worked, as he struggled to put his NEP reforms through over the opposition of the Party's die-hard objectors and the doubts of its uneasy remainder. The ARA's strict accounting procedures, concern for budgets, small staffs, disdain for bureaucracy, its general efficiency—these were now Lenin's own greatest causes. Duranty was aware of this effect of the ARA presence, which he noted in the *New York Times* on October 6, 1921, at a time when Lenin was making his boldest statements about the need for reform: "Internally it is enabling him to put over his new policy and by sheer contrast with the Americans show up the red tape and inefficiency he is anxious to eradicate. Externally it has brought Russia into touch with the one great country that is capable of helping her today."

While the Soviet press was far less pro-ARA than pro-Americanization, still it offered occasional glimpses of how the ARA was seen as a positive influence on Soviet organs—how American relief had, in Duranty's words, "put the Soviet government on its mettle."

Eiduk was credited with one of the strongest examples of this, an *Izvestiia* article of May 13, 1922, in which he praised the ARA's "business-like precision." "The too-evident efficiency of the ARA has stirred up the energy of Soviet office workers as well and especially of conscientious laborers." He pointed to the performance of the transport workers and then, in a momentary fit of hyperbole, stated that even his own apparatus of plenipotentiaries "has been lifted up to a high level."

Very friendly to the ARA was an article signed by "Worker Do-" in *Pravda* on June 10, 1922, in the section "Workers' Life." It described the operations in Moscow, though without mentioning the American relief workers, only the American system as executed by the trained Russian staff: "Walk into any of these kitchens and you will be struck by the cleanliness, accuracy and order. Everything is in shape, weighed out and checked." The author praised as a "novel system of incentive" an ARA practice of awarding "American certificates" to individuals who displayed orderliness and efficiency in ARA-sponsored reconstruction efforts.

Soviet praise of this kind was cited in an ARA administrative division report on the performance of the Russian personnel, which recalled an especially satisfying moment in the mission:

The application of American methods and training and the good accomplished thereby seemed to be particularly noticed on one occasion by Mrs. Kameneva, the wife of Kameneff, one of the leaders of the Communist Party, when she was looking through the offices one day. She expressed great surprise that so few employees could handle such a huge volume of work. And she noted, also with surprise, the absolute order and cleanliness in all departments.

Officials at the Soviet Tea Trust, when they had business to discuss concerning their role in the ARA food package operation, requested that division chief

Burland call upon them in person: "We want to see one of these energetic Americans and find out how they do business."[6]

The most well-publicized instance of Soviet official praise of the ARA as the emblem of American efficiency came near the start of the mission during Kellogg's September 1921 meeting with Kalinin. Kellogg's diary documents the relevant moment as he turned the discussion to the urgency of the relief operation:

I said that not only did the situation demand swift action—but that we Americans were accustomed to move rapidly.

K. (smiling at first and then earnestly) said "Yes—we have heard that and now we know it from personal observation"—& said that he and his colleagues were all impressed by what the ARA had done in the short time its representation had been in Russia & they were gratified by it. . . .

K. then went on to say that in his judgment America was helping Russia in 3 ways by the relief work

1) by material aid of food to starving population

2) by the moral assistance this material aid would engender to help the suffering people have courage to hold out on basis of new hope

3) by the example of the effectiveness of American methods—which would teach the Russians how to help themselves more effectively

Kalinin said evidence of the third influence was already audible in government offices, especially the Foreign Office, where "Americans"—meaning "Russian Americans"—used phrases like "step on the gas" and "don't like him buttin' in." Actually the source of such phrases must have been returned émigrés from America—a different kind of "Russian American"—so American influence was at work even before the ARA arrived.

K. said that not only the Central Govt and the District Govts were observing our methods & effectiveness with interest and appreciation but also the people—& went on to say that what Europe and its politicians and armies had not been able to do, namely win over Russia, America was likely to do with its relief work—and hence (smiling) he and the Moscow govt must look on America as at once the greatest friend but greatest (most dangerous) enemy in that while we saved their children's lives we won their people—intimating that the Russian govt methods would be compared with American energy and effectiveness.

K. then went on to say that in all these things the idealistic elements must not be overlooked—such elements were there and they were as valuable as the material accomplishments.

Kalinin's remarks, which sound as if they must have been spoken at the end of the mission, came before the expansion to adult feeding, the massive corn campaign, the revival of the railroads, and the various reconstruction efforts. Kalinin gives the impression that he and his fellow Bolsheviks viewed the American influence as a welcome contagion, that they would be its willing victims.

After the meeting, Duranty interviewed Kellogg and then, in a dispatch to the *Times*, summarized and polished Kalinin's message:

During the last three years the rest of the world has tried to conquer us in vain. Perhaps it will be you Americans who came here on an errand of mercy who will really win that victory. Where you show us and the Russian people that your methods are better than ours we cannot help trying to adopt them. To that extent Russia will be in a sense Americanized.

The *Times* editors found it irresistible to comment on the irony of this prospect:

If this comes about, it will be but a repetition of the moral of the age-old fable of the competition between the Wind and the Sun in removing the traveler's cloak. The harder the wind blew, the fiercer its blasts, the tighter was the cloak drawn about the traveler's shivering body. When the sun took its turn, "dispersed the vapor and cold," and poured its welcome warmth upon the traveler, overcome by its merciful heat, he cast his cloak on the ground. It is intimated in the dispatch that the belt of red tape, which has held the peasant's Soviet tunic about him has been loosened by the sunshine of efficient mercy, which, in the language of Aesop, "will sooner lay open a poor man's heart than all the threatenings and force of blustering authority."[7]

The imagery says much about how Americans liked to portray their country's assistance to starving Russia, but the analogy breaks down over the true identities of the traveler and his cloak, which would be apparent only at the end of the two-year relief story.

IT WOULD HARDLY BE SURPRISING to find that there was a good deal of curiosity within the Soviet leadership about the man who was the moving force behind the ARA—that is to say, curiosity beyond the enduring suspicions about his motives in Russia. And for a brief moment in the autumn of 1922, it appears that some of the Kremlin leaders, with Lenin leading the way, contemplated the prospect of attracting Hoover to Moscow.

There was no cult of Hoover in Russia commensurate with the popularity of the ARA. Certainly he enjoyed nothing like the exalted status that Henry Ford began to acquire just as the American relief workers were leaving the Soviet Union and *fordizm* was about to become the rage. The reasons for this are self-evident. For one, Ford's mass production assembly line, with its emphasis on narrow specialization and discipline, seemed the quintessence of Taylorist industrial management. Moreover the end product rolling off Ford's assembly line was the sacred automobile.

A more general reason was that aside from his pacifistic causes during the war, Ford was a capitalist entrepreneur pure and simple, which best suited the better-the-enemy-you-know mentality of the Bolsheviks; whereas Hoover had muddied the waters by becoming a statesman and a so-called humanitarian, and both roles were made to serve his famous anti-Bolshevism.

But Lenin's government was desperate for credits and trade and realized that in order to get these things it would have to break the recognition logjam. One man who might singlehandedly be able to bring this about was the one whose own agents were now spread out across Soviet Russia, feeding its citizens and helping to revive its economy. Perhaps direct contact with Hoover himself would produce a breakthrough.

It was Haskell who first raised the idea of bringing Hoover to Moscow. Apparently without Hoover's prior knowledge, he suggested to Lenin during a private meeting in November 1922 that it would be in the Soviet government's best interest to invite the Master of Efficiency himself to Russia to advise it on economic matters. By this time Haskell had become, somewhat to the Chief's embarrassment, a rather outspoken proponent of the idea that the United States government should hook up with Soviet Russia, at least to the extent of establishing trade relations if not granting formal diplomatic recognition.

Nothing came of Haskell's idea, and it is difficult to imagine that anything could have. Since sending the ARA into Russia, Hoover had not softened his antirecognition stance. He agreed with his ARA observers that the Bolsheviks had abandoned their radical economic program, but he felt that they still had some distance to retreat in order to establish a viable system. What he read in the detailed economic reports of the relief workers confirmed him in his belief that Russia still offered no trade or investment opportunities. "Russia is an economic vacuum," he declared in May 1922, echoing Hughes. Granting recognition now would only encourage the Bolsheviks to resist the inevitable return to a normal economic policy.

Toward the end of 1922 as Haskell was meeting with Lenin, Hoover's little book of political and social philosophy, *American Individualism*, appeared in print. About the Soviet experiment he had this to say:

If we throttle the fundamental impulses of man our production will decay. The world in this hour is witnessing the most overshadowing tragedy of ten centuries in the heart-breaking life-and-death struggle with starvation by a nation with a hundred and fifty millions of people. In Russia under the new tyranny a group, in pursuit of social theories, have destroyed the primary self-interest impulse of the individual to production.

There can be little doubt of Hoover's disappointment that the victory over hunger he had led in Russia had not helped bring about the return to normalcy he felt was inevitable—with or, more likely, without the Bolsheviks in power. This outcome had become apparent to him already by spring 1922, and now, one year later, he was absolutely set on getting the ARA out of Russia by summer. At the State Department, Dewitt Clinton Poole of the Russian desk wrote to Hughes on May 4 of a conversation he had just had with Hoover, who informed him that he was terminating operations by June 1: "Mr. Hoover said that he had never been so glad to finish a job as this Russian job; that he was completely disgusted with the Bolsheviks and did not believe that a practical government could ever be worked out under their leadership."[8]

The fact that the ARA was about to shut down its mission entirely with no further reconstruction program and no official U.S.-Soviet contact in its wake lent an air of melancholy to the final banquet sponsored by the ARA, held at the Pink House on June 23 and attended on the Soviet side by Kamenev, Dzerzhinskii, Sokol'nikov, Litvinov, Chicherin, Radek, Lander, and Volodin. Lenin was by this point an invalid; he would be dead within seven months. The American hosts—who took care to call it an "unofficial" event—were Haskell, Quinn, Burland, Lehrs, Telford, Morris, Holden, Brooks, and Gilchriese, joined by the financial editor of the *New York Times*, John Finley.

No stenographic report was taken, but Brooks made a digest of the speeches. Haskell acted as toastmaster and addressed the group six or seven times. The outstanding feature of the Bolsheviks' speeches is the care they took to emphasize Russian and American commonalities and, somewhat at odds with this, to frame the story of the previous twenty-two months as the victory of a grand alliance between the ARA and the Soviet government in a struggle to overcome Russian inefficiency and waste. In short, Karl Marx had not been invited to this banquet table.

After all the actual and affected alarm about Hoover's ulterior motives, now, at the end, these particular Bolsheviks seemed to be sincerely lamenting the fact that their government had failed to make anything more of American relief—neither trade, nor credits, nor official relations. Haskell tried to cheer up the Soviet delegation by saying that the ARA mission might yet lead to U.S. recognition: "The mills of the gods grind slowly at Washington."

Trotsky, who had been careful to keep his distance from the ARA, sent along a brief statement saying he would be out of town but that he wished to praise the "energetic and unselfish" contribution of the Americans, thereby withdrawing the insinuations of a year before. The other part of his message was echoed by his comrades throughout the evening: Soviet Russia—"our country which has suffered so greatly"—asks for normal relations with America.

Chicherin's prepared remarks, delivered in English, were wistful and, as in the following passage, strong on idealism:

The work of the A.R.A. is the work of broad masses of the American people who at a most difficult moment have come to the assistance of the Russian people and have thus laid a firm foundation for the future unalterable relations of friendship and mutual understanding between them. The American nation, which but yesterday took possession of a gigantic virgin continent and turned it into a miracle of most perfect technique of production and culture, can better than any one else understand the similar aspirations and hopes of the peoples of Russia, who have from their bitter past inherited a great part of two continents which had remained in a primitive state as a result of a barbarous regime and oppression in the past.

Grigorii Sokol'nikov, the finance commissar, said that "he personally gained much from his association with the members of the A.R.A. whose efficient methods and work have been a great lesson to all Russians who have come into contact with them. He wished that all Russians would take this lesson to heart and become as efficient as Americans after the true American fashion. Although Russia is now poverty-stricken, it is a country of enormous wealth. The plan of the Soviet Government is to develop this wealth as efficiently as America has developed hers."

Haskell introduced Dzerzhinskii in terms usually reserved for Hoover, saying that there was one guest at the table "who has a worldwide reputation for efficiency, one of the most practical and efficient men in the Government, who always accomplishes what he starts out to do and always keeps his promise." In turn, Dzerzhinskii, whose remarks were characterized as "carefully worded but modest and apparently sincere," praised Haskell for being not only a soldier of peace but a "Knight of the Order of the Heart."

Predictably the most interesting performance of the evening was that of Karl Radek, the Party propagandist and Peck's Bad Boy of the Kremlin. In the summer of 1921 Radek seemed to take special delight in scandalizing Western visitors to his Kremlin office with the statement that in fact the famine would not, as they

had been hearing, lead to the downfall of the Bolshevik regime: "Only famine victims die from famine." A Polish Jew, he admitted that he did not really feel at
home among the Russian *muzhiki* and would have preferred to be off in western
Europe doing propaganda work. It is impossible to introduce the man without remarking on his uncommon physical appearance. George F. Kennan has given a
memorable description of Radek as he looked during the revolutionary period:

He was a short man, of startling and yet not unattractive ugliness, with wide protruding ears, a face framed with a monkey-like fringe of beard (which gave him a
Puck-like aspect), and large yellow teeth from which there incessantly hung an incongruous Dutch pipe. He seemed to love to embellish this exterior with various outlandish forms of clothing. Equally conversant in German, Polish, or Russian (he was
of Polish-Jewish origin), he was a man of great brilliance and wit, coupled with a
breath-taking insolence and a biting and profoundly critical approach to all human
phenomenon [*sic*], great and small.

This was essentially the same Radek the ARA men encountered when they
got to Moscow in 1921, although by then he had acquired a new set of teeth.
Seldes said he "looked like the Ancient Mariner and . . . proved as humorous as
his old-fashioned Cape Cod beard."

When Radek got up to address the banqueters, he began with a disclaimer
that he was speaking as a private individual, a point that shortly became evident.
Brooks wrote a summary of his remarks, which included an unusual discussion of
a familiar question:

When A.R.A. came to Russia everyone of his comrades asked what was the real reason for their coming. This recalled to him the position of young Jews who wished to
go to universities during the Imperial Regime, when Jews were only admitted to universities in certain proportions to Christians. Therefore, when the quota was filled
and when a wealthy Jew wanted his son to enter a university he would assist, financially or otherwise, some young Christian to enter, thus raising the Christian quota
and permitting the entry of his own son. The Russian parents then spent a good deal
of time wondering when the Jew would start to swindle them. This question would
not be necessary in the case of the A.R.A.

This was a rather roundabout way of clearing the name of the ARA; another of
his observations also raised eyebrows:

Mr. Radek said that although he had never been in America he had been following
the American press very closely for a number of years and thought that Europeans in
general judged Americans very wrongly. In Europe the impression is that Americans
are dry business materialists, but he was convinced, mainly through the work of the
A.R.A., that Americans had been badly misjudged and have shown a rare combination of fine business efficiency and moral idealism of the highest order. He had recently read a book by Mr. Hoover on "American Individualism", and he thought that
after viewing the results accomplished by Mr. Hoover and his subordinates that Mr.
Hoover's individualism is a model which every Russian desires to achieve.

Then he went on to illustrate this:

On the streets of Moscow, one sees two kinds of Russian: the first type which
slouches along in a dull stupid manner, dressed in dirty boots, and wearing usually an

oriental cap. The other type are men who walk smartly and energetically through the streets going straight about their business. This second type is now generally called here "the American type" and we look to these new "American" Russians for the future of Russia. Mr. Radek then offered a toast to the 300 Americans of the A.R.A. for their energetic and efficient devotion, even to giving their lives to the work. The way in which the Americans had worked was characteristic of American idealism and he wished to express the thanks of the Government.

The Americans present apparently had no trouble washing down Radek's words with a bottoms-up toast, but the reference to Hoover's *American Individualism* stuck in Burland's throat. As he saw it, Radek had tried to argue that "after all the two philosophies were not as far apart as might be supposed, that Communism was really nothing more than collective individualism. This was a transgression on Marxism, and when asked for an explanation by foreign correspondents, he gave no reply."

Actually, in deflecting such questions, Radek was showing unusual self-restraint. He could easily have parried the reporter's questions and through a clever use of the dialectic bobbed and weaved his way out of that corner, but it probably would have spoiled the good cheer of the occasion. A year later when he was asked about his attitude toward the recent formation of the first-ever British Labour government, his reply was that in the evolution from the monkey to the commissar it was necessary to pass through the stage of the Labour minister.

Radek's cleverness helped to see him through the rough patch of the rout of his confederate Trotsky at the end of the 1920s, and he was able to serve his master Stalin until 1937, at which point he ran out of maneuvering room and was cornered and shot.

The Soviet government returned the ARA's hospitality on July 18 by hosting a banquet of its own, featuring more extended toasts paying tribute to the "unselfish" work of the ARA and the historic Russian-American friendship. On that occasion Krassin was present and invoked the names of Lomonosov, Lobachevsky, and Tolstoy to show that Russia, even Soviet Russia, had much to contribute to humanity "by her participation in the general life of nations."

How much of this Soviet goodwill was sincere is impossible to say. Much depends on the particular Bolshevik; of course Stalin was not present, though had he been he might well have spoken along the same lines. Still, for every moderate Bolshevik seated at the banquet table there were several more die-hards waiting in the wings. Nevertheless a number of the Moscow Americans believed that the friendly atmosphere of the final banquets was further evidence that the ARA episode had sobered the Bolsheviks, moderates and die-hards alike. Ellingston stated it this way:

Isolation and struggle had so distorted the Communist opinion of everything foreign as to render friendly contact almost impossible. By twenty-two months of straightforward dealing and disinterested philanthropy the A.R.A. forced the Soviet leaders in spite of themselves to correct their judgments, which has resulted unavoidably in a greater willingness to live in the family of nations.[9]

Maybe so, but circumstances would make its actuality impossible for almost seven more decades. The reason was that the Bolsheviks could not "correct their judgments" and still be faithful to Marxism-Leninism. It was on this point that Burland based his objection to Radek's banquet toast: "Of course, the innate and complete antagonism between Russian Communism on the one hand, and American individualism on the other, remains an unsolved and unsettled conflict, and was in no way affected by the relief experience."

The traveler had loosened his cloak but had not, and could not, cast it on the ground.

Left: Greeting the arrival of American corn at Vasil'evka, April 10, 1922.

Below: George McClintock and his supplicants.

Right: McClintock
administers relief.

Below: Lining up for corn.

Left: Col. Walter Bell, Ufa.

Below: ARA dining room, Petrograd, 1922. Courtesy of The Alan Mason Chesney Medical Archives of The Johns Hopkins Medical Institutions.

Right above: Gov. Goodrich
meets with villagers in Samara.

Right: The Ufa Americans.
Left to right: Conway Howard,
Denis Murphy, Walter Bell,
and Patrick Verdon.

Below: Russian peasants.

Left: Maxim Gorky,
circa 1920.

Below: Bell among the
Bashkirs, Ufa, 1922.

Top: Ivan Pavlov, *seated, center*, and staff in his Petrograd laboratory; Horsley Gantt is seated second from right. Courtesy of The Alan Mason Chesney Medical Archives of The Johns Hopkins Medical Institutions.

Bottom: Sleigh loaded with ARA supplies.

Left: Soviet President
Mikhail Kalinin addresses
townspeople on the Volga,
1921. Courtesy of the family
of Elmer G. Burland.

Below: Village deserted
on account of famine,
Tsaritsyn.

Top: ARA staff at
Spiridonovka 30.

Right: Mowatt Mitchell,
left, and Haskell, Saratov.

Left: Herbert Hoover:
Master of Efficiency.

Below: ARA food
remittance warehouse,
Moscow.

Above: Central ARA warehouse
at Ufa; Linhart stands far left.

Right: ARA warehouse, Ufa.

ДАР АМЕРИКАНСКОГО НАРОДА

A·R·A

Left: ARA poster: "Gift of the American People."

Below: Carting away an ARA food package. Note the dusting of flour on the dark suit of the recipient.

Right: Feliks Dzerzhinskii.

Below: ARA poster: "America to the Starving People of Russia."

Top: Kiev food remittance station.
Left: Leon G. Turrou, 1921.

Right: Iliodor, the "Mad Monk of Russia."

Below: ARA final banquet, Moscow, June 1923. *Left to right*: Maxim Litvinov, Lev Kamenev, Cyril Quinn, Karl Radek, and People's Commissar of Health N. Semashko.

SINCE THEN

To America this is a passing incident of national duty, undertaken, finished and to be quickly forgotten. The story of it will be told lovingly in Russian households for generations. Through this service America has not only saved millions of lives, but has given impulse to the spiritual and economic recovery of a great nation, and on our own behalf we have created, in the assurance of good will from the Slav races, a great inheritance for our children.

—Colonel William Haskell, 1923

President Hoover has little appeal for the [Russian] man in the street. The enormous task of his American Relief Administration, which transported hundreds of shiploads of grain from the United States and fed nearly eleven million Russians in the days of the darkest famine of 1921 and 1922, seems almost forgotten.

—Major General William Haskell, 1932

In the ship's diary of the U.S.S. *Fox*, a destroyer docked at Odessa to assist the navigation of American food supply ships on the Black Sea, in the entry for March 1, 1922, Commanding Officer Webb Trammel describes a drive out to the cemetery. Soviet Russia was then in its darkest days of famine, and the Odessa cemetery had become an obligatory stop for American naval officers curious to see for themselves the surreal scenes of death they had been hearing about.

En route, Trammell struck up a conversation with his local driver. They communicated in French, which tells us that the man behind the wheel had not long been a chauffeur. The driver asked if other American men-of-war would not follow the food ships and intervene "on behalf of the people." Though fanciful, this idea was hardly unusual among Russians at that moment, not least in the port of call of an American warship, but it was Trammell's first time on shore so he may have been unprepared for the question. No, they would not, he told the driver.

The next few minutes passed in silence while the man behind the wheel absorbed this information, eyes fixed on the road ahead. His passenger would have been distracted by the numerous corpses to be seen along the sides of the road, unfortunates who shared his destination. "*Nous sommes perdus*," the driver broke the silence. Trammell may have wondered if the man was talking about his social class or his countrymen altogether, but whichever it was it took away his spirit. "That was the last thing he said during the trip."[1]

By summer, with the famine defeated, the autumn harvest secured, and the Bolsheviks more firmly in command of the country than ever, few Russians could have harbored illusions of an American military intervention. But because Hoover was not able to have his way and pull his men out all at once, the shock of separation was eased somewhat by being drawn out, with two waves of ARA farewells in the summers of 1922 and 1923.

When the end came, the ARA publicity machine made the most of it, though it preferred lighthearted images of the final farewell: awkward Americans showered with Russian-style kisses and tossed skyward in blankets. It was all rather chin up in the ARA style, whereas the relief workers themselves remembered a "shower of rain and tears" and "Sad goodbyes of a moonlit night."[2]

Their beneficiaries and staff members presented the departing Americans with written expressions of eternal gratitude, trailed by long lists of signatures. Many are adorned with artwork, usually watercolors. Some are by accomplished hands; most are quite crude, notably those painted by children from the homes and hospitals and schools nurtured by American relief. The most compelling tribute in a whole batch of them might consist merely of a few scrawled lines on a torn piece of paper. Among the most affecting are those in Russian verse addressed to "ARA," "Amerika," "Dear Mister Allen," "Kind Mister Barringer," and so on. Hundreds of these made the voyage to America, ending up in various locations across the country.

Those paying tribute want to assure their saviors that the memory of their errand of mercy in Russia's darkest hour will never be extinguished. The American press had no trouble accepting this notion. The *New York Evening World* declared that "ARA" had become part of the Russian language and "will survive for centuries." An American reader might have been slightly misled by this formulation. When they declared of the ARA, as did a Kiev *intelligent*, that "Those three letters will not be forgotten," Soviet Russians pronounced those three letters as two syllables of one word: "Ara."[3]

However it was rendered, even as the American mission was winding down, steps were being taken to erase its memory from the Russian mind. This would not have been evident to American newspaper readers engrossed in articles about the official farewell banquets in Moscow, with their warm toasts and glowing tributes to Hoover and the ARA. The Soviets concluded their ceremony with the presentation to Haskell of a resolution of the Council of People's Commissars, dated July 10, 1923. The Russian text is hand-printed and bordered by an elaborate decorative design that is strong on agrarian imagery and suggestive of traditional Russian iconography, except for the obligatory hammer-and-sickle emblem.

Equally lavish is the resolution's praise of the ARA for "unselfishly" having come to Soviet Russia's aid: "Due to the enormous and entirely disinterested efforts of the A.R.A., millions of people of all ages were saved from death and entire districts and even cities were saved from the horrible catastrophe which threatened them." Never would Soviet citizens forget "the help given them by the American people, through the A.R.A., seeing in it a pledge of the future friendship of the two nations."[4]

Locally as well there were public demonstrations of gratitude on the part of the authorities, most remarkably in Simbirsk, where the *Proletarian Way* published a generous assessment of the ARA's work, which featured portrait sketches of the American relief workers, including the ill-fated Phil Sheild, whose disappearance officially remained a mystery.[5]

Such expressions of goodwill did little to dispel fears over the fate of the ARA's local staffs, past and present, after its departure. Current employees faced the likely prospect of unemployment. Anticipating this, Col. Haskell authorized the distribution of one month's food ration as a bonus—though district supervisors were instinctively inclined toward greater generosity without waiting for Moscow's approval.[6]

In the farewell tributes, it is the children who are most outspoken in their lament over the impending loss of American food, especially the cocoa. Local personnel and their relatives, as well as the staffs of institutions supported by the ARA—several tens of thousands of people in every district—anticipate more profound losses. As part of the ARA "family," these former people had become people once again and now faced a return to their former status.

A larger circle of Russians bemoaned the severance of their country's special connection to America, which, they had become convinced, kept Russia tethered to civilization. The Bolsheviks might have an iron grip on Russia, but the American presence kept their worst excesses in check and would keep the country from sliding back into the abyss. A staff member in Kiev records that a local intellectual—whom he describes as a social worker, a scholar, and an academician—upon learning that the ARA was going to fold up its operations, blurted out: "The d......, then we are all lost."[7] These words, probably spoken in Russian, expressed this particular variation of the Odessa chauffeur's theme.

The retreating relief workers were more focused on the immediate prospects of their former hires. The most dreaded scenario was that with American protection withdrawn, Bolshevik officials would take various forms of revenge. The most dire speculation foresaw a Great Roundup of these former untouchables once the Americans were safely out of the way.

The long-running ARA-Soviet tug-of-war over the inviolability of the native staff was grounds enough for pessimism, but during the final weeks of the mission definite trouble seemed to be brewing. Verbal threats—of the vaguely ominous "Just you wait" variety—were delivered to ARA employees out of American earshot, and there was lately a lot of loose talk in official circles of the dangers of "economic espionage."[8]

Most unsettling to the Moscow chiefs were reports out of Ufa, where the Americans prided themselves on their smooth relations with the government. It seems that while Col. Bell was away in Ekaterinburg, key members of the office personnel had been subject to what Ellingston called "absolutely unjustifiable" searches. If this was a sign of things to come in Ufa, what did it portend for other districts?[9]

One had come to expect the worst in Orenburg, where government relations had been cursed from the outset. According to L'Engle Hartridge, who was winding down the Orenburg show, "No one felt safe at any time and everyone looked forward to our departure with fear, not knowing what treatment from the

Government the future held for them. I myself am most uneasy over their situation and I gravely fear that many of them are going to suffer because of their loyal service with us."

Those recently let go who applied for work at the Central Labor Exchange were told that no former ARA employees could submit applications before September 1. And the government representative made his unwelcome presence felt to the very end:

Orders had been issued by Mr. Rudminsky that there be no public demonstration by children's homes on our departure. However, a few nights before we left, one of the homes wishing to show its appreciation of the work of the A.R.A. gave a highly interesting performance in the local theatre. The performance was given for our benefit but in order to conceal the real purpose the public was charged admission. During the evening, at a moment when the house was completely dark, three little children from the home ran into our box and presented us with a large bouquet of flowers. They hurried out, though, and were gone without a word.

Hartridge says that the American relief workers departed Orenburg "unhonored and unsung"—though only officially. "At the train a memorial of thanks from this same home was put in our compartment, but the children dared do nothing openly themselves."[10]

As soon as the ARA had left, the Blandy Memorial Hospital in Ufa had its sign removed, as did the Blandy Children's Home soon afterward. In Odessa, it was only a matter of time before the Haskell Highway and the Hoover Hospital fell off the proverbial map. This much was expected. But the much-feared St. Bartholomew's Eve of the ARA staff did not materialize, nor were former employees persecuted to a degree beyond what one could reasonably have expected in the circumstances. Which is to say, some scores were settled in the summer of 1923, though just how many is not easy to determine.

Ruhl, who remained in Russia into the autumn, reported only a few arrests, but the ARA network had been dismantled and he could not cover the terrain on his own. Duranty much later recalled a "considerable number," but he was no more reliable a memoirist than a reporter. Seldes, who had left the scene seven months earlier, claimed in one of his several precarious memoirs that in fact every one of the ARA's non-Communist employees was arrested that sorrowful summer of 1923, which would have meant upwards of one hundred thousand prisoners. Seldes was getting ahead of the Soviet story.[11]

However many there were, it only took a few to get the rumor mill turning out stories of arrests or impending arrests. In a case of wishful thinking, *Izvestiia* reported on September 22 that Haskell was about to be named to a senior position in U.S. military intelligence, which seems to have set off a panic in former ARA circles.[12] In April 1924, the Soviet and U.S. press ran stories about an espionage trial in Kiev where an ARA connection had been revealed. The editors of *Laboring Moscow* challenged Secretary of State Hughes to come clean on the matter. Haskell was unimpressed, telling the *Washington Post* that the Bolsheviks were merely "blowing off their steam."[13]

The following month came the verdict in the most prominent of these cases, involving the arrest in Minsk of an ex-ARA employee, Ekaterina Rumiantseva, and an agrarian economist, Professor Katsaurov. Their crime had to do with the submission to district supervisor Charles Willoughby of a report on agricultural conditions in White Russia, which the professor authored and she translated. Such reports were routinely solicited by the ARA, so this was merely a pretext. The prosecutors made great hay of Rumiantseva's gentry background and an alleged connection to White General Wrangel—which was the real point of the exercise. The proceedings were said to have been marked by agitation about American imperialism and innuendo about ARA espionage.

On May 10 the court sentenced Rumiantseva to ten years in solitary confinement, Katsaurov to five years. They sat in a Moscow prison, awaiting transfer to the frozen north. Rumiantseva's health was said to be fast deteriorating. The verdict mobilized the staff at 42 Broadway to mount a quiet but determined drive to win the release of the prisoners through diplomatic channels, both official and unofficial.

Willoughby was tracked down at the *Hattiesburg American*, in Mississippi, and submitted a sworn statement testifying to the innocence of the prisoners. In defense of Rumiantseva's character he testified that on no occasion had she demonstrated any evidence of disloyalty to her country. "On the contrary, it was generally believed by both the American personnel at Minsk headquarters, and a majority of the native employees, that despite Madame Roumianzova's past connections, she was, at the time she was connected with the A. R. A., in the secret employ of the Russian Government as an agent." Willoughby seems genuinely bewildered: *My* spy? I thought she was *your* spy.

As these and other cases lingered into the following year, Hoover could not contain his outrage at the charge of ARA underhandedness. Blowing off his steam, he told the *Washington Evening Star* that the very idea of ARA espionage was ridiculous when one considered that his relief workers had enjoyed unrestricted access to virtually every nook and cranny of Soviet Russia.

The controversy over arrests, such as it was, faded, but the Minsk trial helped to blaze the trail that would eventually become the Communist Party line on the American relief mission: that the ARA had used the cover of philanthropy to engage in the business of espionage. The *Izvestiia* article announcing the Rumiantseva and Katsaurov verdicts did start off by conceding that the ARA's principal activity had been charity, but the title of the article had already made an impression: "Spies of the ARA in the Role of Benefactors."[14]

THE AMERICAN RELIEF WORKERS anticipated their departure with a special kind of dread. They understood that returning home was going to have its drawbacks. Their trepidation was best articulated by the YMCA's Arthur Hillman, whose anonymously authored verse was printed in the "Russian Unit Record" on July 9, 1922, when some had begun to pack their bags. No news or feature item to have appeared in the "Record"—not even the tale of McSweeney's retreat to Moscow without his trousseau—generated such an enthusiastic response from its readers as did the three stanza's of "The Wail of the Homeward Bound."

> I'm going home, sad word,
> To become a member of the common herd.

No private cars on railroad trains;
No pretty girls, no shady lanes;
No crew of servants at beck and call;
None to observe my rise and fall.
A lot of work, few holidays;
No special boats on waterways;
No Cadillacs and fewer Fords;
No clamoring of the hungry hordes.
To ride and have to pay my fare
Is just one difference 'twixt here and there.

The homeward bound ARA man was burdened by the same anxieties that had afflicted returning doughboys in 1918. Many soldiers were from small towns, and having seen a big city or two during their time in the AEF, they were afraid to go back to the farm. Beyond having seen the sights, most had known large experience in Europe—adventure, danger, and romance—on a scale and of an intensity they could not anticipate rediscovering back home. One doughboy wrote the day after the armistice: "[T]he idea of turning back to civilian life seems like an awful jump. I really have got accustomed to fighting, life in the open, running a balloon company with a lot of men, trucks, etc., and it is going to leave a rather gone feeling for a while." Another stated it more concisely a few days later: "Down to earth and job, after voyage on the coat-tails of Fate."[15]

This was roughly how things looked to the retiring ARA man, though his burden was that much greater because he had in most cases been away longer and had tasted the power and privileges enjoyed by an American famine-fighter in an exotic land. He was used to going up against the biggest Bolos in his territory, their secret police included, and often getting his way. He had grown accustomed to being the object of adoring attention by the natives he had rescued, to being toasted as the savior of a nation. On the street all eyes followed him, and he had come to anticipate the excited whispers, "There goes an American."

Now he stood on the brink of anonymity.

I'm going home about the third,
To become a member of the common herd.
To see myself in a Broadway jam,
Where none will know just who I am;
Where I will be quite commonplace,
No following eyes of the populace;
Only a host of vain regrets,
No whispers "eedyot Amerikanets";
No private boxes near the stage;
No speculations on my age;
Where soup is served without the curd
To a simple member of the common herd.

The fact is that when the Germans surrendered, most doughboys wanted to go home right away, and they complained bitterly when the shortage of transport ships delayed their return. It seems otherwise in retrospect partly because a good number of returnees experienced that "rather gone feeling" only upon their arrival back home. Only when confronted with what historian Kennedy, in discussing their plight, calls "the little agonies of ordinary life" did they experience a profound sense of loss.[16]

Although many relief workers professed themselves "fed up on" Russia, to judge by the warm response to Hillman's lament, not a few could see what was coming. Hillman's contribution was to commit to paper scenes from the return to normalcy that might unsettle the ARA man's waking dreams. George Cornick, the Texas doctor, felt that Hillman's little poem hit a bull's eye. He sent a copy home to his sister Amie in San Angelo—to her and not to his parents because he was concerned that the final stanza would send them the wrong message.

I'm going home, Unlucky bird,
To become a member of the common herd.
I've been away a long, long time.
Oh! Home, I fear I am not thine.
I've learned the other ways of life
Without the struggle, without the strife.
On the top o' the world I've sat too long;
It may be right, it may be wrong.
I won't be happy on my homeward trip,
Though I travel on the finest ship.
Forgive me! to have thus demurred
To becoming a member of the common herd.

In his letter to his sister Cornick elaborated on a particular aspect of the approaching transition that Hillman had not spelled out: the fact that

life will be something of a comedown, when I get to a land where I can't go into the office of one of the biggest officials of the place and tell him what he *has to do* if he expects me to work with him. In fact if I should ever forget myself when I return, and talk to individuals in America as I have talked to some of them over here I imagine that someone else will have to pick me up from the floor.[17]

This was also a source of some concern at New York headquarters, which assumed responsibility for easing the ARA man's return by helping him find work. These were still rather difficult economic times in the United States, but the backing of the Chief and the ARA certainly brightened one's job prospects. In fact for the relief worker in good standing, landing a job was usually straightforward; settling down to earth and job was usually not.

The man whose responsibility it was to look after the returning personnel was Frank Page, the ARA secretary at 42 Broadway. He had managed the readjustment phase of earlier missions, but the Russian show, he noticed, produced a severe strain of the syndrome. Bill Kelley, fresh from Ufa in July 1922, was one of his first cases. Kelley was a clever, talented young man, that was plain. But, as Page wrote to Chris Herter, the problem was equally apparent: Kelley was "a little spoiled"—and would probably not make a good subordinate in a low-level job—because he had been a chief in "the big Ufa show."[18]

Page knew that Kelley was hardly a representative case. After all, he had downed tools in Ufa after only six months in order to pursue a career in advertising. More typically, as Page explained to Tommy Burland in Moscow in April 1923, returnees from the Red Planet tended to "wander around for quite a while before they settle down to something." At first nothing seemed quite worthy of them, until they rolled back their expectations, "gradually readjusting themselves to a life of business rather than to being czars in their own particular kingdoms."

Page seems to have hoped to influence Burland and his colleagues to begin decompressing even before they sailed. Still he could not resist relating that Russ Cobb, formerly of the kingdom of Saratov, had "pulled off a stunt." Upon his return he went to work for the Metropolitan Life Insurance Company. The job did not live up to expectations. In fact,

> He hated it. They gave their annual dinner to all employees and Cobb proceeded to take too much to drink and thought he was back bossing his Khirgees and he made two speeches on how damn rotten they ran their business. The next morning he was called into the president's office, of course thinking he was going to be fired. Instead, the president told him that he passed out some mighty good ideas and that he was thereby promoted to the head of the new department in their Chicago office, where he is drawing a pretty good salary and with quite a cheerful outlook.

So the abilities acquired in distant fields of famine were not without their application to the world of business. "Russel Cobb never in the world would have dared to tell the assembled multitude the truth before he had had the Russian experience."[19]

Burland must have indicated to Page that he intended to enter a line of work related to Russia. This seems a natural choice for someone who had occupied the emperor's box for eighteen months, but Page advised against it. "If I were you, and the others abroad, I would try to figure out what I wanted to do, and I wouldn't have a job in relation to Russia as one of the things I wanted to do, for Russia is a dead letter in this country."

Burland ignored this advice, and together with Walter Lyman Brown formed the Lena Gold Fields Company, which in 1925 obtained the largest mining concession granted in Russia since the Revolution.[20] As with most such business ventures in NEP Russia it fizzled out. Nonetheless Burland could claim to have come away a very rich man: on a trip to Moscow in 1924 he married his sweetheart, Katia, a ballerina with the Bolshoi, and brought her to America.

Several other ex–baby feeders attempted to capitalize on their Russia experience, some perhaps hoping to recapture the old glory, but there was no escaping the return to everyday struggle and strife. Their wails about their plight, in commiserative correspondence and conversation, led to the establishment in 1925 of the A.R.A. Association. The idea was to form a veterans' community encompassing all ARA missions, but it was the Russia crowd that inspired the enterprise and dominated its ranks.

That same year saw the inaugural issue of the *A.R.A. Association Review*, which started out ambitiously as a quarterly magazine of opinion carrying serious articles on matters like European reconstruction and international relations, as well as book reviews. There were to be twenty issues in the first ten years and nineteen over the next thirty years, these last prepared and edited by Harold Fleming. The *Review* served as a forum for collective reminiscing, for following the exploits of the Chief, and in the popular "Who's Where" section, for keeping track of each other's doings—and deaths—into old age.

Each issue was given a title, which might indicate the special focus of its contents—"The Slavic Number"—or the advancing age of its readership—"The Waistline Number," "The Short-Winded Number"—but most reflected the state of affairs in the world. Their point is usually obvious, though there is one that brings an American reader up short: "The Victory Number," printed in February 1929. It takes a moment to understand that the victory in question had come the year before with the election of Herbert Hoover as the thirty-first president of the United States. All ARA men, Democrats and Republicans alike, identified with Hoover's triumph. But they, like all Americans, would forever associate the year 1929, the year Hoover entered the White House, with the onset of catastrophe: the Wall Street crash of October, followed by the slide into economic depression, and ultimately the demise of the Chief.

The incongruity takes on a special poignancy because of its ARA context. Hoover's undoing dealt a devastating blow to the organization's ethos. The fundamental values that until 1929 Hoover was seen to embody—American individualism, business efficiency, can-do optimism—were not destroyed, it turned out, but they had lost the aura of invincibility. And the Chief's reputation had gone bust. Over the years, the *Review* would never admit to any doubts, and through the postpresidential decades it continued to profess absolute loyalty to the Chief and express enthusiastic interest in his latest speech or initiative. But sometimes the enthusiasm seems forced—or perhaps this is merely how it looks from here.

So these were especially hard times for ARA veterans—even more so for the old Russia hands because of contemporaneous developments back in the land of Marx and Lenin, where Stalin had chosen capitalism's moment of crisis to attempt a leap into socialism. As the United States gradually became stuck in the mud, the U.S.S.R. forged ahead with a crash industrialization drive under the Five-Year Plan and the wholesale collectivization of agriculture.

Americans were curious to know more about this bold Soviet experiment, and books about the Plan entered the American best-seller lists.[21] The contrast could not have been starker: the dynamic U.S.S.R. versus the depressed U.S.; the Man of Steel outmuscling the Master of Efficiency. Such juxtapositions must have provoked the ARA veteran, whether or not he was out of work. He had, he could tell you, been to Russia—not as some tourist, but as part of the greatest rescue operation of all time. Now, however, with the tables thus turned, the relief episode hardly seemed relevant.

Editor Fleming laced his nostalgia with grim humor, posting this notice in "The Red Ink Number" in January 1932: "Wanted: By a number of former ARA relief workers. A famine, earthquake or pestilence. In going condition. Guaranteed to run indefinitely, or until Prosperity gets around that corner."

After that, the story of Hoover's colossal postwar humanitarian undertaking was obscured by the Depression epic. And should the subject come up, the skeptics now had the upper hand. No longer, as in 1922, did one need to invoke Hoover's anti-Bolshevism, his personal business interests, and American economic nationalism to sap the humanitarianism out of his relief operations. Now, in 1932, Hoover had been exposed as the cold, uncaring president indifferent to the plight of his fellow Americans. Why, Hoover couldn't have had a humanitarian bone in his body if he refused to take measures to help out his own. The subsequent frenzy of New Deal activity clinched the point.

MAJ. GEN. HASKELL VISITED the U.S.S.R. in 1931, as the Soviet government was exhorting its citizens to complete the Five-Year Plan in four years. He had been back once before, in 1925, at which time he had been struck by the large number of orphaned children roaming the streets of Moscow and Leningrad. He guessed that they were survivors of the children's homes he had been so reluctant to enter in 1922—that they were alive thanks to American relief. Concern had been expressed during the mission about the consequences of rescuing millions of children when their parents were dead or doomed. They numbered nearly nine million in 1922, more than half of them between the ages of eight and thirteen. Ragged and barefoot, they roamed the streets in gangs, like wild animals, living in abandoned buildings, in railroad stations—wherever they could find shelter. They survived by begging, bartering, stealing, and prostitution.[22]

In 1925 Haskell could not avoid the sight of these "wild children." By 1931 they had vanished: young adults, they had been mobilized like everyone else for the great socialist offensive.

Haskell arrived one year before the country's next major famine, which is understood to have carried off as many victims as the 1921 famine, this time mostly in Ukraine and the North Caucasus. Nature once again played its part, but the famine of 1932 was largely a man-made disaster. Collectivization meant curtailing private land ownership and otherwise integrating the peasant economy into the planned economy. Peasants naturally resisted, predictably with a special ferocity in Ukraine, and Moscow used famine to break this resistance.

William Henry Chamberlin was one of the first Western reporters to state the matter unequivocally in print: "Of the historical responsibility of the Soviet Government for the famine of 1932–1933 there can be no reasonable doubt." He quotes Kalinin—still the figurehead Soviet president, still the All-Union "elder" to the peasants—sounding much as he did a decade earlier: "The collective farmers this year have passed through a good school. For some this school was quite ruthless."[23]

This time there was to be no dramatic appeal to the world for bread and medicine. Gorky had since returned to Moscow from the West, but he had had to make his peace with the Kremlin, meaning he had been tamed.

Walter Duranty had spent much of the previous ten years in Moscow, earning a Pulitzer Prize in 1932, mainly on the strength of his coverage of the Five-Year Plan. This seems to have given him a stake not simply in keeping the favor of the Kremlin but in upholding the image of a triumphant U.S.S.R., just when famine was threatening to explode it. When his colleagues began to file stories about a famine—or at least the rumors of one—Duranty's reporting turned perverse. It was, he insisted at the harvest of 1933, "sheer absurdity" to speak of starvation when he himself could see "mile after mile of reaped grain in the fields" and "gigantic piles of wheat." He knew better, yet he described village markets as "flowing with eggs, fruit, poultry, vegetables, milk and butter at prices far lower than in Moscow. A child can see that this is not famine but abundance." This in America's newspaper of record.

Duranty was something of a Stalinist true-believer. In his ode to "Red Square," which occupied a full spread in the *Times* on September 18, 1932, he reasoned that

Russians may be hungry and short of clothes and comfort
But you can't make an omelette without breaking eggs.

This last expression, one of Duranty's favorites, was the same formulation that Stalin himself—and others among his Western apologists—used to justify the costs of building socialism.[24]

Haskell's full attention the year before was commanded by the great industrialization drive, then in full swing. In the unpublished memoir he began to write after his return, the country is one big construction site. Measuring the actual progress of the plan involved taking someone else's word for it, but the skeptical general could witness for himself the religious fervor with which the New Russia embraced industrial machinery. He had not forgotten the fanatical worship of the automobile during the famine years, but now, with history in overdrive, the "god of mechanization" seemed insatiable. The thought of it inspires the reticent memoirist to an uncharacteristic outburst: "Radios almost before shoes!"

An inescapable manifestation of this monomania was an obsession with production totals and targets. "More red banners and placards that passed through the Red Square last May Day carried statistics of their bearers' industrial efficiency than slogans of international class war. By nightfall, watchers had become so tired of banners saying '98%,' '102%,' '110% . . . of Our Program Completed', 'Five-Year Plan in Four Years' and so forth, that a good old fashioned 'Down With the Capitalistic Imperialists' banner was a welcome relief."

One of the slogans that naturally caught Haskell's eye declared, "We must not equal, but surpass America." The "Americanization" urge of years past seemed more potent than ever. As Haskell saw it, the obsession with the machine and the fascination with America were, as before, inseparable. Incontestable was the fact that much of the machinery used to power Russia into the future was American-made. "At the giant dam on the Dnieper River which has a potential capacity to produce 810,000 horsepower, one of the largest turbines ever made by the General Electric Company [is] being installed. . . . Oliver, Caterpillar, Holdt and International types of tractors are being uncrated at small stations throughout the country. [They] carry the new standard of Americanization to the furthest front."

With the machines came real live Americans, some associated with the above companies but also a few thousand engineers lured to the U.S.S.R. by the prospect of a well-paying job. The Soviet government aggressively recruited them, valuing their skills and experience. Soviet citizens were equally admiring. Haskell testified: "The American engineer is almost a god in Russia."[25]

Most of these American gods came to the U.S.S.R. to get a job. For some the economic incentive was mixed with idealism and a desire to help build a new world in the Soviet Union. The best remembered of them is John Scott because his gritty 1942 memoir about his experiences, *Behind the Urals*, went on to become a minor classic and is still required reading on American college campuses. Like many of his fellow engineers, Scott applied his skills toward the construction of the "Soviet Pittsburgh," Magnitogorsk, the steel behemoth built from scratch on the eastern slopes of the Ural mountains.

Perhaps someone who crossed Scott's path—who perhaps observed this electric welder going about his business—recalled an American he had come across in an earlier time, and wondered if Col. Walter Bell might not once again come out of the sky. In fact that was roughly what Bell had in mind.

Upon his return to civilization in 1923, Bell had settled in Danbury, Connecticut, where he worked as a purchasing agent for the American Hotel Corporation. This hardly seems a fate worthy of the idol of the Bashkirs. In any case, it appears to have left him considerable mental room in which to wander. The *Philadelphia Record* reported on September 1, 1930, that the colonel "has accepted the invitation of the soviet to put into effect there a colossal scheme of mass feeding of the populace." The U.S.S.R. had not put out a call for famine fighters, but evidently something Bell had read in the newspapers about the Great Soviet Leap inspired him to correspondingly ambitious imaginative heights.

Bell's plan, which seems to have drawn on his experience in the army and the hotel business, envisioned the establishment of central storage stations across the U.S.S.R. from which food would be distributed locally by airplane. The food—presumably none of it American—would be kept fresh using dry ice. If this struck some readers of the *Record* as farfetched, the article reminded them that Bell was highly regarded by the Soviet government for his work in the Urals—"a sort of Pennsylvania of natural resources"—and had been invited by the Kremlin to put his plan into action.[26]

Nothing seems to have come of the dry ice proposition, but still "Ginger" Bell's mind could not rest. In March 1940, he addressed a letter to the A.R.A. Association in New York proposing the formation of what he called a Volunteer Aerial Ambulance Esquadrille, for service in Finland. The Finns were in a bloody Winter War with the Soviet Union, and Bell, now sixty-five, was moved by the spirit of 1915. It was, he conceded, "A pretty big proposition to finance but I think it could be put over."

Bell spent his last years, until his death in 1946, on Clapboard Ridge, outside Danbury. He enclosed several photographs of this rustic homestead in his letter to New York, as though they were intended to prove something. They reveal a simple wooden cottage, whose hearth has been upstaged by a large coal stove. In one winter shot, a pair of white horses is parked just outside the front door, ready to haul away a sleigh bearing two wooden crates. If not for the presence in two of these photographs of the proprietor, a retiring man in a fedora and thick round glasses, jaw clenched on a tobacco pipe—if not for this jolting reminder of the passage of time and the presence of a big old dog instead of a bear cub, one might easily believe they had been taken behind the Urals in the winter of 1922.

In a way, Bell had succeeded in reliving the old days after all, in retirement at a place he called "Dom Nichevo."

HASKELL, MEANWHILE, WAS FORCED to qualify his observation about Soviet reverence for the American engineer with the remark that it did not apply to the occupant of the White House. In fact, "The caricatures of the press have presented him in a rather unfavorable light, and while not despised, he is certainly not a figure loved by the Russian people." This could not have come as a surprise. Leaving aside all the unpleasantness from years past, President Hoover now continued to stand in the way of official U.S. recognition of the Soviet Union, which would be granted only in 1933 after he had been turned out of the White House.

Haskell did not endorse the Chief's point of view on this divisive issue—nor had several other ARA principals, including Goodrich, Golder, Hutchinson, and Fisher. They supported de facto, if not de jure, U.S. recognition—not out of sympathy for the Bolos, they were careful to say, but rather to take away the Soviet alibi of capitalist encirclement. Isolation, they believed, would only keep Bolshevism thriving inside Russia; better to bring it into contact with the outside world, to kill it with kindness.[27]

Defending this minority position in the 1920s entailed some risk. There was always somebody ready to call you a Bolshevik. In those days the accusation was likely to be hurled by a group calling itself the American Defense Society, which labeled Goodrich a Red and declared that Haskell was pro-Communist after Governor Al Smith nominated him to head the National Guard in 1926.

Professional watchdogs were not the only ones on the lookout. When Shafroth returned from Russia in 1922, he too came out in favor of U.S. recognition. This must be what prompted Edgar Rickard, at 42 Broadway, to alert the vice-chairman of the ARA to the fact that Shafroth, who had pioneered American relief to the Volga and fended off intrusive Bolsheviks for nine months in the service of Hoover—that this man had "a distinct communistic leaning." Rickard seems to have arrived at this diagnosis through the same deliberative process he had used to identify wayward relievers suffering from "famine shock"—meaning it was sheer nonsense, but in those early days it was usually no more than that.[28]

The recognition matter was very much on Haskell's mind as he contemplated the dawn of Russia's Iron Age. Although his memoir reached for the Soviet-American commonalities, he understood that, all the talk of the U.S.S.R.'s "Americanization" notwithstanding, the means and end of the Soviet Union's industrial revolution were alien to America. Despite all that imported American machinery and know-how, Russia was going it alone. While careful not to step on the Chief's toes, he could not help but speculate that things might have turned out differently had Washington seized an opportunity during the previous decade. "I . . . have often wondered what change would have resulted in the development of Russia, and whether the Five-Year Plan would have materialized, had the American Government at [that] time assisted Russia in her economic reconstruction, and had we relieved Russia's starvation for capital as we had previously relieved the starvation of millions of her citizens."[29]

There are so many gears turning in Haskell's story that it is a welcome relief to encounter a familiar face. At Autostroy, the automobile plant near Nizhnii Novgorod, the general comes face to face with "Comrade Volodin . . . the prize Russian liar in connection with firebrick he had been commissioned to procure for the repair of the heating plant in A.R.A. headquarters." As far as Haskell knew, Volodin had been convicted of embezzlement and executed, so he seems to have been genuinely "astonished beyond words" to find his old nemesis alive.

"How are you, Colonel?" he said cheerfully. "How are all my friends in the United States?"

I was dumbfounded, and my reply to his greeting was hardly coherent. "Why, Volodin! You here? I'm amazed! I thought you had been shot by the Bolsheviks."

With a sheepish grin as he passed by, he replied: "No, Colonel, I'm very much alive. They haven't shot me—yet."

This omission on the part of the Soviets immediately caused them to fall a number of points in my estimation.[30]

Volodin's number would come up in only a few years, during the Great Terror of 1936 to 1938, when Bolsheviks of several varieties, including some of Lenin's closest colleagues, were made to confess to the most fantastic crimes against the Soviet state—treason, wrecking, sabotage, espionage, assassination—made the defendants in sensational show trials, and either shot or sent to labor camps. Millions of innocents were caught in the whirlwind and met their end in prison cells, cattle cars, and the Gulag.

Dzerzhinskii missed the purge. He had died suddenly in 1926, so he could never be cast as a victim of Soviet terror as well as its first perpetrator. Kamenev was finished off in his jail cell in 1936 with a bullet to the back of the head. Eiduk was similarly dispatched two years later. Lander, who had been suffering from mental illness for many years, passed on during the Terror, though of natural causes. Radek's turn came in 1939. Trotsky received his with the now legendary ice pick, in his Mexican exile in 1940.

The Terror was marked by a morbid xenophobia, which would reach delirious new heights during the dictator's final years. At the trials, meetings and conversations with foreigners—real or concocted, recent or remote—were introduced as evidence that one or another of the accused was an enemy of the people. The ARA episode was not resurrected by the chief prosecutor in this scandalous fashion, though it did come under the scrutiny of the police interrogator. A previous connection with agents of bourgeois "philanthropy"—even the receipt of a food package—might serve to thicken a cloud of suspicion.[31]

Historians cross swords over the extent to which the shadowy figure in the Kremlin orchestrated this macabre ritual. In December 1921, as the U.S. Congress prepared to debate a bill authorizing the shipment of $20 million in food relief to Soviet Russia, Stalin contemplated the dark side of such transactions. He warned a gathering of his fellow Bolsheviks:

[I]t must not be forgotten that the trading and all other sorts of missions and associations that are now pouring into Russia, trading with her and aiding her, are at the same time most efficient spy agencies of the world bourgeoisie, and that, therefore, the world bourgeoisie now knows Soviet Russia, knows her weak and strong sides, better than at any time before, a circumstance fraught with grave danger in the event of new interventionist actions.[32]

The transcript records no applause, but one can assume that his audience sat in agreement. Stalin may have become titanically paranoid in the 1930s, but a virulent xenophobia had long since infected the Bolshevik organism.

As one after another of the principal actors in the Great October Socialist Revolution were exposed as murderous traitors, Soviet history was rewritten accordingly. A growing number of awkward figures and events from the past were simply written out of the sacred text. The ARA did not become one of these "blank spots," though it was usually ignored or merely mentioned, typically in the context of the ongoing effort of the U.S. government to infiltrate the country with spies and wreckers disguised as relief workers.

This interpretation would endure—in harder and softer variations, through successive thaws and ententes—until the waning days of the Soviet Union. The charge of espionage was always either more or less explicit, recognition of actual assistance more or less grudging. By the 1970s, it was enough to cast the majority of relief workers as U.S. Army officers—or cite their enlistment of the "Zionist" Joint Distribution Committee—in order to get the message across.[33]

Haskell confronted none of this during his 1931 sojourn. Nor was he banqueted and toasted as in the old days. Present upheavals were crowding out memories of earlier struggles. Yet the process of forgetting, he sensed, was not entirely natural, as well-informed Russians inquired of him in earnest whether it was true that the American relief workers had merely been taken on as consultants by the Soviet government, much like the recent wave of American engineers.

Within a few years, innocent queries such as this were considered dangerous. Col. J. W. Krueger, a veteran of the U.S. Army and of 42 Broadway, found this out for himself during a brief stay in the summer of 1939. En route he stopped in Danzig, about three weeks before the German attack on Poland, and he says the city showed signs of a "pending upheaval." Leningrad and Moscow seemed oblivious to the gathering storm clouds in the West, but it was hard to say for sure, since the man in the street was not about to unburden himself to a visiting American. Certainly no one was going to risk reminiscing about the old ARA days.

So Krueger had little to offer the old Russia hands in the pages of the ARA *Review* after he got back, although he was able to relate a more gratifying experience on the steamer during the voyage over.[34] In Norway, a Soviet official boarded the ship, and Krueger struck up a conversation, mentioning the ARA—"whereon he placed his arm around my shoulders and exclaimed, 'Oh, the A.R.A.! You are my best friend. You saved my life when I was a little boy.' He then told the story of the A.R.A. to other members of our cruise staff."

Beyond that, there were new buildings sprouting up in Moscow, and Krueger was especially impressed with the extensive renovations going on in the former Petrograd: "and so, within a year or two, Leningrad will no doubt be much easier on the eye."

AS EUROPE DRIFTED INTO WAR, even the most innocently nostalgic letters to the *Review* could not avoid the subject. In autumn 1941, George Townsend's recollection of the Russian winter of 1922 turns into a curse on the Wehrmacht as it advances toward Moscow:

> The northern ports freeze solid.
> The railroads en masse lay down and expire.
> Typhus, cold and famine sweep the country side and there ain't nothing nobody can do about it till Spring, when the miracle of the Russian Easter will resurrect them, a hundred and eighty million or so of mad Russians, ready to have a go at life again.
> Twenty years ago!
> Here's hoping Hitler finds it the same today, not that we love Russia so much, but that we love the U.S.A. the more.

No one seemed to question that Hitler was the greater threat. Still Marshall Tuthill found "the whitewashing of Pal Joey" Stalin in the American press "somewhat nauseating—those of us who thought we were in Russia must have been some other place, or else we met the wrong people."[35] Tuthill must have become apoplectic after the United States entered the war and "Uncle Joe" Stalin's Soviet Union was repackaged into a beacon of democracy. Once again, this time with the help of Hollywood celluloid, Russia had become a fit partner for a league of honour.

As the Eastern front approached the Volga and especially after the great Soviet victory at Tsaritsyn, then known as Stalingrad, here and there Americans recalled the life-saving efforts of two decades earlier and wondered what connection there might be between then and now. Children fed by the ARA had repaid a debt to America, even if unwittingly, by halting the German advance—that was one way to think of it.[36]

The war's end brought something of a resurgence of Hoover-style and -inspired relief and reconstruction activity in Europe, with key roles for some old ARA hands. In 1944 the ARA's Arthur C. Ringland, former mission chief in Constantinople, proposed that the United States undertake a relief operation similar to the ARA's food package program, and this led the following year to the establishment of CARE, the Cooperative for American Remittances to Europe, based on the system Burland had designed for Russia. Burland was present at the creation of CARE, along with fellow ARA men John Speaks and Richard Bonnevalle, under executive director William Haskell.

Two years later, the U.N. General Assembly established the United Nations International Children's Emergency Fund, UNICEF, which was directed during its first eighteen years by the ARA's Maurice Pate.

In June 1947 came the European Recovery Program, better known as the Marshall Plan, which pledged $17 billion in economic assistance to Europe over four years. Aid was offered to the Soviet Union and its Eastern European satellites as well, but the Cold War was getting under way and it was assumed that Moscow would turn the offer down.[37] Equally predictable by now was the hysterical pitch of the rejection. *Pravda* professed to see in the Marshall Plan "the grinning snout of the imperialist beast of prey peeping from behind the coquettishly intertwined olive twigs." *Plain Talk* plucked this quote and used it as a foil for an article by Haskell on "How We Fed the Starving Russians."[38]

A Moscow historical journal, so called, did its part, exposing the Marshall Plan as an attempt to execute the counterrevolutionary strategy that had failed in 1922. "It is difficult to say where Messrs. Shafroth, Allen, Anderson, Willoughby, Landy, McClintock, and Gregg—former agents of Hoover in Soviet Russia—are 'working' now: maybe in Turkey, maybe in Greece, maybe in France, Italy, or Japan."[39]

Stalin's death in 1953 led to a partial relaxation—inside the U.S.S.R. in the form of a "thaw" and internationally in the name of "peaceful coexistence." Travel restrictions to the East bloc were lightened, and Horsley Gantt, the only ARA veteran to maintain a professional connection to Russia, took advantage of the opportunity in 1957 by accepting an invitation to lecture at the Soviet Academy of Sciences. It was his first visit in over two decades. Gantt had returned to Leningrad in 1925 to study with Pavlov and ended up staying most of the next four years. He renewed the association in 1933 and 1935, the year before the great scientist's death.

Gantt continued the work of his mentor at the Pavlovian Laboratory at Johns Hopkins, which he founded in 1929. And he otherwise displayed a special interest in Russian matters, serving as vice-chairman of the Baltimore branch of the Russian War Relief and lending his name to the letterhead of an organization called the Council of American-Soviet Friendship. The title sounds harmless enough in retrospect, but in the early 1950s such societies came under unusually close scrutiny. For some reason, this particular friendship council ended up on the House Un-American Activities Committee's list of disloyal organizations. Gantt was asked to explain himself.

Perhaps there was something to HUAC's indictment because Gantt now claimed that in fact he had earlier written to the head of this organization to have his name removed from its stationery. The trouble was that he had neglected to enclose his letter in the envelope he mailed. This sounds like the kind of innocent absent-mindedness one should expect from great minds, but in those rabidly suspicious times Gantt's excuse gave off a hollow ring of inauthenticity. How, precisely, does one go about mailing an empty envelope, Dr. Gantt? And where was the said letter now? Perhaps Pavlov's dog had ingested it.

In 1953 Gantt was suspended by the Veterans Administration from the directorship of the Pavlovian Laboratory he had established in Perry Point, Maryland, and a formal investigation was begun into his alleged communist sympathies. He was soon cleared and reinstated, and his career then resumed its advance. In 1955 he founded the Pavlovian Society and served for ten years as its president; in 1970 he was nominated for a Nobel Prize in medicine.

The warmer winds that enabled Gantt to reestablish his professional ties in Leningrad and Moscow brought Soviet leaders to the West to engage in summitry and other forms of diplomacy, some of it unorthodox. One such encounter at the White House restored the American relief mission to the front page of the *New York Times*, if only for a day.

The Soviet protagonist in this minor subplot was one Frol Kozlov, first deputy premier of the Soviet Union and rising Kremlin star, who came to Washington in the summer of 1959 and met with President Eisenhower. In the course of their conversation, Kozlov, in rehearsing the argument that the United States had long failed to treat the Soviet Union with due respect, recalled the famine of 1921 and the shameless behavior of the ARA, which had insisted that the Soviet government pay in gold for American relief.

Kozlov might have been able to slide this one by—when it came to details, Ike was no Hoover—but for the recent death of John Foster Dulles. At an official reception that evening, Secretary of State Christian Herter lay in wait for the deputy premier. "I wanted to straighten you out on one matter," the *Times* reporter quotes his opening thrust, delivered "politely but firmly."

Herter could handle himself, but just in case, Vice President Nixon was on the scene to back him up. Three weeks later, Nixon would famously mix it up with Khrushchev at a model American kitchen in Moscow, and he may have hoped to warm up for that contest by sparring a few rounds with the Kremlin contender. The food was a gift, the two Americans reminded Kozlov. No Soviet payment was made or demanded. According to the *Times*, the deputy premier surrendered without a fight. "The question is not one to be discussed," he conceded. "It is not disputed."[40]

This exchange inspired the publication of an article by George Kennan, "Our Aid to Russia: A Forgotten Chapter," in the *New York Times Magazine* on July 19, 1959, which told most readers for the first time the story of the 1921 famine and the American relief.

Khrushchev put the story back in the newspapers that September during his twelve-day tour of the United States. In Los Angeles at a luncheon at the studios of Twentieth Century-Fox, he gave a typically rousing performance. The general secretary of the Communist Party of the Soviet Union had just been informed that contrary to his fervent desire, for security reasons he would not be allowed to visit Disneyland. This seems to have soured his mood that afternoon—although on this occasion he managed to keep his shoes on. Someone in the crowd raised the subject of the ARA, which sparked this translated eruption:

You referred here to the aid extended to Soviet people after the Civil War, during the terrible famine of 1921–1922, when ARA, the American Relief Administration, was set up to aid the starving population. The committee was headed by Herbert Hoover. We remember that well, and we thank you.

But I feel I must raise a "but" on this score. The "but" is that our people remember not only the fact that America helped us through ARA and that as a result thousands of people were saved from starvation in the Volga Region. They also remember that in the hard time after the October Revolution, U.S. troops led by their generals landed on Soviet soil to help the White Guards fight our Soviet system. . . .

Why do I recall all this? For the simple reason that if you and your allies had not landed troops at that time, we would have made short shrift of the White Guards and would have had no Civil War, no ruin and no famine. And you wouldn't have had to help Soviet people through ARA, whose work you have just mentioned.

But even so, even in these circumstances, we thank the Americans for the help they gave us.

There was always a "but," yet the fact is that by Soviet standards this was especially generous. He then closed with a Khrushchevian flourish: "You see how it is, ladies and gentlemen. Please excuse me for these comments. I assure you that I had planned to make a very short and unemotional speech. But I cannot be silent when someone treads on my pet corn, even if he does so after putting a pad on it."[41] After that, the episode slipped back into obscurity.

THOSE WHO SERVED could still resurrect the glory days at their periodic reunions. There were thirty-two over the years, lasting into the 1960s. They included survivors of all the Hoover missions, eventually including veterans of the Belgian operation that had begun it all.

There was only one ARA district reunion, that of Kazan, held on May 15 and 16, 1937, at the Essex House, in Newark, New Jersey, which brought together Wahren, Dear, Turner, Norris, Boyd, Childs, and various spouses. Norris brought his wife, Xenia, and the *Review*, in writing up the occasion, cheerfully recalled that Norris "took a swig of gasoline back in 1922, under the mistaken impression that it was vodka, just before the memorable ceremony of his wedding." At some point in these alcohol-soaked proceedings, someone decided it would be a good idea to share the good cheer with old friends back in the Tatar republic. A waiter was summoned and a telegram sent to the Kazan *Izvestiia*: "We, former members of the A.R.A. in Kazan in 1921-1923, meeting together in reunion for the first time in almost fifteen years, send our most cordial greetings to all our old friends in Kazan with whom we are united in ineffaceable memories." This, in 1937, with the Great Terror in full swing.

On Sunday afternoon, following an extended brunch, Dear and Childs took the train back to Washington. Dear remarked on the fact that six Kazan ARA men had managed to come together fifteen years after the mission, which he thought was a "pretty good record." He wondered, "Where shall we be fifteen years hence?" "Nitchevo," came the reply. "We've got a memory of yesterday and today that will carry us a long way on the road."[42]

Childs continued down the road for another half-century. Along the way he was able to visit the Soviet Union three more times. In 1962 he and Boyd went to Moscow, where they inquired about visas for Kazan but were told that it was a "restricted district." In the time of the Great Famine, when millions starved, typhus raged, and they packed food as a weapon, there was no stopping them. Forty years later they were just two more victims of Intourist.[43]

The Washington, D.C., chapter—which included Fox, Lyon, Barringer, Bonnevalle, Somerville, Walker, Gantt, and Shafroth—proved to be the most active and continued to meet into the late 1960s; otherwise the only gatherings were the official reunions. Usually the Chief was on hand, and it was his death in 1964 that occasioned the final reunion the following year, which also saw the appearance of the final issue of the *Review*, the "Herbert Hoover Number."

The concluding event was held at the Waldorf-Astoria, Hoover's headquarters in his last decades, on the evening of Saturday, April 24. This happened to be the day before Easter—for the faithful a period of abstinence—and Alexis Lapteff, once an ARA employee in Ufa and still a devout Orthodox Christian, says he would not have gone to the reunion had it not been the last. He still intended to make the midnight service, though, so he kept an eye on his watch. As time ran out, he announced to those at his table that he would soon have to take his leave and why, which caused something of an uproar: "Then all at this big round table exclaimed (except few who never were in Russia), what wonderful memories they have of Russian Easter, of Easter service in churches of people greeting each other with three kisses, saying 'Christ is risen', 'Truly He is risen', and of celebration in homes after the service, and some of them made motion of kissing each other."

Fleming was seated at the table, sharing these memories. Hard times had befallen him in recent years. He had lost his wife to an agonizing death, whereupon he "lived for ten months on whiskey till midnight," until his liver gave out. However these circumstances now figured into his calculations, as Lapteff got up to leave, Fleming decided to join him. Lapteff recalls that there was no time to lose: "We came to the church just in time to buy, and to li[gh]t the candles in our hands, and to witness the end of [the] procession of clergy, choir, and the people walking with lit candles, and singing of the resurrection of Christ—three times around the church, in that cool, but calm spring night."[44]

With no more reunions or *Review*, theirs were now individual memories, extinguished one by one into the final decade of the century. As they passed on, probably none could recall—or had ever known—that even before the last American relief workers departed Soviet Russia in 1923, Russian men of science had honored their exploit in a way that placed its memory safely beyond the reach of even the mightiest totalitarian dictator.

This was accomplished through a gift of two minor planets.[45] The first was bestowed by the astronomers at the Pulkova Observatory, in Petrograd, who decided to name their recent discovery, planet no. 916, "America." It may well be that their first choice was unavailable. A year earlier, their colleagues at the Observatory at Simeis in the Crimea, upon discovering planet no. 849, immortalized those three letters, rendered as one Russian word, "Ara."

RIGA AGREEMENT

AGREEMENT BETWEEN THE AMERICAN RELIEF ADMINISTRATION AND THE RUSSIAN SOCIALIST FEDERATIVE SOVIET REPUBLIC

WHEREAS a famine condition exists in parts of Russia, and WHEREAS Mr. Maxim Gorky, with the knowledge of the Russian Socialist Federative Soviet Republic, has appealed through Mr. Hoover to the American people for assistance to the starving and sick people, more particularly the children, of the famine stricken parts of Russia, and

WHEREAS Mr. Hoover and the American people have read with great sympathy this appeal on the part of the Russian people in their distress and are desirous, solely for humanitarian reasons, of coming to their assistance, and

WHEREAS Mr. Hoover, in his reply to Mr. Gorky, has suggested that supplementary relief might be brought by the American Relief Administration to up to a million children in Russia.

THEREFORE it is agreed between the American Relief Administration, an unofficial volunteer American charitable organization under the chairmanship of Mr. Herbert Hoover, hereinafter called the A.R.A., and the Russian Socialist Federative Soviet Republic hereinafter called the Soviet Authorities,

That the A.R.A. will extend such assistance to the Russian people as is within its power, subject to the acceptance and fulfillment of the following conditions on the part of the Soviet Authorities who hereby declare that there is need of this assistance on the part of the A.R.A.

The Soviet Authorities agree:

First: That the A.R.A. may bring into Russia such personnel as the A.R.A. finds necessary in the carrying out of its work and the Soviet Authorities guarantee them full liberty and protection while in Russia. Non-Americans and Americans who have been detained in Soviet Russia since 1917 will be admitted on approval by the Soviet authorities.

Second: That they will, on demand of the A.R.A., immediately extend all facilities for the entry into and exit from Russia of the personnel mentioned in (1) and while such personnel are in Russia the Soviet Authorities shall accord them full liberty to come and go and move about Russia on official business and shall provide them with all necessary papers such as safe-conducts, laissez passer, et cetera, to facilitate their travel.

Third: That in securing Russian and other personnel the A.R.A. shall have complete freedom as to selection and the Soviet Authorities will, on request, assist the A.R.A. in securing same.

Fourth: That on delivery of the A.R.A. of its relief supplies at the Russian ports of Petrograd, Murmansk, Archangel, Novorossisk or other Russian ports as mutually agreed upon, or the nearest practicable available ports in adjacent countries, decision to lie with the A.R.A., the Soviet Authorities will bear all further costs such as discharge, handling, loading and transportation to interior base points in the areas where the A.R.A. may operate. Should demurrage or storage occur at above ports mutually agreed upon as satisfactory such demurrage and storage is for the account of the Soviet Authorities. For purposes of this agreement the ports of Riga, Reval, Libau, Hango and Helsingfors are also considered satisfactory ports. Notice of at least five days will be given to Soviet representatives at respective ports in case the Soviet Authorities are expected to take c.i.f. delivery.

Fifth: That they will at their own expense supply the necessary storage at interior base points mentioned in paragraph (4) and handling and transportation from same to all such other interior points as the A.R.A. may designate.

Sixth: That in all above storage and movement of relief supplies they will give the A.R.A. the same priority over all other traffic as the Soviet Authorities give their own relief supplies, and on demand of the A.R.A. will furnish adequate guards and convoys.

Seventh: That they will give free import re-export and guarantee freedom from requisition to all A.R.A. supplies of whatever nature. The A.R.A. will repay the Soviet Authorities for the expenses incurred by them on re-exported supplies.

Eighth: That the relief supplies are intended for children and the sick, as designated by the A.R.A. in accordance with paragraph (24) and remain the property of the A.R.A. until actually consumed by these children and the sick, and are to be distributed in the name A.R.A.

Ninth: That no individual receiving A.R.A. rations shall be deprived of such local supplies as are given to the rest of the population.

Tenth: That they will guarantee and take every step to insure that relief supplies belonging to the A.R.A. will not go to the general adult population nor to the Army, Navy or Government employees but only to such persons as designated in paragraphs (8) and (24).

Eleventh: That Soviet Authorities undertake to reimburse the A.R.A. in dollars at c.i.f. cost or replace in kind any misused relief supplies.

Twelfth: That the A.R.A. shall be allowed to set up the necessary organizations for carrying out its relief work free from governmental or other interference. The Central and Local Soviet Authorities have the right of representation thereon.

Thirteenth: That the Soviet Authorities will provide:

A. The necessary premises for kitchens, dispensaries and, in as far as possible, hospitals.

B. The necessary fuel and, when available, cooking, distributing and feeding equipment for the same.

C. The total cost of local relief administration, food preparation, distribution, etc., themselves or in conjunction with local authorities. Mode of payment to be arranged at later date.

D. On demand of the A.R.A. such local medical personnel and assistance, satisfactory to the A.R.A., as are needed to efficiently administer its relief.

E. Without cost railway, motor, water or other transportation for movement of relief supplies and of such personnel as may be necessary to efficiently control relief operations. The Soviet Authorities will for the duration of the A.R.A. operations assign to the A.R.A. for the sole use of its personnel, and transport free of cost, such railway carriages as the A.R.A. may reasonably request.

Fourteenth: In localities where the A.R.A. may be operating and where epidemics are raging, the A.R.A. shall be empowered by the Soviet Authorities to take such steps as may be necessary towards the improvement of sanitary conditions, protection of water supply, etc.

Fifteenth: That they will supply free of charge the necessary offices, garages, store-rooms, etc., for the transaction of the A.R.A. business and when available heat, light and water for same. Further that they will place at the disposal of the A.R.A. adequate residential quarters for the A.R.A. personnel in all localities where the A.R.A. may be operating. All such above premises to be free from seizure and requisition. Examination of above premises will not be made except with the knowledge and in presence of the chief of the A.R.A. operations in Russia or his representative and except in case of flagrant delit when examiner will be held responsible in case examination unwarranted.

Sixteenth: That they will give to the A.R.A. complete freedom and priority without cost in the use of existing radio, telegraph, telephone, cable, post, and couriers in Russia and will provide the A.R.A., when available and subject to the consent of competent authorities, with private telegraph and telephone wires and maintenance free of cost.

Seventeenth: To accord the A.R.A. and its American representatives and its couriers the customary diplomatic privileges as to passing the frontiers.

Eighteenth: To supply the A.R.A. free of cost with the necessary gasoline and oil to operate its motor transportation and to transport such motor transportation by rail or otherwise as may be necessary.

Nineteenth: To furnish at the request of the competent A.R.A. Authorities all A.R.A. personnel, together with their impediments and supplies, free transportation in Russia.

Twentieth: To permit the A.R.A. to import and re-export free of duty and requisition such commissary, transport and office supplies as are necessary for its personnel and administration.

Twenty-first: That they will acquaint the Russian people with the aims and methods of the relief work of the A.R.A. in order to facilitate the rapid development of its efficiency and will assist and facilitate in supplying the American people with reliable and non-political information of the existing conditions and the progress of the relief work as an aid in developing financial support in America.

Twenty-second: That they will bear all expenses of the relief operation other than A. Cost of relief supplies at port (See paragraph 4).

B. Direct expenses of American control and supervision of relief work in Russia with exceptions as above. In general they will give the A.R.A. all assistance in their power toward the carrying out of its humanitarian relief operations.

The A.R.A. agrees:

Twenty-third: Within the limits of its resources and facilities to supply, as rapidly as suitable organization can be effected, food, clothing and medical relief to the sick and particularly to the children within the age limits as decided upon by the A.R.A.

Twenty-fourth: That its relief distribution will be to the children and sick without regard to race, religion or social or political status.

Twenty-fifth: That its personnel in Russia will confine themselves strictly to the ministration of relief and will engage in no political or commercial activity whatever. In view of paragraph (1) and the freedom of American personnel in Russia from personal search, arrest and detention, any personnel contravening this will be withdrawn or discharged on the request of the Central Soviet Authorities. The Central Soviet Authorities will submit to the chief officer of the A.R.A. the reasons for this request and the evidence in their possession.

Twenty-sixth: That it will carry on its operations where it finds its relief can be administered most efficiently and to secure best results. Its principal object is to bring relief to the famine stricken areas of the Volga.

Twenty-seventh: That it will import no alcohol in its relief supplies and will permit customs inspection of its imported relief supplies at points to be mutually agreed upon.

The Soviet Authorities having previously agreed as the absolute sine qua non of any assistance on the part of the American people to release all Americans detained in Russia and to facilitate the departure from Russia of all Americans so desiring, the A.R.A. reserves to itself the right to suspend temporarily or terminate all of its relief work in Russia in case of failure on the part of the Soviet Authorities to fully comply with this primary condition or with any condition set forth in the above agreement. The Soviet Authorities equally reserve the right of cancelling this Agreement in case of non-fulfillment of any of the above clauses on the part of the A.R.A.

Made in Riga, August Twentieth, Nineteen hundred and Twenty-one

On behalf of Council of Peoples Commissaries of the Russian Socialist Federative Soviet Republic:

(Signed) Maxim Litvinov,
Assistant Peoples Commissary for Foreign Affairs.

On behalf of the American Relief Administration:

(Signed) Walter Lyman Brown
Director for Europe.

REFERENCE MATTER

For complete authors' names, titles of works, and publication data on works cited in short form in these Notes, consult the Bibliography. The following abbreviations are used in the Notes and Bibliography:

AAR   *A.R.A. Association Review.* 39 issues, 1925–65, Herbert Hoover Presidential Library

ACC   Archibald Cary Coolidge Papers, Harvard University Archives, Correspondence, Box 2

AFSC   American Friends Service Committee Archives, Philadelphia

ARA   American Relief Administration, Russian Operations, Hoover Institution Archives

CON   American Relief Administration 496–97, London Office Russia File, Confidential Letters

CP   James Rives Childs Papers, Hoover Institution Archives

DS   General Records of the Department of State, Record Group 59, National Archives, Washington, D.C.

EWP   Rev. Edmund A. Walsh, S.J., Papers, Lauinger Library, Georgetown University, Washington, D.C.

FGP   Frank A. Golder Papers, Hoover Institution Archives

FRUS   U.S. Department of State, *Papers Relating to the Foreign Relations of the United States, 1921*, vol. 2, Washington, D.C., 1936

GBB   George Barr Baker Papers, Hoover Institution Archives

GCP   George Cornick Papers, Southwest Collection, Texas Tech University, Lubbock, Tex., "Russian Correspondence to Family, 1921–1922"

HFP   Harold Fleming Papers, Hoover Institution Archives

HHP   Herbert Hoover Papers, Hoover Institution Archives

HHPL   Herbert Hoover Presidential Library, West Branch, Iowa

HIA   Hoover Institution Archives, Stanford, Calif.

JDC   Joint Distribution Committee Archives, New York

JGP   James P. Goodrich Papers, Herbert Hoover Presidential Library, West Branch, Iowa

JRC   James Rives Childs Papers, Alderman Library, University of Virginia, Charlottesville

MERSH   Wieczynski, Joseph L., ed., *The Modern Encyclopedia of Russian and Soviet History*, 46 vols., Gulf Breeze, Fla., 1976–87

PS   Personnel Series, Herbert Hoover Presidential Library

PSS   V. I. Lenin, *Polnoe sobranie sochinenii*, 5th ed., 55 vols., Moscow, 1958–65

RED   J. Rives Childs, "Red Days in Russia," ARA 7:12

RUR   "Russian Unit Record," ARA 102:4, 103:1–2

TBP   Thomas C. Barringer Papers, Hoover Institution Archives

TDP   Thomas H. Dickinson Papers, Hoover Institution Archives

WHG   W. Horsley Gantt Papers, Alan Mason Chesney Medical Archives, Johns
         Hopkins Medical Institutions, Baltimore

WPF   W. Parmer Fuller Papers, Hoover Institution Archives

WS   Will Shafroth personal scrapbook

PROLOGUE

1. Shafroth, "The Fact-Story of the Russian Famine," *New York Evening World*,
arts. 2, 4, 6, 8, ARA 81:8.

CHAPTER I

Part epigraph: Ellingston, "Carriage of Philanthropy," 15; McClintock: ARA 70:3.

1. PS 292; ARA 81:8; WS.
2. PS 239.
3. Supply Division History, 10, ARA 64:1.
4. Shafroth, art. 1, ARA 81:8; WS.
5. Kennan, *Russia and the West*, 18–19.
6. Pipes, *Russian Revolution*; Figes, *People's Tragedy*, pt. 3.
7. Malia, *Soviet Tragedy*, 93.
8. Kennan, *Russia and the West*, chs. 5–10; idem, *Decision to Intervene*; Fogelsong,
America's Secret War, chs. 6–7.
9. Pipes, *Russia Under the Bolshevik Regime*, chs. 1–2, 4.
10. Shafroth, art. 1, ARA 81:8; Fisher, *Famine*, 71.
11. Carroll, Sept. 4, 1921, ARA 344:14.
12. Shafroth, Aug. 29, 1921, WS.
13. Carroll, Sept. 4, 1921, ARA 344:14.
14. Shafroth, art. 1, ARA 81:8.
15. Lih, *Bread and Authority*; Pipes, *Russian Revolution*, ch. 16.
16. PSS 36:316–17, 357–64, 374–76, 395–418.
17. Malia, *Soviet Tragedy*, ch. 4.
18. M. Kantor, "K prodovol'stvennoi kampanii," *Vestnik agitatsii i propagandy*,
Nov. 25, 1920.
19. "Moment Is the Mother of Ages," 1, ARA 6:6.
20. "O khlebe," *Kommunisticheskii trud*, Feb. 1, 1921; "Toplivyi krizis v Moskve,"
Izvestiia VTsIK, Feb. 20, 1921.
21. Pipes, *Russian Revolution*, 724; idem, *Russia Under the Bolshevik Regime*, 371;
Malia, *Soviet Tragedy*, 84, 143.
22. Avrich, *Kronstadt 1921*.
23. PSS 44:207–8; *Biulleten' vserossiiskoi konferentsii*, no. 1 (Dec. 19, 1921): 12.
24. Shafroth, art. 1, ARA 81:8; PSS 44:155–75, 193–220.
25. Patenaude, "Bolshevism in Retreat," chs. 4–5.
26. Edmondson, "Soviet Famine Relief Measures," 59–60.
27. Conquest, *Harvest of Sorrow*; Fisher, *Famine*, ch. 21; Golder and Hutchinson,
On the Trail, ch. 1; Edmondson, "Soviet Famine Relief Measures," chs. 1–2.

28. Fisher, *Famine*, 496–505.

29. FRUS, 805.

CHAPTER 2

1. Nash, *Hoover: The Engineer*; Nash, *Hoover: The Humanitarian*; Burner, *Hoover*, chs. 5–6.

2. Burner, *Hoover*, ch. 7; Weissman, *Hoover*, chs. 1–2; Fisher, *Famine*, ch. 1.

3. Burner, *Hoover*, 115–16.

4. Surface and Bland, *American Food in the World War*, 7, 36; Weissman, *Hoover*, 28.

5. Surface and Bland, *American Food in the World War*, 82; Burner, *Hoover*, 116–17.

6. Weissman, *Hoover*, 28; Burner, *Hoover*, 97.

7. Burner, *Hoover*, 341.

8. Weissman, *Hoover*, 29; Burner, *Hoover*, 96; Fisher, *Famine*, 25; Dickinson, "The American Relief Administration: A History of Economic Reconstruction in Europe during the Armistice" (unpublished ms., 1920), vol. 2, ch. 4, [p. 1], TDP.

9. Bane and Lutz (eds.), *Organization of American Relief*, 176–77.

10. Hoover, Mar. 28, 1919, HHP 8; Hoover, "American Relations to Russia," HHP 116.

11. Thompson, *Russia, Bolshevism, and Versailles*, 222–30; Surface and Bland, *American Food in the World War*, 34; Burner, *Hoover*, 125–28.

12. Kennan, *Russia and the West*, 159–61.

13. Hoover to George Barr Baker, Nov. 16, 1925, ARA 344:13.

14. McFadden, *Alternative Paths*, ch. 10; Fisher, *Famine*, ch. 1; Kennan, *Russia and the West*, ch. 10.

15. Kennan, *Russia and the West*, 138, 141.

16. Weissman, *Hoover*, 36–37; Fogelsong, *America's Secret War*, ch. 8.

17. Fisher, *Famine*, ch. 2.

18. Kennan, *Russia and the West*, 206.

19. Schuman, *American Policy Toward Russia*, 200–2, 272–73.

20. FRUS, 806.

21. FRUS, 804–9; U.S.S.R. Ministry of Foreign Affairs, *Dokumenty vneshnei politiki*, 246–47.

22. Fisher, *Famine*, 52–53; FRUS, 807–8.

23. FRUS, 809.

24. Weissman, *Hoover*, ch. 3; Fisher, *Famine*, ch. 3; ARA 22:6, 22:9, 342:9.

25. Coolidge and Lord, *Archibald Cary Coolidge*, 291.

26. Fisher, *Famine*, 54–59.

27. Burner, *Hoover*, 121–25.

28. *Istoricheskii arkhiv*, 76–80; U.S.S.R. Ministry of Foreign Affairs, *Dokumenty vneshnei politiki*, 262–64, 275–81, 781.

29. PSS 53:110–11.

30. Weissman, *Hoover*, 63; ARA 22:6.

31. U.S.S.R. Ministry of Foreign Affairs, *Dokumenty vneshnei politiki*, 275–81.

32. Quinn, ARA 355:1; Brown, Aug. 27, 1921, ARA 22:6; Litvinov, Aug. 13, 1921, in *Istoricheskii arkhiv*, 79.

33. Fisher, *Famine*, 62–67.

34. Fisher, *Famine*, 159–67.

35. Brown, Aug. 27, 1921, ARA 22:6.

36. Gibbons, *Floyd Gibbons*, 152–54; Duranty, *I Write As I Please*, 122–24.

CHAPTER 3

1. GBB 5; Galpin to Herter, Aug. 18, 1921, ARA 337:4; Fuller to Rickard, Jan. 25, 1922, WPF 2:ARA 1922.
2. Kennedy, *Over Here*, 185, 210; Dos Passos, *Three Soldiers*, 399; May, *End of American Innocence*, 378.
3. Dos Passos, *Three Soldiers*, 321.
4. Kennedy, *Over Here*, 152–54.
5. Galpin to Herter, Sept. 23, 1921, ARA 322:8; Brown to Rickard, Aug. 6, 1921, ARA 22:9.
6. Duranty, *I Write As I Please*, 111.
7. ARA 36:6; Shafroth, Sept. 3, 1921, WS; RED, 13.
8. Gregg to Shafroth, Sept. 26, 1921, WS.
9. Shafroth, art. 8, ARA 81:8.
10. Fisher, *Famine*, 83–85; Bowden, Sept. 18, 1921, ARA 73:3; ARA 345:7.
11. Haskell to Brown, Sept. 30, 1921, CON.
12. PS 255.
13. Golder, *War, Revolution, and Peace in Russia*.
14. Shafroth, art. 2, ARA 81:8.
15. Golder and Hutchinson, *On the Trail*, 30–33.
16. Shafroth, art. 2, ARA 81:8; Shafroth, "Inspection Trip to Volga," CON; Shafroth, Sept. 9, 1921, WS.
17. Gregg, Sept. 6, 1921, ARA 29:6.
18. ARA 29:6; WS.
19. Golder and Hutchinson, *On the Trail*, 36–38, 44.
20. Shafroth, art. 2, ARA 81:8.
21. Golder and Hutchinson, *On the Trail*, 32, 56.
22. Mackenzie, *Russia Before Dawn*, 152.
23. Golder and Hutchinson, *On the Trail*, 56–58; Shafroth, art. 4, ARA 81:8.
24. GBB 3.
25. Haskell to Logan, Feb. 17, 1920, ARA, European Operations, HIA 320:1.
26. Hoover to Brown, Aug. 19, 1921, ARA 339:4; Brown to Rickard, July 30, 1921, ARA 69:1; Rickard to Brown, Aug. 2, 1921, ARA 22:9.
27. Haskell, [untitled], Vol. 1, 4–5.
28. Brown, July 30, 1921, ARA 69:1.
29. Kennedy, *Over Here*, 209–10, 224; Hoover, *Memoirs of Capitalism*, 38–39.
30. GBB 3.
31. Gregg to Shafroth, Sept. 26, 1921, WS; Clapp, ARA 107:12.
32. Sellards to Baker, Sept. 28, 1921, PS 292; Haskell to Brown, Sept. 30, 1921, CON; Haskell, [untitled], Vol. 1, 85, 98–99.
33. Haskell to Brown, Sept. 30, Oct. 5, 1921, CON; Haskell to Rickard, Sept. 28, 1921, ARA 95:4.
34. Gregg to Shafroth, Sept. 26, Oct. 7, 1921, WS.
35. Kellogg to Hoover, ARA 327:11; Haskell to Brown, Sept. 30/Oct. 3, 1921, CON; Haskell to Rickard, Sept. 28, 1921, ARA 95:4; Gregg to Shafroth, Oct. 7, 1921, WS.
36. Baker, "Notes on Russia," ARA 336:1.
37. Sellards to Baker, Sept. 28, 1921, PS 292.
38. Carroll to London, Sept. 4, 1921, ARA 344:14; Haskell to Rickard, ARA 94:5.
39. Fisher, *Famine*, 51, n. 5.
40. Hutchinson obituary, *New York Times*, May 23, 1940.
41. Golder to Adams, June 19, 1922, FGP 11:7; Golder and Hutchinson, *On the Trail*, 110.

42. Hutchinson to Brown, Oct. 13, Nov. 9, 1921: ARA 95:6.

43. AAR, Apr. 1, 1925, 13; Hoover to Will H. Hays, Aug. 22, 1921, and Hoover to Goodrich, Sept. 1, 1921, ARA 339:1.

44. ARA 95:3.

45. Haskell to Hoover, Oct. 20, 1921, CON; Nov. 5, 1921, ARA 95:4.

46. Kellogg, ARA 96:5.

47. CON.

48. Degras (comp., ed.), *Soviet Documents on Foreign Policy*, 270–72.

49. Goodrich to Hoover, Nov. 2, 1921, JGP 24; Hutchinson to Brown, Nov. 9, 1921, ARA 95:6.

CHAPTER 4

1. ARA 132:12.

2. Administrative Division History, 6–7, ARA 36:6; ARA 8:5.

3. Fisher, *Famine*, 94.

4. Fisher, *Famine*, 136.

5. Saratov: Kinne, Oct. 7, 1921, ARA 110:9; Lyon: ARA 68:12.

6. Fisher, *America and the New Poland*, 108.

7. Bowden to London, Sept. 18, 1921, ARA 73:3.

8. ARA 72:1.

9. Shafroth, art. 5, ARA 81:8.

10. Simbirsk General Report, III, appendix, doc. 1, ARA 118:4.

11. "Historical Narrative," 10, ARA 99:7.

12. George Cornick, Dec. 30, 1921, GCP; Carroll to London, Sept. 4, 1921, ARA 344:14.

13. Fisher, *Famine*, 98–99.

14. Shafroth, art. 5, ARA 81:8.

15. "Second Year of Operation," II, 20–21, ARA 118:4.

16. Fisher, *America and the New Poland*, 223–37; Fisher, *Famine*, 77.

17. Burland to London, Sept. 11, 1921, ARA 344:14.

18. Weissman, *Hoover*, 13–15, 92–93; PSS 53:24–25, 140–42; Serge, *Memoirs*, 154.

19. Edmondson, "Soviet Famine Relief Measures," chs. 4–5; Fisher, *Famine*, 342.

20. Fisher, *Famine*, 78.

21. RED, 55.

22. Rickard to Brown, Nov. 1, 1921, and Brown to Haskell, Nov. 1, 1921, CON.

23. Haskell to Hoover, Nov. 14, 1921, ARA 339:4.

24. Bowden [Nov. 1921], ARA 100:1.

25. Fisher, *Famine*, 94–95, 102–5.

26. *A.R.A. Bulletin*, ser. 2, no. 45 (1926): 58–59.

27. Fisher, *Famine*, 104–5; Yakovlev, "A.R.A. Men," 10; R. H. Allen, Samara District History, 43, ARA 106:1.

28. Shafroth, art. 5, ARA 81:8.

29. "Historical Narrative," 14, ARA 99:7; Gregg to Moscow, Apr. 23, 1923, ARA 111:2; Elizavetgrad District History, 37–38, ARA 139:3.

30. Lizzy Bach, "Feeding," 3, in Donald Renshaw, Petrograd District History, ARA 76:1.

31. Fisher, *Famine*, ch. 8.

32. Fisher, *Famine*, 432; *American Review* (Aug. 1922): 12, GBB 9; Goodrich to Hoover, Nov. 1, 1921, ARA 95:3; Bowden to London, Sept. 18, 1921, ARA 73:3.

33. Kazan District History, II, 35, ARA 28:1.

34. Ellingston, "Carriage of Philanthropy"; Fisher, *Famine*, ch. 17.
35. Fisher, *Famine*, 120–21.
36. Ellingston, "Carriage of Philanthropy," 10.
37. Fisher, *Famine*, 408.
38. PSS 44:179, 555.
39. Ellingston, "Carriage of Philanthropy," 45; Elizavetgrad District History, 43, ARA 139:3.
40. ARA 8:1; Fisher, *Famine*, 246–47.
41. Fisher, *Famine*, ch. 11.
42. Fisher, *Famine*, 259.
43. Eiduk to Lonergan, Nov. 16, 1921, ARA 19:6.
44. Golder and Hutchinson, *On the Trail*, 113–26; Golder, Dec. 4, 1921, ARA 354:2.
45. Carr, *Bolshevik Revolution*, 135–40, 380–98; Golder and Hutchinson to Haskell, Dec. 4, 1921, ARA 354:2.
46. Carr, *Bolshevik Revolution*, 138.
47. Fisher, *Famine*, 260–61.
48. Eiduk to Lonergan, Nov. 16, 1921, ARA 19:6.
49. Golder and Hutchinson, *On the Trail*, 116.
50. Fisher, *Famine*, 262–63, 266.
51. Haskell to Brown, Dec. 7, 1921, CON.
52. Addendum to [Coolidge] to Golder, Jan. 2, 1922, FGP 12:27.
53. Coolidge, Jan. 2, 1922, ARA 23:2; Fisher, *Famine*, 528–31.
54. K. A. Macpherson, Kiev District History, 3, ARA 141:1; Barringer, May 25, 1923, ARA 138:12.
55. Fisher, *Famine*, 112–15.

CHAPTER 5

1. CON.
2. Weissman, *Hoover*, 67; Burland, "Russian American Contacts," PS 237; *Petlia vmesto khleba*, 9–12.
3. Pipes (ed.), *Unknown Lenin*, 133–34; PSS 53:177–78.
4. Malia, *Soviet Tragedy*, 135.
5. Fisher, *Famine*, 132.
6. RED, 260.
7. Patenaude, "Bolshevism in Retreat," ch. 4.
8. Golder, *War, Revolution, and Peace in Russia*, 133, 280.
9. PSS 53:275–76, 298–99.
10. ARA 22:9.
11. ARA 19:6.
12. Leggett, *Cheka*, 448.
13. Carr, *Bolshevik Revolution*, 179–81.
14. Fisher, *Famine*, 118.
15. Fisher, *Famine*, 127, 120.
16. Eiduk to Lonergan, ARA 72:2.
17. ARA 30:11.
18. ARA 19:6.
19. Shafroth, art. 6, ARA 81:8.
20. Fisher, *Famine*, 124.
21. ARA 22:9.
22. Haskell to Kamenev, Nov. 23, 1921, ARA 21:2.
23. Simbirsk General Report, VII, 8, 10.
24. Bowden [Nov. 1921], ARA 100:1.
25. Coolidge and Lord, *Archibald Cary Coolidge*, 270–305.
26. Coolidge to H. J. Coolidge, Sept. 2, 1921, ACC; Coolidge to Bill [Castle], Dec. 30, 1921, DS file 861.00/9736.
27. Coolidge, Liaison Division History, 3, ARA 52:1.

28. "Our Relations with Mr. Eiduck," Nov. 26, 1921, ARA 94:11.

29. Rickard to Brown, Nov. 28, 1921, CON; Haskell to Hoover, Nov. 14, 1921, ARA 339:4.

30. Mitchell to Brown, Feb. 23, 1922, ARA 23:2; Murphy to Baker, Dec. 12, 1921, GBB 5.

CHAPTER 6

1. Bowden to Haskell, [Jan.] 1922, ARA 21:2.

2. Haskell to Rickard, Feb. 17, 1920, ARA Europe 320:1.

3. Veil, *Adventure's a Wench*, 227; Fuller to Rickard, Jan. 25, 1922, WPF 2:A.R.A. 1922.

4. Brown to Rickard, Oct. 15, 1921, ARA 339:4.

5. Mitchell to Brown, Dec. 20, 1921, CON; Baldwin to Fuller, Dec. 20, 1921, WPF 2:ARA ECF 1921; AAR, Feb. 1929.

6. Brown to Rickard, Oct. 15, 1921, ARA 339:4.

7. Brown to Haskell, Oct. 15, 1921, CON.

8. Brown to Poland, Nov. 9, 1921, CON.

9. Haskell to Hoover, Nov. 14, 1921, ARA 339:4.

10. Hoover, Dec. 5, 1921, ARA 339:4.

11. Rickard to Fuller, Jan. 14, 1922, WPF 2:A.R.A. 1922.

12. GBB 5.

13. Brown to Rickard, Dec. 16, 1921, CON.

14. Brown to Rickard, Oct. 15, 1921, ARA 339:4.

15. Attached to Hoover to Brown, Jan. 31, 1922, ARA 336:7.

16. *Who Was Who in America*, vol. IV, 250; ARA 94:12.

17. Haskell to Brown, Feb. 9, 1922, ARA 318:19.

18. Mitchell to Brown, Feb. 23, 1922, ARA 22:9.

19. Brown to Hoover, Feb. 5, 1922, ARA 318:19.

20. Haskell to Brown, Feb. 15, 1922, ARA 318:19.

21. Haskell, Feb. 5, 1922, and responses, ACC.

22. Coolidge to Haskell, Mar. 9, 1922, ARA 318:19; Rickard to Brown, Mar. 6, 1922, ARA 340:1.

23. Mitchell to Brown, Feb. 23, Feb. 27, 1922, CON.

24. Hoover to Haskell, Feb. 16, 1922, HHPL, Commerce Papers, 255.

25. Haskell to Brown, Jan. 16, 1922, CON.

26. Carroll to Brown, June 1, 1922, CON.

27. Brown to Haskell, Jan. 27, 1922, CON.

28. Mitchell to Brown, Feb. 23, 1922, CON.

29. Goodrich to Hoover, Mar. 6, 1922, ARA 339:2.

30. Mitchell to Brown, Mar. 3, 1922; Special Memorandum no. 66, attached to Brown to Baker, Mar. 16, 1922, ARA 336:1.

31. Brown to Baker, Mar. 16, 1922, ARA 336:1; Rickard to Herter, Apr. 1, 1922, PS 239.

32. Mitchell to Brown, Mar. 11, 1922, ARA 23:2.

CHAPTER 7

1. Brown to Poland, Nov. 9, 1921, CON.

2. Gaddis, *Russia, the Soviet Union and the United States*, ch. 2.

3. Murray, *Red Scare*.

4. U.S. Congress, Senate, *Bolshevik Propaganda.*

5. Fisher, *Famine,* 141.

6. Bailey, *America Faces Russia,* 256.

7. Mcnaughton to Hoover, Oct. 26, 1921, and Hoover to Mcnaughton, Oct. 31, 1921, ARA 307:2; Logan to Hoover, May 24, 1922, and Hoover to Logan, May 29, 1922, ARA 306:11.

8. ARA 349:15.

9. Hoover to Villard, Aug. 17, 1921, ARA 91:2; Hoover to Croly, Sept. 5, 1921, HHPL, Commerce Papers, 30.

10. "New York News Letter," Jan. 28, 1922, ARA 65:1.

11. ARA 322:11, 324:14–18; Fisher, *Famine,* ch. 10.

12. Hoover to Rufus Jones, Feb. 13, 1922, ARA 91:1.

13. Baker to Brown, May 5, 1922, CON.

14. Fisher, *Famine,* 164–66; Hoover to W. K. Thomas, Jan. 26, 1921, and Thomas to Hoover, Jan. 31, 1921, AFSC, General Files, 1921.

15. Sept. 1921 circular, Hoover to Jones, Sept. 21, 1921, and Jones to Hoover, Sept. 16, 1921, AFSC, General Files, 1921; Hoover to Jones, Feb. 13, 1922, ARA 91:1.

16. Hoover to Jones, Nov. 1, 1921, ARA 91:1.

17. ARA New York to London, Mar. 14, 1922, ARA 91:1.

18. Parry Paul to Murray Kentworthy, Nov. 12, 1922, AFSC, General Files, Foreign Service (Russia to Syria) 1922.

19. Fisher, *Famine,* 140.   20. ARA 318:6.

21. Fisher, *Famine,* 144.   22. Baker to Fuller, Dec. 17, 1921, GBB 3.

23. Fisher, *Famine,* 144–46.

24. Kellogg to Baker, HHPL, Commerce Papers, 355.

25. Queen, "American Relief in the Russian Famine," 140–50; Fisher, *Famine,* 149 (n. 14), 477.

26. Haskell to Hoover, Dec. 8, 1921, CON.

27. U.S. Congress, House, *Russian Relief.*

28. U.S. Congress, Senate, *Congressional Record.*

29. Fisher, *Famine,* 144–55, 524.

30. ARA 316:11, 354:7, 309:11.

31. Brown to Hoover, Sept. 16, 1921, ARA 316:11; Burner, 79.

32. ARA 95:4.

33. ARA 317:15, 303:5.

34. Hoover to France, Jan. 12, 1922, ARA 349:12.

35. Haskell to Hoover, Nov. 14, 1921, ARA 339:4; Fisher, *Famine,* 170.

36. Fisher, *Famine,* 154–59; Weissman, *Hoover,* 101.

37. Hoover to Brown, Oct. 28, 1921, ARA 322:13; *Istoricheskii arkhiv,* 81–82.

38. Hoover to Baker, Nov. 19, 1925, ARA 344:13; Forbes, *American Friends and Russian Relief,* 49.

39. Fisher, *Famine,* 171.

CHAPTER 8

1. Hofstra to Haskell, Dec. 27, 1921, ARA 132:12; Shafroth, art. 6, ARA 81:8.

2. Supply Division History, ARA 64:1; Brooks, "Russian Railroads in the National Crisis"; Fleming, "Transportation Difficulties in Soviet Russia," ARA 95:1.

3. C. A. Gaskill Papers, HIA, diary, 5; Hullinger, *Reforging of Russia,* 173–74.

4. Golder, *War, Revolution, and Peace in Russia,* 122.

5. Fisher, *Famine,* 170.

6. Kelley, "Extracts from Letters," 15, 23.

7. Fisher, *Famine*, 173–79; Supply Division History, 14–16, 54, ARA 64:1.

8. Hughes to Sec. of Navy, Sept. 15, 1921, ARA 90:5; Claussen, "American-Soviet Relations," ch. 6; ARA 314:18.

9. Fisher, *Famine*, 179; Quinn to London, Feb. 26, 1922, CON; Supply Division History, 55–57, ARA 64:1.

10. Memorandum of Conference at Moscow Soviet, Mar. 4, 1922, ARA 491:4; Fisher, *Famine*, 183–85; Brown to Rickard, Mar. 25, 1922, ARA 336:7.

11. Fisher, *Famine*, 186–89, 213–16; Kelley, 41.

12. Fisher, *Famine*, 187, 190.

13. Fisher, *Famine*, 190–91; Driscoll, "Historical Narrative," 1–2, ARA 99:7; Driscoll to Bowden, Mar. 29, 1922, ARA 100:1.

14. Fisher, *Famine*, 193–94.

15. Miller to Brown, Mar. 27, 1922, Haskell to Brown, Apr. 1, 1922, and Quinn to London, Mar. 20, 1922, CON.

16. *Istoricheskii arkhiv*, 82–83.

17. Fisher, *Famine*, 194–99; Quinn to London, Apr. 3, 1922, CON; Quinn to London, Apr. 10, 1922, ARA 23:2; Haskell to Eiduk, Apr. 8, 1922, ARA 64:4; *Istoricheskii arkhiv*, 85.

18. CON; Fisher, *Famine*, 199–200.

19. Fisher, *Famine*, 243–44.

20. ARA 64:4; Baker, Apr. 10, 1922, ARA 23:2; ARA 303:4; Mullendore to Baker, May 15, 1922, ARA 336:3; Fisher, *Famine*, 205.

21. Fink, *Genoa Conference*.

22. Haskell to London, Apr. 15, 1922, and Quinn to London, Apr. 3, 1922, CON.

23. "Minutes of the Conference . . . ," attached to Haskell to London, Apr. 15, 1922, CON; Fisher, *Famine*, 201–5; Haskell to Hoover, Apr. 12, 1922, CON.

24. Murphy to Baker, Apr. 16, 1922, ARA 336:2.

25. "Result of Conference . . . " and "Memorandum of Transport Meeting," attached to Haskell to London, Apr. 15, 1922, CON.

26. Fisher, *Famine*, 213–25.

27. ARA 100:1.

28. JGP 16; Kelley, "Extracts from Letters," 44; Fisher, *Famine*, 224.

29. Supply Division History, 54, ARA 64:1.

30. Kelley, "Extracts from Letters," 87; Hale to Herter, Mar. 5, 1922, ARA 305:3; Mackenzie, *Russia Before Dawn*, 127; Cornick, Mar. 3, 1922, GCP.

31. "Observations by a Zone Inspector," ARA 99:6.

32. Hale to Herter, Apr. 24, ARA 305:3; "New York News Letter," Aug. 7, 1922, ARA 65:1.

33. Wolfe, Apr. 24, 1922, ARA 106:6; Fisher, *Famine*, 219, 225.

34. Clapp, ARA 107:12; ARA 121:1; Coleman, May 5, 1922, ARA 68:12; Kelley, "Descriptive Memorandum," 42–43; Kazan District History, 57, ARA 27:12.

35. Report of Conditions, 15, 20, ARA 29:6.

36. Orenburg District History, Sept. 1, 1922, ARA 68:6; Simbirsk General Report, III, 26, IV, 1–2, ARA 118:4.

37. Simbirsk General Report, III, 2, 26; Shafroth to Moscow, May 5, 1922, ARA 97:6; Tsaritsyn District History, ARA 99:8, 17; Bell, Conference of June 16, JGP 16; ARA 8:1.

38. Shafroth, May 16, 1922, ARA 106:6; Buckley, Relief in Orsk Rayon, 7, ARA 68:6; Saratov District History, 69, ARA 109:6; "Press 29," ARA 342:12.

39. Ellingston, "Carriage of Philanthropy," 78.

40. Fisher, *Famine*, 226.

41. Orenburg District History, 29–31; Fisher, *Famine*, 228; Buckley, Relief in Orsk Rayon, ARA 68:6.

CHAPTER 9

1. Golder to Adams, Feb. 7, 1922, FGP 11:7.

2. Rickard to Brown, Mar. 15, 1922, ARA 354:2; Brown to Rickard, Mar. 27, 1922, CON.

3. Wilkinson to Baker, Apr. 11, 1922, ARA 343:3.

4. Fisher, *Famine*, 299–302.

5. RED, 167–68.

6. Shafroth, art. 8, ARA 81:8.

7. Conferences of June 16, June 17, JGP 16.

8. Golder to Adams, June 10, 1922, FGP 11:7.

9. Haskell to Sec. of State [for Hoover], June 24, 1922, ARA 340:1.

10. Fisher to Baker, July 17, 1922, ARA 336:11; Baker to Hoover, July 26, 1922, ARA 336:2; Rickbrown to Chief, July 10, 1922, CON; Goodrich, June 23, 1922, ARA 339:3; ARA 8:1.

11. Childs to Quinn, July 29, 1922, ARA 29:6; Barringer to Page, Aug. 5, 1922, ARA 314:8.

12. Hoover to Hughes, July 28, 1922, ARA 353:1.

13. CON.

14. Fisher to Perrin Galpin, Aug. 3, 1922, ARA 94:14; Barringer to Haskell, Aug. 5, 1922, ARA 137:4; Golder, *War, Revolution, and Peace in Russia*, 209.

15. Ellingston, "Carriage of Philanthropy," 108, 119; Coolidge to Felix Frankfurter, July 11, Aug. 3, 1922, ACC; Haskell to London, Apr. 15, 1922, CON; *Istoricheskii arkhiv*, 89–91; Fisher, *Famine*, 167, 429; Driscoll, "Final Period," 1, ARA 99:7.

16. Fisher, *Famine*, 292–97, 383, 389–90; "Ufa's Inoculation Program," ARA 132:4; Orenburg District History, 31–32.

17. Haskell circular, Sept. 12, 1922, ARA 355:1.

18. Leggett, *Cheka*, 452–53; Baranchenko, "Karl Lander," 200–4.

19. Lander, June 28, attached to Quinn, July 11, 1922, ARA 20:1.

20. Ruhl to Quinn, July 24, 1922, ARA 97:5; Gregg to Moscow, July 22, 1922, ARA 111:3; Quinn to London, Aug. 3, 1922, CON.

21. "Second Year of Operation," 20–21, ARA 118:4.

22. Quinn to London, May 14, 1922, ARA 21:2; Lehrs to Haskell, Sept. 9, 1922, JGP 19.

23. Fisher, *Famine*, 334–42; Haskell to Brown, Oct. 2, Oct. 3, 1922, CON; Ellingston to Fisher, Oct. 7, 1922, ARA 95:2.

24. Haskell to Brown, Oct. 4, 1922, CON.

25. Fisher, *Famine*, 342–48; Childs to Haskell, Oct. 27, Nov. 4, 1922, ARA 26:4.

26. RED, 41; Gregg, "Observations on the Peasants' Attitude Toward the Russian Revolution," Lincoln Hutchinson Papers, 1, HIA; Golder, *War, Revolution, and Peace in Russia*, 265.

27. Coleman, May 15, 1922, ARA 68:12; Simbirsk General Report, VII, 1, ARA 118:4; Bowden, Mar. 10, 1922, ARA 240:1; Stephens, July 21, 1922, ARA 100:1; Hodgson, Sept. 22, 1922, ARA 100:1.

28. Fisher, *Famine*, ch. 14.

29. PSS 45:288; Hoover to C. V. Hibbard, Mar. 23, 1923, ARA 324:14.

30. Ellingston to Quinn, Jan. 23, 1923, Ellingston to Fisher, Jan. 25, 1923, and Ellingston to Fisher, Mar. 15, 1923, ARA 94:13.

31. Simbirsk General Report, IV, 3, "Second Year of Operation," 17–18, and Fleming, Mar. 29, 1923, ARA 106:6; Fisher to Herter, May 1, 1923, ARA 337:1.

32. Ellingston to Fisher, Jan. 4, 1923, ARA 94:13; Quinn, Dec. 28, 1922, CON; Quinn, Jan. 4, 1923, ARA 341:2.

33. Fisher, *Famine*, 353–54; Ellingston to Fisher, Feb. 21, 1923, ARA 94:13.

34. Dailey, Jan. 6, 1923, ARA 20:1; Fisher, *Famine*, 355–60; Ellingston to Fisher, Jan. 16, 1923, ARA 94:13; Quinn to Kamenev, Jan. 16, 1923, attached to Quinn to New York, Jan. 18, 1923, CON.

35. Haskell to Herter, Mar. 6, 1923, ARA 340:3.

36. "Memorandum of Conference," attached to Haskell to Brown, Feb. 28, 1923, CON.

37. Quinn, Jan. 22, 1922, attached to Quinn to New York, Feb. 1, 1923, CON; Baldwin, Feb. 19, 1923, ARA 137:5; Haskell to Brown, Feb. 28, 1923, CON.

38. Hoover to Quinn, Feb. 5, 1923, ARA 314:1; ARA 317:1; Haskell to Herter, Feb. 28, 1923, ARA 340:3.

39. Haskell to Hoover, Mar. 6, 1923, ARA 95:4; Schuman, *American Policy Toward Russia*, 230–31.

40. Haskell to Herter, Mar. 6, 1921, ARA 340:3.

41. Page to Herter, Mar. 15, 1923, HHPL, Commerce Papers, 30.

42. Fisher, *Famine*, 373.

43. "Second Year of Operation," 38, ARA 118:4.

44. Bonnevalle, Mar. 25–Apr. 3, 1923, ARA 106:6.

45. Haskell to Brown, Mar. 1, 1923, CON; Fisher, *Famine*, 391–95.

46. Kelley, Oct. 5, 1922, ARA 81:2; Bell, Ufa-Urals District History, 1, ARA 133:1; Ellingston, "Memorandum for Division Chiefs," Feb. 6, 1923, ARA 48:1; Shafroth, "The New Russia," 49, ARA 349:21; Fleming, "Too little has been made . . . ," 5, HFP; Golder and Hutchinson, *On the Trail*, 18; Dubenetskii, "Opyt izchisleniia," 91; Abramovitch, *Soviet Revolution*, 207.

47. *A.R.A. Bulletin*, ser. 2, no. 28 (1922), 6; "New York News Letter," July 15, 1922, ARA 65:1; Quinn to London, July 2, 1922, ARA 11:4.

48. Kelley to G.L.H., Apr. 20, 1922, FGP 23:5; Hutchinson, Conference of June 17, JGP 16; Fleming to Doris, Nov. 3, 1922, HFP; Fleming, "Trip Through the Volga," 22, ARA 95:1; Mitchell to New York, June 13, 1922, CON.

CHAPTER 10

Part epigraph: Fleming, Jan. 3, 1922, HFP 1:1.

1. Golder, *War, Revolution, and Peace in Russia*, 93; Vail, "Letters from Russia," 22, Edwin H. Vail Papers, HIA; [Henry O. Eversole] to Selskar Gunn, Oct. 8, 1922, Allen Wardwell Papers 7, Bakhmetev Archive, Columbia University, New York.

2. Strong, *I Change Worlds*, 123; Driscoll, "Final Period," 4, ARA 99:7; Orenburg District History, 34, ARA 68:6; Golder to Lutz, July 7, 1922, and Golder to Coolidge, Aug. 13, 1922, FGP 12:27, 13:5.

3. Barringer, May 25, 1923, 5, ARA 138:12; Samara District History, 26, ARA 106:1; Yakovlev, "A.R.A. Men," 11; Childs, Apr. 27, 1922, JRC 20.

4. Haskell, [untitled], Vol. 1, 157; Baker, "Notes on Russia," Feb. 20, 1922, ARA 336:1.

5. Dickinson, ARA 94:12; Rickard to Brown, Apr. 7, 1922, ARA 69:2.

6. DS file 861.48/1977, 861.48/1984; Baker to Hoover, June 12, 1922, ARA 322:14; Ellingston to Fisher, Nov. 16, 1922, ARA 94:13; Sharp, Jan. 16, 1922, A. Ruth Fry Papers 2, Swarthmore College Peace Collection, Swarthmore, Pa.

7. Babine, *Russian Civil War Diary*, 211; Vail, "Letters," 15, AFSC, General Files,

1923; [Elliot], n.d., AFSC, Foreign Service, 1921; A.P.I. Cotterell to A. Ruth Fry, Nov. 25, 1921, and Kentworthy, Nov. 16, 1921, AFSC, General Files, Russia, 1921.

8. Cornick, Apr. 15, 1922, GCP; Cobb, "Extracts," ARA 303:4; Blomquist, "Genesis to Exodus," 3.

9. PS 266; Kelley, "Extracts from Letters," 25, 28, 35, 40, 51, 57, 63, 71, 82; Kelley to G.L.H., Apr. 20, 1922, FGP 23:5.

10. Mitchell to New York, June 13, 1922, CON; Mitchell to Page, Apr. 20, 1923; Lonergan to Ufa, Feb. 6, 1922, PS 233.

11. ARA 70:6; Kelley, "Extracts from Letters," 32–33.

12. Blomquist, 3.

13. [Boris Elperin], "Story of the Ufa District," 7–10, ARA 132:12; Kelley, "Extracts from Letters," 74.

14. ARA 303:4.

15. ARA 354:13; DS file 861.00/9559; Dickinson, "Notes," 5, ARA 94:12; Payne, *Plague*, 75–76; Driscoll, "Historical Narrative," 5, ARA 99:7.

16. Kelley, "Extracts from Letters," 86; Shafroth, art. 4, ARA 81:8.

17. "Among the Dying," 15–16, ARA 118:4; Vasilevskii, *Zhutkaia*, 7; Dickinson, "Notes," 5, ARA 94:12.

18. Gibbs, *Since Then*, 391; Cornick, Apr. 15, 1922, GCP.

19. Golder to Henrietta Eliot, Dec. 22, 1921, FGP 12:35; Kelley, "Extracts from Letters," 17; Clapp, Apr. 16–30, 1922, ARA 107:12.

CHAPTER 11

1. "Manual of Instructions for Child Feeding and Adult Feeding," 21, ARA 27:12; RUR, Jan. 7, 1922; "New York News Letter," Mar. 25, 1922, ARA 64:9; Fleming, June 22, 1922, HFP.

2. Cornick, Dec. 19–26, 1921, GCP; Kelley, "Extracts from Letters," 6; Coolidge and Lord, 282–84; Beeuwkes, May 1923, ARA 69:3.

3. Kelley, "Extracts from Letters," 13; Cornick, Jan. 19, Apr. 15, 1922, GCP.

4. Childs, *Farewell*, 34–35; "Story," 5, ARA 132:12; RED, 171–72; ARA 69:3; Strong, *I Change Worlds*, 118–19.

5. RUR, May 28, 1922; Mackenzie, *Russia Before Dawn*, 158–59; ARA 70:6, 314:13.

6. "Story," 10, ARA 132:12; Ufa-Urals District History, 10, ARA 133:1; Kelley, "Extracts from Letters," 70–74, 79.

7. Kelley, "Extracts from Letters," 68; Bell, May 18, 1922, ARA 70:6; "Ufa Operations," 6, ARA 132:4.

8. Hoover to Brown, May 20, 1922, and Brown to Hoover, May 22, 1922, ARA 314:13.

9. Kelley, "Extracts from Letters," 72; Quinn to London, May 26, 1922, PS 233.

10. Kelley, "Extracts from Letters," 73–74.

CHAPTER 12

1. "Second Year of Operation," III, 60, ARA 118:4; *Chicago Tribune*, Oct. 15, 1921; "Final Period," 3, ARA 99:7; Simbirsk General Report, VII, 60, ARA 118:4; Lyon, in Coolidge and Lord, *Archibald Cary Coolidge*, 282–84.

2. Golder, *War, Revolution, and Peace in Russia*, 145; RUR, Mar. 12, May 14, 1922.

3. Golder to Lutz, Oct. 13, 1921, FGP 13:4; EWP 2:125, diary [Apr. 1922]; Kelley, "Extracts from Letters," 28; Golder, *War, Revolution, and Peace in Russia*, 144; Golder to Quinn, Aug. 29, 1922, ARA 95:2; Barringer, Mar. 15, 1922, TBP 1:3; Blomquist, "Genesis to Exodus," 2.

4. Kelley, "Extracts from Letters," 52–53; Townsend, AAR, May 1965, 33; Babine, *Russian Civil War Diary*, 209; Fisher to Haskell, Oct. 6, 1922, ARA 95:4.

5. Kazan District History, II, 34–35, ARA 27:13; RED, 148; Kelley, "Extracts from Letters," 53; ARA 27:13.

CHAPTER 13

1. RED, 115; Hullinger, *Reforging of Russia*, 84; Townsend, AAR, May 1965, 33; Wilkinson to Baker, Feb. 28, 1922, ARA 510:3; Duranty, *I Write As I Please*, 69–72; Seldes, *You Can't Print That!*, 231; Babine, *Russian Civil War Diary*, 210–11; Orenburg District History, 34, ARA 68:6; Bell to Quinn, Aug. 13, 1922, ARA 69:2; Kelley, "Descriptive Memorandum," 32; Kelley, "Extracts from Letters," 36, 65.

2. Golder, *War, Revolution, and Peace in Russia*, 131; RED, 382.

3. Townsend, AAR, May 1965, 33; Babine, *Russian Civil War Diary*, 207–8; Verdon to Baker, June 13, 1923, ARA 100:1; Haskell, [untitled], Vol. 1, 149S–149T; Golder, *War, Revolution, and Peace in Russia*, 141–42; Golder to Quinn, Aug. 29, Aug. 31, 1922, FGP 23:2; "The Reminiscences of Spurgeon M. Keeny, Sr.," 4:137–38, Oral History Research Office, Columbia University, New York, 1982.

4. Radkey, *Unknown Civil War*.

5. Shafroth, art. 5, ARA 81:8; RUR, Dec. 11, 1921; Kelley, "Extracts from Letters," 1; Brown to Rickard, Dec. 20, 1921, CON; Shafroth, Nov. 28, 1921, ARA 223:2.

6. Barringer, May 25, 1923, 15, ARA 138:12; "General Report," 17, ARA 141:1; PS 267.

7. RUR, July 2, 1922; Tuthill to Haskell, June 11, 1922, ARA 345:6; Fisher to Haskell, Oct. 6, 1922, ARA 95:4; Walter Duranty, "'Amerikansky' Cry Tames a Bandit," *New York Times*, June 30, 1922.

8. ARA 69:4.

9. Veil, *Adventure's a Wench*, 264–65.

10. PS 293, 294; ARA 72:5, 350:2; "Second Year of Operation," III, 61, ARA 118:5; Dalton to Haskell, Oct. 19, 1922, TBP 1:6.

11. John M. Miller to Hoover, Oct. 25, 1922, Herbert W. Jackson to Hoover, Oct. 25, 1922, and Herter to Jackson, Oct. 25, 1922, ARA 350:2; ARA 72:5.

12. Dalton to Haskell, Oct. 19, Oct. 21, 1922, CON; Dalton to Haskell, Nov. 7, 1922, TBP 1:6.

13. RUR, Nov. 5, 1922, ARA 102:4; Godfrey to Matthews, May 13, 1923, PS 254.

CHAPTER 14

1. Vasilevskii, *Zhutkaia*; ARA 94:10.

2. Frank A. Golder Papers, Stanford University Archives, Stanford, Calif., folder 11.

3. Golder, Mar. 11, 1922, FGP 3:6; Vasilevskii, *Zhutkaia*, 7; Strong, *I Change Worlds*, 123; Babine, *Russian Civil War Diary*, 207–13; Yakovlev, 13, ARA 6:6.

4. Orenburg District History, 8–9, ARA 68:6; Fleming, "Russia," 129–30, HFP 1:3; Veil, *Adventure's a Wench*, 239.

5. Kelley to Page, Feb. 23, 1922, PS 266; Wilkinson to London, Feb. 4, 1922, Gilchriese to Wilkinson, Feb. 18, 1922, Wilkinson to Baker, Feb. [19?], 1922, and Wilkinson to Baker, May 29, 1922, ARA 94:10; ARA 510:3.

6. Kelley: ARA 81:2; Dudley Hale to Chris Herter, Apr. 24, 1922, ARA 305:3; Cobb: ARA 303:4; Shafroth to Moscow, Jan. 18, 1922, ARA 267:3; ARA 97:6; Wolfe to Shafroth, Mar. 9, 1922, GBB 9.

7. Haskell, [untitled], Vol. 1, 106A–106G; EWP 2:125; ARA 70:2; TBP 6:1.

CHAPTER 15

1. ARA 69:4.
2. "Historical Narrative," 8–9, ARA 99:7; RUR, Dec. 18, Dec. 25, 1921, and July 24, 1922; GBB 9.
3. Quinn to Page, Apr. 13, 1923, PS 251; Stephens to Moscow, Sept. 25, 1922, ARA 240:1; Cornick, July 10, 1922, and Foy, June 22, 1922, ARA 100:1; Cornick, Dec. 23, 1922, PS 251; Stephens to Quinn, July 21, 1922, ARA 100:1; RUR, Nov. 5, 1922.

CHAPTER 16

1. Blomquist, "Genesis to Exodus," 2; RED, 17; Herriot, *Russie Nouvelle*, 17.
2. Golder, *War, Revolution, and Peace in Russia*, 197; Spewack, *Red Russia Revealed*, 40–41, 46–47; RED, 381.
3. HFP 1:1; Coolidge and Lord, *Archibald Cary Coolidge*, 278–79; Golder, *War, Revolution, and Peace in Russia*, 117.
4. RUR, Apr. 16, 1922.
5. Duranty, *I Write As I Please*, 190; Hullinger, *Reforging of Russia*, 319–23; Ellingston to Fisher, Dec. 26, 1922, ARA 94:13; HFP 1:1; AAR, Feb. 1929, 7–8.
6. Lyon to Donald Renshaw, Dec. 7, 1921, ACC; Clapp, Jan. 12–19, Feb. 1–9, 1922, ARA 107:12.
7. Kelley, "Descriptive Memorandum," 9; Kelley, "Extracts from Letters," 9, 11; "Second Year of Operation," 60, ARA 118:4; Haskell, [untitled], Vol. 1, 149S; "General Report," 4, ARA 141:1.
8. RUR, Jan. 28, 1923, and Oct. 1, 1922; Cornick, Jan. 6, Jan. 31, 1922, GCP; ARA 69:1, 69:4.
9. RED, 320, 211; Cornick, Feb. 9, 1922, GCP; Kelley, "Extracts from Letters," 12; Blomquist, "Genesis to Exodus," 5.

CHAPTER 17

1. Sayler, *Russian Theater*, 288, 294.
2. AAR, May 1965, 33; Fleming, Dec. 16, Nov. 30, Dec. 10, June 10, 1922, HFP 1:1.
3. Sayler, *Russian Theater*, 150–62; Fleming, Dec. 10, Dec. 16, 1922, HFP 1:1; Golder, *War, Revolution, and Peace in Russia*, 252.
4. RED, 178; Fleming, Nov. 15, Dec. 10, 1922, HFP 1:1; Golder, *War, Revolution, and Peace in Russia*, 141, 284–85; Veil, *Adventure's a Wench*, 223–24; Gibbs, *Middle of the Road*, 371; Dickinson, "Russia in the Red Shadows" no. 1, TDP 1; Baker, "Notes on Russia," ARA 336:1; Sayler, *Russian Theater*, 291; Spewack, *Red Russia Revealed*, 46.
5. Hullinger, *Reforging of Russia*, 91–92.
6. Coolidge and Lord, *Archibald Cary Coolidge*, 285–86; Golder, *War, Revolution, and Peace in Russia*, 120, 124–28; Murphy, "Record of a Russian Year," 33–34.
7. Orenburg District History, 34, ARA 68:6; Shafroth, art. 4, ARA 97:6; Kelley, "Extracts from Letters," 10; Cornick, June 8, 1922, GCP.
8. Childs, "Thirty Years in the Near East" (n.d.), 25–26, CP; Childs, *Before the Curtain Falls*, 243; Goodrich diary, Oct. 26, 1921, JPG 17; Gibbs, *Middle of the Road*, 407–8; DS file 861.00/9411, 861.00/9559, 861.00/9751.
9. Sayler, *Russian Theater*, 292; Townsend, AAR, May 1965, 33; Brooks, "Kiev," 5–6, ARA 141:1; RED, 62–63.

CHAPTER 18

1. Yakovlev, "A.R.A. Men," 15.
2. Baker, "Notes on Russia," ARA 336:1; Fleming, Dec. 10, 1922, HFP 1:1; Ellingston to Fisher, Feb. 21, 1923, ARA 94:13; Childs, *Farewell*, 24; Gibbs, *Middle of the Road*, 408.
3. Seroff, *Real Isadora*, 276, 278, 286, 315; Blair, *Isadora*, 296; Sayler, *Russian Theater*, 280–81; Duncan and MacDougall, *Isadora Duncan's Russian Days*, 113; Schneider, *Isadora Duncan*; Duranty, *I Write As I Please*, 238–42.
4. RUR, Feb. 18, Mar. 4, 1923; Blair, *Isadora*, 298; Blomquist, "Genesis to Exodus," 2; Coolidge, Nov. 22, 1921, ACC; Golder, *War, Revolution, and Peace in Russia*, 107, 139.
5. [Mossoloff], "The Moral Spirit of the Russian People," 8, ARA 6:6; Golder, *War, Revolution, and Peace in Russia*, 299; Golder to Adams, Jan. 4, 1923, FGP 11:8; Fleming, June 22, July 3, 1922, HFP 1:1; Babine, *Russian Civil War Diary*, 219; AAR, Feb. 1929, 7–8.
6. Townsend, AAR, May 1965, 33; Golder to Lutz, Jan. 1, 1922, FGP 13:5; Veil, *Adventure's a Wench*, 257, 269; Babine, *Russian Civil War Diary*, 219–20.

CHAPTER 19

1. Fleming letters, HFP 1:1; Fleming, Dec. 10, Dec. 14, 1922, and Aug. 25, 1923, Harold M. Fleming Papers, New York Public Library, 1.
2. AAR, Oct. 1925; Brooks to Fisher, July 5, 1923, ARA 69:2; Veil, *Adventure's a Wench*, 8; Golder to Adams, Sept. 20, 1921, FGP 11:5; Ellingston to Fisher, June 7, 1923, ARA 94:13; RUR, May 14, 1922.
3. Kelley, "Extracts from Letters," 68–70, 90–91; Bell, "Ufa Operations," 9, ARA 132:4; PS 228; Alexis V. Lapteff, "American Relief Administration in Ufa, Russia," 12–13, HIA.
4. ARA 70:2, 72:1.   5. PS 239; ARA 69:4.
6. RUR, May 7, 1922; RED, 193–98.   7. ARA 69:4.
8. Somerville to Mitchell, Sept. 27, 1923, PS 295.
9. Childs, "Between Two Worlds" (n.d.), 101, JRC; Childs letters, JRC 20; Childs, *Credit*, 71, 77; Childs, *Farewell*, 36.
10. RUR, Aug. 20, 1922.

CHAPTER 20

1. Stepanoff to Merrill Spalding, author's possession.
2. Vasilevskii, *Zhutkaia*, 4–5; S. Babayeff, June 3, 1923, ARA 145:1; RED, 115–16.
3. Dalton, Oct. 17, 1922, CON; Godfrey to Beeuwkes, Oct. 17, 1922, private collection of Robert and Mary Ann Swain, Tulsa, Okla.; *New York Times*, Oct. 23, 1922; Dalton, Oct. 19, 1922, CON; Duranty, *I Write As I Please*, 155; Barringer, Mar. 26, 1931, PS 293.
4. PS 278; AAR, Feb. 1929, 7–8; Childs, "Thirty Years in the Near East," 12–14, CP; Childs, *Before the Curtain Falls*, 281–84; Childs, *Farewell*, 40–41; Duranty, *I Write As I Please*, 156–62; Boyd to Moscow, Jan. 29/30, 1923, PS 278; Boyd to Quinn, Feb. 9, 1923, ARA 26:4.
5. RUR, Feb. 4, 1923, Quinn to Page, Mar. 19, 1923, ARA 341:2; Moscow to London, Mar. 9, 1923, Quinn to Walsh, Mar. 15, 1923, and Brown to Murray, June 7, 1923, PS 278.
6. Boyd to Moscow, Jan 29/30, 1923, PS 278; Boyd to Quinn, Feb. 9, 1923, ARA 26:4.

CHAPTER 21

Part epigraph: Hutchinson to Brown, Mar. 29, 1922, CON; Fleming, June 22, 1922, HFP 1:1.

1. Childs to mother, Mar. 3, Mar. 6, 1921, JRC 20; Childs, *Credit*, 46; Childs, *Farewell*, 16; "What Woodrow Wilson Means to Me," JRC 5.
2. JRC 20.
3. CON.
4. DS file 861.00/9671.
5. Rorlich, *Volga Tatars*; Carr, *Bolshevik Revolution*, 314–29.
6. RED, 13–14, 27–29, 34–35; Childs, Oct. 1, 1921, JRC 20; Kellogg: ARA 96:5; Childs, *Farewell*, 28; Murphy, "Record of a Russian Year," 14.
7. Childs, Oct. 1, 1922, Nov. 6, 1921, and July 12, 1922, JRC 20; Ruhl to Haskell, Sept. 16, 1922, ARA 97:5.
8. RED, 293–94; Shafroth, art. 6, ARA 81:8; Ruhl to Haskell, Sept. 16, 1922, ARA 97:5; Kelley, "Extracts from Letters," 92; Childs, *Farewell*, 29; Childs, "Between Two Worlds," 115, JRC.
9. Childs, "Between Two Worlds," 1–3, JRC; Childs, Dec. 8, 1921, and Oct. 14, Dec. 20, 1922, JRC 20.

CHAPTER 22

1. Wahren, Nov. 17, 1921, ARA 29:6.
2. Simbirsk General Report, VII, 37, ARA 118:4.
3. Leggett, *Cheka*, 262–64; MERSH 19:59–60; Pipes, *Russian Revolution*, 611, 773, 802; Duranty, *I Write As I Please*, 40.
4. Fisher, *Famine*, 129.
5. U.S. Congress, Senate, *Bolshevik Propaganda*, 344–45.
6. Haskell, [unititled], Vol. 1, 124; Mackenzie, *Russia Before Dawn*, 102; Pipes, *Bolshevik Revolution*, 802.
7. Golder, *War, Revolution, and Peace in Russia*, 132; Leggett, *Cheka*, 345.
8. Mackenzie, *Russia Before Dawn*, 50; Gibbs, *Middle of the Road*, 335; DS 861.48/1903; Barringer, Aug. 20, 1922, TBP 1:1.
9. RED, 15, 22, 37, 379; Childs, "Thirty Years in the Near East," 20–22, CP.
10. Schapiro, "Role of the Jews," 148–67.
11. Brooks, "Russian Railroads," 52–53; Quinn to Moscow, Feb. 26, 1922, ARA 23:2.
12. Golder, *War, Revolution, and Peace in Russia*, 44; Golder and Hutchinson, *On the Trail*, 208; Gibbs, *Middle of the Road*, 390; Sorokin, *Leaves*, 274; Veil, *Adventure's a Wench*, 219–20.
13. Wahren, Nov. 17, 1921, ARA 29:6; Childs, "Thirty Years in the Near East," 20, CP; RED, 88; Wahren to Moscow (n.d.), ARA 345:6; Rorlich, *Volga Tatars*, 155; Wahren, Apr. 27, 1922, ARA 26:4.

CHAPTER 23

1. RED, 49, 55–57; Childs, *Farewell*, 30; Childs, *Before the Curtain Falls*, 237; Childs, May 18, 1922, JRC 20; Hullinger, *Reforging of Russia*, 94; Childs, "Sleigh Journey," 14–15, ARA 29:6.
2. PS 230; Barringer, May 25, 1923, 1–5, 16, ARA 138:12; Barringer to Page, June 15, 1922, TBP 1:1; Barringer to Page, Aug. 5, 1922, ARA 314:8; Ellingston, "Carriage of

Philanthropy," 13; Barringer to Haskell, Aug. 5, 1922, ARA 137:4; Skvortsov to Barringer, Nov. 20, 1922, and Mar. 24, 1924, TBP 1:3.

3. HHPL, Oral History, 14, George P. Harrington (1969); Harrington to Quinn, Jan. 25, 1923, PS 277; Lander to Quinn, Mar. 30, 1923, ARA 137:5; Quinn to Harrington, Apr. 4, 1923, PS 277; Harrington to Quinn, Apr. 13, 1923, ARA 137:5; Quinn to Lander, Apr. 21, 1923, ARA 137:5; Burland to Lander, May 5, 1923, and Lander to Burland, May 5, 1923, PS 277.

4. Gilchriese to Baker and Wilkinson, May 7, 1923, Murphy to Harrington, May 6, 1923, and Harrington to Moscow, May 6, 1923, PS 277; Ellingston to Fisher, May 10, 1923, ARA 94:13.

5. Burland to Murphy, May 7, 1923, and Burland to Brown, May 8, 1923, PS 277; Harrington to Burland, May 13, 1923, ARA 137:5.

CHAPTER 24

1. TBP 1:1; Barringer to Page, Apr. 13, 1923, TBP 1:11.

2. Gregg, "Survey Conditions," 4, ARA 121:3; Simbirsk General Report, VII, 3, 11, 12, ARA 118:4; Fox to Lonergan, Nov. 28, 1921, Somerville to Lonergan, Nov. 29, 1921, and Tarasov to Haskell, Nov. 20, 1921, PS 295; Fox to Haskell, Dec. 29, 1921, ARA 20:2.

3. "Reception of the ARA," 1, ARA 133:1; "Ufa Operations," 3–4, ARA 132:4; Kelley, "Extracts from Letters," 50.

4. Simbirsk General Report, VII, 18–23, 36–37, 42–46; "Second Year of Operation," 67, ARA 118:4; "The Reminiscences of Spurgeon M. Keeny, Sr.," 4:146–48, Oral History Research Office, Columbia University, New York, 1982.

CHAPTER 25

1. Orenburg District History, 5–6, ARA 68:6; Lyon to Renshaw, [Nov. 1921], Coolidge and Lord, *Archibald Cary Coolidge*, 283; Lyon to Moscow, Apr. 18, 1923, ARA 68:6.

2. Leggett, *Cheka*, 84, 455; Coleman to Moscow, Dec. 14, 1921, ARA 68:12; Lyon to Moscow, Apr. 18, 1923, ARA 68:6; Orenburg District History, 5, 8, ARA 68:6; Duranty, *I Write As I Please*, 29–31.

3. Coleman to Moscow, Dec. 10, 1921, ARA 68:5; Orenburg District History, 6, 11, ARA 68:6; Coleman to Moscow, Jan. 13, 1922, ARA 202:2.

4. Orenburg District History, 1–5, ARA 68:6; Hartridge, 25, ARA 68:6; Coleman to Fisher, July 2, 1922, ARA 65:5; Coleman to Moscow, May 15, 1922, ARA 68:12; Fleming, "Trip Through the Volga," 11, ARA 95:1.

5. Eiduk to Lonergan, Dec. 10, 1921, ARA 20:2; Coleman to Fisher, July 2, 1922, ARA 65:5.

6. Coleman to Klimov, Jan. 31, Apr. 22, May 19, May 23, 1922, ARA 66:8; Orenburg District History, 13–14, 23–24, ARA 68:6; Coleman to Moscow, Apr. 22, May 15, 1922, ARA 68:12.

7. Coleman to Quinn, Apr. 6, 1922, ARA 65:5; Coleman to Klimov, May 20, 1922, ARA 66:8; Coleman to Klimov, July 6, July 12, July 13, 1922, ARA 67:1; Klimov to Coleman, July [?], 1922, ARA 65:5; Orenburg District History, 14, ARA 68:6; Buckley to Baker, June 15, 1922, ARA 344:14.

8. Simbirsk General Report, III, 4, ARA 118:4; Quinn to Coleman, Mar. 5, 1923, and Coleman to Quinn, Mar. 14, 1923, PS 241; AAR, Dec. 1933; Galpin to Fisher, Nov. 16, 1942, PS 304.

9. Coleman to Quinn, July 13, 1922, ARA 204:1; Quinn to Coleman, July 26, 1922,

PS 241; Klimov to Coleman, July 17, 1922, ARA 67:1; Coleman to Haskell, July 17, 1922, ARA 20:1; Orenburg District History, 42, ARA 68:6; ARA 69:4.

10. Hartridge to Moscow, Feb. 1, 1923, ARA 68:12; Hartridge to Rudminsky, Feb. 3, 1923, Hartridge to Moscow, Feb. 11, Feb. 20, 1923, and Hartridge to Baldwin, May 12, 1923, ARA 65:8; Ellingston to Fisher, July 5, 1923, ARA 94:13.

CHAPTER 26

1. Coleman to Fisher, July 2, 1922, and Quinn to Coleman, Sept. 9, 1922, ARA 65:5; Orenburg District History, 15, ARA 68:6; Klimov to Coleman, July 17, 1922, ARA 67:1.

2. ARA 69:4.

3. Studenikin to Eiduk, June 16, 1922, and Hynes to Moscow, June 14, 1922, ARA 20:1; Golder, *War, Revolution, and Peace in Russia*, 348.

4. PS 301; Childs, Nov. 6, 1921, JRC 20; Dear, "Report of Conditions," 1–2, ARA 29:6.

5. Haskell to Brown, Apr. 6, 1922, and Quinn to London, July 1, 1922, CON; PS 303.

6. Murphy, "Record of a Russian Year," 23–24, 60–64; Lonergan to Eiduk, Nov. 21, 1921, and Haskell to Eiduk, Dec. 6, 1921, ARA 21:2; Eiduk to Lonergan, Nov. 29, 1921, ARA 23:1.

7. Lyon to Moscow, Apr. 18, 1923, ARA 68:6; Hale to Herter, Apr. 24, 1922, ARA 305:3; Barringer, "American's Impression," 473.

8. RED, 44–45, 86–96; Wahren to Moscow, Nov. 15, 1921, Eiduk to Haskell, Nov. 20, 1921, and Mouchtaroff to Wahren, Nov. 14, 1921, ARA 23:1; Wahren to Moscow, Nov. 16, 1921, ARA 26:4; Nov. 17, 1921, ARA 29:6; Childs, Nov. 16, 1921, JRC 20; Childs, *Before the Curtain Falls*, 235; Childs, *Farewell*, 29; PS 300.

9. Simbirsk General Report, VII, 14–17, ARA 118:4; ARA 110:5; Gregg to Quinn, July 22, 1922, ARA 111:3.

10. Haskell to Eiduk, Feb. 25, 1922, and Eiduk to Haskell, Mar. 3, 1922, ARA 21:2; Haskell to Eiduk, Mar. 21, 1922, ARA 23:2; Mitchell to Brown, Feb. 27, 1922, ARA 336:1.

11. Shafroth to Lonergan, Mar. 14, 1922, ARA 20:2; Shafroth, art. 5, ARA 81:8; N. F. Gorodnichii, "Maloizvestnaia," 56–58; Shafroth to mother, Mar. 20, 1922, WS; Kogan, "Antisovetskie," 12; Hale to Herter, Apr. 24, 1922, ARA 305:3; Quinn to London, Apr. 3, 1922, CON; Haskell to Eiduk, Mar. 30, 1922, ARA 51:6; Quinn to London, Apr. 10, 1922, ARA 23:2.

12. Allen to Shafroth, May 30, June 30, 1922, WS; Cornick, Apr. 24, 1922, GCP; Simbirsk General Report, VII, 35–36, ARA 118:4; Quinn to London, Apr. 15, 1922, ARA 23:2.

CHAPTER 27

1. Muscat to Childs, June 22, 1922, ARA 30:4; Kennan, *Decision to Intervene*, 38; Brown to Rickard, Aug. 5, 1921, ARA 69:1; Simbirsk General Report, III, 6, ARA 118:4; Administrative Division History, 3, ARA 36:6; "Final Period," 6, ARA 99:7; ARA 70:3.

2. Pate and Walker to Brown, Sept. 22, 1920, ARA 517:3; Ellingston, "Carriage of Philanthropy," 10; "Final Period," 6, ARA 99:7.

3. Childs, *Credit*, 13–14; Childs, Jan. 4, Apr. 6, 1922, JRC 20; Kahn, *Codebreakers*, 327–55; Somerville to Quinn, Sept. 18, 1922, PS 295; Rickard to Brown, Sept. 11, 1922, CON; PS 226; Hale to Herter, Mar. 5, Apr. 24, 1922, ARA 305:3.

4. "What I Saw and What I Know," 6, ARA 141:2; Fleming, "Trip Through the Volga," 1, ARA 95:1; Burland: RUR, Dec. 24, 1922; Fleming, "Russia," 5–6, 9, HFP 1:3.

5. RED, 7, 49, 198–201; Jacobs, "American Relief Administration and My Crime," 15–24; Bowden to Moscow, Jan. 26, 1922, ARA 100:1; "Communications," ARA 90:5; Kinne to Moscow, Oct. 7, 1921, ARA 110:9; Babine, *Russian Civil War Diary*, vii–xxii; Gregg to Moscow, July 22, 1922, ARA 111:3.

6. Ufa-Urals District History, 4, 12, ARA 133:1; Kelley, "Extracts from Letters," 50, 92; PS 248; Hofstra to Shafroth, Nov. 10, 1921, ARA 106:4.

7. Kelley, "Extracts from Letters," 12, 18, 24, 27, 34–36, 43–44, 50; Lapteff, "American Relief Organization in Ufa," 11–14, 20–21; PS 233; ARA 70:6; Bell to Daily, Feb. 22, 1923, PS 231.

8. Murphy, "Record of a Russian Year," 56–57; "Final Period" 6, ARA 99:7; Elizavetgrad District History, 32, ARA 139:3; Duranty, *Search for a Key*, 203–7; "Libbis," 2, ARA 141:1–3; Somerville to Rickard, Oct. 13, 1924, PS 295; ARA 70:3; RUR, Oct. 5, 1922.

9. Fleming, "Trip Through the Volga," 11–12, ARA 95:1; Orenburg District History, 6, 35–36, ARA 68:6; Karlin to Sakharov, June 25, 1922, attached to Coleman to Moscow, July 25, 1922, ARA 204:1; Coleman to Moscow, June 3, 1922, ARA 68:12; Veil, *Adventure's a Wench*, 248–49.

CHAPTER 28

1. Fischer, *Men and Politics*, 64; "Moral Spirit," 7, ARA 6:6; Hullinger, *Reforging of Russia*, 272–77; Sarolea, *Impressions of Soviet Russia*, 10–11; AAR, Feb. 1929; Spewack, *Red Russia Revealed*, 55; Golder, *War, Revolution, and Peace in Russia*, 197, 191.

2. "Second Year of Operation," 17, ARA 118:4; Noggle, *Into the Twenties*, 165; Ellingston to Fisher, Mar. 2, 1923, ARA 94:13; Smith, *Shattered Dream*, 68; Duranty, *I Write As I Please*, 55; Duranty, "'Amerikansky' Cry Tames a Bandit," *New York Times*, June 30, 1922; Fleming, Feb. 15, 1923, HFP 1:1; Duranty, *Search for a Key*, 203–7; Veil, *Adventure's a Wench*, 37.

3. Haskell to Baker, Sept. 22, 1922, ARA 95:4; Blomquist, "Genesis to Exodus," 8; Barringer, "American's Impressions," 474–75; Fleming, "When Russians Were People," 18–20, Fleming Papers, New York Public Library, 1.

4. Ellingston to Fisher, Apr. 4, 1923, ARA 94:13; "Story," 2, ARA 132:12; "Brief Historical Sketches," ARA 132:12; Kelley, "Extracts from Letters," 76; Bell to Krueger, June 9, 1922, ARA 132:12.

5. "On the Edge of Siberia," 9, and "Story," 1–3, ARA 132:12; Iuldashbaev, *Obrazovanie*, 126–27; Hofstra to Haskell, Dec. 27, 1921; Bell to Krueger, June 9, 1922, ARA 132:12; Kelley, "Extracts from Letters," 19; Kelley, "Descriptive Memorandum," 1–4.

6. PS 266; Kelley, "Extracts from Letters," 49–68, 80–81, 90.

7. PS 267; Veil, *Adventure's a Wench*, 238; Babine, *Russian Civil War Diary*, 194, 201–3, 207, 209–12; Herter to Brown, Oct. 12, 1921, PS 241; Cobb, "Extracts," ARA 303:4; Haskell to Brown, Mar. 25, 1922, CON; Mitchell to Brown, Mar. 11, 1922, ARA 23:2; Saratov District History, 90, ARA 109:6; Clapp to Gaskill, May 18, 1922, ARA 114:1; Quinn to London, Aug. 14, 1922, CON; Gregg to Quinn, July 22, 1922, ARA 111:3.

8. Hale to Herter, Apr. 24, 1922, ARA 305:3; ARA 107:12; RED, 58; Baker to Wilkinson, Jan. 27, 1922, PS 226; Fleming, Mar. 31, 1923, Nov. 7, 1922, HFP 1:1; Fleming, "Trip Through the Volga," 26, ARA 95:1; GCP; Kelley, "Extracts from Letters," 86–88; "Story," 9, ARA 132:12.

9. Hynes to Quinn, Aug 3, 1922, ARA 21:2; Litvin to Kohl, July 26, 1922, and Lander to Quinn, July 14, 1922, PS 255; Fisher, 230, 280n; Cobb, "Extracts," ARA 303:4; Quinn to London, Aug. 24, 1922, CON.

CHAPTER 29

1. RED, 12; Golder and Hutchinson, *On the Trail*, 28; Shafroth, art. 1, ARA 81:8; Haskell, [untitled] Vol. 1, 89–90; Soviet Slave: ARA 6:6; Murphy, "Record of a Russian Year," 37–38; Dickinson, art. 4, TDP 1; Francis McCullagh, May 5, 1923, ARA 81:3; Il'f and Petrov, *Golden Calf*, 3–5; Kearny: ARA 70:2; Administrative Division History, 16, ARA 36:6; Barringer, "American's Impression," 214; Duranty, *I Write As I Please*, 189.

2. PS 266; ARA 70:2; Administrative Division History, 14–16, ARA 36:6; ARA 70:2; Supply Memorandum no. 13, Nov. 26, 1921, ARA 64:2; Kearney to Mitchell, Feb. 12, 1923, PS 266; ARA 71:7, 20:1.

3. Barringer, May 25, 1923, 1, ARA 138:12; Golder and Hutchinson, *On the Trail*, 104; Hale to Herter, Apr. 24, 1922, ARA 305:3; Barringer, "American's Impression," 475–76; Elizavetgrad District History, ARA 139:3; Fleming, "Trip through the Volga," 12, 23, ARA 95:1; Mackenzie, *Russia Before Dawn*, 168, 212; RED, 289–90; Kelley, "Extracts from Letters," 54; Goodrich diary, JGP 18; "Conditions in the District," 2, ARA 132:4.

4. Cobb to Gregg, Aug. 7, 1922, ARA 110:9; RUR, Sept. 24, 1922; Ukraine ARA History, ARA 134:11; M. Raskin, 13, ARA 145:3.

5. ARA 69:1, 69:3; Shafroth to Moscow, May 16, 1922, ARA 106:6; Allen, Dec. 10, 1921, ARA 100:1; Golder and Hutchinson, *On the Trail*, 112; Barringer, May 25, 1923, 3–4, ARA 138:12; "Report on the Conference," ARA 73:1; Harrington, 7, ARA 134:11; Haskell to Brown, Oct. 21, 1922, CON; Carroll to London, Sept. 4, 1921, ARA 344:14; Lonergan to Kazan, Oct. 5, 1921, ARA 29:6; Kelley, "Extracts from Letters," 94.

6. [Chukovskii], "One Heart to the Globe," FGP; Wahren to Moscow, Dec. 8, 1922, ARA 73:3; Lander to Quinn, Dec. 22, 1922, ARA 20:1; Baker to Fisher, Jan. 23, 1923, GBB 6: "Rickard"; Jacobs, "American Relief Administration and My Crime," 27; RUR, Apr. 2, 1922; DS file 861.00/9959; Clements: PS 241; Barringer, Mar. 15, 1922, TBP 1:3; DS file 861.00/9559.

7. Hale to Herter, Apr. 24, 1922, ARA 305:3; U.S. Congress, Senate, *Bolshevik Propaganda*, 397, 474, 220; HHPL, Commerce papers, 30; Rickard to Fuller, Jan. 14, 1922, WPF 2; WS; Shafroth, art. 5, ARA 81:8; McCullagh, May 5, 1923, ARA 81:3.

8. Coleman to Sergieve, Apr. 5, 1922, ARA 66:8; Coleman to Quinn, Apr. 6, 1922, and Coleman to Fisher, July 2, 1922, ARA 65:5; Fox to Moscow, Sept. 16, 1922, ARA 121:3; Barringer to Moscow, Apr. 7, 1923, ARA 121:4; Kelley, "Extracts from Letters," 18; Veil, *Adventure's a Wench*, 250–59; Kearney to Lonergan, Feb. 23, 1922, attached to Haskell to Eiduk, Feb. 26, 1922, ARA 294:1.

9. Ellingston to Fisher, May 30, June 7, 1923, ARA 94:13; Lander circular, n.d., TBP 1:1; Skvortsov to Harrington, June 1, 1923, ARA 137:10; Allen to Haskell, June 5, 1923, ARA 106:6; Lander to Haskell, May 22, 1923, and Haskell to Lander, May 26, 1923, ARA 62:4.

CHAPTER 30

1. Childs, Nov. 12, 1921, JRC 20; Cornick, May 5, 1922, GCP; DS file 861.00/9766; Murphy, "Record of a Russian Year," 21, 35, 75; Kelley, "Extracts from Letters," 42; Quinn to London, Apr. 15, 1922, ARA 23:2; Barringer, "American's Impression," 474.

2. PSS 300; ARA 21:2, 322:1.

3. Duranty, *Duranty Reports Russia*, 26–29; Ross, *Russian Soviet Republic*, 279; Fleming, Nov. 7, 1922, HFP 1:1; Seldes, *Tell the Truth*, 140–41; Zhukov to Lander, n.d., attached to Lander to Haskell, Nov. 17, 1922, ARA 73:3; Eiduk to Lonergan, Dec. 26, 1921, ARA 19:6.

4. Golder, *War, Revolution, and Peace in Russia*, 108.

5. RED, 289–93; Childs, July 8, 1922, JRC 20; Kellogg: ARA 96:5; Simbirsk Gen-

eral Report, III, 3, ARA 118:4; Gregg, "Survey Conditions," ARA 121:3; Goodrich diary, 10, JGP 18; Blomquist, "Genesis to Exodus," 6; Mackenzie, *Russia Before Dawn*, 278; Murphy, "Record of a Russian Year," 8–9; Ruhl to Haskell, Sept. 16, 1922, ARA 97:5; Kelley, "Extracts from Letters," 90; ARA 70:1; "My Experiences with the A.R.A.," ARA 141:3; Hoover, *Memoirs of Herbert Hoover*, 21.

6. ARA 69:4; Administrative Division History, 11, ARA 36:6; Seldes, *Tell the Truth*, 129; Kelley, "Extracts from Letters," 5; GCP; Donald Grant Papers, HIA; Shafroth, Aug. 29, 1921, WS; Haskell to Brown, Sept. 30, 1921, CON; Gibbs, 334–39.

7. RED, 291–93; Ruhl to Haskell, Sept. 16, 1922, ARA 97:5; RUR, July 9, 1922; Kelley, "Extracts from Letters," 95; Vail, "Letters," 7, AFSC, General Files, 1923; Kellogg: ARA 96:5; Murphy, "Record of a Russian Year," 5; Fleming, "Trip Through the Volga," 18, ARA 95:1; Veil, *Adventure's a Wench*, 248; Wicksteed, *Life Under the Soviets*, 80.

8. Barringer, "American's Impression," 217; Childs, "Behind the Scenes of History," 35, JRC 1; Mathews to Boyd, May 25, 1923, Haskell to Boyd, June 14, 1923, and Mathews to Haskell, June 18, 22, 25, 1923, ARA 28:4; Veil, *Adventure's a Wench*, 247; Coolidge, "Liaison Work," 8–9, ARA 52:1; Noggle, *Into the Twenties*, 26–27; Fox to Moscow, Mar. 17, 1922, ARA 116:3.

CHAPTER 31

Part epigraph: Macpherson, "General Report," 4, ARA 141:1; Blomquist, "Genesis to Exodus," 7.

1. Kellogg: ARA 96:5; Kelley, "Extracts from Letters," 13–14, 17; Yakovlev, "A.R.A. Men," 5; Jacobs, "American Relief Administration and My Crime," 2; Babayeff, 2, ARA 145:1–2; [Chukovskii], "One Heart to the Globe," FGP.

2. Cobb to Gregg, Aug. 7, 1922, ARA 110:9; Golder, *War, Revolution, and Peace in Russia*, 130; Benoit to Renshaw, May 6, 1923, ARA 302:6; Harrington, 18, ARA 138:12; Barringer to Moscow, Feb. 6, 1923, TBP 1:3; Ellingston, "Carriage of Philanthropy," 45; *New Republic*, Sept. 19, 1923; Haskell to Hoover, Aug. 27, 1923, ARA 340:3.

3. Kazan District History, 66, ARA 27:12; WS; Shafroth, art. 8, ARA 81:8; Gibbs, *Middle of the Road*, 333, 413; Wolfe to Shafroth, Mar. 11, 1922, GBB 9; Dickinson no. 1, TDP 1; ARA 121:1.

4. EWP 2; Hale to Herter, Apr. 24, 1922, ARA 305:3; GBB 3:Gilchriese; Clapp: Saratov District History, 74, ARA 109:6.

5. "Historical Narrative," 9–10, ARA 99:7; Babayeff, 2, ARA 145:1–2; Harrington, 14, ARA 138:12; *Pravda*, July 1, 1923; Golder to Fisher, Jan. 18, 1923, Hoover Institution Records, 94:Golder, Personal Letters.

6. ARA 141:1–3; M. Bulgakov, "Kiev-gorod," 327–36; E. Bredin, "What to Feed the Students," ARA 36:3; Nekrasov, "Po obe storony okeana," 110.

7. Hullinger, *Reforging of Russia*, 189; Harrington, 25, ARA 138:12; Fleming, "Russia," 27, HFP 1:3; Fleming, "Trip Through the Volga," 8–9, ARA 95:1; ARA 141:3.

8. Fisher, *America and the New Poland*, 237; James Rosenberg to Hoover, Feb. 17, 1922, ARA 347:16; Haskell, [untitled] Vol. 1, 30; Ellingston, AAR, Apr. 1, 1925; Fleming, "Russia," 4, HFP 1:3; Ellingston to Fisher Dec. 26, 1922, ARA 94:14; Simbirsk General Report, VII, 15; Ellingston, "Carriage of Philanthropy," 124; WHG 112.

9. Barringer, "American's Impression," 216; Childs, July 22, 1922, JRC 20; Childs, *Farewell*, 42; Harrington, 8, ARA 140:3; Kelley, "Extracts from Letters," 31.

10. Lyon to Moscow, Nov. 22, 1921, ARA 68:12; Barringer to Page, Aug. 5, 1922, ARA 314:8; Ruhl to Haskell, Sept. 16, 1922, ARA 97:5; Kelley, "Descriptive Memorandum," 35–36, 48–49; Kelley, "Extracts from Letters," 17, 19, 80.

11. Barringer, Aug. 20, 1922, TBP 1:1; Fleming, "Russia," 4, HFP 1:3; Fleming, Mar. 31, 1923, and Oct. 18, 1922, HFP 1:1; Bell to Page, Dec. 21, 1922, PS 231; Blomquist, "Genesis to Exodus," 1; Cornick, Mar. 9, 1922, GCP; Haskell to Hoover, Aug. 27, 1923, ARA 340:3.

12. Ellingston, Feb. 6, 1923, and Jan. 31, 1923, ARA 48:1.

CHAPTER 32

1. Duranty, *Duranty Reports Russia*, 32–36; PS 231; "Story," 1, 5, 7, 12, ARA 132:12; Mackenzie, *Russia Before Dawn*, 138; Bell to Page, Dec. 1, 1922, CON; Bell to Krueger, June 9, 1922, ARA 133:1; Kelley, "Descriptive Memorandum," 2, 6–7, 44; Kelley, "Extracts from Letters," 14, 22, 26, 30, 65, 68; Bell to Page, Apr. 12, 1923, and Dec. 21, 1922, PS 231; "Ufa Operations," 10, ARA 132:4.

2. Allen to Shafroth, June 30, 1922, WS; Bell to Page, Dec. 1, 1922, CON; Ellingston to Fisher, Apr. 4, 1923, ARA 94:13; "Story," 13–14, ARA 132:12.

3. ARA 69:3; Duranty, *Duranty Reports Russia*, 32–36; Kelley, "Extracts from Letters," 33–35, 42, 68; Bell to Page, Dec. 21, 1922, CON; Bell to Page, Apr. 12, 1923, PS 231; "Ufa Operations," 2, ARA 132:4; Kelley, "Extracts from Letters," 71; Kelley to Haskell, May 20, 1922, PS 266; ARA 132:12, 69:3; Evelyn Bell, CON.

CHAPTER 33

1. "Story," 4, ARA 132:12; Gibbons: ARA 11:4; Seldes, *Tell the Truth*, 123; Gregg: ARA 29:6; Shafroth, Sept. 21, 1921, WS; Kellogg: ARA 95:6; Spratt, Feb. 28, 1922, ARA 30:1; Childs, *Farewell*, 32; RED, 51; Kelley: ARA 81:2; Sorokin, *Hunger*, 265–70.

2. Barringer, May 11, 1923, TBP 1:1; Duranty, *Duranty Reports Russia*, 20–24, 29; Duranty, *I Write As I Please*, 128–29; "Notes from N.," Oct. 21, 1921, ARA 22:9; Goodrich, Oct. 21, 1921, JGP 18; Goodrich, Nov. 1, 1921, and Goodrich to Hoover, Apr. 3, 1922, ARA 95:3; Childs, "Sleigh Circuit," 2, ARA 29:6.

3. Tolstoy: ARA 11:4; Murphy, "Record of a Russian Year," 27–29; Gor'kii, *O russkom*, 8–9, 16–19, 23, 26, 34–37; [Mossoloff], "Moral Spirit of the Russian People," 1–8, ARA 6:6; PSS 43:228; Riasanovsky, *History of Russia*, 443; Morizet, *Chez Lénine*, 241.

4. MERSH, 15:187–91; Chamberlin, *Confessions*, 106–7; Kellogg: ARA 95:6; Kalinin, *Za eti gody*, 79–99; Harper: ARA 327:8; HHPL, Commerce Papers, 355:Kellogg; GBB 9; Gibbs, *Since Then*, 398.

5. Got'e, *Time of Troubles*, 265; Childs, "Thirty Years in the Near East," 26, CP; Childs, *Farewell*, 25; Childs, *Credit*, 70; Sayler, *Russia*, 101–2; ARA 72:1; Duranty, *I Write As I Please*, 144; Mackenzie, *Russia Before Dawn*, 159–60; Shafroth, June 8, 1922, WS; Dickinson arts. 1, 4, TDP 1.

6. Sarolea, *Impressions of Soviet Russia*, 204–7.

7. Cornick, Sept. 14, 1922, GCP; WHG 2–4, 194; DS file 861.00/11235; "Pavlov's Work in Physiology," ARA 76:6.

8. Sorokin, *Hunger*, 79; Gor'kii, *O russkom*, 17–18; Bechhofer [Roberts], *Through Starving Russia*, 85; *Chronicle of Novgorod*, 54, 76–77.

9. Corcoran, 8–9, GCP; Golder and Hutchinson, *On the Trail*, 43, 64–65; Shafroth, art. 3, ARA 81:8; Golder, *War, Revolution, and Peace in Russia*, 270–75; Duranty, *I Write As I Please*, 131; Sorokin, *Leaves*, 282–91.

10. Golder, *War, Revolution, and Peace in Russia*, 177, 181–83; Gibbs, *Since Then*, 381–82; Hullinger, *Reforging of Russia*, 387–88.

11. Billington, *Icon and the Axe*, 8, 65; Ragsdale, "Constraints of Russian Culture," 70–71.

12. "Effect of Relief Work," 15, ARA 6:6; TBP 1:2; Corcoran, 9–11, GCP; Goodrich, June 24, 1922, ARA 339:3.

CHAPTER 34

1. ARA 48:1; Ellingston, "Carriage of Philanthropy," 19, 34; Murphy, "Record of a Russian Year," 66–67; Mackenzie, *Russia Before Dawn*, 139; "Some Russian Princesses . . . ," ARA 72:1.

2. Haskell, [untitled] Vol. 1, 149-J; Murphy, "Record of a Russian Year," 39–40; Kelley, "Descriptive Memorandum," 18; WS; Hale to Herter, Apr. 24, 1922, ARA 305:3; Clapp: ARA 107:12; Ellingston, "Carriage of Philanthropy," 18; Alsberg to Strauss, Jan. 9, 1923, JDC 449; WHG 112; Spewack, "Moscow Along the Way," *World*, Sept. 8, 1922.

3. Kellogg: ARA 95:6; Ellingston, "Carriage of Philanthropy," 148; "Story," 15–16, ARA 132:12.

4. Cornick, Jan. 19, June 22, 1922, GCP; "Historical Narrative," 7–8, ARA 99:7; Buckley, "Orsk Rayon," 12, ARA 68:6; E. Preobrazhenskii, "Davno pora," *Pravda*, July 28, 1923; Goodrich diary, 10, JGP 18.

5. Hullinger, *Reforging of Russia*, 382; Got'e, *Time of Troubles*, 329; Goldman, *My Disillusionment*, 124; Duranty, *I Write As I Please*, 169–70; Golder, Dec. 22, 1921, FGP 12:35; Golder, *War, Revolution, and Peace in Russia*, 116; RED, 29; Ellingston, "Carriage of Philanthropy," 127; Bowden, Sept. 7, 1921, ARA 345:7.

6. Fleming, July 3, Aug. 1, 1922, HFP 1:1; Fleming to Fisher, Mar. 3, 1923, ARA 95:1; Kelley, "Extracts from Letters," 65; Kelley, "Descriptive Memorandum," 29–30; Kelley to G.L.H., Apr. 20, 1922, FGP 23:5; "General Conditions," 6, ARA 6:6; Fleming to Fisher, Apr. 22, 1923, ARA 95:1; Murphy, "Record of a Russian Year," 7–8; Coolidge and Lord, *Archibald Cary Coolidge*, 276; Brooks, "Russian Railroads," 52; Ellingston, "Carriage of Philanthropy," 18.

7. Haskell, [untitled] Vol. 1, 94–94E; Haskell to Rickard, Sept. 28, 1921, and Haskell to Brown, Oct. 17, 1921, ARA 339:4; Coolidge, "Liaison Work," 8, ARA 52:1; Goodrich: Missiia Norway collection, HIA, 28:23; "Libbis," 2, ARA 141:3; Lyon, Mar. 15, 1923, and Supply Division History, 31, ARA 64:1.

8. Ellingston, "Carriage of Philanthropy," 83; Kelley, "Descriptive Memorandum," 5; Kelley, "Extracts from Letters," 20; Fleming to Fisher, Mar. 3, 1923, ARA 95:1.

9. Fleming, "Trip Through the Volga," 29, ARA 95:1; Blomquist, "Genesis to Exodus," 4; Golder and Hutchinson, *On the Trail*, 42–43; Kelley, "Extracts from Letters," 21; GCP; Fleming, "Moscow," 18, ARA 95:1; Ellingston, "Carriage of Philanthropy," 24; Holden, July 7, 1923, Frank Harvey Holden Papers, HIA.

10. "Libbis," 2, ARA 141:3; Mackenzie, *Russia Before Dawn*, 40, 76, 96, 267; Hullinger, *Reforging of Russia*, 74; Brooks, "Russian Railroads," 52; "Final Period," 4, ARA 99:7; Goodrich diary, Oct. 20, 1921, JGP 18; Goodrich to Hoover, Apr. 3, 1922, ARA 95:3; Coolidge, Nov. 26, 1921, ARA 94:11; Chamberlin, *Confessions*, 68; Fleming, June 1, 1923, HFP 1:1.

11. Kohl, "Early Operations," ARA 89:4; Shafroth, art. 6, ARA 97:6; Brooks, "Russian Railroads," 42; Godfrey, Dec. 1, 1922, ARA 120:4; Chamberlin, *Confessions*, 68; Ragsdale, "Constraints of Russian Culture," 70; Fleming to Fisher, Apr. 22, 1923, ARA 95:1.

CHAPTER 35

1. Ellingston, "Carriage of Philanthropy," 10, 84, 150, 148–50; Duranty, *Duranty Reports Russia*, 23; ARA 48:1; Simbirsk General Report, VII, n.p., ARA 118:4; Ad-

ministrative Division History, 4, ARA 36:6; Mangan: ARA 70:3; "Final Period," 3, ARA 99:7; Verdon, "Second Period," 4, ARA 99:8; Bowden, 1, ARA 99:6; Harrington, 37, ARA 138:12; Saratov District History, 86, ARA 109:6; Raskin, "Nikolaiev," 9, ARA 145:3.

2. Brooks, "Russian Railroads," 1, 91; Ellingston, Feb. 6, 1923, ARA 48:1; Haskell, [untitled], Vol. 1, 39; DS file 861/9959; Ellingston, "Carriage of Philanthropy," 75; Corcoran, 10, GCP; Gibbs, *Ten Years After*, 98, 103.

3. Bell, *End of Ideology*, 226; May, *End of American Innocence*, 132; Haber, *Efficiency and Uplift*, ix–xi, 57, 95, 104–6, 156–59; Kanigel, *One Best Way*; *The Independent*, Mar. 19, 1917; *The Bellman*, Nov. 23, 1918; Hoover, *American Epic*, 30; Kennedy, *Over Here*, 131; Dickinson, II, ch. 1, n.p. [1], TDP.

4. Turner: AAR, May 1965; Golder to Adams, Dec. 10, 1922, FGP 11:7; Mackenzie, *Russia Before Dawn*, 139; Dickinson, "Short Survey," ARA 94:12; Carroll to Brown, May 29, 1922, CON; Mitchell to Brown, Mar. 11, 1922, ARA 23:2; Holden to Fuller, Nov. 3, 1922, WFP.

5. Burland, "Russian American Contacts," 7–8, PS 237; Benoit to Renshaw, May 6, 1923, ARA 302:6; Yakovlev, "A.R.A. Men," 7; Babayeff, 1, ARA 145:1; Rogger, "America in the Russian Mind"; Rogger, "*Amerikanizm.*"

6. "Cherez okean," 1, 3, 5, 12, and "Libbis," 1, ARA 141:3; "Friend of America," 1, ARA 6:6; ARA 141:2; Clapp to Kinne, Nov. 30, 1921, ARA 110:9; Goodrich diary, Oct. 22, 1921, JGP 17; Ruhl, "What the Russians Think of Us"; "Crest," 4, ARA 141:1; *Bednota*, Jan. 17, 1922; Untitled, ARA 141:3, 141:2; "What I Saw and What I Know," 1–2, ARA 127:2.

7. Maitland, Jan. 17, 1923, ARA 18:16; "Historical Narrative," 3–6, ARA 99:7; ARA 33:5; Yakovlev, "A.R.A. Men," 15; PS 226; ARA 148:4.

8. Bowden to London, Sept. 24, 1921, ARA 73:3; [Chukovskii], "One Heart to the Globe," 7–8, FGP; Haines to Hoover, Jan. 19, 1922, and Hoover to Haines, Jan. 23, 1922, ARA 324:7; Lippmann: ARA 91:2.

9. ARA 6:6, 72:1.

10. "Moment Is the Mother of Ages," 9–10, ARA 6:6.

11. Murphy, "Record of a Russian Year," 85; Chukovskii, *Dnevnik*, 198; ARA 141:3; Macpherson, "General Report," 10, ARA 141:1; Haskell, [untitled], Vol. 1, 149-I; Coolidge to Hughes, Dec. 30, 1921, DS file 861.00/9766; Coolidge, Nov. 13, 1921, ACC.

12. Barringer, "American's Impression," 472; Barringer correspondence: TBP 1:1–5.

13. Got'e, *Time of Troubles*, 440; [Chukovskii], "One Heart to the Globe," 5, FGP; Burland to Brown, Feb. 8, 1923, CON; Fisher to Haskell, Oct. 6, 1922, ARA 95:4; "Moral Effects," 5, ARA 11:4; Yakountchakov: ARA 72:1.

CHAPTER 36

1. Noyes, Sept. 6, 1921, ARA 76:5; Ellingston, "Carriage of Philanthropy," 94; Pipes, "Russia's Chance," 29; Brooks, "Russian Railroads," 21; "Moral Effects," 3–4, ARA 11:4; [Mossoloff], "Moral Spirit," 8, ARA 6:6; Fisher, *Famine*, 82; Cornick to mother, Aug. 15, 1922, GCP; Golder, *War, Revolution, and Peace in Russia*, 132.

2. Kellogg in ARA 95:6; Quinn to London, Mar. 22, 1923, ARA 341:2; Rickard, "Millions Fed," 46; Ellingston, "Carriage of Philanthropy," 94–95; Finance and Accounting Division History, 7, ARA 40:1; Haskell to Brown, Feb. 20, 1923, ARA 340:3; Mackenzie, *Russia Before Dawn*, 139–42.

3. Ellingston, "Carriage of Philanthropy," 94; Kelley, "Descriptive Memorandum," 14, 45–47; Kelley, "Extracts fron Letters," 38–43.

4. ARA 23:5; Barringer, Feb. 20, 1923, TBP 1:1; Gregg to Haskell, Sept. 8, 1922, ARA 72:1; Haskell to Hoover, Sept. 8, 1922, ARA 340:2; Ruhl to Haskell, Sept. 16, 1922, ARA 97:5.

5. Goodrich, "Impressions," 61; Finance and Accounting Division History, 64–65, ARA 40:1; Lyon in ARA 94:14; Haskell, [untitled], Vol. 2, 18–22, 25–26.

6. RED, 154–60; Coleman, Apr. 21, 1922, ARA 66:7; Morris, Aug. 5, 1922, ARA 100:1; Kelley, "Extracts from Letters," 23; Lyon, Mar. 15, 1923, ARA 64:1.

CHAPTER 37

1. Vail, "Letters," 66, Vail Papers, HIA; Yakovlev, "A.R.A. Men," 20; "Reception of the A.R.A.," ARA 132:4; Macpherson, "General Report," 24, ARA 141:1; Gaubanoff, May 1, 1922, ARA 99:5; "Moral Effects," 5, ARA 11:4; Pollitz, "Student Feeding," 12, and Swan, "Administrative Division," 7, ARA 76:1; WHG 112; [Chukovskii], "One Heart to the Globe," 5–6, FGP; Kirshner, "Food and Clothing Remittance," 1, ARA 76:1.

2. "General Report," 24, ARA 141:1; Odessa: DS file 861.00/9766; Simbirsk General Report, VII, 71, ARA 118:4; Burland, "Russian American Contacts," 8, PS 237; Ellingston, "Carriage of Philanthropy," 147, 150; "Second Year of Operation," II, 46, ARA 118:4; *Istoricheskii arkhiv*, 89.

3. "General Report," 3, ARA 141:1; "Sic Transit Gloria Mundi," 5, "Across the Ocean," 18, "A Few Sketches from Nature," 5, and "A.R.A.ism," 3, ARA 141:3; "Zheleznodorozhnik," 4–5, ARA 141:1.

4. Carroll to Brown, May 29, 1922, CON; Turrou to Hoover, Apr. 27, 1923, ARA 310:1; Ruhl, "What the Russians Think of Us"; Yakovlev, "A.R.A. Men," 6, 11; "Moral Effects," 5–6, ARA 11:4.

5. Burland, "Russian American Contacts," 3, PS 237; Mitchell to Brown, Aug. 28, 1921, ARA 336:6; Dickinson, art. 1, TDP 1; Haskell, [untitled], Vol. 1, 22; "Interview Between Col. Haskell and Mr. Kameneff, Sept. 8, 1922," 4, JGP 19; Goodrich to Hoover, Apr. 3, 1922, ARA 95:3; Goodrich, "True Communists," 931; Kennedy, *Over Here*, 153; Harding to Hoover, Aug. 12, 1921, HHPL, Herbert Hoover Papers, 235.

6. Hale to Herter, Apr. 24, 1922, ARA 305:3; Rickard, in Weissman, *Hoover*, 25; Hoover to Hughes, Dec. 6, 1921, DS file 661.6215/1; Bloomfield: DS file 102.9102 B62/-; U.S. Congress, House, *Russian Relief*, 39; Burner, *Hoover*, 132–33; Hoover to Brown, Oct. 28, 1921, ARA 322:13; Williams, *American-Russian Relations*, 192–93; Kennedy, *Over Here*, 131, 153–54; Hoover, *American Individualism*, 28–29.

7. Trotsky, in Weissman, *Hoover*, 18–19; "Tov. Trotskii ob otnoshenii Evropy i Ameriki," *Izvestiia*, Aug. 30, 1922; Walker to Moscow, July 19, 1922, ARA 73:3; Simbirsk General Report, VII, 71; Barringer, "American's Impression," 476.

8. RED, 278–89; Pearson, June 14, 1922, Childs to Muscat, June 21, 1922, Muscat to Childs, June 22, 1922, Haskell to Lander, June 30, 1922, and Yakunin, June 27, 1922, ARA 30:4.

CHAPTER 38

1. "A.R.A. Work," ARA 6:6; Buckley, "Orsk Rayon," 4, ARA 68:6; Saratov District History, 89, ARA 109:6; Veil, in Duranty, "Famine Town Honors American," *New York Times*, Dec. 9, 1921; "Zheleznedorozhnik," 3, ARA 141:1; Coleman to Moscow, May 5, 1922, ARA 65:5; Orenburg District History, 20–21, ARA 68:6; Elizavetgrad District History, 30, ARA 139:3.

2. Clapp: ARA 107:12; Golder, *War, Revolution, and Peace in Russia*, 123, 126, 141; Raskin, "Nikolaev," 23, ARA 145:3; Bell to Page, Apr. 12, 1923, PS 231.

3. Coleman to Fisher, July 2, 1922, ARA 65:5; Buckley, "Orsk Rayon," 4, 9, ARA 68:6; Orenburg District History, 20–21, ARA 68:6.

4. Haskell, [untitled], Vol. 1, 158A–158B; Ellingston, "Carriage of Philanthropy," 70; Clapp: ARA 107:12; Kelley, "Descriptive Memorandum," 13.

5. Fisher, *Famine*, 62–67; Bechhofer, *Through Starving Russia*, 120–25; Leighton W. Rogers to Brown, Dec. 21, 1921, CON; Wilbur Thomas to Jane Addams, Oct. 23, 1922, AFSC, General Files:Addams.

6. Haskell to Brown, Dec. 19, 1921, CON; Davenport to Beeuwkes, Dec. 8, 1921, ARA 132:6; Murphy to Baker, Dec. 12/13, 1921, GBB 5; Golder, *War, Revolution, and Peace in Russia*, 123, 147–48, 154, 282; Goodrich to Hoover, Apr. 3, 1922, ARA 95:3; Mitchell to Brown, Mar. 13, 1922, ARA 23:2; Koenker and Bachman (eds.), *Revelations from the Russian Archives*, 555–56.

7. Reynolds, *Nansen*; Mackenzie, *Russia Before Dawn*, 128–29; Quinn to New York, Feb. 1, 1923, CON; Haskell to Herter, Feb. 12, 1923, ARA 340:3; Haskell to Brown, Feb. 20, 1923, CON; Haskell, [untitled], Vol. 2, 31–36.

CHAPTER 39

1. Harrison, *Marooned in Moscow*, 134; Gor'kii, *O russkom*, 28–33; Curtiss, *Russian Church*, chs. 6–7.

2. Pipes (ed.), *Unknown Lenin*, 152–55; Meijer (ed.), *Trotsky Papers*, 688–91; Hullinger, *Reforging of Russia*, 281–90; Golder, *War, Revolution, and Peace in Russia*, 150, 157, 169–70, 204; Mackenzie, *Russia Before Dawn*, 248; Murphy, 52; Duranty, *Duranty Reports Russia*, 57–81.

3. Simbirsk General Report, appendix 3, 23–24, ARA 118:4; Childs, "Sleigh Circuit," 15, ARA 29:6; Billington, *Icon and the Axe*, 6; Ransome, *Russia in 1919*, 95–96; Morizet, *Chez Lénine*, 44; Renshaw, Moscow District History, 10, ARA 35:4.

4. Spewack, "Moscow Along the Way," *World*, Sept. 8, 1922; Mackenzie, *Russia Before Dawn*, 262; Seldes, *Tell the Truth*, 153; Golder, *War, Revolution, and Peace in Russia*, 263; Fleming, Apr. 16, 1923, HFP 1:1; Barringer, "American's Impression," 214–15; Barringer, May 11, 1923, TBP 1:1.

5. Gregg to Moscow, Aug. 10, 1922, ARA 110:9; Saratov District History, 89, ARA 109:6; Clapp: ARA 107:12; Godfrey to Beeuwkes, June 11, 1922, ARA 337:5; Yakovlev, "A.R.A. Men," 20; Hullinger, *Reforging of Russia*, 286; Duranty, *Duranty Reports Russia*, 57–61; Haskell to Hoover, June 24, 1922, ARA 340:1; Lander to Haskell, Oct. 24, 1922, ARA 340:2.

6. Poliakov, *Diversiia*; Fisher, *Famine*, 422–23; Iliodor, *The Mad Monk*; MERSH 14:146–49; Jonge, *Life and Times of Rasputin*; Ellery Rand, "Iliodor Back Again in a New Role," *New York Times*, Dec. 3, 1922; Petrunkevich, Harper, and Golder, *Russian Revolution*, 76–77.

7. Iliodor, *The Mad Monk*, 41; Brownlow, *Behind the Mask*, 360–65; Cornick, Jan. 10, Mar. 24, 1922, GCP.

CHAPTER 40

1. Veil, *Adventure's a Wench*; PS 301.

2. Veil, *Adventure's a Wench*, 227–32, 272, 274; ARA 21:2; Mitchell to Haskell, Oct. 26, 1921, and Haskell to Brown, Nov. 10, 1921, CON; Baker to Fuller, Dec. 17, 1921, GBB 3.

3. Rickard to Brown, Nov. 28, 1921, Brown to Rickard, Dec. 19, 1921, Brown to Haskell, Dec. 19, 1921, Mitchell to Brown, Dec. 20, 1921, Mitchell to Brown, Feb. 23, 1922, Haskell to Brown, Apr. 6, 1922, and Haskell to Brown, Apr. 15, 1922, CON; PS 300.

4. Volodin: ARA 19:6; Mitchell to Brown, Mar. 11, 1922, CON; AAR, Feb. 1929; Quinn to London, July 12, 1922, PS 246; Mitchell to Quinn, Aug. 17, 1922, and Quinn to Mitchell, Aug. 24, 1922, ARA 73:1; Brown to Haskell, Sept. 13, 1922, and Haskell to Brown, Sept. 21, 1922, CON.

5. Gill: PS 254; Duranty, *I Write As I Please*, 53–54; Childs: JRC 20; Childs, "Between Two Worlds," 103, JRC; Kelley, "Extracts from Letters," 22, 46, 52, 93; "Story," 8–9, ARA 132:12; Blandy, May 5, 1922, PS 233; ARA 70:6; Strong, *I Change Worlds*, 179–80.

6. ARA 21:2.

7. Turrou to Mangan, Nov. 2, 1922, PS 274; Haskell to Lander, Nov. 10, 1922, ARA 21:2; Golder to Lutz, Nov. 16, 1922, FGP 13:5; Haskell to Quinn, ARA 20:1.

8. Quinn to Haskell, Dec. 2, 1922, ARA 21:2.

9. Beeuwkes to Quinn, Dec. 4, 1922, and Daley to Quinn, Dec. 5, 1922, ARA 21:2.

10. Lander to Quinn, Dec. 8, 1921, ARA 21:2; Childs, "Between Two Worlds," 124, JRC; Cox: JRC, 16; Childs, Dec. 9, 1922, JRC 20.

11. Lander to Sabine, Jan. 12, 1923, and Quinn to Haskell, Dec. 11, 1922, ARA 21:2; Quinn (cable) to Haskell, Dec. 11, 1922, and Quinn to Haskell, Dec. 21, 1922, CON; Haskell to Quinn (for Lander), Dec. 18, 1922, ARA 360:1; Seldes: ARA 20:1; Baker, n.d., ARA 351:14.

12. Ellingston to Fisher, Dec. 26, 1922, Feb. 28, 1923, ARA 94:13; Burland to Lander, May 18, 1923, ARA 21:2; Frank Harvey Holden Papers, HIA.

13. Burland to Brooks, June 7, 1926, PS 301; Turrou, *Where My Shadow Falls*, 70; Haskell to London, Apr. 12, 1922, and Mitchell to Moscow, Nov. 1, 1922, CON; Janicki to Quinn, Jan. 8, 1923, and Janicki to Daley, Sept. 2, 1924, PS 264; Banetski to Haskell, July 15, 1922, ARA 69:3; Quinn to Page, Mar. 19, 1923, ARA 69:2; Fleming, "Moscow," 3, ARA 95:1; RUR, Aug. 27, 1922; Haskell to Turrou, Feb. 20, 1923, ARA 69:2.

14. Mitchell to Brown, Mar. 8, 1923, ARA 310:1; Quinn to Mitchell, Mar. 8, Mar. 15, 1923, CON; Quinn to Page, Mar. 19, 1923, ARA 69:2; Mitchell to Brown, Mar. 17, 1923, CON; New York to London, Mar. 26, 1923; Quinn to Mitchell (for Brown), Mar. 31, 1923, ARA 310:1; Brown to Haskell, Apr. 4, 1923, CON.

15. Turrou to Hoover, Apr. 27, 1923, Page to Herter, May 14, 1923, and Turrou to Hoover, May 18, 1925, ARA 310:1; Burland to Brooks, June 7, 1926, PS 301.

16. Turrou, *Where My Shadow Falls*, 107, 145–61; "General Haskell and Stern Won't Impugn Turrou," *New York Herald Tribune*, Nov. 22, 1938; "Gen. Haskell at Spy Trial," *Sun*, Nov. 21, 1938; "Turrou Under Fire Again at Spy Trial," *New York Times*, Nov. 22, 1938; PS 301; Turrou, *Nazi Spies*; Tracy and Turrou, *How To Be a G-Man*, 170; AAR, Dec. 1941; Turrou, *Where My Shadow Falls*, 8–9, 142, 211–12; AAR, May 1965.

CHAPTER 41

1. Seldes, *You Can't Print That!*, 233; Hullinger, *Reforging of Russia*, 115; Haskell to Sawtelle, Dec. 9, 1921, PS 259; Hale to Herter, Apr. 24, 1922, ARA 305:3; Jacobs, "American Relief Administration and My Crime," 5; Childs, Nov. 6, 1921, JRC 20; RED, 40; Childs, "Thirty Years in the Near East," 6, CP.

2. Gorodnichii, "Maloizvestnaia," 56–57; Mackenzie, *Russia Before Dawn*, 37; MERSH 10:85–90; Harrison, *Born for Trouble*, 176; Mackenzie, "Real Rulers in Russia Are Old Revolutionists," *New York Globe*, May 24, 1923; Goodrich to Hoover, Apr. 3, 1922, ARA 95:3.

3. Leggett, *Cheka*, 343; Pethybridge, "Railways and Press Communications," 196–97; Golder, *War, Revolution, and Peace in Russia*, 157; Fisher, *Famine*, 206; Brooks, "Russian Railroads," 54–55; Duranty: ARA 340:3; Haskell, [untitled], Vol. 1, 124–26; Fisher to

Darwin P. Kingsley, Nov. 8, 1922, ARA 336:11; Ruhl, "What I've Just Seen in Russia"; Barringer, "American's Impression," 215–16.

4. AAR, Feb. 1929; "Effects of Relief Work," 4–5, ARA 6:6; Duranty, "Russia Opened Up By Famine Crisis," *New York Times*, Oct. 6, 1921; Fisher, 209–10.

5. Stites, *Revolutionary Dreams*, 145–47; *PSS* 36:140–41, 189–90; Haber, *Efficiency and Uplift*, 152; Golder, *War, Revolution, and Peace in Russia*, 265.

6. Brooks, "The Press and Its Message, 231–52; Rogger, "*Amerikanizm*," 384–88, 392, 418; Kazan in ARA 69:3 (Boyd); Administrative Division History, 3–4, ARA 36:6; Ellingston, "Carriage of Philanthropy," 75.

7. Kellogg: ARA 95:6; Duranty, *Duranty Reports Russia*, 19; "Peace Hath Her Victories," *New York Times*, Oct. 7, 1921.

8. Patenaude, "Herbert Hoover's Brush"; Hoover, *American Individualism*, 35–36; Poole to Hughes, May 4, 1923, DS file 861.48/2215.

9. "Digest of Speeches," Quinn to Fisher, June 23, 1923, ARA 20:1; Harrison, *Marooned in Moscow*, 56; Hullinger, *Reforging of Russia*, 35; Kennan, *Decision to Intervene*, 445; Seldes, *Tell the Truth*, 143; Burland, "Russian American Contacts," 9, PS 237; "Proshchanie c ARA," *Izvestiia*, July 20, 1923; Ellingston, "Carriage of Philanthropy," 147.

EPILOGUE

1. Haskell to Hoover, Aug. 27, 1923, ARA 340:3; Haskell, [untitled], Vol. 3, 122–23; DS 861.00/9411.

2. AAR, Feb. 1929.

3. AAR, Oct. 1925; "From Observations of an Inspector," 2, ARA 141:2.

4. Fisher, *Famine*, 398.   5. ARA 121:4.

6. ARA 340:3.   7. "General Conditions," 13, ARA 6:6.

8. Driscoll, "Final Period," 7, ARA 99:7; Verdon to Baker, June 13, 1923, ARA 100:1.

9. Ellingston to Fisher, June 7, 1923, ARA 94:13.

10. Hartridge, 21, 25, ARA 68:6.

11. Lapteff, "American Relief Administration in Ufa," 11; Ruhl to Hoover, Dec. 6–15, 1923, ARA 347:19; Duranty, *I Write As I Please*, 133–34; Seldes, *Truth Behind the News*, 170.

12. Vail, "Letters from Russia," 65, HIA.

13. ARA 543:7.

14. ARA 342:10, 543:7.

15. Kennedy, *Over Here*, 216–17; Noggle, *Into the Twenties*, 9.

16. Kennedy, *Over Here*, 219.   17. Cornick, Oct. 4, 1922, GCP.

18. HHPL, Commerce Papers, 355.   19. Page to Burland, Apr. 9, 1923, PS 237.

20. AAR, July 1, 1925.

21. Filene, *Americans and the Soviet Experiment*, chap. 9.

22. Sabine, Moscow District History, 7–10; Pipes, *Russia Under the Bolshevik Regime*, 320; Figes, *People's Tragedy*, 780–81.

23. Chamberlin, *Russia's Iron Age*, 88–89.

24. Crowl, *Angels in Stalin's Paradise*, ch. 6; Taylor, *Stalin's Apologist*, chaps. 11–12.

25. Haskell, [untitled], Vol. 3, 93–95, 102–8.

26. PS 231.

27. Haskell, [untitled], Vol. 3, 123; Patenaude, "The Strange Death of Soviet Communism."

28. Haskell, [untitled], Vol. 2, 135–37; Rickard to Barnes, July 24, 1923, PS 292.

29. Haskell, [untitled], Vol. 2, 88.

30. Haskell, [untitled], Vol. 3, 29–31.

31. "Materialy fevral'sko-martovskogo plenuma, 5–6; Gorodnichii, "Maloizvest-naia."

32. Stalin, *Works*, 121; Weissman, *Hoover*, 125–26.

33. Weissman, *Hoover*, 184–88; PSS 44:555, n. 86; A. A. Grechko, et al. (eds.), *Istoriia vtoroi mirovoi voiny, 1939–1945*, 226.

34. AAR, Dec. 1939.

35. AAR, Dec. 1941.

36. Bailey, *America Faces Russia*, 255; AAR, Oct. 1953.

37. Gaddis, *Russia*, 186–87.

38. Haskell, "How We Fed the Starving Russians," 15–19.

39. Kogan, "Antisovetskie," 32.

40. Jorden, "Kozlov Confers with Eisenhower on Berlin Crisis," *New York Times*, July 2, 1959.

41. *Khrushchev in America*, 111–12.

42. AAR, Dec. 1937.

43. AAR, May 1965.

44. Lapteff, "American Relief Administration in Ufa," 21.

45. http://cfa-www.harvard.edu/iau/lists/MPNames.html; Edwin B. Frost to Vernon Kellogg, Aug. 20, 1923, HHPL, Commerce Papers, 355.

BIBLIOGRAPHY

ARCHIVAL COLLECTIONS AND PERSONAL PAPERS

Baltimore. The Alan Mason Chesney Medical Archives.
Johns Hopkins Medical Institutions
   W. Horsley Gantt Papers

Cambridge, Mass. Houghton Library. Harvard University
   Archibald Cary Coolidge Papers

Charlottesville, Va. Alderman Library. University of Virginia
   James Rives Childs Papers

Lubbock, Tex. Southwest Collection. Texas Tech University
   George Cornick Papers

New Orleans. Howard–Tilton Memorial Library. Tulane University
   Donald Renshaw Papers

New York. Bakhmetev Archive. Columbia University
   Aleksis V. Laptev Papers
   Allen Wardwell Papers
   American Relief Administration Papers

New York. Jewish Joint Distribution Committee Archives

New York. New York Public Library
   Harold M. Fleming Papers

New York. Oral History Research Office. Columbia University
   The Reminiscences of Spurgeon M. Keeny, Sr. (1982)

Philadelphia. American Friends Service Committee

Stanford, Calif. Green Library. Stanford University
   Frank A. Golder Papers

Stanford, Calif. Hoover Institution Archives. Stanford University
   American Relief Administration, European Operations
   American Relief Administration, Russian Operations
   Nancy Babb Papers
   George Barr Baker Papers
   Thomas C. Barringer Papers
   Philip H. Carroll Papers
   James Rives Childs Papers
   Ethan T. Colton Papers
   Thomas H. Dickinson Papers

Harold H. Fisher Papers
Harold M. Fleming Papers
W. Parmer Fuller Papers
Perry Galpin Papers
C. A. Gaskill Papers
Frank A. Golder Papers
Donald Grant Papers
Charles L. Hall Papers
William N. Haskell Papers
Frank Harvey Holden Papers
Herbert C. Hoover Papers
Lincoln Hutchinson Papers
John F. de Jacobs Papers
Alexis V. Lapteff Papers
Gibbes Lykes Papers
Merle Farmer Murphy Papers
Garner Richardson Papers
Arthur C. Ringland Papers
Edward G. Sabine Papers
Jessica Smith Papers
F. Dorsey Stephens Papers
Leon G. Turrou Papers
Edwin H. Vail Papers
Henry C. Wolfe Papers

Swarthmore, Pa. Friends Historical Library. Swarthmore College

Wilbur Kelsey Thomas Papers

Swarthmore, Pa. Swarthmore College Peace Collection

Jane Addams Papers
A. Ruth Fry Papers

Tulsa, Okla. Robert and Mary Ann Swain

William N. Haskell Papers (private collection)

Washington, D.C. Georgetown University Archives

Rev. Edmund A. Walsh, S.J., Papers

West Branch, Iowa. Herbert Hoover Presidential Library

Belgium-American Educational Foundation files (BAEF)
James P. Goodrich Papers
Oral History Collection
Personnel Series
Secretary of Commerce Papers

PUBLISHED DOCUMENTS AND PAPERS,
COLLECTED LETTERS AND DIARIES

A.R.A. Bulletin. ser. 2; 5 vols. New York, 1921–26. HIA.
[Babine, Alexis]. *A Russian Civil War Diary: Alexis Babine in Saratov, 1917–1922.* Ed. Donald J. Raleigh. Durham, N.C., 1988.
Biulleten' vserossiiskoi konferentsii RKP (bol'sh). nos. 1–5. Moscow, 1921.

Bane, Suda Lorena, and Ralph Haswell Lutz, eds. *Organization of American Relief in Europe, 1918–1919*. Stanford, Calif., 1943.

Chukovskii, K. *Dnevnik, 1901–1929*. Moscow, 1991.

Coolidge, Harold Jefferson, and Robert Howard Lord. *Archibald Cary Coolidge: Life and Letters*. Boston, 1932.

Degras, Jane, comp., ed. *1917–1924*. Vol. 1, *Soviet Documents on Foreign Policy*. London, 1951.

Duncan, Isadora. *Isadora Speaks*. San Francisco, 1981.

Gidney, James B., ed. *Witness to Revolution: Letters from Russia 1916–1919 by Edward T. Heald*. Kent, Ohio, 1972.

[Golder, Frank]. *War, Revolution, and Peace in Russia: The Passages of Frank Golder, 1914–1927*. Comp. and ed. Terence Emmons and Bertrand M. Patenaude. Stanford, Calif., 1992.

Golder, Frank Alfred, and Lincoln Hutchinson. *On the Trail of the Russian Famine*. Stanford, Calif., 1927.

[Got'e, Iu. V.]. *Time of Troubles: The Diary of Iurii Vladimirovich Got'e, Moscow, July 8, 1917, to July 23, 1922*. Trans., ed., and introd. Terence Emmons. Princeton, N.J., 1988.

Istoricheskii arkhiv, no. 6 (1993): 76–95.

Kalinin, M. I. *Za eti gody*. 3 vols. Moscow, 1926–29.

Khrushchev in America. New York, 1960.

Koenker, Diane P. and Ronald D. Bachman, eds. *Revelations from the Russian Archives: Documents in English Translation*. Washington, D.C., 1997.

Lenin, V. I. *Polnoe sobranie sochinenii*. 5th ed.; 55 vols. Moscow, 1958–65.

"Materialy fevral'sko-martovskogo plenuma TsK VKP(b) 1937 goda." *Voprosy istorii*, no. 2 (1995): 3–26.

Meijer, Jan M., ed. *The Trotsky Papers, 1917–1922*. Vol. 2. The Hague, 1971.

Pipes, Richard, ed. *The Unknown Lenin: From the Secret Archive*. New Haven, Conn., 1996.

Stalin, J. V. *Works*. Vol. 5. Moscow, 1953.

Surface, Frank M., and Raymond L. Bland. *American Food in the World War and Reconstruction Period*. Stanford, Calif., 1931.

U.S. Congress. House. *Russian Relief: Hearings Before the Committee on Foreign Affairs on H.R. 9459 and H.R. 9458*. 67th Congress, 2nd session, 1921.

———. Senate. *Bolshevik Propaganda: Hearings Before a Subcommittee of the Judiciary*. 65th Congress, 3rd session, 1919.

———. Senate. *Congressional Record*. 67th Congress, 2nd session, December 21 and 22, 1921. Vol. 62, pt. 1.

U.S. Department of State. *Papers Relating to the Foreign Relations of the United States, 1921*. Vol. 2. Washington, D.C., 1936.

U.S.S.R. Ministry of Foreign Affairs. *Dokumenty vneshnei politiki SSSR*. Vol. 4. Moscow, 1960.

UNPUBLISHED OFFICIAL DOCUMENTS

General Records of the Department of State, Record Group 59.

CONTEMPORARY WORKS, WORKS BY PARTICIPANTS,
AND FICTION

Barringer, Thomas C. "An American's Impression of Soviet Russia." 1923. TBP 1:10.

Bechhofer, C. E. [Roberts, C.E.B.]. *Through Starving Russia*. London, 1921.

Blomquist, Alvin E. "Genesis to Exodus." June 1923. ARA 118:4.

Brooks, Sidney. "Russian Railroads in the National Crisis." *A.R.A. Bulletin*, ser. 2, no. 42 (November 1923): 1–91.

Bulgakov, M. "Kiev-gorod." *Sobranie sochinenii*. Vol. 2. Moscow, 1989.

[Childs, J. Rives]. *Before the Curtain Falls*. Indianapolis, Ind., 1932.

———. *Foreign Service Farewell: My Years in the Near East*. Charlottesville, Va., 1969.

———. *Let the Credit Go: The Autobiography of J. Rives Childs*. New York, 1983.

Colton, Ethan T. *Forty Years with Russians*. New York, 1940.

———. "With the Y.M.C.A. in Revolutionary Russia." *Russian Review* 14 (April 1955): 128–39.

Dos Passos, John. *Three Soldiers*. New York, 1932 [1921].

Dubenetskii, N. "Opyt izchisleniia naseleniia RSFSR i USSR na 1922g." *Biulleten' TsSU* 72 (1923): 89–96.

Dukes, Paul. *Red Dusk and the Morrow*. Garden City, N.Y., 1922.

Duranty, Walter. *Duranty Reports Russia*. New York, 1934.

———. *I Write As I Please*. New York, 1935.

———. *Search for a Key*. New York, 1943.

———. "Ten Years' Struggle to Convert Russia to Communism." *Current History* 27 (November 1927): 153–58.

[Ellingston, John] One Who Served. "The Carriage of Philanthropy." *A.R.A. Bulletin*, ser. 2, no. 43 (December 1923): 1–151.

Fisher, H. H. *America and the New Poland*. New York, 1928.

———. *The Famine in Soviet Russia, 1919–1923: The Operations of the American Relief Administration*. New York, 1927.

Fry, Anna Ruth. *A Quaker Adventure: The Story of Nine Years' Relief and Reconstruction*. London, 1926.

———. *Three Visits to Russia, 1922–25*. London, 1942.

Gef'e, Boris de [Perfilov, B.]. *Chernaia godina*. Tsaritsyn, Russia, 1922.

Gerasimovich, Ivan. *Golod na Ukraini*. Berlin, 1922.

Gibbs, Philip. *The Middle of the Road*. New York, 1923.

———. *Since Then: The Disturbing Story of the World at Peace*. New York, 1930.

———. *Ten Years After: A Reminder*. London, [1925?].

God bor'by s golodom: Uchastie Narodnogo komissariata po prodovol'stviiu v dele pomoshchi golodaiushchim. Moscow, 1922.

God bor'by s golodom, 1921–1922. Kharkov, Ukraine, 1923.

Goldman, Emma. *My Disillusionment in Russia*. Garden City, N.Y., 1923.

———. *My Further Disillusionment in Russia*. Garden City, N.Y., 1924.

Golod i tserkovnye bogatstva. Moscow, 1922.

Goodrich, James P. "The Evolution of Soviet Russia." *International Conciliation*, no. 185 (April 1923): 205–35.

———. "Impressions of the Bolshevik Régime." *Century* (May 1922): 55–65.

———. "The True Communists of Russia." *Current History* (September 1922): 927–32.

Gorev, Mikh. *Otkuda neurozhai i golodovki?* Moscow, 1922.

———. *Tserkovnye bogatstva i golod v Ros[s]ii*, Moscow, 1922.

Gor'kii, Maksim. *O russkom krest'ianstve*. Berlin, 1922.

Harrison, Margaret E. *Born for Trouble: The Story of a Chequered Life*. London, 1936.

———. *Marooned in Moscow*. New York, 1921.

———. *Unfinished Tales from a Russian Prison*. New York, 1923.

Haskell, William N. "How We Fed the Starving Russians." *Plain Talk* (July 1948): 15–19.

————. [untitled]. 3 vols. [1932]. William N. Haskell Papers, HIA.

Herriot, Édouard. *La Russie Nouvelle*. Paris, 1922.

Hoover, Herbert. *American Individualism*. New York, 1923.

————. *An American Epic*. Vol. 2. Chicago, 1960.

————. *The Memoirs of Herbert Hoover: Years of Adventure, 1874–1920*. New York, 1951.

Houghteling, James L., Jr. *A Diary of the Russian Revolution*. New York, 1918.

Hullinger, Edwin Ware. *The Reforging of Russia*. New York, 1925.

Iaroslavskii, Emel'ian. *Pochemu u nas v Rossii golod i kak s nim borot'sia?* Moscow, 1921.

[Iliodor]. *The Mad Monk of Russia: Iliodor. Life, Memoirs, and Confessions of Sergei Michailovich Trufanoff (Iliodor)*. New York, 1918.

Itogi bor'by s golodom v 1921–22gg.: Sbornik statei i otchetov. Moscow, 1922.

Itogi posledgol. Moscow, 1923.

Jacobs, John F. de. "The American Relief Administration and My Crime." Typescript, HIA.

Kameneva, Ol'ga Davydovna. *Kak proletarii vsekh stran pomogaiut golodaiushchim Rossii*. Moscow, 1923.

Kelley, William J. "Descriptive Memorandum on the Work of the A.R.A. District of Ufa." FGP 25:8.

————. "Extracts from the Letters of William J. Kelley." FGP 23:5.

Kniga o golode. Samara, Russia, 1922.

Kondratov, Eduard. *Zhestokii god: Roman*. Kuibyshev [Samara], Russia, 1987.

Kuskova, E. "Mesiats 'soglashatel'stva.'" *Volia Rossii*, nos. 3–5 (1928).

Landfield, Jerome. "The Relief of Starving Russians." *American Review of Reviews* (September 1921): 267–71.

Lapteff, Alexis V. "American Relief Administration in Ufa, Russia." 1971. Typescript, HIA.

McCullagh, Francis. *The Bolshevik Persecution of Christianity*. London, 1924.

Mackenzie, F. A. *Russia Before Dawn*. London, 1923.

Melgounov, Sergey Petrovich. *The Red Terror in Russia*. London, 1926.

Morizet, André. *Chez Lénine et Trotski, Moscou 1921*. Paris, 1922.

Murphy, Merle Farmer. "Record of a Russian Year, 1921–1922." Typescript, HIA.

Nekrasov, Viktor. "Po obe storony okeana." *Novyi mir* 38 (December 1962): 110–52.

O golode: Sbornik statei. Kharkov, Ukraine, 1922.

Payne, Muriel. *Plague, Pestilence and Famine*. London, 1923.

Petlia vmesto khleba: Kak amerikantsy spasaiut golodaiushchikh. Penza, Russia, 1921.

Petrunkevich, Alexander, Samuel Northrup Harper, and Frank Alfred Golder. *The Russian Revolution*. Cambridge, Mass., 1918.

Poliakov, Aleksandr. *Diversiia pod flagom pomoshchi: Povest'-khronika*. Moscow, 1985.

Ponafidine, Emma. "The Famine and the Bolsheviki." *Yale Review* (October 1922): 58–72.

Ransome, Arthur. *Russia in 1919*. New York, 1919.

Reswick, William. *I Dreamt Revolution*. Chicago, 1952.

Rickard, Edgar. "Millions Fed with Your Money." *Our World* (May 1922): 41–48.

Ross, Edward Alsworth. *The Russian Soviet Republic*. New York and London, 1923.

Ruhl, Arthur. "What I've Just Seen in Russia." *Outlook*, July 25, 1923.

————. "What the Russians Think of Us." *New Republic* 36 (September 19, 1923): 95–96.

Sarolea, Charles. *Impressions of Soviet Russia*. 3rd ed. London, 1924.

Sayler, Oliver M. *Russia: White or Red*. Boston, 1919.

————. *The Russian Theater*. New York, 1922.

Seldes, George. *Tell the Truth and Run*. New York, 1953.

————. *The Truth Behind the News, 1918–1928*. London, 1929.

————. *You Can't Print That!* Garden City, N.Y., 1929.

Serge, Victor. *Memoirs of a Revolutionary, 1901–1941*. London, 1963.

Smel'nitskii, Iu. M. *Na Volge*. Kazan, Russia, 1909.

Sorokin, Pitirim. *Hunger as a Factor in Human Affairs*. Gainesville, Fla., 1975 [Petrograd, 1922].

————. *Leaves from a Russian Diary*. New York, 1924.

————. *Man and Society in Calamity*. New York, 1942.

————. *Sovremmenoe sostoianie Rossii*. Prague, 1922.

Spewack, Samuel. *Red Russia Revealed: The Truth About the Soviet Government and Its Methods*. New York, 1923.

Strong, Anna Louise. *I Change Worlds*. New York, 1935.

————. *The First Time in History*. London, 1924.

Tolstoy, Countess Alexandra. *I Worked for the Soviet*. New Haven, Conn., 1934.

Tracy, Tom, and Leon G. Turrou. *How to Be a G-Man*. New York, 1939.

Turrou, Leon G. *Nazi Spies in America*. New York, 1939.

————. *Where My Shadow Falls: Two Decades of Crime Detection*. Garden City, N.Y., 1949.

Vasilevskii, L. M. *Zhutkaia letopis' goloda (samoubiistva i antropofagiia)*. Ufa, Russia, 1922.

Veil, Charles. *Adventure's a Wench: The Autobiography of Charles Veil*. New York, 1934.

Vse-na pomoshch' Povol'zhiu! Samara, Russia, 1922.

Vykhodtsev, S. *Pomoshch inostrantsev golodaiushchim detiam Povol'zhia*. Moscow, 1922.

Yakovlev, Alexey. "The A.R.A. Men and Their Work in a Russian province (1921–1922)." Typescript, ARA 6:6.

Yarovoff, Nikolai. "The Russian Theater Under the Soviet." *Shadowland* (January 1922): 55–62.

SECONDARY BOOKS AND ARTICLES

Abramovitch, Raphael R. *The Soviet Revolution, 1917–1939*. New York, 1962.

Allen, Robert V. *Russia Looks to America: The View to 1917*. Washington, D.C., 1988.

Antisovetskaia interventsiia i ee krakh, 1917–1922. Moscow, 1987.

Asquith, Michael. *Famine: Quaker Work in Russia, 1921–1923*. London, 1943.

Avrich, Paul. *Kronstadt 1921*. Princeton, N.J., 1970.

Bailey, Thomas A. *America Faces Russia*. Ithaca, N.Y. 1950.

Baranchenko, V. E. "Karl Lander." *Voprosy istorii*, no. 1 (1971): 200–4.

Bassow, Whitman. *The Moscow Correspondents: Reporting on Russia from the Revolution to Glasnost*. New York, 1988.

Beatty, Bessie. *The Red Heart of Russia*. New York, 1919.

Bell, Daniel. *The End of Ideology*. Glencoe, Ill., 1960.

Belokorutov, V. I. *Likholet'e: Iz istorii bor'by s golodom v Povolzh'e, 1921–1922gg*. Kazan, Russia, 1976.

Billington, James H. *The Icon and the Axe: An Interpretive History of Russian Culture*. New York, 1970.

Blair, Fredrika. *Isadora: Portrait of the Artist as a Woman*. New York, 1976.

Brooks, Jeffrey. "The Press and Its Message: Images of America in the 1920s and 1930s." In *Russia in the Era of NEP: Explorations in Soviet Society and Culture*. Ed. Sheila Fitzpatrick, Alexander Rabinowitch, and Richard Stites. Bloomington, Ind. 1991.

Brownlow, Kevin. *Behind the Mask of Innocence*. New York, 1990.

Burner, David. *Herbert Hoover: A Public Life*. New York, 1979.

Byrnes, Robert Francis. *Awakening American Education to the World: The Role of Archibald Cary Coolidge, 1866–1928.* Notre Dame, Ind., 1982.

Carr, Edward Hallett. *The Bolshevik Revolution, 1917–1923.* Vol. 1. New York, 1950.

Carter, Huntly. *The New Theatre and Cinema of Soviet Russia.* New York, 1925.

Chamberlin, William Henry. *The Confessions of an Individualist.* New York, 1940.

———. *The Russian Revolution.* 2 vols. New York, 1935.

———. *Russia's Iron Age.* Boston, 1934.

———. *Soviet Russia: A Living Record and a History.* Boston, 1931.

Chemerisskii, I. A. "Iz istorii klassovoi bor'by v 1921g. (Vserossiiskii komitet pomoshchi golodaiushchim)." *Istoricheskie zapiski* 77 (1965): 191–208.

The Chronicle of Novgorod, 1016–1471. Trans. Robert Michell and Nevill Forbes. London, 1914.

Coffman, Edward M. *The War to End All Wars: The American Military Experience in World War I.* New York, 1968.

Conquest, Robert. *The Harvest of Sorrow: Soviet Collectivization and the Terror Famine.* New York, 1986.

Crowl, James William. *Angels in Stalin's Paradise.* Washington, D.C., 1982.

Curtiss, John Shelton. *The Russian Church and the Soviet State, 1917–1950.* Boston, 1953.

Davis, Donald E., and Eugene P. Trani. "The American YMCA and the Russian Revolution." *Slavic Review* 33 (September 1974): 469–91.

Duncan, Irma, and Allan Ross MacDougall. *Isadora Duncan's Russian Days and Her Last Years in France.* New York, 1929.

Edmondson, Charles M. "The Politics of Hunger: The Soviet Response to Famine, 1921." *Soviet Studies* 29 (October 1977): 506–18.

Figes, Orlando. *Peasant Russia, Civil War: The Volga Countryside in Revolution (1917–1921).* Oxford, England, 1989.

———. *A People's Tragedy: The Russian Revolution, 1891–1924.* New York, 1998.

Filene, Peter G. *Americans and the Soviet Experiment, 1917–1933.* Cambridge, Mass., 1967.

Fink, Carole. *The Genoa Conference: European Diplomacy, 1921–1922.* Chapel Hill, N.C., 1984.

Fischer, Louis. *Men and Politics: An Autobiography.* New York, 1941.

Fleming, D. F. *The Cold War and Its Origins, 1917–1960.* Vol. 1. New York, 1961.

Fogelsong, David. *America's Secret War Against Bolshevism: U.S. Intervention in the Russian Civil War.* Chapel Hill, N.C., 1995.

Forbes, John. *American Friends and Russian Relief, 1917–1927.* Philadelphia, 1952.

Gaddis, John Lewis. *Russia, the Soviet Union and the United States: An Interpretive History.* 2nd ed. New York, 1990.

Gibbons, Edward. *Floyd Gibbons: Your Headline Hunter.* New York, 1953.

Giffen, Frederick C. "James Putnam Goodrich and Soviet Russia." *Mid-America* 71 (October 1989): 153–74.

Gorodnichii, N. F. "Maloizvestnaia stranitsa deiatel'nosti ARA v Sovetskoi Rossii." *Voprosy istorii*, no. 12 (1968): 47–58.

Grechko, A. A., et al., eds. *Istoriia vtoroi mirovoi voiny, 1939–1945.* Vol. 1. Moscow, 1973.

Haber, Samuel. *Efficiency and Uplift: Scientific Management in the Progressive Era, 1890–1920.* Chicago and London, 1964.

Harbord, James G. *The American Army in France: 1917–1919.* Boston, 1936.

———. *The American Expeditionary Forces: Its Organization and Accomplishments.* Evanston, Ill., 1929.

Heller, Michel. "Premier avertissement: Un coup de fouet. L'Histoire de l'expulsion des personnalités culturelles hors de l'Union Soviétique en 1922." *Cahiers du Monde russe et soviétique* 20 (April–June 1979): 131–72.

Hoover, Calvin. *Memoirs of Capitalism, Communism, and Nazism.* Durham, N.C., 1965.

Hopkins, George W. "The Politics of Food: United States and Soviet Hungary, March–August, 1919." *Mid-America* 55 (October 1973): 245–70.

Il'f, Ilia, and Evgenii Petrov. *The Golden Calf.* Trans. John H. C. Richardson. New York, 1962.

Ingersoll, Jean M. *Historical Examples of Ecological Disaster: Famine in Russia, 1921–22; Famine in Bechuanland, 1965.* Croton-on-Hudson, N.Y., 1965.

Iuldashbaev, B. *Obrazovanie Bashkirskoi ASSR.* Ufa, Russia, 1958.

Ivanov, Sergei. *La famine en Russie bolcheviste.* Paris, 1924.

Jonge, Alex de. *The Life and Times of Grigorii Rasputin.* New York, 1982.

Kahn, David. *The Codebreakers: The Story of Secret Writing.* New York, 1967.

Kanigel, Robert. *The One Best Way: Frederick Winslow Taylor and the Engine of Efficiency.* New York, 1997.

Kennan, George F. "Our Aid to Russia: A Forgotten Chapter." *New York Times Magazine,* July 19, 1959.

———. *Russia and the West Under Lenin and Stalin.* Boston, 1961.

———. *Russia Leaves the War.* Vol. 1, *Soviet American Relations, 1917–1920.* Princeton, N.J., 1956.

———. *The Decision to Intervene.* Vol. 2, *Soviet American Relations, 1917–1920.* Princeton, N.J., 1958.

Kennedy, David M. *Over Here: The First World War and American Society.* Oxford, England, 1980.

Khenkin, E. M. *Ocherki istorii bor'by Sovetskogo gosudarstva s golodom (1921–1922).* Krasnoiarsk, Russia, 1988.

Kogan, A. N. "Antisovetskie deistviia Amerikanskoi administratsii pomoshchi (ARA) v Sovetskoi Rossii v 1921–1922." *Istoricheskie zapiski* 29 (1949): 3–32.

Lasch, Christopher. *The American Liberals and the Russian Revolution.* New York, 1962.

Leggett, George. *The Cheka: Lenin's Political Police.* Oxford, England, 1981.

Lih, Lars T. *Bread and Authority in Russia, 1914–1921.* Berkeley, Calif., 1990.

Long, James W. "The Volga Germans and the Famine of 1921." *Russian Review* 51 (October 1992): 510–25.

McFadden, David W. *Alternative Paths: Soviets and Americans, 1917–1920.* New York, 1993.

Malia, Martin. *The Soviet Tragedy: A History of Socialism in Russia, 1917–1991.* New York, 1994.

May, Henry F. *The End of American Innocence.* New York, 1959.

Murray, Robert K. *Red Scare: A Study in National Hysteria, 1919–1920.* Minneapolis, Minn., 1955.

Nash, George H. *The Engineer, 1874–1914.* Vol. 1, *The Life of Herbert Hoover.* New Yopkin, 1983.

———. *The Humanitarian, 1914–1917.* Vol. 2, *The Life of Herbert Hoover.* New York, 1988.

———. *Master of Emergencies, 1917–1918.* Vol. 3, *The Life of Herbert Hoover.* New York, 1996.

Noggle, Burl. *Into the Twenties: The United States from Armistice to Normalcy.* Urbana, Ill., 1974.

Patenaude, Bertrand M. "Peasants into Russians: The Utopian Essence of War Communism." *Russian Review* 54 (October 1995): 552–70.

———. "The Strange Death of Soviet Communism: The 1921 Version." In *Reexamining the Soviet Experience: Essays in Honor of Alexander Dallin*. Ed. David Holloway and Norman Naimark. Boulder, Colo., 1996.

Pethybridge, R. W. "Railways and Press Communications in Soviet Russia in the Early NEP Period." *Soviet Studies* 38 (April 1986): 194–206.

Pipes, Richard. *Russia Under the Bolshevik Regime*. New York, 1993.

———. *The Russian Revolution*. New York, 1991.

———. "Russia's Chance." *Commentary* 93:3 (March 1992): 28–33.

Poliakov, Iu. A. *1921-i: Pobeda nad golodom*. Moscow, 1975.

Portnoi, I. L. "Provokatsiia voennykh korablei SShA v Odesskom portu v. 1922g." *Istoricheskii arkhiv*, no. 6 (1960): 183–85.

Queen, George S. "American Relief in the Russian Famine of 1891–1892." *Russian Review* 14 (April 1955): 140–50.

Radkey, Oliver. *The Unknown Civil War in Russia*. Stanford, Calif., 1976.

Ragsdale, Hugh. "The Constraints of Russian Culture." *National Interest* 33 (fall 1993): 68–72.

Reynolds, E. E. *Nansen*. London, 1932.

Rhodes, Benjamin D. "American Relief Operations at Nikolaiev, USSR, 1922–1923." *Historian* 51 (August 1989): 611–26.

———. "Governor James P. Goodrich of Indiana and the 'Plain Facts' About Russia, 1921–1923." *Indiana Magazine of History* 85 (March 1989): 1–30.

Riasanovsky, Nicholas V. *A History of Russia*. 4th ed. New York, 1984.

Rogger, Hans. "America in the Russian Mind—or Russian Discoveries of America." *Pacific Historical Review* 47 (February 1978): 27–51.

———. "*Amerikanizm* and the Economic Development of Russia." *Comparative Studies in History* (July 1981): 382–420.

Rorlich, Azade-Ayse. *The Volga Tatars: A Profile in National Resilience*. Stanford, Calif., 1986.

Rubinshtein, N. L. "Bor'ba Sovetskoi Rossii s golodom 1921 g. i kapitalisticheskie strany." *Istoricheskie zapiski* 22 (1947): 3–41.

Schapiro, Leonard. "The Role of the Jews in the Russian Revolutionary Movement." *Slavonic and East European Review* 40, no. 24 (1961): 148–67.

Schneider, Ilya Ilyich. *Isadora Duncan: The Russian Years*. New York, 1968.

Schuman, Frederick Lewis. *American Policy Toward Russia Since 1917*. New York, 1928.

Scott, John. *Behind the Urals*. Bloomington, Ind., 1973.

Serbyn, Roman. "The Famine of 1921–1923: A Model for 1932–1933?" In *Famine in Ukraine: 1932–1933*. Ed. Roman Serbyn and Bohdan Krawchenko. Edmonton, Canada, 1986.

———. "La première famine en Ukraine et l'Occident (1921–1923)." *L'Est Européen* (April–June 1987): 31–57.

Seroff, Victor. *The Real Isadora*. New York, 1971.

Smith, Gene. *The Shattered Dream: Herbert Hoover and the Great Depression*. New York, 1970.

Stallings, Laurence. *The Doughboys: The Story of the AEF, 1917–1918*. New York, 1963.

Stashevskii, D. N. "Burzhuaznaia literatura SShA ob Amerikanskoi pomoshchi Sovetskoi Rossii." *Voprosi istorii*, no. 4 (1966): 173–80.

———. *Progressivnye sily SShA v bor'be za prisnanie Sovetskogo gosudarstva*. Kiev, 1969.

Stewart, George. *The White Armies of Russia: A Chronicle of Counter-Revolution and Allied Intervention*. New York, 1933.

Stites, Richard. *Revolutionary Dreams: Utopian Vision and Experimental Life in the Russian Revolution*. New York, 1989.

Taylor, S. J. *Stalin's Apologist: Walter Duranty, the New York Times's Man in Moscow*. New York, 1990.

Thompson, John M. *Russia, Bolshevism, and the Versailles Peace*. Princeton, N.J., 1966.

Vel'min, A. "Amerikanskaia pomoshch golodaiushchim v Kieve." *Novyi zhurnal* 59 (1960): 279–85.

Weissman, Benjamin M. *Herbert Hoover and Famine Relief to Soviet Russia, 1921–1923*. Stanford, Calif., 1974.

Who Was Who in America. 13 vols. Chicago, 1943–2000.

Wicksteed, A. *Life Under the Soviets*. London, 1928.

Wieczynski, Joseph L., ed. *The Modern Encyclopedia of Russian and Soviet History*. 46 vols. Gulf Breeze, Fla., 1976–1987.

Williams, William Appleman. *American-Russian Relations, 1781–1947*. New York, 1952.

———. *Some Presidents: Wilson to Nixon*. New York, 1972.

Wilson, Joan Hoff. *Herbert Hoover: A Forgotten Progressive*. Boston, 1975.

———. *Ideology and Economics: U.S. Relations with the Soviet Union, 1918–1933*. Columbia, Mo., 1974.

Wolfe, Bertram D. *The Bridge and the Abyss: The Troubled Friendship of Maxim Gorky and V. I. Lenin*. New York, 1967.

UNPUBLISHED STUDIES

Claussen, Martin Paul. "American-Soviet Relations and the Russian Famine, 1921–1923." Ph.D. dissertation, George Washington University, 1976.

Edmondson, Charles Milton. "Soviet Famine Relief Measures, 1921–1923." Ph.D. dissertation, Florida State University, 1970.

Patenaude, Bertrand Mark. "Bolshevism in Retreat: The Transition to the New Economic Policy, 1920–22." Ph.D. dissertation, Stanford University, 1987.

———. "Herbert Hoover's Brush with Bolshevism." Kennan Institute for Advanced Russian Studies. Occasional Paper no. 248, June 1992.

ACKNOWLEDGMENTS

The Hoover Institution on War, Revolution and Peace on two separate occasions supported my research on this book, in the form of the Title VIII grant that launched it and through its National Fellows Program. The Kennan Institute for Advanced Russian Studies supported a year of research in Washington. The Herbert Hoover Presidential Library provided a travel grant for one of my two visits to West Branch.

I thank Elena Danielson and the staff of the Hoover Institution Archives for generous assistance well beyond the call of duty. Thanks as well to Herbert J. Ellison, Martin Malia, Joan Stevenson, Robert and Mary Ann Swain, Stephen Shafroth, J. Alexis Burland, Norris Pope, and Audrey Southwick, and to Evan S. Connell for *Son of the Morning Star*.

Terence Emmons encouraged me to undertake this project, helped to shape it through the example of his own scholarship and our many conversations about its contents, and otherwise helped sustain me over the years through steadfast support, much of it of the strong, silent type. I am indebted to him for all of this, as well as for two minor planets.